CHRIST FOR THE WORLD

THE HEART OF THE LAMB

BY THE SAME AUTHOR

A Igreja em estado de dialogo. Manhumirim, Brazil: 0 Lutador, 1965.

Le Coeur de Marie, Coeur de l'Eglise. Paris: Lethielleux, 1967.

Padres Profetas e Mistagogos. São Paulo, Brazil: Ed. Paulinas, 1968.

Reinhold Niebuhr, théologien de la communauté mondiale. Paris-Brussels: Desclée de Brouwer, 1969.

The Sacraments and Social Progress. Chicago: Franciscan Herald Press, 1974 (fall).

The publishers express their gratitude to the International Institute of the Heart of Jesus for its generous cooperation in the publication of this book, the first in a projected series on the Sacred Heart of Jesus sponsored by the International Institute.

This is I I H J Publication No. 1.

CHRIST FOR THE WORLD
THE HEART OF THE LAMB
A Treatise on Christology

Bertrand de Margerie S.J.

Translated by Malachy Carroll

FRANCISCAN HERALD PRESS
1434 WEST 51st STREET • CHICAGO, 60609

Christ for the World, The Heart of the Lamb: A Treatise on Christology, by Bertrand de Margerie S.J., translated by Malachy Carroll from *Le Christ pour le monde: Le Coeur de L'Agneau* (Paris: Beauchesne, 1971), originally published in Portuguese, *O Cristo paro o Mundo* (Sao Paulo: Herder, 1971).

Library of Congress Cataloging in Publication Data

Margerie, Bertrand de.
  Christ for the world, the heart of the lamb.

  Translation of Le Christ pour le monde, which was originally published under title: Cristo para o mundo.
  Bibliography: p.
  1. Jesus Christ—Person and offices. 2. Jesus Christ—History of doctrines. I. Title.
BT202.M3313 1974   232   74-1001
ISBN 0-8199-0460-0
ISBN 0-8199-0485-6 (pbk.)

Nihil Obstat:
  Daniel L. Flaherty S.J.
    *Provincial, Chicago Province
    of the Society of Jesus*

Imprimatur:
  Msgr. Richard A. Rosemeyer, J.C.D.
    Vicar General, Archdiocese of Chicago

January 16, 1974

MADE IN THE UNITED STATES OF AMERICA

CONTENTS

KEY TO ABBREVIATIONS

AA: Decree *Apostolicam Actuositatem* of Va-
                tican II
AAS: *Acta Apostolicae Sedis*, Rome, 1919 *seq.*
AG: Decree *Ad Gentes* of Vatican II.
CD: Decree *Christus Dominus* of Vatican II.
DACL: *Dictionnaire d'Archéologie Chrétienne et
                de Liturgie*, Paris, 1924 *seq.*
DB: Denzinger-Bannwarth, *Enchiridion sym-
                bolorum*, Freiburg.
DBS: *Dictionnaire de la Bible, Supplement,*
                Paris, 1928 *seq.*
DC: *Documentation catholique*, Paris.
DH: Decree *Dignitatis Humanae* of Vatican II.
DS: Denzinger-Schönmetzer: *Enchiridion
                symbolorum*, Freiburg, 1963.
DSAM: *Dictionnaire de Spiritualité Ascétique et
                Mystique*, Paris, 1932.
DCT: *Dictionnaire de Théologie Catholique,*
                Paris, 1903 *seq.*
DV: Dogmatic constitution *Dei Verbum* of
                Vatican II.
GS: Pastoral constitution *Gaudium et Spes*
                of Vatican II.
LG: Dogmatic constitution *Lumen Gentium*
                of Vatican II.
NA: Decree *Nostra Aetate* of Vatican II.

NRT:	*Nouvelle Revue Théologique*, Louvain, 1879 *seq*.
OE:	Decree *Orientalium Ecclesiarum* of Vatican II.
OT:	Decree *Optatam Totius* of Vatican II.
PC:	Decree *Perfectae Caritatis* of Vatican II.
PG or MG:	*Patrologia Graeca* (J. P. Migne), Paris, 1857-1866.
PL or ML:	*Patrologia Latina* (J. P. Migne), Paris, 1878-1890.
PO:	Decree *Presbyterorum Ordinis* of Vatican II.
PP:	Encyclical *Populorum Progressio* of Paul VI (1967).
PT:	Encyclical *Pacem in Terris* of John XXIII.
SC:	Constitution *Sacrosanctum Concilium* of Vatican II (1963).
UR:	Decree *Unitatis Redintegratio* of Vatican II.

TRANSLATOR'S NOTE

For most of the Vatican II documents used in this book, the translation is that given in *The Documents of Vatican II*, General Editor: Walter M. Abbott S.J. (America Press and Geoffrey Chapman, 1966). Acknowledgement is made as *Abbott*. Other papal documents and encyclicals, where an English translation is available, are quoted from those published by the Catholic Truth Society of England.

I wish to thank my colleague, Rev. Michael Downey, PH.L., S.T.L., of the Department of Divinity, University of London Institute of Education, Coloma College, West Wickham, Kent, England, who acted as theological adviser throughout this translation.

Malachy Carroll

PREFACE
THE PRINCIPAL THESIS
IN "CHRIST FOR THE WORLD"

When this book first appeared in French (Beauchesne: 1971), it was extensively reviewed, all the reviews being substantially favorable.[1] This has encouraged me, with a view to assisting the reader to its better understanding, to write a special preface for this translation. In it, I summarize the essential theses which the work seeks to present and develop, theses which I believe to be at least in part original. I then go on to indicate the problems which it opens up, and which, as far as I know, are scarcely dealt with anywhere else.

Clearly, the basic thesis of the book is set out in Chapter XI. It concerns the universal co-redemptive mission of the human person, within a Church redeemed and co-redemptive, in union with the Eucharistic Heart of Jesus and with a view to the transsecularization of the world. Every human person has the ability and the splendid vocation to transform and to make fruitful, for all mankind of every period, his trials and his death, by offering them to God, with and through Christ, in the Eucharist, for the salvation of mankind in time and in eternity. Consequently, the Incarnation of the Son of God becomes, in every sense of the world, an *In-humanation*.[2] Through his activity, each and every man can reach out, not just to a limited group (as Cardinal Journet seems to think[3]), but also to the utmost recesses of the human past and to the utmost limits of the human future.

This supplies the solution to the dilemma of Feuerbach and of many of the moderns: either God or man.[4] Already at the natural level,[5] each created person aspires in an obscure way to know and to embrace, within the whole of reality, all other created persons, seen and loved in God; and, to a greater extent, this is initially divinized by the supernatural co-redemptive vocation. The Scriptures direct our attention to this idea: for instance, there are the Deutero-Isaiah and the "corporate personality," the "good thief," and Simon of Cyrene, all symbolic of the destiny of everyman.

This basic thesis is expressed as follows in the present book: "The supernatural activity of each human person reaches out to the extreme limits of space and time. Each person is, in Christ, with Him, through Him, and for Him, an agent of the sacred and universal history of the human race" (p. 263).

The other theses prepare the way for, deploy, and complete this basic thesis of a universal Christian personalism. They can be listed as follows:

1. The pierced and glorified Heart of the Redeemer, willed as Savior of mankind, for His own glory and for that of His Father, is the key to universal history, the latter being the history of love: this is the thesis of the absolute and universal primacy of the Heart of the Lamb of God.

2. Jesus is inseparably the man-through-and-for-others, for the world, and the man-through-and-for-God. Through His human ancestors, through and with His human contemporaries, and for all mankind, He was, as Word made man, ever more and more man. He subordinates all His accidental relations with men to His constitutive relation with the Father as Son of

the Father. He takes up these accidental relations into the uncreated unity of this eternal Relation (144-147).

3. The Christ of the Gospel is the Christ of Nicaea I, only and consubstantial Son of the Father; the Christ of Chalcedon, perfect man, endowed with a rational soul, consubstantial with men; the Christ of Constantinople II, composite and synthetic Person, humanized God; the Christ of Constantinople III, Agent of our salvation by His divine will and through the instrumentality of His divinized human will, in entire submission to this divine will; the Christ of Trent, the Mediator who justifies our sinful free wills through the merits and the satisfactions of His Passion; the Christ of Vatican II—Prophet, Priest, and Recapitulator of mankind (194).

4. In order that, already in His public life, He may be the infallibly exact and true revealer of the Father's secrets, the pre-paschal Christ possesses, in His human intelligence, not only an experimental knowledge of the world but also an infused and prophetic knowledge of the distant and future events, and above all else the vision, in the face of His Father, of all the secrets of human hearts and of the divine will in the course of universal history (206). He is *the Christ-Prophet.*

5. It is here and now, and not merely in the past or in an indeterminate future, that the Spirit of Christ is at work to make the divine word resonate in the Church, and in the world through the Church. Even if it is true that at certain times the *religious language* may be, in its formulation, inadequately adapted to the particular needs of the people of those times, it will never be unintelligible and will always be intelligently listened to. To deny this would be to deny that the Holy Spirit, soul of the Church, is always active in the Church for the salvation of mankind. In relation to this basic statement, possible linguistic revisions are always secondary even when they are desirable, and such revisions are themselves the effect

of the assistance given by the Spirit to the Church of Christ (151-152).

6. The Sacrifice of *the death of the Christ-Priest* is the *sacrament of the sacrifice of all mankind*, the visible and efficacious sign of that sacrifice: Christ dies as a victim of loving holocaust in order to signify what each and every human death should be, and in order to effect in men this invisible and complete oblation. The visible sacrifice of the Mass makes visible on the altar the sacrifice of the Cross, now and henceforth invisible, and it is also the visible and efficacious sign, the sacrament, of the invisible and actual sacrifice of mankind in the measure in which men consent to the sacrifice which Christ has offered and offers in their name, and in the measure in which they associate themselves with this sacrifice of Christ (232-233; 345).

7. The virginity of Christ even unto death was a sacrifice which anticipated this Sacrifice, an act of His human free will by which the Word, far from renouncing the human male sexuality which He had assumed and which was already consecrated by His Inhumanation, consecrated this sexuality anew by unreservedly offering it up to the Father for the salvation of the world. By His celibacy, the only Son ceaselessly offered up to the Father, the conscious and voluntary, though painless, renunciation of an intense and specifically human pleasure of the senses and a lawful emotion of the heart, while uniting, in perfect joy, this renunciation with His future painful death, for the salvation of a sex-endowed humanity which profanes the divinization of its sexuality (280-281). *The celibacy of Jesus forms, therefore, an integral part of His redemptive sacrifice.*

8. Just as the death of Christ was not a disincarnation, a separation between His divine Person and His sacred Humanity, so too His Resurrection, far from being their reunion or a reincarnation, is the glorious and mysterious reanimation of His saving corpse by His created, holy, immortal soul, after their temporary

and real separation, with a view to giving Himself in the Eucharist to each of the baptized (237-238).

9. The risen Christ, *Lord and King*, is the sacrament *par excellence* who consecrates the world by consecrating Himself to the Father for the world. This *consecration of the world*, effected through the mediation of the Church, a priestly and hierarchized people, turns the whole world into a vast sign of God, a sign which gives God through the Church, the latter being the sacrament of salvation. In this way, the whole world becomes a sacrament, in the broad sense, for the man who knows how to read the signs of God. In the light of the transfigured and risen Christ, all things are transfigured in the presence of the Eternal, to the extent to which the mortal condition allows of such a transformation (172-173).

10. Each human person, called to baptism, is not adequately intelligible apart from the mystery of the Cross and of the Resurrection of Jesus. Christ reveals and manifests to man that he will remain eternally a mystery to himself—a mystery whose very incomprehensibility will be appreciated by him only in the beatific vision and the beatifying love as a participation in the inexhaustible incomprehensibility of the divine Love (222-223). *Man is himself a supernatural mystery* in his destiny, both as regards his body called to a glorious resurrection and as regards his soul, immortal by its very nature and supernaturally called to the beatific vision (275).

11. Through and in His Spirit, the Christ-Head incorporates with Himself the Church, in order then to offer the Church, in a homage of filial adoration, to His own Head and Recapitulator, the Father, through and in the same Spirit who is Their Bond (219).

12. There is no such thing as a post-Christian religion; religions which are still non-Christian are already pre-Christian: Christ and His one and universal Church are already active in them, though in a still imperfect way, in order to complete their redemption through the integration in Christ and the Church

of all the authentic values of these religions and of their faithful (38).

13. Through each and every atheist, Christ calls on His Church to do three things: to effect social justice, here and now, through her members; to develop to the utmost the potentialities of logical reason and of knowledge; to purify the faith (60).

14. The Church is the sacrament of salvation, not only because in her we find the Savior, but also because she is the privileged instrument of the Christ-Redeemer in the work of our salvation. The Church has been redeemed only in order that she, in her totality, may be co-redemptive. Redeemed through the Church, Christians are redeemed to the point of becoming her co-redeemers, in a relationship of unequal reciprocity. The Christian has greater need of the Church than the Church has of him. Through him, Christ continues to save the Church.

15. By an act of His human free will, the Man-Jesus has instituted the papacy, in obedience to the salvific design of the Father (cf. Jn. 6, 38-39), in order that all may be one in faith and in mutual love (332), within a prayer adoring the will of the Father (cf. Jn. 8, 29; 17 passim).

16. The *primacy of Peter* is at once a primacy of jurisdiction and a primacy of love. It constitutes *a contingent, limited, temporary and "sacramental"* participation in the *absolute, eternal*, and universal primacy of Jesus Christ, the Alpha and the Omega (cf. Col. 1, 18). Recognition of the dependent and adoring primacy of Peter constitutes a concrete form of the recognition of the absolute and universal Primacy of Christ the Redeemer (297 ff.).

17. Peter's *infallibility* and fullness of power are limited participations in the infallibility and fullness of power of the Man-Jesus, in the service of the infallible act of faith of all the members of the People of God. The charism of infallibility or of infallible service of the truth is a gift through which the Other Paraclete, the Spirit of Truth, pays homage, by glorifying Him,

to the First Paraclete, Jesus Christ, and, through Him, to the Father, because every doctrinal declaration of the Church is Christ-centered and always constitutes a collaboration in the salvific work of the Christ-Prophet, to the glory of the Father (197; 299 ff.; 312 ff.).

18. Like the sacraments and the Scriptures, like all the other ministries, the ministry of Peter will therefore come to an end with the ending of the heavens and the earth. It constitutes one structure of the New Covenant, while carrying a resemblance to the figures of the Old; it is a scaffolding erected before the facade of the Church during the earthly period, and is doomed to disappear on the Last Day when the construction of the Kingdom of Christ will have been completed. Indispensable in our exile for communion in truth and in love, this mortal ministry will die with the language of men and with the sacraments of the Church (312).

19. The *Eucharistic concelebration* by bishops from all parts of the world assembled with the bishop of Rome, is the supreme manifestation on earth, the supreme expression, of *the inner essence of the Church*, in pilgrimage towards her Lord. The pope figures there as vicar of Christ, as sacrament-person of the episcopal collegiality, as model of the pastor of the one flock (330-331).

20. In honoring and adoring the *Eucharistic Heart of Jesus*, the Church expresses her love for the two-fold act of love, eternal and historically past, by which our Redeemer has instituted the Sacrifice and the Sacrament of the Eucharist; and for the twofold act of love—eternal and present, uncreated and divine, but also created, voluntary, and sensible—which leads Him to immolate Himself now and perpetually, through His priests and for our salvation, to the Father, to remain constantly with us in our tabernacles, and to unite Himself physically with each of the baptized in Communion, so that here and now, in us and through us, He may love all men with a sacrificial love.

21. Christ, author and perfecter of the liberating

development, is the Prophet of the growth of mankind, their Priest and their Victim, their Recapitulator. *The Eucharist is the sacrifice of the development:* in It, Christ offers His life to the Father for the supernatural success of the whole human process at whose head He has placed Himself. He constantly redeems His Church to the point of making her the co-redemptrix of the growth of the world; consequently, the whole human universe, even at the natural level, benefits from the bloody sacrifice of the Redeemer (424).

22. Through Communion, Christ effects the temporal and salvific involvement of the Christian. The Eucharist, sacrament of perseverance in fraternal love and in involvement in the service of the temporal development of others, reveals itself as the efficacious sign of the very goal of human growth—the glorious resurrection (Jn. 6, 54). The Eucharist takes on, therefore, the character of *the sacrament of integral human development.* As such, it emerges as being the purpose itself of the In-humanation of the Word. Through the Eucharist, Christ "trans-secularizes" Christians—i.e. He causes them to pass from this world, with Him, to the Father, in the very act through which these Christians commit themselves to live, not for themselves, but for others and for Him-in-the-others (423-424).

23. Christ not only offers to all His disciples, but positively gives to them the supreme "evangelical counsel" of daily Communion when He, who is Himself the Bread of eternal life, makes them ask the Father in His name: "Give us this day our daily bread." The existential choice in favor of the daily breaking of the Eucharistic Bread leads, through the special grace of this sacrament, to the perfection of abnegation, and consequently promotes that self-relinquishment which conditions both personal and social development. That is why, if it is to be fully and supernaturally efficacious, the existential decision to work for the development of all mankind takes the form of a decision to receive Communion daily, when this is practicable. The decision concerning development and

the decision concerning daily Communion, therefore, involve one another. The daily breaking of the Bread of Life affects the whole Christian personality, as its most powerful means of psychological, social, and ontological integration (426-427).

24. The decision concerning sacramental and daily participation in the redemptive death of Christ may be regarded as an "existential macro-decision" which will give meaning and supernatural and eternal efficacy to all the "micro-decisions" taken in the service of human development. It is a decision to offer up one's personal death, a decision reached in inseparable union with the sacrifice of Christ on the Cross as renewed in the Eucharist. *The existential macro-decision concerning daily Communion modulates, therefore, into the existential decision par excellence concerning the co-redemptive oblation of the death to come*, a decision whose ultimate renewal in the final meritorious act of the free will recapitulates all the previous existential decisions and seals them with a definitive seal by conferring on them a meaning which is henceforth immutable, thus constituting *the supreme existential decision* (429-430; 125). "The supernatural activity of each human person reaches out to the extreme limits of space and of time. Each person is, in Christ, with Him, through Him, and for Him, an agent of the sacred and universal history of the human race" (263).

25. Coinciding with the sacrificial death of the last predestined, the Parousia of Jesus will manifest the universal action of His human free will. As instrument of His divine free will, it will transform, "according to the operation whereby also he is able to subdue all things unto himself" (Phil., 3, 21), the whole cosmos in order to make it the abode of the glorified bodies raised up simultaneously with the Parousia. Thus the Parousia will communicate the divine Goodness to the material world, for the benefit of the predestined; *the universe will become the priestly and inseparable garment of the divine Word made human priest.* Far from being a universalizing of the Eucharistic transub-

stantiation, the parousiac transfiguration will coincide
with its definitive disappearance, because it constitutes
the end in every sense of this word (363).

26. Through man's work and for his survival, a
part of the universe has become the bread of his mortal life; then, through the painful work of the Man-
God in His Passion and through the words of His emis-
saries it has become His Body and Blood, the Bread
and the Drink of eternal life, in order finally that this
whole humanized universe, the priestly garment of
the incarnate Word, will allow the eternal and immanent Sun of His divine Person to shine eternally
through it in a ceaseless "diaphany." The whole universe, thus "trans-signified and trans-finalized" by
the created free will and the created soul of the Word,
will cease to be the food and the sustenance of a
yet unperfected mankind, in order to become their
transparent bond, their reward, their glorified extension in total submission to them, the new earth merited
by the sacrifice and by the eating of the Eucharist
(366-367; 387).

27. The decision of the parousiac transformation
will be, in the created will of Jesus, a decision taken in
the unique act of beatifying love which results from
the unique act of the beatific vision in His human intelligence. By the *same and single* act of love through
which, in the first instant of His conception in the
womb of the Immaculate Virgin Mary, He embraced
the salvific will of the Father and instituted the Eucharist at the Last Supper, the Man-Jesus will effect,
through His parousiac decision, the transfiguration of
a cosmos at last in full conformity with the image
and the glory of man and of God, the consummation
of the universe and of history. This unique act of beatifying love effected by the Man-Jesus has never passed
away, and will never do so (363 and 367).

28. In adoring the Eucharistic Heart of Jesus, the
Church loves not only the past and present sacrificial
love of her Savior, which she proclaims until He comes,
but also the twofold loving act of His glorious return,

an eternal divine act and a human and unique act, to come and already present, by which His glorified Heart, forever wounded with love, will subject and assimilate to Himself the entire physical universe, will raise up all hearts, and will manifest perfectly to all His predestined the inexhaustible incomprehensibility of His creative, sacrificial and rewarding love, received from the Father and having the Father's glory as its final purpose.

In loving this Eucharistic and Parousiac Heart, the Church loves the threefold love—sensible, voluntary, and divine—by which this Heart will gather into a consummated unit the universe and herself, in order to recapitulate them in offering them to the Father (388).

In presenting these theses, we have arranged them in a sequence more logical than that in which they appear in the book itself, where the context makes this or that expression more intelligible. No doubt, one or other or even several of these theses may be open to question.

NOTES TO PREFACE

1. I have since developed some of these themes in a brochure: *Le Coeur de l'Agneau de Dieu,* published by the Apostleship of Prayer, Gregorian University Press, Rome, 1972. The numbers used in this preface refer to the pages of the book itself.

2. As one exegete has pointed out, we could and should have cited in our Chapter Eleven, in support of its thesis on the co-redemptive Church, the words of Paul to the Corinthians: "Always bearing about in our body the mortification of Jesus, that the life also of Jesus may be made manifest in our bodies . . . So then death works in us; but life in you" (2 Cor. 4, 10-12).

3. See Chapter XI, however, where we express our great admiration for the theological work of Cardinal Journet.

4. Cf. H. de Lubac S.J.: *Le drame de l'humanisme athée* Paris, 1944.

5. P. 262.

INTRODUCTION
JESUS, YESTERDAY, TODAY,
AND THE SAME FOREVER

At the outset, the reader may rightly expect to be given some information about certain circumstances concerning the origin of this book, its purpose, and the organization of its parts.

In the fall of 1967, the author gave a course of Christology in the English language section of the Faculty of Theology of the University of Saint Paul, Ottawa. Having had occasion to deal in this course with certain current problems and authors, he thought it useful to communicate to the ever increasing body of theological students and to his professional colleagues, both Catholic and non-Catholic, the fruits of his researches not only into these present currents of thought, but also into other aspects, less frequently considered from the same viewpoint, of Catholic Christology. Notably, he has chosen to emphasize the trinitarian bedrock of the christological doctrine, in order to fit in with a course on the Trinity given at the Christo-Rei Faculty of Theology in Sao Leopoldo (Rio Grando do Sul, Brazil).

Christ for the World: this title, borrowed from the Bread of Life discourse (Jn. 6, 51), epitomizes and symbolizes a vision of Christ as Redeemer who, far from being against the world and seeking to condemn it, has come to give Himself to save the world; a vision of Christ present to the world through His Church and His Eucharist, in the dynamism of His divinizing power; a vision, finally, of a Christ who wills to live and grow in every man and in the whole of mankind, for the glory of the Father. The world is the immediate *raison d'être* of Christ.

The Heart of the Lamb: this sub-title intimates that the reader will find several allusions here to the sacrificial love of the Lord, a love which illuminates and transfigures each of the particular christological aspects dealt with. It also serves to synthesize the symbols which have embodied the Christian cult: may one not say that, in general terms, the Christ of the first millenium of our era presents Himself as Shepherd[1] and Lamb, whose Heart reveals itself more manifestly in the course of the second? Finally, the sub-title throws light on the title: Christ gives His flesh "for the life of the world," only by being the Lamb of God who bears and takes away its sin (Jn. 1, 29), by accepting in advance that this sin should pierce, for ever, His Side (Jn. 19, 34-37).

This sub-title also signifies that the author fully adopts the thought expressed by the Sovereign Pontiff to the Society of Jesus: "Will not this cult of the Sacred Heart you are propagating, be for you a most efficacious instrument serving that spiritual and moral renewal of the modern world called for by the Second Vatican Council, and enabling you fruitfully to fulfill your allotted mission to combat atheism?"[2] We hold that, properly understood, this cult is, for reasons both objective and subjective, a source of renewal for theological thought.

Part One attempts to answer the question: Why Jesus? Every vision of Christ is conditioned by the answer given to this question.

But how does Christ appear to those of our contemporaries whose ideas have had the greatest resonance during the past few decades and especially in recent years? What forms have the answers taken which each has given to the question: Why Jesus? How far can we follow them and make our own their christological vision? In what sense can Teilhard, Bultmann, and Bonhoeffer help us to deepen our Catholic Christology? Should we apply to their orientations Lacordaire's idea: "Always, in the heart of man, in the attitudes of mind, in the currents of opinion, in laws, in things and in times, there is a base of operation for God; the great art is to discern it and to make use of it, while placing in the secret and invisible power of God Himself the principle of its courage and of its hope."[3]

Lacordaire has used the decisive word: *to discern.* It signifies that one is not seeking, *a priori* and at all costs, to retain all or to reject all. A certain sympathy in argumentation is, anyhow, a condition of understanding.[4]

Chapter Eight forms a transition between the study of the authors mentioned and the synthetic sounding of the Catholic Christology which is the matter of Part Three. It deals with the relationship between Christology and secularization—a problem which brings home to us the urgent need for a more searching study of the face of Christ such as the Magisterium of the Church has presented it to our view (Chapters Nine and Ten) at Trent and at Vatican II.

In this third part, we have attempted a closer investigation of the mission of the *Agnus Pantocrator* or Master-of-all, the immediate and redemptive finality of His "in-humanation,"* with its historical and sacramental extensions—the Church (including the Pope), the Eucharist, the development. Could one, today, establish contact with Christ while ignoring these extensions? Could not a theologian, writing in a devel-

---

*Translator's note: This term, used a number of times in this book, could be paraphrased as "the becoming embedded in mankind."

oping nation, reflect on the relationship between this
development and the mystery of Jesus?

In the course of this third part, an attempt is made—
a very imperfect attempt, we confess—to show that the
Eucharist is the concrete and living synthesis of the
whole Revelation. The Christ whom people today are
tentatively seeking is the living, present, acting Christ:
the Christ of the Mass, of the Tabernacle, of the
Communion. The Christ for the world is in the world,
seeking (cf. Jn. 4, 23) "true worshippers" who will
worship Him and His Father "in spirit and truth." "In
the Eucharistic Mystery," Pius XII proclaimed in 1954,
"man concretely discovers and experiences his past,
his present, and his future as a unity in Christ. . . .
The secret and the spring of the renewal of social life
is to be found only in the Church, and, through her,
in the Eucharist."[5]

For each of us, for the Church, for pilgrim humanity,
Jesus is the same yesterday, today, tomorrow, and
always. The world, the Church, the human person
evolve and change: Christ "will never die again,"[6]
Christ does not change. The Christ of tomorrow will
be the Christ of yesterday, enhanced by us if we are
faithful to the Christ of today. "Jesus Christ is the
same yesterday and today and for ever" (Heb. 13, 8).
Vatican II "maintains that beneath all changes there
are many realities which do not change and which
have their ultimate foundation in Christ who is the
same yesterday and today, and for ever."[7] Only
Christ, and the Christ of the Eucharist, can satisfy
the basic need of modern man: the need for renewal
and for growth within identity. Without growth, man
falls apart: in the Eucharist, on the contrary, man
is unified that he may unify all things.

It is, in effect, the Eucharist which is "the concrete
realization of that great phrase of Saint Paul's: *Christus heri et hodie, ipse et in saecula: there* the Christ
of the past re-lives, *there* lives the Christ of the present, and *there* the Christ of eternity anticipates His
life."[8]

We would add quite simply that the Christ whom modern man is seeking is also the Christ of tomorrow. In Chapters Fourteen and Fifteen, therefore, we deal with the future which seems to be in store for us, and which anyhow seems to us to be wished for—viz. the cult of the Eucharistic Heart of Jesus. Is it not in the light of this cult that the Church will reveal herself more and more as the Spouse of the Lamb, the city redeemed to become co-redemptrix (Chapter Eleven)?

The above, then, is a short sketch of the themes treated here.

The reader must not expect to find in this work a systematic Christology, or even an exhaustive treatment of the problems discussed, for that is not our aim. Nor must he expect to find a systematic study of the theology of the Eucharist, especially of the problems raised today by certain Dutch theologians; for, equally, that is not our intention here.

We have no illusions about the limitations of this work. However, we do hope that it will serve a useful purpose, and that it will provoke further reflections to extend and prolong what may be original in it (notably on the celibacy of Christ: Chapter Twelve).

At least, we may presume to say with Saint Augustine: "I have attempted . . . not so much to speak with authority of things that I know, as to seek to know them by speaking about them with reverence."[9]

It remains to thank all those who, directly and indirectly, by their prayers, their reflections, their writings, have helped me in the composition of this book. Special thanks are due to the Father Librarians of the University of Saint Paul in Ottawa and of the Cristo-Rei Faculty of Theology in Sao Leopoldo; to the benefactors (relatives and friends) who have sent books to me. Very special thanks are due to Father Jacques Dupuis S.J., professor of dogmatic theology at the scholasticate of Kurseong (India), whose course of Christology, still unpublished, had been of assistance to me (especially with the subjects treated in Chapter One).

Finally, I ask our readers to have the kindness to let me know their reactions, even of a dissenting nature. Such a dialogue would enable us to grow in the knowledge and love of the Truth, who is Christ, and to bear witness to Him, together and in imitation of Him; since He Himself has said: "For this I was born, and for this I have come into the world, to bear witness to the truth . . . I am the truth" (Jn. 18, 37; 14, 6).

Cristo-Rei Faculty of Theology, Sao Leopoldo, RGS, Brazil.
The Feast of Saint Damasus, 11 December 1968.

The Author

NOTES TO INTRODUCTION

1. Cf. a text cited by Dom H. Leclercq, DACL, t. XIII, 2 (1938), col. 2272, art. Pasteur (Bon): "The image of the Good Shepherd was for our fathers in the Faith (the early Christians) what the image of the Crucified is for the faithful of our day." On the Christ-Lamb, see D. H. Leclercq, *ibid.*, t. 1, 1 (1907) col. 877 sq.: art. Agneau; and Mangenot, DTC, t. 1, col. 579-582 (art. Agneau) Paris, 1903.

2. Paul VI, Allocution *Voluimus* to the Society of Jesus: 16 November 1966, AAS, 58 (1966), 1177.

3. Cited by Y.-M.-J. Congar O.P., *Les voies du Dieu vivant,* Paris, 1962, p. 330.

4. We have attempted to apply the same method of discernment to the American Protestant theologian in our book: *Reinhold Niebuhr, théologien de la communauté mondiale* (Desclée de Brouwer, 1969).

5. Pius XII: Allocution *Quest'ora* of 29 May 1954, AAS, 46 (1954), 311-312. The Pope adds: "Priests should orientate orientate all their pastoral and apostolic activity in the light of the Eucharistic sun."

6. Rom. 6, 9.

7. GS, 10, 2.

8. A. Tesnière, *Somme de la prédication eucharistique, le Coeur de Jésus-Christ,* t. II, *La Révélation eucharistique du Sacré-Coeur,* Tourcoing, Brussels, 1904, p. 96.

9. Saint Augustine: *de Trinitate*, I, v, 8.

PART ONE:

WHY JESUS?

1

WHY JESUS CHRIST?
ABSOLUTE AND UNIVERSAL PRIMACY
OF THE CHRIST-REDEEMER

Christ, God's masterpiece, need not ever have come into existence. In teaching us this fundamental truth, the Church shows her respect for the transcendent freedom of God, while at the same time kindling our minds to reflect on the meaning of the Incarnation in the divine plan.

Our claim to know an existent demands several things: primarily, that we know what it is, its essence; but also that we are aware of its *raison d'être*, and even of the fundamental operations or activities by which it attains its ends.

We do not adequately define Jesus by describing Him as the Logos or the incarnate Son of the Father. Really to know the Word and to enjoy more abundantly the eternal life which Jesus has come to give us (cf. Jn. 10, 10), we must also discern, in the luminous darkness of faith, the purpose pursued by Him in His Incarnation.

Too many Christians take for granted the fact of Christ in history and in their own lives, without asking: Why Christ?

To answer this, we must study the Divine Revelation, and in particular, the Scriptures.

3

The New Testament appears to state simultaneously that the world exists for Christ (Col. 1, 15) and that Christ came for our salvation (1 Tim. 1, 15) and for our divinization (Eph. 1, 3-18).

The Magisterium of the Church, the proximate norm of truth for every Christian and especially for the theologian,[1] requires us to profess that the Only Son of God was made flesh for our salvation (Nicene-Constantinople Creed). At the same time, this Magisterium allows full liberty of discussion among differing schools of theological thought, about how this is to be explained.

Does humanity itself exist for Christ, is creation itself ordained to the glory of Christ, or, on the contrary, is Christ ordained to the glory of the human race? Has God willed Christ in an absolute or relative way? Is Christ essentially the Centre of the Universe, or the Redeemer of humanity? We shall first recapitulate the answers given to these questions by the Thomist and Scotist schools, and their traditional expression; we shall then go on to show how certain modern theologians, Thomists and Scotists among others, are leading us towards a more ample and more harmonious solution, partly specified by Vatican II and completely illuminated by the triple love of the Heart of Jesus.

A. Answers of Traditional Thomism and Scotism

A certain traditional Thomism follows Saint Thomas Aquinas in the examination of the hypothesis: had man not sinned, would the Word have been made flesh? The answers lean towards a negative,[2] since here there is a tendency to ascribe to the Incarnation an exclusively redemptive final purpose, ordained to an adequate and superabundant satisfaction offered to God for the salvation of the human race.

It follows from this that the primacy of Christ is a fact of the actual order chosen by God; that this primacy belongs to the Man-God as a corollary of His Incarnation, but fully depends on the historic accident of sin. Without sin, no Christ. Jesus is not a first thought of God, but an after-thought in the divine plan. God initially planned the world without Christ, the latter being subsequently willed as adequate repairer of what had been ruined in Adam.

On the other hand, for traditional Scotism, Christ was not even relatively necessary to the Redemption. God willed the Incarnation independently of sin and of the Redemption, prior to both, in order to be perfectly loved by the Man Jesus, His masterpiece and the *raison d'être* of the universe. To this cosmic role was added, later and accidentally, the redemptive mission.[3]

Had Adam not sinned, the Word would still have been made flesh. Christ is not, therefore, an after-thought in the divine plan, but rather the first and even, in a sense, the sole idea of God. The Blessed Duns Scotus is explicit: "Had neither angel nor man sinned, Christ would have been predestined *in se*, even if no other person except Him had been created." Consequently, the primacy of Christ is not only a *de facto* primacy arising from His redemptive mission, but also a *de jure* primacy. Jesus Christ represents the final, exemplary and even meritorious cause of the creation of the universe.

In a word, the Christ of the Thomist tradition is essentially the Redeemer of an accidentally Christian cosmic order. He is the Christ-for-us. On the other hand, the Christ of the Scotist tradition is willed for His own sake, and the universe, essentially Christian, is willed for Him. He is not for us: we are for Him.

One can appreciate that, when properly posed, the question is not an academic or a merely hypothetical one. What is involved is our existential relationship with the Person of Christ in the actual concrete order— the only order which God has ever had in view and the only one which He has brought into historical existence.

B. Modern Investigations of Thomism and Scotism

1. Before dealing with authors who explicitly rank themselves among the upholders of these traditional

currents of ideas, we turn our attention to certain views held by Scheeben.

This Cologne theologian holds that the Incarnation has taken place for a plurality of purposes polarized by one supreme purpose.

> If we confess in the Creed that the Son of God was made flesh for us men, we do not mean that love for mankind was the primary and the supreme motive of the Incarnation. . . . God could not have willed Christ solely for the creature; Christ is infinitely more precious than all creatures; creatures exist and are loved for His sake, more than He exists and is willed for the sake of creatures. . . . More than in the deliverance and elevation of the creature, the motive of the Incarnation is to be found in the love of God for Himself, who wills to reveal exteriorly His trinitarian glory, in the love of God for Christ to whom He wills to communicate Himself in an infinite manner as to no creature. This is something which we do not exclude, but rather take for granted, when we gratefully confess that the Son of God was made man for us men.[4]

These ideas of Scheeben admirably synthesize the conclusions that must logically be drawn from the declarations of Trent and of Vatican I. Between the two Councils, Saint Lawrence of Brindisi had already, and perhaps more clearly, pointed in the direction Scheeben was to take.

In effect, the triple final purpose of the justification is presented by Trent as "the glory of God and of Christ, and eternal life,"[5] while Vatican I declares anathema those who deny that the world was created for the glory of God.[6] From this we can conclude, resorting to an analogy, that the Incarnation, summit of the creation, has for its immediate purpose eternal life and the salvation of mankind; for its mediate purpose, the glory of Christ; and for its final purpose, the glory of the Father.[7]

Furthermore, Vatican II shows us that these three purposes merge into one purpose: "God is fully glorified provided that men consciously and fully accept His work of salvation which He has accomplished in Christ".[8] The utimate and mediate purposes—the glory of God the Father and of His Christ—are realized only through the attainment of the immediate purpose, the redemptive divinization of mankind.

The same direction is taken by the ideas of Saint Lawrence of Brindisi, Doctor of the Church: the purposes of the Incarnation are the salvation of the world, the glory of Christ, the manifestation of the power of God.[9] In this way, the post-Tridentine Capuchin preacher had already synthesized the views of the *Doctor angelicus* and of the *Doctor Subtilis*, Saint Thomas and the Blessed Duns Scotus.

2. In our time, Father J.-F. Bonnefoy O.F.M. (1897-1958) decidedly and explicitly rejected a part, admittedly a secondary part, of the Scotist view. He held that it was not incidentally that Christ was the Redeemer, and that the Redemption was not a modification of the initial divine plan. Among many possible worlds, Father Bonnefoy argued, God chose to create one in which sin, not willed but merely permitted, constituted the setting for the Redemptive Incarnation.[10] The absolute and universal primacy of the Christ-Redeemer *as man is* thus proclaimed—the primacy of that Christ Jesus who merits, and is the model and reason for existence of all other creatures.[11]

3. Yet more recently, Father Humbert Bouesse O.P. has put forward a parallel argument, but in the opposite direction. He has emphasized the numerous texts of Saint Thomas Aquinas[12] through which, in a variety of ways, the Doctor Angelicus has completed his *Summa Theologica* by presenting other views about the purposes of the Incarnation and about the primacy of Christ.

Let us emphasize, with Father Bouesse, that the redemptive final purpose of the Incarnation, so often set in relief by Saint Thomas, does not signify that

Christ is made subordinate to men or to their salvation.[13] If Christ is primordially Redeemer, He is such for His own glory and for that of His Father: "all are yours; and you are Christ's; and Christ is God's" (1 Cor. 3, 22-23).

The whole christological doctrine, including the primacy of Christ, can be deduced from His ontological structure as Redeemer. It is not, as Duns Scotus held, purely and simply from the mystery of the Word Incarnate, but from His redemptive finality that we may deduce the fact that Jesus Christ is, for all men, the principle of holiness and of glorification.

Bouesse even goes so far as to write:

> God had permitted the fall of the human race in its natural head, with divine foreknowledge and anticipation of the supernatural Head: the Christ-Redeemer. In a sense, the universe was primarily ordained to the glory of the Christ-Reedemer. For it is impossible that, in the primary and unique intention of God's universal Providence, all His works—in the order of their ontological gradation, natural and supernatural—should not have been directed towards the exaltation of that divine masterpiece, the splendid Priest of sinful humanity. Man's sin, which lies at the root of the Incarnation, is conquered and swallowed up in Him who is the culmination and highest expression of human kind. The Christ-Redeemer, dead on the cross for the salvation of mankind, is ultimately greater and more glorious in the eyes of God, and therefore more beneficial for the world which He crowns and perfects, than would have been a Christ who had come merely to complete an innocent world.[14]

For Bouesse, the Christ-Redeemer, masterpiece of God, is also the masterpiece of the universe and of human history, and even (an allusion to the Resurrection) the masterpiece that has structured its own development.[15]

4. In 1961, Father Martelet[16] introduced two important points into the discussion.

On the one hand, he has emphasized the necessary theological function of the imaginary and of hypothetical considerations, showing how by consideration of imaginary situations, even those totally different from the actual situation play a part in theology.

This point has been stressed by the Magisterium of the Church: to recognize what God could have but has not done, is, in the view of the Magisterium, one of the legitimate ways of acknowledging the complete freedom of the whole supernatural order. The encyclical *Humani Generis* points out that there is nothing *per se* impossible and contradictory in the idea of the world and mankind without grace and without Christ, even though there has never been a reality corresponding to such an idea.[17] Far from suppressing Christ by this momentary envisaging of the non-existent, one proves, on the contrary, that one receives Him truly as a Gift deriving solely from God's freely willed love. The hypothesis of a world without Christ is a necessary and paradoxical possibility of Christ's actual existence.

When we consider the purpose of the Incarnation, the consideration of an imaginary situation demonstrates, not in this case that Christ did not have to come, but that having come He takes the first place.

In this sense, traditional Scotism is more profoundly Biblical than Thomism. Saint Thomas regards as potentially normal a point which the Scriptures absolutely ignore—a world of grace without Christ! The Scripture never eliminates Christ from the world, or from the creation, or from the divinization, or from the Redemption. However, Scotism is not completely faithful to the Scriptures, since the former does not connect in any radical way, the Incarnation with the idea of making men sons of God in and through Christ.

Neither Scotism nor Thomism is fully Biblical. The latter envisages as hypothetically possible a non-existence of Christ which the Scriptures never entertain;

the latter masks[18] a redemptive economy always underlined by the Scriptures. The envisaging of the contrary supposition of an unreal hypothesis (Had Adam not sinned . . .) shows the limits of the two systems when confronted with Divine Revelation.

On the other hand, as Suarez well understood, it is precisely this Divine Revelation, in Eph. 1, 3-8, which makes clear to us that the purpose of the Incarnation was to make men sons of God.

In this prologue to Ephesians, Saint Paul clearly appears to be establishing a relationship between the mystery of the Incarnation and that of our filial divinization, of our supernatural adoption as sons of God in the Blood of Christ. The "In-humanation" of the Word finds in sin the reason for its redemptive aspect, and in filial adoption its *raison d'être* as Incarnation.

In short, for Paul, Jesus Christ has as *raison d'être* the justifying and divinizing Redemption of mankind, for his own glory and that of His Father:

> Blessed be the God and Father of our Lord Jesus Christ, who has blessed us in Christ with every spiritual blessing in the heavenly places, even as he chose us in him before the foundation of the world, that we should be holy and blameless before him. He destined us in love to be his sons through Jesus Christ. . . . In him we have redemption through his blood, the forgiveness of our trespasses, according to the riches of his grace . . . for the praise of his glory.[19]

As can be seen, Paul clearly seems to subordinate Redemption and filial adoption to "the praise of his glory"—i.e. the glory of the Father. Suarez enables us to find in Paul the very order of the final purposes of the Incarnation, the order glimpsed by Saint Lawrence of Brindisi.

The divine plan appears to have a number of purposes arranged in this order: the In-humanation of the Word through His insertion into mankind has for its purpose the divinizing redemption of mankind, for the glory of the grace of Christ and, ultimately, for the glory of the Father.

One finds scattered elements of this synthesis in the Fathers of the Church, but these elements had not yet been brought together. Saint Augustine is a notable instance of this: "He who was God becomes man in order to make gods of those who were men";[20] "He descended that we might ascend, and remaining in his own nature he was made a participator of our nature so that, remaining in our nature, we might be made participators in his nature";[21] "Christ dies that the Church may be."[22]

5. The intervention of Father Schillebeeckx, in 1962,[23] further deepened reflection on our subject.

The importance and the profundity of the pre-conciliar christological views of the Flemish theologian lead us to deal with them here in some detail. As will be seen, they bring anthropology and Scripture into harmonious association.

Christ has lived for the Father (cf. Jn. 4, 34). That is His reason for living, and it is our reason too, in Him.

For Christ, to be man is to be *man-with-us (Mitmensch)*. His human involvement is a mission to live for others. The call which affects the human freedom of Christ is a task which concerns life for others from His communion with the Father. There is no point in regarding Christ as Supreme Being existing for His own sake, independently of His task as man-with-us. That would involve a purely Scotist abstraction.

Christ is for mankind (Jn. 3, 16; Rom. 8, 32) and mankind is, yet more profoundly, for Christ (Jn. 17, 1-2; 3, 35; 13, 3).

Being man is not, for Christ, a mere fact, but an ethico-religious mission.

From Biblical expressions such as Son of Man, Messiah, Servant of God, one sees that Christ is, in a supernatural way, all humanity, *the* Man *(der Mensch)*.

This representative function is rooted, not in the hypostatic union as such, but in a particular hypostatic union, in an Incarnation of a determinate kind. In tak-

ing flesh, the Son of God becomes not only man, but
representative man, our representative all in all, the
Messiah—and this in virtue of a vocation *(Berufung)*.

God has constituted the man Jesus as the Church,
in the sense that Jesus gathers all men together into
one people and that His human actions are constitutive
of the Church.

This role of representative of all mankind gathered
together in Him is, for Christ, a vocation which He is
to fulfill in history, gaining through fidelity to this
vocation, the Church as His mystical body. His fulfillment of this task takes the form of human involvement
(Mitmenschlichkeit). In virtue of a disposition of Divine Providence, He is simultaneously Himself and all
of us. The Incarnation is the constituting of the messianic Man: Jesus, Son of God.

It is solely Christ, put to death for our sin but resurrected from the dead, who is the significance and the
convergence point *(Mittelpunkt)* of the creation, of
history, and of the order of grace. The most exalted
meaning of the creation is the Lord-Servant who,
through His fidelity to His mission, has won for us the
Spirit of holiness.

Christ is fully the one and only Lord, but He has
acquired this lordship through His love. It is a primacy
which was for Christ a task to be achieved, confided
to Him by the Father; a primacy which, by His love,
He has wrested from sin, and from His adversary, the
Prince of this world. Every primacy of another kind
is foreign[24] to the Bible (Cf. Col. 1, 15; 1, 18; 1 Pet. 1,
20; Eph. 1, 4).

Involved here are a redemptive divinization and a
divinizing redemption. In Hebrew, *Jesus* means *Redeemer*. I believe, Schillebeeckx insists, only in a true
universal primacy of the Christ-Redeemer. In the other
conceptions, the reality of the intersubjectivity of the
transcendent God with actual men is disregarded.[25]

Sacrificial love is the key to the mystery of the
reality. We owe everything to this love, even our very
existence as men.[26] We must see the Christ concretely

in the Redeemer, not abstractly as the metaphysical masterpiece of God's omnipotence, or as the most perfect adorer—in isolation—of the Father, or as the Omega point of the cosmic evolution.[27]

God the Father, through the Son and in the Spirit, gives Himself as motive and life-force to the Man-Jesus, in order that this Man may live for the salvation of mankind through love for the Father. God also gives Himself to us, in Christ, as our motive and life-force, in order that we may live in the world with our brethren in shared humanity and in communion with the Father.

The Man-Jesus is not the ultimate: He manifests a deeper reality—viz., the inward life of the triune God who, to be God, had no need of us or of Jesus but has willed to be God-for-us in Christ. He is problem-devoid Love involved in problem-beset mankind. It is from the created world and from the history of salvation that we, who are neither immediately nor fully comprehensible to ourselves, contemplate the inward self-intelligibility of God.

All this represents the position taken up by the Flemish Dominican theologian in 1962. Retaining the most valuable attitudes of the Thomist school, while deepening them in the light of valid contributions from modern philosophy, Schillebeeckx showed himself to be a resolute upholder of the absolute ontological primacy of the Christ-Redeemer.

His rightful insistence on the "co-humanity" *(Mitmenschlichkeit)* of Jesus is doubly traditional: it merely expresses in modern terminology what the Council of Chalcedon said about the consubstantiality of Jesus with humanity;[28] and what, much later, Saint Thomas (following Aristotle) said about man as "social animal." It is here, precisely, that the Scotist abstraction falls to pieces—the abstraction which enabled Duns Scotus to entertain the idea of a Christ who would be the only man in existence, without "co-men," the perfect adorer of the Father.

On the eve of Vatican II, one could already discern

the lines of deep agreement which contemporary Catholic theology was already tracing, in spite of numerous individual qualifications.

The convergence-point seems to be acceptance of the absolute ontological primacy, in the divine plan, of the Christ-Redeemer, the Alpha and the Omega of the design of the Creation. There is a greater recognition that neither the Incarnation nor the Redemption is an *a posteriori* accident in the divine plan. This unique economy, *raison d'être* of the Creation, implies the Paschal mystery of the death and resurrection of the Christ-Savior. God has willed in an inseparable way the immolated Lamb and those who were immolating Him and for whom He was immolating Himself. One can and should distinguish between Christ and mankind, but not separate the two; because, in becoming man, the Word willed to be so through man (His ancestors), with and for all men. No one is as much a "social animal" as the Redeemer of human society.

C. Vatican II: Partial Renewal of the Problem: 1964-1965

It was not one of the aims of Vatican II to treat *ex professo* the purposes of the Incarnation. Nonetheless, it has dealt with this matter through numerous allusions to it, especially in the texts promulgated in 1964 and 1965—the decreees on ecumenism and on the missions, the pastoral constitution *Gaudium et Spes*.

The essential progress made by Vatican II is towards a deeper understanding of the social aspects of the Incarnation and of the Redemption. Through this progress, we can understand more clearly the immediate purpose of the In-humanation of the Word, and, consequently, its mediate and final purposes—the glory of the Lamb and that of the Father.

"By His Incarnation, the Son of God has in some fashion united Himself with every man".[29] Why?

The Word was made flesh only by coming to live in the world of men, only by setting up His tent in our midst. His Incarnation is, truly and in every sense of the word, an "in-humanation"; in other words, not only the assumption of a concrete and individual human nature, but also, and thanks to that nature, His insertion, by a new title,[30] into human society. The Word has thus "entered the world's history as a perfect man, taking that history into Himself and summarizing it."[31] Through the in-humanation of the Word, the history of humanity becomes, in a sense, the history itself of the eternal Word of God.[32]

Decidedly, it is to a renewed understanding of the mystery of the Redemption that the Council carries us when it proclaims: "For God's Word, by whom all things were made, was Himself made flesh *so that* as perfect man He might save all men and sum up all things in Himself. . . ."[33] What has revealed the love of God among us is that the only-begotten Son of God has been sent by the Father into the world, *so that*, being made man, the Son might by His redemption of the entire human race give new life to it and unify it."[34]

The affirmation is clear: the union of all men among themselves is an essential aspect of the Redemption, which extends to the material universe. Mankind's sin divided mankind and caused men to lose their domination over the material world at the very moment when this sin set mankind in opposition to God; human reconciliation is therefore an integral part of the Redemption, and the reconciliation of man with God entails the recapitulation of the material universe, subjected anew to God through man and through the Man *par excellence*, Jesus Christ. This is a perfectly Biblical perspective, as the texts cited by the Council prove.[35]

For Vatican II, the coming together and reconciliation of all men in a society of brothers constitutes, therefore, an essential aspect of the purpose pursued by the Word of God when, through His in-humanation, He inserted Himself into this society. God, again says the Council, "*in order* to establish peace or communion be-

tween sinful human beings and Himself, as well as
to fashion them into a fraternal community, determined
to intervene in human history in a way both new and
definitive. For He sent His Son, clothed in our flesh,
in order that through this Son He might snatch men
from the power of darkness and of Satan."[36]

It would be impossible to exaggerate the importance
of these affirmations which explicitly concern the purpose of the redemptive Incarnation. Never before, at
least to the best of my knowledge, has the Magisterium
of the Church, ordinary or extraordinary, presented the
In-humanation of the Word as orientated to the constitution of a fraternal society among men, or to the
recapitulation of the universe, even the physical universe, which is inseparably linked with mankind.

But, it seems to me, this salutary clarification is
concerned only with the immediate purpose of the
Incarnation, and in no way rules out the doctrine outlined above: the intrinsic subordination of this purpose to the mediate purpose of the glory of the Word
incarnate, and to the final purpose of the glory of the
Father. Besides, this subordination is intimated by
Saint Paul in his First Epistle to the Corinthians:
"When all things are subjected to him, then the Son
himself will also be subjected to him who put all
things under him, that God may be everything to every
one" (1 Cor. 15, 28). Moreover, Vatican II twice refers explicitly to this Pauline text.[37]

Furthermore, this purpose-graded distinction of the
ends of the Incarnation enables us to surmount an apparent difficulty already created by certain New Testament texts: if Christ came for our salvation (1 Tim. 1,
15), how can the world be for Christ (Col. 1, 15)?
Everything becomes clear if one discerns that the purpose of our salvation is itself the glory of the Christ-
Savior. Moreover, such clarification of hierarchical
distinctions in no way compels us to distinguish real
and successive stages, in God, of the divine plan; nor
is this divine plan really distinguishable from God
Himself, since it merges with the absolute and mys-

terious incomprehensibility of the transcendent and immanent Love who is the Triune God.

D. The Absolute and Universal Lordship of the Pierced Heart of the Redeemer

The salvation of the world, the glory of the Christ-Son, the glory of the Father—these are all expressions signifying the triumphant expansion of the Divine Charity.

The Word of the Divine Goodness *(Verbum bonitatis)* [38] became a human heart in order to save men, made inhuman through sin, by revealing to them the Heart of the Father. The Heart of the Redeemer symbolizes and expresses His merciful love for us because it signifies the supernatural and mutual love which, by His Spirit, he diffuses in our hearts. It is by leading us to love one another that He saves us.

This mutual love is, however, polarized by the exercise of the first and greatest command. We love men for the love of the Man Jesus, Son of God. The second commandment receives its whole meaning and purpose from the "first," which is "the greatest" (cf. Mt. 22, 38). And this first commandment concerns inseparably the love due to the Son and to the Father, who are one (Jn. 10, 30) in the Spirit. "He who loves me, loves the Father" (cf. Jn. 14, 9).

The salvific love of man follows, therefore, an order inversely parallel to that of God: it rises to the Father through the Son and the members of the Son, as the redemptive love descended from the Father through the Son to men.

At the intersection of this ascension and this descent, is the pierced Heart of the Lord. He wills that we should love men for His love and for that of the Father (cf. Jn. 8, 42; 14, 21). He offers Himself as the model of this triple love. Is He not the first to have loved us as He has loved Himself for love of the Father? When He commands us: "You shall love your neighbor as yourself" (Mt. 22, 39), does not this still amount to demanding that we should imitate Him? No one has ever loved his neighbor as Jesus has done; and has He not loved him as He loved Himself, as He loved His sacred Humanity for the love of the Father?

The love of the Heart of Jesus for others is polarized by His completely disinterested love of Himself, orientated towards the Father. He is the Only Son who is at once towards and "in the bosom of the Father" (Jn. 1, 18)[39] from whom He is eternally born.

And this triple love whose structure is received from the Heart of the Man-God corresponds to the triple purpose of His divine-human being. He has come that men may be saved by loving Him; for His own glory, which is no other than the expansion of His love for and praise of the glory of the Father, who is Love (Jn. 14, 21; Eph. 1, 6, 12; 1 Jn. 4, 8). The world is *for* the pierced Heart of the Christ Redeemer, *for* the Beloved Son who has entered into humanity for the glory of the Father's Love: and in this way the absolute ontological primacy of the Divine Word made human heart presents itself.

It was the happy intuition of the Blessed Duns Scotus to have clearly perceived (though maladroitly, with perhaps unconscious Nestorian connotations)[40] the supreme glorifying value of a finite and created love hypostatically assumed by an infinite love. The only Son loves His Father not only with an eternal and uncreated love, received from Him[41] and breathing with Him *(spirans Amorem)* the personal Love who is the Spirit, but also with a created love, an infused and volitive love which has never ceased since the first moment of His In-humanation and which will never cease; and even with an infused and sensible love, interrupted on Good Friday but resumed at the Resurrection[42] to kindle eternally His human and glorified Heart.

This twofold infused love, of the emotions and of the will, created and assumed by the uncreated Love of the only Son, ceaselessly offers to the Father, ultimate source of all love, the divinized love of His human brethren, thus conferring on this love a value which, in some sort, is infinite. All created loves, all the love poured forth by the Spirit of the Son in the hearts of men throughout the whole course of human history, are thus assumed with this all-embracing history[43] by the only Beloved Son, and offered by Him to the Father in union with His triple divine-human love[44]—which explains why they take on an ineffable and incomprehensible value.

The pierced and glorified Heart of the Redeemer appears, therefore, as indisputably the key to the universal history which is first and foremost the history of Charity. The Heart of the Mediator is the Alpha and the Omega of the universe.

We find this idea already more or less clearly adumbrated in some admirable reflections on the cosmic Adam, the whole man, by Saint Maximus the Confessor, the great theologian of the Incarnation:

> Christ is the great hidden mystery, the blessed end and purpose for which all was created. . . . His eyes fixed on that purpose, God called all things into existence. This goal is the destination where creatures achieve their renewal in God. . . . All the ages have received their origin and their destiny in Christ. This synthesis was already pre-ordained before all the ages: a synthesis of the limited with the infinite, of the Creator with the creature, of repose with movement. In the fullness of time, this synthesis was made manifest in Christ, who was Himself the accomplishment of the designs of God.[45] Christ unites created nature with uncreated Being in love. O wonder of love and of divine tenderness shown to us![46]

In the light of the immolated and triumphant Heart of the Lamb, of the *Agnus pantocrator*, we glimpse, therefore, the possibility, already barely existent, of a fruitful synthesis of the legitimate views held up to now by the different theological schools—a synthesis in perfect harmony with the methodological attitudes of both Saint Thomas[47] and Dune Scotus: "We should love both parties, those whose opinions we reject no less than those whose ideas we follow, since both assist us in the discovery of the truth. It is right, therefore, that we should thank them both."[48]

This synthesis could claim to affirm, through an investigation in depth of the Biblical and patristic data, the absolute and universal primacy of the Heart of the Lamb-Redeemer.[49] Equally, it emphasizes the ultimate character of Jesus Christ, the Alpha who becomes the Omega[50] in being the Mediator *par excellence* and in ceaselessly exercising His transcendent Mediation.

To this we add that the Church, by recognizing and accepting more and more the absolute lordship of the Heart of the Lamb, cooperates in His invisible and visible mission received from the Father. It is through His Spouse that the Alpha becomes the Omega, that the First becomes the Last, and that He who was eternally in the bosom of the Father becomes more and more Him who is in the heart of the world and Him who comes in the clouds of heaven, Him who is the *Pantocrator*, the Master of all things (cf. Rev. 22, 13; 1, 8 and 17).

In proclaiming with increasing emphasis the lordship of the Lamb, the Church becomes more and more His faithful and fruitful Spouse. It is thus that, under the action and the breath of the Spirit, she says repeatedly to Him who is her Temple and her Lamp: "Come" (cf. Rev. 21, 22-23; 22, 17).

NOTES TO CHAPTER ONE

1. Cf. Pius XII, *Humani Generis,* DS, 3884.

2. Saint Thomas Aquinas, *Summa Theologica,* III. 1. 3.

3. In this connection, see: F. Bonnefoy, *Primauté du Christ selon l'Ecriture et la Tradition,* Herder, Rome, 1959; P. Raymond, art. Duns Scot, *Dictionnaire de Théologie catholique,* 4 (1911), col. 1890-1891. Cf. the text cited in note 36.

4. M. J. Scheeben, *Les mystères du Christianisme,* section 64 (Bruges, 1947).

5. DS, 1529.

6. DS, 3025.

7. It is interesting to note the partial parellelism which exists between the purposes of the Incarnation and the purposes of mankind, such as for the latter are presented by Saint Ignatius Loyola in his letter of 7 May to the Jesuit students of Coimbra: ". . . aquello para que fuisteis criados, que es la gloria y honra de Dios, y salvacion vuestra y ayuda de los projimos" (*Obras completas,* Madrid, B.A.C., 1952, p. 722).

8. *Ad gentes divinitus,* par. 7. 3.

9. Cf. the sermons of Saint Lawrence of Brindisi, *Mariale,* p. 84 *sq.;* and the article by Fr. Théodore de A. Chaves: "o Primado de Christo em S. Lourenço de Brindisi," *Revista Eclesiástica Brasileira,* 19 (1957), 590 *seq.*

10. Here, Fr. Bonnefoy (cf. note 3) is in agreement with Saint Lawrence of Brindisi, who interpreted original sin and sin in general in the light of Jn. 11, 4: "But . . . Jesus . . . said: 'This illness is not unto death; it is for the glory of God, so that the Son of God may be glorified by means of it.' "

11. It is also a thesis of the Franciscan school that Christ merited, by His sacrifice on the cross, the creation of the world. There is one serious difficulty about this attractive thesis: it must in every way be admitted that the Lord was not able to merit the creation of His own humanity, and how then could He have merited the creation of the world to which this humanity is attached?

12. Saint Thomas Aquinas: *Summa Theologica,* I. 20. 4. 1, 2; II. II. 2. 7.

13. H. Bouessé O. P., *le Sauveur du Monde,* vol. 1: *Place du Christ* (Chambéry 1951, pp. 103-146). The passage we have in mind here occurs on pp. 126-134: "In fact, Nature has been created with a view to its supernatural completion, because nature is perfected by grace as substance by accident. And every order of grace is divinely orientated to its crowning, as it were, in the Redemptive Incarnation: thus the imperfect is orientated towards the perfect: cf. IV, CG. 27. . . . The highest instance of all is the cause of the others: this latter principle enables us to conclude with the same rigor that, of all the works of God, the Mystery of the Incarnation is the work to which all the others are orientated."

14. H. Bouessé, *op cit.,* pp. 126-134.

15. H. Bouessé, *op. cit.,* p. 116, par. 2.

16. G. Martelet: "le motif de l'Incarnation," in *Problèmes actuels de Christologie,* Paris, 1965, pp. 35-80.

17. Cf. DS, 3891.

18. We note in passing that certain Scotists, at least, would not accept this presentation of the thesis of their schools. In fact, the expression is not a happy one: what Father Martelet really means is that, in the thesis of Duns Scotus, the Redemption seems to be placed on the second plane.

19. Eph. 1, 3-12: this text refers to the redemption in the

blood of Jesus, the immediate end of the Incarnation (and already the synthesis of a multiplicity of ends); to the recapitulation for the glory of Christ, the intermediate end; and finally to the praise and glory of the grace of the Father, the final end. The Suárez commentaries are in his *Opera Omnia,* Vivès, Paris, 1876, t. XVII, disp. V, sect. IV, p. 243.

20. Saint Augustine: "deos facturus qui homines erant, homo factus est qui deus erat." Sermo 192.1; ML 38, 1012.

21. Saint Augustine: "descendit ille ut nos ascenderemus, et manens in natura sua factus est participes naturae nostrae ut nos manentes in natura nostra efficeremur participes naturae ipsius." Epist. 140; ML 33, 541-542.

22. Saint Augustine: "moritur christus ut fiat ecclesia" PL 35, 1463 (In Jo. tr. 9, 10).

23. See *Gott in Welt,* vol. II, Herder, Freiburg, 1964, pp. 43-91: "die Heiligung des Namens Gottes durch die Menschenliebe Jesu des Christus." We do not, however, accept all the ideas put forward by Father Schillebeeckx in this brilliant and profound work. We note in passing that it has, among others, the value of citing different texts of Saint Thomas, which agree with those of Duns Scotus on Christ as the adorer of the Father (*Summa Theologica,* I. II. 102. 3) and as masterpiece of God (*ibid.,* III, 1. 1): p. 80, note 49.

24. We think that this obscure expression refers to what would be primacy of mere power without love. It cannot be denied that, purely as Word Incarnate and even before the accomplishment of his historic task, Christ already possessed a universal primacy and the right to be adored.

25. The reality of this intersubjectivity by no means signifies a perfect reciprocity, impossible between Creator and creature. Man receives his subjectivity from that of God. That is why there is no dialectical relationship between Creator and creature.

26. Perhaps unawares, the author is adopting the thesis of the Scotist school on the sacrifice of Christ on the cross as meritorious cause of the creation of the universe.

27. One recognizes the successive allusions to the Scotist theology and to the Teilhardian vision, both considered as abstractions.

28. DS, 301: dogmatic definition of the Council of Chalcedon: "consubstantialem patri secundum deitatem et consubstantialem nobis secundum humanitatem."

29. *Gaudium et Spes,* 22. 2.

30. The Word was already present in human society as Creator, even before His in-humanation. See note 32 and the text cited there.

31. *Gaudium et Spes,* 38. 1.

32. Cf. Pius XII in a radio-message of Christmas 1957: "The *history of mankind* in the world is most certainly not a

process governed by blind forces: *it is an admirable and vital part of the history itself of the Divine Word.* It had its beginnings in Him and it will fulfill itself through Him on the day of the universal return to the first principle, when the Word Incarnate will offer to the Father, as testimony of His glory, His own redeemed kingdom illuminated by the Spirit of God." (See the original Italian text in AAS 50 (1958), 17).

33. *Gaudium et spes,* 54. 2.

34. *Unitatis redintegratio,* 2 *sub initio.*

35. Jn. 1, 3 and 14; Eph. 1, 10 cited in GC, 38. 1.

36. *Ad gentes divinitus,* 3. 1.

37. See *Lumen Gentium,* 36 and *Ad gentes divinitus,* 2 and 21.

38. Saint Thomas Aquinas: *Summa Theologica,* I. 27. 5. 2; 30. 1. 2; 30. 2. 4. Joining this expression with another used by the Angelic Doctor (*ibid.* 1. 43. 5. 2), one can say that, for him, the Only Son of God is the *"verbum bonitatis spirans amorem."*

39. Father I. de la Potterie S.J. has shown (*Biblica,* 43, 379-387) that Jn. 1, 18 should not be translated: "the only Son, who is in the bosom of the Father," but: "the only Son, who is towards the bosom of the Father"—because one cannot assimilate the preposition *eis,* used here, to the other preposition, *en,* used in Jn. 13, 23.

40. We are referring to the famous explanation of the purpose of the Incarnation given by Duns Scotus: "primo Deus diligit se; secundo diligit se aliis et iste est amor castus; tertio vult se diligi *ab alio* qui potest eum summe diligere loquendo de amore *alicujus extrinseci;* et quarto praevidit unionem illius naturae quae debet eum summe diligere, etsi nullus cecidisset" (Report. III. dist. VII. 5). We admit quite simply that we cannot see how the italicized word: *ab alio, alicujus extrinseci* can escape the charge of Nestorianism. Christ, as Word, is none other than God; His love for the Father is not the love of an outsider (an *extrinsecus*) but of a consubstantial Person; even His human love for the Father is, in the ultimate analysis, the love of a divine Person, since "actus sunt suppositorum." For all that, it is none the less true that the Blessed Duns Scotus deeply grasped all the unique value of the created love of Christ, the divine Person, for His Father.

41. Cf. Saint Thomas Aquinas, *de Potentia,* 10. 4. 8: "nihil prohibet intelligi eundem amorem esse gratuitum ut est patris, debitum vero ut est filii: Idem enim est amor quo pater et quo filius amat; sed hunc amorem filius a patre habet, pater vero a nullo." Here Saint Thomas is adopting the thesis developed by Richard of Saint Victor.

42. Such is the magnificent doctrine put forward by Pius XII in the encyclical *Haurietis Aquas.*

43. Cf. *Gaudium et Spes,* 38. 1.

44. Jesus loves His Father with a divine love, but also with

a human love both volitive and sensible: cf. Pius XII, *Haurietis Aquas,* AAS, 48 (1956), 327-328 and 343, reproduced in DS, 3924-3925.

45. Saint Maximus the Confessor, MG, 90. 612 AB.

46. *Idem,* MG, 91.1308. This text, like the preceding one, figures prominently in H. Urs von Balthasar, *Liturgie cosmique,* Paris, 1947, pp. 203-208.

47. Saint Thomas Aquinas: Commentary on the *Metaphysics of Aristotle,* II, 1 *ad finem*: "priores errantes circa veritatem posterioribus exercitiis occasionem dederunt ut, diligenti discussione habita, veritas limpidius appareret."

48. We have seen this text attributed to Duns Scotus but without exact indication of its source.

49. The orientation here indicated seems to us to be also that of Father Guy de Broglie S.J., notably in the following:

"We must envisage Christ as a being whose essential destiny cannot be achieved otherwise than by the achievement of that of His brethren; and men as having no finality which does not coincide with the glorification in them of the Redeemer-Christ."

This said . . . one cannot regard the Incarnation as a strictly individual fact; one must only see this Incarnation as "relating the Incarnate Word to the created people, who are the indispensable beneficiaries of His condescension. If the Incarnation supposes, as an indispensable explanation, someone towards whom God deigns to abase Himself, it becomes clear that Christ truly finds His specific end in us, and that, in a sense, Christ exists entirely for the greater benefit of His own. We are wholly and irrevocably ordained to His glory, because the supreme glory of a Savior being to save, then, since Christ exists, our destiny becomes one with our destiny to glorify in ourselves Him through whom alone the way of salvation is open to us" (*Dictionnaire de Spiritualité,* II, 1, col. 1679, art. Charité: Paris, 1953).

50. Cf. Y. M. J. Congar O.P., *Esquisse du Mystère de l'Eglise,* Cerf, Paris, 1953, p. 144.

2

THE LORD JESUS
SAVIOR OF THE PRE-CHRISTIANS

Nearly two thousand years after the death and resurrection of Jesus, two thirds of mankind, created and redeemed by Him, are still not incorporated with Him through baptism. They do not belong to the religion founded by the Son of God made man, their brother; on the contrary, many of them subscribe to religions instituted by men.

Vatican II set itself the task of examining anew how they stand as regards the salvation merited by Christ for mankind.

Do the missionaries sent by the Church and, through the Church, by the Son and the Holy Spirit, offer to the non-baptized merely a greater abundance of divine life, or, purely and simply, salvation?

Can the non-baptized be in a state of *visible* and not just *invisible* communion with the Church, sacrament of universal salvation?

Is it right to call such people "non-Christians" if they are actively preparing themselves, under the influence of the grace of Christ, to receive Christianity in all its fullness?

These are the questions which, in inverse order and within the context of the present missionary crisis, we shall attempt to answer, in the light of Vatican II and of the Catholic tradition.

A. Idea of "Pre-Christians"

Vatican II turns its attention to that world which up to now has been labeled "non-Christian," and reconsiders it in the light of the theological vision of the ante-Nicene Fathers, Clement of Alexandria, Justin, and Irenaeus. The Council has taken up again their theology of the universal function of the Logos, always present in the past religious history of mankind.

Saint Justin wrote:

> All those who have lived according to the Word are Christians, even if they have passed for atheists—as, among the Greeks, Socrates, Heraclitus and their like. . . . And there are also those who have lived in contradiction of the Word, have been vicious, enemies of Christ, murderers of the disciples of the Word. On the other hand, those who have lived or are living according to the Word are Christians, intrepid and without fear.[1]

Christ as Logos is at once the source of the partial knowledge of the truth given to all men, and the object and norm of that knowledge. In knowing religious and moral truth, man partially knows Christ; in witnessing to such truth, he participates in the Word.[2]

A little later, Saint Irenaeus stressed simultaneously the perpetual presence of the unique Logos-Son to the world, and the unique significance of the Incarnation: "in giving Himself, Christ brought with Him all newness."[3]

Inspired by these patristic ideas, Vatican II has underlined the idea of "preparation for the Gospel"—an idea which takes on extraordinary importance in the work of the Council.

All the elements of religious truth and of ethical goodness scattered through all the religions and all the systems of philosophy, in all human cultures and modes of existence, are recognized as preparations for the Gospel, seeds of the Word, rays of the Word who illuminates all man and who, through such rays, predisposes them to acknowledge the mystery of His Incarnation and of His Church.

The understandably cautious expression[4] used in the conciliar decree *Ad Gentes* ("these attempts . . . may *sometimes* serve as a guidance course towards the true God, or as a preparation for the gospel") is clarified if one links it with the preceding part of the passage ("this universal design of God for the salvation of the human race is not carried out exclusively in the soul of a man, with a kind of secrecy. Nor is it achieved merely through the multiple endeavors, including religious ones, by which men search for God") and especially if one correlates it with *Gaudium et Spes*, which regards the whole body of true expressions of human culture as preparations for the gospel.

On the one hand, in effect, the passage cited from *Ad Gentes* clearly signifies that the human initiatives[5] at the root of non-revealed religions are integrated in a providential design which makes them means of salvation[6] within a unique and universal design of salvation—i.e. of *the* universal means of salvation[7] which is the unique and universal Church of Christ. Of course, we are referring only to whatever, in these initiatives, is religious truth and ethical goodness. One could regard these human initiatives integrated in the salvific plan, as being responses to other initiatives, initiatives of God and of His grace, and as aspects of a universal partial Revelation of moral and religious truths, accessible or inaccessible to human reason and destined to form a preparation for acceptance of the full Revelation. In the final analysis, whatever truth man perceives or whatever good he does is a gift of the First Cause without whom no second cause can act; equally, one can accept that all the naturally good actions of men are done under the influence of secret actual graces;[8] in fine, one is led to recognize that, in the unique divine plan, all the partial revelations[9] are shaped towards the acceptance of Christ, fullness of the supernatural Revelation.

On the other hand, that qualifying "sometimes" of

Ad Gentes takes on its full significance in the light of
the dogmatic constitution *Lumen Gentium* and of the
pastoral constitution *Gaudium et Spes:* "Whatever
goodness or truth is found among them (i.e. among
Jews, Moslems, idolators, and those who are guiltlessly
ignorant of God) is looked upon by the Church as a
preparation for the gospel. She regards such qualities
as given by Him who enlightens all men so that they
may finally have life."[10] "Among the values of the
culture of today are these: scientific study and strict
fidelity toward truth in scientific research, the necessity of working together with others in technical groups,
a sense of international solidarity, an ever clearer
awareness of the responsibility of experts to aid men
and even to protect them, the desire to make the conditions of life more favorable for all, especially for
those who are deprived of the opportunity to exercise
responsibility or who are culturally poor. All of these
values can provide some preparation for the acceptance
of the message of the gospel—a preparation which can
be animated with divine love by Him who came to save
the world."[11] It is quite clear that if these predominantly ethical data of modern civilization already constitute a preparation for the gospel, one must say the
same about the ethical data and the religious truths
conveyed by the non-revealed religions (conveyed by
means of a supernatural revelation).

It must be maintained that these religions contain
in themselves, and are partially, "seeds of the Word"
by which, according to Vatican II,[12] the Holy Spirit
calls men to Christ. Of course, they are not purely and
simply that, since in them—and the Council admits
this at least by implication[13]—demoniacal seeds are
mixed in with the seeds of the Word. That precisely
is the reason why they need the full Gospel of Christ,
the Word Incarnate, who wills to save the seeds which,
as the Eternal Word, He sows in these religions. This
salvation is none other than Himself fully acknowledged. This amounts to saying that it is by these religions (not by them *alone*, but by them *also*) that the

Spirit of the Word calls men to Christ. They are, there-fore, partially but really, preparations for the gospel, and viewed in this way, they are more properly called *pre-Christian* than *non-Christian*, though they remain the latter through the demoniacal seeds still present in them. To the extent to which they contain and are "rays of the Light that enlightens every man,"[14] they prepare men for the Christ whom they partially ex-press, and therefore rightly deserve the adjective "pre-Christian."

In this respect, their relationship to the perfect Chris-tian religion is analogous to that of the Old Testa-ment[15] to the New. Their rites, in the measure in which they are celebrated by men invincibly ignorant of Christianity, are the occasion of an infusion of grace, of already salutary but non-sacramental grace—that is to say, not fully of a nature to bind man to Christ. They do not cause grace, as do the sacraments; rather does their mode of efficacy resemble that of the sacra-mentals, and one can quite rightly maintain that, like the sacramentals,[16] these rites occasion grace "ex opere orantis et operantis Ecclesiae catholicae," in every case where those who believe in them are in invincible ignorance.

Our thesis is, therefore, clear: the still non-Christian religions are already pre-Christian; Christ and His one and universal Church are already active, though as yet imperfectly, in these religions to secure their redemp-tion through the integration within themselves of all their authentic values and of all their believers. Al-though non-Christian, even anti-Christian, through the demoniacal seeds subsisting in them, these religions are pre-Christian and polarized towards Christ to the extent to which they are and contain the seeds of the Word and the rays of the Light.

Viewed in this way, there is no such thing as a post-Christian religion. Even Islam and the Afro-Brazilian syncretist cults, historically later than Christianity, are still pre-Christian religions; their elements of truth and of goodness are designed, in the providential plan of universal salvation, to prepare their faithful for adherence to Christ and to His one Church. Thus, Christ presents Himself as being, through His Church, the Redeemer of all the religions; as He who purifies all these rays of His light in order to integrate them into the perfect and definite religion which He Himself practices in relation to His Father, under the breath of their common Spirit,[17] in the Eucharist.

It could also be said that, through these partially non-Christian and partially pre-Christian religions, the Humanity of Christ ceaselessly offers itself to the Father in prolonging, through the faithful of these religions, His paschal mystery, in the present form of the covenant made with Noah (Gen. 9, 9-17).[18] Inversely, one can say with Saint Augustine—who, incidentally, was so severe in his *City of God* against everything non-Christian: "What we call today the Christian religion already existed among the Ancients and has never failed to exist since the beginnings of the human race right up to the time when Christ appeared in the Flesh. The true religion, which had existed previously and always, began henceforward to be called the Christian religion."[19] For Saint Augustine and the Fathers of the Church, this true religion embraced all of the just since Abel: "Ecclesia ab Abel."[20]

It can be seen, therefore, that the interpretation here proposed of the decree *Ad Gentes*, and notably of its third paragraph, is more than merely in line with Catholic tradition; it is even the only possible interpretation, since no other makes sense of the positive implications of the text: "The universal design of God is not carried out exclusively in the soul of a man with a kind of secrecy. Nor is it achieved merely through those multiple endeavors, including religious ones, by which men search for God. . . . These attempts need to be enlightened and purified. . . ." The initiative of God and of His grace arouses the religious initiative and activities of men. It is, therefore, only partially but nonetheless really, through Buddhism, Islam, and the other pre-Christian religions that Christ, the sole Savior, saves those who accept His salvation.

B. Partially Visible Communion of Non-Baptized Pre-Christians with the Church, Sacrament of the Universal Salvation

It is "incontestable that graces of salvation exist outside the visible frontiers of the Church, and prior to her fully effective presence."[21] We joyfully acknowledge that a certain number of the non-baptized, being in a state of grace and of charity, are already in communion with the Church without, however, being received into and incorporated with her. A precarious and partial communion, of course, but a very real one. Certainly, the Council does not use the actual word "communion," but has it not this reality in mind?[22]

As formerly Cornelius (Acts, 10), a certain number of the non-baptized of the present day are pre-Christians in a state of grace and of charity. Their condition can be clearly understood through a renewed pondering of the First Letter of Saint John and of Saint Augustine's commentaries on it, and also by a consideration of the spiritual value of the implicit desire for the sacraments.

In reading these texts of the Apostles, how can one fail to apply them to many people of good will who are within though not incorporated with the Church:

> We know that we have passed out of death into life, because we love the brethren. He who does not love remains in death . . . He who loves is born of God and knows God. He who does not love does not know God; for God is love. . . . But if any one has the world's goods and sees his brother in need, yet closes his heart against him, how does God's love abide in him? (1 Jn. 3, 14; 4, 7-8; 3, 17).

Is it not true or at least possible that those of the non-baptized who, under the influence of actual grace,

practice fraternal charity to the needy, are in a state
of supernatural charity? Of course, it is possible to
give away all one has and to deliver one's body to be
burned without having love (cf. 1 Cor. 13, 3), but it
does not follow that none of those who assist their
brethren does have love! It is also true that in Johannine literature the term "brother" designates the
Christians; but why deny that the texts cited above
also apply, by extension, to the non-baptized?

With these texts in mind, then, let us turn to Saint
Augustine's commentary:

> We must devote ourselves to fraternal charity.
> You may say to me: "I have not seen God."
> Could you ever say to me: "I have not seen
> man"? Love your brother. In effect, if you
> love the brother whom you see, you will at the
> same time see God; for you will see the same
> love, and God dwells in it. . . . Let each one
> look again into his own heart: if he finds fra-
> ternal charity there, he has certainly passed
> from death to life.
>
> He who loves his brother must needs love the
> love itself which he shows to him. How could
> he love his brother and not be in love with love?
> And, therefore, does not he who loves love, love
> God? Certainly. In loving love, he loves God—
> for it has just been said by the Apostle that
> God is Love.[23]

Since any truth, if affirmed absolutely, implies the
existence of an unconditional Absolute, fraternal love
is concretely inseparable from the love with which a
man loves himself, and the latter presupposes the absolute and unconditional Love who is God.

By use of a reflective method, therefore, Saint
Augustine aims at disclosing the implications of the
act of fraternal charity. They can be summed up in
one phrase: faith in the divine Love.

Saint John's letter, to which Augustine refers, also
emphasizes that love necessarily manifests itself by
signs: to assist our brothers in need. Fraternal charity

is the visible sign of real love for the invisible God. How can we fail to conclude from this that the charitable non-baptized person loves God above all, at least in an implicit manner, by sacrificing himself for love of his brethren (cf. 1 Jn. 3, 16-26).[24]

His partial communion with the Church, herself a communion in charity, is therefore visibly manifested. Through the exercising of fraternal charity, the non-baptized person signifies to the world both the perfect communion in charity which is the Church, and his own tendency towards the Church through an implicit baptism of desire.

Now, to be more precise, the act of faith and the act of perfect charity constitute this "implicit baptism of desire"[25] through which the non-baptized person is orientated[26] to the Church. Through the baptism of desire, is it not the Eucharist itself which is implicitly desired?[27] For baptism points forward to the Eucharist, the perfect manifestation of the Church on earth.

This could be demonstrated in another way. All those who have charity, which is indivisibly directed to God *and* to man, implicitly desire to fulfill all the divine wishes, and therefore to be incorporated in the Church. One cannot desire God without desiring the Church.

In loving their neighbor with a sacrificial love, the non-baptized who are in a state of grace desire the universal Church. This sacrificial love is visible through the actions which it inspires and which signify it, and therefore their partial communion with the Church is visible. In this respect, then, they are at once within and outside the frontiers of the Church: outside, through absence of the sacramental sign; within, through the presence of a visible sign of desire for the sacramental sign.

Could it not be said that, in the case of a person who loves his neighbor with sacrificial love through fidelity to personal conscience, a pre-Christian religious rite in which he or she participates becomes a new sign, visible and privileged, of implicit adherence to the Church?

Thus, on the one hand—and here we link up with what has been said above—these rites would in a sense be analogous to the sacramentals of this same Church; and, on the other hand, their practice would signify implicit adherence to the Church of Christ in imperfect but real communion with her. Of course, all this presupposes that these rites would not include anything contrary to the natural law.

The Catholic Church, we think, is therefore in partial visible communion with all the sacred rites of the religions of the world in what they present of truth and of good; she makes them in some manner efficacious by her intercession, and she even secures that their participants thereby manifest their will to reciprocal communion with her.

Through their partial and visible communion with her, it is with Christ, the one and universal Savior, perfect adorer of the Father in the Spirit, that they enter into communion, under the influence of grace.

C. The Missionary Proclaiming of Christ and the Salvation of the Non-baptized

Many of the non-baptized in a state of grace are already, therefore, in partial communion, at once invisible and visible, with the one and universal Church, through the loving practice of their own pre-Christian religions. How then can it still be said, as Vatican II emphatically does,[28] not only that the Missions preserve a *raison d'être*, but also that the missionaries bring salvation to these friends and temples of the Father, of the Son, and of their Spirit?

Certain people, as we know, are now inclined to think that the Church does not bring grace or salvation to the non-baptized, but only a greater abundance of divine life, possessed with greater security.

Were that purely and simply true, the aim of the missionary would no longer be the salvation of men, but their perfection. This would make his "going forth" seem to certain people less indispensable and less urgent.

One could answer that a friend of Christ never supposes that his Master is sufficiently loved, and he is always eager to make Him to be loved more intensely and more perfectly. Consequently, even were the above thesis true, it need not serve to cool the zeal of the evangelist.

But one can go further than that. Deeper reflection, favored by the decree *Ad Gentes*, shows that the envoy of the Savior Christ always has in view the present and eternal salvation of him to whom he has been sent, even if such a non-baptized person is already in a state of grace.

This is what the Council has to say:

> Now, since he who does not believe is already judged (cf. Jn. 3; 18), the words of Christ are at one and the same time words of judgment and of grace, of death and of life. For it is only by putting to death what is old that we are able to come to a newness of life. This fact applies first of all to persons, but it holds also for the various goods of the world, which bear the mark both of man's sin and of God's blessing. . . . All stand in need of Christ, their Model, their Mentor, their Liberator, their Savior, their Source of life.[29]

The missionary speaks in the name of Christ, and Christ utters through him His words of judgment and of grace. He is the Judge of those who reject Him as Savior.

Some of the non-baptized could be called "anonymous" Christians in as much as they are unaware both of Christ and of their own implicit Christianity. When such people are confronted with a sufficient[30] presentation of the Gospel, necessarily involving a fresh interior invitation of grace, they find themselves at a crossroads in their life. A new choice opens up before them. Their previous acceptance of the unknown Christ predisposes them to accept the known Christ, without forcing them to do so. They remain free to evade this "kairos" and this obligation. If they reject this word of salvation and refuse baptism, they lose the Christ who by faith was dwelling in their hearts; they become infidels and condemn themselves. Through their own fault "the words of Christ" become a judgment.

If, on the contrary, they accept the words of Christ and seek the baptism which incorporates them sacramentally with Christ and with His Church, their implicit Christianity becomes conscious and explicit; and they grow in the faith, hope, and charity they already possessed; in short, they perform a salvific action and they move towards the consummation of their redemption (cf. Rom. 8, 23). The word is grace and salvation for them.

By adhering fully to Christ, they destroy the "old evil" of their sin and the demonic "old evil" which also darkens the doctrines and rites of their pre-Christian religion.

But there are others besides "anonymous" Christians among the hearers of "the words of Christ." There are also all those whose works are evil, and who, consequently, prefer darkness to light; those who, doing evil, hate the light and turn away from it lest their works be revealed (cf. Jn. 3, 19-26).

An ecclesiology would be invalid were it to ignore the presence of sinners in the Church; equally, no missiological ideas can be formulated on the supposition that all the non-baptized are people of good faith and in a state of grace. To them the words of Jesus also apply: "For the gate is wide and the way is easy, that leads to destruction, and those who enter by it are many. But the gate is narrow and the way is hard, that leads to life, and those who find it are few" (Mt. 7, 13-14).

Christ has come to save those too among the non-baptized who are in a state of mortal sin. Clearly, they are in less favorable conditions for accepting the word and the invitation of Christ than are the non-baptized in a state of grace. Even for the later, however, is it so easy to enter by the narrow gate and to renounce the often attractive errors and seductive malpractices which co-exist with the truths and the graces in their pre-Christian religion? Are they not, like the pharisees, tempted to continue their adherence to them?

All this shows how the non-baptized, whether they have already accepted implicitly the grace of Christ or are still refusing it, are confronted with the offer of salvation and not just of perfection by the evangelizing word. Therefore, there is no incompatibility between the following two statements: grace and even sanctifying grace, is already secretly at work among the non-baptized; and yet the purpose of the Christian missions is their salvation.

But does not this presuppose that one clearly recognizes the earthly precariousness of the ever threatened divinization of those who are not yet fixed forever in adherence to the Immutable? Even those who have already passed from darkness to light and from death to life, still run the risk of hating the light and of preferring to it the darkness of death. If this is true of the baptized, how much more is it true of the non-baptized.

All this amounts to saying that the two thousand million who do not profess to be disciples of Jesus, need His envoys. Through them is effected "the ultimate summons, the call to conversion addressed to the nations before the coming of the Son of Man to judge them."[31] Christ, through the missionaries, is preparing mankind for His return as Judge of the living and of the dead. The preachers of the Gospel are the "instruments of the expected coming of the Son of Man, to invite to conversion."[32]

Through their words, echoes the voice of the Angel of the Apocalypse:

> Then I saw another angel flying in midheaven, with an eternal gospel to proclaim to those who dwell on earth, to every nation and tribe and

> tongue and people; and he said with a loud voice:
> "Fear God and give him glory, for the hour of
> his judgment has come; and worship him who
> made heaven and earth, the sea and the foun-
> tains of water" (Rev. 14, 6-7).

Nor does Revelation leave us in any doubt about
the efficacy of this proclamation of the Gospel "to
every nation and tribe and tongue and people"; in effect, it shows us

> . . . a great multitude which no man could
> number, from every nation, from all tribes and
> peoples and tongues, standing before the throne
> and before the Lamb, clothed in white robes,
> with palm branches in their hands, and crying
> out with a loud voice: "Salvation belongs to
> our God who sits upon the throne, and to the
> Lamb!" (Rev. 7, 9-10).

We may believe and hope that many will wash their
robes and will make "them white in the blood of the
Lamb" (7, 14), without ever having heard the message
of his envoys, but through practicing the works of
love. In this "great multitude" of those "who are written in the Lamb's book of life" (21, 27), will not a
great number of the non-baptized, the blessed of the
Father of Jesus answer Him and say: "Lord, when
did we see thee hungry and feed thee, or thirsty and
give thee drink? And when did we see thee a stranger
and wlcome thee, or naked and clothe thee? And
when did we see thee sick or in prison and visit thee?"
Because they shall have already seen the Lamb face
to face in the depths of the darkness of human misery,
thanks to the light of charity, the King of Glory will
recognize them as His own: "as you did it to one of
the least of these my brethren, you did it to me" (Mt.
25, 31-42). They will then receive as heritage the Kingdom prepared for them "from the foundation of the
world," and they will see perfectly that their earthly
charity towards the brethren, towards the least among
the brethren of the Lord, was also a gift merited by

the blood of the omnipotent Lamb, a gift from the loving Heart of the Mediator.

Thus the Lord Jesus appears as the already actual though embryonic salvation of numberless "pre-Christians." Through His envoys, He proclaims his ever active salvific love. Through the sum total of human culture and more especially by means of the pre-Christian religions, He prepares hearts to love this love, and above all He never ceases to spread it even among those who know nothing of His Incarnation. So it is that He already awakens in many, of all cultures and of every nation, a charity which answers to His own; and so He fulfills His promise: "And I, when I am lifted up from the earth, will draw all men to myself" (Jn. 12, 32). Christ Jesus, present in the least of his brethren, is drawing to Himself, here and now, our contemporaries who are baptized only by implicit desire. Thirsting for them (cf. Mt. 25, 42) and to be loved by them, He inspires them with a thirst for Himself which He wills to quench by giving them visibly the works of charity, and invisibly His Spirit. "If any man thirst, let him come to me and drink" (Jn. 7, 37-39).

As once the gift of tongues,[33] the present gift of charity active among the non-baptized shows that the Spirit springs up and flows from the Heart of the Risen Christ by a kind of preliminary baptism, but in order to lead on to a subsequent baptism (cf. Jn. 7, 37-39 and Acts 10, 47; 11, 15-17). Among the nations there are many Corneliuses, devout men who fear God (Acts 10, 1-2). Vatican II longs to give them the waters of baptism; they have received the Spirit of Love as much as we have! They are only waiting for the messengers of Peter and of the Spirit to declare to them "a message by which (they) will be saved" (Acts, 11, 14). Their waiting will not be in vain: the Word was made flesh to commence with humanity the dialogue of salvation.

NOTES TO CHAPTER TWO

1. Saint Justin, I Apol. XLVI, 1-4.

2. Cf. J. Daniélou S.J., *Message évangélique et culture hellénistique,* Paris, 1961, chap. II, pp. 42-46, to be compared with G. Thils, *Propos et Problème de la théologie des Religions non chrétiennes,* Brussels, 1965, pp. 96-100.

3. Saint Irenaeus, *Adversus Haereses,* "omnem novitatem attulit seipsum afferens," IV. 34. 1.

4. *Ad Gentes,* 3. We say "understandably cautious," since the conciliar emphasis (par. 7 of the same decree) is on the necessity for the missions.

5. Here is the Latin text: ". . . per *incepta* etiam religiosa." The word signifies "enterprises," "projects," with a meaning shaded towards "things begun but not completed." It is therefore well chosen here.

6. In effect, par. 3 of *Ad Gentes* is clarified by par. 3 of *Unitatis Redintegratio:* "The Spirit of Christ has not refrained from using them (the separated Churches and communities) as means of salvation which derive their efficacy from the very fullness of grace and truth entrusted to the Catholic Church. . . . For it is through Christ's Catholic Church alone, which is the all-embracing means of salvation *(generale auxilium salutis),* that the fullness of the means of salvation can be obtained" *(The Documents of Vatican II,* General Editor: Walter M. Abbott S.J., Guild Press, New York, 1966, p. 346. Further references to this English translation will be given as *Abbott).* The non-Christian religions can be regarded, like the still separated Churches, as partial means of salvation in dependence on the general means.

7. This idea (cf. preceding note) will be linked with the definition of the Church as universal sacrament of salvation: "universale salutis sacramentum" *(Lumen Gentium,* 48). Inasmuch as separated Churches and non-Christian religions are partial means of salvation, one could also, though not without a certain awkwardness, describe them as "partial sacraments of salvation."

8. Just as one can also hold that, with the aid of grace, reason also discovers the truths which are naturally accessible to it even without such aid.

9. Cf. G., Thils *op. cit.,* chap. IV, pp. 86-121.

10. *Lumen Gentium,* par. 16.

11 *Gaudium et Spes,* par 57. 6.

12. *Ad Gentes,* 15 and 11. Daniélou, *op. cit.,* pp. 44-45; Thils, *op. cit.,* pp. 96-100, which deals with the origins and meaning of the concept "seeds of the Word." It is highly probable that these *Ad Gentes* allusions to "the seeds of the Word" are at least partly due to the intervention of Msgr. Zoghby in the conciliar debate of 9 November 1964 on the missions: the re-

demptive mission of Christ and of the Church is exercised towards a humanity already "fecundated" by the divine seed, by the seeds of the Word. The messenger of the Gospel casts the seed of the word of God upon souls prepared by the Holy Spirit, souls who have received at their creation the germ of the creative Word. The Church should begin by seeking the divine seed in the nations whom she evangelizes. The Church should not impose upon them a prefabricated Christ. The nations who receive Jesus Christ should be able to express Him, to reincarnate Him, in their own image and likeness, in order that He may be all things to all (cf. *Documentation catholique,* 61, 1964, 1704). It could also be said that the divine seed deposited in the pre-Christian religions, in their elements of truth and goodness, serve to complete the divine seed deposited in every man by his vocation to the supernatural life and to the beatific vision (with the supernatural existential which flows from it and of which K. Rahner speaks); cf *Gaudium et Spes,* 3. 2: "haec sacra synodus, altissimam vocationis hominis profitens et *divinum quoddam semen in eo insertum asseverans;"* 18. 1: *"semen aeternitatis quod in se gerit, ad solam materiam cum irreductibile sit, contra mortem insurgit."* This "eternal seed" inserted in men is the first germ of the Word, to which is then added what the Council calls "the seeds of the Word which lie hidden in their national and religious traditions" (*Ad Gentes,* 11. 2; Abbott, pp. 597-598).

13. *Lumen Gentium,* 16 (Abbott, 35): "But rather often men, deceived by the Evil One, have become caught up in futile reasoning and have exchanged the truth of God for a lie, serving the creature rather than the Creator (Cf. *Rom.* 1: 21, 25)." This text heavily emphasizes (the English "rather often" perhaps insufficiently conveying the force of *saepius*) the elements of corruption which, side by side with and *more often* than the elements which prepare for the Gospel message, insinuate themselves among the non-baptized, and consequently into the heart of their religions.

14. Cf. *Nostra Aetate,* 2. 2 (Abbott, 662): "The Catholic Church rejects nothing which is true and holy in these religions. She looks with sincere respect upon those ways of conduct and of life, those rules and teachings which, though differing in many particulars from what she holds and sets forth, nevertheless often reflect a ray of that Truth which enlightens all men." The allusion to Jn. 1, 9 is clear.

15. By ceaselessly offering the Mass for the salvation of the whole world, and by offering herself entirely for this intention, does not the Church pray implicitly for the spiritual efficacy of the pre-Christian rites?

17. Heb. 9, 14: "Christ . . . through the eternal Spirit, offered himself without blemish to God. . . ."

18. Cf. G. Thils, *op cit.,* pp. 71-79.

19. Saint Augustine, Epist. 102. 12. 5; ML 33, 374-376. Cf. H. Fries, art. Religion, *Encyclopédie de la Foi*, IV, 54 (1967).

20. Cf. *Lumen Gentium, 2 sub fine.*

21. Y. M. J. Congar O.P.: "nécessité de l'activité mission-naire," *Bulletin du Cercle Saint Jean-Baptiste*, VIII. 3, 1968, p. 126. This text reproduces Father Congar's introduction to the *éditions du Cerf* commentary on *Ad Gentes.*

22. Cf. G. Thils, *op. cit.*, p. 180: "All those who are in a state of grace—be they Catholics, Christians, Buddhists, Moslems, Jews—constitute a true spiritual community, a society in the Holy Spirit."

23. Saint Augustine, Commentary on the First Epistle of Saint John: ML 35, 2017-2018 and 2035.

24. Cf. Saint Thomas Aquinas: *de Veritate*, 10. 10. 3.

25. Cf. the letter of the Holy Office to the Archbishop of Boston, 8 August 1949, in DS, 3866-3872. This document explicitly teaches the salvific sufficiency of the implicit desire of baptism informed by perfect charity. We would be inclined to think that the salvific adherence to God can itself be implicit, and conceal itself behind the transparent veil of an adherence in conscience to an absolute ethical obligation, the latter being inexplicable without a personal God: "Conscience is the most secret core and sanctuary of a man. There he is alone with God, whose voice echoes in his depths" (*Gaudium et Spes*, 16; Abbott, 213).

26. The expression is from *Lumen Gentium*, 16.

27. Saint Thomas Aquinas, *Summa Theologica*, 11. 73. 3; cf. B. de Margerie S.J., "Population mondiale, célibat du clergé et évangélisation sacramentelle," *Revue de l'Université d'Ottawa*, 36 (1966), 87-107.

28. *Ad Gentes*, par. 7; cf. Congar, *op. cit.*, p. 126.

29. *Ad Gentes*, par. 8: "verba christi verba sunt simul judicii et gratiae."

30. Cf. the reflections of Francis de Vitoria in his treatise *de Indis* (1532), cited by Journet, *op cit.*, pp. 95-96): "They would have been led to believe only if the Christian faith had been presented to them with a living witness worthy enough to convince them. . . . What they did get was a display of multiple scandals, of horrible crimes, of countless impieties. Consequently, it does not seem to me that the Christian religion has been preached to them with a holiness and probity which would command their adherence."

31. J. Comblin, *Le Christ dans l'Apocalypse* (Paris, 1965), pp. 63-65.

32. *Ibid.*

33. We would readily say that, just as formerly the Holy Spirit manifested the abundance of His presence and His action through the gift of tongues, so today He manifests baptism by implicit desire (which He accords to many who

have not yet received sacramental baptism) through the visible works of fraternal charity; for, are they not "created in Christ Jesus for good works, which God prepared beforehand, that we might walk in them" (Eph. 2, 10)? Do not these works constitute languages understandable by all, languages of fire, inciting the sacramentally baptized to announce to those baptized by desire the Christ by whom the latter are already living? But it remains possible that those baptized by desire will reject the message of the Gospel: cf. the text cited in note 25. N.B. On the doctrine of Vatican II concerning non-Christian religions, the following work should be especially consulted: P. Rossano, *Dizionario del concilio Ecumenico Vaticano Secondo,* Roma, 1969, col. 1693-1703, art. "Religioni non Christiane."

3

THE DIALOGUE OF SALVATION
THE NEED FOR JESUS OF NAZARETH

In the opening chapter, we have considered the purposes of the Incarnation of the Only Son of God, the chief one being so decidedly the divinizing redemption of the human race that we were able, in chapter two, to talk about Jesus as "salvation of the pre-Christians." The present chapter aims at showing how the dialogue between Christians and pre-Christians and also within the Church is an immensely important aspect of this divinizing redemption which is the immediate *raison d'être* of Jesus of Nazareth.

What is the dialogue of salvation? Does Christ speak to the Church through the world and through contemporary atheism? In what different senses is it said that he talks to the world, to atheists, through the Church and through Christians? Can Christians enter into a salvific dialogue with the world without first of all and continually establishing their own dialogue with Christ about and for the salvation of their interlocutors? Furthermore, is this dialogue of salvation, thus widely understood as extending from witness to preaching, the immediate and permanent reason, for the past, present, and immortal In-humanation of the Only Word of the Father in human society?

A. Nature and Place of the Dialogue of Salvation in the Work of the Redemption

The theme of dialogue, thanks notably to Martin Buber,[1] had for several decades already invaded the field of philosophic thought and of contemporary preoccupations in general, when Pope Paul VI decided to "baptize" it and to make it the principal subject of his inaugural encyclical, *Ecclesiam Suam*.

We use the word "baptize"—but strictly speaking it is not as a philosophical concept in its technical sense that the Pope is employing it; it is a current one which he adopts, with certain connotations and presuppositions, to convey the Christian message. Besides, Vatican II has used the concept—and widely encouraged the reality—of the dialogue of salvation.

For Paul VI, the dialogue of salvation is an interior impulse of the love of the Church for the world, an impulse made visible through the proclaiming and the offering of the treasure received from Christ.[2] He cites, as examples of this dialogue, the teachings of Pius XI, of Pius XII, of John XXIII,[3] and presents, as its transcendent source, the salvific will of the Father which is the source of the Revelation of the Son:

> God has sent his Son into the world, not to condemn the world, but that the world may be saved through him (Jn. 3, 17). Here, then, Venerable Brethren, is the noble origin of this dialogue: in the mind of God himself. Religion of its very nature is a certain relationship between God and man. It finds its expression in prayer; and prayer is a dialogue. Revelation, too, that supernatural link which God has established with man, can likewise be looked upon as a dialogue. In the Incarnation and in the Gospel it is God's Word that speaks to us. . . . Indeed the whole history of man's salvation is one long, varied dialogue, which marvelously begins with God and which he prolongs with men in so many different ways. . . . This relationship, this dialogue, which God the Father

initiated and established with us through Christ in the Holy Spirit, is a very real one, even though it is difficult to express in words. We must examine it closely if we want to understand the relationship which we, the Church, should establish and foster with the human race.[4]

Paul VI then continues with a precise description of the origin, the types, and the conditions of this dialogue of salvation whose model is Christ.

One could, therefore, sum up the ideas of Pope Paul on the dialogue of salvation somewhat as follows. It is essentially a conversation in which God speaks to the human race through a supernatural and public[5] Revelation, and in which men make answer to God through Faith and through prayer. The Church is the mediatrix of this dialogue. She presents to men the message which God addresses to them in Jesus Christ, and she presents to the Father, through Jesus, in the Spirit, the believing and prayerful answer of men. What God says to men can be epitomized in the Name, Jesus, the only Word in whom the Father totally expresses Himself and expresses the entire universe. And the obedience of Christ even to the death of the Cross, gathers up all the human answers which are proper to God's design and purpose; for Christ, "the true vine" whose Father is the "vinedresser" (Jn. 15, 1), adheres to the salvific design of the Father in the name of humanity, and without Him no one can produce fruit for salvation.

It can, therefore, be said that, as Mediator of God and of men, Christ *is* the dialogue of salvation because He is the plenitude of salvation. He is not only the Logos, but also the Dialogue; He is the One who, through the duality of His natures in the unity of His Person, is able to speak to men in the name of the Father and answer the Father in their name.

As the Body of Him who is the dialogal Logos,[6] the Church participates in this privilege. In Christ, and in the Prophets and the Apostles, "we may learn the gentle kindness of God, which words cannot express, and how far He has gone in adapting His language with thoughtful concern for our weak human nature";[7] so too should the Church, in offering to men in God's name the dialogue of salvation, assist them to understand the language of God the Revealer, the language of Christ (cf. Jn. 8, 43) intelligible to every man of good will. How should she do so? By explaining this language to them and also by helping them to formulate the answer of their faith in the language of their day, just as "God speaks in sacred Scripture through men in human fashion."[8]

This is a task which the Church, as faithful Spouse of Christ, has never neglected. Nevertheless, men have often rejected the language of the Church, just as they rejected in His lifetime on earth the language of Christ, about which language Vatican II comments: "He revealed the love of the Father and the sublime vocation of man in terms of the most common of social realities and by making use of the speech and the imagery of plain everyday life."[9] It could be said paradoxically but very exactly that the Church would cease to be the Church of Christ if her language were understood, heard, and heeded by *all* those to whom she presents her Lord. For those who receive the grace to hear and to answer within the dialogue of salvation, the rejection of the Church by a certain number of people is a confirming sign of her divine origin.[10]

But these painful facts in no way relieve the Church of the duty constantly to renew, to extend, and to initiate that mysterious and gracious adaptation of the divine language to the language of men which is an integral part of the divine Revelation. She thus models herself on the eternal Word who, on becoming man, expressed Himself in the language of men.

Vatican II has amply confirmed this duty (also voiced by Paul VI),[11] just as it has taken up the reality of the "dialogue of salvation" together with the term itself.

In the Dogmatic Constitution on Divine Revelation, we read:

> Through this revelation, therefore, the invisible God out of the abundance of His love speaks to men as friends *(conversatur)* and lives among them, so that He may invite and take them into fellowship with Himself. . . .[12] Prayer should accompany the reading of sacred Scripture, so that God and man may talk together; for "we speak to Him when we pray; we hear Him when we read the divine sayings."[13]

The purpose of the dialogue of Revelation is the salvation of mankind, to whom Christ speaks through the Church; it is the dialogue of salvation:

> Since it is the mission of the Church to converse with the human society in which she lives, bishops especially are called upon to approach men, seeking and fostering dialogue with them. These conversations on salvation ought to be distinguished for clarity of speech as well as for humility and gentleness so that truth may always be joined with charity, and understanding with love. Likewise they should be characterized by due prudence allied, however, with that trustfulness which fosters friendship and thus is naturally disposed to bring about a union of minds.[14]

There is no salvation without conversion: Christ has preached conversion, the *metanoia* of an interior transformation of the mind and will of man: "Repent, and believe in the gospel" (Mk. 1, 15). The dialogue of salvation practiced by Christ and, in His name, by the Church, inseparably implies the will to announce the Gospel and thus to promote the free conversion of the interlocutor, without "physical pressure," without "external coercion," solely by "the legitimate ways of human friendliness, interior persuasion, and ordinary conversation."[15] As the announcing of indisputable truths and of a necessary salvation, the dialogue of salvation "was" and remains "an appeal of love."[16]

Unlike Montuclard ("we have even abandoned the intention to convert"),[17] Christ and His Church sincerely say to men that they desire their conversion, as an obligation in conscience,[18] this being the purpose of the dialogue of salvation: "Before we can convert the world—as the very condition of converting the world—we must first approach it and speak to it."[19] But, as regards the Church, she opens this dialogue not as an end in itself; she enters into dialogue with those who are willing to listen to her but who explicitly exclude any idea of being converted to her. For, the Church does not exclude the possibility of men knowing her "according to the flesh," or of their having a certain knowledge of the historic Christ, while remaining in invincible ignorance of Christ as Savior[20] and as saving through His Church. Even with these, the dialogue of salvation is possible, whether or not they believe in God.

With the believers of the various religions, "the religious dialogue implies an entry into increasingly intimate communion with the intention of pleasing God; in this light, it is taken for granted that there is love one for another, and that progress is made in the mutual trust inspired by the same love of God." In other words, the dialogue of salvation begins from values held in common by the parties, more especially that supreme value—the love of God. "The intention to please, and to please together, to please more and more, the one, living, and true God, should be the soul of every genuine dialogue with Israel."[21]

With agnostics and atheists, an implicitly religious, ethical dialogue is possible and necessary. Its purpose, too, is to secure the salvation of one's fellow men and to promote the glory of God who pursues that purpose through the Christian believer. It too begins from a value, even a supreme value, held in common—namely, fidelity to the personal conscience and to its imperative that evil is to be avoided and good is to be done. In the measure in which the non-believer ascribes an absolute value to certain imperatives of conscience, he may be regarded as implicitly possessing the salvific faith. The dialogue of salvation takes on, according to particular cases, an ethical or a religious character, or both characters at once.

Can it be said that, because of this will to evangelize or this desire to convert the other, it is reduced to a monologue masked as dialogue? Some have indeed said as much.[22]

This must be resolutely denied. In demanding of his listeners that they repent, Christ spoke to them as free people, taking into account their past, their values, and their aspirations, as is shown by His conversations with Nicodemus and with the Samaritan woman. He was seeking to enrich them as people.

At a deeper level, Christ, as Creator of these people and of all mankind, is the Author of the individual values held by each of them, as well as being Author of the divinizing grace through which each can respond to the offer of salvation. He is the supreme Author of the affirmative response to this offer, a response which nevertheless remains free, spontaneous, personal. It is only within the framework of a classic Protestant conception, which attributes no salvific value to man's collaboration in his salvation—the latter being regarded as the exclusive work of God the Revealer—that the form of the dialogue of salvation could be a disguised monologue. On the other hand, as soon as it is admitted that man cooperates in his own salvation on the basis of a prevenient grace of God, salvation presents itself necessarily in the form of a dialogue.

That the work of Redemption takes the form of a salvific dialogue, emerges with particular clarity in Saint Paul's letters to Timothy: ". . . we have our hope set on the living God, who is the Savior of all men, especially of those who believe. . . . Take heed to yourself and to your teaching; hold to that, for by doing so you will save both yourself and your hearers. . . . Therefore I endure everything for the sake of the elect that they also may obtain the salvation which in Christ Jesus goes with eternal glory" (1 Tm. 4, 10; 4, 16; 2 Tm. 2, 10).

These texts, to which we shall return, show clearly how Saint Paul regarded the place of dialogue in the work of Redemption: Christ saves Timothy by means of his collaboration, through the teaching of the word of God, in the work of salvation, and He saves Timothy's hearers through their adherence to the word of salvation (presented by Timothy), as also through Paul's sufferings in union with His own Passion (Col. 1, 24).

In the design of Christ Jesus, the dialogue of His envoys with others about salvation and about their own salvation, is really an integral part of the mystery of the Redemption. Christ has died in order to make human speech efficacious of eternal salvation.

B. Christ "Speaks" to His Church through the World and through Contemporary Atheism

While it is true that the supernatural and public Revelation of God to the human have definitively ended with the death of the last of the Apostles, it is equally true that the natural, public, cosmo-historical revelation continues to which Saint Paul alludes in Romans 1, 20): "Ever since the creation of the world his invisible nature, namely, his eternal power and deity, has been clearly perceived in the things that have been made."

This manifestation of God conveys, not only His existence, but also His historical designs at the level of the natural order. It is concretely inseparable from these private (and no longer public) manifestations through which the Author of grace wills to help men to associate themselves, in their activities, with His paschal mystery. It is inseparable also from "the signs of the times"—i.e. the wishes of the Eternal concerning the here and now; for, are not these signs an integral part of the natural public revelation which is the "discourse of universal history"?

In *Pacem in Terris*, John XXIII analyzed three signs
of the times: the social improvement in the position
of women ("now taking a part in public life"), of "the
working classes" (who "have gradually gained ground
in economic and public affairs"), and of the colonized
nations (who "have either achieved or are on the way
to achieving independence").[23] Vatican II stresses
in particular the rapid and global transformation of
contemporary life, more dynamic and less static.[24]
Such occurrences, although intrinsically placed at the
level of the "natural" history of the human race, are
also signs given by Him who disposes "the times and
the moments" (Acts 1, 7) in terms of a supernatural
design; signs given by God to the Church, of His designs
concerning the direction which Christian human activity should take in our day. One could cite other
such signs, indicated by John XXIII in his social
encyclicals: equality in the independence and interdependence, the socialization and the "globalization"
of the human person.

It is not only through the Church, but through the
history itself of mankind, that Christ in some sort
discloses His plan of salvation. Vatican II declared this
distinctly: "The People of God believes that it is led
by the Spirit of the Lord, who fills the earth. Motivated
by this faith, it labors to decipher authentic signs of
God's presence and purpose in the happenings, needs,
and desires in which this People has a part along with
other men of our age."[25]

But the God who manifests Himself to the Church
through the "natural" history of mankind, in no way
contradicts the definitively ended supernatural Revelation of salvific truths. While it is true that "Christ
summons the Church, as she goes on her pilgrim way,
to that continual reformation" (under "the influence
of events or of the times") "of which she has need,
insofar as she is an institution of men here on earth,"[26]
it is none the less true that "there can be no question
of reforming the essential nature of the Church or her
basic and necessary structure."[27]

Adapting the terms of Martin Buber, we could therefore say that the eternal and infinitive *Thou* of Christ reveals itself to the *I* of His Spouse, the Church, through the constantly renewed finitude of the Church and of the Word, of the cosmos ceaselessly transformed by the human race that inhabits it; while not forgetting that the creative and conserving Providence of Christ the Savior is constantly active in this universe and in this human race that mediatize His dialogue with the Church.

Now, the world through which God "speaks"[28] to the Church of the twentieth century is in part a world which declares itself atheistic. Although "atheism is a refusal within the mind itself of man, of dialogue between men," and although "the myth of a purifying atheism"[29] must be rejected, it must equally be admitted that *Ecclesiam Suam* and *Gaudium et Spes* constitute a profound and clear recognition, unprecedented in the documents of the Church's Magisterium, of a permissive will of God which allows atheism in order to purify the faith and charity of His Church "at the same time holy and always in need of purification."[30]

This amounts to saying that God "speaks" to the believers and conveys a message to them, not by, but through the atheism of the atheists; just as formerly He made Egypt and Babylon, despite their idolatry, the agents of the merciful justice of God for the purification of Israel. Thus Paul VI shows us the providential function and significance of atheism, "a futile kind of dogmatism which . . . degrades life," while at the same time "striving for a social order which they conceive of as . . . the Absolute and the Necessary," and thereby dooming "to utter destruction any social system based on these principles."[31] The Pope, therefore, sees in atheism quite simply an instrument and, indirectly, a messenger of God. What is the message?

In Pope Paul's view (and the Council[32] was to take up in part the same theme), three main factors explain, without ever justifying, this modern atheism (notably in its Marxist form): "an objection to forms of language and worship which somehow fall short of the ideal"; a generous yearning "for a social order which they regard as the ultimate of perfection"; an enthusiasm "to work out a scientific explanation of the universe by human reasoning," but by a kind which "stops short at a certain point in this inevitable process of reasoning."[33]

Let us take up these factors to show how, in a negative way, they express a triple divine demand which the believer discovers in "the psychological and moral awareness" which Christ aims at developing in him.[34]

Through the atheism of the atheists, God manifests to religious men his salvific will to foster "a more profound and purer presentation of religious truth" than that offered by certain "imperfect forms of language and worship."[35]

In other words, through the atheists, living signs of His will, God invites Catholics to a revision of certain aspects of their religious language.[36] Through the atheists, God invites the non-Catholics "to enquire whether or not God has himself revealed definitely and infallibly how he wishes to be known, loved, and served."[37] The Catholic Church, in her basic structures, is the answer to such an enquiry, even though "the actual image of the Church will never attain to such a degree of perfection, beauty, holiness, and splendor [i.e. in her members and sociological aspects] that it can be said to correspond perfectly with the original conception in the mind of him who fashioned it."[38] Yet she is, through a pilgrim Church, the definitive form of this conception, until the end of time when the sacramental and hierarchic structure of the Church militant, having reached its term, will vanish.

Through the moral values of "solidarity and of compassion" displayed by atheists, through their "anxiety" tinged with "enthusiasm and idealism," through their "dreaming of justice and progress" and their "striving for a social order . . . all but divine," God is inviting Christian to retrace these values to their source; is inviting the Church to renew in herself the spirit of evangelical poverty in order to help the masses, as much as she can, to conquer, in detachment and in the midst of tribulations, any tendency to expect perfect happiness in a terrestrial paradise.[39]

Through the intellectual atheists' desire "to work . . . by human reasoning"—following "rules of logic very similar to those which are taught in the best schools of philosophy" (i.e. of scholastic philosophy—God invites the believers, and, through them, the atheists, to return "finally to the metaphysical and logical assertion of the existence of the supreme God"; to manifest, by use of the method of reflection, His transcendent necessity, which blazes forth when social goals are made aims in themselves and are treated like gods.[40] When the human mind reflects on the process by which work, nature, and society are made gods, and therefore on the essence of this atheistic pantheism we call "Marxism," and when it avoids the opposite pitfall of the idealism which divinizes personal mental activity as final and supreme, "as the measure and source of reality"—then "the training of the mind to scrutinize the truth which lies in the depth of his own awareness" (i.e. the method of reflection) increasingly leads, not only to knowledge of oneself, but to knowledge of the objective reality of the universe, and, through these mediations, to knowledge of the divine presence in both. The mind is an interior mirror, not only of the *I* and of the universe, but above all of the triune God.[41]

Here, then, is the triple call which Christ, Son of the Father, makes to His Church through the negative "sign" of every atheist: to purify faith; to effect social justice as much as possible here and now; and to develop to their fullest the potentialities of logical reason and of knowledge, of which Christ is the supreme source.

Contemporary believers regard atheism as a profound sign which, despite the lack of any formulation normal to supernatural Revelation, serves to complete the natural cosmo-historic[42] revelation through which God manifests to mankind His existence, His goodness, and some of His wishes.

Recourse to the idea and the reality of natural, public, cosmo-historic revelation—ever presently active as distinct from the supernatural Revelation which is terminated in the sense that the latter is "a series of events of the past in which are proposed and deposited truths of faith by which it is intelligibly constituted"[43] —proves fruitful in creating a better understanding of the dialogue of salvation between Christ and the world. The first prepares the second and the dialogue of salvation which expresses it. It is, in its totality, preparation for the Gospel.

The works through which the invisible God conveys Himself to the human intelligence, are not just cosmic, but also historical and human. Through them, the Word prepares the dialogue of salvation. In the divine plan, even the mysterious permitting of evil and of atheism is integrated into this natural revelation.

Saint Paul says to the pagans of Asia Minor: "God did not leave himself without witness, for he did good and gave you from heaven rains and fruitful seasons, satisfying your hearts with food and gladness" (Acts, 14, 17). This is a statement full of meaning for the Church today; for, does it not signify that God, in our era, long after the death of the last of the Apostles, is bearing witness to Himself (therefore also to the world and to the Church) through his gifts of truth and of virtue disseminated in the non-Christian religions, and even in the anti-Christian philosophies and ideologies or movements?

In the light of the inspired words of Saint Paul, should we not take a different view of what distinguishes natural from supernatural revelation? Instead of differentiating them by the presence or absence of a divine witness, ought we not to do so by seeing the manifestation of the *One*[44] God as the proximate purpose of natural revelation, and supernatural revelation as concerned with the disclosing of the *Triune* God in His unity?

In other words, the supernatural Revelation is completely polarized by the proximate and immediate end of the redemptive divinization of the human race, of its elevation to the supernatural life, which is also the purpose, but only the mediate purpose, of the natural revelation.

Thus the believer knows that, since grace does not suppress but perfects nature, it is the same Incarnate Word who "speaks" to him through the natural revelation and who holds with him a dialogue of salvation through the supernatural Revelation.

C. Christ Speaks to the World through the Christians and through the Church

It is not merely a part of His Church that Christ sends as messengers to the world; He sends the whole Church to the whole world. The whole Church is to speak to the world, and open with it the dialogue of salvation.

It is not our intention to discuss here in detail all the aspects of this theme, several of which have already been analyzed or will be examined in subsequent chapters.[45]

Rather, we would here briefly stress the universality of this mission and the conditions for its effective achievement of man's salvation.

"The Church must enter into dialogue with the world in which she lives,"[46] because, first and foremost, she is the voice of the Incarnate Word speaking to the world. As Vatican I proclaimed, she is a great and perpetual reason for believing: is not this to say that her mere visible existence, her holiness, her unity, her catholicity were, are, and will always be a challenge and an answer of the Savior Christ to the world He has come to save?

The Church *is* the dialogue, the dialogue made an institution for the salvation of its hearers. Through it, Christ ceaselessly manifests the power of His Resurrection, His divine-human holiness and unity, the universality of His mission.

Although all her members are not its authentic interpreters, to all members has been confided, for transmission to the whole world, the unique sacred deposit of the word of God, constituted by sacred Tradition and by Holy Scripture.[47]

It is the risen Christ Himself who, by His sacramental action, sends forth all the baptized, all the confirmed, on a mission of salvation. They hold this mission, not only nor above all, from the hierarchic Church, but from Christ Himself, baptizing and confirming through His ministers.[48]

This point emerges clearly from the teaching of Vatican II:

> Since the supreme and eternal Priest, Christ Jesus, wills to continue His witness and serve through the laity too, He vivifies them in His Spirit. . . . For besides intimately associating them with His life and His mission, Christ also gives them a share in His priestly functions for the glory of God and the salvation of men . . . Further, He has shared this power so that by serving Him in their fellow men they might through humility and patience lead their brother men to that King whom to serve is to reign. For, the Lord wishes to spread His kingdom by means of the laity also. . . . The faithful, therefore, must learn the deepest meaning and the value of all creation, and how to relate it to the praise of God. . . .[49]

The commandment of fraternal love is a commandment of the dialogue of salvation, of an incessant and universal dialogue of salvation.

And Christ continues, through Christians and through His Church, to proclaim publicly before the world what He has revealed during His earthly life and, through His Spirit, after His Resurrection. Through Christians, through the Church, the glorious Christ still witnesses to His own past witness. He still says: "He who hears you hears me. . . . I am with you always, to the close of the age." (Lk. 10, 16; Mt. 28, 20).

Vatican II explicitly teaches this permanent accomplishment of the prophetic mission of Christ:

> Christ, the great Prophet, who proclaimed the kingdom of His Father by the testimony of His life and the power of His words, continually fulfils His prophetic office until His full glory is revealed. He does this not only through the hierarchy who teach in His name and with His authority, but also through the laity. For that very purpose He made them His witness and gave them understanding of the faith and the grace of speech (cf. Acts 2, 17-18; Apoc. 19, 10), so that the power of the gospel might shine forth in their daily social and family life . . . Therefore, let the laity strive skilfully to acquire a more profound grasp of revealed truth, and insistently beg of God the gift of wisdom.[50]

The prayer of petition and the study of sacred matters are, therefore, presented to us by the Church as conditions for the exercise of the dialogue of her members with the world, if this dialogue is to be salvific.

We shall return immediately to the first of these conditions. In *Ecclesiam Suam*, Pope Paul indicates several others: a communion of life and of customs with those to whom one speaks; the habit of listening before speaking; "the principle of stressing what we all have in common rather than what divides us"; the recognition and appreciation of what truth the errors contain; perfect orthodoxy of personal conviction and expression; a concern to proclaim the fullness of Christianity and to invite to its acceptance; finally, an awareness of the inexhaustible character of revealed truth.[51]

The extent to which the lay Christian takes care to fulfill these conditions will be the measure of his effectiveness as the mouthpiece of Christ and of His dialogue of salvation.

D. Prayer: Dialogue with Christ for the Salvation of the World

Christ has saved the world through His prayer of desolation in His agony in the garden.

He held a dialogue with His Father in fear and in sadness, but above all in the will to obey Him even unto death, for the salvation of the world.

The Church, in her daily struggle against the prince of this world, needs to speak with Christ, her Spouse and her Head, in order to discern spirits and thus free men still prisoners of error and of evil.

It is in prayer that the Church must hear what the now risen Christ wishes to say to her about or through the world, and must obtain from Him the grace to listen with discernment to the world.

"Indeed, the cultivation of Christian perfection," writes Pope Paul VI, "must still be regarded as the richest source of the Church's spiritual strength. It is the means, so peculiarly its own, whereby the Church basks in the sunlight of Christ's Spirit. . . . It is the Church's surest defense and the cause of its constant renewal of strength amid the difficulties of the secular world."[52]

The vertical dialogue of the Church with the incarnate and adoring Word is the prerequisite and the enabling condition of her reciprocal and horizontal dialogue with the world: "This relationship, this dialogue, which God the Father initiated and established with us through Christ in the Holy Spirit, is a very real one. . . . We must examine it closely if we want to understand the relationship which we, the Church, should establish and foster with the human race."[53]

Even when the horizontal dialogue of salvation is not possible,[54] because men do not want to hear any mention of their Creator and Redeemer, the vertical dialogue of salvation is always possible and efficacious. It is never useless to speak to God about men.

It is by "the apostleship of prayer" that the Church merits for men the grace to listen to the apostles she sends to them. It is this apostleship which enables the visible Church to implement the commandment of universal charity which she has received in her mission to teach the whole world.

This brings us to the happy idea of Father Ramière, nineteenth century founder of the "Apostleship of Prayer," which, even today, continues to orientate the apostolic intercession of millions of the baptized. Here is what he has written:

> Far from being one of the secondary articles of Christian doctrine, the dogma of the limitless power of prayer lies at its very basis, because it is upon this dogma that the limitless extent of the great precept of Charity depends. . . . Upon it rests the unity itself of the society of the children of God, because rational creatures can form a society only to the extent to which they efficaciously assist one another to tend towards their final purpose.[55]

In prayer, the Church fulfills her mission to save the *whole* world; nay more, it is through prayer that the *whole* Church can fulfill this mission. The Church is not only the Church of the saints, but also the Church of the sinners. In His mercy towards sinners and towards the world, the Redeemer still wishes to make use of their prayer for the purpose of the salvation of all men. Those whom grave sin transforms into mortal enemies of Christ are not thereby deprived of His actual graces. While the merit, properly so called, of prayer comes only from charity and is an effect of sanctifying grace, the efficaciousness of this prayer is the effect of actual grace and comes from the faith which the gravely sinful man preserves, and which makes him still a member of the Body of Christ.[56] Is it not very specially through the actual graces of prayer for others, that the Spirit of Christ invites the free adherence of those who are refusing sanctifying grace? So true it is that the dialogue, at once vertical and horizontal, of intercession for others is salvific not only for those who still belong to the communion of the Church, but also for those who have in part betrayed it.

If such is the salvific power even of the sinner who is still a member of the Mystical Body of Christ, what must not be said about that of the Christian, especially the suffering Christian, who is in a state of grace?

Vatican II has linked the progress of the evangelization of the world with the supplication of those who suffer: "It will be the bishop's task to raise up from among his own people, especially the sick and those oppressed by hardship, souls who will offer prayers and penance to God with a generous heart for the evangelization of the world."[57]

Where is the person, where is the Christian who is not, for some reason, "oppressed by hardship"? Thus prayer appears as a co-redemptive dialogue with the one and only Redeemer to secure the perfect outpouring of the graces of Redemption.[58] The evangelization of the world is linked with the loving and suppliant suffering of the Church.

While, in private prayer, efficacious dialogue for the salvation of the world can be opened with Christ, the Church, aware of the superior efficacy of the liturgical prayer which is her official prayer as Spouse of the Redeemer, encourages all her members to the collective or individual recitation of the Divine Office.[59] It is the desire of Vatican II that the people of God show themselves more clearly to the world as a people praying and interceding for it. And did not Pius XI teach that the people of God, in virtue of its common priesthood, should pray for the salvation of the whole world,[60] thereby implying that this sacerdotal people has a mission of mediation in relation to non-baptized humanity?

So we see that the two dialogues of salvation, the vertical and the horizontal, are mutually linked. Christ speaks to the Church through the world, and to the world through the Church. The whole of reality is at once the instrument and the object of this dialogue of salvation. Everything is embraced by the work of redemption; therefore nothing is excluded, especially sin, from this dialogue. The Church speaks about all to all, that Christ may be "all and in all" (cf. Col. 3, 11). More clearly than ever before, Vatican II has focused attention on the catholicity of the dialogue of salvation.

The Catholic Church uses the dialogue of salvation because, first of all, and in dependence on the Word Incarnate, she is "the message of this salvation" (Acts 13, 26). She is the "good" which "the good man," who is God, brings forth from "the good treasure" and the superabundance of His Heart (Mt. 12, 34-35; 19, 17; Mk. 10, 18).

NOTES TO CHAPTER THREE

1. Cf. Martin Buber, *Ich und Du,* Leipzig, 1922.

2. Paul VI, *Ecclesiam Suam,* 61 (1964), 1079 (C.T.S. translation: p. 39).

3. *Ibid.,* 1080: 69 (C.T.S. translations: p. 41).

4. *Ibid.,* 1080-1081 (C.T.S. translation: p 42).

5. The theologians distinguish this public, supernatural Revelation properly so called, from natural revelation, improperly so called. Cf. R. Latourelle S.J., *Théologie de la Révélation,* Bruges, 1966,² pp. 413-416; the author emphasizes that natural revelation, with which we shall deal further on, has not this character of word and of witness (416).

6. By the expression "dialogal Logos," we want to say that the eternal Word is at once the expression of the knowledge which the Father has of Himself, the immanent Logos, and the expression of the salvific knowledge which He has of the created universe, the Logos of the economy of salvation: cf. Saint Thomas Aquinas, *S.T.,* 1. 34. 3; the saint also says, in the *Summa contra Gentiles* that the Son is "Verbum omnium rerum" (IV. 13. 6).

7. *Dei Verbum,* 13 (Abbott, p. 121).

8. *Ibid.,* 12. 1 (Abbott, p. 120).

9. *Gaudium et Spes,* 32. 2 (Abbott, p. 230).

10. Jn. 8; 45; *Lumen Gentium,* 8 and 42.

11. Paul VI, *Eccl. Suam, Loc. cit.,* 1080.

12. *Dei Verbum,* 2 (Abbott, p. 112).

13. *Dei Verbum,* VI, 25 (Abbott, p. 127).

14. Decree *Christus Dominus* on the Bishops' Pastoral Office in the Church, 13. 2 (Abbott, p. 405).

15. Paul VI, *Eccl. Suam, loc. cit.,* 1081. "The dialogue of salvation sprang from the goodness and the love of God. . . .

It was an appeal of love" (C.T.S. translation, p. 43).

16. *Ibid.* The final words are reminiscent of the great revelation of the Sacred Heart of Jesus, in 1675, to Saint Margaret-Mary Alacoque: "I thirst, I burn with desire to be loved" (*Vie et Oeuvres,* Gautey, Paris, 1915,³ t. II, p. 600).

17. A sentence quoted by Msgr. Montini at the Congress of the Apostolate of the Laity (Rome, 1957).

18. Declaration *Dignitatis Humanae* on Religious Freedom, 11 (Abbott, p. 690).

19. Paul VI, *Eccl. Suam, loc. cit.,* 1080 (C.T.S. translation, p. 41).

20. Cf. DS, 3870; *Lumen Gentium,* 16.

21. J.-M. Perrin O.P., *Vie spirituelle,* 115 (1966) pp. 671-673. Father Perrin continues: "One cannot love and respect someone without wishing to tell him completely what one knows to be the truth. In a friendly dialogue, one will convey this truth in a manner which takes careful account of what he thinks, of what he knows, of what he desires, and of how he feels. This attitude rules out the polemical, but also excludes all flattery and all dissimulation of the truth. I love the God you love; so how could we fail to be deeply united?"

22. We give, for example, these two reactions to the encyclical, dialogue is essentially a way of communicating the truth as taught by the Roman Catholic Church. Dialogue, as we understand it, is primarily a sharing in which all receive and all give and through which all are enriched and transformed" (Visser t'Hooft); "Catholic universalism and dialogue which is merely a monologue could do harm to the cause of Church unity," said Msgr. Iakovos, Orthodox Greek Archbishop of America (cf. *Informations catholiques internationales* of 1 Sept. 1964, p. 21). In reality, the views of Paul VI and of Visser t'Hooft are much closer than would at first sight appear: "Before speaking, we must take great care to listen not only to what men say, but more especially to what they have in their heart to say. Only then will we understand them and respect them, and even, as far as possible, agree with them" (*loc. cit.,* 1080: C.T.S. translation, p. 48).

23. John XXIII: *Pacem in Terris,* par. 40-43 (C.T.S. translation, pp. 18-20).

24. *Gaudium et Spes,* 7 and 9. 2, 3.

25. *Gaudium et Spes,* 11. 1 (Abbott, p. 209).

26. *Unitatis redintegratio,* 6. 1 (Abbott, p. 350): "perennem reformationem."

27. Paul VI, *Eccl. Suam, loc cit.,* 1071-1072 (C.T.S. translation, p. 28).

28. We use quotation marks for this word to emphasize the fact that there is question here only of a revelation improperly so called: but a real sign is, nevertheless, involved.

29. Cf. H. Holstein S. J., *Revue de l'Action Populaire,* Sept.

1964, p. 904.

30. *Lumen Gentium,* 8 and 48.3; and also 39.

31. Paul VI, *loc. cit.,* 1087-1088 (C.T.S. translation, pp. 53-55).

32. *Gaudium et Spes,* 20; 19.3.

33. Paul VI, *Eccl. Suam, loc. cit.,* 1088-1089 (C.T.S. translation, p. 55).

34. *Ibid.,* 1062 (C.TS translation, p 13).

35. *Ibid.,* 1088 (C.T.S. translation, p. 55).

36. *Unitatis Redintegratio,* 6: ". . . the formulation of doctrine (which must be carefully distinguished from the deposit itself of faith) . . ." (Abbott, p. 350).

37. Paul VI, *Eccl. Suam,* 1090 (C.T.S. translation, p. 57).

38 *Ibid.,* 1095 (C.T.S. translation, p. 8

39. *Ibid.,* 1088-1089; 1075-1076; *Lumen Gentium,* 8 *sub fine.*

41. *Ibid.,* 1064 (C.T.S. translation, p. 16).

42. Natural revelation is not only cosmic, but also historical, in the sense that it manifests itself through the currents of history; as cosmo-historical, it draws nearer by its object to the supernatural Revelation: cf. Latourelle, *Théologie de la Révélation, Bruges,* 1966,² pp. 30-31.

43. Cf. A. Léonard O.P.: *La parole de Dieu en Jésus-Christ,* Castermann, 1961, pp. 14, 309. The author adds: "This *once for all* (Heb. 10, 10) of the decisive events of Salvation does not exclude the *here and now,* the *today* (Heb. 3, 7-8) of the act of God which arouses adherence to the Faith."

44. Cf. note 5 of this chapter.

45. See especially, chapters 2, 11, 12, 13.

46. Paul VI, *Eccl. Suam,* 1079: "The Church has something to say, a message to give, a communication to make" (C.T.S. translation, p. 40).

47. *Dei Verbum,* 10.

48. Even the non-baptized person who baptizes acts as a minister of the Church, because it is always the Church that administers the sacraments; however, unlike confirmation, baptism is not always conferred by the hierarchic Church. In the case of confirmation, it can be said that the bishop, by the mere fact of confirming, gives the mission of witness of Christ, in the name of Jesus.

49. *Lumen Gentium,* 35-36.

50. LG, 35.

51. Paul VI, ES, *passim.*

52. *Ibid.,* 1069 (C.T.S. translation, p. 23).

53. *Ibid.,* 1091 (C.T.S. translation, p 42).

54. AG, 6. 2, 5.

55. Henri Ramière S.J., *L'Apostolat de laPrière,* Toulouse, 9th edition (undated), chap. 1, art. 3, pp. 51-52.

56. *Ibid.,* chap. 1, art. 6, pp. 68-70.

57. AG, 38. 3 (Abbott, p. 625).

58. See our Chapter XI, B.

59. SC, 100: "Pastors of souls should see to it that the chief hours, especially Vespers, are celebrated in common in church on Sundays and the more solemn feasts. And the laity, too, are encouraged to recite the divine office, either with the priests, or among themselves, or even individually" (Abbott, p. 167).

60. Pius XI, Encyclical *Miserentissimus Redemptor,* AAS, 20 (1928), 171-172: "Christianorum gens universa . . . debet cum pro se tum pro toto humano genere offerre pro peccatis haud aliter propemodum quam sacerdos omnis ac pontifex": the pope then cites Heb. 5, 1. We have already studied this theme in our book: *Padres Profetas e Mistagogos,* São Paulo, 1968, p. 182.

PART TWO:

HOW JESUS?

4

TEILHARD
A COSMIC CHRIST, CONSECRATOR OF THE COSMOS

It would be no exaggeration to say that never before, in the whole Christian era, had the philosophical and theological vision of a Catholic priest been so richly and so rapidly spread as has that of Father Pierre Teilhard de Chardin (1881-1955).

It must be recognized that Teilhard's contribution to Christology has exercised only a slight influence on the ideas of the principal theologians of our day, who work in other categories; yet, despite the difficulties it presents for many readers, this contribution has already exerted a considerable general influence and will, no doubt, continue to do so. Many to whom the message of Jesus has come owe their first idea about His Person to their reading of Teilhard—and there will be many more.

We shall therefore attempt a presentation, necessarily brief and synthetic, of the basic pattern of Teilhardian Christology; then we shall summarize certain difficulties which it creates, by enquiring to what extent the Christ of Teilhard is the Christ of the Gospel and of the Catholic Faith; finally we shall show the merits of his contribution, the horizons which it discovers or renews.

A. The Christological Thesis of Teilhard

We cannot deal here with all the theses; we must therefore choose from among them, and this is not without its disadvantages.

It may be said that Teilhard himself has well summarized his contribution in these lines:

> To formulate a Christology proportionate to the presently recognized dimensions of the Universe—in other words, to acknowledge that Christ, in addition to His strictly human and divine attributes (especially as considered up to now by the theologians), possesses, in virtue of the mechanism of the Incarnation, *Universal* or *cosmic* attributes which make of Him precisely the personal Centre sensed and needed by the Physics and the Metaphysics of Evolution. These perspectives are in striking harmony with the most fundamental texts of Saint John and of Saint Paul, and with the theology of the Greek Fathers.[1]

1. Teilhard here alludes to what he elsewhere calls the third "nature," the "cosmic nature"[2] of Christ. It is above all through this text that his first basic thesis emerges: the Body of Christ is the physical center of the whole material world. For him, Jesus is truly the Word Incarnate, Jesus of Nazareth, and not some vague phantom.

One can, with Father Mooney,[3] distinguish three stages in the affirmation of this thesis.

First of all, there is a premise of a rational kind: "From reason comes his hypothesis of a converging universe, which demands the existence of a transcendent personal Center capable of drawing evolution to its ultimate conclusion by here and now activating the love energy of the world."

Then there is a second premise drawn "from Christian revelation, especially from the letters of Saint Paul." A physical relationship unites the body of Christ, mankind, and the material world: Christ has "a cosmic function . . . by which he is Lord over all of creation."

From these two premises the third immediately follows: "In the present supernatural order . . . Christ must correspond to Omega and fulfill the function of personal Center for the universe, for all that is natural and all that is supernatural." What he (Teilhard) now adds and insists upon in his third affirmation is that, as a consequence, Christ must somehow be a *physical* Center. "He is a personal Center who irradiates His whole influence over the entire process of evolution."

For Teilhard, it is the whole world that has been raised to the supernatural order: everything that God has created, natural or supernatural, has been destined to constitute a single unity, whose center is the Word Incarnate.[4] Christ is "an organic Center for the whole universe; organic Center, i.e. on whom all development, even what is natural, is dependent finally and physically" (*Oeuvres*, IX, 39):[5] here we have the Christ of Teilhard.

As Father Mooney rightly notes, "though Teilhard insisted upon the word 'physical,' he had continual difficulty in giving it a positive content when he applied it to the relationship between the universe and the Body of Christ. The ambiguity of his early essays prompted Maurice Blondel to remark in a 1919 letter that 'a supernaturalism which is purely physical is nonsense.' "[6] In Father Mooney's view, "physical" should be read as meaning "ontological."[7]

2. Teilhard establishes his second christological formula by maintaining that Christ becomes the physical center of the universe through the Eucharistic transubstantiation, which effects a cosmic consecration: "When he says through the priest 'This is my Body,' . . . the priestly action extends itself beyond the transubstantiated Host to the cosmos itself, which the still unfinished Incarnation gradually transforms in the course of the passing centuries."[8] Teilhard simultaneously holds that "the primary body of Christ is

limited to the species of bread and wine" and that that there are "real and physical extensions of the Eucharistic Presence."[9] "In a secondary and generalized, but in a true sense, the sacramental Species are formed by the totality of the world."[10]

In 1955, however, the distinction drawn in the earlier writings between "primary body" and "secondary sense" disappears (at least in appearance) and Teilhard writes in his *Christique:* "And here it is the Eucharistic mystery itself which, before the astonished gaze of the believer, extends itself into the infinite through a truly universal 'transubstantiation,' where the words of consecration fall not only upon the sacrificial bread and wine, but also on the totality of joys and sorrows occasioned in the course of progress by the convergence of the world."[11]

In these conditions, it becomes more understandable that the same *Christique* speaks about "a third nature, in a sense real"[12] of Christ, His cosmic nature. One also understands, in this light, the prayer of *Milieu divin:* "My God, grant that I may adore it (i.e. the Universe) by seeing You hidden within it."[13]

Teilhard has never denied, however, the important clarification he made in a letter of 17 December 1922 to Father A. Valensin: while rejecting the "Spinoza position" (hypostatic union with the whole world), he described that position as "secundum quid vera" and spoke of an "Incarnation ending in the building up of an organic Whole in which the physical union with the divine has degrees."[14] The *Christique* must undoubtedly be read in the light of this letter.

This second thesis illuminates the first; it gives it its full meaning, and it must be recognized as profoundly original in the theological context of the first half of the twentieth century.

3. In a third thesis, Teilhard traces the relationship between Redemption and universe, between suffering and consecration of the world.

Teilhard states his position as follows:

In the dogma of the Redemption, Christian thought and piety have up to now especially stressed (for obvious historical reasons) the idea of expiatory reparation. . . . But, from the beginning, the picture also contained another element (a positive element) of re-construction, or of re-creation. New heavens, a new earth— such were, for an Augustine, the fruit and the prize of the Sacrifice of the Cross. A cross become the sign of growth, as well of redemption, is henceforward the only one with which the world could be signed.[15]

So Teilhard expressed himself in 1942. A little later, in 1944, he completed his idea:

The suffering Christ, without ceasing to be He who bears the sins of the World, and indeed precisely as such, will become more and more for the faithful He who bears and supports the weight of the World in evolution. . . . The Cross, symbol not only of the obscure, regressive face, but also and especially of the conquering and luminous face of the World in genesis; the Cross, symbol of progress and of victory through blunders, deception, and effort; the only Cross, in truth, that we could honestly, proudly, and passionately present to the adoration of a World become conscious of what it was yesterday and what awaits it tomorrow.[16]

Reading these texts, one might be tempted to think that Teilhard sometimes diminished the Cross to a symbol; re-reading them, however, one sees that they contain more than that. A text of 1950 is more satisfying in the sense that it brings out more clearly the positive meaning of the redemption and the co-redemptive mission of the Christian:

". . . the astonishing Christian revelation of a suffering transformable into an expression of love and into a principle of action. Suffering treated as an enemy to be defeated; suffering vigorously combated to the end; and yet, at the same time, suffering rationally and cordially accepted in the measure in which, by wresting us from our egotism and by compensating our deficiencies, it centers us on God. Yes, obscure and repressive suffering itself, erected for the humblest sufferer into a supremely active principle of universal humanization and divinization —such, at its apex, is the prodigious spiritual energy, born of the Cross.[17]

This very beautiful text clearly shows that Teilhard saw in the Sacrifice of the Cross a principle "of humanization and of divinization," and a "supremely active" principle. After some tentative uncertainties of expression,[18] he finally presented the Cross as redemption and as expiatory reparation. If the suffering Christ, precisely as bearing the sins of the world, supports the weight of its evolution, is not this because, ultimately, in Teilhard's view, sin is the greatest obstacle to the evolution and to the progress of the world?[19] Inversely, the Cross of Jesus is indeed for him the supreme principle, whose efficacious cause is that of the humanization and divinization, inconfusible and inseparable, of a humanity wounded by sin but called to a supernatural life. By exalting and because he exalts the "evolutive" Christ, Teilhard never ceases to be an adorer of the Cross, and to demand that men should accept suffering "rationally and cordially" and transform it into an expression of love.

4. Suffering, an expression of love: these words introduce us to a fourth thesis, a corollary of the two preceding ones, but one whose expression by Teilhard shows little consonance with the third. In the extension of his doctrine on the Incarnation and on the Eucharist, it is not surprising that he has elaborated (partly, however, under the influence of his family and religious environment) a very personal expression of the devotion to the Sacred Heart of Jesus. It is above all in his autobiographical work, *Le Coeur de la Matière* (1950, still unpublished) that Teilhard shapes his ideas on this subject. He writes as an epigraph: "In the

Heart of Matter, a Heart of the World, the Heart of a God." A little later, he expresses himself more precisely: "The universalized Heart of Christ coinciding with the heart of amorized matter."[20] It seems, therefore, that there is a perfect identity of meaning among the terms Heart of the World, Heart of Matter (to the extent to which the latter is "amorized") and Heart of God.

Judging by the language of *Milieu divin*, this universalized Heart of Christ could also be identified with the mystical, whole Christ,[21] or rather with the physical extensions of the Eucharist (envisaged in the second thesis). Would Teilhard regard the Eucharist as "amorized matter"? One cannot exclude it.

What is certain, however, is that Teilhard himself warns us against the desire for excessive precision. In *Le Coeur de la Matière*, he writes:

> Historically . . . the cult of the Sacred Heart (or love of Christ), always latent in the Church, was expressed in France, during the *grand siècle*, in a form at once astonishingly alive and yet strangely limited, both in its object ("Reparation") and in its symbol (the Heart of the Savior, expressed in the most strange anatomical contours). Unfortunately, this twofold particularism is still traceable in a liturgy excessively concerned with the idea of sin. . . . But at no time has its influence held the least attraction for my piety.[22]

Teilhard seems, therefore, to reject this[23] (or "a certain"?) version of the devotion to the Sacred Heart, taxed as doubly "particularist," and to prefer in its place a "universalist" version (the universalized Christ —of 1950). A text of 1923 provides the key to this twofold slant, and manifests its unity:

> How strange, my God, are the processes your spirit initiates: When, two centuries ago, your Church began[24] to feel the particular power of your heart, it might have seemed that what

was captivating men's souls was the fact of their finding in you an element even more determined, more circumscribed, than your humanity, as a whole. But now on the contrary a swift reversal is making us aware that your main purpose in this revealing to us of your heart was to enable our love to escape from the constrictions of the too narrow, too precise, too limited image of you which we had fashioned for ourselves. What I discern in your breast is simply[25] a furnace of fire; and the more I fix my gaze on its ardency the more it seems to me that all around it the contours of your body melt away and become enlarged beyond all measure, till the only features I can distinguish in you are those of the face of a world which has burst into flame."[26]

For Teilhard, therefore, it seems that "the Heart of the universalized Christ" is the World itself on fire through the Eucharist; the world become, thanks to the Eucharist, "amorized matter." Such, according to him, would have been the significance which Christ attached, above all else, to His appearances to Saint Margaret Mary and to His message confided to her; and this now (1923) becomes clear to Teilhard in the course of his expedition to inner Mongolia and the Ordos desert. If one may interpret *Messe sur le Monde* and *Le Coeur de la Matière* in the light of the *Christique*, the devotion to the Sacred Heart would, in his view, supply mankind with the means to escape from the narrow and precise limits of the human nature of Christ in order to find His "divine nature" in His "cosmic nature"; and Teilhard saw, as included in his mission, this passing on from particularity to universality in the devotion to the Sacred Heart, since undoubtedly it is first and foremost to him that the true message of these apparitions "becomes evident." The anatomical (i.e. the human) heart and the idea of reparation seem to fade in this devotion, to give place to the Eucharistic amorization of universal matter[24]—the world on fire.

It is curious to note that, in speaking of the Sacred
Heart and of reparation, Teilhard makes no allusion
to the themes of redemption, of the sacrifice of the
Cross, of suffering transformable into an expression of
love and into a principle of union—which he deals with,
however, the very same year in *L'énergie spirituelle de
la souffrance* and by means of which he could have expressed, in their own categories, the ideas of reparation
to and in union with the Heart of Christ. This failure to
bring these ideas together is made yet more strange by
the fact that the final thesis of the Teilhardian Christology, that of the parousiac "pleromization," rather seems
to postulate such a synthesis.

5. In effect, pleromization and Parousia are, for
Teilhard, inseparable from sacrifice, as emerges clearly
in a text of 1919:

> The universal effort of the World can be un-
> derstood as the preparation of a holocaust.
> Through its spiritual acquisitions (in which all
> the others are summed up) the World essentially
> develops a capacity for and a power of adora-
> tion—i.e. of renunciation. The final utilization
> of individual and collective consciousness which
> it elaborates; the supreme act in view of which
> it nourishes, refines and frees them—is their
> voluntary return to God and the willed sacrifice
> of their apparent (or immediate) autonomy. The
> only millenarianism which I envisage is, there-
> fore, that of an age in which Men, having become
> conscious of their complete unity among them-
> selves and of their intimate connection with the
> Rest, will possess the fullness of their soul to
> cast freely into the divine fire. All our work, ul-
> timately, contributes to form the Host on which
> is to descend the divine Fire.[28]

The world's activity is therefore polarized by a final
utilization of collective consciousness. This utilization will be in no sense a suicide, but a holocaust destroying, by a return to God, the tendency of personal
efforts towards an immediate autonomy, though not,

of course, the value of such efforts. Humanity itself will thus become the host on which can descend the Fire of the Parousiac Presence of Christ, who will manifest Himself above all, on the Last Day, as "lightning" (Mat. 24, 27).[29] Thus, again, Teilhard writes in *la Messe sur le Monde:* "The world can never be definitively united with you, Lord, save by a sort of reversal, a turning about, an *excentration*, which must involve the temporary collapse not merely of all individual achievements but even of everything that looks like an advance for humanity."[30]

In Teilhard's conception of the Parousia, therefore, there is a whole sacrificial aspect which, while not being the most original aspect, does assist us to form a correct idea of his contribution. In 1948 he summarized it by saying that "the critical point of human maturation" is "a condition (not truly sufficient, but necessary) of the Christic point of the Parousia."[31]

As emerges clearly in the following extract, the Parousia is for Teilhard the culminating point of the "Christogenesis," of the "cosmogenesis" and of the "plemorization":

> The Parousia will undoubtedly take place when creation has reached the paroxysm of its capacity for union. The unique action of assimilation and synthesis which has been going on since the beginning of time will be revealed at last, and the universal Christ will appear like a flash of lightning amid the clouds of a world which has gradually become sanctified. . . . The monads will rush to their irrevocable destiny . . . some, whose matter has been spiritualized, to the limitless fulfilment of eternal communion; others, whose spirit has become materialized, to the conscious agony of eternal decomposition.
>
> At that moment, Saint Paul tells us (1 Cor. 15, 23ff), when Christ shall have emptied of themselves all the powers of creation (casting aside any factor of dissociation and sur-ani-

mating any force of unity), he will bring to
completion the unification of the universe by
giving himself up to the divine embrace in his
full grown Body, its capacity for union at last
completely fulfilled.

Thus will be constituted the organic complex: God and the world—the Pleroma. We
cannot say this mysterious reality is greater
than God alone, since God has no need of the
world, but neither can we think of it as absolutely unessential without rendering creation
incomprehensible, the Passion of Christ absurd,
and our human effort meaningless.

Et tunc erit finis.

Like an immense wave, Being shall have dominated the agitation of beings. In the midst of
a becalmed Ocean whose every drop of water
shall be conscious of remaining itself, the extraordinary adventure of the world shall reach
its term. The dream of every mystic shall have
found its full and legitimate satisfaction. *Erit
in omnibus omnia Deus.*[32]

In this arresting passage, which includes a reaffir-
mation of an eternal Hell, one is aware of a pretty
constant element in Teilhard's ideas: the accentuation of a *relative* necessity of the creation within the
union of three mysteries (Creation, Incarnation, Redemption) in a single, total mystery. Again we read:

In the World, object of the "Creation," classical metaphysics had accustomed us to seeing a
kind of extrinsic production, the outcome of the
overflowing benevolence, of the supreme effi-
cience of God. Invincibly, and precisely in order
that I might fully act and fully love, I have been
led to see in it now (in accordance with the spirit of Saint Paul) a mysterious product of completion and of fulfilment for the absolute Being
Himself. No longer the participated Being of
extra-positing and of divergence, but the participated Being of pleromization and of convergence.[33]

Since, in our view, what is of first importance

in the World is not "being" but "the union which engenders that being," let us try to substisute, for a metaphysics of *Esse*, a metaphysics of *Unire* (or *Uniri*).[34]

Without creation, something, it seems, would be absolutely lacking to God considered in the plentitude, not of His being, but of His act of Union. For God, then, to create is by definition to unite Himself to His work; that is, to involve Himself in some fashion or other, through incarnation, in the World. Now, to become incarnate, is not this *ipso facto* to participate in the sufferings and the evils inherent in the Many developing painfully towards Unity? Creation, Incarnation, Redemption: viewed in this light, the three mysteries truly become, in the new Christology, but three faces of one and the same basic process, of a fourth mystery . . . which, to distinguish it from the other three, may be called for convenience the mystery of the creative union of the world in God, or Pleromization.[35]

For Teilhard, this "pleromization" is the "mystery of mysteries"[36] and "if I may venture to say so, a little like trinitization."[37] The mystery of pleromization is therefore the mystery of the creative, incarnate and redemptive Word, perfectly recapitulative of the Parousia, which in a sense completes the mystery of the Word producing with His Father the Spirit, their bond of love. For, finally, pleromization and trinitization constitute, or rather will constitute, "the organic complex: God and the World."[38]

Do the mysteries thus united and synthesized by the "mystery of mysteries" remain, for Teilhard, really distinct from one another? That they did not at every period of his life, seems to be proved by two decisive texts, never withdrawn:

— We have already cited the first one: "To create is . . . to involve Himself, through incarnation, in the World; to become incarnate, is not this *ipso facto* to participate in the sufferings and the evils inherent in the Many. . . ?"[39] The creation is presented as being already in itself incarnation, the latter being also, in itself, redemption: "In popular teaching, it is still held that God could become flesh with or without involvement in pain. . . . In my view, it is this conceptual pluralism which, in every hypothesis, it is essential to correct."[40]

— If these texts of 1945 and of 1944 seem clear enough, another of 1934 is clearer still: "In the final analysis, the first and only thing in which I believe is the World (the value, infallibility, and goodness of the World). . . . To that confused faith in a world one and infallible, I abandon myself, to be led wherever it wills." Now, this text is given its full meaning by something Teilhard had already written: "Were I to lose my faith in Christ, in a personal God, . . . I should continue to believe in the World."[41] The world seems indeed to be the "mystery of mysteries."

Teilhard, then, who in 1948 (and already for a considerable time) was elaborating the lineaments of "a new Christology," was, in 1934, giving precedence to a confused faith in the impersonal world over his precise faith in the personal Christ. A Christian can attempt (as has indeed been brilliantly done[42]) to understand this text, but it remains objectively unjustifiable.[43] Even if this particular text does represent an isolated moment in the growth of the author's ideas, the other texts cited above, as well as numerous passages which repeat the same sentiment, show that at times Teilhard did abandon himself to his "confused faith in an infallible World." However, he had in 1923 condemned in advance such an abandonment: ". . . the world travails, not to bring forth from within itself, some supreme reality, but to find its consummation through a union with a pre-existent Being."[44]

Consequently, it can be said that "the organic complex: God and the World" and the pleromization leave intact, at least in many Teilhardian texts, the affirmation of the transcendence of God and of Christ.

It is through this Eucharistic pleromization of the

world by Christ that the consecration of the world is effected which is inseparable from this pleromization. The latter prepares the holocaust of the host on which is to descend the divine fire of the Parousia. It has been said, with every justification, that the Teilhardian Christology is an eschatology.[45]

Before subjecting them to criticism, let us sum up the main Teilhardian affirmations. Christ is the physical and pre-existent center of the material world, through the transubstantiation which makes this world His "secondary" body, acquired at the price of His sacrifice on the cross and subjected to the power of His primary, resurrected body; His heart thus becomes the heart of the world, of matter amorized, His third and cosmic nature; His Parousia, conditioned by human maturation, will bring into perfect existence the pleroma, God-and-the-World, in which the unique mystery of the creative-incarnate-redemptive Word organically unites itself with the mystery of the Trinity. Such are the broad outlines of the "new Christology" of Teilhard. He himself sought to synthesize them in two Pauline texts which he had inscribed on the altar of the chapel at the Peking Institute of Geo-Biology: "Descendit, ascendit ut replerat omnia" (Eph. 4, 10); "ut sit Christus omnia in omnibus" (cf. Col. 3, 11).

B. Critical Reflections

The Christology of Teilhard has been, as have other aspects of his ideas inseparably linked with it, the subject of numerous critiques and especially of much uncritical admiration. However, a certain number of his admirers do keep their critical faculties alert while reading him, and attempt to understand what he sought to say even when they must reject his mode of saying it. We find this attitude in perfect accord with the criteria of judgment set out by Pius XII in 1956.[46]

Recognizing the fact that Teilhard was not a professional theologian,[47] we can nevertheless claim that he has had a theological influence. Is his theological reflection on Christ in line with Revelation and with the teaching of the Church? This is a serious question which must not be evaded. A clear answer would enable us more effectively to distinguish, in the matrix of verbal or conceptual error, the gem of truth, so that we may polish it to its full brilliance.

Let us take up the theses in which we have summarized the Teilhardian Christology.

The first affirms that the body of Christ is the physical center of the material world. The second specifies the means: the Eucharist.

In 1919, Maurice Blondel expressed a pretty radical criticism:

> The danger to be feared here is to suppose, even inadvertently, that the natural order *qua* natural order has a divine stability; that Christ physically plays the role that Pantheism or Monism attributes to the vague and diffuse God with which it is content. There is here a substratum of naturism, of hylozoism, or, indeed, of Hylotheism. . . . It should be maintained that Christ became man for something besides supernaturalization, and that the world, even physically, was divinized without being supernaturalized.[48]

Blondel, therefore, was not at all sure that the language of Teilhard was free from such danger. His ideas, as the citations above on Spinozism[49] show, were untainted by "hylotheism"; but many, if not the majority, of the texts are worded as though the author accepted Spinozism. For instance, had Blondel considered the following text, how could he have read anything but hylotheism into it?—"Jesus, beneath those world-forces, you have become truly and physically everything for me, everything around me, everything within me."[50] One cannot see what distinguishes it from the "Christian Spinozism" which Teilhard explicitly rejected. How many similar passages could not one cite! Reading them undoubtedly led many into a cult of "mystic" adoration of matter. In numerous statements by Teilhard, the world becomes for him, without qualification, the body of Christ. Unlike Saint Paul,[51] when Teilhard speaks of this body, he is thinking much more about the World (nearly always written with a capital W) than about the Church: "It is to your body in this its fullest extension[52]—that is, to the world . . . that I dedicate myself. . . . It is in this dedication, Lord Jesus, I desire to live, in this I desire to die"[53]. . . . "The earth has become for me, beyond itself, the Body of Him who is and of Him who comes."[54]

One perfectly appreciates, therefore, how these Teilhardian texts (or others) led a famous exegete, M. Feuillet, to remind us about the meaning of the Pauline texts which Teilhard loved to stress: "In the letters of the captivity, Christ is increased to the dimensions of the Cosmos, so that nothing in the universe is excluded from His creative and reconciliatory action; but for all that, the cosmos does not become the physical body of Christ."[55] Nor, we may add, does the resurrected Christ become the physical center of the material universe.[56]

This thesis, as Father Fessard rightly observes, would be an "aberration" if one "imagined in mythic fashion an Omega-Christ acting immediately on the cosmic evolution—that is, without its being mediated through Man and through the Noosphere. On the contrary, however, Teilhard always presupposes such mediation."[57] Yes, Teilhard *sometimes* does so, as in "The Divine Milieu,"[58] but not always or even most often.

We cite this text as a sample of many such:

> There is nothing strange about there being a universal physical element in Christ. Each one of us, if we but reflect, is enveloped, aureoled, by an extension of his being as vast as the universe. . . . What we are aware of is only the nucleus which is ourselves. But the interaction

of monads would be incomprehensible if an "aura" did not extend from one to the other, i.e. something proper to each one and common to all. How then are we to imagine the constitution of Christ as cosmic Center of creation? Simply as an extension, a transformation, brought about in the humanity of Jesus, of that "aura" which surrounds every human monad.[59]

Now, it is incorrect to say that the physical domain which extends between people and which is really common to them is proper to each of them. If it is true that the universe is an extension of my body, the latter is radically distinct from it; the universe does not form part of me, and my body is the *totality* of my physical being, not just its "nucleus."

What is said of my body holds good also for that of Christ: the universe is distinct from it. His pre-paschal, non-glorified body, subject to space-time, influenced indirectly all the others; and only some bodies directly; it was not, therefore, unless as to its dignity, the "cosmic center of creation." It would have been so, in a privileged fashion, only if Christ had constantly and universally exercised, physically and as man, His thaumaturgic power, which He did not exercise at all times and which He communicated to His disciples, even as regards the resurrection of the dead.

Similarly, the world does not become a veil of the physical body of the glorified Christ,[60] nor is this body the center of the material universe. The glorified body of Christ has a transcendental relationship with the material universe, and one cannot say that it acts in a direct and physical way on *all* bodies; but, according to many Teilhardian texts,[61] only by such action could it be their center.

These phrases of Teilhard can and should be described, in Father Fessard's well chosen word, as "mythic."

Happily, however, Teilhard has elsewhere given (in 1943) a much more acceptable formulation of his idea:

With the exception of the mystery of "sanctifying grace," the organic side of the Incarnation and therefore the physical conditions to be presupposed have been left in the dark (by the theologians),—all the more readily since the recent and frightening enlargement of the universe around us (in volume, duration, and number) would seem to render quite unimaginable any physical control by the Person of Christ over the totality of the cosmos.[62]

One can and should say that the glorious Body of the risen Christ, numerically identical with His prepaschal, mortal body, presupposes as its physical condition the whole universe, now become in a sense His "secondary" body, if one understands by this expression a distinct extension, ontologically dependent on His "primary" body in view of which it has been created, and subject to the influence of this primary and glorified body when Christ so wills.[63]

Here, therefore, there could be no universal physical presence of the sacred humanity of the Word Incarnate,[64] nor any "vague panchristism." Certain Teilhardian formulations clearly create such ideas in readers' minds favoring a certain "panchristic cosmolatry."[65] Christ has never had and never shall have a "third, cosmic nature"; but His human nature, especially His human freedom, will have a cosmic function at the Parousia—a point to which we shall return later.[66]

We are in full agreement, therefore, with Father Rideau:

> From a viewpoint taking perhaps insufficient account of the substantial connection of matter with spirit and of the free connection of the supernatural with nature, Father Marechal could point out to Teilhard that the "universal" and cosmic function of Christ is less important than His supernatural function of sanctifying souls: "To be thus the key to the whole of nature and 'Savior of the cosmic evolution,' is it not, for

Christ the Savior of souls, a secondary perfection, however necessary and splendid? To perceive this cosmic role, and to have our practice explicitly inspired by it, belongs, it seems to me, to the extension rather than to the essence of our religion." He adds that certain formulas of Teilhard seem to him to invert, at least "effectively," the necessary order of the two aspects, the supernatural and the cosmic, of Christian salvation.[67]

Numerous writers[68] have made similar criticisms of expressions used by Teilhard about the Redemption and about the Cross, and these criticisms contain by implication a stricture on his presentation of the devotion to the Sacred Heart. We have presented his ideas in this matter when (with the aid of its clearest expressions) we were formulating his third thesis—one to which his fourth is unfaithful. This is not surprising, seeing that the formulation given here of the third thesis on the Redemption is very real in Teilhard's works. More frequently the idea is worded, for example, like this: "Christ indeed saves evolution, but should we not add immediately that He is at the same time saved by evolution?"[69]—a formulation which has rightly been found unfortunate.[70] Feuillet observes: "Teilhard seems to prefer Christ the Evolver; but Saint Paul gives emphasis and first prominence to Christ the Redeemer."[71] Teilhard would answer, as indeed he has done, by talking about "evolutive Redemption,"[72] in response to an anonymous accusation: "l'évolution redemptrice du P. Teilhard de Chardin." Teilhard commented: "I absolutely fail to recognize here the expression of my thought: even the title insinuates that I attribute a salvific power of its own to cosmic becoming. My constant preoccupation, on the contrary, has been to irradiate from a personal and transcendent Christ the redemptive properties of the suffering engendered by Evolution."[73]

Admirably precise: evolution, in as much as it concretely involves suffering,[74] becomes a means of the salvific work of Christ. Evolution is not redemptive; it is the Redemption which is evolutive, in the sense that it makes use of evolution—but should we not add: and which saves evolution by orientating it towards the "new earth" merited by the blood of Christ, as indeed Teilhard elsewhere recognizes?[75] Yes, of course; but, in the year of his death, Teilhard writes in quite different terms: "Christianity is the only religion capable (because of the twofold power of its Cross and Resurrection understood in their fullest sense at last) of becoming the moving force of evolution."[76]

Teilhard has benefited, therefore, at least partially, from the criticisms made of his ideas by Father Marechal. He has corrected his idea about the Redemption. Unfortunately, one cannot say the same about his attitude towards the Sacred Heart, the texts for which, being somewhat more sparse, have not attracted the attention of the critics. It must be admitted, however, that before *Haurietis Aquas*, the encyclical published by Pius XII the year after Teilhard's death (1956), the Magisterium of the Church had not yet provided a sufficiently synthetic presentation of this cult, or accentuated the love of the resurrected Heart of Christ. Teilhard's reservations about and dislike of the idea of reparation in this cult can, therefore, be excused, but they remain unjustifiable. Reparation is presented by the encyclicals of Pius XI and Pius XII as an essential element of the worship due to the Sacred Heart. If the resurrected or Eucharistic body of Christ can be called "matter amorized" (and even personally assumed by the Word who is Love), the same cannot be said of matter in general.[77] Such expressions, already criticized in connection with the first two Teilhardian theses, would run the risk of transforming the cult of the Sacred Heart, for many readers, into a concrete expression of a pantheistic cosmolatry. The adoration of the world would thus replace reparation, while making the latter more necessary than ever. . . . One cannot say that Teilhard—on his own admission, so influenced in his youth by the devotion to the Sacred Heart—has much cited or investigated in his writings the Pauline texts on the Redemption, or properly understood or interpreted the message of Paray-le-Monial or of the papal encyclicals which have hearkened back, through Saint Margaret Mary, to the very essence of the doctrine revealed to Saint Paul and, through him, to mankind.[78]

Such incomprehension, such errors of a verbal and even real kind, are traceable to the fact that Teilhard has, at times, allowed his imagination to dominate his intelligence,[79] especially in his conception of original[80] sin or, simply, of sin. In the evolutive Redemption, Jesus is more evolver than Redeemer in Teilhard's view: "Jesus is always He who bears the sins of the world: moral evil is mysteriously compensated by suffering. But, more essentially than that, Jesus is He who structurally overcomes in Himself and for us all, the resistance to spiritual ascent which is inherent in matter."[81] In such a vision of the world, inherent obstacles to evolution seem more important than the offense against God inseparable from sin. A depreciation of reparation and of expiation[82] follows logically from this. We have here a "relative deficiency in the weighing up of sin" and, consequently, of the Redemption, as Father Rideau has clearly shown.[83] And in the measure in which reparation also seeks, beyond a willing and loving acceptance, to endure non-necessary sufferings, through pure desire of identification with the crucified Christ in His suffering, Teilhard was or seems to have been (in his writings, at least) even more remote from the Pauline "folly of the cross." Here one should quote the whole opening chapter of Paul's First Letter to the Corinthians.

At all events, the "preparation of a holocaust,"[84] if not the folly of the cross, is integrated in the "parousiac pleromization" envisaged and exalted by Teilhard. How should we regard this last thesis of the Teilhardian Christology?

In itself, quite clearly the idea of a certain level of

human maturation as the divinely willed condition of Christ's Parousia, contains nothing contrary to Revelation.

Feuillet comments:[85]

> Teilhard gives the impression that the Parousia is dependent upon the development of the cosmos—an idea scarcely in line with Christian tradition.

It is, of course, true that Revelation explicitly says nothing of this kind. But it in no way hinders us from thinking that God Himself has made the Parousia conditional, not on a certain degree of development of the cosmos, but on a certain level of human maturation. This involves merely a simple hypothesis. To the extent to which Teilhard would present it as a certainty, and would neglect to underline that this conditioning is divinely willed, one could not follow him. This, however, does not prevent his hypothesis from remaining extremely rich in suggestion.

As regards the texts we have cited concerning the mystery of the pleromization as "mystery of mysteries" and as synthesis of Creation-Incarnation-Redemption, they also call for a number of qualifications.

Despite declared doubts about his metaphysics of "creative union"—doubts which do not trouble him, however, in the final period of his life[86]—Teilhard was maintaining, even after the encyclical *Humani Generis*,[87] his doctrine concerning the necessity of creation, a doctrine so clearly opposed, at first sight, to the solemn declarations of Vatican I.

To allay any suspicion of overstatement, we invite the reader to compare two affirmations by Teilhard with the texts of Vatican I: "It is not the sense of the Contingency of the created, but the sense of the mutual Completion of the World and of God, which makes Christianity live";[88] "without creation, something, it seems, would be lacking to God considered in the plenitude, not of His being, but of His Act of Union."[89]

Whereas Vatican I proclaimed: "God has created through goodness and in virtue of His omnipotence, not in order to augment His beatitude or to acquire perfection, but in order to manifest His perfection through the gifts He bestows upon creatures. . . . If anyone says that God has created, not through a will free from all necessity, but as necessarily as He loves Himself, let him be anathema."[90]

Nowhere does Teilhard seem to have cited these texts of Vatican I. Did he know of them? It is difficult to accept that he did not, and very surprising that he appears to take so little account of them if they were in his mind. An attempt has been made, not without a degree of success, to show that the contradiction is less drastic than would at first sight appear.[91] In 1945, Teilhard reaffirms that "God is completely self-sufficient"—but goes on to say: "and yet the Universe brings to him something vitally necessary."[92] For him, what would be "absolutely" lacking to God without creation, would not be lacking to Him "in His being," but "in His act of union."[93] All this, while justifying Teilhard's dissatisfaction with his own attempt, remains very vague, and the affirmation of the divine freedom is under-emphasized. For a considerable number of readers fascinated by the style and by the imagery, such formulations imperil faith in the transcendent and absolute freedom of the God-Creator[94] and, consequently, of the Word-Creator.

Why does Teilhard hesitate so much over so necessary an affirmation? The reasons seem to us to be psychological, philosophical, and theological.

At the psychological level, Teilhard fails to appreciate the meaning and the spiritual effects of affirming the contingency of the universe: it is (as he says) "in order that I might fully act and fully love" that Teilhard sought to see the universe as "a mysterious product of completion and of fulfillment for the absolute Being Himself."[95] He asks: "If man is presented with the so-called revelation of his radical inutility, how is he going to avoid distaste for action?"[96]

Contingence in no way signifies uselessness: we have here a strange confusion of ideas. On the contrary, am I not stimulated to love and, consequently, to act, by the awareness that God, having no need of me for His Being or his Beatitude, has yet willed, in the same act by which He wills Himself, to make me participant of His happiness[97] and to be loved by me? Does not Christian Revelation give to each the awareness of a unique place in the divine plan of salvation, and therefore of his radical usefulness, inseparable in fact from his radical non-necessity? Has not Jesus said to His disciples: "By this is my Father glorified, that you bear much fruit . . ." (Jn. 15, 8)? Again, would it not be pride on my part to judge myself necessary to God, thereby appearing to claim that God would not be God did I not exist, or to maintain that I am useless because I am not indispensable?[98]

We believe that if someone had had the courage to direct Teilhard's attention to these presuppositions and consequences of his statements, he would have recognized the untenable and erroneous character of his ideas.

At the philosophical level, Teilhard, instead of seeking to replace[99] the metaphysics of being by the metaphysics of creative union, could have presented a real deepening of the traditional doctrine (which he was still accepting in 1936[100]), had he known the unpublished course of metaphysics of his Louvain friend, Father Charles, who held that Being should be regarded as an act of unification *in se per se*.[101] And it is exactly thus that Teilhard understood the supreme and trinitarian Being of God.[102] A manifest ambiguity: the Being of God is His Nature, unique with unification.

At the theological level, Teilhard thinks of pleromization in relationship with "trinitization."[103] However, his trinitarian reflection is sparse; and this, especially when linked with his declared preference for a deepening of the Christ-Universe relationship over the "Christic-Trinitarian" one,[104] led him to fall more easily into a form of expression tinged with the pantheism to which, on his own admission, he was naturally and for long inclined.[105] Had not Thomas Aquinas, with deep insight, stressed the relative necessity of the revelation of the trinitarian mystery in order that the human mind might more easily avoid emanist pantheism?[106] Teilhard was aware of this point: "If God were not triune, we would find it inconceivable that He could create without immersing Himself completely in the world."[107]

As for the "objective necessity" of the mysteries of the Incarnation and of the Redemption, a text already cited here gives in effect the impression that Teilhard held it, as Smulders maintains.[108] However, Teilhard has elsewhere sufficiently explained his idea: "Creation, Incarnation, Redemption, while each marking a further degree in the absolute freedom of the divine operation, are they not three acts, indissolubly linked in the emergence of participated being?"[109] Certainly, since the indissoluble and freely willed link is a *de facto*, and not a *de jure* one. A highly classic theologian, in the best sense of the term, has written: "If we know how to link together the various mysteries of divine Revelation, it will be seen that basically, in the universe, there is only one integral mystery: the Trinity flowing into the Church, the life of the Father communicated by the Son, in the Spirit, to the whole Mystical Body."[110] We think it is along these lines that the affirmation of Teilhard must be understood. What others call the "one integral mystery" is for him the "organic complex," "the pleroma: God-and-the-world." The expression 'organic complex" is unfortunate and open to different interpretations: the phrase *God-and-the-World* does not signify more of Being than does the single word *God*, but signifies a plurality of beings: God is not the soul of which the world would be the body. But, it seems, Teilhard does not propound any such errors. "For ultimately what Teilhard wants to do in the realm of theology is to rethink the *total* mystery of Christ in terms of *genèse*" (genesis).[111] This project is pretty clearly expressed in a letter of 1951:

> Lately, I have once more become aware that the whole nucleus of my interior outlook depends entirely upon and can be reduced to a simple transposition into dimensions of "cosmogenesis" of the vision which is traditionally expressed in terms of "cosmos." Creation, spirit, evil, God (and, more specifically, original sin, the Cross, the Resurrection, the Parousia, charity . . .), all these ideas, transferred to the dimension of "genesis," become coherent and clear in a way which is astounding.[112]

The Teilhardian project consists, then, in seeking to transpose and to re-formulate a traditional, allegedly static vision, in terms of genesis.

The expressions used call for some investigation.

Can it be truly said that Catholic dogma has expressed God, evil, charity, the death and resurrection of Christ, created spirit and uncreated Spirit, in terms of cosmos, and of static cosmos? This view seems very superficial. Neither the Councils nor the theologians of the past have ignored the movement, the history, the mutability which characterize all creatures. Teilhard himself talked about extending and "developing" a metaphysics of Evolution in line with the "philosophia perennis: primacy of Being, Act and Potency."[113] Such a development does not necessitate any "transposition" involving a rejection of past formulations, but it does not exclude any re-formulation compatible with them and with all the definitive acquisitions in dogmatic expression of revealed truths. This expression transcends the Teilhardian distinction between cosmos and cosmogenesis, and for that very reason, easily meets and survives eventual transformations in our scientific representation of the visible world; it places itself, not at the level of scientific phenomena, but at the level of transphenomenal being and of solidly attested historical facts.

If the transposition attempted by Teilhard aimed at changing the meaning of Catholic dogmas by rejecting the meaning ascribed to them until now by the Church, then such an effort would be indistinguishable from that of Modernism and would be doomed to the same failure.[114] The "new Christology" would be stillborn. If, on the other hand, *to transpose* means to *rethink* and to *re-formulate*, in the cultural context of our time, the christological truths in the expression of which one would retain the ancient and definitively Church-accepted formulations—in other words, remain within the framework of a homogeneous and not heterogeneous evolution of Catholic dogma—then the project, far from being unusual and extravagant, is a *necessary* one. We can even say: the Church adopts it as her own.[115]

Teilhard has constantly rejected Modernism; nevertheless, can one be certain that the theological project of this evolutionist was not, at times, revolutionary, even when he was explicitly affirming his faith in the infallibility of the Church?[116] It must be admitted that the desire for a re-formulation, in terms of *genesis*, of the mystery of an immutable God, Creator "ex nihilo," a God eternal and completely immaterial[117] even though He becomes human flesh, recalls the unhappy attempts of certain "Catholic" theologians of the nineteenth century, condemned by Vatican I,[118] or those of the Modernists. One can scarcely see, at first sight, what else the Teilhardian ideas can precisely signify.[119] No doubt, Teilhard is not especially aiming at an investigation in depth of the eternal generation or genesis of the only born Son. There is no guarantee, moreover, that he was aware of the attempts of Gunther: he never seems to cite Vatican I, and we have seen that he rejects Modernism. One can only conclude, therefore, that this project, such as he was formulating it in 1951, is, at least as regards God, the fruit of spatial images unduly transposed (through lack of self-criticism and the use of the method of analogy) in the affirmation of the Ineffable,[120] as well as being the consequence of an aspect of his metaphysics of creative union.

To say that every Catholic doctrine concerning Christ presupposes a doctrine about Him as God, is to point directly to the extreme fragility of the Teilhardian "new Christology" as regards its fundamental basis. There is no genesis in the divine nature of the eternal God, because He transcends all cosmogenesis, as does also the twofold genesis, divine and human, of the Word Incarnate, Only Son of God and of the Virgin Mary.

The concessions which we are obliged to make, therefore, to the numerous adverse criticisms of both the Teilhardian project and its formulations, enable us more clearly to appreciate the basis for the famous admonition published in 1962 by the Congregation of the Holy Office, not without the explicit and personal approbation of Pope John XXIII: "Apart from matters appertaining to the positive sciences, the works of Father Teilhard de Chardin abound *(scatere)* with such ambiguities, and even with such serious philosophical and theological errors, that they are offensive to Catholic doctrine."[121] It will be noted that the Roman text is directed only at Teilhard's writings, and carefully avoids pronouncing on his own personal convictions. Happily, it is possible to understand correctly the majority of his erroneous formulas, but this does not eliminate the danger to the purity of the Faith resulting from the great popularity of his works. As reported in the *Osservatore Romano*, did not Paul VI, in a sermon of February 1966, speak about the "fantasies" of Teilhard?

However, since nearly [122] all the theses of the Teilhardian Christology contain erroneous aspects, one cannot fail to read with approval the caveat made by Father Grenet:

> It is as deeply unjust to the memory of Father Teilhard as it is seriously imprudent with regard to his readers, to print and circulate without explanation or commentary, and even to

recommend to the general reading public, writings which do not represent his formal and definitive ideas. Such writings, not meant by their author for publication but nevertheless disseminated in this way, are devoured uncritically by incompetent people, and spread by them to the still more incompetent, as representing "the marvelous contribution of the new Teilhardian synthesis" and as meriting the prestige of this great name and the prevailing fashion of this current of ideas. Against such behavior, against such intellectual fraudulence, we may surely be allowed, while expressing our regret that it should happen, to raise our voices in vigorous protest.[123]

In presenting the most important criticisms that have been leveled against the Teilhardian Christology, we have been guided by a concern for honest intellectual objectivity. We have been motivated by the love of truth, by the desire to understand and to defend his theses whenever possible, without seeking to curry general favor by defending Teilhard when he is indefensible, but rather seeking to grasp sympathetically the truths which he loved and which, on his own admission, he has not always felicitously expressed. Let us not be more Teilhardian than Teilhard himself! Let us not be less critical of him through mere respect of persons or through fear of going against the current of approval, for such behavior on our part would be unworthy of him. As Saint Thomas Aquinas saw clearly,[124] to present ideas one judges to be false but without saying so, is to be a false prophet. On the other hand, not to extract from them the part of truth which they contain, is to fall short of the love one owes to truth and to withhold the gratitude due to those who have ventured in order that truth may progress.

C. Merits of the Christological Venture of Teilhard

In presenting the theses of Teilhard which have aroused adverse criticism, we have already had occasion to emphasize many positive elements in his contribution. We can therefore be more brief here. However, we shall return to some of the theses touched on.

It could be said that the fundamental interest of the Teilhardian Christology is at once threefold and single: to confront cosmic and human evolution with the Cross, the Resurrection, the Eucharist, and the Parousia of the Word Incarnate; to show the consecration of the world by the Incarnation; to point towards a magnificent synthesis between, on the one hand, the human and cosmic Pasch (effected by Jesus), and, on the other, the Holy Trinity.

An interest *threefold* and *single*, we have said: because the three elements are all relative to the Pleroma.

Teilhard believed passionately, at the scientific level,[125] in evolution. He has certainly contributed to make possible what Darwin and Hegel had imperiled —a reconciliation between the immutable truths of the Catholic Faith and an evolutive vision of the world. Thus, it is readily admitted that, at least indirectly, he influenced the 1950 encyclical *Humani Generis*.[126] That is no small merit. Thanks to Teilhard, the Church grasps more clearly that creation and evolution are not mutually opposed. His vision of an evolutive Redemption and of the Cross as symbol of human progress, invites us to a deeper understanding of the mysterious relationship which links the cosmos to the Blood of the Lamb, Redeemer of the universe.

It is a relationship of consecration, already anterior, thanks to the Incarnation. Diametrically opposed as is this point to a certain current secularism, it is emphasized by Teilhard to the extreme of denying the existence of the profane: "To repeat: by virtue of the Creation, and, still more, of the Incarnation, *nothing* here below is *profane* for those who know how to see. On the contrary, everything is sacred to the men who can distinguish that portion of chosen being which is subject to Christ's drawing power in the process of consummation."[127]

In the dynamic language of the "parousiac pleromi-

zation," Teilhard had, unknown to himself, been anticipated to some extent by the sixteenth century Catholic
theologians, Cajetan and Lorca, whose language was
not static but ontological and transphenomenal. The
first, a Dominican Cardinal, wrote: "The Incarnation
is a lifting up of the whole universe in one divine Person."[128] The second, in a commentary on the same
text of Saint Thomas Aquinas's *Summa Theologica*,[129]
wrote:

> The Incarnation was also profitable to the
> whole universe. The entire universe, and all
> the natures which it contains, have been in a
> sense lifted up to participation in a divine Per-
> son. Human nature, in effect, is as a link join-
> ing together all natures, and it holds within it-
> self something of each of them. . . . Human na-
> ture having been assumed by the divine Word,
> all the natures have, in a sense, been assumed.
> This lifting up of all the natures by the Incar-
> nation, was pointed out by Saint Paul to the
> Ephesians (1, 10): this summation, this uniting
> of "all things in him" *(anakephalaiosastai)*, sig-
> nifies that the divine Word has assumed all the
> natures, in some sort drawn together and sum-
> mated in man.[130]

Here we certainly have a partial adumbration of what
Teilhard sought to convey by "pleromization"; but
Teilhard, among others, has had the merit of more
clearly grasping the eschatological orientation of the
Pauline summation. In this way, he is also extending
the idea of Saint Gregory of Nyssa who wrote: "The
whole creation becomes a single body."[131] The basic
orientation of the Teilhardian idea concerning the pleromization seems, in this respect, deeply traditional.

But we must add: "The exegete should nevertheless recognize that the ideas of Teilhard have directed
attention to certain less known aspects of the Pauline
Christology. They suggest that man and the cosmos
are not two juxtaposed realities: the universe is human,

man is cosmic (in a certain sense)," writes A. Feuillet.[132]

Although the "cosmic" texts of Saint Paul and the meaning of the word "pleroma" are still and doubtless will long continue to be matters for discussion, a growing number of exegetes[133] are interpreting them in a way which justifies, and in some sort demands, the best elements of the Teilhardian Christology. The Pleroma is the Divinity communicated by the Father to the Son, to the Son Incarnate, and then, through Him and thanks to His *kenosis*, dwelling in His Church and in the universe.[134] The Church is not merely the Body of Christ; precisely because she is the Body of Christ, she is also His Pleroma including in herself the twofold plenitude of God and of the universe. Through man, the universe belongs to the Church[135] and in a sense forms part of it and, for that reason, Saint Paul describes the Church as the fullness of Christ (Eph. 1, 23). Thus, to take up a statement of Teilhard in his project of "transposition" already considered, the various Pauline texts clarify one another and cohere in an amazing way. Some of these texts were very dear to him:

> . . . the Church, which is his body, the fullness of him who fills all in all (Eph. 1, 22-23); For in him the whole fullness of deity dwells bodily, and you have come to fullness of life in him . . . (Col. 2, 9-10); For in him all the fullness of God was pleased to dwell, and through him to reconcile to himself all things, whether on earth or in heaven, making peace by the blood of his cross (Col. 1, 19-20) (in order) to unite all things in him, things in heaven and things on earth (Eph. 1, 10); and to know the love of Christ which surpasses knowledge, that you may be filled with all the fullness of God (Eph. 3, 19); He who descended is he who also ascended far above all the heavens, that he might fill all things (Eph. 4, 10).[136]

If Eph. 1, 10 is compared with 1 Cor. 15, 24-28,

one cannot rule out that the full summation takes place only at the point of the eschatological fullness of time: the fullness, not of time (as in Gal. 4, 4), but of the decisive moments in the history of salvation, could refer still more to the second coming of Christ than to His first coming,[137] and this would also strengthen the Teilhardian thesis of the "parousiac pleromization."

The providential mission of Teilhard could have been, therefore, to assist the Church to a better awareness of the mystery of the Pleroma, an integral part of Revelation. He himself sensed this when he wrote in 1940:

> It is characteristic of the ordinary economy of Christian life that certain elements of revelation which have long lain dormant should suddenly receive a powerful development according to the needs and demands of a new age. It seems to me that in our time this is the role reserved to the great concept of the Christian Pleroma, which is such an integral part of dogma, . . . the mysterious synthesis of the created and the Uncreated—the complete fulfillment (at once qualitative and quantitative) of the universe in God.[138]

It is in the light of the mystery of the Pleroma that we can understand, in part at least, the Teilhardian theory of creative union, which is identical with the pleromization of contingent beings, as Mooney has well shown.[139] As we have already said, it would be erroneous to attempt to apply this theory to the consideration of the eternal and immutable divine Nature; equally, however, we must examine the possibility of using it to secure a better understanding of the creation of the universe in Christ (cf. Eph. 2, 10) and its pleromizing summation by Christ, Mediator between the created pleroma of the World and the Uncreated Pleroma of the Divinity, until He effects their perfect parousiac synthesis.

We need a new Nicaea, says Teilhard in 1955. [140]

He had already voiced this wish in 1918: "With all the intensity of my desire to love God, I also wish that the elements of the truth, universally believed and professed by the Church, about the universal action and presence of God and of Christ, were finally considered together and without attenuation."[141]

It can be said that Vatican II has been, at least to a great extent the New Nicaea which Teilhard desired and which he has influenced in an indirect fashion, in the sense that the Council has taken account of problems raised by him, without however adopting the more specific solutions he suggested. Teilhard's 1918 wish has been partly justified in this text of Vatican II:

> Christ's work of redemption, which essentially concerns the salvation of men, includes also the renewal of the whole temporal order. . . . The spiritual order and the temporal order, although distinct, are linked together in the one divine design; thus God Himself wills, in Christ, to aggregate the whole world in order to make of it a new creature, beginning with this earth and giving it its plentitude on the Last Day. . . . It has pleased God to gather together all existents, both natural and supernatural, into a single whole in Christ, "that in everything he might be pre-eminent" (Col. 1, 18). This purpose is far from depriving the natural order of its autonomy, of its ends, of its own laws, of its means, of its importance for the welfare of man; on the contrary, it renders more perfect the force and the value of this order, while at the same time it raises it to the level of the integral vocation of man here on earth.[142]

The eschatological point of the recapitulation is particularly marked in this text, which also links the Cross of Christ with temporal progress and renewal. But— and here we see the difference between a certain Teilhardian[143] mode of expression and the integrally Christian mode of the Council and of the Church—the text clearly emphasizes that the Redemption is orientated, first and foremost, towards the eternal salvation of mankind.

In conclusion, let us attempt to summarize the element of truths contained in the Teilhardian Christology and in its different theses as we have enumerated them here.

The cosmos, not hypostatically united to the Word, has been indirectly assumed by Him through His prepaschal human body—a body perhaps prepared and conditioned by the whole material evolution of the world of which this body is the *raison d'être*. The universe is the theater of action, direct and indirect, of the glorified body of Christ; it is the sacerdotal garment of the Great High Priest, destined to an eschatological transfiguration under the action of this glorious body. By His blood shed on the Cross, Christ has paid the price of this new earth, the fruit of His sacrifice. The transubstantiation, only very partial,[144] of the universe by the Eucharist enables the Heart of Christ to amorize the hearts of men and to presage the parousiac transfiguration, the new earth. The world is not the third nature (the cosmic nature) of Christ, but the extension of His second nature (His human nature) from which it is distinct. In unifying, through the Church and the Eucharist, men and angels, what is in heaven and what is on earth, Christ, through man, subdues the world more and more to Himself. His Parousia could be conditioned, through a free decision of His own divine will, by humanity's attaining to a degree of temporal progress pre-ordained by Him. Through this progress, interrupted by regressions, is deployed the mystery of the summative Pleromization of the universe by the Word, its Creator, incarnated within it in order to save it—that is, to offer it, perfected and unified, to His Father. Christ is the Mediator of the union, in a distinction without confusion, between, on the one hand, this cosmic, human and ecclesial pleroma, and, on the other, the transcendent and immanent Pleroma of the Holy Trinity.

The world is linked to God by Christ: this is the

basic intuition of Teilhard.[145] More precisely, for Teilhard, it is in the symbol of the Sacred Heart that this linkage is disclosed. Despite his reticences about the element of reparation, he knew how to transform his own suffering into an expression of love, to erect it into an active principle of humanization and of divinization, in preparation for a holocaust, harbinger of the Parousia, in which there is a temporary collapse, not only of his individual achievements, but even of everything that looks like his human advance. When he had consented to the sacrifice of his apparent and immediate autonomy, his work formed the host of his own personality on which was to descend, in a paschal and parousiac death, the Fire of the Resurrected Christ.[146] Thus would be answered, within the heart of the earth, his beloved mother, the prayer[147] he spoke, from the depths of an asiatic desert, to the Heart of the immolated Lamb:

> Lord, lock me up in the deepest depths of your heart; and then, holding me there, burn me, purify me, set me on fire, sublimate me, till I become utterly what you would have me be, through the utter annihilation of my ego.

NOTES TO CHAPTER FOUR

1. Teilhard, text of 1936, *Oeuvres*, t. 9, pp. 161-162.

2. On this theme, see C. F. Mooney S.J.: *Teilhard de Chardin and the Mystery of Christ* (Collins: 1966) pp. 146-147. Further references to this book are given as: Mooney.

3. *Ibid*, pp. 71 *sq*.

4. Mooney, 75.

5. Cf. Mooney, 77: on the word "physical," see note 7.

6. Cited by Mooney, 78-79.

7. Mooney, 85.

8. Unpublished text of 1923, cited by Mooney, 82. The expression, "the still unfinished Incarnation," if taken literally, is clearly inadmissible; but Teilhard is thinking about the universal Christ and the Pleromization, as he regards them.

9. Teilhard, *Mon Univers*, 1924: *Oeuvres*, t. 9, p. 104. Can the world really be a physical extension of the Eucharistic presence? The expression is inadequate: an extension forms

part of what it extends; it would be better to say a presupposition, or a dependence—not physical but ontological. See the next note.

10. Teilhard: *Milieu divin, Oeuvres,* t. 4, pp. 153-154. There too we find the following: "As our humanity assimilates the material world, and as the Host assimilates our humanity, the Eucharistic transformation goes beyond and completes the transubstantiation of the bread on the altar" (English translation: Fontana, p. 125). His use of déborde ("goes beyond") appears to us to be inexact. Cf. note 8.

11. Teilhard: *Le Christique,* 1955, p. 10 (unpublished text cited by Mooney, 87).

12. *Ibid.* p. 9 (Mooney, 177). Teilhard specifies: "nature neither human nor divine, but 'cosmic.' " The only other text of Teilhard on the "cosmic nature" of Christ seems rather to regard it as His human nature at the Resurrected Christ, "ultimate psychic center of universal aggregation" (*Comment je vois:* 1948: unpublished—Mooney: p. 179).

13. Teilhard: *Milieu divin, Oeuvres,* t. 4, p. 172.

14. Letter cited by E. Rideau S.J., *La pensée du P. Teilhard de Chardin,* Paris 1965, p. 396, note 82 (a book here subsequently referred to as: Rideau): "You leave the reader with the impression that the Spinozan position, for example, is *simpliciter mala, falsa.* Why have you not indicated that between the Spinozan "Incarnation" in which the Whole is hypostatically divine, and the "Incarnation" of extrinsicist and cautious theologians in which the Pleroma is merely a social aggregate, there is place for an Incarnation ending in the building up of an organic Whole in which the physical union with the Divine has degrees?" A little later, in the unpublished *Panthéisme et Christianisme* (1923), p. 8, Teilhard makes an extremely important declaration: "This idea of a "hypostatic union' extended to the whole universe (which, we might note, would simply be the pantheism of Spinoza), while not in itself ridiculous or contradictory, is opposed to the whole Christian outlook on individual freedom and personal salvation" (Mooney, note 76, p. 255). It should be noted, however, that this conception would be contradictory if it included under the word "universe" (as normally understood) created persons, for a divine Person can assume a nature, but not a created person. In the universe such as it exists, man's sin, which cannot be imputed to a divine Person, serves to show the impossibility of a cosmic Incarnation, of an "in-cosmization" of the Word. This is what Teilhard has perceived, as is shown by his allusion to "personal salvation."

15. *Le Christ évoluteur* (1942: unpublished). Rideau, 413.

16. Teilhard, *Introduction au Christianisme* (1944: unpublished). Rideau, 413-414.

17. Teilhard, preface to *Energie spirituelle de la souffrance,*

1050, p. 11; cited in *Activation de l'énergie,* p. 256 (Rideau, 497-498).

18. Cf. Rideau, 414, note 125: we see there how Father Marechal, in a letter of 3 July 1934, had helped Teilhard to correct his idea: "If, then, instead of saying: 'The complete and definitive meaning of the Redemption is not more exactly to expiate but to traverse and conquer' . . . one said: 'it is not only to expiate'—I would have no objection in principle against this idea of a redemption both conquering *and* reparatory." (An allusion to the unpublished *Christologie et évolution* of 1933, cited by Rideau, p. 413, in a text already corrected by Teilhard in the light of Marechal's criticism).

19. Teilhard, *Le Coeur de la Matière* (1950: unpublished), p. 27.

21. Cf. Teilhard's idea of the "universal" Christ: "The universal Christ, as I understand Him, is a synthesis of Christ and of the universe, the inevitable full unfolding of the Incarnation": *Comment je crois* (1934: unpublished), p. 22. The text of *Milieu divin* to which we refer is on pp. 140-141: "The mystical Christ, the universal Christ of Saint Paul . . . an expansion of the Christ who was born of Mary and died on the Cross." He is "a development and extension of the Heart of Jesus" (*Comment je crois:* 1934, cited by Mooney p. 73).

22. Teilhard, *Le Coeur de la Matière* (1950: unpublished), partially cited by Rideau, 78. It is all the more interesting to note that, on Teilhard's own admission, the reparatory aspect of the cult of the Heart of Jesus never held the least attraction for him; and yet, in the same autobiographical account, Teilhard writes: "It would be difficult to convey how deeply, with what vehemence and continuity my pre-war religious life developed under the sign and the wonder of the Heart of Jesus" (Rideau, p. 514, note 131).

23. The apparitions of the Sacred Heart of Jesus to Saint Margaret Mary Alacoque took place at Paray-le-Monial.

24. Historical error. It was in the Middle Ages, if not indeed earlier, that the attraction of the Heart of Jesus began to be felt distinctly in the Church: see, for example, what Father Debongnie C.SS.R. wrote about Saint Lutgarde of Aywières (1182-1246) in *Le Coeur,* Etudes Carmélitaines, Paris 1950, 155-158. Furthermore, the Heart of Jesus, "determined, circumscribed," gained the love of souls only as symbol of His not only human but also divine love, and not through an "element more determined, more circumscribed" than His humanity itself. Neither Saint Margaret Mary nor the Church formed an excessively narrow, limited, or precise image of the *infinite* love of the Savior Christ by recognizing in the Heart of Christ His "natural symbol" (cf. DS 3922). One is understandably surprised to find that Teilhard, despite his mother's influence in this respect, so inadequately understood,

behind the clumsy artistic representations, the value of this symbol. Had he read Saint Margaret Mary? We have no evidence that he had. Had he done so, he would have seen that the devotion to the Sacred Heart, far from being something isolated, has its place within the framework of devotion to the Holy Trinity: *Autobiographie,* no. 48 (*Oeuvres,* pub. Gauthey, Paris, 1915³, t. 11). See also P. Blanchard, *Sainte Marguerite-Marie: Experience et Doctrine, Paris* 1961, pp. 190-193.

25. It will be noted that Teilhard keeps, in connection with the Heart of Jesus, only the symbol of fire, and thus eliminates both New Testament symbols of blood and of water (cf. Jn. 19, 34) with all their sacramental significance, as well as the Paray-le-monial symbols, themselves rooted in the Scriptures, of the crown of thorns which surrounds the Sacred Heart and of the Cross which surmounts It: see the text cited in note 33 of our Chapter Nine. Was not such elimination itself symbolic? Would not Teilhard's orientation have been decidedly different, and would it not have correctly channeled his thought, had he adored the Heart of Jesus crowned with thorns, without for all that eliminating the symbol of fire, itself also Biblical?

26. Teilhard, *Hymn of the Universe,* p. 32 (Fontana).

27. Cf. the "Hymn to Matter" (in litany form), one of the first of Teilhard's writing, which was published in *Hymn of the Universe* (Fontana: pp. 63-66).

28. Letter of 29 December 1919 to M. Blondel (Rideau, 359).

29. Cf. Teilhard, *Milieu divin:* "Then the presence of Christ, which has been silently accruing in things, will suddenly be revealed—like a flash of light from pole to pole. . . . Like lightning, like a conflagration, like a flood, the attraction exerted by the Son of Man will lay hold of all the whirling elements in the universe so as to re-write them or subject them to his body" (Fontana, p. 150-151). Can one speak of a presence of *Christ* in things? Would it not be more accurate to say: of the *Word.*

30. Teilhard: *Hymn of the Universe* (Fontana, p. 30).

31. Teilhard: *Trois choses que je vois* (1948: unpublished, p. 4) cited by Mooney, p. 62.

32. *Mon Univers,* 1924: Mooney p. 186.

33. Teilhard: *Le Coeur de la Matière* (1950: p. 30), cited by Rideau, 380, note 30.

34. Teilhard: *Contingence de l'Univers et gout humain de survivre* (1953: unpublished), cited by Rideau, 381, note 30. Teilhard, alas, is no longer following the advice of Father Marechal, and is beginning to use "substitute" instead of "complete"!

35. Teilhard, *Christianisme et Evolution* (1945: unpublished), cited by Rideau, 424, note 158. It will be noted that the creation is treated as a mystery on the same plane as the

Redemptive Incarnation. Catholic theology teaches, however, that the first is not a mystery in the same sense as the second: human reason can demonstrate the existence of a Creator-God, but not of the Redemptive Incarnation, incomprehensible even after its Revelation. By neglecting this distinction, the new Christology of Teilhard is therefore in danger of seeming to nullify the absolute transcendence of Christ in relation to the World.

36. Teilhard, *Comment je vois* (unpublished: 1948, pp. 20-21). Mooney, p. 176.

37. *Ibid.*, pp. 17-19 (Mooney, p. 176). Teilhard has written very little about the mystery of the Trinity, which he ranks among "the fundamental mysteries of Christianity," in the passage cited here. It is one of the weaknesses which explain the limits and the verbal errors of his Christology.

38. Expression taken from text cited in our note 32.

39. Cf. text cited in our note 35.

40. Teilhard, *Comment je vois* (1948: unpublished), par. 31. The "popular" teaching to which Teilhard alludes is the unanimous teaching of Catholic theologians, of which he says, "in every hypothesis it is essential to correct." Teilhard admitted, however, that he was no theologian! Furthermore, this teaching is more shaded than he presents it: cf. Saint Thomas Aquinas, *Summa Theologica*, 11. 16. 2.

41. Teilhard's *Comment je crois* (1929: unpublished). In this connection, see note 40. Already in 1929, Teilhard was writing: "The things in which I believe . . . are: primarily and fundamentally, the value of the World; and secondly, the necessity for some Christ to give to this world a consistency, a heart and a face" (Letter of 15 February 1929: Rideau, 559, note 27). This looks towards that of 1934. Meantime, another was pointing in the same direction: "Henceforward, faith in Christ will be maintained and propagated only through the intermediary of faith in the World" (Letter of 4 May 1931 in *Lettres de voyage,* p. 149; Rideau, 503, note 90). But does the World speak in the name of God? It is Christ who speaks to the world!

42. Henri de Lubac S.J., *La prière du P. Teilhard,* Paris 1964, pp. 145-196.

43. Cf. the declaration of the Council of Trent: ". . . credentes *in primis* a Deo justificari impium per gratiam ejus, per redemptionem quae est in Christo Jesu" (DS, 1526; DB, 798). The first and fundamental object of the faith of the Church is not the world, but Christ the Savior of the world (cf. Jn. 4, 42).

44. Teilhard, *Hymn of the Universe,* pp. 29-30 (Fontana).

45. Cf. G. Crespy, *De la science a la théologie,* Paris-Neuchatel 1965, p. 68: "The Christology of Teilhard is an eschatology, or rather the eschatology reabsorbs, by making them

converge on themselves, all the elements containd elsewhere in Christology."

46. Pius XII, discourse to the ecclesiastical censors, AAS, 48 (1956), 132-133: "The critic should begin with the presumption that what is said or written has a meaning in itself . . . an objective meaning which it is the critic's task to judge. . . . If the objective meaning of the words contains an error, it is the critic's duty to have it noted, even if he has reasons for thinking that its author's subjective line of thought is different and correct. A just and well-wishing critic will, in such a case, suggest a relative verbal correction, in view of who the author is; but for all that, the erroneous objective meaning is not annuled." This amounts to saying that the meaning of the words is governed by an accepted usage which the author cannot modify at will and without clarification; for, language is a phenomenon at once social and personal.

47. Cf. P. Labourdette, *Teilhard de Chardin et la pensée catholique,* Paris 1965, p. 239.

48. Extract from the first memoir of M. Blondel, published by Father de Lubac in *Blondel et Teilhard de Chardin,* Paris 1945, p. 23. Has not Blondel gone straight to the root of the problem? Father de Lubac has made him a partial reply: *ibid.,* note 12, pp. 57-59.

49. See note 14.

50. Teilhard, *Hymn of the Universe,* p. 31.

51. Cf. P. Benoit O.P., *Exégèse et Théologie,* Paris 1961, t. II, p. 136; Mooney, 98-99.

52. As Cardinal Journet points out (*Nova et Vetera,* 1964, p. 309), the original text read: "a votre corps veritable." The alteration could be accounted for by what is said in note 13 of this chapter. On the Church in Teilhard, see Mooney, 159-160.

53. Teilhard, *Hymn of the Universe,* p. 35.

54. Teilhard, *Milieu divin,* t. 4, p. 202.

55. A Feuillet D.S.S., *Le Christ Sagesse de Dieu,* Paris 1966, pp. 380-382.

56. Mooney (see our note 8) says that the word "physical" means "ontological" with Teilhard. We think that this is often true, but not always so, and especially not exclusively so. See the text cited in note 59.

57. G. Fessard S.J., *L'Homme devant Dieu (mélanges de Lubac),* Paris, 1964, t. III, p. 245.

58. *Milieu Divin:* "As our humanity assimilates the material world, and as the Host assimilates our humanity, the Eucharistic transformation goes beyond and completes the transubstantiation of the bread on the altar" (Fontana, p. 125).

59. Teilhard, *Forma Christi,* 1918: quoted by Mooney, 79.

60. Cf. the text quoted in note 50: "Lord Jesus, now that beneath these world-forces. . . ." Taken literally, in their strict

meaning, formulas of this kind, understood as applying not only to the Word, but to the Word Incarnate, will link up with the "ubiquitism" of Luther on the subject of the Eucharist. See note 64.

61. E.g. the following: by His Incarnation, "Christ must needs, without losing His human precision, become co-extensive with the physical immensities of Duration and Space" (*Esquisse d'un Univers personnel*, 1936, *Oeuvres*, t. 6, p. 113); ". . . it becomes conceivable that Christ should radiate physically over the bewildering totality of things; but still more it is inevitable that such radiation should reach a maximum of penetration and activation" (*Le Christique*, 1955, p. 10; Mooney, 86-87). There is nothing to show for certain that Teilhard is here thinking only of the divine nature and the divine person of the Word; he is speaking about Christ, and therefore about the Word Incarnate, in alluding to His "human precision." We think that it is only at the Parousia that the humanity of Christ will act directly on all bodies: we shall discuss this in Chapter Fourteen. The texts we cite here, of 1936 and of 1955, confirm our interpretation of the 1918 text cited at note 59.

62. Teilhard, *Super-humanité, Super-Christ, Super-charité,* 1943, *Oeuvres,* t. 9, pp. 210-211. We agree with the affirmation of a control "by the (divine) Person of Christ," if "control" implies direct action (See Mooney, p. 78).

63. On the ideas of "primary body" and "secondary body," see the texts cited in notes 9 and 10 of the present chapter.

64. This view bears a strong resemblance to the "ubiquitism" of Luther: "Luther ascribed to the body of Christ a participated, repletive presence (omnipresence) of the divinity by reason of the personal union of His human nature with His divinity and of His place at the right hand of the Father, without however this omnipresence enabling us to lay hold on Christ elsewhere than in the Eucharist" (A Michel, *Dictionnaire de Théologie catholique,* Paris, 1950, t. XV, 2, col. 2040: article: "Ubiquisme").

This thesis of ubiquitism had never been explicitly condemned by the Magisterium of the Church before the appearance of the encyclical *Mysterium Fidei* of Pope Paul VI: "Perperam igitur hanc praesentiae rationem aliquis explicet fingendo naturam 'pneumaticam' uti dicunt corporis christi gloriosi ubique praesentem" (AAS 57 (1965) 764). To our knowledge, Teilhard never expressed himself like this.

65. The Teilhardian formulas, or at least some of them, seemed to identify the mystical body and the physical body of Christ: see DS, 3816.

66. In Chapter XIV.

67. Rideau, 344 and 404, note 103: letter of 3 July 1934, already cited.

68. E.g., P. Smulders (*La vision de Teilhard,* Paris, 1965², part II, chap. 7); Rideau, 470: "No trace, in Teilhard, of the definitive destruction of a basic alienation, and of a collective, existential recuperation through the priestly action of Christ; no interpretation of the Cross as that of a pardon and a return to grace."

69. Teilhard, *Le Christique,* 1955, p. 7 (Mooney, 177).

70. *Ibid.*

71. A Feuillet, *Le Christ Sagesse de Dieu,* Paris, 1966, pp. 380-382.

72. Teilhard, *L'étoffe de l'Univers,* 1953, in *l'Activation de l'energie,* p. 405: "Impossible to think of Christ the 'evoluter' without having to re-think the whole of Christology. A functional completion of the One and of the Many is substituted for the creative paternalism to which we were accustomed. The double notion of static Evil and evolutive Redemption correcting or completing the idea of catastrophic Sin and of redemptive Expiation."

73. Teilhard, *Etudes,* 266 (1950), 284.

74. Cf. note 16.

75. Cf. The text to which our note 15 refers; 2 Pet. 3, 13.

76. Teilhard, *Le Christique,* 1955, p. 11 (Mooney, p. 143).

77. Mooney, citing *le Coeur de la Matiere* (1950, pp. 22-23) writes: "In the Heart of Christ there was a 'materialization' of God's love, at once spiritual and tangible, and yet at one and the same time an 'energizing' of that same love" (p. 24).

78. Thus "Crespy complained that Teilhard is never Pauline except in appearance, that he subjects Scripture to himself rather than subjecting himself to Scripture, and that he never sets off from the Bible, even if he does sometimes arrive there" (Feuillet, *op. cit.,* 380-382). There is perhaps some exaggeration in this criticism, at least in regard to the early writings of Teilhard up to and including *Milieu divin.* In 1929, Teilhard criticized the "Pauline" encyclical of Pius XI, *Miserentissimus Redemptor,* in a note of his unpublished *Le sens humain,* p. 16: "There are sentences which strike at the most legitimate hopes of modern man at least as much as did the Syllabus of Errors. We are never going to convert the world with such an outlook" (Mooney, 137). This encyclical deals primarily with reparation to the Heart of Jesus. In it, Pius XI thus described the purpose of this Reparation: "to offer to the uncreated Love a compensation for the indifference, the neglect, the offenses, or the injuries of every kind which may be offered to It." In the encyclical *Haurietis Aquas* (1956), Pius XII condemned the error of those who reject the cult of the Sacred Heart because it demands above all else "penitence, expiation, and many other allegedly passive virtues" (par. 7); cf. in this connection the remarkable study by H. Rondet S.J., "Péché et Réparation dans le culte du Sacré-Coeur," *Cor*

Jesu, Rome, 1959, t. 1, pp. 685-720. It can be said that reparation, already defined here according to Pius XI, finds its charter in Saint Paul's Letter to the Colossians (1, 24): "Now I rejoice in my sufferings for your sake, and in my flesh I complete what is lacking in Christ's affliction for the sake of his body, that is, the Church." In this light, it would be easy to show that joy in Christ crucified is an essential element of reparation, concerned with repairing what Paul elsewhere calls "worldly grief" and inseparable from "godly grief" (2 Cor. 7, 9-11). Teilhard, naturally inclined to a certain pessimism (cf. Mooney, 112-113; 210-211), against which he energetically reacted, had not, it seems, grasped this dialectical linkage between "godly grief" and joy in the Cross, urged by Saint Paul, and tending to exalt reparation to the Sacred Heart. Hence his distaste for a liturgy that seemed to him to be "obsessed with the idea of sin" (cf. the text at note 126). Nevertheless, how could one exaggerate the importance of an "idea" or rather of a *fact* (in which Teilhard, like all of us, was involved) which has issued in the Passion of a Man-God? Today, after the validation in *Haurietis Aquas* of the joy of the resurrected Heart of Christ, the difficulties expressed by Teilhard should disappear, at least in part.

79. Cf. Teilhard, *Le Coeur de la Matière,* 1950, pp. 22-23: "Under the symbol of the 'Sacred Heart' the divine assumed for me the form, the strength, and the properties of an Energy, of a fire. . . . Through its power to become universal, this Fire proved able to invade and impregnate with love the whole atmosphere of the world in which I lived" (Mooney, p. 24). This is certainly a beautiful passage. We cite it as an example of the influence of imagery on Teilhard's reflection. Sometimes, and perhaps here, the imagery tends to dominate the intellectual content rather than to serve it.

80. Cf. Mooney, 141-142.

81. Teilhard, *Christologie et Evolution,* 1933, pp. 7-8 (Mooney, 134-135).

82. Cf. Teilhard, *La vie cosmique,* 1916, *Ecrits du temps de guerre,* pp. 60-61: "Following the 'classical' view, suffering is above all a punishment, an expiation; it is efficacious as sacrifice; it originates from sin and makes reparation for sin. . . . The Cross is the symbol of the pain and toil of evolution rather than the symbol of expiation" (Mooney, 134). Here one notes once again Teilhard's disastrous tendency, which he never completely corrected, to set up his own views in opposition to the traditional doctrine of the Church instead of carrying on this doctrine in a homogeneous direction; from this viewpoint, Teilhard, at the doctrinal level, is "revolutionary" and not "evolutionist."

83. Rideau, 348: "The perspective of the supernatural elevation of nature seems to take precedence over that of repara-

tion. The baptism of Christ in death is not presented as the destruction of human alienation, the pulling down of the wall which, by separating man from God, deprived him also of real communion with his brethren. Teilhard does not seem to have sufficiently emphasized, in the Redemption, its aspect of God's judgment on history, of the condemnation of evil. . . . He adopts a perspective more in line with the logic of his own thinking than with the Biblical data." This final comment seems to be valid for all Teilhard's excursions into the field of theology.

84. Cf. the text to which our note 28 refers.

85. A. Feuillet, *op. cit.,* pp. 380-382.

86. Cf. Mooney, 223-224. Msgr. Bruno de Solages (*Teilhard de Chardin,* Toulouse, 1967, p. 67) notes how Teilhard's confidence in his own metaphysical speculations oscillated: "They began with the *Union créatrice* (1917). Then he moved away from them. . . . Only towards the end of his life, isolated and hardening his attitudes, does he in some texts appear, if I may venture the phrase, to take these attempts seriously."

87. Pius XII, *Humani Generis,* DS, 3890 (DB, 2317).

88. Teilhard, *Contingence de l'Univers et gout humain de survivre* (1953: unpublished). Rideau, 381.

89. Cf. the text to which our note 34 refers. Mooney, 186.

90. Cf. DS, 3002, 3025 (DB, 1783, 1805).

91. Mooney, 174-188. See, however, Smulders, *op. cit.,* part one, appendix one.

92. Teilhard, *Christianisme et Evolution,* 1945, cited by Mooney, p. 176.

93. This phrase shows decisively that the union in question here is not the unity of the Father and the Word in their common Spirit, but that of God with the world. A decided fallacy: how can the union of God with the world create the world? To the best of our knowledge, moreover, one can cite only one text of Teilhard which clearly affirms creation *ex nihilo*—in *Vision du Passé,* 1927, p. 188. One can therefore appreciate the manifest embarrassment in this matter experienced by the annotaters of *Ecrits du temps de guerre,* p. 172.

94. Cf. Teilhard, *Comment je vois* (1948: unpublished), cited by Mooney, 176.

95. Cf. the text to which our note 33 refers.

96. Teilhard, *Contingence de l'Univers et gout humain de survivre* (1953), cited by Mooney, 176.

97. Cf. *ibid.,* p. 379: "the scholastic notion of participation humiliates the man in us; it arouses the indignation of the Christian in me." Showing a deep misunderstanding of the doctrine, not only scholastic, but of the Church herself, Teilhard insists: "God creates through love, say the scholastics. But what, then, is this love, at once inexplicable in its subject and dishonoring for its object, which no need creates (if not

the pleasure of giving for giving's sake)?" (*ibid.*, p. 380). These lines express a proud refusal to adore the mysterious transcendence of the Divine Love.

98. Cf. Lk. 17, 10.

99. Cf. note 18.

100. Teilhard, "Quelques réflexions sur la *Conversion du Monde*": 1936: *Oeuvres*, 9, p. 161: "A first step would be to develop (in the line of the 'Philosophia perennis': primacy of Being, Act, and Potency), a correct Physics and Metaphysics of Evolution."

101. Cited by Rideau, 383, note 34. This is true as regards contingent being, but does not apply to absolute Being, even in the intimate relationships which constitute the divine persons: the Being is exactly identical with the Nature common to the three Divine Persons.

102. Teilhard, *Comment je vois* (1948: unpublished) p. 18: "Even in its primordial depths, the ontological principle taken as the basis of our metaphysics (Teilhard is referring here to the metaphysics of *uniri*) is valid and explicative: God Himself, in a rigorously true sense, exists only by unifying Himself." This is a correct statement as regards the divine Persons, but not as regards their unique nature; it must even be added that the Father and His Word are not parties who unite in order to form the whole of the Holy Spirit or of the divine essence, the opposite of what occurs with a contingent being. Teilhard has transposed in God a principle valid in the created world, without taking sufficient care to distinguish between Persons and Nature and to apply the principles of the analogical method.

103. Teilhard, *Comment je vois:* Rideau, 382, note 33: "Pleromization, that is to say, the realization of participated being by arrangement and totalization, appears as a kind of replication or symmetry of the Trinitization." It seems that with Teilhard there is a subtle distinction between pleromization (the realization of participated being) and Pleroma, an 'organic complex' uniting God and the pleromized World. This would make pleromization a process, and Pleroma its eschatological result.

104. Teilhard, *Christologie et Evolution* (1933: unpublished: cited by Father H. de Lubac S.J. in *Teilhard, Missionnaire et Apologiste*, Toulouse, 1966, p. 39): "It can be said that, throughout the early centuries of the Church, the dominant preoccupations of theology was to determine the position of Christ in relation to the Trinity; but, in our day, its vital interest has become the analysis and definition of the relations of existence and of influence which link Christ and the Universe." This is very true, but we must add that this analysis can be fruitfully carried out only within the authentic Trinitarian doctrine itself. On 14 January 1955, shortly before his

death, Teilhard wrote as follows to Father A. Ravier: "We are reviving, across fifteen hundred years, the great battles of Arianism—with this difference, however, that we are today no longer concerned with specifying the relations between the Christic and the Trinity, but between Christ and a Universe suddenly become fantastically big, formidably organic, and more than probably polyhuman." On 16 February 1955, Teilhard wrote again: "What we need is a new Nicaea" *(ibid.)*.

105. Mooney (p. 81; 179-181) cites and comments on the texts in which Teilhard admits while combating the temptation, notably in oriental religions.

106. Cf. Saint Thomas Aquinas, *Summa Theologica,* 1. 32. 1. 3.

107. Teilhard (unpublished) cited by Massabki, *op. cit.,* p. 139, note 1.

108. Cf. the text to which note 35 refers; and Smulders, *op. cit.,* part two, appendix two, *sub fine.*

109. Teilhard, *Ecrits du temps du guerre,* p. 231 (text of 1918).

110. Philipon O.P., *Seminarium,* 1967, p. 226.

111. Mooney, 62.

112. Teilhard, letter of 1 January 1951, cited by Mooney, 62-63.

113. Teilhard, *Quelques réflexions sur la Conversion du Monde,* 1936, *Oeuvres,* 9, pp. 161-162.

114. Cf. DS, 3020 (DB, 1800); DS, 3549 (DB, 2147).

115. GS, 62. 2: "Furthermore, while adhering to the methods and requirements proper to theology, theologians are invited to seek continually for more suitable ways of communicating doctrine to the men of our time": *semper inquirendum.* The whole paragraph is relevant.

116. Cf. Mooney, 158; but the text, still unpublished, it not cited literally in its most interesting phrases: "To say that the Church is infallible is simply to recognize that it possesses what any living phylum possesses, namely the capacity to find its way through innumerable groping towards maturity and fulfillment. Moreover, it is in perfect conformity with the great law of 'cephalization' which dominates the whole of biological evolution, to localize, as Catholics do, the permanent organ of this phyletic infallibility in the Councils or, by a more developed concentration of the Christian conscience, in the pope (formulating or expressing, not his own ideas, but the mind of the Church)" (cited by Chas. Massabki, *Le Christ, rencontre de deux amours,* Paris, 1962², p. 820). One notes, not only the unconscious wordplay of "cephalization" and "Cephas" or the false attribution of permanence to Councils, which are not a permanent organ of the Church, but above all the expression of an ecclesiology in biological language, without any allusion to the institution of the papacy by Christ—something

quite distinct from "the more advanced concentration of the Christian conscience." Moreover, the infallibility of the Church is traced back, in a style unconsciously Modernist, to that of life ("living organism"), and finally to that of the World (if one links this text with the one cited in note 41), and not to that of God.—The title of the unpublished work is: *Introduction à la vie chrétienne* (1944). Cf. notes 87 and 126.

117. Cf. DS, 3001-3002 (DB, 1782-1783).

118. DS, 3024 (DB, 1804).

119. From this viewpoint, one can understand the reactions of Cardinal Journet followed by Maritain. Both find that, "transposed into the dimensions of cosmogenesis, they (the ideas specified in the Teilhard letter to which our note 112 refers) are no longer Christian except in name; they are meaningful only within a cosmo-theogony of Hegelian type" (J. Maritain, *Le Raysan de la Garonne,* Paris, 1966, pp. 387-3388, citing Journet in *Nova et Vetera,* 1966, p. 150). One has only to place side by side with the Teilhardian list of Christian ideas to be transposed into dimensions of cosmogenesis, this proposition condemned by Pope Saint Pius X in 1907: "progressus scientiarum postulat ut reformentur conceptus christianae de deo, de creatione, de revelatione, de persona verbi incarnati, de redemptione" (DS, 3464; DB, 2064). Apart no doubt from the idea of revelation, Teilhard wanted to "transpose" all the others. One understands how Mooney (203) could maintain that Teilhard had lost the sense of transcendence, even though its concept was never absent from his work. But, unlike the Modernists, he never lost the sense of the historicity of Jesus (Mooney, 71-74). Furthermore, to transpose is not necessarily to reform, in the modernist sense, but could mean to re-formulate within a homogeneous and not heteregeneous evolution of dogma. In this connection, we get at least some reassurance from the following written by Teilhard in 1940: "Theology evolves, not by adding to or subtracting from its content, but by a relative emphasis and de-emphasis in its treatment, the process leading each time to the 'emergence' of a concept or an attitude that is more richly synthetic" (*Le Christ Evoluteur,* 1942, p. 5; Mooney, 198). No doubt the 1951 letter should be read in the light of this statement.

120. Cf. DS, 3001 (DB, 1782): "(deus) supra omnia, quae praeter ipsum sunt et concepi possunt, ineffabiliter excelsus."

121. AAS, 54 (1962), 526: "praetermisso judicio de his quae ad scientias positivas pertinent, in materia philosophica ac theologica satis patet praefata opera (patris Teilhard de Chardin) talibus scatere amiguitatibus, immo etiam gravibus erroribus, ut catholicam doctrinam offendant." Then the Monitum goes on to warn against the dangers in the works of Father Teilhard and of his followers. Father Philippe de la Trinité, in his book: *Rome et Teilhard* (Paris, 1964, p. 23),

states clearly, with the authorization of the Holy Office of which he is a consultor, that the pope has personally approved the Monitum. In May, 1968, Cardinal Garrone confirmed that this Monitum still holds good (Doc. Cath., 65—1968—col. 1054-1055).

We say "nearly," having in mind the thesis on the Redemption, whose Teilhardian formulations, however, apart from from those given here (text cited at note 16) would be far from irreproachable: cf. the text to which note 81 refers.

123. Paul Grenet, *Ami du Clergé*, 78 (1968), 310.

124. Unpublished sermon of 1270, cited by Sprico, *Trinité et vie morale*, Paris, 1957, p. 17.

125. Evolution, far from being just a scientific hypothesis to be accepted, was for Teilhard an article of Faith placed (verbally at least) on the same level as the dogmas of the Catholic Faith; see, for example, this statement as a sample of many: "If we wish to conserve to Christ the very qualities which are the basis of His power and our adoration, we have no alternative but to accept with all their implications the most modern ideas of Evolution" (*Comment je crois:* unpublished, 1934, p. 23). Did it never occur to him that the encyclical *Humani Generis* (DS, 3896; DB, 2327) was aimed at his ideas, when it censured those who were transforming scientific hypotheses into certitudes, without seeming to be in the least aware of the dogmatic difficulties created by the hypothesis of the evolution of the human body from living matter? Teilhard, in fact, as shown by a number of texts, seems to want to extend evolution and to use it to explain the origin, not only of the human body, but also of the soul: "The spirit painfully emerging from it (i.e. matter) through synthesis and centration" (*Oeuvres*, t. 5, pp. 122 *seq.*, 1942). However, an orthodox interpretation can be read into analogous texts, as Msgr. Bruno de Solages (*op. cit.*, p. 289) has shown: it is a question of substituting a more perfect center for a less perfect one: "The soul is created in order to centralize a pre-existent circle."

126. An observation of Father Philippe de la Trinité, *op. cit.*; cf. DS, 3896 (DB, 2327), where it is accepted that the evolution of the human body from matter is reconcilable with creation "ex nihilo" by God.

127. Teilhard, *Milieu divin* (p. 66—Fontana). In reality, it is not a "portion" but the whole of the "being" that is subjected to the power of the resurrected Christ. Everything is sacred in the sense that everything belongs to God, the Creator and Final End of all beings, which keep however their own naturs, their immediate ends, and consequently their relative autonomy, in which latter consists their relative "profaneness."

128. Cajetan: *commentary on the Summa Theologica*, III, 1. 1; cited by Father Mersch, *Le Corps Mystique du Christ*,

t. II, pp. 246-247, Louvain, 1951; see also C. Journet, *Eglise du Verbe incarne,* t. II, pp. 130-131, Paris, 1951. The same author points out elsewhere (*Nova et Vetera,* 1962, p. 49, par. 16) that one cannot speak about the intrinsic divinization of matter, in the sense of participation in "an infinite mode whose perfections are in God."

129. Saint Thomas Aquinas: *Summ Theologica,* III. 1. 1.

130. Lorca, cited by Mersch, *op. cit., ibid.*

131. Saint Gregory of Nyssa: PG, 44, 1317; 44, 441; Mersch, *op. cit.,* t. I, 456.

132. A Feuillet, *op. cit.,* pp. 380-382.

133. Mooney (235—note 62) gives his interpretation as based on Schlier, Benoit, Cerfaux, Warnach, and Dupont. Saint Paul, in Eph. 1, 10, could quite possibly have meant "to present the relationship between Christ and the cosmos as an extension of the physical and sacramental relationship between Christ and the members of his Church" (Mooney 98).

134. Cf. M. Bogdasavich, "Idea of Pleroma in Col. Eph.", *Downside Review,* 83 (1965).

135. "If pléromenoi of Eph. 1, 23 is to be taken in the passive sense (Feuillet) then it is the most complete of the pleroma texts in its statement of the relations between Christ, the Father, and the Church: the Church is Christ's body, the fullness of Him who is filled by the Father (cf. Col. 2, 9; Jo. 14, 20; 17, 22-23). Christ fills the world with the fullness which he has received from the Father (Col. 2, 9). In this sense, Christ is the middle term of the divine economy. For this reason pleroma is applied to Christ in some Pauline texts, to the Church in others. Christ is the pleroma of the Father, and the Church, by its unity with Christ, receives the pleroma from Him." It must be pointed out, however, that Father Benoit does not seem to agree with this exegesis, at least to the extent that pleroma, in his view, also signifies his universe: *Exégèse et Théologie,* Paris, 1961, t. II, pp. 135-153. At all events, the reader will note the convergence of the theme here developed, following Bogdasavich, with what we shall say in Chapter Ten about the recapitulation effected by the Father. Cf. Father Benoit, *Exégèse et Théologie, op. cit.,* p. 149: "In Eph., . . . Paul extends the Church to the dimensions of the Pleroma, thus giving it as it were a cosmic extension: Eph. 1, 3; 4, 13." In this connection, see also Angelicum, 43 (1966), 315.

136. We note that, in Col. 1, 19, as generally in Saint Paul, God signifies the Person of the Father.

137. Cf. Mooney 98-99: "Moreover, the 'fullness of time' in which this Plenitude is to be realized refers most probably to *both* comings of Christ, his Incarnation and the work of Redemption in time and his Parousia at the end of time."

138. Teilhard, *La Parole attendue,* 1940, Cahiers no. 4, p.

26, cited by Mooney, 168. In *Milieu Divin,* Teilhard speaks of "the mysterious Pleroma, in which the substantial *one* and the created *many* fuse without confusion in a *whole* . . ." (p. 122: Fontana).

139. Mooney, 170-171. In particular he cites this text of Teilhard: "The philosophy of creative union . . . is the philosophy of the universe conceived in function of our knowledge of the Mystical Body" (*Mons Univers,* 1940, *Oeuvres,* t. 9, p. 82). In 1944, in *Centrologie,* par. 26, cited by Rideau (380), Teilhard writes: "The fundamental ontological relationship between *being* and *universe* can be expressed in two opposite and no doubt complementary forms: one passive, 'Plus esse est plus a (*or* ex) pluribus uniri' (passive evolution); the other active, 'Plus esse est plus plura unire' (active evolution)." But does not the "plus esse" presuppose originally an "esse"? Does this "creative union" sufficiently respect and adequately express the creative action of God? Rideau seems to have doubts about this: "The inevitable absence (this philosophical problem evades a scientific phenomenology) of a recognition of the creative act for man, burdens the Teilhardian phenomenology with a basic difficulty which emerges when it seeks to complete human history in God" (336); it is the same exigency which Pius XII points out (DS, 3896; DB, 2327): "animas a Deo immediate creari catholica fides nos retinere jubet": we note, however, that Father North S.J. has attempted to investigate this point in *Teilhard and the Creation of the Soul* (Milwaukee, 1967). At all events, it must be emphasized, with Saint Thomas Aquinas, that creation and conservation are really one and the same divine action and that all created things are in motion towards God (*Summa Theologica,* I. 104. 1. 4.; II. II. 1. 7, 8; 2, 8). We shall see later how one can and should hold that Christ, at His Parousia, will exercise an influence over this movement. One can therefore understand, within the "philosophia perennis," if not creative union, at least a pleromization effected by Christ. Blondel, perhaps, best summarizes what Teilhard was attempting to do: the word "*pleroma* could serve to designate the full development of the creative and redemptive design"—and this would make it synonymous with *recapitulation* (letter to Father Valensin, 26 March 1935, *Correspondence,* t. III, 1965, pp. 196-197) and would leave intact the creation of the being of all things by God alone: *Summa Theologica,* I. 45. 5. 1.

140. Teilhard, letter of 16 February 1955, cited by H. de Lubac S.J.: *Teilhard Missionaire et apologiste,* Toulouse, 1966, p. 39.

141. Teilhard, *Ecrits du Temps de Guerre,* p. 279.

142. AA, 5 and 7.

143. Rideau (470) very aptly comments: "The beautiful spirituality of work propounded by Teilhard would have been

enriched by integrating the redemption constituted by the offering up of its constant suffering for the sin itself of human activity and of its historic disorders.'

144. We want to underline in this way Teilhards rejection of a cosmohypostatic union, even through the Eucharist, and also to point out that the transubstantiation affects only the consecrated bread and wine.

145. Crespy, *op. cit.,* p. 24.

146. Here we are repeating phrases from the Teilhardian texts cited in notes 17 and 28; they underline his paschal death in the sense that these thoughts were fostering in him a desire to die on Easter day—a wish which he actually did express a few days before his death. He was granted that wish; he died on Easter Sunday 1955.

147. Cf. Mt. 12, 40: ". . . so will the Son of man be three days and three nights in the heart of the earth. Buried, Teilhard was "locked up within the Heart of Christ, in the sense that the Heart of the Risen Christ is the symbol of the uncreated love of the Word, immense and omnipotent—even in the heart of the earth; but above all, his soul "on fire," "burns" with love for the Word of the divine Goodness, seen, as we hope, face to face, and for His human Heart present in the Eucharist, in so many tabernacles on earth.

148. Teilhard attributes this prayer to an unnamed "servant" of Jesus. It forms, with his commentary on it, the conclusion of "The Mass on the World" (*Hymn of the Universe,* pp. 31-35: Fontana). He also gives the prayer in its original Latin version: "Tu autem Domine mi, include me in imis visceribus Cordis tui. Atque ibi me detine, excoque, expurga, accende, ignifac, sublima, ad purissimum Cordis tui gustum atque placitum, ad puram annihilationem meam." Even if the commentary he makes on it is, in more than one point, open to question, it shows us how richly this prayer had for long nourished his soul. The theme of the universal Christ reappears in it (in this connection, we were unable to consult the book by Father Philippe de la Trinité O.C.D., *Foi au Christ Universal,* Table Ronde, Paris, 1968). We know that "The Mass on the World" originated from Teilhard's reflections during an expedition in central Asia, when he was unable to celebrate Mass. The text creates a special difficulty, common to the major part of Teilhard's writings on this subject, and one which we have not seen clearly analyzed: if, in a certain "pantheism" or "panentheism" the world becomes the body of Christ as a "secondary" body dependent on a "primary" body, the reader, unaware of this distinction made by Teilhard elsewhere (see notes 8 and 9 of this chapter), could gather in all good faith that it is useless to multiply Masses— since the First Mass, celebrated by Christ at the Last Supper, dispenses from any others—and could puzzle about the rea-

sons for Christ's command: "Do this in remembrance of me" (Lk. 22, 19). In other words, repeat what I have done. It is by no means farfetched to suppose such a danger for the reader. It is a striking example of the problem raised by the widespread diffusion of Teilhard's writings—that of the doctrinal and spiritual consequences of defective and sometimes erroneous formulations of an idea which is but rarely beyond reproach. Thus, it is relevant to note that, in the commentary on the prayer reproduced here, a splendid piece of writing, Teilhard unconsciously links up with the Jansenist criticisms against the devotion to the Heart of Jesus: ". . . what was captivating men's souls was the fact of their finding in you an element even more determinate, more circumscribed, than your humanity as a whole" (p. 32—Fontana; cf. the texts to which notes 21-25 refer). Now, what were the Jansenists saying? "The devotees of the Sacred Heart would envisage this Heart separated from the divine Person, and even from the sacred Humanity." They should have known better, since the propagators of this devotion constantly preached the opposite (J. Nouwens M.S.C., *L' Actualité d'un Culte,* reports of the (1955) Congress of the Sacred Heart, Tilburg, 1957, chap. 6: considerations on the Jansenist opposition to the Sacred Heart, p. 63).

Father H. Rondet S.J. has identified the "servant" of Jesus who composed the prayer given and meditated on by Teilhard, as Father G. Druzbicki S.J. (1590-1662). Cf. H. Rondet: "Note sur Teilhard, Druzbicki et la Dévotion au Sacré-Coeur," *Rev. d'Ascétique et de Mystique,* 45 (1969), 451-452.

5

BULTMANN
THE CHRIST OF THE EXISTENTIAL DECISION

We shall now discuss some non-Catholic authors whose christological vision enjoys a considerable vogue at the present time. Although we are far from accepting fully their way of regarding the mystery of the Man Jesus, we nevertheless think that they have a valuable contribution to make to a better understanding of the Savior and a considerable aptitude in making Him known to our contemporaries.

Ranking among the first of these is Bultmann. What does Jesus signify for him. What are his presuppositions? How should a Catholic react to his ideas, and how can a Catholic, through these ideas, renew the testimony of his own fidelity to the one Master?

A. The Christ of Bultmann

The New Testament, according to Bultmann, presents Jesus of Nazareth under the mythological form of Jesus the Christ. Jesus the Rabbi becomes Jesus the Event. The Jesus of history lived as a Jewish Rabbi—but even that is not absolutely certain.[1]

The Christ of faith is a mythically pre-existent being, who appears on earth as a man, works miracles to prove His divinity, dies in expiation of the sins of men and in their place, and destroys the power of death by His Resurrection. According to Bultmann, all this should be regarded as mythic thought and mythological language.

But this language, he holds, has a meaning. The history of Jesus signifies the salvific event of the existential decision in the individual encounter with the transcendent God. We have simply to stop objectifying the representations, while at the same time we keep the profound meaning of the myth. We must re-interpret the myth of Christ precisely in order to be faithful to the word of God.

The New Testament titles of Christ (Son of God, Son of Man, Messiah, Lord, God) are not intended to teach us about Him and about His inmost nature, but are meant to express what He signifies for man. Their meaning is this: in what Jesus says and is, God speaks to us and acts for us. The mere emergence of Jesus invites man to decide for or against God: "Christ is God" would be a false statement if one ascribed an objective meaning to the word "God"; but a correct statement if by "God" one signified the event of the divine action.

For Bultmann, the Heideggerian exegete, the encounter between man and Jesus is summed up as follows:

> If men are standing in the crisis of decision, and if this crisis is precisely the essential characteristic of their humanity, then every hour is the last hour, and we can understand that for Jesus the whole contemporary mythology is pressed into the service of this conception of human existence. Thus he understood and proclaimed his hour as the last hour. This message of the Kingdom of God is absolutely alien to the present-day conception of humanity. . . . Jesus expresses no conception of a human ideal, no thought of a development of human capacities, no idea of something valuable in man as such. . . . The worth of a man is not determined by his human quality . . . but simply by the de-

cision he makes in the here-and-now of his present life.[2]

Bultmann develops this elsewhere by saying that the eschatological event of the Christ is concretely realized only in the here-and-now of the preaching of the Word.[3] We encounter Christ only in the preaching.

The cross of Christ is not an expiatory sacrifice, but a judgment on the world. His resurrection is not the incredible miracle of the re-animation of a corpse; but faith in the resurrection consists in believing that the cross places us in a new situation.

B. The Presuppositions of Bultmann

At the root of Bultmann's Christology, one can clearly discern a whole series of exegetical or metaphysical, even confessional, options. We shall deal briefly with three of these: his idea of the New Testament *Weltanschauung;* his idea of de-mythologization; the influence of Luther.

1. *The world of the New Testament is mythic*

"The whole conception of the world which is in the preaching of Jesus as in the New Testament generally is mythological; i.e., the conception of the world as being structured in three stories, heaven, earth and hell." Man is subjected to the action of supernatural powers: God, angels, devils, miracles. This world is awaiting its end, its judgment, the resurrection. The end of time has come: God has sent His Son.

All this, in Bultmann's view, is mythology. The latter is a primitive science aimed at explaining phenomena and incidents which are strange, curious, surprising, or frightening, by attributing them to supernatural causes, to gods or demons. Myths express man's knowledge that he is not master of the world and of his life. "It may be said that myths give to the transcendent reality an immanent, this-worldly objectivity. Myths give worldly objectivity to that which is unworldly *(Der Mythos objektiviert das Jenseitige zum Diesseitigen)*."[4]

This language is unacceptable to modern man. Science has shown that the division of the world into three stories is a fiction. Progress in the natural sciences has ended faith in angels, in devils,[5] and in miracles.

Nay more, modern man understands himself as the subject of his own activity. He does not accept the New Testament belief that external powers can influence his personal life; he is no longer alienated.

Nevertheless, the New Testament holds a truth which is independent of this mythology, and the task of theology is to de-mythologize the preaching of Christ— a task already begun by the New Testament. "This method of interpretation of the New Testament which tries to recover the deeper meaning behind the mythological conceptions, I call *de-mythologizing*— an unsatisfactory word, to be sure" (*op. cit.*, p. 18).

2. *Demythologization and historicity of the human being*

Bultmann does not seek purely and simply to eliminate the mythology. The aim of his hermeneutic method, he tells us (*op. cit.*, p. 18), "is not to eliminate the mythological statements but to interpret them." Such eliminations would entail the risk of cancelling the message to which we have alluded. That was the error of the liberal theology.

Bultmann seeks to interpret the myths in a critical way; in other words, to distinguish between the objectifying representations of the myth, and the existential signification which these representations embody.

Modern man seeks to understand *himself* in the New Testament, and faith is precisely this self-understanding. The New Testament idea of human existence is summed up in the opposition between the inauthentic life of sin and the authentic life of faith, and in the passage from the one to the other. God invites me to believe that I am a justified sinner. Faith is the decision involved in this passage.

In order to understand what the New Testament is saying to me about God and about myself, I must know, at least implicitly, what is authentic life and authentic death. An explicit knowledge is not required. But it is indispensable if a methodical interpretation of the New Testament is to be given. The existential interpretation of the New Testament presupposes an existential analysis of man.

It is at this point that Heidegger intervenes. In *Sein und Zeit*, he has analyzed the general and formal structures of man, the historicity of the human being. Man is a temporal being who fulfills himself through existential decisions.

3. *Bultmann, disciple of Luther*

If Bultmann ascribes so little importance to the human life and to the destiny of Jesus, this, says Father Bouillard,[6] is because he is a Lutheran. The Christology of Luther is functional; his interest is not in Christ as Christ, but in Christ as existing *for us*. Lutheran Christology does not ascribe an active role to Christ as man in the mystery of the Redemption.[7] Only faith and the divine promise of salvation are important.

With Bultmann, justification by faith is transposed into salvific self-understanding. As he himself explicitly says, "de-mythologizing is the radical application of the doctrine of justification by faith to the sphere of knowledge and thought. Like the doctrine of justification by faith, demythologizing destroys every longing for security. There is no difference between security based on good works and security built on objectifying knowledge. . . . He who abandons every form of security shall find the true security. Man before God has always empty hands" (*op. cit.*, p. 84). Existential philosophy and exegesis become instruments made to contribute to a Lutheran perspective.

C. Critique

1. *NEGATIVE CRITIQUE*

(a) *Myth and demythologization:* if, as Bultman tells us, the New Testament already invites us to demythologize its mythic discourse, does not this mean that, exhaustively considered, this discourse is not mythological?

It is true that the New Testament, like Genesis is another domain, has borrowed some images from the style of the Jewish apocalyptic, and these images are "mythological." But such images are embodied in a discourse which de-mythologizes them. They no longer designate a mythological process, but characterize the salvific work accomplished in Christ and in the faith of the Church. The reference to history changes their meaning, because the discourse which incorporates them expresses judgments through which is manifested the essential cognitive activity of the human mind faced with reality; and these go beyond the sphere of the imagination. The discourse of the New Testament is historical.

(b) *Necessity for a philosophy as an instrument of demythologization within the faith:* it is true that the Christian message would have no significance for us if it did not elucidate the meaning of our existence. If it is to be explicit, such clarification needs some philosophic basis and some help from rational self-understanding on the part of men. Is not this what the Church has constantly held since the Middle Ages? Is not this the reason why she recommends Saint Augustine and Saint Thomas Aquinas? Surely it can be said that, in the Thomistic doctrine of analogy, we have a wonderful instrument for explaining—and, in a sense, for "demythologizing"—the transcendent realities signified by the Biblical text and to be grasped only through the negation of our human way of signifying them. One need only think of the Thomistic explanation of the real (as opposed to notional) relationship between the creature and the Creator, or of the analyses which Saint Thomas gives of the Creation and the Incarnation. He is not beguiled by images, and he is emphatically aware that one cannot speak in the same way about human things and about divine things!

It must be recognized, however, that Bultmann does to some extent see the need for an analogical language in relation to God: "When we speak of God as acting, we mean that we are confronted with God, addressed, asked, judged, or blessed by God. Therefore, to speak in this manner is not to speak in symbols or images, but to speak analogically."[8] But it is abundantly clear that Bultmann's explanation of analogy and of analogical language remains very imperfect when put side by side with that of Saint Thomas Aquinas.[9]

(c) As for *the christological doctrine of Bultmann*, how can it be said that the work of God in Jesus Christ consists *solely* in the transformation of our existence through faith in the message preached? Does this work exhaust itself in the new relationship which binds us to God in Christ? On the contrary, does it not *primarily* consist in a unique relationship of the Man Jesus with God, a relationship which becomes mediative of our relationship with God in faith? If God really acts and really speaks to us through preaching, why should His action in Jesus Christ and in Christ's paschal mystery of death and of resurrection be mythic?

The ideas of mediation, of sign, and of participation are absent from Bultmann's work. His Lutheran faith has taught him that the world of a totally transcendent God is one thing, and the profane world something quite different ("The invisibility of God excludes every myth which tries to make God and His action visible; God withholds Himself from view and observation. . . . Luther has taught us that the world as a whole is indeed a profane place"):[10] therefore, to seek to discover in this world, and not solely in subjective personal experience, the marks of the divine action, shows a lack of faith in the transcendence of God.

2. POSITIVE CRITIQUE

What benefit can Catholic theology derive from Bultmann?—more especially, in connection with Christology? One might suggest two:

(a) *A more acute awareness of the importance of hermeneutics.* Bultmann writes: "We can understand the problem best when we remember that *de-mythologizing is an hermeneutic method,* that is, a method of interpretation or exegesis. . . . Reflection on hermeneutics (the method of interpretation) makes it clear that interpretation, that is exegesis, is always based on principles and conceptions which guide exegesis as pre-suppositions, although interpreters are often not aware of this fact."[11] Is it not, we remark in passing, the method which the Catholic theologian should apply to Bultmann, and which we ourselves have attempted, partially however, to apply to him?

Catholic hermeneutics—as described by Pius XII (encyclical *Divino Afflante,* 1943) and later by Pope Paul (*Dei Verbum,* 1965)[12]—has for its guiding principle the study of the literal sense which the inspired authors had in mind, and which is to be discerned in the light of the culture of their contemporaries and of the literary genres they used.

Besides, this hermeneutics does not admit the presuppositions common to liberal Protestantism, to Modernism, and to Bultmann: i.e. she does not accept the idea that the words and actions attributed to Christ by the Gospels must be considered *a priori* as non-historical on the pretext that they would have been incompatible with the education and with the culture of a man of His time.[13] Consequently, she rejects the gratuitous postulates of naturalism and of immanentism.

The discussions aroused by Bultmann help us to a better grasp of one important matter. Like that of the Councils and of dogma,[14] the language of the New Testament is intelligible to all men of every era, but not necessarily in an immediate way, or even ordinarily. It is bound up, at least in part, with images, representations, mental categories which are not always specifically those of modern man and of modern civilization. We must therefore interpret the New Testament in order to understand it and explain it; we must transpose it into our modern categories in order to make it comprehensible where it is not immediately so. Through and beyond the literalness of the expressions, we must seek to grasp what the inspired authors were conveying to us. In this respect, our task is therefore more difficult than was that of the first century apostles and apologists, at least of those whose mission was directed to the Jewish world.[15]

(b) *A clearer awareness of the inevitably imagist character of human language.* The inspired authors of the New Testament made use at times of "mythic" language in their historical accounts. This was not, however, a concession on their part to a mode of expression with which they could not dispense; they deliberately used this language in order to announce the mystery in the categories which were most accessible to their contemporaries. And this mystery cannot be announced except by using images, which always need to be purified.

However, Bultmann was not entirely unaware of this point. He recognized that heaven is a spatial image of God's transcendence (". . . the transcendent God is imagined as being at an immense distance far above the world. . . . The transcendence of God is imagined by means of the category of space").[16] Does this not amount to saying that man, inserted in space and time, needs to express this insertion, partly identical with his historicity, by means of symbols? Is not this to acknowledge the permanent and continuing value of the Biblical language?[17] And is not Bultmann caught out here in flagrant inconsistency?

D. The Christology of Bultmann, a Call to a Renewal of the Theology of Preaching

Despite his Lutheran "actualism" and his tendency to reduce the divine action to the here-and-now of actually heard preaching, Bultmann rightly emphasizes the importance of the existential encounter between the believer and Christ at the proclamation of the Gospel.

It must be admitted that, until recently, the majority of Catholic theologians had not paid sufficient attention to this salvific encounter. Happily, there is now a renewal of reflection on the role of preaching in the economy of salvation.

As Bultmann stresses, the Cross of Jesus is truly a judgment of God, renewed at each preaching of the Word. The Word of God at once condemns and enlivens. Through the preacher whom He sends, "Christ announces the Christ," to use Saint Augustine's expression.[18] At this proclamation of the Message which constitutes an invitation to man to answer, man is stimulated to renew his existential decision, his choice before God.

The "crisis"[19] or judgment of the existential decision is not the only one, but all the same it is a characteristic manifestation of man at the twofold level of the natural and the supernatural. It should form one of the subjects for theological consideration. Anyhow, just like the discernment of spirits with which it is intimately linked, it constitutes a theme of the patristic tradition, notably in its connection with preaching. Let us therefore remind ourselves of certain essential elements of a Catholic reflection on the function of the salvific dialogue between preacher and hearer in the economy of salvation.[20]

Preaching is a prolonging of the Redemptive Incarnation. In it the preacher invests Christ with an aerial body of words, as the Blessed Virgin Mary had invested Him with human nature.[21] Like the mission of the Savior which it prolongs, preaching constitutes a major mystery of salvation which exceeds human reason: ". . . it pleased God through the folly of what we preach to save those who believe" (1 Cor. 1, 21). Preaching has renewed the face of the earth. Conversion, the effect of Christian faith, is truly the work of preaching, as Pope Benedict XV specifically points out, citing

Saint Paul: "But how are men to call upon him in whom they have not believed? And how are they to believe in him of whom they have not heard? And how are they to hear without a preacher? . . . So faith comes from what is heard, and what is heard comes by the preaching of Christ" (Rom. 10, 14-17).[22]

And with what is the "folly" of the message concerned? With "Christ crucified, a stumbling block to Jews and folly to Gentiles, but to those who are called, both Jews and Greeks, Christ the power of God and the wisdom of God" (1 Cor. 1, 23-24). We can therefore say that preaching is a paschal mystery, not only because of its object and purpose, but also because its appearance (a transitory proclamation by a mortal man) reflects the weakness of the Crucified, while its effect (the construction of the Church and eternal life) reflects the triumphant power of the Risen Lord.

Such are the intermediate and final effects of the proclamation of the Word of Salvation; but its immediate effect is the conversion, the existential decision involving a passage from the inauthentic life of sin to the authentic life of grace, from death to life. Is it not true that a great number of sinners, enemies of the cross of Christ, have been led to take the existential decision *par excellence*, that of conversion, by hearing the word of Christ preached and explained by His messengers?

It is certainly the great merit of Bultmann to have perceived the salvific importance of preaching. It is even curious to note that this provided the starting point of his whole body of ideas: was it not his aim to assist preachers to give sure doctrine to the Christions? One knows the result—the reduction of the Resurrection of Christ to a myth! But this outcome in no way indicates an error in the initial perception of the need for a renewal of preaching; rather does it invite us to think again about its vital importance in the building of the Church.

Moreover, Bultmann has written some very beautiful passages about preaching as the encounter with

God in Jesus Christ. To a very large extent, we can identify with the fine sentiments expressed in the following passage:

> God meets us in His Word, in a concrete word, the preaching instituted in Jesus Christ. . . . It is the word of God which calls man away from his selfishness and from the illusory security which he has built up for himself. It calls him to God, who is beyond the world and beyond scientific thinking. At the same time, it calls man to his true self. For the self of man, his inner life, his personal existence is also beyond the visible world and beyond rational thinking. The Word of God addresses man in his personal existence and thereby it gives him freedom from the world and from the sorrow and anxiety which overwhelm him when he forgets the beyond. By means of science men try to take possession of the world, but in fact the world gets possession of men. We can see in our times to what degree men are dependent on technology, and to what degree technology brings with it terrible consequences. To believe in the Word of God means to abandon all merely human security and thus to overcome the despair which arises from the attempt to find security, an attempt which is always vain.
>
> Faith in this sense, is both the demand of and the gift offered by preaching. Faith is the answer to the message. Faith is the abandonment of man's own security, and the readiness to find security only in the unseen beyond, in God. . . . Genuine freedom is not subjective arbitrariness. It is freedom in obedience.[24]

Here we can see with what clarity Bultmann denounces the real myth of modern man—the myth of the domination of the world by science. When this Prometheus reflects on the matter, should he not discover that he is in the very situation which appears to him, in his hour of technological exaltation, to be that of the man dominated by myth? Like him, he knows quite well that he is not the master of the world or of his own life. Here again and happily, Bultmann is not consistent with his own analysis of myth, because, even in the midst of his negations, he preserves the sense of mystery.

Were Bultmann perfectly consistent with himself and with his notion of myth, he would see that Christian preaching, such as he conceives it, corresponds to his notion of myth: "It may be said that myths give to the transcendent reality an immanent, this-worldly objectivity" (*op. cit.* p. 19). In Bultmann's own terms, we may say that he has "mythologized" preaching at the very time when he was attempting to "de-mythologize" its content.[25] Is not this because he has obscurely perceived that Christian preaching participates in the mysterious character of the transcendent and immanent God which it announces, and, in some manner, makes present? And if preaching is not a myth but a mystery beyond the grasp of pure reason, why cannot the same be said of angels and devils, of miracles and of Christ's Resurrection?

The existential decision of which Bultmann speaks seems, therefore, to be that of the faith which abandons itself to God in order to be finally vanquished by death without any possibility of its triumphing over death. Like the Resurrection of Christ, then, access to the transcendent beatitude is a myth.[26]

On the contrary, according to the Biblical Revelation and the Council of Trent,[27] deeply extended by Karl Rahner,[28] the existential decision *par excellence* is the oblation of the personal death, in union with the sacrifice of Christ on the cross renewed in the Eucharist, and in answer to the message of salvation transmitted by preaching.

It can be said that passive death, the separation of soul from body, is inseparable from active death,[29] the latter being identical with man's final free act of merit or of demerit.

In order that this act may be salvific, it must be linked with the absolutely free grace of final perseverance, "the great gift of God."[30] No one can acquire a strict right to a coincidence of grace with this final existential decision—the decision to place all earthly existence into the hands of the living God; the oblative acceptance of the severance of death in union with that of the dying Christ, Jesus mortal man. It is the supreme grace which Christ, by His death, has merited for those whom He has chosen before the creation of the world: the inmost and ultimate act of the offering of life and death.

This existential decision *par excellence* recapitulates all the preceding decisions and marks them with a definitive seal, conferring on them a meaning which is henceforth immutable.

By this decision, the immortal soul accepts the privation of its body. It offers this privation in expiation and in reparation for its sins. It thus merits eternal life, in a supreme manner. All its prior meritorious acts became definitively so only through this supremely meritorious act. But it can be merited only *de congruo*, through the prayer of supplication, and above all through communion in the "passage" of Christ in the Eucharist, the sacrament of perseverance in charity.

The existential decisions of man are, therefore, enclosed between a first[31] and a final total choice, between a first absolutely free grace of justification and a final supremely gratuitous grace of final perseverance.

It is undeniable that these perspectives which derive from Catholic dogma, offer a much more dramatic view of man's existential decision than does that of Bultmann, for whom immortality is mythological.[32]

For him, it seems to us, man's life and death open on to nothingness; no one decision is more existential than any other, since all decisions are doomed to come to nothing in death, there being no heaven and no hell. The choice is a purely terrestrial one. For the Catholic, the last existential decision is privileged. It constitutes an eternally continuing choice against the gratuitous and merciful love of God the Creator, or, on the contrary, for Him, with Him, and in Him.

Thus, the supreme existential decision of the redeemed man who accepts his gratuitous redemption is indissolubly linked with the supreme existential decision of his Redeemer, the Son of Man: the oblative decision of the redemptive death, the visible sign of the invisible spiritual and corporal sacrifice of predestined humanity.

Now, death can fully attain the dimension here described only if it has been evangelized. The preacher, in celebrating the Eucharistic Sacrifice, announces in an indissoluble way the redemptive death of Christ until He returns (cf. 1 Cor. 11, 26), and the acceptance of his own death offered in union with that of Christ for his hearers. They too, in communicating, announce the death of Christ and the offering of their own death in union with that of the Lord.

In the Mass, the existential decision of the Man-God is renewed and proclaimed. It is recapitulative of all the existential and meritorious decisions of the men of all times, decisions directed not towards nothingness but towards eternal life.

It is during the celebration of the Pasch of the Lord that the preaching of the death and resurrection of the Christian is supremely efficacious of conversion and of existential decision.[33] In the light of the irreversible decision of Christ Jesus, taking on Himself our death and triumphing over it forever, and in the light of the sacramental renewal of this decision, man sees more clearly, in faith, that he has not been created for death but for life, and that, through grace, he is able not only to make successive responses, each decisive for its time, but also and above all (and this is what is lacking in Bultmannian existentialism) to make an irreversible salvific decision.

The word of the cross is the word of life and of reconciliation (1 Cor. 1, 18; Ph. 2, 16; 1 Cor. 5, 19). It proclaims the obligation to die, while at the same time announcing eternal life. The Eucharist is the "feast prepared for all peoples." Through His messengers, Christ unveils in it the mystery veiled by death. And is not this death which "he will destroy for ever," "the mourning veil covering all peoples, and the shroud enwrapping all nations" (Is. 25, 6-8: Jerusalem Bible)?

The veil of the Temple has been rent and the side of the Lamb has been transpierced. "The heart of Jesus is His wisdom which was in the Scriptures. Scripture was sealed: no one understood it. The Lord has been crucified, and His wisdom has liquified like wax, in order that all may understand the Scripture; what was hidden has been revealed, and it is for that reason that the veil of the Temple has been rent," writes Saint Augustine magnificently.[34]

The eternally transpierced heart of the Lord is the sign of His decision to love and to be obedient even unto death, in order to make all men participate in the same decision and to make them exist in a divine way.

NOTES TO CHAPTER FIVE

1. R. Bultmann, *Jesus and the Word,* Scribner, N.Y., 1934, pp. 58 and 61. Note, in the same connection, J. R. Geiselmann: "By the word *Jesus* we designate a personality who belongs to history and who contributes to history; but the word *Christ* is the name of a dignity, since it expresses the action by which God, for our salvation, has intervened in the history of the world" (*Encyclopédie de la Foi,* Paris, 1967, t. II, art. Jesus-Christ, p. 352). See also Cervaux, *Le Christ dans la théologie de Saint Paul,* 1954, pp. 367 and 381; and J. Lebreton S.J.: "From the beginning, Jesus has been the revealer of the Christian dogma as well as being its real object; and for this two-fold reason, it should be said that it is Christ who has made Christology, and not that it is through a Christology, deriving from this or that, that Jesus is made Christ" (*Origines du Dogme de la Trinité,* Paris, 1919⁴, t. I, p. 243).

2. R. Bultmann, *op. cit.* (Fontana), pp. 44-46.

3. R. Bultmann, *Kerugma und Mythos,* t. II, p. 206 (Hamburg, 1952).

4. R. Bultmann, *Jesus Christ and Mythology,* N. Y., 1958, pp. 18-19.

5. Bultmann appears to take for granted that the inspired authors sought to convey, in the name of God, a scientific view of the world—a view which is now obsolete. Many aspects

of his objection disappear when one remembers the words of Leo XIII: "scriptor sacer ea secutus est quae sensibiliter apparent; Spiritum Dei . . . noluisse ista (videlicet—intimam adspectabilium rerum constitutionem) docere homines, nulli saluti profutura" (DS, 3288). In speaking about hell, earth, and heaven, the Scriptures do not claim to give a scientific description. Besides, science is concerned with phenomena, and threefore could never affirm or deny the existence of angels and devils, these being pure spirits.

6. H. Bouillard S.J., *Logique de la Foi,* Paris, 1964, 123-148.

7. Cf. Y. M. J. Congar O.P., *Das Konzil von Chalkedon,* Wuerzburg, 1954, Band III, pp. 457-486: "the Christology of Luther." This is a contribution to a collective work edited by Grillmeier and Bacht.

8. R. Bultmann, *Jesus Christ and Mythology,* pp. 68-69.

9. Bultmann seems to be unacquainted with the three ways of analogy as propounded by Saint Thomas Aquinas: via affirmationis, via negationis, et via eminentiae.

10. Bultmann, *Jesus Christ and Mythology,* pp. 83-85.

11. *Ibid.,* pp. 45-46.

12. Cf. DS, 3236-3830; *Verbum Dei,* par. 12. In this connection, we note, with Cardinal Jean Daniélou: "The authors of the Gospels use literary genres which are those of their contemporaries: the *midrash* (haggadic exegesis), the narration of the lives of the great personages of the Old Testament; the *pesher,* which shows in actual events the fulfillment of the prophesies; the *apocalypse,* which shows them as pre-existent in the eternal design of God. It is through these that the Gospels, far from being denuded of historical value, are on the contrary the expression of an integral history which gives to the events their full dimension. So far, therefore, from nullifying the historical value of the Gospels, a critical attitude does, on the contrary, give to this value its full significance" (*Bulletin du Cercle saint Jean Baptiste,* VII. 2, 1966, pp. 55-56). It can be admitted that the midrashic literary genre is not historical, even though the Evangelists put it to the service of an historical discourse. This has been notably confirmed by the discoveries of the Dead Sea scrolls, showing that what Bultmann regarded as derivatives from Greek Gnosticism was rooted in the Palestinian soil (cf. W. F. Albright, *Bible et vie Chrétienne,* no. 76, 1968, pp. 75-90).

13. Cf. Saint Pius X, *Pascendi,* DS, 3480. *Dei Verbum,* par. 12, in no way contradicts Pope Pius X: the culture of Christ's contemporaries enables us to understand more clearly the meaning of what Christ effectively said and did during His earthly life, and to hold as in no manner impossible or unlikely the words and deeds attributed to Him by the Evangelists.

14. Cf. Paul VI, Enc. *Mysterium Fidei,* AAS, 57 (1965) 758: the Pope points out that the language of the Councils uses

concepts derived from universal and necessary experience.

15. No doubt with Bultmann in mind, Father J. Comblin (*La Résurrection de Jésus,* Paris, 1959) has shown that the Gospel was first proclaimed shortly before the passing of the affective and mythic age which gave place to the rational age of human history. It is to secure a better expression of His revealed message that the Word became man in a particular epoch of history.

16. R. Bultmann, *Jesus Christ and Mythology,* pp. 20 and 22.

17. Thus, the sky will always be a readily understood symbol of God's transcendence. Nevertheless, Psalm 113 (112), verses 4-6, emphasizes that the glory of the Lord is "above the heavens"!

18. Saint Augustine, PL, 39, 1563. Text cited by Pius XII (*Mystici Corporis*).

19. Etymologically, the word "crisis" signifies a decision which presupposes a judgment.

20. Cf. B. de Margerie S.J., *Padres Profetas e Mistagogos,* S. Paulo, 1968, ch. I and II.

21. Pius XII to the Dominican Order, AAS, 38 (1946) 388.

22. Benedict XV, *Humani Generis,* AAS, 9 (1917) 305 *seq.*

23. Notice, in Bultmann, a unilateral insistence on the transcendence of God and, at the same time, by a strange paradox, the implicit negation of the omnipotence of God, who intervenes *in human history* and not just in preaching.

24. R. Bultmann, *Jesus Christ and Mythology,* pp. 78 and 40-41.

25. Because Bultmann sees in preaching an action of God in the world, or, more precisely, in the person: *op. cit.,* p. 68. Also Bultmann would no doubt answer that the personal dimension of subjective existence where God intervenes is not the objective dimension of the world, which remains profane.

26. R. Bultmann, *Jesus Christ and Mythology,* pp. 30-39.

27. DS, 806.

28. K. Rahner S.J., *Ecrits Théologiques,* III, 103-167 (Bruges, 1963).

29. Note that certain exegetes and theologians declare, in the light of 1 Th. 4, 15 *seq.,* that the universality of physical death is uncertain; even if this were so (cf. the formula of the Apostles' Creed which declares that Christ will come "to judge *the living* and the dead"), it remains absolutely certain that, for each individual person, there will be a final free act of merit or of demerit.

30. Cf. DS, 1566.

31. Cf Saint Thomas Aquinas, *Summa Theologica,* I, II,89. 6; the grace of final perseverance can be merited as a merit *de congruo;* it must be acknowledged that this is also possible in the case of an adult who receives the first grace of justification.

The latter could be merited by a merit *de congruo,* under the influence of actual grace.

32. R. Bultmann, *Jesus Christ and Mythology,* pp. 30-31: "Surely both conceptions of transcendent bliss are mythological, the Platonic conception of bliss as philosophical dialogue as well as the Christian conception of blessedness as worship. . . . This (i.e. Christian) faith may be called readiness for the unknown future that God will give. In brief, it means to be open to God's future in the face of death and darkness." Not only does Bultmann *not* affirm immortality, but also without explicitly denying it, he could be said to insinuate that it is improbable: cf. pp. 31-34 where he maintains that Paul and John have de-mythologized the eschatological preaching of Jesus. The ordinary reader will interpret this as a denial of all human life after death. The more astute reader will be less sure about this, but will continue to have something of the same impression. Besides, some incoherence is involved in saying that the immortality of the soul is mythological if one holds, as Bultmann does (cf. note 4) that myth is the reduction of the transcendent and the divine to the human and the immanent. For, on the contrary, does not the doctrine of the immortality of the soul affirm the transcendent as such, in the sense that the immortality of the soul is inseparable from the transcendent God who conserves it? The affirmation of the immortality of the soul, as distinct from the mythic form in in which Bultmann conceives it, does not involve any "immanent, this-worldly objectivity"; the soul is not a sensible, palpable object. On Bultmann's attitude towards mythology, see R. Marlé, *Bultmann et l'interprétation du N.T.,* Paris 1966², pp. 62-71; on the Resurrection of Christ, *ibid.,* pp. 166-170.

33. In effect, it is during the celebration of the holy mysteries, after the sacramental of the collective confession, that the already purified Christian can hear something that will purify him still more (Jn. 15, 3).

34. Saint Augustine (PL, 36, 175) comments as follows on Psalm 22, 15 ("I am poured out like water. . . . My heart is become like wax melting. . . ."): "Cor ipsius Scriptura ipsius, sapientia ipsius quae erat in Scripturis. Clausa erat Scriptura: nemo illam intelligebt. Crucifixus est Dominus et liquaefacta est sicut cera ut omnes infirmi intelligerent scripturam; nam inde et velum templi scissum est quia quod velabatur revelatum est."

6

THE EARLY BONHOEFFER
CHRIST LOGOS ANTI-LOGOS

Eberhard Bethge, close friend of Dietrich Bonhoeffer,
has assembled and carefully reconstructed from notes
taken by students, an unfinished course of Christology[1] given in Berlin in 1933 by the future spiritual
master. It is mainly with this course that we shall be
concerned here in an effort to present his most original perspectives. How did Bonhoeffer envisage the relationship between history and dogma? In what terms
does he pose the question of the identity of Christ, or
see that question posing itself? What, finally, is the
presence of Christ in the community and of the world
in Christ? In connection with these different points,
we shall add the reactions of a Catholic theologian to
reading Bonhoeffer.

We make no claim, therefore, to present a systematic account of the christological theology of Bonhoeffer. Some specialists have already done this,[2]
but it does not seem to us that they have sufficiently
emphasized the new traits;[3] it is this gap we attempt
to fill, with a view to an ecumenical deepening of
Catholic Christology.

A. History and Dogma

Bonhoeffer asks himself to what extent dogmatic
judgments are dependent on historical confirmation.
It is distinctly possible, if not indeed probable, that

he raises this question in the context of Bultmannian "demythologization"[4] and in reaction against it. Two things seem clear to him: that dogmatic theology must be certain about the historicity of Christ, in other words that "the Christ of preaching" and the Christ of history are one and the same; that we must investigate the means of arriving at such certitude—through history alone, or without history? How can the Church become absolutely certain about a fact of history?

Bonhoeffer answers his own question by emphasizing that "it is a characteristic of historical scholarship that it never reckons with the individual fact as an absolute" (*Christology:* Fontana, p. 74). Its absolute necessity can never be demonstrated. "But the historically *(geschichtlich)* fortuitous fact of the life and death of Jesus must be of basic and absolute significance for the church. If he did not live, the church is doomed. So how am I sure of the historical fact of 'Jesus Christ'? Historical investigation and its methods are manifestly transcended here. . . . Historical investigation can never maintain an absolute negative because it can never maintain an absolute positive. . . . Absolute certainty about an historical fact can never be acquired by itself. It remains a paradox. Nevertheless it is constitutive of the Church" *(ibid.).*

"That means," continues Bonhoeffer, "that for the Church an historical fact is not past (i.e. entirely past), but present." And following Kierkegaard, he goes on: "That means that for the church an historical fact is not past, but present; that what is uncertain is the absolute, what is past is present, and what is historical *(das Geschichtliche)* is contemporaneous." This leads on to the question: "But from where does faith receive its sufficient ground to know, when history is uncertain?"—and he answers: "There is only the witness of the Risen One to himself, through which the church bears witness to him as the Historical One *(als den Historischen).* By the miracle of his presence in the church he bears witness to himself here and now as the one who was historical then. . . . The Risen One himself creates belief and so points the way to himself as the Historical One. From here, faith needs no confirmation from history. The confirmation of historical investigation isirrelevant before the self-attestation of Christ in the present. In faith, history is known in the light of eternity. That is the direct access of faith to history" (*ibid.*, p. 75).

Arrived at this stage, Bonhoeffer raises the question: "But does this not open the way for all sorts of heresy?" His answer is quite emphatic: "That is not so, because the self-attestation of Jesus Christ is none other than that which is handed down to us by Scripture, and it comes to us in no other way than by the Word of God (*ibid.*, p. 75). . . . The Risen One encounters us right through the Bible with all its flaws. . . . The historicity of Jesus Christ thus comes under the twofold aspect of history and faith. Bot h aspects are closely associated. The Jesus of history has humbled himself; the Jesus who cannot be grasped by history is the subject of faith in his resurrection" (*ibid.*, p. 76).[5]

Even if, on certain precise and limited points the Catholic theologian cannot subscribe to all Bonhoeffer's ideas or feels obliged to complete them, it is impossible that such rich intuitions should fail to stimulate his own thinking.

Does he not find elsewhere, within his own tradition, ideas which converge with these? Bonhoeffer overlooks but does not specifically deny that statements about historical facts can sometimes claim to have moral certainty; but we can certainly agree that historical certainty, as such, could never be absolute.

At the moment when the Apostles were witnesses of the apparitions of the Risen Christ and were hearing Him bear witness to the truth of His Resurrection, the light of an inner witness of the Word, transcendent and immanent, conferred absolute value on the external witness of which they were the beneficiaries. The immanent, illuminating Word, the sun of the minds of men (to use Augustine's image), was shining *from within* on the external witness of the Incarnate Word.

And this witness was received and accepted, not only by individuals, but by the ecclesial community of the believers, founded and structured by Him, the inward illuminator of its external words and deeds. Each of them had the absolute certainty of faith only within that of the community—of the faith which the triumphant Lamb was producing in the community.

Almost twenty centuries have passed, and the Risen Christ continues to bestow His inner and life-giving light on the Church as a community of faith and a communion in faith, so that she may adhere to the deposit of Revelation of which He "is the Mediator and at the same time the fullness" (Vatican II: *Dei Verbum*, par. 2, 4). He does so through His efficacious actual graces—effacious in fact by faith. If God does not reveal anything new—since the public revelation definitively ended with the death of the last of the Apostles—it is nevertheless still *here and now* that He continues to enlighten us through this Revelation by illuminating its meaning within the depths of our minds: "intima autem per hanc revelationem tam de Deo quam de hominis salute nobis in Christo illuscecit" (*ibid.*, par. 2). It will be noted that the verb "illuscecit" is in the present tense. The same idea recurs in substance a little further on: "Per . . . Traditionem . . . Deus, qui olim locutus est (past tense) sine intermissione cum dilecti Filii sui Sponsa colloquitur (present tense)" (*ibid.*, par. 8 *sub fine*).[6]

It is therefore in and through the mystery of the Church—a mystery with which that of the Scripture is integrated—that the self-attestation of Christ, living witness to His own historicity, is effected. While the Word, the Illuminator of minds, makes known His past history in the light of eternity, He disposes these minds to accept it in the absolute certainty of faith, while subtending by its light the moral certainties of history and of historical affirmations, which therefore keep their interest and their *raison d'être*. The same Light enlightens every man at the natural level and at the supernatural level (cf. Jn. 1, 9). It guides historical investigations and their conclusions based on the authority of human evidence, and it promotes the absolute certainty of the adherence of faith—a certainty which rests only on the sole and infallible witness of God the Revealer.

B. The Identity of Christ

Bonhoeffer then asks himself: "Who is Christ?" In developing the meaning of this question, he makes some subtle and deep reflections, of which the following is a summary.

"The question 'Who?' can only legitimately be put where the person questioned has previously revealed himself and has eradicated the immanent Logos. The question 'Who?' presupposes an answer that has already been given. This means in turn that the christological question can be put scientifically only in the context of the church. It can only be put where the basic presupposition, Christ's claim to be the Logos of God, has been accepted. . . ."

"In the church, in which Christ has revealed himself as the Word of God, the human Logos puts the question: Who are you, Jesus Christ, Word of God, Logos of God? The answer is given, the church receives it anew every day. Faced with all the pretensions of human reason, of the Logos of man, Christ declares that He is the judgment of condemnation on the human reason and on its discourse: 'I am the Truth' means: 'I am the death of the human logos.'"

The question "Who are you?" is therefore the question of the dethroned human reason. *"Who are you?* asks Pilate. Jesus is silent. Man cannot wait for the dangerous answer. The Logos (human) cannot endure the Anti-Logos (i.e. the divine Logos). It knows that one of them must die. So it kills the person of whom it has asked. Because the human Logos does not want to die, the Logos of God, who would be the death of it, must die so that it can live on with its unanswered questions of existence and transcendence. The Logos of God incarnate must be crucified by man's Logos. The one who compelled the dangerous question is killed, the question dies with him."

But what happens if Christ, this Anti-Logos, "this Counter-Word, though killed, rises living and victorious from the death as the ultimate Word of God?. . . . The question ('Who are you?') is reversed and rebounds on the human Logos. 'Who are you, to ask thus?' . . . 'Who are you, who can still only inquire after me when I restore you, justify you, and give you my grace?' The christological question 'Who?' is finally formulated only when this reversed question is also heard. . . . Only God can ask like this." In other words, the Resurrection unfolds its meaning: Christ counters man's question about His identity by posing to men a divine question.[8]

One could sum up these impressive reflections of Bonhoeffer by saying that they seek to present the paschal mystery, the death and the resurrection of the Lord, as dialogue and dialectic between the Logos of God and the Logos of man. Even more relevant in 1973 than in 1933, they constitute a counter-move against the ever recurrent self-idolatry of the human reason, and against the latest claim of rationalism— the reduction of theology to anthropology, the diminution of discourse about God to impassioned affirmation of the perfect self-immanence of man.

They remind the Catholic theologian of a comment by Robert Bellarmine about the "corrupt reason" of man—corrupt not, of course, in its essence, but in its concrete functioning and in its aims. The Logos of God become human Logos, having assumed a human reason perfectly sound and in no way corrupted by the original sin of His human brethren, dethrones the absolute pretensions of the corrupt human reason. The humanized Word is the Redeemer of human reason and of its discourse.

In fact, the created reason which enquires about the identity of Christ and questions Him, is the redeemed human reason which desires the fullness of its own salvation in faith. Even if till now it has not wished to benefit from the application of the merits of the human reason of Christ in the subjective Redemption, it can henceforward pose to Christ its question of identity all the more effectively by being already a beneficiary of the objective redemption of this incarnate Word and of His actual and illuminating graces. For is it not, in effect, the purpose of these graces to divinize human discourse in the discursive act of faith, the dawn of the full moon of the beatifying intuition?

The human reason which poses the christological question is, therefore, never in fact completely estranged from the Church of Christ, even though it remains relatively hostile to her. It is as attracted by the Mystery of Christ, of which the mystery of the Church is the inseparable extension, that the human reason ventures to raise the insistent question about the identity of Christ. Although, in the depths of its most profound corruptions[9] and even without grace, it still has the power and the radical duty to pose this question, it is the grace itself of Christ, constantly or at least periodically offered to its discourse, which strengthens the weaknesses of the human reason and efficaciously incites it to raise the question: 'Who is Christ?' and, with it, that of its relationship to the Christ-Logos. If, despite Bonhoeffer, the christological question can be and is "scientifically" raised "outside" the Church, without any intention of accepting Jesus' affirmation about His own identity—(and how can this be denied without denying the very possibility of the sin of incredulity so constantly stressed in the New Testament?)—this "exteriority" remains wholly relative, since the human reason hostile to the divine Logos is enveloped by His Grace which no resistance discourages. Or, more correctly, this human reason, still hostile, is already secretly restored, justified, divinized, grace-enriched, at least in principle, by the victorious Anti-Logos.

How does this Anti-Logos (i.e. the divine Logos)

manifest itself to the "rationalist" reason which it has dethroned? Within the Christology of Bonhoeffer, the answer is clear: the Risen One speaks to the human reason through the living preaching of the Church: "The word of preaching is the form in which the Logos reaches the human Logos" (*ibid.*, p. 54). It is not just secretly that the Risen One invites it to investigate His own past history; He also urges it to do so, exteriorly and here and now, through His envoys. A complete analysis of the dialectical relationship between the human logos and the divine Anti-Logos, would demand a theology of preaching. Bonhoeffer has sketched such a theology in his *Christology* (52-54, 58, 73). Let it suffice to cite here one of his thoughts in this connection, a thought which contains an exaggeration: "Christ is present as the Risen and Exalted One only in proclamation, and that means at the same time: only by way of a new humiliation."[10] By these words, the young preacher meant that the divine Anti-Logos is hidden under the revealing veil of apparently purely human speech, of a discourse of the human reason.

C. Christ and the World in a State of Reciprocal Immanence

Here we can be more brief, since it would seem that this aspect of the doctrine of Bonhoeffer is better known. But is it not also sometimes distorted?

For our author, it is precisely as the man-for-others that Christ *is* the community, without limiting Himself to acting for it. The community *(Gemeinde)*, far from being merely the recipient of the word of Revelation, is itself Revelation and word of God; and only in the measure in which it is itself word of God, can it understand the word of God. Christ (cf. 1 Cor. 12, 12 cited in the same sense by Pius XII: DS 3806) is the head of the community and Also the community itself.[11]

Thus Bonhoeffer comes increasingly to regard the

community in Christ as in a universal englobing which contains us and the world; and it was in this sense that later on, in a celebrated chapter of his *Ethics*, he would interpret the prologue to Colossians: "Everything has been created in Christ." For him, the world is not divided between Christ and Satan, but belongs entirely to Christ.

Such accentuation of the unity of the divine plan never led him, however, to withdraw an important passage in his Berlin lectures on Christology, concerning the idea of heresy. His high appraisement of the world never, it seems, blinded him to the possibility and the historic reality of heresies.

For him, there is a whole section of Christology whose character is negative: "it establishes and decrees what may *not* be said about Christ" (*ibid.*, p. 77). This is *critical or negative Christology.* "If critical christology is thus concerned with marking out limits," he comments (*ibid.*, p. 78), "that means that it is concerned with the concept of heresy." Sensing that this would cause surprise, Bonhoeffer insisted on it. The following passage has disquieted a number of theologians, Catholic and non-Catholic, who today identify with Bonhoeffer and with all that he stands for:

> We have lost the concept of heresy today because there is no longer a teaching authority *(Lehrautoritaet).* This is a tremendous catastrophe. The present ecumenical councils[12] are not quite councils because the word heresy has been removed from their vocabulary. But there can be no confession without saying, "In the light of Christ, this is true and this is false."

One cannot but pay tribute, with deep sympathy, to this aspiration of a sincere Lutheran to a magisterial authority, for such an aspiration seems to coincide with and to express a profound need felt by the fragile human reason. Is Bonhoeffer not also implying that it is impossible to say the truth about Christ without, *ipso facto*, denouncing the errors which disfigure it?

No doubt, it is for this reason that he adds:

> The concept of heresy belongs necessarily and irrevocably with that of the confession. The doctrine of a confessional church must be contrasted with false doctrine. The Augsburg Confession says clearly: the church condemns.

At this point, he ends by explicitly answering the objection which comes spontaneously to mind:

> We should note here that the concept of heresy emerges from the brotherliness of the church and not from a lack of love. A man acts as a brother towards his fellow only if he does not withhold the truth from him. If I do not tell my neighbor the truth, I treat him as a heathen. If I speak the truth to someone of another opinion, then I am showing him the love that I owe him.[13]

Critical Christology appears, therefore, to be the limit, at once inevitable and necessary, which guarantees the authenticity of the reciprocal real immanence between Christ and the World. For love of the world, the Church must reject a part of what the world says about Christ. In fighting against heresies, the Church manifests to the world the splendor of her love for it.

But does not the explicit recognition of a critical and negative Christology show that, despite the somewhat summary statements of the *Ethics*, Satan does continue to have an influence, permitted by Christ, in a world which is not, however, divided between Christ and him? We touch here on one of the limits of the later evolution of Bonhoeffer: it is rather *de jure* than *de facto* that the world belongs wholly to Christ. The perfect reign of Christ is a mystery yet to come (cf. 1 Cor. 15, 25-28).

This brief account enables us, finally, to sum up the most salient qualities of the Christ of Bonhoeffer. He is at once the One who, in the *here and now* of the Church, bears witness to His historic and past witness; the Risen One who questions the questioning reason which has crucified Him; the victorious Anti-Logos who rejects the heretical discourse of the world concerning Himself, precisely because He loves this world to the point of englobing it in Him.

NOTES TO CHAPTER SIX

1. Dietrich Bonhoeffer, *Gesammelte Schriften,* t. III, Chr. Kaiser Verlag, Munich, 1960, pp. 166-241. English translation: *Christology* (Collins, London, 1966).

2. See, e.g. J. D. Godsey, *The Theology of D. Bonhoeffer,* London, 1963, pp. 264-273; (M. E. Marty ed.) J. Pelikan, *Place of Bonhoeffer,* SCM, London, 1963, pp. 143--166.

3. We are thinking in particular about the penetrating essay by J. Pelikan; see note 2.

4. Cf. J. D. Godsey, *op. cit.,* pp. 275-279.

5 Bonhoeffer, however, has elsewhere (cf. Marty, *op. cit.* p. 146; E. H. Robertson's introduction to Bonhoeffer, *Christology,* p. 13), laid down the principles for an extension beyond the exclusively Biblical position of the encounter with the self-attestation of Christ, by affirming that "the Church is the hidden Christ among us" and that man "exists only through the (ecclesial) community which brings him Christ. . . ."

6. Cf. article: "Doctrine (Development of)" in *New Catholic Encyclopedia* (1967). The distinction between revelation as continually present illumination and as closed body of doctrine is very well presented there.

7. Has Bonhoeffer clearly understood the real meaning of Pilate's question, formulated as "Where are you from?" (Jn. 19, 9). See in this connection the relevant note in the Jerusalem Bible.

8. *Christology,* pp. 29-37.

9. Cf. Pius XII, *Humani Generis,* DS, 3876. This radical power of the reason is not necessarily a proximate and immediate power. Its exercise can meet with serious obstacles, to which Pius XII alludes in the same text.

10. *Christology,* p. 47.

11. The term "Gemeinde" is variously translated by Bonhoeffer specialists: Pelikan (*op. cit.* p. 165, note 6) prefers "church," whereas, later, E. H. Robertson (preface to *Christology,* p. 13) opts for "community."

12. It seems pretty clear that Bonhoeffer is alluding here, not to Vatican I—the "present" would put it out of context, but to ecumenical reunions of international scope.

13. *Christology,* p. 78.

7

THE LATER BONHOEFFER
THE "THIS WORLD" CHRIST, MAN FOR OTHERS

We have seen what profit can be derived from the Christology of the early Bonhoeffer. It is generally admitted that the later Bonhoeffer, the Bonhoeffer of the "Letters from Prison" of 1943-1945, shows development, though without any evidence of clashing with his earlier ideas. The reflections of the prisoner have certainly had a far greater influence on contemporary religious thought than have the lectures of the professor. After a brief recalling of Bonhoeffer's ideas about the powerlessness of Christ, the man of "this world," the man-for-others, we shall show the interest which this new christological horizon holds for the Catholic faith.

A. Christ All-Powerful and Powerless

In his prison cell, Bonhoeffer was experiencing the powerlessness of man, at the very moment when, paradoxically, he was describing the feeling of omnipotence and intoxication of mankind in possession of the technological means to dominate the world.

On 16 July 1944, he wrote:

> So our coming of age forces us to a true recognition of our situation *vis-à-vis God*. God is

teaching us that we must live as men who can
get along very well without him. The God who
is with us is the God who forsakes us (Mark 15,
24). The God who makes us live in this world
without using him as a working hypothesis is
the God before whom we are ever standing. Before God and with him we live without God.
God allows himself to be edged out of the world
and on to the cross. God is weak and powerless
in the world, and that is exactly the way, the
only way, in which he can be with us and help
us. Matthew 8, 17 makes it crystal clear that
it is not by his omnipotence that Christ helps
us, but by his weakness and suffering![1]

It will be noted that, in the last sentence, the
author does not deny, but re-affirms, the divine omnipotence of Christ: in Christ, the omnipotent God has
willed to become powerless. In a series of paradoxical
affirmations, in which Bonhoeffer unintentionally slips
into the style of the mystics and, like some of them,
into certain inexactitudes, we are invited to see in
the very "abandonment" of God the sign of His nearness: the God who abandons us is the powerless and
weak God who, as such, is near us, with us, and assists
us.

This is the decisive difference between Christianity and all religions. Man's religiosity makes
him look in his distress to the power of God in
the world: he uses God as a *Deus ex machina*.
The Bible however directs him to the powerlessness and suffering of God; only a suffering God
can help. To this extent we may say that the
process we have described by which the world
came of age was an abandonment of a false
conception of God, and a clearing of the decks
for the God of the Bible, who conquers power
and space in the world by his weakness. This
must be the starting point for our "worldly"
interpretation.[2]

The God of the religions is the Omnipotent who

never experiences the powerlessness of man; the God of the Bible, says Bonhoeffer, is the Omnipotent who makes His omnipotence known through man by participating in the powerlessness of His rational creature.

The crucified Christ is at once the man abandoned by God and the God-with-us, the Emmanuel. It is He who teaches us to live without God in the world— that is, without a God who would be the instrument of our ambition rather than the transcendent God that He is: that, it seems, is what Bonhoeffer, with the formulas of a "disturbing visionary,"[3] is really saying to us.

Two days later, Bonhoeffer returns to his idea:

> Christians range themselves with God in his suffering: that is what distinguishes them from the heathen. As Jesus asked in Gethsemane, 'Could you not watch with me one hour?' That is the exact opposite of what the religious man expects from God. Man is challenged to participate in the sufferings of God at the hands of a godless world.[4]

It is clear that the imprisoned pastor is expressing above all else his own interior life, his personal way of reacting in terms of his faith to a painful situation. Behind certain paradoxical formulas, one must sense the renewed expression of an attitude which is completely basic and traditional in the history of Christianity: compassion towards the crucified Christ.

"Man is challenged to participate in the sufferings of God at the hands of a godless world. . . . Christians range themselves with God in his suffering: that is what distinguishes them from the heathen." Imprisoned in solitary confinement, in a world partly dominiated by Nazi or Marxist atheism, the Lutheran theologian has ideas reminiscent of Saint Margaret Mary's compassion towards the agonizing Christ, expressed two centuries ago in France.[5] To suffer the passion of God in a godless world, is not this a way of making reparation to God for the crime of anti-theism?

It must be said, however, that this emphasis on such a deeply true point did not make it necessary for Bonhoeffer to say so little about the power of God. While he did perceive that Christ "finds his power in the world through his powerlessness," Bonhoeffer did not probe this idea, or show how the all-powerful grace of the Lord Jesus can always convert in an instant, without violating human freedom, his worst enemies. In our secularized world, He is the same Jesus who still strikes down modern Sauls on new roads to Damascus; Jesus still converts. For the divine omnipotence of the crucified and risen Christ, "the very obstacles are the means of leading men to cooperate freely in their highest ends."[6] The infinite power of God does not show itself only in physical nature, of which He is the Creator, but also in the hearts and wills of man. Did Bonhoeffer acknowledge and reflect on the miracle of conversion?[7] If not, was not this partly because of his Lutheranism.[8]

B. Christ the "Worldly Man," "Man-for-Others"

For Bonhoeffer, Christ is not a "homo religiosus,"[9] or the author of a religion, a deist system of escaping from the world.[10]

In his prison cell, the theologian was elaborating the project of a new Christology. "What do we mean by 'God'? Not in the first place an abstract belief in his omnipotence, etc. That is not a genuine experience of God, but a partial extension of the world. Encounter with Jesus Christ implies a complete orientation of the human being in the experience of Jesus as one whose only concern is for others. This concern of Jesus for others is the experience of transcendence. This freedom from self, maintained to the point of death, (is) the sole ground of his omnipotence, omniscience and ubiquity."[11]

We note that this last sentence, literally inadmissible as signifying that Jesus was not omnipotent before His death, must not be interpreted too strictly: Bonhoeffer is suggesting an "outline for a book," and no doubt he would later have looked at his notes more critically, had he lived to write the book. The basic point of his new orientation is to emphasize that Jesus exists for others, and a little later he adds that Christ ("God in human form") is not "in the Greek divine-human (form) of autonomous man, but man existing for others, and hence the Crucified." From all this, he concludes that "our relation to God (is) . . . a new life for others, through participation in the Being of God".[12] He adds that "the transcendence consists not in tasks beyond our scope and power, but in the nearest thing to hand"—i.e. the service of others.[13]

All this seems to indicate that, for the prisoner Bonhoeffer, the utmost nearness of another person is the supreme manifestation of the transcendence of God. Christ would manifest His Divinity only in an experience of social 'otherness,' or at least predominantly in this way. In short, Jesus would reveal His divine transcendence by His "kenotic" acts of human self-transcendence. By "surpassing" Himself, does not Jesus show that "God is the 'beyond' in the midst of our life."[14]

Nevertheless (or perhaps—or rather—inseparably), Bonhoeffer continues to affirm strongly and magnificently his faith in the divinity of Jesus:

> In Jesus Christ, we believe in God made man, crucified and risen from the death. In the Incarnation, we recognize the love of God for His creature; in the Crucifixion, the judgment of God on all flesh; in the Resurrection, the will of God to raise up a new world. Nothing would be more absurd than to break the link interconnecting these three realities, because the whole is contained in each of them. . . . Incarnation, Cross, and Resurrection should be made manifest in their unity and in their difference.[15]

These lines are cited less often than are the ideas about Jesus existing for others. It is paradoxical that, for many people, the Christology of Bonhoeffer has thus come to be identified with a few notes which were jotted down in what he himself calls a "very crude and sketchy" manner, and which have scarcely any precise and detailed parallels elsewhere in his work. It cannot be denied, however, that they are rich in suggestion; and that is what we shall now show in the light of Catholic Christology and Soteriology.

C. Jesus, Man-for-Others and Man-for-the-Father

Although the expression in no way suffices to designate the mystery of His Person, the presentation of Jesus as "man-for-others" is admissibly Biblical and deserving of praise. It could serve as a précis of Jesus' own words: "For the Son of man also came not to be served but to serve, and to give his life as a ransom for many" (Mk. 10, 15).

We consider that, above all, Jesus was "for others" in His death and in His Resurrection. It might seem surprising that Robinson, an exegete and a professed disciple of Bonhoeffer, did not consider this important aspect of the "for-others-ness" of Jesus. But, in fact, Robinson denies the Church's doctrine which holds that Jesus is for others precisely by the fact that He offers to His Father a "vicarious" satisfaction in the name and in place of all sinners of every era—that He dies to expiate the sins of all men.[16] Jesus has not lived merely for His compatriots and contemporaries, but for all men of all times.

It must be stressed that Jesus was a "man-for-others" precisely because He existed and lived for the Father: "ad Patrem." Reading the Gospels, we even see that at certain moments Christ has not lived for others in a palpably specific way, because at such moments He preferred to pray for them to His Father, and to seek refuge from the multitude in solitude and in silence (Mk. 1, 35; 1, 45). When He did this, Jesus, in our view, was not *less* but *more* for others, for *all* others and not just for *some* others. This solitary prayer for the pre-paschal Christ again shows us that His life for others was completely subordinated to His life for the Father. Jesus lives for others only because this is His Father's will (cf. Jn. 4, 4); as Word, He is eternally and essentially "with" the Father (cf. Jn. 1, 1) and "in the bosom of the Father" (Jn. 1, 18).

Although this twofold expression: "Man-for-others and man-for-God," applied to Jesus, cannot in any way replace that of Chalcedon (which, on the contrary, it presupposes), it must be admitted that the doctrine of the vicarious satisfaction or of the Redemption is latent in these formulas. The whole life of Jesus, and not just His death on the cross, is a work of satisfaction offered to the Father through love for men—for all men of all times; with the twofold signification of purpose and of substitution (Greek: *anti lutron*) attaching to the English word "for." Jesus has lived, died, and risen from the dead for others, and in order that all should live for others, and even in order that all might be enabled, without being dispensed from the necessity of dying, to offer up their death to the Father for others, in Christ and with Christ: "None of us lives to himself, and none of us dies to himself. . . . For to this end Christ died and lived again, that he might be Lord both of the dead and of the living" (Rom. 14, 7-9).

We consider that the Christology of "Jesus, man-for-others," or the Christology of the Servant,[17] opens up another, not less profound horizon. Christ Jesus, as man, is truly a member of the human species and at the same time its Head. The human nature of Christ, like that of any other man and even more so, is intrinsically social.[18] The clear statements of Vatican II about man are valid also for Christ:

> By his innermost nature man is a social being, and unless he relates himself to others he can neither live nor develop his potential. . . . This social life is not something added on to man. Hence, through his dealings with others, through reciprocal duties, and through fraternal dialogue,

he develops all his gifts and is able to rise to his destiny.[19]

As man, Jesus could not fully develop His humanity without the help of human society. The Word has freely willed that His humanity should depend on men for its proper and perfect development; and, again by the sole title of His humanity, Jesus of Nazareth tends to perfect the rest of mankind in the humanity which is common to them and to Him.

Furthermore, Vatican II explicitly makes the point that the Incarnation is in-humanation in the sense of insertion of Christ into human society:

> This communitary character is developed and consummated in the work of Jesus Christ. For the very Word made flesh willed to share in the human fellowship *(humanae consortionis particeps esse voluit)*. He was present at the wedding of Cana, visited the house of Zacchaeus, ate with publicans and sinners. He revealed the love of the Father and the sublime vocation of man in terms of the most common of social realities and by making use of the speech and the imagery of plain everyday life. . . . He chose to lead the life proper to an artisan of His time and place.[20]

High priest chosen from among men (cf. Heb. 5, 1), the Word Incarnate was actively and intrinsically orientated to men and to their salvation, to those men of whom He had need in order that His humanity, ontologically perfected from its first moment of existence, should be perfected within human history. Though Christ was perfect God, and essentially perfect man from the first instant of His In-humanation, one could say of Him that, Son of God though He was, he learned His human condition "through what he suffered" (Heb. 5, 8) and through his human occupation as a carpenter, in order thus to reach the perfect consummation of His humanity (cf. Heb. 2, 10).

Having men for His ancestors, the Word Incarnate

was a man involved with His contemporaries, and a man for all men; He could not fail to be still more man through other men and His relations with them.

But this Word Incarnate had and has a unique Person which is divine. As the Word, Jesus is completely and constantly in relationship to the Father: *ad Patrem*. He is eternally born from the Father as His Only Son, remains always in Him, and is always orientated towards Him. All the actions and feelings of the incarnate and only born Son are for the Father and for His glory: *ad gloriam Patris*. The whole human life, increasingly more humanized and humanizing, of Jesus of Nazareth is intrinsically social, in virtue of a "sociality" not only human but also divine; for this whole life is polarized by the Father, and assumed in the ineffable intimacy of the eternal Son-Father relationship which constitutes the only Person of the Incarnate Word. Consequently, it is by the very fact that He is man through and for men, that Jesus exists and has lived by and for the Father (cf. Jn. 6, 57).[21]

The acts of the human mind and human will of the Man Jesus are simultaneously and hierarchically orientated to the salvation of the brethren and to the glory of God His Father. As man, He turns towards other men by the action of his human mind and will; as only Son and Word of the Father, He is completely towards the Father, and subordinates all His accidental relations with men to His constitutive relation with His Father, because the accidental relations of His sacred Humanity are assumed within the uncreated unity of His eternal relation with the Father.

"The face of Christ the Servant"[22] is the face of this Word and only Son who "worked with human hands, thought with a human mind, acted by human choice, and loved with a human heart";[23] all this in order "to take the world's history up in Himself and summarize it"[24]—the history of all human minds, and of all human hearts. Jesus, man-for-others, is also man-for-the-world. He is that unique Man who, in a conscious and deliberate fashion, has lived from the first instant of His earthly existence,[25] has died and, risen from the dead, still lives for all men of all places and of all times, all being known by His human mind and loved by His human heart in the bosom of the Father. It is thus that He expresses in history and in matter, His eternal life of Sonship in the Father, with the Father and for the Father. Having taken flesh and heart for the life of the world, this Son carries in His Heart this universe which He sustains "by his word of power" (Heb. 1, 3; cf. Jn. 6, 51).

But this Servant Christ would not be truly for others did he not enter into dialogue with them through His disciples here and now, after having personally spread the word of salvation during His earthly life. It is here, undoubtedly, that Bonhoeffer has his most disturbing surprises in store for us.

D. The Language of Jesus, a Non-Religious Language of Deliverance and of Liberation

In one of his letters from prison, which some describe as prophetic, Bonhoeffer wrote as follows:

> It is not for us to foresee the day—but it will come—when men will be called anew to formulate the word of God in such a way that the world will be transformed and renewed by it. This will be a new language, perhaps completely non-religious, but a language of deliverance and of liberation, like the language of Jesus.[26]

With an inner, subjective certainty, therefore, Bonhoeffer foresees the coming of new preachers of the Gospel who will transform and renew the world. Their language could be non-religious (here the certainty wavers). What does this mean?

Another letter throws some light on the matter:

> The time when men could be told everything by means of words, whether theological or simply pious, is over, and so is the time of inwardness and conscience, which is to say the time of

religion as such. We are proceeding towards a time of no religion at all: men as they are now simply cannot be religious any more. Even those who honestly describe themselves as "religious" do not in the least act up to it, and so when they say "religious" they evidently mean something quite different.[27]

As one of his interpreters tells us, this noun "religion" and its adjective "religious" have a pretty vague meaning with Bonhoeffer, who often puts inverted commas around them. However, here at least, our author seems to have in mind, not some magic superstition, but the presuppositions or the expressions of the language of Christian faith and of Christian revelation; he talks about "words theological or pious", about "inwardness and conscience." The time towards which we are moving will be non-religious, Bonhoeffer thinks, precisely because it will no longer be able to endure the pious or theological words, the appeal to conscience or to inwardness.

Another letter serves to confirm this interpretation:

While I often shrink with religious people from speaking of God by name—because that Name somehow seems to me here not to ring true, and I strike myself as rather dishonest (it is especially bad when others start talking in religious jargon: then I dry up almost completely and feel somehow oppressed and ill at ease)—with people who have no religion I am able on occasion to speak of God quite openly and as it were naturally.[29]

Here *religion* and *name of God* are clearly associated together. There can be no disputing this. No doubt, Bonhoeffer is reacting against the pharisaism of certain pious people. This explains but does not justify his tendency, surprising in a believer such as he. Besider, he pursues the idea to its extreme: does he not say that "a secret discipline must be reestablished whereby the *mysteries* of the Christian faith are preserved from profanation" by a certain type of religious language? No doubt, this silence which he is suggesting to the believers is, in his view, a step towards "the new language of deliverance and of liberation" which, he is convinced, will come to formulate anew the word of God; and no doubt too, in his opinion, this language will be the vehicle for speaking "of God quite openly and as it were naturally," as he himself was doing in the evening of his short life.

It remains none the less true that the imprisoned pastor finds, by and large, that men "cannot be religious any more" or understand the explicit language of faith.

Is this true? We do not think so, and we even believe that this is an error with a dire consequence: de-christianization through failure to present the Gospel, on the part of those who could and should be the witnesses to Christ. It is an error partly like that of those who listened to Jesus.

Incontestably, the language of Jesus was indeed, to use Bonhoeffer's phrase, a language of deliverance and of liberation:

> If you continue in my word, you are truly my disciples, and you will know the truth, and the truth will make you free. . . . You seek to kill me, because my word finds no place in you. . . . Why do you not understand what I say? It is because you cannot bear to hear my word. . . . Because I tell the truth, you do not believe me. . . . He who is of God hears the words of God; the reason why you do not hear them is that you are not of God. . . . Truly, truly, I say to you, if any one keeps my word, he will never see death (Jn. 8, 31-51).

As can be seen, the problem of "religious language" is not an entirely new one, and Jesus died because, freely and culpably, His contemporaries refused to hear Him and to understand Him! Sons of the devil, they were not of God, and therefore could not understand the word of His Only Son.

The message of Jesus was rejected by those who listened unreceptively to it, not because it was incomprehensible, but because, by a free choice, they were not in the desired subjective conditions which would have enabled His word "to enter into them"; "for they loved the praise of men more than the praise of God" (Jn. 12, 43).

On the contrary, the language of Jesus is intelligible to men of all periods.[31] As Vatican II very precisely points out: "Jesus revealed the love of the Father and the sublime vocation of men in terms of the most common of social realities and by making use of the speech and the imagery of plain everyday life."[32] Of course, this speech and these images are not always those of our twentieth century, nor are these "social realities" those of our present social life. But those who make the effort of transposition can succeed, on condition however that they are of God and that, consequently, they do not prefer the glory that comes from a technological world, the intoxication of a developed world of which Bonhoeffer speaks, to the hidden glory that comes from the incarnate God in an epoch of collective under-development of the whole of mankind; on condition that they accept the ever offered grace to understand a Word that will never pass away; on condition too, it must be added, that the messengers of the Word Incarnate do not fall silent through lack of faith in the evangelizing will *here and now* of their Lord!

For the hearers who remain in the murk of a culpably deformed conscience, as well as for the messengers who doubt the power of the Risen Christ to "open hearts" to the understanding of His pre-paschal word, the word of salvation rejected or not passed on becomes condemnation:

> If any one hears my sayings and does not keep them, I do not judge him; for I did not come to judge the world but to save the world. He who rejects me and does not receive my

sayings has a judge; the word that I have spoken
will be his judge on the last day (Jn. 12, 47-48).

One cannot really see why the Pharisees should
be regarded as the only people to have freely and culpably rejected, in the course of history, the words of
the Savior, of *their* Savior; could there not be at the
present time, within but also outside the Church, men
and women who are choosing spiritual death in preference to their own liberation? It is therefore impossible
to adduce the differences between the New Testament
cultural context and ours as sufficiently explaining
the rejection of a religious language by a number of
our contemporaries.

In reality, it is not only in some vague future, but
here and now and in every epoch of the New Alliance
between God and men, that the Word of God transforms and renews the world. For, it is not exclusively
in the past or in the future that the Spirit of Christ
is at work to make the divine word resound in the
Church, and in the world through the Church;[34] it
is today (cf. 1 Cor. 12, 10).

Saint Thomas Aquinas had already realized this
most profoundly, when, in dealing with the "charisma
of discourse," he wrote luminously as follows:

> Since the Holy Spirit does not fail in any-
> thing that pertains to the profit of the Church,
> He provides also the members of the Church
> with speech; to the effect that a man not only
> speaks so as to be understood by different peo-
> ple, which pertains to the gift of tongues, but
> also with effect, and this pertains to the grace
> *of the word.* This happens in three ways. First,
> in order to instruct the intellect, and this is the
> case when a man speaks so as *to teach.* Second-
> ly, in order to move the affections, so that a man
> willingly hearkens to the words of God. This
> is the case when a man speaks so as *to please*
> his hearers, not indeed with a view to his own
> favor, but in order to draw them to listen to
> God's word. Thirdly, in order that men may

love that which is signified by the word, and
desire to fulfil it, and this is the case when a
man so speaks as *to sway* his hearers. In order
to effect this the Holy Spirit makes use of the
human tongue as of an instrument; but He it
is who perfects the work within.[53]

Even if it is true that at certain periods in the history of the Church and of mankind, the religious language may be less adapted, in its formulation, to the
particular needs of contemporaries, it will never be
unadapted and—as Saint Thomas clearly perceived—
it will always be heard: to deny this would be to
deny that the Spirit is always the soul of the Church,
and always at work within the Church for the salvation of men. In relation to this basic statement,
possible revisions of language are always secondary,
even when they are desirable; they are also the effect
of the assistance given by the Holy Spirit to the
Church of Christ.

These revisions partly occur under the influence
of the saints whom the same Spirit constantly raises
up in the Church. Her Doctors and her mystics have
not ceased speaking to her about Christ, and will
never cease from doing so. In this connection, it is
enlightening to compare the words of Bonhoeffer quoted above ("While I often shrink with religious people
from speaking of God by name . . . and I strike myself as rather dishonest") and those of the 14th-century
founder of the Jesuates, Blessed John Colombini:

> Everywhere there are more virtues, more
> knowledge and good works than ever, so much
> so that there would be many saints were there
> but charity. But I no longer see this true
> charity which Christ kindles in souls.
> The first remedy for this evil is to speak much
> about Jesus Christ and about His love.
> The more sublimely we speak, the more deeply
> will we feel. The heart is impressed by what
> the tongue expresses. He who talks about the
> world is already chilled, and begins to think like

the world; he who speaks about Christ acquires the mind of Christ.

Know this, dearly beloved, sweet speech about Jesus Christ is the food of the soul, and there is no worse pretension than to bury in silence the gifts of the Lord.

Therefore when the whole world is telling you not to talk about this blessed Name, despise the world, for whoever confesses the name of Christ before men will be confessed by Christ before the Father.[36]

The Blessed Colombini wished his disciples, therefore, "never to lose among themselves the holy art of speaking about God"—an art inseparable from "the art of speaking to God and for God."[37]

One cannot separate, as Bonhoeffer was attempting to do,[38] the "art of speaking to God" from the "art of speaking about God." For the reasons given by the Blessed John Colombini, to neglect the second is to risk losing the first.

But what remains true—and one would like to think that this is the sum total of what Bonhoeffer wished to say—is that the way the Christian talks about Christ should show respect for the freedom of the person he speaks to[39] and for the action of divine grace within him, and should take account of how he already thinks in matters of religion.

As has been well said, "the disappointments sometimes met with in the apostolate arise from an inadequate understanding of the particular situation of the people addressed. . . . Men are never religiously indeterminate."[41]

The Spirit, who ceaselessly animates the sacrificial witness[42] of the Church, is showing her how to speak to the people of our day, in an ever renewed manner, about Jesus the omnipotent Servant who chose to become weak and powerless—the man-for-others and the man-for-the-Father.

NOTES TO CHAPTER SEVEN

1. Bonhoeffer: *Letters and Papers from Prison,* p. 122 (Fontana). The original is called *Widerstand und Ergebung.* It would be more correct to say that Christ assists us both in virtue of His divine omnipotence and in virtue of His voluntary human weakness, meritorious through the intervention of His divine power in our favor; for it is not the human powerlessness of Christ as such which assists us. (In subsequent notes, the German original is indicated as W. E. and the English translation as L. P. P.).

2. W. E., 242; L. P. P., p. 122

3. Title of the final chapter in R. Marlé's *D. Bonhoeffer, témoin de Jésus-Christ parmi ses frères* (Gastermann, 1967) in which the author explains its twofold meaning: p. 123.

4. L. P. P., p. 122.

5. Saint Margaret Mary Alocoque, *Autobiographie,* par. 57; in the *Vie et Oeuvres* of the Saint, edited by Msgr. Gauthey, t. II, Paris, 1915³.

6. Pius XII, encyclical *Summi Pontificatus,* AAS, 31 (1939) 451-452.

7. W. E., 182 (cf. 220-221).

8. The doctrine of extrinsic justification does not favor the recognition of the miraculous character of conversion, precisely because it emphasizes the interior change effected in the free will by grace.

9. W. E., 248: "Another thing is that I have found great help in Luther's advice that we should start out morning and evening prayers by making the sign of the cross. . . . Don't worry, I shan't come out of here a *homo religiosus!*"

10. W. E., 178. Father Marlé (*op. cit.,* pp. 132-122) presents an interesting analysis of the idea of religion in Bonhoeffer. One might question whether the account does not somewhat gloss over its negative aspects.

11. L. P. P., p. 164-165. The original is in the form of notes.

12. *Ibid.,* p. 165.

13. *Ibid.,* p. 165.

14. W. E., 255;L. P. P., 93.

15. Bonhoeffer, *Ethik,* Munich, 1958⁴, p. 83.

16. Cf. J. A. T. Robinson, *Honest to God,* Philadelphia, 1963, p. 79; DS, 1529, 3891.

17. We are here referring to the authors who hold that the entire original Christology of the New Testament, that of the *Acts of the Apostles,* was dominated by the theme of Jesus the Servant, the fulfillment of the Deutero-Isaiah.

18. John XXIII, *Mater et Magister,* 58.

19. *Gaudium et Spes,* 12.2; 25. 1 (Abbott, pp. 211, 224).

20. *Ibid.,* 32.2 (Abbott, p. 230).

21. We know that the original Greek text of Jn. 6, 57 can

be translated in these two ways.

22. Decree *Unitatis Redintegratio,* par. 12 (Abbott, 354).

23. *Gaudium et Spes,* 22. 2 (Abbott, p. 221).

24. *Ibid.,* 38 (Abbott, 236).

25. Cf, Pius XII, *Mystici Corporis,* cited in DS, 3812.

26. W. E., 207.

27. W. E., 178; L. P. P., p. 91. It must be noted that, despite Bonhoeffer, the time of the New Alliance will be one of interiority (cf. Jn. 14, 23: the inhabitation of the Father and the Son in the soul of the disciple) as well as one of witness of conscience (e.g. Rom. 13, 5); one need only glance at a Greek N. T. concordance to see how abundant are the allusions in the sacred text to *suneidêsis;* even at the simple level of human experience, it is clear that the time of conscience will never pass away, and that men will always hear, through the voice of their conscience, the commands and accusations of the divine Judge: cf. *Gaudium et Spes,* 8 and 16.

28. Cf. Marlé, *op. cit.,* p. 132.

29. W. E., 182; L. P. P., p. 92. Notice the contrasting witness of Saint Ignatius of Loyola (sentence 30): "Cum nullo mortalium, licet pessimum, de rebus Dei sermo miscetur, quin plurimum inde lucrum referatur."

30. W. E., 185; L. P. P., p. 95.

31. Cf. our Chapter Five on Bultmann: C.

32. *Guadium et Spes,* 32, 2 (Abbott, p. 230).

33. Cf. Lk., 24, 45.

34. Cf. *Dei Verbum,* 8. 3.

35. *Summa Theologica,* II. II. 177. 1.

36. Cf. Louis Ponnelle, *saint Philippe de Néir,* pp. 157-158, Paris, 1928.

37. *Saint John Baptist de la Salle,* Meditations, 64th meditation—commentary on Mk. 7, 32: "deafness is the usual reason why one remains dumb," adds the saint.

38. W. E., 207: "today our Christian being will consist only of two things: prayer and the practice of good among men."

39. Cf. Paul VI, allocution of 19 June 1968: "Discretion and modesty are necessary in a pluralistic and profane society like ours, for manifestations of a religious nature"; *Dignitatis Humanae* (on religious liberty), par. 14, *sub fine.*

40. *Ibid.*

41. Joseph Comblin, *Le témoignage et l'Esprit,* Paris, 1964, pp. 50-51.

42. *Ibid.,* pp. 50-53: We add the adjective "sacrificial" because we think that it is above all in the celebration of the Eucharistic Sacrifice that the witness of the Church shines forth, including in this celebration all its existential consequences of the irradiation of charity. To this witness is attached, in a mysterious fashion, that of Bonhoeffer himself.

Even in his last days, he was still using a "religious" and Biblical language. Fabian von Schlabrendorff, who occupied the next cell to his, is evidence of this: "How often," he wrote, "did he not slip into my hand a piece of paper on which he had written words of comfort and of faith taken from the Bible" (cf. J. D. Godsey, *The Theology of Dietrich Bonhoeffer,* London, 1960).

8

JESUS CHRIST
AUTHOR OF THE SECULARIZATION OR
OF THE CONSECRATION OF THE WORLD?

Today one often reads or hears it said that Christianity, in direct line from the Old Testament, is at the root of the process of "secularization."[1]

Within nearly all the Christian Churches, there are theologians who are advocates of this tendency. Others resist them, without always adequately justifying their own positions. How the dialectic of world secularization and world consecration is related to the mystery of Christ, is not always brought out sufficiently.

Necessary clarification of this problem is further complicated by questions of terminology. There must be an effort to secure precision and coherence, as well as fidelity to what has been revealed, if one wishes to grasp the profound meaning of the evolution which is occurring here and now.

A. Semantic Preliminaries

We are faced with a complex assemblage of correlative terms: century (saeculum), secularity, secularization, and secularism, on the one hand; sacred, consecration, sacralization, de-sacrilize, sacrifice, and sacrament on the other. The meaning ascribed to these words varies from author to author. By and large, we adopt the most generally accepted meaning, while also

170

noting that, as in any context, antithetical terms clarify one another.

As J. Grand'maison, a Canadian theologian, has very well said, "sacred and profane are two existential dimensions present in all reality. Because it is by its nature relative, the authentically religious 'sacred' is not opposed to the *in se* of the profane, but rather demands it."[2]

By the *sacred* is more usually understood a part of reality—object, place, time, or person—whose use is reserved, in a more or less exclusive way, to the worship of God.[3] For others, the sacred is not "an *in se* like the profane, but a relationship. It should be such that it is distinguished from the profane, but at the same time designates it to consecration. The religious sacred, in contra-distinction to the magical sacred or the taboo sacred,[4] assumes the human condition in its full reality, while leaving to it its full responsibility."[5]

These two conceptions are not, in fact, mutually opposed; rather do they designate two different types of the sacred: the exclusive sacred and the non-exclusive sacred. The meaning of these expressions will appear more clearly in the light of the following distinctions.

"*To sacralize* is in some sort to remove from a reality the specificity of its immediate end, of its primary utility or of its technical fulfillment," leaving to it only its intermediate and ultimate ends.

To consecrate is to unite a dependent reality to the transcendent "beyond" which establishes it in its own independent existence.[6] Such consecration does not in any way remove from the reality involved the specificity of its immediate purpose. Moreover, even when a reality is not only consecrated but also sacralized, it keeps its own nature, even if one cannot use it with a view to its connatural or immediate purpose.

"The *profane* is the real in its own sphere, without its relation to God; the *sacred* is the real in its relation to God. . . . By appropriating the immediate destination of earthly realities in the name of a unique ultimate end, one sacralizes but one does not consecrate."[7]

De-sacralize, secularize, or laicize (terms more or less synonymous) can therefore take on a twofold meaning, according to whether the action they envisage is relative to a sacralization or to a consecration in the distinct sense just defined. A desacralization or secularization could simply indicate the change from an exclusively sacred usage to a usage either sacred or profane; a secularization in the sense of "de-consecration" would in fact be identical with secularism, which we shall define shortly. What needs emphasis at this stage is, to quote Father Audet, that "God transcends both the sacred and the profane, both of which proceed from Him, priority of origin belonging to the profane, not to the sacred. The latter occupies a middle and therefore instrumental position between man and the divine."[8] It is one of the effects of original sin that the sacred seeks to attract to itself the divine transcendence. Now, it is "from this intermediate character of our experience of the divine that the sacred proceeds, at least in its original state."[9] This experience shows itself through the mediation of certain places, of certain times, of certain people. Sin would consist in identifying them with the transcendence to which they should lead us.

Sacrifice is a sacred action which, by carrying the profane into the region reserved to a God-centered usage, effects a *sacralization;* or, if it leaves to the reality concerned its own reality and even its normal usage, a simple *consecration.*

We turn now to our second list of words.

In New Testament language, "this world" designates the aggregate of earthly things in so far as they turn man away from the service of God (cf. Rm. 12, 2; Eph. 2, 2 etc.), and even the kingdom of sin whose head is the devil, whose citizens are worldly men remote from God who reject the grace of the Redemption in favor of and through these earthly things; in short, the present kingdom of Satan as opposed to the future kingdom of God.[10]

Following this line of thought, continued by centuries of Christian reflection, one ends with the canonical definition of *secularization*, as the removal of "consecrated" persons, places, or things from their exclusive or predominant orientation towards "the age to come" in order to reduce them to the service of "this time" (cf. Mk. 10, 30; Mt. 12, 32). It is, more precisely, a return to the world, a regular and voluntary departure from the religious life in a definitive way.[11]

It is readily seen, therefore, that the canonical language is deeply rooted in that of the New Testament. But it is equally certain that the word *secularization* has today taken on a much wider meaning which, however, does not necessarily exclude the original canonical sense.

This new meaning itself comprises various shades of significance more complementary than opposed to one another.

In a first, rather sociological approximation, it is said that secularization is "the phenomenon by which the constitutive realities of human life (political, cultural, scientific, and other realities) tend to establish themselves in an ever increasing freedom from the norms appertaining to the religious or sacred domain."[12] It is immediately obvious that such secularization is not necessarily opposed to consecration as defined above, if the autonomy is merely relative.

Others, such as Cox, author of "The Secular City," would prefer to say—and here we are on the road to the secularism which we shall shortly discuss—that secularization is the almost certainly irreversible historic process by which society and culture are liberated from the tutelage of religious control and from control by rigid metaphysical conceptions of the world.[13] Karl Rahner defines secularization in a more clearly anthropological manner: "development of the world as creation of man . . . ever increasing profaneness of the world by comparison with the epochs when religion, as institution and as social life, the Church, and the world, constituted a relatively homogeneous unit."[14]

Secularism, as opposed to *secularization*, is the "natural perversion" of the latter, according to Gogarten, and even a "secularization which takes itself for its own principle and its own end."[15] According to A. Richardson, the word was first used by G. J. Holyake (1817-1906) in 1851 to designate his philosophical and ethical system which set out to interpret and to regulate life without belief in God, in the Bible, or in a future life. Holyake founded "secular societies." In current usage, the word "secularism" generally signifies the widespread practical tendency to ignore God and all religious matters and observances in order to devote oneself entirely to secular activities.[16] For Reinhold Niebuhr, secularism is "the explicit disavowal of the sacred."[17]

Finally, *secularity* (a term more rarely used than the preceding ones) signifies the quality of what is secular or of a secular, profane, non-sacred action. Such secularity could not subsist if one claimed to sacralize it, but this would not be so if one merely intended to consecrate it.

B. Christ, Author of a Secularization of the World?

Having thus decided on the meaning of the words, we can now more easily establish the relationship between the realities they represent and the Christian mystery.

In relation to a magical sacred or a taboo sacred, in relation to such a process of sacralization as would attribute to persons, places, and times a divine power and would divinize them, it is clear that the Gospel of Christ presents itself as a ferment of "desacralization," of a certain type of desacralization.

Thus, Jesus, in His answer to the Pharisees: "Render therefore to Caesar the things that are Caesar's, and to God the things that are God's" (Mt. 22, 21), clearly signified that Caesar could not be regarded as a god of a pantheon reduced to non-existence: "For although there may be so-called gods in heaven or on earth—as indeed there are many 'gods' and many 'lords'—yet for us there is one God, the Father . . . and one Lord, Jesus Christ . . ." (1 Cor. 8, 5-6). This Pauline text helps us to understand more clearly the exact meaning of the words of Jesus: Caesar is a creature who holds all his power from God, and who will have to give an account of it to God. Caesar is therefore "desacralized, secularized" by Christ. One could say the same about the Temple of Jerusalem (cf. Jn. 4, 21-23) although in a different sense: the Jews did not regard the Temple as God, whereas the pagans divinized many "lords."

Jesus has therefore desacralized the persons, places, and times of the pre-Christian religions.[18] In a more general way, it can be said that He has brought to its term the process of desacralization inaugurated by the Old Testament with regard to the stars and the animals (cf. Gen. 1-2) adored by the peoples who were neighbors to Israel. His sacrifice on the cross, by suppressing all other blood sacrifice, consummated a certain "desacralization" of the universe. The true God "de-divinized" the world.

Within the very heart of the Christian world today, Christ, through His Church, continues this movement of "desacralization."

In effect, throughout the course of her history, the hierarchic Church, in her contact with underdeveloped nations, has been obliged in charity to take on, in a suppletory way, temporal tasks (notably of social assistance) which by their very nature would have been more suitably carried out by the laity. Furthermore, in all periods of history, a certain number of priests have deliberately used their spiritual power to secure temporal domination—the ever recurrent evil of clericalism.

It is always difficult to give up in time a task which has ceased to be suppletory, or to resist the temptation to clericalism. By allowing anti-clerical secularizations, the Spirit of Christ has willed to recall the Church to the purity of her evangelizing mission and to purify her towards that end. In spite of themselves, the persecutors can be the instruments of the glorious Christ (described by Saint John in Revelation) who "desacralizes" an unwarranted extension of an "ecclesiastical sacred" in the interests of a restitution of the secularity of the profane willed by God. May one venture so to regard the "secularization" of the Papal States in the nineteenth century? Did not Pius XII, in 1958, speak of a "healthy laicity" of the State?

There is nothing surprising in all this, if one remembers that the sacred is not identical with the Transcendent, but rather the way to the transcendent. Those appointed to guide others along this way are not, any more than others, exempt from the consequences of original sin. With J. P. Audet, we hold that a false and undue sacralization of the profane is one of its effects. Christ who, as God, is the author and the creator of the secularity of the profane, has come to save it, by the shedding of His redemptive blood, from all illegitimate sacralization. Jesus is the redeemer of the "profaneness" of the world.

Today, through His lay members, Jesus continues this task of redeeming the secularity of the world. Vatican II stresses with a remarkable insistence the "secular quality" which is "proper and special to laymen" and which distinguishes them from those who "by reason of their particular vocation are chiefly and professedly ordained to the sacred ministry."[19] "But the laity, by their very vocation, seek the kingdom of God by engaging in temporal affairs and by ordering them according to the plan of God. They live in the world, that is, in each and in all of the secular professions and occupations. They live in the ordinary circumstances of family and family life, from which the very web of their existence is woven."[20] It will be noted that the Council defines here what it means by *world*. Vatican II elsewhere specifies that the "elements that make up the temporal order . . . the good things of life" constitute the proper object of the activity of the laity, and "not only aid in the attainment of man's ultimate goal but also possess their own intrinsic value." Their "engagement in temporal affairs" constitutes, therefore, for man an intermediate end; such engagement takes on the value of an end.[21] For these temporal goods (life, family, culture, economic affairs, the arts, and the professions, political institutions, international relations, and so forth) are *values* which the Council links up with the dogma of creation:[22] "For by the very circumstance of their having been created, all things are endowed with their own stability, truth, goodness, proper laws, and order . . . For earthly matters and the concerns of faith derive from the same God."

In these conditions, it is not surprising that Vatican II should regard as possible the consecration of the very secularity of the world to God without suppressing that secularity as such: "Thus, as worshippers whose every (lay) deed is holy, the laity can consecrate the world itself to God."[23]

While it is true that Jesus is not the author of a certain secularization running counter to His salvific will;[24] while it is certain that He wills, through and in the Church, to maintain the existence of places, times, and persons consecrated in an exclusive manner to worship;[25] while, in a word, it is true that He wills ceaselessly to build up His Church which is not secular and could never be secularized—it is equally true that it is precisely as Redeemer that He devotes Himself to the renewal and restoration of the full secularity of the world of which He is the Creator. In this work He ceaselessly associates His Church, the co-redemptrix[26] of the secularity and profaneness of the world, as such. Christ, through the Church, ceaselessly wrests from secularism the secularity of the world, in order to orientate it towards "the age to come" (Mt. 12, 32). The full secularity of the world is closely linked with what could be called an "eschatological secularization," with the tireless seeking of "the age to come," which is constantly coming into ours.

In other words, Jesus is not the author of the

secularization described by Cox to the extent to which it signifies freedom from a so-called "metaphysical control" (as if the being of each existent had the power to control itself!) or from control by rigid metaphysical conceptions of the world, as if the data of existence were not subject to the judgment of man, man himself being constantly judged by the transcendent Eternal immanent in all reality! One understands, therefore, why Paul VI, in this connection and on several occasions, has reacted against every attempt to secularize Christianity.[27]

Nor is Jesus the author of secularization in one of the senses ascribed to it by Karl Rahner: "a distancing with regard to the Church." As Vatican II points out: "That the earthly and the heavenly city penetrate each other is a fact accessible to faith alone. It remains a mystery of human history. . . ."[28] The secularization which Jesus promotes through the full secularity of the world, even implies its intimate union with the Church: "She serves as a leaven and as a kind of soul for human society."[29]

Sufficient has been said to show how all this differs from what is ordinarily understood by "secularization." In addition to the fact that it is the canonical sense of the word that still comes readily to mind, at least in Catholic countries, none of the other definitions we have cited and could cite is purely and simply acceptable to a Catholic as regards the reality defined, and the majority are frankly unacceptable. This is not surprising since, as Father Lepargneur[30] has pointed out, the process of secularization is not, in practice, exempt from secularism. In our concrete situation, he insists, one cannot hope for a secularization (in the sense of a promotion of the profane order and of the natural man) without secularism, except as an ideal. Laicization separative from faith and from the Church (as distinct from the healthy laicity validated by Plus XII) is so linked with secularization that we think it impossible to say in an unqualified manner that Christ is the author of the process we see unfolding before our eyes. One could more or less say that Jesus is at the source of certain aspects of certain types of secularization, in the sense (promotion of secularity) previously defined.

Without using the actual word, which is itself becoming an object of magical superstition and of false sacralization for many of our contemporaries, the Council seems to us to have admirably summed up the basic ambiguity of the present phenomenon of secularization when describing the present religious evolution:

> Finally, these new conditions have their impact on religion. On the other hand, a more critical ability to distinguish religion from a magical view of the world and from the superstitions which still circulate, purifies religion and exacts day by day a more personal and explicit adherence to faith. As a result many persons are achieving a more vivid sense of God.
>
> On the other hand, growing numbers of people are abandoning religion in practice. Unlike former days, the denial of God or of religion, or the abandonment of them, are no longer unusual and individual occurrences. For, today it is not rare for such decisions to be presented as requirements of scientific progress or of a certain new humanism.[31]

For the Christian, therefore, secularization should be the object of a "discerning of spirits." While rejecting the atheistic tendency which it implies, one can retain its urgent concern for the purification and promotion of man. But, as we shall see shortly, man can be purified and promoted by and in Christ, only if he agrees to consecrate himself in Him and with Him.

It emerges, then, that the abstract distinction between secularization and secularism is concretely, existentially a fragile one. In fact, at the collective level, there is no secularization without secularism. As the Bishops of the United States said in their Annual Statement in 1947: ". . . there are many men—and their number is daily increasing—who in practice live their lives without recognizing that this is God's world. For the most part they do not deny God. On formal occasions they may even mention His name. . . . But they fail to bring an awareness of their responsibility to God into their thought and actions as individuals and members of society. This, in essence, is what we mean by secularism."

Quite clearly, Jesus Christ has never been, is not now nor ever shall be the inspirer of what in secularization is already secularism. Notably, His message and His action count for nothing in that aspect of secularism which the American Hierarchy very rightly emphasized—viz., the limitation of the spiritual horizon to life on earth.

It must be admitted that the influence of Bultmann, Bonhoeffer, and Teilhard has contributed, in various ways, to the diffusion of a type of "terrestrialism." Bonhoeffer and Teilhard have contributed to this only indirectly and in some sort unintentionally—the first by his devaluation of the religious language of faith[32] of which, however, he has himself made outstanding use; the second by his unbalanced exaltation of the world and of terrestrial tasks within an original eschatology in which he also speaks about death, the cross, and eternal life.[33] Bultmann, however, has contributed to it in a more direct way by allowing doubt to hover over the question of eternal life and not speaking his mind clearly on this subject.[34] In this connection, Bonhoeffer was perhaps unconsciously influenced by Bultmann at the very time when he was verbally reacting against him; by devaluing the religious and theological language, he was discrediting in advance, particularly for superficial readers, what the New Testament can tell us about life after death. Nor does Teilhard completely escape this criticism.[35]

The new religious language, the language of Jesus which Bonhoeffer was seeking, could never eliminate the language of the historical Jesus. The language of the Christ of faith integrates and extends that of the historical Jesus—or anyhow, it does not suppress it.

Now, the attempt at secularization which we are seeing today, is seeking, basically, to "immanentize" the transcendent and to reduce the eschatological to the horizontal present. In this, it is clearly a betrayal of the language of Jesus and of His message—a betrayal, however, which is the reversal of that of a certain early twentieth century Modernism which regarded the message of the Savior as no more than an eschatological discourse.

The Council had already denounced the idea that Jesus could be the author of this type of secularization, an indescribable mixture of silence about the eternal life and of a desire to exclude the Church from human society in the present life:

> The Church has a saving and an eschatological purpose which can be fully attained only in the age to come. . . . Pursuing the saving purpose which is proper to her, the Church not only communicates divine life to men, but in some ways casts the reflected light of that life over the entire earth. . . . Thus, through her individual members and her whole community, the Church believes she can contribute greatly towards making the family of man and its history more human.[36]

Clearly, then, for Vatican II, it is precisely thanks to this pursuit of the "age to come" that the Church and Christ through the Church operate effectively in history. Paul VI has merely pursued this same conciliar line when he denounces secularism, though without naming it, in his "Credo of the people of God":

> We confess that the Kingdom of God, which had its beginnings here on earth in the Church of Christ, is not of this world, whose form is passing, and that its authentic development cannot be measured by the progress of civilization, of science or of technology. The true growth of the Kingdom of God consists in an ever deepening knowledge of the unfathomable riches of Christ, in ever stronger hope in eternal bless-

ings, in an ever more fervent response to the love of God, and in an ever more generous acceptance of grace and holiness by men. But it is this same love that induces the Church to promote persistently the true temporal welfare of men. . . . The urgent solicitude of the Church, the Spouse of Christ, for the needs of men . . . must never be taken to mean that the Church conforms herself to the things of this world, or that her longing for the coming of her Lord and his eternal reign grows cold.[37]

In short, if there is a legitimate "secularization of the Church", it consists above all else in the action by which such secularization is increasingly directed towards the age to come and away "from the present evil age, according to the will of our God Father" (Gal. 1, 4), who wills the temporal and eternal salvation of mankind (1 Tim. 2, 4). *Desecularization* as regards "the present evil age"; *trans-secularization* towards the age to come—such is the aim of the Church's incessant activity in her co-redemptive mission in what concerns the secularity of the world. This *trans-secularization*, this ever renewed passage for one age to another, is the constant Pasch of the Church by which she ceaselessly consecrates herself to the God who has consecrated her in the blood of Christ. Jesus is not the author of the *secularization* of the world, and still less of that of the Church; but He is the author of their paschal *trans-secularization*, which presupposes *certain* "secularizations" and *certain* desecularizations."

C. Jesus Christ, Consecrator of the World?

1. *The Father sanctifies and consecrates the humanity of Jesus by the gift and the anointing of the Spirit: Jesus is the Christ, the Anointed.*

Jesus is He "whom the Father consecrated and sent into the world" (Jn. 10, 36). In what does this "consecration" of the Son by the Father consist? It is permissible to think that it consists in the sanctification[38] of the humanity assumed by the Son through the gift of the Spirit, who, according to the Gospel of Saint John, is the *Holy* Spirit (*Sanctus* Spiritus): "He whom God has sent speaks God's own words: God gives him the Spirit without reserve. The Father loves the Son and has entrusted everything to Him" (Jn. 3, 34-35).[39]

Catholic theology alludes to this sanctification of the humanity of Jesus by the Spirit when it recognizes the existence of sanctifying grace in the created soul of the Incarnate Word;[40] or again when it affirms the triple mission—sacerdotal, prophetic, and kingly— of Jesus, who was anointed[41] by the unction of the Spirit. Jesus is the Christ, consecrated by the Father, sanctified by Him in the Spirit. The unction received at His baptism manifests a prior sanctification.

Thanks to this consecrating sanctification, the prepaschal Jesus is already embryonically what the Christ of the Ascension will be: "a high priest, holy, blameless, unstained, separated from sinners, exalted above the heavens" (Heb. 7, 26),[42] precisely in order that he may be "able for all time to save those who draw near to God through him, since he always lives to make intercession for them" (Heb. 7, 25). The separation of Christ (and, in His image, the "setting apart in a certain sense" of the priest)[43] is functional, fully polarized by a perfect eschatological union.

It is clear that the consecration thus received by the humanity of the Word is the sacred *par excellence* in the economy of the New Alliance. It could be said, in the sense defined earlier,[44] that this consecration has even the effect of "sacralizing" the sacred Humanity, if not straightaway (Jesus was a carpenter for many years) at least when He abandoned His secular trade to respond perfectly to His sacerdotal "vocation," to the call received from the Father, by becoming exclusively the minister of His Gospel even to His death.

The divine "consecrated" One orientates Himself at that moment towards a perfect "consecration" of His own humanity to the Father in the sacrifice of His death, in order that this humanity may become completely a sacrament of the grace and gift of the Spirit to mankind: "Consecrate them in the truth. . . . And for their sake I consecrate myself so that they too may be consecrated in truth" (Jn. 17, 17-19: Jerusalem Bible).

The sacrificial self-sanctification of which Christ speaks here is legitimately translated by the verb *to consecrate*, because, as the note to this text in the Jerusalem Bible points out, the Greek word *agiazein* means "set apart for God, vowed to God." At least as regards Jesus, one would have to translate this verb as 'sacralize" even more than "consecrate," if one wished to be completely faithful to the distinction already considered. Even as regards the question of sanctification or consecration of the disciples, it must be observed with Lagrange:

> The repetition in verse 16 of the affirmation that both Jesus and His disciples "are not of the world" prepares the way for the prayer of verses 17-19. To act on the world without being of it—i.e. safe from its contagion—the disciples must receive a consecration which completes their separation from the world and brings them nearer to God. Chrysostom has indicated the two stages of this consecration: "separate them by the word and by the kerygma," and, more positively: "sanctify them by the gift of the Spirit and of orthodox dogmas." Already, having received the word, the disciples are no longer of the world, but this is only the negative aspect: Jesus asks God to make them participate by virtue of this same word, in the transcendent perfection which is the positive aspect of His holiness. . . . The word "consecration" does not sufficiently express the intimate character of what is done: the disciples are not only "consecrated" to the service of the truth, they are interiorly penetrated and transformed by it.[45]

Even if it is true, as Audet stresses,[46] that a careful distinction must be made between *the holy* and *the sacred,*—since God is holy but transcends the sacred—it is equally true that, in His priestly Prayer, Jesus emphasized how the Father, in sanctifying the Christians by the gift of the Spirit, was separating them from the evil world in which they had perforce to live, and that their acceptance of the word through faith was already separating them from the world, one of whose most characteristic sins is that of incredulity. Such a sanctifying separation reserved them to God: it thus became a consecrating sanctification.

We can now see more clearly the existential closeness to one another of all these ideas which, however, it was necessary to distinguish in an abstract way. This Christ, already sanctified and consecrated by the Father; this Jesus whose soul from the first instant of the Incarnation was completely filled with the Spirit and therefore sacralized, totally and exclusively dedicated to the worship of the Father (cf. Jn. 4, 22-23)—must still sanctify Himself, still consecrate and sacrifice Himself, in order that the Spirit may be able, through His risen and spiritualized body, to send the radiance of His light over all mankind. There is therefore no contradiction between the initial consecration of Jesus (to which Jn. 10, 36 alludes) and His final consecration, evoked in His sacerdotal Prayer. The first was already directed towards the second.

But, clearly, if the second was "necessary" in the divine plan, it was so because Jesus, in taking upon Himself in some sort the whole of human history, the space-time world, in His own flesh made subject to death, was inserting Himself into "this present evil age" (Gal. 1, 4)—"evil" and in that sense "secularized" —in order to "trans-secularize" it in Himself and to make it pass, through the consecration of His own flesh, into the "age to come." In the risen body of the Lord, we have the first fruits and the definitive temple of the Spirit. It is through Him that the Spirit consecrates, and that Christians and the world consecrate themselves.

2. *Christ is the consecrator of the world by His Incarnation and by His Spirit, through the sacraments and the sacramental.*

We understand here the expression "consecration of the world" in the sense given to it by Vatican II, a meaning that, we think, was first admirably worked out by Cardinal Montini in his 1962 pastoral letter to the Church of Milan: "the arduous and most beautiful task of the *consecratio mundi* is to impregnate with Christian principles and with strong natural and supernatural virtues the immense sphere of the lay world."[47]

As we have already seen, Canon Grand'maison, using a different approach, has come to understand *consecration* in the same sense. It does not suppress the secularity of the lay world, but orientates that world towards its supernatural end.

In this sense, it can be said that the word of God and of the universe,[48] by becoming man and above all else by rising from the dead, has consecrated and as it were divinized the universe, His priestly garment. Saint John of the Cross, had already given magnificent expression to this idea:

> According to Saint Paul, the Son of God "reflects the glory of God and bears the very stamp of his nature" (Heb. 1, 3). It must therefore follow that it is solely through this figure of His Son that God has looked upon all things, in giving them their natural being, in bestowing many graces and natural gifts on them, and in completing and perfecting them: "And God looked at all the things that he had made, and he saw that they were good" (Gen. 1, 31). To see them as very good was to make them very good, in the Word, His Son. And not only in looking at them has He bestowed upon them natural being and natural graces, as we have said, but also and solely through this figure of His Son. He has clothed them with beauty by communicating to them supernatural being. This took place when He became man, exalting

Him in the beauty of God and therefore all creatures in Him, in order that in man He might unite Himself with all their natures.[49]

And the saint concluded: "In the exaltation of the Incarnation and the glory of the Resurrection (of His Son) according to the flesh, not only has the Father partly embellished all creatures, but it can also be said that He has completely clothed them with beauty and dignity."

The whole creation, seen by God in His incarnate Son, takes on a new beauty. Everything is consecrated (except, of course, sin) because the whole universe is orientated to the Church, to the glory of the Word Incarnate and, through Him, to that of His Father: a universal consecration by the orientation of the universe towards the one and final supernatural end—the Trinity. The gradual recapitulation of the world and of history is its consecration.[50] As well, of course, as by means unknown to us, Christ Jesus accomplishes this through the sacraments and the sacramentals of the Church.

Christ is the Sacrament *par excellence* who consecrates the world by consecrating Himself to the Father for the world. This consecration of the world, effected through the mediation of the Church, a priestly and hierarchized people, makes the whole world a vast sign of God, a sign which gives God through the Church, sacrament of salvation. In a broad sense, therefore, the whole world becomes a sacrament for the man who knows how to read the signs of God. In the peace and presence of the Eternal, all things are transfigured in the light of the transfigured Christ, as much as this is possible to their mortal condition.[51]

Against the background of, and in order to promote, this cosmic sacramentality linked with the consecration of the world, we have the sacramental consecration (in the strict sense) of Christians by Christ—a consecration which is a setting apart, not a separation, a distinction rather, with a view to the worship of the triune God; a sanctifying consecration which does not impede (on the contrary, indeed) the involvement of consecrated persons in the world, apart of course from any sinful involvement which would violate the engagements assumed at each consecration. And the consecration of the world effected by the incarnate and redemptive Word, is not immediate, but is linked to the consecration of persons, and comes about through the use which Christians, consecrated by God, make of the world.

The basic principle is thus laid down by Vatican II:

> The baptized, by regeneration and the anointing of the Holy Spirit, are consecrated into a spiritual house and a holy priesthood. Thus through all those works befitting Christian men they can offer spiritual sacrifices and proclaim the power of Him who has called them out of darkness into His marvelous light (cf. 1 Pet. 2: 4-10). . . . It is through the sacraments and the exercise of the virtues that the sacred nature and the organic structure of the priestly community is brought into operation.[52]

This twofold baptismal consecration (by grace and by the character),[53] is the initial and basic "setting apart" which conditions any other. It is followed by that of confirmation,[54] and then, according to the various cases, by the sacerdotal[55] or religious[56] consecration, or the quasi-consecration of matrimony.[57] Each of these consecrations constitutes a new functional "setting apart," designed in some way to the good of the whole sacred and priestly community who constitute the people of God, distinct[58] from the peoples of the world whom it must serve; a people that baptism sets apart from all others, without separating it from any.[59]

And this people is set apart precisely in order to bring about, through an indissolubly sacramental and virtuous life, the consecration of the world:

The laity, dedicated to Christ *(Christo dedicati)* and anointed by the Holy Spirit, are marvelously called and equipped to produce in themselves ever more abundant fruits of the spirit. For all their works . . . their daily labor . . . become spiritual sacrifices acceptable to God through Jesus Christ (cf. 1 Pet. 2, 5). During the celebration of the Eucharist, these sacrifices are most lovingly offered to the Father along with the Lord's body. Thus, as worshippers whose every deed is holy, the laity consecrate the world itself to God.[60]

This beautiful description clearly shows us what is the consecration of the world favored and declared necessary by Vatican II. It integrates and synthesizes several elements: on the basis of the initial baptismal consecration (instrumental efficient cause), it is an adoration of the Father by the oblation of all profane and secular activities, in union with the liturgical offering of the consecrated and even sacralized Body of His Son Incarnate. This consecration of the world through that of the secular activities is therefore the goal towards which the baptismal consecration and the Eucharistic consecration both tend. Christ transubstantiates the bread only in order to change hearts, and thus to transfigure this secular world of men. The consecration of the bread and wine, like that of marriage and of the priesthood, far from being the *raison d'être* of the consecration of mankind's secular activities, has on the contrary this latter consecration as its end and purpose. And this end is also attained, though in a secondary manner, by the powerful action of the sacramentals,[61] by which "various occasions in life are rendered holy."[62]

In short, the consecration of the world, a task proper to the laity, is largely linked to and as it were suspended from the whole liturgy of the sacraments and the sacramentals, and through this liturgy is linked to the ministerial priesthood as well as—and especially— to the supreme Priesthood of Christ. It is Christ who, acting by the Spirit within the heart of the laity, consecrates the world by sanctifying their profane activities. Consecrated by the Father as a new tabernacle and a new temple (Jn. 10, 36; 1, 14; 2, 21),[63] He makes the whole world the extension of this temple that He is, the vestibule of the sanctuary of the new and eternal Alliance.

3. *Christ sacralizes certain places, times, and people with a view to the consecration of the whole world.*

We can say with Father Congar[64] that Christ is the quasi-substantial sacred, since as man He is temple, priest, and sacrifice; from Him derives immediately a sacred of the second zone, that of the seven sacraments and of the human situations they engender; from Him also derives, through the mediation of the Church, a sacred of the third zone, the pedagogic sacred of the sacramentals which help us to draw near to Him; finally, from Him as creative Word with the Father and the Spirit, derives the final zone of the sacred—namely, the totality of terrestrial or even cosmic realities, the "age" itself.

Situated, therefore, between the supreme sacred of the humanity of Christ and the cosmic sacred, is the intermediate sacred which links the two. Between the sacrament of the humanity of Christ and the sacrament of the world, there is the mediating sacrament of the salvation of the world, the sacrament of the Church.

In order that the supreme sacred, Jesus Christ, may be able perfectly to consecrate the world, He must partly sacralize it in the mystery of the Church. Furthermore, in order that all space, all historic time, all people may consecrate themselves effectively to Christ, certain places, certain times and certain people must, in virtue of his plan of recapitulation, be reserved to an exclusively sacred usage and precluded, at least in large measure,[65] from profane and temporal usage.

Thus the New Testament recognizes a day of the risen Lord,[66] a day more specially marked by the commemoration of His Pasch; it also recognizes the "setting apart" of certain Christians for the ministry of the Gospel (Rom. 1, 1; Acts 13, 2);[67] finally, although it does not specify that special places are to be explicitly devoted to the new worship in spirit and in truth (cf. Jn. 4, 21-24), nevertheless it does lay down principles which will lead to the setting up of such places, by proclaiming the real presence of Christ in the Eucharist, a non-local[68] presence whose very permanence encourages the Church to consecrate to it special places, exclusively reserved to the worship of her Spouse.

The personal and space-time sacralization is, in the final analysis, a function of the Eucharistic mystery— the mystery of the substantial sacred. The priest is consecrated to the service of the Eucharist and of the communion of the faithful; the churches and the Lord's Day, to the worship of the Lord present in the Eucharist. The intermediate sacred is polarized by the supreme sacred, itself in the service of the life of the world: "The bread which I shall give you for the life of the world is my flesh" (Jn. 6, 51).

It might nevertheless be objected that, as we have seen, the Church presents to us the community of the Christians as "saints" (is not this Paul's terminology?) and as consecrated, without for all that presenting them to us as sacralized, as dedicated to an exclusively sacred usage. Priests, and also monks and nuns, though consecrated people, can in certain cases follow a secular profession:[69] one need only instance the case of the members of the Secular Institutes, who, though not "religious" in the canonical sense of the term, are nevertheless engaged in a "state of perfection" and of more special consecration.

The objection shows that the distinction between "to consecrate" and "to sacralize" is more tenuous than it would at first seem to be. In the context of human activities, this distinction needs to be clarified and in a sense completed by the other one proposed by Grand'maison: "sacred and profane are two existential dimensions present in all reality. The relational nature of the authentically religious sacred is not opposed to the *in se* nature of the profane."[70] Even sacralization does not completely[71] remove from the reality of human activity the specificity of its immediate end. The baptized person, the priest, the religious, remain men. Not all the secular usages of their personal activity are forbidden to them, but only certain usages, and it is thus that their "sacralizing consecration" manifests itself.

Thus, the baptized person is set apart from the non-baptized in view of a Sunday Eucharistic worship, which excludes certain activities incompatible with that worship, and this already involves a certain sacralization within a simple consecration. On the other hand, in certain oriental rites, a man already consecrated by marriage can receive the new consecration of the priesthood, but the celibate who has been ordained a priest cannot marry and keep the usage of the sacred orders; in this sense, he is "sacralized."

It is necessary, therefore, to recognize the analogical character of the ideas of consecration and of sacralization, which are open to a whole gamut of concrete realizations, more or less accentuated from one case to another.

One gets a clearer grasp of this through the historic negations which help us to see the profound link which interconnects all the sacralizing consecrations, while also distinguishing them one from another. Luther sought to desacralize, to secularize at one and the same time, the monastic state, the priesthood, and marriage. He also encouraged bishops, priests, monks and nuns to marry, and declared that marriage was not a sacrament, admitted its dissolution by divorce, and even, in a celebrated case, allowed polygamy.[72] In all these cases, people originally "set apart" with a view to this or that sacred activity to the exclusion of this or that other activity, were encouraged to reject this exclusion or at least to obtain "permission" with regard to it. One might even suspect a profound connection between all these "secularizations" and

Luther's own hostility to the Mass and to the doctrine of transubstantiation (a point to which we shall return), which hostility resulted in his "secularizing" the Christian life of the baptized layman as basically orientated towards the Eucharist, sacrifice and sacrament. This would throw considerable light on the historical origin of a large part of the present day movement of secularization; it would be, as many Protestants acknowledge, a consequence of the sixteenth century Reformation as well as being one of its postulates.

Lutheran tendencies, then, carry the germ of a complete desacralization; but this only makes it all the more striking that, through the use which God's mercy made of certain truths preserved and also of the illogicalness of men, Luther and Lutheranism, as well as the at least moral unanimity of the Christian confessions, have kept consecrated places and times in a manner relatively exclusive of all profane usage: the churches and the Lord's Day. Nay more, Lutheranism and the majority of the Protestant churches still have ministers who do not follow any secular profession. Although not consecrated by a special sacrament, that of Holy Orders, and therefore not distinguished from other baptized persons except at the functional level, they are nontheless set apart from the non-baptized, the latter, in the eyes of the reformed churches, being incapable of exercising this ministry.

Neither in these churches, nor in the Catholic Church, could the Christian life subsist at the collective and sacramental level without specially consecrated places and times. Furthermore, in the Catholic Church, the Christian life could not attain to the fullness willed by Christ, without specially consecrated persons. Pope Paul VI has clearly and firmly reminded us of this.[73]

Such a doctrine of the Church presupposes both a personalist and anthropological idea of the sacred, and a philosophy of a realist, not idealist, kind.

In effect, the correct distinction which Father Congar makes between the different levels of the sacred (quasi-substantial, sacramental, pedagogic and cosmic) fails, perhaps, to stress sufficiently what it nevertheless requires—viz., a personalist polarization. The sacramental, pedagogic, and cosmic sacred is essentially ordained to the voluntary self-consecration and to the partial self-sacralization of *persons*. The "reified" sacred is inter-personal mediation: between human persons, on the one hand, and between them and the incarnate Person of the Word, on the other. The people whom the Word Incarnate sets apart more and more and consecrates in an increasingly special manner through the sacramental life, are not pure spirits but incarnated spirits placed within the world and within history. The consecration of persons, and even more their partial sacralization (in the sense explained), demand a relative spatio-temporal sacralization.

Only an idealist[74] "Weltanschauung" would seek (in vain, however) to separate the inter-personal, cosmic sacred of places and the historic sacred (of specially consecrated times) from the persons whose consecration does not preclude insertion in space and in time.

As against these dissociative tendencies, the Church is so conscious of the grip of the human and Christian person on time-space that she consecrates the churches in which, preeminently, her own mystery[75] is deployed, treating them with the love she bears to living persons.[76] The synthesis between the profane and the sacred (of which Jesus Christ is the instance *par excellence*, as we shall see shortly), still manifests itself in a privileged way in the structure, the vocation, and the charisma proper to Secular Institutes. In them it is made very particularly clear how the secular and the sacred, far from being contradictory and mutually exclusive, are reciprocally harmonious.

> Secular Institutes are not religious communities but they carry with them in the world a

profession of the evangelical counsels which is genuine and complete, and recognized as such by the Church. Their profession confers a consecration on men and women, laity and clergy, who reside in the world. For this reason they should chiefly strive for total self-dedication to God, one inspired by perfect charity. These institutes should preserve their proper and particular character, a secular one, so that they may everywhere measure up successfully to that apostolate which they were designed to exercise, and which is both in the world and, in a sense, of the world.[77]

What, therefore, specially characterizes Secular Institutes is a new consecration following those of baptism and of confirmation; a fresh setting apart with a view to making the Gospel penetrate the world through its very secularity and its profaneness. Secularity for apostolic purposes is itself the object of the sacralizing consecration. What better confirming proof could we have (in conjunction with that of the term *"secular clergy"*) that the profane is of the *in se* order, while the sacred is of the relational order?—that the first concerns the order of immediate finality, and the second that of the ultimate end?

All this puts us, we think, in a better position to understand what Pope Paul VI said to the laity (October 15, 1967):

> We say it with sorrow: there are Catholic writers who lend their support, against the tradition of two centuries in the Church, to the gradual attenuation, even to disappearance, of the sacred character of places, times, and persons.
> Your apostolate . . . goes counter to these currents of ideas. The Council has repeatedly said this to you: the laity "consecrate the world to God," they work for "the sanctification of the world," for "the Christian animation of the world," for "the soundness of institutes and of living conditions in the world": these are

the very expressions of the conciliar documents. And what does all this mean, if not "to re-sacralize" the world by causing it to be filled or filled again with that powerful inspiration of faith in God and in Christ, which can alone lead it to true happiness and salvation?[78]

With the statement of the *fact* of secularization, the Pope contrasts the *obligation* of Christians to re-sacralize the desacralized world through the upholding of the sacred character of places, times, and persons.

4. *Christ sacralizes the Eucharistic bread in order to consecrate the world.*

The doctrine of the New Testament and of the Catholic Church best shows how false is the statement sometimes made that "Christ has abolished the distinction between profane and sacred."

On the contrary, this differentiation reaches its point of culmination in the mystery of the Eucharist, as the Catholic Church has always understood this mystery —viz., that the consecrated bread is no longer common, ordinary bread, it has even ceased to be bread in order to become the Body of Christ. And it is precisely for this reason that the consecrated bread can be said to be sacralized, in the sense that this Bread of Life, the Body of the Lord, can never be put to a non-sacred usage or profaned through being eaten for mere nourishment. It must be "discerned," as Saint Paul said to the Corinthians (1 Cor. 11, 29)—"discerned" from ordinary bread under pain of condemnation by Christ.

In the Eucharist, we have only the Body of Christ, and we no longer have bread; the Catholic doctrine of transubstantiation, as against the Lutheran transubstantiation,[79] shows that there is at least one sector of the real, the Body of Christ under the appearance of bread, where all ontological co-existence of the transcendent and of a non-sacralized profane fails, or where all profane usage of the sacred is excluded, even though the profane hiding the sacred remains visible.

The dogma of the Eucharistic transubstantiation, constantly reaffirmed by the Church for centuries,[80] rules out in advance any possibility of the legitimate secularization of the Church as such. While the hierarchic Church ceaselessly gives us the Eucharist, the latter ceaselessly constructs the Church, the efficacious and sacramental sign of the consecration of the world. To make possible the secularization of the Church as such, Christ would need *not* to have willed a sacred society distinguishable from secular society. However, Revelation tells us that He has willed the distinction, and the most telling sign of this is the mystery of transubstantiation. It must even be said that Christ has willed the constant renewal of this mystery in the course of history, precisely in order to effect constantly what it signifies—viz., the "trans-secularization" of men, and through them of the world, destined to pass together from this age into the age to come.

Until the Parousia, when the distinction between sacred society and secular society will disappear, the *raison d'être* of the first is precisely to make possible and to effect the voluntary self-consecration of the second through the participation of its members in the eucharistic mystery. In instituting the Eucharist, Christ was therefore also instituting the sacrament of Holy Orders, which conditions the Eucharist.

The priest, consecrated by Christ essentially for the exercise of the sacred ministry,[81] is therefore irreducibly distinct from the layman. However, his mission, while not primarily temporal, is not exclusively sacred, in the sense that his indirect contribution to the consecration of the temporal by the laity is decisive. Man of the sacred, the priest is, as such, the spiritual animator of the consecration of the world by the laity. The proper mission of the priest issues into the age, because, by the ministry of the word and by the celebration of the sacraments, it is his duty to assist the laity to sanctify themselves in the exercise of their mission to consecrate the secularity of the world.

In stressing that the primary mission of the priest is to evangelize and that the acme of this mission is eucharistic, Vatican II[82] has pointed the way to a solution of the opposition between, on the one hand, an exclusively sacral concept of the priest and, on the other, a totally secularized concept. Both of these concepts are equally contrary to history and to the plan of Christ. The dilemma is solved by the synthesis suggested by the Council: as minister of the Gospel, the priest is in unceasing contact with the secularity of the world, both by prayer[83] and the word, with a view to making it converge on the altar.

Between the Gospel which he everywhere announces and the altar at which he immolates Him whom he announces in order to give Him as spiritual food, the priest is the man of "the pedagogic sacred" to which Father Congar refers; the man, not only of the sacraments, but also of the sacramentals, with the various blessings which the latter bring to the different secular tasks, consecrating but not sacralizing them.

Within the framework of a truly Catholic idea of the consecration of the world, this is in a very special way the effect of the sacramentals, which are sacred signs instituted by the Church precisely in order to secure the "trans-secularization" they signify.

In passing, we note that these sacramentals, after having been blessed by the Church, keep not only their natural reality but also their profane usage. The blessed bread can be eaten, the blessed water can be drunk, just as ordinary food and drink.

Is it not the priest's vocation, not only to preach the Gospel and to consecrate by baptism and the other sacraments, but also to bless in the name of the triune God who still sees that His creatures are good and proclaims their goodness (cf. the sixfold repetition in Gen. 1)?[84] To bless, is not that to pronounce *good?* By invoking the protection of the God of Heaven, does not the priest exercise a mission to recall frequently to men on earth that, in spite of sin, their enterprises are often good and can become more so? How could it be otherwise, if all the blessings are directed, in one way or another, towards Him who is the link between Heaven and earth, and who is the Blessing *par excellence*, the descendant from Abraham in which all nations are blessed (cf. Gen. 12, 3; Gal. 3, 6-16)?

The hands of the priest bless, absolve, anoint, pour the waters of baptism, elevate and give the Host and the Chalice: they are hands consecrated so that they may consecrate.

Is not the priest, therefore, the permanent sign and instrument, the sacrament of Christ the Consecrator of the world? Christ, the Holy One of God (cf. Jn. 6, 69)—i.e. the One who is consecrated to the Father in an eminent way[85]—does He not continue, through His ministerial priests, to sacralize earthly bread and wine to the point of changing them into His Body and Blood, in order through them to give Himself to the "saints" (cf. Rom. 1, 7) so as to consecrate the world through their secular activities?

If Jesus is the author of a certain secularization of the domain of Caesar and of a world falsely consecrated to non-existent divinities, it is ultimately in order to consecrate this world to His Father by the mediation of His whole Messianic and hierarchized people.

D. The Consecrated Heart of the Consecrator of the World, Synthesis of the Sacred and the Profane

Let us attempt to summarize the results of our enquiry into and reflection on the secularization and the consecration of the world in their relationship with the mystery of Jesus Christ.

The Word of the Father's Goodness, already present by His *presence of enfolding immensity* in the time-space of the cosmos, makes Himself present by a new title, a *presence of in-humanation*, in order to give Himself, through His Spirit, to all created persons, as an eternal Present, in *a presence of the indwelling* of grace[86] by a third and final title,[87] with a view to the praise of the glory of His Father's grace (cf. Eph. 1, 6).

The Word of Goodness thus becomes the sacred and consecrated Heart of the Eucharistic Heart which wills to beat in all human breasts in order to complete their consecration to the glory of His Father, at the same time as, through them, He consecrates the world created by Him. He "amorizes" the world only by amorizing mankind.[88]

But this Heart has consecrated Itself, in all the senses of the word, only through His Spirit.

In a first sense, Jesus has consecrated His Heart by filling and anointing His two-fold human love, sensible and spiritual, with the unction of His Spirit, logically anterior to His Incarnation;[89] an initial consecration, symbolized by the anointing of baptism, and completely orientated towards the final consecration of the sacrificial death by which Jesus has fully submitted His flesh to the irradiation of the Spirit, an irradiation perfectly effected at His Resurrection.

The first of these two consecrations has made Jesus *the Christ*.

Thanks to the second, by which Jesus dedicated Him to the Father in order to be physically filled by their Spirit, He became the Anointed of the Spirit, the Christ.

"God has made him both Lord and Christ, this Jesus whom you crucified" (Acts 2, 36; cf. 4, 27; Heb. 1, 9; Jn. 20, 31). It was at the Resurrection that the Incarnate Word, who had always been Jesus, became perfectly the Christ, in order to be able to make His disciples the anointed ones, "Christians," by giving them the anointing "by the Holy One" so that they would "know everything" (cf. 1 Jn. 2, 20 and 27), and by pouring God's love into their hearts (cf. Rom. 5, 5).

The Word, who was in some sense secularized by entering into "this age" through His Incarnation, was fully consecrated by passing into "the age to come."

In Him, the human element, without ceasing to be such, and without losing its relative[90] spontaneous autonomy—nor, consequently, its "profaneness," its "secularity"—becomes the mediating sacred of all consecration. As D. Lys[91] puts it: "In His being is effected the union of the sacred and the profane, which is the aim of the anointing."

In this personal union, "the absolute distinction between the two natures remains. His transfigured and glorified human nature cannot in any way complete or perfect the Divinity; an eternal impassable chasm divides the two."[92]

In the mystery of Jesus, the Anointed, the Christ, "human nature as He assumed it was not annulled."[93] The same can be said,[94] analogically, about the "secularity of the world": Christ did not destroy but perfected it by consecrating it. His human love, consecrated by the Spirit who is the bond and nucleus of love between Father and Son, has come to consecrate all the legitimate loves and all the loving activities of His brethren.

NOTES TO CHAPTER EIGHT

1. Cf. Harvey Cox, *The Secular City,* New York, 1966[10], p. 21-36.

2. J. Grand'maison, *Le monde et le sacré,* Paris, 1966, t. I, p. 188. One could perhaps express this statement in the language of the traditional philosophy by saying that the profane is identified with the material cause, with the formal cause, and with the immediate or mediate final cause, depending on where the sacred is placed in the line of the ultimate final cause.

3. This sacred usage is conceived as exclusive of any profane usage. Thus a temple would be "profaned" were it used for any other purpose than one pertaining to worship; a religious secularizes himself if he marries; the Lord's day is profaned when the Christian works to the detriment of the worship he should offer to God; the goods of the Church are secularized when the State expropriates them.

4. J. Grand'maison defines "the taboo sacred" as follows: "In all these kinds of prohibitions, the symbols of the numinous

are always persons, things, events, which are or seem to be outside the system of rules, and which threaten the stability of a human condition well defined within its natural and social framework" (*op. cit.*, p. 53).

5. *Ibid.*, p. 78. The author criticizes the definition of the sacred given by Durkheim ("the sacred thing is the one which the profane should not touch and cannot with impunity touch"), basing his criticism on the conclusions reached by specialists in the human sciences of religion, notably by J. Cazeneuve in *Les rites et la condition humaine,* Paris, 1958 (p. 260): "We would not think of denying that the sacred is isolated from the profane by certain interdictions, and that, on the other hand, the profane is sometimes raised to the dignity of the sacred by certain rites of consecration. . . . What we do contest is that it is possible to explicate the consecration and especially the communion merely by defining the sacred in terms of the interdiction which isolates it from the profane. The sacred should be such that it distinguishes itself clearly from the profane, but at the same time calls it to consecration" (Grand'maison, *op. cit.*, p. 55). This point seems to have been overlooked by Father M. D. Chenu O.P. in his article: "Consecratio Mundi," *Nouv. Revue Théologique* 86 (1964), 608-618.

6. J. Grand'maison, *op. cit.*, p. 87. We have slightly modified this author's definition of consecration. Chenu identifies consecration with sacralization.

7. J. Grand'maison, *op. cit.*, p. 199, note 118.

8. J. P. Audet O.P., "Le Sacré et le profane: leur situation en christianisme," in N.R.T., 79 (1957), pp. 54-55.

9. *Ibid.*, p. 36.

10. Cf. J. Bonsirvin S.J., *Les enseignements de Jésus-Christ,* Paris, 1945, p. 94, note 3; L. Bouyer, *Initiation Théologique,* Paris, 1962⁵, t. II, pp. 507-508; in these works, the meaning of the word "kosmos" in John and Paul is discussed; it is very close to the word "age," of which we are more specifically thinking here. In this connection, see: J. Bonsirvin, *Le judaisme palestinien au temps de Jésus-Christ,* Paris, 1934, t. I, pp. 318-319: F. Zorell S.J., *Novi Testamenti Lexicon Graecum,* Paris, 1911: art. "aion." In the NT, "this eon" and "this world" designate the same "present evil age" (Gal. 1, 4).

11. Cf. Codex Juris canonici, art. 638.

12. Definition given by R. Marlé S.J., *Etudes,* 328 (1968), p. 62.

13. Cf. Cox, *The Secular City,* N. Y., 1966¹⁰, pp. 18-20.

14. K. Rahner S.J., "Réflexions théologiques sur le problème de la sécularisation," in *La Théologie du Renouveau,* Paris-Montreal, 1968, t II, p. 257.

15. In this connection, see. R. Marlé S.J., *Etudes,* 328 (1968), 68.

16. A. Richardson, *Procès de la Religion,* 1967, pp. 37-43.

17. A. Reinhold Niebuhr, *Christianity and Power Politics,* N. Y., 1940, pp. 2-3-204.

18. On the meaning of the term "pre-Christian Religions," see our Chapter Two.

19. LG, 31 (Abbott, 57).

20. *Ibid.*

21. AA, 7.

22. GS, 36. 2 (Abbott, 233-234).

23. LG, 34 (Abbott, 60). Cf. GS, 36.

24. Cf. B. Lambert O.P.: "Secularization is the process by which a society breaks with religious ideas, beliefs, and institutions which were governing its existence, in order to constitute itself into an autonomous society and to find an immanent principle for to find an immanent principle for its organization. Secularization is a process of laicization. It is part of its logic to demand the complete elimination of religion, or, if that cannot be done in given circumstances, to confine it to the strictly private domain" (*Vatican II, L'Eglise dans le monde de ce temps,* Paris, 1967, t. II, pp. 149 *seq.*). This definition calls for the following comments. The autonomy of a human society and the fact that it finds in its immanence the principle of its organization, are not irreconcilable with Christianity and with Christian faith among its members, because this autonomy can be relative and not exclude a supreme and transcendent principle of its organization. On the other hand, what is irreconcilable with Christian faith is the elimination of religious ideas and beliefs. Secularization as thus understood is no different from atheism. There is no absolute autonomy of a creature or of a society in relation to God. A pretension of this kind would be a form of atheism.

25. Cf. F. H. Lepargneur O.P., "Secularizaçao e Culto," *Revista Ecclesiástica Brasileira,* 27 (1968).

26. See our Chapter Eleven.

27. Notably in October 1967 at Rome to the Apostolate of the Laity, and on 24th August 1968, in Colombia, when opening the reunion of Latin-American Bishops: "There are those who would secularize Christianity by abandoning its essential reference to religious truth, to supernatural communion with the ineffable and superabundant charity of God towards men. . . . They would, in their view, liberate Christianity itself from this 'form of neurosis which is religion' (H. Cox), banish all preoccupation with theology, give to Christianity a new and wholly pragmatic efficacy—because only in pragmatic terms can its truth be measured, only in such terms can it be rendered acceptable to and efficacious in our modern, profane, and technological civilization."

28. GS, 40.4 (Abbott, 239).

29. GS, 40. 3 (Abbott, 239).

30. F. H. Lepargneur, *op. cit.*, p. 560.

31. GS, 7. 3.

32. See our Chapter Seven, D.

33. Cf. our Chapter Four.

34. Cf. our Chapter Five; Bultmann continues this influence through Robinson.

35. In 1950, Teilhard wrote: "While showing full and deep veneration for the human words of Jesus, may one not observe that the Judeo-Christian faith continues to express itself (and forcefully!) in the Gospel texts in terms of a typically neolithic symbolism?" (cited by Cardinal Journet, *Nova et Vetera,* 1964, p. 306, note 2). By implying that the language of Jesus was some 2,500 years behind that of His contemporaries, Teilhard is really saying that Jesus derived His imagery from an agrarian civilization. One could insist that this symbolism, immediately intelligible to the major part of our contemporaries who still live in the primary rural sector (the underdeveloped countries), will always be intelligible, at least mediately, to people of every period. Besides, what matters is not so much the symbol as the reality symbolized by it. That we here link Teilhard with Bultmann does not mean, however, that we are insensitive to the immense differences between the two; see, in this connection, the interesting observations made by G. Crespy, *La pensée théologique de Teilhard de Chardin,* Paris, 1961, notably pp. 159-186: "For Bultmann, faith is recognition of weakness and abandonment; for Teilhard, it is, in the recognition of weakness and abandonment, impassioned assent to the victorious activity of Christ—a dimension almost totally absent from the Christ of Bultmann" (p. 183); Teilhard's concern with eschatology is also very different from that of Bultmann; for Crespy, however, the Christ of Teilhard "exists within a still mythic body of ideas" (p. 168); precisely because of the eschatology of Teilhard.

36. GS, 40 (Abbott, 239).

37. C.T.S. translation, pp. 13-14.

38. Cf. H. Muehlen, *Der Heilige Geist als Person,* Muenster, 1966², pp. 206-214. PO, 2 interprets Jn 10, 36 as we do.

39. Following Pope Pius XII in *Mystici Corporis* (DS, 3807; DB, 2288) and the Jerusalem Bible, we adopt the "lectio difficilior" of Jn. 2, 34; it is to the Son (incarnate) that the Father gives "the Spirit without reserve." Cf. note 41.

40. Cf., e.g., E. Mersch, *Théologie du Corps Mystique,* Brussels, 1946, t.I, pp. 254-280.

41. Cf. Pius XII, *Mystici Corporis,* AAS, 35 (1943), 206-207 and 219; and H. Muehlen, note 38.

42. Of course, from the first instant of the Incarnation, Jesus was already "holy, blameless, unstained," but not yet perfectly "separated from sinners" since He was still living among them.

43. PO, 3 (Abbott, 536).

44. Cf. the text of J. Grand'maison to which our note 6 refers. If could be said that the initial consecration of Jesus was polarized by His final sacralization.

45. M. J. Lagrange O.P., *Evangile selon saint Jean,* Paris, 1936⁵, pp. 447-448. The remarkable Saint John Chrysostom text is in the saint's commentary on Saint John's Gospel: PG, 59, 443. That the word of Christ which is also the word of the Father, wrests the disciple of Christ from the world precisely to enable him efficaciously to announce this word to the world, is a profound idea which derives directly from the sacerdotal Prayer of Christ: "I have given them your word; and the world has hated them because they are not of the world. . . . I have sent them into the world. . . . I pray also for those who believe in me through their word" (Jn. 17, 14-20). One thus grasps more clearly that, in this prayer, Jesus is consecrating Himself to the Father not only for men, but also in their name, as Father B. Leeming S.J. observes. The latter points out that the word *hagiazô* used in *John* 17, 19, means in the O. T. Greek of the Septuagint the consecrating of a priest or of a prophet to the service of God, or again of an animal to sacrifice. The word has a sacrificial meaning of a complete offering to God and also of consecration, according to Hoskyns (cf. B. Leeming, "Consecration to the Sacred Heart", *Cor Jesu 1,* Rome, 1959, pp. 636-643).

46. Audet, *op. cit.,* p. 54.

z47. *Osservatore Romano,* 23 March 1962; cited by Chenu, *op. cit.,* p. 608.

48. Saint Thomas Aquinas, *Summa contra Gentiles,* IV, 13.

49. Saint John of the Cross, *Spiritual Canticle,* V. 4.

50. Cf. Eph. 1, 10; 1 Cor. 3, 23: "all are yours; and you are Christ's; and Christ is God's."

51. Cf. J. Nadal S.J.: *Christus,* no. 11, 1956, pp. 349-353.

52. LG, 10 and 11.

53. Cf. M. M. Philippon O.P., "Consécration sacerdotale et consécration religieuse," in the review *Vocations,* no. 241, 1968, p. 126.

54. *Ibid.*

55. LG, 28.

56. LG, 45; the religious profession, while not a sacrament, is a sacramental and therefore a means of grace; or more accurately, if one ventures to say so, this sacramental has for its precise purpose to enable the Christian already consecrated by baptism, "to derive more abundant fruit from this baptismal grace" (LG, 44—Abbott, 74).

57. GS, 48. 2, citing Pius XI *(Casti Connubii).*

58. Cf. LG. 9. 2: ". . . this Messianic people, although it does not actually include all men, and may more than once look like a small flock. . . ." The Messianic people of the

New Alliance is distinguished from others by the common good which specifies it—a spiritual and supernatural good held in common—while the peoples of the world are pursuing as nations, a common temporal good intrinsically subordinated, however, to their common supernatural good and to their final end. It could still be said that the people of God are opposed to the people of Satan (cf. Saint Thomas Aquinas: *Summa Theologica*, III. 8. 7 and 8). It is only at the end of history, in the celestial Church, that the distinction between terrestrial peoples and Messianic people will disappear, at the same time as that between the people of God and the people of Satan will crystallize forever: cf LG, 69: Mary intercedes "with her Son . . . until all the peoples of the human family . . . are happily gathered together in peace and harmony into the one People of God. . . ." It would be a serious ecclesiological error to identify, as some have now a tendency to do, the people of God with the people *tout court*.

59. We are adapting to the case of the people of God what PO, 3, says about the setting apart of the priest within the Church.

60. LG, 34.

61. Cf. SC, 60 (Abbott, 158).

62. *Ibid.*

63. Cf. also Nb. 7, 1; according to R. E. Brown S. S. (*The Gospel according to John*, N. Y., 1966, pp. 404, 411, which we are here following), *John* 10, 36 could be a possible allusion to the priesthood of Christ, on the occasion of the Dedication of the Temple.

64. Y. M. J. Congar O.P. *La Liturgie après Vatican II* (commentaire collectif), Paris, 1967, pp. 385-403.

65. As regards the sacred time of the Lord's Day, it is clear that the exclusiveness is not total: the Church does not demand that Christians indulge only in activities of a directly devotional kind on that day, precisely because all human and secular activities can and should be integrated in some way in such devotion (cf. LG, 34).

66. Cf. Rev. 1, 10: "I was in the Spirit on the Lord's day. . . ."

67. Cf. PO, 3.

68. Saint Thomas Aquinas: *Summa Theologica*, III. 76. 5.

69. Cf. LG, 31, which adds that those in holy orders, "by reason of their particular vocation are chiefly and professedly ordained to the sacred ministry." In this connection, we have elsewhere written: "Paul did not follow a profession in the modern sense of contractual insertion into a specific social group with obligations which are proper to it and which take precedence over any others: the Apostle was a self-employed tradesman and did not make tents when he considered it preferable to preach the Gospel or to travel on missionary journeys for that purpose. . . . The Priest *par excellence* of

the New Alliance, Jesus, gave up His carpenter's trade, which he certainly loved, in order to preach the Gospel" (B. de Margerie S.J., *Padres profetas e mistagogos,* São Paulo, 1968, pp. 172-174; *Revue eucharistique du Clergé,* Montreal, 71, 1968, 347-349).

70. Cf. note 2.

71. Cf. the definition to which note 6 refers: *"to sacralize* is in some sort to remove from a reality the specificity of its immediate end. . . ."

72. See in this connection: J. Paquier, DTC, IX, 1 (1926), 1177-1178 and 1274-1283 (article on Luther); E. de Moreau S.J., *Histroire de l'Eglise,* Fliche-Martin, t. 16, *Crise religieuse du XVIᵉ siècle,* Paris, 1950, p. 68. J. Pelikan, "L'Esprit et les structures selon Luther", *La Théologie du Renouveau,* Paris-Montréal, 1968, t. I, pp. 357-374.

73. Cf. note 78.

74. The historic movement of this idealist philosophy coincides in great measure with certain developments with German Protestantism.

75. Cf. UR, 15. 1.

76. Cf. Pie Régamey O.P.: "So important are churches in the eyes of the Church that she consecrates them by the most elaborately rich of all her ceremonies in which she treats them like living persons, and that the aniversary of this dedication is annually celebrated by a feast of the first class" (article: "Edifices du culte" in the encyclopedia *Catholicisme,* Paris, 1952, t. III, col. 1341).

77. PC, 11. 1 (Abbott, 473).

78. Paul VI, discourse of 15 October 1967, *Oss. Romano,* 20 October 1967. It will be noted that, neither here nor elsewhere, does the Pope say anything against the celebration of the Eucharistic Sacrifice in private houses—such celebration having been the exclusive form in the first two centuries. Cf. G. Jacquemet: "we have no proof that buildings exclusively for Christian worship existed before the end of the second century" (article: "Edifices du culte" in the encyclopedia *Catholicisme,* Paris, 1952, t. III, col. 1336).

79. Cf. J. de Baciocchi S.M.: "In ruling out consubstantiation, the Church safeguarded two essential truths: the axis of supreme reference of beings is unique, and links God with the world through Christ; the manifestation of the Redeemer is not juxtaposed with that of the Creator, but includes and fulfills it. Natural religion is included in Christianity and culminates in it. . . . In short, to deny Transubstantiation is to relativize or denature, through Christian sacramentalism, the Incarnation itself. Transubstantiation is not a mystery foreign to that of the Incarnation; it expresses the cosmic import of the union which God seals with His creatures in the unique Person of His incarnate Son" (Encyclopedia *Catho-*

licisme, t. IV, 1956, art. "Eucharistie," col. 650-651). Cf. DTC, art. "Eucharistie," t. V, 2ᵉ partie, col. 1346 *seq.* (1913).

80. See, e.g., Pope Paul the Sixth's "The Credo of the People of God" (30th June 1968): pars. 24-26: C.T.S. English translation.

81. Cf. LG, 31.

82. PO, 4 (primum officium); 2. 4; 5. 2 (Eucharistia culmen evangelizationis).

83. By praying for the evangelization of the world, the Trappist or Carthusian monk contributes powerfully towards it and thus fulfills, in his own special way, his mission of evangelist.

84. Cf. F. X. Durrwell C.SS.R., *La Résurrection de Jésus, mystère de salut,* Lyon-Paris, 1961⁶, pp. 356-357: "The apostolic function of Jesus rests on a consecration and on a mission: '. . . him whom the Father consecrated and sent into the world' (Jn. 10, 36). . . . The disciples as agents of Christ brought to the perfection of His apostolate, receive their investiture by a participation in the twofold sanctification of the Son, that of the first incarnation and that of the glorious incarnation: Jn. 17, 17-19. As with Jesus, the santification of the apostles is a setting apart for God (v. 14-16) and a consecration."

85. Jerusalem Bible, note on Jn. 6, 69.

86. We are using, a partly adapted form, certain distinctions well presented by Cardinal C. Journet in his article: "Dieu proche ou distant?" (*Nova et Vetera,* 1962, p. 61, par. 25 *sub fine*).

87. Without excluding a supreme title: that of the beatific vision towards which sanctifying grace tends.

88. Here we are using the terminology of Teilhard de Chardin; cf. Chapter Four.

89. Cf. H. Muehlen, *op. cit.,* par. 7. 12, pp. 206-207.

90. Cf. DS, 3905 (DB, 2334).

91. D. Lys, "L'onction dans le Bible," *Etudes théol. et relig.,* cahier 29 (1954), p. 50.

92. Cardinal Journet, *op. cit.* (note 77), *ibid.*

93. GS, 22. 2, citing Second and Third Councils of Constantinople (Abbott, 220-221).

94. GS, 38. 1: "Verbum Dei . . . perfectus homo in historiam mundi intravit, eam in *Se assumens*." The last word here is the classic term relative to the Incarnation, properly so called.

PART THREE

THE MISSION OF THE
OMNIPOTENT LAMB.

9

THE CHRIST OF TRENT
PRIEST AND VICTIM,
WHO MERITS, ATONES, AND SANCTIFIES

How, by and large, did the Council of Trent regard the Mystery of Jesus? Here, it seems to us, is a theme which has never been the subject of special analysis and which is nevertheless very important, since the Tridentine vision gave a decisive direction to Catholic theology.

Chalcedon had spoken, in a manner at once definitive and still open to completion, about the Person and the two natures of Christ the Savior.[1] Pope Saint Leo the Great had already given to the Church a magisterial pronouncement on the actions of Christ.[2] More than two centuries later, in 681, the Third Ecumenical Council of Constantinople defined, in a generic way,[3] the existence both of a human free will and of humanly free actions in Christ.

Thus, in a confession of faith which answered to the Revelation of her Lord, the Church had successively acknowledged in Him a divine Person, a human soul, a human nature, a human will, and human actions.[4]

211

The way was thus cleared for a dogmatic consideration of the work and of the specific activity of Christ our Lord—viz., the Redemption and the salvation of mankind, the primary and immediate purpose of His Inhumanation for the glory of the Father.

It is true, of course, that the Church had already deepened her knowledge of her invisible Head, Jesus Christ, in the light of His salvific action. In effect, she had specified the ontological structure of Christ only in reference to the basic axiom: "only what is assumed is saved." But she had not as yet pronounced in a very precise dogmatic way on the redemptive work of Christ Jesus.

The Lutheran heresy, by its negation of the indefectible exercise of the Priesthood of Christ in the Eucharistic sacrifice and in the sacrament of penance, caused the Church to move on from dogmatization concerning the divine Person, the two natures and the faculties of the Word Incarnate, to a dogmatic analysis of His work *par excellence*—justification through the sacraments.

In doing this, the Church was returning to her point of departure. After having known her Savior through His salvific acts (from the acts to the Person: *agere sequitur esse*), she understood them more clearly in the light of the more profound understanding she had meantime acquired of the ontological structure of the Incarnate Word: from the Person to the acts.

For a better grasp of these different points, we must briefly recall the essential features of the Lutheran Christology. We shall then indicate what was the original christological contribution of Trent—namely, the proclamation of the Christ-Mediator who saves mankind by His divine-human actions. Finally, we shall point out the horizon opened by Trent and the future task of an eventual Vatican III—viz., the doctrinal explication of the mystery of the Redemption of a co-redemptive Church, the elaboration of a veritable theology of the Lamb.

A. The Background to the Christ of Luther

The whole Christology of Luther[5] is a doctrine of salvation, a soteriology.

For him, the assumption of our human nature by the Son of God is an assumption of our sin, because this nature is viewed as intimately corrupted in its concrete totality. The key to his christological vision is not, therefore, John 1, 14 ("And the Word became flesh and dwelt among us"), but Paul's Galatians 3, 13: "Christ redeemed us from the curse of the law, having become a curse for us. . . ."[6] The salvific purpose of the Incarnation becomes, for Luther, its very reality. Without personally committing sins, Christ, he holds, assumes my sins, takes them on Himself. He is therefore "the sinner *par excellence*."[7]

Does not this imply an action of the human nature of Christ distinct from His divine action? The Swedish Lutheran theologians do not think so. In their view, Luther has professed a "soteriological monoenergism." In Christ, the human nature would not work in unison with the divine nature and would not be the subject, even by communication, of a salvific mystery of atonement.[8] In the drama of the Redemption, God would be the sole actor. The humanity of Christ would be the theater of a drama which would take place, in reality, within God—the theater of a conflict between His justice and His grace, between His anger and His love.

It follows from this that, for Luther, sacrifice and satisfaction are not offered to God by Christ in His human nature, but it is God Himself who in Christ triumphs over the devil and thus makes satisfaction to Himself. Luther even went so far as to equate the humanity of Christ with the works of faith, and the divinity with the faith itself—with the faith which justifies while the works do not justify.[9] There is in Luther a monophysite tendency which he did not recognize, but which many Lutherans have traced in him. Was it not through that tendency that he appears to have retained only the first four Ecumenical Councils, to the at least implicit exclusion of the fifth (Constantinople II: the composite person of Christ)[10] and of the sixth (Constantinople III: the solemn affirmation of the two wills and of the two actions of Christ)? And was not this monophysitism itself postulated by Luther's refusal to recognize the cooperation of human free will with the grace of God, in the justified man?

The case of Luther serves, therefore, to illustrate the truth of the affirmation of Vatican II concerning "the churches and ecclesial communities which were separated from the Apostolic See of Rome . . . in the West": "We are indeed aware that among them views are held considerably different from the doctrine of the Catholic Church even concerning Christ, God's Word made flesh, and the work of redemption. . . ."[11] It is especially these differences that, as a result of historical circumstances, the Council of Trent had in mind when it gave a partial but still valid answer to the problems posed by Luther, an answer given in the context of the medieval tradition and notably in that of Saint Anselm.

B. The Tridentine Christ: The Mediator

At Trent, the Church proclaimed her faith in the past and present action of Christ as man, mediator of our objective and subjective Redemption (to use concepts belonging, however, to a later period).

Among the "divinely revealed truths," one is "primordial"—namely, that "all who have sinned . . . are justified by his grace as a gift, through the redemption which is in Christ Jesus" (Rom. 3, 23-24).[12] Faith in the Redemption "by the second Adam, Jesus Christ out Savior,"[13] is, therefore, what Vatican II was later to call a fundamental truth in the hierarchy of revealed truths.[14]

"Christ Jesus constantly exercises His action on the justified as does the vine on its branches. This action always precedes, accompanies, and follows their good works. Without it, these works could be in no way agreeable to God or meritorious."[15] Whereas, in fact, "our justice is infused in us by God through the merit of Christ."[16]

The "Redeemer"[17]—we note, in passing, that Paul does not use this word—is recognized as "eternal Priest according to the order of Melchisedech," a Priest "whose priesthood is not ended with death" and who has therefore "left to the Church, His Spouse, a visible sacrifice." Under the "visible signs" of this visible sacrifice, and through visible ministers, the Christ-Priest continues visibly to exercise His invisible priesthood. He "offers Hs body and His blood to God His Father under the species of bread and wine. . . . Having celebrated the old Pasch, He instituted the new Pasch, in memory of His passage from this world to the Father when He redeemed us by the shedding of His blood."[18]

It is enough to compare this text with those of "the great christological Councils," as they are called, to notice the difference of accent. The latter is fundamentally Biblical, and the declarations of Trent are in most cases a tissue of Pauline, or to a lesser extent, Johannine quotations. The aspect deliberately stressed is no longer the consubstantiality of the Word with the Father, His divine nature, but the role assumed by His human nature, which was scarcely considered in the Councils of the patristic period. The Christ of Trent is essentially the blood-stained Savior of men, whom He reconciles with the Father. "All our glory is in Christ, in whom we live (cf. Acts, 17, 28), in whom we merit, in whom we make satisfaction, by producing worthy fruits of penance which draw their power from Him, are by Him offered to the Father, and through Him accepted by the Father."[19] Christ, through passing by means of His own blood from this world to the Father, has become our glorious Pasch, has become the One who, risen from the dead, causes us to follow Him from this world to the Father; and our passage is effected by means of the sacraments, of which the Risen Christ is the principal minister.

One Tridentine text in particular sums up perfectly the Christology of the Council, by synthesizing nearly all its principal ideas:

> The glory of Christ is the purpose of justification. . . . Its meritorious cause is the only and well-beloved Son, our Lord Jesus Christ, who, when we were enemies to Him, and through the exceeding charity with which He has loved us, has merited justification for us on the wood of the Cross through His most holy Passion, and has made satisfaction for us to God the Father. . . . In the act itself of justification, through Jesus Christ in whom he is inserted, man simultaneously receives faith, hope, and charity.[20]

Here, then we have an essential aspect of Tridentine and Catholic teaching: the justification of man through the merits and satisfactions of the crucified Christ, paschal Priest of sinful humanity.

The Christ of Nicaea I was, and is, the only and consubstantial Son of the Father; the Christ of Chalcedon, the perfect man, endowed with a rational soul, consubstantial with us men; the Christ of Constantinople II, a composite and synthetic Person, God humanized; the Christ of Constantinople III, the Effector of our salvation through His divine will, and through His divinized human will in perfect submission to this divine will. The Christ of Trent is the New Adam, who, by the meritorious and satisfactory act accomplished during the Passion by His totally divinized human will, justifies our sinful freedoms, having become our Pasch, our Priest, our Mediator, our Redeemer. This justification operates today within the framework of ecclesial and sacramental actions which arouse our meritorious and satisfactory cooperation in our own salvation.[21]

The evolution of the vocabulary is indicative of a change of accent and a new angle of vision. The patristic and oriental Councils were concerned with consubstantial Person, with nature, and with divinization. Their emphasis was on the *being* of Christ. The Council of Trent—predominantly occidental and Latin, although as ecumenical as the ones already mentioned at which the Latins were scarcely represented—preferred, while retaining fully their language, to stress the human *action* of Christ: sacrifice, merit, satisfaction, all indicate the specifically human action of Him who is, however, the consubstantial Word; and should we not add that the idea of transubstantiation, defined by Trent, is the precise point at which the new language joins the old? Is it not in order to communicate His merits and satisfactions that the consubstantial Word transubstantiates the substances of the bread and wine into those of His body and blood?

In short, Trent has passed from *being to doing*, which still presupposes being and which itself has ontological value as orientated to the completion of being. This is indeed true of the meritorious and satisfactory action of the Tridentine Christ. Dying an unmerited death, He can, and alone can, offer to His Father a work richer in love than the sin of mankind was deserving of hatred, and therefore able to make superabundant satisfaction to the loving and offended Justice of the Creator. At the moment when Jesus, yielding up His spirit, uttered in agony His triumphant cry: "It is finished" (Jn. 19, 30), all men were endowed with grace and glorified, at least potentially, by His infinite merits, and the injured glory of the divine Love was restored by His infinite satisfaction. In a very real sense, there will never be among men any merits other than those of Jesus crucified, nor any satisfaction other than that of the Cross; all other merits, all other satisfaction, derive their value from the Blood of Jesus. That is the message of Trent.[22]

To understand more clearly this message which will always remain in force, and to grasp more firmly the idea of the fruitful and redemptive character of Christ's merits, we must remind ourselves, with Saint Thomas

Aquinas, that merit is "as it were the road to beatitude."[23] Elsewhere, he says: "The merit of a virtuous man consists in the fact that, respising passing goods, he adheres to the final good of all."[24] Merit, like satisfaction, effects therefore an action which reverses the pattern of sin—the latter being a disordered turning to a created good, in contempt of the Creator. In the obedient and loving death of Christ, contempt for earthly life (which is, as it were, the matter of merit), suffering (the matter of satisfaction), and love for the final end (a form of satisfaction and of merit) are perfectly realized; consequently, perfect reparation is made for sin, and divine glory is restored. Since it is a divine Person who merits and makes satisfaction, he does so in an infinite manner.

Through these reflections, we come to realize that Trent inaugurated, at the dogmatic level, the consideration of the ascendent action of the humanity of the incarnate Word, polarized by the glory of the Father. It cannot be said that this point had been considered at any depth by the preceding Councils. Trent went on from their generic affirmation of the existence of a human nature in Christ, to a more specific consideration of its action. Or again, if one prefers, Trent has solemnly[25] defined the Pauline doctrine of the Redemption in certain of its essential points, thanks to Augustine[26] and to Anselm.

The Christ of Trent is not merely the Word made flesh; He is the Mediator who, not only by His being but also by His action, reunites mankind with God. More precisely, this action is the acceptance of a suffering. Trent clearly points out that Catholic dogma is, irreversibly, imbrued with the blood of the Lamb immolated on the Cross. The Church thus shows her wisdom in defining dogmatically "the folly of the cross." May we not hope that the mystery of the Redemption will, at some future time, become the subject of a new doctrinal investigation in depth? Is it possible to think that Trent has not said the last word on this subject? Moreover, is it not difficult, in certain cases, to determine exactly what this Council sought to say and to define?[27]

C. The Horizon Opened by Trent: Redemptive Christ, Co-Redemptive Church

It is in its intimate depths that the soteriological interest of Luther has been understood, retained, integrated by Trent, but without any ontological rejection. The old dogmatic language has been retained: was it not indispensable for the correct understanding of the new language of merit and of satisfaction, Trent's direct answer to Lutheran negations?[28]

It must be recognized that, without Luther, without Anselm, without Augustine, there might not perhaps have been any investigation in depth, at the dogmatic level, of the salvific action of Christ; just as, without Nestorius and Cyril of Alexandria, the Church would not perhaps have defined dogmatically His composite Personality.[29]

But Trent has an even deeper significance. In this Council, far from confining herself to reacting against Luther, the Church has gone far beyond him. In former Councils, she had not pronounced dogmatically on the Person and the natures of Christ just for the luxury of academic speculation, but in order to safeguard her faith and her fidelity as spotless Spouse of the Lamb;[30] so too, in Trent, she does not limit herself to the act (supremely efficacious, however) of contemplating the salvific work of her Savior, but contemplates this work in order to be able to cooperate actively with Him in celebrating His sacramental mysteries, and in order to be able to integrate herself more perfectly in this redemptive act. All the dogmatic definitions, all the doctrinal declarations of the Church, and more especially those concerned with the mystery of the Redemption, have, through and beyond their immediate cultic purpose, a mediate end of cooperation in the salvific work of the Redeemer, with which they are mysteriously integrated.

Such, therefore, is the immortal significance of Trent in the dogmatic itinerary of the pilgrim Church: the divine-human Redeemer, still humanly active, arouses in the Church that He redeems a constantly renewed co-redemptive activity.

We also think, and shall investigate the idea in a later chapter, that a clearer and more precise awareness of the mystery of the Christ-Redeemer and of the co-redemptive Church is one of the destinations towards which the historic pilgrimage of this Church is moving, and at which it will arrive through (or without) an eventual Vatican III.

The modern Councils may be summed up by the key words to which they have given prominence: merit and satisfaction (Trent), supernatural (Vatican I), consecration of the world recapitulated by Christ (Vatican II). In our anthropocentric times, long[31] passed from a cosmic to a human horizon, the divinized Church, redeemed by the merits and by the satisfactory sacrifice of her consubstantial and divine-human Spouse, could still define—or at least doctrinally elucidate—her proper and mysterious coredemptive activity, and the co-redemptive mission of all her members and of all men in and through her.

It seems to us that this difficult domain still awaits adequate doctrinal and even dogmatic development— an essential chapter in the elaboration of a theological anthropology washed in the Blood of the Lamb and written with His Blood. Only a consciously co-redemptive Church can fully effect the humanization and the consecration of the world.

But the Biblical foundations of this anthropology and of this ecclesiological investigation in depth have been pretty generously laid down by Vatican II (as we shall see) and, more immediately to our purpose, by Trent.

One of the many merits of Father Mersch's great book is that it gives us a better appreciation of the anthropological riches germinally contained in the work of Trent.

The Redeemer assumes His fullness in a Mystical Body. Is it conceivable that, at the same time, the act of redemption which is His action *par excellence*—the very act by which He causes this Mystical Body to arise from Himself—should itself not take on His fullness in its actions and its satisfactions?

Christ is essentially and intrinsically Redeemer. Does it not follow that this Mystical Body should also be essentially and intrinsically an immense Redemption and an organism which makes satisfaction?—that the Whole Christ should be Redeemer?[32]

Naclantus, a theologian of the Tridentine period, was sensitively expressing the same idea when he wrote: "It is only in us and through us that Christ completes His task of satisfaction."[33]

In offering to His Father the superabundant satisfaction of His suffering love, Christ manifests His twofold quality of Priest and Victim of His own sacrifice.

So, too, by insisting on the *ever present* Sacrifice of the Priest-Christ, Trent opened the way for the liturgical renewal of the twentieth century in its most profound aspect: the intimate oblation[34] of the human and Christian personality through and with the immolated Lamb, in the Spirit, to the Father.

Without this intimate, socially manifested, consciously exercised participation, the Church would not have been co-redemptrix of a world profaned by sin but re-sacralized by the love of Christians—a love whose source and spring is the Eucharist, the Pasch of the Lord.

By its strong affirmation of the sacrifice and of the real presence of Christ in the Eucharist, Trent guaranteed in advance the efficacious authenticity of the consecration of the world, distinct from and complementary to the Eucharistic consecration.

The Church will deploy the fullness of her co-redemptive activity according to the measure in which Christians exercise, in union with Christ Priest and

Victim, the priestly and victimal office of meriting and of making satisfaction.

Trent embodies, therefore, for all time, the image of Christ as Priest and Victim.

It will ever remain true that

> in Jesus, our divine Mediator and Redeemer, the highest, most universal, most complete state is that of victim—in other words, to avoid all error of ambiguity, the state in which Jesus has carried out the work for which He had come on earth, a work of infinite religion directed towards His Father, a work of perfect expiation for sin and of salvation for our souls.[35]

The contemplation of this basic truth will serve to feed inexhaustibly the co-redemptive activity of the Spouse of the Lamb. In the future as in the past, she will continue to think and speak in that harmonious Tridentine association of Biblical vocabulary (redemption, salvation, sacrifice, victory)[36] and of non-biblical vocabulary (merit and satisfaction). She will continue to teach that Jesus has redeemed us at the cost of His blood; has freed us from the slavery of sin, of death, and of the devil; has made expiation for our sins on the Cross; has offered the sacrifice of His life for our salvation, conquered the powers of darkness and of hell, merited our justification, and made satisfaction for us and for our sins. She will continue to say that it is *thus* that He has introduced us into His Kingdom, the Church, has given us eternal life and raised us up to divine life.[36]

Nay more, it is in terms of these same categories that Christians, anxious to nourish in themselves a coherent and faithful love, will think about their own relationship with the world. It is through these categories that they will express this love, since, however difficult they may seem at first sight, they are irreplaceable and unsurpassable. One can never surpass the Cross of Christ or the language of the cross, the "folly" of God which is wiser than the wisdom of men (cf. 1 Cor. 1, 18-25): "For the word of the cross is folly to those who are perishing, but to us who are being saved it is the power of God."

It is not, therefore, by mere chance or without a deep logic of concepts and of images, that the post-Tridentine Church—with a view to symbolizing definitively this Christ who merits and makes satisfaction through love, in order to redeem mankind by His freely chosen sufferings—has adopted the image of His Heart crowned with thorns and surmounted by a cross, such as was shown to her through Saint Margaret Mary Alacoque. The saint herself had explained perfectly the symbolism of this image so familiar to so many Christians and so ill-understood by many of them:

> On the feast of Saint John the Evangelist after I had received from my divine Savior a grace resembling that given to this beloved disciple at the Last Supper, this divine Heart was represented to me as upon a throne totally enveloped in flame and fire, radiating in all directions, more brilliant than the sun, and transparent like crystal. The wound it received on the Cross appeared distinctly. There were a crown of thorns surrounding this Sacred Heart, and a cross above It; and my divine Savior let me know that these instruments of His Passion signified that the immense love He has for men had been the source of all the sufferings and all the humiliations which He had willed to suffer for us; that, from the first moment of His Incarnation, all these torments and despisings had been present to Him, and that it was from this first moment, when the Cross was, so to speak, implanted in His Sacred Heart, that He henceforth accepted, in order to manifest His love for us, all the humiliations, poverty, sufferings which His sacred humanity had to endure throughout the whole course of His mortal life, and the outrages to which that love is exposed until the end of time in the most holy and the most august Sacrament of the Altar.[37]

In re-reading this admirable description, how can one fail to be reminded of the account of the prophetic vocations of Isaiah and Ezechiel? Does not one find there the same symbolism of love and of suffering? And is not the suffering dominated by the love? Does not the representation of the Heart of Jesus thorn-crowned and cross-surmounted provide the perfect image of the meritorious human love and of the satisfactory Eucharistic charity of the New Adam, our Pasch, such as the Council of Trent presented to us? Does not the crystalline transparence of the Heart of the Redeemer indicate the purity of the love He has for men, to His death and beyond His death, for the glory of the Father—a love, therefore, stronger than death and more powerful than sin? And—a further parallel with the Tridentine doctrine, which presents the glory of Christ as the cause of the justification of which He is the author[38]—has not this pure love itself for its mediate object (mediate between men and the Father), since, in showing to the saint His "ever present Heart emitting flames from every part," the Lord said: "If you but knew how consumed I am with the desire to be loved by men, you would spare no pains to fulfill my wish. . . . I thirst, I burn with desire to be loved."[39] The flames thus come to signify, not only the reparatory love of Christ for men, but also this love as causing His ardent desire to be loved by them, this love being their supreme beatitude.

We can unhesitatingly say, therefore, that the immolated Heart of the Lamb sums up perfectly the Christ of Revelation, presented by the Council of Trent as Priest and paschal Victim,[40] whose love merits our love and makes satisfaction for our sin, which is always a betrayal of the love we owe to the love and mercy of His Father.

NOTES TO CHAPTER NINE

1. DS, 301-302 (DB, 148).

2. DS, 294 (DB, 144): "agit enim utraque forma cum alterius communione quod proprium est: Verbo scilicet operante quod Verbi est et carne exsequente quod carnis est."

3. DS, 553-559 (DB, 289-292).

4. Whereas experience moves from the acts to the Person, the dogmatic way of the Church has gone in the opposite direction.

5. We are here drawing on Y. M. J. Congar O.P., for the Christology of Luther, in the collective work *Chalkedon* (Wuerzburg, 1951, t. III, notably pp. 459-467) published by H. Bacht and A. Grillmeier S.J.

6. See L. Sabourin S.J., *Rédemption sacrificielle*, Bruges, 1961, pp. 81-87, for an excellent historical and exegetical analysis of Luther's development in the interpretation of Gal. 3, 13. The author shows how this exegesis, running counter to Tradition, "quickly reaches the limit of blasphemy." According to Luther, in effect, Christ underwent the pains of hell.

7. Sabourin (*op. cit.* pp. 85-86) summarizes as follows "the Lutheran idea of redemption" in his interpretation of Is. 53, 6 here cited: "Christ, as the Servant, bears the sins of men, not however by expiating them, as the traditional explanation would have it, but in the sense that He is charged with them by juridical imputation."

8. Etymologically, atonement means "at-one-ment."

9. Cf. the Luther text cited by Congar, *op. cit.*, III, p. 467. We note, however, that Luther is also speaking about the merits and satisfactions not of Christians, but of Christ, thus logically presupposing a role for His human freedom.

10. DS, 425 (DB, 216). Cf. Saint John Damascene, *De fide orthodoxa* III, 7 (PG, 94, 1000, and 1008-1009); and A. d'Alès, *De Verbo Incarnato*, Paris, 1930, thesis XIV, pp. 183-187.

11. *Unitatis Redintegratio*, 19-20 (Abbott, 361- 362).

12. DS, 1526 (DB, 799).

13. DS, 1724 (DB, 796).

14. ". . . in Catholic teaching there exists an order or 'hierarchy' of truth, since they vary in their relationship to the foundation of the Christian faith" (UR—Abbott, 354). The Latin text has a singular noun: cum *fundamento* fidei christianae"—a possible allusion to 1 Cor. 3, 11.

15. DS, 1546 (DB, 809).

16. DS, 1547 (DB, 809).

17. DS, 1637 (DB, 874) and elsewhere in the work of Trent.

18. DS, 1740-1741 (DB, 938).

19. DS, 1691 (DB, 904).

20. DS, 1529 (DB, 199).

21. DS, 1582 (DB, 842) and the text cited at note 19.

22. Cf. E. Mersch, *Théologie du Corps Mystique*, Paris, 1944, t. I, pp. 354-355; 359 *seq.*

23. Saint Thomas Aquinas, *Commentary on the Sentences*, II, d; 35, q. 1, a. 3, ad 4; cf. A. D. Sertillanges, *Saint Thomas d'Aquin*, Paris, 1922, t. II, p. 313.

24. Saint Thomas Aquinas, *Summa Theologica*, II. II. 104. 3.

25. Prior to Trent, the Pauline doctrine of the Redemption was professed, as divinely revealed, by the ordinary and universal magisterium of the Church, and this is sufficient to warrant our speaking of it as dogma; but it had not been solemnly defined.

26. It can be sustained that, among the Fathers of the Church, Saint Augustine investigated most closely the Pauline doctrine of justification and of grace, and, in this connection, the mystery of the Redemption.

27. Cf. the article by P. Fransen S.J.: "Réflexions sur l'anathème au concile de Trente," *Ephemerides Theologicae Lovanienses*, 29 (1953), 657-672.

28. Cf. DS, 1548; (DB, 809-810); numerous Biblical texts also contain the doctrine of Christ's merit: Jn. 17, 1-6; Heb. 2, 9-10; Lk. 24, 25-27; Rev. 5, 8-10; and very specially Phil. 2, 6-11: ". . . he humbled himself and became obedient unto death, even death on a cross. *Therefore* God has highly exalted him and bestowed on him the name which is above every name, that . . . every tongue should confess that Jesus Christ is Lord, to the glory of God the Father." Notice that "bestowed" is a translation of the Greek *echarisato* ("to forgive, to do a favor"); "therefore" is a translation of the Greek *dio* which indicates causality. The glory of the Risen Christ is therefore presented by Paul as a recompense for the abasement of His Passion, the object of a merit which is, however, rooted in the absolutely free nature of the grace initially received by Christ: *echarisato*. Whereas the first grace of every other man is merited by Christ, that of Jesus has clearly not been merited by anyone. Finally, if Jesus is Lord *to* the glory of God the Father, this is because the work of the redemption has for its immediate purpose the glorification of the human race, for its intermediate purpose the glory of Christ, and for its final purpose the glory of the Father, as we have shown in Chapter One. A convincing Biblical proof of this is perhaps provided by the Pauline text.

29. The term "personalitas" is applied several times by Saint Thomas Aquinas to the divine person of Jesus; notably in the *Contra Gentiles*, IV. 49.

30. Cf. *Lumen Gentium*, 6. 5: "Ecclesia describitur ut sponsa immaculata Agni immaculati" (Rev. 19, 7; 21, 2 and 9; 22, 17).

31. Cf. Metz, J. B., *Christliche Anthropozentrik*, Kosel, Mu-

nich, 1962; the author attributes this passage at the reflective level, not to Saint Augustine, but to Saint Thomas Aquinas.

32. E. Mersch S. J., *Théologie du Corps Mystique*, Paris-Brussels, 1944, t. I, pp. 355-356.

33. Cited by Mersch, *Le Corps Mystique du Christ*, Louvain, 1933, t. II, p. 256 (note).

34. The dialogue of the vernacular Mass is only a secondary, though highly useful, element of the liturgical renewal; its essential element consists in the conscious participation of the faithful, impossible without intimate oblation.

35. Giraud, *De l'union à Notre-Seigneur dans sa vie de victime, Paris*, 1932[5], chap. 1, pp. 2, 5, 11.

36. We are here drawing on the highly illuminating treatment of the mystery of the Redemption in an unpublished course by Father Paul Hitz C.SS.R., professor at the "Academia Alphonsiana" in Rome.

37. Saint Margaret Mary: Gauthey, *op. cit.*, t. II, p. 567.

38. The Council presents Christ as final cause of justification (DS, 1529; DB, 799) and also as its efficient cause (DS, 1524; DB, 796: justificatio impii . . . translatio . . . per secundum Adam Jesum Christum).

39. Saint Margaret Mary: Gauthey, *op. cit.*, t. II, p. 600. It will be noted that the words of Christ reported by Saint Margaret Mary correspond to certain Gospel phrases in which Christ at least implicitly demands to be loved (Mt. 10, 37; Jn. 14, 21 and 23; 15, 9; 16, 27; 21, 15-17). The primacy accorded by Jesus to the duty of loving Him, in relation to the love due to parents (4th commandment), corresponds to the primacy He accords to the love due to God in relation to that due to the neighbor. By comparing Mt. 10, 37 and Mt. 22, 37 *seq.*, one can see how exact is the commentary of Saint John Chrysostom: Jesus was seeking to indicate to the Pharisees that they were to love Him, to love Him as the closest neighbor and even as their God, more than any other neighbor.

40. In this connection, one is reminded of Bossuet: "There is nothing greater in the universe than Jesus Christ, and there is nothing greater in Jesus Christ than His sacrifice" (*Opuscules de Piété:* réflexions sur l'agonie de Jésus-Christ).

10

THE CHRIST OF VATICAN II

PROPHET, PRIEST, AND RECAPITULATOR

Vatican II did not set out explicitly to provide an elaborated and systematic Christology. However, the Council did refer, and in many ways, to the Mystery of Christ. Its intention was to found in Him a theological anthropology and an ethical renewal.[1]

Thus a result was secured which had not been initially envisaged. Because it took up in their broad outlines the conclusions and the definitions of the great Christological Councils, there is a sense in which, despite a lack of any dogmatic definition in this matter, Vatican II is the most complete and most brilliant of all the Christological Councils in the history of the Church.

We do not aim at dealing adequately here with the Christology of Vatican II, for this would require several volumes. Rather do we seek to trace its essential lines: the Christ of Vatican II is *the* Prophet, *the* Priest, and *the* kingly Recapitulator of the humanity redeemed by Him. Prophetic, priestly, and royal Redeemer of the co-redemptive Church, He illuminates the unsoundable though lesser mystery of man, of each and every man, with the light of His greater mystery as the New Adam.

Naturally, we shall not confine ourselves to merely presenting the *bare* outlines of the conciliar Christology; we shall also attempt to clarify them (at least on certain points) in the light of the traditional Christology and of Scripture.

A. Jesus, Prophet and Revealer

The Dogmatic Constitution on the Church, *Lumen Gentium*, points out the triple mission entrusted by the Father to His only Son: "God sent His Son . . . that He might be Teacher, King, and Priest of all, the Head of the new and universal people of the sons of God."[2]

Master (teacher) or Prophet, Priest, King and Head —these words not only describe the mission of Christ, nor are they just decorative titles, but denote the functions exercised on our behalf, the functions which constitute the final cause (*ut* sit Magister, Rex, et Sacerdos omnium) of the In-humanation of the Word as well as of the modes in which His recapitulative function is exercised. We have here a triple basic datum eminently Biblical and patristic.

The Dogmatic Constitution on Divine Revelation, *Dei Verbum*, teaches that Christ, our Master, is at once the Revealer and the fullness of all Revelation, the subject and the object of the salvific unveiling of the hidden God:

> Christ is the Mediator and at the same time the fullness of all revelation. . . .[3] (God) sent His Son, the eternal Word, who enlightens all men, so that He might dwell among men and tell them the innermost secrets about God *(intima Dei)*. Jesus Christ, therefore, the Word made flesh, sent as "a man to men," "speaks the words of God" (Jn. 3:34), and completes the work of salvation which His Father gave Him to do. To see Jesus is to see His Father. For this reason Jesus perfected revelation by fulfilling it through His whole work of making Himself present and manifesting Himself: through His words

and deeds, His signs and wonders, but especially through His death and glorious resurrection from the dead and final sending of the Spirit of truth. Moreover, He confirmed with divine testimony what revelation proclaimed: that God is with us to free us from the darkness of sin and death and to raise us up to life eternal.

The Christian dispensation, therefore, as the new and definitive covenant, will never pass away, and we now await no further new public revelation before the glorious manifestation of our Lord Jesus Christ.[4]

These lines enable us to grasp the sense in which Christ is the Fullness of Revelation: all revealed truths converge upon Him, and in Him they assume their full dimensions. As only and beloved Son of the Father, and as co-breather, with Him, of Their unique breath of Love, the Holy Spirit, He is, with Them, the divinizer of the humanity to whom He sends His Spirit in the name of the Father. Christ is the Fullness of Revelation because it is in Him and through Him that the redemptive Trinity reveals Itself to the men whom It redeems: ". . . the one and undivided Trinity, which in Christ and through Christ is the fountain and the wellspring of all holiness."[5] Christ is the bond and the nucleus of all the revealed truths: Trinity, Redemption, grace, Church, sacraments, final ends. In revealing Himself, Jesus reveals all mysteries. Since "in him all things hold together" (Col. 1, 17), what wonder that He unveils all in giving Himself? He synthesizes in Himself alone all "the secrets of God."[6]

What needs to be strongly emphasized here is that Christ is Prophet and Revealer as man. It is the human intelligence of the Redeemer that sees the Father, that knows all things[7] in seeing the Father, and that experiences the secrets of the Father in concepts and language intelligible by every generation of mankind. Because He sees the Father, Jesus knows what is in man (cf. Jn. 6, 46 and 2, 25); and thus it is that Father Congar can write as follows:

This supernatural wisdom also enabled Him to know man with all the completeness needed to secure that the humble ideas He put forward and the very simple language in which He expressed them would be man's sufficient and truly inexhaustible nourishment, not only to the end of the world, through centuries of new experiences and fresh discoveries, but also at the profoundest level. . . . Jesus knows the import and the infinite value of His words and of His actions as man.[8]

This, then, is the traditional doctrine of the Catholic Church. In order to be, even during His public life, the infallible Revealer of the Father's secrets, the pre-paschal Christ possessed not only an experiential knowledge of the world, but also a prophetic and infused[9] knowledge of certain distant and future[10] events, and above all the vision in the countenance of His Father of all the secrets of the human heart and of the divine Will throughout all history. Without this face-to-face vision, Christ *as man* could not have loved me and given Himself for me (Gal. 2, 20). His function as Revealer forms an integral part of His mission as Savior: the paschal Christ could not expiate in His human heart sins of which His human mind could have no knowledge, nor could the pre-paschal Christ reveal and express in human terms the design of salvation without a human knowledge absolutely immune from all errors.

It is the Man Jesus who, even before His Resurrection, is the infallible Revealer. An absolute immunity from all error was demanded for the exercise of His mission of absolutely truthful Master. Such absolute immunity, even in statements not immediately connected with His religious mission, required that the soul of Christ should possess the beatific vision as supreme source of infallibility and immutability in the perception of truth. In affirming the pre-paschal infallibility of the Man Jesus, the Catholic Church is simply asserting that He never made an erroneous judgment. It can indeed be admitted that on several points the Man Jesus made no human judgment and spoke as did His contemporaries: for example, Jesus as man had no need to formulate a judgment on the Mosaic authenticity of the Pentateuch![12]

The Man Jesus saw the Father and knew humanly and infallibly what is in man, in all the men whom He had come to save, precisely because, from the first moment of His earthly existence, this Man was not just an ordinary man, but the Word made Man in order to reveal the Father in Himself. In other words, to use the technical language of the theologians, Jesus was really a man, but not merely a man. The authenticity of His humanity is not at all incompatible with his having received, for the exercise of His mission as Revealer, knowledge which the rest of men do not receive because they have no need of it. The prophets of the Old Testament, purely human people, did not need this universal infallibility necessary to Christ for the exercise of His mission of unique Prophet. The same can be said about the prophets and doctors of the New Testament, including the Pope: their infallibility is limited to certain precise cases, and is not constantly active as is that of Jesus, the Divine Person who can never deceive or be deceived.

The exegetes[13] link the prophetic mission of Jesus with His receiving the anointing of the Spirit, at the time of His baptism in the river Jordan. Saint Luke, in his Gospel and in the Acts of the Apostles, presents Jesus as a Prophet "anointed . . . with the Holy Spirit and with power" (Acts 10, 38); as the new Elias sent by the Spirit (Lk. 4, 18) "to preach good news to the poor"; finally, as He who has "received from the Father the promise of the Holy Spirit, which he has pointed out . . ." (Acts 2, 33). It is thus that the God-Prophet Jesus, by accepting to be baptized in His own blood, has merited from the Father the power to pour out on mankind the unction of the Spirit who continues to speak through the prophet-members, through the Christians anointed at confirmation "with the Holy Spirit and with power."

As Father Benoit[14] so well puts the matter, Jesus saw Himself as a Prophet-Revealer who "takes away the sins of the world by bringing to men the light of the knowledge which enables them through His grace to avoid sin: the mission of salvation through the truth." And besides being acknowledged as such, the pre-paschal Jesus Himself claims to be a Prophet: "I must go on my way . . . for, it cannot be that a prophet should perish away from Jerusalem."[15] His prophetic mission was, inseparably, a mission of death for the truth. One appreciates, therefore, why Vatican II has highlighted this title and this mission of Christ by describing Him as "great Prophet."[16]

B. Jesus Priest and Supreme Pontiff

Vatican II, orientated from the outset towards liturgical reform and polarized by a pastoral purpose, had inevitably to consider Christ as Prophet.

As is evident from numerous citations, the doctrine of Vatican II on the priesthood of Christ takes up that of the Epistle to the Hebrews. Indeed, it must be admitted that the Council cites these texts rather than commenting on them. Our best course here, therefore, is to review some basic data of Hebrews on the Priesthood of Christ, with footnote emphasis on the texts cited by the Council.

Drawing on this Epistle, Saint Thomas Aquinas magnificently writes:

> The function of the priest is to be the mediator between God and the people. In effect, he brings sacred things to the people; he is therefore called *sacerdos* in as much as he gives these sacred things. On the other hand, he offers to God the prayers of the people and makes satisfaction in some manner for their sins. Thus the Apostle says: "For every high priest chosen from among men is appointed to act on behalf

of men in relation to God, to offer gifts and sacrifices for sins" (Heb. 5, 1).[17]

In order to offer the priestly sacrifice of our Redemption, the eternal Word of the Father became mortal man and, at the same time, Priest—"a merciful and faithful high priest in the service of God, to make expiation for the sins of the people" (Heb. 2, 17).[17] The humanity of Jesus is therefore sacerdotal in essence and not *per accidens*, as ours can be. Consequently, all the actions of Christ are (mediately or immediately) sacerdotal. They are the actions of Him who is indefectibly Priest in everything He does, and everything is directed to the supreme act of His priesthood, the oblation of His death on the cross: ". . . he has appeared once for all at the end of the age to put away sin by the sacrifice of himself. . . . So Christ (has) been offered once to bear the sins of many . . ." (Heb. 9, 26-28).[18]

Christ is truly the merciful and faithful Priest who mediatizes the relations between God and men: a high priest, holy, blameless, unstained,"[19] perfectly faithful to all the wishes of His Father, having "although he was a Son . . . learned obedience through what he suffered" (Heb. 5, 8).[20] In this very obedience and through it, Christ has merited to become "the source of eternal salvation to all who obey him" (Heb. 5, 9), thus manifesting His mercy towards them. It is this very fidelity towards the Father which makes Him merciful towards men, just as it is also His mercy towards rebellious man which demands of Him faithful obedience to the Father. How could He manifest His compassion towards the people if He did not will to make expiation for their sins" (Heb. 2, 17)?

Now, this "one sacrifice of the New Testament, namely the sacrifice of Christ offering Himself once and for all to His Father as a spotless victim," is "represented and applied in the Sacrifice of the Mass."[21] It is through the Mass and in the Mass that Christ today manifests, in a visible and constant manner, that He continues to exercise His priesthood in its supreme act—*sacrifice*. The Christ of Vatican II is the Priest in actual sacrificial action, who makes continually present, within His Church and among mankind, His Calvary oblation made in their name. It must be clearly stated that the Christ whom the Church continually makes present to the world is first and foremost the Priest and the Victim of the world's salvation, who by His Eucharist enables men to fulfill the new commandment of fraternal love even to self-sacrifice, and thus to transform the social structures of the world.

Any hesitation about accepting this as the doctrine of Vatican II must surely be removed by the following crystal-clear passages:

> Every liturgical celebration, because it is an action of Christ the priest and of His Body the Church, is a sacred action surpassing all others. No other action of the Church can match its claim to efficacy, nor equal the degree of it. . . . The liturgy is the fountain from which all her power flows. . . . The renewal in the Eucharist of the covenant between the Lord and man draws the faithful into the compelling love of Christ and sets them afire. . . . For, the most blessed Eucharist contains the Church's entire spiritual wealth, that is, Christ Himself, our Passover and living bread. Through His very flesh, made vital and vitalizing by the Holy Spirit, He offers life to men. They are thereby invited and led to offer themselves, their labors, and all created things together with Him."[22]

In the Eucharist and through the Eucharist, our High Priest, Christ, who is personally the Covenant of mankind with the Father (cf. Is. 42, 6), renews the ever new and ever eternal alliance which He has established with mankind in His own blood by giving anew to mankind His Spirit.[23] From the Eucharistic Heart of Jesus, there wells up, with His purifying blood, the charity which renews the face of the earth. We shall take up this point in a later chapter. What we wish to stress at the moment is the resumption in another form of the Tridentine doctrine of the "ex opere operato" efficacy of the Eucharist as of the other sacraments: "From the liturgy, therefore, and especially from the Eucharist, as from a fountain, grace is channelled into us; and the sanctification of men in Christ and the glorification of God, towards which all other activities of the Church are directed as toward their goal, are most powerfully achieved."[24] The *virtus* and *efficacia* ascribed to the Christ-Priest acting in the Liturgy and especially in the Eucharist, conveys, though incompletely, the Tridentine idea of "opus operatuf," of an action effected by Christ Himself, as distinct from "opus operantis" or cooperation of the person who consciously and voluntarily receives the sacraments.

The Priest-Christ of Vatican II is not, therefore, a purely and solely passive victim; through the Liturgy, in which Christ "continually exercises His priestly function,"[25] He effects here and now the work of salvation. There is no question of "a bare commemoration of the past,"[26] but of an actual activity.

In this sacramental action, Christ also exercises His priesthood through the word. The Christ of Vatican II is not a silent God who makes no answer to men, but a Preacher, a proclaimer of the good news of His sacrifice, the Word who enters into dialogue with men. He takes the initiative of speaking to them through His messengers specially consecrated for this end,[27] and answers their ever renewed questions: "For, in the liturgy God speaks to His people and Christ is still proclaiming His gospel."[28]

As we have explained elsewhere,[29] it is in a threefold sense that the Word of God still speaks to His people in the Liturgy. He proclaims His word through the priest's reading aloud of the Biblical texts; the homily made by the priest is, as it were, a "second word" commenting on this "first word"; finally, Christ "realizes His word" by the celebration of the sacramental sacrifice of which the purely human minister is His instrument, and of which the words constitute the principal and "formal" part. It is therefore in different ways that Christ, "Priest of the Gospel of God" (cf. Rom. 15, 16),[30] speaks to the Church in the Liturgy.

At the same time as He speaks on earth through His ministers, Christ Jesus "is sitting at the right hand of God, a minister of the sanctuary and of the true tabernacle." The earthly Liturgy constitutes a "vanguard" by which He makes us "participate in the heavenly Liturgy" (cf. Heb. 8, 2).[31] Christ is the "high priest of the good things to come" (Heb. 9, 11). Every earthly cult, even that of the New Testament, is "a copy and shadow of the heavenly" cult (cf. Heb. 8, 5). Christ has "entered once for all into the Holy Place" (cf. Heb. 8, 12)—admirable image of the Being of God, of the spiritual communion of the creatures with the Creator.

The priesthood of Christ is not, therefore, solely a present relationship to the past, to the Cross, to "the oblation made once for all"; it is heavenly, permanent, eternal. Christ will exercise it to the consummation of the world. As a precursor, as a courier, He has passed beyond the veil into the Holy Place (Heb. 6, 20); He is the precursor of mankind in the Holy Place, and men must follow in His footsteps along the road of their eternal destiny. There He exerts the active presence of a worker; there He exercises a Liturgy, an active ministry of the cult, in a permanent way.

This activity of the eternal and celestial Priest-Christ is presented to us as the *raison d'être* of His Resurrection and of His Ascension: "For Christ has entered, not into a sanctuary made with hands, a copy of the true one, but into heaven itself, now to appear in the presence of God on our behalf" (Heb. 9, 24). "He is able to save those who draw near to God through him" only because He makes "intercession for them," and it is precisely for this that "he always lives" (cf.

Heb. 7, 25).[32] Jesus has therefore risen in order to intercede for our salvation, linked with this unceasing heavenly mediation. And the Ascension is the enthronement of the eternal Priest in His new celestial functions, the inauguration of the new liturgy; that is to say, the commencement of the celebration by the Church (and not by Christ alone, as at the Last Supper) of this ever new liturgy, the Mass, "heaven on earth."[33] Thus are consummated at once the priesthood and the sacrifice of Christ, since those for whom it was offered attain and receive its purpose: in other words, they truly draw near to God through grace.[34]

Jesus, the Priest of the heavenly Sanctuary, is not therefore outside the world which He transcends, but, in His glory as the Risen One, He is still towards the world, in the world, and for the world. The Ascension of Jesus is not a leaving of the world, but a taking possession, a mysterious cosmic penetration: the eternal Word made human Priest has "descended into the lower parts of the earth . . . that he might fill all things" (Eph. 4, 9-10). This brings us, therefore, to Christ the Recapitulator, to the royal and cosmic Christ, of whom Vatican II has so eloquently spoken.

C. Jesus: King, Lord, and Recapitulator

The Kingship of Christ which Vatican II offers for our contemplation and as the means of making Him known to men, is the Kingship of the Recapitulation in whom the Father wills to aggregate, unite, and reconcile all things in order that Christ may offer this totality to Him in a homage of filial adoration.

It is in this sense that the Council cites, five times each, two Pauline texts around which is organized its doctrine of the recapitulative Kingship of the Christ-Redeemer: Eph. 1, 10 and 1 Cor. 15, 24-28. This point calls for development.

Not only has the Word of God entered the world's history as a perfect man, taking that history up in Himself and summarizing it,"[35] but also "so that

as perfect man He might . . . sum up all things in Himself"[36]—a purpose twice affirmed.[37] It is in the
light of Christ the Recapitulator that Vatican II sees
the perfect unity of the divine plan, the relative autonomy of the temporal order coordinated with the spiritual order within this one design, or recapitulative design itself finalized by the highlighting of the absolute and universal primacy of the Christ-Redeemer:

> The spiritual and temporal realms, although
> distinct, are so connected in the one plan of
> God, that He Himself intends in Christ to ap-
> propriate the whole universe into a new creation,
> initially here on earth, fully on the last day. . . .
> It has pleased God to unite all things, both
> natural and supernatural, in Christ Jesus "that
> in all things he may have the first place" (Col.
> 1, 18). This destination, however, not only does
> not deprive the temporal order of its indepen-
> dence, its proper goals, laws, resources, and sig-
> nificance for human welfare, but rather per-
> fects the temporal order in its own intrinsic
> strength and excellence and raises it to the level
> of man's total vocation upon earth.[38]

The order of the purposes is therefore clearly marked:
the purpose of the In-humanation of the Word is the
salvific recapitulation of the human universe,[39] and
this is the glorious manifestation of the primacy of
Christ. Does this, however, complete the chain of interrelated purposes? It does not; for Vatican II does
not forget that God the Father, who is the source of
the ascendent movement of the recapitulation, is also
its goal. This emerges clearly when two Pauline texts
are brought together:

> Blessed be the God and Father of our Lord
> Jesus Christ, who . . . has made known to us in
> all wisdom and insight the mystery of his will,
> according to his purpose which he set forth in
> Christ as a plan for the fullness of time, to unite
> all things in him, things in heaven and things on
> earth. . . . Then comes the end, when he delivers

the kingdom to God the Father after destroying
every rule and every authority and power. For,
he must reign until he has put all his enemies
under his feet. The last enemy to be destroyed
is death. "For God has put all things in subjection under his feet." But when it says, "All
things are put in subjection under him," it is
plain that he is excepted who has put all things
under him. When all things are subjected to
him, then the Son himself will also be made subject to him who put all things under him, that
God may be everything to every one (Eph. 1,
3-10; 1 Cor. 15, 24-28).

It is therefore the Father who has willed to unite all
things in his incarnate Son by subjecting all things
to Him. The Father has done so in order that this
Son—become Head and Recapitulator of the universe,
which is the extension and the priestly vestment of
His Body—should finally subject all things to Him
by subjecting Himself to Him. The Kingship of the
Son is a gift from the Father, its purpose being to be
a priestly and cosmic oblation to the Father who is its
origin. Thus is emerges that, besides the recapitulative
kingship of the one and only Son, the monarchy of the
entire Trinity (to use the expression of Pope Saint
Denis) is itself recapitulated in the Person-Summit
of the Father.[40] Christ is a King-Recapitulator within
a trinitarian monarchy of which the Father, in His
turn, is the Recapitulator and the Summit.

Christ must reign over His enemies, must perfectly
vanquish death by raising up all men from death, in
order that He may finally hand back the kingdom to
the Father. This perfect victory over universal death
will be, at the same time, a destruction of all princi-
pality, domination, and power; in other words, the
total reduction to powerlessness, by the universal resurrection, of "him who has the power of death, that
is, the devil," already in a sense reduced to impotence by the death of Christ (cf. Heb. 2, 14-15) who
has delivered "all those who through fear of death

were subject to lifelong bondage"—a fear now devoid of its terror. And since this perfect victory over universal death is a gift of the Father who subjects all things to Him, one understands how it is that the Son subjects Himself to the Father and restores the kingdom to Him; in other words, one understands how it is that, over and above all temporal distinction of before and after, He recognizes that His sacred humanity, like His divine Person of the Word, must be wholly directed towards the Father, the eternal Principle of the trinitarian monarchy. "Without me you can do nothing," Jesus said to His disciples; but He also said: "Truly, truly, I say to you, the Son can do nothing of his own accord, but only what he sees the Father doing" (Jn. 15, 9; 5, 19).

Once again, therefore, we see how the doctrine of Vatican II offers us the same hierarchized purposes of the Incarnation which we have already been given by Saint Lawrence of Brindisi and the Council of Trent.[41] The salvation of the world (including the physical universe from which man is inseparable) for the glory of Christ and to the glory of the Father, the twofold Recapitulation of the universe in Christ and of the Trinity in Itself. This latter aspect has not, it is true, been explicitly dealt with by Vatican II, but it does emerge in the Biblical texts cited by the Council, and in the prior doctrine of the magisterium as presented by Pope Saint Denis; besides, it is clearly implied in a very beautiful conciliar declaration about the Person of the Father—a declaration which, it will be noted, explicitly cites 1 Cor. 15, 28:

> The decree of God the Father flows from that "fountain of love" or charity within God the Father. From Him, who is "the origin without origin," the Son is begotten and the Holy Spirit proceeds through the Son. Freely creating us out of His surpassing and merciful kindness, and graciously calling us moreover to communicate in life and glory with Himself, He has generously poured out His divine goodness and

does not cease to do so. Thus He who made
all things may at last be "all in all" (1 Cor. 15
28), procuring at one and the same time His own
glory and our happiness.[42]

The line of thought in this passage is clear. Everything, whether within or outside the Trinity, flows, in
the final analysis, from the love of the Father as from
its wellspring and source: the Word and the Spirit,
on the one hand, the universe, on the other; and the
Father creates in order to be, through the mediation
of the Son, the Recapitulator "all in all," He who aggregates in Himself all that has been recapitulated in
His Beloved Son.

It is thus that Vatican II presents the doctrine of
the kingly recapitulation of Christ to the glory of the
Father: by His kingship, Jesus Christ is indeed Lord,
but "to the glory of God the Father" (Ph. 2, 11).
Does this idea come only from Saint Paul and Hebrews?
Not so, it seems, because on two occasions[43] the
Council, dealing with the idea of recapitulation, gives
footnotes with references taken from Saint Irenaeus,
the theologian who might well be called the doctor of
the recapitulation.

One cannot, therefore, adequately grasp the concept
of recapitulation, such as the post-Vatican II Church
understands it, without establishing the general outlines of this saint's ideas about it. By a better grasp
of the concept as put forward by Irenaeus, which in
this instance the Church "has made her own,"[44] we
can reach a greater understanding of the mind of the
Church on this subject.

In classical Greek, the noun *anakephalaiôsis* (akin to
képhalé, the head) derives from the verb *anakepha-
laioo*: to comprehend in a summary, to gather together
essential ideas.

Clearly, Eph. 1, 10: "to unite all things in him"
is intimately connected with Eph. 1, 22: "and he has
put all things under his feet and has made him the
head over all things for the church." Recapitulation,

therefore, will designate the orientation of all things towards Christ, in order that they may find their unity in Him.

With Irenaeus, the word is used in this double context, while acquiring its own particular shades of meaning.

Christ sums up what previously existed. "But he was incarnate and made man; and then he summed up (consummated) in himself the long line of the human race, procuring for us a comprehensive salvation, that we might recover in Christ Jesus what in Adam we had lost, namely, the state of being in the image and likeness of God."[45] The incarnate Word sums up the race of Adam, being Himself the second Adam; He aggregates in Himself the totality (pleroma) of its aspects. The sacrifice of Christ appears as taking up and leading to its completion the sacrifice of all those who have preceded Him. In Himself, Christ completes human nature in its concrete and historical reality, He substantially effects, in his person-epitome the salvation of the long series of 72 generations (in 72 nations) stretching from Adam to Himself.

The humanity which Christ aggregates had fallen under the sway of the devil. The recapitulation is a restoration, a re-commencement, a re-creation of the unique creature. The Incarnation is Redemption. The recapitulation implies a special relationship by contrast between the second Adam and the first, saved by Him. Thus, though initially conquered by the devil, the creation of God triumphs.[46]

Thus, with Irenaeus, the recapitulation has a significance at once christological and anthropological (which one finds again in the documents of Vatican II.)[47] It is essentially the completion, the realization within time, of the eternal plan of God, which unfolds itself "infallibly through the vicissitudes of sin and of death, by means of a divine pedagogy, leading mankind in due course to the term of its growth, and causing the instability and weakness of childhood to give place to the consistent strength of the perfect man."[48]

The recapitulation of humanity by Christ even appears, with Irenaeus, as the process in whose course man is created.[49]

The use of the term "recapitulation" by Irenaeus represents, therefore, an attempt to express in a single word the whole Biblical message concerning Christ and His work.[50]

We give two texts of Saint Irenaeus which illustrate this point and which show clearly the two poles, cosmic and trinitarian, of his concept of recapitulation:

> Above all, there is the Father, and He is the Head of Christ;[51] through all, there is the Word, and He is Head of the Church; in all, there is the Spirit, and He is the fountain of living waters.[52] The Lord "consummated all things in himself" by joining man to Spirit and placing Spirit in man. He himself became the source of Spirit, and He gives Spirit to be the source of man's life. For, it is through Spirit that we see and hear and talk.[53]

Christ is therefore the Head of the Church through and in His Spirit, who is the Soul of this Church. It is through this Spirit that He aggregates and incorporates the Church with Himself, in order to offer the Church, in a homage of filial adoration, to His own Head and Recapitulator, the Father, through and in the Spirit who is their Bond.[55]

It is important to note that it is precisely at the point where Vatican II uses the texts of Irenaeus that the Council is stressing the specifically human character of the recapitulative work of Christ. It is not so much as the Word, but rather as *man*, that the Word-made-flesh recapitulates the anthropocentric universe: "The Word of God, before becoming man in order to redeem and to recapitulate all in Himself, was already in the world as the true light that enlightens every man."[56]

In effect, it is through His human body that the incarnate Word is physically linked with the whole universe and with its long history which He assumes. It is by speaking the language of men that the Word of God, made human word, recapitulates the human psyche and the long cultural evolution of mankind. Thanks to the In-humanation of the Word, this cultural evolution, in all its elements of truth and through all its ethical values, finally takes on the revelatory external appearance of its intimate reality as preparation for the Gospel.[57] The progress of mankind pre-figures and prepares the Gospel of God.

As man, Christ is this recapitulation, above all by the hypostatic assuming of a human affectivity and a human heart, in order that God may love men in a human way.

We must recognize here a new and admirable recapitulative nucleus in the work of Christ, a nucleus which the Council, following Saint Paul, does not explicitly state, but does imply: it is preeminently by the proclaiming and practice of the new commandment of fraternal love, received from the Father, that the only Son become Son of Man has consummated His mission as human and cosmic Recapitulator. This is what we must now explain.

Paul, as cited by the Council,[58] develops the idea that all the commandments in the second table of the Law are epitomized in the command: "You shall love your neighbor as yourself."[59] Here is the Pauline text:

> . . . for he who loves his neighbor has fulfilled the law. The commandments, "You shall not commit adultery, You shall not kill, You shall not steal, You shall not covet," and any other commandment, are summed up in this sentence, "You shall love your neighbor as yourself". . . . Therefore love is the fulfilling of the law (Rom. 13, 8-10).

What Saint Paul means is clear: a man can succeed in abstaining habitually from acting against his neighbor and resist the evil impulses and designs which come "out of the heart of man" (cf. Mk. 7, 20-23), only if he adopts as ethical horizon[60]) the love of the neighbor in which are positively epitomized the "you shall not" commandments of God. The Council comments on this Pauline text as follows:

> God, who has fatherly concern for everyone, has willed that all men should constitute one family and treat one another in a spirit of brotherhood. For having been created in the image of God . . . all men are called to one and the same goal, namely, God Himself. For this reason, love for God and the neighbor is the first and greatest commandment. Sacred Scripture, however, teaches us that the love of God cannot be separated from the love of the neighbor: "If there is any other commandment, it is summed up in this saying, Thou shalt love thy neighbor as thyself."[61]

In other words, the final end—viz. the uncreated Love loved above all things—held in common by all the predestined united in unanimity, helps us to grasp that the love of God, and the love of the neighbor which flows necessarily from that love, constitutes in a sense one single commandment—the first and the greatest in relation to all the others.

A single commandment? Does the Council, then, place on the same footing the love due to sinful man and the love due to the Man-God? Yes and no. *Yes*, at the level of the "formal object," of the motive for which we love God and men with a supernatural love, a motive which is none other than the divine claim to love. *No*, at the level of the "material object," of the being who is loved. In the Constitution on the Church, which is dogmatic as well as pastoral, Vatican II specifies, in a manner which leaves no room for confusion between Creator and human creature, the profound reason why love epitomized all the commandments:

> The first and most necessary gift of God is that charity by which we love God above all

things and our neighbor because of God. . . .
For charity, as the bond of perfection and the
fulfillment of the law, rules over all the means
of attaining holiness, gives life to them, and
makes them work. . . . The law of the people of
God is the new commandment to love as Christ
loved us. . . . Since Jesus, the Son of God, manifested His charity by laying down His life for
us, no one has greater love than he who lays
down his life for Christ and his brothers.[62]

The charity which epitomizes, which recapitulates
in itself the commandments, is not just any love, but
the new love manifested to the world in the blood-
sacrifice of Calvary. Since Christ, in giving His life
for His sheep and for the life of the world, obeyed the
order received from His Father, kept His Father's commandments and remained in His love (cf. Jn. 10, 15-19;
6, 51; 15, 10), He can, in giving the new commandment
of sacrificial love, propose Himself as model: "If you
keep my commandments, you will abide in my love,
just as I have kept my Father's commandments and
abide in his love" (Jn. 15, 10). The new commandment of sacrificial love is rooted, therefore, in the
Revelation of the redemptive love of the Father and
of the Son, and it is in the loving oblation of His only
Son that the Father recapitulates all that is in heaven
and all that is on earth (cf. Jn. 13, 34; 3, 16; 15, 13;
Eph. 1, 10).

It is by no means ruled out that—through the practice of the sacrificial love demanded by the new commandment of love which is the fundamental law of
human perfection and therefore of the transformation
of the world[63]—many seeming atheists are mysteriously associated with the Paschal mystery and are thus
recapitulated in the sacrifice of the Son of Man. It
is above all in pouring forth, by His Spirit, sacrificial
love into the hearts of man, that Christ recapitulates
heaven and earth (cf. Rm. 5, 15 and Eph. 1, 10).

In other words, for Paul, for Irenaeus, for Vatican
II, the recapitulation is indeed the work of the Incar-

nation, but above all of the Incarnation as redemptive and divinizing, and not purely and simply of the Incarnation as the assumption of a human mind and body by the Word of God. In His plan, such an assumption without death on the cross, without the assumption of our human death, would not have been recapitulative.

Just as the Resurrection is an integral part of the mystery of the Redemption, so too does the risen and glorious Christ continue, notably through the Eucharis, His recapitulative work, term of which is eschatological. We shall return later to a consideration of the Eucharist as sacrament of the universal eschatological recapitulation, according to the mind of Vatican II. Suffice it here to say that, at the Cross and during the lifetime of the Church, the recapitulative work of Christ, King and Lord, remains uncompleted and in full development towards its consummation.

D. Jesus, Son of Man, Revelatory and Recapitulative Light of Man and of All Men

To fulfill perfectly His mission of Redeemer, that is to say, His mission as Head of all the co-redeemers, Jesus unveils man to himself in his indissolubly personal and social being.

Since this is also a theme we must take up later, a few words will suffice here to show how it synthesizes the teachings of Vatican II on Christ as Prophet, Priest, and lordly Recapitulator.

Christ reveals each human person to that person. In a way itself mysterious, He manifests to each the mystery of His supernatural elevation, which makes each and every man an unfathomable and ineffable mystery.

By the unaided resources of his human reason alone, man would be unable to perceive that he is himself a mystery. But, in fact, this reason has not been abandoned by the Light who creates and illuminates it; it is under the action of the Revealer that man can, if he so wills, discover himself as a mystery. He must, of course, have at least an obscure knowledge of his mysterious character if he is to be judged by God on his acceptance or refusal of his mysterious divinization.

This acceptance or this refusal occurs within a *social* context, within a *social* history: to all men of all the ages of history, the ancient and new[65] commandment of sacrificial love has been obscurely but really intimated by the Word who has eternally willed to sacrifice Himself for all those within time, and through this love to associate them with His Pasch.

In this connection, Vatican II has certainly opened up wide horizons:

> The truth is that only in the light of the incarnate Word does the mystery of man take on light. . . . Christ, the final Adam, by the revelation of the mystery of the Father and His love, fully reveals man to man himself and makes his supreme calling clear. It is not surprising, then, that in Him all the aforementioned truths find their root and attain their crown. . . . The Holy Spirit, in a manner known only to God, offers to every man the possibility of being associated with this paschal mystery.[66]

The individual man is not adequately intelligible apart from the mystery of the cross of Jesus. Christ manifests fully to mankind that any individual man is and remains eternally for himself an incomprehensible mystery, because of his participation in the nature of God which remains eternally incomprehensible by the created mind, even within the beatific vision.[67] To understand himself, he would need to be able to understand fully the intelligibility of God in whose nature he participates, and be able fully to enfold the divine Love who eternally enfolds him through His Son and through His Spirit. It is within the beatifying vision and beatifying love that perfectly divinized man will at last fully grasp the mystery of his own incomprehensibility, and that he will be fully manifested to himself by the Word. Only then, all veils having been removed, will the intellectual creature discover, in its fullness, the sublimity of his vocation, of his call to divinization, of his supernatural elevation, because only then will the Word reveal perfectly in Himself the mystery[68] of the Father and of His love: "For God so loved the world that he gave his only Son . . ." (Jn. 3, 16).

In giving His only Son in the paschal mystery, God wills to associate each and every person with this mystery, in order to reveal fully that the human person was eternally known and spoken in this only Word, loved in their only Spirit, intimately present in the mysteries of the immanent processions of the Godhead.[69] Only the Father knows how the Spirit gives to each and every person the offer to integrate himself in the sacrifice of the Lamb. When the night of history has passed away, the Lamb, temple and lamp of the New Jerusalem, will spread the perfection of His light upon "those who are written in the Lamb's book of life," and His servants will at last see perfectly their face in His, their own face mirrored in and by "the river of the water of life, bright as crystal, flowing from the throne of God and of the Lamb." (Rev. 21, 23 and 27; 22, 1 and 3-5).

The Lamb-Recapitulator is not only the Revealer who discovers the human intelligence to itself by drawing aside the veil which was concealing from it its trinitarian polarization; He is also the Victim and the Savior of human freedom, which He associates (while at the same time respecting it) with His own sacrifice. In His Pasch, in His passage effected once only and for all men, He gathers together and recapitulates all the divinized actions of every created will; and He consummates in unity all those who willingly accept His divinizing offer. The loving holocaust of the death of the Lamb recapitulates all the dead[70] who have willingly passed from the darkness of sin to His immortal light: the Lamb has become "the bright morning star" of an eternal morning (cf. Rev. 2, 28 and 22, 16).

In giving Himself, the Lamb will also give to "those who are written in the Lamb's book of Life," a new heaven and a new earth. He will thus recapitulate all the freely given merits, which they have acquired by the building up of the first earth, "the form" of which has passed away forever (Rev. 22, 1 and 5; 1 Cor. 7, 31) because it was disfigured by their sin.[72] As the eternal Recapitulation of man's cosmic conquest, the Lamb will give to the conqueror "a white stone, with a new name written on the stone which no one knows except him who receives it" (Rev. 2, 17). In giving him this name, the Lamb as He Himself declares "will write on him the name of my God, and the name of the city of my God, the New Jerusalem which comes down from my God out of heaven, and my own new name"—the new name (which He alone is to know, i.e. to penetrate fully) of Word of God. The new name of conqueror, written indelibly by the Lamb on the forehead of His witness, will participate in the character of the name of the Lamb and of the name of His Father—a character beyond the reach of human intelligence (Rev. 2, 17; 3, 12; 3, 5; 14, 1; 19, 12-13). And the Lamb will never "blot his name out of the book of life" (Rev. 3, 5).

In other words, the predestined witness of the Lamb will participate—and already participates—in the mystery and in the eternal incomprehensibility of the Lamb and of His Father, as well in Their sovereign Kingship.

Of his own powers, man was incapable of naming himself by his new and true name; he was incapable of naming the woman. However, in obedience to the divine command, he gave to her the name Eve, and he gave their name to "all the beasts, and all the fowls of the air, and all the cattle of the field"; and he therefore ruled over the creation (Gen. 1, 26; 2, 19-23).

If to this cosmic mastery, he adds "enduring patience and bearing up" for the Lamb's name's sake (Rev. 2, 3), he will see the Lamb Himself writing a new name on his forehead. If the witnesses of the Lamb consent to be pierced with Him by participating in His Pasch, "they will look on him whom they have pierced" (Jn. 19, 37; Za. 12, 10), and will see themselves in Him. The servants of the Lamb will adore Him in the new Jerusalem; they will see His face "like the sun shining in full strength"; they will see His pierced side. His name, henceforward inseparable from their own, will be on their foreheads. Having been placed with the Lamb on His throne, which is also that of the Father, they shall reign with the Lamb "for ever and ever" (Rev. 3, 21; 1, 16; 22, 3-5).

The Christ of Vatican II is "the innocent Lamb,"[74] the Lamb-Recapitulator who "loved with a human heart,"[75] and has thus gathered us together in the unity of His Spirit. This Spirit, sent by the Lamb-Recapitulator, is "the river of the water of life, bright as crystal, flowing from the throne of God and of the Lamb" (Jn. 4, 14; Rev. 22,1). Could not this "throne" be the Cross? Was it not from the side of Jesus crucified, pierced by the lance for our sins, that blood and water flowed—"the water of life" which the man of good will receives as a free gift by drawing near and by placing his hand, with faith, in His side (Jn. 19, 34; Rev. 22, 17; Jn. 20, 27)?

NOTES TO CHAPTER TEN

1. *Gaudium et Spes,* 10. 2.
2. *Lumen Gentium,* 13. 1 (Abbott, 31).
3. *Dei Verbum,* 2 (Abbott,112).
4. *Ibid.,* 4 (Abbott, 113).
5. *Lumen Gentium,* 47 (Abbott, 78).
6. Cf. the texts cited by note 2 of *Verbum Dei,* 2: notably Eph. 1, 3-14. One could cite, with even greater reason perhaps, *Eph.* 3, 1-3, a passage which exalts the mystery of Christ, treated by Saint Paul in a way which seems to make in indeed the synthesis of all the mysteries.

7. Jn. 16, 30; 2, 17.

8. Y. M. F. Congar O.P.: *Jésus-Christ*, Paris, 1966, pp. 64-65. To reinforce this thesis, one could also cite a general principle of the exegesis of Saint John's Gospel, implied by Saint Thomas Aquinas in his commentary of Jn. 2, 25 "what is said here about Christ" (i.e. "He himself knew what was in man") refers not only to His divine knowledge but to His knowledge as a man" *Summa Theologica*, III. 10. 2). Thus, by extension, many affirmations attributed by this Gospel to Jesus Christ, concern not only His divine knowledge or divine Will, but also His human knowledge and His human will. In this connection, see Bernard Leeming, *Cor Jesu*, Rome, 1959, vol. I, pp. 626-634; and especially the same author's "Human knowledge of Christ" in *Irish Theological Quarterly*, 1952, 135 seq., 235 seq.

9. DS, 3924: on the triple knowledge of Christ, the following can be consulted:

E. Mersch S.J.: *Théologie du Corps Mystique*, 1946², t. I, pp. 290-291: the triple knowledge of Christ is intimately related to His divinization by grace; the empirical and social knowledge of Christ is conditioned by language.

B. Leeming S.J.: *Adnotationes de Verbo Incarnato*, Rome, 1936, 319-372.

10. Cf. L. Malevez S.J.: *Nouv. Rev. Théol.*, 88 (1966), 1027-1028; 89 (1967), 113-134, where clear answers are given to certain views put forward by Rahner. Also, in the authors cited in our notes 8 and 9, there is a refutation of certain excessively facile objections made by some modern authors against the traditional doctrine of the triple knowledge of Christ, also defended by the Anglican, Mascall: *Christ, the Christian, and the Church*, London, 1946.

11. Cf. DS, 3432-3435 (DB, 2032-2035). There is an excellent commentary on the modernist propositions denying the infallibility of the Man Jesus, in Lepin: *Christologie*, Paris, 1907.

12. I am here borrowing from a letter to me from Father Leeming (21 December 1967).

13. Cf. J. R. Geiselmann, *Encyclopédie de la Foi*, Paris, 1965, t. II, art.: "Jésus-Christ," pp. 358, 360 and 369; I. de la Potterie S.J., "L'onction du Christ," *Nouv. Rev. Théol.*, 80 (1958), 225-252.

14. Father Benoit O.P., *Revue Biblique* 65 (1958), 269.

15. Lk. 13, 13.

16. Saint Thomas Aquinas, *Summa Theologica*, III. 22. 1, citing Heb. 5, 1, cited five times by Vatican II, notably four times by L. G. (10, 27 and 28).

17. Cited by LG, 8 and PO, 3.

18. Cited by LG, 28, 48 and by AG, 3.

19. Heb. 7, 26, cited by LG, 8 and 39.

20. Cited by LG 28 and PC, 14.

21. LG, 28 (Abbott, 53).

22. SC, 7 and 10 (Abbott, 141, 142); PO, 5. 2 (Abbott, 541).

23. Cf. Saint Thomas Aquinas, *Summa Theologica*, I. II. 106. 1: *"Principaliter* lex nova est ipsa gratia Spiritus Sancti quae datur Christi fidelibus."

24. SC, 10 (Abbott, 142-143).

25. *Ibid.*, 7. 2; PO, 51 adds the words: "on our behalf by the action of His Spirit."

26. Cf. DS, 1753 (DB, 950).

27. LG, 28. 1.

28. SC, 33 (Abbott, 149).

29. B. de Margerie S.J.: "o Sacerdote, ministro da Palavra de Deus na doctrina do Vaticano II," *Revista Eclesiástica Brasileira*, 24 (1964), 687; reproduced in our book *Padres profetas e mistagogos*, S. Paulo, 1968, chap. 2.

30. Cited by PO, 2, 4: this text becomes the key text of the decree harmonizing its evangelizing and its cultic perspective.

31. Cited by SC, 8.

32. LG, 28 and PO 13 cites these texts.

33. An expression used by the tenth-century Russians when they assisted for the first time at the Byzantine Liturgy in Constantinople.

34. In the course of these developments, we are drawing partly on the masterly commentary of P. C. Spicq O.P. on Hebrews (Paris, 1961).

35. GS, 38, 1.

36. *Ibid.*, 45. 2.

37. The affirmation is in effect repeated in GS, 57, 4.

38. AA, 5 and 7 (Abbott, 495, 497).

39. LG, 48, 1—which also explicitly cites Eph. 1, 1 and Col. 1, 20: "cum genere humano universus quoque mundus, qui intime cum homine conjungitur et per eum ad finem suum accedit, perfecte in Christo instaurabitur." GS, 57.4 intimately links salvation and recapitulation, man and cosmos: "antequam caro fieret *ad omnia salvanda* et in Se recapitulanda." The salvation of the cosmos becomes, in and through the salvation of mankind, the immediate purpose of the Incarnation; on the other hand, this pastoral constitution, by extending what is implicit in Saint Paul, attributes the activity of recapitulation to Christ Himself, and not merely to the Father.

40. DS, 112 and 115 (DB, 48 and 51): the author uses the Greek word *sunkephalaioustai,* which is very close to *anakephalaiôsis.*

41. Cf. our Chapter One.

42. AG, 2.

43. LG, 13. 2 (note 12); GS, 57. 2 (note 7).

44. We are referring here to a famous text of Pius XI on Saint Thomas Aquinas: "communem seu universalem Ecclesiae

Doctorem appelandum putemus Thomam cujus doctrinam . . .
suam Ecclesia fecerit" (Enc. *Studiorum Ducem,* AAS, 14
(1923), 314).

45. Saint Irenaeus, *Adversus Haereses,* III, 18. 1; PG. 7 (vol.
I) 932. English translation as in Bettinson: *The Early Christian Fathers* (Oxford, 1956: p. 113).

46. J. Daniélou, *Message évangélique et culture hellénistique,*
Paris-Tournai, 1961, p. 161-167.

47. Cf. GS, 22. 1; 38. 1; 45. 2.

48. L. Escoula S.J.: "le Verbe-Sauveur et Illuminateur chez
saint Irénée," *Nouv. Rev. Thiol.,* 66 (1939), 399, note 11.

49. Cf. Gustav Wingren, *Man and the Incarnation, A Study
in the Biblical Theology of Irenaeus* (English translation from
Swedish: London, 1959, p. 201).

50. *Ibid.,* p. 80. The synthetic aspect of Teilhard's ideas reminds one of Irenaeus. It would be interesting to make a detailed comparison of the two. On the recapitulation in Irenaeus,
the following can be consulted:

Houssiau: *Christologie d'Irénée* (Louvain, 1955, pp. 183-
185, 215-232;

E. Mersch: *Corps mystique de Christ* (Bruges, 1951, t. I,
pp. 317 *seq.*);

J. M. Dufort: "Récapitulation paulinienne dans l'exégèse
des PP.," *Sciences Ecclesiastiques,* 12 (1960), 21-38;

J. Lawson: *Biblical Theology of Irenaeus,* London, 1948,
140-198; and especially:

J. Daniélou (cf. note 46), *op. cit.,* pp. 156-159.

51. Cf. 1. 11, 3: "the head of every man is Christ . . . and
the head of Christ is God" This Pauline text shows the Biblical
foundation for the astonishing statement of Pope Saint Denis,
referred to in note 40 of the present chapter: the Father recapitulates the Trinity in Himself.

52. Saint Irenaeus, *Adversus Haereses,* V, 18. 2; PG, 7 (vol.
III, 1173 (English translation as in Bettinson: "The Early
Christian Fathers," Oxford, 1956).

53. *Ibid.,* V, 20. 2; PG, 7 (vol. II), 1179: "adunans hominem
spiritui et spiritum collocans in homine, ipse caput spiritus factus est; et spiritum dans esse hominis caput; per illum enim
vidimus et audivimus et loquimur." The Word, Breather of
the Spirit, sends Him to men; inasmuch as the Spirit is sent
by the Word to men for their salvation, Christ, as Word, can
be said to be Head of the Spirit whom He gives to His members; He gives to the Spirit to be Head of mankind, since it is
by the gift of the Spirit to men that He is Himself their Head.
It is therefore through the Spirit, our Head, that, with the
eyes of faith, we see Christ; that we hear Christ; and that—
when this Spirit speaks through us, as He did through the Old
Testament prophets—we speak about Christ. To see, to hear,
to speak are all activities which can be attributed equally to

the Head, Christ, and to the Spirit, at once Head and Soul, an image which the Church will prefer. See the following note.

54. Cf. DS, 3807-3080 (DB, 2288); DS, 3327.

55. Cf. DS, 3326; and the profession of faith of Paul VI (30 June 1968).

56. GS, 57. 4. We say: "*not so much as* the Word . . . ," but without denying that the Word as such is recapitulative, in the image of the Father who recapitulates all things in Himself.

57. Cf. AA, 7; GS, 57.

58. *Ibid.,* 24, 1-2; LG, 42. Cf. notes 61 and 62.

59. R. Schnackenburg, *Le message moral du Nouveau Testament,* Lyon, 1963, p. 197.

60. We are here using a deliberately vague expression which merely alludes to the Catholic doctrine: "without grace, not one can observe the natural law completely or for long." One cannot refrain for long from hostile actions if one does not love; one cannot love supernaturally without grace. Habitual or actual grace? We prefer here to avoid being specific on this point; hence our phrase, "ethical horizon."

61. GS, 24. 1 and 2. Cf. Saint Thomas Aquinas, *Summa Theologica,* II. II. 23. 5; 25. 1; 26. 2.

62. LG, 42. 1. 2; 9. 2; 43. 2.

63 GS, 38. 1.

64. *Ibid.,* 22. 5.

65. 1 Jn. 2, 7-8.

66. GS, 22. 1, 5 (Abbott, 220-224).

67. Cf. Saint Thomas Aquinas *Summa Theologica,* I, 12. 7; and Saint John of the Cross, *Spiritual Canticle,* VII. 4 and 9.

68. Cf. DV, 4 *sub fine.*

69. Cf. Saint Thomas Aquinas, *Summa Theologica,* I. 27. 5. 2; 30. 1. 2; 30. 2.4; 37. 2. 3.

70. We shall meet this point again later, admirably dealt with by Father Mersch and By Father Karl Rahner.

71. Cf. DS, 1545 (DB, 809): "vita aeterna . . . gratia . . . et merces."

72. Cf. GS, 39. 1; 1 Cor 7, 31.

73. Cf. E. B. Allo O.P., *l'Apocalypse,* Paris, 1921, p. 280: "it is a name whose full significance cannot be penetrated in the present life; for *oida,* in Johannine usage, means 'to penetrate, to know thoroughly'. . . . This name expresses His essence, which can be penerated only by the divine knowledge." Where there is question of a creature, the new name "designates a renewal of nature. . . . It is always a greater participation in the divine nature, an increase of grace, which can be understood and appreciated, within the depths of his soul, only by him who receives it" (*ibid.,* p. 30, commenting on Rev. 2, 17).

74. GS, 22. 3.

75. *Ibid.,* 22. 2.

11

THE SON OF MAN
REDEEMER OF A COREDEMPTIVE CHURCH

We have attempted to study at some depth the Christological views of Trent and of Vatican II. In pursuance of our purpose in this book—viz., to show how Christ is so completely *for the world* that He allows this world to share in the achievement of its own salvation—we must now deal more fully with the mystery of the Redemption. This word Redemption is very strange at first sight. What does it signify? What is the role of the death and the resurrection of the Lamb of God in the mystery of our redemption? In what sense can it be said that Christ is the Redeemer of the Church? And in what sense, different from but connected with the former, can it be said that the Church is the coredemptrix of the Christians and of the world? In what sense is the Christian called to associate himself with this coredemptive mission of the Church, and how does this task fit in with his mission to complete the creation and to be the architect of the earthly city?

A. The Lamb of God, Redeemer of the Church

The image immediately suggested by the title "Lamb of God" is that of Christ as passively a victim, rather

than that of the work *par excellence* of the Savior.
Nevertheless, Saint John's Gospel proclaims the Good
News of the Sacrifice of the Lamb of God. From the
outset, John transmits the message of his first master,
the Baptist: "The next day he (i.e. John the Baptist)
saw Jesus coming toward him, and said, 'Behold the
Lamb of God, who takes away the sin of the world . . .
this is he who baptizes with the Holy Spirit.' And I
have seen and have borne witness that this is the
Son of God" (Jn. 1, 29-34).

This proclamation of Jesus as the Lamb of God, in
conjunction with the reminder of His prefiguration in
the Old Testament (19, 36), forms the whole framework of Saint John's Gospel. Jesus is the Lamb of God:
this Lamb is *of God*, not only because of His divine
origin—as the bread of heaven He is given by the
Father and He gives His life to the world (cf. Jn. 6,
32-33)—but also by reason of His sacrificial consecration to the Father. He is the Lamb who immolates
Himself to the Father at the same time as He is immolated by men. Called by John, from the very outset, the Lamb of God, He becomes this fully only by
His death. Sanctified and consecrated from the beginning by the Father, He must be sanctified and consecrated yet again in His own blood through His death
(Jn. 10, 36; 17, 19). Just as the darkness is dispelled
by the Light, so sin and death are destroyed through
communion with the Lamb, by participation in the
holiness of His sacrifice. The Lamb dies that the nation and even all mankind may not perish, and to
gather together in the unity of His fold as the Good
Shepherd the children of His Father dispersed throughout the world (Jn. 11, 52; 10, 16). The one Shepherd
leads back the strayed sheep that he has searched the
desert to find, that He may make them into a single
fold by feeding them with His own flesh of the Lamb
become the Bread of life (Jn. 6, 33, 6, 51; 10, 10-11;
10, 16; Lk. 15, 4), with His flesh immolated by them
and for them. The Lamb is the Shepherd who leads
to the springs of the waters of life, to His Heart, where

the sheep drink the Spirit with His Blood (Rev. 14, 17; 22, 1; Jn. 7, 38-39). The Johannine Church is the one fold of the one flock redeemed by the Blood of the one Shepherd become Lamb.

We must carefully note that the Christ whom Saint John presents to us does not limit Himself to wresting His Father's sheep from the thieves that have stolen them and from the demoniacal wolf that has scattered them, but He also gathers them together into a single fold. The salvation which He brings is consummation in unity (cf. Jn. 17 passim).

This Lamb Shepherd of Saint John's Gospel, who gathers all His sheep into the unity of His immolated flesh and blood shed for them, by protecting them from dispersion, fits perfectly with the manner in which Jesus Himself, according to all the Evangelists, presented Himself as the Son of Man.[1] In using this title, however, the Lord transformed its traditional meaning by adding new connotations: He used the enigmatic expression to create an indissoluble association between His mission as glorious and eschatological judge and His mission as suffering Messiah here on earth—and this was something new for His hearers. Was He not thus showing them that the Son of Man, the glorious judge, was identical with the Servant of Yahweh, the Man of Sorrows, and that He was aware of this twofold and inseparable mission? "You will see the Son of man sitting at the right hand of Power, and coming with the clouds of heaven" (Mk. 14, 62); ". . . the Son of man must suffer many things and be rejected by the elders . . ." (Mk. 8, 31); ". . . and whoever would be first among you must be slave of all. For the Son of man also came not to be served but to serve, and to give his life as a ransom for many" (Mk. 10, 44-45)—a ransom given in order to gather all mankind into one people.

This last remark opens up a fresh perspective: the clearly individual meaning which Jesus gives to the expression "Son of Man" does not exclude a collective sense, but rather postulates it. The Son of Man is the model of a sacrificial attitude demanded of all; but He also sacrifices Himself for the sons of men, in order that their sins and their blasphemies may be forgiven them (Mk. 3, 28) and in order that He may be able to identify Himself with each of them to the extent of saying: "I was hungry and you gave me food, I was thirsty and you gave me drink. . . . Truly, I say to you, as you did it to one of the least of these my brethren, you did it to me" (Mt. 25, 35-40).

Already, Jesus is emerging here as the Redeemer of a humanity He wills to associate intimately with His redemptive work; but this is a theme to which we shall return. Was not that the reason why Jesus preferred this title, "Son of Man," to any other? Was He not thus seeking to indicate that the essential earthly mission of the Son of Man would consist in being the suffering Servant, in order that all the sons of men might be able to associate their sacrifices with His? Did He not intend to signify that the Son of Man is the man *par excellence*,[2] man through men, man in order that men should be fully human by being divinized?

He whom John the Baptist presented as the Lamb of God, presented Himself, therefore, as the Son of Man, as He who comes to substitute[3] for men in order then to be able to incorporate them. The Pauline doctrine of the Redemption, a word synonymous in practice with the word "salvation,"[4] synthesizes these two ideas, both so clearly contained in the mystery of the Eucharist. The sacrifice by which Christ substitutes Himself for men in expiation for their sins, is also the sacrifice by which He incorporates them with Himself. The flesh given and the blood shed for their sins, become, in addition to being the food and drink of repentant sinners, the pre-eminent means by which they form with Him one single new man, one single body.

In Saint Paul's view, the salvation which Christ brings is not only the welfare of man, snatched from his wretchedness. Paul specifies exactly the nature of this wretchedness. For the moderns, fallen man is man restored to his proper level by being reduced to the unaided resources of his nature. For Saint Paul, as for Saint John and for the Fathers, he is a slave of the devil. For Paul, Satan is "the spirit of the world" (1 Cor. 2, 12), "the god of this world (who) has blinded the minds of the unbelievers, to keep them from seeing the light of the gospel of the glory of Christ, who is the likeness of God" (2 Cor. 4, 4).[5]

The Redemption, therefore, presents itself as the setting free from a demoniacal captivity. Christ effects it by His death and by His Resurrection. By becoming man, the Word initiates within history the work of man's salvation, a work which He completes by His Pasch. It is important, therefore, to focus more clearly the redemptive role of the death and of the resurrection of the Lamb of God, and the salvific significance of His intermediate corpse state. We offer here some theological reflections on the significance of Good Friday, Holy Saturday, and Easter Sunday in the history of our salvation.

1. *Theology of Good Friday.*

This can be summed up in one proposition: by recapitulating all our deaths, the death of Christ has merited our liberation.

God willed to save mankind by the human act of a God-Man. It was therefore supremely fitting that this God-Man should take on Himself the consequences of the rebellion of human nature: suffering and death.

In the present state of human nature, death has three aspects:

— for human nature, it is rupture, tearing, disintegration, destruction, but not annihilation of its elements;

— for our soul, it is a partial liberation: "For the corruptible body is a load upon the soul: and the earthly habitation presses down the mind that muses upon many things . . . Wretched man that I am! Who will deliver me from this body of death?" (Wis. 9, 15; Rm.

7, 24). Death does not free from the body as such, but from its present state of corruption;

— finally, as regards the human person of the just, death *as a state* is its temporary ontological destrution, but without any destruction of the psychological personality; whereas death *as an act* consists in the final meritorious action of the human will of which it is the consummation. While the death-state is destruction of the human person, the death-act is its fulfillment, the totalization of its previous acts of meritorious freedom, its supreme earthly act which precedes the immutable act of vision. It is in the death-act that the free man takes up a definitive position in relation to the death imposed upon him, the death-state. And the death-act precedes the death-state.

It is *in part only* that death signifies for Christ what it does for us. The death of Christ transcends our purely human deaths. Christ's soul is endowed with immunity from our concupiscences, with an infused prophetic knowledge, and with the beatific vision; hence, death sets Him free only at the level of the space-time conditioning of His acquired and experimental knowledge. It in no way involves any destruction whatsoever of His Person, which is divine. But it does involve the definitive fulfillment of His psychological personality, because this death is the ultimate recapitulative and meritorious action of the human will of the Incarnate Word. One understands, therefore, how Father Mersch could write:

> His death will be the death towards which is directed the history of every individual and the history of mankind; the death which corresponds to the sin of the human race as a whole, to the original sin.
> Death in each individual human life is the point at which that life sums itself up, gathers all together within itself, in order to pass into the beyond. In humanity, the death of Christ will be that. His death is the summation and the consummation of all deaths and of all. It

completes the history of the world even before that history is finished, for it completes the history of every man. . . .

If death is for each man the full realization and final actualization of what he is,[6] the completion of his formation and his passage into the definitive, it must be this too for the Man who is God: *operari sequitur esse.* This peak of the human life of the Man-God is also the peak of His operation, His own act, the act in which He expresses Himself fully[7]. . . . Only the redemptive act in full, not by the exclusion of other acts, but by their inclusion.[8]

Notice Father Mersch's central idea: in recapitulating His whole earthly life, the death of Christ, the loving oblation of His death, is the recapitulation of all the human deaths which seek to associate themselves with His. By offering up His death, Christ offers to the Father the deaths of all those who consent to fall asleep in Him. To use an expression of Augustinian flavor dear to Father de Montcheuil,[9] the sacrifice of His death is the sacrament of the sacrifice of all mankind—that is, its visible and efficacious sign. Christ dies as victim of a loving holocaust, in order to show what the death of each and every man should be, and in order to effect in each and every man this invisible and total oblation. He dies in order to integrate all deaths in His death of unifying love. He dies so that no one may die for himself, but on the contrary for Him, the Lord: "For to this end Christ died . . . that he might be Lord of the dead . . ." (Rm. 14, 9; cf. verses 7 and 8). Thanks to the death of Jesus, every man can conquer death by making his own death a sacrifice of thanksgiving and of expiation of adoring praise and of supplication for the salvation of all the others, and in union with all those who die in Him and for Him. The supreme and decisive act of Christ in His first coming is directed towards the redemptive divinization of all the passings into immortality through death.

Here we have the definitive key to why God allows death, the latter being in itself so essentially contrary to the life-giving plan of the living God of all the living. "For God made not death: neither has he pleasure in the destruction of the living" (Wis. 1, 13). And nevertheless, this God who "made not death" has willed to die. Why is this?

Sin was attachment to the self and to the created world, to the point of despising God the Creator. Salvation will therefore be possible only through an attachment to God to the point of despising the self and the world which is an extension of the personal body—in other words, through death. In order to bestow on us the fullness of His life, Christ had therefore to taste the bitterness of our death: "But we see Jesus . . . made lower than the angels . . . so that by the grace of God he might taste death for every one" (Heb. 2, 9; cf. Jn. 10, 10).

We can therefore better understand all the implications of what Father M. J. Nicolas O.P. writes in the following passage:

> It is more enobling for man to redeem himself, to himself repair the evil he has done, to rehabilitate himself, than to be saved without having to do anything. Hence the economy of salvation is completely dominated, down to its least details, by the idea that *man must save himself*. It is because man is incapable of doing this that God becomes man; but in becoming man, there is no question of His eliminating the part which man himself must take in the Redemption. On the contrary, He will perfect that part and make it fully possible.
>
> Christ did not will to diminish His human suffering through the fact that He is God. He took upon Himself the full burden that a mere man would have had to bear; it was *as man* that He redeemed us. His divinity did not diminish in any way the human burden; that divinity took upon itself this burden, and gave to His human actions the supreme value of in-

finite holiness and the universal import which the most painful of merely human passions could never have attained. God did not become man in order to dispense man from making satisfaction and reparation, but on the contrary to enable him to do so. Herein lies—in so far as we are capable of understanding the deep mystery of the Cross—the reason why the divine Will has linked our salvation with an act which by its nature would involve all that mankind would have to suffer with a view to cleansing itself of its sins.[10]

These ideas are in full accord with the data of the New Testament. Although we must soon return to this point, we recall here that, for Paul, Timothy had to save himself (1 Tim. 4, 16), and that Jesus said *to all:* "If any man would come after me, let him deny himself and take up his cross daily and follow me" (Lk. 9, 23)—even to sharing in my death. It is not only the death of Jesus which is the visible sign of the invisible sacrifice of mankind and its sacrament; it is also His death on the cross which signifies the suffering merited by each sinner, and the painful and loving character of the death which he must accept and offer up by anticipating it every day through mortification and abnegation.

The death of Jesus on the cross is real, not just apparent; it therefore involves a real separation between His soul and His body.

2. Theology of Easter Saturday.

Death is the dissolution and the decomposition of man's composite being (soul and body). It is this decomposition which Christ has willed to undergo in His human nature. We shall deal only briefly here with what happened to the soul of Christ between His death and His resurrection, because this subject has been fully treated by many modern writers.[11] Less attention has been paid to the subject of the corpse of the Word of Life, and it is to this that we direct attention here.

It is the In-humanation itself of the only Son of God which explains the manner in which, by His death, He had ceased to be man. This point has been clearly grasped by Saint Thomas Aquinas:

> It is an article of faith that Christ was truly dead: hence it is an error against faith to assert anything whereby the truth of Christ's death is destroyed. . . . Now it belongs to the truth of the death of man or animal that by death the subject ceases to be man or animal; because the death of a man or animal results from the separation of the soul, which is the formal complement of the man or animal. Consequently to say that Christ was a man during the three days of His death simply and without qualification, is erroneous. Yet it can be said that He was *a dead man* during those three days.[12]

We are here, therefore, at the extreme point of the realism and the kenosis of the Incarnation, now so adequately named: the Word of God was so deeply inserted into humanity that He has temporarily ceased to form part of it; He became man so fully that in death He is no longer so, but only the Word made human soul and the Word made flesh. In this incorruptible corpse of a God who has ceased to be man, we see more clearly how much death dehumanizes, while at the same time it becomes more readily acceptable by us.

But immediately the differences emerge between the corpse of an ordinary man and the Christ-corpse which continues to be the temple of the Word.

Christ willed to participate in the dehumanization of our death, but, as divine eternal Person, He could not undergo its depersonalization. The human person is an individual and composite substance of a rational nature. The separated soul, which is no longer a man, also ceases, by the fact of its separation, to be a human person; but for all that, it does not cease to be an "I," since it remains a violated and incomplete, and therefore depersonalized, "I." On the other hand, the divine "I" is absolutely simple: the "I" of Christ, even of the dead Christ, remains therefore immutably an infinite "I" superior to all violation.

Furthermore, since it has reverted to the cycle of nature, the dehumanized and depersonalized corpse of the saint remains supernaturally powerless; but the dead body of the Word, a corpse powerless any more to merit our salvation, remains all-powerful to apply that salvation. Having fully merited our salvation by death, it remains its instrumental and efficient cause.

Saint Thomas could therefore write:

> In this way Christ's death cannot be the cause of our salvation by way of merit, but only by way of causality, that is to say, inasmuch as the Godhead was not separated from Christ's flesh by death; and therefore, what befell Christ's flesh, even when the soul was departed, was conducive to salvation in virtue of the Godhead united. But the effect of any cause is properly estimated according to its resemblance to the cause. Consequently, since death is a kind of privation of one's own life, the effect of Christ's death is considered in relation to the removal of the obstacles to our salvation: and these are the death of the soul and of the body.[13]

There are therefore at least three ways[14] in which the corpse of Christ mysteriously transcends those of all ordinary mortals: Jesus dead does not cease to be a Person, and to work our salvation precisely by means of this lifeless but incorruptible body which is inseparable from His divine Person as the Word.

It can be said, therefore, that during the "triduum mortis" the Word of God presents Himself as the Link and uncreated Mediator between His immortal and blessed, through deprived, soul, on the one hand, and His dead body on the other. The Word of the divine Goodness continues to assume a Heart which, while it no longer beats with love for us, continues to be the instrument of our salvation—and a wonderfully efficacious instrument, as emerges clearly in the solemn teaching of Saint John the Evangelist (19, 33-35). In order to emphasize, against the already widespread Docetist tendencies, that Jesus really died and really saved us not only by the waters of baptism but also by the Blood of His Passion (cf. 1 Jn. 5, 6), the Evangelist writes that the soldiers "saw that he was already dead" (19, 33) before he records that "one of the soldiers pierced his side with a spear, and at once there came out blood and water" (19, 34). This was the beginning of the pouring forth of the Spirit of the Heart of Jesus, the foundation of the Church.[15] Clearly, John sought to emphasize the efficacious action of the dead Heart of the Redeemer: "He who saw it has borne witness—his testimony is true, and he knows that he tells the truth—that you also may believe" (19, 35).

This is a cry of victory, of the victory of the faith which has conquered the world (cf. 1 Jn. 5, 4-5), a cry which reflects the victorious cry of the agonizing Jesus who has conquered the world and its prince (Mt. 27, 50; Jn. 16, 33). The twofold cry of Jesus and, later on, of the beloved disciple, surely signifies that the devil, while able to destroy temporarily the In-humanation of the Word, was powerless to affect the Incarnation, masterpiece of the eternal Wisdom. From the first instant of His earthly existence, the Word was joined with the flesh, became flesh, in such a way that there could never be any separation from the flesh even by His death.

This death was not, as some perhaps suppose, a separation between the divine Person and the sacred Humanity of the Savior; it merely separated His human and immortal soul from His mortal body. Even after His final breath on Golgotha, the only Son of God has never relinquished either the soul or the body assumed forever, though He did permit their temporary separation for our salvation. Our sins were able to separate the body and soul, but were entirely powerless to destroy the indissoluble unity between the

Word and the separated elements of His humanity.[16] Man's will cannot suppress the masterpiece of God: the love of God for His own humanity and for all humanity is invincible. The death of Christ was not a "disincarnation"; any more than the Resurrection of Christ was a "reincarnation," as the "spirit" movement in the nineteenth century would have had us believe. There is no multiplicity of successive incarnations, but *one* Incarnation of the only Word of God.

3. *Theology of Easter Sunday.*

Since the one Incarnation of the only Son of God has never ceased, His glorious Resurrection, far from being a reunion with a flesh from which in fact He had never been separated, a reincarnation,[17] was the glorious and mysterious reanimation of His saving corpse by His created, holy, immortal and now fully glorified soul. The Resurrection was not the resumption by the Word of a body—which in fact He had never abandoned, but the glorification of His divine corpse, after His body had undergone the ignominies of the Passion. This reanimation was not, as in the case of Lazarus, a temporary one leaving intact the mortality of the reanimated body. On the contrary, is was a definitive glorification.[18] And is not this capital difference magnificently symbolized by Saint John when he points a contrast between Lazarus emerging from the tomb, "his hands and feet bound with bandages, and his face wrapped with a cloth" (11, 44), and the fact that Simon Peter, in the case of Christ, "saw the linen cloths lying, and the napkin, which had been on his head . . . rolled up in a place by itself" (20, 6-7)?

This glorious Resurrection of Jesus is a redemptive act of the Word: ". . . to us who believe in him that raised from the dead Jesus our Lord, who was put to death for our trespasses and raised for our justification" (Rm. 4, 25). It is even the decisive redemptive Act (Heb. 2, 10; 5, 9), and the culminating point of the redemptive sacrifice; for it completes the transform-

ing divinization of the victim, His consummation, thus
becoming "the source of eternal salvation to all those
who obey him" (Heb. 5, 9).

The Resurrection thus appears as the definitive enthronement of the Son of God established forever in
the exercise of His sanctifying power merited by His
death on the cross. His humanity becomes effectively
what it already was in principle: the instrument of
our divinization,[19] through the Eucharist, inseparable
from the Resurrection.

The paschal mystery is that of our passage, with
Jesus, from this world to the glory of the Father.
Christ's "act" of death on Good Friday, His "state"
of death and His real burial on Easter Saturday, His
historical and mysterious resurrection on Easter Sunday, are three indissolubly but distinctly linked stages
of His passage to the Father, a passage which conditions ours. One "telescopes" this distinction only at
the expense of nullifying the twofold reality of the
Word's In-humanation and of our redemption, thus
entailing the risk of a "neo-Docetism."

However, certain distinguished authors[20] are inclined to hold that the death and the resurrection of
Christ could, in reality, have coincided.

In their view, the death of Christ on Good Friday
would have been "relative." His "absolute death"
would have taken place only on Easter Sunday, when
His soul would have abandoned His mortal body in
order to reanimate it as a glorified and spiritualized
body. The witness of the Gospels that Christ was in
the tomb during three days, would serve to symbolize
the incorruptibility of His body.

Such an interpretation appears to contradict directly the Apostles' Creed, which states that the Resurrection occurred on "the third day." The idea of a "relative" death seems very close indeed to that of an
"apparent" death. Does not the denial of an observa-
ble gap of time between "absolute" death and resurrection, endanger the necessary assertion of the separation of soul and body in death, the reality of this death,

and, indirectly, even that of the Resurrection? Could one claim that such an interpretation would have been endorsed by the Evangelists or by the Fathers of the Church?

On the contrary, we hold that they would have rejected it as not in line with the Biblical data. Furthermore, they would have seen it as favoring Docetism.[21] Christ has willed to experience our death in the horror of its real separation between soul and body, and not merely in a glorious semblance. He really died on Good Friday, and it was not the side of a living person that the Roman soldier pierced. We cannot personally accept a re-interpretation which runs counter to the whole historical and dogmatic tradition of the Church, since it no longer admits the resurrection of Christ on the third day in the same sense as does this tradition. Such a heterogeneous development represents regression, not progress.[22] It endangers orthodox belief in the mystery of the Redemption. Its own merit is that it underlines the inseparable character of the death and of the resurrection of Jesus, which nevertheless constitute two different events, even in Biblical language: for example, cf. Mk. 9, 31. It thus helps us, indirectly, to appreciate more clearly the truth so splendidly set in relief by Father Garrigou-Lagrange: the Resurrection is "the visible sign of the invisible victory of the cross."

From this victory, as redeemed and saved by it, the Church was born. Christ the Redeemer and Savior of the Church—this is an idea with which many Christians are insufficiently familiar, and nevertheless it is an integral part of the deposit of Revelation as the Church itself has understood and explained it.

Saint Paul clearly presents it to us, and already shows us its primary and basic meaning: "Christ is the head of the church, his body, and is himself its Savior. . . . Christ loved the Church and gave himself up for her, that he might sanctify her, having cleansed her by the washing of water with the word, that he might present the church to himself in splendor, without spot or wrinkle or any such thing, that she might be holy and without blemish" (Eph. 5, 23-27).

This text, about which so much has been written, indicates the two stages of the redemptive work of Christ as regards the Church: the first stage, on the cross, is that of the objective redemption, when Christ gave Himself up for the Church; the second stage is realized when Christ transforms mankind stained by original and actual sin into a Church "without blemish," by means of the sacrament of baptism. For anyone who compares verses 25 and 27, there can be no doubt that, in Saint Paul's view, it is indeed the Church of earth which is "holy and without blemish" because it has been "sanctified" by Christ in the waters of baptism. The subjective redemption of the Church by Christ occurs when He applies to His members the merits of His Passion. It is thus that Pius XII,[23] without however making a detailed exegesis of the idea, understands the Pauline doctrine, in his encyclical on the Mystical Body of Christ: Christ is the Savior of His Body, the Church, because He is the Savior of the world (Jn. 4, 42) and of all men, but especially of the faithful (1 Tm. 4, 10).

The Fathers of the Church, except Saint Augustine,[24] understood it in this sense, though with a variety of emphasis. They held that the salvific work of Christ in relation to the Church does not alone consist in the baptism given to its members, but is continued beyond this. For Saint Ambrose, for example, leprous humanity becomes, thanks to the waters of baptism, the Church without blemish: "The people must come to the Church. The people, who were strangers and who, before being immersed in the mystic river, were leprous and soiled, are washed by the mysteries of baptism from its blemishes of body and of soul. Then they are no longer lepers; they have begun to be as a virgin without blemish or wrinkle: *immaculata virgo coepit esse sine ruga.*"[25] But Ambrose also shows us the pilgrim Church wounded, not in itself, but in us the members. Thanks to us, its sinful members, the immaculate Church "is symbolized by this woman who comes up behind you, O Lord, touches the fringe of your garment, and says: 'If I only touch his garment, I shall be made well' (Mt. 9, 21). Here we have this Church which confesses its wounds and desires to be made well."[26] About six years previously, Ambrose had clarified in advance the meaning of that last sentence: "It is not in itself but in us that the Church is wounded."[27]

For Ambrose, therefore, Christ is the Savior and the purifier of a Church which desires to be "made well." The Church is already objectively redeemed by the Lord; but it needs His ceaseless application of the merits of His Passion, and consequently, it needs a ceaseless subjective redemption. Though the distributer of the riches of salvation, the Church acknowledges its own need of redemption.

Was it not this that the Lord Jesus wished to bring home to His Church in the Middle Ages, through Saint Francis of Assisi and Saint Catherine of Siena?

The Poverello three times heard the order from above: "Go, Francis, restore my house which is in ruins." The meaning of this eluded him, for he regarded himself as utterly unworthy of great missions. Innocent III understood more clearly the designs of the divine mercy, when in a vision he saw Francis "supporting on his shoulders the Church of the Lateran which was about to crumble."[28]

"Go, Francis, restore my house which is in ruins." Christ has never ceased to save and to build up His indestructible Church (it crumbles only in its sinful members) through its saintly members.

Jesus made Saint Catherine of Siena realize that, by her shortcomings, she was responsible for the sad condition of the Church: "O my soul, throughout your whole existence, you have lost Him, and that is why so much evil, so many calamities have laid waste the world and the holy Church."[29] And the eternal Father said to the saint: "Take your tears and, in union with my other followers, use them to wash the face of my Spouse. I promise you that this will restore her beauty. . . . With these prayers and tears, I desire to wash the face of the Spouse, the holy Church. I have already shown her to you in the image of a woman whose face is soiled and as it were leprous. These soilings are the sins of her ministers and of all Christians. . . ."[30]

For the great Dominican saint, the "leprous" Church is not mankind before baptism,[31] whom Ambrose saw as symbolized by Naaman the Syrian; it is the Church that Christ has already baptized in water, in Blood, and in the Spirit. The sins of its members and ministers stain the holy Church, but do not utterly destroy its holiness. With fine precision, Catherine, reporting the divine words, shows us the Church, not as simply leprous, but "as it were leprous." These soilings remain extrinsic to the Church and do not reach to the inner reality of its mystery. The tears of the saints ceaselessly restore a beauty to the Church, a beauty which in fact it has never lost in the eyes of the angels and of men of good will who look upon it with the eyes of reason and of grace.[32] It is none the less true that the Church does seem to many to be "as it were leprous," that its face needs to be washed by the tears which Christ sheds within it through the eyes of its saints, aware that they have shared in the mystery of evil militating against the communion of love which the Church never ceases to be.[33]

One thus understands how Vatican II could declare in the same breath that the Church is "holy in a way that can never fail" and "always in need of being purified" in the constant pursuit of "penance and renewal."[34] "Spotless spouse of the spotless lamb,"[35] the Church must ceaselessly practice the "metanoia" preached by Christ.[36] Redeemed by Christ as was Mary—that is to say, in a more sublime way than its members were redeemed—the Church, thanks to the intercession of the Virgin who is its transcendent type, cooperates constantly in its own redemption through the very activity by which it distributes to all the fruits of the objective Redemption effected on Calvary. Like Mary, it has been redeemed in order to cooperate in its own redemption by being co-redemptrix of the human race.[37] By working for the salvation of mankind, the Church ceaselessly purifies and saves itself. The Church redeemed is the Church coredeeming.

B. The Church, Co-Redeeming Spouse of the Lamb of God

As we have already emphasized, the Church is the *raison d'être* and the agent of the Redeemer.[38] The new Adam has made this new Eve in His image and likeness: He has willed to make the Church the instrument of His coredemptive work, just as His sacred humanity is the instrument of his divine Word-Person in the accomplishment of the work of salvation. Like this sacred humanity, the Church is a conscious and free instrument in the distribution of the unfathomable riches of the Christ-Redeemer. This theme, already present in the New Testament, has been recently developed by the Magisterium of the Church and by the reflections of the theologians, such developments being a pledge of its future deepening by the redeemed and coredeeming people of the living God.

Saint Mark's Gospel presents the people of the New Covenant as a nation of the redeemed required by their Redeemer to associate themselves intimately with His redemptive death under pain of being excluded from its benefits.

While accepting at Caesarea Philippi the disciples' profession of Messianic faith, through Peter, Jesus nevertheless partly rejected their idea of His Messianic role, and, during a week of systematic instruction (Mk. 8, 31-9, 2), He took pains to show them that the Messiah must suffer and die and that His disciples must prepare themselves for a similar destiny.

The disciples were hearing for the first time the teaching of Jesus about the sufferings of the Son of

Man. They understood and opposed it. Their incomprehension (Mk. 9, 31) was not intellectual, but emotional and religious; for what it clearly said was, not only that the Son of Man must suffer, but also that His disciples must be ready to suffer with Him (Mk. 8, 35). It was because he wished to save his life and not to lose it because of the Son of Man, that Peter "began to rebuke" the Master when He announced His passion and His death. The disciples did not understand how and why their death would promote the Kingdom of God by winning for it the whole world (cf. Mk. 8, 31-36). How could the multitude, who received the same explicit teaching (Mk. 8, 34), be expected to understand it any better?

Nevertheless—and this was a partial success for the teaching of Jesus during His public life—these same disciples were to end by wishing to die with the Master on the eve of His passion (Mk. 14, 31). The outcome was to show, however, how superficial that conviction was. But once converted and after the Resurrection, they were all the more ardent to expound the Master's doctrine and to desire, in union with Him, to give their lives for the multitude (cf. Mk. 10, 45).[39]

As can be seen, a fundamental point of the teaching of Jesus is involved here: the people of God as a whole is called to bear His cross, following the one Redeemer. It is not only for Himself, but also for His whole Mystical Body that the Savior has chosen the cross.[40]

While He alone effected the objective Redemption of the human race, and in this sense is the sole ransome of the multitude, Christ then wills to make use of numerous instruments, in order to distribute the treasures of this Redemption. Such instruments will be the more precious and efficacious the more intimately they are united by prayer and by the word to the one Redeemer. Such is the lesson which emerges from the teaching of Saint Paul in his pastoral Epistles. The theology of the coredemptive Church which they contain, has not yet been properly formulated.[41] For they harmonize and synthesize two series of affirmations.

On the one hand, Paul clearly says to Timothy that "God our Savior desires all men to be saved. . . . For there is one God, and there is one mediator between God and men, the man Jesus Christ, who gave himself as a ransom for all" (1 Tim. 2, 3-6). The work of the Redemption is insistently presented as already accomplished: "God saved us and called us with a holy calling, not in virtue of our works but in virtue of his own purpose and the grace which he gave us in Christ Jesus" (2 Tim. 1, 9). Too much emphasis cannot be placed on the free nature of the grace which precedes the meritorious works. It is the primacy of the Christ Redeemer "come into the world to save sinners."[42]

On the other hand, Paul shows us in these same Epistles how this Redeemer calls into active life the coredemptive Church. Paul, "the foremost of sinners . . . that Christ Jesus came into the world to save" (1 Tim. 1, 15), endures "everything for the sake of the elect, that they also may obtain the salvation which in Christ Jesus goes with eternal glory" (2 Tim. 2, 10).[43] Paul saves them, therefore, not only by suffering, but also by prayer and preaching: "First of all I urge that supplications, prayers, intercessions and thanksgivings be made for all men. . . . This is good, and it is acceptable in the sight of God our Savior" because it is thus that He "desires all men to be saved": the one Mediator calls us to participate by prayer in His mediation (1 Tim. 2, 1-5). But prayer would not be sufficient without the preaching of the word: "Take heed to yourself and to your teaching; hold to that, for by so doing you will save both yourself and your hearers" (1 Tim. 4, 16). Like the Church and, still more, like the Virgin Mary, Paul will save himself by saving the others; like Paul, the Church saves itself by saving the world, through "the message of this salvation" (cf. Acts 13, 26). This message is continued in "the sacred writings which are able to instruct you for salvation through faith in Christ Jesus" (2 Tim.

3, 15). Thus one understands that "the living God" is "the Savior of all men, especially of those who believed" (1 Tim. 4, 10). This ecclesial coredemption realized in Paul and by Paul, this coredemption through suffering, prayer, and preaching, is completely polarized by the baptism whose efficacy it prepares or completes: "God our Savior . . . saved us . . . by the washing of regeneration and renewal in the Holy Spirit" (Tit. 3, 5).

The Pastoral Epistles, then, amply show that the one Mediator, the Savior, has already effected our salvation; but they equally show that it is not the intention of this Savior that the Christian should be saved without his own cooperation, or that His one mediation should exclude dependent and shared mediations through the offering up of the baptized suffering,[44] prayer, and instruction, and especially through the baptism of the non-baptized. Together, these constitute a rich commentary on the basic statement of Saint Paul, which provides the guide lines for ecclesial coredemption: "Now I rejoice in my sufferings for your sake, and in my flesh I complete what is lacking in Christ's afflictions for the sake of his body, that it, the church" (Col. 1, 24). Here Saint Paul explicitly speaks about an individual co-redemption for the benefit of the whole Church, bringing out that every Christian, as a living member of Christ, is in a certain sense savior of the Church, and that through him Christ continues to save the Church (cf. Eph. 5, 23). Saint Thomas Aquinas makes a good comment on this point: "It is necessary that Christ, who has suffered in His own body, should likewise suffer in Paul, His members, and in all the others; and all this, for His body which is the Church, in order that it may be thus redeemed by Christ."[45] But, in the text cited, Paul implicitly affirms that the whole Church, in its justified members, is coredemptive of its sinful members, as well as of all men in general. If Paul can save himself (cf. 1 Tim. 4, 16), then, *a fortiori*, the Church as such can save itself by saving its own members and others. That is why Saint Thomas, who sees in this Pauline text a fresh affirmation of the redemption of the Church by Christ, reads it also as affirming the coredemptive Church: *"I complete what is lacking in Christ's afflictions:* that is, in the afflictions of the whole Church, of which Christ is the Head. . . . God, in His predestination, has decided the measure of the merits which is to accrue to the whole Church . . . and the purest of these merits' are the sufferings of the holy martyrs."

The doctrine of the coredemptive Church, as shown by these commentaries of Saint Thomas[46] and as emerging from the group of Pauline texts we have cited, has solid foundations in the New Testament. We must examine its precise meaning in the light of the Magisterium and of the reflections of modern theologians.

Pius XII has dealt deeply with this theme in his encyclical "The Mystical Body of Christ." Here is the central passage:

> Our Savior wants to be helped by the members of His mystical Body in carrying out the work of Redemption. This is not due to any need or insufficiency in Him, but rather because He has so ordained it for the greater honor of His immaculate Bride. Dying on the Cross, He bestowed upon His Church the boundless treasure of the Redemption without any cooperation on her part; but in the distribution of that treasure He not only shares this work of sanctification with His spotless Bride, but wills it to arise in a certain manner out of her labor. This is truly a tremendous mystery, upon which we can never meditate enough: that the salvation of many souls depends upon the prayers and voluntary mortifications offered for that intention by the members of the mystical Body of Jesus Christ.[47]

Having thus clearly noted the absence of the Church's cooperation in the objective Redemption, and her decisive role as Bride of the Lamb in the subjective Redemption—with all the consequences which flow from this truth for the eternal salvation of so many men and for the responsibility of Christians—Pius XII also deduces from it a negative consequence:

> If there are still many, as unhappily there are, who wander outside the path of Catholic truth and fail to give their free consent to the inspiration of divine grace, this is due to the fact that not only they themselves, but the faithful also, omit to offer to God more fervent prayers for this intention. . . . The greater or less abundance of the gifts of grace depends in no small measure upon our good works by which this rain of heavenly gifts, God's free bounty, is drawn down upon the souls of men.[48]

If these texts are compared with those of Trent which we have already considered,[49] a shift of central emphasis will be noticed from concern with personal coredemption (in the sense of each one's cooperation in his own salvation) to concern with social and ecclesial coredemption. This is not surprising, since the individualism of the Renaissance and of the Reformation created a psychological climate which indirectly influenced many Catholics. When one remembers this, it is even surprising that Trent dealt with the social character of the Eucharist and of merit. It remains true, however, that its main accent was placed on the cooperation of each in his own salvation, much more than on the Christian's collaboration with Christ for the salvation of others. On the other hand, the insistence of modern thought and of the contemporary Church on the social character of human nature and the human person, prepared the ground for an accentuation of the social character of the coredemption, in every sense of that expression: the Church saves its members, and each of the members contributes to the salvation of all the others. Such a development was more systematically called for by the encyclical on the Mystical Body of Christ.

This development culminates in two essential affirmations: by the will of Christ, the subjective Redemption is in a sense born of the Church's activity; and this activity consists of the prayers and voluntary mortifications offered for this intenton by the members of the Church.

It is important to establish the precise meaning of these affirmations within the whole context of the encyclical. It is the grace of the Christ-Redeemer, His intimate action in the Church, which causes the co-redemptive activity of His Spouse, those prayers and those voluntary sacrifices, united with His sacrifice as the Lamb immolated on the Cross, during the Mass which renews that sacrifice.[50] Pius XII presents Christ as the Redeemer and the Savior of a coredemptive Church—a splendid vision, summed up in a sentence borrowed from Clement of Alexandria: "by one and the same means we are both saving and saved."[51]

The little[52] we have said here about the doctrine of Pius XII on the coredemptive Church, shows sufficiently that the Church has gained an increased awareness of this aspect of its mission.

In relation to this matter, how are we to assess the special contribution of Vatican II?

We have already made several allusions to this.[53] In short, one can say that, while not using the actual term, Vatican II is filled with the idea and the reality of the coredemptive Church, even though it does not explicitly take up certain aspects of the doctrine of Pius XII, and even though it considers the subject within a partly different framework—viz., the universal priesthood of the faithful, and the consecration of the world (two ideas about which Pius XII had already spoken, but in a different context). The ethical aspects of the coredemptive activity of the faithful and of the Church are perhaps emphasized more than its ontological reality. Vatican II insists more on *agere* than on *esse*. It clearly indicates that the coredemptive activity affects the temporal order.

The basic principle is that the whole Church must "shoulder the entire saving mission of the Church toward the world."[54] "Upon all the laity, therefore, rests the noble duty of working to extend the divine plan of salvation ever increasingly to all men of every epoch and in every land."[55] The coredemptive mission is therefore that of the whole Church to the whole of mankind, called to be incorporated with it. If each one can fulfill this mission in only a partial way, each can nevertheless contribute in a real way to the salvation of all: "Let each one remember that he can have an impact on all men and contribute to the salvation of the whole world by public worship and prayer as well as by penance and voluntary acceptance of the labors and hardships of life. By such means, does the Christian grow in likeness to the suffering Christ (cf. 2 Cor., 4: 10; Col. 1; 24)."[56]

These considerations remind us that it is not solely or even especially by action, but much more by suffering offered in loving union with the Passion of Christ, that Christians, and the Church in them, fulfill their coredemptive mission, and consecrate the world by saving it. This consecration of the world by the common priesthood of all baptized and confirmed Christians, deploys the powers and the intimate exigencies of the sacrificial consecration of the bread and wine transubstantiated into the body and blood of Christ, at the same time as it draws from it the love without which it could not exist. The consecration of the world by the Christian laity is inseparable from the properly sacrificial consecration through transubstantiation effected by the ministerial priesthood. The two together complete the sacrifice of the coredemptive Church.[57]

That it is especially by its sacrifice that the Church consecrates and saves the world, is a truth which emerges resplendently in the theology of martyrdom[58] and of its human and ecclesial significance, as sketched and encouraged by Vatican II:

Since Jesus, the Son of God, manifested His charity by laying down His life for us, no one has greater love than he who lays down his life for Christ and for his brothers (cf. 1 Jn. 3: 16; Jn. 15: 13). From the earliest times, then, some Christians have been called upon—and some will always be called upon to give this supreme testimony of love to all men, but especially to persecutors. The Church, therefore, considers martyrdom as an exceptional gift and as the highest proof of love. By martyrdom a disciple is transformed into an image of his Master, who freely accepted death on behalf of the world's salvation; he perfects that image even to the shedding of blood. Though few are presented with such an opportunity, nevertheless all must be prepared to confess Christ before man, and to follow Him along the way of the cross through the persecutions which the Church will never fail to suffer.[59]

This is an extraordinarily rich and significant text. It presents martyrdom as a grace, as a "donum" (the word used in the original Latin version)—i.e. a charism bestowed by God for the good of mankind. It affirms that this gift has never been, and never will be, lacking to the Church. The permanence of persecution and of martyrdom is shown to be one of the notes of the true Church of Christ; and we are also told that it is for the salvation of the world that the disciple of Christ accepts death by martyrdom—an acceptance which every such disciple should be prepared to make, and should prepare himself accordingly. How can one fail to conclude that the martyrs to whom the Church constantly gives birth, are the sign and the supreme means of the coredemptive activity of the Church, springing up from its Eucharistic sacrifice? It is in their sacrifice that the sacrifice which the Church offers in celebrating the Mass suceeds in becoming perfectly and universally visible. In vocation, in readiness, in actuality, the whole Church is the Church of the martyrs, the martyrized body of the supreme Martyr, "the faithful

Witness" who, "loves us and has freed us from our sins by his blood" (Rev. 1, 5-6).

Such an interpretation is confirmed by an explicit text of the same Vatican II: "Just as Christ carried out the work of redemption in poverty and under oppression, so the Church is called to follow the same path in communicating to men the fruits of salvation."[60] Here we have a clear statement of the distinction between objective redemption and subjective redemption. The Church is presented as the society which communicates the fruits of the redemption. The expression "coredemptive Church" is not used, but the idea it contains is there all the same, just as it is also implied in the descriptions of the Church as "sacrament of salvation," a key concept of Vatican II. In various ways, the latter is at pains to clarify its significance. "The Church is 'the universal sacrament of salvation,' simultaneously manifesting and exercising the mystery of God's love for man."[61] The Church manifests salvation by being its "mark"— as it has never ceased to be[62] and will never fail to be—and it exercises this salvation by being the Messianic people "used by Christ as an instrument for the redemption of all."[63] It thus resembles *the* Sacrament par excellence, the Humanity of the Redeemer, a humanity which is the sign and the instrument of our salvation. Like this sacred humanity, the Church is a conscious and free instrument in the hands of the saving Word.

It is therefore clear that, for Vatican II, the Church is the salvation of the world, and consequently that the action of this Church saves mankind. However, without creating any opposition between the two, a slight distinction in vocabulary makes a distinction between the language of Vatican II and that of Pius XII. Although the Council has many times referred to the Church as Spouse of Christ, it does not seem to have adopted this metaphor—except perhaps on one occasion[64]—for the precise purpose of expressing the intimate association of Christ with the redemptive work of the Savior. For Vatican II, the Church is rather the conscious instrument which associates it with the Savior in His salvific activity.[65] The emphasis is on the Church as the sacrament of the Redemption rather than on the coredemptive quality of the Church, though the latter is implicitly stated. It all reads as though the Council were seeking to stress that the Church's relationship to and collaboration with Christ, in no way (on the contrary, indeed) suppresses the Church's dependence upon the Lord. We have here a distinction created by a difference of emphasis, but no divergence of doctrine. On the one hand, Pius XII presented the Church as the Spouse of Christ springing from the pierced side of the Lamb,[66] but he never used the term coredemptive Church; on the other, Vatican II does not limit itself to saying that the Church is the instrument of salvation, but states more specifically: "As the salt of the earth and the light of the world (cf. Mt. 5: 13-14), the Church is summoned with special urgency to save and renew every creature."[67] Let us emphasize this: the Church of Vatican II is equally a Church which saves the world "by public worship and prayer and by penance and voluntary acceptance of the labors and hardships of life,"[68] as well as by the martyrdom, actual or merely accepted as possible and risked, of its members. It saves the world by consecrating it through the priestly sacrifice of its faithful in union with the sacrifice of the ministerial priesthood of its clergy. Even though the actual term has not been used, the Church is truly the coredemptive Spouse of the immolated Lamb, in being the sacrament of His free and superabundant Redemption.

A further important point emerges from the teaching of Vatican II. The world which the Church saves is not only that of souls, but also that of the temporal and physical universe. The Church is coredemptive of the temporal order, this being a direct implication of the doctrine pronounced by the Council: "Christ's redemptive work, while of itself directed toward the salvation of man, involves also the renewal of the whole temporal order. Hence the mission of the Church is not only to bring to men the message and grace of Christ, but also to penetrate and perfect the temporal sphere with the spirit of the gospel. . . . Although distinct, these realms (the spiritual and the temporal orders) are . . . connected in the one plan of God."[69] In redeeming man and his temporal activities, the Church saves the universe itself, intimately united with man.[70] The consecration of the world extends to matter as transformed by human labor. It is the Christ-Redeemer who takes possession of the world, bought at the cost of His blood, through the work of man as stimulated by the sacrifice of the Church. The whole universe is colored by the blood of the Lamb and purified by the tears of His Spouse. Such is the climate which pervades Vatican II.

Briefly sketched here, this then is the doctrine which the Church, not without the help of the Holy Spirit, has drawn from the deposit of Revelation in order to offer it for consideration by the theologians. Subject to correction, we think that the theologians have not very systematically investigated this mystery of the coredemptive Church—a mystery which, nevertheless, is so intensively lived by the Spouse of the Lamb. There are, of course, brilliant exceptions; examples are Father Mersch, Cardinal Journet, Father Semmelroth, and Father de Broglie.

Father Mersch is thoroughly alive to the social character of the Redemption. In his *Théologie du Corps Mystique*, he gives a splendid formulation of the problem:

> How could the members of the Redeemer, and of the Redeemer as effecting the act of salvation,[71] fail to be themselves active? They will receive Redemption by becoming one with the Christ who saves them and with the active Redemption. Then, what will they be, in their passive Redemption, but people whose existence

demands to be extended in union with the active Redemption? The act of redemption passes on from the Son of Man to mankind. The unity effected by the Redemption should express itself in the Redemption itself. The redemptive activity will make the members of Christ co-satisfiers and co-repairers of the one Redeemer. This term signifies that the act of the Redeemed enables the Christians truly to make satisfaction. . . .

Would it be conceivable that the Redeemer should assume His fullness in a mystical Body, and yet that the act of redemption which is His supreme act—the precise act in which He causes this mystical body to emanate from Him—should not itself also take on His fullness in the acts and the satisfaction of this body? Christ is essentially and intrinsically Redeemer; must it not follow that this mystical Body should itself also be essentially and intrinsically an immense Redemption . . . that the Whole Christ should be Redeemer?[72]

This eloquent passage is limited, however, to posing the problem of personal co-redemption. This is not surprising, since the author was essentially inspired by the Tridentine teaching, and only slightly, at the speculative level, by "the Apostleship of Prayer."[73]

A few years later, Cardinal Journet dealt with the same problem in a broader way. He extended it to social coredemption, the coredemption through which the Christian cooperates with Christ not only with a view to his own salvation but also for the salvation of others; and, furthermore, to the cooperation of the Church, the new Eve, with the Redeemer. With precision and at depth, this Freiburg theologian has investigated the nature, the subjects and degrees of intensity, the object and its extension, the basis and meaning of the coredemptive activities of the Christians, of the Church and of the Virgin Mary, Mother and Associate of the Redeemer. We shall deal briefly with these points in order to lead up to the conclusions he has reached.

For him, "the meritorious and satisfactory works of the Church represent the most characteristic and most formal aspects of its coredemptive activity. But the Church can be called coredemptive of the world with Christ, in a still wider sense, by reason solely of the impetrative value of its prayer."[74] In this way, the nature of this ecclesial coredemption manifests itself.

What is its subject? The coredemptive mediation of the Church is situated between, on the one hand, the one redemptive mediation, that of Christ, alone capable of meriting in justice the salvation of all men; and, on the other, the coredemptive mediation of the Christians, the latter mediation being entirely dependent on that of Christ from which it draws all its value, and which merits the salvation of others only through a merit de *congruo* based upon love and linking the Christians with Christ. The Christian, in virtue of this love, makes his demand in the name of Christ.[75]

The collective coredemptive mediation of the Church is deployed between the mediation of the Christ-Redeemer and that of the individually co-redemptive Christian. This mediation of the Church is always greater in its fervor than that of members taken individually.

For Journet, the individual coredemptive mediation of the Christian, apart from exceptional cases, does not extend beyond that Christian's contemporaries; the collective mediation of the Church is universal with a relative universality—relative because it is fully valid only for the age in which the Church is fully formed, the eschatological age which is ours since Pentecost, and secures only a part of the graces bestowed on mankind, on all the men of this age; finally, the personal coredemptive mediation of the Virgin Mary is absolutely universal, in the twofold sense that it extends to all people of all the ages and that it secures for them all the graces which derive from the Redemption of Christ. The mediation of the Virgin Mary is therefore anterior and all-embracing in relation to the coredemptive mediation of the Church. She is coredemptrix for the foundation of the Church.[76]

Having thus pinpointed the object of the coredemptive mediation, one can therefore say that the mediation of Christians, of the Church, and of the Virgin Mary, is preceded, originated, and sustained by the one redemptive mediation of Christ.

This brings us to the problem of its basis and, consequently, of its designation. The coredemptive mediation is itself completely borne by the one mediation of the redemption. If the Christ-Head is Redeemer, and if there is a symbiosis between the head and the body, then it must be said that the Church is coredemptive and that, in the measure to which a man becomes a member of Christ and of the Church, he is called to be a coredeemer. To deny this would be to deny the solidarity between the Christians, the Church and Christ.

More profoundly, "the coredemption is to the redemption, the co-merit is to the merit, as participation is to the source—i.e. a taking from without contributing—and as the being of the Universe is to the Being of God: after the creation, say the theologians, there is, intensively, no further being *(non est plus esse)*, there is only a multiplicity of participants in being *(sunt plura entia)*."[77] The doctrine of the ecclesial, individual and collective co-redemption is therefore intimately linked with the ontology of participation. This leads Cardinal Journet to write: "To reject the idea of our coredemption in Christ, through fear of derogating from the redemption of Christ, is not to honor but, on the contrary, to dishonor deeply that redemption. To question the relevance of co-redemption in Christ, on the grounds that the redemption of Christ is sufficient, amounts to challenging the relevance of the being of the universe since the Being of God is sufficient."[78] It is equivalent, therefore, to refusing to accept the design of the Creator-God, and consequently, the design of the Redeemer-God which is one and the same.

To conclude this brief account of Journet's synthesis, we give a concrete illustration involving Jesus, Monica and Augustine, used by this author.

Jesus directly redeems Augustine and Monica, but He arouses the tears of Monica which He unites with His Passion. First and foremost, Augustine's conversion is fully and condignly merited by Christ; and secondarily and *de congruo*, it is fully co-merited by Monica. Augustine's conversion is dependent on the prayers of Monica, these prayers being in turn dependent on the prayers of Christ on the cross. Let it not be said that Monica has contributed nothing; but neither let it be said that what she contributed was not contributed by Christ.[79]

This is a telling illustration, especially if one compares it with that of Stephen, who died after having prayed for Saul, his persecutor (Acts 7, 58. 60; 8, 2-3). It is sufficiently clear that the author of Acts meant us to see in Stephen's prayer a cause of Saul's conversion. Saint Augustine clearly pointed this out.[80] This shows how the coredemptive theology of Saint Paul in his pastoral Epistles, is rooted in a personal experience on which he has reflected in the light of the Spirit. Paul, beneficiary of the prayer of Stephen, would naturally and supernaturally have been led to encourage the Christians to pray for one another (2 Tim. 2, 1-4).

This ends our parenthetic remarks, which were intended to remind us of the basis in Revelation of certain aspects of the doctrine proposed by Cardinal Journet. What about the other subjects?

His justification of an individual and ecclesial coredemption through the intercession of merit and of satisfaction, and also of the term "coredemption" itself, is a solid one. Vatican II, thirteen years after the publication of his *Eglise du Verbe incarné*, has added to the Cardinal's thesis: "No creature could ever be classed with *(connumerari)* the Incarnate Word and Redeemer"—a point which the Cardinal, in line with many theologians, has stressed by carefully distinguishing between coredemption and the mediation of the one Redeemer. "But . . . the unique mediation of the Redeemer does not exclude but rather gives rise among creatures to a manifold cooperation which is but a sharing in this unique source."[81]

Let us add, in the light of what Father P. M. J. Nicolas O.P. has written, certain ideas which link up with the attitude of Vatican II: if one may speak about the Christian's cooperation in his own salvation and in that of his brethren, then why not call him a co-redeemer? What difference is there between the phrase "cooperation of the Church in the (subjective) redemption" of the human race, and the term "coredemptive Church"? The latter term would be ambiguous only if it decisively implied the idea of a "second redeemer," instead of clearly designating a salvation contributing to the redemption of others. "The whole Church," this theologian explicitly adds, "could be called coredemptive because it cooperates in the redemption of men, not only as instrument of the grace of Christ, but also by its own sacrifice."[82]

Saint Paul seems to have been little disturbed by the hesitancies which partly hinder even so great a theologian as Scheeben.[83] An inborn sense of analogy enabled Paul to affirm both that Christ is our Savior and that Timothy must save himself and save others (2 Tim. 1, 10; 1 Tim. 4, 16). He multiplies words containing the prefix "sun" (co-) to describe our intimate association with Christ (Gal. 2, 19; Eph. 3, 6); and it is simply because, although he often speaks of the Redemption, he nowhere refers to Christ as Redeemer (both *redeemer* and *redemptive* being absent from his vocabulary), that he has never called Christians "coredeemers," as he would no doubt have done had he spoken of Christ as "Redeemer." Though Paul does not use the words "Redeemer" and "coredeemer," he was well aware of the realities they express, as we think we have abundantly shown.

Highly controvertible, on the other hand, it seems

to us, in Cardinal Journet's synthesis, is the explicitly stated idea that Christians merit only for a part of mankind and not for the whole human race. We cannot see the reason for such a limitation. Does not the language of the saints, as well as that of the Church itself, demand a broader view?

If, in her letters, Saint Catherine of Siena considered herself to be guilty of the sins of all men (deprived, by their resistance to grace, of the efficacious graces which would have preserved them from sin), did not this imply that she could also merit *(de congruo)* for all men the outpouring of the treasures of the Redemption?[84] Is it not this which the Church implies in the formula which, for centuries, followed the sacramental absolution, and which may still be used today? "May the Passion of our Lord Jesus Christ, the *merits* of the Blessed Virgin Mary and *of all the saints* . . . contribute to the pardon of your sins, increase grace within you, and bring you to eternal life." If therefore the merits of all the saints, including those of the pre-Christian era, obtain subjective redemption, temporal and eternal, for me, why may not I contribute personally to the salvation of all the men of every age, and be to all of them, through my prayers and my merits in Christ, a co-redeemer?

In short, we find no warrant, in the sources of Revelation or in the documents of the Magisterium, for not extending the time-space universality of the influence merited by Christians, by men of a given time and a given place, to the benefit of the subjective redemption of all men. On the contrary, what we find in these documents would lead us to uphold such a universality: we are thinking in particular about the dogma and the mystery of the Communion of Saints, as Pius XII presents them in the encyclical *Mystici Corporis:* ". . . all prayers, even those said in the most private way, have their dignity and their efficacy, and are also of great benefit to the whole mystical Body; for in that Body there can be no good and virtuous deed performed by individual members which does not, through the Communion of Saints, redound also to the welfare of all."[85] While noting that Pius XII indicates no limitation ("the welfare of all," without any qualifications of space or time), we also observe, in developing the ideas proposed elsewhere by the same Pope[86] and by Leo XIII,[87] that this coredemptive vocation of each Christian for the benefit of the whole Communion of Saints is best fulfilled through the eucharistic communion in the immolated Body and Blood of the one Redeemer.

Furthermore, according to a happy distinction suggested by Msgr. Gay, all Christians, by fulfilling the particular and present wishes of God concerning their personal lives, cooperate in fulfilling God's general and universal wish, that is, the recapitulation of all things in Christ (cf. Eph. 1, 10). Every man in a state of grace merits *de congruo* the salvation of all mankind, precisely because he cooperates with the will of God which is fulfilled by the redemptive and recapitulative Incarnation. That Vatican II itself puts forward a similar argument, can be seen by combining two separated statements made in *Lumen Gentium:* "All just men . . . will be gathered together with the Father in the universal Church. . . . It has pleased God, however, to make men holy and save them not merely as individuals without any mutual bonds, but by making them into a single people. . . ."[88] One readily deduces from this that all the elect reciprocally sanctify and save one another, through the grace of Christ which is both redemptive and coredemptive.[89]

As we have already hinted, this theological vision is in harmony with the modern emphasis on the intrinsically social nature of man.[90] It is even in profound harmony with the Thomist doctrine of the human personality: the latter becomes fully itself only by knowing and loving, as much as possible, all other created persons. Universal inter-subjectivity is the bond constitutive in some sort of every created person. We would emphasize that this philosophical view takes on its full significance when seen in the light of its theological extension, which seems to us to be at least intimated by Revelation, and which reason, reflecting in faith, is free to affirm: namely, that every created person is called to participate in the salvific mediation of Christ, who desires to bring all others to the vision and love of His Father. If the person is, initially, a projection vision and love of His Father. If the person is, initially, a projection of knowledge and love by all the others, is not this because their loving vision in God is an aspect of his own salvation, just as he receives a mission to complete them by leading them to this same vision?

In our view, it seems impossible, therefore, to deny this universal coredemption of all by all (a coredemption from which the damned are freely, actively, and passively excluded),[91] without denying the universal vocation, at the twofold level of nature and of grace, of the human person redeemed by the incarnate Word. The Christian, called both to the beatific vision and to the coredemption of the other elect, answers this divine call by making satisfaction in Christ for the just, by praying, and by meriting *de congruo*[92] for mankind of all the ages without exception. The supernatural activity of each human person reaches out, therefore, to the utmost limits of space and of time. Every man is, in Christ, with Him, through Him, and for Him, an agent of the sacred and universal history of the human race.

A twofold objection might, however, be raised at this point. Would not this necessarily involve a total rejection of the idea that the Mother of God has a privileged coredemptive mission; and would it not reduce the coredemptive mission of the Church, Spouse of the Redeemer, to the sum total of the coredemptive missions of its members?

Such conclusions do not follow from the principles we have laid down.

In the first place, it is not certain that the individual or ecclesial coredemption obtains for each person all the graces he receives, even if it is true that it contributes to the salvation of each and every human person. Such a consideration, derived from Cardinal Journet, seems right and proper to us; but we could not insist too much on this aspect of the matter, because of the quantitative appearance of the argument. If it is true that Mary is mediatrix, not only of the divinization of all justified persons, but also of each of the graces received by each one of them, it seems to us even more correct to say that the privileged character of her mediation derives above all else from the fact that she alone has cooperated immediately in the realization itself of the objective Redemption; whence her privileges in the mystery of the subjective Redemption.[93]

We can answer the second objection in the light of the doctrine developed by Father Semmelroth at about the same time as Cardinal Journet was working on his. This difficulty will even provide the opening for a brief discussion of this German Jesuit's ideas about the mystery of the redeemed and coredemptive Church.[94]

The whole Church is coredemptive because it receives, as a whole unit, the fullness of the grace of the Redemption, and distributes it to the individuals who are incorporated in the Church. For the Church is not just the sum total of the redeemed: to maintain the opposite would be to explain the community from the needs of the individual. As the Mystical Body of Christ, the Church is mediative for its members; it is so by the very fact that it inserts men into its community of supernatural life filled with the Pleroma of Christ, and, as the vine does to its branches, communicates to them its life, which is the life of Christ.[95] The Church is mediative, not as a third party, but because as a whole unit it carries the fullness of graces within itself, and the individual participates in that fullness as a member of the Church. Mary is the Church subsisting before all its saints and all its individual members; she is the reality of the idea of the Church as humanity redeemed and coredemptive. It is in the mystery of Mary, mother and super-eminent member of the Church, that the mysterious anteriority of the Church in relation to its members shines forth.

One is thus led to declare that the Church has been redeemed only in order to be coredemptive: "the activity of God in the Redemption consists precisely in enabling humanity to act for itself, to be coredemptive because redeemed."[96]

In this light, we can more deeply understand the great ecclesiological concept of Vatican II: "the Church is the sacrament of salvation," to which we have already alluded. For the Council, this concept means, not only that it is in the Church that we find salvation, but also that it is as the privileged instrument of the Redeemer-Christ that the Church saves us. Far from being confined merely to signifying the Redemption, the Church instrumentally effects salvation at the same time as it symbolizes it. We believe that "the Church, sacrament of salvation" represents a stage which can lead on to a clearer affirmation of the coredemptive Church—Eve actively associated with the second, new and final Adam—on the part of a magisterium which itself participates in this mission of sacramental instrumentality.

It is as contributing to this idea that we interpret the thought of Father Guy de Broglie, even though, to our knowledge at least, he has not investigated in depth this very rich concept. On the horizon of his thought one sees, however, the dawning of the idea of a coredemptive Church regarded as the primary and immediate purpose of the Word in becoming man. The sacrament of salvation appears as the *raison d'être* of the creation He comes to save:

> The Word has come to save us in virtue of our association with His own renunciations and of their continuation in our lives. . . . Christ (is) the Word made flesh in the race of Adam in order to save that race by a life of expiatory renunciation, itself continued and completed by that of His faithful—in order to have that race

by means of the participation of redeemed humanity in His own expiatory renunciation.[97]

The author is, of course, concerned primarily with a personal coredemption, but there is no reason why this text should not be applied also to the social and ecclesial form of this mysterious coredemption.

We can see taking shape, therefore, an acceptance among a certain number of theologians, to which number we could add Father M. de La Taille,[98] of the doctrine of the redeemed and coredemptive Church. Already sufficiently indicated by Saint Thomas Aquinas, it has been clearly expounded by Journet, Semmelroth, and in a lesser way by Mersch and de Broglie. More investigation would no doubt show that a number of others subscribe to the idea. Father N. J. Nicolas has already helped to spread it, his ideas finding an echo in J. Maritain, Thomist philosopher and mystic. The latter expresses as follows his conviction about the future of the idea of coredemption:

> The idea of co-redemption is in fact as old as Christianity and the Mass. It is merely because it merges absolutely with the Christian faith in the redemption that it has taken so long to emerge explicitly (in the late Middle Ages and the subsequent centuries,[99] and above all to find itself denoted by a special word (during the past fifty years, I believe) and conceptualized in an articulated theological doctrine (with the element of controversy which is never lacking in such cases). The word is now completely accepted in the Church[100]. . . . . And it is in accordance with the views expressed by Father Nicolas, I have no doubt, that doctrinal unanimity in question is not for today, it is surely for tomorrow.[101]

Will the Church of the future confirm the views and the desires of Maritain? This is certainly possible for a number of reasons. The Church of Vatican II has established a deeper dialogue with the world; in the words of a celebrated English theologian and philosopher, the Church "has spread out its arms to the world to be crucified by the world." The post-conciliar Church appears as crucified by a new form of persecution, partly unknown in the past: that of a false public opinion, not informed but deformed, both within and outside the Church, by the modern media of communication. It sees its magisterium, its authenticity, its discipline, flouted by many of its sons. Like Christ in Gethsemani, it is experiencing the partial failure of its coredemptive work, and, in the midst of this bitter awareness, it is renewing its faith in the indefectibility of the work of purfication which its glorfied Redeemer accomplishes within it through this persecution. Conscious of the need to continue using fully the modern media for purposes of preaching the Gospel, it cannot but become ever more concerned to immolate itself and to sacrifice itself in union with its Redeemer for the salvation of its persecutors within and without. Faced with the partial failure of the yet necessary use of natural means, it will come to see more clearly the ever necessary need to resort to the supernatural means of its coredemptive mission and, consequently, to clarify its own mission of the breadth of that mission.

It seems to us, however, that two doctrinal investigations in depth could condition the triumph within the Church of the doctrine of coredemption in its various complementary aspects. Is not an effort of thought still needed if we are to secure a better grasp, in so far as this is possible, of the mystery itself of the Redemption? How, on the other hand, could one dissociate the coredemptive mission of the Christian, and especially that of the Church, from their temporal and cosmic repercussions?

We should point out that, despite numerous allusions in Trent and other documents, the extraordinary Magisterium of the Church has not as yet offered us a global view of the mystery of the Redemption,[102] or of its temporal and cosmic consequences.[103]

The Church has never ceased to bow down beneath the Cross of its Savior. In order to become more clearly conscious of its coredemptive mission, it needs to gain a better knowledge of its Redeemer. The mystery of the cross of Christ remains unfathomable for His Spouse; but it is by associating itself more and more with this mystery that the Church will perceive its unfathomable riches. "He who does what is right comes to the light that it may be clearly seen that his deeds have been wrought in God" (Jn. 3, 21). It is by intensifying its coredemptive activity that the Spouse of the Lamb will discover more clearly the basis—the cross of Christ—and the intimate nature of its coredemptive mission, as well as the universal irradiation of that mission.

It is therefore the increase in the love-inspired suffering of the Church which is our principal reason for thinking that it will recognize itself more and more as coredemptive. The continual renewal to which Christ calls it is an ever more painful purification the nearer the Spouse draws to the end of her pilgrimage towards the Redeemer. In this very purification, the Church will recognize more clearly the coredemptive calls of its crucified and glorified Lord. In this light, seeing that sin has injured the temporal without intrinsically corrupting it, and aware of the danger of idolatry of the temporal or "chronolatry," the Christian will transform his temporal activity with saving love. "The temporal is an injured reality which the Christian should love with a redemptive love," writes Mouroux.[104]

The doctrine of the coredemptive Church, far from detaching the Christian from temporal action, is on the contrary the condition of a deeper, more humanly and divinely efficacious, more lasting, and more universal engagement of Christians in modern society. For, by its divine mission, the Church is coredemptive of the temporal, and each of its members participates, in his fashion, in this vocation; whereas the rejection or obscuring of a coredemptive ecclesiology would imperil the full completion of the creation. The Redemption does not destroy the creation, but completes it. Indirectly, but in a real way, the Church is the sacrament of the redemption of the temporal, through its being directly and immediately the sacrament of the salvation of men.

Furthermore, temporal action entails an endurance, a necessary passivity. For that reason also, it should be integrated in the mysterious coredemption which is the Christian's vocation. Teilhard was very conscious of this point, and even went so far as to recognize the value of sickness for the construction and for the health of the world:

> In suffering is hidden, with an extreme intensity, the ascensional force of the world. The important thing is to liberate it by giving it an awareness of what it signifies and what it can do. Ah, what a leap would not the world make towards God, if simultaneously all the sick turned their pain into one shared desire that the Kingdom of God should rapidly mature through the conquest and the organization of the Earth. All the suffering ones of the Earth uniting their sufferings in order that the pain of the World should become one great act of awareness, of sublimation and of union—would not *that* be one of the highest forms that the mysterious work of the Creation could assume for us?[105]

In a very real sense, every Mass provides the answer to Teilhard's wish, as much as the "suffering ones of the Earth" freely will it to do. It is the co-oblation of all the abnegations synthesized in the sacrifice of the Son of Man. The Mass is at once the sacrifice of the Redeemer and the coredemptive oblation of all the redeemed, the salvation of the temporal and of the cosmos as well as of men. It is in the Mass that the Church is supremely expressed as the co-redemptive Bride of the Lamb.

C. Conclusion: The Church with the Chalice at the Foot of the Cross

Let us attempt to summarize the results of our research.

The Lord Jesus, Son and Savior of Mary, redeems, not without its cooperation, the Church, the new Eve born of His pierced side.[106] To the extent to which sinful humanity so desires, He makes of that human kind His immaculate Church, His cooperator.

Through this Church, as voluntary instrument and sacrament of His work of redemption, He applies to men the salvation which He alone won for them on the cross. Through this coredemptive Church, Christ continues to save the world, to the point of making every man of good will a sharer in the universal coredemptive mission of His one Spouse.

At the summit of the pyramid of coredemption, Mary Immaculate cooperates in a unique way in the Redemptive Incarnation and in the foundation of the Church.[107]

Half way up the pyramid, the Church, by its public prayer and its universal sacrifice, cooperates in a much richer way than do all its sinful members in the redemption of each human person.

Constantly emerging at the basis of the pyramid, comes the one who is baptized sacramentally or by desire. His co-redemptive prayer sends out its effects to the extremities of the past and of the future. He thus contributes to the salvation of every human person, just as he himself is saved by the efforts of all the men of good will gathered together by the Son of Man.

Like Him, he saves himself[108] and he saves the others by his loving suffering, by the oblation of his death, in accepting the separation of his soul and body, a separation resulting from his sin, and then their eschatological reunion by the all-powerful transpierced hand of the New Man who is the Life and the Resurrection of the human race.

The mystery of the coredemption is a paschal mystery. Christ, our Pasch (1 Cor. 5, 7) makes every person who is baptized in His blood and in the Fire of His Spirit, a paschal coredeemer.

The one Pasch, the Redeemer, through all the coredeemers, causes the "passing away" of "the form of this world" (1 Cor. 7, 31) which their suffering leads towards "a new heaven and a new earth" (Rev. 21, 1).[109]

Through them also, He renews the face of His Church, ceaselessly washed by the tears of the saints. Through them, above all else, the Church is its own coredemptrix, and, redeemed by the Church, they are redeemed to the point of being coredeemers, in a reciprocity which, however, remains unequal.

The Church is the coredemptrix of Christians, to whom she mints the treasures of the Redemption. The coredemptive Church is the assemblage of the people of God, including its hierarchic and visible heads. The Christian manifests his gratitude to the Church by in his turn saving the Church. It is through him that Christ continues to save the Church. But the reciprocity is of an unequal kind, because the Christian has much more need of the Church than the Church has of him. And yet it remains true that each Christian should save the coredemptive Church.

Saint Catherine of Siena very clearly saw this truth, rooted in the mystery of the Eucharist. Urs von Balthasar has clearly summarized her Eucharistic and coredemptive ecclesiology as follows:

> With Saint Catherine of Siena, the idea of the Church finds its source in the ever renewed shedding of the blood of the cross, which on every occasion accomplishes within the Church a new expiation, sanctifying a new presence of the Bride at the death of her Spouse. Catherine is simply a superior and more personal type of this eucharistic piety which, in writings and in pictures, presents the Mass as "the mysterious wine-press," as the "vine," in the devotions to

the manifestations of the Heart of the Lord, in the cult and the representation of the Church as issued from the wound in Christ's side, which is at the same time the Church with the chalice at the foot of the cross, collecting the blood flowing from the wound.[110]

Issued from the pierced side of the Lamb, the Church is the redeemed Spouse; standing at the foot of the Cross and holding the chalice in which she receives and preserves the Blood which flows from this side, she is the coredemptive Spouse, thirsty for sufferings and humiliations[111] which she drinks with this Blood, for the salvation and for the life of the world. Will it be the mission of an eventual Vatican III to give full precision to the doctrine of the redeemed and coredemptive Church?

NOTES TO CHAPTER ELEVEN

1. Cf. O. Cullmann, *Christology of the New Testament*, London, 1959, p. 290; and pp. 152-164.

2. Cf. Jn. 19, 5 and, 27.

3. Cf. J. Ratzinger, art. "Substitution," *Encyclopédie de la Foi*, Paris 1969, t. IV, pp. 267-277.

4. Cf. J. Gnilka, art. "Rédemption," *Encyc. de la Foi*, IV, 9-13; however, Father J. Galot S.J. points out that Redemption signifies "freedom through a ransom" (cf. Gal. 3, 13; 4, 5)— which, he adds, in no way contradicts the free quality of the divine pardon: "God supplying the ransom by delivering Christ to death." The author concludes: "Thus are harmonized, in Christ, the two ideas of freedom through ransom and freedom freely given" (*Rédemption, Mystère d'Alliance*, Bruges, 1965, pp. 16-18). The idea of salvation does not imply that of ransom; whence the greater precision of the idea of Redemption.

5. Cf. Louis Bouyer, *Les deux économies du gouvernement divin, Initiation Théologique*, t. II, Paris, 1952, pp. 510-513 and 532.

6. Clearly, the expression goes beyond the author's idea: only the glorious resurrection is "the full realization and final actualization" of what every man is. The author simply means that after death no spiritual and meritorious growth is possible and that death marks the limit of the freedom of the human will. Afterwards, there is no further potential in it.

But the expression cited here is tarnished with a certain unintentional idealism.

7. Another inexactitude of expression: what the author says would be correct did he add that, in the case of the Man-God, death is a transitive act; whereas His supreme immanent act is the activity of the beatific vision, accompanied by beatifying love. The decision of the sacrificial death is, in fact, inseparable from the love which accompanies the beatific vision. Cf. Jn. 10, 15; "as the Father knows me and I know the Father; and I lay down my life for the sheep."

8. E. Mersch S.J., *Théologie du Corps Mystique*, Paris, 1946², t. I, pp. 337-343.

9. Y. de Montcheuil S.J., *Mélanges Théologiques*, Paris, 1946, p. 53.

10. M. J. Nicolas O.P., "La corédemption," *Revue Thomiste*, 1947, pp. 30-31. Cited and commented on by J. Maritain, *Le Paysan de la Garonne*, Paris, 1966², pp. 358-359. Father Nicolas is considering an idea of St. Thomas Aquinas: "Christus sustinuit omnem passionem humanam" (*Summa Theologica*, III. 46. 5).

11. See, e.g. *New Catholic Encyclopedia*, Washington, 1967, att: "Descent into Hell"; K. Rahner, *Theological Investigations*, II, 203-217; Danielou, *Théologie du Judéo-Christianisme*, Tournai, 1961. Father Rahner tends to neglect the value of the traditional teaching on this point, and, on the contrary, the Dutch Catechism unexpectedly corrects it, but without naming it.

12. *Summa Theologica*, III. 50. 4 (English Dominican Fathers' translation, pp. 344-345).

13. *Ibid.*, III. 50. 6. In our citation, we have integrated useful observations made in the *ad 1, ad 2,* and *ad 3* sections of this article. Here Saint Thomas is exploiting the idea of instrumental causality to which we shall return in Chapter Fifteen.

14. Cf. *Summa Theologica*, III.

15. Cf. DS, 901 (DB, 480): affirmation of the ecumenical Council of Vienne (1312) and of Pope Pius XII in his encyclical on the Mystical Body: AAS, 35 (1943), 219. Cf. S. Tromp S.J., *Corpus Christi quod est Ecclesia, t.* III, *De Spiritu Christi anima*, Rome, 1960, pp. 55-85. Strictly speaking, the point emphasized here belongs rather to the theology of Good Friday: the piercing of Christ's side did not occur on Holy Saturday.

16. Pius XII alluded to this truth in his paschal message of 1957: *AAS*, 49 (1957), 278. It presupposes, of course, that one admits the separation of soul and body as a fundamental aspect of death. This point has again been emphasized by Pope Paul VI in his profession of faith of 30 June 1968. The doctrine of the indissoluble unity between the Word and the

separated elements of His dead humanity, is very well expressed in the *Spiritual Exercises of Saint Ignatius of Loyola,* par. 219: "When Jesus had breathed His last upon the Cross, His body remained separated from His soul, but without ceasing to be united with the Divinity. . . . His blessed soul, also united to the Divinity, descended into Hell."

17. Cf. T. Mainage, *Religion Spirite,* Paris, 1921, Chap. 1; Bonaventura Kloppenburg O.F.M., *"O Espiritismo no Brasil,"* Petropolis, 1964², Chap. XIV.

18. Saint Thomas Aquinas, *Summa Theologica,* III, 53. 3.

19. Cf. Rm. 1, 4.

20. E. g., R. Troisfontaines, *Je ne meurs pas;* for E. Schillebeeckx (*Révélation et Théologie,* Brussels, 1965, p. 373), a "crypto-heresy" is involved here.

21. Cf. Saint Thomas Aquinas, *Summa Theologica,* III. 53. 2.

22. Cf. DS, 3020, 3043 (DB, 1800, 1818). It seems to us that, if not "in *recto*" at least "in obliquo," the Resurrection of Christ has been defined by the Church as having taken place on the third day.

23. AAS, 35, 1943, 220.

24. See an historical exposition of this question and of the development of Saint Augustine, in C. Journet, *l'Eglise du Verbe incarné,* Bruges, 1951, t. III, pp. 117-1120. The part of truth contained in the Augustinian retractions has been underlined in LG, 48: "For even now on this earth, the Church is marked with a genuine *though imperfect* holiness." Pius XII had expressed this more clearly still: "No one will have failed to notice that the Church militant and especially the civil society of man have not yet reached that full and absolute measure of perfection which answers to the wishes of Jesus Christ . . ." (Enc. *Haurietis Aquas,* par. 66).

25. The text cited here shows in the healing of Naaman the leper, the type of the future salvation of the Gentiles in the Church: *Exp. Evang. sec. Lucam,* IV, 50; PL, 15, 1627.

26. Saint Ambrose, *De poenitentia,* I, 31; PL, 16, 476.

27. Saint Ambrose, *De Virginitate,* VIII, 48; PL, 16, 278; cf. Journet, *op. cit.,* pp. 1116-1117 ("excursus VI sur l'Eglise sans tache ni ride").

28. Pius XI, enc. *Rite Expiatis,* of 30 April 1926, *Actes,* B. Presse, t. III, pp. 198-199.

29. Saint Catherine of Siena: *Dialogue,* t. I, Paris, 1913.

30. *Ibid.,* chap. 15 and 87, pp. 63-64 and 300.

31. Cf. LG, 2: Christ prepares this humanity to become the Church.

32. Cf. GS, 43. 6: "Although by the power of the Holy Spirit the Church has remained the faithful spouse of her Lord and has never ceased to be the sign of salvation on earth . . .": DS, 3013 (DB, 1794). We note here that reason alone, even without the light of grace which it does in fact receive, would

be capable of perceiving the divine origin of the Church.

33. Cf. Saint Ambrose, *Expositio in Ps. 118,* Sermo 17, no. 21; PL, 15, 447: "ipsa jam chartas quae diligendo Deum, ipsius et nomen acceperit, quia Deus charitas est," says the Milan Doctor speaking about the Church.

34. LG, 39; 8. 3 (Abbott, 65 and 24). "Ecclesia semper purificanda" signifies both that the Church must always purify itself and that it is at every moment purified by Christ and by His Spirit.

35. LG, 6. 5. The Church is immaculate because the grace of baptism is preserved by a great number of its members or regained by them through the sacrament of penance. This is the profound meaning of Eph. 5, 23-27. To deny this would be to deny the efficaciousness of the sacrament of baptism.

36. Paul VI, *Ecclesiam Suam,* 1964.

37. Cf. E. Schillebeeckx O.P., *Marie, Mère de la Rédemption,* Paris, 1963, pp. 82-82 and 96-97. The author shows how the Assumption is the culminating point of the redemption of Mary by Christ. The Church, like Mary, is redeemed in a "more sublime" way, because the grace of baptism makes her immaculate in order that she may be coredemptive. The differences should, of course, be also stressed: whereas the leprosy of sin has never touched Mary, it is a leprous mankind that becomes the Church immaculate in love (Eph. 1, 4).

38. See, e.g., Chapter One, C.

39. In this analysis of Saint Mark's Gospel, we are drawing on C. P. Ceroke, "Divinity of Christ in the Gospels," *Catholic Biblical Quarterly,* 24 (1962) 125-133.

40. Cf. Saint Peter Canisius, *Exhortationes Domesticae,* collectae a Schlosser S.J., Ruremundae, 1876, p. 19.

41. This point does not seem to have been dealt with by C. Spicq O.P., *Saint Paul, Les Epitres Pastorales,* Paris, 1947.

42. 1. Tim. 1, 15.

43. Cf. 2 Tim. 3, 12: "Indeed all who desire to live a godly life in Christ Jesus will be persecuted" Now, this must be so for all Christians. By offering up these persecutions, they will contribute to the salvation of their persecutors.

44. Cf. LG, 62.

45. Saint Thomas Aquinas, *Commentary on Saint Paul's Epistle to the Colossians,* I, 24; cited by Cardinal Journet, *L'Eglise du Verbe Incarné,* Paris, 1951, t. II, p. 401.

46. Commenting on the same text *(ibid.),* Saint Thomas Aquinas also shows the need to reject an heretical interpretation: "A superficial reading might lead one to suppose that the Passion of Christ is not enough to redeem us, and that the sufferings of others are added to it by way of complement. But this idea is heretical: the blood of Christ suffices for the redemption, and it would suffice for the redemption of even a multitude of worlds." However, Saint Thomas does not

explicitly make the distinction between objective and subjective redemption, a distinction which enabled Pius XII to throw such light on the doctrine of the (objectively) redeemed and (subjectively) coredemptive Church. It is in the light of this distinction that the Pope, in the same encyclical, shortly after the passage to which our note 48 refers, also explained Col. 1, 24.

47. AAS, 35 (1943) 213; DS, 3805 (Eng. trans.: C.T.S., p. 27).

48. AAS, 35 (1943) 244-245. (C.T.S., p. 60-61). Notice that the first of these two phrases of Pius XII shows the universal truth of the humble self-accusation of Saint Catherine of Siena (cf. note 29) which every Christian should take up on his own account.

49. Cf. Chapter Nine.

50. Pius XII, *Mystici Corporis,* AAS, 9, (1943) 245—C.T.S., p. 35. Earlier, Pius XII recalls a truth already taught by the council of Trent (DB, 938: the Church itself immolates the divine sacrifice.

51. Pius XII, AAS, 35 (1943), 221 cites this very beautiful text of Saint Clement of Alexandria, taken from the Stomates (VII, 2; PG, 9, 413) "ex hénos kai di hénos sozômenoi te kai sôzontes." It is therefore from Christ alone and through Him that we save others. Clements' language is in exact accord with that of Saint Paul in the Pastoral Epistles. We are both saved and saviors.

52. It would be highly interesting to draw up a synthesis of the doctrine of Pius XII on the redemption and the coredemption, in the light of the assemblage of his discourses and messages.

53. Notably in our chapters I, II, III, V, X.

54. LG, 30 (Abbott, 57).

55. LG, 33 (Abbott, 60).

56. AA, 16; cf. *Ad Gentes* 5 (Abbott, 507).

57. On the sacrifice of the Church, see Teixeira-Leite Penido, *O Mistério dos Sacramentos,* Petropolis, 1961², pp. 281-282. One can, however, understand the expression in two connected senses: the Church sacrifices *itself* in union with Christ, at the same time as it sacrifices and immolates its divine Head.

58. On this theology of martyrdom, see:

Karl Rahner S.J.: *Essay on Martyrdom, Theological Writings,* t. III.

Hans Urs von Balthasar: *Cordula ou l'Epreuve décisive,* Paris, 1968.

J. Daniélou S.J., *Essai sur le Mystère de l'Histoire,* Paris, 1953, p. 20: "A theology of martyrdom finds its place in the theology of history as an expression of the conflict between sacred and profane history. Martyrdom there appears as a higher form of the conflict with the powers of evil, as the summit of Christian holiness through transformation in Christ, and as an official promulgation of the Gospel to the representatives of the terrestrial city."

59. LG, 42. 2 (Abbott, 79).

60. LG, 8. 3 (Abbott, 23).

61. GS, 45. 1 (Abbott, 247).

62. GS, 43. 6 (Abbott, 243).

63. LG, 9. 2 (Abbott, 26).

64. GS, 43. 6: "the Church has remained the faithful spouse of her Lord and has never ceased to be the sign of salvation on earth . . ." (Abbott, 245).

65. Pius XII, *Mys. Corp.*, AAS, 35 (1943), 206-207: long before Vatican II Pius XII had already presented the Church, in this encyclical, as instrument of the Redeemer: "In the first moment of the Incarnation, the Son of the Eternal Father had adorned with the fullness of the Holy Spirit the human nature which was substantially united with Himself, that it might be an appropriate instrument of the divinity in the bloody work of the Redemption. In like manner now, in the hour of His precious death, He willed His Church to be enriched with the most complete gifts of the Paraclete, so that in distributing the divine fruits of the Redemption it might be an effective and never-failing instrument of the Incarnate Word" (Eng. trans., C.T.S., p. 21). In distributing the fruits of the Redemption and in meriting to distribute them, the Church does not cease to be an instrument of the Redeemer.

66. *Mys. Corp.*, AAS, 35 (1943), 205.

67. AG, 1.

68. AA, 16 (Abbott, 507).

69. AA, 5 (Abbott, 495).

70. LG, 48. 1.

71. It will be noticed that Father Mersch is not concerned here with the distinction between objective Redemption and subjective Redemption.

72. E. Mersch S.J., *Théologie du Corps Mystique*, Paris, 1946, t. I. pp. 351-356.

73. It should be noted that, in the nineteenth century, Father Ramière, by founding the Apostleship of Prayer, contributed decisively to the change of emphasis from a predominantly individual view of the coredemption to a more clearly social and ecclesial view of it. It is no mere coincidence that the principal editor of the encyclical *Mystici Corporis* was a Jesuit (like Ramière), Father Tromp; it will also be noted that th's encyclical highly praises the Apostleship of Prayer (AAS, 35, 1943, 245). Cf. our Chapter Three.

74. C. Journet, *op. cit.*, t. II, p. 323.

75. Cardinal Journet (*ibid.*, 328-329) rightly distinguishes between the imperfect coredemptive and the eminent co-redemptive members of the Church (the "honest fellows" and

the "perfect friends of God," of whom Tauler spoke). The mere existence of the latter is something more precious and more useful than all the activity of the world, Tauler added (*Sermons,* Paris, 1930, t. II, p. 247).

76. Journet, (*op. cit.,* 411, note 1) here cites Father M. J. Nicolas O.P.; cf. note 82.

77. Journet, *op. cit.,* p. 410.

78. *Ibid.* We have synthesized Journet's ideas as presented in *l'Eglise du Verbe Incarné,* t. II, pp. 321-334 and 398-421.

79. *Ibid.,* pp. 405-410.

80. Saint Augustine, *Sermo* CLXVIII, no. 6, and *Sermo* XLIX, no. 11 (cf. Journet, *op. cit.,* 324). It would be interesting to trace this theme in the Fathers of the Church: the salvific efficaciousness of Stephen's prayer for his executioners, in particular for Saul, and its role in the conversion of Paul. It would even be an easy task to do so, on account of the many homilies on Saint Stephen. Cf. J. P. Audet DSAM IV, 1 (1960) col. 1480-1481 (Art. Etienne).

81. LG, 62.

82. M. J. Nicolas O.P., *Théotokos,* Tournai, 1965, pp. 168-169. Note too, in this connection, that Vatican II says of the laity that they become in the apostolate "cooperatores conscii Dei creatoris, redemptoris et sanctificatoris" (AA, 16); the Council here comes very close to the actual expression "co-redeemers."

83. Cf. M. J. Scheeben, *La Mère Virginale du Sauveur,* Tournai, 1953, pp. 172-173: "The title, coredeemer, gives the impression of a coordination with Christ and a complementing of His power. One should use it only with the explicit qualification, *in a certain sense.*" It is true that Scheeben is talking about Mary, and does not seem to have had Father Nicolas' idea of "generalizing" the expression rather than suppressing it (*op. cit.,* pp. 168-169). On Mary's title of Coredemptrix, see R. Laurentin, *Le Titre de Coredemptrice,* Paris, 1951.

84. See notes 29 and 30 of this chapter. Elsewhere, the saint "regarded herself as the cause of all the evil done throughout the whole world" (*Dialogue,* vol. I, chap. 2); or again, "the occasion and the instrument of all evil. . . . Your people are in the grip of death, darkness envelops Your spouse, principally because of my crimes, mine and not those of other creatures" (*Ibid.,* chap. 13).

85. AAS, 35. (1943): "nihil recte a singulis membris perfici potest quod per sanctorum communionem in universorum quoque salutem non redundet." A clear expression of universal coredemption.

86. In connection with the Eucharistic thanksgiving in the encyclical, *Mediator Dei,* AAS, 39 (1949), 567.

87. DS, 3363 (a remarkable definition of the Communion of Saints).

88. LG, 2 and 9 (Abbott, 16 and 25).

89. Thus, presupposing the divinization of both, it could be said that the first men are coredeemers of the last ones, and reciprocally. This brings out the (in a sense) supra-temporal character of the human person, although the latter is rooted in history. One thus understands more clearly the full scope of the text of Clement of Alexandria cited by Pius XII: "from one alone and by one alone we are both saved and saviors" (see note 51 of this chapter).

90. See S. Tromp S.J., *Corpus Christi quod est Ecclesia,* t. II, *De Christo Capite,* Rome, 1960, p. 397. In the pages which precede and follow, Father Tromp deals in detail with the coredemptive Church.

91. We say *actively* because it is voluntarily that the damned have withheld themselves from the universal coredemption; and *passively,* in the sense that they can no longer benefit by this coredemption.

92. Cf. Y. M. J. Congar O.P., in a remarkably clear article of 1935, reproduced in *les Voies du Dieu vivant,* Paris, 1962, pp. 353-356. This doctrine of the Communion of Saints has been reiterated by the magisterium in the Constitution "Indulgentiarum doctrina" of Paul VI (1st January 1967).

93. We are here using, with modification, some ideas expressed on the occasion of a revision of M. J. Nicolas's book, *Théotokos* (Tournai, 1965) and published in 1968 in the review, *Science et Esprit* (Montréal).

94. Cf. O. Semmelroth S.J., *Maria, Urbild der Kirche,* Wurzburg, 1950.

95. *Ibid.,* pp. 47-48; 61-73. One could complete the answer given here, following Semmelroth, with the following from Journet: "The collective coredemptive mediation of the Church, it too, is measured by its fervor, which can diminish or intensify according to times and places. But always the fervor of the Church is greater than that of each of its members, for it is inspired by an *élan* which comes to it from Pentecost and which is carrying it forward to the great encounter of the Parousia" (*op. cit.,* p. 408). In the final analysis, this is explained by the fact that, as Pius XII points out in *Mystici Corporis* (Eng. trans., C.T.S., p. 51), "public prayer, as proceeding from Mother Church herself, excels beyond any other by reason of the dignity of the Bride of Christ."

96. Semmelroth, *op. cit.,* p. 42. For the preceding phrases, see Semmelroth, pp. 61-73 and 114.

97. G. de Broglie S.J., *Le principe fondamental de la Mariologie,* in *Maria,* t. IV, pp. 318-324, Paris, 1961.

98. M. de La Taille S.J., *Mysterium Fidei,* Paris, 1924, p. 648: "(Christus) universam Ecclesiam adscivit pro tanto sibi coredemptricem pro quanto Redemptionis beneficium non comparamus nobis nisi subofferentes redemptionis pretium:

adeo ut eo magis sit conredemptrix Ecclesia quanto largius est redempta, non uberiorem percipiens functum salutaris sacrificii quam ipsa sibi conciliat ac comparat."

99. See, however, note 80 and note 51.

100. It would be interesting to know when this word was first used with a meaning not exclusively Mariological.

101. J. Maritain, *Le paysan de la Garonne,* Paris, 1966², p. 362. In another work, *De la grace et de l'humanité de Jésus.* (Paris, 1967), pp. 33-45), Maritain has returned to the same theme. Here is a very fine passage from the latter work: "There is only one Cross, that of Jesus, in which all are called to participate. Jesus took upon Himself all sufferings and all sins, all the sufferings of the past, of the present, and of the future, gathered together, concentrated in Him as in a convergent mirror, at the moment when by His sacrifice He became . . . the Head of humanity in the victory over sin. . . . He has made all these sufferings meritorious of eternal life, holy and redemptive in Himself, and coredemptive in the Church, that is at once His Spouse and His Mystical Body. . . . Human suffering has not been abolished, because—through the Blood of Christ and the sorrows of Christ and the merits of Christ, in which they participate—men are with Him the co-authors of their salvation. . . . There we have the idea of the coredemption, which designates an absolutely essential reality of the Mystical Body. All are the redeemed and the coredeemers, both the sinners and the saints, the big flock of the poor stragglers and the small flock of the disciples" *(ibid.,* pp. 44-45). Maritain here expresses some profound ideas, which are, it is true, limited to personal coredemption: the latter is presented as the solution of the problem of evil, as the reason why the Christ-Redeemer did not abolish physical and moral evil; even sinners are coredeemers, and this is true at the level of the *de congruo* merit of the prayer of petition; finally, the expression "co-authors of their salvation" corresponds exactly with the Pauline language of the Pastoral Epistles, which we have already examined.

102. Although the Council of Trent has made many allusions to the mystery of the Redemption (cf. Chapter Nine), it has not given a systematic exposition of this mystery. The ordinary magisterium has dealt with it more methodically, in the encyclical *Haurietis Aquas* of Pius XII (1956). No doubt, the complexity of the problems involved explains the limited treatment of the mystery by the magisterium. See B. Lonergan S.J., *De Verbo incarnato,* Rome, 1964³, pp. 445-593.

103. Cf. LG, 48; GS, 39.

104. J. Mouroux, *Le sens chrétien de l'homme,* Paris, 1948, p. 20.

105. Teilhard, text of 1933, published in *l'Energie Humaine,*

pp. 61-66, and by E. Rideau, *la pensée du P. Teilhard de Chardin,* Paris, 1965, p. 497.

106. LG, 3; cf. the texts cited in note 15 of this chapter.

107. Cf. DS, 3914—3915; 3926.

108. Cf. Heb. 5, 7.

109. Cf. GS, 38. 1.: ". . . the new command of love was the basic law of human perfection and hence of the world's transformation" (Abbott, 236).

110. Hans Urs von Balthasar, *Cordula ou l'Epreuve decisive,* Paris, 1968, pp. 33-34.

111. Cf. the meditation of "the Two Standards" in the *Spiritual Exercises of Saint Ignatius of Loyola,* par. 146-147. The coredemptive Church frees mankind from the slavery of sin only by participating in the Passion and in the kenosis of Christ, meek and humble of heart. It offers salvation to the world only by paying the price of the tears of its confessors and of the blood of its martyrs.

12

THE MYSTERY OF HUMAN SEXUALITY
THE PRIESTLY CELIBACY OF CHRIST

Modern man encounters Christ and His Church in a variety of ways, but perhaps most often when he is confronted with personal problems involving sexual ethics.

However, it would be wrong to limit the Christian view of sexuality to an examination of the demands and the prohibitions of the Natural Law—which can also be called the law of Christ as Creator.[1] In addition, and indeed especially, this view must investigate the connection of these demands and prohibitions with the basis and central truth of the Revelation whose mediator and fullness is Christ.[2]

It is the theologian's bounden duty to examine how the consequences or the presuppositions of Christ's Revelation affect human sexuality. A theology is always situated in the context of a culture; it has neither the right nor the ability to ignore this culture,[3] even when the latter contains inadmissible ideas and practices which are a profanation of human sexuality, as is clearly the case in the present age.

But can we not go further? Can we not say that the men and women of our age will perhaps never grasp the value of Christ's Revelation for their existence, ex-

313

cept through coming to accept it as the light which suffuses and transforms the horizons of their sexuality? Is not this true even for those who have freely chosen a life of consecrated celibacy? Clearly, such abstention from active sexual life does not mean that such people lose the characteristic qualities, both physical and mental, of sexed beings.[4]

In this chapter, we deal therefore with three interrelated mysteries: that Christ is the creator and divinizer of human sexuality; that He redeems this sexuality by His priestly celibacy; and that, as judge, He rewards its virtuous exercise and its consecration.

A. Christ the Creator and Divinizer of Human Sexuality

Since He possesses with the Father and the Holy Spirit one and the same divine nature, Christ ceaselessly creates men and women *ex nihilo*. He endows them with immortal souls (which are sexless, but which "inform" a psychosomatic sexuality) and with sexed mortal bodies. The distinction between the sexes cannot be ascribed to blind chance, or merely to the evolution which would condition this distinction. In the final analysis, it is to be traced to a wise disposition of the Providence of the eternal Word for the human race in which He willed to insert Himself, and which He wills to conserve, with its own cooperation, precisely by means of this sexual differentiation.

God has never created an "a-sexed" human person: everyone is created with a definite sex. Like all material, psychological, or spiritual endowments, sexuality is the object of the Creator's deliberate choice and manifests His wisdom and His power. Every man's sexuality and sexual organs are constantly dependent upon God the Creator both for their existence and for their exercise. No sexual activity can occur without the help of the creative Word. The conceited man who so readily glories in his sexual "potency," can never in fact exercise it without the concurring assistance of Almight God. His vaunted sexual "potency" is simply an abyss of impotence by comparison with the omnipotence of Christ the Creator.[5]

This human sexuality, created by God, is an integral part of the human person. Vatican II speaks in the same breath of the sexuality of man (indoles sexualis hominis[6]) and of the mystery of man.[7] We may therefore legitimately speak, not only about a human sexuality specifically distinct from the sexuality of the brute[8]—a distinction discernible by unaided human reason—but also of a *mystery* of human sexuality which transcends the grasp of mere human reasoning.

In the present state of the human race as raised to the supernatural order—an order lost in the first Adam but restored in the second—it is mankind as a whole, but also each human person, that is a mystery, strictly so called,[9] both in regard to the body as destined for a glorious resurrection, and in regard to the soul as called to the beatific vision.

The human body, at the resurrection, is to receive the beatifying effect of the completed divinization of the soul, fixed in the unchangeable vision and love of the Unchangeable. Since the body is sexed, it is absolutely impossible to deny the indirect divinization of sex and the direct divinization of psychic sexuality[10] through the raising up to eternal life. It may therefore be rightly said that human sexuality shares in the mystery, strictly so called, that is man himself.

This mystery of man remains impenetrable even after the mysteries of man's redemption and supernatural elevation have been revealed. It can, however, be really though not exhaustively grasped by the human mind in the light of analogy with realities man can know, and particularly in the light of its relation to the other revealed mysteries and with its ultimate and supernatural purpose.[11]

In this connection, some reflection on the different purposes of the sexual activity of divinized man will lead to a clearer understanding of what it is.

The immediate purpose of the conjugal act is to be the expression of love between marriage partners; its mediate purpose is the procreation of other human beings in order to propagate the race;[12] finally, its ultimate purpose is the glory of the Father and the Son in as much as They are joined together by the bond of their Love who is the Spirit. In other words, the ultimate purpose of the mystery of this sexual and psychosomatic love is the loving contemplation of the mystery of the purely spiritual love-union of the Father and the Son in the Spirit.[13]

But, in free response to a gift of this Spirit, the human person can choose to abstain from all sexual activity and to consecrate his or her sexuality wholly to God by virginity or celibacy. In such cases, the immediate purpose of this consecration is the good of the Church; its intermediate[14] purpose is the perfection of the consecrated person; its ultimate purpose is the glory of God.

By practice of the acquired and infused virtue of chastity, created and divinized man acknowledges in a concrete way the supreme dominion over his body and soul, over his psychosomatic sexuality, of Him who is both his Creator and his ultimate end. Chastity points him directly towards that end.

The natural law of chastity written by God in man's heart and strengthened and clarified by Christ, inclines and obliges man to seek the vision of God through purity of heart (Rm. 2, 15; Mt. 5, 8 and 27-28). The natural revelation of His natural law (cf. Rm. 2, 15 and 1, 20), like its confirmation by Christ, is merely a complement of the Revelation of the living God concerning Himself as Creator and Lord of the human body. It forms an integral part of the loving, salvific design of Christ as regards the human body. It is ordained to a redemptive revelation.

Lust, the idolatry of the body,[15] a manifestation and punishment of the pride of the spirit (cf. Rm. 1, 24-25), disregards at one and the same time the supreme dominion of the Creator, the aspiration and the "eager longing" of the body itself destined to be resurrected by the incarnate Word, and its ontological destiny to glory (cf. Rm. 8, 19-23; 1 Cor. 15, 21-22).

In every age, but especially today, lust is the most common form in which the practical atheism of many nominal Christians expresses itself: "They profess to know God, but they deny him by their deeds" (Tit. 1, 16). It signifies man's sub-human choice of a purely bestial sexuality, a deliberate dehumanizing of his sexuality (as much as this is possible), and, still more, a complete rebellion, psychic and somatic, against the divine plan to divinize human sexuality. It profanes and prostitutes what was made sacred: "Do you not know that your bodies are members of Christ? Shall I therefore take the members of Christ and make them members of a prostitute?" (1 Cor. 6, 15; cf. vv. 13-20). A sin against Christ's will to divinize human sexuality, it leads us to reflect seriously on the mystery of the Redemption of sexed humanity by the priestly celibacy of the Lord.

B. Christ the Redeemer of Human Sexuality by His Priestly Celibacy, Which Is Continued in the Church

When the Word came into the world to save the sexed humanity which He had created, the body He assumed was in the full sense a male body. In the body of the eternal Word, the sexual element is not only divinized; it can and must be said in the fullest sense that, hypostatically assumed by the Word of God, this human sexuality of a divine Person is adorable. Whereas lust wrongfully adores a purely human sexuality and dehumanizes it by such adoration, it is in Christ alone, come to redeem sexed man, that sexuality is adorable!

The human race had sinned above all else through an arrogant insubordination in sexual matters. Was it not proper, therefore, that the Redeemer should not only divinize human sexuality in a unique way by assuming it, but also that He should effect our salvation by means of a humble virginity unto death?

Everyone accepts as fact the virginal celibacy of

Christ. Very few, however, even among the theologians, have chosen to reflect on the celibacy of the Savior, to probe the nature, origin, and purposes of this celibacy, and to connect it with the mystery of the Redemption.

Why, then, did Christ choose to be a life-long virgin?[16] His is a mysterious celibacy. Was not Jesus a perfect man, perfectly capable of generating without the least disordered inclination, without the smallest imperfection? Furthermore, by instituting the sacrament of Marriage, did He not confirm that the exercise of sexuality is not only not sinful, but is good, holy, meritorious of eternal life? Why, therefore, did the Word choose to assume a sex and yet refrain from any sexual activity in the rigorous sense of the word?[17]

The mere raising of such questions is already sufficient to show how impossible it is to present Christ to the world today without answering them. They show us that the celibacy of Christ is not something to be taken for granted. It was not absolutely necessary; like His work of Redemption and the mystery itself of His Incarnation, of His divine-human being, it was the outcome of a free decision: a free decision which takes its place in the design of His redemptive Incarnation.

We believe there are two main reasons which explain this twofold and free decision, eternal and temporal, of the Word made flesh as a man among men. The Man-Jesus is the only Son of the Father become man in order to effect a Redemption which glorifies the Father.

As only Son of the Father, it was fitting that Jesus, in His humanity, should be only the begetter, spiritually, in the power of the Holy Spirit and in the weakness of a crucified flesh, of adoptive sons of the Father. Being in His sacred humanity purely Son in relation to a God purely Father, and member of a human race on whom His flesh was to confer, not a physical and mortal life, but an immortal participation in His unique divine Sonship, Jesus, come on earth to establish the universal family of God in the Spirit, could not restrict

Himself to the limits of one "family" in the ordinary sense of the word.

It was not fitting that the Son of the Virgin should physically beget a limited number of children, destined in their turn to continue His line; on the contrary, it was for Him to communicate spiritually, without any possible admixture, a participation in His divinely filial life to *all* mankind, including His own ancestors. Neither was it fitting that the same Son of God should be the Creator, the procreator and the New Adam or father according to the Spirit, of men who are His brothers; nor that the Spouse of the universal Church should be, according to the flesh, the husband of a particular woman. Christ's life style, virginal and poor, was designed to manifest His transcendence of the humanity among whom He fully took His place.

Christ's insertion into human kind was not only divinizing but also redemptive. Did not Jesus come to repair the original sin—a sin which, according to some of the Fathers of the Church, was formally a sin of pride and materially a sin of lust? However about this latter point, the life of Jesus, from the first moment of His virginal conception, was entirely dominated by His free decision to die crucified for our eternal salvation.

Saint Thomas Aquinas has set out clearly the concrete consequences of the redemptive purpose of the Incarnation:

> Here, then, was the design of the Son of God in taking upon Himself the nature of man: to show by His actions and His sufferings that men should despise temporal good and temporal evil lest, through a disordered love of temporal things, they diminish their attachment to spiritual things. . . . Christ has endured the weariness of labor, thirst, hunger, corporal punishments in order that we should not turn aside, because of the rigors of this life, from the good ways of virtue, by pursuing earthly pleasures and enjoyments.[18]

In view of the sensual pride by which man profanes his spiritual and physical being, it was supremely right that the Redeemer of human bodies and human souls, after having assumed human flesh in the womb of a Virgin and thus become part of a human family in order to save the whole human family,[19] should have remained a virgin throughout His life. It was not necessary, but supremely fitting—a distinction which shows the free nature of Christ's choice of celibacy.

Of course, in his sacred Humanity, Jesus could not experience any *interior* temptation to any sin of the flesh, or to any other type of sin. But He was perfectly man, able to feel all the normal sentiments which move the heart of a healthy man; and, at the same time, much more than can any other man, He was able to exercise natural control over the pleasures of the senses.[20] If, sometimes, "fallen man becomes bestial in the sexual act, not being able rationally to dominate his voluptuousness and the heat of concupiscence,"[21] this could not possibly have been so with Christ. Consequently, for Jesus—really and not just apparently man—virginal chastity signified a conscious sacrifice, a voluntary renunciation of an intense pleasure of the senses, specifically human and not merely animal, the offering up of an intense and lawful emotion of the heart. It was a free and non-necessary renunciation of an activity and a pleasure which are genuinely human but which, in their turn, are in no way necessary to a man's being fully man. It was a non-painful mortification; temperance and not continence.[22] Apart from this virginity, the Gospels mention no other mortification continued throughout the thirty-three years of the earthly life of Jesus. By affirming, at least implicitly, the virginity of Jesus, they show the prefiguration in act of the death and of the holocaust of the Redeemer.[23]

Yes, the virginity of Jesus "unto death" was a sacrifice which anticipated that death, a sacrifice in the most exact meaning of this word: a free and continuous act by which the Word consecrated to the Father the male sexuality assumed by Him and already on-tologically consecrated by virtue of the hypostatic union. The Son ceaselessly offered this sacrifice to the Father, without any pain, in perfect joy, in union with His future painful death, for the salvation of a sexed humanity which profanes the divinization of its sexuality.

This sacrifice was neither a destruction nor a muti-lation, but truly a consecration of the sexuality of Jesus. Far from being a renunciation by the Man-God of human sexuality, the celibacy of Jesus consti-tuted its salvific offering up for the world. Already made sacred by reason of the Incarnation, the human sexuality of Jesus—which, in Him, was never exclu-sively natural or profane, much less profaned—was further consecrated by a free and continual offering, issuing from the human love of His Heart.

After the death and resurrection of Jesus, His celi-bacy was no doubt understood by His disciples as an anticipation of His death.[24] Today we see even bet-ter perhaps that the virginity of Jesus unto death was an integral part of His redemptive sacrifice.

Jesus willed this celibacy, just as He willed to die scourged, crowned with thorns and crucified, in order to obey the salvific will of the Father. It constituted a free and voluntary acceptance of a mysterious and incomprehensible, but not unintelligible,[25] design of the Father which Christ saw directly through His hu-man intelligence but without being able to exhaust its intelligibility: the will to effect the salvation of mankind through His virginal and obedient death. He knew that the Father could have saved mankind by less difficult means, and that a single act of His own intimate love as the incarnate Son would have been sufficient.[26] He recognized and adored in the plan of the Father's wisdom its incomprehensible transcen-dence in relation to His human and finite intelligence, even though His intelligence was that of a beholder of the divine essence. Before being so for us, His priest-ly and sacrificial celibacy was already an ineffable mystery of love, an incomprehensible call from the Father, for Jesus Himself. And, on His part, there was a response to a call and to a vocation: "I have kept my Father's commandments and abide in his love" (Jn. 15, 10).

This celibacy of loving obedience was yet more free in that Jesus, faced with this wish of the Father, had, in his human will, no possibility of choice. More than any other of the blessed, Jesus as man was free because He secured perfect self-determination by accepting that determination from the Father: "The Father who dwells in me does his works."[27] Knowing perfectly the purpose pursued by His Father, i.e. the glorification of mankind, and identifying Himself intimately and totally with it, Jesus decided to embrace celibacy and death, not because His Father compelled Him to do so, but through a human impulse that was really spontaneous, without possibility of choice, but not without freedom. It was thus that He made His own, in His humanity, the divine choice of the Father.[28]

Christ kept very faithfully His Father's commandment concerning chastity, by consecrating to Him the sexuality which He never exercised. Above all, He offered to the Father His scourging, His crucifixion, and His death on the cross in reparation for all the sins of the flesh—or rather, for the sins of the carnal pride which profanes His work of redemptive divinization of human sexuality.

In this way, the virgin Priest of the New Testament superabundantly recompensed the Father for the crimes deplored by Saint Paul among his pagan contemporaries: not only adultery, but homosexuality (Rm. 1, 24-32). The Lamb of God merited for all people of all eras the actual graces required to observe His law, natural and revealed, concerning sexuality; and, first and foremost, to understand and to love this law.[29] He washed in His Blood all the profanations of baptized bodies.

In looking at the naked and virginal Christ on the

Cross, we are contemplating at once the fruit of human sensuality and the source of the chastity of a new humanity, participating anew in the divine holiness. In the pierced side of the Lord, we see, with the eyes of faith, the source whence there springs, with the blood of the Eucharist and the water of baptism, the sacramental grace of matrimonial consent as well as the grace of holy orders which prolongs the virginal and "virginizing" Sacrifice of the New Covenant. Does not priestly calibacy, too, spring from the Heart of the Lamb?

A glance at the crucified renews, indeed, our understanding of the law of priestly celibacy, the response of the Spouse of the Lamb to the evangelical counsel of perfect priestly chastity.[30]

Since the Priest-Lamb reserved to His spouse all the affectivity of His Heart, was it not fitting that this charismatic law of liberating freedom should be her response to a love as great as this?

Here we return to what we have written elsewhere,[31] in order to consider it at greater length.

The law of celibacy presents itself as a charismatic and liberating law. Presupposing the freely given gift of the free and definitive choice of consecrated celibacy, and the gift both freely given and merited of the continual renewal of this choice—a double charism accorded by the Spirit to certain people—the law of celibacy is itself a free gift which this same Spirit accords to the ecclesial society, both for its own common good and for that of all mankind called to be incorporated in it (cf. 1 Cor. 12, 7). The law of celibacy synthesizes and unifies the charisms of free choice and of fidelity granted to seminarians and to priests, and the charism of strong, humble, and loving ecclesial decision bestowed on the Vicar of Christ, virgin Priest of sensual mankind. Should it not be called a spiritual[32] and liberating law, a pneumatic law, a gift of the Spirit to all those incorporated in Christ crucified, to all those people of whom He is the soul and whom He wills to set more and more free from the slavery of the senses and of the carnal passions? Does it not enable the priest to render a more constant and more universal service to the holy people of God, to that Church that the priest espouses by renouncing carnal and sacramental marriage? Is it not this same liberating and unifying Spirit, the Breath of the immolated and triumphant Lamb, who prompts the candidates to a celibate priesthood, who fosters through the hierarchy the law of celibacy as a law of freedom (cf. Jas. 2, 12), and who inspires all the people of God to pray to Him for an outpouring of all these connected charisms?[33]

No doubt, the ministerial priesthood is not, by its nature, inseparable from celibacy, any more than the Incarnation demanded, in an absolute way, celibacy in the sacred humanity of Jesus. The law of celibacy is not necessary by absolute necessity; but it is a contingent act (and furthermore, a supremely fitting act) of a Church which is free to posit it as the Church is contingent in its own existence.

This law thus reflects the very structure of the mystery of Christ and of the Church, which structure it has as its purpose to validate. Is not the Incarnation a non-necessary act of a necessary God become a contingent man; and is it not freely that Christ has founded this contingent Church that is His *raison d'être*, precisely by being a virgin unto death, through obedience to the salvific and liberating will of the Father? Is not His celibacy as contingent as His earthly existence?

The universe, which perfects itself in and through the Whole Christ, need not have come into existence; and the same is true of Christ and His Church. All three, in their indissoluble unity, are a free gift of the Trinity which alone is necessary. The law, non-necessary but supremely fitting, the "holy and providential"[34] law of ecclesiastical celibacy, shares in the free nature of this triple gift: Christ, the Church, the universe.

He who freely accepts it, by offering himself to the Church to exercise the ministerial priesthood, imitates Christ who, on entering into the world (cf. Heb. 10, 5-14), offered Himself with love to the incomprehensible and eternal will of the Father as regards His celibacy and His death for the salvation of the world. More profoundly, Christ Jesus, invisible Head of the Church, Sovereign High Priest in Heaven, today adores the loving and unfathomable design of His Father concerning priestly celibacy in the Latin rite of the Church in our time, and accomplishes it in His members, through His Spirit. "This profound bond which, in Christ, unites virginity and priesthood, is reflected in those whose destiny it is to participate in the dignity and the mission of the eternal Mediator and Priest."[35] Does not the divine plan shine forth in greater splendor when the paranymph—whose duty it is to introduce the Spouse to the Lamb after having made her beautiful by clothing her "with fine linen, bright and pure," the fine linen being "the righteous deeds of the saints" (Rev. 19, 7-9), the linen having been "made white in the blood of the Lamb" (Rev. 7, 14)—refuses to "defile himself with women" and, remaining a virgin, is able more easily "to follow the Lamb wherever he goes" (Rev. 14, 4)?[36]

In short, it is because the Man-Jesus, through His sufferings and His death, was to be the Redeemer of human sexuality, that He assumed and integrated His priestly celibacy in His composite Personality, to offer that celibacy in sacrifice to the Father and to be the mediator of chastity for mankind. Jesus is at once the source, the model, the goal, and the beatifying joy of the celibacy of His ministers in the Church of today.

C. Christ, Judge and Rewarder of the Practice of Human Sexuality

Human sexuality is divinized by baptism, which constitutes its first consecration in the created person (corresponding to that effected in Jesus by the

Incarnation). Christ consecrates it still further by pouring into human hearts the charism of celibacy or the sacramental charism of marriage. The Man-God has insituted the sacrament of marriage in order to elevate, redeem, and heal the sexual activity of man with a view to the increase of His elect and for the glorification, through their divinized[37] sexual activity, of the sexed bodies of the predestined.

Creator, divinizer, and constant sanctifier (by His sacramental and actual graces) of human sexuality and of its practice, Christ will also be its judge and its eternal rewarder.

On the Last Day, the Lord Jesus, unjustly judged and condemned by human lust, will judge every man on the use he has made of his body and even of his psychic forces. For, is it not true that man's deliberation about the choice of an ultimate purpose[38] and man's basic choice for or against Christ, always shows itself, in a physical manner, in the legitimate use or in the abuse of sex or even in the total abstention from all sexual activity? In fact, there is no sexual behavior without religious significance. It is the sign of humble love of the Christ Creator and Redeemer of the body and of sexuality, or of proved rebellion against Him.

The Christ-Judge will eternally condemn the men and women who, continuously and to the end, have rejected His grace of contrition to purify their sensuality, thus flouting His Precious Blood. The sinner who adores his sexual disorders, freely and culpably condemns himself to eternal damnation.

On the other hand, Christ will raise up and reward the chaste bodies of those who have humbly submitted to His divine will. He will reward with eternal joys, both spiritual and corporal, all the sacrifices made in obedience to His divine law of chastity. Accomplished with the help of the sacramental graces of marriage, and informed by love, does not the conjugal act become, in a sense, a sacred act, a sacrifice? Is it not the matter of the consecration of the world which accompanies the Eucharistic consecration?[39] How could it fail to be rewarded by the greatest human act, the purely spiritual act of the beatific vision?—and by the immortal resurrection of a sexuality which transmits mortal life but cannot itself escape death?

Sexuality as such, envisaged purely and simply, is designed for the multiplying of individuals in order to secure the survival of the species; but human sexuality is destined, beyond all earthly finality, to undergo an incorruptible assumption in a definitively glorified body. It can be seen, therefore, that human sexuality can be called a mystery, strictly speaking, which exceeds the grasp of human intelligence: without any sexual activity, this sex will remain forever in the resurrected body, either ignominiously in the damned, or gloriously in the elect. Glorification or reprobation will not suppress the distinction between the sexes, any more than it will nullify human nature. Just like grace, glory will not destroy the animal nature of man, and much less its specific human qualities, but will perfect their divinization. Specifically human sexuality will be eternally glorified in "a great multitude which no man could number" of men and women "from all tribes and peoples and tongues." "Clothed in white robes, with palm branches in their hands"—symbols of their victory over impurity—they will sing night and day the victory over impurity of the virginal Lamb-Shepherd (cf. Rev. 7, 9-12; 7, 17).

Such endless glory of human sexuality is still to come[40] for the majority of the elect. Implicitly promised in the revelation of the future resurrection of the body, it is a gift of the omnipotent God which man is powerless to procure for himself by his own powers, just as his unaided reason cannot demonstrate its necessity. The faith which accepts and proclaims this gift humbles the carnal pride of man.

But in Mary, Mother of the Redeemer, and in the resurrected Christ, this permanent divinization of human sexuality has already been accomplished. The mystery of the bodily Assumption of the Virgin Mary is the glorification, at the physical level, of the immaculate[41] merits of her perpetual virginity, of her virginal marriage, and of her divine maternity—itself also virginal. The Assumption is the supreme glorification of a purely created sexuality, without any "horizontal" sexual activity involving bodily intercourse; it is at the same time the reward of the unique and "vertical" activity included in the virginal procreation of the Man-God. The sexuality which has given us eternal life could not remain in the bonds of death.[42]

The Resurrection of Christ is a yet more perfect glorification of human sexuality, alone adorable in Him in death as in life,[43] and henceforth assumed in the glory of the Father as were the wounds of His passion. Like the meals of the Risen Christ who had no need to eat,[44] His sexual condition, never to be lost, will manifest forever the truth of His Incarnation and the splendor of a kenosis which in Him alone has rendered adorable even the animality of man whom He came to save.

In Jesus and Mary, there shines forth the virginal and social destiny of human sexuality, an instrument of fraternal charity and a factor in intersubjectivity. The Saducees of all times deserve the answer of Jesus: " 'You are wrong, because you do not understand . . . the power of God. For at the resurrection they neither marry nor are given in marriage, but are like the angels in heaven.' And when the crowd heard it, they were astonished at his teaching" (Mt. 22, 29-33).

Christ could not have taught more clearly the absence of all physico-sexual activity in the life to come. Is "the crowd" today as favorably impressed as were those who heard Jesus? Certainly, for many people, hedonism, the special idolatry of our day,[45] kindles contempt for the promise of an eternally virginal life. No doubt, it is because the majority of men have, and will always have, some difficulty in recognizing the close link between, on the one hand, sex, generation, and death, and, on the other, virginal life and immortality, that Jesus added:

> The sons of this age marry and are given in marriage; but those who are accounted worthy to attain to that age and to the resurrection from the dead neither marry nor are given in marriage, for they cannot die any more, because they are equal to angels and are sons of God, being sons of the resurrection (Lk. 20, 34-36).

Plato said that the act of generation implies the desire for physical survival beyond personal death. The revelation of a personal resurrection could not fail to render yet more desirable an immortal virginity. But, whatever one may wish, there will be no sexual activity after the resurrection, either in heaven or in hell. The virginity of "that age" of the "sons of the resurrection" will ultimately bring to completion that project of total and universal communion of the saved which man and woman had sought here below in marriage, obscurely and partly in vain. The flesh, said Blondel, is a veil that conceals at the same time that it reveals! The virginity of the resurrected in Paradise will be a total communion and a reciprocal immanence among the elect, precisely because it will be an immediate union with the Father, the Son, and the Spirit, seen and loved in translucent souls and bodies: "Then the righteous will shine like the sun in the kingdom of their Father" (Mt. 13, 43). "It is sown a physical body, it is raised a spiritual body" (1 Cor. 15, 44). God being everything to every one" (1 Cor. 15, 28), each created person, human and angelic, will realize his deep-seated wish—to communicate, in light and love, according to the measure of his degree of union with the Absolute Good, with all the others fixed in immutable adherence to the three Persons of the uncreated and inseparable Trinity.

The meaning of the Savior's teaching on the heavenly

virginity of the "sons of the resurrection" who have been "accounted worthy to attain to that age," was admirably expressed by Saint Augustine:

> Knowledge and love are two goods, but love is the greater; because, says the Apostle, although it remains necessary in this life, knowledge will be destroyed, whereas love will never pass away. Thus it will be also with mortal procreation, the reason for marriage: it will be destroyed, whereas abstention from the use of marriage will continue forever.[46]

In other words, the historical discourse of marriage and of human generation will pass away; but virginity or continence, as anticipating the beatific intuition, will continue. Just as the discursive reasoning of human knowledge proceeds from the initial intuition of first principles and ends in the final intuition of the conclusion,[47] the long discourse of the sacred history of the human race proceeds from the call of God, author of marriage, chosen as their ultimate end by the marriage partners, goes through its phrases in succeeding generations, to culminate in the intuitive and merited vision of all the predestined descendants and above all of the Son of Man. The carnal discourse which passes away merits the virginal and imperishable intuition of the only Word who does not pass away. The conjugal act merits its own disappearance in the eschatological plenitude; but the love which penetrates it remains. "The world passes away, and the lust of it; but he who does the will of God abides for ever" (1 Jn. 2, 17).[48]

To this we may add that, to the extent to which sexuality determines the lower psyche of man or woman, at least in its concrete exercise (a view that seems to be generally accepted today), it is impossible to exclude a psycho-sexual activity of the elect, either before or after their resurrection. This is a difficult and obscure point, liable to be ill understood, but none the less true for all that. And, of course, what would thus be affirmed of the elect could not be denied in the case of the Virgin Mother of Christ and of that of Christ Himself. There could be no question, however, of a sexual activity strictly so called, but of the masculine or feminine coloration of the psychological activities of the resurrected person. Notably, one could not deny the permanence of affectivity in the immortal soul, and of an effectivity informed by love in the beatified soul; consequently, how could it be denied that the Heart of Jesus is the physical symbol of the affective love of a masculine being for sexed humanity? If the resurrected humanity of Christ is not a-sexed (which we must affirm to avoid Docetism), it is undeniable that His love for His brethren has a masculine quality, as that of Mary a feminine one. It is this physical and masculine love of the Heart of Christ which is the analogical likeness and the instrument of his twofold spiritual love, human and divine, for us.[49] In contemplating the sensible love of the *Man* Jesus for us, we are able to grasp the eternal love which the uncreated Word bears towards us, and to believe in it.

D. Sexuality, Celibacy, Eucharist, and Kerygma

Enough has been said to show that an investigation of the relations between sexuality and Christology is of interest, is novel, is difficult, but is needed. One of the advantages arising from the current discussions about ecclesiastical celibacy and about the Eucharist, might well be to invite us to such an investigation. In concluding, let us sketch a synthesis[50] of the Christian mystery by starting with priestly celibacy and human sexuality. Since both celibacy and conjugal chastity present problems in the Church and in the world, why not consider them, not as terminal points but as points of departure of the kerygma, of catechetics, and of teaching about the Faith? In the hope of stimulating more expert versions, we would suggest the following formulation:

Many people think that a man who does not marry, who has no children, is not really a man.[51]

The only Son of God has willed to save mankind by becoming man through the free consent of a girl whom He willed to be a virgin, before, during, and after He had been born of her according to the flesh. This only Son, Jesus, has, as God, instituted marriage, and, as God made man, has made it a means of salvation, and of eternal salvation. But He has counselled those who could hear and accept, to preserve virginity through love, in imitation of Himself. He did not marry or have children according to the flesh, though He could have done so; but by His virginity and His death He has begotten all men of good will to a divine, immortal, supernatural life. No one has been more perfectly a man or more human than Jesus, the Creator, Savior, Priest, and Judge of all men.

It is for the purpose of more effectively helping others to be fully men, that the priest, following Jesus, does not marry. To communicate the divine life, he renounces his right to transmit carnal and mortal life. He who marries and has children is a man, especially if he does so for the love of God; he who, for the love of Jesus and in order to proclaim that love to married men, does not himself marry, is yet more a man, because in this respect he is more like the perfect Man, Jesus of Nazareth. Jesus has died and risen from the dead in order that all men may die and be raised in Him and with Him; in order that here and now men may know that virginity is the surest way to indefectible self-identity, to more universal fraternal union, and to more definitive union with the Heart of Jesus.

Of this fraternal union and of this close union with Jesus, the Eucharist is the supremely efficacious sign as well as the most effective realization. The virginal bread of immortal virginity —that is the manner in which Christ presents Himself in the Eucharist.

Through the Eucharist, the Lord Jesus gives to all, including the married, His virginal body and His own chastity, in order that—through the growth of love and of mutual union which is the special fruit of this sacrament—all may be able to cultivate a chaste love. More than any other means, frequent and especially daily Communion effects the integration of sexuality with the whole Christian personality, either through the right use of that sexuality or through continence preserved as the expression of love. During the Mass, Christians offer themselves "as a living sacrifice, holy and acceptable to God" (Rom. 12, 1); they offer their bodies with their sexual activities or abstentions, their efforts to achieve a loving chastity, in union with the gloriously sexed body of the risen Christ.

They offer this chaste and personal sacrifice to the Father, in the Spirit, with the Church, in order to acknowledge the supreme dominion of the creative and redemptive Trinity over their created bodies; in order to give thanks for the gift of these sex-endowed bodies, for the graces of chastity designed to humanize and divinize them perfectly; in order to make reparation for all their sins of impure pride; and finally, to obtain, with chastity, the temporal sanctification and the eternal glorification of their bodies and of their sexuality.

Christians are those who believe that Christ will judge all sexual activity; who hope in Christ as the rewarder of their chastity; who, above all else, love with all the strength of their bodies and of their souls, the Heart of Christ, Savior both of souls and of bodies. Christians are therefore those who "speak upon faith in Jesus Christ," and who discourse "about justice and self-control and future judgment."[52] Through the Christians, God "now commands all men everywhere to repent, because he has fixed a day on which he will judge the world in righteousness by a man whom he has appointed, and of this he has given assurance to all men by raising him from the dead."[53]

NOTES TO CHAPTER TWELVE

1. Saint Paul speaks of the "law of Christ" (Gal. 6, 2) by which we are commanded to bear one another's burdens. The natural law being divine and Christ being God, it can be said that the natural law is the law of Christ. Just as the Redeemer did not come to destroy nature but to divinize it, so too the evangelical law does not suppress but perfects the natural law. One understands, therefore, how the Encyclical *Humanae Vitae* could say: naturalis quoque lex voluntatem Dei declarat, cujus utique fidelis obtemperatio ad aeternam salutem est hominibus necessaria" (par. 4); cf. Mt. 7, 21.

2. DV, 2: UR, 2: Christ is the basis of the Christian faith.

3. Cf. Paul VI: discourse to the international theological congress (1 October 1966): "Theologia . . . expendere debet hanc fidem in vitae actionem adductam ejusque proposita . . . ut solutionem proponat quaestionum quae oriuntur ab ejus comparatione cum vitae usu, cum historia atque cum humana invesigatione. . . . Ipsi (sc. theologi) diligenter interpretando universam nostrae aetatis mentis culturam atque hominum experientiam, contendunt eorum quaestiones perspicere atque dissolvere, luminis ope, quod ab historia salutis manat" (AAS, 58, 1966, 892). See also GS, 62. 7 where something of the same idea can be found; GS, 62. 2; 44. 2.

4. Cf. OT, 10. 3. Celibacy thus appears, not as something negative, but as the most perfect consecration of sexuality, when it is assured definitively by the love of Christ. Celibacy lived in the state of grace, but without the intention to continue indefinitely, would already be a certain consecration. Even marriage is presented by the Council as a consecration of sexuality (GS, 48. 2 citing Pius XI). In the present chapter, we make a distinction between *sex* (physical organ) and *sexuality* (a word which places the emphasis rather on psychological components). It is impossible to identify the lower psyche of man (sensibility, imagination) with that of woman: cf. note 6.

5. Cf. Saint John of the Cross, *Mount Carmel,* I. 4.

6. GS, 51. 3 clearly distinguishes between sexuality and the power to beget, and points out the superiority of both of these in man over sex and sexuality in the brute.

7. GS, 22. 1.

8. GS, 51. 3.

9. DS, 3005, 3016 (DM, 1786, 1796). Man is a mystery only in as much as he participates in "the final and ineffable mystery which surrounds his existence, whence he derives his origin and towards which he tends"—the mystery of the Trinity (cf. NA, 1. 3).

10. Cf. notes 4 and 6 of this chapter. In the strict sense, matter cannot be divinized, since it is incapable of knowing

and loving God. It cannot participate in the intimate operations of the divine life.

11. DS, 3016 (DB, 1796).

12. Cf. DS, 3836 (DB, 2295). The immediate purpose is a means in relation to the mediate purpose, the latter being a means in relation to the intermediate purpose and to the final purpose. The immediate purpose of marriage coincides therefore with one of its secondary purposes, while its mediate purpose is identical with its first purpose. The procreation and upbringing of children is itself, in a sense, directed to the propagation of the species: Cf. Saint Thomas Aquinas: *Summa Theologica*, II. II. 154. 2, commented on by G. de Broglie S.J.: "Pour la morale conjugale traditionelle," *Doctor Communis*, 21 (1968), 117-152.

13. Cf. Saint Thomas Aquinas: *Super Evangelium Joannis lectura*, Marietti, 1952, no. 2214 (in Jo. 17, 11 b). Certain theologians, such as H. Mühlen (*Der Heilige Geist als Person*, Münster, 1967²) rightly suggest an analogy between the generation of the child from two parents as from a single principle, and the procession of the Spirit proceeding from the two Persons of the Father and the Son as from a single principle, as defined by the Council of Florence (DS, 1301; DB, 691). We do not yet know how the majority of theologians will greet this view, which is so much in line with the principle of analogy in theology suggested by Vatican I (DS, 3016; DB, 1796).

14. In his encyclical on the Mystical Body of Christ, Pius XII emphasizes that the Church, like every society, is directed to the good of her members as persons, and not vice versa (as is the case in physical bodies: AAS, 35 (1943), 222; DS, 3810.

15. Cf. AA, 7: "In our own time, moreover, those many who have trusted excessively in the advances of the natural sciences and of technology have fallen into an idolatry of temporal things and have become their slaves rather than their masters." This is especially relevant to the domain of sexuality.

16. An expression used by Pius XII, *Sacra Virginitas*, AAS, 46 (1954), 167.

17. A distinction is drawn between physical sex and psychosomatic sexuality. Jesus willed to assume a masculine sensibility.

18. Saint Thomas Aquinas, *de Rationibus Fidei*, chap. 7.

19. Cf. the neatly worded statement by Saint Jerome: "Vindico Joseph virginem fuisse per Mariam ut e virginali conjugio virgo filius nasceretur" (*Adv. Helv.*, 19; PL, 23, 213). A more developed theological analysis of the significance of the virginal marriage of Mary and Joseph can be found in my book: *Le Coeur de Marie, coeur de l'Eglise*, Lethielleux, Paris, 1967, 25-26.

20. Cf. Saint Thomas Aquinas, *Summa Theologica*, I. 98. 2.

21. *Ibid.*

22. *Ibid.,* III. 7. 2. 3.

23. The Gospels affirm at least implicitly the virginity of Jesus, which is explicitly affirmed by Tradition. Like the Resurrection, the virginity of Jesus is, at once and under different aspects, an historical fact and a mystery. It is not a solemnly defined dogma, but could well become one. One can and should say that it is taught by the ordinary and universal Magisterium of the Church as an incontestable truth, forming part of the deposit of Revelation: it is therefore a non-defined dogma: cf. DS, 3011 (DB, 1792). The considerations here presented on virginity as the continuing sacrifice of Jesus, are partly inspired by G. Jacquemet, enc. *Catholicisme,* art. *"célibat,"* Paris, 1947, col. 763-769.

24. Cf. L. Legrand, M. E. P., *Le virginité dans la Bible,* Paris, 1964, pp. 60-61: "In Luke, Christian celibacy announces the cross."

25. Cf. Saint Thomas Aquinas, *Summa Theologica,* I. 12. 7; and Saint John of the Cross, *Spiritual Canticle,* VII, 4 and 9.

26. Cf. G. Broglie S.J., "Le principe fondamental de la théologie mariale," in *Maria,* t. VI, Paris, 1961, 326-331. Here the author gives a fine analysis of certain problems relative to the virginity of Christ. In a personal letter to the author, Father de Broglie criticized as follows a view of Suárez: "To maintain that, even apart from the hypothesis of the fall, celibacy would be more perfect because the conjugal act would, in any hypothesis, hinder the mind from fixing itself entirely on God, seems to me to be a vain subtlety. Besides the fact that we do not know in what very exalted way the union with God (mystical in form, it seems) could have dominated the life of man in the state of innocence, we should have, on Suárez' argument, to regard as contrary to perfection, all intellectual and physical occupations which in any way absorb the attention, since they too hinder us from fixing our minds entirely on God while we are doing them!"

27. Jn. 14, 10: cf. 10, 32.

28. We can say of the celibate vocation of Christ what Saint Thomas Aquinas says about the Father's commandment concerning the death of His Son: Jesus did not receive an order pure and simple to die, but to die for our salvation *Summa Theologica* III. 18. 5, 6 ad 3m). From this commandment of the Father there resulted an objective necessity which, however, did not hinder the freedom of Christ: choice or the possibility of choice is not essential to that freedom which consists in self-determination: cf. *Summa contra Gen.,* IV. 22: liber sui causa. With perfect knowledge of the purpose fixed by the Father, i.e. the salvation of mankind, and with complete and inner acceptance of this purpose, Christ decided to die, not under any violent pressure from the Father, but through a spontaneous and human impulse of His "voluntas ut ratio,

se determinans et causans" without option or choice: cf. *Summa Theologica,* III. 47. 2. 2. On this point, see B. Leeming, *Adnotationes de Verbo Incarnato,* Rome, 1936. The decision for celibacy is also a free acceptance of what was, on the Father's part, a choice, but was not so for the *human* freedom of Christ.

29. The divine law is fully observed only if it is understood by the mind and loved by the will, as Pope Paul VI points out in *Humanae Vitae* (par. 31).

30. While Christ offers to many the counsel of virginity (to which all are not called, however), we think we can speak in a more special way of a divine counsel of virginity made to those whom Christ calls to the priesthood, in those rites of the Church, in which the law of ecclesiastical celibacy exists: cf. OT, 10, PO, 16. For them, the evangelical counsel has a special quality by reason of the vocation to the priesthood; one can therefore speak of an evangelical counsel of priestly chastity.

31. Cf. B. de Margerie S.J., "La mystérieuse loi charismatique du célibat sacerdotal," *Revue eucharistique du Clergé,* Montréal, 70 (1967), 602-606; or again, we have dealt with certain connected aspects in another article: "Population mondiale, célibat du clergé et évangélisation sacramentelle," *Revue de l'Université d'Ottawa,* 36 (1966), 86-106.

32. Rm. 7, 14; cf. 7, 12.

33. Cf. 1 Cor. 12, 11: "All these are inspired by one and the same Spirit, who apportions to each one individually as he wills."

34. Paul VI, Encyclical *Sacerdotalis Coelibatus* of 24 June 1967, par. 17.

35. *Ibid.,* par. 21.

36. Cf. PO, 16: "Priests profess before men that they desire to dedicate themselves in an undivided way to the task assigned them, namely to betroth the faithful to the one Spouse and to present them as a pure virgin to Christ (2 Cor. 11, 2); they thereby evoke that mysterious marriage which was established by God and will be fully manifested in the future: that of the Church with the one Spouse who is Christ." It can be said, moreover, that priestly celibacy is a sign both of the mystical marriage of the priest with the universal Church and of the spiritual marriage with Christ to which every baptized person is destined even in this world, as Saint John of the Cross teaches.

37. We note in passing that certain theologians, among them Dom Ch. Massabki O.S.B., hold that the first conjugal act of the married couple has a sacramental value, since it alone renders the marriage absolutely indissoluble, not only intrinsically, but also extrinsically (by the authority of the Church) in the case of a marriage between baptized persons. In the

case of the first conjugal act, there is question not only of an action divinized by grace and by the sacramental grace at that, but also of a sacramental action which fully signifies the physical union between the Church and Christ in the Eucharist.

38. Cf. Saint Thomas Aquinas, *Summa Theologica,* I. II. 89. 6.

39. Cf. LG, 34: ". . . their ordinary married and family life . . . become spiritual sacrifices acceptable to God through Jesus Christ (1 Pet. 2, 5). During the celebration of the Eucharist, these sacrifices are most lovingly offered to the Father along with the Lord's Body. In this way, the laity consecrate the world itself to God."

40. We do not, however, exclude other exceptions besides those of Jesus and Mary to which we shall shortly allude; cf. Mt. 27, 52-53: ". . . many bodies of the saints who had fallen asleep were raised, and coming out of the tombs after his resurrection they went into the holy city and appeared to many." Saint Francis de Sales and other theologians believed in a bodily assumption of Saint Joseph, which assumption would not be unconnected with his virginal marriage of which it would be the crowning. It is notable that, unlike her definition of the Immaculate Conception, the Church, in defining the Assumption, did not present it as a singular privilege: cf. DS, 3803 and 3903 (DB, 1641 and 2333). In a sermon reported in the *Osservatore Romano* in May 1960, Pope John XXIII professed his belief in the Assumption of Saint Joseph.

41. Unlike ours, Mary's merits were never tarnished by self-love. This privilege results from her Immaculate Conception.

42. Cf. DS, 3900 (DB, 2331).

43. Cf. our Chapter Eleven.

44.Cf. Saint Thomas Aquinas, *Summa Contra Gen.,* IV. 83: de Christo autem dicendum est quod post resurrectionem comedit, non propter necessitatem, sed ad demonstrandum suae resurrectionis veritatem."

45. Cf. note 15 of this chapter.

46. Saint Augustine, *de Bono conjugali,* VIII. 8 writes: "mortalis generatio destruetur." The Augustine text alludes to 1 Cor. 13, 8. *seq.*

47. Cf. Saint Thomas Aquinas, *Summa Theologica,* I. 79. 8. He deals here with the distinction between *intellectus* and *ratio.*

48. Saint Paul explicitly applies analogous considerations to the conjugal life, in 1 Cor. 7, 29-31: ". . . let those who have wives live as though they had none . . . and those who deal with the world as though they had no dealings with it. For the form of this world is passing away." Cf. 1 Cor. 15, 50: "flesh and blood cannot inherit the kingdom of God." Cf. GS, 39 and the Biblical texts cited there.

49. Cf. DS, 3925: "concipere possumus necessitudines illas arctissimas, quae inter sensibilem amorem physici Cordis Jesu

intercedunt et duplicem amorem, spiritualem quidem, human-
um scilicet et divinum."
 50. We know that Father Karl Rahner and Father F. Varillon regard as important a synthetic presentation of the kerygma
in harmony with the needs of contemporary problems; they have
attempted to give us such a presentation (cf. *Etudes,* 1967).
That of Father Varillon has been published under the title:
Un abrégé de la Foi catholique, Prière et Vie, Toulouse, 1968.
 51. Statement by a native of Tchad, reported by a missionary.
 52. Acts 24, 24-25.
 53. Acts 17, 30-31.

13

THE SOVEREIGN PONTIFF
VICAR OF THE PRIMACY OF CHRIST
IN AND OVER HIS CHURCH

We have seen how the mystery of Christ's celibacy
is at the heart of His work as Redeemer and Recapitulator; and in subsequent chapters, we shall present the
mystery of the Holy Eucharist as the synthesis of this
work of Christ. The present chapter is a convenient
stage at which to investigate the role played by the
papacy in this work—a role which more than ever
before is a subject of interest, attraction, and repulsion
in the dialogue between human history and the eternal Word.

Ours is an epoch in which all structures whether of
human or divine origin, are being challenged; notably,
certain influences on human history radiating from
the priestly celibacy of the Redeemer and from His
Real Presence in the Eucharist. Like them and because of them, the papacy has become a controversial
issue. More than ever for the believer, it seems "a
mystery which creates a problem," and one on which
Christocentric reflection must be directed if we are
to understand the action of the Risen Christ today.

Is not the papacy the incarnation of an "institutional religion" of which mankind has need, as the

American Protestant theologian, Reinhold Niebuhr put it?[1] Is it not, as he also said, "the instrument of unity of a universal Church, preferable to national churches" at the social and racial level?[2]

But an instrument in whose hands? Niebuhr does not say. In the era of ecumenism, we think it useful not to exclude from the area of theological thought, the "cornerstone" which is also "a stone that will make men stumble" (1 Pet. 2, 6-8), but to place it at the center of the mystery of Christ the Redeemer. We do not wish to ignore the doctrine concerning the episcopacy, which constitutes, especially since Vatican II, a lesser difficulty for many of our contemporaries; but because this difficulty is of a slighter nature we do not intend to give this doctrine special attention. We prefer, rather, to investigate the mission which the sovereign pontiff receives from the one Redeemer, in the service of the episcopate and of an entirely coredemptive Church. We hope in this way to make a useful contribution to the cause of Christian unity, which, as we shall see shortly, is the reason why the chair of Peter exists.

Is there a relationship in the economy of salvation —and if so, of what kind—between the "primacy of the pope" and the primacy of Christ the Redeemer? Does the expression "vicar of Christ" serve, in a sense, to sum up this relationship? And, finally, are not the intra-ecclesial hierarchic relationships rooted, through the paschal mystery, in the mystery of the relationship with the Holy Trinity, to which they are designed to lead?

We are seeking to suggest some elements for answers to these questions, in the hope of eliciting from our readers answers of perhaps greater depth.

A. The Primacy of the Sovereign Pontiff in the Service of the Supreme Primacy of Christ the Redeemer

The idea of a "primacy of jurisdiction"[4] and of "love"[5] enjoyed by the pope is an analogical one

which can be fully understood only in the light of
the primacy which the Scriptures accord to Christ.

Saint Paul has placed magnificent emphasis on this
primacy of Christ.

> He is the image of the invisible God, the
> first-born of all creation; for him all things were
> created, in heaven and on earth, visible and
> invisible . . . all things were created through
> him and for him. He is before all things, and in
> him all things hold together. He is the head of
> the body, the church; he is the beginning, the
> first-born from the dead, that in everything he
> might be pre-eminent. For in him all the full-
> ness of God was pleased to dwell, and through
> him to reconcile to himself all things, whether
> on earth or in heaven, making peace by the
> blood of his cross (Col. 1, 15-20).

This text very clearly shows that, for Paul, Christ
held the primacy both as Son-Creator and as Incarnate Son and Redeemer. It is precisely because Christ
is "the first-born of all creation," all things having
been created in Him, through Him and for Him, that
He holds the primacy in all things.[6]

In the Body of the Church of which He is the Head,
Christ also holds the primacy. He has all the more
right to this in that all the fullness of graces and spiritual gifts of this Church come from Him, yet does not
cease to remain with Him when He shares it in a
variety of ways.[7]

Paul can therefore say: "that in everything he
might be preeminent"; in everything, but especially
in the Church. Where would He obtain the primacy,
if not *first and foremost* in the Church? If not first
of all in the Church, where would He be acknowledged
as the first-born Son?

Faced with this fact of Revelation, another such
fact takes on its full meaning. Christ, the first-born
of creation and among the dead, has willed to institute in the Church the primatial function of a man

who would be the first in power for the promotion of
the common good of all His disciples; and did He not
do so in order that, in this way, His own primacy
should be concretely recognized, and that all might
effectively acknowledge that they owe obedience to
Him who, for all, was made obedient even unto the
death of the cross? "Although he was a Son, he
learned obedience through what he suffered; and being
made perfect, he became the source of eternal life to
all who obey him" (Heb. 5, 8-9). Within the framework of the economy of the Incarnation, was it not
fitting that this primacy of Christ should be visibly
manifested to all, and that all should visibly express
their salvific obedience to a single visible and supreme
representative of Christ and of His universal primacy?
That all should do so—including the successors of
the apostles, the bishops of the different countries?

One thus comes to appreciate the harmony of the
divine plan: Christ wills to be acknowledged as exercising supreme power in the service of His Father, and
therefore He institutes, among His disciples, a primacy which to the end of time will be the sign and instrument of His own primacy.[8] Thus, His indefectible
primacy will not only be always acknowledged, but
will also be always exercised in a visible manner—and,
as we shall see, there is a sense in which it can be said
to be exercised in a sacramental way.

Viewed in this light, should not the Catholic doctrine of the full immediate, indefectible, and infallible
primacy of the vicar of Christ, become much easier to
understand?

1. *Full primacy*, first of all. Vatican I had defined
the fullness of the power[9] of the pope over the universal Church, bishops, priests, and faithful. While
confirming this doctrine, Vatican II has specified that
the college of bishops in union with the vicar of Christ
has the same fullness of powers, and that this power of
the college is a participation in the fullness of Christ's
powers over His Church.[10]

Thus Vatican II can be seen to have been concerned with an idea which Saint Robert Bellarmine had magnificently developed: an analogical and Christocentric concept of the fullness of power in the Church and over the Church. Here is the text of the Jesuit doctor of the Church:

> If one compares him with Christ, the sovereign pontiff does not possess the fullness of power, but only a determinate part (suam quamdam portionem) according to the measure of the gift of Christ. For Christ rules the whole church in heaven, in purgatory and on earth; He rules all who were from the beginning of the world, and who will be to its end. He can, therefore, at will, make laws, institute sacraments, and confer grace even without the sacraments. But the pope rules only that part of the Church which is on earth, and this only during his lifetime; he cannot change the laws of Christ, or institute sacraments, or remit sins without sacraments. If, however, one compares the sovereign pontiff with the bishops, one rightly affirms that he has the fullness of power. . . . Only Christ is the principal and perpetual Head of the whole Church. . . . The Church is not the body of Peter or of the pope, who governs it only in a temporary way and in the name of another; the Church is the Body of Christ, who rules it in virtue of His own authority, and forever.[11]

Clearly, for Saint Robert Bellarmine, the pope's power, full by comparison with that of the bishop (the latter's power being full by comparison with that of a parish priest[12]), remains a participation in that of the risen Christ over His Church. The full jurisdiction of the visible head of the Church appears as a partial and necessarily limited manifestation, *hic et nunc*, of the eternal, universal, limitless, and incommunicable power of its invisible Head, Christ Jesus. It is possible that, at some time in the future, the Magisterium of the Church may clearly show that the fullness of the power of the pope and of the college of bishops united with the successor of Peter, is itself a participation in the lordship and the absolute fullness of the salvific power of the risen Christ over the Church. Vatican II has laid down the two premises which point to such a conclusion. Has it not affirmed, on the one hand, the fullness of the power of the pope and of the college of bishops, and, on the other, stated that the power of the college is a participation in that of the Lord? It would only remain to specify that the fullness of power, enjoyed of divine right, by the college of bishops, or its head alone, is itself a participation in another fullness—that of Christ. Would not that be a magnificent conclusion?

The perspective would become wider still if one took ino consideration that the fullness of Christ, in which the hierarchical Church participates, is His pleroma of which Saint Paul speaks in the prologue of his Letter to the Colossians cited above. The power of Christ over His Church is a salvific power, a sanctifying power. The risen Christ, in moving through different degrees of fullness (papal and collegial, on the one hand; episcopal, on the other) of participation, to His full salvific powers, visibly manifests His merciful will to put all Christians in possession of the fullness of the revealed deposit and of the means of salvation, and so of the fullness of God who dwells in Him. In the Church, "which is his body, the fullness of him who fills all in all" (Eph. 1, 23),[13] Christians, thanks to this pleroma of Christ in which the hierarchy participate, share in the fullness of God the Father, in the Spirit (cf. Col. 1, 19; Eph. 3, 19).[14]

We hold, therefore, that the fullness of the pastoral power of jurisdiction enjoyed by the pope and the college of bishops, is to be understood in the context of the Pauline doctrine of the pleroma, and as a participation in that pleroma.

The Bellarmine text cited above gives weight to this interpretation, and even seems to us to hold an invitation which the epoch of Vatican II was no doubt not ready fully to appreciate: with ceasing in any way to establish horizontally the fullness of the pontifical power in relation to that of the individual bishop, we should emphasize its vertical relationship with the pleroma of Christ, and, through this pleroma, with the Father.

Above all, such a way of approaching the ecclesial mystery seems to us to be in perfect conformity with the spirit and the letter of the prologue to Colossians, in which Paul brings together in one whole, the Church as Body of Christ, the primacy of the risen Christ, and the pleroma which dwells in Him. The Church is a function of the paschal pleroma of the Lord. If that is true for the whole Body of Christ, it cannot fail to be particularly true for the "eminent members" of this Body who constitute the hierarchy.

It is in this light that one better understands a fact little noticed up to this point. Following the Gospel of Saint John, the two Vatican Councils,[15] and Pius XII[16] in the interval between them, teach that Jesus conferred the apostolic powers on the Eleven, including Saint Peter, on the day of His Resurrection—and therefore in a paschal context—saying: "As the Father has sent me, even so I send you" (Jn. 20, 21). Saint Robert Bellarmine, drawing his inspiration from Saint Cyril of Alexandria and from Saint John Chrysostom, makes this splendid commentary on these words of the risen Christ:

> As my Father has sent me, even so I send you. The word "as" signifies the grandeur of the power which Christ gave to His disciples: as the Father has given me, in as much as I am man, a very ample and limitless power to rule the Church, even so do I give you a very ample and limitless power. In Christ, this power is limitless because it bears on the whole world and on everything relative to salvation. The same was given to the apostles, with this difference, that they were purely and simply men (puri homines) and therefore they could effec-

tively receive of that fullness only what they were capable of receiving as mere men.[17]

The risen Christ sends His apostles "in power" (Rm. 1, 4) because, in virtue of His paschal mystery, He has effectively received "all authority . . . on earth" (Mt. 28, 18). The pastoral power in the Church is closely connected with the manifestation of the power of the risen Christ.

What we have just said enables us to understand, in the light of Saint John's Gospel, the fullness of power of the college of bishops, but not the fullness of papal power over the bishops *in plenary session.* Answering an objection of Luther, Bellarmine saw in Jn. 21, 15-18, the realization of the promise made in Mt. 16 and the continuation of Jn. 20, 21:

> Jesus says to Peter only: "Feed my sheep," just as it had been to him only that He said: "I will give you the keys of the kingdom of heaven." . . . He received the keys of the kingdom . . . only when he understood the words: "Feed my sheep"; then, even charge over his brother-apostles was confided to him (apostolorum fratrum suorum curi ei commissa est).[18]

In other words, on the Resurrection Day, Peter, like the other apostles and with them, first received the fullness of power over the Christians in general; then (Jn. 21, 15-18), the power to bind and loose even the Ten (Judas had killed himself, and Matthias had not yet been chosen to replace him). Equality in the fullness of *apostolic* power between Peter and the Ten, does not exclude the superiority of the specifically *Patrine* and *papal* power.

Did not Jesus intend, in the episode related by Saint John, to show two things at once: that Peter was to feed, not only the lambs, but also the sheep—i.e. the other apostles; and that, through Peter, He Himself would be their Shepherd and their nurture (cf. Jn. 10, 16; 6, 34-58)?

The full powers given by the Good Shepherd to

Peter and the college of bishops or to Peter alone, remain nevertheless limited. It is the merit of Saint Robert Bellarmine (whose reflections on the episcopate are, however, meager) [19] to have clearly recognized and affirmed these limitations, as we have seen. Only the power of Christ over His Church is limitless.

But it was the very special merit of the Jesuit Doctor that he led us to compare, not so much the respective powers of the pope and the bishops, as their relationship with the salvific omnipotence of the risen Christ. [20]

2. *Immediate primacy:* In this same light, we see more clearly the meaning of the *immediate primacy* of the sovereign pontiff in the visible Church.

In virtue of this power, conferred immediately by Christ, [21] the pope can exercise his universal mission anywhere, without having to defer to the bishop of the diocese in question or seek his permission. To have force and value, his power needs the cooperation or consent of no one whomsoever, neither of the civil power nor even of the universal Church. [22] It could be said, therefore, that this power is immediate in a twofold sense: passively, as received from the risen Lord without any mediation; actively, inasmuch as it can be exercised without any intermediary, on every baptized person.

This immediate primacy logically derives from the fullness already mentioned: since the pope has received a plenary and not partial power over the Church, this power could not be completed in any respect by any person or any thing. [23]

The pope can, therefore, directly exercise his pastoral power of salvific jurisdiction; but this does not necessarily imply that he ought to do so. We have numerous texts of Leo XIII, Pius XI and John XXIII [24] to show that they recognized a twofold obedience of the faithful to the sovereign pontiff—an immediate obedience, and a mediate obedience through and with the bishops. For Pius XI, [25] the bishops are "the golden links" and "joints" (cf. Eph. 4, 15-16:

"knit together by every joint") uniting the faithful among themselves and with the Roman pontiff in the Body of Christ. Yet more clearly, John XXIII says: "One can be united with Christ only in the Church and by the Church, which is His Mystical Body; and one can belong to the Church only through the bishops, the successors of the apostles, in union with the supreme pastor, who is the successor of Peter."[26]

If, therefore, one could do so without risk of misunderstanding or confusion, one might be tempted to distinguish a twofold primacy of the vicar of Christ: *immediate and mediate* over the baptized faithful; *immediate only* over the bishops of the Latin rite and of other rites without patriarchs. It would be necessary to use a more qualified terminology in the case of the Eastern patriarchs, and speak about a quadruple primacy of jurisdiction and of love[27] of the bishop of Rome in what concerns pastoral government[28]: the first, immediate over all the faithful, the bishops and the patriarchs; the second, mediate in a twofold way (through the patriarch and the local ordinary); the third, simply mediate over the bishops (through the patriarch); the fourth, immediate only, over the patriarchs.

We think it important to emphasize that the immediate primacy of the vicar of Christ does not rule out these different types of mediation and of mediate primacy. The pope can exercise his salvific mission without any mediation, but he may also prefer to act through the patriarchs and bishops. His acting through them does not mean, however, that he is in any way bound to do so or must seek any kind of permission; nor does it mean that the bishops are thereby reduced to the status of vicars of the Roman pontiff, whereas they are the vicars of Christ.[29]

In the case of an indirect exercise of the always immediate primacy of the pope (for he does not cease to bind the faithful immediately when, with and through the bishop, he lays an obligation on them), the bishop does not limit himself to transmitting the will of the "first of bishops."[30] He adds his own command to it, and thus binds in his own name. This can enable him to word the papal command somewhat differently, thus, without essential alteration of content, adapting it prudently to a local and particular situation.

Now, the recognition of the twofold exercise, mediate and immediate, of the always immediate primacy of the vicar of Christ, expresses in a concrete way the recognition of the twofold manner in which the Church is governed by Christ, its sole Head[31]: the risen Lord governs it immediately through the outpouring of His actual and efficacious graces, and mediately through the pope and the bishops. In his encyclical on the Mystical Body, Pius XII wrote:

> Our Divine Savior directly and personally governs and guides the society He has founded. In effect, He reigns in the minds and in the hearts of men, bending and inclining at His good pleasure even the most rebellious wills. "The heart of the king is in the hand of the Lord; withersoever he will he shall turn it" (Prov. 21, 1). . . . Without ceasing personally to govern the Church in a mysterious way, Christ also rules over it in a visible manner through him who fulfills His role on earth.[32]

Vatican II, in its turn, emphasizes the fact that "Christ governs the Church through the sovereign pontiff and through the bishops."[33] This mediate action of Christ in no way hinders His simultaneous immediate action—a fact which Vatican II very strongly emphasizes in connection with Mary:

> All the saving influences of the Blessed Virgin on men originate, not from some inner necessity, but from the divine pleasure. They flow forth from the superabundance of the merits of Christ, rest on His mediation, depend entirely on it, and draw all their power from it. In no way do they impede the immediate union of the faithful with Christ. Rather, they foster this union.[34]

Analogically, the immediate primacy of the pope, far from being an obstacle to the immediate action of Christ, serves rather to assist it. It is a mediation instituted by Christ in the service of His own unique mediation. It takes its place eminently within the framework of the general principle re-stated by Vatican II: "The unique mediation of the Redeemer does not exclude but rather gives rise among creatures to a manifold operation which is but a sharing in this unique source."[35]

In the same way, the always immediate character of the pontifical primacy does not preclude but fosters different mediations. Nay more, the fullness itself of the immediate primacy is divinely and intrinsically limited by the need to respect the proper role of the episcopal mediation in a Church governed by Christ alone. The episcopacy is a structure of divine origin which the pope must respect, even though he has the powers to withdraw jurisdiction from this or that bishop. Saint Robert Bellarmine explicitly envisaged this case of legitimate resistance to the pope: "If he sought to depose all the bishops, and thus put the Church in jeopardy."[36] This would amount to an attempt "to destroy the Church."[37] It would then be necessary "to turn to God in prayer, to admonish the said pope with all respect and reverence, to refuse to obey his notoriously unjust commands, and finally to resist him and to nullify the evil intended."[38] He justified this position as follows: "To resist and repel forcefully an unjust violence, one does not need to have authority over the person one resists."[39]

We see, therefore, how clearly the Doctor of the "pontifical monarchy" appreciated the fact that the latter, within the economy of salvation, is in no sense an absolute monarchy, and is unlike that of Christ.

Similarly, the immediate primacy, while it implies that the pope is truly "bishop of the Catholic Church,"[40] does not signify that the pope is "universal bishop," an expression which Saint Gregory the Great indignantly rejected.[41] Alone the supreme visible shepherd of the whole flock, he is not however the only shepherd minding the flock, for he is truly the shepherd of the shepherds; and one of the reasons for the pope's existence is to help the shepherds to fulfill their duties well—to help the bishops to be perfectly such. It is because he is the bishop of bishops, without taking their place, that the pope is not and cannot be the "universal bishop," as the German bishops emphasized in a text solemnly ratified by Pius IX, in answer to Bismarck:

> The pope is bishop of Rome, but not bishop of any other diocese or any other city; he is not bishop of Breslau, or bishop of Cologne, etc. But as bishop of Rome, he is at the same time pope, that is, the shepherd and supreme head of the universal Church, head of all the bishops and all the faithful, and his papal power should be respected and heeded everywhere and always, and not just in special and exceptional circumstances.[43] Holding this position, the pope should be vigilant to ensure that each bishop fulfills his duty throughout the whole territory entrusted to his charge. If a bishop is hindered from doing so, or if some need makes itself felt, the pope has the right and the duty, not in his capacity of bishop of the diocese, but in that of pope, to order everything necessary for the administration of the diocese.[44]

One could also say that one of the purposes (not the only one) of the pope's immediate primacy of salvific jurisdiction is precisely to ensure and to guarantee the salvific exercise of the immediate jurisdiction of the diocesan bishops. Not only, then, does this immediate primacy not preclude mediations, but it even exists to serve the episcopal mission of each and every bishop. That is what Vatican I had already emphatically noted: the pope, as pope, "strengthens, fortifies and defends the episcopal power of the bishops,"[45] not only against wrongful encroachment by the civil authority, but also against their own errors of action, omission, or ignorance.

At the root of this immediate primacy of jurisdiction, there is, therefore, the salvific will of the "eternal Shepherd"[46] as regards the lambs confided to His sheep, and as regards the sheep themselves. Vatican II has made this point very strongly in a text [47] which constitutes an official and very apt interpretation of that of Vatican I concerning the immediate primacy of the pope:

> In this Church of Christ the Roman pontiff is the successor of Peter, to whom Christ entrusted the feeding of His sheep and lambs. Hence by divine institution he enjoys supreme, full, immediate, and universal authority over the care of souls (in curam animarum). Since he is pastor of all the faithful, his mission is to provide for the common good of the universal Church and for the good of the individual churches. He holds, therefore, a primacy of ordinary power over all the churches. For their part, the bishops too have been appointed by the Holy Spirit, and are successors of the apostles as pastors of souls. Together with the supreme pontiff and under his authority, they have been sent to continue throughout the ages the work of Christ, the eternal pastor.

The Council has here very clearly indicated the *raison d'être* of the divine institution of the immediate primacy of the vicar of Christ: the common good of the universal Church, the particular good of each church, and, through them, the perpetuity of the salvific work of Christ Jesus. In a word, the salvation of souls for the glory of Christ: "that in everything he might be pre-eminent" (Col. 1, 18).

An immediate primacy of this kind disconcerts many non-Catholics, even among those who most ardently desire Christian unity. Far from having its origin in human ambition, by which indeed it could neither gain nor preserve recognition, it is to be seen as the result

of the salvific will of the Redeemer. It essentially
exists to manifest the yet more immediate primacy of
Christh.[48] It is "always and everywhere" that the vicar
of Christ should be able to act, and not just in exceptional circumstances, for the salvation of the bishops
and of the faithful, because it is always and everywhere that Christ wills to save mankind. Every attempt to reduce or limit the space-time immediacy or
universality of this primacy of the pope is, in the final
analysis, an attempt to reduce or limit the recognition
of the primacy of the Redeemer and of His rule over
space and history. Such an attempt would be ultimately detrimental to the good of the bishops and to
that of all Christians.

3. *Indefectible primacy.* This primacy will never
end, for the full and immediate primacy of the vicar of
Christ is indefectible within an indefectible Church, in
order to ensure the indefectibility of that Church.

It is the Holy Spirit who ensures the joint and simultaneous indefectibility of the papacy and of the episcopate in communion with the papacy. Vatican II emphasizes this the better to show that the supreme and
universal power of the pope could not suppress the power proper to the bishops: "Their power is not destroyed by the supreme and universal power. On the
contrary, it is strengthened and vindicated thereby,
since the Holy Spirit unfailingly preserves the form of
government established by Christ the Lord in His
Church."[49]

What is the precise content of this indefectibility?
It signifies the perpetuity, identity, and substantial
immutability of the Church in its visible and invisible
elements of divine origin. Already clearly indicated by
Saint Matthew's Gospel (16, 18: "the powers of death
shall not prevail against it"; and 28, 19), it has been
made explicit by the Church against Protestant and
Jansenist denials of its visible indefectibility.[50] It
has been solemnly affirmed by Vatican I: it constitutes one of the two central points of the second chapter
of the Dogmatic Constitution, *Pastor aeternus.* "What

Christ has instituted in the blessed Apostle Peter for the perpetual salvation and for the unceasing good of the Church, must always continue in the Church, which, founded on the rock, will continue in strength, thanks to Christ, until the end of time."[51] The Council therefore anathemizes those who would say that "it is not in virtue of divine ruling, through institution by Christ Himself, that there are successors to Peter perpetually (perpetuos successores) in the primacy of the universal Church."[52]

In concrete and "existential" terms, what does this indefectible perpetuity of the apostolic see signify? It implies that the papacy will never disappear from human history, however powerful in the future may be the persecutions, the apostasies, the heresies, and even the sins of popes and of Catholics generally. Visible to all, there will always be bishops in communion with the bishop of Rome, in order to feed the flock of the one eternal Shepherd. Apart from interregnum periods, there will always be an infallible vicar of Christ in the service of the infallible adherence of the people of God to Revelation, propounded by the Magisterium.

And what does this indefectibility manifest, if not that Christ will never fail His Church?—that He will never leave Christians as "orphans" (cf. Jn. 14, 18), since He will be always present with them through His vicar with whom His vicars are in communion?[53]

We should add, of course, that this perpetuity "of the sacred apostolic primacy in which consists the strength and the solidarity of the whole Church,"[54] is not only *not* a promise of good popes, but shines with particular brilliance through the bad ones. It is indeed through the bad popes, incapable of destroying the Church, that the perpetual presence of the Good Shepherd is manifested. It is to them especially that is directed the inaugural sermon of Saint Robert Bellarmine on his taking possession (28 October 1602) of the archdiocese of Capua. Commenting on Ez. 34, 15: "I will feed my sheep and I will cause them to lie down," he preached charismatically[55] as follows:

Great is the consolation of the sheep who lack a good shepherd through no fault of their own.

God instructs bad shepherds and directs them, in order that they may teach and govern well, even if they themselves have no intention to do so. . . .

God often enlightens an inept and ignorant shepherd, in order that he may rightly direct his sheep, just as, on the contrary, He withholds light from the wise shepherds in order to punish their subjects.

God often makes bad government by shepherds turn out to the good of the subjects. The true fidelity of the subject appears when he honors a bad shepherd because of God, considering only the office he holds. The subjects ponder over the matter and think: "Why has God given us such a bad shepherd? Certainly, He could have given us a good one, or could make him good whom we have. God knows all things; He is the true "Shepherd and Guardian of souls" (1 Pet. 2, 25), and this bad shepherd is His vicar. Why does He tolerate him? Certainly because of our sins." God Himself feeds when He instructs and enlightens His subjects, in order that they may lift their eyes to Christ, the chief Shepherd, if, in his words or in his behavior, the bishop is not governing well. . . . In whatever way God chooses to feed His sheep, he feeds them well, as He has promised: "I will feed them." They are completely safe, the sheep whom God feeds; He never sleeps, and He fears neither the wolf nor the thief. Therefore the Lord has said: "No one is able to snatch them out of the Father's hand" (Jn. 10, 29). But this promise more properly concerns the life to come. Then, in effect, the sheep will be freed, not only out of the grasp of the wolves and of the thieves, but also out of the hand of the mercenaries and of the bad shepherds, and God Himself will feed them with the pasture of the uncreated Word, who gives eternal life.

In other words, the saintly Jesuit Cardinal directs our attention towards the eschatological end (in every sense of the word) of the episcopal office and, consequently, of the papacy. The latter is indefectible throughout history, as is the episcopate in communion with the papacy. But these visible and sacramental structures of the Church will disappear on the Last Day, with the heavens and the earth and with the figure of this world. When Christ has been perfectly manifested to all the elect; when He who is the Alpha and the Omega of history appears in all the glory of His absolutely full and immediate primacy, then there will be no further need of figures, instruments, sacramental anticipations, or sacred powers entrusted to mere men. Christ will be perfectly "all and in all" (Col. 3, 11) and will deliver the Church perfected thanks to the deployment throughout human history of the sacrament of holy orders and of the papacy.

What Vatican II teaches in a general way, applies especially to the papacy: "The pilgrim Church in her sacraments and institutions, which pertain to the present time, takes on the appearance of this passing world."[56] In this sense, the historically indefectible papacy knows and proclaims that it is mortal, like mankind, like history. On the Last Day, the last pope will disappear, just as a sign disappears to give place to the reality which it signifies. The indefectible papacy is an historical and merely historical representation, a transient representation of the Christ who will not pass away. Such a statement is simply an extension of Saint Paul's teaching to the Hebrews concerning the leaders, mortal men and martyrs, of their community: "Remember your leaders, those who spoke to you the word of God; consider the outcome of their life, and imitate their faith. Jesus Christ is the same yesterday and today and for ever." The leaders of the Church disappear, but Christ continues forever, and it is to Him we must attach ourselves.[57]

It could be said that the hierarchy (papacy and episcopate) is a scaffolding, a provisional framework, erec-

ted before the façade of the Church and of humanity
during their pilgrimage through the night of this
world, by the eternal "builder and maker" (cf. Heb.
11, 10), and destined to disappear when the construction is finished, in the light of day.

While the papacy signifies for us the primacy of this
eternal architect of the Church, it also symbolizes
time, the figure of this age which is passing away, human history in pilgrimage towards Christ. In it and
through it, the Church is still a synagogue while being
already the heavenly Jerusalem.[58] Through it, Christ
"secularizes," introduces into the transient world, His
eternal primacy, precisely in order to make men pass
from the present age to the age to come (Mt. 12, 32)
in a salvific "trans-secularization."[59] The papacy is
therefore indissolubly linked with the Pasch of Christ,
which conditions it and whence it derives its strength,
and with the pasch of the Christians, the *raison d'être*
and the purpose of its privileged participation in the
full, immediate, indefectible, and infallible primacy of
its divine Founder.

4. *The infallibility of the pope: gift of the infallible
Man Jesus.*

Since this particular point has never been seriously studied, it is insufficiently noticed that Vatican I
defined the dogma of papal infallibility in an essentially salvific perspective. In this charism of papal
infallibility, the Council saw an expression and instrument of the salvific will of the Redeemer, and defined
it for the salvation of the Christian peoples. This is
equivalent to saying that this infallibility is an integral
part of the mystery of our Redemption, through which
Christ has willed to free us from the slavery of error.

In effect, the actual definition of infallibility was
preceded by an exposé of purposes which constitutes
a passage of high doctrinal value:

> This charism of truth and of indefectible faith
> was divinely conferred on Peter, and on his
> successors in this chair, in order that they might

fulfill their very exalted charge for the salvation of all men; in order that through them the whole flock of Christ might be kept away from the poisonous allure of error, and be fed with heavenly doctrine; finally, in order that, all occasion of schism having been thus suppressed, the whole Church should be conserved in unity and, firmly resting on its foundation, should strongly resist the powers of Hell.[60]

The line of thought is clear. The privilege of a faith without defect or decay is given to Peter's successor for the salvation of the whole world, and, more immediately, in order to maintain the Church in the unity of a unanimous adherence to the revealed truth from which salvation is inseparable. For the human mind ought to reject the poison of error, which would lead to its eternal loss, in order to be saved through the vision of the Truth.

It is abundantly clear, therefore, that Vatican I presents the infallibility of the pope as a manifestation of the merciful love of the Redeemer[61] for the human race. Objectively and logically, the rejection of papal infallibility, according to Vatican I, is synonymous with the rejection or Christ, Master and Redeemer of the wounded[62] intelligence of man.

Having come on earth to save this intelligence, to snatch it from the consequences of eternal blindness attendant upon culpable error, Christ willed to make it infallible through the act of faith in His Revelation,[63] and to make it thus participate in His own Messianic infallibility; and in order that the whole Church should be infallible in the act of faith, He had necessarily to institute an organ to be the infallible expression of His Revelation.

The infallibility of the pope has for its *purpose* the act of infallible and justifying faith of the people of God, of the whole Church; and it is precisely for this reason that it could not have the act of faith as its condition or as the cause of its exercise. Directed to the indefectible divinization of the intelligence of the people of God, its own efficient cause could only be transcendent. It is because it is *for* the people of God that it does not come *from* the people, and that its exercise is not conditioned by the people—except in the sense that they ceaselessly pray for the vicar of Christ.[64] Is not this prayer of the Christians for their Father in Christ, a prolongation, through the action of the Spirit, of the very prayer of Christ Jesus which is at the origin of the indefectible faith of Peter and of his successors (cf. Lk. 22, 32)?

In the light of the above considerations, we can now insert a digression of a more clearly ecclesiological kind by linking together two important Vatican II declarations, one dealing with the infallibility of the Church, the other with that of the pope. The first deals with the infallible and universal consent to the truths of the Faith infallibly and anteriorly defined by the Magisterium, to which the second alludes. This linking of the two declarations shows clearly that the consenting infallibility of the people of God is the *raison d'être* of the "defining" infallibility of the hierarchic Magisterium:

> The body of the faithful as a whole, anointed as they are by the Holy One (cf. Jn. 2: 20, 27), cannot err in matters of belief. Thanks to a supernatural sense of the faith which characterizes the people as a whole, it manifests this unerring quality when, "from the bishops down to the last member of the laity," it shows universal agreement in matters of faith and morals.[65]
> The infallibility with which the Divine Redeemer willed His Church to be endowed in defining a doctrine of faith and morals extends as far as extends the deposit of divine revelation, which must be religiously guarded and faithfully expounded. This is the infallibility which the Roman pontiff, the head of the college of bishops, enjoys in virtue of his office, when, as the supreme shepherd and teacher of all the faithful, who confirms his brethren in their faith

(cf. Lk. 22: 32), he proclaims by a definitive act some doctrine of faith or morals.[66]

We note in passing that the "defining" infallibility in question here is given for the benefit of the whole Church, but only to the Church as a hierarchy. The word "Church" is used, therefore, in a restricted sense. We also note the play on words: the Church *defines* by a *definitive* and irreversible act, a sign of infallible truth. This is made clear by the continuation of the text:

> Therefore his definitions, of themselves and not from the consent of the Church, are justly styled irreformable, for they are pronounced with the assistance of the Holy Spirit, and assistance promised to him in blessed Peter. Therefore they need no approval of others, nor do they allow an appeal to any other judgment. For then the Roman pontiff is not pronouncing judgment as a private person. Rather, as the supreme teacher of the universal Church, as one in whom the charism of the infallibility of the Church herself is individually present, he is expounding or defending a doctrine of Catholic faith. . . . To the resultant definitions the assent of the Church can never be wanting, on account of the activity of that same Holy Spirit, whereby the whole flock of Christ is preserved and progresses in unity of faith.[67]

This important Vatican II text provides an elucidation of Vatican I, whose essential purpose is to show in what sense the previous Council had defined the infallibility of papal definitions "ex sese, non ex consensu Ecclesiae," a formula which had meantime become a stumbling block and which is here confirmed anew. Vatican II, in a way which has perhaps been insufficiently noted, makes a distinction between the *prior non-necessary consent* of the Church (episcopate and people of God) to the pope's definitions, and their *posterior assent* which is necessary, not for the validity of the pontifical act, but for the spiritual good of those who accept it, and which is infallibly guaranteed by the same Spirit who assists the pope in his definitions. We are therefore equally remote from the excesses of the prior consent of the Gallicans, from the Russian "sobornost" (of certain of the Orthodox Christians only, who make the validity of a conciliar act conditional on the adherence of the whole Church), and from every passive vision of the doctrinal attitude of the whole people of God, in whom the Spirit *acts* to arouse an *act* of adherence to the *act* of the definition.

There is a difference, however, between the posterior adherence of the bishops and the assent of the faithful in general, a difference which Vatican II did not stress but equally did not deny. Muzzarelli seems to us to have expressed this difference very clearly:

> Everywhere and always, the bishops keep their original right of judges in the Faith, and they can exercise this right both in relation to the dogmas defined in the General Councils and in relation to those which figure in the constitutions emanating from the Holy See, in order to confirm their truth and to add the force of their own assent. And it is in this that the difference lies between the acceptance made by the bishops and that which emanates from the faithful in general. The first is not only an act of obedience, but also a true judgment in matters of Faith. Hence it is called a canonical and authorized confirmation.[68]

In the eighteenth century, the bishops of France accepted in the way of judgment the bulls of Clement XI vs. Jansenism, and communicated the matter to him in the form with which, it seems, the pope finally declared himself to be satisfied.[69] (The difficulties which could be raised against this doctrine are dealt with in an appendix).

This posterior assent in judicial form is less surprising when one remembers that papal definitions have for their object doctrines already believed in and by the Church to be of divine origin. Although their definition does not need a prior consent of the Church, their matter was already the object of a minimum consent within the Church. The very concept of infallibility implies an accord with Revelation, and with tradition as conserved by the Church. A certain prior consent of the Church is for the pope the sign of the divinely revealed truth he is preparing to define, as for instance in the case of the definition of the Assumption by Pius XII.[70] In this respect, the definitions merely serve to make specific the object of the faith of the Church, of its already existent consent, of which the pope is rightly the infallible judge. One could therefore say that he is infallible, not in virtue of the consent of the Church, but in relationship with this consent and with the Church, and for its good: "non ex consensu Ecclesiae, sed in relatione cum illa."[71] He is the infallible definer of the prior object of Faith and of the prior consent of the Church.[72]

To conclude this digression of a purely ecclesiological nature, it is as well to emphasize that this charism of papal infallibility, the gift of the infallible Man-Jesus,[73] has for its essential object to bear witness to this Man. One can speak of a Christological or Christocentric character of the papal privilege.

Saint Matthew's Gospel (16, 16-17) shows us how, on the day when he made his confession of faith, Simon becomes Peter—i.e. the witness in spirit to the mystery of Christ. He is the witness of Christ, Son of God, before being eye-witness of Christ's resurrection, which has not yet occurred. Underlining this fact, Father Dock adds:

> It is because Simon, in the light of the revelation received from the Father, pronounced the basic truth of the Christian religion, that he is, personally, an authentic prophet of the New Covenant, whose declaration of faith is irreversible in itself, *ex sese*. . . . Peter, from the day of his confession, was constituted a fundamental witness of the Revelation, independently of the

> witness of the other apostles, but not indepen-
> dently of the witness of Christ, the Son of God,
> who confirms the authenticity of Peter's wit-
> ness. . . . Thus the veracity of Peter's confession
> is not dependent on the consent of the apostolic
> college.[74]

Equally, the Gospel clearly highlights the Christocentric conditioning of the promise, and then of the
bestowing of the privilege in this sacrificial and loving
ministry conferred on Peter. It is only after his profession of faith in Christ that he receives the promise
of the keys of the Kingdom; and only after his triple
profession of reparatory love that he effectively received the mission to feed the lambs and the sheep.
The death and the resurrection of the Lord, occurring
between the promise and its fulfillment, emphasizes
the paschal and sacrificial character of the primacy
and of the witness of Peter: ". . . whoever would be
first among you must be slave of all. For the Son of
man also came not to be served but to serve, and to
give his life as a ransom for many" (Mk. 10, 44-45).
This primacy of service and of love implies a primacy
in the witness[76] rendered to the Son of God. The
great proof of love which Peter must give to the risen
Christ, is to be His witness to the lambs and the sheep,
and to the world.

Thus, it emerges that anything which the vicar of
Christ ever defines will always be a truth related in
some way to Christ and to His paschal sacrifice, a
truth professed through love for the living Son of
God and for His glory. Christ is the fullness of Revelation.[77] He communicates the privilege of His infallibility as Revealer only in order to lead men to
adhere infallibly to His Person through adherence to
the truths He reveals concerning Himself and for
His own glory. Such communication is, however, inseparable from His sacrificial prayer: "Simon, Simon
. . . I have prayed for you that your faith may not
fail" (Lk. 22, 32). In order that the infallible Man-

Jesus should, at Caesarea Philippi, confer His own infallibility on Simon Peter, it was necessary that He should consent to die so as to seal it in His blood. The "definatory" infallibility of the pope and of the college of bishops, like the infallibility of the adherence and assent (in faith) of the people of God, is linked with the sacrifice of the one Mediator, and is stained with His blood. This better enables us to understand that faith demands of the human intelligence that it "destroy arguments and every proud obstacle to the knowledge of God, and take every thought captive to obey Christ" (2 Cor. 10, 4-6). The infallibility of the pope is the free gift of Christ to His redeemed and co-redemptive Church, through the faith that justifies.

But if the full, immediate, indefectible, and infallible primacy of the pope is to that extent in the service of that of the Redeemer, is not this because it is in some way sacramental, in the broad sense of the word? Is not this signified by the traditional title, vicar of Christ?

B. The "Sacramental" Primacy of the Vicar of Christ, Instrument of the Redeemer

The relationship we have just analyzed between the primacy of the sovereign pontiff in the pilgrim Church and the absolutely universal primacy of the Christ-Redeemer, is in a sense epitomized and rooted in the very long established title, vicar of Christ.

As applied to the pope, it dates back to at least the twelfth century.[78] It signified and continues to signify the visible representation of a transcendent and heavenly power active here and now in its earthly representative. As we shall demonstrate shortly, the climate of the idea and its framework continue to be those of the here-and-now quality of the action of Christ, operating in His representative.

As Father Congar rightly points out, there is question here of "a highly sacramental, iconological concept, linked with the idea of constant activities of

God and of the heavenly powers within our earthly sphere."[79] In other words, the concept expressed by the term, vicar of Christ, is linked to faith in the earthly activity of the heavenly and glorious Christ. Father Congar adds: "It is also this here-and-now value of vertical descent and activity, which is expressed originally in the famous text of Lk. 10, 16: 'He who hears you hears me, and he who rejects you rejects me.' "[80]

The title was therefore particularly suited to designate the activity of the glorious Christ through a mortal man become the sign and the instrument—let us even say without hesitation, the sacrament—of His full, immediate, indefectible, and infallible primacy. Today, is it not through His visible and universal representative that Christ visibly shows that He is the Master incapable of deceiving or of being deceived, the all-powerful Master who acts and is obeyed within the depths of human hearts?

This is clearly the only meaning ascribed to this title in the official language of the Church; for example, in his encyclical, *Mystici Corporis*, Pius XII writes:

> The divine Redeemer rules His mystical Body also visibly and ordinarily through His vicar on earth. . . . Such was His wisdom that He could in no wise leave the social body of His Church without a visible head. And it cannot be validly objected that by the establishment of a primacy of jurisdiction in the Church, this mystical Body was given two heads. For, in virtue of the primacy, Peter is none other than the vicar of Christ, and therefore this Body has only one principal Head, namely Christ, who, continuing himself to govern the Church invisibly and directly, rules it visibly through His personal representative on earth; so that now, after His glorious ascension into heaven, that Church is built not only on Himself but also on Peter as its visible foundation. That Christ and His vicar constitute only one Head was solemnly taught by our predecessor of immortal memory, Boni-

face VIII, in his apostolic letter, *Unam Sanctam*, and the same doctrine has been constantly repeated by his successors.[82]

Notice that the pope is not presented here as being a mere image of Christ, but decidedly as the human instrument through whom Christ, here and now, visibly governs His Church—i.e. does not limit Himself to an invisible mode of governing. In the mystery of the papacy, the past divine institution by Christ and the ever continuing activity of Christ, are inseparable. As Father Tromp rightly stresses, the title vicar of Christ connotes a physical influence of Christ on His vicar:

> There is a union, not only juridical, but also physical, between Christ and His vicar. Christ exercises an influence of a particular, continual and physical kind on His vicar, in order that the latter, as supreme teacher and as supreme leader, may teach infallibly and govern indefectibly. This union is effected by the Spirit of Christ, who, unique and identical, fills the humanity of Christ and dwells in the sovereign pontiffs with His sevenfold gifts and with all His charisms, thanks to which the vicar of Christ cannot teach false doctrines or take disciplinary measures which are dangerous, harmful, and capable of leading the faithful into error.[83]

The expression, vicar of Christ, ascribes therefore a character in some sense "sacramental" to the action of the sovereign pontiff. We shall shortly return to this point. What we would like to make clear now is that the idea is expressed, not only in the papal language of the encyclicals, but also in the language of the Councils, and particularly in that of Vatican II. Is it not mentioned at least twice in *Lumen Gentium?*[84]

It must be observed, however, that Vatican II has greatly extended, though still along traditional lines, the current usage of the title, by referring also to the bishops as vicars of Christ in their own dioceses.[85]

This is made more remarkable by the fact that the Council of Trent avoided this language.[86] Everything indicates, therefore, that Vatican II sought to direct us towards a more analogical and less univocal use of this fine title, in line with its revaluation of the episcopacy and of the latter's sacramentality, in the strict sense of the word. One thus returns to the language used by a Saint Ignatius Loyola in the sixteenth century, who referred to the sovereign pontiff as "supreme vicar of Christ," to distinguish him from the other vicars of Christ,[87] among whom the saint included religious superiors.[88]

One could say that every priest, every bishop, every religious superior, is, by different rights, the *particular vicar of Christ*, the pope alone being His *universal vicar*. But the bishops, in collegiality and in communion with the pope, are, with him and all together, universal vicars of the Redeemer.

As applied to the pope, however, the title vicar of Christ takes on its full "sacramental" force only in the context of the ecclesiology of Vatican II, centered on the Church viewed as "sacrament of salvation." We have already shown the significance of these terms: the Church is not only the symbol, but also the conscious and voluntary instrument, of the salvation of mankind.[89]

Since visibility is an essential quality of a sacrament, it would be nonsensical to claim that the Church is the sacrament of the salvation of mankind, if at the same time we sought to exclude its visible and hierarchical elements. We must therefore include the papacy and the episcopate in this global sacramentality of the Church, "sacramentality" being understood, of course, in the analogical sense.

In the global sacrament of universal salvation,[90] the pope and the bishops provide, in the manner of an efficacious "sacramentum tantum," the intermediary reality ("res et sacramentum") of visible unity in the profession of the same faith, which faith is itself the intermediary efficient cause of the communion of all

Christians in the divine life through love—the "res tantum" or purpose for which the whole structure of the Church is intended.[91]

As sign and instrument of the visible and invisible unity of the Church in faith and in love, the papacy is, therefore, a sacrament of salvation. Vatican I has made a substantially identical statement, which comes as no surprise to anyone who reads it in the light of the concept of sacrament of salvation as developed by Vatican II. Here is the Vatican I text:

> In order that the episcopate itself should be one and undivided, and in order that the whole body of the faithful should continue in unity of faith and of communion, Christ, giving precedence to the blessed Peter over the other apostles, instituted in him the principle and the visible foundation of this twofold unity.[92]

The significance of this text has been well appreciated and commented on.[93] The papacy has a twofold purpose: an immediate purpose, to preserve the unity of the college; a mediate purpose, to preserve the unity of the whole Church by preserving that of the episcopate. Vatican I is here making splendid use of an idea of Saint Cyprian, from which a good deal of the phrase cited has been borrowed ("episcopatus unitus et indivisus . . . coherentes sibi invicem sacerdotes").[94] We shall shortly consider this purpose of the papacy within the divine plan. Vatican II, in summarizing the text of Vatican I, has placed less emphasis on the hierarchy of these two purposes than did the previous council: "The Roman pontiff, as the successor of Peter, is the perpetual and visible source and foundation of the unity of the bishops and of the multitude of the faithful."[95] Nevertheless, in the two councils, the idea that the pope is a principle of unity (and not merely a sign or ineffectual center) emerges clearly, thus justifying our placing the papacy in the general category of salvific sacramentality. Without ascribing to the vicar of Christ the primacy of love, "in which consists the strength and solidity of the whole Church,"[96] it would be impossible to say what Vatican II proclaims (in a further borrowing from Saint Cyprian, the "doctor of Catholic unity"[97]): "God has gathered together as one all those who in faith look upon Jesus as the author of salvation and the source of unity and peace, and has established them as the Church, that for each and all she may be the visible sacrament of this saving unity."[98]

In the light of this very beautiful text, it can be said that the vicar of Christ is the visible sacrament of the salvific unity of the Church, the efficacious sign of this union in love which saves from hatred and from perdition. The papacy finds the intrinsic and permanent reason for its existence in mutual love, in the reciprocal communion of the bishops, the baptized faithful, and, in the final analysis, all men, since all are called to baptism. It thus appears as the symbol and the concrete recapitulation of the Church itself. Like the Church, the papacy is "a sign and means of intimate union with God and of the unity of the whole human race";[99] and consequently, for each and every person, it is a means and sacrament of salvation, which consists in the exercise of the twofold love of God and of the neighbor.

Of this twofold charity, the Word is, in the mystery of His Inhumanation, the model and the source, as well as being the Mediator. Now, there again the salvific sacramentality of the papacy is made evident. The pope is not directly and immediately the vicar of the Father or of the Spirit, but of the Word made flesh, of the Man-Jesus, King, Priest, and Prophet.[100] He is therefore the instrument of this sacred humanity, the latter being the sacrament *par excellence*. He is the vicar of the Redeemer. Through him the primacy of the Man-Jesus is visibly manifested.

It is from Him that he receives in an immediate way his participation in the primacy, at the very moment when he accepts his election. He does not receive it from men, not even from his electors, or from the

Church: he is not the vicar of the Church, but the vicar of Christ.[101]

This immediate participation takes place through and in the Spirit of Christ, as we have already pointed out, following Father Tromp.[102] It is in a continually renewed outpouring of His Spirit that the Man-Jesus consecrates, by setting him apart for a unique mission, Peter and each of his successors, in order to make each of them the vicar and the instrument of His redemptive primacy. We may properly use here, with Father Philippon, the word *consecration*, since there is a setting apart for a sacred office and, simultaneously, an outpouring of the graces necessary for the exercise of this mission.[103] Here is what this Dominican theologian writes:

> The pope is the man who has the greatest participation in the hierarchic powers of Christ. Like the other bishops, he has received through episcopal consecration the fullness of the sacrament of holy orders; but, in the conclave, on the day of his election, at the very moment of his acceptance of the papacy, he has received directly from Christ, in a direct and invisible manner and in continual dependence on Him, the regency of His Church here on earth. This consecration, of an order at once priestly[104] and royal, makes the pope supreme head of our visible Church, pastor of pastors, vicar of Christ over all the bishops of the world, over all the faithful of the world, and even, virtually, over all men, since all are called to receive the benefits of the Redemption. It is the highest consecration, since it enables a man to participate, as much as a mere man can possibly do . . . in the sovereign royalty of Christ.[105]

In reality, this consecration is not directly of a priestly kind, but of a royal and prophetic nature. It implies the bestowal, not only of the primacy of love, but also of the primacy of infallible witness, of the charism of infallibility which is also given at the very moment when election is accepted. It constitutes the highest earthly participation in the royal and prophetic mission of Jesus, the Anointed of the Spirit. The pope, as vicar of the Man Jesus Christ, is the instrument of Him who is Himself anointed by the Spirit in order to spread that Spirit in the hearts and minds of all men.

Through this consecration, the pope is accredited, is sent on a mission to all the bishops and to all the faithful, by the Son who was Himself sent on a mission by the Father.[106] The pope is therefore sent by the Father and by the Spirit, who sends him to men to whom this Spirit is sent by the Father and by the Son.[107] Vicar of Christ, the pope is simultaneously the vicar and instrument of the Father who anoints, of the Son who is anointed, and of the Spirit who is the Unction.[108] The vicar of Christ cannot but be the vicar of the Trinity. The Trinity that sends him in a highly privileged way, confides to him very particularly the mission to immerse mankind in It through baptism:[109] "Go therefore and make disciples of all nations, baptizing them in the name (or: for the name[110]) of the Father and of the Son and of the Holy Spirit" (Mt. 28, 19).

Vicar of the "Anointer," of the Anointed, and of the Unction, the pope is sent by the Three Divine Persons on a salvific mission to all mankind. This point was strongly made by Gregory XV when he instituted the Congregation for the Propagation of the Faith:

> To Peter only was shown that great sheet, let down from the opened heaven "by four corners upon the earth." Within it were "all kinds of animals and reptiles and birds of the air." A voice then said to him: "Rise, Peter; kill and eat"—words meant to prefigure the task confided to Peter and to his successors: to gather together from the four corners of the earth men of the most varied kind, as though to kill them, i.e. strip them of the old life, and as though to eat them, i.e. change them into members of Peter, visible head of the Church, and thus

make them members of Christ, its invisible Head.[111]

Does this mission, immediately confided by Christ to His vicar in favor of all mankind, even of the non-baptized, signify that the pope—who cannot be, as we have seen, the vicar of the Church, i.e. its instrument, since he is, on the contrary, its visible head—could in no way be the representative of the Church? Vatican II gives a negative answer to this question, and it stresses the fact that "each individual bishop represents his own church, but all of them together in union with the pope represent the entire Church joined in the bond of love, peace, and unity."[112] It gives as the reason for this, that the bishop is the visible principle of the unity of the Church. Reasoning by analogy, we can understand, therefore, that for Vatican II the pope represents the Church, summarizes it in his person, and is its visible image in as much as he is the visible principle of its unity. He is simultaneously the representative of the Christ-Head in relation to the ecclesial community, and the representative of the whole Church in relation to the world. He directly represents the world episcopate in hierarchic communion with him, and, through that episcopate as well as immediately, he represents the whole people of God.

One could push the analysis further and show that the pope is the representative of the Church precisely because he is the vicar and instrument of the Christ-Head. Cannot one say of him, *mutatis mutandis*, what Pius XII said of the priest? "The priest represents the people because he represents the Person of Jesus Christ in as much as He is the Head of all His members and offers Himself for them; and consequently, the priest goes up to the altar as minister of Christ, inferior to Christ but superior to the people."[113] Similarly, the pope represents the Church in as much as he is the vicar and instrument of Christ, Priest, Prophet, and King. Without ever becoming the vicar of the Church which he rules in sacrificing himself for it, the pope, precisely as vicar of Christ, is constituted by Him the representative of the universal Church for each of its members and for the whole of mankind. He is as the bond which unites among themselves all the baptized who acknowledge him, and ultimately, all mankind.

The twofold quality of vicar of Christ and of representative of the universal Church is seen at its clearest when the sovereign pontiff presides at the Eucharistic celebration of the churches. For is it not then that the pope is fully the Shepherd who feeds with most excellent pasture, i.e. with the Body and Blood of the Lamb, the lambs and sheep of the Shepherd become Lamb (cf. Jn. 21, 15-18; Rev. 7, 17)? Is it not then that he confirms His brethren in the Faith, of which the Eucharist is the synthesis?

Father Karl Rahner has thought very deeply about the celebration of the Eucharist as the "becoming-event" of the institutional Church. He writes: "The Church, even as universal, exists and maintains itself in existence only because it is always being fulfilled anew in that unique and total Event, the Eucharist. . . . The local Church is the 'Event' even of this universal Church."[114]

When is such an exact observation more true than on the occasion of a concelebration of local churches, represented by their heads, in the company of the visible head of the universal Church, who presides by divine right "over the whole assembly of charity."[115]

It can indeed be said that this concelebration of the Eucharist over which the pope presides, most clearly evinces the unity of the local churches in the universal Church, which "exists in them and through them,"[116] the hierarchic communion or episcopal collegiality of their heads with the vicar of Christ, and finally, the Eucharistic purpose of the very institution of the papacy.

For, if the Eucharist is the "source and apex of the whole work of preaching the gospel,"[117] the whole doctrinal mission of the pope through which his charism of infallibility is explained, is summed up in the preaching of the Eucharist, synthesis of the whole of Catholic dogma; and his whole pastoral mission, the *raison d'être* of his primacy of jurisdiction and of love, has no other purpose than to lead men to the Eucharist: "Feed my lambs." The Christ whom the pope should announce and give is the Christ really present in the Eucharist: the Christ who is always Priest and Victim. The missionary privileges of the papacy, which we have already emphasized following the Council, are summed up in a privilege of Eucharistic evangelization.

It is all this that comes out clearly in the Mass concelebrated by the vicar of Christ and by the heads of local churches. Slightly modifying a declaration of Vatican II, we could say: "In any community existing around an altar, under the sacred ministry of *bishops assembled with the* sovereign pontiff, there is *most effectually* manifested a symbol of that charity and 'unity of the Mystical Body, without which there can be no salvation.' "[118] We can complement this with an idea of K. Rahner: "At its deepest meaning, the *universal* Church becomes event, in the full sense, only in the local concelebration of the Eucharist *by the heads of particular churches and by the vicar of Christ.*"[119]

While the concelebration by the local pontiffs with the sovereign pontiff[120] symbolizes and realizes most effectively the unity of the love of the whole Mystical Body, it must even be said that it signifies most eloquently the respective purposes which explain the existence of the papacy and of the episcopate. The papacy exists because, in the divine plan, the Church must be both one and universal; whereas the episcopate exists because this same one and universal Church must exist everywhere and make its presence felt in all places. These two complementary structures are necessary in order that everywhere there may be "true adorers of the Father, in the name of Christ, in the Spirit."

The Eucharistic concelebration by the vicars of Christ with *the* vicar of Christ brings out splendidly this truth so neatly formulated by K. Rahner: "The pope is the only one who represents the unity of the whole Church as a totality of local churches, and who does this clearly as of divine right."[123] Such concelebration also shows the coincidence and the convergence of two truly "actualist" visions. Without in any way diminishing the institutional character of the papacy, of the episcopate, and of the Eucharist, this concelebration unites the "unique and total event" of the universal 'Church, i.e. the Eucharist, and the "event" of the invisible government of the Church by the Eucharistic Christ become visible in His vicar and in His vicars.

We are, in a sense, at the meeting place of these two events, when we assist at the papal Mass concelebrated by the bishops of the local churches, who are witnesses in the faith of the construction of the universal Church: "The apostles gathered together the universal Church, which the Lord established on the apostles and built upon blessed Peter, their chief, Christ Jesus Himself remaining the supreme cornerstone."[124]

Peter is the sole "foundation upon rock" on which has been built the house of apostolic witness (cf. Lk. 6, 48; Eph. 2, 20).[125] In the course of the papal concelebration, Christ manifests Himself as the supreme cornerstone, Peter as the rock, and the bishops as the foundation of the witness which the universal Church ceaselessly bears to the Redeemer, in a perfect union of love nourished by the Eucharist. Through the "body of the pastors" united in and by the Body of Christ, it is the "body of the churches" that unveils itself to eyes of faith as being the Mystical Body of the Redeemer.[126]

Nowhere else, perhaps, is the pope more clearly seen to be the vicar of Christ and the head of the apostolic college, the "sacrament-person of this collegiality,"[127] and at the same time the "icon of the Shepherd of the one flock."[128]

C. The Papacy, a Paschal Mystery and a Trinitarian Mystery

In instituting the papacy as the hierarchy of the Church in general, the Man-Jesus took a decision reached in a prayer of sacrificial obedience to the redemptive design of the Father.

It is the episcopal college, it is the whole Church, that Satan has demanded that he might crush them as wheat; but, thanks to the prayer of Christ, a prayer constantly renewed in the Eucharistic sacrifice, the faith of Peter does not fail and his brethren are ceaselessly strengthened by him. Just like his acknowledgement of Christ as the Son of the living God, this indefectibility of faith strengthening his brethren is a gift of the Father to Peter, the Father's answer to the intercession of His only Son.

If it is the Father who has revealed His Son to Peter, it is also the Father who manifests to the only Son His Will to build the Church on the witness of Peter: "For I have not spoken on my own authority; the Father who sent me has himself given me commandment what to say and what to speak. . . . What I say, therefore, I say as the Father has bidden me" (Jn. 12, 49-50), ". . . and the word which you hear is not mine but the Father's who sent me" (Jn. 14, 24).

These declarations of Christ apply with particular force to the words in which He promised Peter the keys of the Kingdom, and then confided to him all His lambs and all His sheep (Mt. 16, 18 sq.; Jn. 21, 15-18).

In instituting Peter's indefectible, infallible, supreme, and immediate primacy of love, Christ has therefore performed an act of obedience to the design of the Father. He has therefore obeyed, even sealing His obedience with His blood, the universal, salvific will of the Father: "I have come down from heaven, not to do my own will, but the will of him who sent me; and this is the will of him that sent me, that I should lose nothing of all that he has given me . . ." (Jn. 6, 38-39).

Just like His own vocation to celibacy, the will of the Father to save the world through a hierarchized Church which would be Christ's own body, was something which the human and finite intelligence of Christ could not fully grasp. It was the free and contingent decision of a necessary God who need not have saved the world or could have done so in another way. It was and still is an aspect of the inscrutable mystery of the will of the Father, an infinite will which no created mind can see or grasp in the way It sees and loves Itself, not even the human mind of a Man-God.

It becomes clear, therefore, why it was that the Man-Jesus, when He instituted His Church, did so as part of a prayer offered in adoration of the inscrutable will of the Father: "I do nothing on my own authority, but speak thus as the Father taught me . . . for I always do what is pleasing to him" (Jn. 8, 28-29).

In instituting the papacy, Christ designed to unite all His sheep in one flock under one supreme and visible shepherd, and to be obeyed through His vicar on earth; but He also wills that His members should unite themselves through this visible representative with Himself, in order that with Him they may obey the Father, and that He may thus be able to continue, through them, the mystery of His obedience offered to the Father for the salvation of the world. "I lay down my life for my sheep. . . . There shall be one flock, one shepherd" (Jn. 10, 15-16).

To state this fact in faith is to prepare the way for a solution of the present ecumenical problem. Will not humble submission to the pope be singularly facilitated when it emerges more clearly, for Catholics in the first place, as a submission with the pope to Christ, with Christ to the Father, in the Spirit?[129]

As we have already said, it is by and in His Spirit that the risen Christ unites to Himself His vicar, to form with him a single head of the Church. The prayer of Christ that Peter's faith may not fail, secures from the Father an outpouring of the charism of infallibility and of the gifts of the Spirit of Light and of Love, not for Peter only, but for all his successors. It is through this prayer (cf. also Jn. 17, 19) that Christ obtained from the Father what Saint Thomas describes for us as follows: "The Son of God consecrates His Church and seals it by the Holy Spirit who is as its character and its seal. . . . Similarly, the vicar of Christ, by his primacy and by his action, in the manner of a faithful minister, preserves the universal Church in subjection to Christ."[130]

It is by remaining *one* in love that the Church subjects itself to Christ, and it is by growing in unity that it grows in submission. Of this unity, the local visible principle is the bishop, the universal visible principle is the pope, the invisible principle being the Spirit of the Father and of the Son, bond of their love and soul of the universal Church. So effective is the seal impressed[131] by Christ on His vicar at the "papal consecration," that this Spirit, supreme bond of the unity of the Mystical Body (cf. Eph. 4, 4), ceaselessly urges the vicar of the Lamb "to confirm all His sheep in faith and to shepherd them in perfect unity." [132] It is through His powerful action that "this Chair presides over the whole assembly of charity and protects legitimate differences while at the same time it ensures that such differences do not hinder unity, but rather contribute to it."[133]

The doctrine of Vatican II also means that the purpose of the papacy coincides with that of the Inhumanation of the Word: namely, the recapitulation of the universe to the glory of the Father. To appreciate this fact, it suffices to compare the two Vatican II texts which deal with these respective purposes.[134] Besides, the coincidence is easy to accept if any one has really grasped that the vicar of Christ is the sacrament of the recapitulative and redemptive primacy of Christ in and over His Church.

Without the papacy, how could the dynamism described by Vatican II be realized? "The Catholic

Church strives energetically and constantly to bring all humanity with all its riches back to Christ its Head in the unity of His Spirit."[135] Of this recapitulation, is not the chair of Peter the chief visible instrument and agent?

But the full efficacy of this constant recapitulative tendency of the papacy depends on its Trinitarian origin and its salvific purpose being widely recognized and acknowledged. Such recognition seems to us impossible without an effort to study deeply the paschal mystery and the mystery of the Trinity. The Trinitarian origin would be of no interest, did the Trinitarian mystery itself appear valueless. Only the desire of the perfect communion with the Father and with the Son, under the breath of the Spirit who is Their communion, will urge us towards hierarchic[136] communion with the vicar of Christ, to obey him in order to obey with him Christ and the Father.

By his mere existence, the sovereign pontiff repeats to each and every man the message of Saint John the Evangelist: "We proclaim to you the eternal life which was with the Father and was made manifest to us . . . so that you may have fellowship with us; and our fellowship is with the Father and with his Son Jesus Christ. And we are writing this that our joy may be complete" (1 Jn. 1, 2-4).

The perfect hierarchic and Eucharistic[137] communion with the vicar of Christ is not an ultimate purpose, but an indispensable means of full horizontal and vertical communion with human, angelic, and divine persons. The pope is not a screen or a limit, but a beacon and a bridge leading towards the eternal life of the Father, the Son, and the Holy Spirit.

The sovereign pontiff is the visible paraclete,[138] instrument of the two invisible Paracletes.[139] The visible head of the Church is its teacher[140] only in order to lead it, by disclosing Him in himself, to its only eternal Teacher and Master, Christ (Mt. 23, 8-10). He is the father of all Christians[141] only in order to help them to bend the knees with him "before the

Father, from whom every family in heaven and on earth is named" (Eph. 4, 14), and to become the adorers in Spirit and in Truth that the Father is seeking (Jn. 4, 23-24).

The vicar of the Man-Jesus is therefore, by that very fact, the ambassador and the instrument of the Father and of their Spirit, the vicar of the redemptive Trinity.

This is surely what Saint Catherine of Siena had in mind when she offered to the heavenly Father this very beautiful prayer[142]:

> O incomprehensible Love, you are always the same! Today, You send your vicar to bring back the children who have gone astray by separating themselves from the obedience of the Church, their mother and your only spouse.
>
> And as formerly to your dear Son, our Savior, it is in anguish and among dangers that You confide to your vicar the mission to snatch these children from the chastisement of disobedience and from the death of sin.
>
> You are in love with the creature. You have sent him your vicar, with the mission to save this sheep in danger. Vouchsafe that I, a miserable sinner, may thank You for this!
>
> In departing from us, You did not leave us orphans. You have left behind You your vicar who gives us the baptism of the Holy Spirit, and this not once only, as with the baptism of water which has washed us once for all. Ceaselessly he purifies us through the holy power which You have given Him, and as the dispenser of your Blood, he wipes away our sins.

The saint, in seeing that the pope is the dispenser of the Blood of Christ, is perfectly in accord with the Gospel, and expresses in her own way the promise of the Savior concerning the power to bind and loose confided to Peter. The power of the keys implies that of remitting sins and even the temporal punishment due to sin—and hence, the power to grant indulgences.

It is not only the power to define the truth, but also that of binding and loosing the conscience of men. Hence it is that Saint Catherine also says that the pope is "the cellarer who holds the keys of the cellar where is stored the holy reserve of your Blood, with the blood of all the martyrs (the value of which derives only from yours)."[143]

So lively an awareness of the splendor of the mission of the Roman pontiff is, with this saint, inseparable from an awareness of all the human weaknesses of him who receives it. The prayer of thanksgiving is followed, therefore, by a prayer of supplication for the vicar of Christ the Redeemer. Saint Catherine offers herself to the Redeemer as a coredemptive victim for the sovereign pontiff:

> Eternal Goodness, enlighten him who is your vicar on earth, in order that he may not love You for himself, or himself for himself, but that he may love You and love himself for your sake.
> If he loves You for himself, we are all lost, for in him is our life and our death, dependent upon his zeal to save us, his lost sheep. If he loves himself and loves You for your sake, we are saved, for we receive from the Good Shepherd an example of how to live.[145]
> Eternal Mercy, make your vicar a devourer of souls, on fire with zeal for your glory, and relying only on You, the infinite and eternal Goodness. Heal through him our infirmities and reinstate your spouse, thanks to his salutary counsels and to his virtuous works. . . . If his dilatoriness offends you, O eternal Love, punish it in my body; I offer my body to You that you may punish it, or even destroy it if such is your good pleasure.[146]

In these texts, we see that, with Saint Catherine, an acute awareness of the salvific mission of the pope in her regard, did not in the least hinder her perception of her own coredemptive mission in regard to the vicar of Christ. We touch here on the supreme expression of a mysterious reciprocity of mutually coredemptive awarenesses, in virtue of which the ambassadors of Christ are in need of being saved through those to whom they are sent; and this need reaches even to the highest earthly degree of the hierarchy.

It thus emerges more clearly that the vicar of Christ is a sacrament of the primacy of redemptive Love in and over Christ's coredemptive Church; that he is, first and foremost, a sign and an instrument of the full primacy of the love of the Redeemer. This triple love of Christ for men has received from the Father all rights over them. He effectively exercises His full power by the outpouring of His efficacious graces. In comparison with the fullness of the power of excellence[147] enjoyed by Christ over His Church, the fullness of the pope's power remains a limited participation through which Christ manifests His unifying and salvific power.

Furthermore, the immediate primacy of the pope is an instrumental sign of a decidedly more immediate primacy of the love of the Word for the created wills which He has redeemed: an absolutely immediate love of the transcendent and immanent Creator, an invisible and visible love which departed from us at the Ascension only in order to remain with us invisibly in the Eucharist, and visibly in His vicar: "elevandus in coelum, amoris sui nobis velut vicarium relinquebat."[148]

The indefectible primacy of the vicar of Redemptive Love shows, by the miracle of its historical permanence despite many shadows and many failures,[149] that this Love will remain with us until the end of the world. The mere existence of the papacy is enough to show any thoughtful man that nothingness does not lie before him, that his destiny is to reach the eternal Love which attracts him ceaselessly towards itself. The indefectibility of the papacy is an incessant call to every man: "Do not fail in love."

Finally, is not the infallible primacy of the vicar of

Christ the means chosen by Christ to signify permanently that He is Himself the immutable Truth inserted, without in any way affecting this immutability into the midst of the movement of human history?—and that at all times He seeks to assuage the thirst for truth which He arouses in the mind of every man?

Yes, Saint Ambrose was right: at the very moment when He ascended into the heavens towards the Father, in order to draw us there after Him, Christ did not leave us orphans, but gave us, with and through His Spirit, the vicar of His full, immediate, indefectible, infallibly redemptive love; the vicar of His Heart and of His peace: "Peace I leave with you; my peace I give to you" (Jn. 14, 27; cf. vv. 14, 18, 26).

In the Eucharistic concelebration of the individual and local vicars with the supreme and universal vicar of Christ, our Pasch, eyes enlightened by faith will see the supreme manifestation on earth of the triune Reality, at once Being and Love: [151]

> I do not pray for these only, but also for those who believe in me through their word, that they may all be one; even as you, Father, are in me, and I in you, that they may be one in us, so that the world may believe that you have sent me. . . . I lay down my life for the sheep. And I have other sheep that are not of this fold; I must bring them also, and they will heed my voice. So there shall be one flock, one shepherd. . . . I am the good shepherd" (Jn. 17, 20-21; 21, 15-17; 10, 15-16; 10, 11).

Appendix on the doctrine of the episcopal judicature.
Some difficulties might be raised against this doctrine:

(a) Vatican I teaches (DS, 3063; DB, 1830) that the Roman pontiff is (by divine right) the supreme judge of the faithful; his judgment cannot be subject to confirmation by any other judgment; it is not lawful to appeal from the pope's judgment to that of an ecumenical council, as if the latter had a superior authority. Under due deference to a more searching analysis of the intentions of the Council, it seems to us that it did not seek to exclude the judgment of canonical confirmation of an episcopate, but rather an examination motivated by doubt or negation. Muzzarelli, pontifical theologian and vigorous opponent of Jansenism, would in no sense accept, however, that this judgment of canonical confirmation could condition the validity and the obligatory nature of the pontifical act. Cf. DS, 638 *sq.*, 861 (DB, 330 *sq.*, 466).

(b) Vatican II (LG, 25. 2) stresses the fallibility of the bishops considered individually, and the same holds good for episcopal conferences. Yes, but this does not hinder them from being judges in matters of faith, even though fallible judges. A bishop is as bound as is a layman by the pontifical magisterium, and yet his acceptance is not merely an act of obedience. The bishop is more than a witness: bishops "are quite rightly called *prelates*, heads of the people whom they govern" (LG, 27—Abbot, 52). The bishop is an authentic teacher and, even apart from the council, a judge (in the first instance) concerning the Faith of which the pope is the supreme judge: LG, 25.

(c) In the eyes of the French bishops of the eighteenth century, the constitutions of the popes were binding on the Church only "when they had been accepted by the body of the pastors" (DTC, III, 1908, 105; art. Clement XI). The pope protested. But he did not deny the more subtle doctrine of Fénelon (taken up by Muzzarelli) and it was with it that he appears to have been satisfied (DTC, XIII, 1, 1936, 1510-1512: art. Quesnel).

NOTES TO CHAPTER THIRTEEN

1. Cf. B. de Margerie S.J., *Reinhold Niebuhr, théologien de la communauté mondiale,* Paris, 1969, pp. 227-228.

2. *Ibid.*

3. This would be as injurious as it would be to exclude consideration of the episcopate from theological thought. In both

cases, this would fall short of the full purpose of the ecumenical dialogue as put forward by Vatican II: "The doctrine concerning the ministers of the Church must therefore be a subject of the dialogue" (UR, 22, 3).

4. The expression "primacy of jurisdiction" is given formal approval through its use by Vatican I (DS, 3064, DM, 1831) as distinct from a mere "office of inspection or of direction."

5. In *Ecclesiam Suam* (AAS, 56, 1964, 656), Paul VI speaks of a "primatum famulatus, ministerii, amoris." Vatican II seems to have avoided the word "jurisdiction" in connection with the primacy.

6. Cf. our Chapter One.

7. Cf. Pius XII, *Mystici Corporis,* AAS, 35 (1943), 215.

8. Cf. 1 Cor. 15, 25 and 24 (we reverse the order of the verses): "For he must reign . . . when he delivers the kingdom to God the Father after destroying every rule and every authority and power." Is it not through Peter that this destruction is ceaselessly effected throughout human history in the warfare against the powers of Hell? (cf. 12 Cor. 10, 4-5).

9. DS, 3064; DB, 1831.

10. LG, 22; 19.

11. Saint Robert Bellarmine, *Controversia III de Summo Pontifice,* Vivès, Paris, 1870, t. I, pp. 483-484.

12. The same text as that cited in note 17.

13. Cf. Chapter Four, note 135.

14. To the texts cited in our Chapter Four, note 135, we may add: the pleroma signifies "concentration in Christ of the sanctifying divine power," according to Cerfaux, *Le Christ dans la théologie de saint Paul,* Paris, 1951, pp. 320-322; Eph. 1, 23 declares that "the Church is filled by Christ, Himself constantly filled by God," according to A. Feuillet, DBS, t. III (1967), col. 37, art. "Plerome."

15. DS, 3050 (DB, 1821); LG, 19.

16. DS, 3806.

17. Saint Robert Bellarmine, sermon of April 25, 1604, *Opera oratoria posthuma,* edited by Father Tromp, Rome, t. V, pp. 196-197.

18. Saint Robert Bellarmine, Controversia III . . . , *op cit.,* pp. 499-500.

19. At the theological, not the pastoral level. Cf. B. de Margerie, "Jésus, Pierre et les Douze suivant Bellarmin," *Sciences ecclésiastiques* 18 (1966), 382 *seq.*

20. Does not this orientation naturally promote the union of all Christians?

21. DS, 3053, 3055 (DB, 1822-1823).

22. DS, 3062 and 3074 (DB, 1829 and 1839).

23. DS, 3064 (DB, 1831).

24. Cited by T. J. Jimenez-Urresti in *La collégialité épiscopale,* le Cerf, Paris, 1965, pp. 242-243.

25. Pius XI, encyclical *Ubi Arcano* of Dec. 23, 1922; *ibid.*, p. 242.

26. AAS, 53 (1961), 466.

27. Cf. E, 7: "nomine vero Patriarchae orientalis venit episcopus, cui competit jurisdictio in omnes episcopos, haul exceptis metropolitis, clerum et populum proprii ritus, ad normam juris et salvo primatu Romani Pontificis." We use the expression "primacy of jurisdiction and of love," in view of LG, 13, 3 (the pope "presides over the whole assembly of charity" —*Abbott*, p. 32), and of the text of Paul VI cited in note 5.

28. OE, 3.

29. LG, 27.

30. Cf. G. Dejaifvre S.J.: "Le premier des évèques," *Nouv. Rev. Théol.*, 1960, 561-579.

31. Cf. Pius XII, *Mystici Corporis*, AAS, 35 (1943), 209: "ipse (Christus) solummodo est qui Ecclesiam regit atque gubernat."

32. *Ibid.*, pp. 207-210.

33. LG, 14. 2 (Abbott, p. 33).

34. LG, 60. 2 (Abbott, 90-91).

35. LG, 62. 2 (Abbott, 92).

36. Cf. J. de la Servière S.J., *La théologie de Bellarmin*, Paris, 1909, p. 267 (text of 1606).

37. Saint Robert Bellarmine, *controversia de Conciliis*, liber II, cap. 19; cf. J. de la Servière, *op. cit.*, p. 167.

38. *Ibid.*, p. 267. In 1607, in his "Recognitiones," the Saint writes: "If the pope commanded what is manifestly vicious or prescribed what is manifestly vicious, one should say with Saint Peter (Acts 5, 29): 'We must obey God rather than men'" (*Recognitiones de Romano Pontifice*, IV, V; cited by Le Bachelet, DTC, art "Bellarmin," col. 591). It must be added that it is impossible that the pope should command the whole Church to commit a sin: the powers of hell shall not prevail against the Church.

39. Same source as the text cited in note 37.

40. The title appended to the pope's signature to conciliar acts, notably those of Vatican II.

41. See numerous texts of Saint Gregory the Great bearing on this matter, in *La collégialité épiscopale*, the work to which note 24 refers.

42. Cf. DS, 3060 (DB, 1827): "Ecclesia Christi . . . unus grex sub uno *summo* pastore," and not "sub uno pastore." The wording is designed to emphasize that the pope is not the only pastor *in* the Church.

43. See an explanation worded differently but apparently amounting to the same thing, by G. Thils in Congar and Dupuy: *L'Episcopat et l'Eglise universelle*, Paris, 1962, p. 705.

44. Complete French translation of this text can be found

in the volume cited in note 43; the German and Latin versions in DS, 3112-3117.

45. DS, 3061 (DB, 1828).

46. This is the title of the Dogmatic Constitution on the Church, promulgated by Vatican I.

47. CD, 2. Cf. LG, 27. 2: "This power which they personally exercise in Christ's name, is proper, ordinary, and immediate, although its exercise is ultimately regulated by the supreme authority of the Church, and can be circumscribed by certain limits, *for the advantage of the Church or of the faithful.* In virtue of this power, bishops have the sacred right and the duty before the Lord, to make laws for their subjects, to pass judgment on them, and to moderate everything pertaining to the ordering of worship and the apostolate" (Abbott, 52). Italics are ours.

48. In his unpublished commentary on the Summa Theologica of Saint Thomas Aquinas, at II. II. 39. 1, Saint Robert Bellarmine distinguishes between the external influence of the pope in proposing the doctrine of faith, and the internal influence of Christ in bestowing the virtue of faith. Cf. S. Tromp S.J., *Corpus Christi quod est Ecclesia,* t. II, *De Christo capite,* Rome, 1960, pp. 436-437.

49. LG, 27. 2, 3. (Abbott, 52).

50. DS, 2601, (DB, 1501); LG, 12. 1.

51. DS, 3056 (DB, 1824).

52. DS, 3058 (DB, 1825).

53. LG, 22 (the pope, vicar of Christ) and 27: "Bishops govern the particular churches entrusted to them as the vicars and ambassadors of Christ" (Abbott, 51).

54. DS, 3052 (DB, 1821).

55. Saint Robert Bellarmine, *Opera omnia posthuma,* ed. Tromp, Rome, t. III, pp. 148-150. We say "charismatically," because the Saint's Latin autobiography amply shows the extraordinary charism of preaching which he was conscious of having received.

56. LG, 48. 3 (Abbott, 79).

57. Heb. 13, 7-8; note in the Jerusalem Bible.

58. This theme, dear to Father Congar (opposition of the already received and of the yet-to-come), has been presented as follows by E. Peterson: "For them (the Fathers) the Synagogue is a *congregation,* the gathering together of a *grex,* and therefore decidedly a natural reality. In the *Ecclesia,* on the contrary, they have recognized the nuance in the use of the term the *ekkalein,* the *evocatio,* the call to come out of the world, to quit the world, its natural structures and its sociological creations" (*Le mystère des Juifs et des Gentils,* p. 10). This book was published in German in 1933 under the title: *Die Kirche aus Juden und Heiden;* cf. Y. Congar, *Crétiens en Dialogue,* Paris, 1964, p. 228.

59. See our Chapter Eight.

60. DS, 3071 (DB, 1837).

61. Cf. DS, 3074 (DB, 1839): "ea infallibilitate pollere, qua *divinus Redemptor* Ecclesiam suam . . . instructam esse voluit."

62. Saint Thomas Aquinas, *Summa Theologica,* I. II. 85. 3.

63. LG, 12; cf. Harent, DTC, t. VI. 1 (1915), col. 369-376, art. "Foi"; Saint Thomas Aquinas, "lumen fidei, quasi sigillatio quaedam Primae Veritatis in mente, non potest fallere sicut Deus non potest decipere vel mentiri" (*in Boet. de Trin.* 3. 1. 4).

64. Pius XII, *Mystici Corporis,* AAS, 35 (1943), 213; DS, 3805.

65. LG, 12. 1. (Abbott, 29).

66. LG, 25. 3 (Abbott, 48-49).

67. *Ibid.* (Abbott, 49).

68. A. Muzzarelli, *De auctoritate R. Pontificis in consiliis generalibus,* t. II, p. 213. A theologian of Pius VII, and disciple of Fénelon; he was like the latter an upholder of the "episcopal judicature" which he sums up in the paragraph quoted here. (Cf. B. D. Dupuy O.P., "La judicature épiscopale," *Rev. des Sc. Phil. et Théol.,* 51 (1967), 245.

69. *Ibid.,* pp. 247-248. The author there indicates his sources. It will be noticed (p. 249) that he does not seem to be aware of the distinction which Vatican II makes between *consensus* and *assensus.* He also cites the examination, not of doubt or negation but of confirmation, of Flavian's book, by the Chalcedon Fathers (*ibid.,* pp. 245-246). See our appendix at the end of this chapter.

70. AAS, 42 (1950), 756 and 769, where there is question of "prope unanima *consensione.*"

71. Formula of the Russian Catholic theologian, Gavriloff.

72. On the advantage of the definitions, see DS, 2802. In saying that the pope is the infallible "definer" of the object of the prior consent of the Church, we are merely expressing in another form what R. Aubert has put so well: "The serious discussions to which the Vatican definition has given rise, have brought out more clearly the distinction between the *sensus ecclesiae,* which the pope, organ of tradition, can never violate; and the *consensus ecclesiae,* which he does not need" (L'ecclésiologie du Concile du Vatican," in: *Le Concile et les Conciles,* Paris, 1960, p. 281). On the same point, but in different terms, see the fine letter of Cardinal Dechamps to Msgr. Ketteler during the Council (July 12, 1870), reproduced in Y. M. J. Congar, *Sainte Eglise,* Paris, 1963, pp. 353-355. We personally would certainly accept what is said there: "non ex consensu praesenti Ecclesiae, sed ex sese, id est, ex charismate sibi a Spiritu Veritatis dato, Romanus Pontifex consensum anteriorem Ecclesiae infallibiliter definit modo tali ut, ex lumine et vi ejusdem Spiritus, haec definitio assensum

posteriorem Ecclesiae infallibiliter obtineat." This presentation, from the viewpoint of temporal unfolding, seems to us to throw light on the discussion.

73. Cf. our Chapter Ten, B.

74. S. Dockx O.P., in *La collégialité épiscopale,* Paris, 1965, p. 327. The author clearly shows the Biblical foundation of "ex sese, non ex consensu Ecclesiae."

75. *Ibid.;* the author sees clearly that "the pastoral power of Peter," like that of the other Apostles, "presupposes his prophetic function"—and, of course, theirs *(ibid.).*

76. Cf. LG, 23, 2: ". . . the successor of Peter, upon whom was imposed in a special way the great duty of spreading the Christian name." (Abbott, 45). The pastoral primacy of love derives from the prophetic primacy in the infallible witness.

77. DV, 2.

78. Cf. Congar, *Saint Eglise,* Paris, 1963, pp. 674 *seq.* The author there sums up an investigation by M. Maccarrone, *Vicarius Christi,* Rome, 1952; cf. Fenton, "Vicarius Christi," *Amer. Eccl. Rev.,* 110 (1944), 458-470.

79. Y. M. J. Congar O.P., in *Problèmes de l'Authorité,* Paris, 1962, pp. 167-168.

80. *Ibid.* It is certainly thus that Pius XII (DS, 3835; DB, 2313) understands this text: Christ speaks today through His Vicar.

81. We think that Father Congar is wrong when he writes: "One fact seems to us to have escaped the attention of Msgr. M. Maccarrone. . . . namely, the way in which the content of the word *vicarius* (Christi) has been really changed, though the word itself continues to be the same. . . . Without this (actualist) value changing, it is overspread by another value . . . i.e. the idea of a power given at the beginning of Christian history by Christ to His Vicar as a representative who was to take His place and who was to transmit the power thus received, according to an historical chain of transmission and of succession." Congar insists: "the actualist or sacramental mystic idea is conjoined with the juridical idea," in the same work *(Problèmes de l'authorité,* pp. 167-168). We hold that in reality no pope transmits to another pope his power of primacy, since in each case the latter is received directly and immediately from Christ (see note 101 of the present chapter) and without having, as it were, to come through the late pope. What remains true, in Father Congar's ideas, is that the pope does succeed Christ in as much as Christ was, during His earthly life, the visible head of the Church; and that the immediate conferring of the pontifical power by Christ signifies the perfect unity of the mystical and juridical aspects of the functions of the "Vicar of Christ." The power was not handed over once for all by Christ, at the beginning of Christian history, to the first pope in order to be transmitted by him to his

successor, and by that successor to his: in each individual instance, it is Christ alone who gives this power directly and immediately. There has therefore been no change of content in the continuing expression "vicarius Christi." On the contrary, the original "actualist" value is still present today, as is shown by the text of Pius XII cited in the previous note.

82. Pius XII, *Mystici Corporis*, AAS, 35 (1943), 211. It will be noted that, for Pius XII, the pope is merely the vicar of Christ, a statement which serves to underline that he is not Christ, but Christ's instrument. We might add: His non-conjoined, but separate, instrument.

83. Cf. S. Tromp S.J., *Corpus Christi quod est Ecclesia*, t. II, *De Christo capite*, Rome, 1960, p. 432; the author here cites DS, 2678 (DB, 1578).

84. LG, 18 and 22; the matter had already been defined at Florence (DS, 1307; DB, 694).

85. LG, 27. 1.

86. Cf. Congar, *Sainte Eglise*, Paris, 1963, p. 675; Maccarrone, *op. cit.*, p. 293.

87. Saint Ignatius Loyola, *Constitutions of the Company of Jesus*, part VII, chap. 1, paragraphs 603, 606, and 607. Congar (*op. cit* in note 86, p. 675) notes that the title *Vicarius Christi* was still being applied to bishops and priests in the sixteenth century.

88. Saint Ignatius Loyola, *Letter on Obedience* (1553), par. 4.

89. See our Chapter Eleven.

90. Cf. LG, 9. 3 and 48. 2.

91. F. A. Sullivan S.J.: "De unitate Ecclesiae," *Gregorianum*, 43 (1962), 519-522.

92. DS, 3051 (DB, 1821).

93. T. J. Jimenez-Urresti, in *La Collégiaté épiscopale*, Paris, 1965, p. 241. The mediate finality in no way hinders the immediate primacy over all the faithful. For it is not only by safeguarding the unity of the episcopate that the pope preserves the unity of the Church; he also does so immediately. This further purpose is thus, in a sense, immediate.

94. Saint Cyprian, *De unitate Ecclesiae*, V (PL, 4, 501); *Epistola*, 66. 8. 3. Cf. A. Dumoustier S.J., Episcopat et union à Rome selon saint Cyprien," *Recherches de Science Religieuse*, 52 (1964), 337-370.

95. LG, 23; the text adds: "The individual bishop, however, is the visible principle and foundation of unity in his particular church." (Abbott, 44). This indicates that it is both mediately and immediately that the pope is the principle of the unity of the whole pilgrim Church—but the visible principle only, since it is the Holy Spirit who is the invisible principle of this unity.

96. DS, 3052 (DB, 1821): "totius Ecclesiae vis ac soliditas."

97. Paul VI (Sept. 15, 1965) called Saint Cyprian "the doctor of the unity of the Church" (*Documentation Catholique,* 1965, col. 1652).

98. LG, 9. 3, citing Saint Cyprian, *Epist.,* 69, 6 (PL, 3, 1142 B).

99. LG, 1.

100. S. Tromp S.J., *op. cit.,* p. 423.

101. *Ibid.;* cf. DS, 2603 (DB, 1503) which condemns as heretical the idea that the Roman Pontiff receives his power over the Church from the Church itself. It is otherwise with a head of State, who receives political power from God through the people.

102. See the text to which note 83 refers.

103. Here one should even use the term "sacralizing consecration" (cf. our Chapter Eight). The idea of a special outpouring of graces at the moment when the newly elected pope accepts his election, is perfectly in line with the doctrine of Saint Thomas (cf. *Summa Theologica,* III. 27. 5: God gives to each the grace befitting his vocation). In view of the salvific universality of the mission of the vicar of Christ, what could be more befitting than that he should receive, at the moment of his papal consecration, a special fullness of graces (cf. Acts 6, 8)? But this, of course, in no way implies that the papacy constitutes an eighth sacrament. It is not the papacy, but the episcopate, which is a sacrament.

104. Equality exists between pope and bishops at the level of Holy Orders. Father Philippon's formula does not seem, therefore, a well chosen one. He may mean, of course, that their power of Orders, equal in its essence, is unequal in its concrete exercise: the "papal consecration" inherent in the election of a new pope means that his power of Orders can no longer be governed in its exercise by any earthly power superior to his own (cf. LG, 27. 2).

105. M. Philippon O.P., "Consécration sacerdotale et consécration religieuse," in *Vocations,* no. 241 (1968), p. 130.

106. Cf. Jn. 17, 18; 20, 21.

107. Cf. Jn. 14, 26; 15, 26; 16, 7; Acts 13, 4.

108. An idea familiar to Saint Irenaeus.

109. Cf. the texts cited by notes 76 and 111.

110. Cf. D. Buzy, *commentaire sur l'Evangile de saint Matthieu,* Paris, 1935, t. IX, p. 386: "the Greek formula of Saint Matthew is to be retained because of the preposition governing the accusative, which seems to suggest a movement of the baptized towards the Trinity (eis to onoma).

111. Gregory XV, bull *Inscrutabile divinae,* June 22, 1622; text cited by S. Tromp S.J. in his edition of the encyclical *Mystici Corporis,* Rome, 1948, Gregorian University, Series theologica, no. 26, p. 106, par. 39. There is a fine commentary there on Acts 10, 11-16.

112. LG, 23. 1 (Abbott, 44).

113. DS, 3850, citing Saint Robert Bellarmine (DB, 2300).

114. K. Rahner, "Quelques réflexions sur les principes constitutionnels de l'Eglise," in *L'Episcopat et l'Eglise universelle,* Paris, 1962, p. 554.

115. LG, 13, 3 (Abbott, 32), citing Saint Ignatius of Antioch, *Epist. ad Rom.*: ". . . Petri cathedrae, quae universo caritatis coetui praesidet."

116. LG, 23. 1 (Abbott, 44).

117. PO, 5. 2. (Abbott, 542).

118. LG, 26; the italics indicate what we have added to the text.

119. K. Rahner, *op. cit.,* ibid. Italics again indicate our additions.

120. Vatican II rarely used this expression. It occurs, however, in CD, 11. We regard it as fitting here, in this context of Eucharistic concelebration.

121. We sum up here, in different words, what Rahner says, *op. cit.,* 555.

122. *Ibid.*

123. *Ibid.,* p. 556.

124. LG, 19.

125. P. Benoit O.P., *Exégèse et Théologie,* Patris, 1961, t. II, p. 270, where the author also says: "Peter is not likened to the constructed foundation of the house, i.e. to this first course of bricks, to this "thémélios of which the other apostles equally form part" (Eph. 2, 20).—On the moment when the words of Jesus recorded in Mt. 16, 18 *seq.,* were spoken, see P. Benoit, *op. cit.,* t. II, pp. 294-295. Interesting in itself, this matter is of secondary importance for dogmatic theology.

126. The expression "corpus ecclesiarum" and "corpus pastorum" (clearly parallels) are used by LG, 23. 2 and 3.

127. Cf. J. Colson, *Episcopat catholique: collégialité et primauté,* Paris, 1963, p. 130: "At the centre of the collegiality of the apostolic successors scattered among all the nations of the world, the bishop of Rome is the personal sacrament of the unity of this collegiality."

128. Formula of Y. M. J. Congar O.P., in *Episcopat et Eglise universelle,* Paris, 1962, p. 258.

129. Cf. Cardinal de Berulle, *Opuscules de Piété,* Paris, 1944, pp. 446-470.

130. Saint Thomas Aquinas, *De erroribus Graecorum,* Opusc. ed. Mandonnet, III, 322.

131. On the symbolism of the Spirit seen as a seal (Eph. 1, 13-14 etc.), see S. Tromp S.J., *Corpus Christi quod est Ecclesia,* t. III, *De Spiritu Christi anima,* Rome, 1960, pp. 133 *seq.*

132. UR, 2. 3.

133. LG, 13. 3. In presenting the proper function of the chair of Peter as a service which guarantees the diversities

and particularities in the Church, Vatican II shows us that it is simultaneously a nucleus of centralization and of decentralization.

134. Cf. our Chapter One: GS, 45; UR, 2; LG, 23. 1.

135. LG, 13. 2 (Abbott, 31).

136. LG, 22. The reference here is to the bishops and to the college of bishops, but the idea is capable of much wider application and may be contrasted with the imperfect, non-hierarchical communion which exists among Christians belonging to confessions or churches still partially separated from Rome and from the Roman Church; UR, 3. This imperfect communion is founded upon valid baptism, whereas hierarchical communion presupposes in addition the unity of faith, of worship, and of government.

137. Cf. UR, 4. 3.

138. In the image of Christ (1 Jn. 2, 1) and of the Holy Spirit (Jn. 15, 26-27), the pope is an advocate who intercedes with the Father—and as such, the "sovereign pontiff"—or who pleads before the tribunal of mankind the cause of the Christians and of the universal Church, by representing it in face of the world. On the idea of Paraclete, see H. M. Dion O.P., "L'origine du titre de Paraclet," *Sciences Ecclésiastiques,* 17 (1965) 143-149.

139. Cf. Jn. 14, 16.

140. DS, 1307 (DB, 694).

141. *Ibid.*

142. This is one of the prayers she composed after a secret audience with Gregory XI at Genoa in October 1376: *Oraisons et Elévations,* French translation by Bernard, pp. 19-24.

143. *Ibid.,* p. 14.

144. Cf. Saint Robert Bellarmine, *Opera oratoria posthuma,* Rome, t. II, p. 120, sermon of Aug. 1, 1604: "It is fitting that we should give thanks to God because He has willed to give us this very solid foundation-stone of the Church, i.e. the supreme pontificate which keeps the whole Church united. Because of it, we are certain that we do not err when we obey and follow him in faith."

145. Saint Catherine of Siena: *op. cit.,* p. 11 *seq.*

146. *Ibid.,* pp. 19-24.

147. The fullness of power of Christ, as Man, over the Church is called a power of excellence. It is the power to determine the deposit of faith, to establish the fundamental law of the Church, to institute the immutable sacraments and ecclesiastical organs. All this is incommunicable, at least *de facto.* Cf. S. Tromp S.J., *Corpus Christi quod est Ecclesia,* t. II, *De Christo Capite,* Rome, 1960, pp. 134 *seq.,* in particular pp. 146-147. Strictly speaking, this incommunicable power is also, as such, incapable of being shared. On the power of ex-

cellence, see note 11 of this chapter and the text to which it refers.

148. Saint Ambrose, *Expos. Ev. sec. Lucam,* par. 175; PL, 15, 1848. The Saint is here commenting on Jn. 21, 15-18. Elsewhere, the Saint expresses the celebrated axiom: "Where Peter is, there is the Church; where the Church is, there is no death, but eternal life" (*Enarr. in Ps.* 40. 30; PL, 14, 1082).

149. Cf. LG, 8, 4: "licet sub umbris, fideliter tamen. . . ." The failures to which we are referring are not, of course, defections from the faith, but infidelities in the exercise of the pastoral mission of the pope.

150. Cf. Pius XII, *Mystici Corporis,* AAS, 35 (1943), 227: there Pius XII underlines the intimate association that exists between the invisible mission of the Spirit and the visible, juridical mission of the Roman Pontiff, between the "arcanam gubernationem" of the first and the "perspicibilem moderationem" of the second. Such an association was willed by Christ.

151. Cf. the *Credo* of Paul VI, June 30, 1968: "Ille est qui est . . . ille est Amor ita ut duo haec nomina Esse et Amor ineffabiliter divinam eandem experimant illius essentiam" (AAS, 60, 1968, par. 9).

152. Cf. the Jerusalem Bible note on Jn. 10, 16 ("I must bring them"): "not to lead them into the Jewish fold, but to gather them together into a flock which Jesus leads to eternal life."

14

THE EUCHARISTIC HEART OF THE LORD:
SYNTHESIS AND CONSUMMATION OF
THE UNIVERSE OF HISTORY AND OF REVELATION

The great spiritual and religious need of our times is that of a broad synthetic vision of the Christian mystery. Such a vision must be developed within an existential context, in the indispensable light which emanates from love. It must arise from one central nucleus which serves to render intelligible all its co-ordinated rays of truth.

There are some non-Catholic, Christian theologians of our age who have attempted such a synthesis; but this cannot be said of any of the best known[1] theologians of the universal and Roman Church.[2] Excessive specialization partly explains, but does not justify, the flinching away from anything which might resemble a *Summa Theologica*. That partly contestable and contested outline sketched by Teilhard de Chardin, who was not a professional theologian, has been acclaimed, notably because of its power to synthesize.

It seems a matter of urgency to us to contribute, if only from afar through pointers and indicators, towards satisfying that basic desire of all who have been baptized in the blood of the Lamb: to recapitulate and unify all realities, as well as all revealed truths, in the pierced Heart of the crucified Christ, in order thus to present fully the mystery of the universal redemption. For the created mind seeks to interpret the universe only in order to transform and to perfect it; the created mind aspires through intellectual activity to take reality into itself, only in order then to express itself outwardly in a world which is capable of receiving its impress, and thus to attain to the face-to-face contemplation of Divine Being, of Divine Love, of Divine Energy which shines forth with its pure light as well as with the diffused light of created reality.

We should therefore like to demonstrate here how the Eucharistic Heart of the Lamb of God could offer to Catholic theology the best initial and completion stages for its systematization: (a) in what concerns the sacrament of the Incarnation and the sacraments of salvation and of grace; (b) in relation to the consummation of the redemption and of the universe; (c) finally, in relation to the Word, Son and Breather, Predestinator, and created[3] and predestined Creator.

A. Meaning of the Cult Rendered to the Eucharistic Heart of Jesus

Both Pius XI and Pius XII regarded the devotion offered to the Heart of Jesus as the "summary of the whole Christian religion," and therefore as "the rule of Christian perfection."[4] Pius XII has clearly shown how this devotion synthesizes all dogma and all morality: "(It) is the cult of the love with which God has loved us through Jesus, while at the same time it is the exercise of the love which we ourselves bear to God and to other men."[5]

In line with this, Vatican II, with splendid insistence, presents "the celebration of the Eucharistic Sacrifice" as "the root, the centre, and the summit of the whole life of the Christian community."[6] The Eucharist, adds the Council, "contains the Church's entire spiritual wealth"[7]; it is "the source and the apex of the whole work of preaching the gospel."[8] Reading these statements of Vatican II and of the earlier popes, the least that one can say is that the Church's magisterium implies that the Eucharistic Sacrifice, on the one hand, and the devotion to the Heart of Jesus, on the other, are both at the centre of the Christian's life and of the life of the Church itself. How could they fail, therefore, to be the radiating centre of their ideas? If the world and the Church have for *raison d'être* the Lord present in a glorious, though hidden, and supremely loving manner in the Eucharist; if the loving action of the Eucharistic Christ is the supreme *raison d'être* of the activity of the Church—then how can we fail to conclude that theological reflection should take as its departure point the Church as it here and now loves and acts in the Eucharist, and should develop a synthesis around this mystery of mysteries, by first placing properly the two poles of attraction indicated here, the Heart of Christ and His Eucharist?

It is still the magisterium which is guiding us in this attempt at a synthesis of two syntheses, when it advocates a "particular devotion to the Eucharistic Heart of Jesus."[9] and also specifies its object:

> We can properly grasp how strong was the love which urged Christ to give Himself to us as spiritual nourishment, only by honoring with a particular devotion the Eucharistic Heart of Jesus, the object of such devotion being to remind us—in the words of our predecessor of blessed memory, Leo XIII—of "the supreme act of love by which our Redeemer, pouring forth all the riches of His Heart, instituted the adorable Sacrament of the Eucharist in order to remain with us until the end of time."[10] And certainly the Eucharist, which He has drawn from the great love of His Heart, is no slight part of that Heart.[11]

The Church, in honoring, even liturgically,[12] the Eucharistic Heart of Jesus, is seeking to adore, love, and praise the twofold act of love, uncreated and created, eternal and temporal, divine and human, by which the incarnate and humanized Word has decided to apply forever the fruits of His redemptive sacrifice by renewing it throughout the course of history; and has thus decided to incorporate mankind with Himself in a union much more intimate than that of the bride with the Spouse, in the power of His Spirit for the glory of His Father. Is it not in the institution of the Eucharist that the three inter-subordinated purposes of the redemptive Incarnation shine forth: the salvation of the world; the exaltation of the Son of Man who draws all things to Himself; the glory of the Father who recapitulates all things in His Beloved Son?

Notice, in effect, the purpose of the institution of the Eucharist according to Pius XII: "in order to remain with us until the end of time"—i.e. until the end of universal history. Why? Christ wills to remain with us precisely in order to save us by applying to us the merits of His Passion, by thus kindling our love for Him, and by being thereby enabled to offer us to His Father in Himself and through Himself. It is our love for the only Son which saves us by glorifying Him, and it is by manifesting to us the riches of His love in the Eucharist that He enables us to love Him and to glorify the Father, supreme source and ultimate object of this love.

If the terms used by Pius XII place special emphasis on the Real Presence, they also apply to the Eucharist as sacrifice and as sacrament, Mass and Communion. In the same encyclical, *Haurietis Aquas*, we also read: "The priesthood and the divine Eucharist are indeed gifts of the Sacred Heart of Jesus. In the Eucharist as sacrament, He gives Himself to men; in the Eucharist as sacrifice, He constantly immolates Himself from the rising of the sun to the going down thereof."[13]

One could maintain, therefore, that this encyclical germinally contains a definition of the object of the worship offered to the Eucharistic Heart of Jesus; a definition wider, in fact, than the one which it actually gives us. This object includes the sacrificial love by which Christ, the Lamb of God, constantly immolates Himself for sinful mankind in all the Masses throughout history: a love which, by renewing the oblation of Calvary, makes it present here and now. It is this very love that we adore in the Eucharistic Heart of the triumphant and ever immolated Lamb.

In this way, one's ideas join up with a still valid current of medieval mysticism, and through the latter, with an Augustinian current.

> Formerly, the devotion[14] placed a primary and almost exclusive stress on the relations of the Eucharist with the Heart of Jesus, envisaged in the very act of His sacrifice on Calvary. . . . The Eucharist was, so to speak, only the Blood of the Heart of Jesus which was shed upon the Cross and through which souls are purified and nourished. The mystery of Jesus considered simply in the Eucharist was not, of course, ignored; but there was a preference for adoring Him there in His precise function of the Victim who continues His sacrifice and who applies that sacrifice to souls.[15]

In the thirteenth century, the mystical writer Ubertino of Casale remarkably specified the relations between the Eucharist and the Sacred Heart within the framework of the Augustinian tradition:

> Every visible sacrifice is the sacrament, that is, the sacred sign, of an invisible sacrifice. Thus the ineffable sacrifice which Christ makes of Himself in the august mystery of our altars and on the altar of the Cross, is the sign of the invisible sacrifice which He continually makes of Himself in the immense temple of His Heart.[16]

The visible sacrifice of the Mass, a sign which represents and applies to us the sacrifice of the Cross now invisible but made visible on the altar, is also, in the light of the same Augustinian tradition, the visible and efficacious sign of the invisible and actual sacrifice of the humanity which consents to what Christ has offered in its name and which associates itself with that offering. During the celebration of the sacred mysteries, Christ offers Himself to the Father as Head of the Church and of humanity, in order to involve every human person in His act of offering. The Heart of Jesus, present in the Eucharist, seeks to enclose within Itself all hearts that consecrate themselves to Him, in order to offer them, in union with Itself, to the Father.[17]

It seems to us, therefore, that, integrally considered, the object of the worship offered by the Church to the Eucharistic Heart of Jesus may be expressed as follows:

> The Church, in honoring and adoring the Eucharistic Heart of Jesus, loves the twofold act of love, eternal and historically past, by which our Redeemer instituted the Sacrifice and the Sacrament of the Eucharist, and the twofold act of love, eternal and actual, uncreated and divine, but also created, voluntary, and sensible,[18] which urges Him to immolate Himself, now and perpetually, by the hands of His priests, to the Father for our salvation, to remain ceaselessly among us in our tabernacles, and to unite Himself physically with each human person in Communion, in order here and now to love all men, in us and through us, with a sacrificial love.

This perspective offers many advantages. It stresses the existential and actual value of the worship offered to the Eucharistic Heart of the Redeemer. The historical aspect (without historicism) accented in the definition of Leo XIII and taken up by Pius XII, is retained but also amplified: it is not only the act of the loving institution of the Eucharist and the permanence of the Real Presence of the triple love of Christ among us, that one adores in this Eucharistic Heart, but also His actual self-offering and His holocaust of ever renewed love. One can thus more readily set in relief the sacramental and ecclesial realism of this devotion: all the dimensions[19] of the Eucharist are contemplated in a cult inseparable from the act of worship by which Christ Himself ceaselessly constructs, builds, and completes His Church by making it grow.[20] Thus the Church adores the vital and life-giving act of love which ceaselessly maintains it in existence and deploys it in space and in time.

To this "vertical" dimension, are joined the "horizontal" advantages of this presentation. If the Eucharistic Heart of Jesus signifies His union of love with each communicant, the worship which is offered to It promotes a ceaselessly increasing irradiation of the sacramental grace proper to the Eucharist: namely, the grace of the dynamic growth of the supernatural and sacrificial fraternal charity which It pours into the world, for the eternal salvation of souls and of bodies. In adoring Christ as sacramental victim, the communicant drinks, with the precious Blood, the ecstatic[21] love which flows from His ever open Heart. The Eucharistic Heart is the Heart of the Lamb who makes each communicant a coredeemer by enabling him to love his remotest neighbor, not only as he loves himself, but also to the extent of the self-sacrifice which characterizes authentic self-love.[22] Such love realizes perfectly the magnificent conclusion of the Epistle of Saint James: "whoever brings back a sinner from the error of his way will save his soul from death and will cover a multitude of sins" (5, 20).

Thus understood, the Eucharistic Heart of the still immolated Lamb is truly the Heart of the Whole Christ, the Heart in which all men of good will, by offering themselves with Him as victims, are consummated in unifying love, in union with the Father and among themselves, through His mediation.[23]

Is there any need to develop at length the Biblical merit of this presentation? It links up very closely with the Johannine vision of Revelation: "Saint John there saw the Lamb in the heavens, in glory, before the throne, the equal of God; 'standing, as though it had been slain'; not slaughtered, but living and bearing the noble scars of the wounds which have caused Its death."[24] (cf. Rev. 5, 6-14). The Lamb of whom

Revelation speaks 29 times is a victim, but "a victim living anew." The immolated paschal Lamb appears in the Johannine poem "as conqueror," and this expression so dear to Saint John signifies "the sovereignty of Christ who dominates history and the world, associated with God in the glorification of the elect."[25] The author of Revelation saw the redemptive Lamb adored in Heaven because of His sacrifice, and giving a participation in His glory to all those who have profited by His Blood for the expiation of their sins.[26]

The integral object of the worship given to the Eucharistic Heart of the Lamb (such as we envisage this object in what seems to us to be a legitimate development of the principles laid down by the magisterium), corresponds well to the double aspect, painful and glorious, of the Lamb of the Johannine Revelation, as well as to the two aspects (death and resurrection) of the paschal mystery.

This integral object seems to be partly implied in the primitive Christian iconography of the Heart of the Lamb: a lamp in the form of a lamb from which there flows an eternal spring of oil in order to bring light and health to men. And in order to signify that it is by the merits of His Passion that the Lamb spreads His gifts, He is represented with a cross on His breast, and with a dove, symbol of the Holy Spirit, hovering over His head. He is laid on an altar or is represented with His side open and bleeding; or again, standing on His throne, while His blood flows from five wounds, joins into one current, and falls into a chalice.[27]

If one seeks to compare the object of this ecclesial devotion to the Eucharistic Heart of Jesus with that of the devotion offered to the Sacred Heart or to the Holy Eucharist, (and such a comparison is as necessary as it is inevitable if we are to understand more clearly the meaning of the Church's attitudes), then the following must be said. On the one hand, "the worship given to the Eucharistic Heart of Jesus does not differ essentially from that given to the Sacred Heart. . . . It is merely that the devotion to the Eucharistic Heart singles out one of Its acts,"[28] namely, the act of love by which Christ institutes the Eucharist, and, we might add, celebrates it as principal minister by immolating Himself anew and by giving Himself in Communion. On the other hand, and in a parallel way, one could say that the worship given to the Eucharistic Heart has the same material object as the worship of the Eucharist, but isolates its formal object—namely, the act of love to which we have just alluded.[29] Together with a certain identity, therefore, there are real differences between these three devotions. They are differences which the Church itself took a long time to perceive clearly. It was through Benedict XV[30] that the individual and specific nature of the devotion to the Eucharistic Heart of Jesus then came to be recognized.

Since this Eucharistic Heart is "the source and the apex of the whole work of preaching the gospel," it is to be expected that It should also be the point of departure and the goal of a systematic theology. *Its point of departure:* could a theology that seeks its source and well spring in reality, find a higher and more acceptable reality than that of the Eucharistic Heart of the Lamb? Is not the theologian who receives Holy Communion, in immediate contact with his Redeemer? *Its goal:* if every course of reflection returns, in its conclusion, to its initial principles and to its basic intuition, will not the theologian, after having considered the data of Divine Revelation in the light of the Eucharistic love, be better able to understand its fullness and its richness? Will he not find that all the rays of Christian dogma converge into the sun of the Eucharist? And will he not be inclined toward this through the sacramental grace of his daily Communions, all of which from the very first are polarized by the last, capable of leading into the pre-beatifying vision of Him who is hidden under the sacramental species?

B. The Eucharistic Heart of Jesus: Synthesizing Symbol of the In-Humanation of the Word, of His Church, and of His Grace

As we have already had occasion to point out, the Incarnation is not only the assumption of an individual human nature; it is also, through this individual nature, an insertion into all humanity, and, in a sense, an assumption of the morally good being and activity of this humanity.

Maurice Blondel grasped very well this "twofold aspect: it is because our persons exist that He (Christ) is a genuine man; but our persons, our human awarenesses, exist only because, in their depths, they rely on and are enlightened by the divine Person of Jesus. There could have been no Man-God, had there been no men-men."[32] In the concrete plan of Providence, there could be no Incarnation which would not be an Inhumanation. Humanity is a condition of Christ, who is the *raison d'être* of the world. There could be no "Christicity" without essential (and not just accidental) relationship with humanity.[33]

The In-humanation of the Word is an entry into the human species. "The whole of human nature is taken on Itself by the Word . . . in order to be united with that nature by means of the individuality which is primary in the order of divinization and of union with God. The individual human nature assumed by God has for its own purpose that of all human nature."[34]

Is there anything so very new in all this? By no means. Saint Thomas Aquinas partly retained the neo-Platonic anthropology which had enabled the Fathers of the Church to develop this theme. Did he not say that "all men are parts and as it were members of human nature; by participation of the species (according to Porphyry) many men are one single man"?[35]

Through His In-humanation, the Word has therefore become neighbor to each one of us, writes Saint Hilary.[36] But it is Saint Cyril of Alexandria whose superb expression of this mystery wins for him the title, Doctor of the In-humanation of the Word. Vatican II cites the following text of his: "For we are all in[37] Christ, and the common person of humanity[38] comes back to life in Him. That is why He is also called the New Adam. . . . For He dwelt among us, who by nature is the Son of God; and therefore in his Spirit we cry out: Abba, Father! But the Word dwells in all, in one temple, namely, that which He assumed for us and from us, that having us all in himself, he might, as Paul says, reconcile all in one body to the Father."[39]

Now, it is this same Saint Cyril who has most clearly shown how, through the Eucharist, the concrete union of the Word with each human person is effected. Through the Eucharist, he says, we become "non-corporal" with the Incarnate Word. In other words, it is in the Eucharistic Communion that the Incarnation becomes fully the In-humanation of the Word, and it is through the Eucharist that He "took up the world's history into Himself," [40] the history of each human person.

But let us listen to the great Doctor of Alexandria himself:

> To unite us, to merge us in unity with God and with one another—even though we are, by our souls and our bodies, separated into distinct personalities—the only Son has invented a means born of His wisdom in accordance with the counsel of the Father.
>
> Through one single body, His own body, He blesses His faithful in the mystic communion, making them con-corporal with Him and with one another.
>
> Who now could separate, who could deprive of their physical union, those who have been joined together through unity in Christ, by means of His unique and blessed body? For if we all eat of one bread, we all form one and the same body (1 Cor. 10, 17). There can be no division in Christ (cf. 1 Cor. 1, 13). . . . All

united in the one Christ through His sacred body, all receiving Him as one and indivisible in our own bodies, We must regard our members as belonging to Him rather than to us.[41]

The Incarnation finds, therefore, its *raison d'être* in the Eucharist through which we are physically with Christ and with one another, belonging to Christ rather than to ourselves. He has taken an individual body only in order through it so unite all the others, and to dwell in them all through this unique body. Here we have a mystery of unity which has its origin in a mysterious love. Does not this unity manifest that Christ, in giving Himself to us in the Eucharist and in uniting us among ourselves through It, does so through love? Does not the Eucharistic Heart of Jesus unveil Itself through the sign of this unity, which reveals His love?

With all this in mind, one more readily understands what Saint Bonaventure wrote eight centuries later:

> I shall say with David: I have found my heart to pray to God (Ps. 5, 8). Yes, I have found the heart of the king, my Lord, my brother and my friend, You excellent Jesus. And then shall I not pray? Oh, yes, I shall pray! For, I say it boldly, His heart is my heart also. . . . Since Christ is my head, must not what belongs to Him belong also to me? . . . The heart of my spiritual leader is truly my heart. It is indeed mine. Jesus and I have but one heart. And what is surprising about this? Had not the multitude of the believers themselves but one heart (Acts 4, 32)?[42]

With even greater reason it could be said that, through the Eucharist, the Heart of Jesus is the vital center of the Whole Christ. It is through the Eucharist that Christ enables the Church to be ever more richly animated by His invisible and uncreated soul, the Spirit of the Father and the Son; and it is through the Eucharist, sacrament of the unity of this Church,[43] that He unites the Church in the love which is His life.

The Christian life is essentially a life of love for the loving Father, in union with His beloved Son, under the breath of the Spirit of Love which pours this love into our hearts (Rm. 5, 5). It is also essentially a sacrificial love for all men. The Church is a community of love and a hierarchic communion of love[44] represented and realized by the "sacrament of the Eucharistic bread."[45] "He who eats my flesh and drinks my blood abides in me, and I in him" (Jn. 6, 56). "We who are many are one body, for we all partake of the one bread" (1 Cor. 10, 17). It is of this unique mystery,[46] which envelops us in divinizing love, that the Eucharistic Heart of Jesus is the symbol.

The Church, sacrament of salvation, primordial sacrament which gives us the other sacraments, was born of the sacrificial decision of Christ, the Lamb of God, who in a sense instituted the Church by the fact that He instituted the Eucharist and immolated Himself in this very institution. At the same time as the Church was born of the pierced Heart of the Lamb, it received from Him the order and the grace to immolate anew its Savior and to immolate itself with Him, as true Spouse of the Lamb. Thanks to the sacrament of Holy Orders, the sacrifice of the Spouse is united with the sacrifice of the Lamb even in celebrating that sacrifice. The love that institutes the Eucharist is the same that institutes the Church as a community of sacrificial life and as a hierarchic society directed by sacrificers whose bounden duty it is to offer themselves as victims of holocaust for the community.[47] It is this ever loving and oblative love which the Church adores in the Eucharistic Heart of the Lamb.

Born of that Heart, the Church preserves numerous links with It.

The Church is a past birth which in a sense renews itself at every Mass and at every moment, since the redemptive Love is the ever present source of its life-giving love.

But, unlike earthly births, this birth is not a separation: the Church remains in the ever open wound of the Heart of its Spouse, as a place of residence where its life grows to fullness. In ceaselessly eating the Flesh and drinking the Blood of its Spouse, the Church remains in Christ, and dwells ever more deeply in His Eucharistic Heart.

Born of Him, living in Him, the Church receives this Eucharistic Heart in order that, through It, the Church may exercise the activities of love which form the basic expression of its life.[48]

In the Church, sacrament of the love that saves, the Eucharistic Heart of Jesus beats with sacrificial and joyous love for the whole world and for His Father. It is the Church which is the mediatrix and the guardian of the ancient and new commandment of fraternal charity, whose efficacious sacramental symbol is the Blood of the Lamb. Faithful Bride, it ceaselessly drinks the Blood which springs from the Heart of its Spouse —the Blood of Love.

The Eucharistic Heart of Jesus is thus the whole Treasure and the whole spiritual riches of the Church.[49] For what the Church recommends to its members and children applies first and foremost to itself: it comes to know the strength of the love which urged and still urges Christ to give Himself for His Church, only by honoring with a special devotion the Eucharistic Heart of this divine Lamb. One may even say that the more the Church comes to appreciate this fact, the more will it express its devotion to the Eucharistic Heart, through which and with which it adores the Father.

In adoring the triple love of the Heart of the Lamb which celebrates and gives the Eucharist, the Church glorifies this same triple love inasmuch as it has instituted and celebrates all the other sacraments, whose end is the Eucharist.[50] It also adores His commandment of twofold sacrificial love of the Father and of its brethren, a commandment whose promulgation He has deliberately associated with the institution of the

Eucharist, sacrifice and sacrament. Finally, it adores the fullness of graces, the pleroma of gifts of the Spirit and of infused virtues which exist in the sacred humanity of the only begotten Son and of which He desires to make all His brethren participants, through the Eucharistic Communion.[51]

In respectfully consuming[52] the Eucharistic Heart of his Redeemer, the Christian knows, at least in an obscure way, that he is collaborating with the Word of Life and of Love to spread and to communicate His In-humanation,[53] to construct His Church, to merit for many men the outpouring of the graces and charisms of the Spirit. "The flesh eaten in the Eucharist is for the Christian a sure testimony that it is for him that Jesus Christ became a man, and for him that He has suffered."[54] In the Eucharistic Communion Christ intimates to the Christian that what Saint Paul said applies also to him: "It is no longer I who live, but Christ who lives in me; and the life I now live in the flesh I live by faith in the Son of God, who loved me and gave himself for me" (Gal. 2, 20).

C. The Eucharistic Heart of Jesus: Special Symbol of His Consummating Love

In celebrating for the last time the Pasch of His ancient covenant and for the first time the Pasch of His new and eternal covenant with the Church, Christ said to His Apostles: "Do this in remembrance of me"; and Saint Paul commented on this command: "For as often as you eat this bread and drink the cup, you proclaim the Lord's death until he comes" (1 Cor. 11, 26).

You also announce, therefore, this coming, this return of Christ: the coming of Christ at the death of each and every person, the coming of Christ at the renewal of all things; the individual and collective Parousia.

The Eucharistic sacrifice is therefore an immolative

and actual remembrance of a past Event and of a future Event, the Pasch of the Head which is prolonged into the Pasch of the members and of the whole universe.

The Eucharistic Heart of Jesus, great High Priest, while symbolizing the past institution and the present celebration of the invisible sacrifice of the Lamb of God, also signifies its human, ecclesial, and cosmic consummation at the Parousia, and announces that beyond all immolation there will be the indefectible oblation of the Whole Christ to the Father, when He submits Himself to Him "who put all things under him, that God may be everything to every one" (cf. 1 Cor. 11, 26, and 15, 24-28). As such, the Eucharistic Heart of Jesus is the symbol of eschatological love, an idea we shall consider more closely. What relationships exist between the Holy Eucharist, on the one hand, and final perseverance, Hell, Purgatory, Heaven, resurrection, and eschatological renewal of the cosmos, on the other.

First of all, the Eucharist is the sacrament of the signal grace of final perseverance in salvific love. No means is more efficacious for obtaining this preeminently free grace of a final act of the human will which is at once free, meritorious, and liberating: "He who eats my flesh and drinks my blood abides in me, and I in him" (Jn. 6, 56). Although Communion cannot merit such a grace absolutely and in strict justice, it can do so with a merit *de congruo;* and the communicant, intimately associated with the prayer of Christ within him, can obtain this perseverance through his persevering supplications. Christ wills to give Himself within time, only in order to give Himself in eternity. Frequent communion with the Eucharistic Heart of Jesus is a sign of perseverance and of predestination. The love of Christ for us within time is the sign of His eternal and merciful will to give us eternal life, and the Eucharistic Heart symbolizes this twofold and unique desire.

However, the Eucharistic Christ does not compel us

to cooperate with His will to save us. He does not impose His divinizing presence on those who obstinately reject His salvific love, but He unveils the eternal presence of an immanent and reprobating Judge. Through their consciences, He condemns them eternally, and ratifies their decision to be separated from Him, a decision signified by their explicit rejection of the Eucharist or of the fraternal love of which, even for non-Christians, the Eucharist is always the source. We cannot with impunity ignore the fact that Jesus has loved us even unto the Cross and the Eucharist, "to the end" (Jn. 14, 1). Eternal Hell is the sanction for despising the Eucharist. It is the "second death": "Truly, truly, I say to you, unless you eat the flesh of the Son of man and drink his blood, you have no life in you" (Jn. 6, 53). Shortly afterwards, Saint John adds: "After this many of his disciples drew back and no longer went about with him" (6, 66).

Twenty years later, Paul severely censured the Christians of Corinth for another abuse of the Eucharist—no longer that of ignoring It, but of receiving It when unworthy to do so. It is precisely because in receiving Communion they were announcing the death of the Lord and His return, that Paul wrote to them as follows:

> Whoever, therefore, eats the bread or drinks the cup of the Lord in an unworthy manner will be guilty of profaning the body and blood of the Lord. . . . For anyone who eats and drinks without discerning the body eats and drinks judgment upon himself. That is why many of you are weak and ill, and some have died. . . . If any one is hungry, let him eat at home, lest you come together to be condemned (1 Cor. 11, 17-34).

Far from being a Communion, to receive the Body of the Lord unworthily separates the soul from Christ in this life and merits an eternal separation. God is not mocked, nor can one mock the gift of His incarnate Son in the Eucharist without changing that gift into a condemnation. One cannot with impunity mock the love of the Eucharist Heart of Jesus, which also shows itself in His anger against and hatred of sin. It is precisely because He loves the Father that Jesus cannot but hate sin. The Heart of Christ, present in the Eucharist, symbolizes not only "His divine love" but also "the sensible emotions which accompany that love: desire, joy, sorrow, fear, and anger, according as His look, His words, and His attitudes express them."[55] The Heart of Christ is therefore the symbol of the reprobating anger of the Lamb (Rev. 19, 15; 6, 16; 14, 10), which is an anger of love.

But the Eucharistic Heart of Jesus, which intercedes on the altars and in the tabernacles of the world for the salvation of all men, is above all the symbol of this praying, supplicating, and purifying love which seeks to purify souls here on earth in order not to have to punish them eternally, or to "tread the wine press of the fury of the wrath of God the Almighty" (Rev. 19, 15). Rather than being the mediator of the Father's anger, He prefers to appease Him through His Eucharistic sacrifice, while purifying with His blood those who drink it. It is one of the effects special to the Eucharist to remit venial sins,[56] and even, consequently, to save the good communicant from purgatory.

All the liturgies of the many rites of the Universal Church contain prayers for the still not fully purified dead.[57] These prayers signify that Christ has died, and today continues to offer up His past death, for the liberation of the suffering Church of purgatory. Much more than did Judas Machabeus, the Eucharistic Heart of Jesus sees the "great grace laid up" for those "who had fallen asleep with godliness," and that is why He ceaselessly renews His expiatory sacrifice "for the dead, that they may be loosed from their sins" (cf. 2 Mach. 12, 45-46).

In venerating this Eucharistic Heart, the pilgrim Church adores Its loving expiation for the sins of the members of the Church suffering, and associates itself with this superabundant satisfaction. Can it not be said that charity towards the dead, concern to win for them and to apply to them the indulgences which reflect and express the painful indulgence of the crucified and agonizing Christ, is the sign of an authentic and supernatural love for the living? "But if any one has the world's goods and sees his brother in need, yet closes his heart against him, how does God's love abide in him?" (1 Jn. 3, 17). Who more urgently needs that help than the Christian who has died with imperfect love and is temporarily unable to enjoy the vision of Love? And how could God's love abide in those who, enjoying the riches and treasure of Christ and of the Church,[58] of the Mass and of Indulgences, nevertheless close their hearts to these paralytics of the spiritual order, by refusing to assist and to deliver them? And it is from Christ received in the Eucharist that the liberating love for the dead proceeds.

But, just as the Immaculate Conception of Mary results from a more sublime expression of the redemptive work of Christ, the same is true of the perfect love which saves from purgatory. Of Itself, the Eucharist frequently received is the sacrament, the efficacious sign, of the immediate entry of the dying Christian into the beatifying vision of the Risen Lord, because It is the sacrament of the fervor of love. From this love which fills the soul of the contemplator of the triune Love, there arises the natural and glorified desire for definitive reunion with the body of which the soul has been (painlessly) deprived. The Communion of the exiled (1 Cor. 5, 6) in the body of the Risen Lord, merits the spiritual vision of this glorious body, instrument of all resurrection, and then Its physical and eternal vision.

Does not this follow from the teaching of Jesus Himself in His discourse on the Bread of Life, and from that of Saint Paul to the Corinthians? "For as by a man came death, by a man has also come the resurrection of the dead" (1 Cor. 15, 21).[59] "He who eats my flesh and drinks my blood has eternal life, and I will raise him up on the last day" (Jn. 6, 54).

How can it be denied that the risen Christ will raise up all the just through love for them and for His Father, and even though a grateful and rewarding love for that love which on earth led them to be partakers of the Eucharist? The glorious resurrection of the just will be, therefore, a visible manifestation of the love (as perfectly shown as possible) which the created and human will of the Resurrected Christ bears to them, and of which the Heart is the parousiac symbol.

To this great manifestation of the human love of Christ, a love which is itself the always inseparable instrument of His divine love; to this glorious resurrection of the bodies of the just, will be added the "resurrection," or more exactly the transfiguration, of the cosmos, their reciprocal bond, through the powerful action of the human will of the Lord. Even now, as the Church teaches, Christ, "sitting at the right hand of the Father, is continually active in the world, leading men to the Church, and through her joining them more closely to Himself and making them partakers of His glorious life by nourishing them with His own body and blood."[60] The present action of the Eucharistic Heart of Jesus is essentially an ecclesial action. Its first effect is the Church, His mystical and social Body. It is in the Church and by the Church, through its sacramental economy, that the Eucharistic Heart of Jesus inaugurates and prepares the final and eschatological transformation of the universe. The world, whose creation is confirmed by Genesis, is a human, anthropocentric world: the consummation of the visible world basically presupposes, therefore, the redemption of man which Christ has effected and effects by His miracles and by His sacraments, the latter being all polarized by the primordial sacrament of the Church.

This "pilgrim Church, in her sacraments and institutions, which pertain to the present times, takes on the appearance of this passing world. She herself dwells among creatures who groan and travail in pain until now and await the revelation of the sons of God (cf.

Rom. 8, 19-22)."[61]   The Church therefore shares in the present condition of the material creation, the latter being polarized by its perfect parousiac consummation which is inseparable from the resurrection of our bodies.

The great exercise of the transforming power of Christ will occur at His Parousia: "We await a Savior, the Lord Jesus Christ, who will change our lowly body to be like his glorious body, by the power which enables him even to subject all things to himself" (Phil. 3, 20-21).

Christ will not limit Himself, therefore, to resurrecting human bodies; He will also transform the material world, making it "a new earth" (2 Pet. 3, 13), precisely in order to adapt it to its new condition as a dwelling for the glorified bodies of the saints. "Since all physical things are in a sense made for man," writes Saint Thomas Aquinas, "it is fitting that at this moment the state of the whole material creation should also be changed, in order that it may be adapted to man's condition then. . . . Since men will be not only delivered from corruption but also clothed in glory, it is proper that the material creation should then also be invested with a certain splendor of glory. Hence it is written: 'Then I saw a new heaven and a new earth' (Rev. 21, 1)."[62]

It is true that no text of the New Testament explicitly attributes to the glorified Christ this transformation of the material world; but the resurrection of the dead (or even of one dead person) is a much greater wonder than the transformation of the whole material universe, and therefore it is reasonable to suppose that the latter is included in "the power which Christ has to raise up the dead and to subject all things to himself." It is a power which the omnipotent Christ will use at the same time as He raises up the dead.

What exactly is the nature of this power possessed by the Man-Jesus to perfect the universe, and to complete the redemption of the universe in that of man?

What can be said on this subject in the light of Catholic tradition?[63]

At the Parousia, the human and created soul of Jesus will reveal itself as being the efficient, instrumental cause of the consummation of the universe. It must be borne in mind that, in effect, the supreme source of all causality and of all efficiency is spiritual: it is the Wisdom of the divine Will. Likewise, in the created order, the highest principles of action are spiritual. The transformation of the universe will result, therefore, from the power, not proper but instrumental, of the human nature, and especially of the human free will of the Man-Jesus, inasmuch as this freedom is the instrument of the divine free will. At the Parousia, the purpose of the human free will of Jesus will be to express the divine Goodness to the material world, for the happiness of predestined mankind, at the very moment when He will glorify mankind by raising up the dead.

In what way is the ultimate transformation of the universe and of nature dependent on the human, immaterial free will of Jesus?

In this exercise of instrumental causality, the principal cause, i.e. the divine nature, unites the instrument —here the human will of Christ—with the effect sought: universal resurrection and transfiguration. (That a spiritual cause, even merely instrumental, can change and transform not only minds but also matter, emerges clearly in the light of the divine causality in general, and, more particularly, in the case of the influence which man's intelligence and will can exert on his physical activities). The divine will of the Incarnate Word will therefore move His human will, which is perfectly obedient to it,[64] by directing this created free will towards all the times and places manifested to the created soul of Christ in the beatifying vision of His own divine Person. Jesus, seeing as the Word His plan of creation and sharing in His human will the universal causality of His divine will, will reach by His created will—the instrument of His divinity—

to all creatures in order to complete them by developing all their potentialities.

It is this magnificent perspective of a universal transformative action of the human free will of Jesus that Saint Thomas Aquinas, developing the thought of Saint Paul (Eph. 1, 10), already sketched centuries ago:

> If we speak of the soul of Christ as it is the instrument of the Word united to Him, it had an instrumental power to effect all the miraculous transmutations ordainable to the end of the Incarnation, which is to re-establish all things that are in heaven and on earth. . . . All other beings are governed by the soul of Christ who is superior to all creatures.[65]

Saint Thomas, therefore, presents the recapitulation of all beings under their Head, Christ, as the purpose itself of His Incarnation, and at the same time the work of His human free will as instrument of the divine action.[66] The ultimate transformation of the universe, orientated to the perfect realization of the purpose of the recapitulative Incarnation, could not escape the powerful, but not omnipotent,[67] human will of the Word made man. Christ will appear as, in the most literal sense of the word, the Savior of the World, the Redeemer of the Universe, finally become an harmonious cosmos[68] to the point of being the priestly[69] garment of the divine Word made human priest. The creation, "subjected to futility" by the first Adam, will be "set free from its bondage to decay" through the created and glorious free will of the only Son of God; it will be made "like his glorious body" after having been like "our lowly body," by the power which this second Adam possesses to subject the whole universe to Himself in order then to subject Himself, at its head, to the Father (Rom. 8, 19-21; Phil. 3, 21; 1 Cor. 15, 27-28).[71] Chaos will at last be cosmos. The consecration of the world will be completed.

As can be seen, even without transposition in terms of Teilhardian *genèse*,[72] it was already possible to reflect deeply on the relations between the cosmos and the Word made flesh, by methodically using the principles laid down by Saint Thomas Aquinas.

Such an undertaking can even claim to have a particular merit: more than on the influence of the glorified body of the Word, it stresses that of His human free will and of His soul divinized by sanctifying grace.[73] It therefore highlights what is most specifically *human* in the cosmic influence of Christ. It presents the parousiac transformation of the physical universe as the divinizing redemption of that universe and as the culminating point of man's salvation by the Man-Jesus; or, if one may so express it,[74] of the salvation of free wills in "cosmic situation" by the loving free will of the Man-Jesus. From this viewpoint, it must be said that, in adoring the Heart of Jesus, the Church adores His love, His threefold love—affective, spiritual, and divine—for the whole physical universe destined to undergo a perfect eschatological humanization. Jesus loves this universe which He creates for men, His brethren; this universe through which He forms bodies destined to resurrection; this universe which He will transfigure in order to reward His brethren for sharing in His Passion.

It must also be stressed that the parousiac transfiguration will be effected at the very moment when the glorified Christ ceases forever to work the miracle of transubstantiation. In the full span of the Church's history on earth, between the Pasch of Christ and the cosmic Pasch, the universe will have been partly transubstantiated but only in order ultimately to become completely transfigured. Through the work of man and for his survival, a *part* of the universe becomes the bread of man[75] and of death[76]—*panis corporalis est panis mortis;* then, through the Passion of the Man-God and through the words of His priests, that bread becomes His body and blood, the Bread and Drink of eternal life; and all this occurs in order that finally the *whole* universe, linked with the glorious Humanity of the Word, may appear as His priestly garment, inseparable and distinct, through which will shine, in an unceasing "diaphany"[77] the eternal and immanent sun of His divine Person, exposing His whole universe to the effulgence of His sacred humanity. Far from being a universalization of the Eucharistic transubstantiation, the latter will come to its end, in both senses of the word "end"; for its purpose was to divinize mankind and not the cosmos as such, since it was *for man's sake* only that Christ came to save this cosmos. Thus the transfiguration of the cosmos will manifest forever the love of the Man-Jesus for His human brethren. It will be at once human and humanizing, divine and divinizing. The Parousia will gloriously proclaim that the cosmic pleroma belongs definitively to the Church, the Body of Christ; it will be the fullness of Christ, including in that fullness the cosmic pleroma.

But, though destined to end at the Parousia, this transubstantiation constitutes here and now the sign, the pledge, the loving promise of that Parousia: "Whenever you eat this bread and drink this cup, you proclaim the death of the Lord until he comes." You proclaim therefore the coming of Him who will declare: "Behold, I make all things new" (Rev. 21, 5). Jesus, whose humanity is now totally divinized by His Resurrection—it was during His earthly life the imperfectly divinized humanity of a God[78]—will raise up in Himself sky, earth, and world,[79] making "the first earth" pass away in order to give us "a new heaven and a new earth" (Rev. 21, 1), in the image of His glorified body. The Head of the Church will become in a visible manner the Head of the Universe.[80]

It can be truly said that the universe—thus incorporated with the Humanity of Christ, as an extension distinct from this Humanity but perfectly subjected to its effulgence and its action—will be completely trans-signified and trans-finalized[81] by the glorified soul of the Word; it will not be transubstantiated, for, unlike the essence of the transubstantiated bread and wine, it will preserve intact its nature, which will not disappear or be changed. The universe will thus cease to be the nourishment and support of a yet imperfect humanity, and will become the recompense and the glorification, as well as the transparent medium, for this same humanity fixed definitively in God. In the present state of the world, matter veils and divides; but matter as transfigured by the glorious Christ will perfectly unite men and reveal them to one another without in any way contributing to their survival. The elect will enjoy, as regards their own bodies and matter in general, a controlling freedom analogous to that of the Risen Christ.

In the created soul of Jesus, the decision of the parousiac transfiguration will be a decision taken in the one act of beatifying love which results from the one act of the beatific vision in His intelligence.[82] Christ will carry out the transformation of the universe by the same act through which, at the first instant of His conception in the virginal womb of Mary, He embraced the universal salvific will of the Father. That act will never pass away.

At the level of the free will which corresponds to that of infused knowledge, this unique act, the most perfect created imitation of and participation in the Pure Act which is the Word in His divine nature, does not preclude a number of successive decisions taken by the glorified humanity of Christ. However, the decision of the Parousia, when time passes into the "aevum" which will mark the end of history, will remain as unique as this passage, identical with the pasch of history itself.[83]

Through love, therefore, the parousiac decision of Christ will effect the consummation of the universe and of history. It will be the supreme event of "the history of the divine Word,"[84] offering to the Father, as testimony to His glory, His own property redeemed and enlightened by the Spirit of God. In the heart of beatifying love, this decision is identical with that of the institution of the Eucharist, even though its material object is distinct and complementary. They both have their place in the one salvific will of Christ, as consequences of His one act of beatific vision. The parousiac decision of the transfiguration of a cosmos at last fully in the image of man and for his glory, will have been justly merited by all the participations by Christians on earth in the Eucharist.[85] In adoring the Eucharist Heart of Jesus, the Church adores His loving oblative decision to renew the face of the earth in order to present it to the Father[86] in an oblation which will never end.

D. Eucharistic Heart and Predestinating Trinity

We can and should apply very specially to the Eucharistic Heart of Jesus, Priest of Mankind, only Son and victim of the Father, what the Spirit of the Father and of the Son teaches us through the Church's magisterium: "The Heart of the Word incarnate is the symbol . . . of the divine love which the Word has in common with the Father and the Holy Spirit. The devotion to the Sacred Heart . . . is certainly none other than the devotion to the divine and human love of the Word incarnate; and, even, none other than the devotion to the love which the Father and the Holy Spirit lavish on sinful men. In effect, as the Angelic Doctor teaches, the love of the Three Divine Persons is the principle of the Redemption. This love flowed into the human will of Jesus Christ and penetrated His adorable Heart, animating it with that same love to such an extent that He willed to shed His blood in order to ransom us from the bondage of sin."[87]

Now, it is indeed through and in the mystery of the Eucharist that, in a concrete and existential way, the Father, the Son and Their Spirit increasingly give Themselves to us. It is the Father who draws us to eat the spiritualized flesh of His Son (Jn. 6, 41-45); or rather, the Father, who is in the Son, enters into us with Him when we receive the Bread of Life (Jn. 14, 10-11; 14, 23; 6, 51). Their Spirit, inseparable from Them, gives Himself with Them to us (Jn. 14, 17).

Through the Eucharistic Communion, we receive the loving presence of the Three divine Guests who have taken possession of our soul—an increasing possession which, however, increasingly respects our human freedom.

In instituting the sacrifice and the sacrament of the Eucharist, Christ made them the sign *par excellence* of the love of the divine Persons for us. In renewing His sacrificial immolation at every Mass, through and for the Church, the Heart of the Redeemer shows us in an ever fresh manner that "the Father did not spare his own Son but gave Him up for us all" (Rom. 8, 32), and that this Son offered Himself as a victim of holocaust to the Father through the Spirit in order to fill us with the fire of this Spirit of Love (cf. Eph. 5, 2; Heb. 9, 14; Lk. 12, 49). The Heart of Jesus present in the Eucharist becomes, when considered in faith, the sign *par excellence* of the Trinitarian love which gives itself to the sinful world through the wound in the side of the Lamb.

The union which Christians effect when they receive the Body of Christ, and thus "eat one another" in fraternal love, is the clearest sign on earth of the union of love that exists among the divine Persons: "Because there is one bread, we who are many are one body, for we all partake of the one bread . . . that they may all be one; even as you, Father, are in me, and I in you, that they also may be one in us, so that the world may believe that you have sent me" ((1 Cor. 10, 17; Jn. 17, 21).

The Eucharist, efficacious sign of the union of the Church in love, is thus seen to be the sign which contains and gives the Trinity, the latter being its source. The dogma of the Eucharist implies that of the Trinity. How could we say what the Eucharistic Christ is, without saying what the Son is and what the Father and the Spirit are? The Eucharistic dogma is the Trinitarian dogma become truth-for-mankind, truth revealed to men in a life communicated to men.[88] In the Eucharist, the Trinity transcendent and immanent to Itself, becomes the Trinity immanent to us men—the Trinity in the economy of salvation.[89] It is in and through the Eucharist that the Christian can ceaselessly grow in the knowledge and possession of the Trinity.

The Christ received in the Eucharist is the only Son of the Father, the Son turned towards the loving Father, towards the bosom of the Father (Jn. 1, 18—Greek) and, with Him, the Breather who, in yielding up the last breath of His human soul, has delivered to us the uncreated Breath (cf. Jn. 19, 30) which proceeds eternally from Himself. In symbolizing the divine love of Christ the Redeemer for us, the Heart of Jesus signifies also the reciprocal love of the divine Persons which eternally conditions Their common love for us, and in which we are already mysteriously included, despite our inescapable contingence, by the unique love, creative and absolute, of the Three Persons. The Eucharist is the visible sign, the sacrament, of the invisible extra-and-intra-trinitarian invisible love of the living God (although in a sense nothing is outside the infinite and immense Trinity). This is what we must attempt to show, if even in a sketchy way. It can be said that the Heart of Jesus symbolizes immediately the divine and loving Person of the incarnate Word, and concomitantly the merciful love of the Father and of the Spirit for the human race—or, to put it more simply, the love of the redemptive Trinity for sinful humanity. But one can also and more profoundly say that the Heart of Jesus symbolizes the personal and eternal love of the only Son for His Father, in as much as it is an answering love to the eternal and personal love of the Father for His only Son; and that from this answering love springs the eternal link of the uncreated *dia*-logue, namely the Spirit who is personal Love. In this connection, the pierced Heart of the immolated Lamb is the immediate symbol (and not merely by concomitance) of the triune Love, of the intra-trinitarian Love which is inseparably (in the sense already defined) extra-trinitarian.

There is nothing arbitrary in this way of putting the matter. In his encyclical, *Haurietis Aquas*, Pius XII wrote: "The Heart of the incarnate Word is rightly seen to be the sign and the principal symbol of this triple love with which the divine Redeemer ceaselessly loves the eternal Father and all mankind."[90] Now, the divine love of the Word for His Father— principle of His twofold human love, spiritual and affective—is a love which is truly personal and not an essential emanation. It is as Son that the Word loves His Father, with a love due to the Father at the same time as given by Him, due to the freely given love which the Father has for the Son; and it is from this reciprocal love—due in one case and freely given in the other—that the Spirit springs, the Spirit who is "the personal Love of the Father and of the Son."[91]

But this mystery of the triune Love symbolized by the Heart of Jesus is also the mystery of the creative Trinity. Pure Act, eternally triune, is creative Act, not necessarily, but eternally and freely. In God, the creative act is not distinguished, except notionally, from the pure and trinitarian Act with which it is really identical. In a mysterious way, created persons are eternally immanent in the mind and love of the uncreated and transcendent Persons.

The Son is the Word, the eternal and uncreated expression through whom the Father expresses to Himself the knowledge He has of His own lovableness and of that of the whole universe, personal and impersonal, created in His image. He is the Word of the Goodness of the Father and of all men destined to be His brethren. In seeing in His Word the transcendent and uncreated archetype of all creatures, their supreme model, the Father creates universal lovableness of the human and non-human world[92] for love of His own Goodness. In speaking Himself in His Word, the Father speaks all things and all persons, including mine. ("One God produced one world by reason of His love for Himself".)[93] The Father wills eternally in love[94] the only Son whom He engenders intellectually by an act of knowledge of His own essence which is Love. Although He does not engender the Word *by* love,[95] the Father lovingly wills and ineffably loves the Word in whom He expresses His lovableness.[96]

The eternal generation of the Son prolongs itself, in some sort, in His temporal mission.[97] The pierced Heart of Jesus, while symbolizing His redemptive mission through obedience even unto the death of the cross, also signifies, in a visible manner, His eternal generation as Word of Love (cf. Jn. 1, 1b and 4, 16) and His eternal relationship of loving oblation to the Father who engenders Him in love. The Son is *from* the Father *(a Patre)* but also *to* the Father *(ad Patrem)*. In engendering Him, the Father gives His Son to the world, and this Son fulfills His mission by giving Himself to His Father for the sake of the world. Sent as victim of expiation for our sins, He becomes our advocate with the Father's love (1 Jn. 2, 1-2; 4 10). The Heart of Jesus symbolizes the temporal mission of the Son, precisely because it also signifies the eternal generation and relationship from which that mission is inseparable. And both are present in the Eucharist: the Father engenders His Son in giving Him to us and in giving Himself with Him; the Son loves His Father in delivering Himself to us for love of Him, and in uniting us in His intratrinitarian unity. The dialogue of love which the Eucharist creates in the Church, shows itself as an extension of the eternal dialogue of the Logos with His Father in the Spirit.

(We do not discuss here the question of the Heart of Jesus as sign of the eternal procession and of the temporal mission of the Holy Spirit, since this will be dealt with in the next chapter).

The Eucharist carries to its culminating point the mission of the Son in as much as Jesus effects in His twofold nature the synthesis of Eternity and Time, of the uncreated divine generation and of the created world; for, in the Eucharistic Communion, are deployed not only the synthesis of the limited and limitless (as Saint Maximus the Confessor had already seen in connection with the Incarnation),[98] but also the synthesis which is, in the most literal sense of the word, a symbiosis. In the sacramental Communion, the union of the divine Persons is united as intimately as possible with that communion of persons re-created in Christ which is the Church. The Eucharist thus realizes a communion of communions, whose one mediator is Christ Jesus. If already, in Christ, "human life-together, essential to each individual person, subsists in the transcendent life-together of the Word in the Trinity,"[99] the Eucharist for its part ensures the divinization of purely human sociability by making it share intimately in the sociability of the divine Persons.

The Eucharistic Heart of Jesus is the symbol of the Trinity as loving us and ransoming us in and through the Eucharist. In paying devotion to this Eucharistic Heart of the immolated Lamb, the Church loves the redemptive love of the Trinity for the Church, the triune Love which is at the root of the institution of the Eucharist, sacrifice and sacrament, by the Man-Jesus: ". . . that they may be one even as we are one, I in them and you in me, that they may become perfectly one, so that the world may know that you have sent me and have loved them even as you have loved me" (Jn. 17, 22-23). Was it not after having given thanks to His Father, in the midst of another prayer, that the Son of Man instituted the Eucharist? Did not the decision to institute the Eucharist occur as a decision reached in prayer? Bearing this in mind, one understands more readily that the love of the Three Persons is the principle, not only of the Redemption, but also of the Eucharist, sacrament of the superabundant and free Redemption. This love penetrates the adorable Heart of Jesus, the human Heart of the beloved Son, making Him will to renew constantly, in an unbloody manner, the sacrifice which ransomed us from the bondage of sin.[100] The act of supreme love by which our Redeemer instituted the Eucharist in order to remain with us until the end of the world, was certainly a twofold act, divine and human, of love for men; but it was entirely orientated and subordinated to the love of His Father.[101] Christ instituted the Eucharist in order to be able to love His Father in His brethren and through His brethren: "As the living Father sent me, and I live because of the Father, so he who eats me will live because of me"—and therefore for the Father for whom I live (cf. Jn. 6, 57).[102] It was in obedience to the salvific will of His Father, in order to keep His commandment, and under the breath of the Spirit who was urging Him to do so (Mk. 1, 12), that Jesus instituted the Eucharist.

Those who, through the Eucharist, often communicate with the Father and the Son in allowing themselves to be drawn by the Father towards the Son, thereby show that they are the elect chosen "before the foundation of the world," to be "holy and blameless" before God, in love (cf. Eph. 1, 4). Is not frequent Communion the sign, not infallible, it is true, but the sign *par excellence,* of freely bestowed predestination in Christ created Creator and predestined Predestinator?

For Saint Augustine, election signifies predestination, that is, "foreknowledge and preparation of the divine benefits by which those are freed who are set free."[104] According to him, predestination in Christ is at once personal and social.[105] His doctrine of predestination is essentially Christological: as the Word, Christ is, in union with the Father, the God who predestines; as man, He is the Head of all His predestined members. As God and only Son of God, Christ predestines and cannot be predestined. But all who are predestined are so in Him and with Him as man; through Him as the only Son of God. The final explanation of the Whole Christ is the love of the Father who predestines Christ to be our Head; the Father predestines all who are His, in and through His only Son. Christ is the first of those who have been freely predestined. Centuries later, Saint Thomas Aquinas said more specifically that Christ is the cause of our predestination, in the sense that the latter must be effected through Christ's help, and that it is one and the same divine will (identical with divine Being, with divine Love) that predestines both Christ and us.[106]

In receiving the Eucharist, we eat in love Him who is the light,[107] the exemplar and the cause of our predestination, as well as being its source and its ultimate end. By the fact that He gives Himself often to us, as Bread of eternal life, and that He associates us with His prayer as Mediator in order that we may persevere in love, Christ manifests, as much as possible, His eternal predestinating love and His efficacious will to give Himself to us beyond death. "He who eats my flesh and drinks my blood has eternal life, and I will raise him up at the last day."[108] This is a gift which will crown both the merit of eating the Eucharist and especially the absolutely free nature of the first grace which leads to it and of the last grace which causes the elect to abide in Christ forever.[109] Nay more, even the grace of Christ which has merited the Christian's first grace and last grace is itself rooted in the absolutely free gift of Himself to His own humanity, which the Word made at the first moment of His earthly existence. Christ, who has merited our salvation and carried out the divine design of predestination of the elect, was unable to merit either our predestination or His own, both originating in a single decision of the absolutely free love of the divine Word in relation to the Whole Christ.

The Eucharistic Heart of Jesus is therefore the earthly sign of the salvific omnipotence of merciful and also freely given Love: the earthly sign only, since the Eucharist will cease to exist at the general Resurrection, there being then no further need to nourish and sustain our dcision to love and serve Christ. But the Heart of Christ, forever wounded and open, will not cease to exist.

Before returning to the latter point in the conclusion to this chapter, we must more precisely describe the relationship between the free character and the remunerative character of the divine love for men, notably in the mystery of the Eucharist.

On the one hand, as we have already said, the free nature of the grace, and especially the absolutely free nature of the grace initially received by Christ, is at the origin of all our merits, which grow to their fullness through our frequent reception of the Eucharist.

On the other hand, the meritorious act *par excellence* consists in this receiving of the Eucharist from the motive of pure love, without concerning ourselves primarily with the rewards for doing so. Such receiving deserves to be called a *free* human act, the answer to the perfectly free nature of the divine love for us. Just as God has loved us through pure generosity, and without the least need to do so, we in return love Him with a pure love when we are not induced "to honor God through personal self-interest concerning body or soul, the present life or eternal life, but to do so because of the Goodness of God in Himself."[110]

Such purity of love given freely to God who has freely loved us before any possibility of a return of love by us, shines forth most resplendently in the consecration of reparation to the Heart of Jesus and in the Eucharistic Communion, the latter being the Christian's supreme sharing in the consecration of reparation which this Heart offers to the Father. Through Communion, in us and through us Christ completes His consecration to His Father as the victim (of expiation and of reparation) sacrificed for our salvation. "And for their sake I consecrate myself, that they also may be consecrated in truth. . . . God sent his Son to be the expiation for our sins" (Jn. 17, 19; 1 Jn. 4, 19).

In the mystery of the Eucharist, sacrifice and sacrament, we see a fusion of "the great duties of the Catholic religion: love and expiation,"[111] and also of the aims of devotion to the Sacred Heart of Jesus: consecration and reparation.

The Johannine idea of "selfless love," to use Dom Warnach's expression,[112] shows in a remarkable way that the freely given love of the reparatory consecration, in the context of the Eucharistic mystery, is supremely meritorious.

Saint John's Gospel and the philosophy of personality illuminate one another. A person genuinely achieves what is best in him, and does so in an integral way, only through the giving of himself to other people. A person is loved in proportion to the success with which he attains to this supreme value of the giving of self. The free nature of his doing so "motivates"[113] his love. This, according to Christ in Saint John's Gospel, is the "selfless motivation" of the love of the Father and of the Son for us, and preeminently of the love of the Father for the Son: "For this reason the Father loves me, because I lay down my life, that I may take it again; if a man loves me . . . my Father will love him; the Father Himself loves you, because you have loved me; he who loves me will be loved by my Father, and I will love him and manifest myself to him" (Jn. 10, 17; 14, 23; 16, 27; 14, 21).

In other words, it is the active response of the only Son and of the adopted sons that the Father seeks through His benevolent love. At first sight, it might seem that the eternal and uncreated love of the Father and of the Son for their creatures depends, as if through the addition of a new dimension, on the love of men for Them; or that the love of the Father for His Son is partly conditioned by the return of love which the sacred humanity of the only Son makes to His Father.[114] In reality, as Saint Thomas Aquinas has clearly shown in his commentaries on Saint John's Gospel,[115] no one can merit by his good works the uncreated and eternal love of God, a freely given love which is indeed the source of all merit; but man, and preeminently the Man-Jesus, can merit the effect of the divine love, viz. glorification. Ordinary men can merit growth in grace, but not the first grace or an increase of the already infinite love of God for them. We must therefore understand the Johannine texts presented by Dom Warnach, as expressing Christ's solemn affirmation concerning two points: the death of the Son through love for the Father is a sign of the ineffable love of the Father for the Son, because the Son could not offer His life unless the Father willed that He should do so; furthermore, Christ as man, in dying for love of the Father, merited from the Father the manifestation of the Father's love, which manifestation is the glorification of His body: "For this reason the Father loves me, because I lay down my life, that I may take it again." This "taking again" manifests the love of the Father, who was the original source of the gift and who now rewards it. In an analogous way it can be said that, when we love the Son, the Father loves us in the sense that He manifests to us that, in the final analysis, our love for the Son comes from the Father Himself, who is completely "ad Filium." Has not Jesus also said: "In that day you will know that I am in my Father, and you in me, and I in you" (Jn. 14, 20)?

Through Saint Thomas, therefore, himself inspired by the Augustinian tradition, we see that this "selfless motivation" of the Johannine agapé is none other than the merit, through a love freely given in the first instance, of its own growth. Only in this way is it possible to reconcile the texts cited with another text of the same Saint John: "In this is love, not that we loved God but that He loved us and sent his son to be the expiation for our sins" (1 Jn. 4, 10). Saint Thomas Aquinas makes this point explicitly.[117]

It is equally true that God has willed from eternity the free nature itself of the love for Himself which He freely gives us, thus in a sense inserting us into the reciprocity of the freely given love which exists between Him and His only Son. It is this free nature of our love for Him that He wills to reward.

Now, such a dialectic of freely given love emerges preeminently in the mystery of the Cross, which is renewed by the Eucharistic sacrifice. Has not Christ instituted and does He not celebrate the Mass, as principal Priest, precisely in order to show us the extent of His freely given love for the free nature of the

Father's love for Him and for the human race? In His flesh and in His blood, through the Mass, He has given us the strength and the means to love God with a pure and free love which does not seek earthly rewards thereby, and which is even resolved not to aspire primarily towards heavenly rewards—without, of course, committing the error of despising them.[118] From this viewpoint, the object of the worship which the Church pays to the Eucharistic Heart of Jesus must surely be His pure and freely given love for the Father and for men; and that its fruit must be our sharing in this pure love, the sacramental grace proper to the Eucharist. A final point should be made: since Christ's sacrificial love which we honor in honoring His Eucharistic Heart, is a freely given gift of the Father, then, in the final analysis, the object of this devotion is the love of the Father for the Son and for the world: "For God so loved the world that he gave his only Son, that whoever believes in Him should not perish but have eternal life" (Jn. 3, 16).

One sees, therefore, that through the sheer internal consistency of Christian dogma, the worship paid to the Eucharistic Heart of Jesus blends into the worship due to the merciful love of the Trinity for sinful mankind. To the undeserved hatred which sin directs against the Father and the Son (cf. Jn. 15, 22-26), these two devotions make the answer of freely given love. Against the sinful but finite will of man, is opposed the infinite and omnipotent salvific will of the Father and of the Son, which is expressed in the Eucharist.

Within this one salvific will, infinitely simple and identical with the Pure Act which is the Trinity, one must distinguish—by a notional distinction which shows its effects in created reality—between God's *relative* love and His *absolute* love for His rational creatures.

In commenting on these words of Jesus: "He who loves me will be loved by my Father, and I will love him and manifest myself to him" (Jn. 14, 21), Saint Thomas Aquinas recognized that, as regards their created effects, one cannot simply regard, as one and the same, the love by which God wills a particular good to one creature (i.e. relative love) and the love by which He wills all good—or the absolute love which expresses itself as the giving of self without reservation.[119] Through this second love, the Father and the Son come to dwell in the soul which They make holy. This is a privileged love, whereas God loves all His creatures with a relative love: as Saint Thomas explicitly stresses, God loves in this way even the devils, since He gives them the relative benefits of life, intelligence, and existence (ut vivant, et intelligant, et sint). Like the human damned, the angelical damned are loved by God with a love that is even merciful, in the sense that He does not punish them as much as they deserve.[120]

In the infinite simplicity of the trinitarian Love, the universal salvific will is identical, really identical, mysteriously identical, with the absolute predestinating will of a number of the elect—a number whose size is unknown but which does not coincide with the number of rational creatures.[121]

In dying to fulfill the salvific will of the Father in relation to all creatures, Christ has saved the predestined, while adoring the permissive will of His Father as regards the loss of the angelic and the human damned. This is an unfathomable mystery which causes the weak human reason to fear and tremble, but also and especially to hope. It is a mystery of love which is not really distinguishable from the mystery of the new and eternal Alliance between God and men, renewed at every Mass by the one Mediator. The predestined Predestinator adores in this mystery of love the predestinating will of the Father, the Father's merciful will, while fulfilling the part of it which belongs to Him. The Cross and the Mass are inseparable from the predestinating Love which gives itself in the Eucharist as a sign and pledge of eternal and absolute giving of God Himself to His predestined. The Eucharistic Heart of Jesus is the Heart of merciful predestinating love.

E. The Temporal and Eternal Manifestation of the Heart of the Lamb, Symbol of the Pleroma

In his encyclical, *Haurietis Aquas*, Pius XII explicitly presents the Heart of Jesus as the symbol of the Pleroma of which Saint Paul speaks in the Letters of the Captivity: " '(You have power) to know the love of Christ which surpasses knowledge, that you may be filled with all the fullness of God' (Eph. 4, 19). Of this fullness of God *containing all things* (italics ours), the Heart of Christ Jesus is indeed the most beautiful image: a fullness of mercy, proper to the New Testament, in which appear the goodness of God our Savior and His love for men."[122]

This is a highly significant text. In it, Pius XII emphasizes, not only that the Heart of Jesus is a symbol of the Fullness of God, but that it is the symbol *par excellence* of that Fullness. He identifies this fullness with the divine Mercy, but explicitly states that it contains all created realities, and this is in perfect accord with the various shades of the word "pleroma" in the Pauline Epistles, such as we have already considered them.[123] The pleroma of God contains the universe and the Church, the universe which is itself destined to an eschatological integration in the Church and whose ecclesial integration has, in a mysterious way, already begun in the sacraments. This universe and this Church are, in a sense, immanent in the infinite pleroma of the triune God, of the divinity which flows from the Father through the Son in the Spirit, in order to give itself to the world in the measure in which the later, despite its finitude and its sin, is capable of receiving it.

The magisterium presents, therefore, the Heart of Christ as the indirect symbol of the cosmic pleroma and of the ecclesial pleroma—of the cosmos and of the Church as they are in God and from God; but primarily as the symbol of the infinite mercy of the divine pleroma which is at the origin and the end of the cosmo-ecclesial pleroma.

In the same encyclical, Pius XII implies that the Heart of Christ is also the symbol of the fullness of the graces which are in the Word incarnate: he does so by citing[124] Jn. 1, 16: "And from his fullness we have all received, grace upon grace." He affirms this more explicitly in the words: "Placed in His Heart as in a casket of great price, our Savior carries immense treasures of merits, the fruits of His threefold triumph (over the devil, over sin, over death), and He distributes them generously to the redeemed human race. It is this consoling truth which Saint Paul expresses in the words: 'Therefore it is said, "When he ascended on high he led a host of captives, and he gave gifts to men." ' . . . He who descended is he who also ascended far above all the heavens, that he might fill all things (Eph. 4, 8-10)."

Pius XII places a very special emphasis, therefore, on the Heart of Jesus as symbol of the pleroma of the graces of the Man-God. This point, among others, differentiates between the ways in which Teilhard and Pius XII, in documents published almost at the same time, regarded the Heart of Jesus as symbol of the pleroma. We do not find so clear a formulation in Teilhard, though his idea is implied in what he writes.

With Teilhard, the accent is entirely placed on the cosmic and finite pleroma in process of pleromization under the action of Christ. With Pius XII, the accent is primarily on the infinite divine pleroma of the mercy of the Word, as in a sense containing within it, in its immensity, the finitude of the cosmo-ecclesial pleroma; and then on the mediating (rather than intermediary) pleroma of the graces which are in the sacred Humanity of the Word.

Of all these pleromas, the Heart of Jesus is the symbol and the bond. It directly and immediately symbolizes only the divine pleroma and the pleroma of graces; while it symbolizes in only an indirect and mediate way the cosmo-ecclesial pleroma—the cosmic pleroma which derives from the divine pleroma and the ecclesial pleroma which derives from the pleroma of graces. It symbolizes this cosmo-ecclesia pleroma as contained in the immensity of the pleroma of the divine nature, creative and redemptive of the universe and of the Church. It could be said that this Heart connotes them still more than it symbolizes them. After all, the Church is the pleroma *of Christ* (Eph. 1, 23).

The divine and infinite love of the Word of the divine Goodness fills the finite universe; the human love, spiritual and affective, of the incarnate Word fills the Church. In these distinct senses, the universe and the Church are contained in the Heart of the Word made flesh. Christ is less in the universe than the universe is in Christ. Even if one considers particularly the humanity of Christ, one can say that the universe is in the human and wounded Heart of the glorified Christ in as much as it is no longer the universe which acts upon this Heart—as in the case of the pre-paschal Christ—but this Heart which acts upon it, since It is the symbol of the voluntary and totally divinized affectivity of the Man-God, who reaches out to the whole universe by His powerful action, but remains entirely distinct from it.

In adoring the Eucharistic Heart of the incarnate Word, the Church therefore adores the past and constantly renewed historic act by which the infinite pleroma of His divine nature wills to fill with Himself and with His activity the cosmic and finite pleroma, making His ecclesial pleroma share in the fullness of His graces (Col. 2, 9; Eph. 4, 10; 1, 23; Jn. 1, 14b), in order, finally, that "the whole fullness of the deity" may dwell "bodily" in us (Col. 2, 9b).

Christ is therefore the pleroma that ceaselessly "pleromizes" His Church, and thus recapitulates the cosmos. The pleromization[126] of the Church occurs preeminently through the Eucharistic sacrifice. It is in offering itself as a holocaust in union with Christ, and in immolating itself, that the Church increasingly becomes the fullness of Christ, His pleroma. It is in the light of the Eucharist that we must understand this beautiful statement of Vatican II's *Dogmatic Consti-*

tution on the Church: "Christ fills the Church, which is His Body and His fullness, with His divine gifts (cf. Eph. 1, 22-23) so that she may grow and reach all with the fullness of God" (cf. Eph. 3, 19).

It is in the Eucharist that Christ, the Lamb of God, fulfills here on earth the promise which He linked with the institution and the first celebration of the Sacrifice of the New Alliance: "He who has my commandments and keeps them, he it is who loves me; and he who loves me will be loved by my Father, and I will love him and manifest myself to him" (Jn. 14, 21).

The Eucharist is the sacrament, that is, the visible sign, by which Christ manifests, and causes to be experienced, not only His affective love, but also His spiritual and supra-sensible love, human and divine, to him who eats His flesh and drinks His blood. The Eucharistic Heart of Jesus is the supreme visible sign of the fullness of merciful love which is in Christ.

This Eucharistic manifestation has been set in splendid relief by Saint Bonaventure and the authors of the Franciscan school.

For the Seraphic Doctor,[128] the Eucharist is the sacrament of mystical experience. In Communion, the well-disposed recipient perceives the benign nature of the divinity and this is the gift of wisdom in action. Through Eucharistic incorporation with Christ, he tastes the sweetness of the Savior, a sweetness exceeding that of honey. With the Lamb of the true Pasch, he passes from this world to eternal life: "He who eats my flesh and drinks my blood has eternal life" (Jn. 6, 54).

A little later, in the fourteenth century, Raoul de Biberach[129] deals magnificently with the threefold manifestation of Christ, the way to the Trinity: Christ Jesus manifested Himself in the Creation, in the Incarnation, in the Eucharist.

First of all, Christ manifests Himself (to eyes of faith) in the Creation. But the contemplation of the universe, even with faith, does not yield an experimental knowledge of God.[130]

Then the Lord manifests Himself in the Incarnation: even faith, however, does not give us this experimental knowledge, since the event is outside our experience. Finally, Jesus manifests Himself in the Eucharist: the grace of experiencing Christ is the special gift of the Eucharist. In the Holy Sacrament, Christ is the way to the Trinity. It is this for man's senses (thanks to the sacramentality of the sacramental species which orientate towards divine things); for man's intelligence, since the Eucharistic mystery demands perfect faith; and for man's will, which in this sacrament reaches Christ through ardent love.

If this manifestation meets with no obstacle, it should normally lead the communicant to spiritual marriage with Christ, living and acting in the Eucharist to purify him, to enlighten him, and to transform him as completely as possible. For is not the Eucharist the sacrament of the mystic marriage with the immolated and triumphant Lamb.

Whatever may be the extent of Christ's manifestation of Himself to him who no longer forms but one body, one Heart, and one soul with Him, such manifestation remains enveloped in the obscurity of faith and lacks "the clear vision that belongs to the life to come."[131] Nay more, it serves to make more lively the desire for this perfect manifestation which will mark the beatific vision.

We have already shown in what sense the Eucharistic Heart of Jesus is a very special symbol of His consummating love. We must now show why it is that the Heart of the Redeemer will remain, even after the Parousia, the indefectible symbol of the incomprehensible pleroma of the divine mercy, even in the midst of the beatific vision.

At first sight, this statement may seem absurd. How could the eternally pierced Heart of the Lord preserve a symbolizing function in the context of face-to-face vision? Up to the resurrection of all hearts, the symbolism is readily acceptable. But afterwards? Let us recall what we have already said several times:

the Word of the divine Goodness, even seen face to face, will nevertheless remain eternally beyond our complete comprehension. It can never be known by us, even in the midst of the beatific vision, in the manner in which It knows Itself—i.e. exhaustively.

It can therefore be said that the wounded Heart of the Risen Lord will forever remain the natural and glorified symbol of the incomprehensibility of the creative, redemptive, and remunerative love of the only Son, of His Father, and of Their Spirit.

We must add that, even after the ending of the whole sacramental and Eucharistic economy of the earthly Church, this Heart of the Lamb will, in a real sense, be the Eucharistic Heart, the Heart whose love will remain incomprehensibly transcendent to every created mind.

There will still be place in eternity and in the beatific vision for the most beautiful symbol ever to issue out of human history and finite time. The Heart of Jesus, His Eucharistic Heart, is an eschatological[132] symbol in every sense of the word: it indicates, promises, and contains an eternal love, and in eternity it will still indicate the ineffable incomprehensibility of this infinite love.

With the forever pierced side of the Lamb in one's mind, one understands how Saint Francis de Sales could write:

> In the glory of Heaven, after the motif of the divine goodness known and considered in itself, that of the death of the Savior will have the greatest power to delight beyond measure the blessed in God; in sign of which, at the transfiguration, which was a foretaste of glory, Moses and Elias spoke with him "of his decease which he was to accomplish in Jerusalem" (Lk. 9, 31).[133]

It is in the light of the lamp that "is the Lamb" (Rev. 21, 23), that the elect will see face to face how incomprehensible was and remains the love which the Father and the Son have shown to them in the darkness of their exile, and now manifests to them in blinding clarity. In returning to their first principle, they taste the eternal pleasure given to the Father and the Son by the death of Christ, ineffably signified by the wound in His side.[134] It is in the death of His beloved Son that the Father finds His whole pleasure.

The worship of the pierced Heart of Christ will never cease, therefore, either in the pilgrim Church or even in the Church triumphant.[135] After having adored in faith this sign of the merciful love of their Savior, the elect, seeing with the eyes of the bodies raised up by Him, the glorified wound in His side, will discover, with the illuminated eyes of the soul, the divine love of which they were the object and whose continuing incomprehensibility will be their ceaseless joy.

The whole universe will appear to them as the garment, radiant with light, of the transfigured and "transfiguring" Christ. This cosmic and priestly garment, "dazzling white" (cf. Lk. 9, 29; Mt. 17, 2), will be forever the new earth merited by the sacrifice and by the eating of the Eucharist. The keeping of the new commandment of love will have resulted in the renewal and transforming of the world, even of the physical world.[136]

We are now able, in concluding this chapter, to complete as follows the definition of the object of the worship paid by the Church to the Eucharistic Heart of Jesus:

> In adoring the Eucharistic Heart of Jesus, the Church loves the past and present sacrificial love of its Savior, which it announces until He comes; but it also loves the twofold act of love of His return in glory, an act eternal and to come, divine and human, by which His glorified Heart, forever wounded with love, will subject to Himself and assimilate to Himself the whole physical universe, will raise up all hearts, and will manifest perfectly to all His elect the inexhaustible incomprehensibility of His creative, sacrificial, and remunerative love received from

the Father and having the Father's glory as its ultimate purpose.[137]

In loving this Eucharistic and "parousiac" Heart, the Church loves the threefold love—affective, voluntary, and divine—through which He will gather together in a consummated unity the universe and the Church in it, by recapitulating them for the glory of the Father.[138]

NOTES TO CHAPTER FOURTEEN

1. Neither K. Rahner nor Schillebeeckx. A less prominent theologian, Dom Charles Massabki O.S.B. has published a synthesis of Catholic theology, *Le Christ recontre de deux amours,* Paris, 1962. Among non-Catholics, one can instance the syntheses of Karl Barth *(Dogmatic)* and of Tillich *(Systematic Theology).* That of Barth remains, however, uncompleted.

2. An expression of Vatican I (DS, 3001; DB, 1782).

3. Cf. DS, 536 (DB, 285): "secundum quod Deus est creavit Mariam, secundum quod homo creatus est a Maria."

4. AAS, 48 (1956), 313; a point specifically made in pars. 69 and 73 of the encyclical *Haurietis Aquas:* "absolutissima, si usum et exercitationem spectes, professio christianae religionis."

5. *Ibid.,* par. 71.

6. CD, 30; PO, 6. Cf. Paul VI: "The Eucharist has a power of doctrinal synthesis. . . . The whole of the Revelation is concentrated at this point, the most mysterious and most luminous of our faith. . . . And existential synthesis: in the sacrament, every virtue finds its nourishment" (Discourse of 21 August, 1968).

7. PO, 5 (Abbott, p. 541).

8. PO, 5 (Abbott, p. 542).

9. "Peculiari modo Eucharistici Cordis Jesu cultum fovendo": cf. note 11.

10. Leo XIII, *Acta,* 22 (1903), 307 *seq.*

11. Pius XII, *Haurietis Aquas,* AAS, 48 (1956), 351, par. 82.

12. Benedict XV granted a Mass of the Eucharistic Heart of Jesus "pro aliquibus locis," celebrated on the Thursday following the Feast of the Sacred Heart. See AAS, 13 (1921), 515. On the history of the devotion to the Eucharistic Heart of Jesus, see: L. Rayez, A. de Bonhomme: art. "Eucharistique (Coeur)," DSAM, IV. 2 (1961), 1648-1653; D. Castelain: *De cultu eucharistici Cordis Jesu,* Paris, 1928; A. Hamon, *Histoire de la dévotion au Sacré-Coeur,* Paris, 1940, t. 5, pp. 247-254;

R. Brouillard, art. "Coeur Eucharistique de Jésus," *Catholicisme,* t. II, Paris, 1949. On the relations between Eucharist and Sacred Heart, see note 29, and L. Garriguet, *Eucharistie et Sacré-Coeur,* Paris, 1925, pp. 305-310.

13. Pius XII, *Haurietis Aquas,* par. 43.

14. That is: to the Eucharistic Heart of Jesus.

15. Hilaire de Barenton, *La dévotion au Sacré-Coeur,* Paris, 1944, pp. 229-230.

16. Ubertino of Casale, *Arbor vitae crucifixae,* cited by de Barenton, *op. cit.,* p. 230; 81-84.

17. Cf. this text of Saint Augustine, cited by PO, 2: ". . . the entire commonwealth of the redeemed . . . (should) be offered as a universal sacrifice to God through the High Priest who in His Passion offered His very Self for us that we might be the body of so exalted a Head" (Abbott, p. 536). Father de Montcheuil has rightly directed attention to the importance of this idea of the Mass as sacrament of the sacrifice of humanity, the visible sign of its invisible sacrifice.

18. Cf. *Haurietis Aquas,* par. 67.

19. That is to say, the Eucharist as sacrifice (Mass) and transitory sacrament (Communion) and permanent sacrament (Real Presence in the tabernacle).

20. LG, 17; UR, 15.

21. We mean: the supernatural love which inclines towards the total giving of the self to God through fraternal charity, in accordance with the teaching of 1 John; only thus can the intimate indwelling of the Three Divine Persons reveal itself (cf. 1 Jn. 3, 18. 23. 24; Jn. 14, 21-23). The passage to sacrifical exteriority conditions the return to the interiority of the transcendent God.

22. Cf. Saint Thomas Aquinas, *Summa Theologica,* II. II. 25. 4. 3; 25. 7.

23. We recall that the growth of the twofold love of God and of the neighbor is the proper fruit of the Eucharist, sacrament of the fervor of love.

24. Mangenot, *Dictionnaire de Théologie Catholique,* 1, 1 (1923), art. "Agneau."

25. Y. M. J. Congar, *Mystère du Temple,* Paris, 1958, p. 247.

26. Mangenot, cf. note 24. One could even say that, in Saint John's view, all the faithful participate here on earth in the sacrifice and in the glory of the immolated and triumphant Lamb: "Feed my lambs" (Jn. 21, 15; cf. Rev. 7, 17); they are all the lambs of whom the Lamb is the supreme spehherd—the lambs of the Lamb.

27. Mangenot, cf. note 24. In 1891, the Holy Office expressed its disapproval of images which showed, in the midst of a host, a heart surmounted with flames, or hosts falling from the Heart of Jesus on to a paten: cf. Hamon, *op. cit.,* pp. 248-249. On the other hand, no objection could be made against

the images representing Jesus and His Heart burning with love for men, having before Him a chalice and bread: the Heart of Jesus instituting the Eucharist.

28. Hamon, *op. cit.*, p. 253. Besides, is it not to be expected that the very origin of the Christian liturgy should be the object of a liturgical celebration?

29. In 1949, Pius XII specified as follows the difference between devotion to the Sacred Heart and devotion to the Eucharist: "These two salvific devotions cannot be confused as to their object, or their motive, or their end, or their origin. . . . One honors the love of the Lord under the natural symbol of His Heart; the other adores this flesh and this blood in which this love is entirely given to us" (AAS, 41 (1949, 331). It could be said that the devotion to the Eucharistic Heart of Jesus isolates, in the devotion to the Heart of Jesus, one of His acts; and, in the Eucharistic devotion, its formal object. These devotions are not, therefore, purely and simply identical with one another.

30. Benedict XV promoted the devotion to the Eucharistic Heart of Jesus throughout his whole reign (see Castelain and Hamon, *op. cit.*, pp. 251-252). He declared: "I shall myself propagate this devotion. . . . It is the jewel of the devotion to the Sacred Heart. . . . The devotion to the Eucharistic Heart will be a source of graces for souls; *it will spread more and more in the Church* (*ibid.*, p. 252). There is a prophetic accent in this declaration, and it is our fervent wish that the present book may in some way contribute to the realization of this prophecy.

31. Cf. the teaching of God the Father to Saint Catherine of Siena, *Dialogue* XIII (43): "The just who have lived in charity and who die in love . . . see the happiness which I have prepared for them. . . . They thus taste eternal life before they have left their mortal remains, before the soul is separated from the body." The perfect taste their destined beatitude even before leaving the body at the moment of death, whereas the imperfect enter into purgatory.

32. Cited by R. Marlé S.J., *Au coeur de la crise moderniste,* Paris, 1960, p. 240.

33. Cf. G. Martelet S.J., in *Problèmes actuels de Christologie,* Paris, 1965, p. 42.

34. M. J. Nicolas O.P., *ibid,* p 82 It will be noted that the author expresses an idea which is in line with Greek patristic thought as taken up by Saint Thomas Aquinas; he does not say that all human persons are seized by the Word. Human persons having been corrupted by original sin only because of nature, Christ first repairs this nature in order fully to repair the human persons at the glorious Resurrection; cf. the following note.

35. Saint Thomas Aquinas, In Romanos 5, lectio III, par.

410: Marietti, Rome, 1953. It is in the context of original sin that the text cited here occurs.

36. Saint Hilary on Mt. 19, 5: Christus "omnium nostrum corpus assumpsit et unicuique nostrum assumpti corporis ratione factus est proximus" (PL, 9, 1025).

37. Saint Cyril of Alexandria, author of this text, in thus interpreting Jn. 1, 14 (Mersch translates as *en* rather than the customary *parmi*) highlights that it should be interpreted in conjunction with Jn. 17, 21, 23. In the prologue, it is probable that John already intended to allude to the immanence of Christ *in* us through grace and the Eucharist. It is especially important to compare this use of the preposition *in* with numerous analogues of Jn. 15: allegory of the Vine.

38. On this Platonic view and on the unity of the human species, see L. Malevez S.J., "l'Eglise dans le Christ," *Recherches de Science Religieuse,* 25 (1935), pp. 260 and 418; R. Arnou S.J., art. "Platonisme des Pères," *Dictionnaire de Théologie catholique,* XII, 2347 (1935).

39. Saint Cyril of Alexandria, in Jn. 1, 14 (PG, 73, 161-164) cited by Mersch, *op. cit.,* vol. I, pp. 516-517, Paris, 1951; and by AG, 7. 3.

40. GS, 38. 1.

41. Saint Cyril of Alexandria, in Jn. 11, 11 (PG, 74, 560): cited by Mersch, *op. cit.,* p. 505. Cyril explicitly refers to Eph. 3, 6 where Paul speaks of nations "con-corporal" (sussôma) of the promise of God in Christ. The term in Pauline, not coined by Cyril, who eloquently adds: "If we are all concorporal one with another *in Christ,* and not just one with another but also with Him who comes *in* us through his flesh, how could we not all be one, and one in one another, and in Christ?"

42. Saint Bonaventure, *Vitis Mystica,* chap. III.

43. Saint Thomas Aquinas, *Summa Theologica,* III. 73. 2, *sed contra;* III. 73. 3; III. 80. 4 and 5. 2.

44. LG, 8 (communitas) and 9 (communio).

45. LG, 3.

46. Cf. NA, 1: ". . . that ultimate and unutterable mystery which engulfs our being, and whence we take our rise, and whither our journey leads us" (Abbott, p. 661).

47. Cf. DS, 1739-1741 (DB, 938); DS, 3847; LG, 11. 1.

48. We are drawing here on G. de Broglie S.J.: *Le Sacré-Coeur et la doctrine du Corps Mystique* (Apostolat de la prière, Toulouse, 1946); and on certain patristic texts, notably of Saint Ambrose: "cubiculum Ecclesiae corpus est Christi" (*in Ps.* 118, sermo I, par. 16; PL, 15, 1271; the text is an allusion to Mt. 6, 6: the wounds of Christ constitute the room into which one must retire to pray to the Father in secret); and on Saint Jerome: "De Christo et Ecclesia omnis credentium multitudo generata est. Quae unum Ecclesiae corpus effecta, rursum in latere Christi ponitur, et costae locum replet,

et unum viri corpus efficitur" (in Eph. 5, 31; PL, 26, 569).

49. PO, 5. 2 (citing Saint Thomas Aquinas, Summa Theologica, III. 65. 3. 1; 79. 1).

50. PO, 5. 2: "sacramenta, sicut et omnia ecclesiastica ministeria et opera apostolatus, cum Sacra Eucharistica cohaerent et ad eam ordinantur."

51. Cf. Jn. 1, 16; Pius XII, Myst. Corp., par. 47; in this pleroma adored by the Church, there also figure the actual graces received by Christ or transmitted by Him inasmuch as they are all identical with Pure Act, with God who is Love and Light (1 Jn. 4, 16; 1. 5). All this is also implied in the worship rendered by the Church to the Eucharistic Heart of Jesus.

52. Cf. the original meaning of the Greek verb, trôgôn, used in Jn. 6, 54.

53. An allusion to Bossuet's famous definition of the Church: "le Christ répandru et communiqué."

54. Bossuet, Méditations sur l'Evangile, part 1, la Cène, 48th day.

55. Pius XII, Haurietis Aquas, par. 32, AAS, 48 (1956), 327. The Pope here cites this text of Saint Thomas Aquinas (Summa Theologica, I. II. 48. 4) which he applies to Christ: "the turmoil of anger spreads to the exterior of the body, especially to those parts where the influence of the heart is most powerfully felt, as the eyes, the face, the tongue." The cult of the Sacred Heart signifies for the Church, therefore, the cult of the holy anger of Christ: cf. Jn. 2, 15 seq.; Mk. 3, 5. One sees how free the Church is from the sentimentalities sometimes attributed to it: cf. Haurietis Aquas, par. 38: "The Heart of Jesus trembled with a holy indignation" (Latin text, 330).

56. Cf. Saint Thomas Aquinas, Summa Theologica, III. 79. 4.

57. Our reference is to those who have not yet made full satisfaction to the loving and salvific justice of God, and have not paid all the temporal punishment due to their venial sins.

58. This treasury of the Church is Christ Himself, "in whom are abundantly the satisfactions and the merits of His redemption," as Paul VI says in the apostolic constitution Indulgentiarum Dominus, 11, par. 5, AAS, 59 (1967), 11-12. The text specifies in what sense the merits of the saints also form part of this treasury.

59. Paul VI, in fact, does not speak explicitly about the link between earthly Eucharist an glorious Resurrection. One can maintain, however, that he does so implicitly or negatively in I Cor. 11, 27, by leaving it to be inferred that unworthy Communion merits eternal damnation.

60. LG, 48. 2. It is clear that the worship paid by the Church to the Eucharist Heart of Jesus has also for its object the constant Eucharistic attraction exercised by the glorified Christ,

who ceaselessly wills to convert mankind.

61. LG, 48. 3 (Abbott, 79).

62. Saint Thomas Aquinas, *Summa con. Gen.,* IV. 97.

63. Here and in the following paragraphs, we are following the fine article by John H. Wright S.J., "The Consummation of the Universe in Christ," (*Gregorianum,* 39 1958), 285-294. We consider that this short article has made a very important contribution to the development of a "cosmic Christology."

64. Cf. the declarations of Constantinople III (681) on the complete divinization of the human will of Jesus, united with but distinct from His divine will: DS, 556 (DB, 291).

65. Saint Thomas Aquinas, *Summa Theologica,* 13. 2; 59. 6. 3. The soul of Christ has therefore the power to effect the transfiguration and even the miraculous transformations of the whole physical universe, in the measure in which such changes are orientated to the recapitulative purpose of the Incarnation.

66. Note that the recapitulation, even in its material aspect, is therefore the work of the created and immaterial free will of the Man-God.

67. Saint Thomas Aquinas (*Summa Theologica,* III. 13. 2) specifies that only God can create or annihilate, and this is something which the human soul of Christ could not do, even instrumentally.

68. Clearly, a world in the grip of "futility," and "decay" (Rm. 8, 20-21) is not yet a properly orientated and harmonious cosmos. The whole creation is "groaning in travail" to bring forth this cosmos in which the power of Christ will transform it.

69. Saint Thomas Aquinas clearly teaches that men have merited the glorification of the universe: "this glory, the irrational and insensible bodies have certainly not merited; but man has merited that it should be bestowed on the universe, inasmuch as this glory contributes to increase the glory of man. Thus someone could merit that decorations be placed on his coat, without the coat itself having merited them." (*Summa Theologica,* Supplement, III. 91. 1). The universe is therefore represented by Saint Thomas as man's garment. This is a very rich image, which implies that the universe is a garment fashioned by man. The universe is also presented as due to be glorified as a result of man's merits and for his glory. These merits are, of course, rooted in the merit of the Passion of Christ, The Priest of the cosmos. It is therefore correct to say that the final cosmos, succeeding to the initial chaos, will be the priestly garment of Christ, a garment completely dyed in His Blood.

70. Cf. Saint Augustine, *Enarr. in Ps.* 109, 4 (PL, 37, 1459): "as born of the Father, God with God, He is co-eternal with Him who engendered Him. He is not Priest; but He is Priest

because of the Victim whom He has received from us and whom He offers for us."

71. It will be noted that in these three Pauline texts, the same Greek verb is used: "hupotassein," meaning "to subject."

72. Cf. a Teilhard text referred to in our note 112 to Chapter Four.

73. The theologians are unanimous in saying that Christ has been divinized, in His created soul, through sanctifying grace. Cf. Saint Thomas Aquinas, *Summa Theologica*, II. 7. 1. 1: "quia cum unitate personae remanet distinctio naturarum, anima Christi non est per suam essentiam divina. Unde oportet quod fiat divina per participationem, quae est secundum gratiam." This enables Father Fransen S.J. to observe very exactly: "Christ has divinized His own human nature in humanizing it"—i.e. in causing it to grow to its full and perfect development (*Problèmes de l'Autorité*, Paris, 1961, p. 62).

74. We mean that these free wills are not only limited, but that they are also conditioned by the interplay of secondary causes which constitute the whole of the created world.

75. Clearly, bread is not a substance in exactly the same way as we apply the word to natural things on which man has not worked. Bread is a substance whose existence as such depends on man's labor and whose purpose is to be man's food. In a more proximate and immediate way than do many other substances, it fulfills the purpose of the whole physical universe—i.e. to serve man. However, in transforming wheat into bread by his labor, man does not create the substance of bread (cf. J. de Finance S.J., *Connaissance de l'Etre*, Paris, 1966, pp. 250-285).

76. Cf. the commentary of Saint Thomas Aquinas on Jn. 6, 35: "I am the bread of life": "panis corporalis est panis mortis qui non competit nisi ad restaurandum defectum mortalitatis, unde et solum in hac vita mortali necessarius est. Non dat vitam set tantum praeexistentem sustentat ad tempus" (*Super Evang. S. Joannis lectura*, Marietti, Turin, 1952, par. 914.

77. One knows that Father Teilhard de Chardin regarded the universe as a "diaphany" or transparency of God. See *Milieu Divin*, p. 162: "Not Your Epiphany, Jesus, but Your diaphany."

78. Cf. Saint Ambrose: "Tunc secundum carnem homo, nunc per omnia Deus" (PL, 16, 1341).

79. Cf. Saint Ambrose: "Resurrexit in Eo mundus, resurrexit in Eo coelum, resurrexit in Eo terra" (PL, 16, 1354).

80. Cf. Col. 1, 18—and the commentary on it by Father Lamarche S.J. in *Le Christ vivant*, Paris, 1966, p. 70: "Is not Christ called both Head of the Church and Head of the universe? This use of the same word for both ideas shows quite properly the one and only saving action exerted by

Christ over the Church and the universe; but this identity of verbal usage does not exclude real differences. It is in a privileged manner that Christ is the Head of the Church, since the Church alone is the part of the universe that becomes assimilated to Christ's body and which is given the title, (Mystical) Body of Christ. Through its growth, the Church is to take on the dimensions of the universe." It is therefore in an imperfect manner only that the physical universe forms part, here and now, of the Church; it will be fully part of it at the Parousia.

81. We are referring here to the declarations of Paul VI in the encyclical *Mysterium Fidei,* AAS, 57 (1965), 766: "Peracta transsubstantiatione, species panis et vini novam procul dubio induunt significationem, novumque finem, cum amplius non sint communis panis et communis potus, sed signum rei sanctae signumque spiritualis alimoniae; sed ideo novam induunt significationem et novam finem, quia novam continent 'realitatem,' quam merito *ontologicam* dicimus." Cf. *ibid.,* p. 755. At the Parousia, it will be not only the species of bread and wine, but the whole universe, that will be "trans-signified" and "trans-finalized" without preliminary transubstantiation.

82. Cf. Saint Thomas Aquinas, *Compendium Theol.,* I. 149.

83. On *aevum,* see Saint Thomas Aquinas, *Summa Theologica,* I. 10. 5. 1, 2; Michel A., DTC, V. 1 (1913), art. *"Eternité,"* col. 912-921.

84. Pius XII, Christmas 1957, AAS, 50 (1958) 17. Cf. also H. de Lubac S.J.: *La pensée religieuse du P. Teilhard de Chardin,* Paris, 1962, pp. 185-200.

85. Thus, the human free will conditions, in the providential plan, not necessarily the hour of the Parousia, but the existence itself of the cosmic consequences of this supreme event, which is identical with the Second Coming of the Son of Man. Communion with the Transfigurator merits the cosmic Transfiguration.

86. The words "until he comes" (1 Cor. 11, 26) must be read in the light of 15, 24-28, of the same Epistle: in order to subject all things to the Father.

87. Pius XII, *Haurietis Aquas,* par. 33 and 54: AAS, 48 (1956), 327, 338.

88. Cf. Mersch S.J., *op. cit.,* t. II, p. 13. Cf. Jn. 6, 45-57

89. Cf. K. Rahner's thesis on the identity of the immanent Trinity and of the economic Trinity: *Mysterium Salutis,* Köln, 1961, t. II, pp. 327-329 and 370 *seq.*

90. Pius XII, AAS, 48 (1956), 327.

91. *Ibid.,* 310 (par. 3).

92. Saint Thomas Aquinas, *Summa Theologica,* I. 34. 2.

93. *Ibid.,* I. 32. 1. 1.

94. *Ibid.,* I. 41. 2.

95. *Ibid.* I. 41. 2. 2 (commentary on Col. 1, 13: the "beloved Son"). This doctrine of Saint Thomas is not a dogma of the Catholic Faith.

96. In this connection, Saint Thomas Aquinas has coined the splendid expression: "Verbum bonitatis" (*ibid.*, I. 27. 5. 2).

97. *Ibid.*, I. 43. 2. 2: "missio includit processionem aeternam, et aliquid addit, sc. temporalem effectum."

98. Saint Maximus the Confessor, PG, 90, 612 AB.

99. Mersch S.J., *op. cit.*, t. I, p. 285.

100. Cf. the second text referred to in note 87 of this chapter.

101. LG, 42 1; cf. Chapter Ten, C.

102. M. J. Lagrange O.P. (*Evangele selon saint Jean*, Paris, 1948⁸, pp. 185-187) translates the Greek "dia" here as *pour* and not *par*.

103. Cf. 1 Jn. 1, 3; Jn. 6, 44.

104. Saint Augustine, *de dono perseverantiae*, 14. 35; ML, 45, 1014.

105. *Ibid.*, 24. 67 (ML, 45, 1034): "Et illum et nos praedestinavit; quia et in illo ut esset caput nostrum et in nobis ut ejus corpus essemus, non praecessura merita nostra, sed opera sua futura praescivit." It is regrettable that Hans Urs von Balthasar, in his beautiful book, *Elizabeth de la Trinité* (Paris, 1960, pp. 37-87, notably 67-69), has seen fit to contrast social predestination and individual predestination, and to reject the latter. The doctrine of an irreducibly personal predestination cannot be set aside.

106. Saint Thomas Aquinas, *Summa Theologica*, III. 24. 4.

107. In his *De Praedestinatione Sanctorum*, 15, 30 (ML, 44, 981): "Est praeclarissimum lumen praedestinationis et gratiae ipse Salvator, Mediator Dei et hominum, Christus Jesus." On which Saint Thomas Aquinas splendidly comments: "Dicitur lumen praedestinationis et gratiae inquantum per ejus praedestinationem et gratiam manifestatur nostra praedestinatio" (*Summa Theologica*, III. 24. 3, *sed contra*): our predestination as members is manifested in that of our Head.

108. Jn. 6, 54.

109. Cf. DS, 1532, 1540, 1541, 1566 (DB, 801, 805, 806, 826).

110. Pius XII, *Haurietis Aquas*, par. 74 (AAS, 48, 1956, 346-347). The Pope adds: "In the devotion to the Sacred Heart, exterior works of piety are not given the first place, and its essential element does not consist in the benefits to be obtained; for if Christ the Lord saw fit to guarantee such benefits by private promises, this was done in order to urge men to fulfill with greater fervor the great duties of the Catholic religion—namely, love and expiation, and thereby to provide in the best possible way for their own spiritual growth." One notices the subtle quality of the idea: nothing is more effective than the pure love which relegates to the

second place, while not eliminating, temporal or spiritual personal interest. The idea and practice of reparation fosters this pure love.

111. See the text cited in the preceding note. On reparation, the following are useful: H. Rondet S.J.: "Le péché et la réparation dans le culte du Sacré-Coeur," in *Cor Jesu*, Rome, 1959, t. I, pp. 683-720; P. Hartmann S.C.J.: *Le sens plénier de la réparation du péché*, Apostolat de le Réparation, Louvain, 1955, pp. 250-293.

112. Dom Victor Warnach O.S.B., *Agape, die Liebe als Grundmotiv der Neutestamentlichen Theologie*, Düsseldorf, 1951. We are acquainted with Dom Warnach's ideas thanks to an article by B. Dumoulin, "Epistémologie et Théologie trinitaire," *Rex. des Sc. Relig.*, 41 (1967), 331-340.

113. Saint Thomas Aquinas reminds us, however, that this motivation must not be understood in an anthropomorphic manner (*Summa Theologica*, 19. 4): "(Deus) vult ergo hoc esse propter hoc; sed non propter hoc vult hoc." One could question whether the authors mentioned in the preceding note have sufficiently avoided this pitfall.

114. In reality, the human love of the Man-Jesus for His Father is still a gift of the Father to His only Son, just as is His divine love.

115. Saint Thomas Aquinas, *Super Evangelium S. Joannis Lectura, in Jo.* 10, 17 (Marietti, Rome, 1952, par. 1422): "Ipsam Dei delectionem nullus mereri potest sed effectum divinae delectionis mereri possumus per bona opera nostra. . . . Evidens signum delectionis est quod homo ex caritate faciat Dei mandata." What is involved here is a proof of the love of God for this man.

116. Saint Augustine makes this splendid commentary on Jn. 16, 27 ("The Father himself loves you because you have loved me"): "Hinc ergo factum est ut diligeremus quia delecti sumus. Prorsus donum Dei est diligere Deum. Ipse ut diligeretur dedit qui non dilectus dilexit. . . . Amat nos Pater quia nos amamus Filium: cum a Patre et a Filio acceperimus ut et Patrem amemus et Filium: diffundit enim caritatem in cordibus nostris amborum Spiritus (Rm. 5, 5), per quem Spiritum et Patrem amamus et Filium et quem Spiritum cum Patre amamus et Filio. Amorem itaque nostrum pium quo colimus Deum fecit Deus et vidit quia bonum est, ideo quippe amavit ipse quod fecit. Sed in nobis non faceret quod amaret nisi antequam id faceret nos amaret" (In Joannem, *tract.* 102. 5; PL, 35, 1898).

117. Saint Thomas Aquinas commentates on Jn. 16, 27 in the light of 1 Jn. 4, 10 (read as against the Vulgate which adds an adverb, "*prior* dilexit," absent from the original Greek text): "Probatio non est per causam sed est per signum, quia hoc ipsum quod nos Deum diligimus est signum quod ipse

amat nos. . . . Amare Christum inquantum a Deo exivit satis est evidens signum amoris Dei. Qui ergo amat Christum quia a Deo exivit amor ejus praecipue retorquetur in Deum Patrem: non autem si amat Christum inquantum hominem." This is an admirable observation, singularly relevant in our own day!

118. Cf. note 110 of this chapter.

119. Saint Thomas Aquinas, *Super Ev. S. Jo. lect., in Jo. 14, 21* (Marietti, Rome, 1952, par. 1936): a distinction drawn between "dilectio secundum quid" ("vult aliquod bonum particulare") and "dilectio simpliciter" ("omne bonum, ut habeat ipsum Deum"). The Saint adds: "Deus autem omnia causata diligit secundum quid quia omni creaturae vult aliquid bonum, etiam ipsis daemonibus, ut sc. vivant, et intelligant, et sint." Clearly, the absolute love of the giving of self without conditions is predestinating love.

120. Saint Thomas Aquinas, *Summa Theologica,* I. 21. 4. 1; *de Potentia,* 5. 4. 6.

121. Cf. C. Boyer S.J., *De gratia* (Rome, 1930, p. 273, par. 365): the doctrine of predestination "ante praevisa merita," upheld by Saint Robert Bellarmine following Saint Augustine, does not run counter to "congruism." What we say here is inspired more directly by Saint Thomas Aquinas's commentary on 1 Tm. 2, 4 ("God our Savior desires all men to be saved") where the Angelic Doctor presents the commentary of Saint John Damascene: God wills with an antecedent willing the salvation of all, and with a consequent willing the salvation of the predestined: *super Epist. Pauli Lectura, t.* II, in 1 Tm., par. 62.

122. Pius XII, *Haurietis Aquas,* par. 64 (AAS, 48, 1956, 341-342: "cujus *omnia complectentis* plenitudinis Dei clarissima imago est ipsum Cor Christi Jesu: plenitudinem dicimus misericordiae, quae propria est Novi Testamente." The word "complecti" can have two meanings: "to embrace" and "to contain." The first meaning, no doubt implied here *in recto,* in no way excludes the second, at least *in obliquo.*

123. Cf. Chapter Four, note 135.

124. Pius XII, *Haurietis Aquas,* par. 21 (AAS, 48, 1956, 321).

125. *Ibid.,* par. 47 (Latin text, p. 334).

126. We are using a Teilhardian term, fully applicable to the Humanity of Christ if one considers its activity in relation to the Church.

127. LG, 7. 8.

128. Saint Bonaventure, "Sermo de Corpore Christi," *Opera,* t. 5 (Quarrachi, 1891, pp. 553-566); discussed by E. Longpré O.F.M. in "Eucharistie et union mystique selon la spiriutalité franciscaine" (*Rev. d'Ascétique et de Mystique,* 25 (1949), 310-318.

129. See Longpré, *art. cit.,* pp. 322-327; and also the same author's article, "Eucharistie et expérience mystique," in

DSAM, t. IV, col. 1598-1601 (Paris, 1961).

130. A certain, perhaps unilateral, interpretation of Teilhard would tend to deny this.

131. Saint John of the Cross, *The Living Flame of Love,* third strophe, *sub fine.* In *The Spiritual Canticle* (strophe 27, no 2) this saint defines the spiritual marriage in a way which corresponds perfectly with the effect proper to the Eucharist when the communicant places no obstacle in the way of grace: "It is a complete transformation within the Beloved, a transformation in which the parties give themselves one to the other completely in a union of love as perfect as is possible in this life." Complete transformation, reciprocal union, mutual possession: these too are the effects of the sacramental grace of the Eucharist.

132. "Eucharistic Heart" is a symbolic expression, like that of "Heart of Jesus." Both expressions signify the loving person of Christ. If the former adds a shade of meaning to the latter, both use one of the words of the basic vocabulary of men, the word "heart," a word which designates a whole human composite, the innermost center of the person. The eschatological character of the symbol of the Eucharistic Heart results from the structure itself of the sacrament of the Eucharist, a sacrament which announces the glory to come and is its "prognostic" sign (Saint Thomas Aquinas, *Summa Theologica,* III. 64. 3).

133. Saint Francis de Sales: conclusion to "Treatise on the love of God."

134. Blessed Ruysbroeck, *L'anneau ou la pierre brillante,* chap. 12, published as an appendix to *L'ornement de noces spirituelles, Brussels,* 1920, p. 269.

135. After the Parousia, the Heart of Christ as such "will not cease to beat with its steady and peaceful rhythm (imperturbabile ac placido pulsu moveri) and still to signify the threefold love through which the Son of God is united to His heavenly Father and with the whole community of men"—because men will again be composites of bodies and souls, except that the bodies will be perfectly translucent signs of the souls. The quotation in the above sentence is from *Haurietis Aquas,* par. 34 (Latin text, pp. 328-329). Already in this first relationship, the Heart of Christ will continue to symbolize His threefold love. As wounded visibly and forever wounded, It will symbolize this love in an even stricter sense: through the visible wound, we shall see the incomprehensible character of the formerly invisible but henceforth visible wound of love (cf. *ibid.,* par. 52; Latin text, p. 337). Furthermore, Saint Thomas Aquinas (*Summa Theologica,* III. 54. 4. 3) clearly explains that Christ's body could change only by a new death: "unde patet quod cicatrices quas Christus post resurrectionem in suo corpore ostendit, numquam postmodum ab illius corpore

sunt remotae." The wound in Christ's side will be the sign of a suffering once undergone and never to return.

136. Cf. GS, 38. 1.

137. One could say that the Eucharistic Heart will remain forever the natural, even glorified, symbol of the trinitarian love. On the symbol, see K. Rahner S.J., *Schriften zur Theologie,* Koeln, 1960, t. IV, pp. 275-312.

138. We here define the object of the devotion paid by the Church to the Eucharistic Heart as the *twofold* act of Christ in instituting the Eucharist. A consequence both of the traditional doctrine concerning the divine-human works of Christ, and of the Church's condemnation of monoergism, is involved here (Cf. A. Michel, DTC, XV, 1, 1950, 205-216: art. *"théandrique, operation,"* and also DS, 268).

15

THE EUCHARISTIC HEART OF JESUS
GIVER OF THE OTHER PARACLETE,
THE SPIRIT OF TRUTH

A theme which has long exercised the minds of theologians is that concerning the relations between the (incarnate) Word and the Holy Spirit. To investigate this theme is certainly the most splendid of undertakings, but also the most difficult if one is to avoid certain brilliant but false formulations.

This theme can be dealt with in a basically trinitarian manner, or primarily from the viewpoint of Christology. It is the latter that we choose here.

Is it the Holy Spirit who sends Christ, or is it Christ who gives the Spirit? Is it Christ the Word or Christ the Word Incarnate who gives Him? What relation exists between the mystery of the Eucharist and the gift of the Spirit of Truth and of Love? Is the Holy Spirit symbolized by the Heart of Jesus? Has the Spirit played a role in the development of the cult of this Heart and, more especially, of this Eucharistic Heart?

Let us atempt to answer these questions in order, and to establish the connection between the answers; for it is through careful attention to the inter-relationships between mysteries that theology progresses.[1]

455

A. The Eucharistic Heart of Jesus, Giver of the "Other Paraclete" (Jn. 14, 16)

It cannot be denied that the Holy Spirit has formed the Man-Jesus; for does not the Apostles' Creed proclaim that Christ was born of the Holy Spirit and of the Virgin Mary?

The Scriptures also show us that Christ was "driven" and sent by the Holy Spirit: "And Jesus, full of the Holy Spirit, returned from the Jordan, and was led by the Spirit for forty days in the wilderness" (Lk. 4, 1): ". . . he saw the heavens opened and the Spirit descending upon him like a dove. . . . The Spirit immediately drove him out into the wilderness" (Mk. 1, 10-12): "And Jesus returned in the power of the Spirit into Galilee, and . . . he came to Nazareth . . . and he went to the synagogue . . . and there was given to him the book of the prophet Isaiah. He opened the book and found the place where it was written, 'The Spirit of the Lord is upon me, because he has anointed me to preach good news to the poor. He has sent me to proclaim release to the captive and recovering of sight to the blind . . .' " (Lk. 4, 14-18).

Thus Christ presents Himself to us as the Emissary of the Spirit, as His Anointed, consecrated by the Unction, which is the Spirit Himself[2] and, although born of the Holy Spirit (cf. Lk. 1, 35), as having been filled by this Spirit in a new way[3] at His baptism, with a view to His mission.

However, the same Gospel of Saint Luke shows us the risen Christ promising to send the Spirit promised by the Father (Lk. 24, 49). The Gospel of Saint John, while in line with the synoptic Gospels as regards the descent of the Holy Spirit on Christ at His baptism, emphasizes the Christ who promises, breathes, sends the Spirit in whom He baptizes (Jn. 1, 32-34; 15, 26; 16, 7; 20, 22).

It is clear, therefore, that the Christ of Saint John's Gospel is much more He who sends the Spirit, than He who is sent by this Spirit.

Saint Thomas Aquinas is in perfect harmony with the Gospel and with his own doctrine of the mission of the Divine Persons, a doctrine itself also rooted in this datum, when he refuses to see, in Saint Luke's expressions concerning the sending of Christ by the Spirit, the indication of a sending, properly so called, of the Son by the Third Divine Person.[4]

Clearly, it is impossible that the Spirit, proceeding from the only Son to whom He owes His eternal origin, could be the origin of that Son. On the other hand, however, there is nothing to prevent our saying that the Holy Spirit, like the Father and the Son, is the principle of the redemptive work accomplished by Christ.

On the contrary, the Son sends the Spirit in the strictest sense of the verb. The Word, Co-breather with the Father of their only Spirit, sends this Spirit to men, in an extension of His uncreated act of breathing Him. The same Word of the divine Goodness, in perfect union with His Father, loves Their common lovableness, and thus eternally produces their Spirit of Love—the Spirit whom They both send, in the absolute simplicity of the same eternity, to mortal men. The Holy Spirit is eternally sent in time.

Some theologians[5] have recently affirmed that Christ *as man* gives and sends the Spirit to men. They have interpreted in this sense the statement in Saint John's Gospel: ". . . he breathed on them, and said to them. 'Receive the Holy Spirit' " (20, 22). These theologians, it seems to us, do not express themselves very happily.

In effect, the eternal procession is connoted by the temporal mission.[6] If the Man-Jesus, precisely as man, gave and sent the Spirit, this would necessarily imply that the Creator would proceed from the creature, and thereby God's transcendence would be destroyed. But we are not to be taken as saying that all is false in these theologians' statement.

Saint Thomas Aquinas has splendidly developed

the element of truth which it contains. Focusing on an idea of Saint Augustine, he writes:

> To give grace or the Holy Spirit belongs to Christ as He is God, authoritatively; but instrumentally it belongs also to Him as man, inasmuch as His manhood is the instrument of His Godhead. And hence by the power of the Godhead His actions were beneficial—i.e., by causing grace in us, both meritoriously and efficiently. But Augustine denies that Christ as man gives the Holy Spirit authoritatively. Even other saints are said to give the Holy Spirit instrumentally, or ministerially . . .[7]

One notes his distinction: the Man-Jesus gives the Spirit, but it is not as *man*[8] that He does so; He gives the Spirit "inasmuch as His manhood is the instrument of His Godhead" in the work of Redemption. The Man-Jesus, who in the unity of His Person is the Word of God, breathes and sends the Spirit whom His "manhood" does not breathe or send. The humanity of Jesus gives the Spirit, not on the mere authority of His human nature, but on the authority of that nature as assumed by a divine Person.[9]

Or, if one prefers, the humanity of Christ is only the instrumental cause, and not the secondary cause, of the giving of the Spirit. In this connection, we remind outselves that the instrumental action as such does not belong to the instrument, whereas the action of the secondary cause is truly its own, though of course in absolute dependence on the primary Cause.[10]

Clearly, the humanity of the Risen Christ is the instrument of the gift of the Spirit in a different although similar way, by comparison with the instrumentality of the saints to which the Angelic Doctor refers in the text quoted above. The human free will of Christ is a primary instrumental cause, while His psychological or physical powers actuated by this free will, are secondary instrumental causes; whereas the ministers of the sacraments are distinct instrumental causes.

If Jesus, as man, receives the Spirit and, as man assumed by the Word, i.e. through His humanity as instrument of the Word, gives this Spirit, it is purely and simply as the Word that He gives Him, as being the eternal origin of the Spirit and as He who sends the Spirit in time. But, as Father de Guillou rightly emphasizes,[11] it is the incarnate Word, in the unity of His being, who sends this Spirit.

Another Dominican theologian, Father Guérard des Lauriers, also focuses this point and a part of the matter in question:

> Although it is as God that Christ sends the Spirit, nevertheless the human nature subsists in the Word producing the Spirit—in this very act which belongs to the Person of the Word and which produces the Spirit. . . . Using the language of psychology, we could also say that the sacred humanity is completely present to the Word that breathes the Spirit, and that this sacred humanity thus assists in the breathing which it does not produce in a human way, but in which it subsists inasmuch as this humanity has been assumed by the Divinity.
>
> The intuition of Saint Cyril, expressed in the formula which now reads strangely, "mia phusis tou logou sesarkôménè," tends to link up with this mystery. Because of refinements established since his day, we no longer say that Christ has a unitary nature,[13] but that He is a reality one and incarnate, that is, admitting of human nature. Consequently, in accordance with the unity and with the wholeness of Christ's Being, this reality always underlies every operation which emanates from it. Although they are distinct, Christ's two natures do not divide His *esse*: this *esse* belongs formally to the Word, but it remains true that the sacred humanity does not have an *esse* which could be part of this simple *esse*. It follows that, in fact, the sacred humanity is inseparable from whatever subsists in accordance with this simple *esse*, and in particular inseparable from the divine opera-

tion by which the Holy Spirit proceeds and is sent.[14]

It must be maintained, therefore, that inasmuch as Christ is a reality one and incarnate, His human nature, especially after the Resurrection,[15] cannot be excluded from the sending of the Holy Spirit.

We can now take the matter further, with Dom H. M. Diepen and in the light of the encyclical *Haurietis Aquas:*

> The sacred Humanity is the instrumental cause of the pouring forth of the Holy Spirit. . . . The Paraclete proceeds eternally from the uncreated Love of the Son. The hypostatic union of the human will of Christ with this divine Love, and the harmonious unity of the Person of the Incarnate Word, make His human heart the special instrument for the pouring forth of the Paraclete. It is by His human intelligence that Christ communicates to us the mysteries which He contemplates in the bosom of the Father; equally, it is through His Sacred Heart that He gives the Spirit who proceeds from His eternal Love.[16]

This being so, one understands how Pius XII could write: "love is the gift of the Heart of Christ and of His Spirit"[17]; "est enim haec caritas Jesu Cordis ejusque Spiritus donum." Thus Pius XII regards the Holy Spirit as the Spirit of the Heart of Jesus. He connects this with the explicit doctrine of Christ Himself, showing us how the Church drinks the Spirit and the rivers of living waters which flow from the Heart of Christ, to whom the Church, thanks to the "inestimable gift" of the devotion to this Heart, can manifest a more ardent love:

> Enriched with this inestimable gift, the Church can manifest to its divine founder a more ardent love, and thus realize more fully this wish which Saint John ascribes to Christ Himself: "On the last day of the feast, the great day, Jesus stood

up and proclaimed, 'If anyone thirst, let him come to me and drink. He who believes in me, as Scripture has said, *Out of his heart shall flow rivers of living water.*' Now this he said about the Spirit, which those who believed in him were to receive" (Jn. 7, 37-39). Those who were listening to Him would surely have associated this promise of a spring of "living water" flowing from His side, with the prophetic words of Isaiah, Ezechiel, and Zechariah concerning the Messianic kingdom, and also with the symbolic stone which miraculously emitted a jet of water when Moses struck it.[20]

Thus, as Pius XII quite clearly informs us, the Holy Spirit "flows from the side of Christ." A little further on, he develops magnificently the Gospel image: "He alone, the Word made flesh, full of grace and truth, come among men crushed with the weight of their sins and their miseries, can cause to spring from His human nature, hypostatically united with His divine Person, a spring of living water to irrigate the parched earth of humanity, so as to make of it a flourishing and fertile garden."[21] The garden is, clearly, the Church as irrigated by the River of life "flowing from the throne of God and of the Lamb" (Rev. 22, 1).

These texts provide the New Testament basis for Pius XII's statement that the Paraclete is the Spirit of Jesus, the Breath of the Heart of Jesus. This complements by contrast another statement in the same encyclical: the Spirit that flows from the side of the crucified Christ is also He whose operation has formed the Heart of Jesus in the womb of the Virgin Mary.[22]

Dom Piepen has well synthesized these different aspects:

> The Holy Spirit is, by personal attribute, the immanent product of the uncreated love of Christ. He is, by appropriation, the efficient principle of His created love and of His Heart. He is, by personal attribute, the supreme gift of Christ—the gift merited by His human love,

spread by His divine love and by His human love and even by His human heart: the Gift, therefore, of the triple love of Christ; in short, the Gift of the Sacred Heart.[23]

It is therefore the human and sensible love of the Redeemer which gives and spreads, under the sacramental symbols of water and of blood, and as the instrument of the divine and supra-sensible Word, the Holy Spirit that is the immanent product of His uncreated love. The human love of a divine Person gives the divine fruit of His divine Love.

The pierced Heart of Jesus is therefore the symbol and the sign of the Spirit of Love whom It gives and contains.[24] This Heart is, for sinful mankind who resist It, the most evocative sign of the love of the Spirit of Truth.

To be precise, the Heart of Jesus instrumentally gives the Holy Spirit as Spirit of Truth and loving Revealer of hidden mysteries, through the sacramental charisms of confirmation and of the episcopate.[25]

But these sacraments are polarized by the Eucharist, their *raison d'être*. Confirmation involves, above all, a declaration of faith in the mystery which brings together all the other mysteries: the Eucharist.[26] The episcopate as sacrament signifies and instrumentally realizes the unity around the Eucharistic table.[27] On the other hand, the Heart of Jesus—which, as instrument of the Word, spreads the Spirit—acts now in the Church preeminently through the mystery of the Eucharist. Through the Eucharist, the Heart of the Lamb comes "to re-activate" the sacramental graces of confirmation and of the episcopate. In the Eucharist, Christ immolates Himself anew and offers Himself to the Father in order to fill us with Their Spirit, in Communion. It is preeminently through the Eucharist that we receive and drink the Spirit (cf. 1 Cor., 12, 13).[28] To use a favorite image of the Greek Fathers, and notably of Saint John Damascene,[29] the Eucharist is the burning coal of the Divinity in which glows the

Fire of the Spirit which Christ came to kindle (cf. Is. 6, 6-7; Lk. 12, 49). Scheeben has dealt splendidly and at considerable length with this theme of the Christ who, through the Eucharist, regales us and fills us with His Spirit.[30]

We can say without hesitation, therefore, that the Eucharistic Heart of Jesus gives to the pilgrim Church the Spirit of Truth, the other Paraclete. It immolates Itself in order to give this Spirit to the Church (cf. Jn. 14, 16) in the sacramental sign of Its Blood. This is at once a gift by last will and testament and a gift of the living, if one may use (as indeed the New Testament does) legal terms in relation to this mystery. And the Eucharistic Heart gives the Paraclete in the Eucharist. Precisely as sacramental, our Communions are therefore spiritual in the sense that they enable us to commune with the Holy Spirit through the spiritualized flesh of Christ. Each of our sacramental and spiritual (in every sense of this latter adjective[31]) Communions quicken in us the gifts of faith-grounded love which are received at our confirmation. Although in itself the flesh can achieve nothing, the Spirit vivifies through the flesh of Christ, the Word made flesh, delivered for the life of the world— a life which cannot be obtained if one does not eat this spiritualized flesh (Jn. 6, 63; 1, 14; 6, 51. 54. 57; 1 Cor. 15, 44).[32]

It might be objected that, while all this is true, the love that is grounded on faith is a gift which is appropriated to the Holy Spirit, and which is also given by the Father and the Son. Yes, indeed. But Saint Thomas defines "appropriation" as "a manifestation of the divine Persons by the use of essential attributes": its function therefore is to manifest the personal attribute of a divine Person.[33] In specially attributing to the Holy Spirit the gift of the love that is grounded on faith, we give real expression to the idea that the Third Person is the Breath of the reciprocal Love of the Father and of the Son—the personal Love in God, the fruit of the Love which the Father and the Son have, as a single principle, for their own Truth; and that therefore the Third Person is the Spirit of Truth. Consequently, in saying that the Eucharist Heart of the Lamb gives the Spirit of Truth, we are proclaiming the lovable splendor of the truth of the trinitarian mystery.

One thus understands more clearly how Vatican II could say: "Christ is now at work in the hearts of men through the energy of His Spirit."[34] But, reciprocally, it is equally true to say—and this is something we have now to consider—that the Spirit of Jesus draws men to the Eucharistic Heart, symbol of the Paraclete's love for errant mankind.

B. The Spirit of Truth Draws Mankind to the Heart and the Eucharistic Heart of Jesus

Among the many ways in which the Holy Spirit assists the Church of which He is the soul, we must certainly include the schools of spirituality and the growth of Catholic worship.

The whole history of the birth and gradual growth of the cult of the Sacred Heart of Jesus unveils to eyes of faith the action of the Spirit who glorifies Christ (cf. Jn. 16, 14).

Bearing in mind what "appropriation" means, as we have seen above, one readily accepts that this progress can be appropriated in a special way to the Spirit of Love. If, with Pius XII, one acknowledges the cult of the Sacred Heart as an inestimable gift which enables the Church to love its Spouse more perfectly, how can one fail to attribute the origin of this cult to Him who is the personal Love between the Father and the Son?

The Spirit is the author of the Scriptures which already invite us, at least implicitly, to cultivate this devotion to the Heart of Jesus.[35] The same Spirit has aroused the medieval mystics (Bonaventure, Catherine of Siena, Suss), and then those of the Counter-Reformation (John Eudes, Margaret Mary), through whom this cult has gradually developed, first among the spiritual élite, then among the Catholic masses; but the latter development really took place only when the Holy See took up a decisive attitude towards it.

In connection with this long history, one can also accept as true the general observation made by Father Holstein as regards the "pneumatic" origin of the development of the dogma:

> The special grace bestowed by the Holy Spirit on the Catholic hierarchy, is that of discerning and judging the Christian sense of the faithful, of recognizing tradition in that sense, and of explicitly proclaiming the lived faith when the Spirit judges that the time is ripe.
>
> The same Spirit who inspired Scripture in order to give us the Revelation, inspires[36] the Church in its complex and infrangible unity, to understand this Scripture in order that it may grasp fully the Revelation contained therein, and accept it in faith. He inspires the devotion of the faithful by giving them the sense of faith; and He enlightens the theologians that they may formulate, justify, clarify this faith which they themselves protect and of which they are living examples. And He gives to the magisterium to proclaim the living Tradition of which He is the faithful interpreter.[37]

Today, we can more clearly see that the Spirit of the Father was urging, first the faithful, then the magisterium, towards the Heart of the Son. After having induced the private cult, He aroused the explicit public cult of the pierced Heart of the Redeemer. This stage reached its culmination in 1856, when Pius IX extended to the universal Church (of the Latin rite) the feast of the Sacred Heart. Then, thanks to a great collective effort of Catholic theologians who had prepared the way, the magisterium, in 1928 and in 1956, was able to specify in memorable encyclicals the doctrinal import of this cult. In this very homogeneous evolution, the Spirit has been constantly active.

An analogous pattern of development could be traced in connection with the private cult and the public cult of the Eucharistic Heart of Jesus, in the Church. Initially, early in the second half of the nineteenth century, the time when it blossomed, it met with some resistance. Nevertheless, by 1890, one could already count 14 pontifical documents favorable to the devotion to the Eucharistic Heart.[38] After new restrictive measures taken by the Holy See, measures now lapsed except for one of them,[39] the Church introduced the feast of the Eucharistic Heart of Jesus, not automatically to the whole Church, however.[40] Then, in the encyclical *Haurietis Aquas*, the Church solemnly recognized the duty of the cult to the Eucharistic Heart. Let us recall lines we have already quoted, in order to consider them in a new context:

> One cannot readily accept the strength of the love which urged Christ to give Himself to us as spiritual food, except through honoring with a particular cult the Eucharistic Heart of Jesus.[41]

Clearly, we have a real duty to grasp, as perfectly as possible, the strength of this oblative and sacrificial love which is at the origin of our Eucharistic eating of Christ. Consequently, the cult, at least private, of the Eucharistic Heart, and a particular cult which gives more specific focus to the more general cult of the Heart of Jesus, is also a real and delightful obligation recognized and accepted by us in grateful love. However, this does not rule out a previous statement in another document of the Holy See: "The cult of the Sacred Heart in the Eucharist is not more perfect than that of the Eucharist, nor is it different from the cult of the Sacred Heart."[42] But the text of Pius XII, carrying as it does the more solemn authority of an encyclical, stresses more clearly perhaps that a cult involves "an essential attitude of religion and of love, characterizing our relations with God in Christ."[43]

The cult of the Eucharistic Heart of Jesus serves to complete and to specify the cult of the Sacred Heart, by particularizing it.

Such a cult would not be approved or made public in the Church or presented as obligatory by the Church, unless through the action of the Spirit of Love, of that eternal Spirit in whom and under whose pressure the incarnate Son offers Himself to the Father. The help the Spirit gives to the Church, His body that He ceaselessly animates, shows itself in the progressive and increasing approbation of this devotion leading up to this "particular cult."

What is the design thus pursued by the Spirit, who comes from the Father and the Son and who glorifies Them both? Although no one knows "whither . . . goes" anyone "who is born of the Spirit" (cf. Jn. 3, 8) or the Church born of Him, we nevertheless hear the voice of the Spirit through and with the Church. It seems to us that first the progress and then the solemn approval of the ecclesial cult of the Eucharistic Heart constitute for the theologian a "sign of the times." These things signify what the Spirit wills for the Church of our age—namely, that there should be concentrated theological reflection and heightened spiritual life centered on the mystery of the Eucharist, synthesis of Revelation, in the ardent light of love. While the devotion to the Eucharistic Heart is not more sublime than the devotion simply to the Sacred Heart, nevertheless the first more effectively promotes theological synthesis.

It even seems to us that the complex symbolism of the Eucharistic Heart, to which we shall return shortly, links up in the scope of its synthesis with the basic intuitions of Cyril of Alexandria. The two words, "Eucharistic Heart," sensitively express, of course in a different context, what the great Doctor of the Incarnation had in mind: a unified vision of the Trinity, of the Redemptive Incarnation and of the Church, bringing these mysteries together in that of the Eucharist. It is this unified vision which our era is yearning to recover, and it could well be the will of the Holy Spirit that we should re-discover it under the symbolism of the Eucharistic Heart, in the light of Saint Cyril. It is useful therefore to recall and to consider some of his texts.

The primordial idea of Sain Cyril is that the Spirit leads us to the Son, who is present in the Eucharist and through whom we have, together, access to the Father. "Our return to God, which is achieved through Christ our Savior, occurs only in the communion and the sanctification of the Spirit. It is the Spirit who raises us to the Son and thus unites us with God. In receiving Him into our souls, we become participants and communicants in the divine nature. We receive Him through the Son, and, in the Son, we receive the Father."[44]

The Spirit leads us to the only Son, but it is the Son who gives us the Spirit. Is not that exactly what we have brought out when dealing with the relationship between the Spirit, the Eucharist, and ourselves?

In Saint Cyril's view, the Son "receives" the Spirit in order to give Him to us: "Although He possesses the Spirit, it is nevertheless said that the Spirit has been given to the Son in order that, in the Son, we should all receive the Spirit. It is with this aim that the Son assumes the descent from Abraham and that He becomes like in all things to His brethren. It is not for Himself that He, the only Son, receives the Holy Spirit, because the Spirit is to Him, in Him, and through Him."[45]

Saint Cyril holds that we are spiritually united with Christ through His Spirit, and physically united with Him through the eating of His flesh. In the same way, we are united one with another. Again, Saint Cyril writes:

> First Christ comes physically, as man, mingling and uniting Himself with us through the mystic communion; but spiritually also, as God, through the power and love of His Spirit, who

comes within us to infuse us with a new life and to make us sharers of His divine nature.[46]

It is interesting to notice the parallelism (of Platonic tinge) between the flesh and the Spirit shown by this text, a parallelism to which Cyril seems to hold, though this does not lead him to maintain the existence of an organic union between the two, or of an instrumental causality of the physical union with the Eucharistic Christ in relation to the pouring forth of the Spirit in us. Like Augustine, Cyril seems to ignore the idea of instrumental causality.[47] Underlying what he says,[48] and indeed serving as an horizon to his thought, is the idea that the physical breath, itself spiritualized, of the Risen Christ exhales the Spirit. Or, in our categories and in accordance with our symbolism (in which the nature of man and the Biblical language blend harmoniously), it is the Eucharistic and spiritualized Heart of Christ, the Anointed of the Spirit,[49] that gives us this Spirit in and through the Blood that still flows from It.

Whatever one might say about he anthropology of Saint Cyril and the way it conditions his theology, it remains true that he brought together, in the harmony of a splendid synthesis, the mysteries of the Trinity, of the Redemptive Incarnation, of the Eucharist, of grace, and of the Church, viewed together in the light of Saint John, on whose Gospel he is, with Augustine, the most pleasing of commentators. We believe that the Spirit of the Lamb, desiring to restore to the Church of the twentieth century a global vision recapitulated in all its aspects through a single symbol, has led the Church to declare the need for a particular cult of the Eucharistic Heart of Jesus.

This symbol, we have said, is complex. We shall see why the Eucharistic Heart is a very attractive and highly rich symbol of the mystery of the love of the Person of the Paraclete, in His eternal procession and in His temporal mission.

First, let us remind ourselves[50] that already the

Heart of Jesus signifies (though indirectly[51]) the eternal and reciprocal[52] Love between the Father and the Son, from which springs eternally the personal Love who is Their Spirit: an eternal intra-divine Love which is the condition and the origin of the love of the Holy Spirit for the sinful human race. "The cult of the Sacred Heart is none other than the cult of the love which the Holy Spirit lavishes upon sinful men", writes Pius XII.[53] The human heart of the incarnate Word is a much more expressive symbol of the love of the "other Paraclete" (Jn. 14, 16) than is that of the dove, of water, of wind, or of fire. On the one hand, human love better symbolizes the intra-divine and extra-divine personal Love than do these cosmic things; and on the other hand, human love inclues in itself or connotes nearly all those things which it places at its service or through which it expresses itself. If the Heart of Jesus is an indirect image of the Breath of the Father and of the Son, one could say that the human breath of the Heart of the Risen Jesus, with the love that produces it, is the most direct image of that divine Breath. The breath through which Jesus has willed to represent to us the Person of His Spirit, is, with man, a yearning sigh by which his love, and therefore his heart, overflows, produced as it is by the intensity of his love. The Holy Spirit is a Breath of Love who issues from the Father and from the Son,[55] and whom the human heart of the Son gives and spreads when His Resurrection, by the power of this divine Spirit, has made Him "the last Adam become a life-giving spirit" (cf. 1 Cor. 15, 44-45). It can be said that Christ, by deliberately and freely[56] choosing in fidelity to the whole Biblical tradition the symbol of His human and loving[57] breath in order to designate the Third Person of the Trinity, was intending to link Him with the natural symbol of His own human heart as the direct expression of His love, and as the indirect expression of the love of this Spirit.

If already the symbol of the Heart of Jesus carries a rich pneumatological significance, even richer is that of the Eucharistic Heart. With the symbol of the heart, the expression associates the not less anthropological symbol of the spiritualized bread and wine of the Eucharistic mystery which is a sacrament—i.e. the visible sign of an invisible reality. In uniting among themselves the hearts of the communicants, so as to make them to be as "one heart" (Acts 4, 32), the Eucharistic Heart of Jesus symbolizes the Spirit, who is the consubstantial[58] and invisible communion between the Father and the Son. Con-corporal and consanguine one with the other, consummated in one because they eat the flesh of the Son of man and drink His Blood, they are thus an instrument through whom the world believes that the Father has sent His Son and that these Two are one in and through the Spirit (cf. Jn. 6 and 17, *passim*). The Eucharistic Heart symbolizes the Spirit of Love who loves the world to which He is sent by the Father and the Son, from whom He proceeds and whose bond of unity He is. It is a symbolism whose medium is the symbolic mystery of the unity of the Church, image of the unity of the triune God in the Spirit as well as being its effect.

But the Eucharistic Heart is not only the "visible"[59] sign of "the unity of the Spirit in the bond of peace" (Eph. 4, 3); this Heart is also the Mediator containing and giving this Spirit. This is what, in full continuity with the Eastern and Western patristic tradition,[60] the new canons of the Latin rite bring out: "In nourishing ourselves with the Body and Blood of Your Son, may we be filled with His Spirit, so as to become visibly one body and one soul in Christ."[61] The liturgy itself, therefore, bears witness to this truth that the Blood of Christ fills us with His Spirit. There is nothing surprising in this, since Jesus already implied as much: "He who eats my flesh and drinks my blood has eternal life. . . . If anyone thirst, let him come to me and drink. He who believes in me, as Scripture has said, 'Out of his heart shall flow rivers of living water' " (Jn. 6, 54; 7, 37-39). The Blood that flows from the Heart of the Lamb is presented by Him as a symbol of His Spirit—as a sacramental symbol that not only signifies but also contains this Spirit.[62] The Blood is therefore a direct symbol, the Heart an indirect symbol, of the Spirit.

The New Testament also indicates to us that the wine, like blood but in a very different manner, is the symbol of the Holy Spirit (Eph. 5, 18; Acts 2, 13). The wine, a product of man's work on something which is the free gift of God, supplies the matter which the words of Christ, in the power of the Spirit, transubstantiate into His precious Blood. Wine intoxicates: the Blood of Christ, in which we drink the Spirit, produces the ecstasy of love. The Eucharistic and bloody Heart of Christ, in signifying and giving the Spirit, connotes the cosmos from which It derives its conditions of existence and which aspires, through It, to its transfiguration. This Heart also connotes the Church which It fills with the Spirit and which It associates through this pouring forth of the Spirit, with Its redemptive sacrifice. Finally, It connotes Its own Parousia through which, by transfiguring the world, it will consummate the Church, fully unweiling to it the Spirit who is its soul and its life-giving drink.

We see more clearly, therefore, why the Spirit leads the Church to adore His own symbol in the Eucharistic Heart of the Redeemer. Does He not thus offer to the Church a particularly rich sign of His love, a daily renewed sign of the communion of the Father and the Son that is the Spirit Himself, of the Redemptive Incarnation, of the Church as a communion-in-love of all the coredeemers, and of the cosmos which He creates and transfigures, first by the love which He pours into human hearts, and then definitively on the Last Day through the humanity of His Anointed? For all these mysteries are symbolized and brought together in the Eucharistic Heart of the Redeemer.

When one considers the matter, is not the way in which the private and public cult of the Eucharistic Heart of the Lamb has grown up in the Church, a singular manifestation of the merciful love of the Spirit for the Church? Does not this cult present the Spirit, already a Gift of the Heart of Jesus, as a new and inestimate Gift of this immolated Lamb to His Spouse? —a more particular Gift within the general gift of His Heart? In fostering this devotion, we enable the Church "to manifest to its divine founder a more ardent love,"[63] and to drink more copiously the Spirit that flows, with the Blood, from His ever open Heart.

It is in connection with the Eucharistic Heart that these words of Paul VI are verified more particularly:

> In the Sacred Heart of Jesus are to be found the origin and the principle of the sacred liturgy, since this Heart is the holy temple of God whence there rises up to the Father the sacrifice of expiation which can save those who through it come to God (cf. Heb. 7, 25). Furthermore, it is this Heart that incites the Church to seek every means by which our separated brethren may come into full unity with the Chair of Peter, and by which even those who are not yet Christians may also know with us the only true God, and Jesus Christ whom He has sent (Jn. 17, 3).

Was Cardinal Amette, Archbishop of Paris, wrong when he wrote in 1903: "The cult to the Eucharistic Heart is the purest and fullest blossoming of the devotion to the Sacred Heart"?[65] Was Benedict XV misled when he prophesied: "The devotion to the Eucharistic Heart will be a source of graces for souls; it will spread more and more in the Church"?[66] Did not Pius XII validate this prophecy when, in formally recognizing this cult with all the solemnity of an encyclical, he used these words which we again quote: "One cannot readily grasp the strength of the love which urged Christ to give Himself to us as spiritual food, except through honoring with a particular cult the Eucharistic Heart of Jesus"? More than even, will not the Church of the future concentrate its dogmatic, liturgical, and moral effort on that sun which, through the Spirit, ceaselessly enlightens and enfolds it—the sun that is the Eucharistic Heart of Jesus, the Lamb of God?

Appendix: Eucharist and Holy Spirit according to Scheeben

The Eucharist realizes above all the most real and most perfect external mission of the Divine Persons.

> The Holy Spirit, Spirit of the Son, is united in a very real way with the body of the Son in whom He reposes and dwells. Similarly, He comes to us in this body, in order to unite Himself with us and to communicate Himself to us. In the body of the Logos that He fills, we receive the Holy Spirit at the very source, so to speak, whence it springs; like the blood, the Holy Spirit spreads Himself from the Heart into the other members, from the real body of the Logos into the members of His mystical Body who are substantially united with Him. . . .
>
> The distinction and the relationship between the mission of the Son and that of the Holy Spirit are, as we have already indicated, already expressed in the Eucharistic species. The species of wine (symbol of the blood) with its liquidity, its warmth, its comforting and pleasant bouquet, its enlivening quality, represents the Holy Spirit, whose procession is a springing up from the Father and the Son, and whose mission is a pouring forth which is in itself the river and the sweet odor of the divine life. This species represents him as the wine that springs up from the Logos as from a divine cluster of grapes, the wine of ardent love, of strength and of life, of intoxicating beatitude, the wine that has been pressed out in the sacred blood of the human heart of the Logos by the great strength of His love, that has been spread over the world and poured into us in this blood.

Although the Holy Spirit is sent by the Son and comes to us in the Son, He is nevertheless, by the strongest of appropriations, the channel through whom the Son is introduced into us.

As the Breath of His love, He urges the Son to give Himself to us in the Incarnation and in the Eucharist; as the fire of His sanctifying and unifying ardor, He effects within the womb of the Virgin the origin, the hypostatic union, and the holiness of the human nature of the Son; and, in the Eucharist, the transformation of earthly substances into those of His Flesh and His Blood. After the hypostatic union and the transubstantiation, He dwells with His warmth and His vital force in the flesh and blood of the Son of God from whom He proceeds, and He fills them with His essence in order to sanctify and to glorify them. In the Eucharist, above all, He glorifies and spiritualizes them, as a burning coal, so that they themselves appear as fire, as pure spirit. He makes use of this flesh and blood as of an instrument to manifest His sanctifying and glorifying power to all those who enter into contact with them; as of an organ to communicate Himself to all those who receive this flesh and this blood.

The body of Christ has *sprung* from the fire of the Holy Spirit, as a spiritual gift which God gives to us and which we in our turn offer in sacrifice. It is *penetrated* and *enfolded* by the Holy Spirit who glorifies and spiritualizes it, in such a way that the fire and the kindled coals appear to be one and the same. Finally, the body of Christ overflows with the Holy Spirit, spreading His sweet odor in the Mass, and His life-living power in Communion.

Those relations of the Eucharist with the Holy Spirit are best expressed by the image of the glowing coal, an image by which the Eastern Fathers and the liturgies love to designate the Eucharist. The very name *Eucharist* already indicates these relations, for does it not mean *the preeminent gift*, which flows from the Holy Spirit, Himself the gift *par excellence*, the gift that contains the Holy Spirit, with His essence and His power? How beautiful and meaningful was not the ancient custom of reserving the Eucharist in the *peristerium*, a dove-shaped vase, symbolizing the Holy Spirit! How well this symbolizes the Holy Spirit who brings to us the gift contained in this vase, and who dwells in this gift with His essence and His power, enfolding and penetrating it as the fire enfolds and penetrates the coal.

M. J. Scheeben, *Les Mystères du Christianisme*, Bruges, 1947, par. 73, pp. 532-534. On the peristerium, see: H. Leclercq, "Colombe eucharistique" in *Diction. d'Archéologie chrétienne et de Liturgie*, t. III, Paris, 1913, col. 2231-2234.

NOTES TO CHAPTER FIFTEEN

1. Cf. DS, 3016 (DB, 1796). The principle enunciated is very specially valid for examining the links between redemptive Incarnation and Trinity.

2. See Chapter Ten, note 13, and the text to which it refers. Pius XII teaches that the Son of God adorned His soul with this Spirit of grace and of Truth already in the immaculate womb of the Virgin (AAS, 35, 1943, 219).

3. It must be accepted that the humanity of Christ was filled from the first moment of its existence with the Holy Spirit who dwelt in it. Saint Thomas Aquinas held that no increase of grace occurred in Christ. J. Maritain thinks, however, that the grace of the *Christus viator,* complete of its kind, "did not cease to grow throughout His earthly life" (*De la Grace et de l'Humanité de Jesus,* Bruges, 1967, p. 89). If that is true, then baptism would have been a specific moment of that growth. If not, it may be admitted that the sacred Humanity of Jesus received, at that moment, a transient actual grace more closely preparing Him for the mission of His public life. It is therefore that He appears "full of the Holy Spirit" (Lk. 4, 1).

4. Saint Thomas Aquinas, *Summa Theologica,* I. 43. 8; cf. I, 43. 2. 3.

5. See, e.g., E. Schillebeeckx O.P., "Ascension and Pentecost," *Worship* 35 (1961), 352 ff.; E. Mersch, *op. cit.,* t. II, pp. 124-241.

6. Cf. H. F. Dondaine O.P., in his edition of the treatise *La Trinité* in the *Summa Theologica* of Saint Thomas Aquinas, Paris, Cerf, 1946, t. II, pp. 425-431.

7. Saint Thomas Aquinas, *Summa Theologica,* III. 8. 1. 1. Saint Thomas gently contradicts Saint Augustine who, it seemed to him, always ignored the idea of instrumental causality. In his commentary on Gal. 3, 5, Saint Thomas specifies: "Spiritus Sanctus datur a solo Patre et Filio secundum quod ejus auctoritatem habent, non quidem dominii sed originis, quia ab utroque procedit" (*Super Ep. S. Pauli lectura,* I, Marietti, Rome, 1953, p. 594, par. 127). If, in this sense, the Holy Spirit does not Himself give Himself, it is not surprising that in the same connection, Christ as man cannot give the Holy Spirit. Saint Augustine deals with the subject in his *De Trinitate,* I. 12 and XV. 26. For him, the Risen Christ's act of breathing on the Apostles signifies that the Spirit proceeds eternally from the divine Person of the Son, but not that the Spirit is sent by the incarnate Word, or even given by Him as man. The idea of instrumental causality was to enable Saint Thomas to be the faithful interpreter of all the shades of meaning in the sacred text.

8. We mean: in as much as His humanity would be the *secondary* cause of such a gift.

9. Cf. the "rules of preaching" developed by Catholic theology concerning Christ, for example in the *Summa Theologica* of Saint Thomas Aquinas, III. 16. 5, 10.

10. On instrumental causality as distinct from secondary causality, see J. de Finance S.J., *Connaissance de l'Etre,* Paris-Bruges, 1966, par. 94, pp. 388-389. It must also be observed that, in the case considered here, the instrument used by the divine Person of the Word is a supernatural instrument causing an effect which infinitely exceeds it, just as it exceeds all the forces of nature. Cf. Saint Thomas Aquinas, III. 19. 1, 2; 48. 6.

11. M. J. Le Guillou O.P., encyclopedia *Catholicisme,* art. "Esprit-Saint," Paris, 1954, t. IV, col. 492.

12. A formula which Father Guérard de Lauriers, not without reason, prefers to translate as "a single and incarnate nature," and not as "a single nature incarnate." However, notice one important and rarely emphasized point: the local Lateran Council, in 649, of whose doctrinal authority we are aware because of the approbation of Pope Saint Martin I, retained and interpreted the famous formula of Saint Cyril concerning the "one nature," at the same time as it admitted the two-natures (diphysite) formula of Chalcedon (DS, 505-506; DB, 258-259): "incarnata dicitur nostra substantia perfecte in Christo Deo et indiminute absque tantummodo peccato significata." The Copts had no need, therefore, to renounce the *formula* of Saint Cyril in order to be restored to full communion with the Roman Church, but only to interpret this formula in a restricted sense. On these problems, which have been given renewed attention recently, cf. the contributions

of Heyer, Karmiris, Nersoyan, in *Monde non crétien,* 77 (1966), 3-56; and of Msgr. Emilianos (*Lutheran World,* Saint Louis, 1966). In the light of Lateran, 649, and of Saint Martin I, long after Chalcedon, it does not seem exact to write, as does Father Guérard des Lauriers: "we no longer say that Christ possesses one nature." We should rather write that we no longer say *only* that. An important ecumenical problem is involved.

13. See the end of the preceding note.

14. Father G. des Lauriers O.P., cited by Father Le Guillou; cf. note 11. Father des Lauriers rightly stresses that, while there are two *operations* in the incarnate Word, there is in Him only one *operant.* This is what Saint Cyril had profoundly grasped. The Dominican theologian also introduces an idea which is very true: Christ as man enjoys the beatifying vision of the eternal breathing of the Spirit, through His own divine Person as the Word, but He cannot entitatively share in it as man. In this connection, see the fine interpretation of Saint John of the Cross (*Living Flame,* str. 4, verses 4-6) given by J. Maritain, *Les Degés du Savoir,* chap. IX, par. 15, Paris, 1959⁶, pages 749-753. Finally, in answer to Father des Lauriers' profound reflections on the unity of the *esse* of Christ as an explanation of the exactitude of Saint Cyril's intuition ("a reality one and incarnate"), one could not put forward the famous text of Saint Thomas Aquinas concerning the "esse secundarium" of Christ as man, because Maritain also very clearly shows (*ibid.,* pp. 868-872) that, according to the same Saint Thomas, there is only one *esse personale* in Christ, the *esse secundarium* being merely a temporal and created *esse* proper to human nature. Cf. Saint Thomas Aquinas, *de Unione Verbi incarnati,* 4. 1. Through the *esse secundarium,* the Person of the Word exists, not purely and simply, but humanly.

15. Cf. Jn. 7, 39; on this point, see F. X. Durwell C.SS.R., *La Résurrection de Jésus, Mystère de Salut,* Paris, 1961⁶, pp. 102-110.

16. H. M. Diepen O.S.B., "L'Esprit du Coeur de Jesus," *Cor Jesu,* Rome, 1959, I, 188.

17. Pius XII, *Haurietis Aquas,* AAS, 48 (1959) 335: note that "ejus" refers to "cordis" and not merely to "Jesus." In this connection, let us note the following fine commentary by Father Diepen: "The eternal procession of the Third Person, immanent end of the Love of the Father and of the Son, is the principal idea in the phrase which already surprises us much less than at first sight: the Spirit of the Heart of Jesus." (*op. cit.,* I, 173). The Spirit is *of t*he Heart of Jesus because of the threefold love of Christ, but especially because of His divine love.

18. It is well known that the encyclical has set aside the

Vulgate punctuation and adopted that suggested by recent exegetical and patristic studies (cf. K. Rahner, S.J., *Biblica*, 22, 1941, pp. 269-302; the article is entitled "Flumina de ventre Christi"). Nevertheless, it is not entirely exact to write (Diepen, *op. cit.*, I, 152) that the Scriptural citation indicated by Jn. 7, 38, cannot be found in the Old Testament if one accepts the Vulgate punctuation and if one supposes that the "rivers of living water" flow from the "belly" of the believer: Is. 58, 11 would suffice to justify Jn. 7, 38; but it must be recognized that the believer, not his "belly," is presented by this text as a spring "of living water." Anyhow, Jn. 7, 38, should be read in the light of Jn. 4, 14: the Heart of Jesus is "a spring of water" which makes the believer, in its likeness, a derivative source.

19. Here is the Latin text on this important point: "ipse (Jesus) 'aquae vivae' fontem pollicebatur *e suo sinu oriturum.*" The italics are ours. Cf. note 20.

20. Pius XII, *Haurietis Aquas,* 48 (1956), 310. From Jn. 7, 38-39, as properly understood by Tradition and by the magisterium (Pius XII), it emerges therefore that Christ Himself invites us to drink the Spirit flowing from His pierced Heart (cf. Jn. 19, 37), to venerate His wounds (cf. 20, 27), and especially the wound in His side. The public Revelation, understood and interpreted by Saint John, already showed Christ's desire to see His Heart an object of adoring worship, at least an implicit desire for this. Up to now, it seems, what we state here has not been made the subject of an analytical study, or even of an effort of precise focus.

21. Pius XII, *Haurietis Aquas,* AAS, 48 (1956), 320. The arid and dried up soil of sinful humanity becomes, thanks to the baptismal water which flows from the Heart of Christ, the paradise of the holy Church.

22. *Ibid.,* par. 24 (AAS, 48, 1956, 323).

23. Diepen, *op. cit.,* I, 189.

24. In giving the Spirit, the Heart (divine or human) does not relinquish Him; for the Spirit is present in the Son by virtue of the mystery of circuminsession, and He dwells in the human soul of the incarnate Word.

25. Diepen, *op. cit.,* I, 185-186. Dom Diepen here probes in an original way the traditional doctrine of the visible mission of the Spirit. The Council (AG, 4) has taken up the traditional doctrine of Saint Leo the Great and of Leo XIII: "Doubtless, the Holy Spirit was already at work in the world before Christ was glorified; but, on the day of Pentecost, He came down upon the disciples . . . and the gospel began to spread upon the nations . . ." (Abbott, pp. 587-588). Dom Diepen has shown convincingly that this visible mission of the Spirit not only signifies that He was poured forth more abundantly in a quantitative sense, but also implies a quali-

tatively new doctrinal nuance of love; cf. 1 Jn. 2, 20-21. 27;
1 Cor. 2, 11-16.

26. Cf. PO, 5. 2.

27. Cf. LG, 23.1; 26. 1.

28. An interpretation dear to Saint John Chrysostom. Cf.
J. Lecuyer, *Le sacrifice de la Nouvelle Alliance,* Lyon, 1962,
p. 262; PG, 61, 251 *(In 1 Cor., Hom.* 30, 2).

29. Saint John Damascene, *De fide orthodoxa,* IV. 13. PG,
94, 1149.

30. Scheeben, *Les mystères du Christianisme,* Bruges, 1947,
V, chap. 18, par. 75. We give extracts from this in an appendix.
To mark the importance of this theme, let it suffice to recall
here, with Scheeben, the ancient custom of reserving the
Blessed Sacrament in a "peristerium" or ciborium in the form
of a dove, symbol of the Spirit who gives the Eucharist.

31. Desire, inspired by the Spirit, to eat the spiritualized
flesh of Christ, and to receive the Holy Spirit through the
Body of Christ. Cf. DS, 1648 (DB, 881).

32. In citing these texts, we are of course aware that 1 Cor.
15, 44 uses the Greek word "soma," whereas the Johannine
texts use the word "sarx." But this point is secondary to our
line of thought here.

33. Saint Thomas Aquinas, *Summa Theologica,* I. 39. 7; *de
Veritate,* 7. 3.

34. GS, 38. 1. (Abbott, 236).

35. Cf. note 20 of this chapter.

36. The author is not using the word in the technical sense,
reserved to the Bible, of which however there is question in
the preceding words. It would be more accurate to speak of
assistance.

37. H. Holstein S.J., in a work edited by H. du Manoir S.J.,
Maria (Paris, 1961, t. VI, p. 290). Notice on this occasion
the complexity of the basis of the worship due to the Sacred
Heart of Jesus: on the one hand, the encyclical, *Haurietis
Aquas,* presents this Heart as "the most impressive *natural*
symbol of the love which the divine Redeemer continues to
feel for the human race" (par. 50; Latin text, p. 341); on the
other hand, it shows in *"Scripture and Tradition* the profound
source of this devotion" (par. 64; Latin text, p. 341). It presupposes, therefore, that right reason, concretely enlightened
by grace, recognizes, in the midst of a correct anthropological
vision, the "natural symbolism" of the heart. One may hold
that here too Revelation has been the occasion, not to say the
cause, of an anthropological deepening, as in the case of the
Augustinian considerations on the trinitarian structure of the
human soul, created in the image of the living God.

38. Cf. A. Hamon S.J., *Histoire de la Dévotion au Sacré-
Coeur,* Paris, 1940, t. V, p. 248.

39. Cf. A. Rayez and A. de Bonhomme, DSAM, IV 2, art.

"Eucharistique (Coeur)," col. 1651, published in 1961. On the one measure which still exists, see our chapter XIV, note 27.

40. This feast is allowed to the dioceses which request it. Suppressed in the course of the liturgical reform, it has been reestablished with the same conditions and is celebrated in Brazil. See Chap. XIV, note 12.

41. Pius XII, *Haurietis Aquas,* par. 82; AAS, 48 (1956), 351: "Nec facile percipere erit vim amoris, quo Christus compulsus nobis se ipse exhibuit spirituale alimentum, nisi peculiari modo Eucharistici Cordis Jesu cultum fovendo."

42. Declaration of the Holy Office, 27 May 1891, cited by Rayez and Bonhomme, DSAM, IV. 2, (1961) col. 1651, art. "Eucharistique (Coeur)." We note that, nevertheless, the declaration of Leo XIII in 1901 and that of Pius XII in 1956 (citing, however, his predecessor) have shifted the ground of the problem, because the Eucharistic Heart is not purely and simply identical with the Sacred Heart in the Eucharist, since the first expression also connotes the past decision which led to the loving institution of the Holy Eucharist. In this connection, it would not be wrong to say that the devotion to the Sacred Heart is, in a sense, more perfect than that of the Eucharist.

43. An expression of J. Jacques S.C.J., in "Culte et Théologie du Sacré-Coeur," *Année Théologique,* 8 (1947), 274; cited by Father Hartman S.C.J., *Le sens plénier de la réparation du péché,* Louvain, 1955, pp. 254-255. Although Vatican II (LG, 51) speaks of "the authentic cult of the saints" (Abbott, p. 84), the word *cult* is generally used with a more clearly theological meaning than the word "devotion." The saints have a right only to "dulia," the Sacred Heart to a cult of "latria" or adoration.

44. Saint Cyril of Alexandria, in Jo. 11, 10; PG. 74, 545. See E. Mersch S.J., *Le Corps Mystique du Christ,* Paris, 1951³, t. I. p. 520.

45. Saint Cyril of Alexandria, *in Jo.,* V, 2; PG, 73, 753-756; cf. Mersch, *op. cit.,* p. 515.

46. Cyril, *in Jo.* 11, 12; PG, 74, 564-565; cf. Mersch, *op. cit.,* pp. 508-509.

47. Cf. however PG, 76, 1163 B.

48. In his commentary on Jn. 20, 22 (PG, 74, 710; cf. 76, 1188), Saint Cyril, not without reason, says that the action of the Risen Christ, in symbolizing by His breathing on the disciples the gift of His Holy Spirit to them, signifies that the Spirit proceeds from the Father through the Son. He very clearly implies (PG, 76, 1188) that the flesh of Christ gives the Spirit. See S. Tromp, *De Christo Capite,* Rome, 1960, pp. 215-226.

49. Cf. Saint Irenaeus, *Adversus Haereses,* III. 18. 3; PL, 7, 234: "In Christi enim nomine subauditur qui unxit et ipse

qui unctus est et ipsa unctio in qua unctus est. Et unxit quidem Pater, unctus est vero Filius, in Spiritu qui est unctio."
50. Cf. chap. XIV, D.
51. In a direct way, the Heart of Jesus symbolizes the human and divine love of the incarnate Word; indirectly, It symbolizes the love of the Father and of the Son, which love is the principle of the human love of the incarnate Word.
52. Pius XII, *Haurietis Aquas*, par. 49 (Latin text, p. 335: "mutuus amor Personalis Patris erga Filium et Filii erga Patrem").
53. *Ibid.*, par. 54 (Latin text, p. 338).
54. Cf. J. Guillet S.J., DSAM, IV, 2 (1961), col. 1246-1247: art. *"Esprit-Saint dans l'Ecriture."*
55. We are here closely following M. J. Scheeben, *Les Mystères du Christianisme*, Bruges, 1947, chap. II, par. 10, pp. 59, 63-64. His explanation could be correlated with those of Saint Thomas Aquinas (*Summa con. Gen.*, IV, chap. 23, par. 1; or par. 3592 of the Marietti Edition, Rome, 1961): "nomen spiritus a respiratione animalium sumptum videtur in qua aer cum quodam motu infertur et emittitur. Unde nomen spiritus ad omnem impulsum et motum vet cujuscumque aerei corporis trahitur et sic ventus dicitur spiritus. . . . Quia aer invisibilis est, translatum est ulterius spiritus nomen ad omnes virtutes et substantias invisibiles et motivas. Et propter hoc et anima sensibilis et angeli et Deus spiritus dicuntur; et proprie Deus per modum amoris procedens quia amor virtutem quandam motivam insinuat" (Book IV, chap. 23, par. 1—or par. 3592 of the Marietti edition, Rome, 1961). The text is enlightening. Saint Thomas clearly understood the original connection between the term "Holy Breath" which Jesus uses to describe the Third Person of the Trinity, and the word "breath" as applied to animal respiration. He thus opens the way to a more clearly anthropological understanding of this term: the animal breath in accordance with which the Holy Spirit is so designated, is a human breath, because man is the animal *par excellence* who understands the other animals by reference to himself. The Old Testament describes the wind as the "breath from the nostrils of Yahweh" (Ex. 15, 8) seen in terms of a man who breathes: it is with this in mind that we must understand the expression "Breath (or Spirit) of God," and therefore the expression "Holy Spirit" in the New Testament. We can thus more readily understand how Jesus could refer to the Spirit as His Holy Breath, and why He willed to give It by breathing on His disciples, since Jesus knows Himself to be God equal to the Father. On the meaning of the word "Spirit" (Ruah), see Ceuppens O.P., *Theologica biblica*, t. II, Rome, 1949, p. 48 *seq.* The connection which Saint Thomas made between animal breath, analogously affirmed of God, and affective and loving impulses, and pulsa-

tions, is itself not without foundation in the New Testament
(cf. 1 Cor. 4, 2; 6, 17; 11 Cor. 12, 18; Eph. 4, 3; Phil. 1, 27); we
thank Father P. B. Kipper S.J. who pointed out this fact to
us. It is not surprising, therefore, that the mode in which the
risen Christ gave the Spirit, His Holy Breath—and, with the
Spirit, the power to forgive sins—was that of the exhalation
that is part of the process of breathing.

56. Cf. Father Congar's remark quoted in Chapter Ten,
note 8.

57. In the context of the citations given in note 55, it will
be noticed that, just before breathing on His disciples in giving them the Spirit, Jesus showed them the open wound in
His side, a source of great joy for them (Jn. 20, 20-22). The
Evangelist thus implies anew (cf. Jn. 7, 39; 19, 34-37) that
the Spirit is a gift of the pierced Heart of the glorified Christ;
and, we remark in passing, that the disciples, on the very day
of the Resurrection, see with joy Him whom they have
pierced (identical Greek verb used in Jn. 19, 37, and 20, 20).
Above all, in clearly affirming the connection between the
gift of the Divine Breath and the Risen Christ's exhaling of
the breath He has resumed (cf. Jn. 19, 30, and 20, 22), the
Evangelist gives us to understand that all his other statements
concerning the Holy Spirit must be understood in the light
of this manifestation of the glorious Christ. The Holy Spirit
is the Breath sent by Jesus as Word and given by Him as Word
made flesh, because, in dying, He has delivered up to the
Father His purely human breath, and, through and with
this purely human breath, the Divine Breath whom He
breathes eternally.

58. Saint Augustine says, on the one hand, that the Holy
Spirit is "communio" between the Father and the Son (in Jo.
tract., 105) and, on the other, that He is "caritas substantialis
et consubstantialis amborum" (in Jo. tract., 105, 3; PL, 1904 d).

59. The Eucharistic species, on the one hand, and the Eucharistic Communion of the faithful, on the other, are, properly
speaking, the visible sign of the unity of the Spirit (the species
being considered from the viewpoint of the breaking of one
and the same consecrated bread). The visibility of the
Eucharistic Heart supposes the mediation of the "eyes of
faith" (cf. Eph. 1, 18), just as today the "visibility" of the
Heart of Jesus supposes it. This sign comes into the category
of the "prophecy" intelligible to the unbeliever or the unini-
tiated through a mystagogy (cf. 1 Cor. 14, 22-25) which unveils in this Eucharistic Heart the present and active sign
of the whole Christian mystery and of the "pleroma." It is
precisely this which constitutes its superiority as sign in relation to the already very rich significance of the Heart of Jesus,
a sign which does not accentuate in the same way (though it
too accentuates) the real and actual presence among us of

Christ and of His loving sacrifice, as the nucleus of the whole synthesis (real and logically established) of the Christian mystery. It could be said that the Eucharistic Heart of Jesus is preeminently the "totalizing sign" of this mystery. It combines the purely anthropological sign of *heart* with the cosmo-anthropological sign of *bread and wine.* In isolating one aspect of what It signifies (cf. chap. 14, texts cited in notes 29 and 30) and in having a more particular object, this Eucharistic Heart more clearly manifests the totality of the pleroma, and consequently its value in preaching the Gospel is greater (cf. note 42 of this chapter).

60. Cf., e.g., Saint Fulgence de Ruspe: PL, 65, 184-192; 788-791; 769; 812.

61. Latin text of the third Eucharistic anaphora ("concede, ut qui Corpore et Sanguine Filii tui reficimur, Spiritu ejus Sancto repleti, unum corpus et unus spiritus inveniamur in Christo") published on 23 May 1968.

62. One understands, therefore, how Saint John Chrysostom could say that the Eucharist is the breast of the mystery of the Spirit—a breast at which, like children, we drink the grace of the Spirit (quoted by Scheeben, *Mystères du Christianisme,* V, XVIII, par 75, note 19): "hom. de S. Philogonio."

63. Cf. the text of Pius XII cited in note 20 of this chapter.

64. Letter addressed by Paul VI to the superiors general of the religious institutes vowed to the cult of the Sacred Heart (25 May 1965). This letter does not appear to have been published by AAS, but it is contained in the *Actes Pontificaux* of Paul VI, no. 148 (Bellarmin, Montreal).

65. Cardinal Amette, *Revue de l'Adoration Réparatrice,* 1903, p. 138; cited by R. Brouillard, encyclopedia *Catholicisme,* 1949, t. II, col. 1282 (art. "Coeur Euch.").

66. Cf. Chapter Fourteen, note 30.

67. Cf. note 41 of this chapter.

16

THE LAMB OF GOD
DEVELOPMENT OF THE HUMANITY OF CHRIST
AND HIS CONSECRATING SACRIFICE

We have seen how Christ unites Himself with the Church through the Eucharist and in the Holy Spirit. Like its invisible Head, this Church is "for the life of the world." It ceaselessly associates itself with the work of Christ. However, the world of which, thanks to Him, the Church is the coredeemer, is a world in evolution, in growth. What is the relationship between this development and the sacrifice of the Church in the Eucharist mystery? How are we to understand the idea and the reality of this development at its different levels? In answering these questions, in inverse order, we shall have occasion to sum up the results of our inquiry into the mystery of Christ the Redeemer, or at least some of these results. This will logically lead to a statement of the absolute need for an existential decision in favor of the Redeemer and of the coredemptive activity, the basic and obligatory vocation of every human person. We mean the decision concerning human and Eucharistic development.

A. The Development of Man, of Humanity, and of the Church

By his encyclical *Populorum Progressio* ("On Fostering the Development of Peoples"), Paul VI has certainly helped the Church to a better understanding both of the importance and of the meaning of development. He has thus opened up new paths to theological reflection on earthly matters, on the historicity of man, and on humanism.

In gathering together the scattered data which this encyclical offers us concerning development, we begin with the following idea:

> In order to be authentic, development must be complete, integral; that is, it must promote the good of every man and of the whole man. . . . In the design of God, every man is called upon to develop and fulfill himself, for every life is a vocation. At birth, everyone is granted, in germ, a set of aptitudes and qualities for him to bring to fruition. This coming to maturity, which will be the result of education received from the environmental and personal efforts, will allow each man to direct himself towards the destiny intended for him by his Creator. Endowed with intelligence and freedom, he is responsible for his fulfillment as he is for his salvation. He is aided, or sometimes impeded, by those who educate him and those with whom he lives, but each one remains, whatever be these influences affecting him, the principal agent of his own success or failure. By the unaided[1] effort of his own intelligence and will, each man can grow in humanity, can enhance his personal worth, can become more a person.[2]

Development is, therefore, something which reaches well beyond any considerations of economic demands or productivity. It is essentially a person's vocation to human growth; it is therefore a mission, a responsibility, a duty. Each will have to account to God for his success or his failure. Man is not born fully developed, but born with a mission to achieve his own fulness. "As Pascal has said so well: 'Man infinitely surpasses man.' "[3] In other words, the inner man developed to his full personal potential should be regarded as the masterpiece of mankind.

It is to every human person, considered in the concrete fullness of his nature as aided by grace, that the parable of the talents applies. Each receives, as his initial capital, natural and supernatural, a "set of aptitudes and qualities for him to bring to fruition" through "the education received from the environmental and personal effort,"[4] these being the conditions for the success of the project of man and of the plan of God.

Such a vision of man as bound in conscience to be the architect of his own development, links up, while surpassing and extending it, with what Stalin said on 4 May 1936: "Man is the most valuable capital." Paul VI shows us that no man is deprived, at birth, of his capital of *humanity* without which all other capital would be useless, and with which—despite deficiencies as regards economic resources or instruction, and even if "impeded by those who educate him and those with whom he lives"[5]—every man can reach those inseparable degrees of human growth and of supernatural holiness to which Providence calls him.

It emerges clearly, therefore, that socio-economic underdevelopment cannot prevent any individual from realizing his human and spiritual betterment. Man is never the slave of his environment. Inseparably a social, rational, and religious animal as he is, his freedom is not and cannot be suppressed by others. Every man remains always free to become more a man.

On the basis of such a conviction, it is easier to promote a "true humanism . . which is open to the Absolute," and consequently to secure "the fully-rounded development of the whole man and of all men."[6] This "new humanism" cannot be cut away from "the higher values of love and friendship, of prayer and contemplation."[7] For is it not in prayer and contemplation that man finds the strength to love his fellow-men, and the freedom to grow humanly and spiritually despite environmental obstacles?

To every man, grace offers this invitation to liberating prayer; for in himself every man is "open to the Absolute," and therefore capable of growth, of development, of humanization. Grace can also "open to" the transcendent Absolute, and therefore introduce to full humanism even those who deliberately close themselves against the Absolute which is inviting them. Should it not be said that it belongs to efficacious grace to open gently to the Absolute those who, not without doing violence to the most profound aspirations of their nature, have closed themselves against it? Needless to say, such grace would in no way violate their human freedom of choice.

In the light of the Biblical and Catholic doctrine of supernatural elevation and of efficacious grace, one already grasps more readily the content and the significance of "transcendent humanism."[8] Man cannot be fully man without the grace which divinizes him; for, in divinizing, grace humanizes. A man who, rejecting the idea of divinizing help, sought to be "man and more than man," would fall to a sub-human level.

In "transcendent humanism," therefore, we have a real fusion—but without confusion of identity—of the growth, humanization, and divinization of the human person. Integral development is identical with full and transcendent humanism; this twofold reality supposes, however, an inner tension in him who lives it. What man, tempted by his evil inclinations, has not experienced to what extent "the exclusive pursuit of possessions becomes an obstacle to individual fulfillment and to man's true greatness"?[9]

In order "to be more," it is often necessary to fight against the selfish desire to have more, in order that others may "have more" and "be more." Often, richness of being presupposes poverty of actual, and especially of desired, possessions. More precisely, the efficaciousness of my desire to have more for others, will often be linked with the mortification of my greed to have more for myself. "For you know the grace of our Lord Jesus Christ, that though he was rich, yet for your sake he became poor, so that by his poverty you might become rich," writes Saint Paul (2 Cor. 8, 9).

Already, from this viewpoint, one can weigh and consider a truth to which we shall return: namely, that there is no development, no growth of man and of humanity, without sacrifice. "Being more" sometimes demands "having more," but more often it demands "having less."[10]

The same sacrificial tension is found in Saint Paul. On the one hand, as we have seen, he presents Christ as increasing our being by Himself having less; on the other hand, he invites Christians "to grow up in every way into him who is the head, into Christ" (Eph. 4, 15), and he prays that the Colossians "may abound more and more, with knowledge and all discernment" (Col. 1, 9). On behalf of the Christians of Philippi, he gives us the perfect prayer of earthly development polarized by an eschatological vision:

> And it is my prayer that your love may abound more and more, with knowledge and all discernment, so that you may approve what is excellent, and may be pure and blameless, for the day of Christ, filled with the fruits of righteousness which come through Jesus Christ, to the glory and praise of God (Phil. 1, 9-11).

In these Pauline texts, one sees how the Revelation of the Mystery of Christ sharpens and makes sublime the natural desire of man in any age, which Paul VI sums up in the qualities relevant to our own times: "in brief, to seek to do more, know more, and have more in order to be more."[11] Is there not a divinization of *doing* in the works of charity, of *knowing* in faith, of *having* in the hope that anticipates possession, *being* in the grace inseparable from charity? Could one separate the aspiration to full earthly development and the thirst for a permanent divinization? Can one talk about the first, but remain silent about the second?

In no circumstances, however, must this necessary eschatological insistence be taken as a warrant to diminish the earthly aspect of development, for which, in reality, it provides both basis and encouragement. With development integrally considered, underdevelopment is contrasted in both its material and its moral aspecs: 'the lack of material necessities for those who are without the minimum essential for life; the moral deficiencies of those who are mutilitated by selfishness."[12]

In the midst of the integral vision of transcendent humanism, it is clear that the worst underdevelopment is not that of the victims of "undeserved misery," but much more that of men who mutilate their own humanity by exploiting the misery of others. The moral underdevelopment of the economically developed nations could reduce their *being* in inverse ratio to the increase of their *having*.

Far removed from all philosophical idealism and from empty pretension to consider the soul in complete abstraction from the body and from society, the very idea of development here recalled in the light of the teaching of Paul VI implies the physical side of man who aspires to "subsistence, health and fixed employment,"[13] and who ought so to aspire, not only for himself, but also for others.

A Christian and integral vision of development overcomes, therefore, the twofold danger of dualist Platonism and of monist materialism: the first would claim to be interested only in spiritual growth; the second, only in economic growth. The Christian vision looks to "the fully-rounded development of the whole man and of all men."

Society today has collective duties towards the society of the future. An exclusive pursuit of possessions on our part, could injure the specifically human quality of generations to come. The inner tension already mentioned is accompanied by an historical tension.

The Church, composed as it is of people belonging to different generations, encounters through them the same tensions. "Sharing the noblest aspirations of men and suffering when she sees them not satisfied, the Church wishes to help them to attain their full flowering, and that is why she offers men what she possesses as her characteristic attribute: a global vision of man and of the human race."[14]

If the Church wishes to help men to attain their full flowering, is not this because through that flowering the Church yearns to achieve its own fullness? Is not the pilgrim Church a Church in process of development, a Church with an obligation to grow in numbers and in quality? Is it not "the body that upbuilds itself in love," by laboring to "grow up in every way into him who is the head, into Christ"? If it organizes its "saints, for the work of ministry, for building up the body of Christ," is not this because at the end we must all come together "to build up together that perfect Man of whom Saint Paul speaks 'who realizes the fullness of Christ'" (Eph. 4, 12-16).[15]

The intense interest which the Church takes in development can be fully understood only in the light of an ever greater awareness that it has itself a duty to grow for the glory of its Head. It too, at its own supernatural level, wishes and must wish "to do more, to know more, and to have more in order to be more" until it finally reaches its fullness on the last day of its earthly history.

The development of mankind and even that of each individual person involve the growth of the Church—although, of course, the Church is not to be confused with humanity, or any of its members, or any man. Pauline ecclesiology, especially in the Epistle to the Ephesians, is an ecclesiology of development. This is not surprising; for, is not Paul's missionary companion, Saint Luke, the evangelist of the growth of Christ as well as being the historian of the growth in numbers and quality of the Church whose infancy (still continuing as long as history endures) imitates that of its Master?

Let us recall, substituting the present tense for the

past,[16] the principal texts of Saint Luke about the growth of the Church and of Christ: "And the word of God increases; and the number of the disciples greatly. . . . So the word of the Lord grows and prevails mightily" (Acts 6, 7; 19, 20). Such growth of the Church, the Body of Christ, in the course of its pilgrimage, signifies in the final analysis that Christ grows through it. Incomplete, in a sense, He grows towards His full eschatological stature: "And the child grows and becomes strong filled with wisdom; and the favor of God is upon him. . . . And Jesus increases in wisdom and in stature, and in favor with God and man" (Lk. 2, 40. 52: changed to present tense). Does not Saint Luke take pleasure in describing the growth of the historic Christ in order to underline its mystical and ecclesial extension in human history?

Is it not from its own continual growth that the Church is particularly able to grasp and promote the integral development of man and of humanity, that is to say, the growth of Christ in them?

It might be objected, however, that the history of the Church is not one of unbroken progress, but one marked at times by setbacks. At a certain level of events, this cannot be denied. But these setbacks provide the matter and the occasion for an invisible progress in depth. By accepting the permissive will of God concerning apostasies, heresies, schisms, the Church progresses in submission to the Redeemer. This explains why Vatican II could very clearly declare: "Seeking after the glory of Christ, the Church becomes more like her exalted model, and continually progresses in faith, hope, and charity, searching out and doing the will of God in all things."[17]

A Church which proclaims its continual progress in its most intimate and most essential activity, is a Church always unsatisfied with the degree of growth to which it has already attained. For it, growth is a duty recognized as such. Consequently, is not the Church particularly fitted to present to the world the obligation of integral development? Who could refuse to a Church in constant and humble growth, the right to invite men to become one with its own development, in the progress of its faith, its hope, and its charity?

One must even carry the matter further by saying, not only that the Church works its own growth through human development insofar as the latter signifies a transcendent humanism, but also that the aspect of earthly progress involved in this development is of great importance for the growth of Christ, though they remain distinct.[18]

Since the idea of development is greater than that of earthly progress, it can be said that the growth of the reign of Christ, which transcends the latter, does not transcend the former.

This amounts to affirming, both of the development with which *Populorum Progressio* is concerned and of the growth of the reign of the Redeemer, that we can say with Saint Paul:

> I planted, Apollos watered, but God gave the growth. So neither he who plants nor he who waters is anything, but only God who gives the growth. He who plants and he who waters are equal, and each shall receive his wages according to his labor. For we are fellow workers for God; you are God's field, God's building (1 Cor. 3, 6-9).

Through the secondary causes, the first Cause and supreme author of development is God, the Father of Our Lord Jesus Christ. The growth of man is the work of the Father, his Creator. Not only does He call man to *self-development* as an obligation in conscience, but by watering with the water of His Spirit the "branches" of Jesus, "the true Vine," the Father who is "the vinedresser" develops them and causes them to bear fruit (cf. Jn. 15, 1-4). The work of development, undertaken in Christ, deserves wages because it constitutes a cooperation with God. It is the Father who, with His two hands, the Son and the Spirit,[19] enables man to "do more, to know more, and to have more, in order to be more."

The words of Jesus, "Apart from me you can do nothing" (Jn. 15, 5), also apply to integral development. Without Christ's grace, there is no fully human development.

This is not surprising, since development is synonymous with growth of the extensions of Christ's humanity. But, just as Christ had to pass by means of death from the "less human conditions" of His prepaschal life to the "more human conditions" of His life as the Risen Lord, so too man will achieve self-development only by passing through self-abnegation, through uniting himself with the Pasch of the Redeemer.

B. Development and Eucharistic Sacrifice

A Christian vision of the development presupposes reflection on death, which is its means *par excellence*.

This statement may at first sight seem a complex paradox, for is not death the definitive negation of all growth and of all progress? How can it be said that it is the means *par excellence* of development?

It suffices to remind ourselves, however, in the light of the dead and risen Christ, that death is the condition and the price of the final and definitive blossoming of that "set of aptitutes and qualities" which every man received "at birth," if we may use the already quoted words of Paul VI.[20] How can one forget the answer of Jesus: "Truly, truly, I say to you, unless a grain of wheat falls into the earth and dies, it remains alone; but if it dies, it bears much fruit" (Jn. 12, 24)? Without the resurrection of the body, there is no enduring growth, no definitive development.

Is not the resurrection of the body the development *par excellence* which Christ brings to the world? The beatific vision accorded to souls? Without and prior to this resurrection, where is one to find the perfection of "being more" to which man aspires? Are not all the other desires polarized by a natural desire to conquer death and to see God?[21]

The acceptance of death is linked, therefore, with the desire of the human person for self-growth and self-blossoming. In *Populorum Progressio*, Paul VI implicitly noted this fact: "This road towards a greater humanity requires effort and sacrifice; but suffering itself, accepted for the love of our brethren, favors the progress of the entire human family. Christians know that union with the sacrifice of our Savior contributes to the building up of the Body of God in its plenitude: the assembled People of God."[22]

In the Eucharistic sacrifice, we see the harmonizing of the acceptance of death and of the fight for life and for survival, on earth and beyond the earth, personal and collective.

I can offer the death of Christ and my own death only "for the life of the world" (Jn. 6, 51). "And he died for all, that those who live might live no longer for themselves but for him who for their sake died and was raised" (2 Cor. 5, 15).

To participate in the Mass, to receive Communion, is not this to signify publicly a constantly renewed engagement to work for he peace, the growth, the development of men?—and all this for the glory of Christ who has died and risen from the dead for their sake?

The Eucharist is the sacrament of fraternal love: it signifies and effects this love in the communicants. "By this we know love, that he laid down his life for us; and we ought to lay down our lives for the brethren. But if anyone has the world's goods and sees his brother in need, yet closes his heart against him, how does God's love abide in him?" (1 Jn. 3, 16-17).

Through the Eucharist, Christ abides in him who receives It. Christ enters into him in order to love other men with a sacrificial love; He opens the heart of him who eats His flesh and drinks His blood. Through Communion, Christ effects the temporal and salvific engagement of the Christian, but without confining Himself to signifying it.

It is thus that the Eucharist, sacrament of perseverance in fraternal love and in involvement with other men's temporal development, shows itself to be the efficacious sign of the very goal of human growth—

namely, the glorious resurrection. "He who eats my flesh and drinks my blood has eternal life, and I will raise him up at the last day" (Jn. 6, 54).

One gathers from this that Christ has specially emphasized, not the temporal or purely individual aspect of human development, but its eternal and social mystery: "Do not labor for the food which perishes, but for the food which endures to eternal life, which the Son of man will give to you; for on him has God the Father set his seal" (Jn. 6, 27)—i.e. the seal of His Holy Spirit.[23] Is not the Eucharist this food? And should not the Christian labor to nourish Christ who is hungry in men (cf. Mt. 25, 35-40), and hungry to grow in them through the Eucharist?

The Eucharist, therefore, assumes the aspect of the sacrament of integral human development.

As such, it becomes the immediate end of the In-humanation of the Word. By inserting Himself as the Word Incarnate into human society in order to unite and recapitulate mankind in Himself, the Word became the promoter of the development of man, such development being the *raison d'être* of His Incarnation.

Having come "that they may have life, and have it abundantly" (Jn. 10, 10), the Lord Jesus, through the efforts of His members to promote the development of each and every man, wills to lead the pre-Christians to recognize Him, in the Eucharist, as their salvation and their life.

The dialogue for and about development thus globally considered, becomes an integral part of the dialogue of salvation for which the Word was made human word and transubstantiating word.

In the heart of this development, the cosmos becomes transfigured, as Christ, through the Eucharist, increasingly assumes the world and human history. In this way, the best of the Teilhardian vision is realized.

Through His own existential choice of a redemptive death, a decision clearly manifested at the Last Supper, Christ merited, founded, and polarized the existential decision of the Christian. This latter decision, far from being that of a faith almost devoid of content, as Bultmann supposes, is a decision to opt for human and divine growth. We shall return shortly to this point.

As the Word whose language condemns the deceitful word of men,[25] the anti-logos Logos, Christ is therefore precisely the man-for-others, the man devoted in an exemplary way to the full growth of all the others, for the glory of the Father. In proportion as, following Christ's example, he sacrifices himself for the growth of his brethren, the Christian becomes with Christ, as Bonhoeffer would have him to be, a "man-for-others."

Preeminently, it is Christ Himself, in His Eucharist, who makes the Christian a "man-for-others." In consecrating him to Himself, he "transsecularizes" him and makes him pass with Himself to the Father, in the same act by which the Christian engages himself to live, not for himself, but for others and for Christ-in-the-others.

Christ, author and consummator of this development, is the Prophet of the growth of humanity, its Priest and its Victim, its Recapitulator. He redeems His Church to the poitn of making it the coredemptrix of the world's growth. For the same purpose, He extends through and in the Church, His sacrificial celibacy and His primacy of love.

The Eucharistic Heart of Jesus is, therefore, through His Spirit, the active nucleus of human development.

The growth of the world is dependent on the sacrifice of the Lamb, even if the existence of the universe is not dependent on that sacrifice.[26]

Thus it emerges that all the themes developed in this book converge on and meet in the Eucharist, sacrifice and sacrament of human development.

The Eucharist is the sacrifice of human development in the sense that in it Christ offers His life to the Father for the supernatural success of the human enterprise at whose head He has placed Himself. Consequently, it is the whole human universe, even at the natural level, that benefits from the bloody sacrifice of the Redeemer.

The Eucharist is also the sacrifice of the development *in* love, just as it is the efficacious sign of the growth *of* love in this world. It signifies and effects the passage from less human to more human conditions. It does so by promoting and vivifying the twofold existential decision of the Christian who aims to labor at the construction of the earthly city while at the same time he seeks to become increasingly one flesh and one victim with Christ, our Pasch, through frequent Communion.

C. The Existential Decision of Human Development

If "human fulfillment constitutes, as it were, a summary of our duties,"[27] it should be made the object of a free, deliberate, and constantly renewed choice.

The decision to seek self-fulfillment and to help others to fulfill themselves for the glory of God, is the concrete expression of the love of the heavenly Father and of one's brethren. In this connection, Bultmann's idea holds good: "The worth of a man is not determined by his human quality . . . but simply by the decision he makes in the here-and-now of his present life."[28]

Faced with the increasing gap between the developed and the under-developed countries, faced with the hunger, ignorance, and misery of innumerable people, should not each ask himself the questions put by Paul VI: "Is he prepared to support out of his own pocket works and undertakings organized in favor of the most destitute? Is he ready to pay higher taxes so that the public authorities can intensify their efforts in favor of development? Is he ready to pay a higher price for imported goods so that the producer may be more justly rewarded? Or to leave his country, if necessary and if he is young, in order to assist in this development of the young nations?"[29] In short, is he prepared to assist in "building a world where every man, no matter what his race, religion, or nationality, can live a fully human life"?[30]

To devote oneself to development is to opt for a

hard, personal poverty directed to the improvement of the lot of others.

When the Christian accepts the obligation to promote development, he works at one and the same time for the building up of the world and for the building up of the Church, because the growth of man and the growth of the Church go hand in hand, as we have shown in the early part of this chapter.

When one has properly grasped that the Eucharist is characterized by a dynamism of love, it becomes clear that frequent reception of this "sacrament of development" is the supreme mediate factor which decides the temporal efficaciousness of our engagement.[31]

This latter especially needs the fire of charity, whose nucleus is communion with the Eucharistic Heart of Jesus.

Is it not through eating the flesh and drinking the blood of the immolated and triumphant Lamb that the Christian will find the strength to immolate himself with Him to the Father, for the development of others? How could he himself grow without the Eucharist?

To be fully efficacious, the existential decision to work for the development of all is perfected by a decision to receive Communion daily, where this is possoble. By anyone given to theological reflection, daily Communion is seen to be the supreme evangelical counsel given (and not just offered) to all by Christ when He directed that, in His name, we should ask His Father: "Give us each day our daily bread" (Lk. 11, 3).[32]

Much more than are the three counsels recognized as such by Christian tradition, the evangelical counsel of daily Communion (which, anyhow, these other three promote) is capable of leading to the perfection of love, the soul of human development. It is the counsel of growth.

The existential choice in favor of the daily breaking of the Eucharistic Bread is a sacrificial choice. It leads to perfect abnegation, and therefore promotes that self-denial which conditions both personal and social development.

The Eucharistic Christ desires to be the daily bread of our love for one another, of our fraternal union, and therefore of our growth together for the lifting up of the world.

For the Catholic, therefore, the decision for development and the decision to receive Communion daily, involve one another.

It behoves us, for ourselves and for others, to make the sun of daily Communion shine forth as a value which affects the whole personality; as the most powerful factor for promoting the psychological, social, and ontological integration of the human personality; as, in a sense, a supreme value of this earthly life. We must do this, if we wish to help towards the efficacious and definitive crystalization of the redeemed human free will.

Is not daily Communion the best means to achieve the very purpose of our creation, the *raison d'être* of our earthly life—namely, the praise and service of Christ the Redeemer in the fulfillment of the twofold command of love?

If a man desires to love Jesus Christ above all things, can he reasonably deprive Christ of the opportunity to enter into him, and through him to glorify the Father and to serve His brethren? And this, day after day? On the other hand, would not the absence of a desire for daily Communion be the sign that some created being, and especially he "self," is loved more than Jesus?

The free, definitive, constantly renewed decision to receive Communion daily in order to increase in oneself the love of God and the love of the neighbor for God's sake, is, on the contrary, the existential decision *par excellence* whose dynamism entails a multiplicity of successive decisions to promote human development, even in its earthly aspects.

A means of socio-ecclesial integration, daily Communion is also a factor promoting the psychological and ontological integration of the human and Christian personality.

Modern man often feels cut away from his past and

threatened by his future. The remedy which the Eucharist brings to this ever recurrent disintegration resulting from the human condition, has been admirably analyzed by Pope Pius XII:

> For many, the present is simply the wild rush of a torrent which sweeps men, like so much detritus, into the dark night of a future in which they will lose themselves with the very current that carries them along.
>
> Only the Church can lead men back from that darkness to the light; only the Church can give them awareness of a vigorous past, mastery of the present, confidence in the future. . . .
>
> On our countless altars, do we not daily see Christ, the divine Victim, whom arms reach out from end to end of the world, to enfold and embrace, at once in its past, in its present and in its future, the whole of human society? . . .
>
> In the holy Mass, men come to a greater awareness of their sinful past, and at the same time gain the immense blessings received in this memorial of Calvary—this memorial of the most sublime event in the history of mankind. They can receive the strength needed to free themselves from the deepest misery of the present, the misery of daily sins, and this to such an extent that even the most hardened feel the breath of the personal love of the God of Mercy. Their eyes are lifted towards a secure future, towards the consummation of time in the victory of the Lord, who is there on the altar; the victory of that Judge who one day will pronounce the final and definitive sentence. . . .
>
> In the holy Mass, therefore, the Church makes its greatest contributions to the building of human Society.[33]

Through the communicants, the Eucharistic Christ is the leaven in the dough of human society. By immersing them daily in the eternity of Christ, the daily Communion of these communicants saves their past, become a meritorious source of eternal life; helps them to become, at the cost of their own self-sacrifices, "the slaves of all" (cf. Mt. 10, 44) and the servants of the growth of the world; and even assures, as much as this is possible to the unstable free will of men, their final perseverance in divine love. Alienated as we partly are from our past and our future, it in some sort restores past and present to us, and in this way likens us to God with whom there is neither past nor future.[34] It divinizes both the temporal and the social structure of the created mind.

In these conditions, one understands why the Church, precisely because she is aware that "human fulfillment" constitutes, as it were, "a summary of our duties" (PP, 16), invites her children to eat daily the fruit of the Tree of Life at her "marriage supper of the Lamb," at the nuptial and sacrificial feast of the Mass (cf. Rev. 19, 9; 22, 2). The Church invites us to divinize, daily and with growing intensity, our imaginations, our sensibilities, our intellects, and our free wills through intimate contact with the human imagination, sensibility, intellect, and free will of Christ the Redeemer. In a sense, it can be said that the whole apostolic pedagogy of the Church and that of its most living members, are methodically directed towards securing a free, deliberate, personal, definite, and increasingly deepened resolution to work, through and thanks to daily Communion, for the global development, human and supernatural, of all men.

To the technicians and the builders of the earthly city, the Church says: "It is neither daily Mass nor daily Communion that deflects you from your work or from your studies; in fact, the contrary is true. There can be no serious and sustained work without mortification of the passions, of the imagination, and of the sensual appetites; there can be no mortification of the lower psyche without frequent participation, through the Eucharist, in the death of Christ. If every day you receive Him who is eternal Light and eternal Wisdom, Him who is the Lord of the world and even of His enemies, Him who is the supreme author of the organic growth of mankind, you will gain a greater understanding and mastery of the earth in the service of man." The decision to participate sacramentally and daily in the redemptive death of Christ, may be considered to be the "existential macro-decision" which gives meaning and supernatural efficacy to all the "microdecisions" to promote human development, while at the same time it anticipates and prepares for the supreme decision concerning coredemptive death.[35]

Is it not because this Eucharistic decision is constantly taken and renewed throughout the whole world by countless men and women, that the Church, as Vatican II says, continually grows in faith, in hope, and in charity?

Should it not also be said that, at least indirectly, this decision is the source of that progress of human history which the Providence of Christ, Creator and Redeemer, links organically with the progress of His Church?

To those who fail to see this relative progress, through fixing their eyes on the partial and periodic regressions which they witness, we answer with Paul VI:

> It may be that these persons are not realistic enough, and that they have not perceived the dynamism of a world which desires to live more fraternally—a world which, in spite of its ignorance, its mistakes, and even its sins, its relapses into barbarism, and its wanderings far from the road of salvation, is, even unawares, taking slow but sure steps towards its Creator. ... Civilizations are born, develop, and die. But humanity is advancing along the path of history like the waves of a rising tide encroaching gradually on the shore.[36]

For the believer, there can be no doubt about the connection, on the one hand, between this "rising tide" and this dynamism of human history, and, on the other, the active and frequent participation in the Eucharistic sacrifice. One must, of course, distinguish the different levels of the growth of the world, but one cannot separate them, or ignore the influence of the Eucharist on the concrete unfolding of human history.[37]

The connection between the growth of the Church and the decision concerning Eucharistic development is more obvious. Through the Eucharist, the Good News, the Gospel, of which the Eucharist as we have seen is the summary and the synthesis, bears fruit and is developed throughout the whole world (cf. Col. 1, 6); thanks to the Eucharist, numerous Christians are "bearing fruit in every good work and increasing in the knowledge of God" (Col. 1, 10); because they more frequently and more fervently eat the Body of Christ, they increasingly attach themselves "to the Head, from whom the whole body, *nourished* and knit together through its joints and ligaments, *grows* with a growth that is from God" (Col. 2, 19). Thanks to the Eucharistic growth of the grain of mustard seed of the Church in its beginning, the "smallest of all seeds . . . becomes a tree, so that the birds of the air"—i.e. the nations—"come and make nests in its branches" (Mt. 13, 31-32; Ez. 17, 23; Deut. 4, 9-18). Christ, received frequently in the Eucharist, enfolds in His arms, through His Church, the whole of human history.

The adult Christian's decision to seek development through the Eucharist, enables the Church to fulfill the ancient command: "Increase and multiply, and fill the earth, and subdue it" (Gn. 1, 28), which command Christ came, not to abolish, but to fulfill in a new command: "Fill all things . . . that God may be everything to every one" (Eph. 4, 10; 1 Cor. 15, 27-28).[38] This decision is the seed sown in good soil: it brings forth "grain, growing up and increasing and yielding . . . a hundredfold" (Mk. 4, 8). It is the principal factor of the "Eucharistic pleromization of the world" through which the Church is constantly and increasingly filled with Christ, "the fullness of him who fills all in all" (Eph. 1, 23).[39]

The decision to receive Communion daily, a decision taken as a means to promote the self-development of others,[40] amounts almost to entry into a state of life; it is, in a sense, a public profession of the desire for the perfection of love. In this respect, it constitutes a voluntary setting apart[41] in the midst of the People of God and for that people, a development of the consecration inaugurated by baptism. It is the Christian's response to the prayer that Christ offered for him to the Father: "And for their sake I consecrate myself, that they may be consecrated in truth" (Jn. 17, 19)—that is, that they may agree to share in my own consecration.

Jesus is He whom the Father has marked with His seal—that is, with His Spirit; and whom He has consecrated and sent into the world in order that He might consecrate Himself, as "the first-born of all creation," under the breath of this same Spirit.[42] Human development is the fruit of His consecrating sacrifice. The initial consecration of Christ, the Anointed of the Spirit, is orientated towards the sacrifice,[43] polarized by the final consecration of the world, of all mankind. John the Baptist had to decrease in order that Jesus might increase (Jn. 3, 30) to the sacrifice of Himself for the growth of the Church and of the world. Jesus is the bloody Victim for our development. The Lamb of God died in order that we might also agree to be victims for the lifting up of the world. There can be no development, no growth, without sacrifice and without abnegation. The consecration received by the Christian in baptism and confirmation, orientates him towards the sacrifices demanded for personal and social development, just as Christ's consecration by His Father, in the Spirit, orientated Him towards His paschal sacrifice and towards the return to the Father, a return in which He incorporates the fruits of His kenosis.[44]

In the final analysis, does not development mean the building up by all men of good will, in union with Christ, of that perfect Man grown to full age in whom is realized the fullness of Christ—i.e. the Church, the Whole Christ, this Church which, in a sense, includes the cosmos and, *a fortiori*, the natural order of human growth in its totality?[45] But can one separate from his paschal inclusion of human growth in the development towards the pleroma, the no less paschal decrease to which Saint John the Baptist referred: "He must increase, but I must decrease" (Jn. 3, 30)? Is not human development secured by the simultaneous operation of a certain law of decrease (of the old man) and of the natural and supernatural law of increase of the new man? In order that Christ may grow, we must, in various and complementary respects, decrease and increase. The decision to receive Communion daily is therefore a coredemptive decision which brings both these laws into play, provided that it is regarded and lived as something which raises and divinizes a man's professional and social life.[46]

This decision is therefore the choice of a coredemptive existence which inserts into the Eucharistic Sacrifice the development which it stimulates. It manifests and intensifies the will to share in the sacrifice of the Lamb of God for the consecration of the world. It is already a sacrificial consecration to the development of the Church and of the world.

* * * * *

Thanks be to you, Eucharistic heart of Jesus, for having willed to place Yourself at the head of a world in growth and in development, through the sacrifice of Your Pasch.

Praise be to You for ceaselessly immolating Yourself and for offering at every moment Your flesh for the life of the world (cf. Jn. 6, 51).

You are the living Bread that came down from Heaven that we might eat It and never die (cf. Jn. 6, 50). In receiving Your testimony and Your Eucharistic offering, we bear witness "that God is true" (cf. Jn. 3, 33).

We offer and consecrate ourselves as vicims to Your hunger and Your thirst to grow in us and in all mankind.

To You, creative and redemptive Bread, we give completely our being, our freedom, our work, our whole activity.

Come within us, as the Expiator of capitalist greed and Marxist atheism, as the Repairer of our selfishness. Be to us the daily Bread of our growth together. Come, Son of Man, to work within us, not for the food that perishes, but in order to satisfy fully the hunger of men with an eternal food which You freely give to us. For it is You that the Father has marked with His seal, the Holy Spirit (cf. Jn. 6, 27).

Lamb of God, You have come from the Father into the world: through us, take now this world into Your Heart which enfolds it and which is towards the Father's bosom (Jn. 1, 18).[47]

Appendix: The Significance and the Limits of the Evangelical Counsel of Daily Communion

Certain readers may be surprised to read in this final chapter: "Daily Communion is the most powerful factor of the social, psychological, and ontological integration of the human person."

I do not mean, however, any and every type of daily Communion; for example, of the daily Communion received hastily and casually, without deep respect; or of the type where the communicant is indulging in a kind of spiritual egoism, having a *tête-à-tête* with Jesus in the Host, while ignoring the "horizontal" consequences which daily Communion ought to entail.

Nor am I unaware of the very real danger that the quality of a Christian life might come to be reckoned by the number of Communions, without any thought for the necessary awareness, the preparation, and thanksgiving (normally of fifteen minutes duration for an adult).

I am also aware of the norms laid down by the moralists when they were commenting on the decisions of Saint Pius X; for example, here is what Cappello wrote:

"The confessor should refuse permission for frequent Communion to those who habitually omit a serious preparation and a suitable thanksgiving, in accordance with the strength, conditions, and duties of each person; because they show that they do not approach the sacred Table with due deliberation and that therefore they lack the proper dispositions. . . . The faithful who desire to communicate frequently should seek the judgment or advice of the confessor, who, in this domain, holds a declarative and non-imperative authority. The confessor may, *per accidens*, forbid frequent Communion if it cannot be practiced without detriment to the duties of the penitent's state in life" (*De Sacramentis*, Rome, 1928, t.I., par. 511-512).

But in our day, when religious sociologists are everywhere noting the drop in frequent Communion, I wanted to show the meaning of this evangelical counsel in the twofold history, temporal and salvific, of the human race.

NOTES TO CHAPTER SIXTEEN

1. "Unaided" must be read here as referring to the absence of aid from social influences, as the context clearly shows. There is, of course, no suggestion of the absence of divine aid.

2. Paul VI, *Populorum Progressio,* par. 15 (C.T.S. translation). Further reference to this encyclical in the notes will appear as PP.

3. PP, par. 42, quoting *Pensées*, no. 434, ed. Brunschvicg.

4. PP, 15. Cf. Mt. 25, 14-20.

5. PP, 15. This paragraph, stressing the responsibility of each man for his own destiny, for his success or his failure, even in an underdeveloped milieu, might seem to contradict what is said in par 6: ". . . to seek to do more, know more, and have more, in order to be more: that is what men aspire to now when a greater number of them are condemned to live in conditions that make this lawful desire illusory." There is certainly an element of tension between these two paragraphs, but not of contradiction. Paragraph 6 does not say that no progress is possible for the majority of men who live in the underdeveloped countries. It merely says that *all* the types of lawful progress which they could desire are, in the present circumstances, impossible for them. Furthermore, there is always a supernatural level of development which is largely independent of the natural level.

6. PP, 42.

7. PP, 20, citing Maritain.

8. PP, 16.

9. PP, 19; cf. 18.

10. Cf. PP, 24.

11. PP, 6; cf. note 5.

12. PP, par. 21.

13. PP, par. 6.

14. PP, par. 13.

15. PP, par. 28.

16. Our doing so can be justified: on the one hand, it is in line with the profound sense envisaged by Saint Luke, for whom the history of the Church which he gives us is, in a sense, a prophecy and a paradigm; on the other, it is in line with the interpretation of the New Testament presupposed, at least implicitly, by LG, 65; cf. the following note.

17. LG, 65. In his " 'Credo' of the People of God," Paul VI explains the precise meaning of this progress of the Church: "The true growth of the Kingdom of God cannot be measured by the progress of civilization, of science or of technology: it consists in an ever deepening knowledge of the unfathomable riches of Christ, in ever stronger hope in eternal blessings, in an ever more fervent response to the love of God, and in an ever more generous acceptance of grace and holiness by men" (C.T.S. translation, pp. 13-14).

18. GS, 39. 2.

19. Saint Irenaeus's image: *Adv. Haer.* IV. 20. 1 (MG, 7, 1032).

20. PP, 15.

21. Cf. Rom. 8, 21; cf. B. de Margerie S.J., *R. Niebuhr, théologien de la communauté mondiale,* Desclée de Brouwer, Bruges, 1969, Part 3, Chap. II, par. 1, 2.

22. PP, 79.

23. This is the interpretation of this verse in the Jerusalem Bible. It is in full conformity with Eph. 1, 13-14; 4, 30; 2 Cor. 1, 22.

24. Cf, Chapter One, C.

25. Cf. Jn. 8, 44. 45.

26. Cf. Chapter One, note 11.

27. PP, 16.

28. The final sentence of the text to which note 2 of our Chapter Five refers. Bultmann also says there that "Jesus expresses no conception of a human ideal, no thought of a development of human capacities"; but how would he interpret the parable of the talents (Mt. 25, 14-30) and other Gospel texts?

29. PP, 47.

30. *Ibid.*

31. The *temporal efficacy* of our engagement, we say here: what we mean is that *(other things being equal, however)* he who receives the Eucharist can efficaciously deploy his qualities and natural virtues more readily than others can do.

Cf. the text of Pius XII and that of John XXIII cited in note 37; see also B. de Margerie S.J., *A Igreja em stado de diálogo,* Manhumirun, Brazil, 1965, pp. 303-353.

32. In the light of Jn. 14, 13; 16, 23-27, it is clear that the Christian recites the "Our Father" in the name of Jesus and in union with Him. Besides, the patristic and ecclesiastical tradition has rightly interpreted the request for daily bread in a Eucharistic manner; see the decree *Sacra Tridentina Synodus,* approved by Pius X, 20 December 1905 (*Actes de saint Pie X,* Paris, Bonne Presse, t. II, pp. 252-253). We have dealt fully with this subject in an article, "Rythme eucharistique et pastorale contemporaine," *Rev. Eucharistique du Clergé* (Montreal), 69 (1966), 257-278. We have there attempted to suggest how to present at the present time the evangelical counsel of daily Communion, against the wiles of the prince of the world. Here, within the framework of a fresh presentation, we take up again in part some of the ideas dealt with there.

33. Pius XII, allocution, "La Elevatezza" of 20 February 1945; AAS, 38 (1946), 150-151.

34. Cf. Saint Thomas Aquinas, *Commentaries on the Sentences,* 1 *Sent.* 8. 1. 1.

35. Cf. our Chapter Five, sub fine.

36. PP, 79 and 17.

37. Cf. John XXIII, citing Pius XII, in 1960: AAS, 52 (1960), 402: "The Eucharist is a mystery of physical life: directly, of eternal physical life, because, as Jesus assures us, those who receive It with proper dispositions are certain to have a glorious resurrection on the last day; indirectly, of temporal physical life, because, in developing the Christian life and good moral behavior, It preserves the recipients from the many infirmities which contaminate the body and torment the life of sin" (cf. note 31).

38. Cf. L. Ligier S.J., *Péché d'Adam et Péché du Conde,* Paris, 1961, t. II, p. 342: the author here shows how Saint Paul, in the Epistles of the Captivity, has paraphrased Gn. 1, 28 (*ibid.,* note 81)—a text of Gn. cited by PP, 22.

39. Cf. Chapter Four, note 135; Chapter Thirteen, note 14.

40. Cf. PP, 34: "Man is truly man in as far as, master of his own acts and judge of their worth, he is author of his own advancement, in keeping with the nature which was given to him by his Creator, and whose possibilities and exigencies he himself freely assumes." One cannot "develop" others, but one can and should help them to develop themselves. The concept of development is inseparable from that of responsibility.

41. "Set apart," that is, *de facto,* not *de jure:* this counsel of daily Communion is offered to all, given to all, but accepted and practiced only by a minority. We speak here of "the desire for the perfection of love" and not necessarily of the

subjectively efficacious tendency towards it; because the decree, *Sancta Tridentina Synodus,* already cited, has reminded us that to receive Communion it is not indispensable (however highly desirable) to be free from all deliberate venial sin. We say that the habit of daily Communion constitutes almost a state of life, because "the fruits of daily Communion are incomparably more abundant than those of weekly or monthly Communion" (*ibid.;* see my article, already cited, pp. 260-261). Now, the decision concerning daily Communion is the choice to seek assured continuity of spiritual progress, and, in this respect, can be regarded as, in a sense, the entry into a state of life—one which would be no other than that to which the baptized person aspires in virtue of the very dynamism of the baptismal grace, completely polarized by the Eucharist. The Eucharist is the sacrament which produces, *ex opere operato,* the perfection of love, fundamental law of Christian action. The remission of venial sins is one of the special fruits of the Eucharist, sacrament of the fervor of love. Daily Communion does not presuppose perfect holiness, since Its purpose is to confer this on him who places no obstacle in its way. "Because you are constantly sinning, receive Communion constantly," Saint Ambrose says in substance (*De Sacramentis* IV, 6, par. 28).

42. Cf. Jn. 10, 36; Col. 1, 15; Lk. 4, 1.

43. Westcott, cited by R. E. Brown S.S. (*The Gospel according to John,* Anchor Bible, N.Y. 1966, p. 261), thus interprets Jn. 6, 27 in the light of 10, 36: "consecration to sacrifice."

44. Cf. this very beautiful text of Gerson: "Exivit (Christus) secundum animam per creationis emanationem et ad Deum vadit per sui et aliorum omnium in Deum revolutionem intelligibilem; et sicut omnia quodammodo a Deo accepit in sua creatione dum propter eam facta sunt omnia, sic omnia refert in Deum dilective proportionnaliter satis ad primum exitum et reditum aeternalem" (Sermon *A Deo exivit,* edited by A. Combes, *Essai sur la critique de Ruysbroeck par Gerson,* Paris, 1945, t. I, p. 648).

45. Cf. the interpretation of Saint Paul by Father Benoit, Chapter Four, note 135.

46. Cf. John XXIII, in *Pacem in Terris:* "It is necessary that human beings, in the intimacy of their own consciences, should so live and act in their temporal lives as to create a synthesis between scientific, technical, and professional elements on the one hand, and spiritual values on the other" (C.T.S. translation, p. 54). It is precisely for this purpose that we end this book on Christology with an invitation to Christian and human action. Contemplative reflection should issue in action which transforms the world. This is also the undoubted aim of Paul VI in PP, about which one could read

P. E. Charbonneau, *Desenvolvimento dos Povos,* Herder, S. Paulo (Brazil), 1967 (303 pages).

47. We are adopting the translation of Jn. 1, 18 given by I. de la Potterie in *Biblica,* 43 (1962), 379-387.

BIBLIOGRAPHY

A. D'ADHEMAR, S.J., *De Verbo Incarnato*, Paris, 1930.
E. B. ALLO, O.P., *L'Apocalypse*, Paris, 1921.
ST. AUGUSTIN, *de Trinitate*, Bibliothèque Augustinienne, Paris, 1955.
— *in Joannem* (M. L. 35).
H. DE BARENTON, O.F.M.CAP., *La dévotion au Sacré-Coeur*, Paris, 1914.
ST. R. BELLARMIN, S.J., *Controversia de Summo Pontifice*, Vivès, Paris, 1870.
— *Opera oratoria posthuma*, Rome, 1940, *sq*, 9 vol.
P. BENOIT, O.P., *Exégèse et Théologie*, Paris, 1961, 2 vol.
D. BONHOEFFER., *Résistance et Soumission*, Genève, 1967.
— *Christology*, London, 1966.
F. BONNEFOY, O.F.M., *Primauté du Christ selon l'Ecriture et la Tradition*, Herder, Rome, 1959.
H. BOUESSE, O.P., *Le Sauveur de Monde*, t. I, Place du Christ, Chambéry, 1951.
H. BOUILLARD, S.J., *Logique de la foi*, Paris, 1964.
L. BOUYER., *Les deux économies du gouvernement divin, Initiation Théologique* t. II, Paris, 1952.
G. DE BROGLIE, S.J., *Le principe fondamental de la Mariologie, Maria*, t. VI, Paris, 1961.
R. BROWN, S.S., *The Gospel according to John*, N.Y, 1966.
R. BULTMANN, *Jésus Christ and Mythology*, N.Y, 1958.
STE. CATHERINE DE SIENNE, *Dialogue*, éd. Hurtaud, Paris, 1913.
L. CERFAUX, *Le Christ dans la théologie de Saint Paul*, Paris, 1954.
Collectiff, *La Collégialité épiscopale*, Paris, 1965.
Collectif, *La Parole de Dieu en Jésus-Christ*, Castermann, Tournai, 1961.

513

Collectif, *Cor Jesu*, ouvrage dirigé par A. BEA, S.J., Rome, 1959, 2 vols.

J. COLSON, *Episcopat catholique : collégialité et primauté*, Paris, 1963.

J. COMBLIN, *Le Christ dans l'Apocalypse*, Paris, 1965.

Concile Oécuménique Vatican II; Constitutions, décrets, déclarations. Ed. Bilingue, Centurion, Paris, 1967.

Y. M. J. CONGAR, O.P., *Mystère du Temple*, Paris, 1958.

— *Voies du Dieu vivant*, Paris, 1962.

— *Esquisse du Mystère de l'Eglise*, Paris, 1953.

— *Jésus-Christ*, Paris. 1966.

— *Sainte Eglise*, Paris, 1963.

— *Episcopat et Eglise universelle*, Paris, 1962.

G. CRES-Y, *De la Science à la Théologie*, Paris-Neuchatel, 1965.

O. CULLMANN, *Christology of the New Testament*, London, 1959.

J. DANIELOU, S.J., *Message évangélique et culture hellénistique*, Paris, 1961.

— *Théologie du Judéo-Christianisme*, Tournai, 1961.

— *Essai sur le mystère de l'Histoire*, Paris, 1953.

J. M. DUFORT, S.J., *Récapitulation paulinienne dans l'exégèse des Pères*, Sciences Ecclésiastiques, 12 (1960) 21-38.

F. X. DURRWELL, C.SS.R., *La Résurrection de Jésus, Mystère du salut*, Paris, 1961.

A. FEUILLET, *Le Christ Sagesse de Dieu*, Paris, 1966.

J. DE FINANCE, S.J., *Connaissance de l'Etre*, Paris, 1966.

H. FRIES, *Encyclopédie de la foi*, 4 vol., Paris, 1967.

J. GALOT, *Rédemption, Mystère d'Alliance*, Bruges, 1965.

GIRAUD, *De l'Union à Notre Seigneur dans sa vie de victime*, Paris, 1932.

J. D. GODSEY, *Theology of Dietrich Bonhoeffer*, London, 1963.

Gott in Welt, (Festgabe fuer K. Rahner) Freiburg, 1958.

P. HARTMANN, S.C.J., *Le sens plénier de la réparation du péché*, Louvain, 1955.

HOUSSIAU, *Christologie d'Irénée*, Louvain, 1955.

ST. IRENEE, *Adversus Haereses*.

C. JOURNET, CARDINAL, *l'Eglise du Verbe Incarné*, Bruges, 1951.

B. KLOPPENBURG, O.F.M., *O espiritismo no Brasil*, Petropolis, 1964.

M. J. LAGRANGE, O.P., *Evangile selon Saint Jean*, Paris, 1948.

LAMARCHE, *Le Christ vivant*, Paris, 1966.

M. DE LA TAILLE, S.J., *Mysterium Fidei*, Paris, 1924.

R. LATOURELLE, S.J., *Théologie de la Révélation*, Bruges, 1966.

J. LAWSON, *Biblical theology of Irenaeus*, London, 1948.

J. LEBRETON, S.J., *Origine du dogme de la Trinité*, Paris, 1919.

J. LECUYER, C.S.SP., *Le sacrifice de la Nouvelle Alliance*, Lyon, 1962.

B. LEEMING, S.J., *Adnotationes de Verbo Incarnato*, Rome, 1936.

L. LIGIER, S.J., *Péché d'Adam et Péche du Monde*, Paris, 1961, 2 vol.

B. LONERGAN, S.J., *De Verbo Incarnato*, Rome, 1964.

E. LONGPRE, O.F.M., *Eucharistie et expérience mystique, DSAM*, t. IV, Paris, 1961.

H. DE LUBAC, S.J., *La prière du P. Tielhard*, Paris, 1964.

— *Blondel et Teilhard de Chardin*, Paris, 1965.

— *Teilhard, Missionnaire et Apologiste*, Toulouse, 1966.

B. DE MARGERIE, S.J., R. NIEBUHR, *théologien de la communauté mondiale*, Paris-Brussels, 1969.

— *Le Coeur de Marie, Coeur de l'Eglise*, Paris, 1967.

— *A Igreja em estado de dialogo*, Manhumirim, Brazil, 1965.

— *Padres Profetas e Mistagogos*, S. Paulo, 1968.

STE. MARGUERITE-MARIE ALACOQUE, *Vie et Oeuvre*, éd. Gauthey, Paris, 1915.

J. MARITAIN, *De la grace et de l'humanité de Jésus*, Bruges, 1967.

— *Le paysan de la Garonne*, Paris, 1966.

R. MARLE, S.J., *Bultmann et l'interprétation du Nouveau Testament*, Paris, 1966.

— *D. Bonhoeffer, témoin de Jésus-Christ parmi ses frères*, Tournai, 1967.

E. MASCALL, *Christ, the Christian and the Church*, London, 1946.

CH. MASSABKI, DOM, O.S.B., *Le Christ rencontre de deux amours*, Paris, 1962.

R. C. McCREARY, O.F.M. CAP., *Christ the Savior according to St. Lawrence of Brindisi*, Laurentianum 4 (1963) 401-430.

— *The Redemptive Incarnation according to St. Lawrence of Brindisi*, Laurentianum 6 (1965) 315-328.

— *The glorification of Christ in the Thought of St Lawrence*, Laurentianum 10 (1969) 401-412.

E. MERSCH, S.J., *Théologie du Corps Mystique*, Paris-Bruxelles, 1944.

— *Le Corps Mystique du Christ*, Louvain, 1933.

J. B. METZ, *Christliche Anthropozentrik*, Munich, 1962.

C. F. MOONEY, S.J., *Teilhard de Chardin et le Mystère du Christ*, Paris, 1968. (Original work published in English, N.Y, 1966).

H. MUHLEN, *Der Heilige Geist als Person*, Munster, 1967.

M. J. NICOLAS, O.P., *Théotokos*, Tournai, 1965.

P. NORTH, S.J., *Teilhard and the Creation of the Soul*, Milwaukee, 1967.

M. PENIDO, TEIXEIRA-LEITE, *O mistério des Sacramentos*, Petropolis, 1961.

PHILLIPPE DE LA TRINITE, O.C.D., *Rome et Teilhard*, Paris, 1964.

Problèmes actuels de christologie, ouvrage publié sous la direction de H. Bouessé, O.P., Paris, 1965.

K. RAHNER, S.J., *Ecrits Théologiques*, Bruges.

H. RAMIERE, S.J., *L'Apostolat de la Prière*, Toulouse, 9ᵉ éd.

E. RIDEAU, S.J., *La Pensée du P. Teilhard de Chardin*, Paris, 1965.

L. SABOURIN, S.J., *Rédemption Sacrificielle*, Bruges, 1961.

M. J. Scheeben, *Les Mystères du Christianisme*, Bruges, 1947.

E. Schillebeeckx, o.p., *Marie, Mère de la Rédemption*, Paris, 1963.

— *Révélation et théologie*, Bruxelles, 1965.

R. Schnackenburg, *Le Message moral du N.T.*, Lyon, 1963.

O. Semmelroth, s.j., *Maria, Urbild der Kirche*, Wurzburg, 1950.

P. Smulders, s.j., *La vision de Teilhard*, Paris, 1965.

P. Teilhard de Chardin, s.j., *Oeuvres*, Seuil, Paris, 9 vols.

G. Thils, *Propos et problèmes de la Théologie des religionsnon chrétiennes*, Bruxelles, 1965.

St. Thomas d'Aquin, *Summa Theologiae*, Alba, Paulinae, Rome, 1962.

S. Tromp, s.j., *Corpus Christi quod est Ecclesia*, t. II., *de Christo Capite*, t. III., *de spiritu Christi anima*, Rome, 1960.

H. Urs von Balthasar, *Liturgie cosmique*, Paris, 1947.

G. Wingren, *Man and the Incarnation*, A study in the bibliocal theology of Irenaeus, London, 1959.

INDEX

A

Abel, 30
Adam, 243, 249, 275, 296
Afro-Brazilian syncretist cults, 29
Agnostics, 49
Agnus pantocrator, 19
Albright, W. F., author, 137
Allo, E. B., author, 256
Ambrose, St., 272-274, 305, 306, 384, 395, 445, 448
Amette, Cardinal, Archbishop of Paris, 473, 484
Anakephalaiosastai, 98
Anakephalaiosis, 242, 254
Anselm, St., 214, 218, 219
Apostles' Creed, 270
Arianism, 114
Aristotle, 13
Arnou, R., author, 445
Ascension of Christ, 183, 237, 238
Asia Minor, 56
Assumption of Mary, 328, 338, 363
Assumption of St. Joseph, 338
Atheism, xxvi, 44, 49, 53-55, 153, 247, 317, 507
Aubert, R., author, 389
Audet, J. P., author, 172, 176, 184, 202, 205, 309
Augsburg Confession, 149
Augustine, St., xxix, xxx, 11, 22, 30-32, 42, 136, 138, 139, 142, 218, 219, 226, 227, 290, 305, 309, 330, 338, 400, 428, 443, 447, 450-452, 457, 469, 477, 483

B

Babylon, 53
Bacht, T., author, 137, 225
Baciocchi, J. de, author, 207
Baptism, 33, 272
Barenton, H. de, author, 443
Barth, K., author
Bellarmine, St. Robert, 145, 344,346, 348, 351, 355-357, 386-388, 393-394, 452
Benoit, P., author, 108, 117, 233, 253, 511
Berlin, 140, 148
Bernard, author, 394
Berulle, Cardinal P. de, 393
Bethge, E., author, 140
Bettinson, author, 255
Biberach, R. de, author, 438
Bishops of France, 362, 385
Bismarck, 352
Blanchard, P., author, 106
Blondel, M., author, 70, 82, 106, 108, 118, 405
Bogdasavich, M., author, 117
Bonaventure, St., 407, 438, 445, 452, 464
Bonhoeffer, D., author, xxvii, 140-169, 180
early, 140-150
later, 151-169
Bonhomme, A. de, author, 442, 480, 481
Bonnefoy, J. F., author, 7, 20, 21
Bonsirvin, J., author, 202
Bossuet, 227, 446
Bouesse, H., author, 7, 8, 21
Bouillard, H., author, 125, 137

517

SECOND EDITION

MATHEMATICS and CALCULUS with APPLICATIONS

MARGARET L. LIAL / CHARLES D. MILLER

American River College

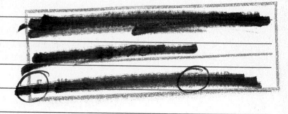

SCOTT, FORESMAN AND COMPANY

Glenview, Illinois   London, England

To the Student

A *Student Solutions Manual* to accompany this textbook is available from your college bookstore. The detailed step-by-step solutions in the manual can help you study and understand the course material by providing additional correct examples for the odd-numbered exercises.

Cover and chapter opener artworks are from *The Spirit of Colors: The Art of Karl Gerstner,* Henri Stierlin, editor. Photographs by Alexander von Steiger, Basel. © 1981 by The Massachusetts Institute of Technology. Reproduced with permission.

Cover: Karl Gerstner. *Color Relief 10,* Turquoise, Intro Version, 1966/1968. Nitrocellulose on masonite, 1640 × 1640 unframed. Dresdner Bank, Dortmund. **Extended application symbols:** artwork first appearing on page 31: Karl Gerstner. From the series *Aperspective 3* (The Large Sliding Mirror Picture), 1953/55; page 99: Karl Gerstner. *Color Sound 1C,* Intro Version, 1968–1972, 1973; page 102: Karl Gerstner. *Carro 64,* alterable object, 1956/61; page 112: Karl Gerstner. *AlgoRhythm 1,* alterable object of 7 plates, 1969–1970.

Library of Congress Cataloging in Publication Data

Lial, Margaret L.
    Mathematics and calculus with applications.

    Includes index.
    1. Mathematics—1961–   .   I. Miller, Charles
David.   II. Title.
QA37.2.L5 1985   510   84-23554
ISBN 0-673-15896-9

345678910-RRC-9089888786

PREFACE

This revised edition of *Mathematics and Calculus with Applications* is designed to be useful to the student and helpful for the instructor. For the student we have written a book with explanations and examples that are clear, direct, and to the point. The exercises are carefully graded in difficulty with examples corresponding to the exercises. Abundant applied problems and extended applications show students how mathematics is used in job situations. For the instructor, we have produced a comprehensive instructional package.

The text is carefully laid out to match standard courses. Each section includes only those topics that an instructor would normally expect to find.

Mathematics and Calculus with Applications, Second Edition, presents the topics for a one-year course in finite mathematics and calculus for students majoring in management, a social science, or a life science. The book can also be used for separate courses in finite mathematics and calculus.

The prerequisite is three to four semesters of high school algebra or the equivalent. For those students who may not have studied algebra recently, an algebra review is included at the beginning of the book. This review can be discussed in class or left for reference, as desired.

PEDAGOGICAL FEATURES

Exercise sets are extensive, with a wide range of difficulty from drill problems to challenging applied problems. Almost every exercise set includes applications to management and biology.

Examples clearly illustrate the techniques and concepts presented. Numbering nearly 450, the examples prepare students for success with the exercises.

Applications are included in examples and exercise sets to motivate student interest. Our applications are practical, varied, and interesting.

Extended applications are included throughout the book in appropriate spots. These extended applications answer the question, ''Why are we studying this?'' Students can see the utility of the mathematics by learning how it is used at Southern Pacific or Upjohn, for example.

FORMAT

A **second color** is used pedagogically. Important rules, definitions, theorems, and equations are enclosed in colored boxes and highlighted with a title in the margin.

Color is also used to **annotate** and **clarify** troublesome areas and in the artwork to clarify processes and procedures.

CONTENT FEATURES

In-depth coverage and **logical sequencing** of topics give students a thorough course in both finite mathematics and calculus.

Linear programming has been expanded into two chapters. One introduces the topic with the intuitive graphical method; the other presents the simplex method. The coverage includes a discussion of duality theory.

Mathematics of Finance is a self-contained chapter following the topics on finite mathematics and preceding the chapters on the calculus, permitting coverage as desired. This chapter has been updated to reflect current interest rates. A new section on sequences offers more complete coverage of annuities and amortization.

Systems of linear equations and their solutions are presented before matrices to better motivate matrix theory and demonstrate the power of matrix methods.

Complete coverage of calculus is included. Students are given a thorough introduction to this key portion of mathematics.

Complete coverage of probability provides students with a superior introduction to this difficult topic.

Exponential and logarithmic functions are covered in Chapter 12. The non-calculus sections of the chapter may be covered at any point after Chapter 1.

Chapters were written for maximum flexibility of course design. Chapter interdependence is as follows:

Chapter 1, Functions and Graphs, has no prerequisite. (The non-calculus portions of the chapter on exponential and logarithmic functions may be covered at any time after Chapter 1.)

Chapter 2, Matrix Theory, depends on Chapter 1.

Chapters 3 and 4, on linear programming, depend on Chapters 1 and 2.

Chapter 5, Sets and Counting, depends on Chapter 1.

Chapter 6, Probability, requires Chapter 5.

Chapters 7 and 8, the applications of probability, depend on Chapter 6.

Chapter 9, Mathematics of Finance, depends on Chapter 1.

Chapters 10 through 16, the calculus chapters, require Chapter 1.

SUPPLEMENTS

Instructor's Manual. This manual features answers to even-numbered exercises, together with an extensive test bank.

Student Solutions Manual. This booklet, available for purchase by students, features complete solutions to all odd-numbered exercises.

Computer applications. Donald Coscia has prepared a softbound textbook packaged to include a diskette (in Apple II and IBM-PC versions). The programs allow students to solve meaningful problems without the difficulties of extensive arithmetic calculations. This book bridges the gap between the text and the computer by providing additional explanations and additional exercises for solution using a micro-computer. Appropriate computer exercises in this text are identified with the symbol shown in the margin.

Acknowledgments

Many instructors helped us prepare this revision. In particular, we would like to thank

Yousef Alavi, Western Michigan University
John Beachy, University of Washington
Steven Bellenot, Florida State University
Richard Bieberich, Ball State University
Orville Bierman, University of Wisconsin—Eau Claire
Robert Blefko, Western Michigan University
James L. Buckley, University of Alabama in Birmingham
Joseph Buckley, Western Michigan University
Ronald M. Davis, Northern Virginia Community College
Robert Eicken, Illinois Central College
Garret Etgen, University of Houston
Joseph Faber, East Tennessee State University
Carolyn Funk, Thornton Community College
James Hall, University of Wisconsin—Madison
Robert Heal, University of California—Berkeley
Christopher Hee, Eastern Michigan University
David Hinde, Rock Valley College
Louis Hoelzle, Bucks County Community College
Charles Johnson, Louisiana State University
Eleanor Kendrick, San Jose City College
Marty McCaskey, Western Michigan University
Sandy McKaig, American River College
Curtis McKnight, University of Oklahoma
Walter Roth, University of North Carolina
Daniel Scanlon, Orange Coast College
Glenn Seseske, Quinnipiac College
Nancy Shoemaker, Oakland University
Donna Smith, American River College
Martha Stewart, University of North Carolina
Gary Walls, University of Southern Mississippi
Lee Witt, Western Michigan University
Dennis Zill, Loyola Marymount College.

Finally, we must thank Marge Prullage, Kayla Cohen, and Janet Tilden, editors who contributed a great deal to the finished book.

Margaret L. Lial
Charles D. Miller

CONTENTS

CHAPTER 11

Applications of the Derivative   517

CHAPTER 12

Exponential and Logarithmic Functions   593

CHAPTER 13

Integration   651

Order of Operations

Absolute Value

Solution of Linear Equations

Inequalities

Solution of Linear Inequalities

Polynomials

Factoring

Quadratic Equations

Quadratic Inequalities

Rational Expressions

Integer Exponents

Roots

Radicals

Rationalizing the Denominator

This algebra review is designed for self-study: you can either study it all at once, or use it as a reference when needed throughout the course. Since this is a review, answers to all exercises are given in the answer section at the back of the book.

Order of Operations

To avoid possible ambiguity when working problems with real numbers, use the following *order of operations,* which has been generally agreed on as the most useful. (This order of operations is used by computers and many calculators.)

Order of Operations

1. First, do any work inside parentheses or brackets.
2. Do multiplications or divisions, in order, from left to right.
3. Do additions or subtractions, in order, from left to right.
4. If the problem involves a fraction bar, treat the numerator and the denominator separately.

EXAMPLE

Use the order of operations given above to simplify the following.

(a) $6 \div 3 + 2 \cdot 4 = 2 + 2 \cdot 4 = 2 + 8 = 10$

(b) $\dfrac{-9(-3) + (-5)}{2(-8) - 5(3)} = \dfrac{27 + (-5)}{-16 - 15} = \dfrac{22}{-31} = -\dfrac{22}{31}$

EXERCISES

Simplify each of the following using the order of operations given above. Round to the nearest thousandth in Exercises 9–10.

1. $(-9 + 4 \cdot 3)(-7)$

2. $-15(-8 - 4 \div 2)$

3. $-(-13 - 8) - [(-4 - 5) - (-8 + 15)]$

4. $[8 - (-7 - 19)] + (-4 - 11) - (-7 - 2)$

5. $\dfrac{-8 + (-4)(-6) \div 12}{4 - (-3)}$

6. $\dfrac{15 \div 5 \cdot 4 \div 6 - 8}{-6 - (-5) - 8 \div 2}$

7. $\dfrac{17 \div (3 \cdot 5 + 2) \div 8}{-6 \cdot 5 - 3 - 3(-11)}$

8. $\dfrac{-12(-3) + (-8)(-5) + (-6)}{17(-3) + 4 \cdot 8 + (-7)(-2) - (-5)}$

9. $\dfrac{-9.23(5.87) + 6.993}{1.225(-8.601) - 148(.0723)}$

10. $\dfrac{189.4(3.221) - 9.447(-8.772)}{4.889[3.177 - 8.291(3.427)]}$

Absolute Value

Distance is always given as a nonnegative number. For example, the distance from 0 to -2 on a number line is 2, the same as the distance from 0 to 2. We say that 2 is the absolute value of both numbers, 2 and -2. By definition, the **absolute value** of a number a is the distance on the number line from a to 0. Write the absolute value of a as $|a|$. For example, the distance on the number line from 9 to 0 is 9, as is the distance from -9 to 0 (See Figure 1), making $|9| = 9$ and $|-9| = 9$.

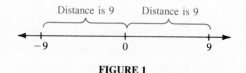

Distance is 9   Distance is 9

-9 0   9

FIGURE 1

The definition of absolute value can be stated more formally.

Absolute Value

For a real number a,

$$|a| = a \quad \text{if } a \geq 0$$
$$|a| = -a \quad \text{if } a < 0.$$

The second part of this definition requires a little care. If a is a *negative* number, then $-a$ is a *positive* number. Thus, for any value of a, we have $|a| \geq 0$.

EXAMPLE

Find each of the following.

(a) $|5|$

$5 > 0$, so $|5| = 5$.

(b) $|-5| = 5$

(c) $-|-5| = -(5) = -5$

(d) $|0| = 0$

(e) $|-4 - 7| = |-11| = 11$ ◾

EXERCISES

Evaluate each of the following.

11. $|6 - 4|$ **12.** $-|12 + (-8)|$ **13.** $|8 - (-9)|$ **14.** $|8| - |-4|$

15. $-|-4| - |-1 - 14|$ **16.** $|3 - 17|$ **17.** $|-6 + (-15)|$ **18.** $|-3 - (-2)|$

19. $|-9| - |-12|$ **20.** $-|6| - |-12 - 4|$

Solution of Linear Equations

One of the main uses of algebra is to solve equations. An **equation** states that two expressions are equal. Examples of equations include $x + 6 = 9$, $4y + 8 = 12$, and $9z = -36$. The letter in each equation, the unknown, is called the **variable.**

Equations which can be written in the form $ax + b = c$, where a, b, and c are real numbers, with $a \neq 0$, are called **linear equations.** Examples of linear equations include $5y + 9 = 16$, $8x = 4$, and $-3p + 5 = -8$. Equations that are *not* linear include absolute value equations, such as $|x| = 4$.

The following properties are used to help solve linear equations.

Properties of Real Numbers

For all real numbers a, b, and c,

$a(b + c) = ab + ac.$ Distributive property

If $a = b$, then $a + c = b + c.$ Addition property of equality

(The same number may be added to both sides of an equation.)

If $a = b$, then $ac = bc.$ Multiplication property of equality

(The same number may be multiplied on both sides of an equation.)

| **EXAMPLE** | Solve $\dfrac{r}{10} - \dfrac{2}{15} = \dfrac{3r}{20} - \dfrac{1}{5}$. |

To solve this equation, first eliminate all denominators by multiplying both sides of the equation by a **common denominator,** a number which can be divided (with no remainder) by each denominator in the equation. Here the denominators are 10, 15, 20, and 5. Each of these numbers can be divided into 60, so that 60 is a common denominator. Multiply both sides of the equation by 60 and use the distributive property. (If a common denominator cannot be found easily, all the denominators in the problem can be multiplied together to find one.)

$$\frac{r}{10} - \frac{2}{15} = \frac{3r}{20} - \frac{1}{5}$$

$$60\left(\frac{r}{10} - \frac{2}{15}\right) = 60\left(\frac{3r}{20} - \frac{1}{5}\right)$$

$$60\left(\frac{r}{10}\right) - 60\left(\frac{2}{15}\right) = 60\left(\frac{3r}{20}\right) - 60\left(\frac{1}{5}\right)$$

$$6r - 8 = 9r - 12$$

Add $-6r$ and 12 to both sides.

$$6r - 8 + (-6r) + 12 = 9r - 12 + (-6r) + 12$$

$$4 = 3r$$

Multiply both sides by 1/3 to get

$$r = \frac{4}{3}. \quad \blacksquare$$

EXERCISES

Solve each equation. Round solutions to the nearest hundredth in Exercises 31–36.

21. $.2m - .5 = .1m + .7$

22. $\dfrac{5}{6}k - 2k + \dfrac{1}{3} = \dfrac{2}{3}$

23. $3r + 2 - 5(r + 1) = 6r + 4$

24. $2[m - (4 + 2m) + 3] = 2m + 2$

25. $\dfrac{3x - 2}{7} = \dfrac{x + 2}{5}$

26. $\dfrac{x}{3} - 7 = 6 - \dfrac{3x}{4}$

27. $\dfrac{m}{2} - \dfrac{1}{m} = \dfrac{6m + 5}{12}$

28. $-\dfrac{3k}{2} + \dfrac{9k - 5}{6} = \dfrac{11k + 8}{k}$

29. $\dfrac{4}{x - 3} - \dfrac{8}{2x + 5} + \dfrac{3}{x - 3} = 0$

30. $\dfrac{5}{2p + 3} - \dfrac{3}{p - 2} = \dfrac{4}{2p + 3}$

31. $9.06x + 3.59(8x - 5) = 12.07x + .5612$

32. $-5.74(3.1 - 2.7p) = 1.09p + 5.2588$

33. $\dfrac{2.5x - 7.8}{3.2} + \dfrac{1.2x + 11.5}{5.8} = 6$

34. $\dfrac{4.19x + 2.42}{.05} - \dfrac{5.03x - 9.74}{.02} = 1$

35. $\dfrac{2.63r - 8.99}{1.25} - \dfrac{3.90r - 1.77}{2.45} = r$

36. $\dfrac{8.19m + 2.55}{4.34} - \dfrac{8.17m - 9.94}{1.04} = 4m$

Inequalities

To write that one number is greater than or less than another number, use the following symbols.

Inequality Symbols

$<$ means *is less than*	$\leq$ means *is less than or equal to*
$>$ means *is greater than*	$\geq$ means *is greater than or equal to*

EXAMPLE

(a) $3 < 7$

(b) $5 \geq 5$, since $5 = 5$

(c) $|-2| < |-9|$

(d) $-2 > -9$ ▪

EXERCISES

In each of the following exercises, fill in the blank with either $=$, $<$, or $>$.

37. -4 _____ -1

39. $-|7|$ _____ $|7|$

41. $|-2 + 8|$ _____ $|2 - 8|$

43. $|3| \cdot |-5|$ _____ $|3(-5)|$

45. $|3 - 2|$ _____ $|3| - |2|$

38. $-(-9)$ _____ -5

40. $|6 - (-4)|$ _____ $|-4 - 6|$

42. $|3 + 1|$ _____ $|-3 - 1|$

44. $|3| \cdot |2|$ _____ $|3(2)|$

46. $|5 - 1|$ _____ $|5| - |1|$

Solution of Linear Inequalities

An equation states that two expressions are equal; an **inequality** states that they are unequal. A **linear inequality** is an inequality which can be simplified to the form $ax < b$. (Throughout this section, we usually make statements only for $<$, but they are equally valid for $>$, $\leq$, or $\geq$.) Linear inequalities are solved by means of the following properties.

Properties of Inequality

For all real numbers a, b, and c,

    1. if $a < b$, then $a + c < b + c$;

    2. if $a < b$, and if $c > 0$, then $ac < bc$;

    3. if $a < b$, and if $c < 0$, then $ac > bc$.

Pay careful attention to part (3): if both sides of an inequality are multiplied by a negative number, the direction of the inequality symbol must be reversed. For example, if we start with the true statement $-3 < 5$ and multiply both sides by the *positive* number 2, we get

$$-3 \cdot 2 < 5 \cdot 2$$

or
$$-6 < 10,$$

still a true statement. On the other hand, if we start with $-3 < 5$ and multiply both sides by the *negative* number -2, we get a true result only if we reverse the direction of the inequality symbol:

$$-3 < 5$$
$$-3(-2) > 5(-2)$$
$$6 > -10.$$

EXAMPLE

Solve $4 - 3y \le 7 + 2y$. Graph the solution.
First add -4 to both sides.

$$4 - 3y + (-4) \le 7 + 2y + (-4)$$
$$-3y \le 3 + 2y$$

Add $-2y$ to both sides. Remember that *adding* to both sides never changes the direction of the inequality symbol.

$$-3y + (-2y) \le 3 + 2y + (-2y)$$
$$-5y \le 3$$

Multiply both sides by $-1/5$. Since $-1/5$ is negative, we must change the direction of the inequality symbol.

$$-\frac{1}{5}(-5y) \ge -\frac{1}{5}(3)$$

$$y \ge -\frac{3}{5}$$

To **graph** the solution, start with a number line as in Figure 2. Place a heavy dot at $-3/5$, since $-3/5$ is a part of the solution. The solution includes all real numbers greater than or equal to $-3/5$. Indicate this process with a heavy arrow to the right. ■

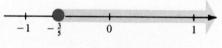

FIGURE 2

EXAMPLE

Solve $-2 < 5 + 3m < 20$. Graph the solution.

The inequality $-2 < 5 + 3m < 20$ says that $5 + 3m$ is *between* -2 and 20. Solve this inequality with an extension of the properties given above. Work as follows, first adding -5 to each part.

$$-2 + (-5) < 5 + 3m + (-5) < 20 + (-5)$$
$$-7 < 3m < 15$$

Now multiply each part by $1/3$.

$$-\frac{7}{3} < m < 5$$

A graph of the solution is given in Figure 3; here open circles are used to show that $-7/3$ and 5 are *not* part of the graph.   ▇

FIGURE 3

EXERCISES

Solve each inequality and graph the solution.

47. $-3p - 2 \geq 1$

48. $6k - 4 < 3k - 1$

49. $m - (4 + 2m) + 3 < 2m + 2$

50. $-2(3y - 8) \geq 5(4y - 2)$

51. $3p - 1 < 6p + 2(p - 1)$

52. $x + 5(x + 1) > 4(2 - x) + x$

53. $-7 < y - 2 < 4$

54. $8 \leq 3r + 1 \leq 13$

55. $-4 \leq \dfrac{2k - 1}{3} \leq 2$

56. $-1 \leq \dfrac{5y + 2}{3} \leq 4$

57. $\dfrac{3}{5}(2p + 3) \geq \dfrac{1}{10}(5p + 1)$

58. $\dfrac{8}{3}(z - 4) \leq \dfrac{2}{9}(3z + 2)$

59. $8.0413z - 9.7268 < 1.7251z - 0.25250$

60. $3.2579 + 5.0824k > 0.76423k + 6.280619$

Polynomials

A **polynomial** is an expression of the form

$$a_n x^n + a_{n-1} x^{n-1} + \cdots + a_1 x + a_0,$$

where $a_0, a_1, a_2, \ldots, a_n$ are real numbers, n is a natural number, and $a_n \neq 0$. Examples of polynomials include

$$5x^4 + 2x^3 + 6x, \qquad 8m^3 + 9m^2 - 6m + 3, \qquad 10p, \qquad \text{and} \qquad -9.$$

When we write $9p^4$, the entire expression is called a **term,** the number 9 is called the **coefficient,** p is the **variable,** and 4 is the **exponent.** The expression p^4 means $p \cdot p \cdot p \cdot p$, while p^2 means $p \cdot p$, and so on.

Polynomials can be added or subtracted by using the distributive property. For example,

$$12y^4 + 6y^4 = (12 + 6)y^4 = 18y^4$$

and

$$-2m^2 + 8m^2 = (-2 + 8)m^2 = 6m^2.$$

The polynomial $8y^4 + 2y^5$ cannot be further simplified.

Two terms having the same variable and the same exponent are called **like terms;** other terms are called **unlike terms.** Only like terms may be added or subtracted. To subtract polynomials, use the fact that $-(a + b) = -a - b$. The next example shows how to add and subtract polynomials.

EXAMPLE

Add or subtract as indicated.

(a) $(8x^3 - 4x^2 + 6x) + (3x^3 + 5x^2 - 9x + 8)$

Combine like terms.

$$(8x^3 - 4x^2 + 6x) + (3x^3 + 5x^2 - 9x + 8)$$
$$= (8x^3 + 3x^3) + (-4x^2 + 5x^2) + (6x - 9x) + 8$$
$$= 11x^3 + x^2 - 3x + 8$$

(b) $(-4x^4 + 6x^3 - 9x^2 - 12) + (-3x^3 + 8x^2 - 11x + 7)$
$$= -4x^4 + 3x^3 - x^2 - 11x - 5$$

(c) $(2x^2 - 11x + 8) - (7x^2 - 6x + 2)$
$$= (2x^2 - 11x + 8) + (-7x^2 + 6x - 2)$$
$$= -5x^2 - 5x + 6 \quad \blacksquare$$

The distributive property is also used when multiplying polynomials. For example, the product of $8x$ and $6x - 4$ is found as follows.

$$8x(6x - 4) = 8x(6x) - 8x(4) = 48x^2 - 32x$$

The product of $3p - 2$ and $5p + 1$ can be found by using the distributive property twice:

$$(3p - 2)(5p + 1) = (3p - 2)(5p) + (3p - 2)(1)$$
$$= 3p(5p) - 2(5p) + 3p(1) - 2(1)$$
$$= 15p^2 - 10p + 3p - 2$$
$$= 15p^2 - 7p - 2.$$

EXERCISES

Perform each operation.

61. $(2x^2 - 6x + 11) + (-3x^2 + 7x - 2)$

62. $(-4y^2 - 3y + 8) - (2y^2 - 6y - 2)$

63. $-3(4q^2 - 3q + 2) + 2(-q^2 + q - 4)$

64. $2(3r^2 + 4r + 2) - 3(-r^2 + 4r - 5)$

65. $(.613x^2 - 4.215x + 0.892) - .47(2x^2 - 3x + 5)$

66. $.83(5r^2 - 2r + 7) - (7.12r^2 + 6.423r - 2)$

67. $-9m(2m^2 + 3m - 1)$

68. $(6k - 1)(2k - 3)$

69. $(5r - 3s)(5r + 4s)$

70. $(9k + q)(2k - q)$

71. $\left(\frac{2}{5}y + \frac{1}{8}z\right)\left(\frac{3}{5}y + \frac{1}{2}z\right)$

72. $\left(\frac{3}{4}r - \frac{2}{3}s\right)\left(\frac{5}{4}r + \frac{1}{3}s\right)$

73. $(.012x - .17)(.3x + .54)$

74. $(6.2m - 3.4)(.7m + 1.3)$

75. $(3p - 1)(9p^2 + 3p + 1)$

76. $(2p - 1)(3p^2 - 4p + 5)$

77. $(2m + 1)(4m^2 - 2m + 1)$

78. $(k + 2)(12k^3 - 3k^2 + k + 1)$

79. $(m - n + k)(m + 2n - 3k)$

80. $(r - 3s + t)(2r - s + t)$

Factoring

Multiplication of polynomials can be performed using the distributive property. The reverse process, where a polynomial is written as a product of other polynomials, is called **factoring.** For example, one way to factor the number 18 is to write it as the product $9 \cdot 2$. When 18 is written as $9 \cdot 2$, both 9 and 2 are called **factors** of 18. It is true that $18 = 36 \cdot 1/2$, but we do not call 36 and 1/2 factors of 18; we restrict our attention only to integer factors. Integer factors of 18 are

$$2, 9; \quad -2, -9; \quad 6, 3; \quad -6, -3; \quad 18, 1; \quad -18, -1.$$

To factor the algebraic expression $15m + 45$, start with the two terms, $15m$ and 45. Each of these terms can be divided by 15. In fact, $15m = 15 \cdot m$ and $45 = 15 \cdot 3$. We then use the distributive property to write

$$15m + 45 = 15 \cdot m + 15 \cdot 3 = 15(m + 3).$$

Both 15 and $m + 3$ are factors of $15m + 45$. Since 15 divides into all terms of $15m + 45$ (and is the largest number that will do so), 15 is the **greatest common factor** for the polynomial $15m + 45$. The process of writing $15m + 45$ as $15(m + 3)$ is called **factoring out** the greatest common factor.

EXAMPLE

Factor out the greatest common factor.

(a) $12p - 18q$

Both $12p$ and $18q$ are divisible by 6. Therefore,

$$12p - 18q = 6 \cdot 2p - 6 \cdot 3q = 6(2p - 3q).$$

(b) $8x^3 - 9x^2 + 15x$

Each of these terms is divisible by x.

$$8x^3 - 9x^2 + 15x = (8x^2) \cdot x - (9x) \cdot x + 15 \cdot x$$
$$= x(8x^2 - 9x + 15) \quad \blacksquare$$

A polynomial may not have a greatest common factor (other than 1), and yet may still be factorable. For example, the polynomial $x^2 + 5x + 6$ can be factored as $(x + 2)(x + 3)$. To see that this is correct, find the product $(x + 2)(x + 3)$; you should get $x^2 + 5x + 6$.

If we are given a polynomial such as $x^2 + 5x + 6$, how do we know that it is the product $(x + 2)(x + 3)$? There are two different ways to factor a polynomial of three terms such as $x^2 + 5x + 6$, depending on whether the coefficient of x^2 is 1, or a number other than 1. If the coefficient is 1, proceed as shown in the following example.

EXAMPLE

Factor $y^2 + 8y + 15$.

Since the coefficient of y^2 is 1, factor by finding two numbers whose *product* is 15, and whose *sum* is 8. Use trial and error to find these numbers. Begin by listing all pairs of integers having a product of 15. As you do this, also form the sum of the numbers.

Products	Sums
$15 \cdot 1 = 15$	$15 + 1 = 16$
$5 \cdot 3 = 15$	$5 + 3 = 8$
$(-1) \cdot (-15) = 15$	$-1 + (-15) = -16$
$(-5) \cdot (-3) = 15$	$-5 + (-3) = -8$

The numbers 3 and 5 have a product of 15 and a sum of 8. Thus, $y^2 + 8y + 15$ factors as

$$y^2 + 8y + 15 = (y + 3)(y + 5).$$

We can also write the answer as $(y + 5)(y + 3)$. $\quad \blacksquare$

If the coefficient of the squared term is *not* 1, work as shown in the next example.

EXAMPLE

Factor $2x^2 + 9xy - 5y^2$.

The factors of $2x^2$ are $2x$ and x; the possible factors of $-5y^2$ are $-5y$ and y, or $5y$ and $-y$. Try various combinations of these factors until one works (if, indeed, any work). Let's try the product $(2x + 5y)(x - y)$. Multiply:

$$(2x + 5y)(x - y) = (2x + 5y)(x) - (2x + 5y)(y)$$
$$= 2x^2 + 5xy - 2xy - 5y^2$$
$$= 2x^2 + 3xy - 5y^2.$$

This product is not the one we want. So try another combination:

$$(2x - y)(x + 5y) = (2x - y)(x) + (2x - y)(5y)$$
$$= 2x^2 - xy + 10xy - 5y^2$$
$$= 2x^2 + 9xy - 5y^2.$$

This combination led to the correct polynomial; thus

$$2x^2 + 9xy - 5y^2 = (2x - y)(x + 5y). \quad \blacksquare$$

Four special types of factorizations occur so often that we shall list them for future reference.

Special		
Factorizations	$x^2 - y^2 = (x + y)(x - y)$	**Difference of two squares**
	$x^2 + 2xy + y^2 = (x + y)^2$	**Perfect square**
	$x^3 - y^3 = (x - y)(x^2 + xy + y^2)$	**Difference of two cubes**
	$x^3 + y^3 = (x + y)(x^2 - xy + y^2)$	**Sum of two cubes**

EXAMPLE

Factor each of the following.

(a) $64p^2 - 49q^2 = (8p)^2 - (7q)^2 = (8p + 7q)(8p - 7q)$

(b) $x^2 + 36$ cannot be factored.

(c) $x^2 + 12x + 36 = (x + 6)^2$

(d) $9y^2 - 24yz + 16z^2 = (3y - 4z)^2$

(e) $y^3 - 8 = y^3 - 2^3 = (y - 2)(y^2 + 2y + 4)$

(f) $m^3 + 125 = m^3 + 5^3 = (m + 5)(m^2 - 5m + 25)$

(g) $8k^3 - 27z^3 = (2k)^3 - (3z)^3 = (2k - 3z)(4k^2 + 6kz + 9z^2) \quad \blacksquare$

EXERCISES

Factor each of the following. If a polynomial cannot be factored, write "cannot be factored." Factor out the greatest common factor as necessary.

81. $8a^3 - 16a^2 + 24a$

82. $3y^3 + 24y^2 + 9y$

83. $25p^4 - 20p^3q + 100p^2q^2$

84. $60m^4 - 120m^3n + 50m^2n^2$

85. $m^2 + 9m + 14$

86. $x^2 + 4x - 5$

87. $z^2 + 9z + 20$

88. $b^2 - 8b + 7$

89. $a^2 - 6ab + 5b^2$

90. $s^2 + 2st - 35t^2$

91. $y^2 - 4yz - 21z^2$

92. $6a^2 - 48a - 120$

93. $3m^3 + 12m^2 + 9m$

94. $2x^2 - 5x - 3$

95. $3a^2 + 10a + 7$

96. $2a^2 - 17a + 30$

97. $15y^2 + y - 2$

98. $21m^2 + 13mn + 2n^2$

99. $24a^4 + 10a^3b - 4a^2b^2$

100. $32z^5 - 20z^4a - 12z^3a^2$

101. $x^2 - 64$

102. $9m^2 - 25$

103. $121a^2 - 100$

104. $9x^2 + 64$

105. $z^2 + 14zy + 49y^2$

106. $m^2 - 6mn + 9n^2$

107. $9p^2 - 24p + 16$

108. $a^3 - 216$

109. $8r^3 - 27s^3$

110. $64m^3 + 125$

Quadratic Equations

An equation of the form $ax + b = c$ is a linear equation; an equation with 2 as the highest exponent is a **quadratic equation.**

Quadratic Equation

> If a, b, and c are real numbers with $a \neq 0$, then
> $$ax^2 + bx + c = 0$$
> is a **quadratic equation.**

(Why is the restriction $a \neq 0$ necessary?) A quadratic equation written in the form $ax^2 + bx + c = 0$ is said to be in **standard form.**

The simplest way to solve a quadratic equation, but a way that is not always easily applied, is factoring. This method depends on the **zero-factor property.**

Zero-factor Property

> If a and b are real numbers, with $ab = 0$, then
> $$a = 0 \text{ or } b = 0 \text{ or both.}$$

EXAMPLE

Solve $6r^2 + 7r = 3$.

First write the equation in standard form.

$$6r^2 + 7r - 3 = 0$$

Now factor $6r^2 + 7r - 3$ to get

$$(3r - 1)(2r + 3) = 0.$$

By the zero-factor property, the product $(3r - 1)(2r + 3)$ can equal 0 only if

$$3r - 1 = 0 \quad \text{or} \quad 2r + 3 = 0.$$

Solve each of these equations separately to find that the solutions of the original equation are 1/3 and $-3/2$. Check these solutions by substituting them back in the original equation. ■

If a quadratic equation cannot be solved easily by factoring, use the *quadratic formula* (the derivation of which is given in most algebra books).

Quadratic Formula

The solutions of the quadratic equation $ax^2 + bx + c = 0$, where $a \neq 0$, are given by
$$x = \frac{-b \pm \sqrt{b^2 - 4ac}}{2a}.$$

EXAMPLE

Solve $x^2 - 4x - 5 = 0$ by the quadratic formula.

The equation is already in standard form (it has 0 alone on one side of the equals sign) so that we can identify the letters a, b, and c of the quadratic formula. The coefficient of the squared term gives the value of a; here $a = 1$. Also, $b = -4$ and $c = -5$. (Be careful to get the correct signs.) Substitute these values into the quadratic formula.

$$x = \frac{-(-4) \pm \sqrt{(-4)^2 - 4(1)(-5)}}{2(1)} \qquad \text{Let } a = 1, \ b = -4, \ c = -5$$

$$= \frac{4 \pm \sqrt{16 + 20}}{2} \qquad (-4)^2 = (-4)(-4) = 16$$

$$x = \frac{4 \pm 6}{2} \qquad \sqrt{16 + 20} = \sqrt{36} = 6$$

The $\pm$ sign represents the two solutions of the equation. To find all of the solutions, first use $+$ and then use $-$.

$$x = \frac{4 + 6}{2} = \frac{10}{2} = 5 \qquad \text{or} \qquad x = \frac{4 - 6}{2} = \frac{-2}{2} = -1$$

The two solutions are 5 and -1. ▪

EXAMPLE

Solve $x^2 + 1 = 4x$.

First add $-4x$ to both sides, to get 0 alone on the right side.

$$x^2 - 4x + 1 = 0$$

Now identify the letters a, b, and c. Here $a = 1$, $b = -4$, and $c = 1$. Substitute these numbers into the quadratic formula.

$$x = \frac{-(-4) \pm \sqrt{(-4)^2 - 4(1)(1)}}{2(1)}$$

$$= \frac{4 \pm \sqrt{16 - 4}}{2}$$

$$= \frac{4 \pm \sqrt{12}}{2}$$

To simplify the solutions, write $\sqrt{12}$ as $\sqrt{4 \cdot 3} = \sqrt{4} \cdot \sqrt{3} = 2\sqrt{3}$. Substituting $2\sqrt{3}$ for $\sqrt{12}$ gives

$$x = \frac{4 \pm 2\sqrt{3}}{2}$$

$$= \frac{2(2 \pm \sqrt{3})}{2} \qquad \text{Factor } 4 \pm 2\sqrt{3}$$

$$x = 2 \pm \sqrt{3}.$$

The two solutions are $2 + \sqrt{3}$ and $2 - \sqrt{3}$.

The exact values of the solutions are $2 + \sqrt{3}$ and $2 - \sqrt{3}$. Decimal approximations of these solutions (to the nearest thousandth) are

$$2 + \sqrt{3} \approx 2 + 1.732 = 3.732$$

and

$$2 - \sqrt{3} \approx 2 - 1.732 = .268. \quad \blacksquare$$

EXERCISES

In Exercises 111–122, solve each equation by factoring.

111. $(y - 5)(y + 4) = 0$ **112.** $x^2 + 5x + 6 = 0$ **113.** $r^2 - 5r - 6 = 0$

114. $a^2 + 5a = 24$ **115.** $x^2 = 3 + 2x$ **116.** $m^2 + 16 = 8m$

117. $2k^2 - k = 10$ **118.** $6x^2 - 5x = 4$ **119.** $m(m - 7) = -10$

120. $9x^2 - 16 = 0$ **121.** $z(2z + 7) = 4$ **122.** $12y^2 - 48y = 0$

In Exercises 123–134, use the quadratic formula to solve each equation. If the solutions involve square roots, give both the exact and approximate solutions.

123. $3x^2 - 5x + 1 = 0$ **124.** $2m^2 = m + 4$ **125.** $p^2 + p - 1 = 0$

126. $k^2 - 10k = -20$ **127.** $2x^2 + 12x + 5 = 0$ **128.** $2r^2 - 7r + 5 = 0$

129. $6k^2 - 11k + 4 = 0$ **130.** $x^2 + 3x = 10$ **131.** $2x^2 = 3x + 5$

132. $2x^2 - 7x + 30 = 0$ **133.** $3k^2 + k = 6$ **134.** $5m^2 + 5m = 0$

Quadratic Inequalities

A **quadratic inequality** is an inequality of the form $ax^2 + bx + c > 0$ (or $<$, or $\leq$, or $\geq$). The highest exponent is always 2. Examples of quadratic inequalities include

$$x^2 - x - 12 < 0, \qquad 3y^2 + 2y \geq 0, \qquad \text{and} \qquad m^2 \leq 4.$$

A method of solving quadratic inequalities is shown in the next few examples.

EXAMPLE

Solve the quadratic inequality $x^2 - x - 12 < 0$.

Since $x^2 - x - 12 = (x - 4)(x + 3)$, the given inequality is really the same as

$$(x - 4)(x + 3) < 0.$$

We want the product of $x - 4$ and $x + 3$ to be negative. The product will be negative if the two factors $x - 4$ and $x + 3$ have opposite signs. The factor $x - 4$ is positive when $x - 4 > 0$, or $x > 4$. Thus, $x - 4$ is negative if $x < 4$. In the same way, $x + 3$ is positive when $x > -3$ and negative when $x < -3$. This information is shown on the *sign graph* of Figure 4.

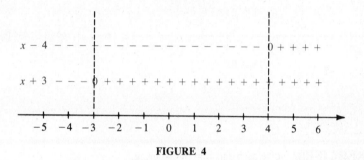

FIGURE 4

We said above that the product $(x - 4)(x + 3)$ will be negative when $x - 4$ and $x + 3$ have opposite signs. From the sign graph of Figure 4, these expressions have opposite signs whenever x is between -3 and 4. The solution is thus given by $-3 < x < 4$. A graph of this solution is shown in Figure 5. ■

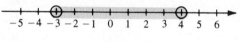

FIGURE 5

EXAMPLE

Solve the quadratic inequality $r^2 + 3r \geq 4$.

First rewrite the inequality so that one side is 0.

$$r^2 + 3r \geq 4$$
$$r^2 + 3r - 4 \geq 0 \qquad \textbf{Add } -4 \textbf{ to both sides}$$

Factor $r^2 + 3r - 4$ as $(r + 4)(r - 1)$. The factor $r + 4$ is positive when $r > -4$ and negative when $r < -4$. Also, the factor $r - 1$ is positive when $r > 1$ and negative when $r < 1$. Use this information to produce the sign graph of Figure 6. The product $(r + 4)(r - 1)$ will be positive when $r + 4$ and $r - 1$ have the same signs, either both positive or both negative. From Figure 6 the solution is seen to include those numbers less than or equal to -4, together with those numbers greater than or equal to 1. This solution is written

$$r \leq -4 \quad \text{or} \quad r \geq 1.$$

A graph of the solution is given in Figure 7. ■

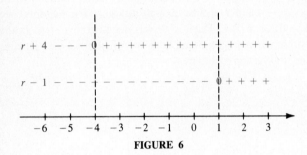

FIGURE 6

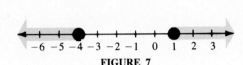

FIGURE 7

EXERCISES

Solve each of the following quadratic inequalities. Graph each solution.

135. $(m + 2)(m - 4) < 0$

136. $(t + 6)(t - 1) \geq 0$

137. $y^2 - 3y + 2 < 0$

138. $2k^2 + 7k - 4 > 0$

139. $q^2 - 7q + 6 \leq 0$

140. $2k^2 - 7k - 15 \leq 0$

141. $6m^2 + m > 1$

142. $10r^2 + r \leq 2$

143. $2y^2 + 5y \leq 3$

144. $3a^2 + a > 10$

145. $x^2 \leq 25$

146. $p^2 - 16p > 0$

Rational Expressions

Many algebraic fractions are **rational expressions,** which are quotients of polynomials with nonzero denominators. Examples include

$$\frac{8}{x - 1}, \qquad \frac{3x^2 + 4x}{5x - 6}, \qquad \text{and} \qquad \frac{2 + \dfrac{1}{y}}{y} = \frac{2y + 1}{y^2}.$$

Methods for working with rational expressions are summarized in the following box.

Properties of

Rational

Expressions

For all mathematical expressions P, $Q \neq 0$, R, and $S \neq 0$,

1. $\dfrac{P}{Q} = \dfrac{PS}{QS}$ **Fundamental property**

2. $\dfrac{P}{Q} \cdot \dfrac{R}{S} = \dfrac{PR}{QS}$ **Multiplication**

3. $\dfrac{P}{Q} + \dfrac{R}{Q} = \dfrac{P + R}{Q}$ **Addition**

4. $\dfrac{P}{Q} - \dfrac{R}{Q} = \dfrac{P - R}{Q}$ **Subtraction**

5. $\dfrac{P}{Q} \div \dfrac{R}{S} = \dfrac{P}{Q} \cdot \dfrac{S}{R}$, $R \neq 0$.   **Division**

EXAMPLE

Write each rational expression in lowest terms.

(a) $\dfrac{8x + 16}{4} = \dfrac{8(x + 2)}{4} = \dfrac{4 \cdot 2(x + 2)}{4} = 2(x + 2)$

Here we first factored $8x + 16$. The answer could also be written as $2x + 4$, if desired.

(b) $\dfrac{k^2 + 7k + 12}{k^2 + 2k - 3} = \dfrac{(k + 4)(k + 3)}{(k - 1)(k + 3)} = \dfrac{k + 4}{k - 1}$

The answer cannot be further reduced. ■

EXAMPLE

Perform each operation.

(a) $\dfrac{3y + 9}{6} \cdot \dfrac{18}{5y + 15}$

Factor where possible, then multiply numerators and denominators and reduce to lowest terms.

$$\dfrac{3y + 9}{6} \cdot \dfrac{18}{5y + 15} = \dfrac{3(y + 3)}{6} \cdot \dfrac{18}{5(y + 3)} = \dfrac{3 \cdot 18(y + 3)}{6 \cdot 5(y + 3)}$$

$$= \dfrac{3 \cdot 6 \cdot 3(y + 3)}{6 \cdot 5(y + 3)} = \dfrac{3 \cdot 3}{5} = \dfrac{9}{5}$$

(b) $\dfrac{m^2 + 5m + 6}{m + 3} \cdot \dfrac{m}{m^2 + 3m + 2} = \dfrac{(m + 2)(m + 3)}{m + 3} \cdot \dfrac{m}{(m + 2)(m + 1)}$

$$= \dfrac{m(m + 2)(m + 3)}{(m + 3)(m + 2)(m + 1)} = \dfrac{m}{m + 1}$$

(c) $\dfrac{9p - 36}{12} \div \dfrac{5(p - 4)}{18}$

$= \dfrac{9p - 36}{12} \cdot \dfrac{18}{5(p - 4)}$ **Invert and multiply**

$= \dfrac{9(p - 4)}{12} \cdot \dfrac{18}{5(p - 4)} = \dfrac{27}{10}$

(d) $\dfrac{4}{5k} - \dfrac{11}{5k}$

As property (4) above shows, when two rational expressions have the same denominators, we subtract by subtracting the numerators.

$$\frac{4}{5k} - \frac{11}{5k} = \frac{4 - 11}{5k} = -\frac{7}{5k}$$

(e) $\dfrac{7}{p} + \dfrac{9}{2p} + \dfrac{1}{3p}$

These three denominators are different; we cannot add until the denominators are the same. A common denominator into which p, $2p$, and $3p$ all divide is $6p$. Rewrite each rational expression, using property (1), so the denominator is $6p$.

$$\frac{7}{p} + \frac{9}{2p} + \frac{1}{3p} = \frac{6 \cdot 7}{6 \cdot p} + \frac{3 \cdot 9}{3 \cdot 2p} + \frac{2 \cdot 1}{2 \cdot 3p}$$

$$= \frac{42}{6p} + \frac{27}{6p} + \frac{2}{6p}$$

$$= \frac{42 + 27 + 2}{6p} = \frac{71}{6p} \quad \blacksquare$$

EXERCISES

In Exercises 147–158, write each rational expression in lowest terms.

147. $\dfrac{7z^2}{14z}$

148. $\dfrac{25p^3}{10p^2}$

149. $\dfrac{8k + 16}{9k + 18}$

150. $\dfrac{3(t + 5)}{(t + 5)(t - 3)}$

151. $\dfrac{8x^2 + 16x}{4x^2}$

152. $\dfrac{36y^2 + 72y}{9y}$

153. $\dfrac{m^2 - 4m + 4}{m^2 + m - 6}$

154. $\dfrac{r^2 - r - 6}{r^2 + r - 12}$

155. $\dfrac{x^2 + 3x - 4}{x^2 - 1}$

156. $\dfrac{z^2 - 5z + 6}{z^2 - 4}$

157. $\dfrac{8m^2 + 6m - 9}{16m^2 - 9}$

158. $\dfrac{6y^2 + 11y + 4}{3y^2 + 7y + 4}$

In Exercises 159–182, perform the indicated operation.

159. $\dfrac{9k^2}{25} \cdot \dfrac{5}{3k}$

160. $\dfrac{15p^3}{9p^2} \div \dfrac{6p}{10p^2}$

161. $\dfrac{a + b}{2p} \cdot \dfrac{12}{5(a + b)}$

162. $\dfrac{a - 3}{16} \div \dfrac{a - 3}{32}$

163. $\dfrac{2k + 8}{6} \div \dfrac{3k + 12}{2}$

164. $\dfrac{9y - 18}{6y + 12} \cdot \dfrac{3y + 6}{15y - 30}$

165. $\dfrac{4a + 12}{2a - 10} \div \dfrac{a^2 - 9}{a^2 - a - 20}$

166. $\dfrac{6r - 18}{9r^2 + 6r - 24} \cdot \dfrac{12r - 16}{4r - 12}$

167. $\dfrac{k^2 - k - 6}{k^2 + k - 12} \cdot \dfrac{k^2 + 3k - 4}{k^2 + 2k - 3}$

168. $\dfrac{m^2 + 3m + 2}{m^2 + 5m + 4} \div \dfrac{m^2 + 5m + 6}{m^2 + 10m + 24}$

169. $\dfrac{2m^2 - 5m - 12}{m^2 - 10m + 24} \div \dfrac{4m^2 - 9}{m^2 - 9m + 18}$

170. $\dfrac{6n^2 - 5n - 6}{6n^2 + 5n - 6} \cdot \dfrac{12n^2 - 17n + 6}{12n^2 - n - 6}$

171. $\dfrac{a + 1}{2} - \dfrac{a - 1}{2}$

172. $\dfrac{3}{p} + \dfrac{1}{2}$

173. $\dfrac{2}{y} - \dfrac{1}{4}$

174. $\dfrac{1}{6m} + \dfrac{2}{5m} + \dfrac{4}{m}$

175. $\dfrac{1}{m - 1} + \dfrac{2}{m}$

176. $\dfrac{6}{r} - \dfrac{5}{r - 2}$

177. $\dfrac{8}{3(a - 1)} + \dfrac{2}{a - 1}$

178. $\dfrac{2}{5(k - 2)} + \dfrac{3}{4(k - 2)}$

179. $\dfrac{2}{x^2 - 2x - 3} + \dfrac{5}{x^2 - x - 6}$

180. $\dfrac{2y}{y^2 + 7y + 12} - \dfrac{y}{y^2 + 5y + 6}$

181. $\dfrac{3k}{2k^2 + 3k - 2} - \dfrac{2k}{2k^2 - 7k + 3}$

182. $\dfrac{4m}{3m^2 + 7m - 6} - \dfrac{m}{3m^2 - 14m + 8}$

Integer Exponents

Recall that $a^2 = a \cdot a$, while $a^3 = a \cdot a \cdot a$, and so on. In this section we give a more general meaning to the symbol a^n.

Definition of **Exponent**	If n is a natural number, then $$a^n = a \cdot a \cdot a \ldots a,$$ where a appears as a factor n times.

We call n the **exponent** in a^n, and a the **base.** This definition can be extended by defining a^n for *zero* and *negative* integer values of n.

Zero and Negative **Exponents**	If a is any nonzero real number, and if n is a positive integer, then $$a^0 = 1 \quad \text{and} \quad a^{-n} = \dfrac{1}{a^n}.$$

(The symbol 0^0 is meaningless.)

EXAMPLE

(a) $6^0 = 1$

(b) $(-9)^0 = 1$

(c) $3^{-2} = \dfrac{1}{3^2} = \dfrac{1}{9}$

(d) $9^{-1} = \dfrac{1}{9^1} = \dfrac{1}{9}$

(e) $\left(\dfrac{3}{4}\right)^{-1} = \dfrac{1}{\left(\frac{3}{4}\right)^1} = \dfrac{1}{\frac{3}{4}} = \dfrac{4}{3}$ ▪

By using the definitions of exponents given above, we could prove the following.

Properties of

Exponents

For any integers m and n, and any real numbers a and b for which the following exist,

1. $a^m \cdot a^n = a^{m+n}$ 4. $(ab)^m = a^m \cdot b^m$

2. $\dfrac{a^m}{a^n} = a^{m-n}$ 5. $\left(\dfrac{a}{b}\right)^m = \dfrac{a^m}{b^m}.$

3. $(a^m)^n = a^{mn}$

RATIONAL EXPRESSIONS ALSO

EXAMPLE

Use the properties of exponents to simplify each of the following. Leave answers with positive exponents. Assume all variables represent positive real numbers.

(a) $7^4 \cdot 7^6 = 7^{4+6} = 7^{10}$ Property (1)

(b) $\dfrac{9^{14}}{9^6} = 9^{14-6} = 9^8$ Property (2)

(c) $\dfrac{r^9}{r^{17}} = r^{9-17} = r^{-8} = \dfrac{1}{r^8}$ Property (2)

(d) $(2m^3)^4 = 2^4 \cdot (m^3)^4 = 16m^{12}$ Properties (3) and (4)

(e) $(3x)^4 = 3^4 \cdot x^4$ Property (4)

(f) $\left(\dfrac{9}{7}\right)^6 = \dfrac{9^6}{7^6}$ Property (5)

(g) $\dfrac{2^{-3} \cdot 2^5}{2^4 \cdot 2^{-7}} = \dfrac{2^2}{2^{-3}} = 2^{2-(-3)} = 2^5$

(h) $2^{-1} + 3^{-1} = \dfrac{1}{2} + \dfrac{1}{3} = \dfrac{5}{6}$ ▪

EXERCISES

Evaluate the expressions in Exercises 183–198. Write all answers without exponents.

183. 8^{-2} **184.** 3^{-4} **185.** 6^{-3} **186.** 5^0

187. $(-12)^0$ **188.** $2^{-1} + 4^{-1}$ **189.** -2^{-4} $= -\frac{1}{2^4} = \frac{1}{16}$ **190.** $(-2)^{-4}$

191. $-(-3)^{-2}$ **192.** $-(-3^{-2})$ **193.** $\left(\dfrac{5}{8}\right)^2$ **194.** $\left(\dfrac{6}{7}\right)^3$

195. $\left(\dfrac{1}{2}\right)^{-3}$ **196.** $\left(\dfrac{1}{5}\right)^{-3}$ **197.** $\left(\dfrac{2}{7}\right)^{-2}$ **198.** $\left(\dfrac{4}{3}\right)^{-3}$

Simplify the expressions in Exercises 199–214. Assume all variables represent positive real numbers. Write answers with only positive exponents.

199. $\dfrac{7^5}{7^9}$ **200.** $\dfrac{3^{-4}}{3^2}$ **201.** $\dfrac{2^{-5}}{2^{-2}}$ **202.** $\dfrac{6^{-1}}{6}$

203. $4^{-3} \cdot 4^6$ **204.** $\dfrac{8^9 \cdot 8^{-7}}{8^{-3}}$ **205.** $\dfrac{10^8 \cdot 10^{-10}}{10^4 \cdot 10^2}$ **206.** $\left(\dfrac{5^{-6} \cdot 5^3}{5^{-2}}\right)^{-1}$

207. $\dfrac{x^4 \cdot x^3}{x^5}$ **208.** $\dfrac{y^9 \cdot y^7}{y^{13}}$ **209.** $\dfrac{(4k^{-1})^2}{2k^{-5}}$ **210.** $\dfrac{(3z^2)^{-1}}{z^5}$

211. $\dfrac{2^{-1}x^3y^{-3}}{xy^{-2}}$ **212.** $\dfrac{5^{-2}m^2y^{-2}}{5^2 m^{-1}y^{-2}}$ **213.** $\left(\dfrac{a^{-1}}{b^2}\right)^{-3}$ **214.** $\left(\dfrac{2c^2}{d^3}\right)^{-2}$

Evaluate each expression in Exercises 215–220, assuming that $a = 2$ and $b = -3$.

215. $a^{-1} + b^{-1}$ **216.** $b^{-2} - a$

217. $\dfrac{2b^{-1} - 3a^{-1}}{a + b^2}$ **218.** $\dfrac{3a^2 - b^2}{b^{-3} + 2a^{-1}}$

219. $\left(\dfrac{a}{3}\right)^{-1} + \left(\dfrac{b}{2}\right)^{-2}$ **220.** $\left(\dfrac{2b}{5}\right)^2 - 3\left(\dfrac{a^{-1}}{4}\right)$

Roots

We have discussed and given meaning to expressions of the form a^m for all nonzero real numbers a and all *integer* values of m, both positive and negative. Now we define a^m for *rational* values of m. We first look at an expression of the form $a^{1/n}$, where n is a positive integer. We want any meaning that we assign to $a^{1/n}$ to be consistent with the properties given above. For example, we know that for any real number a, and integers m and n, $(a^m)^n = a^{mn}$. If this property is to hold for the expression $a^{1/n}$, we must have

$$(a^{1/n})^n = a^{(1/n)n} = a^1 = a,$$

or $$(a^{1/n})^n = a.$$

Thus, the nth power of $a^{1/n}$ must be a. For this reason, $a^{1/n}$ is an **nth root** of a. For example, $a^{1/2}$ denotes a second root, or **square root** of a, while $a^{1/3}$ is the third root, or **cube root,** of a.

EXAMPLE

(A calculator will be helpful here.)

(a) $121^{1/2} = 11$, since 11 is positive and $11^2 = 121$

(b) $625^{1/4} = 5$, since $5^4 = 625$

(c) $256^{1/4} = 4$

(d) $64^{1/6} = 2$

(e) $27^{1/3} = 3$

(f) $(-32)^{1/5} = -2$

(g) $128^{1/7} = 2$

(h) $(-49)^{1/2}$ is not a real number. ■

We have now defined a^m for all integer values of m and all exponents of the form $a^{1/n}$, where n is a positive integer. To extend the definition of a^m to include all rational values of m, we make the following definition.

Definition of $a^{m/n}$

For all real numbers a for which the indicated roots exist, and for any rational number m/n,

$$a^{m/n} = (a^{1/n})^m.$$

EXAMPLE

(a) $27^{2/3} = (27^{1/3})^2 = 3^2 = 9$

(b) $32^{2/5} = (32^{1/5})^2 = 2^2 = 4$

(c) $64^{4/3} = (64^{1/3})^4 = 4^4 = 256$

(d) $25^{3/2} = (25^{1/2})^3 = 5^3 = 125$ ■

All the properties for integer exponents given above also apply to rational exponents, as long as we restrict the base to positive real numbers.

EXAMPLE

(a) $\dfrac{27^{1/3} \cdot 27^{5/3}}{27^3} = \dfrac{27^{1/3+5/3}}{27^3} = \dfrac{27^2}{27^3} = 27^{2-3} = 27^{-1} = \dfrac{1}{27}$

(b) $m^{2/3}(m^{7/3} + 2m^{1/3}) = m^{2/3+7/3} + 2m^{2/3+1/3} = m^3 + 2m$ ■

EXERCISES

Write each number in Exercises 221–232 without exponents.

221. $81^{1/2}$ **222.** $27^{1/3}$ **223.** $8^{2/3}$ **224.** $1000^{2/3}$

225. $32^{2/5}$ **226.** $-125^{2/3}$ **227.** $\left(\dfrac{4}{9}\right)^{1/2}$ **228.** $\left(\dfrac{64}{27}\right)^{1/3}$

229. $16^{-5/4}$ **230.** $625^{-1/4}$ **231.** $\left(\dfrac{27}{64}\right)^{-1/3}$ **232.** $\left(\dfrac{121}{100}\right)^{-3/2}$

Simplify each expression in Exercises 233–250. Write all answers with only positive exponents. Assume all variables represent positive real numbers.

233. $2^{1/2} \cdot 2^{3/2}$ **234.** $27^{2/3} \cdot 27^{-1/3}$ **235.** $\dfrac{4^{2/3} \cdot 4^{5/3}}{4^{1/3}}$

236. $\dfrac{3^{-5/2} \cdot 3^{3/2}}{3^{7/2} \cdot 3^{-9/2}}$ **237.** $\dfrac{7^{-1/3} \cdot 7 r^{-3}}{7^{2/3} \cdot (r^{-2})^2}$ **238.** $\dfrac{12^{3/4} \cdot 12^{5/4} \cdot y^{-2}}{12^{-1} \cdot (y^{-3})^{-2}}$

239. $\dfrac{6 k^{-4} \cdot (3 k^{-1})^{-2}}{2^3 \cdot k^{1/2}}$ **240.** $\dfrac{8 p^{-3} \cdot (4 p^2)^{-2}}{p^{-5}}$ **241.** $\dfrac{a^{4/3} \cdot b^{1/2}}{a^{2/3} \cdot b^{-3/2}}$

242. $\dfrac{x^{1/3} \cdot y^{2/3} \cdot z^{1/4}}{x^{5/3} \cdot y^{-1/3} \cdot z^{3/4}}$ **243.** $\dfrac{k^{-3/5} \cdot h^{-1/3} \cdot t^{2/5}}{k^{-1/5} \cdot h^{-2/3} \cdot t^{1/5}}$ **244.** $\dfrac{m^{7/3} \cdot n^{-2/5} \cdot p^{3/8}}{m^{-2/3} \cdot n^{3/5} \cdot p^{-5/8}}$

245. $\dfrac{k^{3/2} \cdot k^{-1/2}}{k^{1/4} \cdot k^{3/4}}$ **246.** $\dfrac{m^{2/5} \cdot m^{3/5} \cdot m^{-4/5}}{m^{1/5} \cdot m^{-6/5}}$ **247.** $\dfrac{x^{-2/3} \cdot x^{4/3}}{x^{1/2} \cdot x^{-3/4}}$

248. $\dfrac{-4 a^{1/2} \cdot a^{2/3}}{a^{-5/6}}$ **249.** $\dfrac{8 y^{2/3} y^{-1}}{2^{-1} y^{3/4} \cdot y^{-1/6}}$ **250.** $\dfrac{9 \cdot k^{1/3} \cdot k^{-1/2} \cdot k^{-1/6}}{k^{-2/3}}$

Radicals

Above, we defined $a^{1/n}$ as the nth root of a, for appropriate values of a and n. An alternate notation for $a^{1/n}$ uses **radicals.**

Radicals	If n is an even natural number and $a > 0$, or n is an odd natural number, then $$a^{1/n} = \sqrt[n]{a}.$$

The symbol $\sqrt[n]{}$ is a **radical sign,** the number a is the **radicand,** and n is the **index** of the radical. The familiar symbol $\sqrt{a}$ is used instead of $\sqrt[2]{a}$.

EXAMPLE   (a) $\sqrt[4]{16} = 16^{1/4} = 2$

(b) $\sqrt[5]{-32} = -2$

(c) $\sqrt[3]{1000} = 10$

(d) $\sqrt[6]{\dfrac{64}{729}} = \dfrac{2}{3}$ ▩

With $a^{1/n}$ written as $\sqrt[n]{a}$, we can also write $a^{m/n}$ using radicals.

$$a^{m/n} = (\sqrt[n]{a})^m \qquad \text{or} \qquad a^{m/n} = \sqrt[n]{a^m}$$

Also, all the familiar laws of exponents can be written with radicals.

Properties of

Radicals

Let a and b be real numbers and m and n natural numbers such that $\sqrt[n]{a}$ and $\sqrt[n]{b}$ are real numbers. Then

1. $(\sqrt[n]{a})^n = a$

2. $\sqrt[n]{a^n} = \begin{cases} |a| & \text{if } n \text{ is even} \\ a & \text{if } n \text{ is odd} \end{cases}$

3. $\sqrt[n]{a} \cdot \sqrt[n]{b} = \sqrt[n]{ab}$

4. $\dfrac{\sqrt[n]{a}}{\sqrt[n]{b}} = \sqrt[n]{\dfrac{a}{b}} \qquad (b \neq 0)$

5. $\sqrt[m]{\sqrt[n]{a}} = \sqrt[mn]{a}.$

Property (3) can be used to simplify certain radicals. For example, since $48 = 16 \cdot 3$,

$$\sqrt{48} = \sqrt{16 \cdot 3} = \sqrt{16} \cdot \sqrt{3} = 4\sqrt{3}.$$

EXAMPLE

(a) $\sqrt{1000} = \sqrt{100 \cdot 10} = \sqrt{100} \cdot \sqrt{10} = 10\sqrt{10}$

(b) $\sqrt{128} = \sqrt{64 \cdot 2} = 8\sqrt{2}$

(c) $\sqrt{108} = 6\sqrt{3}$

(d) $\sqrt[3]{54} = \sqrt[3]{27 \cdot 2} = \sqrt[3]{27} \cdot \sqrt[3]{2} = 3\sqrt[3]{2}$

(e) $\sqrt{288m^5} = \sqrt{144 \cdot m^4 \cdot 2m} = 12m^2\sqrt{2m}$

(f) $2\sqrt{18} - 5\sqrt{32} = 2\sqrt{9 \cdot 2} - 5\sqrt{16 \cdot 2}$

$$= 2\sqrt{9} \cdot \sqrt{2} - 5\sqrt{16} \cdot \sqrt{2}$$

$$= 2(3)\sqrt{2} - 5(4)\sqrt{2} = -14\sqrt{2}$$ ▩

EXERCISES

Simplify in Exercise 251–272. Assume all variables represent positive real numbers.

251. $\sqrt[3]{125}$

252. $\sqrt[4]{1296}$

253. $\sqrt[5]{-3125}$

254. $\sqrt{50}$

255. $\sqrt{2000}$

256. $\sqrt{32y^5}$

257. $7\sqrt{2} - 8\sqrt{18} + 4\sqrt{72}$

258. $4\sqrt{3} - 5\sqrt{12} + 3\sqrt{75}$

259. $2\sqrt{5} - 3\sqrt{20} + 2\sqrt{45}$

260. $\sqrt{50} - 8\sqrt{8} + 4\sqrt{18}$

261. $6\sqrt{27} - 3\sqrt{12} + 5\sqrt{48}$

262. $3\sqrt{28} - 4\sqrt{63} + \sqrt{112}$

263. $3\sqrt[3]{16} - 4\sqrt[3]{2}$

264. $\sqrt[3]{2} - \sqrt[3]{16} + 2\sqrt[3]{54}$

265. $2\sqrt[3]{3} + 4\sqrt[3]{24} - \sqrt[3]{81}$

266. $\sqrt[3]{32} - 5\sqrt[3]{4} + 2\sqrt[3]{108}$

267. $\sqrt{2x^3y^2z^4}$

268. $\sqrt{98\,r^3s^4t^{10}}$

269. $\sqrt[3]{16z^5x^8y^4}$

270. $\sqrt[4]{x^8y^7z^{11}}$

271. $\sqrt{a^3b^5} - 2\sqrt{a^7b^3} + \sqrt{a^3b^9}$

272. $\sqrt{p^7q^3} - \sqrt{p^5q^9} + \sqrt{p^9q}$

Rationalizing the Denominator

The next example shows how to *rationalize* (remove all radicals from) the denominator in an expression containing radicals.

EXAMPLE

Simplify each of the following expressions by rationalizing the denominator.

(a) $\dfrac{4}{\sqrt{3}}$

To rationalize the denominator, multiply by $\sqrt{3}/\sqrt{3}$ (or 1) so that the denominator of the product is a rational number.

$$\frac{4}{\sqrt{3}} \cdot \frac{\sqrt{3}}{\sqrt{3}} = \frac{4\sqrt{3}}{3}$$

(b) $\dfrac{1}{1 - \sqrt{2}}$

The best approach here is to multiply both numerator and denominator by the number $1 + \sqrt{2}$. Doing so gives

$$\frac{1}{1 - \sqrt{2}} = \frac{1(1 + \sqrt{2})}{(1 - \sqrt{2})(1 + \sqrt{2})} = \frac{1 + \sqrt{2}}{1 - 2} = -1 - \sqrt{2}.$$

EXERCISES

Rationalize the denominator in Exercises 273–286. Assume all radicands represent positive real numbers.

273. $\dfrac{5}{\sqrt{7}}$

274. $\dfrac{-2}{\sqrt{3}}$

275. $\dfrac{-3}{\sqrt{12}}$

276. $\dfrac{4}{\sqrt{8}}$

277. $\dfrac{3}{1-\sqrt{5}}$

278. $\dfrac{5}{2-\sqrt{6}}$

279. $\dfrac{-2}{\sqrt{3}-\sqrt{2}}$

280. $\dfrac{1}{\sqrt{10}+\sqrt{3}}$

281. $\dfrac{1}{\sqrt{r}-\sqrt{3}}$

282. $\dfrac{5}{\sqrt{m}-\sqrt{5}}$

283. $\dfrac{y-5}{\sqrt{y}-\sqrt{5}}$

284. $\dfrac{z-11}{\sqrt{z}-\sqrt{11}}$

285. $\dfrac{\sqrt{x}+\sqrt{x+1}}{\sqrt{x}-\sqrt{x+1}}$

286. $\dfrac{\sqrt{p}+\sqrt{p^2-1}}{\sqrt{p}-\sqrt{p^2-1}}$

Rationalize the *numerator* in Exercises 287–292. Assume all radicands represent positive real numbers.

287. $\dfrac{1+\sqrt{2}}{2}$

288. $\dfrac{1-\sqrt{3}}{3}$

289. $\dfrac{\sqrt{x}}{1+\sqrt{x}}$

290. $\dfrac{\sqrt{p}}{1-\sqrt{p}}$

291. $\dfrac{\sqrt{x}+\sqrt{x+1}}{\sqrt{x}-\sqrt{x+1}}$

292. $\dfrac{\sqrt{p}+\sqrt{p^2-1}}{\sqrt{p}-\sqrt{p^2-1}}$

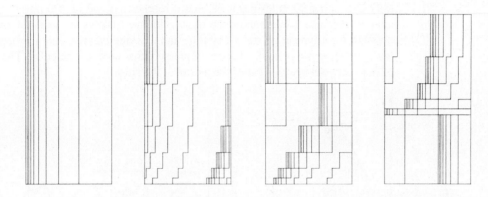

FUNCTIONS
AND GRAPHS

Karl Gerstner. Drawings from *The Golden-Sectioned Pillar*, alterable object, 1956/57.

The graph on the left in Figure 1 is from *Road and Track* magazine.* The graph shows the speed in miles per hour at time t in seconds for a Porsche 928 as it accelerates from rest. For example, the graph shows that 15 seconds after starting, the car is going 90 miles per hour, and it reaches a speed of 100 miles per hour after 19 seconds. The graph on the right in Figure 1 shows the variation in blood pressure for a typical person.† (Systolic and diastolic pressures are the upper and lower limits in the periodic changes in pressure that produce the pulse. The length of time between peaks is called the period of the pulse.)

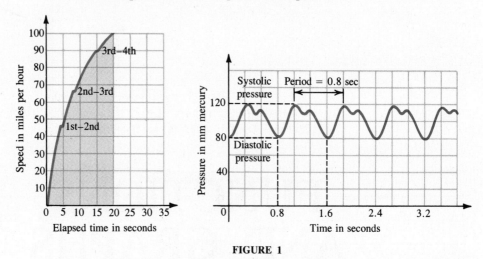

FIGURE 1

Both graphs of Figure 1 are graphs of **functions,** which are rules or procedures giving just *one value* of one of the variables from a given value of the other variable. Functions are useful in applications because only one value is produced: the car above is not going two different speeds after 10 seconds, and a person has only one blood pressure at a particular instant.

Functions are very useful in setting up **mathematical models,** mathematical descriptions of real-world situations. Constructing a mathematical model of a given situation requires a solid understanding of the situation to be modeled, along with a good knowledge of the possible mathematical ideas that can be used to construct the model. This chapter discusses a variety of functions useful in modeling.

1.1   Functions

Suppose X is the set of all students studying this book every Monday evening at the local pizza parlor. Let Y be the set of integers between 0 and 100. To each student in set X can be associated a number from Y which represents the score the student received on the last test. Typical associations between students in set X and scores in set Y are shown in Figure 2.

*From *Road & Track,* April and May 1978. Reprinted with permission.
†From *Calculus for the Life Sciences* by Rodolfo De Sapio. Copyright © 1976, 1978 by W. H. Freeman and Company. Reprinted by permission.

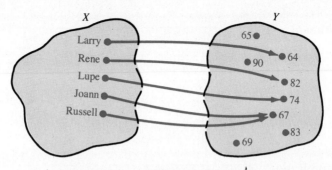

FIGURE 2

Another association might be set up between amounts of money deposited in a bank account, and the amounts of interest earned by the deposits in one year at 12% interest. Typical associations are shown in Figure 3.

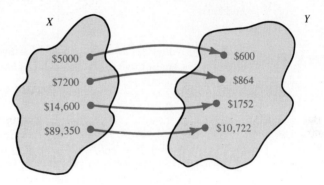

FIGURE 3

In this second example, a formula could be used to show how the numbers in set X are used to obtain the numbers in set Y. If x is a dollar amount from set X, then the interest earned, the corresponding number in set Y, can be found with the formula

$$y = .12 \times x,$$

or

$$y = .12x.$$

In this example, x, the amount of money deposited, is called the **independent variable,** while y is the **dependent variable.** (The amount of interest earned *depends* on the amount of money deposited.) When a specific number, say 2000, is substituted for x, then y takes on *one* specific value—in this case, $.12 \times 2000 = 240$. The variable y is said to be a *function* of x.

Definition of	A **function** is a rule which assigns to each element from one set exactly one
Function	element from another set.

In almost every use of functions in this book, the "rule" mentioned in the box will be given by an equation, such as the equation $y = .12x$ above.

Domain and Range	The set of all possible values for the independent variable in a function is called
	the **domain** of the function: the set of all possible values for the dependent
	variable is the **range.**

The domain and range may or may not be the same set. For example, in the function of Figure 2, the domain is a set of students, and the range is a set of integers. In the function of Figure 3, both the domain and range are a set of positive numbers.

EXAMPLE 1	Do the following represent functions? (Assume x represents the independent variable, an assumption we shall make throughout this book.) Give the domain and range of any functions.

(a) $y = -4x + 11$

For a given value of x, calculating $-4x + 11$ produces exactly one value of y. (For example, if $x = -7$, then $y = -4(-7) + 11 = 39$.) Since one value of the independent variable leads to exactly one value of the dependent variable, $y = -4x + 11$ is a function. Both x and y may take on any real number values at all, so both the domain and range here are the set of all real numbers.

(b) $y^2 = x$

Suppose $x = 36$. Then $y^2 = x$ becomes $y^2 = 36$, from which $y = 6$ or $y = -6$. Since one value of the independent variable can lead to two values of the dependent variable, $y^2 = x$ does not represent a function.   ▧

We shall make the following *agreement on domains*.

Agreement on	Unless otherwise stated, assume that the domain of all functions defined by an
Domains	equation is the largest set of real numbers that are meaningful replacements for
	the independent variable.

For example, suppose

$$y = \frac{-4x}{2x - 3}.$$

Any real number can be used for x except $x = 3/2$, which makes the denominator equal 0. By the agreement on domains, the domain of this function will be assumed to be the set of all real numbers except 3/2.

Function Notation The letters f, g, or h are frequently used to represent functions. For example, we might use f to name the function defined by $y = 5 - 3x$, or

$$f: \quad y = 5 - 3x.$$

For a given value of x in the domain of f, there is exactly one corresponding value of y in the range. To emphasize that y is obtained by applying function f to the element x, replace y with the symbol $f(x)$, read "f of x" or "f at x." Here x is the independent variable; either y or $f(x)$ represents the dependent variable.

Using $f(x)$ to replace y in the function $y = 5 - 3x$ gives

$$f(x) = 5 - 3x.$$

By choosing 2 as a value of x, $f(x)$ becomes $5 - 3 \cdot 2 = 5 - 6 = -1$, written

$$f(2) = -1.$$

In a similar manner,

$$f(-4) = 5 - 3(-4) = 17, \qquad f(0) = 5, \qquad f(-6) = 23,$$

and so on.

EXAMPLE 2

Let $g(x) = -x^2 + 4x - 5$. Find each of the following.

(a) $g(3)$

Replace x with 3.

$$g(3) = -3^2 + 4 \cdot 3 - 5 = -9 + 12 - 5 = -2$$

(b) $g(a)$

Replace x with a to get

$$g(a) = -a^2 + 4a - 5.$$

This replacement of one variable with another is important in later chapters.

(c) $g(x + h) = -(x + h)^2 + 4(x + h) - 5$

$$= -(x^2 + 2xh + h^2) + 4(x + h) - 5$$

$$= -x^2 - 2xh - h^2 + 4x + 4h - 5$$

(d) $g\left(\frac{2}{r}\right) = -\left(\frac{2}{r}\right)^2 + 4\left(\frac{2}{r}\right) - 5 = -\frac{4}{r^2} + \frac{8}{r} - 5$ ■

Interval Notation   When writing the domain of a function, we might refer to sets such as the set of all real numbers less than 4. This set can be written in **interval notation** as $(-\infty, 4)$. The symbol ∞ (the symbol for infinity) is not a real number—it shows that the interval includes *all* real numbers less than 4. Examples of other sets written in interval notation are shown in the following table. Square brackets are used when the given number is part of the interval. Whenever two real numbers a and b are used to write an interval, it is always assumed that $a < b$.

Type of Interval	*Interval*	*Interval Notation*	*Graph*
open interval	$a < x$	(a, ∞)	
	$a < x < b$	(a, b)	
	$x < b$	$(-\infty, b)$	
half-open interval	$a \le x$	$[a, \infty)$	
	$a < x \le b$	$(a, b]$	
	$a \le x < b$	$[a, b)$	
	$x \le b$	$(-\infty, b]$	
closed interval	$a \le x \le b$	$[a, b]$	

EXAMPLE 3

Find the domain and range for each of the following functions.

(a) $f(x) = x^2$

Any number may be squared, so the domain is the set of all real numbers. Since $x^2 \ge 0$ for every value of x, the range, written in interval notation, is $[0, \infty)$.

(b) $f(x) = \sqrt{6 - x}$

A square root can be found only for nonnegative numbers. The expression $6 - x$ takes on nonnegative values only when $6 - x \ge 0$, or $6 \ge x$. This makes the domain $(-\infty, 6]$. The range is $[0, \infty)$.

(c) $f(x) = \sqrt{2x^2 + 5x - 12}$.

The domain of f includes only those values of x satisfying $2x^2 + 5x - 12 \ge 0$.

Consult the algebra review for a discussion of the methods for solving a quadratic inequality. Using these methods and interval notation produces the domain

$$(-\infty, -4] \cup [3/2, \infty).* \quad \blacksquare$$

Graphs Any value of x in the domain of a function defined by $y = f(x)$ produces a value for y. This pair of numbers, one for x and one for y, can be written as an **ordered pair** (x, y) or $(x, f(x))$.

For example, let $y = f(x) = 8 + x^2$. If $x = 1$, then $f(1) = 8 + 1^2 = 9$, producing the ordered pair $(1, 9)$. (Always write the value of the independent variable first.) If $x = -3$, then $f(-3) = 8 + (-3)^2 = 17$, giving $(-3, 17)$. Other ordered pairs for this function include $(0, 8)$, $(-1, 9)$, $(2, 12)$, and so on.

It is often useful to draw a graph of the ordered pairs produced by a function using a **Cartesian coordinate system,** as shown in Figure 4. The horizontal number line, or **x-axis,** represents the elements from the domain of the function, while the vertical or **y-axis** represents the elements from the range. The point where the number lines cross is the zero point on both lines; this point is called the **origin.**

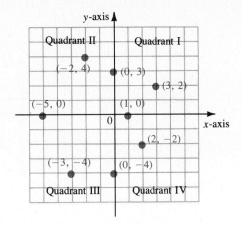

FIGURE 4

To plot points corresponding to ordered pairs, proceed as in the following example. Locate the point $(-2, 4)$ by starting at the origin and counting 2 units to the left on the horizontal axis, and 4 units upward parallel to the vertical axis. This point is shown in Figure 4, along with several other sample points. The number -2 is the **x-coordinate** and 4 is the **y-coordinate** of $(-2, 4)$.

The x-axis and y-axis divide the graph into four parts or **quadrants.** For example, Quadrant I includes all those points whose x- and y-coordinates are both positive. The quadrants are numbered as shown in Figure 4. The points of the axes themselves belong to no quadrant. The set of points corresponding to the ordered pairs of a function is called the **graph** of the function.

---

*The *union* of sets A and B, written $A \cup B$, is defined as the set of all elements in A or B or both.

EXAMPLE 4

Let $f(x) = 3 - 2x$, with domain $\{-2, -1, 0, 1, 2, 3, 4\}$. Graph the ordered pairs produced by this function.

If $x = -2$, then $f(-2) = 3 - 2(-2) = 7$, giving the ordered pair $(-2, 7)$. In a similar way, we can complete the following table.

x	-2	-1	0	1	2	3	4
y	7	5	3	1	-1	-3	-5
Ordered pair	$(-2, 7)$	$(-1, 5)$	$(0, 3)$	$(1, 1)$	$(2, -1)$	$(3, -3)$	$(4, -5)$

These ordered pairs are graphed in Figure 5. ■

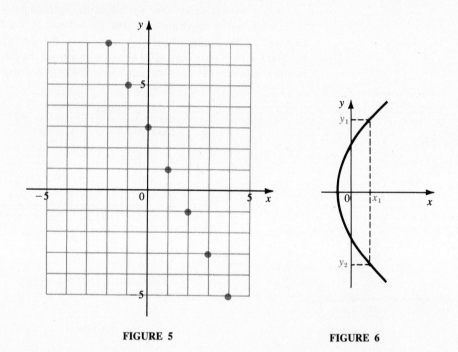

FIGURE 5   FIGURE 6

For a graph to be the graph of a function, each value of x from the domain must lead to exactly one value of y. In the graph of Figure 6, the domain value x_1 leads to *two* y-values, y_1 and y_2. Since the given x-value corresponds to two different y-values, this graph is not the graph of a function. This example suggests the **vertical line test** for the graph of a function.

Vertical Line Test

If a vertical line intersects a graph in more than one point, then the graph is not the graph of a function.

1.1 EXERCISES

List the ordered pairs obtained from the functions in Exercises 1–18 if the domain is $\{-2, -1, 0, 1, 2, 3\}$. Graph each set of ordered pairs. Give the range.

1. $y = x - 1$

2. $y = 2x + 3$

3. $y = -4x + 9$

4. $y = -6x + 12$

5. $y = -x - 5$

6. $y = -2x - 3$

7. $2x + y = 9$

8. $3x + y = 16$

9. $2y - x = 5$

10. $6x - y = -3$

11. $y = x(x + 1)$

12. $y = (x - 2)(x - 3)$

13. $y = x^2$

14. $y = -2x^2$

15. $y = \dfrac{1}{x + 3}$

16. $y = \dfrac{-2}{x + 4}$

17. $y = \dfrac{3x - 3}{x + 5}$

18. $y = \dfrac{2x + 1}{x + 3}$

Which graphs in Exercises 19–24 represent functions?

19.

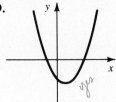

20.

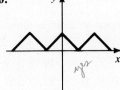

21.

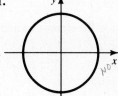

22.

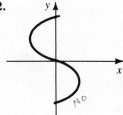

23.

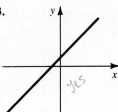

24.

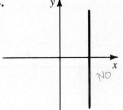

For each of the functions in Exercises 25–32, find **(a)** $f(4)$; **(b)** $f(-3)$; **(c)** $f(-1/2)$;
(d) $f(a)$; **(e)** $f(2/m)$.

25. $f(x) = 3x + 2$

26. $f(x) = 5x - 6$

27. $f(x) = -x^2 + 5x + 1$

28. $f(x) = -x^2 - x + 5$

29. $f(x) = \dfrac{2x + 1}{x - 2}$

30. $f(x) = \dfrac{3x - 5}{2x + 3}$

31. $f(x) = (x + 1)(x + 2)$

32. $f(x) = (x + 3)(x - 4)$

For each graph in Exercises 33–36, find the indicated function values: **(a)** $f(-2)$ **(b)** $f(0)$
(c) $f(1/2)$ **(d)** $f(4)$.

33.

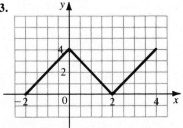

34.

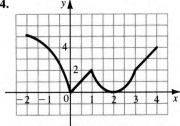

35.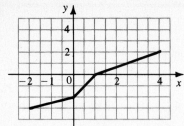

36.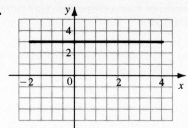

Let $f(x) = 6x - 2$ and $g(x) = x^2 - 2x + 5$. Find values for Exercises 37–46.

37. $f(m - 3)$

38. $f(2r - 1)$

39. $g(r + h)$

40. $g(z - p)$

41. $g\left(\dfrac{3}{q}\right)$

42. $g\left(-\dfrac{5}{z}\right)$

43. $f[g(2)]$

44. $g[f(-1)]$

45. $g\left[f\left(\dfrac{1}{2}\right)\right]$

46. $f\left[g\left(\dfrac{2}{3}\right)\right]$

Write each of the expressions in Exercises 47–54 in interval notation. Graph each interval.

47. $-1 < x < 4$

48. $x \geq -3$

49. $x < 0$

50. $8 > x > 3$

51. $2 > x \geq 1$

52. $-4 \geq x > -5$

53. $-9 > x$

54. $6 \leq x$

Using the variable x, write each of the intervals in Exercises 55–62 as an inequality.

55. $(-4, 3)$

56. $[2, 7)$

57. $(-\infty, -1]$

58. $(3, \infty)$

59.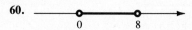
$\qquad\qquad -2 \qquad\quad 6$

60.
$\qquad\qquad\qquad\quad 0 \qquad\quad 8$

61.
$\qquad\qquad\qquad -4$

62.
$\qquad\qquad\qquad\quad 3$

Give the domain of the functions in Exercises 63–80.

63. $f(x) = 2x$

64. $f(x) = x + 2$

65. $f(x) = x^4$

66. $f(x) = (x - 2)^2$

67. $f(x) = \sqrt{16 - x^2}$

68. $f(x) = |x - 1|$

69. $f(x) = (x - 3)^{1/2}$

70. $f(x) = (3x + 5)^{1/2}$

71. $f(x) = \dfrac{2}{x^2 - 4}$

72. $f(x) = \dfrac{-8}{x^2 - 36}$

73. $f(x) = \sqrt{\dfrac{3}{x^2 + 25}}$

74. $f(x) = \sqrt{\dfrac{6}{x^2 + 121}}$

75. $f(x) = -\sqrt{\dfrac{2}{x^2 + 9}}$

76. $f(x) = -\sqrt{\dfrac{5}{x^2 + 36}}$

77. $f(x) = \sqrt{x^2 - 4x - 5}$

78. $f(x) = \sqrt{x^2 + 7x + 10}$

79. $f(x) = -\sqrt{6x^2 + 7x - 5}$

80. $f(x) = \sqrt{15x^2 + x - 2}$

Give both the domain and the range of the functions in Exercises 81–84.

81.

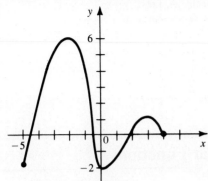

82.

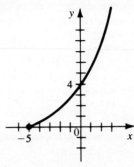

83.

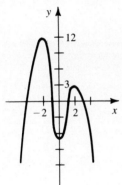

84.

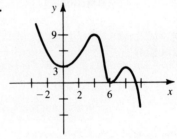

For each of the functions in Exercises 85–92 find: **(a)** $f(x + h)$; **(b)** $f(x + h) - f(x)$; **(c)** $\dfrac{f(x + h) - f(x)}{h}$.

85. $f(x) = x^2 - 4$

86. $f(x) = 8 - 3x^2$

87. $f(x) = 6x + 2$

88. $f(x) = 4x - 11$

89. $f(x) = 2x^3 + x^2$

90. $f(x) = -4x^3 - 8x$

91. $f(x) = \dfrac{1}{x}$

92. $f(x) = -\dfrac{1}{x^2}$

93. A chain-saw rental firm charges \$7 per day or fraction of a day to rent a saw, plus a fixed fee of \$4 for resharpening the blade. Let $S(x)$ represent the cost of renting a saw for x days. Find each of the following.

(a) $S\left(\dfrac{1}{2}\right)$ **(b)** $S(1)$

(c) $S\left(1\dfrac{1}{4}\right)$ **(d)** $S\left(3\dfrac{1}{2}\right)$

(e) $S(4)$ **(f)** $S\left(4\dfrac{1}{10}\right)$ **(g)** $S\left(4\dfrac{9}{10}\right)$

(h) A portion of the graph of $y = S(x)$ is shown here. Explain how the graph could be continued.

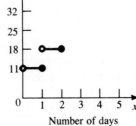

94. To rent a midsized car from one agency costs \$40 per day or fraction of a day. If you
pick up the car in Boston and drop it off in Utica, there is a fixed \$40 charge. Let
$C(x)$ represent the cost of renting the car for x days, taking it from Boston to Utica.
Find each of the following.

(a) $C\left(\dfrac{3}{4}\right)$ **(b)** $C\left(\dfrac{9}{10}\right)$ **(c)** $C(1)$ **(d)** $C\left(1\dfrac{5}{8}\right)$

(e) $C\left(2\dfrac{1}{9}\right)$ **(f)** Graph the function $y = C(x)$.

1.2   Linear Functions

Many practical situations can be described (at least approximately) with a **linear
function.**

Linear Function

> A function f is **linear** if
> $$f(x) = ax + b,$$
> for real numbers a and b.

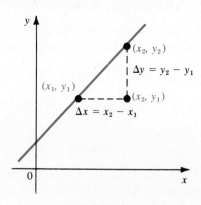

FIGURE 7

We shall see that, as the name implies, every linear function has a graph that
is a straight line. An important characteristic of a straight line is its *slope*, a numerical measure of the steepness of the line. To find this measure, start with the line
through the two distinct points (x_1, y_1) and (x_2, y_2), as shown in Figure 7. (Assume
$x_1 \neq x_2$.) The difference

$$x_2 - x_1$$

is called the *change in x* and written with the symbol Δx (read "delta x"), where Δ is the Greek letter delta. In the same way, the *change in y* is

$$\Delta y = y_2 - y_1.$$

The slope of a nonvertical line is defined as the quotient of the change in y and the change in x.

Definition of Slope

> The **slope** m of the line through the distinct points (x_1, y_1) and (x_2, y_2) is
>
> $$m = \frac{\Delta y}{\Delta x} = \frac{y_2 - y_1}{x_2 - x_1}.$$

Using similar triangles we can show that the slope does not depend on which pair of points on the line is chosen. That is, the same slope will be obtained for any two points on the line.

The slope of a line can be found only if the line is nonvertical, because $x_2 \neq x_1$ for a nonvertical line, so that the denominator $x_2 - x_1 \neq 0$. The slope of a vertical line is not defined.

EXAMPLE 1

Find the slope of the line through each of the following pairs of points.

(a) $(-4, 8), (2, -3)$

Let us choose $x_1 = -4$, $y_1 = 8$, $x_2 = 2$, and $y_2 = -3$. Then $\Delta y = -3 - 8 = -11$ and $\Delta x = 2 - (-4) = 6$. By definition, the slope is $m = \Delta y/(\Delta x) = -11/6$.

(b) $(2, 7)$ and $(2, -4)$

A sketch shows that the line through $(2, 7)$ and $(2, -4)$ is vertical. As mentioned above, the slope of a vertical line is undefined. (An attempt to use the definition of slope here would produce a zero denominator.)

(c) $(5, -3)$ and $(-2, -3)$

By the definition of slope,

$$m = \frac{-3 - (-3)}{-2 - 5} = 0. \quad \blacksquare$$

By drawing a graph, the line of Example 1(c) can be seen to be horizontal, which suggests that the slope of a horizontal line is 0.

In summary,

> The slope of a horizontal line is 0.
> The slope of a vertical line is not defined.

Figure 8 shows lines of various slopes. As suggested by the figure, a line with a positive slope goes up from left to right, but a line with a negative slope goes down.

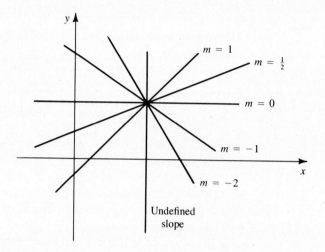

FIGURE 8

EXAMPLE 2

Graph the line going through $(-1, 5)$ and having slope $-5/3$.

First locate the point $(-1, 5)$ as shown in Figure 9. Since the slope of this line is $-5/3$, a change of 3 units horizontally produces a change of -5 units vertically, giving a second point, which is used to complete the graph. ■

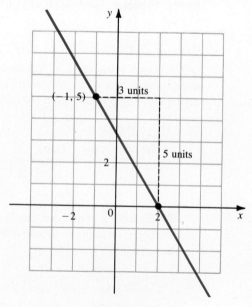

FIGURE 9

Equations of a Line   The slope of a line, together with a point that the line goes through, can be used to find an equation of the line. The procedure for finding the equation depends on whether or not the line is vertical. The vertical line through the point $(a, 0)$ goes through all points of the form (a, y), making the equation $x = a$.

Vertical Line

> An equation of the vertical line through the point $(a, 0)$ is $x = a$.

Let m be the slope of a nonvertical line. Assume that the line goes through the fixed point (x_1, y_1). Let (x, y) represent any other point on the line. The point (x, y) can be on the line if and only if the slope of the line through (x_1, y_1) and (x, y) is m; that is, if

$$\frac{y - y_1}{x - x_1} = m.$$

Multiplying both sides by $x - x_1$ gives

$$y - y_1 = m(x - x_1).$$

In summary,

Point-Slope Form

> The line with slope m passing through the point (x_1, y_1) has an equation
> $$y - y_1 = m(x - x_1).$$
> This equation is called the **point-slope form** of the equation of a line.

EXAMPLE 3

Write an equation of each line.

(a)   through $(-4, 1)$ with slope -3.

Use the point-slope form of the equation of a line with $x_1 = -4$, $y_1 = 1$, and $m = -3$.

$$\begin{aligned}
y - 1 &= -3[x - (-4)] \\
&= -3(x + 4) \\
&= -3x - 12 \\
y &= -3x - 11 \quad \text{or} \quad 3x + y = -11.
\end{aligned}$$

(b)   through $(-3, 2)$ and $(2, -4)$.

First find the slope with the definition of slope:

$$m = \frac{-4 - 2}{2 - (-3)} = \frac{-6}{5}.$$

We can use either $(-3, 2)$ or $(2, -4)$ for (x_1, y_1). Choosing $x_1 = -3$ and $y_1 = 2$ gives

$$y - 2 = \frac{-6}{5}[x - (-3)]$$

$$5(y - 2) = -6(x + 3)$$

$$5y - 10 = -6x - 18$$

$$5y = -6x - 8 \quad \text{or} \quad 6x + 5y = -8.$$

Verify that using $(2, -4)$ instead of $(-3, 2)$ leads to the same result. ▣

Any value of x where a graph crosses the x-axis is called an **x-intercept** for the graph. Any value of y where the graph crosses the y-axis is called a **y-intercept** for the graph. The graph in Figure 10 has x-intercepts x_1, x_2, and x_3 and y-intercept y_1. As suggested by the graph, x-intercepts can be found by letting $y = 0$, while letting $x = 0$ identifies y-intercepts.

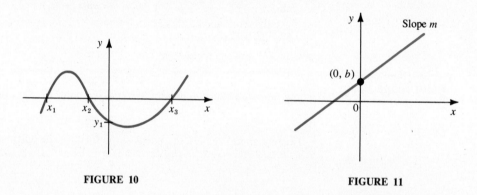

FIGURE 10   FIGURE 11

Figure 11 shows a line with y-intercept b; the line goes through $(0, b)$. If the slope of the line is m, then by the point-slope form, an equation of the line is

$$y - y_1 = m(x - x_1)$$

$$y - b = m(x - 0)$$

$$y = mx + b.$$

This result, which shows both the slope and the y-intercept, is the **slope-intercept form** of the equation of a line. Reversing these steps shows that any equation of the form $y = mx + b$ has a graph that is a line with slope m and going through the point $(0, b)$.

The line with slope m passing through the point $(0, b)$ has an equation
$$y = mx + b.$$
This equation is called the **slope-intercept form** of the equation of a line.

This result, together with the fact that vertical lines have equations of the form $x = k$, shows that every line has an equation of the form $ax + by + c = 0$, where a and b are not both 0. Conversely, assuming $b \neq 0$ and solving $ax + by + c = 0$ for y gives $y = (-a/b)x - c/b$. By the result above, this equation is a line with slope $-a/b$ and y-intercept $-c/b$. If $b = 0$, solve for x to get $x = -c/a$, a vertical line. In any case, the equation $ax + by + c = 0$ has a straight line for its graph.

If a and b are not both 0, then the equation $ax + by + c = 0$ has a line for its graph. Also, any line has an equation of the form $ax + by + c = 0$.

EXAMPLE 4

Graph $3x + 2y = 6$.
    By the work above, this equation has a line for its graph. Two distinct points on the line are enough to locate the graph. The intercepts often provide the necessary points. To find the x-intercept, let $y = 0$ to get

$$3x + 2(0) = 6$$
$$3x = 6$$
$$x = 2.$$

The x-intercept is 2. Let $x = 0$ to find that the y-intercept is 3. These two intercepts were used to get the graph shown in Figure 12.

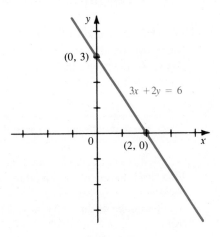

FIGURE 12

Alternatively, solve $3x + 2y = 6$ for y to get

$$3x + 2y = 6$$
$$2y = -3x + 6$$
$$y = -\frac{3}{2}x + 3.$$

By the slope-intercept form, the graph of this equation is the line with y-intercept 3 and slope $-3/2$. (This means the line goes down 3 units for each 2 units it goes to the right.) ▦

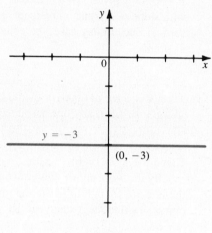

FIGURE 13

Graph $y = -3$.

To have an x-intercept there must be a value of x that makes $y = 0$. Here, however, $y = -3 \neq 0$. This means the line has no x-intercept, which can happen only if the line is parallel to the x-axis (see Figure 13). ▦

One application of slopes involves deciding whether two lines are parallel. Since two parallel lines are equally "steep," they should have the same slope. Also, two lines with the same "steepness" are parallel.

Parallel Lines

> Two nonvertical lines are parallel if and only if they have the same slope.

EXAMPLE 6

Find the equation of the line through the point $(3, 5)$ and parallel to the line $2x + 5y = 4$.

The slope of $2x + 5y = 4$ is found by writing the equation in slope-intercept form.

$$2x + 5y = 4$$

$$y = -\frac{2}{5}x + \frac{4}{5}$$

This result shows that the slope is $-2/5$. Since the lines are parallel, $-2/5$ is also the slope of the line whose equation is needed. This line goes through $(3, 5)$. Substituting $m = -2/5$, $x_1 = 3$, and $y_1 = 5$ into the point-slope form gives

$$y - y_1 = m(x - x_1)$$

$$y - 5 = -\frac{2}{5}(x - 3)$$

$$5(y - 5) = -2(x - 3)$$

$$5y - 25 = -2x + 6$$

$$2x + 5y = 31. \quad \blacksquare$$

As mentioned above, two nonvertical lines are parallel if and only if they have the same slope. It turns out that two lines having slopes with a product of -1 are perpendicular. A proof of this fact, which depends on similar triangles from geometry, is given in Exercise 66 below.

Perpendicular Lines

> Two lines, neither of which is vertical, are perpendicular if and only if their slopes have a product of -1.

EXAMPLE 7

Find the slope of the line L perpendicular to the line with equation $5x - y = 4$. To find the slope, write $5x - y = 4$ in slope-intercept form:

$$y = 5x - 4.$$

The slope is 5. Since the lines are perpendicular, if line L has slope m, then

$$5m = -1$$

$$m = -\frac{1}{5}. \quad \blacksquare$$

Supply and Demand   Linear functions are often good choices for **supply and demand curves.** Typically, as the price of an item increases, the demand for the item decreases, while the supply increases. (There are exceptions, such as cosmetics, medicine, and dog food.)

EXAMPLE 8

Suppose an economist studies the supply and demand for a product over a number of years and concludes that the price, p, and the demand, x, in appropriate units and for an appropriate domain, are related by

$$\text{Demand:} \quad p = 60 - \frac{3}{4}x,$$

with the price and the supply related by

$$\text{Supply:} \quad p = \frac{3}{4}x.$$

(a) Find the demand at a price of $40.

Start with the demand function

$$p = 60 - \frac{3}{4}x,$$

and replace p with 40.

$$40 = 60 - \frac{3}{4}x.$$

Solve this equation to find x; going through the necessary steps gives

$$\frac{80}{3} = x.$$

At a price of $40, 80/3 units will be demanded, giving the ordered pair (80/3, 40).

(b) Graph $p = \frac{3}{4}x$.

Use the ordered pairs (80, 60) and (16, 12) to get the supply graph shown in Figure 14.

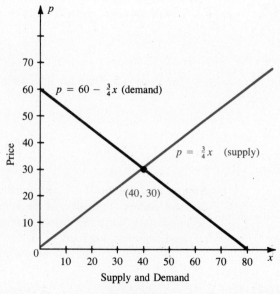

FIGURE 14

In our example, supply and demand are given by

$$p = \frac{3}{4}x \quad \text{and} \quad p = 60 - \frac{3}{4}x,$$

respectively. To find a price where supply and demand are equal, solve the equation

$$\frac{3}{4}x = 60 - \frac{3}{4}x,$$

getting $x = 40.$

Supply and demand will be equal when $x = 40$: this happens at a price of

$$p = \frac{3}{4}x$$

$$p = \frac{3}{4}(40) = 30,$$

or \$30. (Find the same result by using the demand function.) If the price of the item is more than \$30 the supply will exceed the demand. At a price less than \$30, the demand will exceed the supply. Only at a price of \$30 will demand and supply be equal. For this reason, \$30 is called the *equilibrium price*. When the price is \$30, demand and supply both equal 40 units, the *equilibrium supply* or *equilibrium demand*. ▪

Generalizing, the **equilibrium price** of a commodity is the price found at the point where the supply and demand graphs for that commodity cross. The **equilibrium demand** is the demand at that same point; the **equilibrium supply** is the supply at that point.

1.2 EXERCISES

Find the slope of each line in Exercises 1–14 that has a slope.

1. through $(4, 5)$ and $(-1, 2)$

2. through $(5, -4)$ and $(1, 3)$

3. through $(8, 4)$ and $(8, -7)$

4. through $(1, 5)$ and $(-2, 5)$

5. $y = 2x$

6. $y = 3x - 2$

7. $5x - 9y = 11$

8. $4x + 7y = 1$

9. $x = -6$

10. the x-axis

11. the line parallel to $2y - 4x = 7$

12. the line perpendicular to $6x = y - 3$

13. through $(-1.978, 4.806)$ and $(3.759, 8.125)$

14. through $(11.72, 9.811)$ and $(-12.67, -5.009)$

Write an equation of each line in Exercises 15–28.

15. through $(1, 3)$, $m = -2$

16. through $(2, 4)$, $m = -1$

17. through $(6, 1)$, $m = 0$

18. through $(-8, 1)$, undefined slope

19. through $(4, 2)$ and $(1, 3)$

20. through $(8, -1)$ and $(4, 3)$

21. through $(0, 3)$ and $(4, 0)$

22. through $(-3, 0)$ and $(0, -5)$

23. x-intercept 3, y-intercept -2

24. x-intercept -2, y-intercept 4

25. vertical, through $(-6, 5)$

26. horizontal, through $(8, 7)$

27. through $(-1.76, 4.25)$, with slope -5.081

28. through $(5.469, 11.08)$, with slope 4.723

Graph the lines in Exercises 29–42.

29. through $(-1, 3)$ $m = 3/2$

30. through $(-2, 8)$, $m = -1$

31. through $(3, -4)$, $m = -1/3$

32. through $(-2, -3)$, $m = -3/4$

33. $3x + 5y = 15$

34. $2x - 3y = 12$

35. $4x - y = 8$

36. $x + 3y = 9$

37. $x + 2y = 0$

38. $3x - y = 0$

39. $x = -1$

40. $y + 2 = 0$

41. $y = -3$

42. $x = 5$

Write an equation for each of the lines in Exercises 43–50.

43. through $(-1, 4)$, parallel to $x + 3y = 5$

44. through $(2, -5)$, parallel to $y - 4 = 2x$

45. through $(3, -4)$, perpendicular to $x + y = 4$

46. through $(-2, 6)$, perpendicular to $2x - 3y = 5$

47. x-intercept -2, parallel to $y = 2x$

48. y-intercept 3, parallel to $x + y = 4$

49. the line with y-intercept 2 and perpendicular to $3x + 2y = 6$

50. the line with x-intercept $-2/3$ and perpendicular to $2x - y = 4$

51. Do the points $(4, 3)$, $(2, 0)$, and $(-18, -12)$ lie on the same line? (Hint: find the equation of the line through two of the points.)

52. Find k so that the line through $(4, -1)$ and $(k, 2)$ is (a) parallel to $3y + 2x = 6$, (b) perpendicular to $2y - 5x = 1$.

53. Use slopes to show that the quadrilateral with vertices at $(1, 3)$, $(-5/2, 2)$, $(-7/2, 4)$, and $(2, 1)$ is a parallelogram.

54. Use slopes to show that the square with vertices at $(-2, 3)$, $(4, 3)$, $(4, -1)$, and $(-2, -1)$ has diagonals which are perpendicular.

55. Let the supply and demand functions for a product be given by

$$\text{supply: } p = \frac{2}{5}x \quad \text{and} \quad \text{demand: } p = 100 - \frac{2}{5}x.$$

(a) Graph these on the same axes.

(b) Find the equilibrium demand.

(c) Find the equilibrium price.

56. Let the supply and demand functions for sugar be given by

$$\text{supply: } p = 1.4x - .6 \quad \text{and} \quad \text{demand: } p = -2x + 3.2.$$

(a) Graph these on the same axes.

(b) Find the equilibrium demand.

(c) Find the equilibrium price.

Many real-world situations can be approximately described by a straight-line graph. One way to find the equation of such a straight line is to use two typical data points from the graph and the point-slope form of the equation of a line. In Exercises 57–60, assume that the data can be approximated fairly closely by a straight line. Use the given information to find an equation of the line. Find the slope of each of the lines.

57. A company finds that it can make a total of 20 small trailers for $13,900, while 10 of the trailers cost $7500. Let y be the total cost to produce x trailers.

58. When a certain industrial pollutant is introduced into a river, the reproduction of catfish declines. In a given period of time, three tons of the pollutant results in a fish population of 37,000. Also, 12 tons of pollutant produce a fish population of 28,000. Let y be the fish population when x tons of pollutant are introduced into the river.

59. According to research done by the political scientist James March, if the Democrats win 45% of the two-party vote for the House of Representatives, they win 42.5% of the seats. If the Democrats win 55% of the vote, they win 67.5% of the seats. Let y be the percent of seats won, and x the percent of the two-party vote.

60. If the Republicans win 45% of the two-party vote, they win 32.5% of the seats (see Exercise **59**). If they win 60% of the vote, they get 70% of the seats. Let y represent the percent of the seats, and x the percent of the vote.

61. A person's tibia bone goes from ankle to knee. A male with a tibia 40 cm in length will have a height of 177 cm, while a tibia 43 cm in length corresponds to a height of 185 cm.
   (a) Write a linear equation showing how the height of a male, h, relates to the length of his tibia, t.
   (b) Estimate the height of a male having a tibia of length 38 cm; 45 cm.
   (c) Estimate the length of the tibia for a height of 190 cm.

62. The radius bone goes from the wrist to the elbow. A female whose radius bone is 24 cm long would be 167 cm tall, while a radius of 26 cm corresponds to a height of 174 cm.
   (a) Write a linear equation showing how the height of a female, h, corresponds to the length of her radius bone, r.
   (b) Estimate the height of a female having a radius of length 23 cm; 27 cm.
   (c) Estimate the length of a radius bone for a height of 170 cm.

63. To rent a midsized car costs $27 per day or fraction of a day. If you pick up the car in Lansing and drop it in West Lafayette, there is a fixed $25 dropoff charge. Let $C(x)$ represent the cost of renting the car for x days, taking it from Lansing to West Lafayette. Find each of the following.
   (a) $C(3/4)$ **(b)** $C(9/10)$ **(c)** $C(1)$
   (d) $C\left(1\frac{5}{8}\right)$ **(e)** $C(2.4)$ **(f)** Graph $y = C(x)$.
   (g) Is C a function?   **(h)** Is C a linear function?

64. Use similar triangles from geometry to show that the slope of a line is the same, no matter which two distinct points on the line are chosen to compute it.

65. Suppose that $(0, b)$ and (x_1, y_1) are distinct points on the line $y = mx + b$. Show that $(y_1 - b)/x_1$ is the slope of the line, and that $m = (y_1 - b)/x_1$.

66. To prove that two perpendicular lines, neither of which is vertical, have slopes with a product of -1, go through the following steps. Let line L_1 have equation $y = m_1x + b_1$, and let line L_2 have equation $y = m_2x + b_2$. Assume that L_1 and L_2

are perpendicular and complete right triangle *MPN* as shown in the figure. Prove each of the following statements.

(a) *MQ* has length m_1

(b) *QN* has length $- m_2$

(c) triangles *MPQ* and *PQN* are similiar

(d) $m_1/1 = 1/- m_2$ and $m_1 m_2 = -1$.

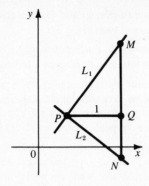

1.3   Linear Mathematical Models

Throughout this book, we set up mathematical models which are mathematical descriptions of real-world situations. In this section, we look at situations which lead to linear functions as mathematical models.

Sales Analysis   It is common to compare the change in sales of two companies by comparing the rates at which these sales change. If the sales of the two companies can be approximated by linear functions, the work of the last section can be used to find rates of change. For example, the chart below shows sales in two different years for two different companies.

Company	Sales in 1982	Sales in 1985
A	$10,000	$16,000
B	5000	14,000

The sales of Company A increased from $10,000 to $16,000 over this 3-year period, for a total increase of $6000, making the average rate of change of sales

$$\frac{\$6000}{3} = \$2000 \text{ per year.}$$

Suppose a study of past records suggests that the sales of Company A have increased linearly (that is, that the sales can be closely approximated by a linear function). To find a linear equation describing the sales, we might decide to let $x = 0$ represent 1982, so that 1985 corresponds to $x = 3$. Then, by the chart above, the sales of Company A go through the points (0, 10,000) and (3, 16,000). The slope of the line through these points is

$$\frac{16,000 - 10,000}{3 - 0} = 2000,$$

the same as the annual rate of change found above. Using the point-slope form of the equation of a line,

$$y - 10{,}000 = 2000(x - 0)$$
$$y = 2000x + 10{,}000$$

gives the equation describing the sales of Company A.

Assume that the sales of Company B have also increased linearly. Then its sales can be described by a line through (0, 5000) and (3, 14,000), leading to

$$y = 3000x + 5000,$$

as the equation describing the sales of Company B. The average annual rate of change of sales is $3000.

As the example suggests, the average rate of change is the same as the slope of the line. This is always true for data that can be modeled with a linear function.

EXAMPLE 1

Suppose that a researcher has concluded that a dosage of x grams of a certain stimulant causes a rat to gain

$$y = 2x + 50$$

grams of weight, for appropriate values of x. If the researcher administers 30 grams of the stimulant, how much weight will the rat gain?

Let $x = 30$. The rat will gain

$$y = 2(30) + 50 = 110$$

grams of weight.

The average rate of change of weight gain with respect to the amount of stimulant is given by the slope of the line. The slope of $y = 2x + 50$ is 2, so that the difference in weight gain when the dose is varied by 1 gram is 2 grams. ■

Cost Analysis The cost of manufacturing an item commonly consists of two parts. The first is **fixed cost** for designing the product, setting up a factory, training workers, and so on. Within broad limits, the fixed cost is constant for a particular product and does not change as more items are made. The second part is a *cost per item* for labor, materials, packing, shipping, and so on. The total value of this second cost does depend on the number of items made.

EXAMPLE 2

Suppose that the cost of producing clock-radios can be approximated by

$$C(x) = 12x + 100,$$

where $C(x)$ is the cost in dollars to produce x radios. The cost to produce 0 radios is

$$C(0) = 12(0) + 100 = 100,$$

or $100. This sum, $100, is the fixed cost.

Once the company has invested the fixed cost into the clock-radio project, what then will be the additional cost per radio? As an example, we first find the cost of a total of 5 radios:

$$C(5) = 12(5) + 100 = 160,$$

or $160. The cost of 6 radios is

$$C(6) = 12(6) + 100 = 172,$$

or $172.

The sixth radio itself costs $172 − $160 = $12 to produce. In the same way, the 81st radio costs $C(81) − C(80) = \$1072 − \$1060 = \$12$ to produce. In fact, the $(n + 1)$st radio costs

$$C(n + 1) - C(n) = [12(n + 1) + 100] - [12n + 100] = 12$$

or $12, to produce. The number 12 is also the slope of the cost function, $C(x) = 12x + 100$.

In economics, the cost of producing an additional item is called the *marginal cost* of that item. In the clock-radio example, the marginal cost of each radio is $12. ▪

The work of Example 2 can be generalized. Suppose the total cost to make x items is given by the cost function $C(x) = mx + b$. The fixed cost is found by letting $x = 0$:

$$C(0) = m \cdot 0 + b = b;$$

the fixed cost is b dollars. The marginal cost of the $(n + 1)$st item is

$$C(n + 1) - C(n),$$

or

$$\begin{aligned} C(n + 1) - C(n) &= [m(n + 1) + b] - [mn + b] \\ &= mn + m + b - mn - b \\ &= m, \end{aligned}$$

the slope of $C(x) = mx + b$.

Cost Function

In a cost function of the form $C(x) = mx + b$, m represents the **marginal cost** per item and b the **fixed cost.** Conversely, if the fixed cost of producing an item is b and the marginal cost is m, then the **cost function,** $C(x)$, for producing x items, is $C(x) = mx + b$.

EXAMPLE 3

In a certain city, a taxi company charges riders a fixed charge of $1.50 plus $1.80 per mile. Write a cost function, $C(x)$, which is a mathematical model for a ride of x miles.

Here the fixed cost is $b = 1.50$ dollars, with a marginal cost of $m = 1.80$ dollars. The cost function, $C(x)$, is

$$C(x) = 1.80x + 1.50.$$

For example, a taxi ride of 4 miles will cost $C(4) = 1.80(4) + 1.50 = 8.70$, or $8.70. Each additional mile causes the cost to increase by $1.80. ▪

EXAMPLE 4

The marginal cost for raising a certain type of frog for laboratory study is $12 per unit of frogs, while the cost to produce 100 units is $1500. Find the cost function, $C(x)$, if we know it is linear.

Since the cost function is linear, it can be expressed in the form $C(x) = mx + b$. The marginal cost is $12 per unit, which gives the value for m, leading to $C(x) = 12x + b$. To find b, use the fact that the cost of producing 100 units of frogs is $1500, or $C(100) = 1500$. Substituting $x = 100$ and $C(x) = 1500$ into $C(x) = 12x + b$ gives

$$C(x) = 12x + b$$
$$1500 = 12 \cdot 100 + b$$
$$1500 = 1200 + b$$
$$300 = b.$$

The model is given by $C(x) = 12x + 300$. The fixed cost is $300. ▪

Break-even Analysis   A company can make a profit only if the revenue received from its customers exceeds the cost of producing its goods and services. The point at which revenue just equals cost is the **break-even point.**

EXAMPLE 5

A firm producing poultry feed finds that the total cost, $C(x)$, of producing x units is given by

$$C(x) = 20x + 100.$$

The revenue, $R(x)$, from selling x units at $24 per unit is the product of the price per unit and the number of units sold, or

$$R(x) = 24x.$$

The firm will just break even (no profit and no loss), as long as revenue just equals cost, or $R(x) = C(x)$. Substituting for $R(x)$ and $C(x)$ gives

$$24x = 20x + 100,$$

from which $x = 25$. The firm breaks even by selling 25 units.

The graphs of $C(x) = 20x + 100$ and $R(x) = 24x$ are shown in Figure 15. The break-even point is shown on the graph. If the company produces more than 25 units (if $x > 25$), it makes a profit while if $x < 25$ it loses money.

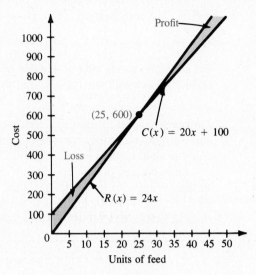

FIGURE 15

1.3 EXERCISES

1. Suppose the sales of a particular brand of electric guitar satisfy the relationship

$$S(x) = 300x + 2000,$$

where $S(x)$ represents the number of guitars sold in year x, with $x = 0$ corresponding to 1982. Find the sales in each of the following years.

(a) 1984   **(b)** 1985   **(c)** 1986   **(d)** 1982

(e) Find the annual rate of change of the sales.

2. Let $N(x) = -5x + 100$ represent the number of bacteria (in thousands) present in a certain tissue culture at time x, measured in hours, after an antibacterial spray is introduced into the environment. Find the number of bacteria present at each of the following times.

(a) $x = 0$ **(b)** $x = 6$ **(c)** $x = 20$

(d) What is the hourly rate of change in the number of bacteria? Interpret the negative sign in the answer.

3. Let $R(x) = -8x + 240$ represent the number of students present in a large business calculus class, where x represents the number of hours of study required weekly. Find the number of students present at each of the following levels of required study.

(a) $x = 0$ **(b)** $x = 5$ **(c)** $x = 10$

(d) What is the rate of change of the number of students in the class with respect to the number of hours of study? Interpret the negative sign in the answer.

(e) The professor in charge of the class likes to have exactly 16 students. How many hours of study must he require in order to have exactly 16 students?

4. Assume that the sales of a certain appliance dealer are approximated by a linear function. Suppose that sales were $850,000 in 1980 and $1,262,500 in 1985. Let $x = 0$ represent 1980.

(a) Find the equation giving the dealer's yearly sales.

(b) What were the dealer's sales in 1983?

(c) Estimate sales in 1988.

5. Assume that the sales of a certain automobile parts company are approximated by a linear function. Suppose that sales were $200,000 in 1978, and $1,000,000 in 1985. Let $x = 0$ represent 1978 and $x = 7$ represent 1985.

(a) Find the equation giving the company's yearly sales.

(b) Find the sales in 1980.

(c) Estimate the sales in 1987.

6. In psychology, the just-noticeable-difference (JND) for some stimulus is defined as the amount by which the stimulus must be increased so that a person will perceive it as having just barely been increased. For example, suppose a research study indicates that a line 40 centimeters in length must be increased to 42 cm before a subject thinks that it is longer. In this case, the JND would be $42 - 40 = 2$ cm. In a particular experiment, the JND is given by

$$y = 0.03x,$$

where x represents the original length of the line and y the JND. Find the JND for lines having the following lengths.

(a) 10 cm   **(b)** 20 cm   **(c)** 50 cm   **(d)** 100 cm

(e) Find the rate of change in the JND with respect to the original length of the line.

Write a cost function for Exercises 7–10. Identify all variables used.

7. A chain saw rental firm charges $12 plus $1 per hour.

8. A trailer-hauling service charges $45 plus $2 per mile.

9. A parking garage charges 50¢ plus 35¢ per half-hour.

10. For a one-day rental, a car rental firm charges $44 plus 28¢ per mile.

Assume that each of Exercises 11–18 can be expressed as a linear cost function. Find the appropriate cost function in each case.

11. Fixed cost, $100; 50 items cost $1600 to produce.

12. Fixed cost, $400; 10 items cost $650 to produce.

13. Fixed cost, $1000; 40 items cost $2000 to produce.

14. Fixed cost, $8500; 75 items cost $11,875 to produce.

15. Marginal cost, $50; 80 items cost $4500 to produce.

16. Marginal cost, $120; 100 items cost $15,800 to produce.

17. Marginal cost, $90; 150 items cost $16,000 to produce.

18. Marginal cost, $120; 700 items cost $96,500 to produce.

19. The manager of a local restaurant told us that his cost function for producing coffee is $C(x) = .097x$, where $C(x)$ is the total cost in dollars of producing x cups. (He is ignoring the cost of the coffee pot and the cost of labor.) Find the total cost of producing the following numbers of cups.

    (a) 1000 cups
    (b) 1001 cups
    (c) Find the marginal cost of the 1001st cup.
    (d) What is the marginal cost for *any* cup?

20. In deciding whether or not to set up a new manufacturing plant, company analysts have decided that a reasonable function for the total cost to produce x items is

    $$C(x) = 500,000 + 4.75x.$$

    (a) Find the total cost to produce 100,000 items.
    (b) Find the marginal cost of the items to be produced in this plant.

Let $C(x)$ be the total cost to manufacture x items. Then the quotient $(C(x))/x$ is the **average cost** per item. Use this definition in Exercises 21 and 22.

21. $C(x) = 800 + 20x$; find the average cost per item if x is

    (a) 10   (b) 50   (c) 200.

22. $C(x) = 500,000 + 4.75x$; find the average cost per item if x is

    (a) 1000   (b) 5000   (c) 10,000.

23. The cost to produce x units of wire is $C(x) = 50x + 5000$, while the revenue is $R(x) = 60x$. Find the break-even point and the revenue at the break-even point.

24. The cost to produce x units of squash is $C(x) = 100x + 6000$, while the revenue is $R(x) = 500x$. Find the break-even point.

You are the manager of a firm. You are considering the manufacture of a new product, so you ask the accounting department to produce cost estimates and the sales department to produce sales estimates. After you receive the data, you must decide whether or not to go ahead with production of the new product. Analyze the data in Exercises 25–28 (find a break-even point) and then decide what you would do.

25. $C(x) = 85x + 900$; $R(x) = 105x$; not more than 38 units can be sold.

26. $C(x) = 105x + 6000$; $R(x) = 250x$; not more than 400 units can be sold.

27. $C(x) = 70x + 500$; $R(x) = 60x$ (Hint: what does a negative break-even point mean?)

28. $C(x) = 1000x + 5000$; $R(x) = 900x$.

The solid lines in the graphs of Exercises 29 and 30 show the estimated sales in millions of cars and trucks for General Motors and for Ford.* The dashed lines show the estimated break-even points for these same two companies. Use the graphs to estimate the numbers of cars and trucks on which the following companies will make a profit in 1983.

---

*Chicago Tribune Graphic: "Factory Sales, Break-Even Point in Auto Industry" from "Automakers Learn a Lesson in Numbers" by James Mateja, *Chicago Tribune,* October 24, 1982. Copyright © 1982 Chicago Tribune. Used with permission.

29.

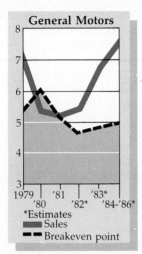

General Motors

*Estimates
▬ Sales
▬▬ Breakeven point

30.

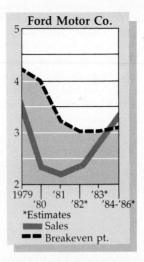

Ford Motor Co.

*Estimates
▬ Sales
▬▬ Breakeven pt.

31. Most people are not very good at estimating the passage of time. Some people's estimations are too fast, and others, too slow. One psychologist has constructed a mathematical model for actual time as a function of estimated time: if y represents actual time and x estimated time, then

$$y = mx + b,$$

where m and b are constants that must be determined experimentally for each person. Suppose that for a particular person, $m = 1.25$ and $b = -5$. Find y if x is

(a) 30 minutes **(b)** 60 minutes **(c)** 120 minutes **(d)** 180 minutes.

32. Suppose that for another person, $m = .85$ and $b = 1.2$. Find y if x is

(a) 15 minutes **(b)** 30 minutes **(c)** 60 minutes **(d)** 120 minutes.

For this same person, find x if y is

(e) 60 minutes **(f)** 90 minutes.

EXTENDED

APPLICATION

Marginal Cost—Booz, Allen & Hamilton

Booz, Allen & Hamilton is a large management consulting firm.* One of the services they provide to client companies is profitability studies, in which they show ways in which the client can increase profit levels. The client company requesting the analysis presented in this case is a large producer of a staple food. The company buys from farmers, and then processes the food in its mills, resulting in a finished product. The company sells both at retail under its own brands, and in bulk to other companies who use the product in the manufacture of convenience foods.

*This case was supplied by John R. Dowdle of the Chicago office of Booz, Allen & Hamilton. Reprinted by permission.

The client company has been reasonably profitable in recent years, but the management retained Booz, Allen And Hamilton to see whether its consultants could suggest ways of increasing company profits. The management of the company had long operated with the philosophy of trying to process and sell as much of its product as possible, since, they felt, this would lower the average processing cost per unit sold. However, the consultants found that the client's fixed mill costs were quite low, and that, in fact, processing extra units made the cost per unit start to increase. (There are several reasons for this: the company must run three shifts, machines break down more often, and so on.)

In this application, we shall discuss the marginal cost of two of the company's products. The marginal cost (cost of producing an extra unit) of production for product A was found by the consultants to be approximated by the linear function

$$y = .133x + 10.09,$$

where x is the number of units produced (in millions) and y is the marginal cost. (Here the marginal cost is not a constant, as it was in the examples of the text.)

For example, at a level of production of 3.1 million units, an additional unit of product A would cost about

$$y = .133(3.1) + 10.09 \approx \$10.50.^*$$

At a level of production of 5.7 million units, an extra unit costs $10.85. Figure 16 shows a graph of the marginal cost function from $x = 3.1$ to $x = 5.7$, the domain over which the function above was found to apply.

The selling price for product A is $10.73 per unit, so that, as shown on the graph that follows, the company was losing money on many units of the product that it sold. Since the selling price could not be raised if the company was to remain competitive, the consultants recommended that production of product A be cut.

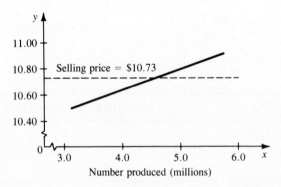

FIGURE 16

For product B, the Booz, Allen And Hamilton consultants found a marginal cost function given by

$$y = .0667x + 10.29,$$

with x and y as defined above. Verify that at a production level of 3.1 million units, the marginal cost is about $10.50; while at a production level of 5.7 million units, the mar-

---

*The symbol $\approx$ means *approximately equal to*.

ginal cost is about $10.67. Since the selling price of this product is $9.65, the consultants again recommended a cutback in production.

The consultants ran similar cost analyses of other products made by the company, and then issued their recommendation to the company: The company should reduce total production by 2.1 million units. The analysts predicted that this would raise profits for the products under discussion from $8.3 million annually to $9.6 million—which is very close to what actually happened when the client took the advice.

EXERCISES

1. At what level of production, x, was the marginal cost of a unit of product A equal to the selling price?

2. Graph the marginal cost function for product B from $x = 3.1$ million units to $x = 5.7$ million units.

3. Find the number of units for which marginal cost equals the selling price for product B.

4. For product C, the marginal cost of production is
$$y = .133x + 9.46.$$
   (a) Find the marginal cost at a level of production of 3.1 million units; of 5.7 million units.

   (b) Graph the marginal cost function.

   (c) For a selling price of $9.57, find the level of production for which the cost equals the selling price.

1.4 Quadratic Functions

We have seen that a linear function has the form
$$f(x) = ax + b,$$
for real numbers a and b. Including a term with x^2 produces a **quadratic function.**

Quadratic Function

> A **quadratic function** has the form
> $$f(x) = ax^2 + bx + c,$$
> where a, b, and c are real numbers, with $a \neq 0$.

(Why do we need the restriction $a \neq 0$?) Perhaps the simplest quadratic function is $f(x) = x^2$, with $a = 1$, $b = 0$, and $c = 0$. To graph this function, choose several values of x and find the corresponding values of $f(x)$. Plot the resulting ordered pairs $(x, f(x))$, and draw a smooth curve through them, as in Figure 17. This graph is called a **parabola.** Every quadratic function has a parabola as its graph. The lowest (or highest) point on a parabola is the **vertex** of the parabola. The vertex of the parabola in Figure 17 is $(0, 0)$.

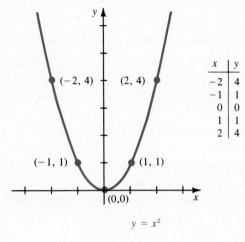

x	y
-2	4
-1	1
0	0
1	1
2	4

$y = x^2$

FIGURE 17

$y = x^2 - 4$

$(0, -4)$

FIGURE 18

If the graph of Figure 17 were folded in half along the y-axis, the two halves of the parabola would match exactly. This means that the graph of a quadratic function is *symmetric* to a vertical line through the vertex: this line is the **axis** of the parabola.

There are many real-world instances of parabolas. For example, cross sections of spotlight reflectors or radar dishes form parabolas. Also, a projectile thrown in the air follows a parabolic path.

EXAMPLE 1

Graph $y = x^2 - 4$.

Each value of y will be 4 less than the corresponding value of y in $y = x^2$. The graph of $y = x^2 - 4$ has the same shape as that of $y = x^2$ but is 4 units lower. See Figure 18. The vertex of the parabola (on this parabola, the *lowest* point) is at $(0, -4)$. The axis of the parabola is the vertical line $x = 0$. ▪

EXAMPLE 2

Graph $y = (x - 4)^2$.

By choosing values of x and finding the corresponding values of y, this parabola is seen to be moved 4 units to the right when compared with the graph of $y = x^2$. The vertex is at $(4, 0)$. The axis is the vertical line $x = 4$. See Figure 19. ▪

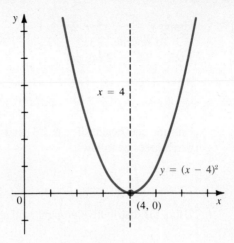

$x = 4$

$y = (x - 4)^2$

$(4, 0)$

FIGURE 19

Graph $y = -(x + 3)^2 + 1$.

This parabola is shifted 3 units to the left and 1 unit up compared to $y = x^2$. Because of the minus sign in front of the squared quantity, the graph opens downward. The vertex, $(-3, 1)$, is the highest point on the graph. The axis is the line $x = -3$. See Figure 20. ▢

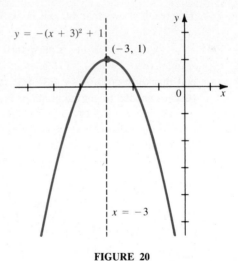

$y = -(x + 3)^2 + 1$

$(-3, 1)$

$x = -3$

FIGURE 20

Completing the Square   The vertex and axis of a parabola can be found quickly if the equation of the parabola is in the form

$$y = a(x - h)^2 + k,$$

for real numbers $a \neq 0$, h and k. An equation not given in this form can be converted by a process called *completing the square*. This process is explained next.

EXAMPLE 4

Graph $y = -3x^2 - 2x + 1$.

To rewrite $-3x^2 - 2x + 1$ in the form $a(x - h)^2 + k$, first factor -3 from $-3x^2 - 2x$ to get

$$y = -3\left(x^2 + \frac{2}{3}x\right) + 1.$$

Half the coefficient of x is 1/3, and $(1/3)^2 = 1/9$. Add and subtract 1/9 inside the parentheses as follows:

$$y = -3\left(x^2 + \frac{2}{3}x + \frac{1}{9} - \frac{1}{9}\right) + 1.$$

Using the distributive property and simplifying gives

$$y = -3\left(x^2 + \frac{2}{3}x + \frac{1}{9}\right) - 3\left(-\frac{1}{9}\right) + 1$$

$$= -3\left(x^2 + \frac{2}{3}x + \frac{1}{9}\right) + \frac{4}{3}.$$

Factor to get

$$y = -3\left(x + \frac{1}{3}\right)^2 + \frac{4}{3}.$$

This result shows that the axis is the vertical line

$$x + \frac{1}{3} = 0 \quad \text{or} \quad x = -\frac{1}{3}$$

and that the vertex is $(-1/3, 4/3)$. Use these results and plot additional ordered pairs as needed to get the graph of Figure 21.   ■

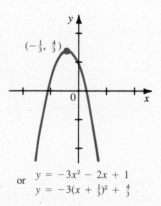

or
$y = -3x^2 - 2x + 1$
$y = -3(x + \frac{1}{3})^2 + \frac{4}{3}$

FIGURE 21

The examples of this section suggest the following result.

Parabolas

> When the equation of a parabola is written in the form
>
> $$y = a(x - h)^2 + k$$
>
> the vertex is (h, k). The axis is the vertical line $x = h$.

The parabola opens up if $a > 0$ and down if $a < 0$. If $a > 0$, then k is the minimum value of the function; if $a < 0$, k is the maximum. If $|a| > 1$, the parabola is "thinner" than $y = x^2$, but it is "fatter" than $y = x^2$ if $0 < |a| < 1$.

The fact that the vertex of a parabola of the form $y = ax^2 + bx + c$ is the highest or lowest point on the graph can be used in applications to find a maximum or a minimum value.

EXAMPLE 5

Ms. Whitney owns and operates Aunt Emma's Pie Shop. She has hired a consultant to analyze her business operations. The consultant tells her that her profit $P(x)$ from the sale of x units of pies is given by

$$P(x) = 120x - x^2.$$

How many units of pies should be made in order to maximize the profit? What is the maximum possible profit?

The profit function can be rewritten as $P(x) = -x^2 + 120x + 0$. Complete the square to rewrite $P(x)$ as

$$P(x) = -(x - 60)^2 + 3600.$$

The graph of P is a parabola with vertex at (60, 3600) and opening downward. Since the parabola opens downward, the vertex leads to *maximum* profit. Figure 22 shows the portion of the profit function in quadrant I. (Why is quadrant I the only one of interest here?) The maximum profit of $3600 is reached when 60 units of pies are produced. In this case, profit increases as more pies are made up to 60 units and then decreases as more pies are made past this point. ▪

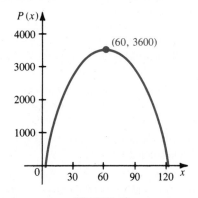

FIGURE 22

1.4 EXERCISES

1. Graph functions a–d on the same coordinate system.

   (a) $f(x) = 2x^2$ (b) $f(x) = 3x^2$ (c) $f(x) = \frac{1}{2}x^2$ (d) $f(x) = \frac{1}{3}x^2$

   (e) How does the coefficient affect the shape of the graph?

2. Graph functions a–d on the same coordinate system.

   (a) $y = \frac{1}{2}x^2$ (b) $y = -\frac{1}{2}x^2$ (c) $y = 4x^2$ (d) $y = -4x^2$

   (e) What affect does the minus sign have on the graph?

3. Graph functions a–d on the same coordinate system.

   (a) $f(x) = x^2 + 2$ (b) $f(x) = x^2 - 1$ (c) $f(x) = x^2 + 1$ (d) $f(x) = x^2 - 2$

   (e) How do these graphs differ from the graph of $f(x) = x^2$?

4. Graph functions a–d on the same coordinate system.

   (a) $f(x) = (x - 2)^2$ (b) $f(x) = (x + 1)^2$ (c) $f(x) = (x + 3)^2$ (d) $f(x) = (x - 4)^2$

   (e) How do these graphs differ from the graph of $f(x) = x^2$?

Graph the parabolas in Exercises 5–18. Give the vertex and axis of each.

5. $y = (x - 2)^2$

6. $y = (x + 4)^2$

7. $y = (x + 3)^2 - 4$

8. $y = (x - 5)^2 - 4$

9. $y = -2(x + 3)^2 + 2$

10. $y = -3(x - 2)^2 + 1$

11. $y = -\frac{1}{2}(x + 1)^2 - 3$

12. $y = \frac{2}{3}(x - 2)^2 - 1$

13. $y = x^2 - 2x + 3$

14. $y = x^2 + 6x + 5$

15. $y = -x^2 - 4x + 2$

16. $y = -x^2 + 6x - 6$

17. $y = 2x^2 - 4x + 5$

18. $y = -3x^2 + 24x - 46$

For each function in Exercises 19–22, find several points on the graph and then sketch the graph.

19. $y = .14x^2 + .56x - .3$

20. $y = .82x^2 + 3.24x - .4$

21. $y = -.09x^2 - 1.8x + .5$

22. $y = -.35x^2 + 2.8x - .3$

23. Glenview Community College wants to construct a rectangular parking lot on land bordered on one side by a highway. It has 320 feet of fencing which it will use to fence off the other three sides. What should be the dimensions of the lot if the enclosed area is to be a maximum? (Hint: let x represent the width of the lot and let $320 - 2x$ represent the length. Graph the area parabola, $A = x(320 - 2x)$, and investigate the vertex.)

24. What would be the maximum area that could be enclosed by the college's 320 feet of fencing if it decided to close the entrance by enclosing all four sides of the lot? (See Exercise 23.)

25. George runs a sandwich shop. By studying data concerning his past costs, he has found that the cost of operating his shop is given by

$$C(x) = 2x^2 - 20x + 360$$

where $C(x)$ is the daily cost in dollars to make x units of sandwiches. Find the number of units George must sell to minimize the cost. What is the minimum cost?

26. The revenue of a charter bus company depends on the number of unsold seats. If the revenue $R(x)$, is given by
$$R(x) = 5000 + 50x - x^2,$$
where x is the number of unsold seats, find the maximum revenue and the number of unsold seats which produce maximum revenue.

27. The number of mosquitoes, $M(x)$, in millions, in a certain area of Kentucky depends on the June rainfall, x, in inches, approximately as follows.
$$M(x) = 10x - x^2$$
Find the rainfall that will produce the maximum number of mosquitoes.

28. If an object is thrown upward with an initial velocity of 32 feet per second, then its height after t seconds is given by
$$h = 32t - 16t^2.$$
Find the maximum height attained by the object. Find the number of seconds it takes the object to hit the ground.

29. Find two numbers whose sum is 20 and whose product is a maximum. (Hint: Let x and $20 - x$ be the two numbers, and write an equation for the product.)

30. A charter flight charges a fare of $200 per person plus $4 per person for each unsold seat on the plane. If the plane holds 100 passengers, and if x represents the number of unsold seats, find the following.

    (a) An expression for the total revenue received for the flight. (Hint: Multiply the number of people flying, $100 - x$, by the price per ticket.)

    (b) The graph for the expression of part (a).

    (c) The number of unsold seats that will produce the maximum revenue.

    (d) The maximum revenue.

31. The demand for a certain type of cosmetic is given by
$$p = 500 - x,$$
where p is the price in dollars when x units are demanded.

    (a) Find the revenue, $R(x)$, that would be obtained at a price of x. (Hint: Revenue = demand $\times$ price.)

    (b) Graph the revenue function, $R(x)$.

    (c) From the graph of the revenue function, estimate the price that will produce maximum revenue.

    (d) What is the maximum revenue?

32. Between the months of June and October, the percent of maximum possible chlorophyll production in a leaf is approximated by $C(x)$, where
$$C(x) = 10x + 50.$$
Here x is time in months with $x = 1$ representing June. From October through December, $C(x)$ is approximated by
$$C(x) = -20(x - 5)^2 + 100,$$
with x as above. Find the percent of maximum possible chlorophyll production in each of the following months: (a) June   (b) July   (c) September
(d) October   (e) November   (f) December.

33. Use your results from Exercise 32 to sketch a graph of $y = C(x)$, from June through December. In what month is chlorophyll production a maximum?

34. An arch is shaped like a parabola. It is 30 m wide at the base and 15 m high. How wide is the arch 10 m from the ground?

35. A culvert is shaped like a parabola, 18 cm across the top and 12 cm deep. How wide is the culvert 8 cm from the top?

36. Let x be in the interval $[0, 1]$. Use a graph to suggest that the product $x(1 - x)$ is always less than or equal to $1/4$. For what values of x does the product equal $1/4$?

1.5   Polynomial and Rational Functions

In the previous sections we discussed linear and quadratic functions and found their graphs. Both these functions are special types of **polynomial functions.**

Polynomial Function

> A **polynomial function** of degree n, where n is a nonnegative integer, is a function of the form
>
> $$f(x) = a_n x^n + a_{n-1} x^{n-1} + \ldots + a_1 x + a_0,$$
>
> where $a_n, a_{n-1}, \ldots, a_1$, and a_0 are real numbers, with $a_n \neq 0$.

For $n = 1$, a polynomial function takes the form

$$f(x) = a_1 x + a_0,$$

a linear function. A linear function, therefore, is a polynomial function of degree 1. (An exception: a linear function of the form $f(x) = a_0$ for a real number a_0 is a polynomial function of degree 0.) A polynomial function of degree 2 is a quadratic function.

Now we need to investigate the graphs of polynomial functions of degree 3 or more. Accurate graphs of many polynomial functions require the methods of calculus, to be discussed later. In this section we shall plot points in order to get a reasonable sketch of the graph.

Perhaps the simplest polynomial functions of higher degree are those of the form $f(x) = x^n$, so we graph some of these first. For example, to graph $f(x) = x^3$, find several ordered pairs that satisfy $y = x^3$, then plot them and connect the points with a smooth curve. The graph of $f(x) = x^3$ is shown as a black curve in Figure 23. This same figure also shows the graph of $f(x) = x^5$ in color.

We can sketch graphs of $f(x) = x^4$ and $f(x) = x^6$ in a similar manner. Figure 24 shows $f(x) = x^4$ as a black curve and $f(x) = x^6$ in color. These graphs have symmetry about the y-axis as does the graph of $f(x) = ax^2$ for a nonzero real number a.

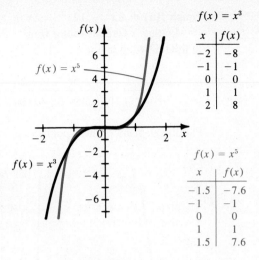

$f(x) = x^3$

x	$f(x)$
-2	-8
-1	-1
0	0
1	1
2	8

$f(x) = x^5$

x	$f(x)$
-1.5	-7.6
-1	-1
0	0
1	1
1.5	7.6

FIGURE 23

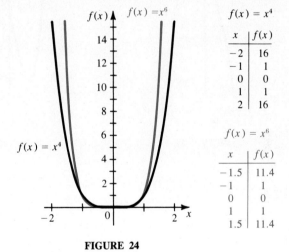

$f(x) = x^4$

x	$f(x)$
-2	16
-1	1
0	0
1	1
2	16

$f(x) = x^6$

x	$f(x)$
-1.5	11.4
-1	1
0	0
1	1
1.5	11.4

FIGURE 24

As with the graph of $f(x) = ax^2$, the value of a in $f(x) = ax^n$ affects the width of the graph. When $|a| > 1$, the graph is "thinner" than the graph of $f(x) = x^n$; when $0 < |a| < 1$, the graph is "fatter."

We mentioned above that the only method currently available for graphing polynomial functions of degree 3 or more is by plotting points. For the rest of the graphing examples, we let x take on integer values from -3 through 3. By plotting the resulting points we hope to get a reasonable sketch of the graph.

EXAMPLE 1

Graph $f(x) = 8x^3 - 12x^2 + 2x + 1$.

Letting x take on values from -3 through 3 leads to the values of $f(x)$ given in the following table.

x	-3	-2	-1	0	1	2	3
$f(x)$	-329	-115	-21	1	-1	21	115

Plotting as many of these points as convenient gives the graph of Figure 25.

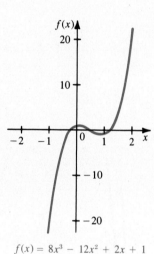

$f(x) = 8x^3 - 12x^2 + 2x + 1$

FIGURE 25

$f(x) = 3x^4 - 14x^3 + 54x - 3$

FIGURE 26

EXAMPLE 2

Graph $f(x) = 3x^4 - 14x^3 + 54x - 3$.

Complete a table of ordered pairs.

x	-3	-2	-1	0	1	2	3
$f(x)$	456	49	-40	-3	40	41	24

See the graph in Figure 26.

As suggested by the graphs above, the domain of a polynomial function is the set of all real numbers. The range of a polynomial function of odd degree is also the set of all real numbers. Some typical graphs of polynomial functions of odd degree are shown in Figure 27. These graphs suggest that for every polynomial function f of odd degree there is at least one real value of x that makes $f(x) = 0$. Such a value of x is called a **real zero** of f; these values are also the x-intercepts of the graph.

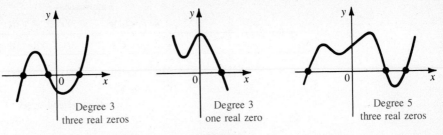

Degree 3
three real zeros

Degree 3
one real zero

Degree 5
three real zeros

FIGURE 27

Polynomial functions of even degree have a range that takes either the form $(-\infty, k]$ or the form $[k, \infty)$ for some real number k. Figure 28 shows two typical graphs of polynomial functions of even degree.

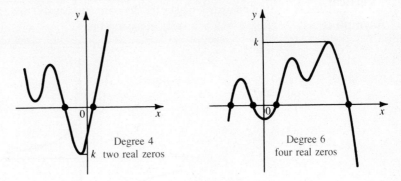

Degree 4
k two real zeros

Degree 6
four real zeros

FIGURE 28

Rational Functions   A function of the form

$$f(x) = \frac{p(x)}{q(x)}, \text{ with } q(x) \neq 0,$$

and where $p(x)$ and $q(x)$ are polynomial functions, is called a **rational function.** Since any values of x such that $q(x) = 0$ are excluded from the domain, a rational function usually has a graph with one or more breaks.

EXAMPLE 3   Graph $y = \dfrac{2}{1 + x}$.

This function is undefined for $x = -1$, since -1 leads to a 0 denominator. For this reason, the graph of this function will not intersect the vertical line $x = -1$. Since x can take on any value except -1, the values of x can approach -1 as closely as desired from either side of -1.

x approaches −1

x	−.5	−.8	−.9	−.99	↓ −1.01	−1.1	−1.2	−1.5
$1 + x$	.5	.2	.1	.01	−.01	−.1	−.2	−.5
$y = \dfrac{2}{1 + x}$	4	10	20	200	−200	−20	−10	−4

↑
$|y|$ **gets larger and larger**

The table above suggests that as x gets closer and closer to -1 from either side, the sum $1 + x$ gets closer and closer to 0, and $|2/(1 + x)|$ gets larger and larger. The vertical line $x = -1$ approached by the curve is called a **vertical asymptote.** ▩

Vertical	If a number k makes the denominator equal 0 in a rational function, then the
Asymptote	line $x = k$ is a **vertical asymptote.***

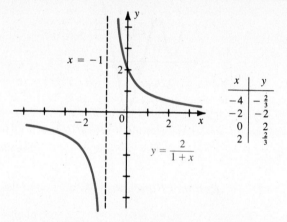

x	y
-4	$-\frac{2}{3}$
-2	-2
0	2
2	$\frac{2}{3}$

FIGURE 29

As $|x|$ gets larger and larger, $y = 2/(1 + x)$ gets closer and closer to 0 as shown in the table below.

x	−101	−11	−2	0	9	99
$1 + x$	−100	−10	−1	1	10	100
$y = \dfrac{2}{1 + x}$	−.02	−.2	−2	2	.2	.02

Whenever the values of y approach some number k as $|x|$ gets larger and larger, the line $y = k$ is a **horizontal asymptote.** As the table suggests, $y = 0$ is a horizontal

---

*Actually, we should make sure that $x = k$ does not also make the numerator 0. If both the numerator and denominator are 0, then there may be no vertical asymptote at k.

asymptote in our example. By using the asymptotes and plotting the intercept and a few points (shown with the figure), we get the graph of Figure 29.

EXAMPLE 4

Graph $y = \dfrac{3x + 2}{2x + 4}$.

The value $x = -2$ makes the denominator 0, with the line $x = -2$ a vertical asymptote. To find a horizontal asymptote, let x get larger and larger, as in the following chart.

x	$y = \dfrac{3x + 2}{2x + 4}$	Ordered pair
10	$\dfrac{32}{24} = 1.33$	(10, 1.33)
20	$\dfrac{62}{44} = 1.41$	(20, 1.41)
100	$\dfrac{302}{204} = 1.48$	(100, 1.48)
100,000	$\dfrac{300,002}{200,004} = 1.49998$	(100,000, 1.49998)

The chart suggests that as x gets larger and larger, $(3x + 2)/(2x + 4)$ gets closer and closer to 1.5, or 3/2, with the line $y = 3/2$ a horizontal asymptote. Use a calculator to show that as x gets more negative and takes on the values -10, -100, -1000, $-100,000$, and so on, the graph again approaches the line $y = 3/2$. Using these asymptotes and plotting several points leads to the graph of Figure 30. ▪

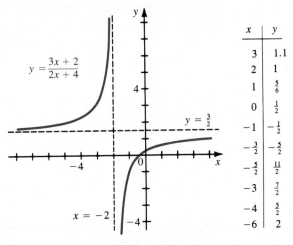

x	y
3	1.1
2	1
1	$\frac{5}{6}$
0	$\frac{1}{2}$
-1	$-\frac{1}{2}$
$-\frac{3}{2}$	$-\frac{5}{2}$
$-\frac{5}{2}$	$\frac{11}{2}$
-3	$\frac{7}{2}$
-4	$\frac{5}{2}$
-6	2

FIGURE 30

In Example 4 above, we found that $y = 3/2$ is a horizontal asymptote for the rational function $y = (3x + 2)/(2x + 4)$. An equation for the horizontal asymptote also can be found by solving $y = (3x + 2)/(2x + 4)$ for x. To do this, first multiply both sides of the equation by $2x + 4$. This gives

$$y(2x + 4) = 3x + 2$$

or
$$2xy + 4y = 3x + 2.$$

Collect all terms containing x on one side of the equation:

$$2xy - 3x = 2 - 4y.$$

Factor out x on the left and solve for x.

$$x(2y - 3) = 2 - 4y$$

$$x = \frac{2 - 4y}{2y - 3}$$

This form of the equation shows that y cannot take on the value 3/2. This means that the line $y = 3/2$ is a horizontal asymptote.

EXAMPLE 5

In many situations involving environmental pollution, much of the pollutant can be removed from the air or water at a fairly reasonable cost, but the last small part of the pollutant can be very expensive to remove.

Cost as a function of the percentage of pollutant removed from the environment can be calculated for various percentages of removal, with a curve fitted through the resulting data points. This curve then leads to a mathematical model of the situation. Rational functions are often a good choice for these **cost-benefit models.**

For example, suppose a cost-benefit model is given by

$$y = \frac{18x}{106 - x},$$

where y is the cost (in thousands of dollars) of removing x percent of a certain pollutant. The domain of x is the set of all numbers from 0 to 100 inclusive; any amount of pollutant from 0% to 100% can be removed. To remove 100% of the pollutant here would cost

$$y = \frac{18(100)}{106 - 100} = 300,$$

or $300,000. Check that 95% of the pollutant can be removed for $155,000, 90% for $101,000, and 80% for $55,000. Using these points, as well as others that could be obtained from the function above, gives the graph shown in Figure 31. ■

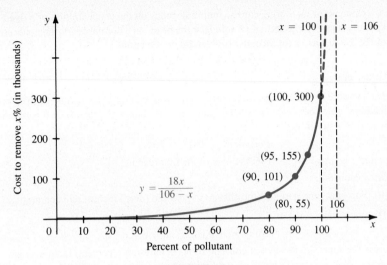

FIGURE 31

1.5 EXERCISES

In Exercises 1–20, sketch the graph of each polynomial function by replacing x, in turn, with the integers from -3 through 3.

1. $f(x) = (x + 1)^3$

2. $f(x) = x^3 + 1$

3. $f(x) = x^3 - 7x - 6$

4. $f(x) = x^3 + x^2 - 4x - 4$

5. $f(x) = x^4 - 5x^2 + 6$

6. $f(x) = x^3 - 3x^2 - x + 3$

7. $f(x) = 6x^3 + 11x^2 - x - 6$

8. $f(x) = x^4 - 2x^2 - 8$

9. $f(x) = x^4 + x^3 - 2$

10. $f(x) = 6x^4 - x^3 - 23x^2 + 4x + 12$

11. $f(x) = 8x^4 - 2x^3 - 47x^2 - 52x - 15$

12. $f(x) = x^3 - 4x^2 - 5x + 18$

13. $f(x) = x^3 + 3x^2 - 9x - 11$

14. $f(x) = -x^3 + 4x^2 + 3x - 8$

15. $f(x) = -x^3 + 6x^2 - x - 14$

16. $f(x) = 2x^3 + 4x - 1$

17. $f(x) = 2x^3 + 4x + 1$

18. $f(x) = x^4 - 4x^3 + 3x - 2$

19. $f(x) = 2x^4 - 3x^3 + 4x^2 + 5x - 1$

20. $f(x) = -x^4 - 2x^3 + 3x^2 + 3x + 5$

Find the horizontal and vertical asymptotes for each of the rational functions in Exercises 21–32. Draw the graph of each function.

21. $y = \dfrac{-4}{x - 3}$

22. $y = \dfrac{-1}{x + 3}$

23. $y = \dfrac{2}{3 + 2x}$

24. $y = \dfrac{4}{5 + 3x}$

25. $y = \dfrac{3x}{x - 1}$

26. $y = \dfrac{4x}{3 - 2x}$

27. $y = \dfrac{x + 1}{x - 4}$

28. $y = \dfrac{x - 3}{x + 5}$

29. $y = \dfrac{1 - 2x}{5x + 20}$

30. $y = \dfrac{6 - 3x}{4x + 12}$

31. $y = \dfrac{-x - 4}{3x + 6}$

32. $y = \dfrac{-x + 8}{2x + 5}$

33. A technique for measuring cardiac output depends on the concentration of a dye after a known amount is injected into a vein near the heart. In a normal heart, the concentration of the dye at time x (in seconds) is given by the function

$$g(x) = -.006x^4 + .140x^3 - .053x^2 + 1.79x.$$

Graph $g(x)$.

34. The pressure of the oil in a reservoir tends to drop with time. By taking sample pressure readings, petroleum engineers have found that the change in pressure in a particular oil reservoir is given by

$$P(t) = t^3 - 25t^2 + 200t,$$

where t is time in years from the date of the first reading.

(a) Graph $P(t)$.

(b) For what time period is the change in pressure (drop) increasing? decreasing?

35. The polynomial function

$$A(x) = -0.015x^3 + 1.058x$$

gives the approximate alcohol concentration (in tenths of a percent) in an average person's bloodstream x hours after drinking about eight ounces of 100 proof whiskey. The function is approximately valid for x in the interval $[0, 8]$.

(a) Graph $A(x)$.

(b) Using the graph you drew for part (a), estimate the time of maximum alcohol concentration.

(c) In one state, a person is legally drunk if the blood alcohol concentration exceeds .15%. Use the graph of part (a) to estimate the period in which this average person is legally drunk.

36. During the early part of the 20th century, the deer population of the Kaibab Plateau in Arizona experienced a rapid increase, because hunters had reduced the number of natural predators. The increase in population depleted the food resources and eventually caused the population to decline. For the period from 1905 to 1930, the deer population was approximated by

$$D(x) = -.125x^5 + 3.125x^4 + 4000,$$

where x is time in years from 1905.

(a) Use a calculator to find enough points to graph $D(x)$.

(b) From the graph, over what period of time (from 1905 to 1930) was the population increasing? relatively stable? decreasing?

37. Suppose the average cost per unit, $C(x)$, in dollars, to produce x units of margarine is given by

$$C(x) = \frac{500}{x + 30}.$$

(a) Find $C(10)$, $C(20)$, $C(50)$, $C(75)$, and $C(100)$.

(b) Which of the intervals $(0, \infty)$ or $[0, \infty)$ would be a more reasonable domain for C? Why?

(c) Graph $y = C(x)$.

38. In a recent year, the cost per ton, y, to build an oil tanker of x thousand deadweight tons is approximated by

$$y = \frac{110,000}{x + 225}.$$

(a) Find y for $x = 25$, $x = 50$, $x = 100$, $x = 200$, $x = 300$, and $x = 400$.

(b) Graph the function.

39. Suppose a cost-benefit model (see Example 5) is given by

$$y = \frac{6.5x}{102 - x},$$

where y is the cost in thousands of dollars of removing x percent of a certain pollutant. Find the cost of removing the following percents of pollutants.

(a) 0%   (b) 50%   (c) 80%   (d) 90%

(e) 95%   (f) 99%   (g) 100%

(h) Graph the function.

40. Suppose a cost-benefit model is given by

$$y = \frac{6.7x}{100 - x},$$

where y is the cost in thousands of dollars of removing x percent of a given pollutant. Find the cost of removing each of the following percents of pollutants.

(a) 50%   (b) 70%   (c) 80%   (d) 90%

(e) 95%   (f) 98%   (g) 99%

(h) Is it possible, according to this function, to remove *all* the pollutant?

(i) Graph the function.

41. Antique car fans often enter their cars in a *concours d'elegance* in which a maximum of 100 points can be awarded to a particular car. Points are awarded for the general attractiveness of the car. Based on a recent article in *Business Week,* we constructed the following mathematical model for the cost, in thousands of dollars, of restoring a car so that it will win x points.

$$C(x) = \frac{10x}{49(101 - x)}$$

Find the cost of restoring a car so that it will win

(a) 99 points;   (b) 100 points.

42. To calculate the drug dosage for a child, pharmacists may use the formula

$$d(x) = \frac{Dx}{x + 12},$$

where x is the child's age in years and D is the adult dosage. Let $D = 70$, the adult dosage of the drug Naldecon.

(a) What is the vertical asymptote for this function?

(b) What is the horizontal asymptote for this function?

(c) Graph $d(x)$.

43. In electronics, the circuit gain is given by

$$G(R) = \frac{R}{r + R},$$

where R is the resistance of a temperature sensor in the circuit and r is a constant. Let $r = 1000$ ohms.

(a) Find any vertical asymptotes of the function.

(b) Find any horizontal asymptotes of the function.

(c) Graph $G(R)$.

Exercises 44 and 45 refer to the *Laffer curve,* originated by the economist Arthur Laffer. It has been a center of controversy. An idealized version of this curve is shown here.

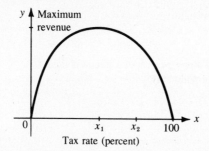

According to this curve, increasing a tax rate, say from x_1 percent to x_2 percent on the graph, can actually lead to a decrease in government revenue. All economists agree on the endpoints—0 revenue at tax rates of both 0% and 100%, but there is much disagreement on the location of the rate x_1 that produces maximum revenue.

44. Suppose an economist studying the Laffer curve produced the rational function

$$y = \frac{60x - 6000}{x - 120}$$

where y is government revenue in millions from a tax rate of x percent, with the function valid for $50 \le x \le 100$. Find the revenue from a tax rate of

(a) 50%   **(b)** 60%   **(c)** 80%   **(d)** 100%.

(e) Graph the function.

45. Suppose our economist studies a different tax, this time producing

$$y = \frac{80x - 8000}{x - 110}$$

with y giving government revenue in tens of millions of dollars for a tax rate of x percent, with the function valid for $55 \le x \le 100$. Find the revenue from a tax rate of

(a) 55%   **(b)** 60%   **(c)** 70%   **(d)** 90%   **(e)** 100%

(f) Graph the function.

We can find approximate maximum or minimum values of polynomial functions on given intervals as follows: Evaluate the function at the left endpoint of the given interval. Then add 0.1 to the value of x and reevaluate the polynomial. Keep doing this until the right endpoint of the interval is reached. Then identify the approximate maximum and minimum value for the polynomial on the interval. Use this procedure in Exercises 46–50.

46. $y = x^3 + 4x^2 - 8x - 8, [-3.8, -3]$

47. $y = x^3 + 4x^2 - 8x - 8, [0.3, 1]$

48. $y = 2x^3 - 5x^2 - x + 1, [-1, 0]$

49. $y = x^4 - 7x^3 + 13x^2 + 6x - 28, [-2, -1]$

50. $y = x^4 - 7x^3 + 13x^2 + 6x - 28, [2, 3]$

Get a table of ordered pairs for the following functions over the given interval at intervals of .5. Then graph the function.

51. $f(x) = x^3 + 3x^2 - 2x + 1; [-3, 1.5]$

52. $f(x) = -3x^4 - 2x^3 + x^2 + x; [-3, 1.5]$

53. $f(x) = \frac{-2x^2}{x^2 - 10}; [-6, 2]$

54. $f(x) = \frac{5x + 4}{2x^2 - 1}; [-4, 6]$

Find the horizontal asymptotes for the functions in Exercises 55–58. Use this information together with the vertical asymptotes and a few ordered pairs to sketch the graph of each function.

55. $f(x) = \dfrac{-2x^2 + x - 1}{2x + 3}$

56. $f(x) = \dfrac{3x + 2}{x^2 - 4}$

57. $f(x) = \dfrac{2x^2 - 5}{x^2 - 1}$

58. $f(x) = \dfrac{4x^2 - 1}{x^2 + 1}$

1.6   Algebra of Functions

In this section we see how to combine two or more functions to obtain a new function. Such combining of functions is called the **algebra of functions.**

Given two functions f and g, their **sum**, written $f + g$, is defined as

$$(f + g)(x) = f(x) + g(x),$$

for all x such that both $f(x)$ and $g(x)$ exist. Similar definitions can be given for the difference, $f - g$, product, $f \cdot g$, and quotient, f/g, of functions; however, the quotient,

$$\left(\frac{f}{g}\right)(x) = \frac{f(x)}{g(x)},$$

is defined only for those values of x where both $f(x)$ and $g(x)$ exist and $g(x) \neq 0$.

Operations on Functions

Let f and g be functions. Let x be in both the domain of f and the domain of g. Then the sum, difference, product, and quotient of f and g are defined as follows:

$$(f + g)(x) = f(x) + g(x) \qquad \text{sum}$$
$$(f - g)(x) = f(x) - g(x) \qquad \text{difference}$$
$$(f \cdot g)(x) = f(x) \cdot g(x) \qquad \text{product}$$
$$\left(\frac{f}{g}\right)(x) = \frac{f(x)}{g(x)}, \quad \text{if } g(x) \neq 0. \qquad \text{quotient}$$

EXAMPLE 1

Let $f(x) = 3x^2 - 4x + 1$ and $g(x) = -4x + 6$. Find each of the following.

(a) $(f + g)(2)$

Since $f(2) = 3 \cdot 2^2 - 4 \cdot 2 + 1 = 12 - 8 + 1 = 5$, and $g(2) = -4 \cdot 2 + 6 = -2$,

$$(f + g)(2) = f(2) + g(2) = 5 + (-2) = 3.$$

We could also find $(f + g)(2)$ by first finding $(f + g)(x)$:

$$(f + g)(x) = (3x^2 - 4x + 1) + (-4x + 6) = 3x^2 - 8x + 7.$$

Replacing x with 2 gives the same result for $(f + g)(2)$.

(b) $(f \cdot g)(-1)$

First, $f(-1) = 3 + 4 + 1 = 8$, and $g(-1) = 4 + 6 = 10$, with

$$(f \cdot g)(-1) = 8 \cdot 10 = 80.$$

(c) $\left(\dfrac{f}{g}\right)(3) = \dfrac{f(3)}{g(3)} = \dfrac{3 \cdot 3^2 - 4 \cdot 3 + 1}{-4 \cdot 3 + 6} = \dfrac{16}{-6} = -\dfrac{8}{3}.$

(d) $\left(\dfrac{f}{g}\right)\left(\dfrac{3}{2}\right)$ cannot be found since $g\left(\dfrac{3}{2}\right) = -4 \cdot \dfrac{3}{2} + 6 = 0.$ ■

EXAMPLE 2

Let $f(x) = 8x - 9$ and $g(x) = \sqrt{2x - 1}$.

(a) $(f + g)(x) = f(x) + g(x) = 8x - 9 + \sqrt{2x - 1}$

(b) $(f - g)(x) = f(x) - g(x) = 8x - 9 - \sqrt{2x - 1}$

(c) $(f \cdot g)(x) = f(x) \cdot g(x) = (8x - 9)\sqrt{2x - 1}$

(d) $\left(\dfrac{f}{g}\right)(x) = \dfrac{f(x)}{g(x)} = \dfrac{8x - 9}{\sqrt{2x - 1}}$

The domain of f is the set of all real numbers, while the domain of $g(x) = \sqrt{2x - 1}$ includes just those real numbers that make $2x - 1 \geq 0$; that is, the interval $[1/2, \infty)$. The domain of $f + g$, $f - g$, and $f \cdot g$ is thus $[1/2, \infty)$. With f/g, the restriction that the denominator not be 0 means that 1/2 must be excluded from the domain. The domain of f/g is $(1/2, \infty)$. ■

The following box summarizes the domains of $f + g$, $f - g$, $f \cdot g$, and f/g. (Recall: the intersection of two sets is the set of all elements belonging to *both* of the sets.)

For functions f and g, the domains of $f + g$, $f - g$, and $f \cdot g$ are made up of all real numbers in the intersection of the domains of f and g, while the domain of f/g is made up of those real numbers in the intersection of the domains of f and g that do not make $g(x) = 0$.

Composition of Functions   The sketch in Figure 32 shows a function f which assigns to each element x of set X some element y of set Y. Suppose also that a function g takes each element of set Y and assigns a value z of set Z. By using both

f and g, an element x in X is assigned to an element z in Z. The result of this process is a new function h, which takes an element x in X and assigns to it an element z in Z.

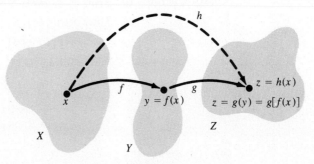

FIGURE 32

This function h is called the *composition* of functions g and f, written $g \circ f$, and defined as follows.

Composite Function

> Let f and g be functions. The **composite function,** or **composition,** of g and f is
> $$(g \circ f)(x) = g[f(x)],$$
> for all x in the domain of f such that $f(x)$ is in the domain of g.

EXAMPLE 3

Let $f(x) = 2x - 1$ and $g(x) = \sqrt{3x + 5}$. Find the following.

(a) $(g \circ f)(4)$

Since $(g \circ f)(4) = g[f(4)]$, find $f(4)$ first.
$$f(4) = 2 \cdot 4 - 1 = 8 - 1 = 7.$$

Then
$$(g \circ f)(4) = g[f(4)] = g[7] = \sqrt{3 \cdot 7 + 5} = \sqrt{26}.$$

(b) $(f \circ g)(4)$

By definition, $(f \circ g)(4) = f[g(4)]$. Since $g(4) = \sqrt{3 \cdot 4 + 5} = \sqrt{17}$,
$$(f \circ g)(4) = f[g(4)] = 2 \cdot \sqrt{17} - 1 = 2\sqrt{17} - 1.$$

(c) $f[g(-2)]$ does not exist since -2 is not in the domain of g. ■

EXAMPLE 4

Let $f(x) = 4x + 1$ and $g(x) = 2x^2 + 5x$. Find each of the following.

(a) $(g \circ f)(x)$

By definition, $(g \circ f)(x) = g[f(x)]$. Using the given functions,

$$
\begin{aligned}
(g \circ f)(x) &= g[f(x)] \\
&= g[4x + 1] \\
&= 2(4x + 1)^2 + 5(4x + 1) \\
&= 2(16x^2 + 8x + 1) + 20x + 5 \\
&= 32x^2 + 16x + 2 + 20x + 5 \\
&= 32x^2 + 36x + 7.
\end{aligned}
$$

(b) $(f \circ g)(x)$

By the definition above, with f and g interchanged, $(f \circ g)(x)$ becomes $f[g(x)]$, making

$$
\begin{aligned}
(f \circ g)(x) &= f[g(x)] \\
&= f[2x^2 + 5x] \\
&= 4(2x^2 + 5x) + 1 \\
&= 8x^2 + 20x + 1. \quad \blacksquare
\end{aligned}
$$

As this example shows, it is not always true that $f \circ g = g \circ f$. (In fact, it is rare to find two functions f and g such that $f \circ g = g \circ f$. See Exercises 37–42.) The domain of both composite functions given in Example 4 is the set of all real numbers.

EXAMPLE 5

Find functions f and g so that the functions given below equal the composition of f and g.

(a) $h(x) = \sqrt{4x + 5}$

If $f(x) = \sqrt{x}$ and $g(x) = 4x + 5$, then

$$h(x) = f[g(x)] = (f \circ g)(x).$$

(b) $h(x) = 2(x - 1)^3 + 5(x - 1)^2 + 4$.

Let $f(x) = 2x^3 + 5x^2 + 4$, and let $g(x) = x - 1$. Then

$$h(x) = f[g(x)] = (f \circ g)(x).$$

There could be different functions f and g whose compositions would also equal $h(x)$. $\blacksquare$

1.6 EXERCISES

In Exercises 1–8, find $f + g$, $f - g$, $f \cdot g$, and f/g. Give the domain of each.

1. $f(x) = 4x - 1$, $g(x) = 6x + 3$
2. $f(x) = 9 - 2x$, $g(x) = -5x + 2$
3. $f(x) = 3x^2 - 2x$, $g(x) = x^2 - 2x + 1$
4. $f(x) = 6x^2 - 11x$, $g(x) = x^2 - 4x - 5$
5. $f(x) = \sqrt{2x + 5}$, $g(x) = \sqrt{4x - 9}$
6. $f(x) = \sqrt{11x - 3}$, $g(x) = \sqrt{2x - 15}$
7. $f(x) = 4x^2 - 11x + 2$, $g(x) = x^2 + 5$
8. $f(x) = 15x^2 - 2x + 1$, $g(x) = 16 + x^2$

Let $f(x) = 4x^2 - 2x$ and let $g(x) = 8x + 1$. Find each of the following.

9. $(f + g)(3)$
10. $(f + g)(-5)$
11. $(f \cdot g)(4)$
12. $(f \cdot g)(-3)$
13. $\left(\dfrac{f}{g}\right)(-1)$
14. $\left(\dfrac{f}{g}\right)(4)$
15. $(f + g)(m)$
16. $(f - g)(2k)$
17. $(f \circ g)(2)$
18. $(f \circ g)(-5)$
19. $(g \circ f)(2)$
20. $(g \circ f)(-5)$
21. $(f \circ g)(k)$
22. $(g \circ f)(5z)$

Find $f \circ g$ and $g \circ f$ in Exercises 23–36.

23. $f(x) = 8x + 12$, $g(x) = 3x - 1$
24. $f(x) = -6x + 9$, $g(x) = 5x + 7$
25. $f(x) = 5x + 3$, $g(x) = -x^2 + 4x + 3$
26. $f(x) = 4x^2 + 2x + 8$, $g(x) = x + 5$
27. $f(x) = -x^3 + 2$, $g(x) = 4x$
28. $f(x) = 2x$, $g(x) = 6x^2 - x^3$
29. $f(x) = \dfrac{1}{x}$, $g(x) = x^2$
30. $f(x) = \dfrac{2}{x^4}$, $g(x) = 2 - x$
31. $f(x) = \sqrt{x + 2}$, $g(x) = 8x^2 - 6$
32. $f(x) = 9x^2 - 11x$, $g(x) = 2\sqrt{x + 2}$
33. $f(x) = \dfrac{1}{x - 5}$, $g(x) = \dfrac{2}{x}$
34. $f(x) = \dfrac{8}{x - 6}$, $g(x) = \dfrac{4}{3x}$
35. $f(x) = \sqrt{x + 1}$, $g(x) = \dfrac{-1}{x}$
36. $f(x) = \dfrac{8}{x}$, $g(x) = \sqrt{3 - x}$

In Exercises 37–42, show that $(f \circ g)(x) = x$ and $(g \circ f)(x) = x$.

37. $f(x) = 8x$, $g(x) = \dfrac{1}{8}x$
38. $f(x) = \dfrac{3}{4}x$, $g(x) = \dfrac{4}{3}x$
39. $f(x) = 8x - 11$, $g(x) = \dfrac{x + 11}{8}$
40. $f(x) = \dfrac{x - 3}{4}$, $g(x) = 4x + 3$
41. $f(x) = x^3 + 6$, $g(x) = \sqrt[3]{x - 6}$
42. $f(x) = \sqrt[5]{x - 9}$, $g(x) = x^5 + 9$

In Exercises 43–48, a function h is given. Find functions f and g such that $h(x) = (f \circ g)(x)$. Many such pairs of functions exist.

43. $h(x) = (6x - 2)^2$
44. $h(x) = (11x^2 + 12x)^2$
45. $h(x) = \sqrt{x^2 - 1}$
46. $h(x) = \dfrac{1}{x^2 + 2}$
47. $h(x) = (3x^2 - 1)^4 + 2(3x^2 - 1)^3$
48. $h(x) = (x + 2)^3 - 3(x + 2)^2$

49. Suppose the population P of a certain species of fish depends on the number x (in hundreds) of a smaller kind of fish which serves as its food supply, so that

$$P(x) = 2x^2 + 1.$$

Suppose, also, that the number x (in hundreds) of the smaller species of fish depends upon the amount a (in appropriate units) of its food supply, a kind of plankton. Suppose

$$x = f(a) = 3a + 2.$$

Find $(P \circ f)(a)$, the relationship between the population P of the large fish and the amount a of plankton available.

50. Suppose the demand for a certain brand of vacuum cleaner is given by

$$D(p) = \frac{-p^2}{100} + 500,$$

where p is the price in dollars. If the price, in terms of the cost, c, is expressed as

$$p(c) = 2c - 10,$$

find the demand in terms of the cost.

51. An oil well off the Gulf Coast is leaking, with the leak spreading oil over the surface as a circle. At any time t, in minutes, after the beginning of the leak, the radius of the circular oil slick on the surface is $r(t) = 4t$ feet. Let $A(r) = \pi r^2$ represent the area of a circle of radius r. Find and interpret $(A \circ r)(t)$.

52. When a thermal inversion layer is over a city (such as happens often in Los Angeles), pollutants cannot rise vertically but are trapped below the layer and must disperse horizontally. Assume that a factory smokestack begins emitting a pollutant at 8 A.M. Assume that the pollutant disperses horizontally, forming a circle. If t represents the time, in hours, since the factory began emitting pollutants ($t = 0$ represents 8 A.M.), assume that the radius of the circle of pollution is $r(t) = 2t$ miles. Let $A(r) = \pi r^2$ represent the area of a circle of radius r. Find and interpret $(A \circ r)(t)$.

Let f and g be polynomial functions each of degree 4. Find the degree of the functions in Exercises 53–55.

53. $f + g$ **54.** $f - g$ **55.** $f \cdot g$

56. Let $f(x) = x/(x - 1)$ for $x \neq 1$. Show that $(f \circ f)(x) = x$. Graph f.

A function f is **even** if $f(-x) = f(x)$ for all x in the domain of f. A function f is **odd** if $f(-x) = -f(x)$ for all x in the domain of f. Decide whether the functions in Exercises 57–64 are *even, odd,* or *neither.*

57. $f(x) = x^2$ **58.** $f(x) = x^3$

59. $f(x) = x^3 - x$ **60.** $f(x) = x^4 + x^2 + 5$

61. $f(x) = 2x + 3$ **62.** $f(x) = |x|$

63. $f(x) = \dfrac{5}{x - 6}$ **64.** $f(x) = \dfrac{8}{x}$

65. Prove: if f is any function, then $g(x) = \frac{1}{2}[f(x) + f(-x)]$ is even.

66. Prove: if f is any function, then $h(x) = \frac{1}{2}[f(x) - f(-x)]$ is odd.

67. Use the results of Exercises 65 and 66 to show that any function may be expressed as the sum of an odd function and an even function.

Prove the statements in Exercises 68–71.

68. The sum of two even functions is even.

69. The product of two even functions is even.

70. The sum of two odd functions is odd.

71. The product of two odd functions is even.

72. What can you say about the sum of an odd and an even function? Give examples.

KEY WORDS		
	mathematical model	equilibrium supply
	function	fixed cost
	independent variable	marginal cost
	dependent variable	break-even point
	domain	quadratic function
	range	parabola
	interval notation	vertex
	Cartesian coordinate system	completing the square
	x-axis	polynomial function
	y-axis	real zero
	quadrant	rational function
	vertical line test	vertical asymptote
	linear function	horizontal asymptote
	slope	cost-benefit model
	point-slope form	algebra of functions
	slope-intercept form	composition of functions
	supply and demand curves	

Chapter 1   REVIEW EXERCISES

List the ordered pairs obtained from each of the following if the domain of x for each exercise is $\{-3, -2, -1, 0, 1, 2, 3\}$. Graph each set of ordered pairs. Give the range.

1. $2x - 5y = 10$

2. $3x + 7y = 21$

3. $y = (2x + 1)(x - 1)$

4. $y = (x + 4)(x + 3)$

5. $y = -2 + x^2$

6. $y = 3x^2 - 7$

7. $y = \dfrac{2}{x^2 + 1}$

8. $y = \dfrac{-3 + x}{x + 10}$

9. $y + 1 = 0$

10. $y = 3$

In Exercises 11–14, find **(a)** $f(6)$, **(b)** $f(-2)$, **(c)** $f(-4)$, **(d)** $f(r+1)$.

11. $f(x) = 4x - 1$ **12.** $f(x) = 3 - 4x$

13. $f(x) = -x^2 + 2x - 4$ **14.** $f(x) = 8 - x - x^2$

15. Let $f(x) = 5x - 3$ and $g(x) = -x^2 + 4x$. Find each of the following.

   (a) $f(-2)$ **(b)** $g(3)$ **(c)** $g(-4)$ **(d)** $f(5)$

   (e) $g(-k)$ **(f)** $g(3m)$ **(g)** $g(k-5)$ **(h)** $f(3-p)$

   (i) $f[g(-1)]$ **(j)** $g[f(2)]$

16. Assume that it costs 30¢ to mail a letter weighing one ounce or less, with each additional ounce, or portion of an ounce, costing 27¢. Let $C(x)$ represent the cost to mail a letter weighing x ounces. Find the cost of mailing a letter of the following weights.

   (a) 3.4 ounces   **(b)** 1.02 ounces

   (c) 5.9 ounces   **(d)** 10 ounces

   (e) Graph C.   **(f)** Give the domain and range for C.

Graph each of the following.

17. $y = 4x + 3$ **18.** $y = 6 - 2x$

19. $3x - 5y = 15$ **20.** $2x + 7y = 14$

21. $x + 2 = 0$ **22.** $y = 1$

23. $y = 2x$ **24.** $x + 3y = 0$

25. The supply and demand for a certain commodity are related by

$$\text{supply: } p = 6x + 3; \quad \text{demand: } p = 19 - 2x,$$

where p represents the price at a supply or demand, respectively, of x units. Find the supply and the demand when the price is

   (a) 10   **(b)** 15   **(c)** 18.

   (d) Graph both the supply and the demand functions on the same axes.

   (e) Find the equilibrium price.

   (f) Find the equilibrium supply; the equilibrium demand.

26. For a particular product, 72 units will be supplied at a price of 6, while 104 units will be supplied at a price of 10. Write a supply function for this product.

In Exercises 27–34, find the slope for each line that has a slope.

27. through $(-2, 5)$ and $(4, 7)$ **28.** through $(4, -1)$ and $(3, -3)$

29. through the origin and $(11, -2)$ **30.** through the origin and $(0, 7)$

31. $2x + 3y = 15$ **32.** $4x - y = 7$

33. $x + 4 = 9$ **34.** $3y - 1 = 14$

In Exercises 35–46, find an equation for each line.

35. through $(5, -1)$, slope 2/3   **36.** through $(8, 0)$, slope $-1/4$

37. through $(5, -2)$ and $(1, 3)$ **38.** through $(2, -3)$ and $(-3, 4)$

39. undefined slope, through $(-1, 4)$ **40.** slope 0, through $(-2, 5)$

41. no x intercept, y intercept 3/4

42. through $(2, -1)$ parallel to $3x - y = 1$

43. through $(0, 5)$, perpendicular to $8x + 5y = 3$

44. through $(2, -10)$, perpendicular to a line with undefined slope

45. through $(3, -5)$ parallel to $y = 4$

46. through $(-7, 4)$, perpendicular to $y = 8$

Graph the lines in Exercises 47–50.

47. through $(2, -4)$, $m = 3/4$

48. through $(0, 5)$, $m = -2/3$

49. through $(-4, 1)$, $m = 3$

50. through $(-3, -2)$, $m = -1$

Find the linear cost functions in Exercises 51–53.

51. eight units of paper cost $300; fixed cost is $60

52. twelve units cost $445; 50 units cost $1585

53. thirty units cost $1500; 120 units cost $5640

54. The cost of producing x units of a product is $C(x)$, where

$$C(x) = 20x + 100.$$

The product sells for $40 per unit.

(a) Find the break-even point.

(b) What revenue will the company receive if it sells just that number of units?

Graph each of the following.

55. $y = x^2 - 4$

56. $y = 6 - x^2$

57. $y = 3(x + 1)^2 - 5$

58. $y = -\frac{1}{4}(x - 2)^2 + 3$

59. $y = x^2 - 4x + 2$

60. $y = -3x^2 - 12x - 1$

61. $f(x) = x^3 + 5$

62. $f(x) = 1 - x^4$

63. $f(x) = 2x^3 - 11x^2 - 2x + 2$

64. $f(x) = x^3 - 3x^2 - 4x - 2$

65. $f(x) = x^4 - 4x^3 - 5x^2 + 14x - 15$

66. $f(x) = x^4 + x^3 - 7x^2 - x + 6$

67. $f(x) = \dfrac{8}{x}$

68. $f(x) = \dfrac{2}{3x - 1}$

69. $f(x) = \dfrac{4x - 2}{3x + 1}$

70. $f(x) = \dfrac{6x}{(x - 1)(x + 2)}$

Let $f(x) = 3x^2 - 4$ and $g(x) = x^2 - 3x - 4$. Find each of the following.

71. $(f + g)(x)$

72. $(f \cdot g)(x)$

73. $(f - g)(4)$

74. $(f + g)(-4)$

75. $(f + g)(2k)$

76. $(f \cdot g)(1 + r)$

77. $(f/g)(3)$

78. $(f/g)(-1)$

79. Give the domain of $(f \cdot g)(x)$.

80. Give the domain of $(f/g)(x)$.

Let $f(x) = \sqrt{x - 2}$ and $g(x) = x^2$. Find each of the following.

81. $(f \circ g)(x)$

82. $(g \circ f)(x)$

83. $(f \circ g)(-6)$

84. $(f \circ g)(2)$

85. $(g \circ f)(3)$

86. $(g \circ f)(24)$

SYSTEMS OF LINEAR EQUATIONS AND MATRICES

Karl Gerstner. From the series *Aperspective 3* (The Large Sliding Mirror Picture), 1953/55.

Many mathematical models involve more than one equation that must be satisfied. A set of equations related in this way is called a **system of equations.** Any solutions of the equations in the set that satisfy all the equations are solutions of the system. After discussing systems, this chapter introduces the idea of a **matrix,** and shows how matrices are used to solve systems of linear equations.

2.1   Systems of Linear Equations

An animal feed is made from three ingredients: corn, soybeans, and cottonseed. One unit of each ingredient provides the number of units of protein, fat, and fiber shown in the table. For example, the entries in the first row, .25, .4, and .3, mean that one unit of corn provides twenty-five hundredths (one fourth) of a unit of protein, four tenths of a unit of fat, and three tenths of a unit of fiber. Suppose we need to know the number of units of each ingredient that should be used to make a feed which contains 22 units of protein, 28 units of fat, and 18 units of fiber.

	Protein	Fat	Fiber
Corn	.25	.4	.3
Soybeans	.4	.2	.2
Cottonseed	.2	.3	.1

To find out, let x represent the number of units of corn; y, the number of units of soybeans; and z, the number of units of cottonseed which are required. Since the total amount of protein is to be 22 units,

$$.25x + .4y + .2z = 22.$$

Also, for the 28 units of fat,

$$.4x + .2y + .3z = 28,$$

and, for the 18 units of fiber,

$$.3x + .2y + .1z = 18.$$

To solve the problem, values of x, y, and z must be found that satisfy this system of equations. Verify that $x = 40$, $y = 15$, and $z = 30$ is a solution of the system, since these numbers satisfy all three equations. In fact, this is the only solution of this system. Many practical problems lead to such systems of equations. In this chapter, we consider methods for solving these systems of first-degree equations.

A **first degree equation** in n unknowns is any equation of the form

$$a_1x_1 + a_2x_2 + \cdots + a_nx_n = k,$$

where a_1, a_2, $\cdots$, a_n and k are all real numbers. Each of the three equations from the animal feed problem is a first degree equation in 3 unknowns. The **solution** of the first degree equation

$$a_1x_1 + a_2x_2 + \cdots + a_nx_n = k$$

is a sequence of numbers s_1, s_2, $\cdots$, s_n, such that

$$a_1s_1 + a_2s_2 + \cdots + a_ns_n = k.$$

The solution may be written between parentheses as $(s_1, s_2, \cdots, s_n)$. For example, $(1, 6, 2)$ is a solution of the equation $3x_1 + 2x_2 - 4x_3 = 7$, since $3(1) + 2(6) - 4(2) = 7$.

A first-degree equation in two unknowns has a graph which is a straight line. For this reason, first-degree equations are also called **linear equations.** In this section we develop a method of solving a system of first degree equations. Although our discussion will be confined to equations with only a few variables, the methods of solution can be extended to systems with many variables.

Because the graph of a linear equation in two variables is a straight line, there are three possibilities for the solution of a system of two linear equations in two variables.

1. The two graphs are lines intersecting at a single point. The coordinates of this point give the solution of the system. [See Figure 1(a).]
2. The graphs are distinct parallel lines. When this is the case, the system is **inconsistent;** that is, there is no solution common to both equations. [See Figure 1(b).]
3. The graphs are the same line. In this case, the equations are said to be **dependent,** since any solution of one equation is also a solution of the other. There are an infinite number of solutions. [See Figure 1(c).]

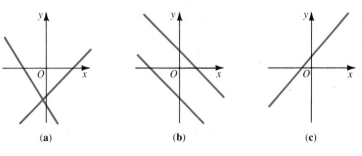

(a)   (b)   (c)

FIGURE 1

In larger systems, with more equations and more variables, there also may be exactly one solution, an infinite number of solutions, or no solution. In any system, if all the equations are dependent, the system will have an infinite number of solutions. If no solution satisfies every equation in the system, the system is inconsistent.

Transformations   To solve a linear system of equations, properties of algebra are used to change the system until a simpler equivalent system is found. An **equivalent system** is one that has the same solutions as the given system. Three transformations can be applied to a system to get an equivalent system:

Transformations

of a System

1. **exchanging any two equations;**
2. **multiplying both sides of an equation by any nonzero real number;**
3. **adding to any equation a multiple of some other equation.**

Use of these transformations leads to an equivalent system because each transformation can be reversed or "undone," allowing a return to the original system.

EXAMPLE 1

Solve the system

$$3x - 4y = 1 \tag{1}$$
$$2x + 3y = 12. \tag{2}$$

We want to get a system of equations which is equivalent to the given system, but simpler. If the equations are transformed so that the variable x disappears from one of them, the value of y can be found. First, use the second transformation to multiply both sides of equation (1) by 2. This gives the equivalent system

$$6x - 8y = 2 \tag{3}$$
$$2x + 3y = 12. \tag{2}$$

Now, using the third transformation, multiply both sides of equation (2) by -3, and add the result to equation (3).

$$(6x - 8y) + (-3)(2x + 3y) = 2 + (-3)(12)$$
$$6x - 8y - 6x - 9y = 2 - 36$$
$$-17y = -34$$
$$y = 2$$

The result of these steps is the equivalent system

$$3x - 4y = 1 \tag{1}$$
$$y = 2. \tag{4}$$

To find the value of x, substitute 2 for y in equation (1) to get

$$3x - 4(2) = 1$$
$$3x - 8 = 1$$
$$x = 3.$$

The solution of the given system is (3, 2). The graphs of both equations of the system are shown in Figure 2. The graph suggests that (3, 2) satisfies both equations of the system. ■

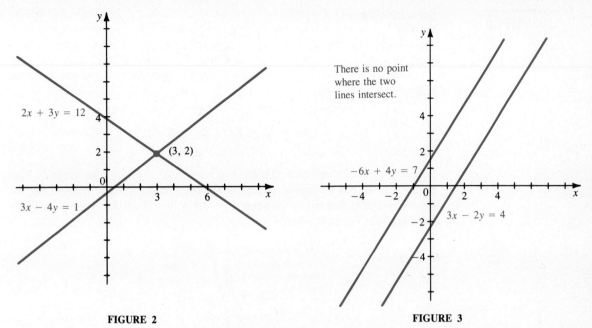

FIGURE 2   **FIGURE 3**

Since the method of solution in Example 1 results in the elimination of one variable from an equation of the system, it is called the **elimination method** for solving a system.

EXAMPLE 2

Solve the system

$$3x - 2y = 4$$
$$-6x + 4y = 7.$$

Eliminate x by multiplying the first equation by 2 and adding the result to the second equation.

$$2(3x - 2y) + (-6x + 4y) = 2(4) + 7$$
$$6x - 4y - 6x + 4y = 8 + 7$$
$$0 = 15$$

The new system is

$$3x - 2y = 4$$
$$0 = 15. \qquad \text{**False**}$$

In the second equation, both variables have been eliminated with the result a false statement, a signal that these two equations have no common solution. This system is inconsistent and has no solution. As Figure 3 shows, the graph of the system is made up of two distinct parallel lines. ∎

EXAMPLE 3

Solve the system

$$-4x + y = 2$$
$$8x - 2y = -4.$$

To eliminate x, multiply both sides of the first equation by 2 and add the result to the second equation.

$$2(-4x + y) + (8x - 2y) = 2(2) + (-4)$$
$$-8x + 2y + 8x - 2y = 4 - 4$$
$$0 = 0$$

This true statement indicates that the two equations have the same graph, which means that there is an infinite number of solutions for the system. In this case, all the ordered pairs that satisfy the equation $-4x + y = 2$ (or $8x - 2y = -4$) are solutions. See Figure 4. ■

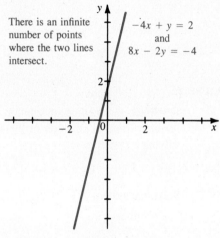

There is an infinite number of points where the two lines intersect.

$-4x + y = 2$
and
$8x - 2y = -4$

FIGURE 4

Several steps are needed to use the elimination method to solve a system of three equations with three variables, as shown in Example 4.

EXAMPLE 4

Solve the system

$$2x + y - z = 2 \qquad \qquad \textbf{(1)}$$
$$x + 3y + 2z = 1 \qquad \qquad \textbf{(2)}$$
$$x + y + z = 2. \qquad \qquad \textbf{(3)}$$

Begin by eliminating one variable from one pair of equations. Suppose we choose to eliminate x from equations (2) and (3) by multiplying both sides of equation (3) by -1 and then adding the two equations vertically.

$$x + 3y + 2z = 1 \qquad \qquad \textbf{(2)}$$
$$\underline{-x - y - z = -2}$$
$$2y + z = -1 \qquad \qquad \textbf{(4)}$$

Now eliminate x from another pair of equations, say (1) and (2). This can be done by multiplying both sides of equation (2) by -2 and adding the result to equation (1).

$$2x + y - z = 2 \qquad \textbf{(1)}$$
$$\underline{-2x - 6y - 4z = -2}$$
$$-5y - 5z = 0 \qquad \textbf{(5)}$$

Equations (4) and (5) are now used to eliminate another variable. Multiplying both sides of equation (5) by 1/5 and adding the result to equation (4) eliminates z.

$$2y + z = -1 \qquad \textbf{(4)}$$
$$\underline{-y - z = 0} \qquad \textbf{(6)}$$
$$y \quad\;\; = -1$$

Now substitute for y in equation (6) to get

$$-y - z = 0$$
$$-(-1) - z = 0$$
$$1 - z = 0$$
$$z = 1.$$

Finally, substituting $y = -1$ and $z = 1$ into one of the original equations, say equation (1), gives

$$2x + (-1) - (1) = 2$$
$$2x - 2 = 2$$
$$2x = 4$$
$$x = 2.$$

The solution is $(2, -1, 1)$. ▪

The Echelon Method   Although the elimination method can be used to solve systems with more than two equations, it is a complicated process even for systems of three variables. A more systematic approach, using matrix notation (discussed later in this chapter), makes it possible to solve systems of equations by computer. In the next example we solve the system of Example 4 again to illustrate the new method.

EXAMPLE 5

Solve the system

$$2x + y - z = 2 \qquad \textbf{(1)}$$
$$x + 3y + 2z = 1 \qquad \textbf{(2)}$$
$$x + y + z = 2. \qquad \textbf{(3)}$$

We want to replace the given system with an equivalent system from which the solution is easily found. In the new system, the coefficient of x in the first equation should be 1. Use the first transformation to exchange equations (1) and (2). (We could have multiplied both sides of equation (1) by 1/2 instead.) The new system is

$$x + 3y + 2z = 1 \tag{2}$$
$$2x + y - z = 2 \tag{1}$$
$$x + y + z = 2. \tag{3}$$

To get a new second equation without x, multiply each term of equation (2) by -2 and add the results to equation (1). This gives

$$-5y - 5z = 0. \tag{4}$$

Multiply both sides of equation (4) by $-1/5$ to make the coefficient of y equal to 1.

$$y + z = 0 \tag{5}$$

We now have the equivalent system

$$x + 3y + 2z = 1 \tag{2}$$
$$y + z = 0 \tag{5}$$
$$x + y + z = 2. \tag{3}$$

Get a new third equation without x by multiplying both sides of equation (2) by -1 and adding the results to equation (3). The result is

$$-2y - z = 1. \tag{6}$$

Now multiply both sides of equation (5) by 2 and add to equation (6) to get

$$z = 1. \tag{7}$$

The original system has now led to the equivalent system

$$x + 3y + 2z = 1 \tag{2}$$
$$y + z = 0 \tag{5}$$
$$z = 1. \tag{7}$$

From equation (7) we know $z = 1$. Substitute 1 for z in equation (5) to get $y = -1$. Finally substitute 1 for z and -1 for y in equation (2) to get $x = 2$, and the solution of the system, $(2, -1, 1)$. ∎

This method, where the system is rewritten in the form suggested by equations (2), (5), and (7), is sometimes called the **echelon method.** In summary, to solve a linear system in n variables by the echelon method, perform the following steps using the three transformations.

The Echelon Method of Solving a Linear System	1. Make the coefficient of the first variable equal to 1 in the first equation and 0 in the other equations. 2. Make the coefficient of the second variable equal to 1 in the second equation and 0 in all remaining equations. 3. Make the coefficient of the third variable equal to 1 in the third equation and 0 in all remaining equations. 4. Continue in this way until the last equation is of the form $x_n = k$, where k is a constant.

Parameters The systems of equations discussed so far have had the same number of equations as variables. Such systems have either one solution, no solution, or an infinite number of solutions. However, sometimes a mathematical model leads to a system of equations with fewer equations than variables. Such systems always have an infinite number of solutions or no solution.

EXAMPLE 6

Solve

$$2x + 3y + 4z = 6 \qquad \textbf{(1)}$$
$$x - 2y + z = 9 \qquad \textbf{(2)}$$
$$3x - 6y + 3z = 27. \qquad \textbf{(3)}$$

Since the third equation here is a multiple of the second equation, this system really has only the two equations

$$2x + 3y + 4z = 6 \qquad \textbf{(1)}$$
$$x - 2y + z = 9. \qquad \textbf{(2)}$$

Exchange the two equations so that the coefficient of x is 1 in the first equation of the system. This gives

$$x - 2y + z = 9 \qquad \textbf{(2)}$$
$$2x + 3y + 4z = 6. \qquad \textbf{(1)}$$

To get a new second equation without x, multiply both sides of equation (2) by -2 and add to equation (1). The result is

$$7y + 2z = -12.$$

Multiply both sides of this equation by 1/7. The new system is

$$x - 2y + z = 9 \qquad \textbf{(2)}$$
$$y + \frac{2}{7}z = \frac{-12}{7}. \qquad \textbf{(3)}$$

Since we have only two equations, we can go no further. To complete the solution, solve equation (3) for y.

$$y = \frac{-2}{7}z - \frac{12}{7}$$

Now substitute the result for y in equation (2), and solve for x.

$$x - 2y + z = 9 \qquad \textbf{(2)}$$
$$x - 2\left(\frac{-2}{7}z - \frac{12}{7}\right) + z = 9$$
$$x + \frac{4}{7}z + \frac{24}{7} + z = 9$$
$$7x + 4z + 24 + 7z = 63$$
$$7x + 11z = 39$$
$$7x = -11z + 39$$
$$x = \frac{-11}{7}z + \frac{39}{7}$$

We now have both x and y expressed in terms of z. Each choice of a value for z leads to values for x and y. For example,

if $z = 1$,   then $x = -\dfrac{11}{7} \cdot 1 + \dfrac{39}{7} = 4$ and $y = -\dfrac{2}{7} \cdot 1 - \dfrac{12}{7} = -2$;

if $z = -6$,   then $x = 15$ and $y = 0$;

if $z = 0$,   then $x = \dfrac{39}{7}$ and $y = \dfrac{-12}{7}$.

Since x and y are both given in terms of z, the variable z is called a **parameter.** There is an infinite number of solutions for the original system, since z can take on an infinite number of values. The set of solutions may be written

$$\left\{ \left(\frac{-11}{7}z + \frac{39}{7}, \frac{-2}{7}z - \frac{12}{7}, z \right) \right\}.$$

By solving the original system in a different way, we could make x or y the parameter. ▪

Example 6 discussed a system with one more variable than equations. If there are two more variables than equations, there usually will be two parameters, and so on. What if there are fewer variables than equations? For example, consider the system

$$\begin{array}{lr} 2x + 3y = 8 & \textbf{(1)} \\ x - y = 4 & \textbf{(2)} \\ 5x + y = 7, & \textbf{(3)} \end{array}$$

which has three equations and two variables. Since each of these equations has a line as its graph, there are various possibilities: three lines that intersect at a common point, three lines that cross at three different points, three lines of which two are the same line so that the intersection would be a point, three lines of which two are parallel so that the intersection would be two different points, three lines which are all parallel so that there would be no intersection, and so on. As in the case of n equations with n variables, the possibilities result in a unique solution, no solution, or an infinite number of solutions.

To solve the system using the echelon method, begin by exchanging equations (1) and (2) to get a 1 for the coefficient of x in the first equation.

$$\begin{array}{lr} x - y = 4 & \textbf{(2)} \\ 2x + 3y = 8 & \textbf{(1)} \\ 5x + y = 7 & \textbf{(3)} \end{array}$$

Now multiply both sides of equation (2) by -2 and add the result to equation (1) to get $5y = 0$. The new system is

$$\begin{array}{lr} x - y = 4 & \textbf{(2)} \\ 5y = 0 & \textbf{(4)} \\ 5x + y = 7. & \textbf{(3)} \end{array}$$

Multiply both sides of equation (4) by 1/5 to get $y = 0$. Substituting $y = 0$ leads to $x = 4$ in equation (2) and $x = 7/5$ in equation (3), a contradiction. This contradiction shows that the system has no solution.

Applications   If the mathematical techniques of this text are to be useful, you must be able to apply them to practical problems. To do this, always begin by reading the problem carefully. Then identify what must be found. Each unknown quantity should be represented by a variable. It is a good idea to *write down* exactly what each variable represents. Then reread the problem, looking for all necessary data. Write that down, too. Finally, look for one or more sentences which lead to equations or inequalities. The next example illustrates these steps.

EXAMPLE 7

A bank teller has a total of 70 bills, of five-, ten- and twenty-dollar denominations. The number of fives is three times the number of tens, while the total value of the money is $960. Find the number of each type of bill.

Let x be the number of fives, y the number of tens, and z the number of twenties. Then, since the total number of bills is 70,

$$x + y + z = 70.$$

Also the number of fives, x, is 3 times the number of tens, y.

$$x = 3y$$

Finally, the total value is $960. The value of the fives is $5x$, of the tens is $10y$, and of the twenties is $20z$, so that

$$5x + 10y + 20z = 960.$$

Rewriting the second equation as $x - 3y = 0$ gives the system

$$
\begin{array}{lr}
x + \quad y + \quad z = 70 & \textbf{(1)} \\
x - \quad 3y \qquad\quad = 0 & \textbf{(2)} \\
5x + 10y + 20z = 960. & \textbf{(3)}
\end{array}
$$

To solve by the echelon method, first eliminate x from equation (2). Do this by multiplying both sides of equation (1) by -1 and adding to equation (2). Then multiply both sides of the result by $-1/4$. The new system is

$$
\begin{array}{lr}
x + \quad y + \quad z = 70 & \textbf{(1)} \\
y + \dfrac{1}{4}z = \dfrac{35}{2} & \textbf{(4)} \\
5x + 10y + 20z = 960. & \textbf{(3)}
\end{array}
$$

Use a similar procedure to eliminate x from equation (3) to get the system

$$
\begin{array}{lr}
x + y + \quad z = 70 & \textbf{(1)} \\
y + \dfrac{1}{4}z = \dfrac{35}{2} & \textbf{(4)} \\
5y + 15z = 610. & \textbf{(5)}
\end{array}
$$

To eliminate y from equation (5), multiply both sides of equation (4) by -5 and add to equation (5). The final equivalent system is

$$x + y + z = 70 \tag{1}$$

$$y + \frac{1}{4}z = \frac{35}{2} \tag{5}$$

$$\frac{55}{4}z = \frac{1045}{2}. \tag{6}$$

Equation (6) gives $z = 38$. Substituting this result into equation (5) gives $y = 8$, and finally, from equation (1), $x = 24$. The teller had 24 fives, 8 tens, and 38 twenties. Check this answer in the words of the original problem. ■

2.1 EXERCISES

Use the elimination method to solve the systems of two equations in two unknowns in Exercises 1–16. Check your answers.

1. $x + y = 9$
$2x - y = 0$

2. $4x + y = 9$
$3x - y = 5$

3. $5x + 3y = 7$
$7x - 3y = -19$

4. $2x + 7y = -8$
$-2x + 3y = -12$

5. $3x + 2y = -6$
$5x - 2y = -10$

6. $-6x + 2y = 8$
$5x - 2y = -8$

7. $2x - 3y = -7$
$5x + 4y = 17$

8. $4m + 3n = -1$
$2m + 5n = 3$

9. $5p + 7q = 6$
$10p - 3q = 46$

10. $12s - 5t = 9$
$3s - 8t = -18$

11. $6x + 7y = -2$
$7x - 6y = 26$

12. $2a + 9b = 3$
$5a + 7b = -8$

13. $3x + 2y = 5$
$6x + 4y = 8$

14. $9x - 5y = 1$
$-18x + 10y = 1$

15. $4x - y = 9$
$-8x + 2y = -18$

16. $3x + 5y + 2 = 0$
$9x + 15y + 6 = 0$

In Exercises 17–20, first multiply both sides of each equation by its common denominator to eliminate the fractions. Then use the elimination method to solve. Check your answers.

17. $\dfrac{x}{2} + \dfrac{y}{3} = 8$
$\dfrac{2x}{3} + \dfrac{3y}{2} = 17$

18. $\dfrac{x}{5} + 3y = 31$
$2x - \dfrac{y}{5} = 8$

19. $\dfrac{x}{2} + y = \dfrac{3}{2}$
$\dfrac{x}{3} + y = \dfrac{1}{3}$

20. $x + \dfrac{y}{3} = -6$
$\dfrac{x}{5} + \dfrac{y}{4} = -\dfrac{7}{4}$

In Exercises 21–34, use the echelon method to solve each of the systems of three equations in three unknowns. Check your answers.

21. $x + y + z = 2$
$2x + y - z = 5$
$x - y + z = -2$

22. $2x + y + z = 9$
$-x - y + z = 1$
$3x - y + z = 9$

23. $x + 3y + 4z = 14$
$2x - 3y + 2z = 10$
$3x - y + z = 9$

24. $4x - y + 3z = -2$
$3x + 5y - z = 15$
$-2x + y + 4z = 14$

25. $x + 2y + 3z = 8$
$3x - y + 2z = 5$
$-2x - 4y - 6z = 5$

26. $3x - 2y - 8z = 1$
$9x - 6y - 24z = -2$
$x - y + z = 1$

27. $2x - 4y + z = -4$
$x + 2y - z = 0$
$-x + y + z = 6$

28. $4x - 3y + z = 9$
$3x + 2y - 2z = 4$
$x - y + 3z = 5$

29. $x + 4y - z = 6$
$2x - y + z = 3$
$3x + 2y + 3z = 16$

30. $3x + y - z = 7$
$2x - 3y + z = -7$
$x - 4y + 3z = -6$

31. $5m + n - 3p = -6$
$2m + 3n + p = 5$
$-3m - 2n + 4p = 3$

32. $2r - 5s + 4t = -35$
$5r + 3s - t = 1$
$r + s + t = 1$

33. $a - 3b - 2c = -3$
$3a + 2b - c = 12$
$-a - b + 4c = 3$

34. $2x + 2y + 2z = 6$
$3x - 3y - 4z = -1$
$x + y + 3z = 11$

Solve the systems of equations in Exercises 35–40. Let x be the parameter.

35. $5x + 3y + 4z = 19$
$3x - y + z = -4$

36. $3x + y - z = 0$
$2x - y + 3z = -7$

37. $x + 2y + 3z = 11$
$2x - y + z = 2$

38. $-x + y - z = -7$
$2x + 3y + z = 7$

39. $x + y - z + 2w = -20$
$2x - y + z + w = 11$
$3x - 2y + z - 2w = 27$

40. $4x + 3y + z + 2w = 1$
$-2x - y + 2z + 3w = 0$
$x + 4y + z - w = 12$

Solve each of the systems of equations in Exercises 41–46.

41. $5x + 2y = 7$
$-2x + y = -10$
$x - 3y = 15$

42. $9x - 2y = -14$
$3x + y = -4$
$-6x - 2y = 8$

43. $x + 7y = 5$
$4x - 3y = 2$
$-x + 2y = 10$

44. $-3x - 2y = 11$
$x + 2y = -14$
$5x + y = -9$

45. $x + y = 2$
$y + z = 4$
$x + z = 3$
$y - z = 8$

46. $2x + y = 7$
$x + 3z = 5$
$y - 2z = 6$
$x + 4y = 10$

Write a system of equations for Exercises 47–52; then solve the system.

47. A working couple earned a total of $4352. The wife earned $64 per day; the husband earned $8 per day less. Find the number of days each worked if the total number of days worked by both was 72.

48. Midtown Manufacturing Company makes two products, plastic plates and plastic cups. Both require time on two machines: a batch of plates—one hour on machine A and two hours on machine B; a batch of cups—three hours on machine A and one hour on machine B. Both machines operate 15 hours a day. How many batches of each product can be produced in a day under these conditions?

49. A company produces two models of bicycles, model 201 and model 301. Model 201 requires 2 hours of assembly time and model 301 requires 3 hours of assembly time. The parts for model 201 cost $25 per bike and the parts for model 301 cost $30 per bike. If the company has a total of 34 hours of assembly time and $365 available per day for these two models, how many of each can be made in a day?

50. Juanita invests $10,000, received from her grandmother, in three ways. With one part, she buys mutual funds which offer a return of 8% per year. The second part, which amounts to twice the first, is used to buy government bonds at 9% per year. She puts the rest in the bank at 5% annual interest. The first year her investments bring a return of $830. How much did she invest in each way?

51. To get the necessary funds for a planned expansion, a small company took out three loans totaling $25,000. The company was able to borrow some of the money at 16%. They borrowed $2000 more than one-half the amount of the 16% loan at 20%, and the rest at 18%. The total annual interest on the loans was $4440. How much did they borrow at each rate?

52. The business analyst for Midtown Manufacturing wants to find an equation which can be used to project sales of a relatively new product. For the years 1982, 1983, and 1984 sales were \$15,000, \$32,000, and \$123,000 respectively.

(a) Graph the sales for the years 1982, 1983, and 1984 letting the year 1982 equal 0 on the x-axis. Let the values on the vertical axis be in thousands. [For example, the point (1983, 32,000) will be graphed as (1, 32).]

(b) Find the equation of the straight line $ax + by = c$ through the points for 1982 and 1984.

(c) Find the equation of the parabola $y = ax^2 + bx + c$ through the three given points.

(d) Find the projected sales for 1987 first by using the equation from part (b) and second, by using the equation from part (c). If you were to estimate sales of the product in 1987 which result would you choose? Why?

In Exercises 53 and 54, find the value of k for which each system has a single solution, then find the solution of the system.

53.
$$\begin{aligned}
4x \quad\quad + 8z &= 12 \\
2y - \quad z &= -2 \\
3x + \quad y + \quad z &= -1 \\
x + \quad y - kz &= -7
\end{aligned}$$

54.
$$\begin{aligned}
2x + \quad y + \quad z &= 4 \\
3y + \quad z &= -2 \\
x + \quad y - \quad z &= -3 \\
4x \quad\quad + kz &= 8
\end{aligned}$$

2.2 Solution of Linear Systems by
the Gauss-Jordan Method

In the last section the echelon method was used to solve linear systems of equations. Since the variables are always the same, we really need to keep track of just the coefficients and the constants. For example, let's look at the system we solved in Examples 4 and 5 of the previous section,

$$\begin{aligned}
2x + \quad y - \quad z &= 2 \\
x + 3y + 2z &= 1 \\
x + \quad y + \quad z &= 2.
\end{aligned}$$

This system can be written in an abbreviated form as

$$\begin{bmatrix} 2 & 1 & -1 & 2 \\ 1 & 3 & 2 & 1 \\ 1 & 1 & 1 & 2 \end{bmatrix}.$$

Such a rectangular array of numbers enclosed by brackets is called a **matrix** (plural: **matrices**). Each number in the array is an **element** or **entry.** To separate the constants in the last column of the matrix from the coefficients of the variables, use a vertical line, producing the following **augmented matrix.**

$$\left[\begin{array}{ccc|c} 2 & 1 & -1 & 2 \\ 1 & 3 & 2 & 1 \\ 1 & 1 & 1 & 2 \end{array}\right]$$

The rows of the augmented matrix can be transformed in the same way as the equations of the system, since the matrix is just a shortened form of the system. The **row operations** on the augmented matrix which correspond to the transformations of systems of equations are given in the following theorem.

Row Operations

For any augmented matrix of a system of equations, the following operations produce the augmented matrix of an equivalent system:

1. interchanging any two rows;
2. multiplying the elements of a row by any nonzero real number;
3. adding a multiple of the elements of one row to the corresponding elements of some other row.

Row operations, like the transformations of systems of equations, are reversible. If they are used to go from matrix A to matrix B, then it is possible to use row operations to transform B back into A. In addition to their use in solving equations, row operations are very important in the simplex method of Chapter 4.

By the first row operation, the matrix

$$\begin{bmatrix} 1 & 3 & 5 & 6 \\ 0 & 1 & 2 & 3 \\ 2 & 1 & -2 & -5 \end{bmatrix} \quad \text{becomes} \quad \begin{bmatrix} 0 & 1 & 2 & 3 \\ 1 & 3 & 5 & 6 \\ 2 & 1 & -2 & -5 \end{bmatrix}$$

by interchanging the first two rows. Row three is left unchanged.

The second row operation allows us to change

$$\begin{bmatrix} 1 & 3 & 5 & 6 \\ 0 & 1 & 2 & 3 \\ 2 & 1 & -2 & -5 \end{bmatrix} \quad \text{to} \quad \begin{bmatrix} -2 & -6 & -10 & -12 \\ 0 & 1 & 2 & 3 \\ 2 & 1 & -2 & -5 \end{bmatrix}$$

by multiplying the elements of the first row of the original matrix by -2. Note that rows two and three are left unchanged.

Using the third row operation,

$$\begin{bmatrix} 1 & 3 & 5 & 6 \\ 0 & 1 & 2 & 3 \\ 2 & 1 & -2 & -5 \end{bmatrix} \quad \text{becomes} \quad \begin{bmatrix} -1 & 2 & 7 & 11 \\ 0 & 1 & 2 & 3 \\ 2 & 1 & -2 & -5 \end{bmatrix}$$

after first multiplying each element in the third row of the original matrix by -1 and then adding the results to the corresponding elements in the first row of that matrix. Work as follows.

$$\begin{bmatrix} 1 + 2(-1) & 3 + 1(-1) & 5 + (-2)(-1) & 6 + (-5)(-1) \\ 0 & 1 & 2 & 3 \\ 2 & 1 & -2 & -5 \end{bmatrix} = \begin{bmatrix} -1 & 2 & 7 & 11 \\ 0 & 1 & 2 & 3 \\ 2 & 1 & -2 & -5 \end{bmatrix}$$

Again rows two and three are left unchanged, *even though the elements of row three were used to transform row one.*

The Gauss-Jordan Method The *Gauss-Jordan method* is an extension of the echelon method of solving systems. Before the Gauss-Jordan method can be used, the system must be in proper form: the terms with variables should be on the left and the constants on the right in each equation, with the variables in the same order in each equation. The following example illustrates the use of the Gauss-Jordan method to solve a system of equations.

EXAMPLE 1

Solve the system

$$3x - 4y = 1 \tag{1}$$
$$5x + 2y = 19. \tag{2}$$

The system is already in the proper form. The solution procedure is parallel to the echelon method of Section 2.1, except for the last step. We show the echelon method on the left below and the Gauss-Jordan method on the right. First, write the augmented matrix for the system.

Echelon Method

$$3x - 4y = 1 \tag{1}$$
$$5x + 2y = 19 \tag{2}$$

Multiply both sides of equation (1) by 1/3 so that x has a coefficient of 1.

$$x - \frac{4}{3}y = \frac{1}{3} \tag{3}$$
$$5x + 2y = 19 \tag{2}$$

Eliminate x from equation (2) by adding -5 times equation (3) to equation (2).

$$x - \frac{4}{3}y = \frac{1}{3} \tag{3}$$
$$\frac{26}{3}y = \frac{52}{3} \tag{4}$$

Multiply both sides of equation (4) by 3/26 to get $y = 2$.

$$x - \frac{4}{3}y = \frac{1}{3} \tag{3}$$
$$y = 2 \tag{5}$$

Substitute $y = 2$ into equation (3) and solve for x to get $x = 3$.

$$x = 3 \tag{6}$$
$$y = 2 \tag{5}$$

Gauss-Jordan Method

$$\left[\begin{array}{cc|c} 3 & -4 & 1 \\ 5 & 2 & 19 \end{array}\right]$$

Using row operation (2), multiply each element of row 1 by 1/3.

$$\left[\begin{array}{cc|c} 1 & -\frac{4}{3} & \frac{1}{3} \\ 5 & 2 & 19 \end{array}\right]$$

Using row operation (3), add -5 times the elements of row 1 to the elements of row 2.

$$\left[\begin{array}{cc|c} 1 & -\frac{4}{3} & \frac{1}{3} \\ 0 & \frac{26}{3} & \frac{52}{3} \end{array}\right]$$

Multiply the elements of row 2 by 3/26, using row operation (2).

$$\left[\begin{array}{cc|c} 1 & -\frac{4}{3} & \frac{1}{3} \\ 0 & 1 & 2 \end{array}\right]$$

Multiply the elements of row 2 by 4/3 and add to the elements of row 1 (row operation (3)).

$$\left[\begin{array}{cc|c} 1 & 0 & 3 \\ 0 & 1 & 2 \end{array}\right]$$

The solution of the system, (3, 2), can be read directly from the last column of the final matrix. ■

In the final matrix above, the columns to the left of the vertical line were transformed into the 2×2 identity matrix. When using row operations to transform the matrix, it is best to work column by column from left to right. For each column, the first change should produce a 1 in the proper position. Next, perform the steps that give zeros in the remainder of the column. Then proceed to the next column in the matrix.

EXAMPLE 2

Use the Gauss-Jordan method to solve the system

$$x + 5z = -6 + y$$
$$3x + 3y = 10 + z$$
$$x + 3y + 2z = 5.$$

First, rewrite the system in proper form as follows.

$$x - y + 5z = -6$$
$$3x + 3y - z = 10$$
$$x + 3y + 2z = 5$$

Begin the solution by writing the augmented matrix of the linear system.

$$\begin{bmatrix} 1 & -1 & 5 & | & -6 \\ 3 & 3 & -1 & | & 10 \\ 1 & 3 & 2 & | & 5 \end{bmatrix}$$

Our method of solution will be to use row transformations to rewrite this matrix in the form

$$\begin{bmatrix} 1 & 0 & 0 & | & m \\ 0 & 1 & 0 & | & n \\ 0 & 0 & 1 & | & p \end{bmatrix},$$

where m, n, and p are real numbers. From this final form of the matrix, the solution can be read: $x = m$, $y = n$, and $z = p$.

There is already a 1 for the first element in column one. To get 0 for the second element in column one, multiply each element in the first row by -3 and add the results to the corresponding elements in row two (using row operation (3)).

$$\begin{bmatrix} 1 & -1 & 5 & | & -6 \\ 0 & 6 & -16 & | & 28 \\ 1 & 3 & 2 & | & 5 \end{bmatrix}$$

To change the last element in column one to 0, multiply each element in the first row by -1 and add each result to the corresponding elements of the third row (again using row operation (3)).

$$\begin{bmatrix} 1 & -1 & 5 & | & -6 \\ 0 & 6 & -16 & | & 28 \\ 0 & 4 & -3 & | & 11 \end{bmatrix}$$

This transforms the first column. Transform the second and third columns in a similar manner.

$$\begin{bmatrix} 1 & -1 & 5 & | & -6 \\ 0 & 1 & -\frac{8}{3} & | & \frac{14}{3} \\ 0 & 4 & -3 & | & 11 \end{bmatrix}$$ Second row multiplied by $\frac{1}{6}$ [row operation (2)]

$$\begin{bmatrix} 1 & 0 & \frac{7}{3} & | & -\frac{4}{3} \\ 0 & 1 & -\frac{8}{3} & | & \frac{14}{3} \\ 0 & 4 & -3 & | & 11 \end{bmatrix}$$ Second row added to first row [row operation (3)]

$$\begin{bmatrix} 1 & 0 & \frac{7}{3} & | & -\frac{4}{3} \\ 0 & 1 & -\frac{8}{3} & | & \frac{14}{3} \\ 0 & 0 & \frac{23}{3} & | & -\frac{23}{3} \end{bmatrix}$$ -4 times second row added to third row [row operation (3)]

$$\begin{bmatrix} 1 & 0 & \frac{7}{3} & | & -\frac{4}{3} \\ 0 & 1 & -\frac{8}{3} & | & \frac{14}{3} \\ 0 & 0 & 1 & | & -1 \end{bmatrix}$$ Third row multiplied by $\frac{3}{23}$ [row operation (2)]

$$\begin{bmatrix} 1 & 0 & 0 & | & 1 \\ 0 & 1 & -\frac{8}{3} & | & \frac{14}{3} \\ 0 & 0 & 1 & | & -1 \end{bmatrix}$$ $-\frac{7}{3}$ times third row added to first row [row operation (3)]

$$\begin{bmatrix} 1 & 0 & 0 & | & 1 \\ 0 & 1 & 0 & | & 2 \\ 0 & 0 & 1 & | & -1 \end{bmatrix}$$ $\frac{8}{3}$ times third row added to second row [row operation (3)]

The linear system associated with the final augmented matrix is

$$\begin{aligned} x & = 1 \\ y & = 2 \\ z & = -1, \end{aligned}$$

and the solution is $(1, 2, -1)$. ▪

In summary, the Gauss-Jordan method of solving a linear system requires the following steps.

The Gauss-Jordan Method of Solving a Linear System

1. Write all equations with variable terms on the left and constants on the right. Be sure the variables are in the same order in all equations.
2. Write the augmented matrix that corresponds to the system.
3. Use row operations to transform the first column so that the first element is 1 and the remaining elements are 0.
4. Use row operations to transform the second column so that the second element is 1 and the remaining elements are 0.
5. Use row operations to transform the third column so that the third element is 1 and the remaining elements are 0.
6. Continue in this way until the last row is in the form $[0 \quad 0 \quad 0 \ldots 0 \quad 1 \mid k]$, where k is a constant.

EXAMPLE 3

Use the Gauss-Jordan method to solve the system

$$x + y = 2$$
$$2x + 2y = 5.$$

Begin by writing the augmented matrix.

$$\begin{bmatrix} 1 & 1 & | & 2 \\ 2 & 2 & | & 5 \end{bmatrix}$$

The first element in column one is already 1. To get a 0 for the second element in column one, multiply the numbers in row one by -2 and add the results to the corresponding elements in row two.

$$\begin{bmatrix} 1 & 1 & | & 2 \\ 0 & 0 & | & 1 \end{bmatrix}$$

The next step is to get a 1 for the second element in column two. Since this is impossible, we cannot go further. This matrix leads to the system

$$x + y = 2$$
$$0x + 0y = 1.$$

Since the second equation is $0 = 1$, the system is inconsistent and has no solution. The row $\begin{bmatrix} 0 & 0 & | & 1 \end{bmatrix}$ is a signal that the given system is inconsistent. ▪

EXAMPLE 4

Use the Gauss-Jordan method to solve the system

$$x + 2y - z = 0$$
$$3x - y + z = 6$$
$$-2x - 4y + 2z = 0.$$

The augmented matrix is

$$\begin{bmatrix} 1 & 2 & -1 & | & 0 \\ 3 & -1 & 1 & | & 6 \\ -2 & -4 & 2 & | & 0 \end{bmatrix}.$$

The first element in column one is 1. Use row operations to get zeros in the rest of column one.

$$\begin{bmatrix} 1 & 2 & -1 & | & 0 \\ 0 & -7 & 4 & | & 6 \\ -2 & -4 & 2 & | & 0 \end{bmatrix}$$

$$\begin{bmatrix} 1 & 2 & -1 & | & 0 \\ 0 & -7 & 4 & | & 6 \\ 0 & 0 & 0 & | & 0 \end{bmatrix}$$

The row of all zeros in the last matrix is a signal that two of the equations (the first and last) are dependent. Continuing, multiply row 2 by $-1/7$.

$$\begin{bmatrix} 1 & 2 & -1 & | & 0 \\ 0 & 1 & -\frac{4}{7} & | & -\frac{6}{7} \\ 0 & 0 & 0 & | & 0 \end{bmatrix}$$

Finally, add -2 times row 2 to row 1.

$$\begin{bmatrix} 1 & 0 & \frac{1}{7} & \bigg| & \frac{12}{7} \\ 0 & 1 & -\frac{4}{7} & \bigg| & -\frac{6}{7} \\ 0 & 0 & 0 & \bigg| & 0 \end{bmatrix}$$

This is as far as we can go with the Gauss-Jordan Method. To complete the solution write the equations that correspond to the first two lines of the matrix.

$$x \quad + \frac{1}{7}z = \frac{12}{7}$$

$$y - \frac{4}{7}z = -\frac{6}{7}$$

Solving the first equation for x and the second equation for y gives

$$x = -\frac{1}{7}z + \frac{12}{7} \quad \text{and} \quad y = \frac{4}{7}z - \frac{6}{7}.$$

The solution may be written

$$\left\{ \left(-\frac{1}{7}z + \frac{12}{7}, \frac{4}{7}z - \frac{6}{7}, z \right) \right\}. \quad \blacksquare$$

Although the examples have used only systems with two equations and variables or three equations and variables, the Gauss-Jordan method can be used for any system with n equations and n variables. In fact, it can be used with n equations and m variables, as Example 4 illustrated. The system in Example 4 actually had just two equations with three variables. The method does become tedious even with three equations and three variables. However, it is very suitable for use by computers. A computer can produce the solution to a fairly large system very quickly.*

2.2 EXERCISES

Write the augmented matrix for each of the systems in Exercises 1–10. **Do not solve.**

1. $2x + 3y = 11$
$\quad x + 2y = 8$

2. $3x + 5y = -13$
$\quad 2x + 3y = -9$

3. $x = 6 - 5y$
$\quad\quad\quad y = 1$

4. $7y = 1 - 2x$
$\quad 5x = -15$

5. $2x + y + z = 3$
$\quad 3x - 4y + 2z = -7$
$\quad x + y + z = 2$

6. $4x - 2y + 3z = 4$
$\quad 3x + 5y + z = 7$
$\quad 5x - y + 4z = 7$

---

*See D. R. Cosica, *Computer Applications for Finite Mathematics and Calculus*, Scott, Foresman and Company, 1986.

7.
$$y = 2 - x$$
$$2y = -4 - z$$
$$z = 2$$

8. $x = 6$
$$y = 2 - 2z$$
$$x = 6 + 3z$$

9. $x = 5$
$$y = -2$$
$$z = 3$$

10. $x = 8$
$$y + z = 6$$
$$z = 2$$

Write the system of equations associated with each of the augmented matrices in Exercises 11–16. **Do not solve.**

11. $\begin{bmatrix} 1 & 0 & | & 2 \\ 0 & 1 & | & 3 \end{bmatrix}$

12. $\begin{bmatrix} 1 & 0 & | & 5 \\ 0 & 1 & | & -3 \end{bmatrix}$

13. $\begin{bmatrix} 2 & 1 & | & 1 \\ 3 & -2 & | & -9 \end{bmatrix}$

14. $\begin{bmatrix} 1 & -5 & | & -18 \\ 6 & 2 & | & 20 \end{bmatrix}$

15. $\begin{bmatrix} 1 & 0 & 0 & | & 2 \\ 0 & 1 & 0 & | & 3 \\ 0 & 0 & 1 & | & -2 \end{bmatrix}$

16. $\begin{bmatrix} 1 & 0 & 1 & | & 4 \\ 0 & 1 & 0 & | & 2 \\ 0 & 0 & 1 & | & 3 \end{bmatrix}$

Use the Gauss-Jordan method to solve the systems of equations in Exercises 17–42.

17. $x + y = 5$
$x - y = -1$

18. $x + 2y = 5$
$2x + y = -2$

19. $x + y = -3$
$2x - 5y = -6$

20. $3x - 2y = 4$
$3x + y = -2$

21. $2x = 10 + 3y$
$2y = 5 - 2x$

22. $y = 5 - 4x$
$2x = 3 - y$

23. $2x - 5y = 10$
$4x - 5y = 15$

24. $4x - 2y = 3$
$-2x + 3y = 1$

25. $2x - 3y = 2$
$4x - 6y = 1$

26. $x + 2y = 1$
$2x + 4y = 3$

27. $6x - 3y = 1$
$-12x + 6y = -2$

28. $x - y = 1$
$-x + y = -1$

29. $x + y = -1$
$y + z = 4$
$x + z = 1$

30. $x - z = -3$
$y + z = 9$
$x + z = 7$

31. $x + y - z = 6$
$2x - y + z = -9$
$x - 2y + 3z = 1$

32. $x + 3y - 6z = 7$
$2x - y + 2z = 0$
$x + y + 2z = -1$

33. $y = x - 1$
$y = 6 + z$
$z = -1 - x$

34. $x = 1 - y$
$2x = z$
$2z = 2 - y$

35. $x - 2y + z = 5$
$2x + y - z = 2$
$-2x + 4y - 2z = 2$

36. $3x + 5y - z = 0$
$4x - y + 2z = 1$
$-6x - 10y + 2z = 0$

37. $2x + 3y + z = 9$
$4x - y + 3z = -1$
$6x + 2y - 4z = -8$

38. $3x + 2y - z = -16$
$6x - 4y + 3z = 12$
$3x + 3y + z = -11$

39. $5x - 4y + 2z = 4$
$10x + 3y - z = 27$
$15x - 5y + 3z = 25$

40. $4x - 2y - 3z = -23$
$-4x + 3y + z = 11$
$8x - 5y + 4z = 6$

41. $x + 2y - w = 3$
$2x + 4z + 2w = -6$
$x + 2y - z = 6$
$2x - y + z + w = -3$

42. $x + 3y - 2z - w = 9$
$2x + 4y + 2w = 10$
$-3x - 5y + 2z - w = -15$
$x - y - 3z + 2w = 6$

43. At rush hours, substantial traffic congestion is encountered at the traffic intersections shown in the figure. (The streets are all one way.)

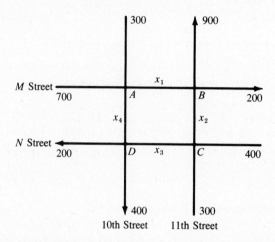

The city wishes to improve the signals at these corners so as to speed the flow of traffic. The traffic engineers first gather data. As the figure shows, 700 cars per hour come down M Street to intersection A; 300 cars per hour come to intersection A on 10th Street. A total of x_1 of these cars leave A on M Street, while x_4 cars leave A on 10th Street. The number of cars entering A must equal the number leaving, so that

$$x_1 + x_4 = 700 + 300$$

or

$$x_1 + x_4 = 1000.$$

For intersection B, x_1 cars enter B on M Street, and x_2 cars enter B on 11th Street. The figure shows that 900 cars leave B on 11th while 200 leave on M. We have

$$x_1 + x_2 = 900 + 200$$

$$x_1 + x_2 = 1100.$$

At intersection C, 400 cars enter on N Street, 300 on 11th Street, while x_2 leave on 11th Street and x_3 leave on N Street. This gives

$$x_2 + x_3 = 400 + 300$$

$$x_2 + x_3 = 700.$$

Finally, intersection D has x_3 cars entering on N and x_4 entering on 10th. There are 400 leaving D on 10th and 200 leaving on N, so that

$$x_3 + x_4 = 400 + 200$$

$$x_3 + x_4 = 600.$$

(a) Use the four equations to set up an augmented matrix, and then use the Gauss-Jordan method to solve it. (Hint: keep going until you get a row of all zeros.)

(b) Since you got a row of all zeros, the system of equations does not have a unique solution. Write three equations, corresponding to the three nonzero rows of the matrix.

(c) Solve each of the equations for x_4.

(d) One of your equations should have been $x_4 = 1000 - x_1$. What is the largest possible value of x_1 so that x_4 is not negative? What is the largest value of x_4 so that x_1 is not negative?

(e) Your second equation should have been $x_4 = x_2 - 100$. Find the smallest possible value of x_2 so that x_4 is not negative.

(f) For the third equation, $x_4 = 600 - x_3$, find the largest possible values of x_3 and x_4 so that neither variable is negative.

(g) Look at your answers for parts (d)–(f). What is the maximum value of x_4 so that all the equations are satisfied and all variables are nonnegative? Of x_3? Of x_2? Of x_1?

44. A manufacturer purchases a part for use at both of its two plants—one at Roseville, California, the other at Akron, Ohio. The part is available in limited quantities from two suppliers. Each supplier has 75 units available. The Roseville plant needs 40 units and the Akron plant requires 75 units. The first supplier charges $70 per unit delivered to Roseville and $90 per unit delivered to Akron. Corresponding costs from the second supplier are $80 and $120. The manufacturer wants to order a total of 75 units from the first, less expensive, supplier, with the remaining 40 units to come from the second supplier. If the company spends $10,750 to purchase the required number of units for the two plants, find the number of units that should be purchased from each supplier for each plant as follows:

(a) Assign variables to the four unknowns.

(b) Write a system of five equations with the four variables. (Not all equations will involve all four variables.)

(c) Use the Gauss-Jordan method to solve the system of equations.

Solve the linear systems in Exercises 45–48.

45. $2.1x + 3.5y + 9.4z = 15.6$
$6.8x - 1.5y + 7.5z = 26.4$
$3.7x + 2.5y - 6.1z = 18.7$

46. $9.03x - 5.91y + 2.68z = 29.5$
$3.94x + 6.82y + 1.53z = 35.4$
$2.79x + 1.68y - 6.23z = 12.1$

47. $10.47x + 3.52y + 2.58z - 6.42w = 218.65$
$8.62x - 4.93y - 1.75z + 2.83w = 157.03$
$4.92x + 6.83y - 2.97z + 2.65w = 462.3$
$2.86x + 19.1\ y - 6.24z - 8.73w = 398.4$

48. $28.6x + 94.5y + 16.0z - 2.94w = 198.3$
$16.7x + 44.3y - 27.3z + 8.9w = 254.7$
$12.5x - 38.7y + 92.5z + 22.4w = 562.7$
$40.1x - 28.3y + 17.5z - 10.2w = 375.4$

In Exercises 49–52, write a system of equations and then solve it.

49. Natural Brand plant food is made from three chemicals. The mix must include 10.8% of the first chemical and the other two chemicals must be in the ratio of 4 to 3 as measured by weight. How much of each chemical is required to make 750 kilograms of the plant food?

50. Three species of bacteria are fed three foods, I, II, and III. A bacterium of the first species consumes 1.3 units each of foods I and II and 2.3 units of food III each day. A bacterium of the second species consumes 1.1 units of food I, 2.4 units of food II, and 3.7 units of food III each day. A bacterium of the third species consumes 8.1 units of I, 2.9 units of II, and 5.1 units of III each day. If 16,000 units of I, 28,000 units of II, and 44,000 units of III are supplied each day, how many of each species can be maintained in this environment?

51. A lake is stocked each spring with three species of fish, A, B, and C. Three foods, I, II, and III, are available in the lake. Each fish of species A requires 1.32 units of food I, 2.9 units of food II, and 1.75 units of food III on the average each day. Species B fish each require 2.1 units of food I, .95 unit of food II, and .6 unit of food III daily. Species C fish require .86, 1.52, and 2.01 units of I, II, and III per day, respectively. If 490 units of food I, 897 units of food II, and 653 units of food III are available daily, how many of each species should be stocked?

52. A company produces three combinations of mixed vegetables which sell in one kilogram packages. Italian style combines .3 kilogram of zucchini, .3 of broccoli, and .4 of carrots. French style combines .6 kilogram of broccoli and .4 of carrots. Oriental style combines .2 kilogram of zucchini, .5 of broccoli, and .3 of carrots. The company has a stock of 16,200 kilograms of zucchini, 41,400 kilograms of broccoli, and 29,400 kilograms of carrots. How many packages of each style should they prepare to use up their supplies?

2.3   Basic Matrix Operations

In the last section we saw how a matrix is used to represent a system of linear equations. The study of matrices has been of interest to mathematicians for some time. Recently, however, the use of matrices has gained greater importance in the fields of management, natural science, and social science because matrices provide such a convenient way to organize data, as Example 1 demonstrates.

EXAMPLE 1

The EZ Life Company manufactures sofas and armchairs in three models, A, B, and C. The company has regional warehouses in New York, Chicago, and San Francisco. In its August shipment, the company sends 10 model A sofas, 12 model B sofas, 5 model C sofas, 15 model A chairs, 20 model B chairs, and 8 model C chairs to each warehouse.

To organize this data, we might first list it as follows.

sofas	10 model A	12 model B	5 model C
chairs	15 model A	20 model B	8 model C

Alternatively, we might tabulate the data in a chart.

		Model A	Model B	Model C
Furniture	Sofas	10	12	5
	Chairs	15	20	8

With the understanding that the numbers in each row refer to the furniture type (sofa, chair) and the numbers in each column refer to the model (A, B, C), the same information can be given by a matrix, as follows.

$$M = \begin{bmatrix} 10 & 12 & 5 \\ 15 & 20 & 8 \end{bmatrix} \quad \blacksquare$$

Matrices are classified by their **order** (or **dimension**), that is, by the number of rows and columns that they contain. For example, matrix M above has two rows and three columns. This matrix is of **order** 2×3 (read "2 by 3") or **dimension** 2×3. By definition, a matrix with m rows and n columns is of **order** $m \times n$. The number of rows is always given first.

EXAMPLE 2

(a)   The matrix $\begin{bmatrix} 6 & 5 \\ 3 & 4 \\ 5 & -1 \end{bmatrix}$ is of order 3×2.

(b) $\begin{bmatrix} 5 & 8 & 9 \\ 0 & 5 & -3 \\ -4 & 0 & 5 \end{bmatrix}$ is of order 3×3.

(c) $\begin{bmatrix} 1 & 6 & 5 & -2 & 5 \end{bmatrix}$ is of order 1×5.

(d) $\begin{bmatrix} 3 \\ -5 \\ 0 \\ 2 \end{bmatrix}$ is of order 4×1. $\blacksquare$

A matrix with the same number of rows as columns is called a **square matrix.** The matrix in Example 2(b) above is a square matrix.

A matrix containing only one row is called a **row matrix.** The matrix in Example 2(c) is a row matrix, as are

$$[5 \quad 8], \qquad [6 \quad -9 \quad 2], \qquad \text{and} \qquad [-4 \quad 0 \quad 0 \quad 0].$$

A matrix of only one column, as in Example 2(d), is a **column matrix.** Two matrices are **equal** if they are of the same order and if each pair of corresponding elements is equal. By this definition, the matrices

$$\begin{bmatrix} 2 & 1 \\ 3 & -5 \end{bmatrix} \qquad \text{and} \qquad \begin{bmatrix} 1 & 2 \\ -5 & 3 \end{bmatrix}$$

are not equal (even though they contain the same elements and are of the same order) since the corresponding elements differ.

EXAMPLE 3

(a)   From the definition of equality given above, the only way that the statement

$$\begin{bmatrix} 2 & 1 \\ p & q \end{bmatrix} = \begin{bmatrix} x & y \\ -1 & 0 \end{bmatrix}$$

can be true is if $2 = x$, $1 = y$, $p = -1$, and $q = 0$.

(b)   The statement

$$\begin{bmatrix} x \\ y \end{bmatrix} = \begin{bmatrix} 1 \\ 4 \\ 0 \end{bmatrix}$$

can never be true, since the two matrices are of different order. (One is 2×1 and the other is 3×1.) ▪

Addition   The matrix given in Example 1,

$$M = \begin{bmatrix} 10 & 12 & 5 \\ 15 & 20 & 8 \end{bmatrix},$$

shows the August shipment from the EZ Life plant to its New York warehouse. If matrix N below gives the September shipment to the same warehouse, what is the total shipment for each item of furniture for these two months?

$$N = \begin{bmatrix} 45 & 35 & 20 \\ 65 & 40 & 35 \end{bmatrix}$$

If 10 model A sofas were shipped in August and 45 in September, then altogether $10 + 45 = 55$ model A sofas were shipped in the two months. The other corresponding entries can be added in a similar way, to get a new matrix, call it Q, which represents the total shipment for the two months.

$$Q = \begin{bmatrix} 55 & 47 & 25 \\ 80 & 60 & 43 \end{bmatrix}$$

It is convenient to refer to Q as the sum of M and N.

The way these two matrices were added illustrates the following definition of addition of matrices.

Addition of

Matrices

> **The sum** of two $m \times n$ matrices X and Y is the $m \times n$ matrix $X + Y$ in which each element is the sum of the corresponding elements of X and Y.

It is important to remember that only matrices with the same order or dimension can be added.

EXAMPLE 4

Find each sum when possible.

(a) $\begin{bmatrix} 5 & -6 \\ 8 & 9 \end{bmatrix} + \begin{bmatrix} -4 & 6 \\ 8 & -3 \end{bmatrix} = \begin{bmatrix} 5 + (-4) & -6 + 6 \\ 8 + 8 & 9 + (-3) \end{bmatrix} = \begin{bmatrix} 1 & 0 \\ 16 & 6 \end{bmatrix}$

(b) The matrices

$$A = \begin{bmatrix} 5 & 8 \\ 6 & 2 \end{bmatrix} \quad \text{and} \quad B = \begin{bmatrix} 3 & 9 & 1 \\ 4 & 2 & 5 \end{bmatrix}$$

are of different orders. Therefore, the sum $A + B$ does not exist. ▪

EXAMPLE 5

The September shipments from the EZ Life Company to the New York, San Francisco, and Chicago warehouses are given in matrices N, S, and C below.

$$N = \begin{bmatrix} 45 & 35 & 20 \\ 65 & 40 & 35 \end{bmatrix}, \quad S = \begin{bmatrix} 30 & 32 & 28 \\ 43 & 47 & 30 \end{bmatrix}, \quad C = \begin{bmatrix} 22 & 25 & 38 \\ 31 & 34 & 35 \end{bmatrix}$$

What was the total amount shipped to the three warehouses in September?

The total of the September shipments is represented by the sum of the three matrices N, S, and C.

$$N + S + C = \begin{bmatrix} 45 & 35 & 20 \\ 65 & 40 & 35 \end{bmatrix} + \begin{bmatrix} 30 & 32 & 28 \\ 43 & 47 & 30 \end{bmatrix} + \begin{bmatrix} 22 & 25 & 38 \\ 31 & 34 & 35 \end{bmatrix}$$

$$= \begin{bmatrix} 97 & 92 & 86 \\ 139 & 121 & 100 \end{bmatrix}$$

For example, this sum shows that the total number of model C sofas shipped to the three warehouses in September was 86. ▪

The **additive inverse** (or **negative**) of a matrix X is the matrix $-X$ in which each element is the additive inverse of the corresponding element of X. If

$$A = \begin{bmatrix} 1 & 2 & 3 \\ 0 & -1 & 5 \end{bmatrix} \quad \text{and} \quad B = \begin{bmatrix} -2 & 3 & 0 \\ 1 & -7 & 2 \end{bmatrix},$$

then by the definition of the additive inverse of a matrix,

$$-A = \begin{bmatrix} -1 & -2 & -3 \\ 0 & 1 & -5 \end{bmatrix} \quad \text{and} \quad -B = \begin{bmatrix} 2 & -3 & 0 \\ -1 & 7 & -2 \end{bmatrix}.$$

By the definition of matrix addition, for each matrix X the sum $X + (-X)$ is a **zero matrix,** O, whose elements are all zeros. There is an $m \times n$ zero matrix for each pair of values of m and n. Zero matrices have the following **identity property:** If O is an $m \times n$ zero matrix, and A is any $m \times n$ matrix, then

$$A + O = O + A = A.$$

Subtraction   The **subtraction** of matrices is defined in a manner comparable to subtraction for real numbers.

Subtraction of Matrices	For two $m \times n$ matrices X and Y, the **difference** of X and Y, or $X - Y$, is the matrix defined by $$X - Y = X + (-Y).$$

With A, B, and $-B$ as defined above,

$$A - B = A + (-B) = \begin{bmatrix} 1 & 2 & 3 \\ 0 & -1 & 5 \end{bmatrix} + \begin{bmatrix} 2 & -3 & 0 \\ -1 & 7 & -2 \end{bmatrix}$$

$$= \begin{bmatrix} 3 & -1 & 3 \\ -1 & 6 & 3 \end{bmatrix}.$$

According to this definition, matrix subtraction can be performed by subtracting corresponding elements.

EXAMPLE 6

(a) $[8 \quad 6 \quad -4] - [3 \quad 5 \quad -8] = [5 \quad 1 \quad 4]$

(b)   The matrices

$$\begin{bmatrix} -2 & 5 \\ 0 & 1 \end{bmatrix} \quad \text{and} \quad \begin{bmatrix} 3 \\ 5 \end{bmatrix}$$

have different orders and cannot be subtracted.   ▨

EXAMPLE 7

During September the Chicago warehouse of the EZ Life Company shipped out the following numbers of each model.

$$K = \begin{bmatrix} 5 & 10 & 8 \\ 11 & 14 & 15 \end{bmatrix}$$

What was the Chicago warehouse inventory on October 1, taking into account only the number of items received and sent out during the month?

The number of each kind of item received during September is given by matrix C from Example 5; the number of each model sent out during September is given by matrix K. The October 1 inventory will be represented by the matrix $C - K$:

$$\begin{bmatrix} 22 & 25 & 38 \\ 31 & 34 & 35 \end{bmatrix} - \begin{bmatrix} 5 & 10 & 8 \\ 11 & 14 & 15 \end{bmatrix} = \begin{bmatrix} 17 & 15 & 30 \\ 20 & 20 & 20 \end{bmatrix}.$$ ▨

2.3 EXERCISES

Mark each of the statements in Exercises 1–6 as *true* or *false*. If false, tell why.

1. $\begin{bmatrix} 1 & 3 \\ 5 & 7 \end{bmatrix} = \begin{bmatrix} 1 & 5 \\ 3 & 7 \end{bmatrix}$

2. $\begin{bmatrix} 1 \\ 2 \\ 3 \end{bmatrix} = [1 \quad 2 \quad 3]$

3. $\begin{bmatrix} x \\ y \end{bmatrix} = \begin{bmatrix} 3 \\ 5 \end{bmatrix}$ if $x = 3$ and $y = 5$.

4. $\begin{bmatrix} 3 & 5 & 2 & 8 \\ 1 & -1 & 4 & 0 \end{bmatrix}$ is a 4×2 matrix.

5. $\begin{bmatrix} 1 & 9 & -4 \\ 3 & 7 & 2 \\ -1 & 1 & 0 \end{bmatrix}$ is a square matrix.

6. $\begin{bmatrix} 2 & 4 & -1 \\ 3 & 7 & 5 \\ 0 & 0 & 0 \end{bmatrix} = \begin{bmatrix} 2 & 4 & -1 \\ 3 & 7 & 5 \end{bmatrix}$

Find the order of each matrix in Exercises 7–12. Identify any square, column, or row matrices.

7. $\begin{bmatrix} -4 & 8 \\ 2 & 3 \end{bmatrix}$

8. $\begin{bmatrix} -9 & 6 & 2 \\ 4 & 1 & 8 \end{bmatrix}$

9. $\begin{bmatrix} -6 & 8 & 0 & 0 \\ 4 & 1 & 9 & 2 \\ 3 & -5 & 7 & 1 \end{bmatrix}$

10. $[8 \quad -2 \quad 4 \quad 6 \quad 3]$

11. $\begin{bmatrix} 2 \\ 4 \end{bmatrix}$

12. $[-9]$

Find the values of the variables in Exercises 13–18.

13. $\begin{bmatrix} 2 & 1 \\ 4 & 8 \end{bmatrix} = \begin{bmatrix} x & 1 \\ y & z \end{bmatrix}$

14. $\begin{bmatrix} -5 \\ y \end{bmatrix} = \begin{bmatrix} -5 \\ 8 \end{bmatrix}$

15. $\begin{bmatrix} x + 6 & y + 2 \\ 8 & 3 \end{bmatrix} = \begin{bmatrix} -9 & 7 \\ 8 & k \end{bmatrix}$

16. $\begin{bmatrix} 9 & 7 \\ r & 0 \end{bmatrix} = \begin{bmatrix} m - 3 & n + 5 \\ 8 & 0 \end{bmatrix}$

17. $\begin{bmatrix} -7 + z & 4r & 8s \\ 6p & 2 & 5 \end{bmatrix} + \begin{bmatrix} -9 & 8r & 3 \\ 2 & 5 & 4 \end{bmatrix} = \begin{bmatrix} 2 & 36 & 27 \\ 20 & 7 & 12a \end{bmatrix}$

18. $\begin{bmatrix} a + 2 & 3z + 1 & 5m \\ 4k & 0 & 3 \end{bmatrix} + \begin{bmatrix} 3a & 2z & 5m \\ 2k & 5 & 6 \end{bmatrix} = \begin{bmatrix} 10 & -14 & 80 \\ 10 & 5 & 9 \end{bmatrix}$

In Exercises 19–28 perform the indicated operations where possible.

19. $\begin{bmatrix} 1 & 2 & 5 & -1 \\ 3 & 0 & 2 & -4 \end{bmatrix} + \begin{bmatrix} 8 & 10 & -5 & 3 \\ -2 & -1 & 0 & 0 \end{bmatrix}$

20. $\begin{bmatrix} 1 & 5 \\ 2 & -3 \\ 3 & 7 \end{bmatrix} + \begin{bmatrix} 2 & 3 \\ 8 & 5 \\ -1 & 9 \end{bmatrix}$

21. $\begin{bmatrix} 1 & 5 & 7 \\ 2 & 2 & 3 \end{bmatrix} + \begin{bmatrix} 4 & 8 & -7 \\ 1 & -1 & 5 \end{bmatrix}$

22. $\begin{bmatrix} 2 & 4 \\ -8 & 1 \end{bmatrix} + \begin{bmatrix} 9 & -3 \\ 8 & 5 \end{bmatrix}$

23. $\begin{bmatrix} 1 & 3 & -2 \\ 4 & 7 & 1 \end{bmatrix} + \begin{bmatrix} 3 & 0 \\ 6 & 4 \\ -5 & 2 \end{bmatrix}$

24. $\begin{bmatrix} 1 & 3 & -2 \\ 4 & 7 & 1 \end{bmatrix} - \begin{bmatrix} 3 & 6 & -5 \\ 0 & 4 & 2 \end{bmatrix}$

25. $\begin{bmatrix} 2 & 8 & 12 & 0 \\ 7 & 4 & -1 & 5 \\ 1 & 2 & 0 & 10 \end{bmatrix} - \begin{bmatrix} 1 & 3 & 6 & 9 \\ 2 & -3 & -3 & 4 \\ 8 & 0 & -2 & 17 \end{bmatrix}$

26. $\begin{bmatrix} 2 & 1 \\ 5 & -3 \\ -7 & 2 \\ 9 & 0 \end{bmatrix} + \begin{bmatrix} 1 & -8 & 0 \\ 5 & 3 & 2 \\ -6 & 7 & -5 \\ 2 & -1 & 0 \end{bmatrix}$

27. $\begin{bmatrix} -4x + 2y & -3x + y \\ 6x - 3y & 2x - 5y \end{bmatrix} + \begin{bmatrix} -8x + 6y & 2x \\ 3y - 5x & 6x + 4y \end{bmatrix}$

28. $\begin{bmatrix} 4k - 8y \\ 6z - 3x \\ 2k + 5a \\ -4m + 2n \end{bmatrix} - \begin{bmatrix} 5k + 6y \\ 2z + 5x \\ 4k + 6a \\ 4m - 2n \end{bmatrix}$

Using matrices $O = \begin{bmatrix} 0 & 0 \\ 0 & 0 \end{bmatrix}$, $P = \begin{bmatrix} m & n \\ p & q \end{bmatrix}$, $T = \begin{bmatrix} r & s \\ t & u \end{bmatrix}$, and $X = \begin{bmatrix} x & y \\ z & w \end{bmatrix}$, verify the statements in Exercises 29–34.

29. $X + T$ is a 2×2 matrix (Closure property)

30. $X + T = T + X$ (Commutative property of addition of matrices)

31. $X + (T + P) = (X + T) + P$ (Associative property of addition of matrices)

32. $X + (-X) = 0$ (Inverse property of addition of matrices)

33. $P + O = P$ (Identity property of addition of matrices)

34. Which of the above properties are valid for matrices that are not square?

35. When John inventoried his screw collection, he found that he had 7 flathead long screws, 9 flathead medium, 8 flathead short, 2 roundhead long, no roundhead medium, and 6 roundhead short. Write this information first as a 3×2 matrix and then as a 2×3 matrix.

36. At the grocery store, Miguel bought 4 quarts of milk, 2 loaves of bread, 4 chickens, and an apple. Mary bought 2 quarts of milk, a loaf of bread, 5 chickens, and 4 apples. Write this information first as a 2×4 matrix and then as a 4×2 matrix.

37. A dietician prepares a diet specifying the amounts a patient should eat of four basic food groups: group I, meats; group II, fruits and vegetables; group III, breads and starches; group IV, milk products. Amounts are given in "exchanges" which represent 1 ounce (meat), 1/2 cup (fruits and vegetables), 1 slice (bread), 8 ounces (milk), or other suitable measurements.

 (a) The number of "exchanges" for breakfast for each of the four food groups respectively are 2, 1, 2, and 1; for lunch, 3, 2, 2, and 1; and for dinner, 4, 3, 2, and 1. Write a 3×4 matrix using this information.

 (b) The amounts of fat, carbohydrates, and protein (in appropriate units) in each food group respectively are as follows.

> Fat: 5, 0, 0, 10
> Carbohydrates: 0, 10, 15, 12
> Protein: 7, 1, 2, 8

 Use this information to write a 4×3 matrix.

 (c) There are 8 calories per exchange of fat, 4 calories per exchange of carbohydrates, and 5 calories per exchange of protein; summarize this data in a 3×1 matrix.

38. At the beginning of a laboratory experiment, five baby rats measured 5.6, 6.4, 6.9, 7.6, and 6.1 centimeters in length, and weighed 144, 138, 149, 152, and 146 grams respectively.

 (a) Write a 2×5 matrix using this information.

 (b) At the end of two weeks, their lengths were 10.2, 11.4, 11.4, 12.7, and 10.8 centimeters, and they weighed 196, 196, 225, 250, and 230 grams. Write a 2×5 matrix with this information.

(c) Use matrix subtraction and the matrices found in (a) and (b) to write a matrix which gives the amount of change in length and weight for each rat.

(d) The following week the rats gained as shown in the matrix below.

$$\begin{matrix} \text{Length} \\ \text{Weight} \end{matrix} \begin{bmatrix} 1.8 & 1.5 & 2.3 & 1.8 & 2.0 \\ 25 & 22 & 29 & 33 & 20 \end{bmatrix}$$

What were their lengths and weights at the end of this week?

2.4   Multiplication of Matrices

In work with matrices, a real number is called a **scalar.**

Product of a

Matrix and a Scalar

> The **product** of a scalar k and a matrix X is the matrix kX, each of whose elements is k times the corresponding element of X.

For example,

$$(-3) \begin{bmatrix} 2 & -5 \\ 1 & 7 \end{bmatrix} = \begin{bmatrix} -6 & 15 \\ -3 & -21 \end{bmatrix}.$$

Finding the product of two matrices is more involved. However, such multiplication is important in solving practical problems. To understand the reasoning behind matrix multiplication, it may be helpful to consider another example concerning the EZ Life Company discussed in Section 2.3. Suppose sofas and chairs of the same model are often sold as sets with matrix W showing the number of each model set in each warehouse.

$$\begin{array}{c} \\ \text{New York} \\ \text{Chicago} \\ \text{San Francisco} \end{array} \begin{array}{ccc} A & B & C \\ \begin{bmatrix} 10 & 7 & 3 \\ 5 & 9 & 6 \\ 4 & 8 & 2 \end{bmatrix} \end{array} = W$$

If the selling price of a model A set is $800, of a model B set $1000, and of a model C set $1200, the total value of the sets in the New York warehouse is found as follows.

Type	Number of sets		Price of set		Total
A	10	×	$800	=	$8000
B	7	×	$1000	=	$7000
C	3	×	$1200	=	$3600
					$18,600
					(Total for New York)

The total value of the three kinds of sets in New York is $18,600.

The work done in the table above is summarized as follows:

$$10(\$800) + 7(\$1000) + 3(\$1200) = \$18,600.$$

In the same way, the Chicago sets have a total value of

$$5(\$800) + 9(\$1000) + 6(\$1200) = \$20,200,$$

and in San Francisco, the total value of the sets is

$$4(\$800) + 8(\$1000) + 2(\$1200) = \$13,600.$$

We can write the selling prices as a column matrix, P, and the total value in each location as a column matrix V.

$$\begin{bmatrix} 800 \\ 1000 \\ 1200 \end{bmatrix} = P \qquad \begin{bmatrix} 18,600 \\ 20,200 \\ 13,600 \end{bmatrix} = V$$

Look at the elements of W and P; multiplying the first, second, and third elements of the first row of W by the first, second, and third elements respectively of the column matrix P and then adding these products gives the first element in V. Doing the same thing with the second row of W gives the second element of V; the third row of W leads to the third element of V, suggesting that it is reasonable to write the product of matrices

$$W = \begin{bmatrix} 10 & 7 & 3 \\ 5 & 9 & 6 \\ 4 & 8 & 2 \end{bmatrix} \qquad \text{and} \qquad P = \begin{bmatrix} 800 \\ 1000 \\ 1200 \end{bmatrix}$$

as

$$WP = \begin{bmatrix} 10 & 7 & 3 \\ 5 & 9 & 6 \\ 4 & 8 & 2 \end{bmatrix} \begin{bmatrix} 800 \\ 1000 \\ 1200 \end{bmatrix} = \begin{bmatrix} 18,600 \\ 20,200 \\ 13,600 \end{bmatrix} = V.$$

The product was found by multiplying the elements of the *rows* of the matrix on the left and the corresponding elements of the *column* of the matrix on the right, and then finding the sum of these separate products. Notice that the product of a 3×3 matrix and a 3×1 matrix is a 3×1 matrix.

The **product** AB of an $m \times n$ matrix A and an $n \times k$ matrix B is found as follows. Multiply each element of the *first row* of A by the corresponding element of the *first column* of B. The sum of these n products is the *first row, first column* element of AB. Similarly, the sum of the products found by multiplying the elements of the *first row* of A times the corresponding elements of the *second column* of B gives the *first row, second column* element of AB, and so on.

Product of an

Two Matrices

Let A be an $m \times n$ matrix and let B be an $n \times k$ matrix. To find the ith row, jth column element of the **product matrix** AB, multiply each element in the ith row of A by the corresponding element in the jth column of B. The sum of these products will give the row i, column j element of AB. The product matrix AB is of order $m \times k$.

EXAMPLE 1

Find the product AB given

$$A = \begin{bmatrix} 2 & 3 & -1 \\ 4 & 2 & 2 \end{bmatrix} \quad \text{and} \quad B = \begin{bmatrix} 1 \\ 8 \\ 6 \end{bmatrix}.$$

Step 1. Multiply the elements of the first row of A and the corresponding elements of the column of B.

$$\begin{bmatrix} 2 & 3 & -1 \\ 4 & 2 & 2 \end{bmatrix} \begin{bmatrix} 1 \\ 8 \\ 6 \end{bmatrix} \quad 2 \cdot 1 + 3 \cdot 8 + (-1) \cdot 6 = 20$$

Therefore, 20 is the first row entry of the product matrix AB.

Step 2. Multiply the elements of the second row of A with the corresponding elements of B.

$$\begin{bmatrix} 2 & 3 & -1 \\ 4 & 2 & 2 \end{bmatrix} \begin{bmatrix} 1 \\ 8 \\ 6 \end{bmatrix} \quad 4 \cdot 1 + 2 \cdot 8 + 2 \cdot 6 = 32$$

The second row entry of the product is 32.

Step 3. Write the product as a column matrix using the two entries found above.

$$AB = \begin{bmatrix} 2 & 3 & -1 \\ 4 & 2 & 2 \end{bmatrix} \begin{bmatrix} 1 \\ 8 \\ 6 \end{bmatrix} = \begin{bmatrix} 20 \\ 32 \end{bmatrix} \quad \blacksquare$$

EXAMPLE 2

Find the product CD given

$$C = \begin{bmatrix} -3 & 4 & 2 \\ 5 & 0 & 4 \end{bmatrix} \quad \text{and} \quad D = \begin{bmatrix} -6 & 4 \\ 2 & 3 \\ 3 & -2 \end{bmatrix}.$$

Step 1.

$$\begin{bmatrix} -3 & 4 & 2 \\ 5 & 0 & 4 \end{bmatrix} \begin{bmatrix} -6 & 4 \\ 2 & 3 \\ 3 & -2 \end{bmatrix} \quad (-3) \cdot (-6) + 4 \cdot 2 + 2 \cdot 3 = 32$$

Step 2.

$$\begin{bmatrix} -3 & 4 & 2 \\ 5 & 0 & 4 \end{bmatrix} \begin{bmatrix} -6 & 4 \\ 2 & 3 \\ 3 & -2 \end{bmatrix} \quad (-3) \cdot 4 + 4 \cdot 3 + 2 \cdot (-2) = -4$$

Step 3.

$$\begin{bmatrix} -3 & 4 & 2 \\ 5 & 0 & 4 \end{bmatrix} \begin{bmatrix} -6 & 4 \\ 2 & 3 \\ 3 & -2 \end{bmatrix} \quad 5 \cdot (-6) + 0 \cdot 2 + 4 \cdot 3 = -18$$

Step 4.

$$\begin{bmatrix} -3 & 4 & 2 \\ 5 & 0 & 4 \end{bmatrix} \begin{bmatrix} -6 & 4 \\ 2 & 3 \\ 3 & -2 \end{bmatrix} \quad 5 \cdot 4 + 0 \cdot 3 + 4 \cdot (-2) = 12$$

Step 5. The product is

$$CD = \begin{bmatrix} -3 & 4 & 2 \\ 5 & 0 & 4 \end{bmatrix} \begin{bmatrix} -6 & 4 \\ 2 & 3 \\ 3 & -2 \end{bmatrix} = \begin{bmatrix} 32 & -4 \\ -18 & 12 \end{bmatrix}.$$

Here the product of a 2×3 matrix and a 3×2 matrix is a 2×2 matrix. ■

As the definition of matrix multiplication shows,

> **the product AB of two matrices A and B can be found only if the number of columns of A is the same as the number of rows of B.**

The final product will have as many rows as A and as many columns as B.

EXAMPLE 3

Suppose matrix A is 2×2 and matrix B is 2×4. Can the product AB be calculated? What is the order of the product?

The following diagram helps decide the answers to these questions.

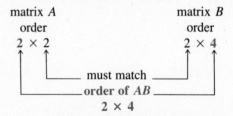

The product of A and B can be found because A has two columns and B has two rows. The order of the product is 2×4. ■

EXAMPLE 4

Find BA given

$$A = \begin{bmatrix} 1 & -3 \\ 7 & 2 \end{bmatrix} \quad \text{and} \quad B = \begin{bmatrix} 1 & 0 & -1 \\ 3 & 1 & 4 \end{bmatrix}.$$

Since B is a 2×3 matrix and A is a 2×2 matrix, the product BA cannot be found. ▪

EXAMPLE 5

A contractor builds three kinds of houses, models A, B, and C, with a choice of two styles, Spanish or contemporary. Matrix P shows the number of each kind of house planned for a new 100-home subdivision. The amounts for each of the exterior materials depend primarily on the style of the house. These amounts are shown in matrix Q. (Concrete is in cubic yards, lumber in units of 1000 board feet, brick in 1000's, and shingles in units of 100 square feet.) Matrix R gives the cost in dollars for each kind of material.

$$
\begin{array}{c}
\\
\text{Model A} \\
\text{Model B} \\
\text{Model C}
\end{array}
\begin{array}{cc}
\text{Spanish} & \text{Contemporary}
\end{array}
\begin{bmatrix}
0 & 30 \\
10 & 20 \\
20 & 20
\end{bmatrix} = P
$$

$$
\begin{array}{c}
\\
\text{Spanish} \\
\text{Contemporary}
\end{array}
\begin{array}{cccc}
\text{Concrete} & \text{Lumber} & \text{Brick} & \text{Shingles}
\end{array}
\begin{bmatrix}
10 & 2 & 0 & 2 \\
50 & 1 & 20 & 2
\end{bmatrix} = Q
$$

$$
\begin{array}{c}
\\
\text{Concrete} \\
\text{Lumber} \\
\text{Brick} \\
\text{Shingles}
\end{array}
\begin{array}{c}
\text{Cost per unit}
\end{array}
\begin{bmatrix}
20 \\
180 \\
60 \\
25
\end{bmatrix} = R
$$

(a)   What is the total cost of these materials for each model house?

To find the cost for each model, first find PQ, which shows the amount of each material needed for each model house.

$$
PQ = \begin{bmatrix} 0 & 30 \\ 10 & 20 \\ 20 & 20 \end{bmatrix} \begin{bmatrix} 10 & 2 & 0 & 2 \\ 50 & 1 & 20 & 2 \end{bmatrix}
$$

$$
= \begin{array}{c} \\ \\ \\ \end{array}
\begin{array}{cccc}
\text{Concrete} & \text{Lumber} & \text{Brick} & \text{Shingles}
\end{array}
\begin{bmatrix}
1500 & 30 & 600 & 60 \\
1100 & 40 & 400 & 60 \\
1200 & 60 & 400 & 80
\end{bmatrix}
\begin{array}{c}
\text{Model A} \\
\text{Model B} \\
\text{Model C}
\end{array}
$$

Now multiply PQ and R, the cost matrix, to get the total cost of the exterior materials for each model house.

$$
\begin{bmatrix}
1500 & 30 & 600 & 60 \\
1100 & 40 & 400 & 60 \\
1200 & 60 & 400 & 80
\end{bmatrix}
\begin{bmatrix}
20 \\
180 \\
60 \\
25
\end{bmatrix}
=
\begin{bmatrix}
72,900 \\
54,700 \\
60,800
\end{bmatrix}
\begin{array}{c}
\text{Model A} \\
\text{Model B} \\
\text{Model C}
\end{array}
$$

(b)   How much of each of the four kinds of material must be ordered?

The totals of the columns of matrix PQ will give a matrix whose elements represent the total amounts of each material needed for the subdivision. Let us call this matrix T, and write it as a row matrix.

$$T = [3800 \quad 130 \quad 1400 \quad 200]$$

(c)   What is the total cost for exterior material?

For the total cost of all the exterior materials, find the product of matrix T, the matrix showing the total amounts of each material, and matrix R, the cost matrix. (To multiply these and get a 1×1 matrix, representing total cost, we must multiply a 1×4 matrix by a 4×1 matrix. This is why T was written as a row matrix in (b) above.)

$$TR = [3800 \quad 130 \quad 1400 \quad 200] \begin{bmatrix} 20 \\ 180 \\ 60 \\ 25 \end{bmatrix} = [188,400].$$

(d)   Suppose the contractor builds the same number of homes in five subdivisions. Calculate the total amount of each exterior material for each model for all five subdivisions.

Multiply PQ by the scalar 5, as follows.

$$5 \begin{bmatrix} 1500 & 30 & 600 & 60 \\ 1100 & 40 & 400 & 60 \\ 1200 & 60 & 400 & 80 \end{bmatrix} = \begin{bmatrix} 7500 & 150 & 3000 & 300 \\ 5500 & 200 & 2000 & 300 \\ 6000 & 300 & 2000 & 400 \end{bmatrix}$$

We can introduce a notation to help us keep track of the quantities a matrix represents. For example, we can say that matrix P, from Example 5, represents models/styles, matrix Q represents styles/materials, and matrix R represents materials/cost. In each case, write the meaning of the rows first and the columns second. In the product PQ of Example 5, the rows of the matrix represented models and the columns represented materials. Therefore, the matrix product PQ represents models/materials. Note that the common quantity, styles, in both P and Q was eliminated in the product PQ. By this method, the product $(PQ)R$ represents models/cost.

In practical problems this notation helps decide in which order to multiply matrices so that the results are meaningful. In Example 5(c) either RT or TR could have been found. However, since T represents subdivisions/materials and R represents materials/cost, the product TR gives subdivisions/cost.

2.4 EXERCISES

In Exercises 1–8, the dimensions of two matrices A and B are given. Find the dimensions of the product AB and the product BA, whenever these products exist.

1. A is 2×2, B is 2×2 **2.** A is 3×3, B is 3×3 **3.** A is 4×2, B is 2×4

4. A is 3×1, B is 1×3 **5.** A is 3×5, B is 5×2 **6.** A is 4×3, B is 3×6

7. A is 4×2, B is 3×4 **8.** A is 7×3, B is 2×7

Let

$$A = \begin{bmatrix} -2 & 4 \\ 0 & 3 \end{bmatrix} \quad \text{and} \quad B = \begin{bmatrix} -6 & 2 \\ 4 & 0 \end{bmatrix}.$$

Find each of the following.

9. $2A$ **10.** $-3B$ **11.** $-4B$

12. $5A$ **13.** $-4A + 5B$ **14.** $3A - 10B$

Find each of the matrix products in Exercises 15–26 where possible.

15. $\begin{bmatrix} 1 & 2 \\ 3 & 4 \end{bmatrix} \begin{bmatrix} -1 \\ 7 \end{bmatrix}$ **16.** $\begin{bmatrix} -1 & 5 \\ 7 & 0 \end{bmatrix} \begin{bmatrix} 6 \\ 2 \end{bmatrix}$

17. $\begin{bmatrix} 2 & 2 & -1 \\ 3 & 0 & 1 \end{bmatrix} \begin{bmatrix} 0 & 2 \\ -1 & 4 \\ 0 & 2 \end{bmatrix}$ **18.** $\begin{bmatrix} -9 & 2 & 1 \\ 3 & 0 & 0 \end{bmatrix} \begin{bmatrix} 2 \\ -1 \\ 4 \end{bmatrix}$

19. $\begin{bmatrix} 1 & 2 \\ 3 & 4 \end{bmatrix} \begin{bmatrix} -1 & 5 \\ 7 & 0 \end{bmatrix}$ **20.** $\begin{bmatrix} -1 & 5 \\ 7 & 0 \end{bmatrix} \begin{bmatrix} 1 & 2 \\ 3 & 4 \end{bmatrix}$

21. $\begin{bmatrix} -2 & -3 & 7 \\ 1 & 5 & 6 \end{bmatrix} \begin{bmatrix} 1 \\ 2 \\ 3 \end{bmatrix}$ **22.** $\begin{bmatrix} 6 \\ 5 \\ 4 \end{bmatrix} \begin{bmatrix} -1 & 1 & 1 \end{bmatrix}$

23. $\left(\begin{bmatrix} 4 & 3 \\ 1 & 2 \\ 0 & -5 \end{bmatrix} \begin{bmatrix} 2 & -2 \\ 1 & -1 \end{bmatrix} \right) \begin{bmatrix} 10 \\ 0 \end{bmatrix}$ **24.** $\begin{bmatrix} 4 & 3 \\ 1 & 2 \\ 0 & -5 \end{bmatrix} \left(\begin{bmatrix} 2 & -2 \\ 1 & -1 \end{bmatrix} \begin{bmatrix} 10 \\ 0 \end{bmatrix} \right)$

25. $\begin{bmatrix} 2 & -2 \\ 1 & -1 \end{bmatrix} \left(\begin{bmatrix} 4 & 3 \\ 1 & 2 \end{bmatrix} + \begin{bmatrix} 7 & 0 \\ -1 & 5 \end{bmatrix} \right)$ **26.** $\begin{bmatrix} 2 & -2 \\ 1 & -1 \end{bmatrix} \begin{bmatrix} 4 & 3 \\ 1 & 2 \end{bmatrix} + \begin{bmatrix} 2 & -2 \\ 1 & -1 \end{bmatrix} \begin{bmatrix} 7 & 0 \\ -1 & 5 \end{bmatrix}$

27. Let

$$A = \begin{bmatrix} -2 & 4 \\ 1 & 3 \end{bmatrix} \quad \text{and} \quad B = \begin{bmatrix} -2 & 1 \\ 3 & 6 \end{bmatrix}.$$

(a) Find AB.   (b) Find BA.

(c) Did you get the same answer in parts (a) and (b)? Do you think that matrix multiplication is commutative?

(d) In general, for matrices A and B such that AB and BA both exist, does AB always equal BA?

Given matrices

$$P = \begin{bmatrix} m & n \\ p & q \end{bmatrix}, \quad X = \begin{bmatrix} x & y \\ z & w \end{bmatrix}, \quad T = \begin{bmatrix} r & s \\ t & u \end{bmatrix},$$

verify that the statements in Exercises 28–32 are true. The statements are valid for any matrices whenever matrix multiplication and addition can be carried out. This, of course, depends on the *order* of the matrices.

28. $(PX)T = P(XT)$ (Associative property: see Exercises 23 and 24.)

29. $P(X + T) = PX + PT$ (Distributive property: see Exercises 25 and 26.)

30. PX is a 2×2 matrix (Closure property)

31. $k(X + T) = kX + kT$ for any real number k

32. $(k + h)P = kP + hP$ for any real numbers k and h

33. Let I be the matrix $I = \begin{bmatrix} 1 & 0 \\ 0 & 1 \end{bmatrix}$, and let matrices P, X, and T be defined as above.

(a) Find IP, PI, IX.

(b) Without calculating, guess what the matrix IT might be.

(c) Suggest a reason for naming a matrix such as I an *identity* matrix.

34. The Bread Box, a small neighborhood bakery, sells four main items: sweet rolls, bread, cake, and pie. The amount of eggs or of certain other main ingredients (in cups) required to make these items is given in matrix A.

$$A = \begin{array}{c} \\ \\ \\ \\ \end{array} \begin{array}{ccccc} \text{Eggs} & \text{Flour} & \text{Sugar} & \text{Shortening} & \text{Milk} \\ \left[\begin{array}{ccccc} 1 & 4 & \frac{1}{4} & \frac{1}{4} & 1 \\ 0 & 3 & 0 & \frac{1}{4} & 0 \\ 4 & 3 & 2 & 1 & 1 \\ 0 & 1 & 0 & \frac{1}{3} & 0 \end{array}\right] & & & & \end{array} \begin{array}{l} \text{Sweet rolls (dozen)} \\ \text{Bread (loaves)} \\ \text{Cake (1)} \\ \text{Pie (1)} \end{array}$$

The cost (in cents per egg or per cup) for each ingredient when purchased in large lots and in small lots is given by matrix B.

$$\begin{array}{c} \text{Cost} \\ \text{Large lot \quad Small lot} \end{array}$$

$$B = \begin{bmatrix} 5 & 5 \\ 8 & 10 \\ 10 & 12 \\ 12 & 15 \\ 5 & 6 \end{bmatrix} \begin{array}{l} \text{Eggs} \\ \text{Flour} \\ \text{Sugar} \\ \text{Shortening} \\ \text{Milk} \end{array}$$

(a) Use matrix multiplication to find a matrix representing the comparative costs per item under the two purchase options.

Suppose a day's orders consist of 20 dozen sweet rolls, 200 loaves of bread, 50 cakes, and 60 pies.

(b) Represent these orders as a 1×4 matrix and use matrix multiplication to write as a matrix the amount of each ingredient required to fill the day's orders.

(c) Use matrix multiplication to find a matrix representing the costs under the two purchase options to fill the day's orders.

35. In Exercise 37, Section 2.3, label the matrices found in parts (a), (b), and (c) respectively X, Y, and Z.

(a) Find the product matrix XY. What do the entries of this matrix represent?

(b) Find the product matrix YZ. What do the entries represent?

36. Show that the system of linear equations

$$\begin{aligned} 2x_1 + 3x_2 + x_3 &= 5 \\ x_1 - 4x_2 + 5x_3 &= 8 \end{aligned}$$

can be written as the matrix equation

$$\begin{bmatrix} 2 & 3 & 1 \\ 1 & -4 & 5 \end{bmatrix} \begin{bmatrix} x_1 \\ x_2 \\ x_3 \end{bmatrix} = \begin{bmatrix} 5 \\ 8 \end{bmatrix}.$$

Solve the system and substitute into the matrix equation to check the results.

37. Let $A = \begin{bmatrix} 1 & 2 \\ -3 & 5 \end{bmatrix}$, $\quad X = \begin{bmatrix} x_1 \\ x_2 \end{bmatrix}$, and $\quad B = \begin{bmatrix} -4 \\ 12 \end{bmatrix}$.

Show that the equation $AX = B$ represents a linear system of two equations in two unknowns. Solve the system and substitute into the matrix equation to check your results.

Use the following matrices to find the matrix products in Exercises 38–44.

$$A = \begin{bmatrix} 2 & 3 & -1 & 5 & 10 \\ 2 & 8 & 7 & 4 & 3 \\ -1 & -4 & -12 & 6 & 8 \\ 2 & 5 & 7 & 1 & 4 \end{bmatrix} \qquad B = \begin{bmatrix} 9 & 3 & 7 & -6 \\ -1 & 0 & 4 & 2 \\ -10 & -7 & 6 & 9 \\ 8 & 4 & 2 & -1 \\ 2 & -5 & 3 & 7 \end{bmatrix}$$

$$C = \begin{bmatrix} -6 & 8 & 2 & 4 & -3 \\ 1 & 9 & 7 & -12 & 5 \\ 15 & 2 & -8 & 10 & 11 \\ 4 & 7 & 9 & 6 & -2 \\ 1 & 3 & 8 & 23 & 4 \end{bmatrix} \qquad D = \begin{bmatrix} 5 & -3 & 7 & 9 & 2 \\ 6 & 8 & -5 & 2 & 1 \\ 3 & 7 & -4 & 2 & 11 \\ 5 & -3 & 9 & 4 & -1 \\ 0 & 3 & 2 & 5 & 1 \end{bmatrix}$$

38. AC **39.** CD **40.** DC **41.** CA **42.** Is $AC = CA$?

43. Is $CD = DC$?

44. Find $C + D$, $(C + D)B$, CB, DB, and $CB + DB$. Does $(C + D)B = CB + DB$?

EXTENDED
APPLICATION

Routing

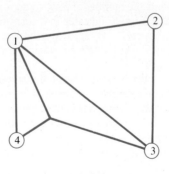

FIGURE 1

The diagram in Figure 1 shows the roads connecting four cities. Another way of representing this information is shown in matrix A, where the entries represent the number of roads connecting two cities without passing through another city.* For example, from

---

*Taken from Hugh G. Campbell, *Matrices With Applications,* © 1968, p. 50—51. Reprinted by permission of Prentice-Hall, Inc., Englewood Cliffs, N.J.

the diagram we see that there are two roads connecting city 1 to city 4 without passing through either city 2 or 3. This information is entered in row 1, column 4 and again in row 4, column 1 of matrix A.

$$A = \begin{bmatrix} 0 & 1 & 2 & 2 \\ 1 & 0 & 1 & 0 \\ 2 & 1 & 0 & 1 \\ 2 & 0 & 1 & 0 \end{bmatrix}$$

Note that there are 0 roads connecting each city to itself. Also, there is one road connecting cities 3 and 2.

How many ways are there to go from city 1 to city 2, for example, by going through exactly one other city? Since we must go through one other city, we must go through either city 3 or city 4. On the diagram in Figure 1, we see that we can go from city 1 to city 2 through city 3 in 2 ways. We can go from city 1 to city 3 in 2 ways and then from city 3 to city 2 in one way, giving the $2 \cdot 1 = 2$ ways to get from city 1 to city 2 through city 3. It is not possible to go from city 1 to city 2 through city 4, because there is no direct route between cities 4 and 2.

Now multiply matrix A by itself, to get A^2. Let the first row, second column entry of A^2 be b_{12}. (We use a_{ij} to denote the entry in the i-th row and j-th column of matrix A.) The entry b_{12} is found as follows.

$$\begin{aligned} b_{12} &= a_{11}a_{12} + a_{12}a_{22} + a_{13}a_{32} + a_{14}a_{42} \\ &= 0 \cdot 1 + 1 \cdot 0 + 2 \cdot 1 + 2 \cdot 0 \\ &= 2. \end{aligned}$$

The matrix A^2 gives the number of ways to travel between any two cities by passing through exactly one other city. The first product $0 \cdot 1$ in the calculations above represents the number of ways to go from city 1 to city 1 (0) and then from city 1 to city 2 (1). The 0 result indicates that such a trip does not involve a third city. The only non-zero product $(2 \cdot 1)$ represents the two routes from city 1 to city 3 and the one route from city 3 to city 2 which result in the $2 \cdot 1$ or 2 routes from city 1 to city 2 by going through city 3.

Similarly, A^3 gives the number of ways to travel between any two cities by passing through exactly two cities. Also, $A + A^2$ represents the total number of ways to travel between two cities with at most one intermediate city.

The diagram can be given many other interpretations. For example, the lines could represent lines of mutual influence between people or nations; they could represent communication lines such as telephone lines.

EXERCISES

1. Use matrix A from the text to find A^2. Then answer the following questions.

(a) How many ways are there to travel from city 1 to city 3 by passing through exactly one city?

(b) How many ways are there to travel from city 2 to city 4 by passing through exactly one city?

(c) How many ways are there to travel from city 1 to city 3 by passing through at most one city?

(d) How many ways are there to travel from city 2 to city 4 by passing through at most one city?

2. Find A^3. Then answer the following questions.

    (a) How many ways are there to travel between cities 1 and 4 by passing through exactly two cities?

    (b) How many ways are there to travel between cities 1 and 4 by passing through at most two cities?

3. A small telephone system connects three cities. There are four lines between cities 3 and 2, three lines connecting city 3 with city 1 and two lines between cities 1 and 2.

    (a) Write a matrix B to represent this information.

    (b) Find B^2.

    (c) How many lines which connect cities 1 and 2 go through exactly one other city (city 3)?

    (d) How many lines which connect cities 1 and 2 go through at most one other city?

4. The figure shows four southern cities served by Delta Airlines.

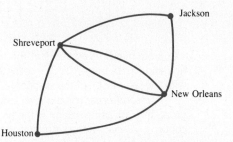

    (a) Write a matrix to represent the number of non-stop routes between cities.

    (b) Find the number of one-stop flights between Houston and Jackson.

    (c) Find the number of flights between Houston and Jackson which require at most one stop.

    (d) Find the number of one-stop flights between New Orleans and Houston.

5. The figure shows a food web. The arrows indicate the food sources of each population. For example, cats feed on rats and on mice.

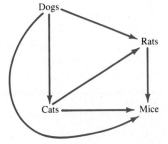

    (a) Write a matrix C in which each row and corresponding column represents a population in the food chain. Enter a one when the population in a given row feeds on the population in the given column and a zero otherwise.

    (b) Calculate and interpret C^2.

6. Find A^2, B^2, and C^2 for the matrices used in these problems.

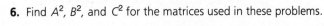

EXTENDED

APPLICATION

Contagion

Suppose that three people have contracted a contagious disease.* A second group of five people may have been in contact with the three infected persons. A third group of six people may have been in contact with the second group. We can form a 3×5 matrix P with rows representing the first group of three and columns representing the second group of five. We enter a one in the corresponding position if a person in the first group has contact with a person in the second group. These direct contacts are called *first-order contacts*. Similarly we form a 5×6 matrix Q representing the first-order contacts between the second and third group. For example, suppose

$$P = \begin{bmatrix} 1 & 0 & 0 & 1 & 0 \\ 0 & 0 & 1 & 1 & 0 \\ 1 & 1 & 0 & 0 & 0 \end{bmatrix} \quad \text{and} \quad Q = \begin{bmatrix} 1 & 1 & 0 & 1 & 1 & 1 \\ 0 & 0 & 0 & 0 & 1 & 0 \\ 0 & 0 & 0 & 0 & 0 & 0 \\ 0 & 1 & 0 & 1 & 0 & 0 \\ 1 & 0 & 0 & 0 & 1 & 0 \end{bmatrix}.$$

From matrix P we see that the first person in the first group had contact with the first and fourth persons in the second group. Also, none of the first group had contact with the last person in the second group.

A *second-order contact* is an indirect contact between persons in the first and third group through some person in the second group. The product matrix PQ indicates these contacts. Verify that the second row, fourth column entry of PQ is 1. That is, there is one second-order contact between the second person in group 1 and the fourth person in group 3. Let a_{ij} denote the element in the i-th row and j-th column of the matrix PQ. By looking at the products which form a_{24} below, we see that the common contact was with the fourth individual in group 2. (The p_{ij} are entries in P, and the q_{ij} are entries in Q.)

$$\begin{aligned} a_{24} &= p_{21}q_{14} + p_{22}q_{24} + p_{23}q_{34} + p_{24}q_{44} + p_{25}q_{54} \\ &= 0 \cdot 1 \quad + 0 \cdot 0 \quad + 1 \cdot 0 \quad + 1 \cdot 1 \quad + 0 \cdot 1 \\ &= 1 \end{aligned}$$

The second person in group 1 and the fourth person in group 3 both had contact with the fourth person in group 2.

This idea could be extended to third-, fourth-, and larger order contacts. It indicates a way to use matrices to trace the spread of a contagious disease. It could also pertain to the dispersal of ideas or anything that might pass from one individual to another.

EXERCISES

1. Find the second-order contact matrix PQ mentioned in the text.

2. How many second-order contacts were there between the second contagious person and the third person in the third group?

*Reprinted by permission of Stanley I. Grossman and James E. Turner from *Mathematics for the Biological Sciences* (New York: Macmillan Publishing Company, Inc., 1974). See also Stanley I. Grossman, *Finite Mathematics with Applications to Business, Life Sciences, and Social Sciences* (Belmont, CA: Wadsworth Publishing Company, 1983), p. 103.

3. Is there anyone in the third group who has had no contacts at all with the first group?

4. The totals of the columns in *PQ* give the total number of second-order contacts per person, while the column totals in *P* and *Q* give the total number of first-order contacts per person. Which person has the most contacts, counting both first- and second-order contacts?

5. Find the matrix product in Exercise 1.

2.5 Matrix Inverses

In Section 2.3, we defined a zero matrix which has properties similar to those of the real number zero, the identity for addition. The real number 1 is the identity element for multiplication: for any real number a, $a \cdot 1 = 1 \cdot a = a$. In this section, we define an *identity matrix I* which has properties similar to those of the number 1. This identity matrix is then used to find the multiplicative inverse of any square matrix which has an inverse.

If I is to be the identity matrix, the products AI and IA must both equal A. This means that an identity matrix exists only for square matrices. Otherwise, IA and AI could not both be found. The **2 × 2 identity matrix** which satisfies these conditions is

$$I = \begin{bmatrix} 1 & 0 \\ 0 & 1 \end{bmatrix}.$$

To check that I, as defined above, is really the 2 × 2 identity matrix, let

$$A = \begin{bmatrix} a & b \\ c & d \end{bmatrix}.$$

Then AI and IA should both equal A.

$$AI = \begin{bmatrix} a & b \\ c & d \end{bmatrix}\begin{bmatrix} 1 & 0 \\ 0 & 1 \end{bmatrix} = \begin{bmatrix} a(1) + b(0) & a(0) + b(1) \\ c(1) + d(0) & c(0) + d(1) \end{bmatrix} = \begin{bmatrix} a & b \\ c & d \end{bmatrix} = A$$

$$IA = \begin{bmatrix} 1 & 0 \\ 0 & 1 \end{bmatrix}\begin{bmatrix} a & b \\ c & d \end{bmatrix} = \begin{bmatrix} 1(a) + 0(c) & 1(b) + 0(d) \\ 0(a) + 1(c) & 0(b) + 1(d) \end{bmatrix} = \begin{bmatrix} a & b \\ c & d \end{bmatrix} = A$$

This verifies that I has been defined correctly. (It can also be shown that I is the only 2 × 2 identity matrix.)

The identity matrices for 3 × 3 matrices and 4 × 4 matrices, respectively, are

$$I = \begin{bmatrix} 1 & 0 & 0 \\ 0 & 1 & 0 \\ 0 & 0 & 1 \end{bmatrix} \quad \text{and} \quad I = \begin{bmatrix} 1 & 0 & 0 & 0 \\ 0 & 1 & 0 & 0 \\ 0 & 0 & 1 & 0 \\ 0 & 0 & 0 & 1 \end{bmatrix}.$$

By generalizing, an $n \times n$ identity matrix can be determined for any value of n.

Recall that the multiplicative inverse of the nonzero real number a is $1/a$. The product of a and its multiplicative inverse $1/a$ is 1. Now we try to do a similar thing with matrices: given a matrix A, can we find a matrix A^{-1} (read "A-inverse") satisfying both

$$AA^{-1} = I \quad \text{and} \quad A^{-1}A = I?$$

It turns out that we often can find this matrix inverse A^{-1}, using the row operations of Section 2.2. Before doing this, we might mention that the symbol A^{-1} does not mean $1/A$; the symbol A^{-1} is just the notation for the inverse of matrix A. Also, only square matrices can have inverses. If an inverse exists, it is unique. That is, any given square matrix has no more than one inverse. The proof of this is left to Exercise 50 of this section.

As an example, let us find the inverse of

$$A = \begin{bmatrix} 2 & 4 \\ 1 & -1 \end{bmatrix}.$$

Let the unknown inverse matrix be

$$A^{-1} = \begin{bmatrix} x & y \\ z & w \end{bmatrix}.$$

By the definition of matrix inverse, $AA^{-1} = I$, or

$$AA^{-1} = \begin{bmatrix} 2 & 4 \\ 1 & -1 \end{bmatrix}\begin{bmatrix} x & y \\ z & w \end{bmatrix} = \begin{bmatrix} 1 & 0 \\ 0 & 1 \end{bmatrix}.$$

By matrix multiplication,

$$\begin{bmatrix} 2x + 4z & 2y + 4w \\ x - z & y - w \end{bmatrix} = \begin{bmatrix} 1 & 0 \\ 0 & 1 \end{bmatrix}.$$

Setting corresponding elements equal gives the system of equations

$$2x + 4z = 1 \tag{1}$$
$$2y + 4w = 0 \tag{2}$$
$$x - z = 0 \tag{3}$$
$$y - w = 1. \tag{4}$$

Since equations (1) and (3) involve only x and z, while equations (2) and (4) involve only y and w, these four equations lead to two systems of equations,

$$\begin{array}{c} 2x + 4z = 1 \\ x - z = 0 \end{array} \quad \text{and} \quad \begin{array}{c} 2y + 4w = 0 \\ y - w = 1. \end{array}$$

Writing the two systems as augmented matrices gives

$$\begin{bmatrix} 2 & 4 & | & 1 \\ 1 & -1 & | & 0 \end{bmatrix} \quad \text{and} \quad \begin{bmatrix} 2 & 4 & | & 0 \\ 1 & -1 & | & 1 \end{bmatrix}.$$

Each of these systems can be solved by the Gauss-Jordan method. However, since the elements to the left of the vertical bar are identical, the two systems can be combined into one matrix

$$\left[\begin{array}{cc|cc} 2 & 4 & 1 & 0 \\ 1 & -1 & 0 & 1 \end{array}\right]$$

and solved simultaneously as follows. Exchange the two rows to get a 1 in the upper left corner.

$$\left[\begin{array}{cc|cc} 1 & -1 & 0 & 1 \\ 2 & 4 & 1 & 0 \end{array}\right]$$

Multiply row one by -2 and add the results to row two to get

$$\left[\begin{array}{cc|cc} 1 & -1 & 0 & 1 \\ 0 & 6 & 1 & -2 \end{array}\right].$$

Now, to get a 1 in the second row, second column position, multiply row two by 1/6.

$$\left[\begin{array}{cc|cc} 1 & -1 & 0 & 1 \\ 0 & 1 & \frac{1}{6} & -\frac{1}{3} \end{array}\right]$$

Finally, add row two to row one to get a 0 in the second column above the 1.

$$\left[\begin{array}{cc|cc} 1 & 0 & \frac{1}{6} & \frac{2}{3} \\ 0 & 1 & \frac{1}{6} & -\frac{1}{3} \end{array}\right]$$

The numbers in the first column to the right of the vertical bar give the values of x and z. The second column gives the values of y and w. That is,

$$\left[\begin{array}{cc|cc} 1 & 0 & x & y \\ 0 & 1 & z & w \end{array}\right] = \left[\begin{array}{cc|cc} 1 & 0 & \frac{1}{6} & \frac{2}{3} \\ 0 & 1 & \frac{1}{6} & -\frac{1}{3} \end{array}\right]$$

so that

$$A^{-1} = \left[\begin{array}{cc} x & y \\ z & w \end{array}\right] = \left[\begin{array}{cc} \frac{1}{6} & \frac{2}{3} \\ \frac{1}{6} & -\frac{1}{3} \end{array}\right].$$

To check, multiply A by A^{-1}. The result should be I.

$$AA^{-1} = \left[\begin{array}{cc} 2 & 4 \\ 1 & -1 \end{array}\right]\left[\begin{array}{cc} \frac{1}{6} & \frac{2}{3} \\ \frac{1}{6} & -\frac{1}{3} \end{array}\right] = \left[\begin{array}{cc} \frac{1}{3}+\frac{2}{3} & \frac{4}{3}-\frac{4}{3} \\ \frac{1}{6}-\frac{1}{6} & \frac{2}{3}+\frac{1}{3} \end{array}\right] = \left[\begin{array}{cc} 1 & 0 \\ 0 & 1 \end{array}\right] = I.$$

Verify that $A^{-1}A = I$, also. Finally,

$$A^{-1} = \left[\begin{array}{cc} \frac{1}{6} & \frac{2}{3} \\ \frac{1}{6} & -\frac{1}{3} \end{array}\right].$$

Finding an Inverse

Matrix

> To obtain A^{-1} for any $n \times n$ matrix A for which A^{-1} exists, follow these steps.
> 1. Form the augmented matrix $[A|I]$, where I is the $n \times n$ identity matrix.
> 2. Perform row operations on $[A|I]$ to get a matrix of the form $[I|B]$.
> 3. Matrix B is A^{-1}.

EXAMPLE 1

Find A^{-1} if $A = \begin{bmatrix} 1 & 0 & 1 \\ 2 & -2 & -1 \\ 3 & 0 & 0 \end{bmatrix}$.

Write the augmented matrix $[A|I]$.

$$[A|I] = \begin{bmatrix} 1 & 0 & 1 & | & 1 & 0 & 0 \\ 2 & -2 & -1 & | & 0 & 1 & 0 \\ 3 & 0 & 0 & | & 0 & 0 & 1 \end{bmatrix}$$

Since 1 is already in the upper left-hand corner as desired, begin by selecting the row operation which will result in a 0 for the first element in row two. Multiply row one by -2 and add the result to row two. This gives

$$\begin{bmatrix} 1 & 0 & 1 & | & 1 & 0 & 0 \\ 0 & -2 & -3 & | & -2 & 1 & 0 \\ 3 & 0 & 0 & | & 0 & 0 & 1 \end{bmatrix}.$$

To get 0 for the first element in row three, multiply row one by -3 and add to row three. The new matrix is

$$\begin{bmatrix} 1 & 0 & 1 & | & 1 & 0 & 0 \\ 0 & -2 & -3 & | & -2 & 1 & 0 \\ 0 & 0 & -3 & | & -3 & 0 & 1 \end{bmatrix}.$$

To get 1 for the second element in row two, multiply row two by $-1/2$, obtaining the new matrix

$$\begin{bmatrix} 1 & 0 & 1 & | & 1 & 0 & 0 \\ 0 & 1 & \frac{3}{2} & | & 1 & -\frac{1}{2} & 0 \\ 0 & 0 & -3 & | & -3 & 0 & 1 \end{bmatrix}.$$

To get 1 for the third element in row three, multiply row three by $-1/3$, with the result

$$\begin{bmatrix} 1 & 0 & 1 & | & 1 & 0 & 0 \\ 0 & 1 & \frac{3}{2} & | & 1 & -\frac{1}{2} & 0 \\ 0 & 0 & 1 & | & 1 & 0 & -\frac{1}{3} \end{bmatrix}.$$

To get 0 for the third element in row one, multiply row three by -1 and add to row one, which gives

$$\begin{bmatrix} 1 & 0 & 0 & | & 0 & 0 & \frac{1}{3} \\ 0 & 1 & \frac{3}{2} & | & 1 & -\frac{1}{2} & 0 \\ 0 & 0 & 1 & | & 1 & 0 & -\frac{1}{3} \end{bmatrix}.$$

To get 0 for the third element in row two, multiply row three by $-3/2$ and add to row two.

$$\begin{bmatrix} 1 & 0 & 0 & | & 0 & 0 & \frac{1}{3} \\ 0 & 1 & 0 & | & -\frac{1}{2} & -\frac{1}{2} & \frac{1}{2} \\ 0 & 0 & 1 & | & 1 & 0 & -\frac{1}{3} \end{bmatrix}$$

From the last transformation, the desired inverse is

$$A^{-1} = \begin{bmatrix} 0 & 0 & \frac{1}{3} \\ -\frac{1}{2} & -\frac{1}{2} & \frac{1}{2} \\ 1 & 0 & -\frac{1}{3} \end{bmatrix}.$$

Confirm this by forming the products $A^{-1}A$ and AA^{-1}, both of which should equal I. ▪

EXAMPLE 2

Find A^{-1} if $A = \begin{bmatrix} 2 & -4 \\ 1 & -2 \end{bmatrix}$.

Using row operations to transform the first column of the augmented matrix

$$\begin{bmatrix} 2 & -4 & | & 1 & 0 \\ 1 & -2 & | & 0 & 1 \end{bmatrix}$$

results in the following matrices.

$$\begin{bmatrix} 1 & -2 & | & \frac{1}{2} & 0 \\ 1 & -2 & | & 0 & 1 \end{bmatrix}$$

$$\begin{bmatrix} 1 & -2 & | & \frac{1}{2} & 0 \\ 0 & 0 & | & -\frac{1}{2} & 1 \end{bmatrix}$$

At this point, the matrix should be transformed so that the second element of row two will be 1. Since that element is now 0, there is no way to complete the desired transformation.

What is wrong? Just as the real number 0 has no multiplicative inverse, some matrices do not have inverses. Matrix A is an example of a matrix that has no inverse: there is no matrix A^{-1} such that $AA^{-1} = A^{-1}A = I$. ▪

Solving Systems of Equations with Inverses Matrices were used to solve systems of linear equations by the Gauss-Jordan method in Section 2.2. Another way to use matrices to solve linear systems is to write the system as a matrix equation $AX = B$, where A is the matrix of the coefficients of the variables of the system, X is the matrix of the variables, and B is the matrix of the constants. Matrix A is called the **coefficient matrix.**

To solve the matrix equation $AX = B$, first see if A^{-1} exists. Assuming A^{-1} exists and using the facts that $A^{-1}A = I$ and $IX = X$ gives

$$\begin{aligned} AX &= B \\ A^{-1}(AX) &= A^{-1}B \qquad \text{Multiply both sides by } A^{-1} \\ (A^{-1}A)X &= A^{-1}B \\ IX &= A^{-1}B \\ X &= A^{-1}B. \end{aligned}$$

When multiplying by matrices on both sides of a matrix equation, be careful to multiply in the same order on both sides of the equation, since multiplication of matrices is not commutative (unlike multiplication of real numbers).

Solving a System

$AX = B$ Using

Matrix Inverses

To solve a system of equations $AX = B$ where A is the matrix of coefficients, X is the matrix of variables, and B is the matrix of constants, first find A^{-1}. Then $X = A^{-1}B$.

This method is most practical in cases where several systems with the same coefficient matrix, but different constants, are to be solved. Then just one inverse matrix must be found.

EXAMPLE 3

Use the inverse of the coefficient matrix to solve the linear system

$$2x - 3y = 4$$
$$x + 5y = 2.$$

To represent the system as a matrix equation, use the coefficient matrix of the system together with the matrix of variables and the matrix of constants.

$$A = \begin{bmatrix} 2 & -3 \\ 1 & 5 \end{bmatrix}, \qquad X = \begin{bmatrix} x \\ y \end{bmatrix}, \qquad \text{and} \qquad B = \begin{bmatrix} 4 \\ 2 \end{bmatrix}.$$

The system can then be written in matrix form as the equation $AX = B$ since

$$AX = \begin{bmatrix} 2 & -3 \\ 1 & 5 \end{bmatrix}\begin{bmatrix} x \\ y \end{bmatrix} = \begin{bmatrix} 2x - 3y \\ x + 5y \end{bmatrix} = \begin{bmatrix} 4 \\ 2 \end{bmatrix} = B.$$

To solve the system, first find A^{-1}. Do this by using row operations on matrix $[A|I]$ to get

$$\begin{bmatrix} 1 & 0 & \frac{5}{13} & \frac{3}{13} \\ 0 & 1 & -\frac{1}{13} & \frac{2}{13} \end{bmatrix}.$$

From this result,

$$A^{-1} = \begin{bmatrix} \frac{5}{13} & \frac{3}{13} \\ -\frac{1}{13} & \frac{2}{13} \end{bmatrix}.$$

Next, find the product $A^{-1}B$.

$$A^{-1}B = \begin{bmatrix} \frac{5}{13} & \frac{3}{13} \\ -\frac{1}{13} & \frac{2}{13} \end{bmatrix}\begin{bmatrix} 4 \\ 2 \end{bmatrix} = \begin{bmatrix} 2 \\ 0 \end{bmatrix}$$

Since $X = A^{-1}B$,

$$X = \begin{bmatrix} x \\ y \end{bmatrix} = \begin{bmatrix} 2 \\ 0 \end{bmatrix}.$$

The solution of the system is $(2, 0)$. ∎

EXAMPLE 4

Use the inverse of the coefficient matrix to solve the system

$$-x - 2y + 2z = 9$$
$$2x + y - z = -3$$
$$3x - 2y + z = -6.$$

The needed matrices are

$$A = \begin{bmatrix} -1 & -2 & 2 \\ 2 & 1 & -1 \\ 3 & -2 & 1 \end{bmatrix}, \quad X = \begin{bmatrix} x \\ y \\ z \end{bmatrix}, \quad \text{and} \quad B = \begin{bmatrix} 9 \\ -3 \\ -6 \end{bmatrix}.$$

To find A^{-1}, start with matrix

$$[A|I] = \begin{bmatrix} -1 & -2 & 2 & | & 1 & 0 & 0 \\ 2 & 1 & -1 & | & 0 & 1 & 0 \\ 3 & -2 & 1 & | & 0 & 0 & 1 \end{bmatrix}$$

and use row operations to get $[I|A^{-1}]$, from which

$$A^{-1} = \begin{bmatrix} \frac{1}{3} & \frac{2}{3} & 0 \\ \frac{5}{3} & \frac{7}{3} & -1 \\ \frac{7}{3} & \frac{8}{3} & -1 \end{bmatrix}.$$

Now find $A^{-1}B$.

$$A^{-1}B = \begin{bmatrix} \frac{1}{3} & \frac{2}{3} & 0 \\ \frac{5}{3} & \frac{7}{3} & -1 \\ \frac{7}{3} & \frac{8}{3} & -1 \end{bmatrix} \begin{bmatrix} 9 \\ -3 \\ -6 \end{bmatrix} = \begin{bmatrix} 1 \\ 14 \\ 19 \end{bmatrix}$$

Since $X = A^{-1}B$,

$$X = \begin{bmatrix} x \\ y \\ z \end{bmatrix} = \begin{bmatrix} 1 \\ 14 \\ 19 \end{bmatrix}.$$

From this result, $x = 1$, $y = 14$, $z = 19$ and the solution is (1, 14, 19.)

2.5 EXERCISES

In Exercises 1–8, decide whether or not the given matrices are inverses of each other. (Check to see if their product is the identity matrix I.)

1. $\begin{bmatrix} 2 & 3 \\ 1 & 1 \end{bmatrix}$ and $\begin{bmatrix} -1 & 3 \\ 1 & -2 \end{bmatrix}$

2. $\begin{bmatrix} 5 & 7 \\ 2 & 3 \end{bmatrix}$ and $\begin{bmatrix} 3 & -7 \\ -2 & 5 \end{bmatrix}$

3. $\begin{bmatrix} 2 & 1 \\ 3 & 2 \end{bmatrix}$ and $\begin{bmatrix} 2 & 1 \\ -3 & 2 \end{bmatrix}$

4. $\begin{bmatrix} -1 & 2 \\ 3 & -5 \end{bmatrix}$ and $\begin{bmatrix} -5 & -2 \\ -3 & -1 \end{bmatrix}$

5. $\begin{bmatrix} 1 & 2 & 0 \\ 0 & 1 & 0 \\ 0 & 1 & 0 \end{bmatrix}$ and $\begin{bmatrix} 1 & -2 & 0 \\ 0 & 1 & 0 \\ 0 & -1 & 1 \end{bmatrix}$

6. $\begin{bmatrix} 0 & 1 & 0 \\ 0 & 0 & -2 \\ 1 & -1 & 0 \end{bmatrix}$ and $\begin{bmatrix} 1 & 0 & 1 \\ 1 & 0 & 0 \\ 0 & -1 & 0 \end{bmatrix}$

7. $\begin{bmatrix} 1 & 3 & 3 \\ 1 & 4 & 3 \\ 1 & 3 & 4 \end{bmatrix}$ and $\begin{bmatrix} 7 & -3 & -3 \\ -1 & 1 & 0 \\ -1 & 0 & 1 \end{bmatrix}$

8. $\begin{bmatrix} -1 & 0 & 2 \\ 3 & 1 & 0 \\ 0 & 2 & -3 \end{bmatrix}$ and $\begin{bmatrix} -\frac{1}{5} & \frac{4}{15} & -\frac{2}{15} \\ \frac{3}{5} & \frac{1}{5} & \frac{2}{5} \\ \frac{2}{5} & \frac{2}{15} & -\frac{1}{15} \end{bmatrix}$

Find the inverse, if it exists, for each of the matrices in Exercises 9–24.

9. $\begin{bmatrix} 1 & -1 \\ 2 & 0 \end{bmatrix}$

10. $\begin{bmatrix} -1 & 2 \\ -2 & -1 \end{bmatrix}$

11. $\begin{bmatrix} 3 & -1 \\ -5 & 2 \end{bmatrix}$

12. $\begin{bmatrix} -1 & -2 \\ 3 & 4 \end{bmatrix}$

13. $\begin{bmatrix} -6 & 4 \\ -3 & 2 \end{bmatrix}$

14. $\begin{bmatrix} 5 & 10 \\ -3 & -6 \end{bmatrix}$

15. $\begin{bmatrix} 1 & 0 & 0 \\ 0 & -1 & 0 \\ 1 & 0 & 1 \end{bmatrix}$

16. $\begin{bmatrix} 1 & 0 & 1 \\ 0 & -1 & 0 \\ 2 & 1 & 1 \end{bmatrix}$

17. $\begin{bmatrix} -1 & -1 & -1 \\ 4 & 5 & 0 \\ 0 & 1 & -3 \end{bmatrix}$

18. $\begin{bmatrix} 2 & 0 & 4 \\ 3 & 1 & 5 \\ -1 & 1 & -2 \end{bmatrix}$

19. $\begin{bmatrix} 1 & 2 & 3 \\ -3 & -2 & -1 \\ -1 & 0 & 1 \end{bmatrix}$

20. $\begin{bmatrix} 2 & 0 & 4 \\ 1 & 0 & -1 \\ 3 & 0 & -2 \end{bmatrix}$

21. $\begin{bmatrix} 2 & 4 & 6 \\ -1 & -4 & -3 \\ 0 & 1 & -1 \end{bmatrix}$

22. $\begin{bmatrix} 2 & 2 & -4 \\ 2 & 6 & 0 \\ -3 & -3 & 5 \end{bmatrix}$

23. $\begin{bmatrix} 1 & -2 & 3 & 0 \\ 0 & 1 & -1 & 1 \\ -2 & 2 & -2 & 4 \\ 0 & 2 & -3 & 1 \end{bmatrix}$

24. $\begin{bmatrix} 1 & 1 & 0 & 2 \\ 2 & -1 & 1 & -1 \\ 3 & 3 & 2 & -2 \\ 1 & 2 & 1 & 0 \end{bmatrix}$

Solve each of the systems of equations in Exercises 25–32 by using the inverse of the coefficient matrix.

25. $2x + 3y = 10$
    $x - y = -5$

26. $-x + 2y = 15$
    $-2x - y = 20$

27. $2x + y = 5$
    $5x + 3y = 13$

28. $-x - 2y = 8$
    $3x + 4y = 24$

29. $-x + y = 1$
    $2x - y = 1$

30. $3x - 6y = 1$
    $-5x + 9y = -1$

31. $-x - 8y = 12$
    $3x + 24y = -36$

32. $x + 3y = -14$
    $2x - y = 7$

Solve each of the systems of equations in Exercises 33–40 by using the inverse of the coefficient matrix. The inverses for the first four problems are found in Exercises 17, 18, 21, and 22 above.

33. $-x - y - z = 1$
    $4x + 5y = -2$
    $y - 3z = 3$

34. $2x + 4z = -8$
    $3x + y + 5z = 2$
    $-x + y - 2z = 4$

35. $2x + 4y + 6z = 4$
    $-x - 4y - 3z = 8$
    $y - z = -4$

36. $2x + 2y - 4z = 12$
    $2x + 6y = 16$
    $-3x - 3y + 5z = -20$

37. $x + 2y + 3z = 5$
    $2x + 3y + 2z = 2$
    $-x - 2y - 4z = -1$

38. $x + y - 3z = 4$
    $2x + 4y - 4z = 8$
    $-x + y + 4z = -3$

39. $2x - 2y = 5$
    $4y + 8z = 7$
    $x + 2z = 1$

40. $x + z = 3$
    $y + 2z = 8$
    $-x + y = 4$

Solve the systems of equations in Exercises 41–42 by using the inverse of the coefficient matrix. The inverses were found in Exercises 23 and 24.

41.
$$\begin{aligned} x - 2y + 3z \quad\quad &= 4 \\ y - z + w &= -8 \\ -2x + 2y - 2z + 4w &= 12 \\ 2y - 3z + w &= -4 \end{aligned}$$

42.
$$\begin{aligned} x + y \quad\quad + 2w &= 3 \\ 2x - y + z - w &= 3 \\ 3x + 3y + 2z - 2w &= 5 \\ x + 2y + z \quad\quad &= 3 \end{aligned}$$

Let $A = \begin{bmatrix} a & b \\ c & d \end{bmatrix}$. Show that statements 43–45 are true.

43. $IA = A$

44. $AI = A$

45. $A \cdot O = O$

46. Find A^{-1}. (Assume $ad - bc \neq 0$.) Show that $AA^{-1} = I$.

47. Show that $A^{-1}A = I$.

48. Using the definitions and properties listed in this section, show that for square matrices A and B of the same order, if $AB = O$ and if A^{-1} exists, then $B = O$.

49. The Bread Box Bakery sells three types of cakes, each requiring the amounts of the basic ingredients shown in the following matrix.

$$\begin{array}{cc} & \begin{array}{ccc} \text{I} & \text{II} & \text{III} \end{array} \\ \begin{array}{l} \text{Flour (cups)} \\ \text{Sugar (cups)} \\ \text{Eggs} \end{array} & \begin{bmatrix} 2 & 4 & 2 \\ 2 & 1 & 2 \\ 2 & 1 & 3 \end{bmatrix} \end{array}$$

To fill its daily orders for these three kinds of cake, the bakery uses 72 cups of flour, 48 cups of sugar, and 60 eggs.

(a) Write a 3 × 1 matrix for the amounts used daily.

(b) Let the number of daily orders for cakes be a 3 × 1 matrix X with entries x_1, x_2, and x_3. Write a matrix equation which you can solve for X, using the given matrix and the matrix from part (a).

(c) Solve the equation you wrote in part (b) to find the number of daily orders for each type of cake.

50. Prove that, if it exists, the inverse of a matrix is unique. Hint: Assume there are two inverses B and C for some matrix A, so that $AB = BA = I$ and $AC = CA = I$. Multiply the first equation by C and the second by B.

Use matrices C and D to find the inverses in Exercises 51–54.

$$C = \begin{bmatrix} -6 & 8 & 2 & 4 & -3 \\ 1 & 9 & 7 & -12 & 5 \\ 15 & 2 & -8 & 10 & 11 \\ 4 & 7 & 9 & 6 & -2 \\ 1 & 3 & 8 & 23 & 4 \end{bmatrix} \qquad D = \begin{bmatrix} 5 & -3 & 7 & 9 & 2 \\ 6 & 8 & -5 & 2 & 1 \\ 3 & 7 & -4 & 2 & 11 \\ 5 & -3 & 9 & 4 & -1 \\ 0 & 3 & 2 & 5 & 1 \end{bmatrix}$$

51. C^{-1}

52. $(CD)^{-1}$

53. D^{-1}

54. Is $C^{-1}D^{-1} = (CD)^{-1}$?

Solve the matrix equation $AX = B$ for X, given A and B as follows.

55.
$$A = \begin{bmatrix} 2 & 3 & 5 \\ 1 & 7 & 9 \\ -3 & 2 & 10 \end{bmatrix} \qquad B = \begin{bmatrix} 3 \\ 4 \\ 1 \end{bmatrix}$$

56.
$$A = \begin{bmatrix} 2 & 5 & 7 & 9 \\ 1 & 3 & -4 & 6 \\ -1 & 0 & 5 & 8 \\ 2 & -2 & 4 & 10 \end{bmatrix} \qquad B = \begin{bmatrix} 3 \\ 7 \\ -1 \\ 5 \end{bmatrix}$$

57.
$$A = \begin{bmatrix} 3 & 2 & -1 & -2 & 6 \\ -5 & 17 & 4 & 3 & 15 \\ 7 & 9 & -3 & -7 & 12 \\ 9 & -2 & 1 & 4 & 8 \\ 1 & 21 & 9 & -7 & 25 \end{bmatrix} \qquad B = \begin{bmatrix} -2 \\ 5 \\ 3 \\ -8 \\ 25 \end{bmatrix}$$

EXTENDED APPLICATION   Code Theory

Governments need sophisticated methods of coding and decoding messages. One example of such an advanced code uses matrix theory. Such a code takes the letters in the words and divides them into groups. (Each space between words is treated as a letter; punctuation is disregarded.) Then, numbers are assigned to the letters of the alphabet. For our purposes, let the letter *a* correspond to 1, *b* to 2, and so on. We let the number 27 correspond to a space between words.

For example, the message

mathematics is for the birds

can be divided into groups of three letters each.

mat   hem   ati   cs-   is-   for   -th   e-b   ird   s--

Note that we used "-" to represent a space between words. We now write a column matrix for each group of three symbols using the corresponding numbers, as determined above, instead of letters. For example, the letters *mat* can be encoded as

$$\begin{bmatrix} 13 \\ 1 \\ 20 \end{bmatrix}.$$

The coded message then is the set of 3 × 1 column matrices.

$$\begin{bmatrix} 13 \\ 1 \\ 20 \end{bmatrix} \begin{bmatrix} 8 \\ 5 \\ 13 \end{bmatrix} \begin{bmatrix} 1 \\ 20 \\ 9 \end{bmatrix} \begin{bmatrix} 3 \\ 19 \\ 27 \end{bmatrix} \begin{bmatrix} 9 \\ 19 \\ 27 \end{bmatrix} \begin{bmatrix} 6 \\ 15 \\ 18 \end{bmatrix} \begin{bmatrix} 27 \\ 20 \\ 8 \end{bmatrix} \begin{bmatrix} 5 \\ 27 \\ 2 \end{bmatrix} \begin{bmatrix} 9 \\ 18 \\ 4 \end{bmatrix} \begin{bmatrix} 19 \\ 27 \\ 27 \end{bmatrix}$$

We can further complicate the code by choosing a matrix which has an inverse, in this case a 3 × 3 matrix, call it *M,* and find the products of this matrix and each of the

above column matrices. (Note that the size of each group, the assignment of numbers to letters, and the choice of matrix M must all be predetermined.)
Suppose

$$M = \begin{bmatrix} 1 & 3 & 3 \\ 1 & 4 & 3 \\ 1 & 3 & 4 \end{bmatrix}.$$

If we find the products of M and the column matrices above, we have a new set of column matrices,

$$\begin{bmatrix} 76 \\ 77 \\ 96 \end{bmatrix} \begin{bmatrix} 62 \\ 67 \\ 75 \end{bmatrix} \text{ and so on.}$$

The entries of these matrices can then be transmitted to an agent as the message *76, 77, 96, 62, 67, 75,* and so on.

The agent receiving the message divides it into groups of numbers and forms each group into a column matrix. After multiplying each column matrix by the matrix M^{-1}, the message can be read.

Although this type of code is relatively simple, it is actually difficult to break. Many ramifications are possible. For example, a long message might be placed in groups of 20, thus requiring a 20×20 matrix for coding and decoding. Finding the inverse of such a matrix would require an impractical amount of time if calculated by hand. For this reason some of the largest computers are used by government agencies involved in coding.

EXERCISES

1. Let $M = \begin{bmatrix} 4 & -1 \\ 2 & 6 \end{bmatrix}$

(a) Use M to encode the message: *Meet at the cave.* Use 2×1 matrices.

(b) What matrix should be used to decode the message?

2. Let $M = \begin{bmatrix} -1 & 2 \\ 2 & -5 \end{bmatrix}.$

Encode the message: *Attack at dawn unless too cold.*

3. Matrix M from Exercise 2 was used to encode the following message. Decode it.

$$\begin{bmatrix} -17 \\ 33 \end{bmatrix} \begin{bmatrix} 26 \\ -72 \end{bmatrix} \begin{bmatrix} 53 \\ -133 \end{bmatrix} \begin{bmatrix} 21 \\ -54 \end{bmatrix} \begin{bmatrix} 41 \\ -103 \end{bmatrix} \begin{bmatrix} 35 \\ -97 \end{bmatrix} \begin{bmatrix} 29 \\ -77 \end{bmatrix} \begin{bmatrix} -15 \\ 24 \end{bmatrix} \begin{bmatrix} 39 \\ -98 \end{bmatrix}$$

4. Finish encoding the message given in the text.

2.6   Input-Output Models

Nobel prize winner Wassily Leontief developed an interesting application of matrix theory to economics. His matrix models for studying the interdependencies in an economy are called *input-output* models. In practice these models are very complicated with many variables. We discuss only simple examples with few variables.

Input-output models are concerned with the production and flow of goods (and perhaps services). In an economy with n basic commodities, or sectors, the production of each commodity uses some (perhaps all) of the commodities in the economy as inputs. The amounts of each commodity used in the production of one unit of each commodity can be written as an $n \times n$ matrix A, called the **technological** or **input-output matrix** of the economy.

EXAMPLE 1

Suppose a simplified economy involves just three commodity categories: agriculture, manufacturing, and transportation, all in appropriate units. Production of 1 unit of agriculture requires 1/2 unit of manufacturing and 1/4 unit of transportation. Production of 1 unit of manufacturing requires 1/4 unit of agriculture and 1/4 unit of transportation; while production of 1 unit of transportation requires 1/3 unit of agriculture and 1/4 unit of manufacturing. Give the input-output matrix of this economy.

The matrix is shown below.

$$
\begin{array}{c}
\\
\text{Agriculture} \\
\text{Manufacturing} \\
\text{Transportation}
\end{array}
\begin{array}{ccc}
\text{Agric.} & \text{Manuf.} & \text{Trans.}
\end{array}
\left[
\begin{array}{ccc}
0 & \frac{1}{4} & \frac{1}{3} \\
\frac{1}{2} & 0 & \frac{1}{4} \\
\frac{1}{4} & \frac{1}{4} & 0
\end{array}
\right] = A
$$

The first column of the input-output matrix represents the amount of each of the three commodities consumed in the production of 1 unit of agriculture. The second column gives the corresponding amounts required to produce 1 unit of manufacturing, and the last column gives the amounts needed to produce one unit of transportation. (Although it is perhaps unrealistic that production of a unit of each commodity requires none of that commodity, the simpler matrix involved is useful for our purposes.) ▨

Another matrix used with the input-output matrix is the matrix giving the amount of each commodity produced, called the **production matrix,** or the matrix of gross output. In an economy producing n commodities, the production matrix can be represented by a column matrix X with entries $x_1, x_2, x_3, \ldots, x_n$.

EXAMPLE 2

In Example 1, suppose the production matrix is

$$
X = \begin{bmatrix} 60 \\ 52 \\ 48 \end{bmatrix}.
$$

Then 60 units of agriculture, 52 units of manufacturing and 48 units of transportation are produced. As 1/4 unit of agriculture is used for each unit of manufacturing produced, $1/4 \times 52 = 13$ units of agriculture must be used up in the "production" of manufacturing. Similarly, $1/3 \times 48 = 16$ units of agriculture will be used up in the "production" of transportation. Thus $13 + 16 = 29$ units of agriculture are used for production in the economy. Look again at the matrices A and X. Since X gives the number of units of each commodity produced and A gives the amount (in units) of each commodity used to produce one unit of the various commodities, the matrix product AX gives the amount of each commodity used up in the production process.

$$AX = \begin{bmatrix} 0 & \frac{1}{4} & \frac{1}{3} \\ \frac{1}{2} & 0 & \frac{1}{4} \\ \frac{1}{4} & \frac{1}{4} & 0 \end{bmatrix} \begin{bmatrix} 60 \\ 52 \\ 48 \end{bmatrix} = \begin{bmatrix} 29 \\ 42 \\ 28 \end{bmatrix}$$

From this result 29 units of agriculture, 42 units of manufacturing, and 28 units of transportation are used up to produce 60 units of agriculture, 52 units of manufacturing, and 48 units of transportation. ▪

We have seen that the matrix product AX represents the amount of each commodity used up in the production process. The remainder (if any) must be enough to satisfy the demand for the various commodities from outside the production system. In an n-commodity economy, this demand can be represented by a **demand matrix** D with entries $d_1, d_2, \ldots, d_n$. The difference between the production matrix, X, and the amount, AX, used up in the production process must equal the demand, D, or

$$D = X - AX.$$

In Example 2,

$$D = \begin{bmatrix} 60 \\ 52 \\ 48 \end{bmatrix} - \begin{bmatrix} 29 \\ 42 \\ 28 \end{bmatrix} = \begin{bmatrix} 31 \\ 10 \\ 20 \end{bmatrix},$$

so that production of 60 units of agriculture, 52 units of manufacturing, and 48 units of transportation would satisfy a demand of 31, 10, and 20 units of each, respectively.

Another way to state the relationship between production, X, and demand, D, is to express X as $X = D + AX$. In practice, A and D usually are known and X must be found. That is, we need to decide on the amounts of production necessary to satisfy the required demands. Matrix algebra can be used to solve the equation $D = X - AX$ for X.

$$D = X - AX$$
$$D = IX - AX$$
$$D = (I - A)X$$

If the matrix $I - A$ has an inverse, then

$$X = (I - A)^{-1}D.$$

EXAMPLE 3

Suppose, in the 3-commodity economy of Examples 1 and 2, there is a demand for 516 units of agriculture, 258 units of manufacturing, and 129 units of transportation. What should production of each commodity be?

The demand matrix is

$$D = \begin{bmatrix} 516 \\ 258 \\ 129 \end{bmatrix}.$$

To find the production matrix X, first calculate $I - A$.

$$I - A = \begin{bmatrix} 1 & 0 & 0 \\ 0 & 1 & 0 \\ 0 & 0 & 1 \end{bmatrix} - \begin{bmatrix} 0 & \frac{1}{4} & \frac{1}{3} \\ \frac{1}{2} & 0 & \frac{1}{4} \\ \frac{1}{4} & \frac{1}{4} & 0 \end{bmatrix} = \begin{bmatrix} 1 & -\frac{1}{4} & -\frac{1}{3} \\ -\frac{1}{2} & 1 & -\frac{1}{4} \\ -\frac{1}{4} & -\frac{1}{4} & 1 \end{bmatrix}$$

Use row operations to find the inverse of $I - A$ (the entries are rounded to two decimal places).

$$(I - A)^{-1} = \begin{bmatrix} 1.40 & .50 & .59 \\ .84 & 1.36 & .62 \\ .56 & .47 & 1.30 \end{bmatrix}$$

Since $X = (I - A)^{-1}D$,

$$X = \begin{bmatrix} 1.40 & .50 & .59 \\ .84 & 1.36 & .62 \\ .56 & .47 & 1.30 \end{bmatrix} \begin{bmatrix} 516 \\ 258 \\ 129 \end{bmatrix} = \begin{bmatrix} 928 \\ 864 \\ 578 \end{bmatrix}.$$

(Entries have been rounded to the nearest whole numbers).

The last result shows that production of 928 units of agriculture, 864 units of manufacturing, and 578 units of transportation is required to satisfy demands of 516, 258, and 129 units respectively. ■

EXAMPLE 4

An economy depends on two basic products, wheat and oil. To produce 1 metric ton of wheat requires .25 metric tons of wheat and .33 metric tons of oil. Production of 1 metric ton of oil consumes .08 metric tons of wheat and .11 metric tons of oil. Find the production which will satisfy a demand of 500 metric tons of wheat and 1000 metric tons of oil.

The input-output matrix, A, and $I - A$ are

$$A = \begin{bmatrix} .25 & .08 \\ .33 & .11 \end{bmatrix} \quad \text{and} \quad I - A = \begin{bmatrix} .75 & -.08 \\ -.33 & .89 \end{bmatrix}.$$

Next, calculate $(I - A)^{-1}$.

$$(I - A)^{-1} = \begin{bmatrix} 1.39 & .13 \\ .51 & 1.17 \end{bmatrix} \quad \text{(rounded)}$$

To find the production matrix X, use the equation $X = (I - A)^{-1}D$, with

$$D = \begin{bmatrix} 500 \\ 1000 \end{bmatrix}.$$

The production matrix is

$$X = \begin{bmatrix} 1.39 & .13 \\ .51 & 1.17 \end{bmatrix} \begin{bmatrix} 500 \\ 1000 \end{bmatrix} = \begin{bmatrix} 815 \\ 1425 \end{bmatrix}.$$

Production of 815 metric tons of wheat and 1425 metric tons of oil are required to satisfy the indicated demand. ▪

The model we have discussed is referred to as an **open model,** since it allows for a surplus from the production equal to D. In the **closed model,** all the production is consumed internally in the production process so that $X = AX$. There is nothing left over to satisfy any outside demands from other parts of the economy, or from other economies. In this case, the sum of each column in the input-output matrix equals one.

To solve the equation $X = AX$ for X, first let O represent an n-row column matrix with each element equal to 0. Write $X = AX$ or $X - AX = O$: then

$$IX - AX = O,$$

$$(I - A)X = O.$$

The system of equations which corresponds to $(I - A)X = O$ does not have a single unique solution. However, it can be solved in terms of a parameter. As we saw in Section 2.1, this means there are infinitely many solutions.

EXAMPLE 5

Use matrix A below to find the production of each commodity in a closed model.

$$A = \begin{bmatrix} \frac{1}{2} & \frac{1}{4} & \frac{1}{3} \\ 0 & \frac{1}{4} & \frac{1}{3} \\ \frac{1}{2} & \frac{1}{2} & \frac{1}{3} \end{bmatrix}$$

Find the value of $I - A$, then set $(I - A)X = O$ to find X.

$$I - A = \begin{bmatrix} \frac{1}{2} & -\frac{1}{4} & -\frac{1}{3} \\ 0 & \frac{3}{4} & -\frac{1}{3} \\ -\frac{1}{2} & -\frac{1}{2} & \frac{2}{3} \end{bmatrix}$$

$$(I - A)X = \begin{bmatrix} \frac{1}{2} & -\frac{1}{4} & -\frac{1}{3} \\ 0 & \frac{3}{4} & -\frac{1}{3} \\ -\frac{1}{2} & -\frac{1}{2} & \frac{2}{3} \end{bmatrix} \begin{bmatrix} x_1 \\ x_2 \\ x_3 \end{bmatrix} = \begin{bmatrix} 0 \\ 0 \\ 0 \end{bmatrix}$$

Multiply to get

$$\begin{bmatrix} \frac{1}{2} x_1 - \frac{1}{4} x_2 - \frac{1}{3} x_3 \\ 0 x_1 + \frac{3}{4} x_2 - \frac{1}{3} x_3 \\ -\frac{1}{2} x_1 - \frac{1}{2} x_2 + \frac{2}{3} x_3 \end{bmatrix} = \begin{bmatrix} 0 \\ 0 \\ 0 \end{bmatrix}.$$

From the last matrix equation, we get the following system.

$$\frac{1}{2} x_1 - \frac{1}{4} x_2 - \frac{1}{3} x_3 = 0$$

$$\frac{3}{4} x_2 - \frac{1}{3} x_3 = 0$$

$$-\frac{1}{2} x_1 - \frac{1}{2} x_2 + \frac{2}{3} x_3 = 0$$

Solving the system with x_3 as the parameter gives the solution of the system which can be written as

$$x_1 = \tfrac{8}{9} x_3$$
$$x_2 = \tfrac{4}{9} x_3$$
$$x_3 \quad \text{arbitrary.}$$

If $x_3 = 9$, then $x_1 = 8$ and $x_2 = 4$, with the production of the three commodities in the ratio $8:4:9$. ▪

2.6 EXERCISES

Find the production matrix for the following input-output and demand matrices using the open model.

1. $A = \begin{bmatrix} .5 & .4 \\ .25 & .2 \end{bmatrix} \quad D = \begin{bmatrix} 2 \\ 4 \end{bmatrix}$

2. $A = \begin{bmatrix} .2 & .04 \\ .6 & .05 \end{bmatrix} \quad D = \begin{bmatrix} 3 \\ 10 \end{bmatrix}$

3. $A = \begin{bmatrix} .1 & .03 \\ .07 & .6 \end{bmatrix} \quad D = \begin{bmatrix} 5 \\ 10 \end{bmatrix}$

4. $A = \begin{bmatrix} .01 & .03 \\ .05 & .05 \end{bmatrix} \quad D = \begin{bmatrix} 100 \\ 200 \end{bmatrix}$

5. $A = \begin{bmatrix} .4 & 0 & .3 \\ 0 & .8 & .1 \\ 0 & .2 & .4 \end{bmatrix} \quad D = \begin{bmatrix} 1 \\ 3 \\ 2 \end{bmatrix}$

6. $A = \begin{bmatrix} .1 & .5 & 0 \\ 0 & .3 & .4 \\ .1 & .2 & .1 \end{bmatrix} \quad D = \begin{bmatrix} 10 \\ 4 \\ 2 \end{bmatrix}$

In Exercises 7 and 8, refer to Example 4.

7. If the demand is changed to 690 metric tons of wheat and 920 metric tons of oil, how many units of each commodity should be produced?

8. Change the technological matrix so that production of 1 ton of wheat requires 1/5 metric ton of oil (and no wheat), and the production of 1 metric ton of oil requires 1/3 metric ton of wheat (and no oil). To satisfy the same demand matrix, how many units of each commodity should be produced?

In Exercises 9–12, refer to Example 3.

9. If the demand is changed to 516 units of each commodity, how many units of each commodity should be produced?

10. Suppose 1/3 unit of manufacturing (no agriculture or transportation) is required to produce 1 unit of agriculture, 1/4 unit of transportation is required to produce 1 unit of manufacturing, and 1/2 unit of agriculture is required to produce 1 unit of transportation. How many units of each commodity should be produced to satisfy a demand of 1000 units for each commodity?

11. Suppose 1/4 unit of manufacturing and 1/2 unit of transportation are required to produce 1 unit of agriculture, 1/2 unit of agriculture and 1/4 unit of transportation to produce 1 unit of manufacturing, and 1/4 unit of agriculture and 1/4 unit of manufacturing to produce one unit of transportation. How many units of each commodity should be produced to satisfy a demand of 1000 units for each commodity?

12. If the technological matrix is changed so that 1/4 unit of manufacturing and 1/2 unit of transportation are required to produce 1 unit of agriculture, 1/2 unit of agriculture and 1/4 unit of transportation are required to produce 1 unit of manufacturing, and 1/4 unit each of agriculture and manufacturing are required to produce 1 unit of transportation, find the number of units of each commodity which should be produced to satisfy a demand for 500 units of each commodity.

13. A primitive economy depends on two basic goods, yams and pork. Production of 1 bushel of yams requires 1/4 bushel of yams and 1/2 of a pig. To produce 1 pig requires 1/6 bushel of yams. Find the amount of each commodity which should be produced to get

(a) 1 bushel of yams and 1 pig;

(b) 100 bushels of yams and 70 pigs.

14. Use the input-output matrix

$$\begin{array}{cc} & \text{yams} \quad \text{pigs} \\ \begin{array}{c} \text{yams} \\ \text{pigs} \end{array} & \left[\begin{array}{cc} \frac{1}{4} & \frac{1}{2} \\ \frac{3}{4} & \frac{1}{2} \end{array} \right] \end{array}$$

and the closed model to find the ratios of yams and pigs produced.

Find the ratios of products A, B, and C, using a closed model.

15.

$$\begin{array}{c} \quad\quad A \quad B \quad C \\ \begin{array}{c} A \\ B \\ C \end{array} \left[\begin{array}{ccc} .3 & .1 & .8 \\ .5 & .6 & .1 \\ .2 & .3 & .1 \end{array} \right] \end{array}$$

16.

$$\begin{array}{c} \quad\quad A \quad B \quad C \\ \begin{array}{c} A \\ B \\ C \end{array} \left[\begin{array}{ccc} .2 & .1 & .5 \\ .4 & .3 & .4 \\ .4 & .6 & .1 \end{array} \right] \end{array}$$

Solve the following input-output problems.

17.

$$A = \left[\begin{array}{cccc} .25 & .25 & .25 & .05 \\ .01 & .02 & .01 & .1 \\ .3 & .3 & .01 & .1 \\ .2 & .01 & .3 & .01 \end{array} \right] \quad D = \left[\begin{array}{c} 2930 \\ 3570 \\ 2300 \\ 580 \end{array} \right]$$

18.

$$A = \left[\begin{array}{cccc} .2 & .1 & .2 & .2 \\ .3 & .05 & .07 & .02 \\ .1 & .03 & .02 & .01 \\ .05 & .3 & .05 & .03 \end{array} \right] \quad D = \left[\begin{array}{c} 5000 \\ 1000 \\ 8000 \\ 500 \end{array} \right]$$

19. A simple economy depends on three commodities: oil, corn, and coffee. Production of one unit of oil requires .1 unit of oil, .2 unit of corn, and no units of coffee. To produce one unit of corn requires .2 unit of oil, .1 unit of corn, and .05 unit of coffee. To produce one unit of coffee requires .1 unit of oil, .05 unit of corn, and .1 unit of coffee. Find the gross production required to give a net production of 1000 units each of oil, corn, and coffee.

EXTENDED
APPLICATION

Leontief's Model of the American Economy

In the April 1965 issue of *Scientific American,* Leontief explained his input-output system, using the 1958 American economy as an example.* He divided the economy into 81 sectors, grouped into six families of related sectors. In order to keep the discussion reasonably simple, we will treat each family of sectors as a single sector and so, in effect, work with a six sector model. The sectors are listed in Table 1.

The workings of the American economy in 1958 are described in the input-output table (Table 2) based on Leontief's figures. We will demonstrate the meaning of Table 2 by considering the first left-hand column of numbers. The numbers in this column mean that 1 unit of final nonmetal production requires the consumption of 0.170 unit of (other) final nonmetal production, 0.003 unit of final metal output, 0.025 unit of basic metal products, and so on down the column. Since the unit of measurement that Leontief used for this table is millions of dollars, we conclude that the production of $1 million worth of final nonmetal production consumes $0.170 million, or $170,000, worth of other final nonmetal products, $3000 of final metal production, $25,000 of basic metal products, and so on. Similarly, the entry in the column headed FM and opposite S of 0.074 means that $74,000 worth of output from the service industries goes into the production of $1 million worth of final metal products, and the number 0.358 in the column headed E and opposite E means that $358,000 worth of energy must be consumed to produce $1 million worth of energy.

Table 1

Sector	Examples
Final nonmetal (FN)	Furniture, processed food
Final metal (FM)	Household appliances, motor vehicles
Basic metal (BM)	Machine-shop products, mining
Basic nonmetal (BN)	Agriculture, printing
Energy (E)	Petroleum, coal
Services (S)	Amusements, real estate

Table 2

	FN	FM	BM	BN	E	S
FN	0.170	0.004	0	0.029	0	0.008
FM	0.003	0.295	0.018	0.002	0.004	0.016
BM	0.025	0.173	0.460	0.007	0.011	0.007
BN	0.348	0.037	0.021	0.403	0.011	0.048
E	0.007	0.001	0.039	0.025	0.358	0.025
S	0.120	0.074	0.104	0.123	0.173	0.234

By the underlying assumption of Leontief's model, the production of n units (n = any number) of final nonmetal production consumes $0.170n$ unit of final nonmetal output, $0.003n$ unit of final metal output, $0.025n$ unit of basic metal production, and so on. Thus, production of $50 million worth of products from the final nonmetal section of the 1958 American economy required $(0.170)(50) = 8.5$ units ($8.5 million) worth of final nonmetal output, $(0.003)(50) = 0.15$ unit of final metal output, $(0.025)(50) = 1.25$ units of basic metal production, and so on.

Example 1

According to the simplified input-output table for the 1958 American economy, how many dollars worth of final metal products, basic nonmetal products, and services are required to produce $120 million worth of basic metal products?

Each unit ($1 million worth) of basic metal products requires 0.018 unit of final metal products because the number in the BM column opposite FM is 0.018. Thus, $120 million, or 120 units, requires $(0.018)(120) = 2.16$ units, or $2.16 million of final metal products. Similarly, 120 units of basic metal production uses $(0.021)(120) = 2.52$ units of basic nonmetal production and $(0.104)(120) = 12.48$ units of services, or $2.52 million and $12.48 million of basic nonmetal output and services, respectively.

The Leontief model also involves a *bill of demands,* that is, a list of requirements for units of output beyond that required for its inner workings as described in the input-output table. These demands represent exports, surpluses, government and individual consumption, and the like. The bill of demands for the simplified version of the 1958 American economy we have been using was (in millions)

FN	$99,640
FM	$75,548
BM	$14,444
BN	$33,501
E	$23,527
S	$263,985

We can now use the methods developed above to answer the question: how many units of output from each sector are needed in order to run the economy and fill the bill of demands? The units of output from each sector required to run the economy and fill the bill of demands is unknown, so we denote them by variables. In our example, there are six quantities which are, at the moment, unknown. The number of units of final nonmetal production required to solve the problem will be our first unknown, because this sector is represented by the first row of the input-output matrix. The unknown quantity of final nonmetal units will be represented by the symbol x_1. Following the same pattern, we represent the unknown quantities in the following manner:

x_1 = units of final nonmetal production required,

x_2 = units of final metal production required,

x_3 = units of basic metal production required,

x_4 = units of basic nonmetal production required,

x_5 = units of energy required,

x_6 = units of services required.

These six numbers are the quantities we are attempting to calculate.

To find these numbers, first let A be the 6×6 matrix corresponding to the input-output table.

$$A = \begin{bmatrix} 0.170 & 0.004 & 0 & 0.029 & 0 & 0.008 \\ 0.003 & 0.295 & 0.018 & 0.002 & 0.004 & 0.016 \\ 0.025 & 0.173 & 0.460 & 0.007 & 0.011 & 0.007 \\ 0.348 & 0.037 & 0.021 & 0.403 & 0.011 & 0.048 \\ 0.007 & 0.001 & 0.039 & 0.025 & 0.358 & 0.025 \\ 0.120 & 0.074 & 0.104 & 0.123 & 0.173 & 0.234 \end{bmatrix}$$

A is the input-output matrix. The bill of demands leads to a 6×1 demand matrix D, and X is the matrix of unknowns.

$$D = \begin{bmatrix} 99{,}640 \\ 75{,}548 \\ 14{,}444 \\ 33{,}501 \\ 23{,}527 \\ 263{,}985 \end{bmatrix} \quad \text{and} \quad X = \begin{bmatrix} x_1 \\ x_2 \\ x_3 \\ x_4 \\ x_5 \\ x_6 \end{bmatrix}$$

Now we need to find $I - A$.

$$I - A = \begin{bmatrix} 1 & 0 & 0 & 0 & 0 & 0 \\ 0 & 1 & 0 & 0 & 0 & 0 \\ 0 & 0 & 1 & 0 & 0 & 0 \\ 0 & 0 & 0 & 1 & 0 & 0 \\ 0 & 0 & 0 & 0 & 1 & 0 \\ 0 & 0 & 0 & 0 & 0 & 1 \end{bmatrix} - \begin{bmatrix} 0.170 & 0.004 & 0 & 0.029 & 0 & 0.008 \\ 0.003 & 0.295 & 0.018 & 0.002 & 0.004 & 0.016 \\ 0.025 & 0.173 & 0.460 & 0.007 & 0.011 & 0.007 \\ 0.348 & 0.037 & 0.021 & 0.403 & 0.011 & 0.048 \\ 0.007 & 0.001 & 0.039 & 0.025 & 0.358 & 0.025 \\ 0.120 & 0.074 & 0.104 & 0.123 & 0.173 & 0.234 \end{bmatrix}$$

$$= \begin{bmatrix} 0.830 & -0.004 & 0 & -0.029 & 0 & -0.008 \\ -0.003 & 0.705 & -0.018 & -0.002 & -0.004 & -0.016 \\ -0.025 & -0.173 & 0.540 & -0.007 & -0.011 & -0.007 \\ -0.348 & -0.037 & -0.021 & 0.597 & -0.011 & -0.048 \\ -0.007 & -0.001 & -0.039 & -0.025 & 0.642 & -0.025 \\ -0.120 & -0.074 & -0.104 & -0.123 & -0.173 & 0.766 \end{bmatrix}$$

Find the inverse (actually an approximation) by the methods of this chapter.

$$(I - A)^{-1} = \begin{bmatrix} 1.234 & 0.014 & 0.006 & 0.064 & 0.007 & 0.018 \\ 0.017 & 1.436 & 0.057 & 0.012 & 0.020 & 0.032 \\ 0.071 & 0.465 & 1.877 & 0.019 & 0.045 & 0.031 \\ 0.751 & 0.134 & 0.100 & 1.740 & 0.066 & 0.124 \\ 0.060 & 0.045 & 0.130 & 0.082 & 1.578 & 0.059 \\ 0.339 & 0.236 & 0.307 & 0.312 & 0.376 & 1.349 \end{bmatrix} .$$

Therefore, $X = (I - A)^{-1}D =$

$$\begin{bmatrix} 1.234 & 0.014 & 0.006 & 0.064 & 0.007 & 0.018 \\ 0.017 & 1.436 & 0.057 & 0.012 & 0.020 & 0.032 \\ 0.071 & 0.465 & 1.877 & 0.019 & 0.045 & 0.031 \\ 0.751 & 0.134 & 0.100 & 1.740 & 0.066 & 0.124 \\ 0.060 & 0.045 & 0.130 & 0.082 & 1.578 & 0.059 \\ 0.339 & 0.236 & 0.307 & 0.312 & 0.376 & 1.349 \end{bmatrix} \begin{bmatrix} 99{,}640 \\ 75{,}548 \\ 14{,}444 \\ 33{,}501 \\ 23{,}527 \\ 263{,}985 \end{bmatrix} = \begin{bmatrix} 131{,}161 \\ 120{,}324 \\ 79{,}194 \\ 178{,}936 \\ 66{,}703 \\ 426{,}542 \end{bmatrix} .$$

From this result,

$$x_1 = 131,161$$
$$x_2 = 120,324$$
$$x_3 = 79,194$$
$$x_4 = 178,936$$
$$x_5 = 66,703$$
$$x_6 = 426,542$$

In other words, by this model 131,161 units ($131,161 million worth) of final non-metal production, 120,324 units of final metal output, 79,194 units of basic metal products, and so on are required to run the 1958 American economy and completely fill the stated bill of demands.

EXERCISES

1. A much simplified version of Leontief's 42 sector analysis of the 1947 American economy divides the economy into just three sectors: agriculture, manufacturing, and the household (i.e., the sector of the economy which produces labor). It consists of the following input-output table:

	Agriculture	Manufacturing	Household
Agriculture	0.245	0.102	0.051
Manufacturing	0.099	0.291	0.279
Household	0.433	0.372	0.011

The bill of demands (in billions of dollars) is

Agriculture	2.88
Manufacturing	31.45
Household	30.91.

(a) Write the input-output matrix A, the demand matrix D, and the matrix X.
(b) Compute $I - A$. (c) Check that

$$(I - A)^{-1} = \begin{bmatrix} 1.454 & 0.291 & 0.157 \\ 0.533 & 1.763 & 0.525 \\ 0.837 & 0.791 & 1.278 \end{bmatrix}$$

is an approximation to the inverse of $I - A$ by calculating $(I - A)^{-1}(I - A)$.
(d) Use the matrix of part (c) to compute X. (e) Explain the meaning of the numbers in X in dollars.

2. An analysis of the 1958 Israeli economy* is here simplified by grouping the economy into three sectors: agriculture, manufacturing, and energy. The input-output table is the following.

	Agriculture	Manufacturing	Energy
Agriculture	0.293	0	0
Manufacturing	0.014	0.207	0.017
Energy	0.044	0.010	0.216

Exports (in thousands of Israeli pounds) were

Agriculture	138,213
Manufacturing	17,597
Energy	1,786

(a) Write the input-output matrix A and the demand (export) matrix D. *(b)* Compute $I - A$. *(c)* Check that

$$(I - A)^{-1} = \begin{bmatrix} 1.414 & 0 & 0 \\ 0.027 & 1.261 & 0.027 \\ 0.080 & 0.016 & 1.276 \end{bmatrix}$$

is an approximation to the inverse of $I - A$ by calculating $(I - A)^{-1}(I - A)$. *(d)* Use the matrix of part *(c)* to determine the number of Israeli pounds worth of agricultural products, manufactured goods, and energy required to run this model of the Israeli economy and export the stated value of products.

KEY WORDS

system of equations
first degree equation in *n* unknowns
inconsistent system
dependent equations
equivalent system
elimination method
echelon method
parameter
matrix
element (entry)
augmented matrix
row operations
Gauss-Jordan method

dimension (order)
square matrix
row matrix
column matrix
zero matrix
scalar
identity matrix
multiplicative inverse of a matrix
input-output matrix
production matrix
demand matrix

---

*Wassily Leontief, *Input-Output Economics* (New York: Oxford University Press, 1966), pp. 54—57.

Chapter 2   REVIEW EXERCISES

Solve each of the systems in Exercises 1–4 by the echelon method.

1. $2x + 3y = 10$
$-3x + y = 18$

2. $\dfrac{x}{2} + \dfrac{y}{4} = 3$

$\dfrac{x}{4} - \dfrac{y}{2} = 4$

3. $2x - 3y + z = -5$
$x + 4y + 2z = 13$
$5x + 5y + 3z = 14$

4. $x - y \qquad = 3$
$2x + 3y + z = 13$
$3x \qquad - 2z = 21$

Write each of Exercises 5–8 as a system of equations and solve.

5. An office supply manufacturer makes two kinds of paper clips, standard, and extra large. To make 1000 standard paper clips requires 1/4 hour on a cutting machine and 1/2 hour on a machine which shapes the clips. One thousand extra large paper clips require 1/3 hour on each machine. The manager of paper clip production has four hours per day available on the cutting machine and six hours per day on the shaping machine. How many of each kind of clip can he make?

6. Jane Schmidt plans to buy shares of two stocks. One costs $32 per share and pays dividends of $1.20 per share. The other costs $23 per share and pays dividends of $1.40 per share. She has $10,100 to spend and wants to earn dividends of $540. How many shares of each stock should she buy?

7. The Waputi Indians make woven blankets, rugs, and skirts. Each blanket requires 24 hours for spinning the yarn, 4 hours for dying the yarn, and 15 hours for weaving. Rugs require 30, 5, and 18 hours, and skirts 12, 3, and 9 hours respectively. If there are 306, 59, and 201 hours available for spinning, dying, and weaving respectively, how many of each item can be made? (Hint: Simplify the equations you write, if possible, before solving the system.)

8. An oil refinery in Tulsa sells 50% of its production to a Chicago distributor, 20% to a Dallas distributor, and 30% to an Atlanta distributor. Another refinery in New Orleans sells 40% of its production to the Chicago distributor, 40% to the Dallas distributor, and 20% to the Atlanta distributor. A third refinery in Ardmore sells the same distributors 30%, 40%, and 30% of its production. The three distributors received 219,000, 192,000, and 144,000 gallons of oil respectively. How many gallons of oil were produced at each of the three plants?

Solve the systems in Exercises 9–13 by the Gauss-Jordan method.

9. $2x + 4y = -6$
$-3x - 5y = 12$

10. $x + 2y = -9$
$4x + 9y = 41$

11. $x - y + 3z = 13$
$4x + y + 2z = 17$
$3x + 2y + 2z = 1$

12. $x + \qquad - 2z = 5$
$3x + 2y \qquad = 8$
$-x \qquad + 2z = 10$

13. $3x - 6y + 9z = 12$
$-x + 2y - 3z = -4$
$x + y + 2z = 7$

In Exercises 14–17, find the order of the matrices, find the values of any variables, and identify any square, row, or column matrices.

14. $\begin{bmatrix} 2 & 3 \\ 5 & q \end{bmatrix} = \begin{bmatrix} a & b \\ c & 9 \end{bmatrix}$

15. $\begin{bmatrix} 2 & x \\ y & 6 \\ 5 & z \end{bmatrix} = \begin{bmatrix} a & -1 \\ 4 & 6 \\ p & 7 \end{bmatrix}$

16. $[m \quad 4 \quad z \quad -1] = [12 \quad k \quad -8 \quad r]$

17. $\begin{bmatrix} a+5 & 3b & 6 \\ 4c & 2+d & -3 \\ -1 & 4p & q-1 \end{bmatrix} = \begin{bmatrix} -7 & b+2 & 2k-3 \\ 3 & 2d-1 & 4l \\ m & 12 & 8 \end{bmatrix}$

18. The activities of a grazing animal can be classified roughly into three categories: grazing, moving, and resting. Suppose horses spend 8 hours grazing, 8 moving, and 8 resting; cattle spend 10 grazing, 5 moving and 9 resting; sheep spend 7 grazing, 10 moving, and 7 resting; and goats spend 8 grazing, 9 moving, and 7 resting. Write this information as a 4 × 3 matrix.

19. The New York Stock Exchange reports in the daily newspapers give the dividend, price to earnings ratio, sales (in hundreds of shares), last price, and change in price for each company. Write the following stock reports as a 4 × 5 matrix. American Telephone & Telegraph: 5, 7, 2532, 52 3/8, −1/4. General Electric: 3, 9, 1464, 56, +1/8. Mobil Oil: 2.50, 5, 4974, 41, −1 1/2. Sears: 1.36, 10, 1754, 18 7/8, +1/2.

Given the matrices

$$A = \begin{bmatrix} 4 & 10 \\ -2 & -3 \\ 6 & 9 \end{bmatrix}, \qquad B = \begin{bmatrix} 2 & 3 & -2 \\ 2 & 4 & 0 \\ 0 & 1 & 2 \end{bmatrix}, \qquad C = \begin{bmatrix} 5 & 0 \\ -1 & 3 \\ 4 & 7 \end{bmatrix},$$

$$D = \begin{bmatrix} 6 \\ 1 \\ 0 \end{bmatrix}, \qquad E = [1 \quad 3 \quad -4], \qquad F = \begin{bmatrix} -1 & 4 \\ 3 & 7 \end{bmatrix}, \qquad G = \begin{bmatrix} 2 & 5 \\ 1 & 6 \end{bmatrix},$$

find each of the following which exists.

20. $A + C$ **21.** $2G - 4F$ **22.** $3C + 2A$ **23.** $B - A$

24. $2A - 5C$ **25.** AF **26.** AC **27.** DE

28. ED **29.** BD **30.** EA **31.** F^{-1}

32. B^{-1} **33.** $(A + C)^{-1}$

Find the inverse of each of the following matrices that has an inverse.

34. $\begin{bmatrix} 2 & 1 \\ 5 & 3 \end{bmatrix}$ **35.** $\begin{bmatrix} -4 & 2 \\ 0 & 3 \end{bmatrix}$ **36.** $\begin{bmatrix} 2 & 0 \\ -1 & 5 \end{bmatrix}$ **37.** $\begin{bmatrix} 6 & 4 \\ 3 & 2 \end{bmatrix}$

38. $\begin{bmatrix} 2 & -1 & 0 \\ 1 & 0 & 1 \\ 1 & -2 & 0 \end{bmatrix}$ **39.** $\begin{bmatrix} 2 & 0 & 4 \\ 1 & -1 & 0 \\ 0 & 1 & -2 \end{bmatrix}$

40. $\begin{bmatrix} 1 & 3 & 6 \\ 4 & 0 & 9 \\ 5 & 15 & 30 \end{bmatrix}$ **41.** $\begin{bmatrix} 2 & 3 & 5 \\ -2 & -3 & -5 \\ 1 & 4 & 2 \end{bmatrix}$

Solve the matrix equation $AX = B$ for X using the matrices in Exercises 42–45.

42. $A = \begin{bmatrix} 2 & 4 \\ -1 & -3 \end{bmatrix}$, $B = \begin{bmatrix} 8 \\ 3 \end{bmatrix}$

43. $A = \begin{bmatrix} 1 & 3 \\ -2 & 4 \end{bmatrix}$, $B = \begin{bmatrix} 15 \\ 10 \end{bmatrix}$

44. $A = \begin{bmatrix} 1 & 0 & 2 \\ -1 & 1 & 0 \\ 3 & 0 & 4 \end{bmatrix}$, $B = \begin{bmatrix} 8 \\ 4 \\ -6 \end{bmatrix}$

45. $A = \begin{bmatrix} 2 & 4 & 0 \\ 1 & -2 & 0 \\ 0 & 0 & 3 \end{bmatrix}$, $B = \begin{bmatrix} 72 \\ -24 \\ 48 \end{bmatrix}$

46. A printer has three orders for pamphlets which require three kinds of paper as shown in the following matrix.

Orders

		I	II	III
	High-grade	10	5	8
Paper	Medium-grade	12	0	4
	Coated	0	10	5

The printer has on hand 3170 sheets of high-grade paper, 2360 sheets of medium-grade paper, and 1800 sheets of coated paper. All the paper must be used in preparing the order.

(a) Write a 3×1 matrix for the amounts of paper on hand.

(b) Write a matrix of variables to represent the number of pamphlets that must be printed in each of the three orders.

(c) Write a matrix equation using the given matrix and your matrices from parts (a) and (b).

(d) Solve the equation from part (c).

Solve each of the following systems of equations by inverses.

47. $2x + y = 5$
$3x - 2y = 4$

48. $5x + 10y = 80$
$3x - 2y = 120$

49. $x + y + z = 1$
$2x + y = -2$
$3y + z = 2$

Find the production matrix given the following input-output and demand matrices.

50. $A = \begin{bmatrix} .01 & .05 \\ .04 & .03 \end{bmatrix}$ $D = \begin{bmatrix} 200 \\ 300 \end{bmatrix}$

51. $A = \begin{bmatrix} .2 & .1 & .3 \\ .1 & 0 & .2 \\ 0 & 0 & .4 \end{bmatrix}$ $D = \begin{bmatrix} 500 \\ 200 \\ 100 \end{bmatrix}$

52. An economy depends on two commodities, goats and cheese. It takes 2/3 of a unit of goats to produce 1 unit of cheese and 1/2 unit of cheese to produce 1 unit of goats.

(a) Write the input-output matrix for this economy.

(b) Find the production required to satisfy a demand of 400 units of cheese and 800 units of goats.

LINEAR PROGRAMMING: THE GRAPHICAL METHOD

Karl Gerstner. From the series *Aperspective 3* (The Large Sliding Mirror Picture), 1953/55.

Many realistic problems involve inequalities—a factory can manufacture *no more* than 12 items on a shift, or a medical researcher must interview *at least* a hundred patients to be sure that a new treatment for a disease is better than the old treatment. *Linear inequalities* of the form $ax + by \leq c$ (or with $\geq$, $<$, or $>$ instead of $\leq$) can be used in a process called *linear programming* to *optimize* (find the maximum or minimum for) a given situation.

In this chapter we look at some linear programming problems that can be solved by graphical methods. Then, in Chapter 4, we discuss the *simplex method*, a general method for solving linear programming problems with many variables.

3.1   Graphing Linear Inequalities

As mentioned above,

Linear Inequality

A **linear inequality** in two variables has the form

$$ax + by \leq c$$

for real numbers a, b, and c, with a and b not both 0.

While our definitions and theorems are usually given for $\leq$, keep in mind that $\leq$ may be replaced with $\geq$, $<$, or $>$.

EXAMPLE 1

Graph the linear inequality $3x - 2y \leq 6$.

Because of the "$=$" portion of $\leq$, the points of the line $3x - 2y = 6$ satisfy the linear inequality $3x - 2y \leq 6$ and are part of its graph. As in Chapter 1, find the intercepts by first letting $x = 0$ and then letting $y = 0$; use these points to get the graph of $3x - 2y = 6$ shown in Figure 1.

The points on the line satisfy "$3x - 2y$ *equals* 6." To locate the points satisfying "$3x - 2y$ *is less than* or equal to 6," first solve $3x - 2y \leq 6$ for y.

$$3x - 2y \leq 6$$

$$-2y \leq -3x + 6$$

$$y \geq \frac{3}{2}x - 3$$

(Recall that multiplying both sides of an inequality by a negative number reverses the direction of the inequality symbol.)

As shown in Figure 2, the points *above* the line $3x - 2y = 6$ satisfy

$$y > \frac{3}{2}x - 3,$$

while those below the line satisfy

$$y < \frac{3}{2}x - 3.$$

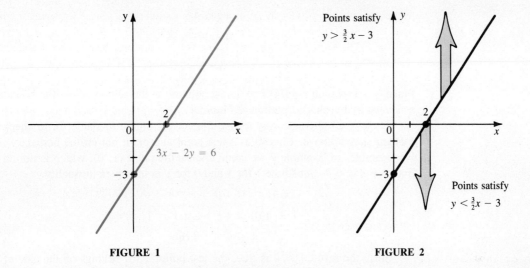

FIGURE 1   FIGURE 2

The line itself is the **boundary.** In summary, the inequality $3x - 2y \leq 6$ is satisfied by all points *on or above* the line $3x - 2y = 6$. Indicate the points above the line by shading, as in Figure 3. The line and shaded region of Figure 3 make up the graph of the linear inequality $3x - 2y \leq 6$. ▪

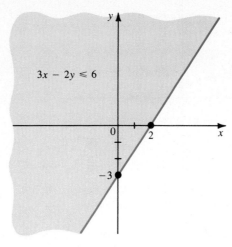

FIGURE 3

EXAMPLE 2

Graph $x + 4y < 4$.

The boundary here is the line $x + 4y = 4$. Since the points on this line do not satisfy $x + 4y < 4$, the line is drawn dashed, as in Figure 4. To decide whether to shade the region above the line or the region below the line, solve for y.

$$x + 4y < 4$$

$$4y < -x + 4$$

$$y < -\frac{1}{4}x + 1$$

Since y is less than $(-1/4)x + 1$, the solution is the region below the boundary, as shown by the shaded portion of Figure 4. ■

There is an alternate way to find the correct region to shade, or to check the method shown above. Choose as a test point any point not on the boundary line. For example, in Example 2 we could choose the point $(1, 0)$, which is not on the line $x + 4y = 4$. Substitute 1 for x and 0 for y in the given inequality.

$$x + 4y < 4$$

$$1 + 4(0) < 4 \qquad \text{Let } x = 1, \ y = 0$$

$$1 < 4 \qquad \textbf{True}$$

Since the result $1 < 4$ is true, the test point $(1, 0)$ belongs on the side of the line where all the points satisfy $x + 4y < 4$. For this reason, shade the side containing $(1, 0)$, as in Figure 4. Choosing a different test point, such as $(1, 5)$, would produce a false result when substituted into the given inequality. In this case, shade the side of the line *not including* the test point.

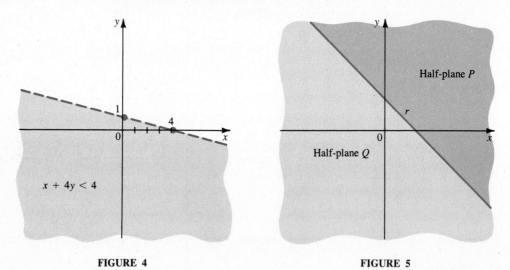

FIGURE 4   FIGURE 5

As the examples above suggest, the graph of a linear inequality is a region in the plane, perhaps including the line which is the boundary of the region. Each of the shaded regions is an example of a **half-plane,** a region on one side of a line. For example, in Figure 5 line r divides the plane into half-planes P and Q. The points of r belong to neither P nor Q. Line r is the boundary of each half-plane.

EXAMPLE 3

Graph $x \leq -1$.

Recall that the graph of $x = -1$ is the vertical line through $(-1, 0)$. To decide which half-plane belongs to the solution, choose a test point. If we choose $(2, 0)$, and replace x with 2, we get a false statement:

$$x < -1$$

$$2 < -1. \quad \textbf{False}$$

The correct half-plane is the one that does *not* contain $(2, 0)$; it is shaded in Figure 6. ▪

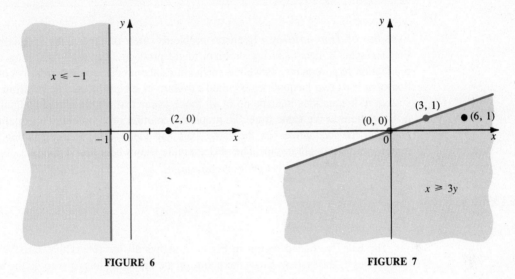

FIGURE 6   **FIGURE 7**

EXAMPLE 4

Graph $x \geq 3y$.

Start by graphing the boundary, $x = 3y$. If $x = 0$, then $y = 0$, giving the point $(0, 0)$. Setting $y = 0$ would produce $(0, 0)$ again. To get a second point on the line, choose another number for x. Choosing $x = 3$ gives $y = 1$, with $(3, 1)$ a point on the line $x = 3y$. The points $(0, 0)$ and $(3, 1)$ lead to the line graphed in Figure 7. To decide on which half-plane to shade, let us choose $(6, 1)$ as a test point. (Any point that is not on the line $x = 3y$ may be used.) Replacing x with 6 and y with 1 in the original inequality gives a true statement, so the half-plane containing $(6, 1)$ is shaded, as shown in Figure 7. ▪

Let us now summarize the steps in graphing a linear inequality.

Graphing a Linear Inequality

1. Draw the graph of the boundary line. Make the line solid if the inequality involves $\leq$ or $\geq$; make the line dashed if the inequality involves $<$ or $>$.

2. Decide which half-plane to shade: either
   (a) solve the inequality for y; shade the region above the line if $\geq$, below if $\leq$, or
   (b) choose any point not on the line as a test point; shade the half-plane that includes the test point if the test point satisfies the original inequality; otherwise, shade the half-plane on the other side of the boundary line.

Systems of Inequalities   Realistic problems often involve many inequalities. For example, a manufacturing problem might produce inequalities resulting from production requirements, as well as inequalities about cost requirements. A collection of at least two inequalities is called a **system of inequalities.** The **solution** of a system of inequalities is made up of all those points that satisfy all the inequalities of the system at the same time. To graph the solution of a system of inequalities, graph all the inequalities on the same axes and identify, by heavy shading, the region common to all graphs. The next example shows how this is done.

EXAMPLE 5

Graph the system

$$y < -3x + 12$$
$$x < 2y.$$

The heavily shaded region in Figure 8 shows all the points that satisfy both inequalities of the system. Since the points on the boundary lines are not in the solution, the boundary lines are dashed.

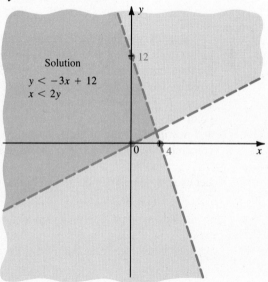

FIGURE 8

The heavily shaded region of Figure 8 is sometimes called the **region of feasible solutions,** or just the **feasible region,** since it is made up of all the points that satisfy (are feasible for) each inequality of the system.   ■

EXAMPLE 6

Graph the feasible region for the system

$$2x - 5y \leq 10$$
$$x + 2y \leq 8$$
$$x \geq 0$$
$$y \geq 0.$$

On the same axes, graph each inequality by graphing the boundary and choosing the appropriate half-plane. Then find the feasible region by locating the overlap of all the half-planes. This feasible region is shaded in Figure 9. The inequalities $x \geq 0$ and $y \geq 0$ restrict the feasible region to the first quadrant.   ■

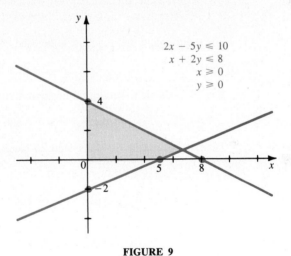

$$2x - 5y \leq 10$$
$$x + 2y \leq 8$$
$$x \geq 0$$
$$y \geq 0$$

FIGURE 9

Applications   As we shall see in the rest of this chapter, many realistic problems lead to systems of linear inequalities. The next example is typical of such problems.

EXAMPLE 7

Midtown Manufacturing Company makes plastic plates and cups, both of which require time on two machines. A unit of plates requires one hour on machine A and two on machine B, while a unit of cups requires three hours on machine A and one on machine B. Each machine is operated for at most 15 hours per day. The profit on each unit of plates is $250 and on each unit of cups is $400. How many units of plates and cups should be manufactured to maximize the total profit?

Start by making a chart which summarizes the given information.

	Number Made	Time on Machine A	Time on Machine B	Profit Per Unit
Plates	x	1	2	$250
Cups	y	3	1	$400
Maximum Time Available		15	15	

Here x represents the number of units of plates to be made, and y represents the number of units of cups.

On machine A, x units of plates require a total of $1 \cdot x = x$ hours while y units of cups require $3 \cdot y = 3y$ hours. Since machine A is available no more than 15 hours a day,

$$x + 3y \leq 15.$$

The requirement that machine B be used no more than 15 hours a day gives

$$2x + y \leq 15.$$

It is not possible to produce a negative number of cups or plates, so that

$$x \geq 0 \qquad \text{and} \qquad y \geq 0.$$

The feasible region for our system of inequalities is shown in Figure 10.

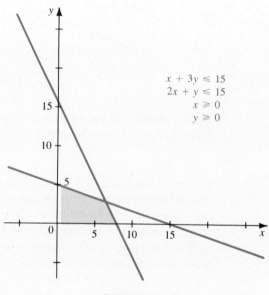

$$x + 3y \leq 15$$
$$2x + y \leq 15$$
$$x \geq 0$$
$$y \geq 0$$

FIGURE 10

3.1 EXERCISES

Graph the linear inequalities in Exercises 1–26.

1. $x + y \leq 2$
2. $y \leq x + 1$
3. $x \geq 3 + y$
4. $y \geq x - 3$
5. $4x - y < 6$
6. $3y + x > 4$
7. $3x + y < 6$
8. $2x - y > 2$
9. $x + 3y \geq -2$
10. $2x + 3y \leq 6$
11. $4x + 3y > -3$
12. $5x + 3y > 15$
13. $2x - 4y < 3$
14. $4x - 3y < 12$
15. $x \leq 5y$
16. $2x \geq y$
17. $-3x < y$
18. $-x > 6y$
19. $x + y \leq 0$
20. $3x + 2y \geq 0$
21. $y < x$
22. $y > -2x$
23. $x < 4$
24. $y > 5$
25. $y \leq -2$
26. $x \geq 3$

Graph the feasible region for the systems of inequalities in Exercises 27–40.

27. $x + y \leq 1$
    $x - y \geq 2$

28. $3x - 4y < 6$
    $2x + 5y > 15$

29. $2x - y < 1$
    $3x + y < 6$

30. $x + 3y \leq 6$
    $2x + 4y \geq 7$

31. $-x - y < 5$
    $2x - y < 4$

32. $6x - 4y > 8$
    $3x + 2y > 4$

33. $x + y \leq \quad 4$
    $x - y \leq \quad 5$
    $4x + y \leq -4$

34. $3x - 2y \geq \quad 6$
    $x + \quad y \leq -5$
    $y \leq \quad 4$

35. $-2 < x < 3$
    $-1 \leq y \leq 5$
    $2x + y < 6$

36. $-2 < x < 2$
    $y > 1$
    $x - y > 0$

37. $2y + x \geq -5$
    $y \leq 3 + x$
    $x \geq 0$
    $y \geq 0$

38. $2x + 3y \leq \quad 12$
    $2x + 3y > \quad -6$
    $3x + \quad y < \quad 4$
    $x \geq \quad 0$
    $y \geq \quad 0$

39. $3x + 4y > 12$
    $2x - 3y < \quad 6$
    $0 \leq y \leq \quad 2$
    $x \geq \quad 0$

40. $0 \leq \quad x \leq \quad 9$
    $x - 2y \geq \quad 4$
    $3x + 5y \leq 30$
    $y \geq \quad 0$

41. A small pottery shop makes two kinds of planters, glazed and unglazed. The glazed type requires 1/2 hour to throw on the wheel and 1 hour in the kiln. The unglazed type takes 1 hour to throw on the wheel and 6 hours in the kiln. The wheel is available for at most 8 hours a day and the kiln is available for at most 20 hours per day. The profit on each glazed pot is $1.50 and on each unglazed pot $1.00. How many of each kind of pot should be produced in order to maximize profit?

    (a) Complete this chart.

	Number	Wheel	Kiln	Profit on each
Glazed	x			$1.50
Unglazed	y			$1.00

    Maximum Hours
    Available

    (b) Set up a system of inequalities and graph the feasible region.

42. Carmella and Walt produce handmade shawls and afghans. They spin the yarn, dye it, and then weave it. A shawl requires 1 hour of spinning, 1 hour of dyeing, and 1 hour of weaving. An afghan needs 2 hours of spinning, 1 of dyeing, and 4 of weaving. They make a $16 profit per shawl and a $20 profit per afghan. Together, they spend at most 8 hours spinning, 6 hours dyeing, and 14 hours weaving. How many of each item should they make to maximize profit?

(a) Complete this chart.

		Hours for:			
	Number	Spinning	Weaving	Dyeing	Profit on each
Shawls	x				$16
Afghans	y				$20
Maximum Hours Available		8	6	14	

(b) Set up a system of inequalities and graph the feasible region.

43. The California Almond Growers have 2400 boxes of almonds to be shipped from their plant in Sacramento to Des Moines and San Antonio. The Des Moines market needs at least 1000 boxes, while the San Antonio market must have at least 800 boxes. Let x = the number of boxes to be shipped to Des Moines and y = the number of boxes to be shipped to San Antonio.

(a) Write a system of inequalities to express the conditions of the problem.

(b) Graph the feasible region of the system.

44. A cement manufacturer produces at least 3.2 million barrels of cement annually. He is told by the Environmental Protection Agency that his operation emits 2.5 pounds of dust for each barrel produced. The EPA has ruled that annual emissions must be reduced to 1.8 million pounds. To do this the manufacturer plans to replace the present dust collectors with two types of electronic precipitators. One type would reduce emissions to .5 pounds per barrel and would cost 16¢ per barrel. The other would reduce the dust to .3 pounds per barrel and would cost 20¢ per barrel. The manufacturer does not want to spend more than .8 million dollars on the precipitators. He needs to know how many barrels he should produce with each type.

(a) Let x = the number of barrels in millions produced with the first type and y = the number of barrels in millions produced with the second type. Write inequalities to express the manufacturer's restrictions.

(b) Graph the feasible region of the system.

3.2   Mathematical Models for Linear Programming

Many mathematical models designed to solve problems in business, biology, and economics involve finding the optimum value (either the maximum or the minimum) of a function, subject to certain restrictions. In a **linear programming** problem, we must find the maximum or minimum value of a function, called the **objec-**

tive function, while satisfying a set of restrictions, or **constraints,** given by linear inequalities.

In this section we see how to set up linear programming problems in two variables. In the next section we will solve such problems.

EXAMPLE 1

A farmer raises only geese and pigs. She wants to raise no more than 16 animals including no more than 10 geese. She spends $5 to raise a goose and $15 to raise a pig, and has $180 available for this project. Find the maximum profit she can make if each goose produces a profit of $6 and each pig a profit of $20.

Let x represent the number of geese to be produced, and let y represent the number of pigs. Start by summarizing the information of the problem in a table.

	Number	Cost to Raise	Profit Each
Geese	x	$5	$6
Pigs	y	$15	$20

Maximum Funds Available	$180

Use this table to write the necessary constraints. Since the total number of animals cannot exceed 16, the first constraint is

$$x + y \leq 16.$$

"No more than 10 geese" leads to

$$x \leq 10.$$

The cost to raise x geese at $5 per goose is $5x$ dollars, while the cost for y pigs at $15 each is $15y$ dollars. Since only $180 is available,

$$5x + 15y \leq 180.$$

The number of geese and pigs cannot be negative:

$$x \geq 0, \quad y \geq 0.$$

The farmer wants to know the number of geese and the number of pigs that should be raised for maximum profit. Each goose produces a profit of $6, and each pig, $20. If z represents total profit, then

$$z = 6x + 20y.$$

In summary, the mathematical model for the given linear programming problem is as follows:

maximize	$z = 6x + 20y$	**(1)**
subject to:	$x + y \leq 16$	**(2)**
	$x \leq 10$	**(3)**
	$5x + 15y \leq 180$	**(4)**
	$x \geq 0, y \geq 0$	**(5)**

Here $z = 6x + 20y$ is the objective function, while inequalities (2)–(4) are the constraints.

Using the methods of the previous section, graph, as in Figure 11, the feasible region for the system of inequalities (2)–(5).

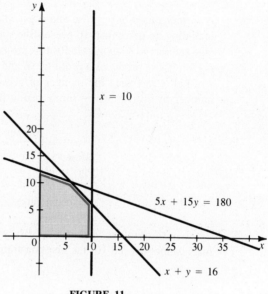

FIGURE 11

Any value in the feasible region of Figure 11 will satisfy all the constraints of the problem. However, in most problems only one point in the feasible region will lead to maximum profit. In the next section, we will see that maximum profit is found by looking at all the *corner points* in the feasible region; a **corner point** is a point in the feasible region where the boundary lines of two constraints cross. The feasible region of Figure 11 has been redrawn in Figure 12, with all the corner points identified.

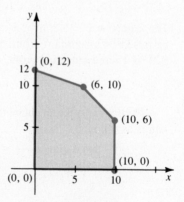

FIGURE 12

Since corner points occur where two straight lines cross, the coordinates of the corner point are the solution of a system of linear equations. For example, the corner point (6, 10) of Figure 12 is found by solving the system

$$x + y = 16$$
$$5x + 15y = 180.$$

By the methods of Chapter 2, the solution of this system is (6, 10). ▪

EXAMPLE 2

An office manager needs to purchase new filing cabinets. He knows that Ace cabinets cost \$40 each, require 6 square feet of floor space, and hold 8 cubic feet of files. On the other hand, each Excello cabinet costs \$80, requires 8 square feet of floor space, and holds 12 cubic feet. His budget permits him to spend no more than \$560 on files, while the office has room for no more than 72 square feet of cabinets. The manager desires the greatest storage capacity within the limitations imposed by funds and space. How many of each type cabinet should he buy?

Let x represent the number of Ace cabinets to be bought and let y represent the number of Excello cabinets. Summarize the information of the problem in a table.

	Number	Cost of each	Space required	Storage capacity
Ace	x	\$40	6 sq ft	8 cu ft
Excello	y	\$80	8 sq ft	12 cu ft
Maximum Available		\$560	72 sq ft	

The constraints imposed by cost and space are as follows.

$$40x + 80y \le 560 \quad \text{cost}$$
$$6x + 8y \le 72 \quad \text{floor space}$$

Since the number of cabinets cannot be negative, $x \ge 0$ and $y \ge 0$. The objective function to be maximized gives the amount of storage capacity provided by some combination of Ace and Excello cabinets. From the information in the table, the objective function is

$$\text{storage space} = z = 8x + 12y.$$

In summary, the given problem has produced the mathematical model

$$\text{maximize} \quad z = 8x + 12y$$
$$\text{subject to:} \quad 40x + 80y \le 560$$
$$6x + 8y \le 72$$
$$x \ge 0, \quad y \ge 0.$$

A graph of the feasible region is shown in Figure 13. Three of the corner points can be identified from the graph as (0, 0), (0, 7), and (12, 0). The fourth corner point, labeled Q in the figure, can be found by solving the system of equations

$$40x + 80y = 560$$
$$6x + 8y = 72.$$

Solve this system to find that Q is the point (8, 3). ▪

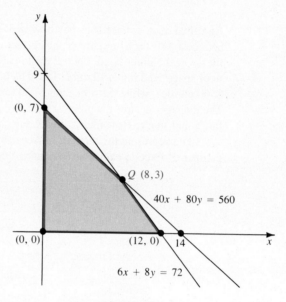

FIGURE 13

EXAMPLE 3

Certain laboratory animals must have at least 30 grams of protein and at least 20 grams of fat per feeding period. These nutrients come from food A, which costs 18¢ per unit and supplies 2 grams of protein and 4 of fat, and food B, with 6 grams of protein and 2 of fat, costing 12¢ per unit. Food B is bought under a long term contract requiring that at least 2 units of B be used per serving. How much of each food must be bought to produce minimum cost per serving?

Let x represent the amount of food A needed, and y the amount of food B. Use the given information to produce the following table.

Food	Number of units	Grams of protein	Grams of fat	Cost
A	x	2	4	18¢
B	y	6	2	12¢
Minimum Required		30	20	

The mathematical model is

$$\text{minimize} \quad z = .18x + .12y$$
$$\text{subject to:} \quad 2x + 6y \geq 30$$
$$4x + 2y \geq 20$$
$$y \geq 2$$
$$x \geq 0, \ y \geq 0.$$

(The constraint $y \geq 0$ is redundant because of the constraint $y \geq 2$.) A graph of the feasible region is shown in Figure 14.

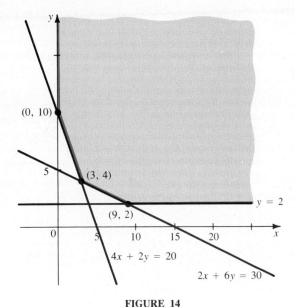

FIGURE 14

The feasible region in Figure 14 is an **unbounded** feasible region—the region extends indefinitely to the upper right. With this region it would not be possible to *maximize* the objective function, because the total cost of the food could always be increased by encouraging the animals to eat more. ■

3.2 EXERCISES

Write Exercises 1–6 as linear inequalities. Identify all variables used. (Not all the information is used in Exercises 5 and 6.)

1. Product A requires 2 hours on machine I, while product B needs 3 hours on the same machine. The machine is available at most 45 hours per week.

2. A cow requires a third of an acre of pasture and a sheep needs a quarter acre. A rancher wants to use at least 120 acres of pasture.

3. John needs at least 25 units of vitamin A per day. Green pills provide 4 units and red pills provide 1.

4. Sandra spends 3 hours selling a small computer and 5 hours selling a larger model. She works no more than 45 hours per week.

5. Coffee costing $6 a pound is to be mixed with coffee costing $5 a pound to get at least 50 pounds of a mixture.

6. A tank in an oil refinery holds 120 gallons. The tank contains a mixture of light oil worth $1.25 per gallon and heavy oil worth $.80 per gallon.

In Exercises 7–16, set up a mathematical model, graph the feasible region, and identify all corner points. Do not try to solve the problem.

7. A manufacturer of refrigerators must ship at least 100 refrigerators to its two West coast warehouses. Each warehouse holds a maximum of 100 refrigerators. Warehouse A holds 25 refrigerators already, while warehouse B has 20 on hand. It costs $12 to ship a refrigerator to warehouse A and $10 to ship one to warehouse B. How many refrigerators should be shipped to each warehouse to minimize cost? What is the minimum cost?

8. Mark, who is ill, takes vitamin pills. Each day he must have at least 16 units of vitamin A, 5 units of vitamin B_1, and 20 units of vitamin C. He can choose between pill #1 which contains 8 units of A, 1 of B_1, and 2 of C, and pill #2 which contains 2 units of A, 1 of B_1, and 7 of C. Pill #1 costs 15¢ and pill #2 costs 30¢. How many of each pill should he buy in order to minimize his cost? What is the minimum cost?

9. A machine shop manufactures two types of bolts. Each can be made on any of three groups of machines, but the time required on each group differs, as shown in the table below.

		Machine groups		
		I	II	III
Bolts	Type 1	.1 minute	.1 minute	.1 minute
	Type 2	.1 minute	.4 minute	.15 minute

Production schedules are made up one day at a time. In a day, there are 240, 720, and 160 minutes available, respectively, on these machines. Type 1 bolts sell for 10¢ and type 2 bolts for 12¢. How many of each type of bolt should be manufactured per day to maximize revenue? What is the maximum revenue?

10. Seall Manufacturing Company makes color television sets. It produces a bargain set that sells for $100 profit and a deluxe set that sells for $150 profit. On the assembly line the bargain set requires 3 hours, while the deluxe set takes 5 hours. The cabinet shop spends one hour on the cabinet for the bargain set and 3 hours on the cabinet for the deluxe set. Both sets require 2 hours of time for testing and packing. On a particular production run the Seall Company has available 3900 work hours on the assembly line, 2100 work hours in the cabinet shop, and 2200 work hours in the testing and packing department. How many sets of each type should it produce to make maximum profit? What is the maximum profit?

11. The manufacturing process requires that oil refineries must manufacture at least two gallons of gasoline for every one of fuel oil. To meet the winter demand for fuel oil, at least 3 million gallons a day must be produced. The demand for gasoline is no more than 6.4 million gallons per day. If the refinery sells gasoline for $1.25 per gallon, and fuel oil for $1 per gallon, how much of each should be produced to maximize revenue? Find the maximum revenue.

12. In a small town in South Carolina, zoning rules require that the window space (in square feet) in a house be at least one-sixth of the space used up by solid walls. The cost to heat the house is 2¢ for each square foot of solid walls and 8¢ for each square foot of windows. Find the maximum total area (windows plus walls) if $16 is available to pay for heat.

13. A candy company has 100 kilograms of chocolate-covered nuts and 125 kilograms of chocolate-covered raisins to be sold as two different mixes. One mix will contain half nuts and half raisins and will sell for $6 per kilogram. The other mix will contain 1/3 nuts and 2/3 raisins and will sell for $4.80 per kilogram. How many kilograms of each mix should the company prepare for maximum revenue?

14. Ms. Oliveras was given the following advice. She should supplement her daily diet with at least 6000 USP units of vitamin A, at least 195 milligrams of vitamin C, and at least 600 USP units of vitamin D. Ms. Oliveras finds that Mason's Pharmacy carries Brand X vitamin pills at 5¢ each and Brand Y vitamins at 4¢ each. Each Brand X pill contains 3000 USP units of A, 45 milligrams of C, and 75 USP units of D, while the Brand Y pills contain 1000 USP units of A, 50 milligrams of C, and 200 USP units of D. What combination of vitamin pills should she buy to obtain the least possible cost? What is the least possible cost per day?

15. Sam, who is dieting, requires two food supplements, I and II. He can get these supplements from two different products, A and B, as shown in the following table.

		Supplement (grams per serving)	
		I	II
Product	A	3	2
	B	2	4

Sam's physician has recommended that he include at least 15 grams of each supplement in his daily diet. If product A costs 25¢ per serving and product B costs 40¢ per serving, how can he satisfy his requirements most economically? Find the minimum cost.

16. A small country can grow only two crops for export, coffee and cocoa. The country has 500,000 hectares of land available for the crops. Long-term contracts require that at least 100,000 hectares be devoted to coffee and at least 200,000 hectares to cocoa. Cocoa must be processed locally, and production bottlenecks limit cocoa to 270,000 hectares. Coffee requires two workers per hectare, with cocoa requiring five. No more than 1,750,000 people are available for these crops. Coffee produces a profit of $220 per hectare, and cocoa a profit of $310 per hectare. How many hectares should the country devote to each crop in order to maximize the profit? Find the maximum profit.

3.3   Solving Linear Programming Problems Graphically

In the last section we saw how to set up a linear programming problem by writing an objective function and the necessary constraints. We then graphed the feasible region and identified all corner points. In this section we complete this process and go on to solve the linear programming problems. The method of solving these problems from the graph of the feasible region is explained in the next example.

EXAMPLE 1

Solve the following linear programming problem:

$$\text{maximize} \quad z = 2x + 5y$$
$$\text{subject to:} \quad 3x + 2y \le 6$$
$$-2x + 4y \le 8$$
$$x \ge 0, \ y \ge 0.$$

The feasible region is graphed in Figure 15. The coordinates of point A, (1/2, 9/4), can be found by solving the system

$$3x + 2y = 6$$
$$-2x + 4y = 8.$$

Every point in the feasible region satisfies all the constraints. However, we want to find those points that produce the maximum possible value of the objective function. To see how to find this maximum value, let us add to the graph of Figure 15 lines which represent the objective function $z = 2x + 5y$ for various sample values of z. If we choose the values 0, 5, 10, and 15 for z, the objective function becomes (in turn)

$$0 = 2x + 5y, \qquad 5 = 2x + 5y, \qquad 10 = 2x + 5y, \qquad 15 = 2x + 5y.$$

These four lines are graphed in Figure 16. (Why are all the lines parallel?) The figure shows that z cannot take on the value 15 because the graph for $z = 15$ is entirely outside the feasible region. The maximum possible value of z will be obtained from a line parallel to the others and between the lines representing the objective function when $z = 10$ and $z = 15$. The value of z will be as large as possible and all constraints will be satisfied, if this line just touches the feasible region. This occurs at point A. We found above that A has coordinates (1/2, 9/4). The value of z at this point is

$$z = 2x + 5y = 2\left(\frac{1}{2}\right) + 5\left(\frac{9}{4}\right) = 12\frac{1}{4}.$$

The maximum possible value of z is 12 1/4. Of all the points in the feasible region, A leads to the largest possible value of z. ∎

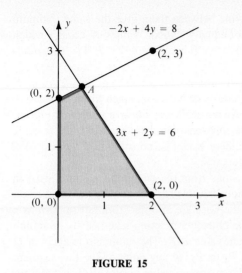

FIGURE 15

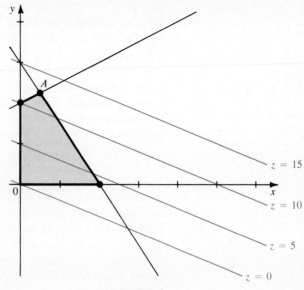

FIGURE 16

EXAMPLE 2

Solve the linear programming problem

$$\text{minimize} \quad z = 2x + 4y$$
$$\text{subject to:} \quad x + 2y \geq 10$$
$$3x + y \geq 10$$
$$x \geq 0, \, y \geq 0.$$

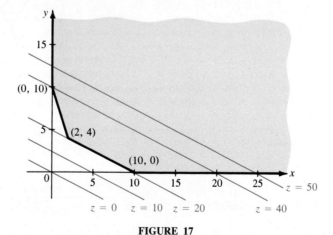

FIGURE 17

Figure 17 shows the feasible region and the lines that result when z in the objective function is replaced by 0, 10, 20, 40, and 50. The line representing the objective function touches the region of feasible solutions when $z = 20$. Two corner points, (2, 4) and (10, 0), lie on this line. In this case, both (2, 4) and (10, 0) as well as all the points on the boundary line between them give the same optimum value of z. There is an infinite number of equally "good" values of x and y which give the same minimum value of the objective function $z = 2x + 4y$. This minimum value is 20. ▪

The feasible region in Example 1 above is *bounded*, since the region is enclosed by boundary lines on all sides. As we shall see, linear programming problems with bounded regions always have solutions. On the other hand, the feasible region in Example 2 is *unbounded* and there would be no solution if we had tried to *maximize* the value of the objective function.

We can draw some general conclusions from the method of solution used in Examples 1 and 2. Figure 18 shows various feasible regions and the lines that result from various values of z. (We assume the lines are in order from left to right as z increases.) In part (a) of the figure, the objective function takes on its minimum value at corner point Q and its maximum value at P. The minimum is again at Q in part (b), but the maximum occurs at P_1 or P_2, or any point on the line segment connecting them. Finally, in part (c), the minimum value occurs at Q, but the objective function has no maximum value because the feasible region is unbounded.

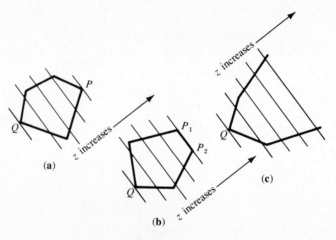

FIGURE 18

The preceding discussion suggests the truth of the **corner point theorem.**

Corner Point	If an optimum value (either a maximum or a minimum) of the objective function exists, it will occur at one or more of the corner points of the feasible region.
Theorem	

This theorem simplifies the job of finding an optimum value: First, graph the feasible region and find all corner points. Then test each corner point in the objective function. Finally, identify the corner point producing the optimum solution. For unbounded regions, you must decide whether or not the required optimum can be found; see Example 2.

With the theorem, we could have solved the problem in Example 1 by identifying the four corner points of Figure 15: (0, 0), (0, 2), (1/2, 9/4), and (2, 0). We would then substitute each of the four points into the objective function, $z = 2x + 5y$ to identify the corner point that produces the maximum value of z.

Corner Point	Value of $z = 2x + 5y$
(0, 0)	$2(0) + 5(0) = 0$
(0, 2)	$2(0) + 5(2) = 10$
$(\frac{1}{2}, \frac{9}{4})$	$2(\frac{1}{2}) + 5(\frac{9}{4}) = 12\frac{1}{4}$ (maximum)
(2, 0)	$2(2) + 5(0) = 4$

From these results, the corner point (1/2, 9/4) yields the maximum value of 12 1/4. This is the same result found earlier.

EXAMPLE 3

Sketch the feasible region for the following set of constraints.

$$3y - 2x \geq 0$$
$$y + 8x \leq 52$$
$$y - 2x \leq 2$$
$$x \geq 3$$

Then find the maximum and minimum values of the objective function

$$z = 5x + 2y.$$

The graph in Figure 19 shows that the feasible region is bounded. Use the corner points from the graph to find the maximum and minimum values of the objective function.

Corner point	Value of $z = 5x + 2y$
(3, 2)	$5(3) + 2(2) = 19$ (minimum)
(6, 4)	$5(6) + 2(4) = 38$
(5, 12)	$5(5) + 2(12) = 49$ (maximum)
(3, 8)	$5(3) + 2(8) = 31$

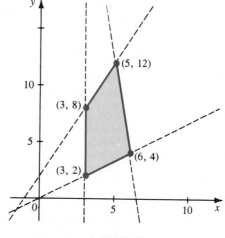

FIGURE 19

The minimum value of $z = 5x + 2y$ is 19 at the corner point (3, 2). The maximum value is 49 at (5, 12). ◼

We shall end this section by completing the solution of Example 2 from the last section.

EXAMPLE 4

An office manager needs to purchase new filing cabinets. He knows that Ace cabinets cost $40 each, require 6 square feet of floor space, and hold 8 cubic feet of files. On the other hand, each Excello cabinet costs $80, requires 8 square feet of floor space, and holds 12 cubic feet. His budget permits him to spend no more than $560 on files, while the office has room for no more than 72 square feet of cabinets. The manager desires the greatest storage capacity within the limitations imposed by funds and space. How many of each type of cabinet should he buy?

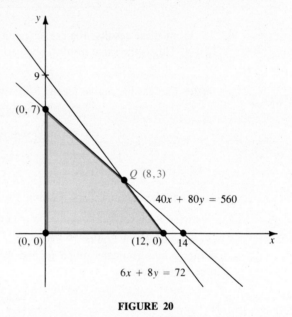

FIGURE 20

Figure 20 repeats the feasible region and corner points found in Example 2 of the previous section. Now test these four points in the objective function to determine the maximum value of z. The results are shown in the table.

Corner point	Value of $z = 8x + 12y$
(0, 0)	0
(0, 7)	84
(12, 0)	96
(8, 3)	100 (maximum)

The objective function, which represents storage space, is maximized when $x = 8$ and $y = 3$. The manager should buy 8 Ace cabinets and 3 Excello cabinets. ▪

Let us now summarize the steps in solving a linear programming problem by the graphical method.

Solving a Linear Programming Problem	1. Write the objective function and all necessary constraints.
	2. Graph the feasible region.
	3. Identify all corner points.
	4. Find the value of the objective function at each corner point.
	5. For a bounded region, the solution is given by the corner point producing the optimum value of the objective function.
	6. For an unbounded region, check that a solution actually exists. If it does, it will occur at a corner point.

3.3 EXERCISES

Exercises 1–6 show regions of feasible solutions. Use these regions to find maximum and minimum values of each given objective function.

1. $z = 3x + 5y$

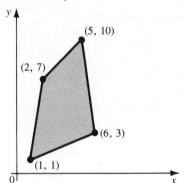

2. $z = 6x + y$

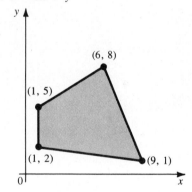

3. $z = .40x + .75y$

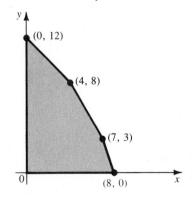

4. $z = .35x + 1.25y$

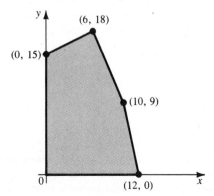

5. $z = 2x + 3y$

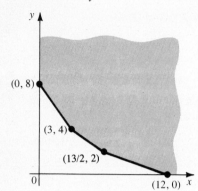

6. $z = 5x + 6y$

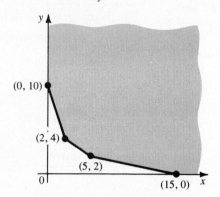

Use graphical methods to solve problems 7–14.

7. Maximize $\quad z = 5x + 2y$
$\quad$ subject to: $\quad 2x + 3y \le 6$
$\quad\quad\quad\quad\quad\quad 4x + \ y \le 6$
$\quad\quad\quad\quad\quad\quad x \ge 0, y \ge 0$

8. Minimize $\quad z = x + 3y$
$\quad$ subject to: $\quad x + \ y \le 10$
$\quad\quad\quad\quad\quad\quad 5x + 2y \ge 20$
$\quad\quad\quad\quad\quad\quad -x + 2y \ge 0$
$\quad\quad\quad\quad\quad\quad x \ge 0, y \ge 0$

9. Maximize $\quad z = 2x + y$
$\quad$ subject to: $\quad 3x - y \ge 12$
$\quad\quad\quad\quad\quad\quad x + y \le 15$
$\quad\quad\quad\quad\quad\quad x \ge 2, y \ge 5$

10. Maximize $\quad z = x + 3y$
$\quad$ subject to: $\quad 2x + 3y \le 100$
$\quad\quad\quad\quad\quad\quad 5x + 4y \le 200$
$\quad\quad\quad\quad\quad\quad x \ge 10, y \ge 20$

11. Maximize $\quad z = 4x + 2y$
$\quad$ subject to: $\quad x - y \le 10$
$\quad\quad\quad\quad\quad\quad 5x + 3y \le 75$
$\quad\quad\quad\quad\quad\quad x \ge 0, y \ge 0$

12. Maximize $\quad z = 4x + 5y$
$\quad$ subject to: $\quad 10x - \ 5y \le 100$
$\quad\quad\quad\quad\quad\quad 20x + 10y \ge 150$
$\quad\quad\quad\quad\quad\quad x \ge 0, y \ge 0$

13. Find values of $x \ge 0$ and $y \ge 0$ which maximize $z = 10x + 12y$ subject to each of the following sets of constraints.

(a) $x + \ y \le 20$
$\quad x + 3y \le 24$

(b) $3x + \ y \le 15$
$\quad\ x + 2y \le 18$

(c) $2x + 5y \ge 22$
$\quad 4x + 3y \le 28$
$\quad 2x + 2y \le 17$

14. Find values of $x \ge 0$ and $y \ge 0$ which minimize $z = 3x + 2y$ subject to each of the following sets of constraints.

(a) $10x + \ 7y \le 42$
$\quad\ 4x + 10y \ge 35$

(b) $6x + 5y \ge 25$
$\quad 2x + 6y \ge 15$

(c) $\ x + 2y \ge 10$
$\quad 2x + \ y \ge 12$
$\quad\ x - \ y \le 8$

In Exercises 15–24, complete the solution of the problems that were set up in Exercises 7–16 of the previous section.

15. A manufacturer of refrigerators must ship at least 100 refrigerators to its two West coast warehouses. Each warehouse holds a maximum of 100 refrigerators. Warehouse A holds 25 refrigerators already, while warehouse B has 20 on hand. It costs $12 to ship a refrigerator to warehouse A and $10 to ship one to warehouse B. How many refrigerators should be shipped to each warehouse to minimize cost? What is the minimum cost?

16. Mark, who is ill, takes vitamin pills. Each day he must have at least 16 units of vitamin A, 5 units of vitamin B_1, and 20 units of vitamin C. He can choose between pill #1 which contains 8 units of A, 1 of B_1, and 2 of C, and pill #2 which contains 2 units of A, 1 of B_1, and 7 of C. Pill #1 costs 15¢ and pill #2 costs 30¢. How many of each pill should he buy in order to minimize his cost? What is the minimum cost?

17. A machine shop manufactures two types of bolts. Each can be made on any of three groups of machines, but the time required on each group differs, as shown in the table below.

		Machine groups		
		I	II	III
Bolts	Type 1	.1 minute	.1 minute	.1 minute
	Type 2	.1 minute	.4 minute	.5 minute

Production schedules are made up one day at a time. In a day there are 240, 720, and 160 minutes available, respectively, on these machines. Type 1 bolts sell for 10¢ and type 2 bolts for 12¢. How many of each type of bolt should be manufactured per day to maximize revenue? What is the maximum revenue?

18. Seall Manufacturing Company makes color television sets. It produces a bargain set that sells for $100 profit and a deluxe set that sells for $150 profit. On the assembly line the bargain set requires 3 hours, while the deluxe set takes 5 hours. The cabinet shop spends one hour on the cabinet for the bargain set and 3 hours on the cabinet for the deluxe set. Both sets require 2 hours of time for testing and packing. On a particular production run the Seall Company has available 3900 work hours on the assembly line, 2100 work hours in the cabinet shop, and 2200 work hours in the testing and packing department. How many sets of each type should it produce to make maximum profit? What is the maximum profit?

19. The manufacturing process requires that oil refineries must manufacture at least two gallons of gasoline for every one of fuel oil. To meet the winter demand for fuel oil, at least 3 million gallons a day must be produced. The demand for gasoline is no more than 6.4 million gallons per day. If the refinery sells gasoline for $1.25 per gallon, and fuel oil for $1 per gallon, how much of each should be produced to maximize revenue? Find the maximum revenue.

20. In a small town in South Carolina, zoning rules require that the window space (in square feet) in a house be at least one-sixth of the space used up by solid walls. The cost to heat the house is 2¢ for each square foot of solid walls and 8¢ for each square foot of windows. Find the maximum total area (windows plus walls) if $16 is available to pay for heat.

21. A candy company has 100 kilograms of chocolate-covered nuts and 125 kilograms of chocolate-covered raisins to be sold as two different mixes. One mix will contain half nuts and half raisins and will sell for $6 per kilogram. The other mix will contain 1/3 nuts and 2/3 raisins and will sell for $4.80 per kilogram. How many kilograms of each mix should the company prepare for maximum revenue? Find the maximum revenue.

22. Ms. Oliveras was given the following advice. She should supplement her daily diet with at least 6000 USP units of vitamin A, at least 195 milligrams of vitamin C, and at least 600 USP units of vitamin D. Ms. Oliveras finds that Mason's Pharmacy carries Brand X vitamin pills at 5¢ each and Brand Y vitamins at 4¢ each. Each Brand X pill contains 3000 USP units of A, 45 milligrams of C, and 75 USP units of D, while

Brand Y pills contain 1000 USP units of A, 50 milligrams of C, and 200 USP units of D. What combination of vitamin pills should she buy to obtain the least possible cost? What is the least possible cost per day?

23. Sam, who is dieting, requires two food supplements, I and II. He can get these supplements from two different products, A and B, as shown in the following table.

		Supplement (grams per serving)	
		I	II
Product	A	3	2
	B	2	4

Sam's physician has recommended that he include at least 15 grams of each supplement in his daily diet. If product A costs 25¢ per serving and product B costs 40¢ per serving, how can he satisfy his requirements most economically? Find the minimum cost.

24. A small country can grow only two crops for export, coffee and cocoa. The country has 500,000 hectares of land available for the crops. Long-term contracts require that at least 100,000 hectares be devoted to coffee and at least 200,000 hectares to cocoa. Cocoa must be processed locally, and production bottlenecks limit cocoa to 270,000 hectares. Coffee requires two workers per hectare, with cocoa requiring five. No more than 1,750,000 people are available for these crops. Coffee produces a profit of $220 per hectare, and cocoa a profit of $310 per hectare. How many hectares should the country devote to each crop in order to maximize the profit? Find the maximum profit.

The importance of linear programming is shown by the inclusion of linear programming problems on most examinations for Certified Public Accountant. Answer the following questions from one such examination.*

The Random Company manufactures two products, Zeta and Beta. Each product must pass through two processing operations. All materials are introduced at the start of Process No. 1. There are no work in process inventories. Random may produce either one product exclusively or various combinations of both products subject to the following constraints:

	Process No. 1	Process No. 2	Contribution Margin Per Unit
Hours required to produce one unit of:			
Zeta	1 hour	1 hour	$4.00
Beta	2 hours	3 hours	5.25
Total capacity in hours per day	1,000 hours	1,275 hours	

A shortage of technical labor has limited Beta production to 400 units per day. There are no constraints on the production of Zeta other than the hour constraints in the above schedule. Assume that all relationships between capacity and production are linear.

---

*Material from *Uniform CPA Examinations and Unofficial Answers*, copyright © 1973, 1974, 1975 by the American Institute of Certified Public Accountants, Inc., is reprinted with permission.

25. Given the objective to maximize total contribution margin, what is the production constraint for Process No. 1?

    a. Zeta + Beta $\leq$ 1,000.

    b. Zeta + 2 Beta $\leq$ 1,000.

    c. Zeta + Beta $\geq$ 1,000.

    d. Zeta + 2 Beta $\geq$ 1,000.

26. Given the objective to maximize total contribution margin, what is the labor constraint for production of Beta?

    a. Beta $\leq$ 400.   **c.** Beta $\leq$ 425.

    b. Beta $\geq$ 400.   **d.** Beta $\geq$ 425.

27. What is the objective function of the data presented?

    a. Zeta + 2 Beta = \$9.25.

    b. \$4.00 Zeta + 3(\$5.25) Beta = Total Contribution Margin.

    c. \$4.00 Zeta + \$5.25 Beta = Total Contribution Margin.

    d. 2(\$4.00) Zeta + 3(\$5.25) Beta = Total Contribution Margin.

KEY WORDS

system of inequalities	constraints
half-plane	region of feasible solutions
boundary	corner point
linear inequality	bounded
objective function	unbounded

Chapter 3   REVIEW EXERCISES

Graph each of the linear inequalities in Exercises 1–6.

1. $y \geq 2x + 3$ **2.** $3x - y \leq 5$ **3.** $3x + 4y \leq 12$

4. $2x - 6y \geq 18$ **5.** $y \geq x$ **6.** $y \leq 3$

Graph the solution of each of the systems of inequalities in Exercises 7–12. Find all corner points.

7. $x + y \leq 6$ **8.** $4x + y \geq 8$ **9.** $-4 \leq x \leq 2$

      $2x - y \geq 3$ $2x - 3y \leq 6$ $-1 \leq y \leq 3$

                                                              $x + y \leq 4$

10. $2 \leq x \leq 5$ **11.** $x + 3y \geq 6$ **12.** $x + 2y \leq 4$

       $1 \leq y \leq 7$ $4x - 3y \leq 12$ $2x - 3y \leq 6$

       $x - y \leq 3$ $x \geq 0$ $x \geq 0$

                                  $y \geq 0$ $y \geq 0$

Set up a system of inequalities for problems 13 and 14; then graph the solution of the system.

13. A bakery makes both cakes and cookies. Each batch of cakes requires two hours in the oven and three hours in the decorating room. Each batch of cookies needs one and a half hours in the oven and two thirds of an hour in the decorating room. The oven is available no more than 15 hours a day, while the decorating room can be used no more than 13 hours a day.

14. A company makes two kinds of pizza, basic and plain. Basic contains cheese and beef, while plain contains onions and beef. The company sells at least three units a day of basic, and at least two units of plain. The beef costs $5 per unit for basic, and $4 per unit for plain. They can spend no more than $50 per day on beef. Dough for basic is $2 per unit, while dough for plain is $1 per unit. The company can spend no more than $16 per day on dough.

Use the given regions to find the maximum and minimum values of the objective function $z = 2x + 4y$.

15.

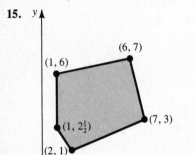

16.

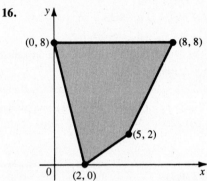

Use the graphical method to solve Exercises 17–22.

17. Maximize $z = 2x + 4y$
    subject to: $3x + 2y \leq 12$
                   $5x + y \geq 5$
                   $x \geq 0,\ y \geq 0$

18. Minimize $z = 3x + 2y$
    subject to: $8x + 9y \geq 72$
                   $6x + 8y \geq 72$
                   $x \geq 0,\ y \geq 0$

19. Minimize $z = 4x + 2y$
    subject to: $x + y \leq 50$
                   $2x + y \geq 20$
                   $x + 2y \geq 30$
                   $x \geq 0,\ y \geq 0$

20. Maximize $z = 4x + 3y$
    subject to: $2x + 7y \leq 14$
                   $2x + 3y \leq 10$
                   $x \geq 0,\ y \geq 0$

21. How many batches of cakes and cookies should the bakery of Exercise 13 make in order to maximize profits if cookies produce a profit of $20 per batch and cakes produce a profit of $30 per batch?

22. How many units of each kind of pizza should the company of Exercise 14 make in order to maximize profits if basic sells for $20 per unit and plain for $15 per unit?

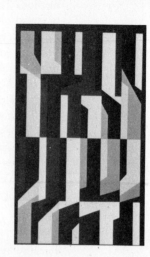

LINEAR PROGRAMMING: THE SIMPLEX METHOD

Karl Gerstner. From the series *Aperspective 1* (The Endless Spiral at a Right Angle), 1952–1956.

In the previous chapter, we solved linear programming problems by the graphical method. This method illustrates the basic ideas of linear programming, but it is practical only for problems with two variables. For problems with more than two variables, or with two variables and many constraints, the simplex method is used.

The simplex method starts with the selection of one corner point (often the origin) from the feasible region. Then, in a systematic way, another corner point is found which improves the value of the objective function. Finally, an optimum solution is reached or it can be seen that none exists.

The simplex method requires a number of steps. We have divided the presentation of these steps into two parts. First, in Section 4.1, we set up the problem and begin the method, and then, in Section 4.2, we complete the method.

4.1 Slack Variables and the Pivot

Because the simplex method is used for problems with many variables, it is usually not convenient to use letters such as x, y, z, or w as variable names. Instead, the symbols x_1 (read "x-sub-one"), x_2, x_3, and so on, are used. These variable names lend themselves easily to use on the computer. In the simplex method, all constraints must be expressed in the linear form

$$a_1x_1 + a_2x_2 + a_3x_3 + \ldots \leq b$$

where x_1, x_2, x_3, . . . are variables and a_1, a_2, . . . , b are constants.

We shall first discuss the simplex method for linear programming problems in *standard maximum form*.

Standard Maximum Form	A linear programming problem is in **standard maximum form** if **1.** the objective function is to be maximized; **2.** all variables are nonnegative ($x_i \geq 0$); **3.** all constraints involve $\leq$; **4.** the constants in the constraints are all nonnegative ($b \geq 0$).

(In Sections 4.3 and 4.4 we discuss problems which do not meet all of these conditions.)

Begin the simplex method by converting the constraints, which are linear inequalities, into linear equations. Do this by adding a nonnegative variable, called a **slack variable**, to each constraint. For example, convert the inequality $x_1 + x_2 \leq 10$ into an equation by adding the slack variable x_3, to get

$$x_1 + x_2 + x_3 = 10, \qquad \text{where } x_3 \geq 0.$$

The inequality $x_1 + x_2 \leq 10$ says that the sum $x_1 + x_2$ is less than or perhaps equal to 10. The variable x_3 "takes up any slack" and represents the amount by which $x_1 + x_2$ fails to equal 10. For example, if $x_1 + x_2$ equals 8, then x_3 is 2. If $x_1 + x_2 = 10$, the value of x_3 is 0.

EXAMPLE 1

Restate the following linear programming problem by introducing slack variables.

$$\begin{aligned} \text{maximize} \quad & z = 3x_1 + 2x_2 + x_3 \\ \text{subject to:} \quad & 2x_1 + x_2 + x_3 \leq 150 \\ & 2x_1 + 2x_2 + 8x_3 \leq 200 \\ & 2x_1 + 3x_2 + x_3 \leq 320 \end{aligned}$$

with $x_1 \geq 0$, $x_2 \geq 0$, $x_3 \geq 0$.

Rewrite the three constraints as equations by adding slack variables x_4, x_5, and x_6, one for each constraint. By this process, the problem is restated as

$$\begin{aligned} \text{maximize} \quad & z = 3x_1 + 2x_2 + x_3 \\ \text{subject to:} \quad & 2x_1 + x_2 + x_3 + x_4 = 150 \\ & 2x_1 + 2x_2 + 8x_3 + x_5 = 200 \\ & 2x_1 + 3x_2 + x_3 + x_6 = 320 \end{aligned}$$

with $x_1 \geq 0$, $x_2 \geq 0$, $x_3 \geq 0$, $x_4 \geq 0$, $x_5 \geq 0$, $x_6 \geq 0$. ▪

Adding slack variables to the constraints converts a linear programming problem into a system of linear equations. These equations should have all variables on the left of the equals sign and all constants on the right. All the equations of Example 1 satisfy this condition except for the objective function, $z = 3x_1 + 2x_2 + x_3$, which may be written with all variables on the left as

$$-3x_1 - 2x_2 - x_3 + z = 0.$$

Now the equations of Example 1 can be written as the augmented matrix

$$\begin{array}{ccccccc} x_1 & x_2 & x_3 & x_4 & x_5 & x_6 & z \\ \left[\begin{array}{ccccccc|c} 2 & 1 & 1 & 1 & 0 & 0 & 0 & 150 \\ 2 & 2 & 8 & 0 & 1 & 0 & 0 & 200 \\ 2 & 3 & 1 & 0 & 0 & 1 & 0 & 320 \\ \hline -3 & -2 & -1 & 0 & 0 & 0 & 1 & 0 \end{array}\right] \end{array}$$

indicators

This matrix is called the **initial simplex tableau.** The numbers in the bottom row, which are from the objective function, are called **indicators** (except for the 0 at the far right). The column headed z will never change in all our future work, and will be omitted from now on.

EXAMPLE 2

Set up the initial simplex tableau for the following problem:

A farmer has 100 acres of available land which he wishes to plant with a mixture of potatoes, corn, and cabbage. It costs him $400 to produce an acre of potatoes, $160 to produce an acre of corn, and $280 to produce an acre of cabbage. He has a maximum of $20,000 to spend. He makes a profit of $120 per acre of potatoes, $40 per acre of corn, and $60 per acre of cabbage. How many acres of each crop should he plant to maximize his profit?

Summarize the given information as follows.

Crop	Number of acres	Cost per acre	Profit per acre
Potatoes	x_1	$400	$120
Corn	x_2	160	40
Cabbage	x_3	280	60
Maximum available	100	$20,000	

If the number of acres allotted to each of the three crops is represented by x_1, x_2, and x_3, respectively, then the constraints of the example can be expressed as

$$x_1 + x_2 + x_3 \leq 100 \quad \text{(number of acres)},$$
$$400x_1 + 160x_2 + 280x_3 \leq 20{,}000 \quad \text{(production costs)},$$

where x_1, x_2, and x_3 are all nonnegative. The first of these constraints says that $x_1 + x_2 + x_3$ is less than or perhaps equal to 100. Use x_4 as the slack variable, giving the equation

$$x_1 + x_2 + x_3 + x_4 = 100.$$

Here x_4 represents the amount of the farmer's 100 acres that will not be used. (x_4 may be 0 or any value up to 100.)

In the same way, the constraint $400x_1 + 160x_2 + 280x_3 \leq 20{,}000$ can be converted into an equation by adding a slack variable, x_5:

$$400x_1 + 160x_2 + 280x_3 + x_5 = 20{,}000.$$

The slack variable x_5 represents any unused portion of the farmer's $20,000 capital. (Again, x_5 may be any value from 0 to 20,000.)

The objective function represents the profit. The farmer wants to maximize

$$z = 120x_1 + 40x_2 + 60x_3.$$

We have now set up the following linear programming problem:

$$\text{maximize} \quad z = 120x_1 + 40x_2 + 60x_3$$
$$\text{subject to:} \quad x_1 + x_2 + x_3 + x_4 = 100$$
$$400x_1 + 160x_2 + 280x_3 + x_5 = 20{,}000.$$

with $x_1 \geq 0$, $x_2 \geq 0$, $x_3 \geq 0$, $x_4 \geq 0$, $x_5 \geq 0$. Rewrite the objective function as $-120x_1 - 40x_2 - 60x_3 + z = 0$, with the initial simplex tableau as follows.

$$
\begin{array}{ccccc}
x_1 & x_2 & x_3 & x_4 & x_5 \\
\end{array}
$$

$$
\left[
\begin{array}{ccccc|c}
1 & 1 & 1 & 1 & 0 & 100 \\
400 & 160 & 280 & 0 & 1 & 20{,}000 \\
\hline
-120 & -40 & -60 & 0 & 0 & 0
\end{array}
\right]
$$

Since the x_4 and x_5 columns in this tableau make up the identity matrix, these variables are called **basic variables.** If we let $x_4 = 100$ (the entry to the far right in the row where the x_4 column has a 1), and let $x_5 = 20{,}000$, the system of equations

$$
\begin{aligned}
x_1 + x_2 + x_3 + x_4 &= 100 \\
400x_1 + 160x_2 + 280x_3 + x_5 &= 20{,}000
\end{aligned}
$$

becomes

$$
\begin{aligned}
x_1 + x_2 + x_3 + 100 &= 100 \\
400x_1 + 160x_2 + 280x_3 + 20{,}000 &= 20{,}000
\end{aligned}
$$

or

$$
\begin{aligned}
x_1 + x_2 + x_3 &= 0 \\
400x_1 + 160x_2 + 280x_3 &= 0.
\end{aligned}
$$

Since $x_1 \ge 0$, $x_2 \ge 0$, and $x_3 \ge 0$, the only possible solution for this last system of equations is $x_1 = 0$, $x_2 = 0$, and $x_3 = 0$. This solution, which corresponds to the origin of the region of feasible solutions, is hardly optimal—it produces a profit of $0 for the farmer. In the next section we use the simplex method to start with this solution and improve it to find the maximum possible profit. ■

EXAMPLE 3

Read a solution from the matrix below.

$$
\begin{array}{ccccc}
x_1 & x_2 & x_3 & x_4 & x_5 \\
\end{array}
$$

$$
\left[
\begin{array}{ccccc|c}
2 & 1 & 8 & 5 & 0 & 27 \\
9 & 0 & 3 & 12 & 1 & 45 \\
\hline
-2 & 0 & -4 & 0 & 0 & 0
\end{array}
\right]
$$

The variables x_2 and x_5 are basic variables. The 1 in the x_2 column is in the first row. This means that $x_2 = 27$ (the far right number in the first row). Also, $x_5 = 45$. Letting $x_2 = 27$ and $x_5 = 45$ forces x_1, x_3, and x_4 to be zero. The solution is thus $x_1 = 0$, $x_2 = 27$, $x_3 = 0$, $x_4 = 0$, and $x_5 = 45$. ■

Pivots   Solutions read directly from the initial simplex tableau are seldom, if ever, optimal. It is necessary to proceed to other solutions (corresponding to other corner points of the feasible region) until an optimum solution is found. To get these other solutions, use the row transformations of Chapter 2 to change the tableau by "pivoting" about one of the nonzero entries of the tableau. Pivoting, explained in the next example, produces a new tableau leading to another solution of the system of equations obtained from the original problem.

EXAMPLE 4

Pivot about the indicated 2 of the initial simplex tableau

$$
\begin{array}{cccccc}
x_1 & x_2 & x_3 & x_4 & x_5 & x_6 \\
\end{array}
$$

$$
\left[
\begin{array}{cccccc|c}
2 & 1 & 1 & 1 & 0 & 0 & 150 \\
2 & 2 & 8 & 0 & 1 & 0 & 200 \\
2 & 3 & 1 & 0 & 0 & 1 & 320 \\
-3 & -2 & -1 & 0 & 0 & 0 & 0
\end{array}
\right].
$$

To pivot about the indicated 2, change x_1 into a basic variable by getting a 1 where the 2 is now and changing all other entries in the x_1 column to 0. Start by multiplying each entry of row 1 by 1/2.

$$
\begin{array}{cccccc}
x_1 & x_2 & x_3 & x_4 & x_5 & x_6 \\
\end{array}
$$

$$
\left[
\begin{array}{cccccc|c}
1 & \frac{1}{2} & \frac{1}{2} & \frac{1}{2} & 0 & 0 & 75 \\
2 & 2 & 8 & 0 & 1 & 0 & 200 \\
2 & 3 & 1 & 0 & 0 & 1 & 320 \\
-3 & -2 & -1 & 0 & 0 & 0 & 0
\end{array}
\right]
$$

Now get 0 in row 2, column 1 by multiplying each entry in row 1 by -2 and adding the result to the corresponding entry in row 2.

$$
\begin{array}{cccccc}
x_1 & x_2 & x_3 & x_4 & x_5 & x_6 \\
\end{array}
$$

$$
\left[
\begin{array}{cccccc|c}
1 & \frac{1}{2} & \frac{1}{2} & \frac{1}{2} & 0 & 0 & 75 \\
0 & 1 & 7 & -1 & 1 & 0 & 50 \\
2 & 3 & 1 & 0 & 0 & 1 & 320 \\
-3 & -2 & -1 & 0 & 0 & 0 & 0
\end{array}
\right]
$$

Change the 2 in row 3, column 1 to a 0 by a similar process.

$$
\begin{array}{cccccc}
x_1 & x_2 & x_3 & x_4 & x_5 & x_6 \\
\end{array}
$$

$$
\left[
\begin{array}{cccccc|c}
1 & \frac{1}{2} & \frac{1}{2} & \frac{1}{2} & 0 & 0 & 75 \\
0 & 1 & 7 & -1 & 1 & 0 & 50 \\
0 & 2 & 0 & -1 & 0 & 1 & 170 \\
-3 & -2 & -1 & 0 & 0 & 0 & 0
\end{array}
\right]
$$

Finally, change the indicator -3 to 0 by multiplying each entry in row 1 by 3 and adding the result to the corresponding entry in row 4.

$$
\begin{array}{cccccc}
x_1 & x_2 & x_3 & x_4 & x_5 & x_6 \\
\end{array}
$$

$$
\left[
\begin{array}{cccccc|c}
1 & \frac{1}{2} & \frac{1}{2} & \frac{1}{2} & 0 & 0 & 75 \\
0 & 1 & 7 & -1 & 1 & 0 & 50 \\
0 & 2 & 0 & -1 & 0 & 1 & 170 \\
0 & -\frac{1}{2} & \frac{1}{2} & \frac{3}{2} & 0 & 0 & 225
\end{array}
\right]
$$

This simplex tableau gives the solution $x_1 = 75$, $x_2 = 0$, $x_3 = 0$, $x_4 = 0$, $x_5 = 50$, and $x_6 = 170$. Substituting these results into the objective function gives $z = 225$. (The value of z is always the number in the lower right-hand corner.) ■

In the simplex method, this process is repeated until an optimum solution is found, if one exists. In the next section, we discuss how to decide where to pivot to improve the value of the objective function. We also show how to tell when an optimum solution has been reached or does not exist.

4.1 EXERCISES

Convert each of the inequalities in Exercises 1–4 into equations by adding a slack variable.

1. $x_1 + 2x_2 \leq 6$

2. $3x_1 + 5x_2 \leq 100$

3. $2x_1 + 4x_2 + 3x_3 \leq 100$

4. $8x_1 + 6x_2 + 5x_3 \leq 250$

For Exercises 5–8, **(a)** determine the number of slack variables needed; **(b)** name them; **(c)** use slack variables to convert each constraint into a linear equation.

5. Maximize $z = 10x_1 + 12x_2$

subject to: $4x_1 + 2x_2 \leq 20$
$5x_1 + x_2 \leq 50$
$2x_1 + 3x_2 \leq 25$

and $x_1 \geq 0$, $x_2 \geq 0$.

6. Maximize $z = 1.2x_1 + 3.5x_2$

subject to: $2.4x_1 + 1.5x_2 \leq 10$
$1.7x_1 + 1.9x_2 \leq 15$

and $x_1 \geq 0$, $x_2 \geq 0$.

7. Maximize $z = 8x_1 + 3x_2 + x_3$

subject to: $7x_1 + 6x_2 + 8x_3 \leq 118$
$4x_1 + 5x_2 + 10x_3 \leq 220$

and $x_1 \geq 0$, $x_2 \geq 0$, $x_3 \geq 0$.

8. Maximize $z = 12x_1 + 15x_2 + 10x_3$

subject to: $2x_1 + 2x_2 + x_3 \leq 8$
$x_1 + 4x_2 + 3x_3 \leq 12$

and $x_1 \geq 0$, $x_2 \geq 0$, $x_3 \geq 0$.

Write the solution that can be read from Exercises 9–12.

9.

$$\begin{array}{ccccc} x_1 & x_2 & x_3 & x_4 & x_5 \\ \end{array}$$
$$\left[\begin{array}{ccccc|c} 2 & 2 & 0 & 3 & 1 & 15 \\ 3 & 4 & 1 & 6 & 0 & 20 \\ \hline -2 & -1 & 0 & 1 & 0 & 10 \end{array}\right]$$

10.

$$\begin{array}{ccccc} x_1 & x_2 & x_3 & x_4 & x_5 \\ \end{array}$$
$$\left[\begin{array}{ccccc|c} 0 & 2 & 1 & 1 & 3 & 5 \\ 1 & 5 & 0 & 1 & 2 & 8 \\ \hline 0 & -2 & 0 & 1 & 1 & 10 \end{array}\right]$$

11.

$$\begin{array}{cccccc} x_1 & x_2 & x_3 & x_4 & x_5 & x_6 \\ \end{array}$$
$$\left[\begin{array}{cccccc|c} 6 & 2 & 1 & 3 & 0 & 0 & 8 \\ 2 & 2 & 0 & 1 & 0 & 1 & 7 \\ 2 & 1 & 0 & 3 & 1 & 0 & 6 \\ \hline -3 & -2 & 0 & 2 & 0 & 0 & 12 \end{array}\right]$$

12.

$$\begin{array}{cccccc} x_1 & x_2 & x_3 & x_4 & x_5 & x_6 \\ \end{array}$$
$$\left[\begin{array}{cccccc|c} 0 & 2 & 0 & 1 & 2 & 2 & 3 \\ 0 & 3 & 1 & 0 & 1 & 2 & 2 \\ 1 & 4 & 0 & 0 & 3 & 5 & 5 \\ \hline 0 & -4 & 0 & 0 & 4 & 3 & 20 \end{array}\right]$$

Pivot as indicated in the simplex tableau in Exercises 13–18. Read the solution from the final result.

13.

$$\begin{array}{ccccc} x_1 & x_2 & x_3 & x_4 & x_5 \\ \end{array}$$
$$\left[\begin{array}{ccccc|c} 1 & 2 & 4 & 1 & 0 & 56 \\ 2 & 2 & 1 & 0 & 1 & 40 \\ \hline -1 & -3 & -2 & 0 & 0 & 0 \end{array}\right]$$

14.

$$\begin{array}{ccccc} x_1 & x_2 & x_3 & x_4 & x_5 \\ \end{array}$$
$$\left[\begin{array}{ccccc|c} 5 & 4 & 1 & 1 & 0 & 50 \\ 3 & 3 & 2 & 0 & 1 & 40 \\ \hline -1 & -2 & -4 & 0 & 0 & 0 \end{array}\right]$$

15.

x_1	x_2	x_3	x_4	x_5	x_6	
2	2	1	1	0	0	12
1	2	3	0	1	0	45
3	1	1	0	0	1	20
−2	−1	−3	0	0	0	0

16.

x_1	x_2	x_3	x_4	x_5	x_6	
4	2	3	1	0	0	22
2	2	5	0	1	0	28
1	3	2	0	0	1	45
−3	−2	−4	0	0	0	0

17.

x_1	x_2	x_3	x_4	x_5	x_6	
1	1	1	1	0	0	60
3	1	2	0	1	0	100
1	2	3	0	0	1	200
−1	−1	−2	0	0	0	0

18.

x_1	x_2	x_3	x_4	x_5	x_6	x_7	
1	2	3	1	1	0	0	115
2	1	8	5	0	1	0	200
1	0	1	0	0	0	1	50
−2	−1	−1	−1	0	0	0	0

Introduce slack variables as necessary and then write the initial simplex tableau for the linear programming problems in Exercises 19–24.

19. Find $x_1 \geq 0$ and $x_2 \geq 0$ such that

$2x_1 + 3x_2 \leq 6$
$4x_1 + x_2 \leq 6$

and $z = 5x_1 + x_2$ is maximized.

20. Find $x_1 \geq 50$ and $x_2 \geq 50$ such that

$2x_1 + 3x_2 \leq 100$
$5x_1 + 4x_2 \leq 200$

and $z = x_1 + 3x_2$ is maximized.

21. Find $x_1 \geq 0$ and $x_2 \geq 0$ such that

$x_1 + x_2 \leq 10$
$5x_1 + 2x_2 \leq 20$
$x_1 + 2x_2 \leq 36$

and $z = x_1 + 3x_2$ is maximized.

22. Find $x_1 \geq 0$ and $x_2 \geq 0$ such that

$x_1 + x_2 \leq 10$
$5x_1 + 3x_2 \leq 75$

and $z = 4x_1 + 2x_2$ is maximized.

23. Find $x_1 \geq 0$ and $x_2 \geq 0$ such that

$3x_1 + x_2 \leq 12$
$x_1 + x_2 \leq 15$

and $z = 2x_1 + x_2$ is maximized.

24. Find $x_1 \geq 0$ and $x_2 \geq 0$ such that

$10x_1 + 4x_2 \leq 100$
$20x_1 + 10x_2 \leq 150$

and $z = 4x_1 + 5x_2$ is maximized.

Set up Exercises 25–30 for solution by the simplex method; that is, express the linear constraints and objective function, add slack variables, and set up the initial simplex tableau.

25. A candy company has 100 kilograms of chocolate-covered nuts and 125 kilograms of chocolate-covered raisins to be sold as two different mixtures. One mix will contain half nuts and half raisins and will sell for $6 per kilogram. The other mix will contain 1/3 nuts and 2/3 raisins, and will sell for $4.80 per kilogram. How many kilograms of each mix should the company prepare for maximum revenue? (This is Exercise 13, Section 3.2.)

26. Seall Manufacturing Company makes color television sets. It produces a bargain set that sells for $100 profit and a deluxe set that sells for $150 profit. On the assembly line the bargain set requires 3 hours' work, while the deluxe set takes 5 hours. The cabinet shop spends one hour on the cabinet for the bargain set and 3 hours on the cabinet for the deluxe set. Both sets require 2 hours of time for testing and packing. On a particular production run the Seall Company has available 3900 work hours on the assembly line, 2100 work hours in the cabinet shop, and 2200 work hours in the testing and packing department. How many sets of each type should it produce to make maximum profit? What is the maximum profit? (See Exercise 10, Section 3.2.)

27. A small boat manufacturer builds three types of fiberglass boats: prams, runabouts, and trimarans. The pram sells at a profit of $75, the runabout at a profit of $90, and the trimaran at a profit of $100. The factory is divided into two sections. Section A does the molding and construction work, while section B does the painting, finishing and equipping. The pram takes 1 hour in section A and 2 hours in section B. The runabout takes 2 hours in A and 5 hours in B. The trimaran takes 3 hours in A and 4 hours in B. Section A has a total of 6240 hours available and section B has 10,800 hours available for the year. The manufacturer has ordered a supply of fiberglass that will build at most 3000 boats, figuring the average amount used per boat. How many of each type of boat should be made to produce maximum profit? What is the maximum profit?

28. Caroline's Quality Candy Confectionery is famous for fudge, chocolate cremes, and pralines. Its candy-making equipment is set up to make 100-pound batches at a time. Currently there is a chocolate shortage and the company can get only 120 pounds of chocolate in the next shipment. On a week's run, the confectionery's cooking and processing equipment is available for a total of 42 machine hours. During the same period the employees have a total of 56 work hours available for packaging. A batch of fudge requires 20 pounds of chocolate while a batch of cremes uses 25 pounds of chocolate. The cooking and processing take 120 minutes for fudge, 150 minutes for chocolate cremes, and 200 minutes for pralines. The packaging times measured in minutes per one pound box are 1, 2, and 3 respectively, for fudge, cremes, and pralines. Determine how many batches of each type of candy the confectionery should make, assuming that the profit per pound box is 50¢ on fudge, 40¢ on chocolate cremes, and 45¢ on pralines. What is the maximum profit?

29. A cat breeder has the following amounts of cat food: 90 units of tuna, 80 units of liver, and 50 units of chicken. To raise a Siamese cat, the breeder must use 2 units of tuna, 1 of liver, and 1 of chicken per day, while raising a Persian cat requires 1, 2, and 1 units respectively per day. If a Siamese cat sells for $12, while a Persian cat sells for $10, how many of each should be raised in order to obtain maximum gross income? What is the maximum gross income?

30. Banal, Inc. produces art for motel rooms. Its painters can turn out mountain scenes, seascapes, and pictures of clowns. Each painting is worked on by three different artists, T, D, and H. Artist T works only 25 hours per week, while D and H work 45 and 40 hours per week, respectively. Artist T spends 1 hour on a mountain scene, 2 hours on a seascape, and 1 hour on a clown. Corresponding times for D and H are 3, 2, and 2 hours, and 2, 1, and 4 hours, respectively. Banal makes $20 on a mountain scene, $18 on a seascape, and $22 from a clown. The head painting packer can't stand clowns, so that no more than 4 clown paintings may be done in a week. Find the number of each type of painting that should be made weekly in order to maximize profit. Find the maximum possible profit.

4.2   Solving Maximization Problems

We have learned how to prepare a linear programming problem for solution by first converting the constraints to linear equations with slack variables. We then wrote the coefficients of the variables from the linear equations as an augmented matrix. Finally, we used the pivot to go from one vertex of the region of feasible solutions to another.

Now we are ready to put all this together and produce an optimum value for the objective function. To see how this is done, let us complete the example about the farmer. (Recall Example 2 from Section 4.1.)

In the previous section we set up the following simplex tableau.

$$
\begin{array}{ccccc}
x_1 & x_2 & x_3 & x_4 & x_5 \\
\end{array}
$$

$$
\left[
\begin{array}{ccccc|c}
1 & 1 & 1 & 1 & 0 & 100 \\
\hline
400 & 160 & 280 & 0 & 1 & 20{,}000 \\
\hline
-120 & -40 & -60 & 0 & 0 & 0
\end{array}
\right]
$$

This tableau leads to the solution $x_1 = 0$, $x_2 = 0$, $x_3 = 0$, $x_4 = 100$, and $x_5 = 20{,}000$. These values produce a value of 0 for z. Since a value of 0 for the farmer's profit is not an optimum, we try to improve this value.

The coefficients of x_1, x_2, and x_3 in the objective function are nonzero, so the profit could be improved by making any one of these variables take on a non-zero value in a solution. To decide which variable to use, look at the indicators in the initial simplex tableau above. The coefficient of x_1, -120, is the "most negative" of the indicators. This means that x_1 has the largest coefficient in the objective function, so that profit is increased the most by increasing x_1.

If x_1 is nonzero in the solution, then x_1 will be a basic variable. This means that either x_4 or x_5 no longer will be a basic variable. To decide which variable will no longer be basic, start with the equations of the system,

$$
\begin{aligned}
x_1 + x_2 + x_3 + x_4 &= 100 \\
400x_1 + 160x_2 + 280x_3 \qquad + x_5 &= 20{,}000.
\end{aligned}
$$

and solve for x_4 and x_5 respectively.

$$
\begin{aligned}
x_4 &= 100 - x_1 - x_2 - x_3 \\
x_5 &= 20{,}000 - 400x_1 - 160x_2 - 280x_3
\end{aligned}
$$

Only x_1 is being changed to a nonzero value; both x_2 and x_3 keep the value 0. Replacing x_2 and x_3 with 0 gives

$$
\begin{aligned}
x_4 &= 100 - x_1 \\
x_5 &= 20{,}000 - 400x_1.
\end{aligned}
$$

Since both x_4 and x_5 must remain nonnegative, there is a limit to how much the value of x_1 can be increased. The equation $x_4 = 100 - x_1$ (or $x_4 = 100 - 1x_1$) shows that x_1 cannot exceed 100/1, or 100. The second equation, $x_5 = 20{,}000 - 400x_1$, shows that x_1 cannot exceed 20,000/400, or 50. To satisfy both these conditions, x_1 cannot exceed 50, the smaller of 50 and 100. If we let x_1 take the value 50, then $x_1 = 50$, $x_2 = 0$, $x_3 = 0$, and $x_5 = 0$. Since $x_4 = 100 - x_1$, then

$$
x_4 = 100 - 50 = 50.
$$

This solution gives a profit of

$$
\begin{aligned}
z &= 120x_1 + 40x_2 + 60x_3 + 0x_4 + 0x_5 \\
&= 120(50) + 40(0) + 60(0) + 0(50) + 0(0) = 6000.
\end{aligned}
$$

The same result could have been found from the initial simplex tableau given above. To use the tableau, select the most negative indicator. (If no indicator is negative, then the value of the objective function cannot be improved.)

$$
\begin{array}{ccccc}
x_1 & x_2 & x_3 & x_4 & x_5 \\
\end{array}
$$

$$
\left[
\begin{array}{ccccc|c}
1 & 1 & 1 & 1 & 0 & 100 \\
400 & 160 & 280 & 0 & 1 & 20{,}000 \\
\hline
-120 & -40 & -60 & 0 & 0 & 0 \\
\end{array}
\right]
$$

↑—most negative indicator

The most negative indicator identifies the variable whose value is to be made nonzero. To find the variable which is now basic and which will become nonbasic, calculate the quotients that were found above. Do this by dividing each number from the right side of the tableau by the corresponding number from the column with the most negative indicator.

Quotients

$$100/1 = 100$$

smaller → $$20{,}000/400 = 50$$

$$
\begin{array}{ccccc}
x_1 & x_2 & x_3 & x_4 & x_5 \\
\end{array}
$$

$$
\left[
\begin{array}{ccccc|c}
1 & 1 & 1 & 1 & 0 & 100 \\
400 & 160 & 280 & 0 & 1 & 20{,}000 \\
\hline
-120 & -40 & -60 & 0 & 0 & 0 \\
\end{array}
\right]
$$

The smaller quotient is 50, from the second row. This identifies 400 as the pivot. Use 400 as pivot, and the appropriate row transformations, to get the second simplex tableau as follows: get 1 in the pivot position by multiplying each element of the second row by 1/400. Then multiply each of the entries in the second row by -1 and add the results to the corresponding entries in the first row, to get a 0 above the pivot. Get a 0 below the pivot, as the first indicator, in a similar way. The new tableau is

$$
\begin{array}{ccccc}
x_1 & x_2 & x_3 & x_4 & x_5 \\
\end{array}
$$

$$
\left[
\begin{array}{ccccc|c}
0 & .6 & .3 & 1 & -.0025 & 50 \\
1 & .4 & .7 & 0 & .0025 & 50 \\
\hline
0 & 8 & 24 & 0 & .3 & 6000 \\
\end{array}
\right]
$$

and the solution read from this tableau is

$$x_1 = 50, \quad x_2 = 0, \quad x_3 = 0, \quad x_4 = 50, \quad x_5 = 0,$$

the same result found above. The entry 6000 (in color) in the lower right corner of the tableau gives the value of the objective function for this solution:

$$z = \$6000.$$

None of the indicators in the final simplex tableau is negative, which means that the value of z cannot be improved beyond $6000. To see why, recall that the last row gives the coefficients of the objective function. Including the coefficient of 1 for the z column which was dropped gives

$$0x_1 + 8x_2 + 24x_3 + 0x_4 + .3x_5 + z = 6000,$$

or $\qquad z = 6000 - 0x_1 - 8x_2 - 24x_3 - 0x_4 - .3x_5.$

Since x_2, x_3, and x_5 are zero, $z = 6000$, but if any of these three variables were to increase, z would decrease.

This result suggests that the optimal solution has been found as soon as no indicators are negative. As long as an indicator is negative, the value of the objective function can be improved. Just find a new pivot and repeat the process until no negative indicators remain.

We can finally state the solution to the problem about the farmer: the optimum value of z is 6000, where $x_1 = 50$, $x_2 = 0$, $x_3 = 0$, $x_4 = 50$, and $x_5 = 0$. That is, the farmer will make a maximum profit of \$6000 by planting 50 acres of potatoes. Another 50 acres should be left unplanted. It may seem strange that leaving assets unused can produce a maximum profit, but such results actually occur often.

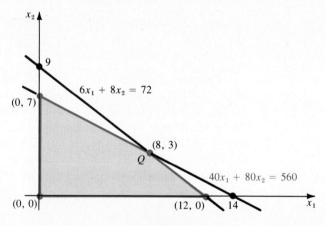

FIGURE 1

EXAMPLE 1

To compare the simplex method with the geometric method, use the simplex method to solve the problem in Example 2, Section 3.2. The graph is shown again in Figure 1. The objective function to be maximized was

$$z = 8x_1 + 12x_2. \qquad \text{(storage space)}$$

(Since we are using the simplex method, we use x_1 and x_2 as variables instead of x and y.) The constraints were as follows:

$$40x_1 + 80x_2 \leq 560 \qquad \text{(cost)}$$
$$6x_1 + 8x_2 \leq 72 \qquad \text{(floor space)}$$
$$x_1 \geq 0, \; x_2 \geq 0.$$

Add a slack variable to each constraint.

$$40x_1 + 80x_2 + x_3 \qquad = 560$$
$$6x_1 + 8x_2 \qquad + x_4 = 72.$$

Write the initial simplex tableau.

$$
\begin{array}{cccc}
x_1 & x_2 & x_3 & x_4 \\
\end{array}
$$
$$
\left[
\begin{array}{cccc|c}
40 & 80 & 1 & 0 & 560 \\
6 & 8 & 0 & 1 & 72 \\
\hline
-8 & -12 & 0 & 0 & 0
\end{array}
\right]
$$

This tableau leads to the solution $x_1 = 0$, $x_2 = 0$, $x_3 = 560$, and $x_4 = 72$, with $z = 0$, which corresponds to the origin in Figure 1. The most negative indicator is -12. The necessary quotients are

$$\frac{560}{80} = 7 \qquad \text{and} \qquad \frac{72}{8} = 9.$$

The smaller quotient is 7, giving 80 as the pivot. Use row transformations to get the new tableau.

$$
\left[
\begin{array}{cccc|c}
\frac{1}{2} & 1 & \frac{1}{80} & 0 & 7 \\
2 & 0 & -\frac{1}{10} & 1 & 16 \\
\hline
-2 & 0 & \frac{3}{20} & 0 & 84
\end{array}
\right]
$$

The solution from this tableau is $x_1 = 0$, $x_2 = 7$, $x_3 = 0$, and $x_4 = 16$, with $z = 84$, which corresponds to the corner point $(0, 7)$ in Figure 1. Because of the indicator -2, the value of z can be improved. Use the 2 in row 2, column 1 as pivot to get the final tableau.

$$
\left[
\begin{array}{cccc|c}
0 & 1 & \frac{3}{80} & -\frac{1}{4} & 3 \\
1 & 0 & -\frac{1}{20} & \frac{1}{2} & 8 \\
\hline
0 & 0 & \frac{1}{20} & 1 & 100
\end{array}
\right]
$$

Here the solution is $x_1 = 8$, $x_2 = 3$, $x_3 = 0$, and $x_4 = 0$, with $z = 100$. This solution, which corresponds to the corner point $(8, 3)$ in Figure 1, is the same as the solution found earlier.

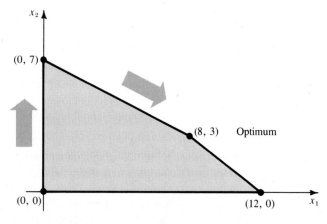

FIGURE 2

As we have seen, each simplex tableau above gave a solution corresponding to one of the corner points of the feasible region. As shown in Figure 2, the first solution corresponded to the origin, with $z = 0$. By choosing the appropriate pivot, we moved systematically to a new corner point, $(0, 7)$, which improved the value of z to 84. The next tableau took us to $(8, 3)$, producing the optimum value of $z = 100$. There was no reason to test the last corner point, $(12, 0)$, since the optimum value of z was found before that point was reached. ◼

The next example shows how to handle zero or a negative number in the column containing the pivot.

EXAMPLE 2

Find the pivot for the following initial simplex tableau.

$$
\begin{array}{ccccc}
x_1 & x_2 & x_3 & x_4 & x_5 \\
\end{array}
$$

$$
\left[
\begin{array}{ccccc|c}
1 & -2 & 1 & 0 & 0 & 100 \\
3 & 4 & 0 & 1 & 0 & 200 \\
5 & 0 & 0 & 0 & 1 & 150 \\
\hline
-10 & -25 & 0 & 0 & 0 & 0 \\
\end{array}
\right]
$$

The most negative indicator is -25. To find the pivot, find the quotients formed by the entries in the right-most column and in the x_2 column: $100/(-2)$, $200/4$, and $150/0$. Since division by 0 is meaningless, disregard the quotient $150/0$, which comes from the equation

$$5x_1 + 0x_2 + 0x_3 + 0x_4 + x_5 = 150.$$

If $x_1 = 0$, the equation reduces to

$$0x_2 + x_5 = 150 \quad \text{or} \quad x_5 = 150 - 0x_2.$$

Since the pivot is in the x_2 column, x_5 cannot be 0. In general, disregard quotients with a 0 denominator.

The quotients predict the value of a variable in the solution, and thus cannot be negative. In this example, the quotient $100/(-2) = -50$ comes from the equation

$$x_1 - 2x_2 + x_3 + 0x_4 + 0x_5 = 100.$$

For $x_1 = 0$, this becomes

$$x_3 = 100 + 2x_2.$$

If x_3 is to be nonnegative, then

$$100 + 2x_2 \geq 0$$

$$x_2 \geq -50.$$

Since x_2 must be nonnegative anyway, this equation tells us nothing new. For this reason, disregard negative quotients also.

The only usable quotient is $200/4 = 50$, making 4 the pivot. If all the quotients are either negative or have zero denominators, no optimum solution will be found. The quotients, then, determine whether or not an optimum solution exists. ◼

Let us now summarize the steps involved in solving a standard maximum linear programming problem by the simplex method.

Simplex Method

1. Determine the objective function.

2. Write all necessary constraints.

3. Convert each constraint into an equation by adding slack variables.

4. Set up the initial simplex tableau.

5. Locate the most negative indicator. If there are two such indicators, choose either.

6. Form the necessary quotients to find the pivot. Disregard any negative quotients or quotients with a 0 denominator. The smallest nonnegative quotient gives the location of the pivot. If all quotients must be disregarded, no maximum solution exists.* If two quotients are equally the smallest, let either determine the pivot.†

7. Transform the tableau so that the pivot becomes 1 and all other numbers in that column become 0.

8. If the indicators are all positive or 0, this is the final tableau. If not, go back to Step 5 above and repeat the process until a tableau with no negative indicators is obtained.

9. Read the solution from this final tableau. The maximum value of the objective function is the number in the lower right corner of the final tableau.

Although linear programming problems with more than a few variables would seem to be very complex, in practical applications many entries in the simplex tableau are zeros.

4.2 EXERCISES

In Exercises 1–6, the initial tableau of a linear programming problem is given. Use the simplex method to solve each problem.

1.

$$\begin{array}{ccccc} x_1 & x_2 & x_3 & x_4 & x_5 \end{array}$$

$$\left[\begin{array}{ccccc|c} 1 & 2 & 4 & 1 & 0 & 8 \\ 2 & 2 & 1 & 0 & 1 & 10 \\ \hline -2 & -5 & -1 & 0 & 0 & 0 \end{array}\right]$$

2.

$$\begin{array}{ccccc} x_1 & x_2 & x_3 & x_4 & x_5 \end{array}$$

$$\left[\begin{array}{ccccc|c} 2 & 2 & 1 & 1 & 0 & 10 \\ 1 & 2 & 3 & 0 & 1 & 15 \\ \hline -3 & -2 & -1 & 0 & 0 & 0 \end{array}\right]$$

*Some special circumstances are noted at the end of Section 4.3.

†It may be that the first choice of a pivot does not produce a solution. In that case, try the other choice.

3.

$$
\begin{array}{ccccc}
x_1 & x_2 & x_3 & x_4 & x_5 \\
\end{array}
$$

$$
\left[
\begin{array}{ccccc|c}
1 & 3 & 1 & 0 & 0 & 12 \\
2 & 1 & 0 & 1 & 0 & 10 \\
1 & 1 & 0 & 0 & 1 & 4 \\
\hline
-2 & -1 & 0 & 0 & 0 & 0 \\
\end{array}
\right]
$$

4.

$$
\begin{array}{cccccc}
x_1 & x_2 & x_3 & x_4 & x_5 & x_6 \\
\end{array}
$$

$$
\left[
\begin{array}{cccccc|c}
2 & 2 & 1 & 1 & 0 & 0 & 50 \\
1 & 1 & 3 & 0 & 1 & 0 & 40 \\
4 & 2 & 5 & 0 & 0 & 1 & 80 \\
\hline
-2 & -3 & -5 & 0 & 0 & 0 & 0 \\
\end{array}
\right]
$$

5.

$$
\begin{array}{cccccc}
x_1 & x_2 & x_3 & x_4 & x_5 & x_6 \\
\end{array}
$$

$$
\left[
\begin{array}{cccccc|c}
2 & 2 & 8 & 1 & 0 & 0 & 40 \\
4 & -5 & 6 & 0 & 1 & 0 & 60 \\
2 & -2 & 6 & 0 & 0 & 1 & 24 \\
\hline
-14 & -10 & -12 & 0 & 0 & 0 & 0 \\
\end{array}
\right]
$$

6.

$$
\begin{array}{ccccc}
x_1 & x_2 & x_3 & x_4 & x_5 \\
\end{array}
$$

$$
\left[
\begin{array}{ccccc|c}
3 & 2 & 4 & 1 & 0 & 18 \\
2 & 1 & 5 & 0 & 1 & 8 \\
\hline
-1 & -4 & -2 & 0 & 0 & 0 \\
\end{array}
\right]
$$

Use the simplex method to solve Exercises 7–14.

7. Maximize $z = 4x_1 + 3x_2$

subject to: $2x_1 + 3x_2 \leq 11$
$x_1 + 2x_2 \leq 6$,

and $x_1 \geq 0$, $x_2 \geq 0$

8. Maximize $z = 2x_1 + 3x_2$

subject to: $3x_1 + 5x_2 \leq 29$
$2x_1 + x_2 \leq 10$,

and $x_1 \geq 0$, $x_2 \geq 0$

9. Maximize $z = 10x_1 + 12x_2$

subject to: $4x_1 + 2x_2 \leq 20$
$5x_1 + x_2 \leq 50$
$2x_1 + 2x_2 \leq 24$

and $x_1 \geq 0$, $x_2 \geq 0$.

10. Maximize $z = 1.2x_1 + 3.5x_2$

subject to: $2.4x_1 + 1.5x_2 \leq 10$
$1.7x_1 + 1.9x_2 \leq 15$

and $x_1 \geq 0$, $x_2 \geq 0$.

11. Maximize $z = 8x_1 + 3x_2 + x_3$

subject to: $x_1 + 6x_2 + 8x_3 \leq 118$
$x_1 + 5x_2 + 10x_3 \leq 220$

and $x_1 \geq 0$, $x_2 \geq 0$, $x_3 \geq 0$.

12. Maximize $z = 12x_1 + 15x_2 + 5x_3$

subject to: $2x_1 + 2x_2 + x_3 \leq 8$
$x_1 + 4x_2 + 3x_3 \leq 12$

and $x_1 \geq 0$, $x_2 \geq 0$, $x_3 \geq 0$.

13. Maximize $z = x_1 + 2x_2 + x_3 + 5x_4$

subject to: $x_1 + 2x_2 + x_3 + x_4 \leq 50$
$3x_1 + x_2 + 2x_3 + x_4 \leq 100$

and $x_1 \geq 0$, $x_2 \geq 0$, $x_3 \geq 0$, $x_4 \geq 0$.

14. Maximize $z = x_1 + x_2 + 4x_3 + 5x_4$

subject to: $x_1 + 2x_2 + 3x_3 + x_4 \leq 115$
$2x_1 + x_2 + 8x_3 + 5x_4 \leq 200$
$x_1 + x_3 \leq 50$

and $x_1 \geq 0$, $x_2 \geq 0$, $x_3 \geq 0$, $x_4 \geq 0$.

Set up and solve Exercises 15–20 by the simplex method.

15. A biologist has 500 kilograms of nutrient A, 600 kilograms of nutrient B, and 300 kilograms of nutrient C. These nutrients will be used to make 4 types of food, whose contents (in percent of nutrient per kilogram of food) and whose "growth values" are as shown below.

Food	Nutrient (%)			Growth value
	A	B	C	
P	0	0	100	90
Q	0	75	25	70
R	37.5	50	12.5	60
S	62.5	37.5	0	50

How many kilograms of each food should be produced in order to maximize total growth value? Find the maximum growth value.

16. A baker has 150 units of flour, 90 units of sugar, and 150 of raisins. A loaf of raisin bread requires 1 unit of flour, 1 of sugar and 2 of raisins, while a raisin cake needs 5, 2, and 1 units, respectively. If raisin bread sells for 35¢ a loaf and raisin cake for 80¢ each, how many of each should be baked so that gross income is maximized? What is the maximum gross income?

17. A candy company has 100 kilograms of chocolate-covered nuts and 125 kilograms of chocolate-covered raisins to be sold as two different mixtures. One mix will contain half nuts and half raisins and will sell for $6 per kilogram. The other mix will contain 1/3 nuts and 2/3 raisins, and will sell for $4.80 per kilogram. How many kilograms of each mix should the company prepare for maximum revenue? (See Exercise 25, Section 4.1.) Find the maximum revenue.

18. Caroline's Quality Candy Confectionery is famous for fudge, chocolate cremes, and pralines. Its candy-making equipment is set up to make 100-pound batches at a time. Currently there is a chocolate shortage and the company can get only 120 pounds of chocolate in the next shipment. On a week's run, the confectionery's cooking and processing equipment is available for a total of 42 machine hours. During the same period the employees have a total of 56 work hours available for packaging. A batch of fudge requires 20 pounds of chocolate while a batch of cremes uses 25 pounds of chocolate. The cooking and processing take 120 minutes for fudge, 150 minutes for chocolate cremes, and 200 minutes for pralines. The packaging times measured in minutes per one pound box are 1, 2, and 3, respectively for fudge, cremes and pralines. Determine how many batches of each type of candy the confectionery should make, assuming that the profit per pound box is 50¢ on fudge, 40¢ on chocolate cremes, and 45¢ on pralines. Also, find the maximum profit for the week. (See Exercise 28, Section 4.1.)

19. A manufacturer of bicycles builds one-, three-, and ten-speed models. The bicycles need both aluminum and steel. The company has available 91,800 units of steel and 42,000 units of aluminum. The one-, three-, and ten-speed models need respectively 17, 27, and 34 units of steel, and 12, 21, and 15 units of aluminum. How many of each type of bicycle should be made in order to maximize profit if the company makes $8 per one-speed bike, $12 per three-speed, and $22 per ten-speed? What is the maximum possible profit?

20. A political party is planning a half-hour television show. The show will have 3 minutes of direct requests for money from viewers. Three of the party's politicians will be on the show—a senator, a congresswoman, and a governor. The senator, a party "elder statesman," demands that he be on at least twice as long as the governor. The total time taken by the senator and the governor must be at least twice the time taken by the congresswoman. Based on a pre-show survey, it is believed that 40, 60, and 50 (in thousands) viewers will watch the program for each minute the senator, congresswoman, and governor, respectively are on the air. Find the time that should be alloted to each politician in order to get the maximum number of viewers. Find the maximum number of viewers.

The next two problems come from past CPA examinations.* Select the appropriate answer for each question.

---

21. The Ball Company manufactures three types of lamps, labeled A, B, and C. Each lamp is processed in two departments, I and II. Total available man-hours per day for departments I and II are 400 and 600, respectively. No additional labor is available. Time requirements and profit per unit for each lamp type is as follows:

	A	B	C
Man-hours in I	2	3	1
Man-hours in II	4	2	3
Profit per unit	$5	$4	$3

The company has assigned you as the accounting member of its profit planning committee to determine the numbers of types of A, B, and C lamps that it should produce in order to maximize its total profit from the sale of lamps. The following questions relate to a linear programming model that your group has developed.

(a) The coefficients of the objective function would be
- **(1)** 4, 2, 3.   **(2)** 2, 3, 1.
- **(3)** 5, 4, 3.   **(4)** 400, 600.

(b) The constraints in the model would be
- **(1)** 2, 3, 1.   **(2)** 5, 4, 3.
- **(3)** 4, 2, 3.   **(4)** 400, 600.

(c) The constraint imposed by the available man-hours in department 1 could be expressed as
- **(1)** $4X_1 + 2X_2 + 3X_3 \leq 400.$ **(2)** $4X_1 + 2X_2 + 3X_3 \geq 400.$
- **(3)** $2X_1 + 3X_2 + 1X_3 \leq 400.$ **(4)** $2X_1 + 3X_2 + 1X_3 \geq 400.$

22. The Golden Hawk Manufacturing Company wants to maximize the profits on products A, B, and C. The contribution margin for each product follows:

Product	Contribution margin
A	$2
B	$5
C	$4

The production requirements and departmental capacities, by departments, are as follows:

Department	Production requirements by product (hours)			Departmental capacity (total hours)
	A	B	C	
Assembling	2	3	2	30,000
Painting	1	2	2	38,000
Finishing	2	3	1	28,000

(a) What is the profit-maximization formula for the Golden Hawk Company?
- **(1)** $2A + $5B + $4C = X (where X = profit)   **(2)** 5A + 8B + 5C ≤ 96,000
- **(3)** $2A + $5B + $4C ≤ X   **(4)** $2A + $5B + $4C = 96,000

(b) What is the constraint for the Painting Department of the Golden Hawk Company?

    (1) $1A + 2B + 2C \geq 38{,}000$ **(2)** $\$2A + \$5B + \$4C \geq 38{,}000$

    (3) $1A + 2B + 2C \leq 38{,}000$ **(4)** $2A + 3B + 2C \leq 30{,}000$

Determine the constraints and the objective function for Exercises 23 and 24, then solve each problem.

23. A manufacturer makes two products, toy trucks and toy fire engines. Both are processed in four different departments, each of which has a limited capacity. The sheet metal department can handle at least $1\frac{1}{2}$ times as many trucks as fire engines. The truck assembly department can handle at most 6700 trucks per week, while the fire engine assembly department assembles at most 5500 fire engines weekly. The painting department, which finishes both toys, has a maximum capacity of 12,000 per week. If the profit is $8.50 for a toy truck and $12.10 for a toy fire engine, how many of each item should the company produce to maximize profit?

24. The average weights of the three species stocked in the lake referred to in Section 2.2, Exercise 51 are 1.62, 2.14, and 3.01 kilograms for species A, B, and C, respectively. If the largest amounts of food that can be supplied each day are given as in Exercise 51, how should the lake be stocked to maximize the weight of the fish supported by the lake?

4.3 Mixed Constraints

So far we have used the simplex method only to solve standard maximum linear programming problems. In this section we extend this work to include linear programming problems with mixed $\leq$ and $\geq$ constraints. Then we see how solving these problems gives a method of solving minimum problems. (An alternate approach to minimum problems is given in the next section.)

Problems with $\leq$ and $\geq$ Constraints   Suppose a new constraint is added to the farmer problem from Example 2 of Section 4.1: to satisfy orders from regular buyers, the farmer must plant a total of at least 60 acres of the three crops. This constraint introduces the new inequality

$$x_1 + x_2 + x_3 \geq 60.$$

As before, this inequality must be rewritten as an equation in which the variables all represent nonnegative numbers. The inequality $x_1 + x_2 + x_3 \geq 60$ means that

$$x_1 + x_2 + x_3 - x_6 = 60$$

for some nonnegative variable x_6. (Remember that x_4 and x_5 are the slack variables in the problem.)

The new variable, x_6, is called a **surplus variable.** The value of this variable represents the excess number of acres (over 60) which may be planted. Since the total number of acres planted is to be no more than 100 but at least 60, the value of x_6 can vary from 0 to 40.

We must now solve the system of equations

$$
\begin{aligned}
x_1 + \quad x_2 + \quad x_3 + x_4 \qquad\qquad\qquad &= \quad 100 \\
400x_1 + 160x_2 + 280x_3 \qquad\quad + x_5 \qquad\qquad &= \quad 20{,}000 \\
x_1 + \quad x_2 + \quad x_3 \qquad\qquad - x_6 \qquad &= \quad 60 \\
-120x_1 - \quad 40x_2 - \quad 60x_3 \qquad\qquad\qquad + z &= \quad 0
\end{aligned}
$$

with x_1, x_2, x_3, x_4, x_5, and x_6 all nonnegative.

Set up the initial simplex tableau. (The z column is omitted as before.)

$$
\begin{array}{cccccc}
x_1 & x_2 & x_3 & x_4 & x_5 & x_6 \\
\end{array}
$$

$$
\left[
\begin{array}{cccccc|c}
1 & 1 & 1 & 1 & 0 & 0 & 100 \\
400 & 160 & 280 & 0 & 1 & 0 & 20{,}000 \\
1 & 1 & 1 & 0 & 0 & -1 & 60 \\
\hline
-120 & -40 & -60 & 0 & 0 & 0 & 0
\end{array}
\right]
$$

This tableau gives the solution

$$
x_1 = 0, \quad x_2 = 0, \quad x_3 = 0, \quad x_4 = 100, \quad x_5 = 20{,}000, \quad x_6 = -60.
$$

But this is not a feasible solution, since x_6 is negative. All the variables in any feasible solution must be nonnegative.

When a negative value of a variable appears, use row operations to transform the matrix until a solution is found in which all variables are nonnegative. The difficulty is caused by the -1 in row three of the matrix. We do not have the third column of the usual 3×3 identity matrix. To get around this, use row transformations to change a column that has nonzero entries (such as the x_1, x_2, or x_3 columns) to one in which the third row entry is 1 and the other entries are 0. The choice of a column is arbitrary. Let's choose the x_2 column and if this choice does not lead to a feasible solution, try one of the other columns.

The third row entry in the x_2 column is already 1. Using row transformations to get 0's in the rest of the column gives the following tableau.

$$
\begin{array}{cccccc}
x_1 & x_2 & x_3 & x_4 & x_5 & x_6 \\
\end{array}
$$

$$
\left[
\begin{array}{cccccc|c}
0 & 0 & 0 & 1 & 0 & 1 & 40 \\
240 & 0 & 120 & 0 & 1 & 160 & 10{,}400 \\
1 & 1 & 1 & 0 & 0 & -1 & 60 \\
\hline
-80 & 0 & -20 & 0 & 0 & -40 & 2400
\end{array}
\right]
$$

This tableau gives the solution

$$
x_1 = 0, \quad x_2 = 60, \quad x_3 = 0, \quad x_4 = 40, \quad x_5 = 10{,}400, \quad \text{and} \quad x_6 = 0,
$$

which is feasible. The process of applying row transformations to get a feasible solution is called *phase I* of the solution. In *phase II*, the simplex method is applied as usual. The pivot is 240:

$$
\begin{array}{cccccc}
x_1 & x_2 & x_3 & x_4 & x_5 & x_6 \\
\end{array}
$$

$$
\left[
\begin{array}{cccccc|c}
0 & 0 & 0 & 1 & 0 & 1 & 40 \\
240 & 0 & 120 & 0 & 1 & 160 & 10{,}400 \\
\hline
1 & 1 & 1 & 0 & 0 & -1 & 60 \\
-80 & 0 & -20 & 0 & 0 & -40 & 2400 \\
\end{array}
\right]
$$

$$
\begin{array}{cccccc}
x_1 & x_2 & x_3 & x_4 & x_5 & x_6 \\
\end{array}
$$

$$
\left[
\begin{array}{cccccc|c}
0 & 0 & 0 & 1 & 0 & 1 & 40 \\
1 & 0 & .5 & 0 & .004 & .667 & 43.3 \\
\hline
0 & 1 & .5 & 0 & -.004 & -1.667 & 16.7 \\
0 & 0 & 20 & 0 & .32 & 13.4 & 5864 \\
\end{array}
\right]
\quad \text{(rounded)}
$$

The second matrix above has been obtained from the first by standard row operations; some numbers in it have been rounded.

This final tableau gives

$$
x_1 = 43.3, \quad x_2 = 16.7, \quad x_3 = 0, \quad x_4 = 40, \quad x_5 = 0, \quad \text{and} \quad x_6 = 0.
$$

For maximum profit with this new constraint, the farmer should plant 43.3 acres of potatoes, 16.7 acres of corn, and no cabbage. Forty acres of the 100 available should not be planted. The profit will be \$5864, less than the \$6000 profit if he planted only 50 acres of potatoes. Because of the additional constraint that at least 60 acres must be planted, the profit is reduced.

EXAMPLE 1

Maximize $\quad z = 10x_1 + 8x_2$

subject to: $\quad 4x_1 + 4x_2 \geq 60$

$$
2x_1 + 5x_2 \leq 120
$$

and $x_1 \geq 0, \ x_2 \geq 0$.

Add slack or surplus variables to the contraints as needed to get the system

$$
\begin{aligned}
4x_1 + 4x_2 - x_3 & &= 60 \\
2x_1 + 5x_2 &+ x_4 &= 120 \\
-10x_1 - 8x_2 & + z &= 0.
\end{aligned}
$$

Now write the first simplex tableau.

$$
\begin{array}{cccc}
x_1 & x_2 & x_3 & x_4 \\
\end{array}
$$

$$
\left[
\begin{array}{cccc|c}
4 & 4 & -1 & 0 & 60 \\
2 & 5 & 0 & 1 & 120 \\
\hline
-10 & -8 & 0 & 0 & 0 \\
\end{array}
\right]
$$

The solution here,

$$
x_1 = 0, \quad x_2 = 0, \quad x_3 = -60, \quad \text{and} \quad x_4 = 120,
$$

is not feasible, because of the -60. In phase I, use row transformations to modify the tableau to produce a feasible solution. We need a column with 1 in the first row and 0's in the rest of the rows. Let us choose the x_1 column. Multiply the entries in the first row by 1/4 to get 1 in the top row of the column. Then use row transformations to get 0's in the other rows of that column.

$$
\begin{array}{cccc}
x_1 & x_2 & x_3 & x_4 \\
\end{array}
$$

$$
\left[
\begin{array}{cccc|c}
1 & 1 & -\frac{1}{4} & 0 & 15 \\
0 & 3 & \frac{1}{2} & 1 & 90 \\
\hline
0 & 2 & -\frac{5}{2} & 0 & 150
\end{array}
\right]
$$

This solution,

$$x_1 = 15, \quad x_2 = 0, \quad x_3 = 0, \quad \text{and} \quad x_4 = 90,$$

is feasible, so phase I is complete. Perform phase II by completing the solution in the usual way. The pivot is 1/2. The next tableau is

$$
\begin{array}{cccc}
x_1 & x_2 & x_3 & x_4 \\
\end{array}
$$

$$
\left[
\begin{array}{cccc|c}
1 & \frac{5}{2} & 0 & \frac{1}{2} & 60 \\
0 & 6 & 1 & 2 & 180 \\
\hline
0 & 17 & 0 & 5 & 600
\end{array}
\right].
$$

No indicators are negative, so we have found the optimum value of the objective function:

$$z = 600 \quad \text{when } x_1 = 60 \quad \text{and} \quad x_2 = 0. \quad \blacksquare$$

The approach discussed above is used to solve problems where the constraints are mixed $\leq$ and $\geq$ inequalities. The method also can be used to solve a problem where the constant term is negative. (This is not likely to happen in an application, however.)

Minimization Problems   We defined a standard maximum linear programming problem earlier in this chapter. Now we can define a **standard minimum linear programming problem:**

Standard Minimum Form	A linear programming problem is in **standard minimum form** if

A linear programming problem is in **standard minimum form** if
1. the objective function is to be minimized;
2. all variables are nonnegative;
3. all constraints involve $\geq$;
4. the constants in the constraints are all nonnegative.

The difference between maximum and minimum problems is in conditions 1 and 3: in standard minimum problems the objective function is to be *minimized*, and all constraints must have $\geq$ instead of $\leq$.

Standard minimum problems can be solved with the method of surplus variables presented above. To solve a minimum problem, first observe that the minimum of an objective function is the same number as the *maximum* of the *negative* of the function, as suggested by Figure 3.

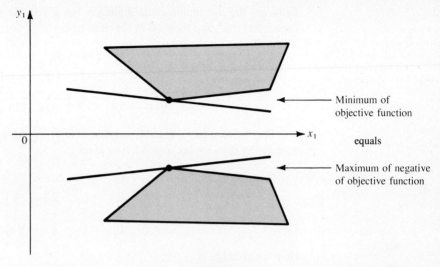

FIGURE 3

The next example illustrates this process. We use y_1 and y_2 as variables, and w for the objective function as a reminder that this is a minimum problem.

EXAMPLE 2

Minimize $w = 3y_1 + 2y_2$

subject to: $y_1 + 3y_2 \geq 6$
                $2y_1 + y_2 \geq 3$

and $y_1 \geq 0, \quad y_2 \geq 0$.

Change this to a maximization problem by letting z equal the *negative* of the objective function: $z = -w$. Then find the *maximum* value of z.

$$z = -w = -3y_1 - 2y_2$$

The problem can now be stated as follows.

maximize $z = -3y_1 - 2y_2$

subject to: $y_1 + 3y_2 \geq 6$
                $2y_1 + y_2 \geq 3$

and $y_1 \geq 0, \ y_2 \geq 0$.

For phase I of the solution, add surplus variables and set up the first tableau.

$$\begin{array}{cccc}
y_1 & y_2 & y_3 & y_4 \\
\end{array}$$
$$\left[\begin{array}{cccc|c}
1 & 3 & -1 & 0 & 6 \\
2 & 1 & 0 & -1 & 3 \\
\hline
3 & 2 & 0 & 0 & 0
\end{array}\right]$$

The solution, $y_1 = 0$, $y_2 = 0$, $y_3 = -6$, and $y_4 = -3$, contains negative numbers. Row transformations must be used to get a tableau with a feasible solution.

Let's use the y_1 column since it already has a 1 in the first row. First, get a 0 in the second row, and then a 0 in the third row.

$$
\begin{array}{cccc}
y_1 & y_2 & y_3 & y_4
\end{array}
$$

$$
\begin{bmatrix}
1 & 3 & -1 & 0 & | & 6 \\
0 & -5 & 2 & -1 & | & -9 \\
0 & -7 & 3 & 0 & | & -18
\end{bmatrix}
$$

This tableau has a feasible solution. Now, in phase II, complete the solution as usual by the simplex method. The pivot is -5.

$$
\begin{array}{cccc}
y_1 & y_2 & y_3 & y_4
\end{array}
$$

$$
\begin{bmatrix}
1 & 0 & \frac{1}{5} & -\frac{3}{5} & | & \frac{3}{5} \\
0 & 1 & -\frac{2}{5} & \frac{1}{5} & | & \frac{9}{5} \\
0 & 0 & \frac{1}{5} & \frac{7}{5} & | & -\frac{27}{5}
\end{bmatrix}
$$

Here the solution is

$$
y_1 = \frac{3}{5}, \quad y_2 = \frac{9}{5}, \quad y_3 = 0, \quad \text{and } y_4 = 0.
$$

This solution is feasible, and the tableau has no negative indicators. Since $z = -27/5$ and $z = -w$, then $w = 27/5$ is the minimum value, which is obtained when $y_1 = 3/5$ and $y_2 = 9/5$. ▪

Let us summarize the steps involved in the phase I and phase II method used to solve nonstandard problems in this section.

Solving Nonstandard Problems	
	1. If necessary, convert the problem to a maximum problem.
	2. Add slack variables and subtract surplus variables as needed.
	3. Write the initial simplex tableau.
	4. If the solution from this tableau is not feasible, use row transformations to get a feasible solution (phase I).
	5. After a feasible solution is reached, solve by the simplex method (phase II).

We certainly have not covered all the possible complications that can arise in using the simplex method. Some of the difficulties include the following:

1. Some of the constraints may be *equations* instead of inequalities. In this case, *artificial variables* must be used.
2. Occasionally, a transformation will cycle—that is, produce a "new" solution which was an earlier solution in the process. These situations are known as *degeneracies* and special methods are available for handling them.
3. It may not be possible to convert a nonfeasible basic solution to a feasible basic solution. In that case, no solution can satisfy all the constraints. Graphically, this means there is no region of feasible solutions.

(These difficulties are covered in more detail in advanced texts. One example of a text that you might find helpful is *An Introduction to Management Science*, Third Edition, by David R. Anderson, Dennis J. Sweeney, and Thomas A. Williams, 1982, West Publishing Company.)

Two linear programming models in actual use, one on making ice cream, the other on merit pay, are presented at the end of this chapter. These models illustrate the usefulness of linear programming. In most real applications, the number of variables is so large that these problems could not be solved without the use of a method, like the simplex method, which can be adapted to a computer.

4.3 EXERCISES

Rewrite each system of inequalities, adding slack variables or subtracting surplus variables as necessary.

1. $2x_1 + 3x_2 \le 8$
$x_1 + 4x_2 \ge 7$

2. $5x_1 + 8x_2 \le 10$
$6x_1 + 2x_2 \ge 7$

3. $x_1 + x_2 + x_3 \le 100$
$x_1 + x_2 + x_3 \ge 75$
$x_1 + x_2 \quad\ \ge 27$

4. $2x_1 \quad\ + x_3 \le 40$
$x_1 + x_2 \quad\ \ge 18$
$x_1 \quad\ + x_3 \ge 20$

Convert Exercises 5–8 into maximization problems.

5. Minimize $w = 4x_1 + 3x_2 + 2x_3$
subject to: $x_1 + x_2 +\ x_3 \ge 5$
$x_1 + x_2 \quad\ \ge 4$
$2x_1 + x_2 + 3x_3 \ge 15$
and $x_1 \ge 0,\ x_2 \ge 0,\ x_3 \ge 0$.

6. Minimize $w = 8x_1 + 3x_2 + x_3$
subject to: $7x_1 + 6x_2 +\ 8x_3 \ge 18$
$4x_1 + 5x_2 + 10x_3 \ge 20$
and $x_1 \ge 0,\ x_2 \ge 0,\ x_3 \ge 0$.

7. Minimize $w = x_1 + 2x_2 + x_3 + 5x_4$
subject to: $x_1 + x_2 +\ x_3 + x_4 \ge 50$
$3x_1 + x_2 + 2x_3 + x_4 \ge 100$
and $x_1 \ge 0,\ x_2 \ge 0,\ x_3 \ge 0,\ x_4 \ge 0$.

8. Minimize $w = x_1 + x_2 + 4x_3$
subject to: $x_1 + 2x_2 + 3x_3 \ge 115$
$2x_1 +\ x_2 +\ x_3 \le 200$
$x_1 \quad\ + x_3 \ge 50$
and $x_1 \ge 0,\ x_2 \ge 0,\ x_3 \ge 0$.

Use the simplex method to solve Exercises 9–14.

9. Find $x_1 \ge 0$ and $x_2 \ge 0$ such that
$x_1 + 2x_2 \ge 24$
$x_1 +\ x_2 \le 40$
and $z = 12x_1 + 10x_2$ is maximized.

10. Find $x_1 \ge 0$ and $x_2 \ge 0$ such that
$3x_1 + 4x_2 \ge 48$
$2x_1 + 4x_2 \le 60$
and $z = 6x_1 + 8x_2$ is maximized.

11. Find $x_1 \ge 0$, $x_2 \ge 0$, and $x_3 \ge 0$ such that
$x_1 + x_2 + x_3 \le 150$
$x_1 + x_2 + x_3 \ge 100$
and $z = 2x_1 + 5x_2 + 3x_3$ is maximized.

12. Find $x_1 \ge 0$, $x_2 \ge 0$, and $x_3 \ge 0$ such that
$x_1 + x_2 + 2x_3 \le 38$
$2x_1 + x_2 +\ x_3 \ge 24$
and $z = 3x_1 + 2x_2 + 2x_3$ is maximized.

13. Find $x_1 \geq 0$ and $x_2 \geq 0$ such that

$$x_1 + x_2 \leq 100$$
$$x_1 + x_2 \geq 50$$
$$2x_1 + x_2 \leq 110$$

and $z = 2x_1 + 3x_2$ is maximized.

14. Find $x_1 \geq 0$ and $x_2 \geq 0$ such that

$$x_1 + 2x_2 \leq 18$$
$$x_1 + 3x_2 \geq 12$$
$$2x_1 + 2x_2 \leq 24$$

and $z = 5x_1 + 10x_2$ is maximized.

Solve each of the following by the two-phase method.

15. Find $y_1 \geq 0$, $y_2 \geq 0$ such that

$$10y_1 + 5y_2 \geq 100$$
$$20y_1 + 10y_2 \geq 150$$

and $w = 4y_1 + 5y_2$ is minimized.

16. Minimize $w = 3y_1 + 2y_2$ subject to

$$2y_1 + 3y_2 \geq 60$$
$$y_1 + 4y_2 \geq 40$$

and $y_1 \geq 0$, $y_2 \geq 0$.

17. Minimize $w = 2y_1 + y_2 + 3y_3$ subject to

$$y_1 + y_2 + y_3 \geq 100$$
$$2y_1 + y_2 \qquad \geq 50$$

and $y_1 \geq 0$, $y_2 \geq 0$, $y_3 \geq 0$.

18. Minimize $w = 3y_1 + 2y_2$ subject to

$$y_1 + 2y_2 \geq 10$$
$$y_1 + y_2 \geq 8$$
$$2y_1 + y_2 \geq 12$$

and $y_1 \geq 0$, $y_2 \geq 0$.

Use the simplex method to solve Exercises 19–25.

19. Brand X Canners produce canned whole tomatoes and tomato sauce. This season, they have available 3,000,000 kilograms of tomatoes for these two products. To meet the demands of regular customers, they must produce at least 80,000 kilograms of sauce and 800,000 kilograms of whole tomatoes. The cost per kilogram is $4 to produce canned whole tomatoes and $3.25 to produce tomato sauce. How many kilograms of tomatoes should they use for each product to minimize cost?

20. Sam, who is dieting, requires two food supplements, I and II. He can get these supplements from two different products, A and B, as shown in the table.

Supplement
(grams per serving)

		I	II
Product	A	3	2
	B	2	4

Sam's physician has recommended that he include at least 15 grams of each supplement in his daily diet. If product A costs 25¢ per serving and product B costs 40¢ per serving, how can he satisfy his requirements most economically? Find the minimum cost. (See Exercise 15, Section 3.2.)

21. Mark, who is ill, takes vitamin pills. Each day he must have at least 16 units of vitamin A, 5 units of vitamin B_1, and 20 units of vitamin C. He can choose between pill #1 which costs 10 cents and contains 8 units of A, 1 of B_1, and 2 of C, and pill #2 which costs 20 cents and contains 2 units of A, 1 of B_1, and 7 of C. How many of each pill should he buy in order to minimize his cost? (See Exercise 8, Section 3.2.)

22. A brewery produces regular beer and a lower-carbohydrate "light" beer. Steady customers of the brewery buy 12 units of regular beer and 10 units of light beer. While setting up the brewery to produce the beers, the management decides to produce extra beer, beyond that needed to satisfy the steady customers. The cost per unit of regular beer is $36,000 and the cost per unit of light beer is $48,000. The number of units of light beer should not exceed twice the number of units of regular beer. At least twenty additional units of beer can be sold. How much of each type beer should be made so as to minimize total production costs?

23. The chemistry department at a local college decides to stock at least 800 small test tubes and 500 large test tubes. It wants to buy at least 1500 test tubes to take advantage of a special price. Since the small tubes are broken twice as often as the larger, the department will order at least twice as many small tubes as large. If the small test tubes cost 15¢ each and the large ones, made of a cheaper glass, cost 12¢ each, how many of each size should they order to minimize cost?

24. Topgrade Turf lawn seed mixtures contain three types of seeds: bluegrass, rye, and bermuda. The costs per pound of the three types of seed are 20¢, 15¢, and 5¢. In each mixture there must be at least 20% bluegrass seed and the amount of bermuda must be no more than the amount of rye. To fill current orders, the company must make at least 5000 pounds of the mixture. How much of each kind of seed should be used to minimize cost?

25. A biologist must make a nutrient for her algae. The nutrient must contain the three basic elements D, E, and F, and must contain at least 10 kilograms of D, 12 kilograms of E, and 20 kilograms of F. The nutrient is made from three ingredients, I, II, and III. The quantity of D, E, and F in one unit of each of the ingredients is as given in the following chart.

One unit of ingredient	Contains the following elements in kilograms			Cost of one unit of ingredient
	D	E	F	
I	4	3	0	4
II	1	2	4	7
III	10	1	5	5

How many units of each ingredient are required to meet her needs at minimum cost?

Determine the constraints and the objective function for Exercises 26 and 27, then solve each problem.

26. Natural Brand plant food is made from three chemicals. (See Section 2.2, Exercise 49.) In a batch of the plant food there must be at least 81 kilograms of the first chemical and the other two chemicals must be in the ratio of 4 to 3. If the three chemicals cost $1.09, $.87, and $.65 per kilogram, respectively, how much of each should be used to minimize the cost of producing at least 750 kilograms of the plant food?

27. A company is developing a new additive for gasoline. The additive is a mixture of three liquid ingredients, I, II, and III. For proper performance, the total amount of additive must be at least 10 ounces per gallon of gasoline. However, for safety reasons, the amount of additive should not exceed 15 ounces per gallon of gasoline. At least 1/4 ounce of ingredient I must be used for every ounce of ingredient II and at least 1 ounce of ingredient III must be used for every ounce of ingredient I. If the cost of I, II, and III is $.30, $.09, and $.27 per ounce, respectively, find the mixture of the three ingredients which produces the minimum cost of the additive. How much of the additive should be used per gallon of gasoline?

Solve the following linear programming problem, which has both "greater than" and "less than" constraints.

28. A popular soft drink called Sugarlo, which is advertised as having a sugar content of no more than 10%, is blended from five ingredients, each of which has some sugar content. Water may also be added to dilute the mixture. The sugar content of the ingredients and their costs per gallon are given below.

	Ingredient					
	1	2	3	4	5	Water
Sugar content (%)	.28	.19	.43	.57	.22	0
Cost ($/gal.)	.48	.32	.53	.28	.43	.04

At least .01 of the content of Sugarlo must come from ingredients 3 or 4, .01 must come from ingredients 2 or 5, and .01 from ingredients 1 or 4. How much of each ingredient should be used in preparing 15,000 gallons of Sugarlo to minimize the cost?

4.4   Duality (Optional)

An interesting connection exists between standard maximum and standard minimum problems. It turns out that any solution of a standard maximum problem produces the solution of an associated standard minimum problem, and vice-versa. Each of these associated problems is called the **dual** of the other. One advantage of duals is that standard minimum problems can be solved by the simplex methods already discussed. Let us explain the idea of a dual with an example. (This is similar to Example 2 of the previous section; compare this method of solution with the one given there.)

EXAMPLE 1

Minimize $w = 8y_1 + 16y_2$
subject to: $y_1 + 5y_2 \geq 9$
                     $2y_1 + 2y_2 \geq 10$
and $y_1 \geq 0,$ $y_2 \geq 0.$

(As mentioned earlier, we use y_1 and y_2 as variables and w as the objective function as a reminder that this is a minimum problem.) Without considering slack variables just yet, write the augmented matrix of the system of inequalities, and include the coefficients of the objective function (not their negatives) as the last row in the matrix.

$$\begin{bmatrix} 1 & 5 & 9 \\ 2 & 2 & 10 \\ 8 & 16 & 0 \end{bmatrix}$$

Look now at the following new matrix, obtained from the one above by interchanging rows and columns.

$$\begin{bmatrix} 1 & 2 & 8 \\ 5 & 2 & 16 \\ 9 & 10 & 0 \end{bmatrix}$$

The *rows* of the first matrix (for the minimizing problem) are the *columns* of the second matrix.

The entries in this second matrix could be used to write the following standard maximum linear programming problem (again ignoring the fact that the numbers in the last row are not negative):

$$\text{maximize} \qquad z = 9x_1 + 10x_2$$
$$\text{subject to:} \qquad x_1 + 2x_2 \le 8$$
$$5x_1 + 2x_2 \le 16$$

with all variables nonnegative.

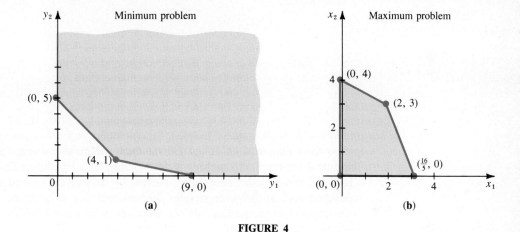

(a) **(b)**

FIGURE 4

Figure 4(a) shows the graphical solution to the minimum problem given above, while Figure 4(b) shows the solution of the maximum problem produced by exchanging rows and columns.

Corner point	$w = 8y_1 + 16y_2$		*Corner point*	$z = 9x_1 + 10x_2$	
(0, 5)	80		(0, 0)	0	
(4, 1)	**48**	minimum	(0, 4)	40	
(9, 0)	72		**(2, 3)**	**48**	maximum
			$(\frac{16}{5}, 0)$	28.8	

The minimum is 48 when $\qquad$ The maximum is 48 when
$$y_1 = 4, \ y_2 = 1. \qquad\qquad x_1 = 2, \ x_2 = 3$$

The two feasible regions in Figure 4 are different and the corner points are different, but the values of the objective functions are equal—both are 48. An even closer connection between the two problems is shown by using the simplex method to solve the maximum problem given above.

Maximum Problem

$$
\begin{array}{cccc}
x_1 & x_2 & x_3 & x_4 \\
\end{array}
$$

$$
\left[\begin{array}{cccc|c}
1 & 2 & 1 & 0 & 8 \\
5 & 2 & 0 & 1 & 16 \\
\hline
-9 & -10 & 0 & 0 & 0
\end{array}\right]
$$

$$
\begin{array}{cccc}
x_1 & x_2 & x_3 & x_4 \\
\end{array}
$$

$$
\left[\begin{array}{cccc|c}
\frac{1}{2} & 1 & \frac{1}{2} & 0 & 4 \\
4 & 0 & -1 & 1 & 8 \\
\hline
-4 & 0 & 5 & 0 & 40
\end{array}\right]
$$

$$
\begin{array}{cccc}
x_1 & x_2 & x_3 & x_4 \\
\end{array}
$$

$$
\left[\begin{array}{cccc|c}
0 & 1 & \frac{5}{8} & -\frac{1}{8} & 3 \\
1 & 0 & -\frac{1}{4} & \frac{1}{4} & 2 \\
\hline
0 & 0 & 4 & 1 & 48
\end{array}\right]
$$

The maximum is 48 when

$$x_1 = 2, \; x_2 = 3.$$

Notice that the solution to the *minimum problem* is found in the bottom row of the final simplex tableau for the maximum problem. This result suggests that standard minimum problems can be solved by forming the dual standard maximum problem, solving it by the simplex method, and then reading the solution for the minimum problem from the bottom row of the final simplex tableau. ▪

Before using this method to actually solve a minimum problem, let us find the duals of some typical linear programming problems. The process of exchanging the rows and columns of a matrix, which is used to find the dual, is called **transposing** the matrix, and each of the two matrices is the **transpose** of the other.

EXAMPLE 2

Find the transpose of each matrix.

(a)

$$
A = \begin{bmatrix}
2 & -1 & 5 \\
6 & 8 & 0 \\
-3 & 7 & -1
\end{bmatrix}.
$$

Write the rows of matrix A as the columns of the transpose.

$$
\text{transpose of } A = \begin{bmatrix}
2 & 6 & -3 \\
-1 & 8 & 7 \\
5 & 0 & -1
\end{bmatrix}
$$

(b) the transpose of $\begin{bmatrix} 1 & 2 & 4 & 0 \\ 2 & 1 & 7 & 6 \end{bmatrix}$ is $\begin{bmatrix} 1 & 2 \\ 2 & 1 \\ 4 & 7 \\ 0 & 6 \end{bmatrix}$. ▪

EXAMPLE 3

Write the dual of the following standard maximum linear programming problems.

(a) Maximize $\quad z = 2x_1 + 5x_2$

subject to: $\quad x_1 + x_2 \leq 10$
$$2x_1 + x_2 \leq 8$$

and $x_1 \geq 0, \quad x_2 \geq 0$.

Begin by writing the augmented matrix for the given problem.

$$\begin{bmatrix} 1 & 1 & | & 10 \\ 2 & 1 & | & 8 \\ 2 & 5 & | & 0 \end{bmatrix}$$

Form the transpose of this matrix, to get

$$\begin{bmatrix} 1 & 2 & | & 2 \\ 1 & 1 & | & 5 \\ 10 & 8 & | & 0 \end{bmatrix}.$$

The dual problem is stated from this second matrix as follows (using y instead of x):

Minimize $\quad w = 10y_1 + 8y_2$

subject to: $\quad y_1 + 2y_2 \geq 2$
$$y_1 + y_2 \geq 5$$

and $y_1 \geq 0, \quad y_2 \geq 0$.

(b)

Given problem	*Dual*

Given problem
Minimize $\quad w = 7y_1 + 5y_2 + 8y_3$

subject to:
$$3y_1 + 2y_2 + y_3 \geq 10$$
$$y_1 + y_2 + y_3 \geq 8$$
$$4y_1 + 5y_2 \qquad \geq 25$$

and $y_1 \geq 0, \quad y_2 \geq 0, \quad y_3 \geq 0$.

Dual
Maximize $\quad z = 10x_1 + 8x_2 + 25x_3$

subject to:
$$3x_1 + x_2 + 4x_3 \leq 7$$
$$2x_1 + x_2 + 5x_3 \leq 5$$
$$x_1 + x_2 \qquad \leq 8$$

and $x_1 \geq 0, x_2 \geq 0, x_3 \geq 0$. ■

In Example 3, all the constraints of the given standard maximum problems were $\leq$ inequalities, while all those in the dual minimum problems were $\geq$ inequalities. This is generally the case; inequalities are reversed when the dual problem is stated.

The following table shows the close connection between a problem and its dual.

Given Problem	*Dual Problem*
m variables	n variables
n constraints	m constraints
coefficients from objective function	constants
constants	coefficients from objective function

The next theorem, whose proof requires advanced methods, guarantees that a standard minimum problem can be solved by forming a dual standard maximum problem.

Theorem of Duality

> The objective function w of a minimizing linear programming problem takes on a minimum value if and only if the objective function z of the corresponding dual maximizing problem takes on a maximum value. The maximum value of z equals the minimum value of w.

This method is illustrated in the following example. (This is Example 2 of the previous section; compare this solution with the one given there.)

EXAMPLE 4

Minimize $w = 3y_1 + 2y_2$

subject to: $y_1 + 3y_2 \geq 6$
$$2y_1 + y_2 \geq 3$$

and $y_1 \geq 0, \quad y_2 \geq 0$.

Use the given information to write the matrix

$$\begin{bmatrix} 1 & 3 & | & 6 \\ 2 & 1 & | & 3 \\ \hline 3 & 2 & | & 0 \end{bmatrix}.$$

Transpose to get the following matrix for the dual problem.

$$\begin{bmatrix} 1 & 2 & | & 3 \\ 3 & 1 & | & 2 \\ \hline 6 & 3 & | & 0 \end{bmatrix}$$

Write the dual problem from this matrix, as follows:

$$\text{maximize} \quad z = 6x_1 + 3x_2$$
$$\text{subject to:} \quad x_1 + 2x_2 \leq 3$$
$$3x_1 + x_2 \leq 2$$

and $x_1 \geq 0, \quad x_2 \geq 0$.

Solve this standard maximum problem using the simplex method. Start by introducing slack variables to give the system

$$
\begin{aligned}
x_1 + 2x_2 + x_3 \qquad\qquad &= 3 \\
3x_1 + x_2 \qquad + x_4 \quad &= 2 \\
-6x_1 - 3x_2 - 0x_3 - 0x_4 + z &= 0
\end{aligned}
$$

with $x_1 \geq 0, \quad x_2 \geq 0, \quad x_3 \geq 0, \quad x_4 \geq 0$.

The first tableau for this system is given below, with the pivot as indicated.

$$
\begin{array}{cccccc}
 & & x_1 & x_2 & x_3 & x_4 \\
\text{Quotients} & & & & & \\
3/1 = 3 & \begin{bmatrix} 1 & 2 & 1 & 0 & | & 3 \\ \boxed{3} & 1 & 0 & 1 & | & 2 \\ \hline -6 & -3 & 0 & 0 & | & 0 \end{bmatrix} \\
2/3 & & & & &
\end{array}
$$

The simplex method gives the following final tableau.

$$
\begin{array}{cccc}
x_1 & x_2 & x_3 & x_4 \\
\begin{bmatrix} 0 & 1 & \frac{3}{5} & -\frac{1}{5} & | & \frac{7}{5} \\ 1 & 0 & -\frac{1}{5} & \frac{2}{5} & | & \frac{1}{5} \\ \hline 0 & 0 & \frac{3}{5} & \frac{9}{5} & | & \frac{27}{5} \end{bmatrix}
\end{array}
$$

The last row of this final tableau shows that the solution of the given *standard minimum problem* is as follows:

The minimum value of $w = 3y_1 + 2y_2$, subject to the given constraints, is 27/5 and occurs when $y_1 = 3/5$ and $y_2 = 9/5$.

The minimum value of w, 27/5, is the same as the maximum value of z. ▩

Let us summarize the steps in solving a standard minimum linear programming problem by the method of duals.

Solving Minimum Problems With Duals

1. Find the dual standard maximum problem.
2. Solve the maximum problem using the simplex method.
3. The minimum value of the objective function w is the maximum value of the objective function z.
4. The optimum solution is given by the entries in the bottom row of the columns corresponding to the slack variables.

Further Uses of the Dual   The dual is useful not only in solving minimum problems, but also in seeing how small changes in one variable will affect the value of the objective function. For example, suppose an animal breeder needs at least 6 units per day of nutrient A and at least 3 units of nutrient B and that the breeder can choose between two different feeds, feed 1 and feed 2. Find the minimum cost for the breeder if each bag of feed 1 costs $3 and provides 1 unit of nutrient A and 2 units of B, while each bag of feed 2 costs $2 and provides 3 units of nutrient A and 1 of B.

If y_1 represents the number of bags of feed 1 and y_2 represents the number of bags of feed 2, the given information leads to

$$\text{minimize} \quad w = 3y_1 + 2y_2$$
$$\text{subject to:} \quad y_1 + 3y_2 \geq 6$$
$$2y_1 + y_2 \geq 3$$

and $y_1 \geq 0, \quad y_2 \geq 0.$

This standard minimum linear programming problem is the one we solved in Example 4 of this section. In that example, we formed the dual and reached the following final tableau:

$$
\begin{array}{cccc}
x_1 & x_2 & x_3 & x_4 \\
\end{array}
$$
$$
\left[\begin{array}{cccc|c}
0 & 1 & \frac{3}{5} & -\frac{1}{5} & \frac{7}{5} \\
1 & 0 & -\frac{1}{5} & \frac{2}{5} & \frac{1}{5} \\
0 & 0 & \frac{3}{5} & \frac{9}{5} & \frac{27}{5}
\end{array} \right].
$$

This final tableau shows that the breeder will obtain minimum feed costs by using 3/5 bag of feed 1 and 9/5 bag of feed 2 per day, for a daily cost of 27/5 = 5.40 dollars.

The top two numbers in the right-most column give the **imputed costs** in terms of the necessary nutrients. From the final tableau, $x_2 = 7/5$ and $x_1 = 1/5$, which means that a unit of nutrient A costs 1/5 = .20 dollars, while a unit of nutrient B costs 7/5 = 1.40 dollars. The minimum daily cost, $5.40, is found by the following procedure.

$$(\$.20 \text{ per unit of A}) \times (6 \text{ units of A}) = \$1.20$$
$$+ (\$1.40 \text{ per unit of B}) \times (3 \text{ units of B}) = \underline{\$4.20}$$
$$\$5.40 \text{ total}$$

These two numbers from the dual, $.20 and $1.40, also allow the breeder to estimate feed costs for "small" changes in nutrient requirements. For example, an increase of one unit in the requirement for each nutrient would produce a total cost of

$$
\begin{array}{ll}
\$5.40 & (6 \text{ units of A, 3 of B}) \\
.20 & (\text{an extra unit of A}) \\
\underline{1.40} & (\text{extra of B}) \\
\$7.00 & \text{total per day.}
\end{array}
$$

The numbers .20 and 1.40 are called the **shadow values** of the nutrients.

4.4 EXERCISES

Find the transpose of each matrix in Exercises 1–4.

1. $\begin{bmatrix} 1 & 2 & 3 \\ 3 & 2 & 1 \\ 1 & 10 & 0 \end{bmatrix}$

2. $\begin{bmatrix} 2 & 5 & 8 & 6 & 0 \\ 1 & -1 & 0 & 12 & 14 \end{bmatrix}$

3. $\begin{bmatrix} -1 & 4 & 6 & 12 \\ 13 & 25 & 0 & 4 \\ -2 & -1 & 11 & 3 \end{bmatrix}$

4. $\begin{bmatrix} 1 & 11 & 15 \\ 0 & 10 & -6 \\ 4 & 12 & -2 \\ 1 & -1 & 13 \\ 2 & 25 & -1 \end{bmatrix}$

State the dual problem for Exercises 5–8.

5. Maximize $z = 4x_1 + 3x_2 + 2x_3$

subject to: $x_1 + x_2 + x_3 \le 5$
$x_1 + x_2 \quad\quad \le 4$
$2x_1 + x_2 + 3x_3 \le 15$

and $x_1 \ge 0, \quad x_2 \ge 0, \quad x_3 \ge 0.$

6. Maximize $z = 8x_1 + 3x_2 + x_3$

subject to: $7x_1 + 6x_2 + 8x_3 \le 18$
$4x_1 + 5x_2 + 10x_3 \le 20$

and $x_1 \ge 0, \quad x_2 \ge 0, \quad x_3 \ge 0.$

7. Minimize $w = y_1 + 2y_2 + y_3 + 5y_4$

subject to: $y_1 + y_2 + y_3 + y_4 \ge 50$
$3y_1 + y_2 + 2y_3 + y_4 \ge 100$

and $y_1 \ge 0, \quad y_2 \ge 0, \quad y_3 \ge 0, \quad y_4 \ge 0.$

8. Minimize $w = y_1 + y_2 + 4y_3$

subject to: $y_1 + 2y_2 + 3y_3 \ge 115$
$2y_1 + y_2 + 8y_3 \ge 200$
$y_1 \quad\quad + y_3 \ge 50$

and $y_1 \ge 0, \quad y_2 \ge 0, \quad y_3 \ge 0.$

Use the simplex method to solve Exercises 9–14.

9. Find $y_1 \ge 0$ and $y_2 \ge 0$ such that

$2y_1 + 3y_2 \ge 6$
$2y_1 + y_2 \ge 7$

and $w = 5y_1 + 2y_2$ is minimized.

10. Find $y_1 \ge 0$ and $y_2 \ge 0$ such that

$3y_1 + y_2 \ge 12$
$y_1 + 4y_2 \ge 16$

and $w = 2y_1 + y_2$ is minimized.

11. Find $y_1 \ge 0$ and $y_2 \ge 0$ such that

$10y_1 + 5y_2 \ge 100$
$20y_1 + 10y_2 \ge 150$

and $w = 4y_1 + 5y_2$ is minimized.

12. Minimize $w = 3y_1 + 2y_2$

subject to: $2y_1 + 3y_2 \ge 60$
$y_1 + 4y_2 \ge 40$

and $y_1 \ge 0, \quad y_2 \ge 0.$

13. Minimize $w = 2y_1 + y_2 + 3y_3$

subject to: $y_1 + y_2 + y_3 \ge 100$
$2y_1 + y_2 \quad\quad \ge 50$

and $y_1 \ge 0, \quad y_2 \ge 0, \quad y_3 \ge 0.$

14. Minimize $w = 3y_1 + 2y_2$

subject to: $y_1 + 2y_2 \ge 10$
$y_1 + y_2 \ge 8$
$2y_1 + y_2 \ge 12$

and $y_1 \ge 0, \quad y_2 \ge 0.$

Exercises 15 and 17 are repeated from the previous section. Solve them with the method of duals and compare the solutions with Exercises 19 and 21 in Section 4.3.

15. Brand X Canners produce canned whole tomatoes and tomato sauce. This season, they have available 3,000,000 kilograms of tomatoes for these two products. To meet the demands of regular customers, they must produce at least 80,000 kilograms of sauce

and 800,000 kilograms of whole tomatoes. The cost per kilogram is $4 to produce canned whole tomatoes and $3.25 to produce tomato sauce. How many kilograms of tomatoes should they use for each product to minimize cost?

16. Sam, who is dieting, requires two food supplements, I and II. He can get these supplements from two different products, A and B, as shown in the following table.

$$\begin{array}{c} \textit{Supplement} \\ \text{(grams per serving)} \\ \begin{array}{cc} \text{I} & \text{II} \end{array} \\ \textit{Product} \quad \begin{array}{c} A \\ B \end{array} \begin{bmatrix} 3 & 2 \\ 2 & 4 \end{bmatrix} \end{array}$$

Sam's physician has recommended that he include at least 15 grams of each supplement in his daily diet. If product A costs 25¢ per serving and product B costs 40¢ per serving, how can he satisfy his requirements most economically?

17. Mark, who is ill, takes vitamin pills. Each day he must have at least 16 units of vitamin A, 5 units of vitamin B_1, and 20 units of vitamin C. He can choose between pill #1 which costs 10 cents and contains 8 units of A, 1 of B_1, and 2 of C, and pill #2 which costs 20 cents and contains 2 units of A, 1 of B_1, and 7 of C. How many of each pill should he buy in order to minimize his cost?

18. Refer to the example at the end of the section on minimizing the daily cost of feeds.

   (a) Find a combination of feeds that will cost $7.00 and give 7 units of A and 4 units of B.

   (b) Use the dual variables to predict the daily cost of feed if the requirements change to 5 units of A and 4 units of B. Find a combination of feeds to meet these requirements at the predicted price.

19. A small toy manufacturing firm has 200 squares of felt, 600 ounces of stuffing, and 90 feet of trim available to make two types of toys, a small bear and a monkey. The bear requires 1 square of felt and 4 ounces of stuffing. The monkey requires 2 squares of felt, 3 ounces of stuffing, and 1 foot of trim. The firm makes $1 profit on each bear and $1.50 profit on each monkey. The linear program to maximize profit is

$$\begin{aligned} \text{maximize} \quad & x_1 + 1.5x_2 = z \\ \text{subject to:} \quad & x_1 + 2x_2 \leq 200 \\ & 4x_1 + 3x_2 \leq 600 \\ & x_2 \leq 90 \end{aligned}$$

The final simplex tableau is

$$\begin{bmatrix} 0 & 1 & .8 & -.2 & 0 & | & 40 \\ 1 & 0 & -.6 & .4 & 0 & | & 120 \\ 0 & 0 & -.8 & .2 & 1 & | & 50 \\ 0 & 0 & .6 & .1 & 0 & | & 180 \end{bmatrix}$$

   (a) What is the corresponding dual problem?

   (b) What is the optimal solution to the dual problem?

   (c) Use the shadow values to estimate the profit the firm will make if their supply of felt increases to 210 squares.

   (d) How much profit will the firm make if their supply of stuffing is cut to 590 ounces and their supply of trim is cut to 80 feet?

20. Refer to the problem about the farmer solved at the beginning of Section 4.2.

    (a) Give the dual problem.

    (b) Use the shadow values to estimate the farmer's profit if land is cut to 90 acres but capital increases to $21,000.

    (c) Suppose the farmer has 110 acres but only $19,000. Find the optimum profit and the planting strategy that will produce this profit.

Determine the constraints and the objective function for Exercises 21 and 22, then solve each problem by the simplex method.

21. Natural Brand plant food is made from three chemicals. In a batch of the plant food there must be at least 81 kilograms of the first chemical and the other two chemicals must be in the ratio of 4 to 3. If the three chemicals cost $1.09, $.87, and $.65 per kilogram, respectively, how much of each should be used to minimize the cost of producing at least 750 kilograms of the plant food?

22. A company is developing a new additive for gasoline. The additive is a mixture of three liquid ingredients, I, II, and III. For proper performance, the total amount of additive must be at least 10 ounces per gallon of gasoline. However, for safety reasons, the amount of additive should not exceed 15 ounces per gallon of gasoline. At least 1/4 ounce of ingredient I must be used for every ounce of ingredient II and at least 1 ounce of ingredient III must be used for every ounce of ingredient I. If the cost of I, II, and III is $.30, $.09, and $.27 per ounce, respectively, find the mixture of the three ingredients which produces the minimum cost of the additive. How much of the additive should be used per gallon of gasoline?

EXTENDED   Making Ice Cream*

APPLICATION

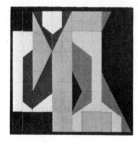

The first step in the commercial manufacture of ice cream is to blend several ingredients (such as dairy products, eggs, and sugar) to obtain a mix which meets the necessary minimum quality restrictions regarding butterfat content, serum solids, and so on.

Usually, many different combinations of ingredients may be blended to obtain a mix of the necessary quality. Within this range of possible substitutes, the firm desires the combination that produces minimum total cost. This problem is quite suitable for solution by linear programming methods.

A "mid-quality" line of ice cream requires the following minimum percentages of constituents by weight:

fat	16%
serum solids	8%
sugar solids	16%
egg solids	.35%
stabilizer	.25%
emulsifier	.15%
Total	40.75%

---

*From *Linear Programming in Industry: Theory and Application, An Introduction* by Sven Danø, Fourth revised and enlarged edition. Copyright © 1974 by Springer-Verlag/Wein. Reprinted by permission of Springer-Verlag New York, Inc.

Ingredients	1	2	3	4	5	6	7	8	9
	40% cream	23% cream	Butter	Plastic cream	Butter oil	4% milk	Skim condensed milk	Skim milk powder	Liquid sugar
Cost ($/lb)	.298	.174	.580	.576	.718	.045	.052	.165	.061
Constituents									
(1) Fat	.400	.230	.805	.800	.998	.040			
(2) Serum solids	.054	.069		.025		.078	.280	.970	
(3) Sugar solids									.707
(4) Egg solids									
(5) Stabilizer									
(6) Emulsifier									

The balance of the mix is water. A batch of mix is made by blending a number of ingredients, each of which contains one or more of the necessary constituents, and nothing else. The chart above shows the possible ingredients and their costs.

In setting up the mathematical model, use $c_1, c_2, \ldots, c_{14}$ as the cost per unit of the ingredients, and $x_1, x_2, \ldots, x_{14}$ for the quantities of ingredients. The table shows the composition of each ingredient. For example, one pound of ingredient 1 (the 40% cream) contains .400 pounds of fat and .054 pounds of serum solids, with the balance being water.

The ice cream mix is made up in batches of 100 pounds at a time. For a batch to contain 16% fat, at least $100(.16) = 16$ pounds of fat is necessary. Fat is contained in ingredients 1, 2, 3, 4, 5, 6, 10, and 11. The requirement of at least 16 pounds of fat produces the constraint

$$.400x_1 + .230x_2 + .805x_3 + .800x_4 + .998x_5 + .040x_6 + .500x_{10}$$
$$+ .625x_{11} \geq 16.$$

Similar constraints can be obtained for the other constituents. Because of the minimum requirements, the total of the ingredients will be at least 40.75 pounds, or

$$x_1 + x_2 + \ldots + x_{13} \geq 40.75.$$

The balance of the 100 pounds is water, making $x_{14} \leq 59.25$.

The table shows that ingredients 12 and 13 must be used—there is no alternate way of getting these constituents into the final mix. For a 100 pound batch of ice cream, $x_{12} = .25$ pound and $x_{13} = .15$ pound. Removing x_{12} and x_{13} as variables permits a substantial simplification of the model: the problem is now reduced to the following system of four constraints:

$$.400x_1 + .230x_2 + .805x_3 + .800x_4 + .998x_5 + .040x_6 + .500x_{10}$$
$$+ .625x_{11} \geq 16$$

$$.054x_1 + .069x_2 + .025x_4 + .078x_6 + .280x_7 + .970x_8 \geq 8$$

$$.707x_9 + .100x_{10} \geq 16$$

$$.350x_{10} + .315x_{11} \geq .35$$

Ingredients	10	11	12	13	14	Requirements
	Sugared egg yolk	Powdered egg yolk	Stabilizer	Emulsifier	Water	
Cost ($/lb)	.425	1.090	.600	.420	0	
Constituents						
(1) Fat	.500	.625				16
(2) Serum solids						8
(3) Sugar solids	.100					16
(4) Egg solids	.350	.315				.35
(5) Stabilizer			1			.25
(6) Emulsifier				1		.15

The objective function, which is to be minimized, is

$$c = .298x_1 + .174x_2 + \ldots + 1.090x_{11}.$$

As usual, $x_1 \geq 0$, $x_2 \geq 0, \ldots, x_{14} \geq 0$.

Solving this linear programming problem with the simplex method gives

$$x_2 = 67.394, \qquad x_8 = 3.459, \qquad x_9 = 22.483, \qquad x_{10} = 1.000.$$

The total cost of these ingredients is $14.094. To this, we must add the cost of ingredients 12 and 13, producing total cost of

$$14.094 + (.600)(.250) + (.420)(.150) = 14.307,$$

or $14.307.

EXERCISES

1. Find the mix of ingredients needed for a 100-pound batch of the following grades of ice cream.
   a. "generic," sold in a white box, with at least 14% fat and at least 6% serum solids (all other ingredients the same);
   b. "premium," sold with a funny foreign name, with at least 17% fat and at least 16.5% sugar solids (all other ingredients the same).

 2. Solve the example in the text by using a computer.

EXTENDED
APPLICATION

Merit Pay—The Upjohn Company

Individuals doing the same job within the management of a company often receive different salaries. These salaries may differ because of length of service, productivity of an individual worker, and so on. However, for each job there is usually an established minimum and maximum salary.

Many companies make annual reviews of the salary of each of their management employees. At these reviews, an employee may receive a general cost of living increase, an increase based on merit, both, or neither.

In this case, we look at a mathematical model for distributing merit increases in an optimum way.* An individual who is due for salary review may be described as shown in the figure below. Here i represents the number of the employee whose salary is being reviewed.

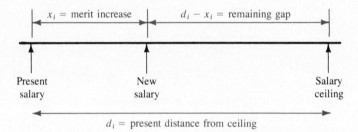

Here the salary ceiling is the maximum salary for the job classification, x_i is the merit increase to be awarded to the individual ($x_i \geq 0$), d_i is the present distance of the current salary from the salary ceiling, and the difference, $d_i - x_i$, is the remaining gap.

We let w_i be a measure of the relative worth of the individual to the company. This is the most difficult variable of the model to actually calculate. One way to evaluate w_i is to give a rating sheet to a number of co-workers and supervisors of employee i. An average rating can be obtained and then divided by the highest rating received by an employee with that same job. This number then gives the worth of employee i relative to all other employees with that job.

The best way to allocate money available for merit pay increases is to minimize

$$\sum_{i=1}^{n} w_i(d_i - x_i).$$

This sum is found by multiplying the relative worth of employee i and the distance of employee i from the salary gap, after any merit increase. Here n represents the total number of employees who have this job. The one constraint here is that the total of all merit increases cannot exceed P, the total amount available for merit increases. That is,

$$\sum_{i=1}^{n} x_i \leq P.$$

---

*Based on part of a paper by Jack Northam, Head, Mathematical Services Department, The Upjohn Company, Kalamazoo, Michigan.

Also, the increases for an employee must not put that employee over the maximum salary. That is, for employee i,

$$x_i \le d_i.$$

We can simplify the objective function, using rules from algebra.

$$\sum_{i=1}^{n} w_i(d_i - x_i) = \sum_{i=1}^{n} (w_i d_i - w_i x_i)$$

$$= \sum_{i=1}^{n} w_i d_i - \sum_{i=1}^{n} w_i x_i$$

For a given individual, w_i and d_i are constant. Therefore, $w_i d_i$ is some constant, say Z, and

$$\sum_{i=1}^{n} w(d_i - x_i) = Z - \sum_{i=1}^{n} w_i x_i.$$

We want to minimize the sum on the left; we can do so by *maximizing* the sum on the right. (Why?) Thus, the original model simplifies to maximizing

$$\sum_{i=1}^{n} w_i x_i,$$

subject to

$$\sum_{i=1}^{n} x_i \le p \quad \text{and} \quad x_i \le d_i$$

for each i.

Here are the current salary information and job evaluation averages for six employees who have the same job. The salary ceiling is $1700 per month.

Employee number	Evaluation average	Current salary
1	570	$1600
2	500	$1550
3	450	$1500
4	600	$1610
5	520	$1530
6	565	$1420

1. Find w_i for each employee by dividing that employee's evaluation average by the highest evaluation average.

2. Use the simplex method to find the merit increase for each employee. Assume that p is 400.

KEY WORDS

simplex method	dual
slack variable	surplus variable
basic feasible solution	phase I
pivot	phase II
simplex tableau	transpose

Chapter 4   REVIEW EXERCISES

For Exercises 1–4, (a) select appropriate variables, (b) write the objective function, (c) write the constraints as inequalities.

1. Roberta Hernandez sells three items, A, B, and C, in her gift shop. Each unit of A costs her $5 to buy, $1 to sell and $2 to deliver. For each unit of B, the costs are $3, $2 and $1 respectively, and for each unit of C the costs are $6, $2, and $5 respectively. The profit on A is $4, on B it is $3, and on C, $3. How many of each should she get to maximize her profit if she can spend $1200 to buy, $800 on selling costs, and $500 on delivery costs?

2. An investor is considering three types of investment: a high risk venture into oil leases with a potential return of 15%, a medium risk investment in bonds with a 9% return, and a relatively safe stock investment with a 5% return. He has $50,000 to invest. Because of the risk, he will limit his investment in oil leases and bonds to 30% and his investment in oil leases and stock to 50%. How much should he invest in each to maximize his return assuming investment returns are as expected?

3. The Aged Wood Winery makes two white wines, Fruity and Crystal, from two kinds of grapes and sugar. The wines require the following amounts of each ingredient per gallon and produce a profit per gallon as shown below.

	Grape A (bushels)	Grape B (bushels)	Sugar (pounds)	Profit (dollars)
Fruity	2	2	2	12
Crystal	1	3	1	15

The winery has available 110 bushels of grape A, 125 bushels of grape B, and 90 pounds of sugar. How much of each wine should be made to maximize profit?

4. A company makes three sizes of plastic bags: 5 gallon, 10 gallon and 20 gallon. The production time in hours for cutting, sealing, and packaging a unit of each size is shown below.

size	cutting	sealing	packaging
5 gallon	1	1	2
10 gallon	1.1	1.2	3
20 gallon	1.5	1.3	4

There are at most 8 hours available each day for each of the three operations. If the profit on a unit of 5-gallon bags is $1, 10-gallon bags is $.90, and 20-gallon bags is $.95, how many of each size should be made per day?

For Exercises 5–8, (a) add slack variables or subtract surplus variables, and (b) set up the initial simplex tableau.

5. Maximize $z = 5x_1 + 3x_2$

subject to: $2x_1 + 5x_2 \le 50$
$x_1 + 3x_2 \le 25$
$4x_1 + x_2 \le 18$
$x_1 + x_2 \le 12$

and $x_1 \ge 0, x_2 \ge 0$.

6. Maximize $z = 25x_1 + 30x_2$

subject to: $3x_1 + 5x_2 \le 47$
$x_1 + x_2 \le 25$
$5x_1 + 2x_2 \le 35$
$2x_1 + x_2 \le 30$

and $x_1 \ge 0, x_2 \ge 0$.

7. Maximize $z = 5x_1 + 8x_2 + 6x_3$

subject to: $x_1 + x_2 + x_3 \le 90$
$2x_1 + 5x_2 + x_3 \le 120$
$x_1 + 3x_2 \ge 80$

and $x_1 \ge 0, x_2 \ge 0, x_3 \ge 0$.

8. Maximize $z = 2x_1 + 3x_2 + 4x_3$

subject to: $x_1 + x_2 + x_3 \ge 100$
$2x_1 + 3x_2 \le 500$
$x_1 + 2x_3 \le 350$

and $x_1 \ge 0, x_2 \ge 0, x_3 \ge 0$.

Use the simplex method to solve the maximizing linear programming problems with initial tableaus as given in Exercises 9–12.

9.

x_1	x_2	x_3	x_4	x_5	
1	2	3	1	0	28
2	4	1	0	1	32
−5	−2	−3	0	0	0

10.

x_1	x_2	x_3	x_4	
2	1	1	0	10
1	3	0	1	16
−2	−3	0	0	0

11.

x_1	x_2	x_3	x_4	x_5	x_6	
1	2	2	1	0	0	50
3	1	0	0	1	0	20
1	0	2	0	0	−1	15
−5	−3	−2	0	0	0	0

12.

x_1	x_2	x_3	x_4	x_5	
3	6	−1	0	0	28
1	1	0	1	0	12
2	1	0	0	1	16
−1	−2	0	0	0	0

Convert the problems of Exercises 13–15 into maximization problems.

13. Minimize $w = 10x_1 + 15x_2$

subject to: $x_1 + x_2 \ge 17$
$5x_1 + 8x_2 \ge 42$

and $x_1 \ge 0, x_2 \ge 0$.

14. Minimize $w = 20x_1 + 15x_2 + 18x_3$

subject to: $2x_1 + x_2 + x_3 \ge 112$
$x_1 + x_2 + x_3 \ge 80$
$x_1 + x_2 \ge 45$

and $x_1 \ge 0, x_2 \ge 0, x_3 \ge 0$.

15. Minimize $w = 7x_1 + 2x_2 + 3x_3$

subject to: $x_1 + x_2 + 2x_3 \ge 48$
$x_1 + x_2 \ge 12$
$x_3 \ge 10$
$3x_1 + x_3 \ge 30$

and $x_1 \ge 0, x_2 \ge 0, x_3 \ge 0$.

The tableaus in Exercises 16–20 are the final tableaus of minimizing problems. State the solution and the minimum value of the objective function for each problem.

16.

$$
\begin{array}{cccccc}
x_1 & x_2 & x_3 & x_4 & x_5 & x_6 \\
\end{array}
$$

$$
\left[
\begin{array}{cccccc|c}
1 & 0 & 0 & 3 & 1 & 2 & 12 \\
0 & 0 & 1 & 4 & 5 & 3 & 5 \\
0 & 1 & 0 & -2 & 7 & -6 & 8 \\
\hline
0 & 0 & 0 & 5 & 7 & 3 & -172 \\
\end{array}
\right]
$$

17.

$$
\begin{array}{cccccc}
x_1 & x_2 & x_3 & x_4 & x_5 & x_6 \\
\end{array}
$$

$$
\left[
\begin{array}{cccccc|c}
0 & 0 & 3 & 0 & 1 & 1 & 2 \\
1 & 0 & -2 & 0 & 2 & 0 & 8 \\
0 & 1 & 7 & 0 & 0 & 0 & 12 \\
0 & 0 & 1 & 1 & -4 & 0 & 1 \\
\hline
0 & 0 & 5 & 0 & 8 & 0 & -62 \\
\end{array}
\right]
$$

18.

$$
\begin{array}{ccccc}
x_1 & x_2 & x_3 & x_4 & x_5 \\
\end{array}
$$

$$
\left[
\begin{array}{ccccc|c}
5 & 1 & 0 & 7 & -1 & 100 \\
-2 & 0 & 1 & 1 & 3 & 27 \\
\hline
12 & 0 & 0 & 7 & 2 & -640 \\
\end{array}
\right]
$$

19. Solve Exercise 1.

20. Solve Exercise 2.

21. Solve Exercise 3.

22. Solve Exercise 4.

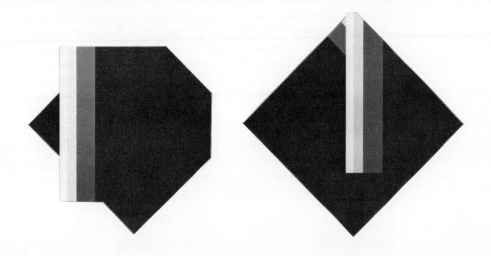

SETS AND COUNTING

Karl Gerstner. From the series *Progressive Penetration* (Finite-Infinite Series), 1960. Pierburg Collection, Neus, West Germany.

We have used sets from time to time throughout this book. Now in this chapter we present a more detailed discussion of sets. The terminology and concepts of sets have proved to be very useful. Sets, which are collections of objects, help to clarify and classify many mathematical ideas, making them easier to understand. Sets are particularly useful in presenting the topics of probability. The principles of counting, discussed later in this chapter, will also be needed to find probabilities.

5.1   Sets

Think of a **set** as a collection of objects. We could form a set containing one of each type of coin now put out by the government. Another set might be made up of all the students in your class. In mathematics, sets are often made up of numbers. The set consisting of the numbers 3, 4, and 5 is written

$$\{3, 4, 5\},$$

with set braces, $\{\ \}$, enclosing the numbers belonging to the set. The numbers 3, 4, and 5 are called the **elements** or **members** of this set. To show that 4 is an element of the set $\{3, 4, 5\}$ use the symbol $\in$ and write

$$4 \in \{3, 4, 5\}.$$

Also, $5 \in \{3, 4, 5\}$. To show that 8 is *not* an element of this set, place a slash through the symbol.

$$8 \notin \{3, 4, 5\}$$

Sets are often named with capital letters, so that if

$$B = \{5, 6, 7\},$$

then, for example, $6 \in B$ and $10 \notin B$.

Two sets are **equal** if they contain the same elements. The sets $\{5, 6, 7\}$, $\{7, 6, 5\}$, and $\{6, 5, 7\}$ all contain exactly the same elements and are equal. In symbols,

$$\{5, 6, 7\} = \{7, 6, 5\} = \{6, 5, 7\}.$$

Sets which do not contain exactly the same elements are *not equal*. For example, the sets $\{5, 6, 7\}$ and $\{7, 8, 9\}$ do not contain exactly the same elements and are not equal. This is written as follows:

$$\{5, 6, 7\} \neq \{7, 8, 9\}.$$

Sometimes we are more interested in a common property of the elements in a set, rather than a list of the elements. This common property can be expressed by using **set-builder notation:** the set

$$\{x \mid x \text{ has property } P\}$$

(read ''the set of all elements x such that x has property P'') represents the set of all elements x having some stated property P.

EXAMPLE 1

Write the elements belonging to each of the following sets.

(a) $\{x \mid x$ is a counting number less than 5$\}$

The counting numbers less than 5 make up the set $\{1, 2, 3, 4\}$.

(b) $\{x \mid x$ is a state that touches Florida$\}$ = $\{$Alabama, Georgia$\}$ ▨

When discussing a particular situation or problem, we can identify a **universal set** that contains all the elements appearing in any set used in that particular problem. The letter U is used to represent the universal set.

For example, when discussing the set of company employees who favor a certain pension proposal, the universal set might be the set of all company employees. In discussing the types of species found by Charles Darwin on the Galápagos Islands, the universal set might be the set of all species on all Pacific islands.

Sometimes every element of one set also belongs to another set. For example, if

$$A = \{3, 4, 5, 6\}$$

and

$$B = \{2, 3, 4, 5, 6, 7, 8\},$$

then every element of A is also an element of B. This means that A is a **subset** of B, written $A \subset B$. For example, the set of all presidents of corporations is a subset of the set of all executives of corporations.

EXAMPLE 2

Decide whether the following statements are true or false.

(a) $\{3, 4, 5, 6\} = \{4, 6, 3, 5\}$

Both sets contain exactly the same elements; the sets are equal. The given statement is true. (The fact that the elements are in a different order doesn't matter.)

(b) $\{5, 6, 9, 10\} \subset \{5, 6, 7, 8, 9, 10, 11\}$

Every element of the first set is also an element of the second, making the given statement true. ▨

Figure 1 shows a set A which is a subset of a set B. The rectangle represents the universal set, U. Such diagrams, called **Venn diagrams,** are used to help clarify relationships among sets.

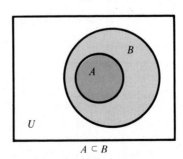

$A \subset B$

FIGURE 1

By the definition of subset, the **empty set** (which contains no elements) is a subset of every set. That is, if A is any set, and the symbol $\varnothing$ represents the empty set, then $\varnothing \subset A$. Also, the definition of subset can be used to show that every set is a subset of itself: that is, if A is any set, then $A \subset A$. In summary,

---

For any set A,

$$\varnothing \subset A \qquad \text{and} \qquad A \subset A.$$

EXAMPLE 3

List all possible subsets for each of the following sets.

(a) $\{7, 8\}$

There are four subsets of $\{7, 8\}$:

$$\varnothing, \quad \{7\}, \quad \{8\}, \quad \{7, 8\}.$$

(b) $\{a, b, c\}$

There are eight subsets of $\{a, b, c\}$:

$$\varnothing, \quad \{a\}, \quad \{b\}, \quad \{c\}, \quad \{a, b\}, \quad \{a, c\}, \quad \{b, c\}, \quad \{a, b, c\}. \quad ■$$

The **cardinal number** of a set is the number of distinct elements in the set. The cardinal number of the set A is written $n(A)$. For example, the set

$$A = \{a, b, c, d, e\}$$

has cardinal number 5, written

$$n(A) = 5.$$

Since the empty set has no elements, its cardinal number is 0, by definition. Thus, $n(\varnothing) = 0$.

EXAMPLE 4

Give the cardinal number of each of the following sets.

(a) $B = \{2, 5, 7, 9, 10, 12, 15\}$.

This set has seven elements, so $n(B) = 7$.

(b) $C = \{x, y, z\}$.

Since set C has three elements, $n(C) = 3$. ■

In Example 3, we found all the subsets of $\{7, 8\}$ and all the subsets of $\{a, b, c\}$ by trial and error. An alternate method uses a **tree diagram,** a systematic way of listing all the subsets of a given set. Figures 2(a) and (b) show tree diagrams for finding the subsets of $\{7, 8\}$ and $\{a, b, c\}$.

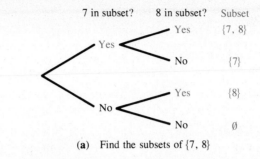

(a)   Find the subsets of {7, 8}

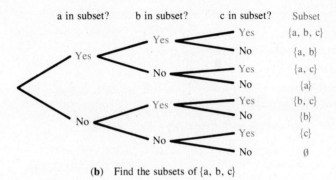

(b)   Find the subsets of {a, b, c}

FIGURE 2

Examples and tree diagrams similar to the ones above suggest the following rule, which we prove in Section 5.5.

A set of n distinct elements has 2^n subsets.

EXAMPLE 5

Find the number of subsets for each of the following sets.

(a)   {3, 4, 5, 6, 7}

This set has five elements; thus it has 2^5 or 32 subsets.

(b)   {−1, 2, 3, 4, 5, 6, 12, 14}

This set has 8 elements and therefore has 2^8 or 256 subsets.

(c)   ∅

The empty set has 0 elements, and $2^0 = 1$ subset. (Compare this result with Exercise 39 below.) ▪

5.1 EXERCISES

Write *true* or *false* for Exercises 1–18.

1. $3 \in \{2, 5, 7, 9, 10\}$

2. $6 \in \{-2, 6, 9, 5\}$

3. $1 \in \{3, 4, 5, 1, 11\}$

4. $12 \in \{19, 17, 14, 13, 12\}$

5. $9 \notin \{2, 1, 5, 8\}$

6. $3 \notin \{7, 6, 5, 4\}$

7. $\{2, 5, 8, 9\} = \{2, 5, 9, 8\}$

8. $\{3, 0, 9, 6, 2\} = \{2, 9, 0, 3, 6\}$

9. $\{5, 8, 9\} = \{5, 8, 9, 0\}$

10. $\{3, 7, 12, 14\} = \{3, 7, 12, 14, 0\}$

11. {all counting numbers less than 6} = {1, 2, 3, 4, 5, 6}

12. {all whole numbers greater than 7 and less than 10} = {8, 9}

13. {all whole numbers not greater than 4} = {0, 1, 2, 3}

14. {all counting numbers not greater than 3} = {0, 1, 2}

15. $\{x \mid x$ is a whole number, $x \leq 5\} = \{0, 1, 2, 3, 4, 5\}$

16. $\{x \mid x$ is an integer, $-3 \leq x < 4\} = \{-3, -2, -1, 0, 1, 2, 3, 4\}$

17. $\{x \mid x$ is an odd integer, $6 \leq x \leq 18\} = \{7, 9, 11, 15, 17\}$

18. $\{x \mid x$ is an even counting number, $x \leq 9\} = \{0, 2, 4, 6, 8\}$

Let
$$A = \{2, 4, 6, 8, 10, 12\} \quad D = \{2, 10\}$$
$$B = \{2, 4, 8, 10\} \quad U = \{2, 4, 6, 8, 10, 12, 14\}$$
$$C = \{4, 10, 12\}$$

Write *true* or *false* for Exercises 19–34.

19. $A \subset U$

20. $C \subset U$

21. $D \subset B$

22. $D \subset A$

23. $A \subset B$

24. $B \subset C$

25. $\varnothing \subset A$

26. $\varnothing \subset \varnothing$

27. $\{4, 8, 10\} \subset B$

28. $\{0, 2\} \subset D$

29. $D \not\subset B$

30. $A \not\subset C$

31. There are exactly 32 subsets of A.

32. There are exactly 16 subsets of B.

33. There are exactly 6 subsets of C.

34. There are exactly 4 subsets of D.

Find the number of subsets for each of the sets in Exercises 35–42.

35. {4, 5, 6}

36. {3, 7, 9, 10}

37. {5, 9, 10, 15, 17}

38. {6, 9, 1, 4, 3, 2}

39. $\{\varnothing\}$

40. {0}

41. $\{x \mid x$ is a counting number between 6 and 12}

42. $\{x \mid x$ is a whole number between 8 and 12}

Give the cardinal number of each of the sets in Exercises 43–48.

43. {m, p, q, n}

44. {a, b, c, d, e, f}

45. {1, 2, 3}

46. {0}

47. $\varnothing$

48. $\{0, \varnothing\}$

49. A candy bar of a certain size contains 220 calories. Suppose you eat two of these candy bars and then decide to exercise and get rid of the calories. A list of possible exercises shows the following information.

Exercise	Abbreviation	Calories per hour
Sitting around	s	100
Light exercise	l	170
Moderate exercise	m	300
Severe exercise	e	450
Very severe exercise	u	600

The universal set here is $U = \{s, l, m, e, u\}$. Find all subsets of U (with no element listed twice) that will burn off the calories from the candy bars in **(a)** one hour; **(b)** two hours.

50. The list below includes the producers of most (93%) of the hazardous wastes in the United States.

Let x be the number associated with an industry in the table opposite. The universal set is $U = \{1, 2, 3, 4, 5, 6\}$. List the elements of the following subsets of U.

(a) $\{x|\text{the industry produces more than 15% of the wastes}\}$.

(b) $\{x|\text{the industry produces less than 5% of the wastes}\}$.

(c) Find all subsets of U containing industries which produce a total of at least 50% of the waste.

Industry	%
Inorganic Chemicals (1)	11
Organic Chemicals (2)	34
Electroplating (3)	12
Petroleum Refining (4)	5
Smelting and Refining (5)	26
Textiles Dyeing and Finishing (6)	5

5.2   Set Operations

Given a set A and a universal set U, the set of all elements of U which do *not* belong to A is called the **complement** of set A. For example, if set A is the set of all the female students in a class, and U is the set of all students in the class, then the complement of A would be the set of all male students in the class. The complement of set A is written A'. (Read: "A-prime.") The Venn diagram of Figure 3 shows a set B. Its complement, B', is shown in color.

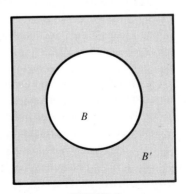

FIGURE 3

EXAMPLE 1

Let $U = \{1, 2, 3, 4, 5, 6, 7\}$, $A = \{1, 3, 5, 7\}$, and $B = \{3, 4, 6\}$. Find each of of the following sets.

(a) A'

Set A' contains the elements of U that are not in A.

$$A' = \{2, 4, 6\}$$

(b) $B' = \{1, 2, 5, 7\}$

(c) $\emptyset' = U$ and $U' = \emptyset$ ▪

Given two sets A and B, the set of all elements belonging to both set A and set B is called the **intersection** of the two sets, written $A \cap B$. For example, the elements that belong to both $A = \{1, 2, 4, 5, 7\}$ and $B = \{2, 4, 5, 7, 9, 11\}$ are 2, 4, 5, and 7, so that

$$A \cap B = \{1, 2, 4, 5, 7\} \cap \{2, 4, 5, 7, 9, 11\} = \{2, 4, 5, 7\}.$$

The Venn diagram of Figure 4 shows two sets A and B; their intersection, $A \cap B$, is shown in color.

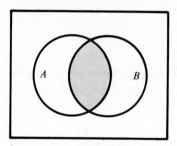

FIGURE 4

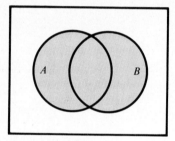

FIGURE 5

EXAMPLE 2

(a) $\{9, 15, 25, 36\} \cap \{15, 20, 25, 30, 35\} = \{15, 25\}$

The elements 15 and 25 are the only ones belonging to both sets.

(b) $\{-2, -3, -4, -5, -6\} \cap \{-4, -3, -2, -1, 0, 1, 2\} = \{-4, -3, -2\}$ ▪

Two sets that have no elements in common are called **disjoint sets.** For example, there are no elements common to both $\{50, 51, 54\}$ and $\{52, 53, 55, 56\}$, so that these two sets are disjoint, and

$$\{50, 51, 54\} \cap \{52, 53, 55, 56\} = \emptyset.$$

The result of this example can be generalized: for any sets A and B, if A and B are disjoint sets then $A \cap B = \emptyset$.

The set of all elements belonging to either set A or set B or both is called the **union** of the two sets, written $A \cup B$. For example,

$$\{1, 3, 5\} \cup \{3, 5, 7, 9\} = \{1, 3, 5, 7, 9\}.$$

The Venn diagram of Figure 5 shows two sets A and B, with their union, $A \cup B$, shown in color.

EXAMPLE 3

(a) Find the union of $\{1, 2, 5, 9, 14\}$ and $\{1, 3, 4, 8\}$.
  Begin by listing the elements of the first set, $\{1, 2, 5, 9, 14\}$. Then include any elements from the second set that are not already listed. Doing this gives

$$\{1, 2, 5, 9, 14\} \cup \{1, 3, 4, 8\} = \{1, 2, 3, 4, 5, 8, 9, 14\}.$$

(b) $\{1, 3, 5, 7\} \cup \{2, 4, 6\} = \{1, 2, 3, 4, 5, 6, 7\}.$ ▪

Finding the complement of a set, the intersection of two sets, or the union of two sets are examples of **set operations.** These are similar to operations on numbers, such as addition, subtraction, multiplication, and division.
  The next box summarizes the various operations on sets.

Operations on Sets

Let A and B be any sets with U the universal set.

Then

  the **complement** of A, written A', is

$$A' = \{x \,|\, x \notin A \text{ and } x \in U\};$$

  the **intersection** of A and B is

$$A \cap B = \{x \,|\, x \in A \text{ and } x \in B\};$$

  the **union** of A and B is

$$A \cup B = \{x \,|\, x \in A \text{ or } x \in B\}.$$

EXAMPLE 4

The table below gives the current dividend, price-to-earnings ratio (the quotient of the price per share and the annual earnings per share), and price change at the end of a day for six companies, as listed on the New York Stock Exchange.

Stock	Dividend	Price to earnings ratio	Price change
ATT	5	6	$+\frac{1}{8}$
GE	3	9	0
Hershey	1.4	6	$+\frac{3}{8}$
IBM	3.44	12	$-\frac{3}{8}$
Mobil	3.40	6	$-1\frac{5}{8}$
RCA	1.80	7	$-\frac{1}{4}$

Let set A include all stocks with a dividend greater than \$3, B all stocks with a price to earnings ratio of at least 10, and C all stocks with a positive price change. Find the following.

(a) A'

Set A' contains all the listed stocks outside set A, those with a dividend less than or equal to \$3, so $A' = \{$GE, Hershey, RCA$\}$.

(b) $A \cap B$

The intersection of A and B will contain those stocks that offer a dividend greater than \$3 *and* have a price to earnings ratio of at least 10.

$$A \cap B = \{\text{IBM}\}$$

(c) $A \cup C$

We want the set of all stocks with a dividend greater than \$3 *or* a positive price change (or both).

$$A \cup C = \{\text{ATT, Hershey, IBM, Mobil}\} \quad \blacksquare$$

5.2 EXERCISES

Write *true* or *false* for Exercises 1–12.

1. $\{5, 7, 9, 19\} \cap \{7, 9, 11, 15\} = \{7, 9\}$

2. $\{8, 11, 15\} \cap \{8, 11, 19, 20\} = \{8, 11\}$

3. $\{2, 1, 7\} \cup \{1, 5, 9\} = \{1\}$

4. $\{6, 12, 14, 16\} \cup \{6, 14, 19\} = \{6, 14\}$

5. $\{3, 2, 5, 9\} \cap \{2, 7, 8, 10\} = \{2\}$

6. $\{8, 9, 6\} \cup \{9, 8, 6\} = \{8, 9\}$

7. $\{3, 5, 9, 10\} \cap \varnothing = \{3, 5, 9, 10\}$

8. $\{3, 5, 9, 10\} \cup \varnothing = \{3, 5, 9, 10\}$

9. $\{1, 2, 4\} \cup \{1, 2, 4\} = \{1, 2, 4\}$

10. $\{1, 2, 4\} \cap \{1, 2, 4\} = \varnothing$

11. $\varnothing \cup \varnothing = \varnothing$

12. $\varnothing \cap \varnothing = \varnothing$

Let $U = \{2, 3, 4, 5, 7, 9\}$, $X = \{2, 3, 4, 5\}$, $Y = \{3, 5, 7, 9\}$, and $Z = \{2, 4, 5, 7, 9\}$. Find each of the sets in Exercises 13–26.

13. $X \cap Y$

14. $X \cup Y$

15. $Y \cup Z$

16. $Y \cap Z$

17. $X \cup U$

18. $Y \cap U$

19. X'

20. Y'

21. $X' \cap Y'$

22. $X' \cap Z$

23. $Z' \cap \varnothing$

24. $Y' \cup \varnothing$

25. $X \cup (Y \cap Z)$

26. $Y \cap (X \cup Z)$

Let $U = \{$all students in this school$\}$
  $M = \{$all students taking this course$\}$
  $N = \{$all students taking accounting$\}$
  $P = \{$all students taking zoology$\}$
Describe each of the following sets in words.

27. M'

28. $M \cup N$

29. $N \cap P$

30. $N' \cap P'$

31. $M \cup P$

32. $P' \cup M'$

Given $U = \{1, 2, 3, 4, 5, 6, 7, 8, 9, 10\}$, $P = \{2, 4, 6, 8, 10\}$, $Q = \{4, 5, 6\}$, and $R = \{4\}$, find the cardinal number of the sets in Exercises 33–40.

33. $P \cup Q$ **34.** $P \cap Q$ **35.** P' **36.** Q'

37. $P' \cap Q$ **38.** $P \cup R'$ **39.** $P \cup (R \cap Q)$ **40.** $P \cap (R \cup Q)$

Refer to Example 4 in the text. Describe each of the sets in Exercises 41–46 in words. Then list the elements of each set.

41. B' **42.** C' **43.** $B \cap C$ **44.** $A \cup B$

45. $(A \cap B)'$ **46.** $(A \cup C)'$

47. The lists below show some symptoms of an overactive thyroid and an underactive thyroid.

Underactive thyroid	Overactive thyroid
Sleepiness, s	Insomnia, i
Dry hands, d	Moist hands, m
Intolerance of cold, c	Intolerance of heat, h
Goiter, g	Goiter, g

(a) Find the smallest possible universal set U that includes all the symptoms listed.

Let N be the set of symptoms for an underactive thyroid, and let O be the set of symptoms for an overactive thyroid. Find each of the following sets.

(b) O' **(c)** N' **(d)** $N \cap O$ **(e)** $N \cup O$ **(f)** $N \cap O'$

48. Let A and B be sets with cardinal numbers $n(A) = a$ and $n(B) = b$, respectively. Answer *true* or *false* for the following statements:

(a) $n(A \cup B) = n(A) + n(B)$;   **(b)** $n(A \cup B) = n(A) + n(B) - n(A \cap B)$.

5.3 Venn Diagrams

Venn diagrams were used in the last section to help in understanding set union and intersection. The rectangular region of a Venn diagram represents the universal set U. Including only a single set A inside the universal set, as in Figure 6, divides U into two regions. Region 1 represents those elements of U outside set A, while region 2 represents those elements belonging to set A. (Our numbering of these regions is arbitrary.)

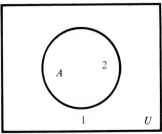

One set leads to 2 regions
(numbering is arbitrary)

FIGURE 6

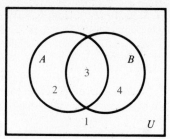

Two sets lead to 4 regions
(numbering is arbitrary)

FIGURE 7

The Venn diagram of Figure 7 shows two sets inside U. These two sets divide the universal set into four regions. As labeled in Figure 7, region 1 includes those elements outside of both set A and set B. Region 2 includes those elements belonging to A and not to B. Region 3 includes those elements belonging to both A and B. Which elements belong to region 4? (Again, the labeling is arbitrary.)

EXAMPLE 1   Draw Venn diagrams similar to Figure 7 and shade the regions representing the following sets.

(a) $A' \cap B$

Set A' contains all the elements outside of set A. As labeled in Figure 7, A' is made up of regions 1 and 4. Set B is made up of the elements in regions 3 and 4. The intersection of sets A' and B, the set $A' \cap B$, is made up of the elements in the region common to regions 1 and 4 and regions 3 and 4. The result, region 4, is shaded in Figure 8.

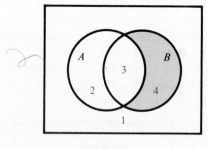

FIGURE 8

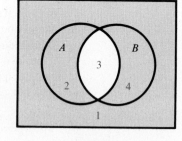

FIGURE 9

(b) $A' \cup B'$

Again, set A' is represented by regions 1 and 4, while B' is made up of regions 1 and 2. To find $A' \cup B'$, identify the elements belonging to either regions 1 and 4 or to regions 1 and 2. The result, regions 1, 2, and 4, is shaded in Figure 9. ■

Venn diagrams can also be drawn with three sets inside U. These three sets divide the universal set into eight regions, which can be numbered (arbitrarily) as in Figure 10.

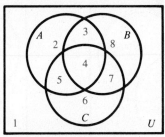

Three sets lead to 8 regions

FIGURE 10

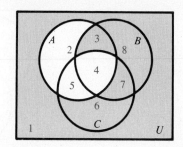

FIGURE 11

EXAMPLE 2

Shade $A' \cup (B \cap C')$ on a Venn diagram.

First find $B \cap C'$. Set B is made up of regions 3, 4, 7, and 8, while C' is made up of regions 1, 2, 3, and 8. The overlap of these regions, the set $B \cap C'$, is made up of regions 3 and 8. Set A' is made up of regions 1, 6, 7, and 8. The union of regions 3 and 8 and regions 1, 6, 7, 8 is regions 1, 3, 6, 7 and 8, which are shaded in Figure 11. ▨

Applications   Venn diagrams and the cardinal number of a set can be used to solve problems that result from surveying groups of people. As an example, suppose a group of 60 freshman business students at a large university was surveyed, with the following results.

19 of the students read *Business Week;*
18 read *The Wall Street Journal;*
50 read *Fortune;*
13 read *Business Week* and *The Journal;*
11 read *The Journal* and *Fortune;*
13 read *Business Week* and *Fortune;*
 9 read all three.

Let us use this data to help answer the following questions.
(a) How many students read none of the publications?
(b) How many read only *Fortune?*
(c) How many read *Business Week* and *The Journal,* but not *Fortune?*

Many of the students are listed more than once in the data above. For example, some of the 50 students who read *Fortune* also read *Business Week.* The 9 students who read all three are counted in the 13 who read *Business Week* and *Fortune,* and so on.

We can use a Venn diagram, as shown in Figure 12 on the next page, to better illustrate this data. Since 9 students read all three publications, begin by placing 9 in the area that belongs to all three regions, as shown in Figure 13. Of the 13 students who read *Business Week* and *Fortune* 9 also read *The Journal.* Therefore,

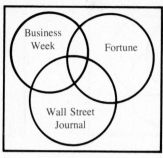

FIGURE 12

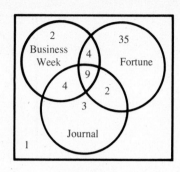

FIGURE 13

only $13 - 9 = 4$ read just *Business Week* and *Fortune*. Place the number 4 in the area of Figure 13 common to *Business Week* and *Fortune* readers. In the same way, place 4 in the region common only to *Business Week* and *The Journal*, and 2 in the region common only to *Fortune* and *The Journal*.

We know 19 students read *Business Week*. However, we have already placed $4 + 9 + 4 = 17$ readers in the region representing *Business Week*. The balance of this region will contain only $19 - 17 = 2$ students. These 2 students read *Business Week* only—not *Fortune* and not *The Journal*. In the same way, 3 students read only *The Journal* and 35 read only *Fortune*.

A total of $2 + 4 + 3 + 4 + 9 + 2 + 35 = 59$ students are placed in the three circles of Figure 13. Since 60 students were surveyed, $60 - 59 = 1$ student reads none of the three publications, and 1 is placed outside all three regions.

We can now use Figure 13 to answer the questions asked above.

(a) Only 1 student reads none of the three publications.
(b) From Figure 13, there are 35 students who read only *Fortune*.
(c) The overlap of the regions representing *Business Week* and *The Journal* shows that 4 students read *Business Week* and *The Journal* but not *Fortune*.

EXAMPLE 3

Jeff Friedman is a section chief for an electric utility company. The employees in his section cut down tall trees, climb poles, and splice wire. Friedman reported the following information to the management of the utility.

Of the 100 employees in my section,
45 can cut tall trees;
50 can climb poles;
57 can splice wire;
28 can cut trees and climb poles;
20 can climb poles and splice wire;
25 can cut trees and splice wire;
11 can do all three;
9 can't do any of the three (management trainees).

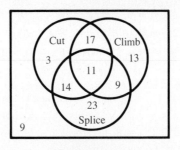

FIGURE 14

The data supplied by Friedman lead to the numbers shown in Figure 14. Add all the numbers from the regions to get the total number of employees:

$$9 + 3 + 14 + 23 + 11 + 9 + 17 + 13 = 99.$$

Friedman claimed to have 100 employees, but his data indicates only 99. The management decided that Friedman didn't qualify as a section chief, and reassigned him as a nightshift meter reader in Guam. (Moral: he should have taken this course.) ▪

Note that in both examples above, we started in the innermost region, the intersection of the three categories. This is usually the best way to begin solving these problems.

5.3 EXERCISES

Use a Venn diagram similar to Figure 7 to show each of the sets in Exercises 1–8.

1. $B \cap A'$ **2.** $A \cup B'$ **3.** $A' \cup B$ **4.** $A' \cap B'$

5. $B' \cup (A' \cap B')$ **6.** $(A \cap B) \cup B'$ **7.** U' **8.** $\emptyset'$

Use a Venn diagram similar to Figure 10 to show each of the sets in Exercises 9–16.

9. $(A \cap B) \cap C$ **10.** $(A \cap C') \cup B$

11. $A \cap (B \cup C')$ **12.** $A' \cap (B \cap C)$

13. $(A' \cap B') \cap C$ **14.** $(A \cap B') \cup C$

15. $(A \cap B') \cap C$ **16.** $A' \cap (B' \cup C)$

17. If $n(A) = 5$, $n(B) = 8$, and $n(A \cap B) = 4$, what is $n(A \cup B)$?

18. If $n(A) = 12$, $n(B) = 27$, and $n(A \cup B) = 30$, what is $n(A \cap B)$?

19. Suppose $n(B) = 7$, $n(A \cap B) = 3$, and $n(A \cup B) = 20$. What is $n(A)$?

20. Suppose $n(A \cap B) = 5$, $n(A \cup B) = 35$, and $n(A) = 13$. What is $n(B)$?

Draw a Venn diagram and use the given information to fill in the number of elements for each region.

21. $n(U) = 38$, $n(A) = 16$, $n(A \cap B) = 12$, $n(B') = 20$

22. $n(A) = 26$, $n(B) = 10$, $n(A \cup B) = 30$, $n(A') = 17$

23. $n(A \cup B) = 17$, $n(A \cap B) = 3$, $n(A) = 8$, $n(A' \cup B') = 21$

24. $n(A') = 28$, $n(B) = 25$, $n(A' \cup B') = 45$, $n(A \cap B) = 12$

25. $n(A) = 28$, $n(B) = 34$, $n(C) = 25$, $n(A \cap B) = 14$, $n(B \cap C) = 15$, $n(A \cap C) = 11$, $n(A \cap B \cap C) = 9$, $n(U) = 59$

26. $n(A) = 54$, $n(A \cap B) = 22$, $n(A \cup B) = 85$, $n(A \cap B \cap C) = 4$, $n(A \cap C) = 15$, $n(B \cap C) = 16$, $n(C) = 44$, $n(B') = 63$

27. $n(A \cap B) = 6$, $n(A \cap B \cap C) = 4$, $n(A \cap C) = 7$, $n(B \cap C) = 4$, $n(A \cap C') = 11$, $n(B \cap C') = 8$, $n(C) = 15$, $n(A' \cap B' \cap C') = 5$

28. $n(A) = 13$, $n(A \cap B \cap C) = 4$, $n(A \cap C) = 6$, $n(A \cap B') = 6$, $n(B \cap C) = 6$, $n(B \cap C') = 11$, $n(B \cup C) = 22$, $n(A' \cap B' \cap C') = 5$

Use Venn diagrams to answer the following questions.

29. Jeff Friedman, of Example 3 in the text, was again reassigned, this time to the home economics department of the electric utility. He interviewed 140 people in a suburban shopping center to find out some of their cooking habits. He obtained the following results. Should he be reassigned yet one more time?

> 58 use microwave ovens;
> 63 use electric ranges;
> 58 use gas ranges;
> 19 use microwave ovens and electric ranges;
> 17 use microwave ovens and gas ranges;
> 4 use both gas and electric ranges;
> 1 uses all three;
> 2 cook only with solar energy.

30. Toward the middle of the harvesting season, peaches for canning come in three types: earlies, lates, and extra lates, depending on the expected date of ripening. During a certain week, the following data was recorded at a fruit delivery station.

> 34 trucks went out carrying early peaches;
> 61 had late peaches;
> 50 had extra lates;
> 25 had earlies and lates;
> 30 had lates and extra lates;
> 8 had earlies and extra lates;
> 6 had all three;
> 9 had only figs (no peaches at all).

(a) How many trucks had only late variety peaches?

(b) How many had only extra lates?

(c) How many had only one type of peaches?

(d) How many trucks in all went out during the week?

31. A chicken farmer surveyed his flock with the following results. The farmer had

> 9 fat red roosters;
> 2 fat red hens;
> 37 fat chickens;
> 26 fat roosters;
> 7 thin brown hens;
> 18 thin brown roosters;
> 6 thin red roosters;
> 5 thin red hens.

Answer the following questions about the flock. Hint: you need a Venn diagram with regions for fat, for male (a rooster is a male, a hen is a female), and for red (assume that brown and red are opposites in the chicken world). How many chickens were

(a) fat? **(b)** red? **(c)** male? **(d)** fat, but not male?

(e) brown, but not fat? **(f)** red and fat?

32. Country-western songs emphasize three basic themes: love, prison, and trucks. A survey of the local country-western radio station produced the following data.

12 songs were about a truck driver who was in love while in prison;

13 about a prisoner in love;

28 about a person in love;

18 about a truck driver in love;

3 about a truck driver in prison who was not in love;

2 about a prisoner who was not in love and did not drive a truck;

8 about a person out of jail who was not in love, and did not drive a truck;

16 about truck drivers who were not in prison.

(a) How many songs were surveyed?

Find the number of songs about

(b) truck drivers; **(c)** prisoners; **(d)** truck drivers in prison;

(e) people not in prison; **(f)** people not in love.

33. After a genetics experiment, the number of pea plants having certain characteristics was tallied, with the results as follows.

22 were tall;

25 had green peas;

39 had smooth peas;

9 were tall and had green peas;

17 were tall and had smooth peas;

20 had green peas and smooth peas;

6 had all three characteristics;

4 had none of the characteristics.

(a) Find the total number of plants counted.

(b) How many plants were tall and had peas which were neither smooth nor green?

(c) How many plants were not tall but had peas which were smooth and green?

34. Human blood can contain either no antigens, the A antigen, the B antigen, or both the A and B antigens. A third antigen, called the Rh antigen, is important in human reproduction, and again may or may not be present in an individual. Blood is called type A-positive if the individual has the A and Rh, but not the B antigen. A person having only the A and B antigens is said to have type AB-negative blood. A person having only the Rh antigen has type O-positive blood. Other blood types are defined in a similar manner. Identify the blood type of the individuals in regions (a)–(g) below.

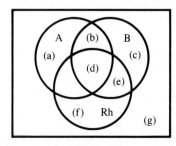

35. (Use the diagram from Exercise 34.) In a certain hospital, the following data were recorded.

> 25 patients had the A antigen;
> 17 had the A and B antigens;
> 27 had the B antigen;
> 22 had the B and Rh antigens;
> 30 had the Rh antigen;
> 12 had none of the antigens;
> 16 had the A and Rh antigens;
> 15 had all three antigens.

How many patients

(a) were represented?

(b) had exactly one antigen?

(c) had exactly two antigens?

(d) had O-positive blood?

(e) had AB-positive blood?

(f) had B-negative blood?

(g) had O-negative blood?

(h) had A-positive blood?

36. A survey of 80 sophomores at a western college showed that

> 36 take English;
> 32 take history;
> 32 take political science;
> 16 take political science and history;
> 16 take history and English;
> 14 take political science and English;
> 6 take all three.

How many students:

(a) take English and neither of the other two?

(b) take none of the three courses?

(c) take history, but neither of the other two?

(d) take political science and history, but not English?

(e) do not take political science?

37. The following table shows the number of people in a certain small town in Georgia who fit in the given categories.

Age	Drink vodka (V)	Drink bourbon (B)	Drink gin (G)	Totals
21–25 (Y)	40	15	15	70
26–35 (M)	30	30	20	80
over 35 (O)	10	50	10	70
Totals	80	95	45	220

Using the letters given in the table, find the number of people in each of the following sets.

(a) $Y \cap V$

(b) $M \cap B$

(c) $M \cup (B \cap Y)$

(d) $Y' \cap (B \cup G)$

(e) $O' \cup G$

(f) $M' \cap (V' \cap G')$

38. The following table shows the results of a survey in a medium-sized town in Tennessee. The survey asked questions about the investment habits of local citizens.

Age	Stocks (S)	Bonds (B)	Savings accounts (A)	Totals
18–29 (Y)	6	2	15	23
30–49 (M)	14	5	14	33
50 or over (O)	32	20	12	64
Totals	52	27	41	120

Using the letters given in the table, find the number of people in each of the following sets.

(a) $Y \cap B$ **(b)** $M \cup A$ **(c)** $Y \cap (S \cup B)$

(d) $O' \cup (S \cup A)$ **(e)** $(M' \cup O') \cap B$

For the statements of Exercises 39–42 draw Venn diagrams for the sets on each side of the equals sign. Show that the Venn diagrams are the same.*

39. $(A \cup B)' = A' \cap B'$

40. $(A \cap B)' = A' \cup B'$

41. $A \cap (B \cup C) = (A \cap B) \cup (A \cap C)$

42. $A \cup (B \cap C) = (A \cup B) \cap (A \cup C)$

43. Let $n(A)$ represent the number of elements in set A. Verify that $n(A \cup B) = n(A) + n(B) - n(A \cap B)$ for sets $A = \{1, 2, 3, 4, 5\}$ and $B = \{3, 5, 7\}$.

44. Do you think the statement in Exercise 43 is true for all sets A and B?

5.4 Permutations and Combinations

After making do with your old automobile for several years, you finally decide to replace it with a new small super-economy model. You drive over to Ned's New Car Emporium to choose the car that's just right for you. Once there, you find that you can select from 5 models, each with 4 power options, a choice of 8 exterior color combinations and 3 interior colors. How many different new cars are available to you? Problems of this sort are best solved by the counting principles discussed in this section. These counting methods are very useful in probability.

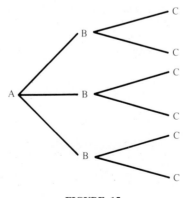

FIGURE 15

*The statements in Exercises 39 and 40 are known as De Morgan's Laws. They are named for the English mathematician Augustus De Morgan (1806–71).

Let us begin with a simpler example. If there are three roads from town A to town B and two roads from town B to town C, in how many ways can we travel from A to C by way of B? For each of the three roads from A there are two different routes leading from B to C, making $3 \cdot 2 = 6$ different ways for the trip, as shown in Figure 15. This example illustrates a general principle of counting, called the **multiplication principle.**

Multiplication Principle

Suppose n choices must be made, with

$$m_1 \text{ ways to make choice 1,}$$
$$m_2 \text{ ways to make choice 2,}$$

and so on, with

$$m_n \text{ ways to make choice } n.$$

Then there are

$$m_1 \cdot m_2 \cdot \cdot \cdot m_n$$

different ways to make the entire sequence of choices.

Using this multiplication principle, there are

$$5 \cdot 4 \cdot 8 \cdot 3 = 480$$

ways of selecting a new car at Ned's.

EXAMPLE 1

A teacher has 5 different books that he wishes to arrange side by side. How many different arrangements are possible?

Five choices will be made, one for each space which will hold a book. Any of the five possible books could be chosen for the first space. There are four possible choices for the second space, since one book has already been placed in the first space, three possible choices for the third space, and on. By the multiplication principle, the number of different possible arrangements is $5 \cdot 4 \cdot 3 \cdot 2 \cdot 1 = 120$. ■

The use of the multiplication principle often leads to products such as $5 \cdot 4 \cdot 3 \cdot 2 \cdot 1$. For convenience, the symbol $n!$ (read "n factorial") is used for such products. By definition,

n-factorial

For any natural number n,

$$n! = n(n - 1)(n - 2) \cdot \cdot \cdot (3)(2)(1).$$

With this symbol, the product $5 \cdot 4 \cdot 3 \cdot 2 \cdot 1$ can be written as $5!$. Also, $3! = 3 \cdot 2 \cdot 1 = 6$. The definition of $n!$ could be used to show that

$n[(n - 1)!] = n!$ for all natural numbers $n \geq 2$. It is helpful if this result also holds for $n = 1$. This can only happen if $0!$ is defined to equal 1:

$$0! = 1.$$

EXAMPLE 2

Suppose the teacher in Example 1 wishes to place only 3 of the 5 books on his desk. How many arrangements of 3 books are possible?

　　The teacher again has 5 ways to fill the first space, 4 ways to fill the second space, and 3 ways to fill the third. Since he wants to use only 3 books, only 3 spaces can be filled (3 events) instead of 5, for $5 \cdot 4 \cdot 3 = 60$ arrangements. ∎

Permutations　The answer 60 in Example 2 is called the number of permutations of 5 things taken 3 at a time. A **permutation** of r (where $r \geq 1$) elements from a set of n elements is any arrangement, *without repetition*, of the r elements. The number of permutations of n things taken r at a time (with $r \leq n$) is written $P(n, r)$. Based on the work in Example 2 above, $P(5, 3) = 5 \cdot 4 \cdot 3 = 60$. Factorial notation can be used to express this product as follows.

$$5 \cdot 4 \cdot 3 = 5 \cdot 4 \cdot 3 \cdot \frac{2 \cdot 1}{2 \cdot 1} = \frac{5 \cdot 4 \cdot 3 \cdot 2 \cdot 1}{2 \cdot 1} = \frac{5!}{2!} = \frac{5!}{(5 - 3)!}$$

This example illustrates the general rule of permutations which is stated in the following box.

Permutations

> If $P(n, r)$ (where $r \leq n$) is the number of permutations of n elements taken r at a time, then
>
> $$P(n, r) = \frac{n!}{(n - r)!}.$$

　　The proof of this rule follows the discussion of Example 2 above. There are n ways to choose the first of the r elements, $n - 1$ ways to choose the second, and $n - r + 1$ ways to choose the rth element. This makes

$$P(n, r) = n(n - 1)(n - 2) \cdot \cdot \cdot (n - r + 1).$$

Now multiply on the right by $(n - r)!/(n - r)!$.

$$P(n, r) = n(n - 1)(n - 2) \cdot \cdot \cdot (n - r + 1) \cdot \frac{(n - r)!}{(n - r)!}$$

$$= \frac{n(n - 1)(n - 2) \cdot \cdot \cdot (n - r + 1)(n - r)!}{(n - r)!}$$

$$= \frac{n!}{(n - r)!}.$$

　　To find $P(n, r)$, either the result in the box or direct application of the multiplication principle may be used, as the following example shows.

EXAMPLE 3

Find the number of permutations of 8 elements taken 3 at a time.

Since 3 choices are to be made, the multiplication principle gives $P(8, 3) = 8 \cdot 7 \cdot 6 = 336$. Alternatively, use the formula above to get

$$P(8, 3) = \frac{8!}{(8 - 3)!} = \frac{8!}{5!} = \frac{8 \cdot 7 \cdot 6 \cdot 5!}{5!} = 8 \cdot 7 \cdot 6 = 336 \quad \blacksquare$$

Combinations   In Example 2 above, we found that there are 60 ways that a teacher can arrange 3 of 5 different books on his desk. That is, there are 60 permutations of 5 things taken 3 at a time. Suppose now that the teacher does not wish to arrange the books on his desk, but rather wishes to choose, without regard to order, any 3 of the 5 books for a book sale to raise money for his school. In how many ways can he do this?

At first glance, we might say 60 again, but this is incorrect. The number 60 counts all possible *arrangements* of 3 books chosen from 5. However, the following arrangements would all lead to the same set of three books being given to the book sale.

> mystery-biography-textbook   biography-textbook-mystery
> mystery-textbook-biography   textbook-biography-mystery
> biography-mystery-textbook   textbook-mystery-biography

The list shows 6 different *arrangements* of 3 books, but only one *set* of 3 books. A subset of items selected *without regard to order* is called a **combination**. The number of combinations of 5 things taken 3 at a time is written $\binom{5}{3}$.

To evaluate $\binom{5}{3}$, start with the $5 \cdot 4 \cdot 3$ *permutations* of 5 things taken 3 at a time. Since order doesn't matter, and each subset of 3 items from the set of 5 items can have its elements rearranged in $3 \cdot 2 \cdot 1 = 3!$ ways, $\binom{5}{3}$ can be found by dividing the number of permutations by 3!, or

$$\binom{5}{3} = \frac{5 \cdot 4 \cdot 3}{3!} = \frac{5 \cdot 4 \cdot 3}{3 \cdot 2 \cdot 1} = 10.$$

There are 10 ways that the teacher can choose 3 books for the book sale. Generalizing this discussion gives the following formula for the number of combinations of n elements taken r at a time:

$$\binom{n}{r} = \frac{P(n, r)}{r!}.$$

A more useful version of this formula can be found as follows.

$$\binom{n}{r} = \frac{P(n, r)}{r!}$$

$$= \frac{n!}{(n - r)!} \cdot \frac{1}{r!}$$

$$= \frac{n!}{(n - r)!\, r!}$$

This last form is the most useful for calculation. The steps above lead to the following result.

Combinations

> **If $\binom{n}{r}$ is the number of combinations of n elements taken r at a time, then**
> $$\binom{n}{r} = \frac{n!}{(n-r)!\,r!}.$$

The table of combinations in the Appendix gives the values of $\binom{n}{r}$ for $n \le 20$.

EXAMPLE 4

How many committees of 3 people can be formed from a group of 8 people?

A committee is an unordered set, so we want $\binom{8}{3}$, which can be found with the formula in the box.

$$\binom{8}{3} = \frac{8!}{5!3!} = \frac{8 \cdot 7 \cdot 6 \cdot 5 \cdot 4 \cdot 3 \cdot 2 \cdot 1}{5 \cdot 4 \cdot 3 \cdot 2 \cdot 1 \cdot 3 \cdot 2 \cdot 1} = \frac{8 \cdot 7 \cdot 6}{3 \cdot 2 \cdot 1} = 56. \quad \blacksquare$$

EXAMPLE 5

From a group of 30 employees, 3 are to be selected to work on a special project.

(a) In how many different ways can the employees be selected?

Here we wish to know the number of 3-element combinations that can be formed from a set of 30 elements. (We want combinations, not permutations, since order within the group of 3 doesn't matter.)

$$\binom{30}{3} = \frac{30!}{27!3!} = \frac{30 \cdot 29 \cdot 28 \cdot 27!}{27! \cdot 3 \cdot 2 \cdot 1}$$

$$= \frac{30 \cdot 29 \cdot 28}{3 \cdot 2 \cdot 1}$$

$$= 4060$$

There are 4060 ways to select the project group.

(b) In how many ways can the group of 3 be selected if one particular person must work on the project?

Since one person has already been selected for the project, the problem is reduced to selecting 2 more people from the remaining 29 employees.

$$\binom{29}{2} = \frac{29!}{27!2!} = \frac{29 \cdot 28 \cdot 27!}{27! \cdot 2 \cdot 1} = \frac{29 \cdot 28}{2 \cdot 1} = 29 \cdot 14 = 406$$

In this case, the project group can be selected in 406 ways. $\quad \blacksquare$

The formulas for permutations and combinations given in this section will be very useful in solving probability problems in the next chapter. Difficulty in using these formulas often comes from being unable to select between them. In the next examples, we concentrate on recognizing which formulas to use.

EXAMPLE 6

A manager must select 4 employees for promotion: 12 employees are eligible.

(a)   In how many ways can the four be chosen?

Since there is no reason to differentiate among the 4 who are selected, use combinations.

$$\binom{12}{4} = \frac{12!}{4!8!} = 495$$

(b)   In how many ways can 4 employees be chosen (from 12) to be placed in 4 different jobs?

In this case, once a group of 4 is selected, they can be assigned in many different ways (or arrangements) to the 4 jobs. Therefore, this problem requires permutations.

$$P(12, 4) = \frac{12!}{8!} = 11,880 \quad \blacksquare$$

EXAMPLE 7

In how many ways can a full house of aces and eights (3 aces and 2 eights) be dealt in five card poker?

Here, we are not interested in the arrangement of the three aces or the two eights. Use combinations and the multiplication principle. There are $\binom{4}{3}$ ways to get 3 aces from the 4 aces in the deck, and $\binom{4}{2}$ ways to get 2 eights. The number of ways to get 3 aces and 2 eights is

$$\binom{4}{3} \cdot \binom{4}{2} = 4 \cdot 6 = 24. \quad \blacksquare$$

EXAMPLE 8

In how many ways can a flush be dealt in five-card poker? (A flush is a five-card hand of the same suit.)

The total number of ways that 5 cards of a particular suit of 13 cards can be dealt is $\binom{13}{5}$. Since the arrangement of the five cards is not important, use combinations. There are four different suits, so the multiplication principle gives

$$4 \cdot \binom{13}{5} = 4 \cdot 1287 = 5148$$

ways to deal a 5-card flush. $\quad \blacksquare$

The following table outlines the similarities of permutations and combinations as well as their differences.

Permutations	Combinations
Number of ways of selecting r items out of n items	
Repetitions are not allowed	
Order is important	Order is not important
Arrangements of r items from a set of n items	Subsets of r items from a set of n items
$P(n, r) = \dfrac{n!}{(n - r)!}$	$\dbinom{n}{r} = \dfrac{n!}{(n - r)!r!}$

It should be stressed that not all counting problems lend themselves to either of these techniques. Whenever a tree diagram or the multiplication principle can be used directly, then use it.

5.4 EXERCISES

Evaluate the factorials, permutations, and combinations in Exercises 1–12.

1. $P(4, 2)$

2. $3!$

3. $\binom{8}{3}$

4. $7!$

5. $P(8, 1)$

6. $\binom{8}{1}$

7. $4!$

8. $P(4, 4)$

9. $\binom{12}{5}$

10. $\binom{10}{8}$

11. $P(13, 2)$

12. $P(12, 3)$

You can use a computer to find values for Exercises 13–20.

13. $P(25,12)$

14. $P(38,17)$

15. $P(14,5)$

16. $P(17,12)$

17. $\binom{21}{10}$

18. $\binom{34}{25}$

19. $\binom{25}{16}$

20. $\binom{30}{15}$

21. How many different two-card hands can be dealt from an ordinary deck (52 cards)?

22. How many different four-card hands can be dealt from an ordinary deck?

23. Five cards are marked with the numbers 1, 2, 3, 4, and 5, then shuffled, and two cards are drawn. How many different two-card combinations are possible?

24. Marbles are drawn without replacement from a bag containing 15 marbles.
   (a) How many samples of 2 marbles can be drawn?
   (b) How many samples of 4 marbles can be drawn?
   (c) If the bag contains 3 yellow, 4 white, and 8 blue marbles, how many samples of 2 marbles can be drawn in which both marbles are blue?

25. Use the multiplication principle to decide how many 7-digit telephone numbers are possible if the first digit cannot be zero and
   (a) only odd digits may be used;
   (b) the telephone number must be a multiple of 10 (that is, it must end in zero);
   (c) the telephone number must be a multiple of 100;
   (d) the first three digits are 481;
   (e) no repetitions are allowed?

26. How many different license numbers consisting of 3 letters followed by 3 digits are possible?

27. In a club with 8 men and 11 women members, how many 5-member committees can be chosen that have **(a)** all men; **(b)** all women; **(c)** 3 men and 2 women.

28. Five cards are drawn from an ordinary deck. In how many ways is it possible to draw
   (a) all red cards;
   (b) all face cards (face cards are the Jack, Queen, and King);
   (c) no face card;
   (d) exactly 2 face cards;
   (e) 1 heart, 2 diamonds, and 2 clubs.

29. If a baseball coach has 5 good hitters and 4 poor hitters on the bench and chooses 3 players at random, in how many ways can he choose at least 2 good hitters?

30. A technical institute gives 12 different introductory courses, with each course given for a week. Of these courses, 5 do not require a knowledge of mathematics. If you take a course a week for three weeks, and don't repeat a course, how many arrangements are possible that do not require a knowledge of mathematics?

31. A bag contains 5 black, 1 red, and 3 yellow jelly beans; you reach in and select 3. How many samples are possible in which the jelly beans are

(a) all black;   (b) all red;

(c) all yellow;   (d) 2 black, 1 red;

(e) 2 black, 1 yellow; (f) 2 yellow, 1 black;

(g) 2 red, 1 yellow.

32. A crate of 25 apples has 5 rotten ones. How many samples of 3 apples might be drawn

(a) from the crate?

(b) in which all three are rotten?

(c) with two good apples and one rotten apple?

33. How many different types of homes are available if a builder offers a choice of 5 basic plans, 3 roof styles, and 2 exterior finishes?

34. An auto manufacturer produces 7 models, each available in 6 different colors, with 4 different upholstery fabrics, and 5 interior colors. How many varieties of the auto are available?

35. How many different 4-letter radio station call letters can be made

(a) if the first letter must be K or W and no letter may be repeated?

(b) if repeats are allowed (but the first letter is K or W)?

(c) How many 4-letter call letters (starting with K or W) with no repeats end in R?

36. A business school gives one section each of typing, shorthand, transcription, business English, technical writing, and accounting. In how many ways can a student arrange a schedule if 3 courses are taken and none of the sections overlap?

37. In how many ways can an employer select 2 new employees from a group of 4 applicants?

38. Hal's Hamburger Hamlet sells hamburgers with cheese, relish, lettuce, tomato, mustard, or catsup. How many different kinds of hamburgers can be made using any three of the extras?

39. A group of 7 workers decides to send a delegation of 2 to their supervisor to discuss their grievances.

(a) How many delegations are possible?

(b) If it is decided that a particular employee must be in the delegation, how many different delegations are possible?

(c) If there are 2 women and 5 men in the group, how many delegations would include at least 1 woman?

40. In how many ways can 7 of 10 monkeys be arranged in a row for a genetics experiment?

41. A group of 3 students is to be selected from a group of 12 students to take part in a special class in cell biology.

(a) In how many ways can this be done?

(b) In how many ways can the group which will *not* take part be chosen?

42. In an experiment on plant hardiness, a researcher gathers 6 wheat plants, 3 barley plants, and 2 rye plants. She wishes to select 4 plants to test.

(a) In how many ways can this be done?

(b) In how many ways can this be done if exactly 2 wheat plants must be included?

43. In an experiment on social interaction, 6 people will sit in 6 seats in a row. In how many ways can this be done?

44. A couple has narrowed down the choice of a name for their new baby to 3 first names and 5 middle names. How many different first and middle name arrangements are possible?

45. A session at a management meeting is to be made up of 5 presentations, 2 on motivation, 2 on stress, and 1 on the foreign threat. In how many ways may the presentations be arranged?

46. How many different license plate numbers can be formed using 3 letters followed by 3 digits if no repeats are allowed?

47. How many license plate numbers (see Exercise 46) are possible if there are no repeats and either numbers or letters can come first?

48. An economics club has 30 members. If a committee of 4 is to be selected, in how many ways can it be done?

49. A city council is composed of 5 liberals and 4 conservatives. A delegation of 3 is to be selected to attend a convention.

(a) How many delegations are possible?

(b) How many delegations could have all liberals?

(c) How many delegations could have 2 liberals and 1 conservative?

(d) If one member of the council serves as mayor, how many delegations which include the mayor are possible?

50. The coach of the Morton Valley Softball Team has 6 good hitters and 8 poor hitters. He chooses 3 hitters at random.

(a) In how many ways can he choose 2 good hitters and 1 poor hitter?

(b) In how many ways can he choose all good hitters?

51. How many 5-card poker hands are possible with a regular deck of 52 cards?

52. How many 5-card poker hands with all cards from the same suit are possible?

53. How many 13-card bridge hands are possible with a regular deck of 52 cards?

54. How many 13-card bridge hands with 4 aces are possible?

55. Eleven drugs have been found to be effective in the treatment of a disease. It is believed that the sequence in which the drugs are administered is important in the effectiveness of the treatment. In how many orders can 5 of the 11 drugs be administered?

56. A biologist is attempting to classify 52,000 species of insects by assigning 3 initials to each species. Is it possible to classify all the species in this way? If not, how many initials should be used?

5.5   The Binomial Theorem (Optional)

Evaluating the expression $(x + y)^n$ for various values of n gives a family of expressions, called **expansions,** which are important in the study of mathematics generally, and in particular in the study of probability (in the next chapter). For example,

$$(x + y)^1 = x + y$$
$$(x + y)^2 = x^2 + 2xy + y^2$$
$$(x + y)^3 = x^3 + 3x^2y + 3xy^2 + y^3$$
$$(x + y)^4 = x^4 + 4x^3y + 6x^2y^2 + 4xy^3 + y^4$$
$$(x + y)^5 = x^5 + 5x^4y + 10x^3y^2 + 10x^2y^3 + 5xy^4 + y^5.$$

Inspection of these expansions shows a pattern. Let us try to identify the pattern so that we can write a general expression for $(x + y)^n$.

First, each expansion begins with x raised to the same power as the binomial itself. That is, the expansion of $(x + y)^1$ has first term x^1, that of $(x + y)^2$ starts with x^2, while $(x + y)^3$ has first term x^3, and so on. The last term in each expansion is y raised to the same power as the binomial. Based on this, the expansion of $(x + y)^n$ should begin with x^n and end with the term y^n.

Also, the exponents on x decrease by 1 in each term after the first, while the exponents on y, beginning with y in the second term, increase by 1 in each succeeding term, with the *variables* in the expansion of $(x + y)^n$ having the following pattern:

$$x^n, \quad x^{n-1}y, \quad x^{n-2}y^2, \quad x^{n-3}y^3, \quad \ldots, \quad x^2y^{n-2}, \quad xy^{n-1}, \quad y^n.$$

This pattern shows that the sum of the exponents on x and y in each term is n. For example, in the third term above, the variable is $x^{n-2}y^2$, and the sum of the exponents, $n - 2 + 2$, is n.

Now let us try to find a pattern for the *coefficients* in the terms of the expansions shown above. In the product

$$(x + y)^5 = (x + y)(x + y)(x + y)(x + y)(x + y), \quad\quad (*)$$

the variable x occurs 5 times, once in each factor. To get the first term of the expansion, form the product of these 5 x's to get x^5. The product x^5 can occur in just one way, by taking an x from each factor in (*), so that the coefficient of x^5 is 1. We can get the term with x^4y in more than one way. For example, the x's could come from the first 4 factors and the y from the last factor, or the x's might be taken from the last 4 factors and the y from the first, and so on. Since there are 5 factors of $x + y$ in (*), from which exactly 4 x's must be selected for the term x^4y, there are

$\binom{5}{4} = 5$ of the x^4y terms. Therefore, the term x^4y has coefficient 5. In this manner, combinations can be used to find the coefficients for each term of the expansion:

$$(x + y)^5 = x^5 + \binom{5}{4}x^4y + \binom{5}{3}x^3y^2 + \binom{5}{2}x^2y^3 + \binom{5}{1}xy^4 + y^5.$$

The coefficient 1 of the first and last terms could be written $\binom{5}{5}$ or $\binom{5}{0}$ to complete the pattern.

Generalizing from this special case, the coefficient for any term of $(x + y)^n$ in which the variable is $x^{n-r}y^r$ is $\binom{n}{n-r}$. The **binomial theorem** gives the general binomial expansion.

Binomial Theorem

> **For any positive integer n,**
>
> $$(x + y)^n = \binom{n}{n}x^n + \binom{n}{n-1}x^{n-1}y + \binom{n}{n-2}x^{n-2}y^2$$
>
> $$+ \binom{n}{n-3}x^{n-3}y^3 + \cdots + \binom{n}{1}xy^{n-1} + \binom{n}{0}y^n.$$

A proof of the binomial theorem requires the method of mathematical induction. Details are given in most college algebra texts.

EXAMPLE 1

Write out the binomial expansion of $(a + b)^7$.
Use the binomial theorem.

$$(a + b)^7 = a^7 + \binom{7}{6}a^6b + \binom{7}{5}a^5b^2 + \binom{7}{4}a^4b^3 + \binom{7}{3}a^3b^4$$
$$+ \binom{7}{2}a^2b^5 + \binom{7}{1}ab^6 + b^7$$
$$= a^7 + 7a^6b + 21a^5b^2 + 35a^4b^3 + 35a^3b^4$$
$$+ 21a^2b^5 + 7ab^6 + b^7 \quad \blacksquare$$

EXAMPLE 2

Expand $\left(a - \dfrac{b}{2}\right)^4$

Use the binomial theorem to write

$$\left(a - \frac{b}{2}\right)^4 = \left[a + \left(-\frac{b}{2}\right)\right]^4$$

$$= a^4 + \binom{4}{3}a^3\left(-\frac{b}{2}\right) + \binom{4}{2}a^2\left(-\frac{b}{2}\right)^2 + \binom{4}{1}a\left(-\frac{b}{2}\right)^3 + \left(-\frac{b}{2}\right)^4$$

$$= a^4 + 4a^3\left(-\frac{b}{2}\right) + 6a^2\left(\frac{b^2}{4}\right) + 4a\left(-\frac{b^3}{8}\right) + \frac{b^4}{16}$$

$$= a^4 - 2a^3b + \frac{3}{2}a^2b^2 - \frac{1}{2}ab^3 + \frac{1}{16}b^4. \quad \blacksquare$$

Pascal's Triangle   Another method for finding the coefficients of the terms in a binomial expansion is by ***Pascal's triangle,*** in Figure 16. The nth row in the triangle gives the coefficients for the expansion of $(x + y)^n$. To see this, compare the numbers in the rows shown below with the coefficients of the expansions given at the beginning of this section. Each number in the triangle is found by adding the two numbers directly above it. Two illustrations of this are shown in color on the triangle below. A disadvantage of this method of finding coefficients is that the entire triangle must be produced down to the row which gives the desired coefficients.

```
            1
          1   1
        1   2   1
      1   3   3   1
    1   4   6   4   1
  1   5   10  10   5   1
```

FIGURE 16

The binomial theorem can be used to prove the following result, used in Section 5.1.

A set of n distinct elements has 2^n subsets.

We will illustrate the proof for $n = 6$. Subsets of a set of 6 elements can be chosen as follows: there are $\binom{6}{6}$ subsets with 6 elements, $\binom{6}{5}$ subsets with 5 elements, $\binom{6}{4}$ subsets with 4 elements and so on. Altogether there are

$$\binom{6}{6} + \binom{6}{5} + \binom{6}{4} + \binom{6}{3} + \binom{6}{2} + \binom{6}{1} + \binom{6}{0}$$

subsets. By the binomial theorem,

$$(x + y)^6 = \binom{6}{6}x^6 + \binom{6}{5}x^5y + \binom{6}{4}x^4y^2 + \binom{6}{3}x^3y^3 + \binom{6}{2}x^2y^4$$
$$+ \binom{6}{1}xy^5 + \binom{6}{0}y^6.$$

If $x = 1$ and $y = 1$,

$$(1 + 1)^6 = \binom{6}{6} \cdot 1^6 + \binom{6}{5} \cdot 1^5 \cdot 1 + \binom{6}{4} \cdot 1^4 \cdot 1^2 + \binom{6}{3} \cdot 1^3 \cdot 1^3$$
$$+ \binom{6}{2} \cdot 1^2 \cdot 1^4 + \binom{6}{1} \cdot 1 \cdot 1^5 + \binom{6}{0} \cdot 1^6$$

or $$2^6 = \binom{6}{6} + \binom{6}{5} + \binom{6}{4} + \binom{6}{3} + \binom{6}{2} + \binom{6}{1} + \binom{6}{0}.$$

Thus the total number of subsets of a set of 6 elements is $2^6 = 64$. In the general case, using the binomial theorem in the same way,

$$2^n = \binom{n}{n} + \binom{n}{n-1} + \binom{n}{n-2} + \cdots + \binom{n}{0},$$

so the total number of subsets is 2^n.

EXAMPLE 3

The Yummy Yogurt Shoppe offers either chocolate or vanilla yogurt with a choice of 3 fruit toppings, chocolate topping, and chopped nuts. How many different servings are possible with one flavor of yogurt and any combination of toppings?

Use the multiplication principle first. There are really 2 basic choices—a flavor of yogurt and a combination of toppings. A flavor can be selected in 2 ways. The 4 toppings plus nuts form a set of 5 elements. The number of different subsets which can be selected from a set of 5 elements is 2^5, making the number of different servings

$$2 \cdot 2^5 = 2^6 = 64. \quad \blacksquare$$

5.5 EXERCISES

Write out the binomial expansion and simplify the terms in Exercises 1–6.

1. $(m + n)^4$

2. $(p - q)^5$

3. $(3x - 2y)^6$

4. $(2x + t^3)^4$

5. $\left(\dfrac{m}{2} - 3n\right)^5$

6. $\left(2p + \dfrac{q}{3}\right)^3$

In Exercises 7–10, write out the first four terms of the binomial expansion and simplify.

7. $(p + q)^{10}$

8. $(r + 5)^9$

9. $(a + 2b)^{15}$

10. $(3c + d)^{12}$

11. How many different subsets can be chosen from a set of ten elements?

12. How many different subsets can be chosen from a set of eight elements?

13. How many different pizzas can be chosen if you can have cheese, beef, sausage, pepper, tomatoes, and onion?

14. How many different vanilla sundaes can be chosen if the available trimmings are chocolate, strawberry, apricot, pineapple, peanuts, walnuts, and pecan crunch?

15. How many different school programs can be selected from 20 course offerings if at least two courses and no more than six courses can be selected? (Assume no courses overlap.)

16. How many different committees can be selected from a group of 16 people if the committee must have between 2 and 5 people (inclusive)?

17. A buffet offers 4 kinds of salad to any of which can be added sliced beets, bean sprouts, chopped egg, and sliced mushrooms. How many different salads are possible?

18. The buffet in Exercise 17 offers 3 meat and 2 fish entrees. How many different entree combinations are possible?

KEY WORDS

$\{\}\quad\in\{1,2,3\}$

set	disjoint sets
element (member)	union
set-builder notation	set operations
universal set	multiplication principle
$\{1\}\subset$ subset $\{1,2,3\}$	factorial
Venn diagram	permutations
empty set $\subset$ of everything	combinations
tree diagram	expansion
complement	binomial theorem
intersection	

$\{1,2,3,4\}$ # of $C = 2^{\#\in}$ ex $2^4 = 16$

Chapter 5   REVIEW EXERCISES

Write *true* or *false* for Exercises 1–10.

1. $9 \in \{8, 4, -3, -9, 6\}$ F

2. $4 \notin \{3, 9, 7\}$

3. $2 \notin \{0, 1, 2, 3, 4\}$

4. $0 \in \{0, 1, 2, 3, 4\}$

5. $\{3, 4, 5\} \subset \{2, 3, 4, 5, 6\}$

6. $\{1, 2, 5, 8\} \subset \{1, 2, 5, 10, 11\}$

7. $\{3, 6, 9, 10\} \subset \{3, 9, 11, 13\}$

8. $\varnothing \subset \{1\}$ T

9. $\{2, 8\} \not\subset \{2, 4, 6, 8\}$

10. $0 \subset \varnothing$ F

List the elements in the sets in Exercises 11–14. Give the cardinal number of each set.

11. $\{x \mid x$ is a counting number more than 5 and less than 8$\}$ $\#\in$

12. $\{x \mid x$ is an integer, $-3 \le x < 1\}$

13. $\{$all counting numbers less than five$\}$ 0 NOT counting # (0 is whole #)

14. $\{$all whole numbers not greater than 2$\}$

Let $U = \{a, b, c, d, e, f, g\}$, $K = \{c, d, f, g\}$, and $R = \{a, c, d, e, g\}$. Find the following.

15. the number of subsets of K

16. the number of subsets of R

17. K'

18. R'

19. $K \cap R$

20. $K \cup R$

21. $(K \cap R)'$

22. $(K \cup R)'$

23. $\varnothing'$

24. U'

Let $U = \{$all employees of the K.O. Brown Company$\}$
 $A = \{$employees in the accounting department$\}$
 $B = \{$employees in the sales department$\}$
 $C = \{$employees with at least 10 years in the company$\}$
 $D = \{$employees with an MBA degree$\}$

Describe the sets of Exercises 25–30 in words.

25. $A \cap C$

26. $B \cap D$

27. $A \cup D$

28. $A' \cap D$

29. $B' \cap C'$

30. $(B \cup C)'$

Draw Venn diagrams for Exercises 31–34.

31. $A \cup B'$

32. $A' \cap B$

33. $(A \cap B) \cup C$

34. $(A \cup B)' \cap C$

A telephone survey of television viewers revealed the following information. Use this information for Exercises 35–38.

    20 watch situation comedies
    19 watch game shows
    27 watch movies
     5 watch both situation comedies and game shows
     8 watch both game shows and movies
    10 watch both situation comedies and movies
     3 watch all three
     6 watch none of these

35. How many viewers were interviewed?

36. How many viewers watch comedies and movies but not game shows?

37. How many viewers watch only movies?

38. How many viewers watch comedies and game shows but not movies?

39. In how many ways can 6 business tycoons line up their golf carts at the country club?

40. In how many ways can a sample of 3 oranges be taken from a bag of a dozen oranges?

41. In how many ways can a selection of 2 pictures from a group of 5 different pictures be arranged in a row on a wall?

42. In how many ways can the pictures of Exercise 41 be arranged if a certain one must be first?

43. In a Chinese restaurant the menu lists 8 items in column A and 6 items in column B. To order a dinner, the diner is told to select 3 items from column A and 2 from column B. How many dinners are possible?

44. A spokesperson is to be selected from each of 3 departments in a small college. If there are 7 people in the first department, 5 in the second department, and 4 in the third department, how many different groups of 3 representatives are possible?

45. Write out the binomial expansion of $(2m + n)^5$.

46. Write out the first 3 terms of the binomial expansion of $(a + b)^{16}$.

47. Write out the first 4 terms of the binomial expansion of $(x - y/2)^{20}$.

48. How many different sums can be formed from combinations of two or more of the numbers 2, 5, 10, and 13?

49. How many different collections can be formed from a set of 8 old coins, if each collection must contain at least 2 coins?

50. How many sets of three or more books can be formed from a collection of six books?

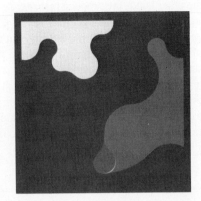
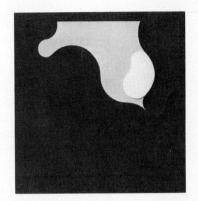

PROBABILITY

Karl Gerstner. From the series *AlgoRhythm 3*, 1973. Roche AG, Basel.

If you go to a supermarket and buy five pounds of peaches at 54¢ per pound, you can easily find the *exact* price of your purchase: $2.70. Such a purchase is **deterministic:** the result can be found *exactly*.

On the other hand, the produce manager of the market is faced with the problem of ordering peaches. The manager may have a good estimate of the number of pounds of peaches that will be sold during the day, but there is no way to know exactly. The number of items that customers will purchase during a day is **random:** the number needed cannot be predicted exactly.

A great many problems that come up in applications of mathematics are random phenomena—those for which exact prediction is impossible. The best that can be done is to construct a mathematical model that gives the *probability* of certain events. The basics of probability are discussed in this chapter, with applications of probability discussed in succeeding chapters.

6.1   Sample Spaces

In probability, each repetition of an experiment is called a **trial.** The possible results of each trial are **outcomes.** An example of a probability experiment is the tossing of a coin. Each trial of the experiment (each toss) has two possible outcomes, heads and tails, abbreviated h and t, respectively. If the two outcomes, h and t, are equally likely to occur, then the coin is not "loaded" to favor one side over the other. Such a coin is called **fair.** For a coin that is not loaded, this "equally likely" assumption is made for each trial.

Since *two* equally likely outcomes are possible, h and t, and just *one* of them is heads, we would expect that a coin tossed many, many times would come up heads approximately 1/2 of the time. We also would expect that the more times the coin was tossed, the closer the occurrence of heads should be to 1/2.

Suppose an experiment could be repeated again and again under unchanging conditions. Suppose the experiment is repeated n times, and that a certain outcome happens m times. The ratio m/n is called the **relative frequency** of the outcome after n trials.

If this ratio m/n approaches closer and closer to some fixed number p as n gets larger and larger, then p is called the **probability** of the outcome. If p exists, then

$$p \approx \frac{m}{n}$$

as n gets larger and larger.

This approach to probability is consistent with most people's intuitive feeling as to the meaning of probability—a way of measuring the likelihood of occurrence of a certain outcome. For example, since 1/4 of the cards in an ordinary deck are diamonds, we would assume that if we drew a card from a well-shuffled deck, kept track of whether it was a diamond or not, and then replaced the card in the deck, after a large number of repetitions of the experiment about 1/4 of the cards drawn would be diamonds.

This definition of probability, on the other hand, has the disadvantage of not being precise, since it uses phrases such as "approaches closer and closer" and "gets larger and larger." In the first few sections of this chapter a more precise meaning is given to the terms associated with probability.

The probability of heads on a single toss of a fair coin is 1/2. This is written

$$P(h) = \frac{1}{2}.$$

Also, $P(t) = 1/2$.

EXAMPLE 1

Suppose we spin the spinner of Figure 1.

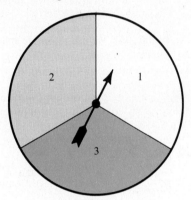

FIGURE 1

(a) Find the probability that it will point to 1.

A natural assumption is that if this spinner were spun many, many times, it would point to 1 about 1/3 of the time, so that

$$P(1) = \frac{1}{3}.$$

(b) Find the probability that it will point to 2.

Since 2 is one of three possible outcomes, $P(2) = 1/3$. ▪

An ordinary die is a cube whose six faces show the numbers 1, 2, 3, 4, 5, and 6. If the die is not "loaded" to favor certain faces over others, then any one of the six faces is equally likely to come up when the die is rolled.

EXAMPLE 2

(a) If a single fair die is rolled, find the probability of rolling the number 4.

Since one out of six faces shows a 4, $P(4) = 1/6$.

(b) Using the same die, find the probability of rolling the number 6.

Since one out of six faces shows a 6, $P(6) = 1/6$. ▪

Sample Space   Sometimes we are interested in a result that is satisfied by more than one of the possible outcomes. To find the probability that the spinner in Example 1 will point to an odd number, notice that two of the three possible outcomes are odd numbers, 1 and 3, with

$$P(\text{odd}) = \frac{2}{3}.$$

The set of all possible outcomes for an experiment is the **sample space** for the experiment. A sample space for the experiment of tossing a coin is made up of the two outcomes, heads (h) and tails (t). If S represents this sample space, then

$$S = \{h, t\}.$$

In the same way, the sample space for tossing a single fair die is

$$\{1, 2, 3, 4, 5, 6\}.$$

EXAMPLE 3

(a)   For the purposes of a certain public opinion poll, people are classified as young, middle-aged, or older, and as male or female. The sample space for this poll would be a set of ordered pairs:

{(young, male), (young, female), (middle-aged, male),
(middle-aged, female), (older, male), (older, female)}.

(b)   A firm can run its assembly line at a low, medium, or high rate. With each speed, the firm may find 1%, 2%, or 3% of the items from the line defective. Placing the line speed first in an ordered pair, and the rate of defectives second, gives the sample space

{(low, 1%), (low, 2%), (low, 3%), (medium, 1%), (medium, 2%),
(medium, 3%), (high, 1%), (high, 2%), (high, 3%)}.

(c)   A manufacturer tests automobile tires by running a tire until it fails or until tread depth reaches a certain unsafe level. The number of miles that the tire lasts, m, is recorded. At least in theory, m can be any nonnegative real number, so that the sample space is

$$\{m \mid m \geq 0\}.$$

However, for a particular type of tire, there would be practical limits on m, so that the sample space might then be

$$\{m \mid 0 \leq m \leq 50{,}000\}. \quad \blacksquare$$

An **event** is a subset of a sample space. If the sample space for tossing a coin is $S = \{h, t\}$, then one event is $E = \{h\}$, which represents the outcome "heads." For the sample space of tossing a single fair die, $\{1, 2, 3, 4, 5, 6\}$, one event is $\{2, 4, 6\}$, or "the number showing on top is even."

EXAMPLE 4

An experiment consists of studying all possible families having exactly three children. Let *b* represent "boy" and *g* represent "girl."

(a)　Write a sample space for the experiment.

　　A family can have three boys, written *bbb*, three girls, *ggg*, or various combinations, such as *bgg*. The sample space is made up of all such outcomes (there are eight).

$$S = \{bbb,\ bbg,\ bgb,\ gbb,\ bgg,\ gbg,\ ggb,\ ggg\}.$$

(b)　Write event *H*, "the family has exactly two girls."

　　Families can have exactly two girls with either *bgg*, *gbg*, or *ggb*, so that event *H* is

$$H = \{bgg,\ gbg,\ ggb\}.$$

(c)　Write the event *J*, "the family has three girls."

　　Only *ggg* satisfies this condition, so

$$J = \{ggg\}. \quad ■$$

　　In Example 4(c), event *J* had only one possible outcome, *ggg*. Such an event, with only one possible outcome, is a **simple event.** If event *E* equals the sample space *S*, then *E* is a **certain event.** If event *E* = ∅, then *E* is an **impossible event.**

EXAMPLE 5

Suppose a die is rolled. As we have seen, the sample space is {1, 2, 3, 4, 5, 6}.

(a)　The event "the die has a four showing" is a simple event, {4}. The event has only one possible outcome.

(b)　The event "the number showing is less than ten" equals the sample space, *S* = {1, 2, 3, 4, 5, 6}. This event is a certain event; if a die is rolled the number showing (either 1, 2, 3, 4, 5, or 6), must be less than ten.

(c)　The event "the die has 7 showing" is the empty set, ∅; this event is impossible. ■

　　Events are sets, so the union, intersection, and complement of events can be formed.

EXAMPLE 6

A die is tossed; let *E* be the event "the number showing is more than 3", and let *F* be the event "the number showing is even." Then

$$E = \{4, 5, 6\} \quad \text{and} \quad F = \{2, 4, 6\}.$$

(a)　*E* ∩ *F* is the event "the number showing is more than 3 *and* is even", the outcomes common to *both E* and *F*.

$$E \cap F = \{4, 6\}.$$

(b) $E \cup F$ is the event "the number showing is more than 3 *or* is even", the outcomes of E or F, or both.

$$E \cup F = \{2, 4, 5, 6\}.$$

(c) Event E' is the event "the number showing is *not* more than 3"; the elements of the sample space that are *not* in E. (Event E' is the *complement* of event E.)

$$E' = \{1, 2, 3\}.$$

The sketches of Figure 2 show the events $E \cap F$, $E \cup F$, and E'. ■

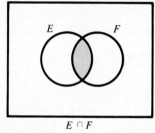 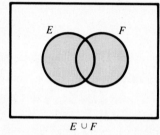 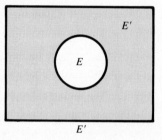

FIGURE 2

Two events that cannot both occur at the same time, such as both a head and a tail on the same toss of a coin, are **mutually exclusive events.** The events A and B are mutually exclusive events if $A \cap B = \emptyset$.

EXAMPLE 7

Let $S = \{1, 2, 3, 4, 5, 6\}$, the sample space for tossing a die. Let $E = \{4, 5, 6\}$, and let $G = \{1, 2\}$. Then E and G are mutually exclusive events since they have no outcomes in common: $E \cap G = \emptyset$. See Figure 3. ■

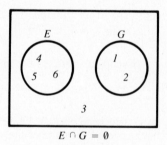

$E \cap G = \emptyset$

FIGURE 3

In summary:

Events	Let E and F be events for a sample space S. Then

$E \cap F$ occurs when both E and F occur;
$E \cup F$ occurs when either E or F or both occur;
E' occurs when E does not occur;
E and F are mutually exclusive if $E \cap F = \varnothing$.

Remember that a simple event has only one possible outcome.

6.1 EXERCISES

Write sample spaces for the experiments in Exercises 1–12. (The sample spaces in Exercises 11–12 are infinite.)

1. Choose a month of the year.

2. Pick a day in April.

3. Ask a student how many points she earned on a recent 80-point test.

4. Ask a person how many hours (to the nearest hour) he watched television yesterday.

5. The management of an oil company must decide whether to go ahead with a new oil shale plant, or cancel it.

6. A record is kept for three days about whether a particular stock goes up or down.

7. The length of life of a light bulb is measured to the nearest hour; the bulbs never last more than 5000 hours.

8. Toss a coin and roll a die.

9. Toss a coin four times.

10. A box contains five balls, numbered 1, 2, 3, 4, and 5. A ball is drawn at random, the number on it recorded, and the ball replaced. After shaking the box, a second ball is drawn, and its number is recorded.

11. A coin is tossed until a head appears.

12. A die is rolled, but only "odd" (1, 3, 5) or "even" (2, 4, 6) is recorded. Roll the die until odd appears.

13. A die is tossed twice, with the tosses recorded as ordered pairs. Write the
    (a) sample space;
    (b) event F, the first die is 3;
    (c) event G, the sum of the dice is 8;
    (d) event H, the sum of the dice is 13.

14. One urn contains four balls, labeled 1, 2, 3, and 4. A second urn contains five balls, labeled 1, 2, 3, 4, and 5. An experiment consists of taking one ball from the first urn, and then taking a ball from the second urn. Find the

   (a) sample space;

   (b) event E, the first ball is even;

   (c) event F, the second ball is even;

   (d) event G, the sum of the numbers on the two balls is 5;

   (e) event H, the sum of the numbers on the two balls is 1.

15. A coin is tossed until two heads appear, or until the coin is tossed five times, whichever comes first. Write the

   (a) sample space;

   (b) event E, the coin is tossed exactly two times;

   (c) event F, the coin is tossed exactly three times;

   (d) event G, the coin is tossed exactly five times, without getting two heads.

16. A committee of two people is selected from five executives, Abbot, Babbit, Coats, Dickson, and Ellsberg. Write the

   (a) sample space;

   (b) event E, Coats is on the committee;

   (c) event F, Dickson and Ellsberg are not both on the committee;

   (d) event G, both Abbot and Coats are on the committee.

17. The management of a firm wishes to check on the opinions of its assembly line workers. To do this, the workers are first divided into various categories. Define events E, F, and G as follows.

> E: worker is female
> F: worker has worked less than five years
> G: worker contributes to a voluntary retirement plan

Describe each of the following events in words.

   (a) E' **(b)** F' **(c)** $E \cap F$

   (d) $F \cup G$ **(e)** $E \cup G'$ **(f)** $F' \cap G'$

18. For a medical experiment, people are classified as to whether they smoke, have a family history of heart disease, and are overweight. Define events E, F, and G as follows.

> E: person smokes
> F: person has a family history of heart disease
> G: person is overweight

Describe each of the following events in words.

   (a) G' **(b)** $E \cup F$ **(c)** $F \cap G$

   (d) $E' \cap F$ **(e)** $E \cup G'$ **(f)** $F' \cup G'$

Decide if the events in Exercises 19–24 are mutually exclusive.

19. Owning a car and owning a truck.

20. Wearing glasses and wearing sandals.

21. Being married and being over 30 years old.

22. Being a teen-ager and being over 30 years old.

23. Rolling a die once and getting a 4 and an odd number.

24. A person being both male and a postal worker.

25. If E is an event, must E and E' be mutually exclusive?

26. Let E and F be mutually exclusive events. Let F and G be mutually exclusive events. Must E and G be mutually exclusive events?

27. Suppose E and F are mutually exclusive events. Must E' and F' be mutually exclusive events?

28. Suppose E and F are mutually exclusive events. Must E and $(E \cup F)'$ be mutually exclusive events?

29. A person is taking accounting and business law. Let E be the event that the student passes accounting, and let F be the event that the student passes business law. Write each of the following using E, F, $\cup$, $\cap$, and $'$, as needed. The student

(a) fails accounting;   (b) passes both;

(c) fails both;   (d) passes accounting but not business law;

(e) passes exactly one course; (f) passes at least one course.

30. Let E and F be events. Write the following, using $\cap$, $\cup$, or $'$, as needed.

(a) E does not happen   (b) neither happens   (c) both happen

(d) E happens, but not F (e) one or the other happens, but not both

31. Let $S = \{r, s, t\}$. Write all events associated with S.

32. Let $S = \{1, 2, 3, 4, \ldots, n\}$, where n is a positive integer. How many different events could be obtained from S?

6.2   Basics of Probability

Given a sample space S, we now need to assign to each event that can be obtained from S a number, called the **probability of the event.** This number will indicate the relative likelihood of the various events. In the remainder of this chapter, attention is restricted to sample spaces with a *finite* number of elements.

For events that are *equally likely*, the probability of the event can be found from the following **basic probability principle:**

Basic Probability Principle

Let a sample space S have n possible equally likely outcomes.
Let event E contain m of these outcomes, all distinct. Then the **probability** that event E occurs, written $P(E)$, is

$$P(E) = \frac{m}{n}.$$

This same result can also be given in terms of the cardinal number of a set. (Recall from Chapter 5 that $n(E)$ represents the number of elements in a finite set E.) With the same assumptions given above,

$$P(E) = \frac{n(E)}{n(S)}.$$

EXAMPLE 1

Suppose a single fair die is rolled. The sample space is $S = \{1, 2, 3, 4, 5, 6\}$. Set S contains 6 outcomes, all of which are equally likely. (This makes $n = 6$ in the box above.) Find the probability of the following outcomes.

(a) $E = \{1, 2\}$.

Event E contains two elements, so

$$P(E) = \frac{2}{6} = \frac{1}{3}.$$

By this result, a 1 or 2 will show up on a single die about 1/3 of the time.

(b) An even number is rolled.

Let event $F = \{2, 4, 6\}$ be the event "an even number is rolled." Event F contains three elements, so

$$P(F) = \frac{3}{6} = \frac{1}{2}.$$

(c) The die shows a 7.

A die can never show 7. If G is this event, then $G = \varnothing$, and

$$P(G) = \frac{0}{6} = 0.$$

This event is impossible. ■

EXAMPLE 2

If a single playing card is drawn at random from an ordinary 52-card bridge deck, find the probability of each of the following events.

(a) An ace is drawn.

There are four aces in the deck, out of 52 cards, so

$$P(\text{ace}) = \frac{4}{52} = \frac{1}{13}.$$

(b) A face card is drawn.

Since there are 12 face cards,

$$P(\text{face card}) = \frac{12}{52} = \frac{3}{13}.$$

(c) A spade is drawn.

The deck contains 13 spades, so

$$P(\text{spade}) = \frac{13}{52} = \frac{1}{4}.$$

(d) A spade or a heart is drawn.

Besides the 13 spades, the deck contains 13 hearts, so

$$P(\text{spade or heart}) = \frac{26}{52} = \frac{1}{2}. ■$$

EXAMPLE 3

The manager of a department store has decided to make a study on the size of purchases made by people coming into the store. To begin, he chooses a day that seems fairly typical and gathers the following data. (Purchases have been rounded to the nearest dollar, with sales tax ignored.)

Amount of Purchase	Number of Customers
$0	158
$1–$5	94
$6–$9	203
$10–$19	126
$20–$49	47
$50–$99	38
$100 and over	53

First, the manager might add the numbers of customers to find that 719 people came into the store that day. Of these 719 people, $126/179 \approx .175$ made a purchase of at least $10 but no more than $19. Also, $53/719 \approx .074$ of the customers spent $100 or more. Thus, the probability (on this given day) that a customer entering the store will spend from $10 to $19 is .175, and the probability that the customer will spend $100 or more is .074. Probabilities for the various purchase amounts can be assigned in the same way, giving the results of the following table.

Size of Purchase	Probability
$0	.220
$1–$5	.131
$6–$9	.282
$10–$19	.175
$20–$49	.065
$50–$99	.053
$100 and over	.074
Total	1.000

From the table, .282 of the customers spend from $6 to $9, inclusive—over a quarter of the customers. Since this price range attracts so many customers, perhaps the store's advertising should emphasize items in, or near, this price range.

The manager should use this table of probabilities to help in predicting the results on other days only if the manager is reasonably sure that the day when the measurements were made is fairly typical of the other days the store is open—for example, on the last few days before Christmas the probabilities might be quite different.   ▪

Probability Distributions   In Example 3 the outcomes were various purchase amounts, and a probability was assigned to each outcome. By this process, a **probability distribution** can be set up; that is, to each possible outcome of an experiment, a number, called the *probability* of that outcome, is assigned.

As we have seen, one way to think of these probabilities is as relative frequencies; that is, for a large number of sales days of the type measured in the table, approximately 13% of all purchases would be in the $1–$5 range, approximately 28% in the $6–$9 range, and so on.

EXAMPLE 4

Set up a probability distribution for the number of girls in a family with three children.

Start by writing the sample space, which shows the possible number of boys and girls in a family of three children, $S = \{bbb, bbg, bgb, gbb, bgg, gbg, ggb, ggg\}$. Let event E_0 be "the family has no girls;" from the sample space, $E_0 = \{bbb\}$.

In a similar way, let $E_1 = \{bbg, bgb, gbb\}$, $E_2 = \{bgg, gbg, ggb\}$, and $E_3 = \{ggg\}$. Sample space S has eight possible outcomes, and event E_1, for example, has three elements, giving $P(E_1) = 3/8$. Doing the same thing for the other events gives the following probability distribution.

Number of Girls	Probability
0	1/8
1	3/8
2	3/8
3	1/8
Total	1

(Here we assume that the probability of having a girl baby and a boy baby is equal. This assumption is not quite exact in actual fact, but the correct fraction is not far from 1/2.)

The probability distributions that were set up above suggest the following properties of probability. (Recall that a simple event contains only one possible outcome.)

Properties of Probability

Let $S = \{s_1, s_2, s_3, \ldots, s_n\}$ be the sample space obtained from the union of the n distinct simple events $\{s_1\}, \{s_2\}, \{s_3\}, \ldots, \{s_n\}$ with associated probabilities $p_1, p_2, p_3, \ldots, p_n$. Then

1. $0 \le p_1 \le 1, 0 \le p_2 \le 1, \cdots, 0 \le p_n \le 1$
   (All probabilities are between 0 and 1, inclusive.);
2. $p_1 + p_2 + p_3 + \cdots + p_n = 1$;
   (The sum of all probabilities for a sample space is 1.);
3. $P(S) = 1$;
4. $P(\varnothing) = 0$.

The Addition Principle   Suppose event E is the union of several simple events, say

$$E = \{s_1, s_2, s_3\} = \{s_1\} \cup \{s_2\} \cup \{s_3\}.$$

To find $P(E)$, the probability of event E, add the probabilities for each of the simple events making up E. For $E = \{s_1, s_2, s_3\}$,

$$P(E) = P(\{s_1\}) + P(\{s_2\}) + P(\{s_3\}).$$

The generalization of this result is called the *addition principle:*

Addition Principle

> Suppose $E = \{s_1, s_2, s_3, \cdots, s_m\}$, where $\{s_1\}, \{s_2\}, \{s_3\}, \cdots, \{s_m\}$ are distinct simple events. Then
>
> $$P(E) = P(\{s_1\}) + P(\{s_2\}) + P(\{s_3\}) + \cdots + P(\{s_m\}).$$

The addition rule *does not necessarily apply* to the addition of probabilities of events that are not simple. For example, the sum of the probability of getting at least 4 on a single roll of a die, and the probability of getting an even number on a single roll is *not* equal to the probability of getting at least 4 or an even number on a single roll. That is, $P(\text{at least } 4) = P(4, 5, \text{ or } 6) = 1/2$, $P(\text{even number}) = P(2, 4, \text{ or } 6) = 1/2$, and $P(\text{at least 4 or even}) = P(2, 4, 5, \text{ or } 6) = 2/3$, with $P(\text{at least } 4) + P(\text{even number}) \neq P(\text{at least 4 or even})$.

EXAMPLE 5

Refer to Example 3 and find the probability that a customer spends at least $6 but less than $50.

This event is the union of three simple events, spending from $6 to $9, spending from $10 to $19, or spending from $20-$49. The probability of spending at least $6 but less than $50 can thus be found by the addition principle.

$P(\text{spending at least \$6 but less than \$50})$

$$= P(\text{spending \$6-\$9}) + P(\text{spending \$10-\$19}) + P(\text{spending \$20-\$49})$$

$$= .282 + .175 + .065 = .522. \quad \blacksquare$$

Let us now extend the addition rule to events that are not necessarily simple events, but that are mutually exclusive events. Suppose that E and F are mutually exclusive events, with $E = \{s_1, s_2, \cdots, s_n\}$, and $F = \{t_1, t_2, \cdots, t_m\}$, where $\{s_1\}, \{s_2\}, \cdots, \{s_n\}$ and $\{t_1\}, \{t_2\}, \cdots, \{t_m\}$ are simple events. Then

$$P(E) + P(F) = P(\{s_1, s_2, \cdots, s_n\}) + P(\{t_1, t_2, \cdots, t_m\})$$

$$= P(\{s_1\}) + P(\{s_2\}) + \cdots + P(\{s_n\})$$
$$+ P(\{t_1\}) + P(\{t_2\}) + \cdots + P(\{t_m\})$$

$$= P(\{s_1, s_2, \cdots, s_n, t_1, t_2, \cdots, t_m\})$$

$$= P(E \cup F).$$

Addition for Mutually Exclusive Events	For *mutually exclusive* events E and F, $$P(E \cup F) = P(E) + P(F).$$

EXAMPLE 6

Use the probability distribution of Example 4 to find the probability that a family with three children has at least two girls.

Event E, "the family has at least two girls," is the union of two mutually exclusive events, "the family has two girls," and "the family has three girls." By the result in the box,

$$P(E) = P(\text{at least two girls}) = P(2 \text{ girls}) + P(3 \text{ girls})$$

$$= \frac{3}{8} + \frac{1}{8} = \frac{1}{2}. \quad \blacksquare$$

Recall that the set of all outcomes in a sample space that do not belong to an event E is called the *complement* of E, written E'. For example, in the experiment of drawing a single card from a well-shuffled deck of 52 cards, let E be the event "the card is an ace." Then E' is the event "the card is not an ace." Using this definition of E', for any event E from a sample space S,

$$E \cup E' = S \quad \text{and} \quad E \cap E' = \varnothing.$$

Since $E \cap E' = \varnothing$, events E and E' are mutually exclusive, so that

$$P(E \cup E') = P(E) + P(E').$$

However, $E \cup E' = S$, the sample space, and $P(S) = 1$. Thus

$$P(E \cup E') = P(E) + P(E') = 1,$$

giving two alternate and useful results:

Complements	$$P(E) = 1 - P(E') \quad \text{and} \quad P(E') = 1 - P(E).$$

EXAMPLE 7

In a particular experiment, $P(E) = 2/7$. Find $P(E')$.

$$P(E') = 1 - P(E) = 1 - \frac{2}{7} = \frac{5}{7} \quad \blacksquare$$

The next example shows that it is sometimes easier to find $P(E)$ by first finding $P(E')$, and then finding $P(E) = 1 - P(E')$.

EXAMPLE 8

In Example 3 above, find the probability that a customer spends less than $100.

Let E be the event "a customer spends less than $100". From the table of Example 3,

$$P(E) = .220 + .131 + .282 + .175 + .065 + .053 = .926.$$

We can also find $P(E)$ by noting that if E is the event "a customer spends less than $100," then E' is the event "a customer spends $100 and over." From the table, $P(E') = .074$, and

$$P(E) = 1 - P(E') = 1 - .074 = .926.$$

Here $P(E)$ is easier to calculate as $1 - P(E')$. ◾

Odds   Sometimes probability statements are given in terms of *odds*, a comparison of $P(E)$ with $P(E')$:

Odds

> The **odds in favor** of an event E is defined as the ratio of $P(E)$ to $P(E')$, or
>
> $$\frac{P(E)}{P(E')}.$$

EXAMPLE 9

Suppose the weather forecaster says that the probability of rain tomorrow is 1/3. Find the odds in favor of rain tomorrow.

Let E be the event "rain tomorrow." Then E' is the event "no rain tomorrow." Since $P(E) = 1/3$, we have $P(E') = 2/3$. By the definition of odds,

$$\text{odds in favor of rain} = \frac{1/3}{2/3} = \frac{1}{2}, \quad \text{written} \quad 1 \text{ to } 2, \quad \text{or} \quad 1:2.$$

On the other hand, the odds that it will *not* rain are

$$\frac{2/3}{1/3} = \frac{2}{1}, \quad \text{written} \quad 2 \text{ to } 1, \quad \text{or} \quad 2:1. \quad ◾$$

If we know that the odds in favor of an event are, say, 3 to 5, then the probability of the event is 3/8, while the probability of the complement of the event is 5/8. (Odds of 3 to 5 indicate 3 outcomes in favor of the event out of a total of 8 outcomes.) In general, if the odds favoring event E are m to n, then

$$P(E) = \frac{m}{m + n} \quad \text{and} \quad P(E') = \frac{n}{m + n}.$$

EXAMPLE 10

The odds that a particular bid will be the low bid are 4 to 5. Find the probability that the bid will be the low bid.

Odds of 4 to 5 show 4 favorable chances out of $4 + 5 = 9$ chances altogether:

$$P(\text{bid will be low bid}) = \frac{4}{4 + 5} = \frac{4}{9}.$$

There is a 5/9 chance that the bid will *not* be the low bid. ◾

Subjective Probabilities   The formulas above let us find the probability of an event that can be repeated exactly, again and again. However, we also would like to be able to assign probabilities to many occurrences that cannot be exactly repeated. For example, we might want to give the probability of rain on the day planned for the company picnic, or the probability that the earnings of a firm will increase by 30%, or the probability that a given number of pounds of peaches will be sold on a given day (as mentioned in the introduction to this chapter). The probabilities for these events are known as **subjective probabilities,** and must be assigned, if at all, on the basis of personal judgment. A sales manager may use past experience to assign a probability to the success of the current July sale, but since this year's sale can never be exactly like that of past or future Julys, it is still a subjective assignment of probability.

In many cases, no information is available and probability must be assigned on the basis of hunches or expectations. In fact, sometimes it is necessary to assign probabilities to events that will happen only once.

One difficulty with subjective probability is that different people may assign different probabilities to the same event. Nevertheless, subjective probabilities can be assigned to many occurrences where the objective approach to probability cannot be used. In a later chapter, we illustrate the use of subjective probability in more detail.

6.2 EXERCISES

A single fair die is rolled. Find the probability of the events in Exercises 1–4.

1. a 2

2. an odd number

3. a number less than 5

4. a number greater than 2.

A card is drawn from a well-shuffled deck of 52 cards. Find the probability of drawing

5. a 9;

6. a black card;

7. a black 9;

8. a heart;

9. the 9 of hearts;

10. a face card.

A single fair die is rolled. Find the odds in favor of rolling

11. the number 5;

12. 3, 4, or 5;

13. 1, 2, 3, or 4;

14. some number less than 2.

List the simple events whose union forms each of the events in Exercises 15–18.

15. getting an even number on a roll of a die

16. drawing a card that is both a heart and a face card from an ordinary deck

17. a record is made of whether a company's annual profit goes up, down, or stays the same

18. a batch of 7 items was checked, and the number of defectives recorded

An experiment is conducted for which the sample space is $S = \{s_1, s_2, s_3, s_4, s_5\}$. Which of the probability distributions in Exercises 19–24 is possible for this experiment? If a distribution is not possible, tell why.

19.

Outcomes	s_1	s_2	s_3	s_4	s_5
Probability	.09	.32	.21	.25	.13

20.

Outcomes	s_1	s_2	s_3	s_4	s_5
Probability	.92	.03	0	.02	.03

21.

Outcomes	s_1	s_2	s_3	s_4	s_5
Probability	$\frac{1}{3}$	$\frac{1}{4}$	$\frac{1}{6}$	$\frac{1}{8}$	$\frac{1}{10}$

22.

Outcomes	s_1	s_2	s_3	s_4	s_5
Probability	$\frac{1}{5}$	$\frac{1}{3}$	$\frac{1}{4}$	$\frac{1}{5}$	$\frac{1}{10}$

23.

Outcomes	s_1	s_2	s_3	s_4	s_5
Probability	.64	$-.08$	.30	.12	.02

24.

Outcomes	s_1	s_2	s_3	s_4	s_5
Probability	.05	.35	.5	.2	$-.3$

The table below gives a certain golfer's probabilities of scoring in various ranges on a par-70 course.

Range	Probability
below 60	.01
60–64	.08
65–69	.15
70–74	.28
75–79	.22
80–84	.08
85–89	.06
90–94	.04
95–99	.02
100 or more	.06

In a given round, find the probability that the golfer's score will be

25. 90 or higher;

26. below par of 70;

27. in the 70's;

28. in the 90's;

29. not in the 60's;

30. not in the 60's or 70's.

31. Find the odds in favor of the golfer shooting below par.

32. Find the odds against the golfer shooting in the 70s.

Fransisco has set up the following probability distribution for the number of hours it will take him to finish his homework.

Hours	1	2	3	4	5	6
Probability	.05	.10	.20	.40	.10	.15

Find the probability that his homework will take

33. fewer than 3 hours;

34. 3 hours or less;

35. more than 2 hours;

36. at least 2 hours;

37. more than 1 hour and less than 5 hours;

38. 8 hours.

A marble is drawn from a box containing 3 yellow, 4 white, and 8 blue marbles. Find the probability of drawing

39. a yellow marble;

40. a blue marble;

41. a white marble.

For this same marble experiment, find the odds in favor of drawing a

42. yellow marble;   **43.** blue marble;   **44.** white marble.

45. Find the odds of not drawing a white marble.

46. The probability that a company will make a profit this year is .74. Find the odds against the company making a profit.

47. If the odds that it will rain are 4 to 7, what is the probability of rain?

48. If the odds that a given candidate will win an election are 3 to 2, what is the probability that the candidate will lose?

The probability distribution for a given experiment having sample space $S = \{s_1, s_2, s_3, s_4, s_5, s_6\}$ is shown here.

Outcomes	s_1	s_2	s_3	s_4	s_5	s_6
Probability	.17	.03	.09	.46	.21	.04

Let $E = \{s_1, s_2, s_5\}$, and let $F = \{s_4, s_5\}$. Find each of the following probabilities.

49. $P(E)$ **50.** $P(F)$ **51.** $P(E \cap F)$ **52.** $P(E \cup F)$ **53.** $P(E' \cup F')$ **54.** $P(E' \cap F)$

Which of the following are examples of subjective probability?

55. the probability of heads on five consecutive tosses of a coin

56. the probability that a freshman entering college will graduate with a degree

57. the probability that a person is allergic to penicillin

58. the probability of drawing an ace from a standard deck of 52 cards

59. the probability that a person will get lung cancer from smoking cigarettes

60. a weather forecaster predicts a 70% chance of rain tomorrow

61. a gambler claims that on a roll of a fair die, $P(\text{even}) = 1/2$

62. a surgeon gives a patient a 90% chance of a full recovery

63. a bridge player has a 1/4 chance of being dealt a diamond

64. a forest ranger states that the probability of a short fire season this year is only 3 in 10

65. On page 134 of Roger Staubach's autobiography, *First Down, Lifetime to Go*, Staubach makes the following statement regarding his experience in Vietnam: "Odds against a direct hit are very low but when your life is in danger, you don't worry too much about the odds." Is this wording consistent with our definition of odds, for and against? How could it have been said so as to be technically correct?

One way to solve a probability problem is to repeat the experiment (or a simulation of the experiment) many times, keeping track of the results. Then the probability can be approximated using the basic definition of the probability of an event E: $P(E) = m/n$, where m favorable outcomes occur in n trials of an experiment. This is called the *Monte Carlo* method of finding probabilities. Suppose a coin is tossed five times. Use the Monte Carlo method to approximate the probabilities in Exercises 66 and 67. Then calculate the theoretical probabilities using the methods of the text and compare the results.

66. $P(4 \text{ heads})$ **67.** $P(2 \text{ heads}, 1 \text{ tail}, 2 \text{ heads})$ (in the order given)

Use the Monte Carlo method to approximate the following probabilities if four cards are drawn from 52.

68. $P(\text{any two cards and then two kings})$ **69.** $P(\text{two kings})$

EXTENDED	**Making a First Down**

APPLICATION

A first down is desirable in football—it guarantees four more plays by the team making it, assuming no score or turnover occurs in the plays. After getting a first down, a team can get another by advancing the ball at least ten yards. During the four plays given by a first down, a team's position will be indicated by a phrase such as "third and 4," which means that the team has already had two of its four plays, and that 4 more yards are needed to get the 10 yards necessary for another first down. An article in a management journal* offers the following results for 189 games of a recent National Football League season. "Trials" represents the number of times a team tried to make a first down, given that it was currently playing either a third or a fourth down. Here n represents the number of yards still needed for a first down.

n	Trials	Successes	Probability of making first down with n yards to go
1	543	388	
2	327	186	
3	356	146	
4	302	97	
5	336	91	

EXERCISES

1. Complete the table.

2. Why is the sum of the answers in Exercise 1 not equal to 1?

6.3   Extending the Addition Rule

We saw in the previous section that for mutually exclusive events E and F,

$$P(E \cup F) = P(E) + P(F). \tag{1}$$

This result can now be extended to *any* two events E and F.

*Reprinted by permission of Virgil Carter and Robert Machols, "Optimal Strategies on Fourth Down," *Management Science*, Vol. 24, No. 16, December 1978, copyright © 1978 The Institute of Management Sciences.

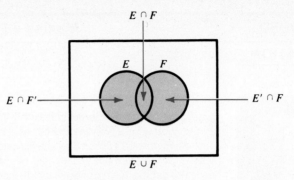

FIGURE 4

To obtain this more general result, take the region $E \cup F$ of Figure 4 and break it into three disjoint regions: that part of E not including F, $E \cap F'$; the intersection, $E \cap F$; and that part of F not including E, $E' \cap F$. By this process, $E \cup F$ becomes

$$E \cup F = (E \cap F') \cup (E \cap F) \cup (E' \cap F).$$

Since all three of the sets on the right are disjoint, use an extension of property (1) above to get

$$P(E \cup F) = P(E \cap F') + P(E \cap F) + P(E' \cap F). \tag{2}$$

As illustrated by Figure 4,

$$E = (E \cap F') \cup (E \cap F) \qquad \text{and} \qquad F = (E' \cap F) \cup (E \cap F)$$

so that, by (1) above,

$$P(E) = P(E \cap F') + P(E \cap F) \tag{3}$$

and

$$P(F) = P(E' \cap F) + P(E \cap F). \tag{4}$$

From (3),

$$P(E \cap F') = P(E) - P(E \cap F) \tag{5}$$

and from (4),

$$P(E' \cap F) = P(F) - P(E \cap F). \tag{6}$$

Substituting from equations (5) and (6) into equation (2) gives

$$P(E \cup F) = P(E) + P(F) - P(E \cap F). \tag{7}$$

This result is called the *extended addition principle*.

Extended Addition Principle	For any two events E and F from a sample space S, $$P(E \cup F) = P(E) + P(F) - P(E \cap F).$$

Notice the similarity of this result to the formula for the number of elements in the union of two sets, given in Chapter 5.

EXAMPLE 1

If a single card is drawn from an ordinary deck, find the probability that it will be red or a face card.

Let R and F represent the events "red" and "face card" respectively. Then

$$P(R) = \frac{26}{52}, \qquad P(F) = \frac{12}{52}, \qquad \text{and} \qquad P(R \cap F) = \frac{6}{52}.$$

(There are six red face cards in a deck.) By the extended addition principle,

$$P(R \cup F) = P(R) + P(F) - P(R \cap F)$$

$$= \frac{26}{52} + \frac{12}{52} - \frac{6}{52}$$

$$= \frac{32}{52} = \frac{8}{13}. \quad \blacksquare$$

EXAMPLE 2

Suppose two fair dice are rolled. Find each of the following probabilities.

(a) The first die shows a 2 or the sum is 6 or 7

The sample space for the throw of two dice is shown in Figure 5. The two events are labeled A and B. From the diagram,

$$P(A) = \frac{6}{36}, \qquad P(B) = \frac{11}{36}, \qquad \text{and} \qquad P(A \cap B) = \frac{2}{36}.$$

By the extended addition principle,

$$P(A \cup B) = P(A) + P(B) - P(A \cap B),$$

$$P(A \cup B) = \frac{6}{36} + \frac{11}{36} - \frac{2}{36} = \frac{15}{36} = \frac{5}{12}.$$

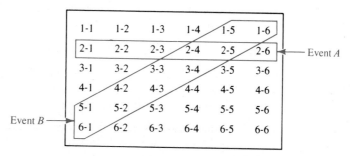

FIGURE 5

(b)   the sum is 11 or the second die is 5

P(sum is 11) = 2/36, P(second die is 5) = 6/36, and P(sum is 11 and second die is 5) = 1/36, so

$$P\text{(sum is 11 or second die is 5)} = \frac{2}{36} + \frac{6}{36} - \frac{1}{36} = \frac{7}{36}. \quad \blacksquare$$

EXAMPLE 3

The personnel director at a medium sized manufacturing company has received 20 applications from people applying for a job as plant manager. Of these 20 people, 8 have MBA degrees, 9 have previous related experience, and 5 have both MBA degrees and experience. Find the probability that a given candidate has an MBA degree or previous related experience.

Use M for "has degree" and E for "has experience." As stated, $P(M) =$ 8/20, $P(E) =$ 9/20, and $P(M \cap E) =$ 5/20, with

$$P(M \cup E) = \frac{8}{20} + \frac{9}{20} - \frac{5}{20} = \frac{12}{20} = \frac{3}{5}. \quad \blacksquare$$

EXAMPLE 4

Susan is a college student who receives heavy sweaters from her aunt at the first sign of cold weather. The probability that a sweater is the wrong size is .47, the probability that it is a loud color is .59, and the probability that it is both the wrong size and a loud color is .31. Let W represent the event "wrong size," while L represents "loud color." Place the given information on a Venn diagram by starting with .31 in the intersection of the regions for W and L. Event W has probability .47. Since .31 has already been placed inside the intersection of W and L,

$$.47 - .31 = .16$$

goes inside region W, but outside the intersection of W and L. In the same way,

$$.59 - .31 = .28$$

goes inside the region for L, and outside the overlap.

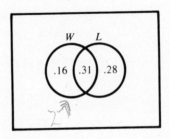

FIGURE 6

(a)   Find the probability that the sweater is the correct size and not a loud color.

Using regions W and L, this event becomes $W' \cap L'$. From the Venn diagram of Figure 6, the labeled regions have probability

$$.16 + .31 + .28 = .75.$$

Since the entire region of the Venn diagram is assumed to have probability 1, the region outside W and L, or $W' \cap L'$, has probability

$$1 - .75 = .25.$$

The probability is .25 that the sweater is the correct size and not a loud color.

(b) Find the probability that the sweater is the correct size or is not loud.

The region $W' \cup L'$ has probability

$$.25 + .16 + .28 = .69. \quad \blacksquare$$

6.3 EXERCISES

Two dice are rolled. Find the probability of rolling the sums in Exercises 1–14.

1. 2

2. 4

3. 5

4. 6

5. 8

6. 9

7. 10

8. 13

9. 9 or more

10. less than 7

11. between 5 and 8

12. not more than 5

13. not less than 8

14. between 3 and 7

One card is drawn from an ordinary deck of 52 cards. Find the probability of drawing

15. a 9 or a 10;

16. red or a 3;

17. a 9 or black 10;

18. a heart or black;

19. less than 4 (count aces as 1s);

20. a diamond or a 7;

21. a black card or an ace;

22. a heart or a jack.

Ms. Elliott invites ten relatives to a party: her mother, two aunts, three uncles, two brothers, one male cousin, and one female cousin. If the chances of any one guest arriving first are equally likely, find the probability that the first guest to arrive is

23. a brother or uncle;

24. a brother or cousin;

25. a brother or her mother;

26. an uncle or a cousin;

27. a male or a cousin;

28. a female or a cousin.

The numbers 1, 2, 3, 4, and 5 are written on slips of paper and two slips are drawn at random without replacement. Find each of the following probabilities.

29. the sum of the numbers is 9

30. both numbers are even

31. the sum of the numbers is 5 or less

32. one of the numbers is even or greater than 3

33. the first number is 2 or the sum is 6

34. the sum is 5 or the second number is 2

35. A student feels that her probability of passing accounting is .74, of passing mathematics is .39, and that her probability of passing both courses is .25. Find the probability that the student passes at least one course.

36. Suppose that 8% of a certain batch of calculators have a defective case, and that 11% have defective batteries. Also, 3% have both a defective case and defective batteries. A calculator is selected from the batch at random. Find the probability that the calculator has a good case and good batteries.

The table below shows the probability that a customer of a department store will make a purchase in the indicated range.

Cost	Probability
below $2	.07
$2–$4.99	.18
$5–$9.99	.21
$10–$19.99	.16
$20–$39.99	.11
$40–$69.99	.09
$70–$99.99	.07
$100–$149.99	.08
$150 or over	.03

Find the probability that a customer makes a purchase which is

37. less than $5;   **38.** $10 to $69.99;   **39.** $20 or more;

40. more than $4.99;   **41.** less than $100;   **42.** $100 or more.

Suppose $P(E) = .26$, $P(F) = .41$, and $P(E \cap F) = .17$. Use a Venn diagram to help find each of the following.

43. $P(E \cup F)$ **44.** $P(E' \cap F)$ **45.** $P(E \cap F')$ **46.** $P(E' \cup F')$

Let $P(Z) = .42$, $P(Y) = .38$, and $P(Z \cup Y) = .61$. Find each of the following probabilities.

47. $P(Z' \cap Y')$ **48.** $P(Z' \cup Y')$ **49.** $P(Z' \cup Y)$ **50.** $P(Z \cap Y')$

Color blindness is an inherited characteristic which is sex-linked, so that it is more common in males than in females. If M represents male and C represents red-green color blindness, we use the relative frequencies of the incidence of males and of red-green color blindness as probabilities to get $P(C) = .049$, $P(M \cap C) = .042$, $P(M \cup C) = .534$. Find the following.

51. $P(C')$ **52.** $P(M)$ **53.** $P(M')$

54. $P(M' \cap C')$ **55.** $P(C \cap M')$ **56.** $P(C \cup M')$

Gregor Mendel, an Austrian monk, was the first to use probability in the study of genetics. In an effort to understand the mechanism of character transmittal from one generation to the next in plants, he counted the number of occurrences of various characteristics. Mendel found that the flower color in certain pea plants obeyed this scheme:

Pure red crossed with pure white produces red.

The red offspring received from its parents genes for both red (R) and white (W) but in this case red is *dominant* and white *recessive,* so the offspring exhibits the color red. However, the offspring still carries both genes, and when two such offspring are crossed, several things can happen in the third generation. The table below, which is called a *Punnet square,* shows the possibilities.

		2nd parent	
		R	W
	R	RR	RW
1st parent	W	WR	WW

Use the fact that red is dominant over white to find

57. P(red);   **58.** P(white).

Mendel found no dominance in snapdragons, with one red gene and one white gene producing pink-flowered offspring. These second generation pinks, however, still carry one red and one white gene, and when they are crossed, the next generation still yields the Punnet square above. Find

59. P(red);   **60.** P(pink);   **61.** P(white).

(Mendel verified these probability ratios experimentally and did the same for many character units other than flower color. His work, published in 1866, was not recognized until 1890.)

   In most animals and plants, it is very unusual for the number of main parts of the organism (arms, legs, toes, flower petals, etc.) to vary from generation to generation. Some species, however, have *meristic variability,* in which the number of certain body parts varies from generation to generation. One researcher studied the front feet of certain guinea pigs and produced the following probabilities.*

$$P(\text{only four toes, all perfect}) = .77$$
$$P(\text{one imperfect toe and four good ones}) = .13$$
$$P(\text{exactly five good toes}) = .10$$

Find the probability of each of the following events.

62. no more than four good toes

63. five toes, whether perfect or not

64. Let E, F, and G be events from a sample space S. Show that
$$P(E \cup F \cup G) = P(E) + P(F) + P(G) - P(E \cap F) - P(E \cap G) - P(F \cap G)$$
$$+ P(E \cap F \cap G).$$

   (Hint: let $H = E \cup F$ and use equation (7).)

65. A group of three people, each with a different type of hat, decides to exchange hats. To do so, they toss their hats into a pile. Each person then takes a hat at random. Find the probability that at least one person gets his own hat.

66. Prove equation (2) in this section.

Approximate the following probabilities, using the Monte Carlo method.

67. A jeweler received 8 identical watches each in a box marked with the serial number of the watch. An assistant, who does not know that the boxes are marked, is told to polish the watches and then put them back in the boxes. She puts them in the boxes at random. What is the probability that she gets at least one watch in the right box?

68. A check room attendant has 10 hats but has lost the numbers identifying them. If he gives them back randomly, what is the probability that at least 2 of the hats are given back correctly?

---

*From "An Analysis of Variability in Guinea Pigs" by J. R. Wright in *Genetics* 19, pp. 506–536. Reprinted by permission.

6.4   Applications of Counting

In Chapter 5 we studied permutations and combinations—ways of counting the number of outcomes for various kinds of experiments. In this section we use these methods of counting to help solve problems in probability. The solution to many of these problems depends on the basic probability principle of Section 6.2:

> Let a sample space S have n possible equally likely outcomes, and let event E contain m of these outcomes, all distinct elements. The probability that event E occurs is

$$P(E) = \frac{m}{n}.$$

EXAMPLE 1

From a group of 22 employees, 4 are to be selected to present a list of grievances to management.

(a)   In how many ways can this be done?

We must select 4 employees from a group of 22; this can be done in $\binom{22}{4}$ ways. From Section 5.4,

$$\binom{22}{4} = \frac{22!}{4!18!} = \frac{22(21)(20)(19)}{4(3)(2)(1)} = 7315.$$

There are 7315 ways to choose 4 people from 22.

(b)   One of the employees is Jill Streitsel; the group agrees that she must be one of the 4 people chosen. Find the probability that Streitsel will be among the 4 chosen.

If Streitsel must be one of the 4 people, the problem reduces to finding the number of ways that the additional 3 employees can be chosen. The 3 are chosen from 21 employees; this can be done in

$$\binom{21}{3} = \frac{21!}{3!18!} = \frac{21(20)(19)}{3(2)(1)} = 1330$$

ways. The probability that Streitsel will be one of the 4 employees chosen is

$$P(\text{Streitsel is chosen}) = \frac{1330}{7315} \approx .182.$$

The probability that she will *not* be chosen is $1 - .182 = .818.$ ∎

EXAMPLE 2

When shipping diesel engines abroad, it is common to pack 12 engines in one container which is then loaded on a rail car and sent to a port. Suppose that a company has received complaints from its customers that many of the engines arrive in nonworking condition. To help solve this problem, the company decides to make a spot check of containers after loading—the company will test 3 engines from a container at random; if any of the 3 are nonworking, the container will not be shipped until each engine in it is checked. Suppose a given container has 2 nonworking engines, and find the probability that the container will not be shipped.

The container will not be shipped if the sample of 3 engines contains 1 or 2 defective engines. If P(1 defective) represents the probability of exactly 1 defective engine in the sample, then

$$P(\text{not shipping}) = P(\text{1 defective}) + P(\text{2 defectives}).$$

There are $\binom{12}{3}$ ways to choose the 3 engines for testing:

$$\binom{12}{3} = \frac{12!}{3!9!} = \frac{12(11)(10)}{3(2)(1)} = 220.$$

There are $\binom{2}{1}$ ways of choosing 1 defective engine from the 2 in the container, and for each of these ways, there are $\binom{10}{2}$ ways of choosing 2 good engines from among the 10 in the container. This makes

$$\binom{2}{1}\binom{10}{2} = \frac{2!}{1!1!} \cdot \frac{10!}{2!8!} = 2(45) = 90$$

ways of choosing a sample of 3 engines containing one defective, with

$$P(\text{1 defective}) = \frac{90}{220}.$$

There are $\binom{2}{2}$ ways of choosing 2 defective engines from the 2 defective engines in the container, and $\binom{10}{1}$ ways of choosing 1 good engine from among the 10 good engines, for

$$\binom{2}{2}\binom{10}{1} = \frac{2!}{2!0!} \cdot \frac{10!}{1!9!} = 1(10) = 10$$

ways of choosing a sample of 3 engines containing 2 defectives. Finally,

$$P(\text{2 defectives}) = \frac{10}{220}$$

and

$$P(\text{not shipping}) = P(\text{1 defective}) + P(\text{2 defectives})$$

$$= \frac{90}{220} + \frac{10}{220} = \frac{100}{220} \approx .455.$$

The probability is $1 - .455 = .545$ that the container *will* be shipped, even though it has 2 defective engines. The management must decide if this probability is acceptable; if not, it may be necessary to test more than three engines from a container. ▪

Instead of finding the sum $P(1 \text{ defective}) + P(2 \text{ defectives})$, the result in Example 2 could be found as $1 - P(\text{no defectives})$.

$$P(\text{not shipping}) = 1 - P(\text{no defectives in sample})$$

$$= 1 - \frac{\binom{2}{0}\binom{10}{3}}{\binom{12}{3}}$$

$$= 1 - \frac{1(120)}{220}$$

$$= 1 - \frac{120}{220} = \frac{100}{220} \approx .455$$

EXAMPLE 3

In a common form of the card game *poker*, a hand of 5 cards is dealt to each player from a deck of 52 cards. There are a total of

$$\binom{52}{5} = \frac{52!}{5!47!} = 2,598,960$$

such hands possible. Find each of the following probabilities.

(a) a hand containing only hearts, called a *heart flush*

There are 13 hearts in a deck, with

$$\binom{13}{5} = \frac{13!}{5!8!} = \frac{13(12)(11)(10)(9)}{5(4)(3)(2)(1)} = 1287$$

different hands containing only hearts. The probability of a heart flush is

$$P(\text{heart flush}) = \frac{1287}{2,598,960} = \frac{33}{66,640} \approx .000495.$$

(b) a flush of any suit

There are 4 suits in a deck, so

$$P(\text{flush}) = 4 \cdot P(\text{heart flush}) = 4 \cdot \frac{33}{66,640} \approx .00198.$$

(c) a full house of aces and eights (3 aces and 2 eights)

There are $\binom{4}{3}$ ways to choose 3 aces from among the 4 in the deck, and $\binom{4}{2}$ ways to choose 2 eights.

$$P(3 \text{ aces, } 2 \text{ eights}) = \frac{\binom{4}{3} \cdot \binom{4}{2}}{2,598,960} = \frac{1}{108,290} \approx .00000923.$$

(d) any full house (3 cards of one value, 2 of another)

The 13 values in a deck give 13 choices for the first value, leaving 12 choices for the second value (order *is* important here, since a full house of aces and eights is not the same as a full house of eights and aces). From part (c), the probability for any *particular* full house is $1/108,290$; the probability of *any* full house is

$$P(\text{full house}) = 13 \cdot 12 \cdot \left(\frac{1}{108,290}\right) = \frac{156}{108,290} \approx .00144. \quad \blacksquare$$

EXAMPLE 4

Suppose a group of n people is in a room. Find the probability that at least 2 of the people have the same birthday.

Here we refer to the month and the day, not necessarily the same year. Also, ignore leap years, and assume that each day in the year is equally likely as a birthday. Let us first find the probability that *no 2 people* among 5 people have the same birthday. There are 365 different birthdays possible for the first of the 5 people, 364 for the second (so that the people have different birthdays), 363 for the third, and so on. The number of ways the 5 people can have different birthdays is the number of permutations of 365 things (days) taken 5 at a time, or

$$P(365, 5) = 365 \cdot 364 \cdot 363 \cdot 362 \cdot 361.$$

The number of ways that the 5 people can have the same or different birthdays is

$$365 \cdot 365 \cdot 365 \cdot 365 \cdot 365 = (365)^5.$$

Finally, the *probability* that none of the 5 people have the same birthday is

$$\frac{P(365, 5)}{(365)^5} = \frac{365 \cdot 364 \cdot 363 \cdot 362 \cdot 361}{365 \cdot 365 \cdot 365 \cdot 365 \cdot 365} \approx .973.$$

The probability that at least 2 of the 5 people *do* have the same birthday is $1 - .973 = .027$.

We can extend this same result for more than 5 people. Generalizing, the probability that no 2 people among n people have the same birthday is

$$\frac{P(365, n)}{(365)^n}.$$

The probability that at least 2 of the n people *do* have the same birthday is

$$1 - \frac{P(365, n)}{(365)^n}.$$

The following table shows this probability for various values of n.

Number of People, n	Probability that Two Have the Same Birthday
5	.027
10	.117
15	.253
20	.411
22	.476
23	.507
25	.569
30	.706
35	.814
40	.891
50	.970
365	1

The probability that 2 people among 23 have the same birthday is .507, a little more than half. Many people are surprised at this result—somehow it seems that a larger number of people should be required. ■

6.4 EXERCISES

A shipment of 9 typewriters contains 2 defectives. Find the probability that a sample of the following size, drawn from the 9, will not contain a defective.

1. 1   **2.** 2   **3.** 3   **4.** 4

Refer to Example 2. The management feels that the probability of .545 that a container will be shipped even though it contains 2 defectives is too high. They decide to increase the sample size chosen. Find the probability that a container will be shipped even though it contains 2 defectives if the sample size is increased to

5. 4;   **6.** 5.

A basket contains 6 red apples and 4 yellow apples. A sample of 3 apples is drawn. Find the probability that the sample contains

7. all red apples;   **8.** all yellow apples;

9. 2 yellow and 1 red apple;   **10.** more red than yellow apples.

Two cards are drawn at random from an ordinary deck of 52 cards.

11. How many two card hands are possible?

Find the probability that the two card hand contains

12. two aces;   **13.** at least one ace;

14. all spades;   **15.** two cards of the same suit;

16. only face cards;   **17.** no face cards;

18. no card higher than 8 (count ace as 1).

Twenty-six slips of paper are each marked with a different letter of the alphabet, and placed in a basket. A slip is pulled out, its letter recorded (in the order in which the slip was drawn), and the slip replaced. This is done 5 times. Find the probabilities that the "word" formed

19. is "chuck";   **20.** starts with p;

21. has all different letters;   **22.** contains no x, y, or z.

Find the probability of the following hands at poker. Assume aces are either high or low.

23. royal flush (5 highest cards of a single suit)

24. straight flush (5 in a row in a single suit, but not a royal flush)

25. four of a kind (4 cards of the same value)

26. straight (5 cards in a row, not all of the same suit) with ace either high or low

A bridge hand is made up of 13 cards from a deck of 52. Set up the probability that a hand chosen at random

27. contains only hearts;   **28.** has 4 aces;

29. contains exactly 3 aces and exactly 3 kings;

30. has 6 of one suit, 5 of another, and 2 of another.

31. Set up the probability that at least 2 of the 39 Presidents of the United States have had the same birthday.

32. Estimate the probability that at least 2 of the 100 U.S. Senators have the same birthday.

33. Give the probability that 2 of the 435 members of the House of Representatives have the same birthday.

34. Show that the probability that in a group of n people *exactly one* pair have the same birthday is

$$\binom{n}{2} \cdot \frac{P(365,\ n-1)}{(365)^n}.$$

35. To win a contest, a player must match 4 movie stars with his or her baby picture. Suppose this is done at random. Find the probability of getting no matches correct; of getting exactly 2 correct.

36. A contractor has hired a decorator to send 3 different sofas out to the contractor's model homes each week for a year. The contractor does not want exactly the same 3 sofas sent out twice. Find the minimum number of sofas that the decorator will need.

37. An elevator has 4 passengers and stops at 7 floors. It is equally likely that a person will get off at any one of the 7 floors. Find the probability that no 2 passengers leave at the same floor.

Exercises 38–44 involve the idea of a *circular permutation:* the number of ways of arranging distinct objects in a circle. The number of ways of arranging n distinct objects in a line is $n!$, but there are fewer ways for arranging the n items in a circle since the first item could be placed in any of n locations.

38. Show that the number of ways of arranging n distinct items in a circle is $(n-1)!$.

Find the number of ways of arranging the following number of distinct items in a circle.

39. 4   **40.** 7   **41.** 10

Use the idea of a circular permutation for Exercises 42–44.

42. Suppose that 8 people sit at a circular table. Find the probability that 2 particular people are sitting next to each other.

43. A keyring contains 7 keys; one black, one gold, and 5 silver. If the keys are arranged at random on the ring, find the probability that the black key is next to the gold key.

44. A circular table for a board of directors has 10 seats for the 10 attending members of the board. The chairman of the board always sits closest to the window. The vice president for sales, who is currently out of favor, will sit 3 positions to the chairman's left, since the chairman doesn't see so well out of his left eye. The chairman's daughter-in-law will sit opposite him. All other members take seats at random. Find the probability that a particular other member will sit next to the chairman.

45. Rework Exercises 23–26 using the Monte Carlo method to approximate the answers with $n = 25$. Since each hand has 5 cards, you will need $25 \cdot 5 = 125$ random numbers to "look at" 25 hands. Compare these experimental results with the theoretical results.

46. Rework Exercises 27–30 using the Monte Carlo method to approximate the answers with $n = 20$. Since each hand has 13 cards, you will need $20 \cdot 13 = 260$ random numbers to "look at" 20 hands.

6.5   Conditional Probability

The training manager for a large stockbrokerage firm has noticed that some of the firm's brokers use the firm's research advice, while other brokers tend to go with their own feelings of which stocks will go up. To see if the research department is better than just the feelings of the brokers, the manager conducted a survey of 100 brokers, with results as shown in the following table.

	Picked Stocks that Went Up	Didn't Pick Stocks that Went Up	Totals
Used research	30	15	45
Didn't use research	30	25	55
Totals	60	40	100

Letting A represent the event "picked stocks that went up," and letting B represent the event "used research," we can find the following probabilities.

$$P(A) = \frac{60}{100} = .6 \qquad P(A') = \frac{40}{100} = .4$$

$$P(B) = \frac{45}{100} = .45 \qquad P(B') = \frac{55}{100} = .55$$

Suppose we want to find the probability that a broker using research will pick stocks that go up. From the table above, of the 45 brokers who use research, 30 picked stocks that went up, with

$$P(\text{broker who uses research picks stocks that go up}) = \frac{30}{45} = .667.$$

This is a different number than the probability that a broker picks stocks that go up, .6, since we have additional information (the broker uses research) which reduced the sample space. In other words, we found the probability that a broker picks stocks that go up, A, given the additional information that the broker uses research, B. This is called the *conditional probability* of event A, given that event B has occurred, written $P(A|B)$. In the example above,

$$P(A|B) = \frac{30}{45},$$

which can be written as

$$P(A|B) = \frac{30/100}{45/100} = \frac{P(A \cap B)}{P(B)}$$

where $P(A \cap B)$ represents, as usual, the probability that both A and B will occur.

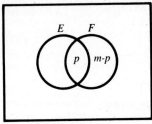

Event F has a total of m elements

FIGURE 7

Let us generalize this result. Assume that E and F are two events for a particular experiment. Assume that the sample space S for this experiment has n possible equally likely outcomes. Suppose event F has m elements, while $E \cap F$ has p elements ($p \le m$). Using the fundamental principle of probability,

$$P(F) = \frac{m}{n} \quad \text{and} \quad P(E \cap F) = \frac{p}{n}.$$

We now want $P(E|F)$, the probability that E occurs given that F has occurred. Since we assume F has occurred, look only at the m elements inside F. (See Figure 7). Of these m elements, there are p elements where E also occurs, since $E \cap F$ has p elements. This makes

$$P(E|F) = \frac{p}{m}.$$

Divide numerator and denominator by n to get

$$P(E|F) = \frac{\dfrac{p}{n}}{\dfrac{m}{n}} = \frac{P(E \cap F)}{P(F)}.$$

This result is actually chosen as the definition of conditional probability.

Definition of Conditional Probability

The **conditional probability** of event E given event F, written $P(E|F)$, is

$$P(E|F) = \frac{P(E \cap F)}{P(F)}, \qquad P(F) \ne 0.$$

EXAMPLE 1

Use the information given in the chart at the beginning of this section to find the following probabilities.

(a) $P(B|A)$

By the definition of conditional probability,

$$P(B|A) = \frac{P(B \cap A)}{P(A)}.$$

In the example, $P(B \cap A) = 30/100$, and $P(A) = 60/100$, with

$$P(B|A) = \frac{30/100}{60/100} = \frac{1}{2}.$$

If a broker picked stocks that went up, then the probability is 1/2 that the broker used research.

(b) $P(A'|B)$

$$P(A'|B) = \frac{P(A' \cap B)}{P(B)} = \frac{15/100}{45/100} = \frac{1}{3}.$$

(c) $P(B'|A')$

$$P(B'|A') = \frac{P(B' \cap A')}{P(A')} = \frac{25/100}{40/100} = \frac{5}{8}. \quad \blacksquare$$

Venn diagrams can be used to illustrate problems in conditional probability. A Venn diagram for Example 1, in which the probabilities are used to indicate the number in the set defined by each region, is shown in Figure 8. In the diagram, $P(B|A)$ is found by reducing the sample space to just set A. Then $P(B|A)$ is the ratio of the number in that part of set B which is also in A to the number in set A, or $.3/.6 = .5$.

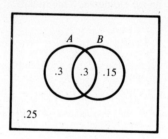

FIGURE 8

EXAMPLE 2

Two fair coins were tossed, and it is known that at least one was heads. Find the probability that both were heads.

The sample space has four equally likely outcomes, $S = \{hh, ht, th, tt\}$. Define two events:

$$E_1 = \text{at least one head}, \quad \text{or } E_1 = \{hh, ht, th\}.$$
$$E_2 = \text{two heads}, \quad \text{or } E_2 = \{hh\}.$$

Since there are four equally likely outcomes, $P(E_1) = 3/4$. Also, $P(E_1 \cap E_2) = 1/4$. We want the probability that both were heads, given that at least one was a head; that is, we want to find $P(E_2|E_1)$. Use the definition above.

$$P(E_2|E_1) = \frac{P(E_2 \cap E_1)}{P(E_1)} = \frac{1/4}{3/4} = \frac{1}{3} \quad \blacksquare$$

In the definition of conditional probability given earlier, we can multiply both sides of the equation for $P(E|F)$ by $P(F)$ to get the following **product rule** for probability:

Product Rule

For any events E and F,

$$P(E \cap F) = P(F) \cdot P(E|F).$$

The product rule gives us a method for finding the probability that events E and F both occur, as illustrated by the next few examples.

EXAMPLE 3

A class is 2/5 women and 3/5 men. Of the women, 25% are business majors. Find the probability that a student chosen at random is a woman business major.

Let B and W represent the events "business major" and "woman," respectively. We want to find $P(B \cap W)$. By the product rule,

$$P(B \cap W) = P(W) \cdot P(B|W).$$

Using the given information, $P(W) = 2/5 = .4$ and $P(B|W) = .25$. Thus

$$P(B \cap W) = .4(.25) = .10. \quad \blacksquare$$

EXAMPLE 4

A company needs to hire a new director of advertising. It has decided to try to hire either person A or person B, who are assistant advertising directors for its major competitor. In trying to decide between A and B, the company does research on the campaigns managed by either A or B (no campaign is managed by both), and finds that A is in charge of twice as many advertising campaigns as B. Also, A's campaigns have satisfactory results three out of four times, while B's campaigns have satisfactory results only two out of five times. Suppose one of the competitor's advertising campaigns (managed by A or B) is selected. Find the probabilities of the following events.

(a)   A is in charge of an advertising campaign that produces satisfactory results.

First construct a *tree diagram* showing the various possible outcomes for this experiment, as in Figure 9. (Recall the discussion of tree diagrams in Section 5.1.) Since A does twice as many jobs as B, the probabilities of A and B having done the job are 2/3 and 1/3 respectively, as shown on the first stage of the tree. The second stage shows four different conditional probabilities. The ratings for the advertising campaigns are S (satisfactory) and U (unsatisfactory). For example, along the branch from B to S,

$$P(S|B) = \frac{2}{5}$$

since B has satisfactory results in 2 out of 5 campaigns.

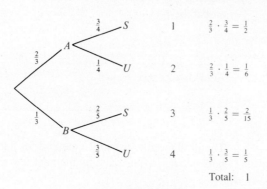

Executive   Campaign   Branch   Probability

FIGURE 9

Each of the four composite branches in the tree is numbered, with its probability given on the right. At each point where the tree branches, the sum of the probabilities is 1. The event that A has a campaign with a satisfactory result (event $A \cap S$) is associated with branch 1, so

$$P(A \cap S) = \frac{1}{2}.$$

(b)   B runs the campaign and produces satisfactory results.

This event, $B \cap S$, is shown on branch 3:

$$P(B \cap S) = \frac{2}{15}.$$

(c)   The campaign is satisfactory.

The result S combines branches 1 and 3, so

$$P(S) = \frac{1}{2} + \frac{2}{15} = \frac{19}{30}.$$

(d)   The campaign is unsatisfactory.

Event U combines branches 2 and 4, so

$$P(U) = \frac{1}{6} + \frac{1}{5} = \frac{11}{30}.$$

Alternatively, $P(U) = 1 - P(S) = 1 - 19/30 = 11/30$.

(e)   Either A runs the campaign or the results are satisfactory (or both).

Event A combines branches 1 and 2, while event S combines branches 1 and 3. Thus, we use branches 1, 2, and 3.

$$P(A \cup S) = \frac{1}{2} + \frac{1}{6} + \frac{2}{15} = \frac{4}{5} \quad \blacksquare$$

The next three examples could be worked with combinations, as explained in the previous section. In this section we show an alternate approach, using tree diagrams and conditional probability.

EXAMPLE 5

From a box containing 3 white, 2 green, and 1 red marble, two marbles are drawn one at a time without replacing the first before the second is drawn. Find the probability that one white and one green marble are drawn.

A tree diagram showing the various possible outcomes is given in Figure 10. In this diagram, W represents the event "drawing a white marble" and G represents "drawing a green marble." On the first draw, $P(W$ on the 1st$) = 3/6 = 1/2$ because 3 of the 6 marbles in the box are white. On the second draw, $P(G$ on the 2nd$|W$ on the 1st$) = 2/5$. One white marble has been removed, leaving 5, of which 2 are green.

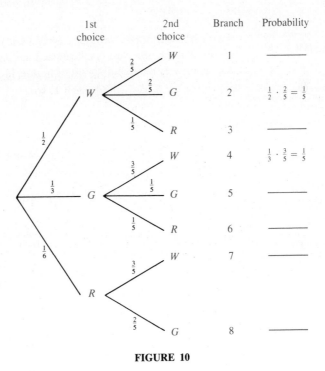

FIGURE 10

Now we want to find the probability of drawing one white marble and one green marble. This event can occur in two ways: drawing a white marble first and then a green one (branch 2 of the tree diagram), or drawing a green marble first and then a white one (branch 4). For branch 2,

$$P(W \text{ on 1st}) \cdot P(G \text{ on 2nd}|W \text{ on 1st}) = \frac{1}{2} \cdot \frac{2}{5} = \frac{1}{5}.$$

For branch 4, where the green marble is drawn first,

$$P(G \text{ on 1st}) \cdot P(W \text{ on 2nd}|G \text{ on 1st}) = \frac{1}{3} \cdot \frac{3}{5} = \frac{1}{5}.$$

Since the two events are mutually exclusive, the final probability is the sum of these two probabilities, or

$$P(\text{one } W, \text{ one } G) = P(W \text{ on 1st}) \cdot P(G \text{ on 2nd}|W \text{ on 1st})$$

$$+ P(G \text{ on 1st}) \cdot P(W \text{ on 2nd}|G \text{ on 1st}) = \frac{2}{5}. \quad \blacksquare$$

The product rule is often helpful with *stochastic processes,* where the outcome of an experiment depends on the outcomes of previous experiments. For example, the outcome of a draw of a card from a deck depends on any cards previously drawn. (Stochastic processes are studied in more detail in a later chapter.)

EXAMPLE 6   Two cards are drawn without replacement from an ordinary deck. Find the probability that the first card is a heart and the second card is red.

Start with the tree diagram of Figure 11.

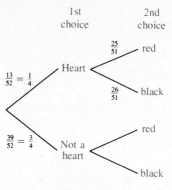

FIGURE 11

On the first draw, since there are 13 hearts in the 52 cards, the probability of drawing a heart is $13/52 = 1/4$. On the second draw, since a heart has been drawn already, there are 25 red cards in the remaining 51 cards. Thus, the probability of drawing a red card on the second draw, given that the first is a heart, is $25/51$. Therefore,

$$P(\text{heart on first and red on second})$$

$$= P(\text{heart on first}) \cdot P(\text{red on second}|\text{heart on first})$$

$$= \frac{1}{4} \cdot \frac{25}{51} = \frac{25}{204} \approx .1225. \quad \blacksquare$$

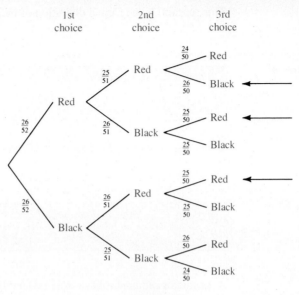

FIGURE 12

EXAMPLE 7

Three cards are drawn without replacement from an ordinary deck. Find the probability that exactly two of the cards are red.

Here we need a tree diagram with three stages, as shown in Figure 12. The three branches indicated with arrows produce exactly two red cards from the three draws. Multiply the probabilities along each of these branches and then add.

$$P(\text{exactly two red cards}) = \frac{26}{52} \cdot \frac{25}{51} \cdot \frac{26}{50} + \frac{26}{52} \cdot \frac{26}{51} \cdot \frac{25}{50} + \frac{26}{52} \cdot \frac{26}{51} \cdot \frac{25}{50}$$

$$= \frac{50{,}700}{132{,}600} = \frac{13}{34} \approx .382. \quad \blacksquare$$

Independent Events Suppose a fair coin is tossed and gives heads. The probability of heads on the next toss is still 1/2; the fact that heads was obtained on a given toss has no effect on the outcome of the next toss. Coin tosses are *independent events,* since knowledge of the outcome of one toss does not help decide on the outcome of the next toss. Rolls of a fair die are independent events; the fact that a 2 came up on one roll does not help increase our knowledge of the outcome of the next roll. On the other hand, the events "today is cloudy" and "today is rainy" are *dependent events;* if we know that it is cloudy, we know that there is an increased chance of rain.

If events E and F are independent, then the knowledge that E has occurred gives us no (probability) information about the occurrence or nonoccurrence of event F. That is, $P(F)$ is exactly the same as $P(F|E)$, or

$$P(F|E) = P(F).$$

This, in fact, is the formal definition of independent events:

Definition of Independent Events	E and F are **independent events** if $$P(F \mid E) = P(F).$$

Using this definition, the product rule can be simplified for independent events.

Product Rule	If E and F are independent events, then $$P(E \cap F) = P(E) \cdot P(F).$$

EXAMPLE 8

A calculator requires a key-stroke assembly and a logic circuit. Assume that 99% of the key-stroke assemblies are satisfactory and 97% of the logic circuits are satisfactory. Find the probability that a finished calculator will be satisfactory.

If the failure of a key stroke assembly and the failure of a logic circuit are independent events, then

P(satisfactory calculator)

$\qquad = P$(satisfactory key-stroke assembly) $\cdot$ P(satisfactory logic circuit)

$\qquad = (.99)(.97) \approx .96.$

The probability of a defective calculator is $1 - .96 = .04.$ ▪

EXAMPLE 9

When black-coated mice are crossed with brown-coated mice, a pair of genes, one from each parent, determines the coat color of the offspring. Let b represent the gene for brown and B the gene for black. If a mouse carries either one B gene and one b gene (Bb or bB) or two B genes (BB), the coat will be black. If the mouse carries two b genes (bb), the coat will be brown. Find the probability that a mouse born to a brown-coated female and a black-coated male who is known to carry the Bb combination will be brown.

To be brown-coated, the offspring must receive one b gene from each parent. The brown-coated parent carries two b genes, so that the probability of getting one b gene from the mother is 1. The probability of getting one b gene from the black-coated father is 1/2. Therefore, since these are independent events, the probability of a brown-coated offspring from these parents is $1 \cdot 1/2 = 1/2.$ ▪

It is common for students to confuse the ideas of *mutually exclusive* events and *independent* events. Events E and F are mutually exclusive if $E \cap F = \emptyset$. For example, if a family has exactly one child, the only possible outcomes are $B = \{\text{boy}\}$ and $G = \{\text{girl}\}$. These two events are mutually exclusive. However, the events are *not* independent, since $P(G|B) = 0$ (if a family with only one child has a boy, the probability it has a girl is then 0). Since $P(G|B) \neq P(G)$, the events are not independent.

Of all the families with exactly *two* children, the events $G_1 = \{$first child is a girl$\}$ and $G_2 = \{$second child is a girl$\}$ are independent, since $P(G_2|G_1)$ equals $P(G_2)$. However, G_1 and G_2 are not mutually exclusive, since $G_1 \cap G_2 = \{$both children are girls$\} \neq \varnothing$.

The only way to show that two events E and F are independent is to show that $P(F|E) = P(F)$.

6.5 EXERCISES

If a single fair die is rolled, find the probability of rolling

1. a 2, given that the number rolled was odd;

2. a 4, given that the number rolled was even;

3. an even number, given that the number rolled was 6.

If two fair dice are rolled, find the probability of rolling

4. a sum of 8, given the sum was greater than 7;

5. a sum of 6, given the roll was a "double" (two identical numbers);

6. a double, given that the sum was 9.

If 2 cards are drawn without replacement from an ordinary deck, find the probability that

7. the second is a heart, given that the first is a heart;

8. they are both hearts;

9. the second is black, given that the first is a spade;

10. the second is a face card, given that the first is a jack.

If 5 cards are drawn without replacement from an ordinary deck, find the probability that all the cards are

11. diamonds;

12. diamonds, given that the first and second were diamonds;

13. diamonds, given that the first four were diamonds;

14. clubs, given that the third was a spade;

15. the same suit.

A smooth-talking young man has a 1/3 probability of talking a policeman out of giving him a speeding ticket. The probability that he is stopped for speeding during a given weekend is 1/2. Find the probability that

16. he will receive no speeding tickets on a given weekend;

17. he will receive no speeding tickets on 3 consecutive weekends.

Slips of paper marked with the digits 1, 2, 3, 4, and 5 are placed in a box and mixed well. If two slips are drawn (without replacement), find the probability that

18. the first is even and the second is odd;

19. the first is a 3 and the second a number greater than 3;

20. both are even;

21. both are marked 3.

Two marbles are drawn without replacement from a jar with 4 black and 3 white marbles. Find the probability that

22. both are white;

23. both are black;

24. the second is white given that the first is black;

25. the first is black and the second is white;

26. one is black and the other is white.

The Midtown Bank has found that most customers at the tellers' windows either cash a check or make a deposit. The chart below indicates the transactions for one teller for one day.

	Cash Check	No Check	Totals
Make deposit	50	20	70
No deposit	30	10	40
Totals	80	30	110

Letting C represent "cashing a check" and D represent "making a deposit," express each of the following probabilities in words and find its value.

27. $P(C|D)$ **28.** $P(D'|C)$ **29.** $P(C'|D')$

30. $P(C'|D)$ **31.** $P[(C \cap D)']$

A pet shop has 10 puppies, 6 of them males. There are 3 beagles (1 male), 1 cocker spaniel (male), and 6 poodles. Construct a table similar to the one above and find the probability that one of these puppies, chosen at random, is

32. a beagle;   **33.** a beagle, given that it is a male;

34. a male, given that it is a beagle;   **35.** a cocker spaniel, given that it is a female;

36. a poodle, given that it is a male;   **37.** a female, given that it is a beagle.

A bicycle factory runs two assembly lines, A and B. If 95% of line A's products pass inspection, while only 90% of line B's products pass inspection, and 60% of the factory's bikes come off assembly line B (the rest off A), find the probability that one of the factory's bikes did not pass inspection and came off

38. assembly line A;   **39.** assembly line B.

40. Both of a certain pea plant's parents had a gene for red and a gene for white flowers. (See the exercises for Section 6.3.) If the offspring has red flowers, find the probability that it combined a gene for red and a gene for white (rather than two for red).

Assuming that boy and girl babies are equally likely, fill in the remaining probabilities on the tree diagram and use the information to find the probability that a family with three children has all girls, given that

41. the first is a girl;

42. the third is a girl;

43. the second is a girl;

44. at least two are girls;

45. at least one is a girl.

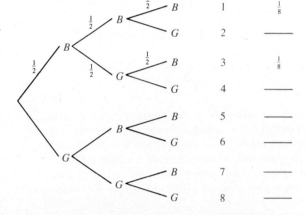

The following table shows frequencies for red-green color blindness, where *M* represents male and *C* represents color-blind. Use this table to find the following probabilities.

46. $P(M)$ **47.** $P(C)$

48. $P(M \cap C)$ **49.** $P(M \cup C)$

50. $P(M|C)$ **51.** $P(C|M)$

52. $P(M'|C)$

	M	M'	Totals
C	.042	.007	.049
C'	.485	.466	.951
Totals	.527	.473	1.000

53. Are the events *C* and *M* described above dependent?

54. A scientist wishes to determine if there is any dependence between color blindness (*C*) and deafness (*D*). Given the probabilities listed in the table below, what should his findings be? (See Exercises 46–53.)

	D	D'	Totals
C	.0004	.0796	.0800
C'	.0046	.9154	.9200
Total	.0050	.9950	1.0000

The Motor Vehicle Department has found that the probability of a person passing the test for a driver's license on the first try is .75. The probability that an individual who fails on the first test will pass on the second try is .80, and the probability that an individual who fails the first and second tests will pass the third time is .70. Find the probability that an individual

55. fails both the first and second tests;

56. will fail three times in a row;

57. will require at least two tries to pass the test.

According to a booklet put out by Frontier Airlines, 98% of all scheduled Frontier flights actually take place. (The other flights are cancelled due to weather, equipment problems, and so on.) Assume that the event that a given flight takes place is independent of the event that another flight takes place.

58. Elizabeth Thornton plans to visit her company's branch offices; her journey requires three separate flights on Frontier. What is the probability that all these flights will take place?

59. Based on the reasons we gave for a flight to be cancelled, how realistic is the assumption of independence that we made?

60. In one area, 4% of the population drives a luxury car. However, 17% of the CPAs drive a luxury car. Are the events "drive a luxury car" and "person is a CPA" independent?

61. Corporations where a computer is essential to day-to-day operations, such as banks, often have a second backup computer in case of failure by the main computer. Suppose there is a .003 chance that the main computer will fail in a given time period, and a .005 chance that the backup computer will fail while the main computer is being repaired. Assume these failures represent independent events, and find the fraction of the time that the corporation can assume it will have computer service. How realistic is our assumption of independence?

62. A key component of a space rocket will fail with a probability of .03. How many such components must be used as backups to ensure the probability that at least one of the components will work is .999999?

In searching for a new drug with commercial possibilities, drug company researchers use the ratio

$$N_S : N_A : N_p : 1.$$

That is, if the company gives preliminary screening to N_S substances, it may find that N_A of them are worthy of further study, with N_P of these surviving into full scale development. Finally, 1 of the substances will result in a marketable drug. Typical numbers used by Smith, Kline, and French Laboratories in planning research budgets might be 2000 : 30 : 8 : 1.* Use this ratio in the following exercises.

63. Suppose a compound has been chosen for preliminary screening. Find the probability that the compound will survive and become a marketable drug.

64. Find the probability that the compound will not lead to a marketable drug.

65. Suppose the number of such compounds receiving preliminary screening is a. Set up the probability that none of them produces a marketable drug. (Assume independence throughout these exercises.)

66. Use your results from Exercise 65 to set up the probability that at least one of the drugs will prove marketable.

67. Suppose now that N scientists are employed in the preliminary screening, and that each scientist can screen c compounds per year. Set up the probability that no marketable drugs will be discovered in a year.

68. Set up the probability that at least one marketable drug will be discovered.

---

*Reprinted by permission of E. B. Pyle, III, B. Douglas, G. W. Ebright, W. J. Westlake, A. B. Bender, "Scientific Manpower Allocation to New Drug Screening Programs," *Management Science*, Vol. 19, No. 12, August 1973, copyright © 1973 The Institute of Management Sciences.

For the following exercises, evaluate your answer in Exercise 68 for the following values of N and c. Use a calculator with a y^x key, or a computer.

69. $N = 100$, $c = 6$

70. $N = 25$, $c = 10$

Let E and F be events which are neither the empty set nor the sample space S. Identify the following as true or false.

71. $P(E|E) = 1$ **72.** $P(E|E') = 1$ **73.** $P(\varnothing|F) = 0$

74. $P(S|E) = P(E)$ **75.** $P(F|S) = P(F)$ **76.** $P(E|F) = P(F|E)$

77. $P(E|E \cap F) = 0$ **78.** If $P(E|F) = P(E \cap F)$, then $P(F) = 1$

79. Let E and F be mutually exclusive events such that $P(F) > 0$. Find $P(E|F)$.

80. If $E \subset F$, where $E \neq \varnothing$, find $P(F|E)$ and $P(E|F)$.

81. Let F_1, F_2, and F_3 be a set of pairwise mutually exclusive events (that is, $F_1 \cap F_2 = \varnothing$, $F_1 \cap F_3 = \varnothing$, and $F_2 \cap F_3 = \varnothing$), with sample space $S = F_1 \cup F_2 \cup F_3$. Let E be any event. Show that
$$P(E) = P(F_1) \cdot P(E|F_1) + P(F_2) \cdot P(E|F_2) + P(F_3) \cdot P(E|F_3).$$

82. Show that for three events E, F, and G,
$$P(E \cap F \cap G) = P(E) \cdot P(F|E) \cdot P(G|E \cap F).$$

6.6 Bayes' Formula

Suppose the probability that a person gets lung cancer, given that the person smokes a pack or more of cigarettes daily, is known. For a research project, it might be necessary to know the probability that a person smokes a pack or more of cigarettes daily, given that the person has lung cancer. More generally, if $P(E|F)$ is known for two events E and F, can $P(F|E)$ be found? It turns out that it can, using the formula to be developed in this section. To find this formula, let us start with the product rule:

$$P(E \cap F) = P(E) \cdot P(F|E),$$

which can also be written as $P(F \cap E) = P(F) \cdot P(E|F)$. From the fact that $P(E \cap F) = P(F \cap E)$,

$$P(E) \cdot P(F|E) = P(F) \cdot P(E|F),$$

or $$P(F|E) = \frac{P(F) \cdot P(E|F)}{P(E)}. \tag{1}$$

Given the two events E and F, if E occurs, then either F also occurs or F' also occurs. The probabilities of $E \cap F$ and $E \cap F'$ can be expressed as follows.

$$P(E \cap F) = P(F) \cdot P(E|F)$$
$$P(E \cap F') = P(F') \cdot P(E|F')$$

Since $(E \cap F) \cup (E \cap F') = E$ (because F and F' form the sample space),

$$P(E) = P(E \cap F) + P(E \cap F')$$

or $$P(E) = P(F) \cdot P(E|F) + P(F') \cdot P(E|F').$$

From this, equation (1) produces the following result, a special case of Bayes' Formula, which is discussed in more generality later in this section.

Bayes' Formula

(Special Case)

$$P(F|E) = \frac{P(F) \cdot P(E|F)}{P(F) \cdot P(E|F) + P(F') \cdot P(E|F')}. \qquad (2)$$

EXAMPLE 1

For a fixed length of time, the probability of worker error on the production line is .1, the probability that an accident will occur when there is a worker error is .3, and the probability that an accident will occur when there is no worker error is .2. Find the probability of a worker error if there is an accident.

Let A represent the event of an accident, and let E represent the event of worker error. From the information above,

$$P(E) = .1, \qquad P(A|E) = .3, \qquad \text{and} \quad P(A|E') = .2.$$

These probabilities are shown on the tree diagram of Figure 13.

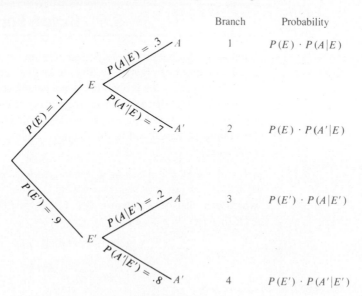

	Branch	Probability
A	1	$P(E) \cdot P(A|E)$
A'	2	$P(E) \cdot P(A'|E)$
A	3	$P(E') \cdot P(A|E')$
A'	4	$P(E') \cdot P(A'|E')$

FIGURE 13

Find $P(E|A)$ using equation (2) above:

$$P(E|A) = \frac{P(E) \cdot P(A|E)}{P(E) \cdot P(A|E) + P(E') \cdot P(A|E')}$$

$$= \frac{(.1)(.3)}{(.1)(.3) + (.9)(.2)} = \frac{1}{7}.$$

In a similar manner, the probability that an accident is not due to worker error is $P(E'|A)$, or

$$P(E'|A) = \frac{P(E') \cdot P(A|E')}{P(E') \cdot P(A|E') + P(E) \cdot P(A|E)}$$

$$= \frac{(.9)(.2)}{(.9)(.2) + (.1)(.3)} = \frac{6}{7}. \blacksquare$$

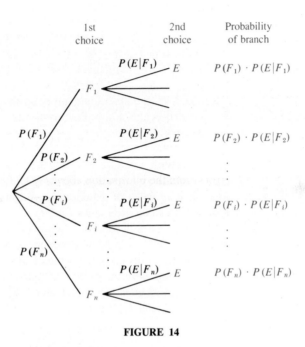

	1st choice	2nd choice	Probability of branch

FIGURE 14

Equation (2) above can be generalized to more than two possibilities. To do so, use the tree diagram of Figure 14. This diagram shows the paths that can produce some event E. We assume that the events $F_1, F_2, \cdots, F_n$ are pairwise mutually exclusive events (that is, events which, taken two at a time, are disjoint) whose union is the sample space, and that E is an event that has occurred.

To find the probability $P(F_i|E)$, where $1 \le i \le n$, divide the probability for the branch containing $P(E|F_i)$ by the sum of the probabilities of all the branches producing event E. That is,

Bayes' Formula

$$P(F_i|E) = \frac{P(F_i) \cdot P(E|F_i)}{P(F_1) \cdot P(E|F_1) + P(F_2) \cdot P(E|F_2) + \cdots + P(F_n) \cdot P(E|F_n)}.$$

This result is known as **Bayes' Formula,** after the Reverend Thomas Bayes, whose paper on probability was published a little over two hundred years ago.

The basic statement of Bayes' Formula can be daunting. Actually, it is easier to remember the formula by thinking of the tree diagram that produced it. Go through the following steps.

Using Bayes' Formula

1. Start a tree diagram with branches representing events $F_1, F_2, \cdots, F_n$. Label each branch with its corresponding probability.
2. From the end of each of these branches, draw a branch for event E. Label this branch with the probability of getting to it, $P(E|F_i)$.
3. You now have n different paths that result in event E. Next to each path, put its probability—the product of the probabilities that the first branch occurs, $P(F_i)$, and that the second branch occurs, $P(E|F_i)$; that is, the product $P(F_i) \cdot P(E|F_i)$.
4. The desired probability is given by the probability of the branch you want, divided by the sum of the probabilities of all the branches producing event E.

EXAMPLE 2

Based on past experience, a company knows that an experienced machine operator (one or more years of experience) will produce a defective item 1% of the time. People with some experience (up to one year) have a 2.5% defect rate, while new people have a 6% defect rate. At any one time, the company has 60% experienced employees, 30% with some experience, and 10% new employees. Find the probability that a particular defective item was produced by a new operator.

Let E represent the event "an item is defective," with F_1 representing "item was made by an experienced operator," F_2 "item was made by a person with some experience," and F_3 "item was made by a new employee." Then

$$P(F_1) = .60 \qquad P(E|F_1) = .01$$
$$P(F_2) = .30 \qquad P(E|F_2) = .025$$
$$P(F_3) = .10 \qquad P(E|F_3) = .06.$$

We need to find $P(F_3|E)$, the probability that an item was produced by a new operator, given that it is defective. First, draw a tree diagram using the given information, as in Figure 15. The steps leading to event E are shown in heavy type.

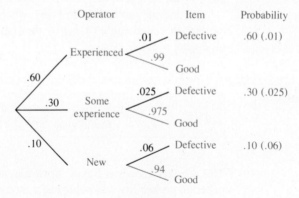

FIGURE 15

Find $P(F_3|E)$ with the bottom branch of the tree in Figure 15; divide the probability for this branch by the sum of the probabilities of all the branches leading to E, or

$$P(F_3|E) = \frac{.10(.06)}{.60(.01) + .30(.025) + .10(.06)} = \frac{.006}{.0195} = \frac{4}{13}.$$

In a similar way

$$P(F_2|E) = \frac{.30(.025)}{.60(.01) + .30(.025) + .10(.06)} = \frac{.0075}{.0195} = \frac{5}{13}.$$

Finally, $P(F_1|E) = 4/13$. Check that $P(F_1|E) + P(F_2|E) + P(F_3|E) = 1$. (That is, the defective item was made by *someone*.) ▪

EXAMPLE 3

A manufacturer buys items from six different suppliers. The fraction of the total number of items obtained from each supplier, along with the probability that an item purchased from that supplier is defective, is shown in the following chart.

Supplier	Fraction of Total Supplied	Probability of Defective
1	.05	.04
2	.12	.02
3	.16	.07
4	.23	.01
5	.35	.03
6	.09	.05

Find the probability that a defective item came from supplier 5.

Let F_1 be the event that an item came from supplier 1, with F_2, F_3, F_4, F_5, and F_6 defined in a similar manner. Let E be the event that an item is defective. We want to find $P(F_5|E)$. By Bayes' Formula (draw a tree),

$$P(F_5|E) = \frac{(.35)(.03)}{(.05)(.04)+(.12)(.02)+(.16)(.07)+(.23)(.01)+(.35)(.03)+(.09)(.05)}$$

$$= \frac{.0105}{.0329} \approx .319.$$

There is about a 32% chance that a defective item came from supplier 5. ▪

6.6 EXERCISES

For two events M and N, $P(M) = .4$, $P(N|M) = .3$, and $P(N|M') = .4$. Find each of the following.

1. $P(M|N)$ **2.** $P(M'|N)$

For mutually exclusive events R_1, R_2, R_3, we have $P(R_1) = .05$, $P(R_2) = .6$, and $P(R_3) = .35$. Also, $P(Q|R_1) = .40$, $P(Q|R_2) = .30$, and $P(Q|R_3) = .60$. Find each of the following.

3. $P(R_1|Q)$ **4.** $P(R_2|Q)$ **5.** $P(R_3|Q)$ **6.** $P(R_1'|Q)$

Suppose you have three jars with the following contents: 2 black balls and 1 white ball in the first; 1 black ball and 2 white balls in the second; and 1 black ball and 1 white ball in the third. One jar is to be selected, and then one ball is to be drawn from the selected jar. If the probabilities of selecting the first, second, or third jar are 1/2, 1/3, and 1/6 respectively, find the probability that if a white ball is drawn, it came from

7. the second jar   **8.** the third jar.

The following table shows the fraction of the population in various income levels, as well as the probability that a person from that income level will take an airline flight within the next year.

Income Level	Proportion of Population	Probability of a Flight During the Next Year
$0–$5999	12.8%	.04
$6000–$9999	14.6%	.06
$10,000–$14,999	18.5%	.07
$15,000–$19,999	17.8%	.09
$20,000–$24,999	13.9%	.12
$25,000 and over	22.4%	.13

If a person is selected at random from an airline flight, find the probability that the person has an income level of

9. $10,000–$14,999;   **10.** $25,000 and over.

The following table shows the proportion of people over 18 who are in various age categories, along with the probability that a person in a given age category will vote in a general election.

Age	Proportion of Voting Age Population	Probability of a Person of This Age Voting
18–21	11.0%	.48
22–24	7.6%	.53
25–44	37.6%	.68
45–64	28.3%	.64
65 or over	15.5%	.74

Suppose a voter is picked at random. Find the probability that the voter is in the following age categories.

11. 18–21   **12.** 65 or over

Of all the people applying for a certain job, 70% are qualified, and 30% are not. The personnel manager claims that she approves qualified people 85% of the time; she approves an unqualified person 20% of the time. Find each of the following probabilities.

13. A person is qualified if he or she was approved by the manager.

14. A person is unqualified if he or she was approved by the manager.

A building contractor buys 70% of his cement from supplier A, and 30% from supplier B. A total of 90% of the bags from A arrive undamaged, while 95% of the bags from B come undamaged. Give the probability that a damaged bag is from supplier

15. A;

16. B.

The probability that a customer of a local department store will be a "slow pay" is .02. The probability that a "slow pay" will make a large down payment when buying a refrigerator is .14. The probability that a person who is not a "slow pay" will make a large down payment when buying a refrigerator is .50. Suppose a customer makes a large down payment on a refrigerator. Find the probability that the customer is

17. a "slow pay;"

18. not a "slow pay."

Companies A, B, and C produce 15%, 40%, and 45% respectively of the major appliances sold in a certain area. In that area, 1% of the Company A appliances, 1 1/2% of the Company B appliances, and 2% of the Company C appliances need service within the first year. Suppose a defective appliance is chosen at random; find the probability that it was manufactured by Company

19. A;

20. B.

On a given weekend in the fall, a tire company can buy television advertising time for a college football game, a baseball game, or a professional football game. If the company sponsors the college game, there is a 70% chance of a high rating, a 50% chance if they sponsor a baseball game, and a 60% chance if they sponsor a professional football game. The probability of the company sponsoring these various games is .5, .2, and .3, respectively. Suppose the company does get a high rating; find the probability that it sponsored

21. a college game;

22. a professional football game.

According to readings in business publications, there is a 50% chance of a booming economy next summer, a 20% chance of a mediocre economy, and a 30% chance of a recession. The probabilities that a particular investment strategy will produce a huge profit under each of these possibilities are .1, .6, and .3 respectively. Suppose it turns out that the strategy does produce huge profits; find the probability that the economy was

23. booming;

24. in recession.

25. The probability that a person with certain symptoms has hepatitis is .8. The blood test used to confirm this diagnosis gives positive results for 90% of those who have the disease and 5% of those without the disease. What is the probability that an individual with the symptoms who reacts positively to the test has hepatitis?

A recent issue of *Newsweek* described a new test for toxemia, a disease that affects pregnant women. To perform the test, the woman lies on her left side and then rolls over on her back. The test is considered positive if there is a 20 mm rise in her blood pressure within one minute. The article gives the following probabilities, where T represents having toxemia at some time during the pregnancy, and N represents a negative test.

$$P(T'|N) = .90, \quad \text{and} \quad P(T|N') = .75.$$

Assume that $P(N') = .11$, and find each of the following.

26. $P(N|T)$

27. $P(N'|T)$

28. In a certain county, the Democrats have 53% of the registered voters, 12% of whom are under 21. The Republicans have 47% of all registered voters, of whom 10% are under 21. If Kay is a registered voter who is under 21, what is the probability that she is a Democrat?

Let F, G, and H be nonempty events with $F \cap G = \emptyset$, $F \cap H = \emptyset$, and $G \cap H = \emptyset$.
Let $S = F \cup G \cup H$. Let E be any event. Prove each of the following.

29. $P(E) = P(E \cap F) + P(E \cap G) + P(E \cap H)$

30. $P(E) = P(E|F) \cdot P(F) + P(E|G) \cdot P(G) + P(E|H) \cdot P(H)$

EXTENDED

APPLICATION

Medical Diagnosis

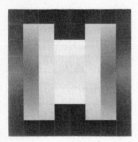

When a patient is examined, information, typically incomplete, is obtained about his state of health. Probability theory provides a mathematical model appropriate for this situation, as well as a procedure for quantitatively interpreting such partial information to arrive at a reasonable diagnosis.*

To do this, we list the states of health that can be distinguished in such a way that the patient can be in one and only one state at the time of the examination. For each state of health H, we associate a number $P(H)$ between 0 and 1 such that the sum of all these numbers is 1. This number $P(H)$ represents the probability, before examination, that a patient is in the state of health H, and $P(H)$ may be chosen subjectively from medical experience, using any information available prior to the examination. The probability may be most conveniently established from clinical records, that is, a mean probability is established for patients in general, although the number would vary from patient to patient. Of course, the more information that is brought to bear in establishing $P(H)$, the better the diagnosis.

For example, limiting the discussion to the condition of a patient's heart, suppose there are exactly 3 states of health, with probabilities as follows:

	State of health H	$P(H)$
H_1	patient has a normal heart	.8
H_2	patient has minor heart irregularities	.15
H_3	patient has a severe heart condition	.05

Having selected $P(H)$, the information of the examination is processed. First, the results of the examination must be classified. The examination itself consists of observing the state of a number of characteristics of the patient. Let us assume that the examination for a heart condition consists of a stethoscope examination and a cardiogram. The outcome of such an examination, C, might be one of the following:

C_1—stethoscope shows normal heart
and cardiogram shows normal heart;

C_2—stethoscope shows normal heart
and cardiogram shows minor irregularities,

and so on.

*This example is based on "Probabilistic Medical Diagnosis," Roger Wright, from *Some Mathematical Models in Biology,* Robert M. Thrall, ed., rev. ed., (The University of Michigan, 1967), by permission of Robert M. Thrall.

It remains to assess for each state of health H the conditional probability $P(C|H)$ of each examination outcome C using only the knowledge that a patient is in a given state of health. (This may be based on the medical knowledge and clinical experience of the doctor.) The conditional probabilities $P(C|H)$ will not vary from patient to patient, so that they may be built into a diagnostic system, although they should be reviewed periodically.

Suppose the result of the examination is C_1. Let us assume the following probabilities:

$$P(C_1|H_1) = .9$$
$$P(C_1|H_2) = .4$$
$$P(C_1|H_3) = .1.$$

Now, for a given patient, the appropriate probability associated with each state of health H, after examination, is $P(H|C)$ where C is the outcome of the examination. This can be calculated by using Bayes' Formula. For example, to find $P(H_1|C_1)$—that is, the probability that the patient has a normal heart given that the examination showed a normal stethoscope examination and a normal cardiogram—we use Bayes' Formula as follows:

$$P(H_1|C_1) = \frac{P(C_1|H_1)P(H_1)}{P(C_1|H_1)P(H_1) + P(C_1|H_2)P(H_2) + P(C_1|H_3)P(H_3)}$$

$$= \frac{(.9)(.8)}{(.9)(.8) + (.4)(.15) + (.1)(.05)} \approx .92.$$

Hence, the probability is about .92 that the patient has a normal heart on the basis of the examination results. This means that in 8 out of 100 patients, some abnormality will be present and not be detected by the stethoscope or the cardiogram.

EXERCISES

1. Find $P(H_2|C_1)$.

2. Assuming the following probabilities, find $P(H_1|C_2)$:
   $$P(C_2|H_1) = .2, \qquad P(C_2|H_2) = .8, \qquad P(C_2|H_3) = .3.$$

3. Assuming the probabilities of Exercise 2, find $P(H_3|C_2)$.

6.7 Bernoulli Trials

Many probability problems are concerned with experiments in which an event is repeated many times. For example, we might want to find the probability of getting 7 heads in 8 tosses of a coin, or hitting a target 6 times out of 6, or finding 1 defective item in a sample of 15 items. Probability problems of this kind are called **repeated trials** problems, or **Bernoulli processes.** In each case, some outcome is designated a success, and any other outcome is considered a failure. Thus, if the probability of a success in a single trial is p, the probability of failure will be $1 - p$. Repeated trials problems, or *binomial problems*, must satisfy the following conditions.

Bernoulli Trials

1. The same experiment is repeated several times.
2. There are only two possible outcomes, success and failure.
3. The repeated trials are independent.
4. The probability of each outcome remains the same for each trial.

Let us consider the solution of a problem of this type. Suppose we want to find the probability of getting 5 ones on 5 rolls of a die. The probability of getting a one on 1 roll is 1/6, while the probability of any other result is 5/6.

$$P(5 \text{ ones on } 5 \text{ rolls}) = P(1) \cdot P(1) \cdot P(1) \cdot P(1) \cdot P(1) = \left(\frac{1}{6}\right)^5$$
$$\approx .00013$$

Now, let us find the probability of getting a one exactly 4 times in 5 rolls of the die. The desired outcome for this experiment can occur in more than one way, as shown below, where s represents getting a success (a one), and f represents getting a failure (any other result).

$$
\begin{array}{ccccc}
s & s & s & s & f \\
s & s & s & f & s \\
s & s & f & s & s \\
s & f & s & s & s \\
f & s & s & s & s \\
\end{array}
$$

The probability of each of these five outcomes is

$$\left(\frac{1}{6}\right)^4 \left(\frac{5}{6}\right).$$

Since the five outcomes represent mutually exclusive alternative events, add the five probabilities.

$$P(4 \text{ ones in } 5 \text{ rolls}) = 5\left(\frac{1}{6}\right)^4 \left(\frac{5}{6}\right) = \frac{5^2}{6^5} \approx .0032$$

In the same way, we can compute the probability of rolling a one exactly 3 times in 5 rolls of a die. The probability of any one way of achieving 3 successes and 2 failures will be

$$\left(\frac{1}{6}\right)^3 \left(\frac{5}{6}\right)^2.$$

Again the desired outcome can occur in more than one way. Let the set {1, 2, 3, 4, 5} represent the first, second, third, fourth, and fifth tosses. The number of 3-element subsets of this set will correspond to the number of ways in which 3 successes and 2 failures can occur. Using combinations, there are $\binom{5}{3}$ such subsets.

Since $\binom{5}{3} = 5!/(3!2!) = 10$,

$$P(3 \text{ ones in 5 rolls}) = 10 \left(\frac{1}{6}\right)^3 \left(\frac{5}{6}\right)^2 = \frac{250}{6^5} \approx .032.$$

Suppose now that the probability of a success on one trial of a Bernoulli experiment is p, and the probability of exactly x successes in n repeated trials is needed. It is possible that the x successes could come first, followed by $n - x$ failures:

$$\underbrace{s \quad s \quad s \cdots s}_{x \text{ successes, then}} \quad \underbrace{f \quad f \cdots f.}_{n - x \text{ failures}} \tag{1}$$

The probability of this result is

$$P(s \quad s \quad s \cdots s \quad s \quad f \quad f \cdots f)$$

$$= \underbrace{P(s) \cdot P(s) \cdot P(s) \cdots P(s)}_{x \text{ factors}} \cdot \underbrace{P(f) \cdot P(f) \cdots P(f)}_{n - x \text{ factors}}$$

$$= \underbrace{p \cdot p \cdot p \cdots p}_{x \text{ factors}} \cdot \underbrace{(1 - p) \cdot (1 - p) \cdots (1 - p)}_{n - x \text{ factors}}$$

$$= p^x (1 - p)^{n-x}.$$

The x successes could also be obtained by rearranging the letters in (1) above. There are $\binom{n}{x}$ ways of choosing the x places where the s's occur and the $n - x$ places where the f's occur, so the probability of exactly x successes is

$$\binom{n}{x} p^x (1 - p)^{n-x}.$$

A summary follows.

Probability In a Bernoulli Experiment

If p is the probability of success in a single trial of a Bernoulli experiment, the probability of x successes and $n - x$ failures in n independent repeated trials of the experiment is

$$\binom{n}{x} \cdot p^x \cdot (1 - p)^{n-x}.$$

EXAMPLE 1

The advertising agency which handles the Diet Supercola account thinks that 40% of all consumers prefer this product over its competitors. Suppose a sample of 6 people is chosen. Assume that all responses are independent of each other. Find the probability of the following.

(a) Exactly 3 of the 6 people prefer Diet Supercola.

In this example, $P(\text{success}) = P(\text{prefer Diet Supercola}) = .4$. The sample is made up of 6 people, so $n = 6$. To find the probability that exactly 3 people prefer this drink, let $x = 3$.

$$P(\text{exactly 3}) = \binom{6}{3}(.4)^3(1 - .4)^{6-3}$$
$$= 20(.4)^3(.6)^3$$
$$= 20(.064)(.216)$$
$$= .27648$$

(b) None of the 6 people prefer Diet Supercola.

Let $x = 0$.

$$P(\text{exactly 0}) = \binom{6}{0}(.4)^0(1 - .4)^6 = 1(1)(.6)^6 \approx .0467 \quad \blacksquare$$

EXAMPLE 2

At a certain school in northern Michigan, 80% of the students ski. If 5 students at this school are selected, and their responses are independent, then the probability that exactly 1 of the 5 students skis is

$$P(\text{exactly 1}) = \binom{5}{1}(.8)^1(.2)^4 = .0064,$$

while the probability that exactly four of the five students ski is

$$P(\text{exactly 4}) = \binom{5}{4}(.8)^4(.2)^1 = .4096. \quad \blacksquare$$

EXAMPLE 3

Find each of the following probabilities.

(a) the probability of getting exactly seven heads in eight tosses of a fair coin

The probability of success, getting a head in a single toss, is 1/2. The probability of a failure, getting a tail, is $1 - 1/2 = 1/2$. Thus,

$$P(\text{7 heads in 8 tosses}) = \binom{8}{7}\left(\frac{1}{2}\right)^7\left(\frac{1}{2}\right)^1 = 8\left(\frac{1}{2}\right)^8 = .03125.$$

(b) the probability of 2 fours in 8 rolls of a die

The probability of success, a 4, is 1/6, while the probability of failure (a number other than 4), is 5/6.

$$P(\text{2 fours in 8 tosses}) = \binom{8}{2}\left(\frac{1}{6}\right)^2\left(\frac{5}{6}\right)^6 \approx .2605 \quad \blacksquare$$

EXAMPLE 4

Assuming that selection of items for a sample can be treated as independent trials, find the probability of the occurrence of one defective item in a random sample of 15 items from a production line, if the probability that any one item is defective is .01.

The probability of success (a defective item), is .01, while the probability of failure (an acceptable item) is .99. This makes

$$P(\text{1 defective in 15 items}) = \binom{15}{1}(.01)^1(.99)^{14}$$

$$= 15(.01)(.99)^{14}$$

$$\approx .130. \quad \blacksquare$$

EXAMPLE 5

A new style of shoe is sweeping the country. In one area, 30% of all the shoes are of this type. Assume that these sales are independent events, and find the following probabilities.

(a) Of 10 people who buy shoes, at least 8 buy the new shoe style.

Let success be "buy the new style", so that $P(\text{success}) = .3$. For at least 8 people out of 10 to buy the shoe, it must be sold to 8, 9, or 10 people, with

$$P(\text{at least 8}) = P(8) + P(9) + P(10)$$

$$= \binom{10}{8}(.3)^8(.7)^2 + \binom{10}{9}(.3)^9(.7)^1 + \binom{10}{10}(.3)^{10}(.7)^0$$

$$\approx .0014467 + .0001378 + .0000059$$

$$= .0015904.$$

(b) Of 10 people who buy shoes, no more than 7 buy the new shoe style.

"No more than 7" means 0, 1, 2, 3, 4, 5, 6, or 7 people buy the shoe. We could add $P(0)$, $P(1)$, and so on, but it is easier to use the formula $P(E) = 1 - P(E')$. The complement of "no more than 7" is "8 or more." Finally,

$$P(\text{no more than 7}) = 1 - P(\text{8 or more})$$

$$= 1 - .0015904 \qquad \text{(answer from part (a))}$$

$$= .9984096. \quad \blacksquare$$

The Probability of k Trials for m Successes   In the rest of this section, we will find the probability that k trials will be needed to guarantee m successes in a Bernoulli experiment. As an example, suppose that a salesperson in a very competitive business makes a sale in one client visit out of five, so $P(\text{sale}) = .2$. The probability of a sale on the first call is .2. The probability that the *first* sale will be on the *second* call is

$$P(\text{no sale on first}) \cdot P(\text{sale on second}) = .8(.2) = .16.$$

The probability that the *first* sale will be on the *third* call is

$$(.8)^2(.2) = .128.$$

Generalizing, the probability that the first sale will be on the kth call is

$$(.8)^{k-1}(.2).$$

<table>
<tr><td>**EXAMPLE 6**</td><td>How many calls must this salesperson make to have an 80% chance of making a sale?</td></tr>
</table>

There is a .2 chance of making a sale on the first call, a .16 chance of making the first sale on the second call, a .128 chance of making the first sale on the third call, and so on. The probability of a sale by the kth call is the sum of all the probabilities of sales on calls 1, 2, 3, $\cdots$, k. A calculator gives the results of the following table.

Call Number	Probability That First Sale is on That Call	Total of all Probabilities up to and Including This Call
1	$(.8)^0(.2) = .2$	.2
2	$(.8)^1(.2) = .16$	.36
3	$(.8)^2(.2) = .128$	.488
4	$(.8)^3(.2) = .1024$	.5904
5	$(.8)^4(.2) \approx .082$	$\approx .672$
6	$(.8)^5(.2) \approx .066$	$\approx .738$
7	$(.8)^6(.2) \approx .052$	$\approx .790$
8	$(.8)^7(.2) \approx .042$	$\approx .832$

The salesperson must make 8 calls to have an 80% chance of making one sale. ◼

This result can be generalized: let p be the probability of success on one trial in a Bernoulli experiment. Then to find the probability that k trials will be needed to guarantee m successes, we must assume the kth trial was a success, and that $m - 1$ successes were distributed in some order among the other $k - 1$ trials. The desired probability is thus

$$\left[\binom{k-1}{m-1} p^{(m-1)} \cdot (1 - p)^{(k-1)-(m-1)} \right] \cdot p$$

or

$$\binom{k-1}{m-1} p^m \cdot (1 - p)^{k-m}.$$

<table>
<tr><td>**EXAMPLE 7**</td><td>Find the probability that the salesperson of Example 6 will require 9 calls to make 3 sales.</td></tr>
</table>

Let $k = 9$ and $m = 3$. We know that $p = .2$. The desired probability is

$$\binom{9-1}{3-1}(.2)^3(1 - .2)^{9-3} = \binom{8}{2}(.2)^3(.8)^6 \approx .0587. \quad ◼$$

6.7 EXERCISES

Suppose that a family has 5 children. Also, suppose that the probability of having a girl is 1/2. Find the probability that the family will have

1. exactly 2 girls;

2. exactly 3 girls;

3. no girls;

4. no boys;

5. at least 4 girls;

7. no more than 3 boys;

6. at least 3 boys;

8. no more than 4 girls.

A die is rolled 12 times. Find the probability of rolling

9. exactly 12 ones;

11. exactly 1 one;

13. no more than 3 ones;

10. exactly 6 ones;

12. exactly 2 ones;

14. no more than 1 one.

A coin is tossed 5 times. Find the probability of getting

15. all heads;

17. no more than 3 heads;

16. exactly 3 heads;

18. at least 3 heads.

A factory tests a random sample of 20 transistors for defectives. The probability that a particular transistor will be defective has been established by past experience to be .05.

19. What is the probability that there are no defectives in the sample?

20. What is the probability that the number of defectives in the sample is at most 2?

A company gives prospective employees a 6-question multiple-choice test. Each question has 5 possible answers, so that there is a 1/5 or 20% chance of answering a question correctly just by guessing. Find the probability of answering, by chance,

21. exactly 2 questions correctly;

23. at least 4 correctly;

22. no questions correctly;

24. no more than 3 correctly.

25. Over the last decade, 10% of all clients of J. K. Loss & Company have lost their life savings. Suppose a sample of 3 of the current clients of the firm is chosen. Assuming independence, find the probability that exactly one of the 3 clients will lose everything.

According to a recent article in a business publication, only 20% of the population of the United States has never had a Big Burg hamburger at a major fast-food chain. Assume independence and find the probability that in a random sample of 10 people

26. exactly 2 never had a Big Burg;

28. 3 or fewer never had a Big Burg;

27. exactly 5 never had a Big Burg;

29. 4 or more *have* had a Big Burg.

A new drug cures 70% of the people taking it. Suppose 20 people take the drug; find the probability that

30. exactly 18 are cured;

32. at least 17 are cured;

31. exactly 17 are cured;

33. at least 18 are cured.

In a 10-question multiple-choice biology test with 5 choices for each question, a student who did not prepare guesses on each item. Find the probability that he answers

34. exactly 6 questions correctly;

36. at least 8 correctly;

35. exactly 7 correctly;

37. less than 8 correctly.

Assume that the probability that a person will die within a month after a certain operation is 20%. Find the probability that in 3 such operations

38. all 3 people survive;

40. at least 2 people survive;

39. exactly 1 person survives;

41. no more than 1 person survives.

Six mice from the same litter, all suffering from a vitamin A deficiency, are fed a certain dose of carrots. If the probability of recovery under such treatment is .70, find the probability that

42. none recover;

44. all recover;

43. exactly 3 of the 6 recover;

45. no more than 3 recover.

46. In an experiment on the effects of a radiation dose on cells, a beam of radioactive particles is aimed at a group of 10 cells. Find the probability that 8 of the cells will be hit by the beam, if the probability that any single cell will be hit is .6. (Assume independence.)

47. The probability of a mutation of a given gene under a dose of 1 roentgen of radiation is approximately 2.5×10^{-7}. What is the probability that in 10,000 genes, at least 1 mutation occurs?

48. A new drug being tested causes a serious side effect in 5 out of 100 patients. What is the probability that no side effects occur in a sample of 10 patients taking the drug?

An economist feels that the probability that a person at a certain income level will buy a new car this year is .2. Find the probability that among 12 such people,

49. exactly 4 buy a new car;

51. no more than 3 buy a new car;

50. exactly 6 buy a new car;

52. at least 3 buy a new car.

Find the probability that the following numbers of tosses of a fair coin will be required to obtain three heads.

53. 5   **54.** 6   **55.** 8   **56.** 10

Find the probability that the following numbers of rolls of a fair die will be required to get 4 fives.

57. 6   **58.** 10   **59.** 12   **60.** 16

The probability that a given exploration team sent out by a mining company will find commercial quantities of iron ore is .15. How many such teams must the company send out to have the following probabilities of finding ore?

61. 60%   **62.** 75%   **63.** 80%

64. Suppose we find the probability of r successes out of n trials for a Bernoulli experiment having probability p. Show that the result is the same as for the probability of $n - r$ successes out of n trials for a Bernoulli experiment having probability $1 - p$.

Calculate each of the probabilities in Exercises 65–68.

65. A flu vaccine has a probability of 80% of preventing a person who is inoculated from getting flu. A county health office inoculates 134 people. What is the probability that

(a) exactly 10 of them get the flu?

(b) no more than 10 get the flu?

(c) none of them get the flu?

66. The probability that a male will be color-blind is .042. What is the probability that in a group of 53 men

(a) exactly five are color-blind?

(b) no more than five are color-blind?

(c) at least 1 is color-blind?

67. The probability that a certain machine turns out a defective item is .05. What is the probability that in a run of 75 items

   (a) exactly 5 defectives are produced?

   (b) no defectives are produced?

   (c) at least 1 defective is produced?

68. A company is taking a survey to find out if people like their product. Their last survey indicated that 70% of the population like their product. Based on that, of a sample of 58 people, what is the probability that

   (a) all 58 like the product?

   (b) from 28 to 30 (inclusive) like the product?

KEY WORDS		
	experiment	simple event
	trial	certain event
	outcome	impossible event
	sample space	mutually exclusive events
	probability distribution	probability of an event
	addition principle	stochastic processes
	complement of an event	independent events
	odds	dependent events
	subjective probability	Bayes' formula
	conditional probability	repeated trials
	tree diagram	Bernoulli experiments
	product rule	binomial problems
	event	

Chapter 6   REVIEW EXERCISES

Write sample spaces for the following.

1. a die is rolled

2. a card is drawn from a deck containing only the thirteen spades

3. the weight of a person is measured to the nearest half pound; the scale will not measure more than 300 pounds

4. a coin is tossed four times

An urn contains five balls labeled 3, 5, 7, 9, and 11, respectively, while a second urn contains four red and two green balls. An experiment consists of pulling one ball from each urn, in turn. Write each of the following.

5. the sample space

6. event E, the first ball is greater than 5

7. event F, the second ball is green

8. Are the outcomes in the sample space equally likely?

A company sells typewriters and copiers. Let E be the event "a customer buys a typewriter," and let F be the event "a customer buys a copier." Write each of the following using $\cap$, $\cup$, or $'$ as necessary.

9. A customer buys neither

10. A customer buys at least one

When a single card is drawn from an ordinary deck, find the probability that it will be

11. a heart;

12. a red queen;

13. a face card;

14. black or a face card;

15. red, given it is a queen;

16. a jack, given it is a face card;

17. a face card, given it is a king.

Find the odds in favor of a card drawn from an ordinary deck being

18. a club

19. a black jack

20. a red face card or a queen

A sample shipment of five swimming pool filters is chosen at random. The probability of exactly 0, 1, 2, 3, 4, or 5 filters being defective is given in the following table.

Number Defective	0	1	2	3	4	5
Probability	.31	.25	.18	.12	.08	.06

Find the probability that the following number of filters is defective.

21. no more than 3

22. at least 3

The square shows the four possible (equally likely) combinations when both parents are carriers of the sickle cell anemia trait. Each carrier parent has normal cells (N) and trait cells (T).

		2nd Parent	
		N_2	T_2
1st Parent	N_1		$N_1 T_2$
	T_1		

23. Complete the table.

24. If the disease occurs only when two trait cells combine, find the probability that a child born to these parents will have sickle cell anemia.

25. The child will carry the trait but not have the disease if a normal cell combines with a trait cell. Find this probability.

26. Find the probability that the child is neither a carrier nor has the disease.

Find the probability for the following sums when two fair dice are rolled.

27. 8

28. 0

29. at least 10

30. no more than 5

31. odd and greater than 8

32. 12, given it is greater than 10

33. 7, given that at least one die is 4

34. at least 9, given that at least one die is 5

Suppose $P(E) = .51$, $P(F) = .37$, and $P(E \cap F) = .22$. Find each of the following probabilities.

35. $P(E \cup F)$

36. $P(E \cap F')$

37. $P(E' \cup F)$

38. $P(E' \cap F')$

A basket contains 4 black, 2 blue, and 5 green balls. A sample of 3 balls is drawn. Find the probability that the sample contains

39. all black balls;

40. all blue balls;

41. 2 black balls and 1 green ball;

42. exactly 2 black balls;

43. 2 green and 1 blue ball;

44. exactly 1 blue ball.

Suppose two cards are drawn without replacement from an ordinary deck of 52. Find the probability that

45. both cards are red;

46. both cards are spades;

47. at least one card is a spade;

48. the second card is red given that the first card was a diamond;

49. the second card is a face card, given that the first card was not;

50. the second card is a five, given that the first card was the five of diamonds.

The table below shows the results of a survey of 1000 new or used car buyers of a certain model car.

	Satisfied	Not Satisfied	Totals
New	300	100	400
Used	450	150	600
Totals	750	250	1000

Let S represent the event "satisfied", and N the event "bought a new car." Find each of the following.

51. $P(N \cap S)$

52. $P(N \cup S')$

53. $P(N|S)$

54. $P(N'|S)$

55. $P(S|N')$

56. $P(S'|N')$

Of the appliance repair shops listed in the phone book, 80% are competent and 20% are not. A competent shop can repair an appliance correctly 95% of the time; an incompetent shop can repair an appliance correctly 60% of the time. Suppose an appliance was repaired correctly. Find the probability that it was repaired by

57. a competent shop;

58. an incompetent shop.

Suppose an appliance was repaired incorrectly. Find the probability that it was repaired by

59. a competent shop;

60. an incompetent shop.

61. Box A contains 5 red balls and 1 black ball; box B contains 2 red and 3 black balls. A box is chosen, and a ball is selected from it. The probability of choosing box A is 3/8. If the selected ball is black, what is the probability that it came from box A?

62. Find the probability that the ball in Exercise 61 came from box B, given that it is red.

Suppose a family plans six children, and the probability that a particular child is a girl is 1/2. Find the probability that the family will have

63. exactly 3 girls;

64. all girls;

65. at least 4 girls;

66. no more than 2 boys.

A certain machine used to manufacture screws produces a defective rate of .01. A random sample of 20 screws is selected. Find the probability that the sample contains

67. exactly 4 defective screws;   **68.** exactly 3 defective screws;

69. no more than 4 defective screws.

70. *Set up* the probability that the sample has 12 or more defective screws. (Do not evaluate.)

71. An oil company finds oil with 14% of the wells that it drills. How many wells must the company drill to have the following probabilities of finding oil?

   (a) 2/3   **(b)** 3/4

72. *Randomized Response Method for Getting Honest Answers to Sensitive Questions.**
Basically, this is a method to guarantee an individual that answers to sensitive questions will be anonymous, thus encouraging a truthful response. This method is, in effect, an application of the formula for finding the probability of an intersection and operates as follows. Two questions A and B are posed, one of which is sensitive and the other not. The probability of receiving a "yes" to the nonsensitive question must be known. For example, one could ask

   A: Does your Social Security number end in an odd digit? (Nonsensitive)
   B: Have you ever intentionally cheated on your income taxes? (Sensitive)

We know that P(answer yes|answer A) $= 1/2$. We wish to approximate P(answer yes| answer B). The subject is asked to flip a coin and answer A if the coin comes up heads and otherwise to answer B. In this way, the interviewer does not know which question the subject is answering. Thus, a "yes" answer is not incriminating. There is no way for the interviewer to know whether the subject is saying "Yes, my Social Security number ends in an odd digit" or "Yes, I have intentionally cheated on my income taxes." The percentage of subjects in the group answering "yes" is used to approximate P(answer yes).

   (a) Use the fact that the event "answer yes" is the union of the event "answer yes and answer A" with the event "answer yes and answer B" to prove that

$$P(\text{answer yes}|\text{answer B})$$
$$= \frac{P(\text{answer yes}) - P(\text{answer yes}|\text{answer A}) \cdot P(\text{answer A})}{P(\text{answer B})}$$

   (b) If this technique is tried on 100 subjects and 60 answered "yes," what is the approximate probability that a person randomly selected from the group has intentionally cheated on income taxes?

CHAPTER 7

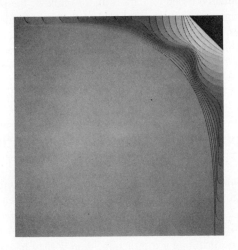

STATISTICS AND PROBABILITY DISTRIBUTIONS

Karl Gerstner. From the series *Color Form*, Archetypal Conversion Cycle, 1970–1975, 1977. Paul Gredinger Collection, Düsseldorf.

Statistics deals with the collection and summarization of data, and methods of drawing conclusions about a population based on data from a sample of the population. Statistical models have become increasingly useful in a variety of fields—for example, manufacturing, government, agriculture, medicine, the social sciences, and in all types of research. In this chapter we give a brief introduction to some of the key topics from statistical theory.

7.1   Basic Properties of Probability Distributions

Random Variables   A bank is interested in improving its services to the public. The manager decides to begin by finding the amount of time tellers spend on each transaction. She decides to time the transactions to the nearest minute. To each transaction, then, will be assigned one of the numbers 0, 1, 2, 3, 4, · · ·. That is, if T represents the experiment of timing a transaction, then T may take on any of the values from the list 0, 1, 2, 3, 4, · · ·. Since the value that T takes on for a particular transaction is random, T is called a *random variable*.

Random Variable

> A **random variable** is a function that assigns a real number to each outcome of an experiment.

It is common to use upper case letters, such as X or Y, for random variables. Lower case letters, such as x or y, are then used for a particular value of the random variable.

Probability Distributions   Suppose that the bank manager finds the times for 75 different transactions, with results as shown in Table 1. As the table shows, the shortest transaction time was 1 minute, with 3 transactions of 1-minute duration. The longest time was 10 minutes. Only one transaction took that long.

In Table 1, the ten values assumed by the random variable T are listed in the first column and the number of occurrences corresponding to each of these values, the **frequency** of that value, is given in the second column. Table 1 is an example of a **frequency distribution,** a table listing the frequencies for each value a random variable may assume.

Now suppose that several weeks after starting new procedures to speed up transactions, the manager takes another survey. This time she includes 57 transactions, and she records their times as shown in the frequency distribution of Table 2.

Table 1

Time	Frequency
1	3
2	5
3	9
4	12
5	15
6	11
7	10
8	6
9	3
10	1
	Total: 75

Table 2

Time	Frequency
1	4
2	5
3	8
4	10
5	12
6	17
7	0
8	1
9	0
10	0
	Total: 57

Do the results in Table 2 indicate an improvement? It is hard to compare the two tables, since one is based on 75 transactions and the other on 57. To make them comparable, we can add a column to each table which will give the relative frequency of each transaction time. These results are shown in Tables 3 and 4. Where necessary, decimals are rounded to the nearest hundredth. To find a **relative frequency,** divide each frequency by the total of the frequencies. Here the individual frequencies are divided by 75 or 57 respectively.

Table 3

Time	Frequency	Relative Frequency
1	3	$\frac{3}{75} = .04$
2	5	$\frac{5}{75} \approx .07$
3	9	$\frac{9}{75} = .12$
4	12	$\frac{12}{75} = .16$
5	15	$\frac{15}{75} = .20$
6	11	$\frac{11}{75} \approx .15$
7	10	$\frac{10}{75} \approx .13$
8	6	$\frac{6}{75} = .08$
9	3	$\frac{3}{75} = .04$
10	1	$\frac{1}{75} \approx .01$

Table 4

Time	Frequency	Relative Frequency
1	4	$\frac{4}{57} \approx .07$
2	5	$\frac{5}{57} \approx .09$
3	8	$\frac{8}{57} \approx .14$
4	10	$\frac{10}{57} \approx .18$
5	12	$\frac{12}{57} \approx .21$
6	17	$\frac{17}{57} \approx .30$
7	0	$\frac{0}{57} = 0$
8	1	$\frac{1}{57} \approx .02$
9	0	$\frac{0}{57} = 0$
10	0	$\frac{0}{57} = 0$

Whether the differences in relative frequency between the distributions in Tables 3 and 4 are interpreted as desirable or undesirable depends on management goals. If the manager wanted to eliminate the most time-consuming transactions, the results appear to be desirable. However, before the new procedures were followed, the largest relative frequency of transactions, .20 of all transactions, was for a transaction of 5 minutes. After the new procedures, the largest relative frequency, .30, corresponds to a transaction of 6 minutes. At any rate, the results shown in the two tables are easier to compare using relative frequencies.

The relative frequencies of Tables 3 and 4 can be considered as probabilities. A table, such as Table 3 or Table 4, which gives the set of possible values of a random variable, along with the corresponding probabilities, is called a **probability distribution.** The sum of the probabilities shown in a probability distribution must always be 1. (The sum in an actual distribution may vary slightly from 1 due to rounding.)

EXAMPLE 1

Many plants have seed pods with a variable number of seeds. One variety of green beans has no more than 6 seeds per pod. Suppose that examination of 30 such bean pods gave the results shown in Table 5. Here the random variable X tells the number of seeds per pod. Give a probability distribution for these results.

The probabilities are found by computing the relative frequencies. A total of 30 bean pods were examined, so each frequency should be divided by 30 to get the probabilities shown in the distribution of Table 6. Some of the results have been rounded to the nearest hundredth.

Table 5

X	Frequency
0	3
1	4
2	6
3	8
4	5
5	3
6	1
Total:	30

Table 6

X	Frequency	Probability
0	3	$\frac{3}{30} = .10$
1	4	$\frac{4}{30} \approx .13$
2	6	$\frac{6}{30} = .20$
3	8	$\frac{8}{30} \approx .27$
4	5	$\frac{5}{30} \approx .17$
5	3	$\frac{3}{30} = .10$
6	1	$\frac{1}{30} \approx .03$
Total:	30	

As shown in Table 6, the probability that the random variable X takes on the value 2 is 6/30, or .20. This is often written as

$$P(X = 2) = .20.$$

Also, $P(X = 5) = .10$, and $P(X = 6) \approx .03$. ▪

Instead of writing the probability distribution of the number of seeds as a table, we could write the same information as a set of ordered pairs:

$$\{(0, .10), (1, .13), (2, .20), (3, .27), (4, .17), (5, .10), (6, .03)\}.$$

There is just one probability for each value of the random variable. Thus, a probability distribution defines a function, called a **probability distribution function,** or, simply, a **probability function.** We shall use the terms "probability distribution" and "probability function" interchangeably. The function described in

Example 1 is a **discrete function,** since it has a finite number of ordered pairs. A **continuous** probability distribution function has an infinite number of values of the random variable, corresponding to an interval on the number line. Continuous probability distribution functions are discussed in Section 7.4.

The information in a probability distribution is often displayed graphically in a special kind of bar graph called a **histogram.** The bars all have the same width. The heights of the bars are determined by the frequencies. A histogram for the data of Table 3 is given in Figure 1. A histogram shows important characteristics of a distribution which may not be evident in tabular form, such as the relative sizes of the probabilities and any symmetry in the distribution.

The area of the bar above $T = 1$ in Figure 1 is the product of 1 and .04, or $.04 \times 1 = .04$. Since each bar has a width of 1, its area is equal to the probability which corresponds to that value of T. The probability that a particular value will occur is thus given by the area of the appropriate bar of the graph. For example, the probability of a transaction time less than four minutes is the sum of the areas for $T = 1$, $T = 2$, and $T = 3$. This area, shown in color in Figure 2, corresponds to 23% of the total area, since

$$P(T < 4) = P(T = 1) + P(T = 2) + P(T = 3)$$
$$= .04 + .07 + .12 = .23.$$

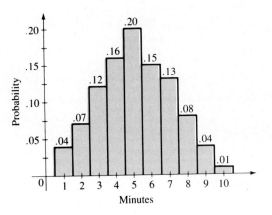

FIGURE 1

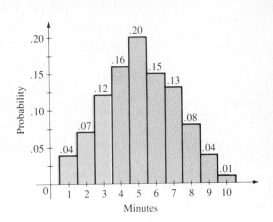

FIGURE 2

EXAMPLE 2

Construct a histogram for the probability distribution of Example 1. Then find the area which gives the probability that the number of seeds will be more than 4.

A histogram for this distribution is shown in Figure 3. The portion of the histogram in color represents

$$P(X > 4) = P(X = 5) + P(X = 6)$$
$$= .10 + .03 = .13,$$

or 13% of the total area. ▧

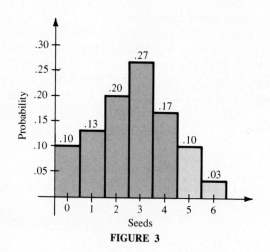

FIGURE 3

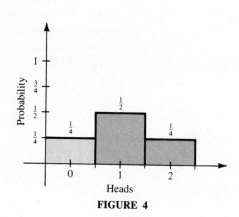

FIGURE 4

EXAMPLE 3

(a) Give the probability distribution for the number of heads showing when two coins are tossed.

Let X represent the random variable, number of heads. Then X can take on the values 0, 1, or 2. Now find the probability of each outcome. The results are shown in Table 7.

Table 7

x	$P(X = x)$
0	$\frac{1}{4}$
1	$\frac{1}{2}$
2	$\frac{1}{4}$

(b) Draw a histogram for the distribution of Table 7. Which bars represent the probability that at least one coin comes up heads?

The histogram is shown in Figure 4. The portion in color represents

$$P(X \geq 1) = P(X = 1) + P(X = 2) = \frac{3}{4}. \quad ▧$$

7.1 EXERCISES

In Exercises 1–6, (a) give the probability distribution, and (b) sketch its histogram.

1. In a seed-viability test 50 seeds were placed in 10 rows of five seeds each. After a period of time, the number which germinated in each row were counted with the following results.

Number Germinated	Frequency
0	0
1	0
2	1
3	3
4	4
5	2
Total:	10

2. At a large supermarket during the 5-o'clock rush, the number of customers waiting in each of 10 check-out lines was counted. The results are shown below.

Number Waiting	Frequency
2	1
3	2
4	4
5	2
6	0
7	1
Total:	10

3. At a training program for police officers, each member of a class of 25 took 6 shots at a target. The total number of bullseyes are shown in the table below.

Number of Bullseyes	Frequency
0	0
1	1
2	0
3	4
4	10
5	8
6	2
Total:	25

4. A class of 42 students took a 10-point quiz. The frequency of scores is given below.

Number of Points	Frequency
5	2
6	5
7	10
8	15
9	7
10	3
Total:	42

5. Five mice are inoculated against a disease. After an incubation period, the number who contract the disease is noted. The experiment is repeated 20 times, with the results shown at the side.

Number With the Disease	Frequency
0	3
1	5
2	6
3	3
4	2
5	1
Total:	20

6. The telephone company kept track of the calls for the correct time during a 24-hour period for two weeks. The results are shown at right.

Number of Calls	Frequency
28	1
29	1
30	2
31	3
32	2
33	2
34	2
35	1
Total:	14

For each of the experiments in Exercises 7–12, let X determine a random variable, and use your knowledge of probability to prepare a probability distribution.

7. Four coins are tossed and the number of heads is observed each time.

8. Two dice are rolled and the total number of points is noted.

9. Three cards are drawn from a deck. The number of aces is counted.

10. Two balls are drawn from a bag in which there are 4 white balls and 2 black balls. The number of black balls is counted.

11. A ballplayer with a batting average of .290 comes to bat 4 times in a game. The number of hits is counted.

12. Five cards are drawn from a deck. The number of black threes is counted.

For Exercises 13–18, draw a histogram and shade the region which gives the indicated probability.

13. Exercise 7; $P(X \leq 2)$

14. Exercise 8; $P(X \geq 11)$

15. Exercise 9; P(at least one ace)

16. Exercise 10; P(at least one black ball)

17. Exercise 11; $P(X = 2 \text{ or } X = 3)$

18. Exercise 12; $P(1 \leq X \leq 2)$

19. The frequency with which letters occur in a large sample of any written language does not vary much. Therefore, determining the frequency of each letter in a coded message

is usually the first step in deciphering it. The percent frequencies of the letters in the English language are as follows.

Letter	%	Letter	%	Letters	%
E	13	S, H	6	W, G, B	1.5
T	9	D	4	V	1
A, O	8	L	3.5	K, X, J	0.5
N	7	C, U, M	3	Q, Z	0.2
I, R	6.5	F, P, Y	2		

Use the introductory paragraph of this exercise as a sample of the English language. Find the percent frequency for each letter in the sample. Compare your results with the frequencies given above.

20. The following message is written in a code in which the frequency of the symbols is the main key to the solution.

)? − − 8)) y * + 8506 * 3 × 6 ; 4 ?* 7* & × * −6.48 ( ) 985)?

(8 + 2: ;48) 81 & ?(;46 *3)y *;48 & (+8(* 509 + & 8 () 8 = 8

(5* − 8 − 5(81 ? 098 ;4 & +)& 15 * 50:)6)6 *; ? 6;6 & * 0? − 7

(a) Find the frequency of each symbol.

(b) By comparing the high-frequency symbols with the high-frequency letters in English, and the low-frequency symbols with the low-frequency letters, try to decipher the message. (Hint: Look for repeated two-symbol combinations and double letters for added clues. Try to identify vowels first.)

7.2 Expected Value

In working with experimental data, it is often useful to have a typical or "average" number that represents the entire set of data. For example, we compare our heights and weights to those of the typical or "average" person on weight charts. Students are familiar with the "class average" and their own "average" at any time in a given course.

In a recent year, a citizen of the United States could expect to complete about 12 years of school, to be a member of a household earning $20,091 per year, and to live in a household of 2.7 people. What do we mean here by "expect"? Many people have completed less than 12 years of school; many others have completed more. Many households have less income than $20,091 per year; many others have more. The idea of a household of 2.7 people is a little hard to swallow. The numbers all refer to *averages*. When the term "expect" is used in this way, it refers to *mathematical expectation*, which we shall see is a kind of average.

The **arithmetic mean,** or **average,** of a set of numbers is the sum of the numbers in the set, divided by the total number of numbers. To write the sum of the n numbers $x_1, x_2, x_3, \cdots, x_n$ in a compact way, use **summation notation:** using the Greek letter Σ (sigma), the sum $x_1 + x_2 + x_3 + \cdots + x_n$ is written

$$x_1 + x_2 + x_3 + \cdots + x_n = \sum_{i=1}^{n} x_i.$$

The symbol $\bar{x}$ (read x-bar) is used to represent the mean, so that the mean of the n numbers $x_1, x_2, x_3, \cdot\cdot\cdot, x_n$ is

$$\bar{x} = \frac{\sum\limits_{i=1}^{n} x_i}{n}.$$

For example, the mean of the set of numbers 2, 3, 5, 6, 8 is

$$\frac{2 + 3 + 5 + 6 + 8}{5} = \frac{24}{5} = 4.8.$$

What about an average value for a random variable? Can we use the mean to find it? As an example, let us find the average number of offspring for a certain species of pheasant, given the probability distribution in Table 8.

Table 8

Number of Offspring	Frequency	Probability
0	8	.08
1	14	.14
2	29	.29
3	32	.32
4	17	.17
Total:	100	

We might be tempted to find the typical number of offspring by averaging the numbers 0, 1, 2, 3, and 4, which represent the numbers of offspring possible. This won't work, however, since the various numbers of offspring do not occur with equal probability: for example, 3 offspring are much more common than 0 or 1 offspring. The differing probabilities of occurrence can be taken into account with a **weighted average,** found by multiplying each of the possible numbers of offspring by its corresponding probability, as follows:

$$\text{typical number of offspring} = 0(.08) + 1(.14) + 2(.29) + 3(.32) + 4(.17)$$
$$= 0 + .14 + .58 + .96 + .68$$
$$= 2.36.$$

Based on the data above, the typical family of pheasants has 2.36 offspring.

It is certainly not possible for a pair of pheasants to produce 2.36 offspring. However, if the number of offspring produced by many different pairs of pheasants are found, then the average, or the mean, of these numbers will be about 2.36.

We can use the idea of this example to define the mean, or expected value, of a probability distribution. This is done as follows.

Expected Value

> Suppose the random variable X can take on the n values $x_1, x_2, x_3, \cdots,$ x_n. Also, suppose the probabilities that each of these values occurs are respectively $p_1, p_2, p_3, \cdots, p_n$. Then the **expected value** of the random variable is
>
> $$E(X) = x_1p_1 + x_2p_2 + x_3p_3 + \cdots + x_np_n.$$

The symbol μ (the Greek letter mu) is used for the expected value of the random variable X. As in the example above, the expected value of a random variable may be a number which can never occur on any one trial of the experiment.

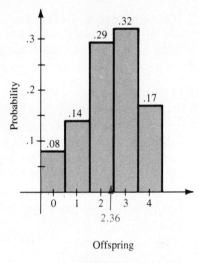

FIGURE 5

Physically, the expected value of a probability distribution represents a balance point. Figure 5 shows a histogram for the distribution of the pheasant offspring. If the histogram is thought of as a series of weights with magnitudes represented by the heights of the bars, then the system would balance if supported at the point corresponding to the expected value.

EXAMPLE 1

The local church decides to raise money by raffling a microwave oven worth $400. A total of 2000 tickets are sold at $1 each. Find the expected value of winning for a person who buys one ticket in the raffle.

Here the random variable represents the possible amounts of net winnings, where net winnings = amount of winning − cost of ticket. The net winnings of the person winning the oven are $400 (amount of winning) − $1 (cost of ticket) = $399. The net winnings for each losing ticket are $0 − $1 = −$1.

The probability of winning is 1 in 2000, or 1/2000, while the probability of losing is 1999/2000. See Table 9.

Table 9

Outcome (net winning)	Probability
$399	$\dfrac{1}{2000}$
−$1	$\dfrac{1999}{2000}$

The expected winnings for a person buying one ticket are

$$399\left(\frac{1}{2000}\right) + (-1)\left(\frac{1999}{2000}\right) = \frac{399}{2000} - \frac{1999}{2000} = -\frac{1600}{2000} = -.80.$$

On the average, a person buying one ticket in the raffle will lose $.80, or 80¢.

It is not possible to lose 80¢ in this raffle—you either lose $1, or you win a $400 prize. However, if you bought tickets in many such raffles over a long period of time, you would lose 80¢ per ticket, on the average. ■

EXAMPLE 2

What is the expected number of girls in a family having exactly three children?

Some families with three children will have 0 girls, others will have 1 girl, and so on. We need to find the probabilities associated with 0, 1, 2, or 3 girls in a family of three children. To find these probabilities, first write the sample space S of all possible three-child families: $S = \{ggg, ggb, bgg, gbb, bgb, bbg, bbb, gbg\}$. This sample space gives the probabilities shown in Table 10, assuming that the probability of a girl at each birth is 1/2.

Table 10

Outcome (number of girls)	Probability
0	$\frac{1}{8}$
1	$\frac{3}{8}$
2	$\frac{3}{8}$
3	$\frac{1}{8}$

The expected number of girls can now be found by multiplying each outcome (number of girls) by its corresponding probability and finding the sum of these values.

$$\text{expected number of girls} = 0 \cdot \frac{1}{8} + 1 \cdot \frac{3}{8} + 2 \cdot \frac{3}{8} + 3 \cdot \frac{1}{8}$$

$$= \frac{3}{8} + \frac{6}{8} + \frac{3}{8}$$

$$= \frac{12}{8} = \frac{3}{2} = 1.5$$

On the average, a three-child family will have 1.5 girls. ■

EXAMPLE 3

Each day Donna and Mary toss a coin to see who buys the coffee (40¢ a cup). One tosses and the other calls the outcome. If the person who calls the outcome is correct, the other buys the coffee; otherwise the caller pays. Find Donna's expected winnings.

Assume that an honest coin is used, that Mary tosses the coin, and that Donna calls the outcome. The possible results and corresponding probabilities are shown below.

		Possible Results		
Result of toss	H	H	T	T
Call	H	T	H	T
Caller wins?	Yes	No	No	Yes
Probability	$\frac{1}{4}$	$\frac{1}{4}$	$\frac{1}{4}$	$\frac{1}{4}$

Donna wins a 40¢ cup of coffee whenever the results and calls match, and loses a 40¢ cup when there is no match. Her expected winnings are

$$(.40)\left(\frac{1}{4}\right) + (-.40)\left(\frac{1}{4}\right) + (-.40)\left(\frac{1}{4}\right) + (.40)\left(\frac{1}{4}\right) = 0.$$

On the average, over the long run, Donna neither wins nor loses. ▪

A game with an expected value of 0 (such as the one of Example 3) is called a **fair game.** Casinos do not offer fair games. If they did, they would win (on the average) $0, and have a hard time paying the help! Casino games have expected winnings for the house that vary from 1.5 cents per dollar to 60 cents per dollar. Exercises 18–21 at the end of the section ask you to find the expected winnings for certain games of chance.

The idea of expected value can be very useful in decision making, as shown by the next example.

EXAMPLE 4

At age 50, you receive a letter from the Mutual of Mauritania Insurance Company. According to the letter, you must tell the company immediately which of the following two options you will choose: take $20,000 at age 60 (if you are alive, $0 otherwise) or $30,000 at age 70 (again, if you are alive, $0 otherwise). Based only on the idea of expected value, which should you choose?

Life insurance companies have constructed elaborate tables showing the probability of a person living a given number of years into the future. From a recent such table, the probability of living from age 50 to age 60 is .88, while the probability of living from age 50 to 70 is .64. The expected values of the two options are given below.

First option: $(20,000)(.88) + (0)(.12) = 17,600$

Second option: $(30,000)(.64) + (0)(.36) = 19,200$

Based strictly on expected values, choose the second option. ▪

7.2 EXERCISES

Find the expected value for each of the random variables in Exercises 1–4.

1.

x	2	3	4	5
$P(X = x)$	.1	.4	.3	.2

2.

y	4	6	8	10
$P(Y = y)$	.4	.4	.05	.15

3.

z	9	12	15	18	21
$P(Z = z)$	.14	.22	.36	.18	.10

4.

x	30	32	36	38	44
$P(X = x)$	.31	.30	.29	.06	.04

Find the expected value for the random variable X having probability functions graphed as in Exercises 5–8.

5.

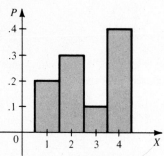

6.

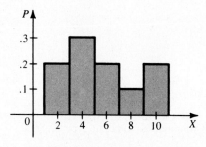

7.

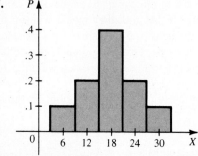

8.

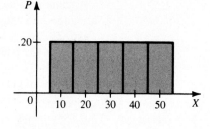

9. A raffle offers a first prize of $100, and two second prizes of $40 each. One ticket costs $1, and 500 tickets are sold. Find the expected winnings for a person who buys one ticket. Is this a fair game?

10. A raffle offers a first prize of $1000, two second prizes of $300 each, and twenty prizes of $10 each. If 10,000 tickets are sold at 50¢ each, find the expected winnings for a person buying one ticket. Is this a fair game?

Many of the following exercises use the ideas of combinations, which were discussed in Chapter 5.

11. If 3 marbles are drawn from a bag containing 3 yellow and 4 white marbles, what is the expected number of yellow marbles in the sample?

12. If 5 apples in a barrel of 25 apples are known to be rotten, what is the expected number of rotten apples in a sample of 2 apples?

13. A delegation of 3 is selected from a city council made up of 5 liberals and 4 conservatives.

(a) What is the expected number of liberals on the committee?

(b) What is the expected number of conservatives?

14. From a group of 2 women and 5 men, a delegation of 2 is selected. Find the expected number of women in the delegation.

15. In a club with 20 senior and 10 junior members, what is the expected number of junior members on a 3-member committee?

16. If 2 cards are drawn at one time from a deck of 52 cards, what is the expected number of diamonds?

17. Suppose someone offers to pay you $5 if you draw 2 diamonds in the game of Exercise 16. He says that you should pay 50¢ for the chance to play. Is this a fair game?

Find the expected winnings for the games of chance described in Exercises 18–21.

18. In one form of roulette, you bet $1 on "even." If one of the 18 even numbers comes up, you get your dollar back, plus another one. If one of the 20 noneven (18 odd, 0, and 00) numbers comes up, you lose.

19. In another form of roulette, there are only 19 noneven numbers (no 00).

20. Numbers is an illegal game where you bet $1 on any three-digit number from 000 to 999. If your number comes up, you get $500.

21. In one form of the game Keno, the house has a pot containing 80 balls, each marked with a different number from 1 to 80. You buy a ticket for $1 and mark one of the 80 numbers on it. The house then selects 20 numbers at random. If your number is among the 20, you get $3.20 (for a net winning of $2.20).

22. Use the assumptions of Example 3 to find Mary's expected winnings. If Mary tosses and Donna calls, is it still a fair game?

23. Suppose one day Mary brings a two-headed coin and uses it to toss for the coffee. Since Mary tosses, Donna calls.

(a) Is this still a fair game?

(b) What is Donna's expected gain if she calls heads?

(c) If she calls tails?

24. Find the expected number of girls in a family of four children.

25. Find the expected number of boys in a family of five children.

26. Jack must choose at age 40 to inherit either $25,000 at age 50 (if he is still alive) or $30,000 at age 55 (if he is still alive). If the probabilities for a person of age 40 to live to be 50 and 55 are .90 and .85, respectively, which choice gives him the larger expected inheritance?

27. An insurance company has written 100 policies of $10,000, 500 of $5000, and 1000 policies of $1000 on people of age 20. If experience shows that the probability of dying during the twentieth year of life is .001, how much can the company expect to pay out during the year the policies were written?

28. A builder is considering a job which promises a profit of $30,000 with a probability of .7 or a loss (due to bad weather, strikes, and such) of $10,000 with a probability of .3. What is the expected profit?

29. Experience has shown that a ski lodge will be full (160 guests) during the Christmas holidays if there is a heavy snow pack in December, while a light snowfall in December means that they will have only 90 guests. What is the expected number of guests if the probability for a heavy snow in December is .40? (Assume that there must either be a light snowfall or a heavy snowfall.)

30. A magazine distributor offers a first prize of $100,000, two second prizes of $40,000 each, and two third prizes of $10,000 each. A total of 2,000,000 entries are received in the contest. Find the expected winnings if you submit one entry to the contest. If it would cost you 25¢ in time, paper, and stamps to enter, would it be worth it?

31. A local used-car dealer gets complaints about his cars, as shown in the following table.

Number of complaints per day	0	1	2	3	4	5	6
Probability	.01	.05	.15	.26	.33	.14	.06

Find the expected number of complaints per day.

32. I can take one of two jobs. With job A, there is a 50% chance that I will make $60,000 per year after 5 years, and a 50% chance of making $30,000. With job B, there is a 30% chance that I will make $90,000 per year after 5 years and a 70% chance that I will make $20,000. Based strictly on expected value, which job should I take?

33. Levi Strauss and Company* uses expected value to help its salespeople rate their accounts. For each account, a salesperson estimates potential additional volume and the probability of getting it. The product of these gives the expected value of the potential, which is added to the existing volume. The totals are then classified as A, B, or C as follows: below $40,000, class C; between $40,000 and $55,000, class B; above $55,000, class A. Complete the following chart for one of its salespeople.

Account Number	Existing Volume	Potential Additional Volume	Probability of Getting It	Expected Value of Potential	Existing Volume + Expected Value of Potential	Class
1	$15,000	$10,000	.25	$2,500	$17,500	C
2	40,000	0	—	—	40,000	C
3	20,000	10,000	.20			
4	50,000	10,000	.10			
5	5,000	50,000	.50			
6	0	100,000	.60			
7	30,000	20,000	.80			

34. At the end of play in a major golf tournament, two players, an "old pro" and a "new kid," are tied. Suppose first prize is $80,000 and second prize is $20,000. Find the expected winnings for the old pro if

(a) both players are of equal ability,

(b) the new kid will freeze up, giving the old pro a 3/4 chance of winning.

35. In a certain animal species, the probability that a healthy adult female will have no offspring in a given year is .31, while the probability of 1, 2, 3, or 4 offspring are respectively .21, .19, .17, and .12. Find the expected number of offspring.

---

*This example was supplied by James McDonald, Levi Strauss and Company, San Francisco.

36. According to an article in a magazine not known for its accuracy, a male decreases his life expectancy by one year, on the average, for every point that his blood pressure is above 120. The average life expectancy for a male is 76 years. Find the life expectancy for a male whose blood pressure is

   (a) 135;   **(b)** 150;   **(c)** 115;   **(d)** 100.

   (e) Suppose a certain male has a blood pressure of 145. Find his life expectancy. How would you interpret the result to him?

37. One of the few methods that can be used in an attempt to cut the severity of a hurricane is to *seed* the storm. In this process, silver iodide crystals are dropped into the storm. Unfortunately, silver iodide crystals sometimes cause the storm to *increase* its speed. Wind speeds may also increase or decrease even with no seeding. The probabilities and amounts of property damage in the following tree diagram are from an article by R. A. Howard, J. E. Matheson, and D. W. North, "The Decision to Seed Hurricanes."*

   (a) Find the expected amount of damage under each option, "seed" and "do not seed."

   (b) To minimize total expected damage, what option should be chosen?

	Change in wind speed	Property damage (millions of dollars)
0.038	+32%	335.8
0.143	+16%	191.1
Seed 0.392	0	100.0
0.255	−16%	46.7
0.172	−34%	16.3
0.054	+32%	335.8
0.206	+16%	191.1
Do not seed 0.480	0	100.0
0.206	−16%	46.7
0.054	−34%	16.3

---

*"The Decision to Seed Hurricanes," Howard, R. A. et al., *Science,* Vol. 176, pp. 1191–1202, Fig. 7, 16 June 1972. Copyright © 1972 by the American Association for the Advancement of Science. Reprinted by permission of the American Association for the Advancement of Science and SRI International, Menlo Park, California.

38. A contest at a fast-food restaurant offered the following cash prizes and probabilities of winning on one visit.

Prize	Probability
$100,000	$\dfrac{1}{176,402,500}$
$25,000	$\dfrac{1}{39,200,556}$
$5000	$\dfrac{1}{17,640,250}$
$1000	$\dfrac{1}{1,568,022}$
$100	$\dfrac{1}{282,244}$
$5	$\dfrac{1}{7056}$
$1	$\dfrac{1}{588}$

Suppose you spend $1 to buy a bus pass that lets you go to 25 different restaurants in the chain and pick up entry forms. Find your expected value.

EXTENDED

APPLICATION

Optimal Inventory for a Service Truck

For many different items it is difficult or impossible to take the item to a central repair facility when service for the item is required. Washing machines, large television sets, office copiers, and computers are only a few examples of such items. Service for items of this type is commonly performed by sending a repair person to the item, with the person driving to the item in a truck containing various parts that might be required in repairing the item. Ideally, the truck should contain all the parts that might be required in repairing the item. However, most parts would be needed only infrequently, so that inventory costs for the parts would be high.

An optimum policy for deciding on the parts to stock on a truck would require that the probability of not being able to repair an item without a trip back to the warehouse for needed parts be as low as possible, consistent with minimum inventory costs. An analysis similar to the one below was developed at the Xerox Corporation.*

To set up a mathematical model for deciding on the optimum truck stocking policy, let us assume that a broken machine might require one of 5 different parts (we could assume any number of different parts—we use 5 to simplify the notation). Suppose also that the probability that a particular machine requires part 1 is p_1, that it requires part 2 is p_2, and so on. Assume also that the failure of different part types are independent, and that at most one part of each type is used on a given job.

Suppose that, on the average, a repair person makes N service calls per time period.

*Reprinted by permission of Stephen Smith, John Chambers, and Eli Shlifer, "Optimal Inventories Based on Job Completion Rate for Repairs Requiring Multiple Items," *Management Science*, Vol. 26, No. 8, August 1980, copyright © 1980 The Institute of Management Sciences.

If the repair person is unable to make a repair because at least one of the parts is unavailable, there is a penalty cost, L, corresponding to wasted time for the repair person, an extra trip to the parts depot, customer unhappiness, and so on. For each of the parts carried on the truck, an average inventory cost is incurred. Let H_i be the average inventory cost for part i, where $1 \le i \le 5$.

Let M_1 represent a policy of carrying only part 1 on the repair truck, M_{24} represent a policy of carrying only parts 2 and 4, with M_{12345} and M_0 representing policies of carrying all parts and no parts, respectively.

For policy M_{35}, carrying parts 3 and 5 only, the expected cost per time period per repair person, written $C(M_{35})$, is

$$C(M_{35}) = (H_3 + H_5) + NL[1 - (1 - p_1)(1 - p_2)(1 - p_4)].$$

(The expression in brackets represents the probability of needing at least one of the parts not carried, 1, 2, or 4 here.) As further examples, $C(M_{125})$ is

$$C(M_{125}) = (H_1 + H_2 + H_5) + NL[1 - (1 - p_3)(1 - p_4)],$$

while
$$C(M_{12345}) = (H_1 + H_2 + H_3 + H_4 + H_5) + NL[1 - 1]$$
$$= H_1 + H_2 + H_3 + H_4 + H_5,$$

and
$$C(M_0) = NL[1 - (1 - p_1)(1 - p_2)(1 - p_3)(1 - p_4)(1 - p_5)].$$

To find the best policy, evaluate $C(M_0)$, $C(M_1)$, $\cdots$, $C(M_{12345})$ and choose the smallest result. (A general solution method is in the *Management Science* paper.)

Example

Suppose that for a particular item, only 3 possible parts might need to be replaced. By studying past records of failures of the item, and finding necessary inventory costs, suppose that the following values have been found.

p_1	p_2	p_3	H_1	H_2	H_3
.09	.24	.17	$15	$40	$9

Suppose $N = 3$ and L is $54. Then, as an example,

$$C(M_1) = H_1 + NL[1 - (1 - p_2)(1 - p_3)]$$
$$= 15 + 3(54)[1 - (1 - .24)(1 - .17)]$$
$$= 15 + 3(54)[1 - (.76)(.83)]$$
$$\approx 15 + 59.81$$
$$= 74.81.$$

Thus, if policy M_1 is followed (carrying only part 1 on the truck), the expected cost per repair person per time period is $74.81. Also,

$$C(M_{23}) = H_2 + H_3 + NL[1 - (1 - p_1)]$$
$$= 40 + 9 + 3(54)[.09]$$
$$= 63.58,$$

so that M_{23} is a better policy than M_1. By finding the expected values for all other possible policies (see the exercises below), the optimum policy may be chosen. ∎

EXERCISES

1. Refer to the example above and find each of the following.

   (a) $C(M_0)$ **(b)** $C(M_2)$ **(c)** $C(M_3)$ **(d)** $C(M_{12})$

   (e) $C(M_{13})$ **(f)** $C(M_{123})$.

2. Which policy leads to lowest expected cost?

3. In the example above, $p_1 + p_2 + p_3 = .09 + .24 + .17 = .50$. Why is it not necessary that the probabilities add to 1?

4. Suppose an item to be repaired might need one of n different parts. How many different policies would then need to be evaluated?

EXTENDED APPLICATION

Bidding on a Potential Oil Field—Signal Oil

Signal Oil, with headquarters in Los Angeles, is a major petroleum company. In this example we use probability and expected values to help determine the best bid price for a new off-shore oil field. The company has used all the modern methods of oil exploration to help interpret the economic potential of each tract.*

    Two uncontrollable (and therefore uncertain) variables dominate a problem of this type: (a) the amount of commercial oil reserves that might be found in a tract, and (b) the length of time that would be required to develop and begin commercial production using these reserves. Another important variable is the amount to be bid for the right to develop the tract. Although the bid is a variable, it is not subject to uncertainty, but is under the control of the company. The company must analyze the effects of bids of various sizes along with the variables involving uncertainty so that the proper bid can be made.

    The following chart shows the probabilities of various events. Commercial production includes events B_2, B_3, and B_4. Note that commercial production is given a 20% chance of occurring, with an 80% chance of the occurrence of less than a commercially profitable level of oil reserves.

	Oil Reserves	
Event B_j	*Millions of Barrels*	*Chance of Occurrence*
B_1	0.0	.80
B_2	19.0	.06
B_3	25.5	.10
B_4	30.6	.04

*This example was supplied by Kenneth P. King, Senior Planning Analyst, Signal Oil Company.

Any delay in beginning the commercial development of the field adversely affects the overall profitability of the project. This delay can be caused by seasonal weather variation in the offshore area, together with its relative isolation and the uncertainty of drilling rig availability. Beginning development in a shorter-than-normal time would require a concerted speedup effort that would incur cost increases over the normal period of development. This additional cost, however, is somewhat offset by the fact that the income from the field would be received sooner. The chart below shows the probabilities of various lengths of time required for commercial development to begin.

Years From Bid to Start of Drilling		
Event A_i	Years	Chance of Occurrence
A_1	2	.75
A_2	1	.13
A_3	3	.12

The time required for drilling to begin is independent of the quantity of reserves in the field. Hence, for each possible value of i and j, we have

$$P(A_i \text{ and } B_j) = P(A_i) \cdot P(B_j).$$

For example, $P(2 \text{ years' delay and } 25.5 \text{ million barrels}) = P(A_1 \text{ and } B_3) = P(A_1) \cdot P(B_3) = (.75)(.10) = .075$. The chart below shows the probabilities for all possible cases, along with the payoffs to the company for different bid levels.

		Payoff (in millions of dollars)				
Case	Event	Probability	$0 Bid	$2	$5	$10
1	A_1 and B_1	.600	−1.1	−2.3	−4.0	−6.9
2	A_1 and B_2	.045	10.4	8.4	5.4	0.4
3	A_1 and B_3	.075	17.0	15.0	12.0	7.0
4	A_1 and B_4	.030	22.2	20.2	17.2	12.2
5	A_2 and B_1	.104	−1.1	−2.3	−4.0	−6.9
6	A_2 and B_2	.008	13.2	11.2	8.2	3.2
7	A_2 and B_3	.013	21.5	19.5	16.5	11.5
8	A_2 and B_4	.005	27.7	25.7	22.7	17.7
9	A_3 and B_1	.096	−1.1	−2.3	−4.0	−6.9
10	A_3 and B_2	.007	7.5	5.5	2.5	−2.5
11	A_3 and B_3	.012	13.0	11.0	8.0	3.0
12	A_3 and B_4	.005	17.5	15.5	12.5	7.5
	Total:	1.000				

Now the company must calculate the expected value for each different bid level. For example, the expected value at a bid level of $2 million is given by

$E(\text{bid of } \$2 \text{ million}) = (-2.3)(.600) + (8.4)(.045)$

$+ (15.0)(.075) + \cdots + (15.5)(.005).$

If the expected values for various possible bid levels are found in the same way and plotted, we get the graph in the following figure. Using techniques from mathematics of finance (the payoffs above are actually present values), the company knows that the expected value of a profitable bid must be $0 or more. As shown in the figure, this means that $3.5 million is the most the company can bid for this particular tract.

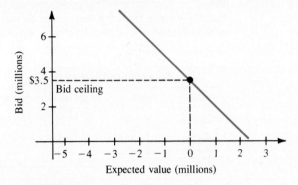

1. Calculate E(bid of $2 million).

2. Calculate E(bid of $5 million).

7.3   Variance and Standard Deviation

The mean of a distribution gives us an average value of the distribution, but the mean tells us nothing about the *spread* of the numbers in the distribution. For example, suppose seven measurements of the thickness (in cm) of a copper wire produced by one machine were

$$.010, \quad .010, \quad .009, \quad .008, \quad .007, \quad .009, \quad .010,$$

and seven measurements of the same type of wire produced by another machine were

$$.014, \quad .004, \quad .013, \quad .005, \quad .009, \quad .004, \quad .014.$$

The mean of both samples is .009, yet the two samples are quite dissimilar; the amount of dispersion or variation within the samples is different. In addition to the mean, we need another kind of measure, which describes the variation of the numbers in a distribution.

Since the mean represents the center of the distribution, one way to measure the variation within a set of numbers might be to find the average of their distances from the mean. That is, if the numbers are $x_1, x_2, \cdot \cdot \cdot, x_n$ and the mean is $\bar{x}$, we might first find the differences $x_1 - \bar{x}, x_2 - \bar{x}, \cdot \cdot \cdot, x_n - \bar{x}$, and then find the mean of the differences. However, it turns out that the sum of these differences is always 0, so that their mean would also be 0. To see why, look at the four numbers x_1, x_2, x_3, x_4 having mean $\bar{x}$. The sum of the four differences is

$$\sum_{i=1}^{4} (x_i - \bar{x}) = (x_1 - \bar{x}) + (x_2 - \bar{x}) + (x_3 - \bar{x}) + (x_4 - \bar{x})$$
$$= x_1 + x_2 + x_3 + x_4 - 4(\bar{x})$$

By definition, $\bar{x} = (x_1 + x_2 + x_3 + x_4)/4$, giving

$$\bar{x} = x_1 + x_2 + x_3 + x_4 - 4\left(\frac{x_1 + x_2 + x_3 + x_4}{4}\right)$$
$$= 0.$$

While we proved this result only for four values, the proof could be extended to any finite number of values.

Since the sum of the differences from the mean is always 0, the mean of these differences also would be 0—not a good measure of the variability of a distribution. It turns out that a very useful measure of variability is found by *squaring* the differences from the mean.

For example, let us use the seven measurements given above,

$$.010, \quad .010, \quad .009, \quad .008, \quad .007, \quad .009, \quad .010.$$

The mean of these numbers is .009. Subtracting the mean from each of the seven values gives the differences

$$.001, \quad .001, \quad 0, \quad -.001, \quad -.002, \quad 0, \quad .001.$$

(Check that the sum of these differences is 0.) Now square each difference, getting

$$.000001, .000001, \quad 0, \quad .000001, \quad .000004, \quad 0, \quad .000001.$$

Next, find the mean of these squares, which is .00000114 (rounded).

This number, the mean of the squares of the differences, is called the **variance** of the distribution. If X is the random variable for the distribution, then the variance is written $\text{Var}(X)$. The variance gives a measure of the variation of the numbers in the distribution, but, since we used the squared differences to get it, the size of the variance does not reflect the actual amount of variation. To correct this problem, another measure of variation is used, the **standard deviation,** which is the square root of the variance. The symbol σ (the Greek lower case sigma) is used for standard deviation. The standard deviation of the distribution discussed above is

$$\sigma = \sqrt{.00000114} \approx .001.$$

EXAMPLE 1

Find the standard deviation of the seven measurements of copper wire produced by the second machine in the example above.

It is best to arrange the work in columns as in Table 11.

Table 11

x	$x - \bar{x}$	$(x - \bar{x})^2$
.014	.005	.000025
.004	− .005	.000025
.013	.004	.000016
.005	− .004	.000016
.009	0	0
.004	− .005	.000025
.014	.005	.000025
	Total:	.000132

As we have seen, the column $x - \bar{x}$ always should have a sum of 0. This is a good way to check your work at that point. To get the variance, divide the sum of the $(x - \bar{x})^2$ column by the number of values in the set, seven in this case. Then take the square root to get the standard deviation.

$$\text{variance} = \frac{.000132}{7} \approx .0000189$$

$$\sigma = \sqrt{.0000189} \approx .004$$

Both measures of variation, the variance and the standard deviation, are larger for this sample than for the first sample, showing that the first machine produces copper wire with less variation than the second. ▪

Variance is defined as follows:*

Variance; Standard Deviation

The **variance** of a set of n numbers $x_1, x_2, x_3, \cdots x_n$, with mean $\bar{x}$, is

$$\mathbf{Var}(x) = \frac{\Sigma(x - \bar{x})^2}{n}.$$

The **standard deviation** of the set is

$$\sigma = \sqrt{\frac{\Sigma(x - \bar{x})^2}{n}}.$$

Variation for a probability distribution is measured in a similar way.

---

*These formulas sometimes have $n - 1$ instead of n in the denominator. Some calculators which compute variance and standard deviation use n, and others use $n - 1$. Be sure to check how your calculator works before using it for the exercises.

Variance for a	If a random variable X takes on the n values x_1, x_2, x_3, $\cdots$, x_n with
Probability	respective probabilities p_1, p_2, p_3, $\cdots$, p_n, and if its expected value is
Distribution	$E(X) = \mu$, then the **variance** of X is

$$\text{Var}(X) = p_1(x_1 - \mu)^2 + p_2(x_2 - \mu)^2 + \cdots + p_n(x_n - \mu)^2.$$

The **standard deviation** of X is

$$\sigma = \sqrt{\text{Var}(X)}.$$

EXAMPLE 2

Find the variance and the standard deviation of the number of pheasant offspring given the following probability distribution.

Table 12

X	p_i
0	.08
1	.14
2	.29
3	.32
4	.17

In Section 7.2, we found the mean of this distribution, $\mu = 2.36$. To use the formula in the box it is easiest to work in columns as in Example 1.

Table 13

X	p_i	$x_i - \mu$	$(x_i - \mu)^2$	$p_i(x_i - \mu)^2$
0	.08	-2.36	5.57	.45
1	.14	-1.36	1.85	.26
2	.29	$-.36$	.13	.04
3	.32	.64	.41	.13
4	.17	1.64	2.69	.46
			Total:	1.34

The total of the last column gives the variance, 1.34. To find the standard deviation, take the square root of the variance.

$$\sigma = \sqrt{1.34} \approx 1.16 \quad \blacksquare$$

Chebyshev's Theorem   Suppose we know only the mean, or expected value, μ of a distribution, along with the standard deviation σ. What then can be said about the values of the distribution? For example, if σ is very small, we would expect most of the values of the distribution to be close to μ, while a larger value of σ would suggest more spread in the values. One estimate of the fraction of values that lie within a specified distance of the mean is given by **Chebyshev's Theorem,** named after the Russian mathematician P. L. Chebyshev, 1821–94.

Chebyshev's Theorem

For any distribution of numbers with mean μ and standard deviation σ, the probability that a number will lie within k standard deviations of the mean is at least

$$1 - \frac{1}{k^2}.$$

That is,

$$P(\mu - k\sigma \leq X \leq \mu + k\sigma) \geq 1 - \frac{1}{k^2}.$$

EXAMPLE 3

By Chebyshev's Theorem, at least

$$1 - \frac{1}{3^2} = 1 - \frac{1}{9} = \frac{8}{9},$$

or about 89%, of the numbers in any distribution lie within 3 standard deviations of the mean. Figure 6 shows a geometric interpretation of this result.   ■

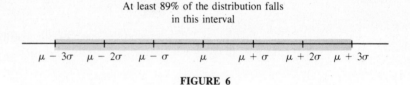

At least 89% of the distribution falls
in this interval

$\mu - 3\sigma \quad \mu - 2\sigma \quad \mu - \sigma \quad \mu \quad \mu + \sigma \quad \mu + 2\sigma \quad \mu + 3\sigma$

FIGURE 6

Suppose a distribution has mean 52 and standard deviation 3.5. Then "3 standard deviations" is $3 \times 3.5 = 10.5$, and "three standard deviations from the mean" is

$$52 - 10.5 \quad \text{to} \quad 52 + 10.5,$$

or $41.5 \quad \text{to} \quad 62.5.$

By Example 3, at least 89% of the values in this distribution will lie between 41.5 and 62.5.

Chebyshev's Theorem gets much of its importance from the fact that it applies to *any* distribution—only the mean and the standard deviation must be known. Other results given later produce more accurate estimates, but only with additional information about the distribution.

EXAMPLE 4

The Forever Power Company claims that their batteries have a mean life of 26.2 hours with a standard deviation of 4.1 hours. In a shipment of 100 batteries, about how many will have a life within 2 standard deviations of the mean—that is, between $26.2 - (4.1 \times 2) = 18$ and $26.2 + (4.1 \times 2) = 34.4$ hours?

Use Chebyshev's Theorem with $k = 2$. At least

$$1 - \frac{1}{2^2} = 1 - \frac{1}{4} = \frac{3}{4},$$

or 75%, of the batteries should have a life within 2 standard deviations of the mean. At least $75\% \times 100 = 75$ of the batteries can be expected to last between 18 and 34.4 hours. ▪

7.3 EXERCISES

Find the standard deviation for each of the sets of numbers in Exercises 1–6.

1. 42; 38; 29; 74; 82; 71; 35

2. 122; 132; 141; 158; 162; 169; 180

3. 241; 248; 251; 257; 252; 287

4. 51; 58; 62; 64; 67; 71; 74; 78; 82; 93

5. 3; 7; 4; 12; 15; 18; 19; 27; 24; 11

6. 15; 42; 53; 7; 9; 12; 28; 47; 63; 14

Find the variance and standard deviation for each of the following probability distributions.

7.

x_i	2	3	4	5
p_i	.1	.3	.4	.2

8.

x_i	10	20	30	40
p_i	.1	.5	.3	.1

9.

x_i	.01	.02	.03	.04	.05
p_i	.1	.5	.2	.1	.1

10.

x_i	100	105	110	115	120
p_i	.01	.08	.20	.50	.21

Find the standard deviation of the random variable in each of the following problems. (See Exercises 11–14 in Section 7.2.)

11. The number of yellow marbles, if 3 marbles are drawn from a bag containing 3 yellow and 4 white marbles.

12. The number of rotten apples, if 2 apples are drawn from a barrel of 25 apples, 5 of which are known to be rotten.

13. The number of liberals on a committee of 3 selected from a city council made up of 5 liberals and 4 conservatives.

14. The number of women in a delegation of 2 selected from a group of 2 women and 5 men.

Exercises 15 and 16 give histograms of two probability distributions. Decide from the graphs without any calculations which distribution has the greatest variance.

15.

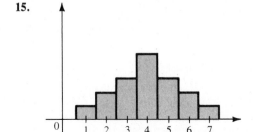

(a)

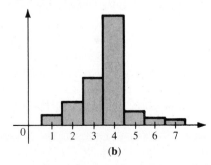

(b)

16.

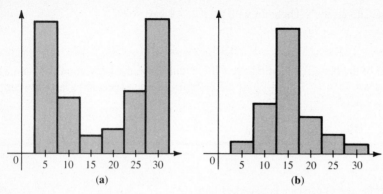

For Exercises 17 and 18, the histogram of a probability distribution is given. Calculate the variance.

17.

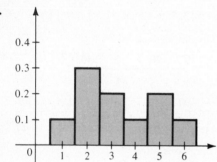

18.

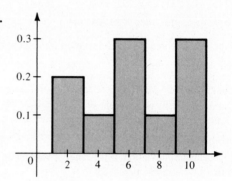

19. Use Chebyshev's Theorem to find the fraction of a distribution that lies within the following numbers of standard deviations from the mean.

(a) 2   (b) 4   (c) 5

20. A probability distribution has an expected value of 50 and a standard deviation of 6. Use Chebyshev's Theorem to tell what percent of the numbers lie between each of the following values.

(a) 38 and 62   (b) 32 and 68   (c) 26 and 74   (d) 20 and 80

(e) less than 38 or more than 62   (f) less than 32 or more than 68

21. The weekly wages of the seven employees of Harold's Hardware Store are $180, $190, $240, $256, $300, $360, and $714.

(a) Find the mean and standard deviation of this distribution.

(b) How many of the seven employees earn within one standard deviation of the mean?

(c) How many earn within two standard deviations of the mean?

(d) What does Chebyshev's Theorem give as the number earning within two standard deviations of the mean?

22. The Forever Power Company conducted tests on the life of its batteries and those of a competitor (Brand X). They found that their batteries had a mean life in hours of 26.2 with a standard deviation of 4.1 (see Example 4). Their results for a sample of 10 Brand X batteries were as follows: 15, 18, 19, 23, 25, 25, 28, 30, 34, 38.

(a) Find the mean and standard deviation for Brand X batteries.

(b) Which batteries have a more uniform life in hours?

(c) Which batteries have the highest average life in hours?

23. The Quaker Oats Company conducted a survey to determine if a proposed premium, to be included in their cereal, was appealing enough to generate new sales.* Four cities were used as test markets, where the cereal was distributed with the premium, and four cities as control markets, where the cereal was distributed without the premium. The eight cities were chosen on the basis of their similarity in terms of population, per capita income, and total cereal purchase volume. The results were as follows.

<table>
<tr><th colspan="3">Percent Change in Average
Market Shares Per Month</th></tr>
<tr><td rowspan="4">Test cities</td><td>1</td><td>+18</td></tr>
<tr><td>2</td><td>+15</td></tr>
<tr><td>3</td><td>+7</td></tr>
<tr><td>4</td><td>+10</td></tr>
<tr><td rowspan="4">Control cities</td><td>1</td><td>+1</td></tr>
<tr><td>2</td><td>-8</td></tr>
<tr><td>3</td><td>-5</td></tr>
<tr><td>4</td><td>0</td></tr>
</table>

(a) Find the mean of the change in market share for the four test cities.

(b) Find the mean of the change in market share for the four control cities.

(c) Find the standard deviation of the change in market share for the test cities.

(d) Find the standard deviation of the change in market share for the control cities.

(e) Find the difference between the means of (a) and (b). This difference represents the estimate of the percent change in sales due to the premium.

(f) The two standard deviations from (c) and (d) were used to calculate an "error" of ± 7.95 for the estimate in (e). With this amount of error, what is the smallest and largest estimate of the increase in sales?

On the basis of the interval estimate of part (f) the company decided to mass produce the premium and distribute it nationally.

24. Show that the formula for variance given in the text can be rewritten as

$$\frac{1}{n^2}[n \cdot \Sigma(x^2) - (\Sigma x)^2].$$

Use a computer to solve the problems in Exercises 25–28.

25. Twenty-five laboratory rats used in an experiment to test the food value of a new product made the following weight gains in grams:

5.25	5.03	4.90	4.97	5.03
5.12	5.08	5.15	5.20	4.95
4.90	5.00	5.13	5.18	5.18
5.22	5.04	5.09	5.10	5.11
5.23	5.22	5.19	4.99	4.93

Find the mean gain and the standard deviation of the gains.

---

*This example was supplied by Jeffery S. Berman, Senior Analyst, Marketing Information, Quaker Oats Company.

26. An assembly-line machine turns out washers with the following thicknesses in mm.

1.20	1.01	1.25	2.20	2.58	2.19
1.29	1.15	2.05	1.46	1.90	2.03
2.13	1.86	1.65	2.27	1.64	2.19
2.25	2.08	1.96	1.83	1.17	2.24

Find the mean and standard deviation of these thicknesses.

27. The prices of pork bellies futures on the Chicago Mercantile Exchange over a period of several weeks were as follows:

48.25	48.50	47.75	48.45	46.85
47.10	46.50	46.90	46.60	47.00
46.35	46.65	46.85	47.20	46.60
47.00	45.00	45.15	44.65	45.15
46.25	45.90	46.10	45.82	45.70
47.05	46.95	46.90	47.15	47.10

Find the mean and standard deviation.

28. A medical laboratory tested 21 samples of human blood for acidity on the pH scale with the following results.

7.1	7.5	7.3	7.4	7.6	7.2	7.3
7.4	7.5	7.3	7.2	7.4	7.3	7.5
7.5	7.4	7.4	7.1	7.3	7.4	7.4

Find the mean and standard deviation.

7.4   The Normal Distribution

The bank transaction times in the example of Section 7.1 were timed to the nearest minute. Theoretically at least, they could have been timed to the nearest tenth of a minute, or hundredth of a minute, or even more accurately. Actually it is possible for the transaction times to take on any real number value greater than 0. As mentioned earlier, a distribution in which the random variable can take any real number value within some interval is a **continuous distribution.**

   The distribution of heights (in inches) of college freshmen women is another example of a continuous distribution, since these heights include infinitely many possible measurements, such as 53, 58.5, 66.3, 72.666 . . . , and so on. Figure 7 shows the continuous distribution of heights of college freshmen women. Here the most frequent heights occur near the center of the interval shown.

   Another continuous curve, which approximates the distribution of yearly incomes in the United States, is shown in Figure 8. From the graph, it can be seen that the most frequent incomes are grouped near the low end of the interval. This kind of distribution, where the peak is not at the center, is called **skewed.**

   Many different experiments produce probability distributions which come from a very important class of continuous distributions called **normal probability distributions.** The distribution shown in Figure 7 is approximately a normal distribution,

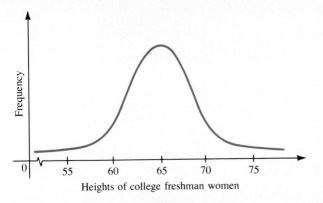

Heights of college freshman women

FIGURE 7

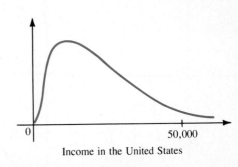

Income in the United States

FIGURE 8

while the one of Figure 8 is not. The distribution of the lengths of the leaves of a certain tree would approximate a normal distribution, as should the distribution of the actual weights of cereal boxes that have an average weight of 16 ounces.

Each normal probability distribution has associated with it a bell-shaped curve, such as the one in Figure 9. This curve, called a **normal curve,** is symmetric about a vertical line drawn through the mean, μ. Vertical lines drawn at points $+1\sigma$ and -1σ from the mean show where the direction of "curvature" of the graph changes. (For those who have studied calculus, these points are the inflection points of the graph.)

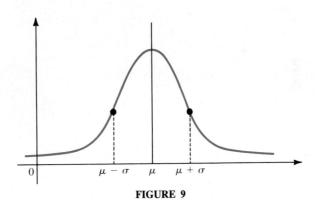

FIGURE 9

A normal curve never touches the x-axis—it extends indefinitely in both directions. The area under a normal curve is always the same: 1. If the value of the mean μ is fixed, changing the value of σ will change the shape of the normal curve. A larger value of σ produces a "flatter" normal curve, while smaller values of σ produce more values near the mean, which results in a "taller" normal curve. See Figure 10.

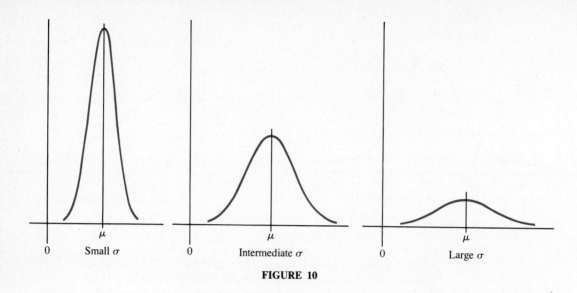

FIGURE 10

An experiment which has normally distributed outcomes and its associated normal curve are connected by the fact that the probability that an experiment produces a result between *a* and *b* is equal to the area under the normal curve from *a* to *b*. That is, the shaded area in Figure 11 gives the probability that the experimental outcome is between *a* and *b*. (Notice how the work under discussion in this section is related to the work with histograms in Section 7.1. Refer to pages 302 to 304.)

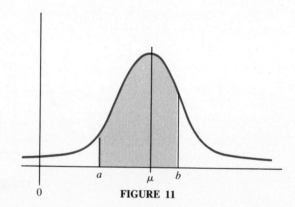

FIGURE 11

Since a normal curve is symmetric about the mean, and since the total area under a normal curve is 1, the probability that a particular outcome is below the mean is 1/2. A normal curve comes from a continuous distribution, with an infinite number of possible values, so that the probability of the occurrence of any particular value is 0.

Probabilities for a Normal Probability Distribution

Let X be a random variable with a normal probability distribution. Then

1. $P(a \leq X \leq b)$ is the area under the associated normal curve between a and b;
2. $P(X < \mu) = 1/2$;
3. $P(X > \mu) = 1/2$;
4. $P(X = x) = 0$ for any real number x;
5. $P(X < x) = P(X \leq x)$ for any real number x.

Part (5) follows from part (4).

The equation of the normal curve having mean μ and standard deviation σ is given by

$$y = \frac{1}{\sigma \sqrt{2\pi}} \, e^{-[(x-\mu)/\sigma]^2/2},$$

where $e \approx 2.7182818$. To find probabilities from normal curves, we would need to use this equation, along with calculus. Doing so would produce an infinite number of different tables, one for each pair of values of μ and σ. We get around this problem by using just one table, the table for the normal curve where $\mu = 0$ and $\sigma = 1$, to find values for any normal curve.

The normal curve having $\mu = 0$ and $\sigma = 1$ is called the **standard normal curve.** The normal curve table in the Appendix gives the areas under the standard normal curve, along with a sketch of the curve. The values in this table include the total area under the standard normal curve to the left of the number z.

EXAMPLE 1

Find the following areas from the table for the standard normal curve.

(a) to the left of $z = 1.25$.

Look up 1.25 in the normal curve table. The corresponding area is .8944, so the shaded area shown in Figure 12 is .8944. This area represents 89.44% of the total area under the normal curve.

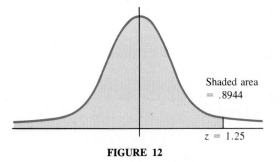

Shaded area = .8944

$z = 1.25$

FIGURE 12

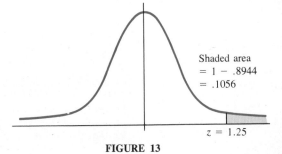

Shaded area = 1 − .8944 = .1056

$z = 1.25$

FIGURE 13

(b)   to the right of $z = 1.25$.

In part (a) we found that the area to the left of $z = 1.25$ is .8944. The total area under the normal curve is 1, so that the area to the right of $z = 1.25$ is

$$1 - .8944 = 1.0000 - .8944 = .1056.$$

See Figure 13 on page 331, where the shaded area represents 10.56% of the total area under the normal curve.

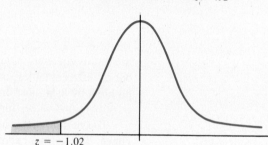

$z = .92$

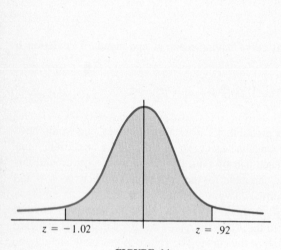

$z = -1.02$ $z = .92$ $z = -1.02$

FIGURE 14   **FIGURE 15**

(c)   between $z = -1.02$ and $z = .92$

To find this area, shaded in Figure 14, start with the area to the left of $z = .92$ and subtract the area to the left of $z = -1.02$. See Figure 15. The result is .8212 − .1539 = .6673.   ▨

If a normal distribution does not have $\mu = 0$ and $\sigma = 1$, use the following theorem, which is stated without proof.

Area Under a Normal Curve	Suppose a normal distribution has mean μ and standard deviation σ. The area under the associated normal curve that is to the left of the value x is exactly the same as the area to the left of $$z = \frac{x - \mu}{\sigma}$$ for the standard normal curve.

Using this result, the normal curve table can be used for *any* normal curve with any values of μ and σ. The number z in the theorem is called a **z-score.**

EXAMPLE 2

A normal distribution has mean 46 and standard deviation 7.2. Find the following areas under the associated normal curve.

(a) to the left of 50

Find the appropriate z-score using $x = 50$, $\mu = 46$, and $\sigma = 7.2$. Round to the nearest hundredth.

$$z = \frac{50 - 46}{7.2} = \frac{4}{7.2} \approx .56$$

From the table, the desired area is .7123.

(b) to the right of 39

$$z = \frac{39 - 46}{7.2} = \frac{-7}{7.2} \approx -.97$$

The area to the *left* of $z = -.97$ is .1660, so that the area to the *right* is

$$1 - .1660 = .8340.$$

(c) between 32 and 43

Find z-scores for both values.

$$z = \frac{32 - 46}{7.2} = \frac{-14}{7.2} \approx -1.94 \qquad \text{and} \qquad z = \frac{43 - 46}{7.2} = \frac{-3}{7.2} \approx -.42$$

Start with the area to the left of $z = -.42$ and subtract the area to the left of $z = -1.94$, which gives

$$.3372 - .0262 = .3110. \quad \blacksquare$$

The z-scores are actually standard deviation multiples—that is, a z-score of 2.5 corresponds to a value 2.5 standard deviations above the mean. Looking up $z = 1.00$ and $z = -1.00$ in the table shows that

$$.8413 - .1587 = .6826,$$

or 68.26%, of the area under a normal curve lies within one standard deviation of the mean. Also,

$$.9772 - .0228 = .9544,$$

or 95.44% of the area lies within two standard deviations of the mean. These results, summarized in Figure 16 (page 334), can be used to get a quick estimate of results when working with normal curves.

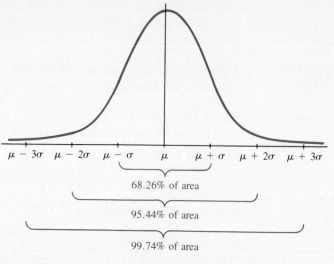

68.26% of area

95.44% of area

99.74% of area

FIGURE 16

EXAMPLE 3

Suppose that the average salesperson for Dixie Office Supplies drives $\mu = 1200$ miles per month in a company car, with standard deviation $\sigma = 150$ miles. Assume that the number of miles driven is closely approximated by a normal curve. Find the percent of all drivers traveling

(a)   between 1200 and 1600 miles per month.

First find the number of standard deviations above the mean that corresponds to 1600 miles. This is done by finding the z-score for 1600.

$$z = \frac{x - \mu}{\sigma}$$

$$= \frac{1600 - 1200}{150} \qquad \text{Let } x = 1600, \quad \mu = 1200, \quad \sigma = 150$$

$$= \frac{400}{150}$$

$$z \approx 2.67$$

From the table, the area to the left of $z = 2.67$ is .9962. Since $\mu = 1200$, the value 1200 corresponds to $z = 0$, the area to the left of $z = 0$ is .5000, and

$$.9962 - .5000 = .4962,$$

or 49.62% of the drivers travel between 1200 and 1600 miles per month. See Figure 17.

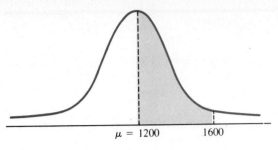

$\mu = 1200$ 1600

FIGURE 17

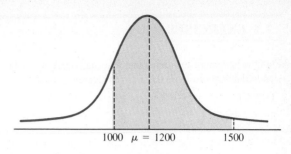

1000 $\mu = 1200$ 1500

FIGURE 18

(b) between 1000 and 1500 miles per month.

As shown in Figure 18, z-scores for both $x = 1000$ and $x = 1500$ are needed.

For $x = 1000$,   For $x = 1500$,

$$z = \frac{1000 - 1200}{150} \qquad\qquad z = \frac{1500 - 1200}{150}$$

$$= \frac{-200}{150} \qquad\qquad\qquad = \frac{300}{150}$$

$$z \approx -1.33 \qquad\qquad\qquad z = 2.00$$

From the table, $z = -1.33$ leads to an area of .0918, while $z = 2.00$ corresponds to .9772. A total of .9772 − .0918 = .8854, or 88.54%, of all drivers travel between 1000 and 1500 miles per month. ▪

Suppose a normal distribution has $\mu = 1000$ and $\sigma = 150$. Then the method of this section can be used to show that 95.44% of all values lie within 2 standard deviations of the mean; that is, between

$1000 - (2 \times 150) = 700$ and $1000 + (2 \times 150) = 1300.$

Chebyshev's Theorem (Section 7.3) says that *at least*

$$1 - \frac{1}{2^2} = 1 - \frac{1}{4} = \frac{3}{4},$$

or 75% of the values lie between 7000 and 1300. The difference between 95.44% and at least 75%, from Chebyshev's Theorem, comes from the fact that Chebyshev's Theorem applies to *any* distribution, while the methods of this section apply only to *normal* distributions. Thus it should not be surprising that having more information (a normal distribution) should produce more accurate results (95.44% instead of "at least 75%.")

7.4 EXERCISES

Find the percent of the area under a normal curve between the mean and the number of standard deviations from the mean in Exercises 1–8.

1. 2.50 **2.** 1.68 **3.** 0.45 **4.** 0.81

5. −1.71 **6.** −2.04 **7.** 3.11 **8.** 2.80

Find the percent of the total area under the normal curve between the z-scores in Exercises 9–16.

9. $z = 1.41$ and $z = 2.83$

10. $z = 0.64$ and $z = 2.11$

11. $z = -2.48$ and $z = -0.05$

12. $z = -1.74$ and $z = -1.02$

13. $z = -3.11$ and $z = 1.44$

14. $z = -2.94$ and $z = -0.43$

15. $z = -0.42$ and $z = 0.42$

16. $z = -1.98$ and $z = 1.98$

Find a z-score satisfying the following conditions. (Hint: use the table backwards.)

17. 5% of the total area is to the left of z

18. 1% of the total area is to the left of z

19. 15% of the total area is to the right of z

20. 25% of the total area is to the right of z

A certain type of light bulb has an average life of 500 hours, with a standard deviation of 100 hours. The length of life of the bulb can be closely approximated by a normal curve. An amusement park buys and installs 10,000 such bulbs. Find the total number that can be expected to last

21. at least 500 hours;

22. less than 500 hours;

23. between 500 and 650 hours;

24. between 300 and 500 hours;

25. between 650 and 780 hours;

26. between 290 and 540 hours;

27. less than 740 hours;

28. more than 300 hours;

29. more than 790 hours;

30. less than 410 hours.

A box of oatmeal must contain 16 ounces. The machine that fills the oatmeal boxes is set so that, on the average, a box contains 16.5 ounces. The boxes filled by the machine have weights that can be closely approximated by a normal curve. What fraction of the boxes filled by the machine are underweight if the standard deviation is

31. .5 ounce; **32.** .3 ounce; **33.** .2 ounce; **34.** .1 ounce?

The chickens at Colonel Thompson's Ranch have a mean weight of 1850 grams with a standard deviation of 150 grams. The weights of the chickens are closely approximated by a normal curve. Find the percent of all chickens having weights

35. more than 1700 grams;

36. less than 1800 grams;

37. between 1750 grams and 1900 grams;

38. between 1600 grams and 2000 grams;

39. less than 1550 grams;

40. more than 2100 grams.

In nutrition, the Recommended Daily Allowance of vitamins is a number set by the government as a guide to an individual's daily vitamin intake. Actually, vitamin needs vary drastically from person to person, but the needs are very closely approximated by a normal curve. To calculate the Recommended Daily Allowance, the government first finds the average need for vitamins among people in the population, and the standard deviation. The Recommended Daily Allowance is then defined as the mean plus 2.5 times the standard deviation.

41. What percentage of the population will receive adequate amounts of vitamins under this plan?

Find the recommended daily allowance for the vitamins in Exercises 42–44.

42. mean = 1800 units, standard deviation = 140 units

43. mean = 159 units, standard deviation = 12 units

44. mean = 1200 units, standard deviation = 92 units

Assume the distributions in Exercises 45–52 are all normal, and use the areas under the normal curve given in the table to answer the questions.

45. A machine produces bolts with an average diameter of .25 inches and a standard deviation of .02 inches. What is the probability that a bolt will be produced with a diameter greater than .3 inches?

46. The mean monthly income of the trainees of an engineering firm is $1200 with a standard deviation of $200. Find the probability that an individual trainee earns less than $1000 per month.

47. A machine that fills quart milk cartons is set up to average 32.2 ounces per carton, with a standard deviation of 1.2 ounces. What is the probability that a filled carton will contain less than 32 ounces of milk?

48. The average contribution to the campaign of Polly Potter, a candidate for city council, was $50 with a standard deviation of $15. How many of the 200 people who contributed to Polly's campaign gave between $30 and $100?

49. At the Discount Market, the average weekly grocery bill is $32.25 with a standard deviation of $9.50. What are the largest and smallest amounts spent by the middle 50% of this market's customers?

50. The mean clotting time of blood is 7.45 seconds with a standard deviation of 3.6 seconds. What is the probability that an individual's blood clotting time will be less than 7 seconds or greater than 8 seconds?

51. The average size of the fish in Lake Amotan is 12.3 inches with a standard deviation of 4.1 inches. Find the probability of catching a fish there longer than 18 inches.

52. To be graded extra large, an egg must weigh at least 2.2 ounces. If the average weight for an egg is 1.5 ounces with a standard deviation of .4 ounces, how many of five dozen eggs would you expect to grade extra large?

One professor uses the following grading system for assigning letter grades in a course.

Grade	Score in Class
A	greater than $\mu + \frac{3}{2}\sigma$
B	$\mu + \frac{1}{2}\sigma$ to $\mu + \frac{3}{2}\sigma$
C	$\mu - \frac{1}{2}\sigma$ to $\mu + \frac{1}{2}\sigma$
D	$\mu - \frac{3}{2}\sigma$ to $\mu - \frac{1}{2}\sigma$
F	below $\mu - \frac{3}{2}\sigma$

What percent of the students receive the following grades?

53. A   **54.** B   **55.** C

56. Do you think this system would be more likely to be fair in a large freshman class in psychology or in a graduate seminar of five students? Why?

A teacher gives a test to a large group of students. The results are closely approximated by a normal curve. The mean is 74, with a standard deviation of 6. The teacher wishes to give A's to the top 8% of the students and F's to the bottom 8%. A grade of B is given to the next 15%, with D's given similarly. All other students get C's. Find the bottom cutoff (rounded to the nearest whole number) for the following grades. (Hint: use the table in the Appendix backwards.)

57. A   **58.** B   **59.** C   **60.** D

Use a computer to find the following probabilities by finding the comparable area under a standard normal curve.

61. $P(1.372 \leq X \leq 2.548)$ **62.** $P(-2.751 \leq X \leq 1.693)$ **63.** $P(X > -2.476)$

64. $P(X < 1.692)$ **65.** $P(X < -.4753)$ **66.** $P(X > .2509)$

Use a computer to find the following probabilities for a distribution with a mean of 35.693 and a standard deviation of 7.104.

67. $P(12.275 < X < 28.432)$ **68.** $P(X > 38.913)$

69. $P(X < 17.462)$ **70.** $P(17.462 \leq X \leq 53.106)$

EXTENDED
APPLICATION

Inventory Control

A department store must control its inventory carefully.* It should not reorder too often, because it then builds up a large warehouse full of merchandise, which is expensive to hold. On the other hand, it must reorder sufficiently often to be sure of having sufficient stock to meet customer demand. The company desires a simple chart that can be used by its employees to determine the best possible time to reorder merchandise. The merchandise level on hand will be checked periodically. At the end of each period, if the level on hand is less than some predetermined level given in the chart, which considers sales rate and waiting time for orders, the item will be reordered. The example uses the following variables.

F = frequency of stock review (in weeks)
r = acceptable risk of being out of stock (in percent)
P = level of inventory at which reordering should occur
L = waiting time for order to arrive (in weeks)
S = sales rate in units per week
M = minimum level of merchandise to guarantee that the probability of being out of stock is no higher than r
z = z-score (from table of cumulative distribution) corresponding to r

Goods should not be reordered until inventory on hand has declined to a level less than the rate of sales per week, S, times the sum of the number of weeks until the next stock review, F, and the expected waiting time in weeks, L, plus a minimum level of merchandise, M, necessary to guarantee that the probability of being out of stock is no higher than r. That is, $P = S(F + L) + M$.

---

*Example supplied by Leonard W. Cooper, Operations Research Project Director, Federated Department Stores.

To find M, which depends on S, F, and L, we shall assume that both sales and waiting time are normally distributed. With this assumption, a formula from more advanced statistics courses permits us to write $M = z\sqrt{2S(F + L)}$, where z is the z-score (from the table) corresponding to r, and $\sqrt{2S(F + L)}$ is the standard deviation of normally distributed deviations in sales rate and waiting time.

Combining these two formulas, we have

$$P = S(F + L) + z\sqrt{2S(F + L)}.$$

Suppose the firm wishes to be 95% sure of having goods to sell, so that $r = 5\%$. From the table, we find $z = 1.64$. Hence, for $r = 5\%$,

$$P = S(F + L) + 1.64\sqrt{2S(F + L)}.$$

Based on this formula, the chart below was prepared.

REORDER LEVELS (P) Reorder merchandise when inventory on hand falls below the levels given in the chart. $r = 5\%$, $F = 1$ week						
Rate of Sales (S) (Units/Week)	Waiting Time in Weeks for Order (L)					
	1	**2**	**3**	**4**	**5**	**6**
9	28	39	50	61	71	81
10	30	43	55	66	78	89
11	33	46	59	72	85	97
12	35	50	64	78	92	105
13	38	54	69	84	99	113
14	40	57	83	89	105	121
15	43	61	78	95	112	129

$r = 5\%$, $F = 4$ weeks						
Rate of Sales (S) (Units/Week)	Waiting Time in Weeks for Order (L)					
	1	**2**	**3**	**4**	**5**	**6**
1	10	12	13	15	16	17
2	17	20	23	25	28	30
3	24	28	32	35	39	43
4	30	35	40	45	50	55

By using the chart, if an item is reviewed every 4 weeks ($F = 4$), the waiting time for a reorder is 3 weeks ($L = 3$), and the rate of sales is 2 per week ($S = 2$), then the item should be reordered when the number on hand falls at or below 23.

EXERCISES

1. Suppose an item is reviewed weekly, and the waiting time for a reorder is 4 weeks. If the average sales per week of the item is 12 units, and the current inventory level is 85 units, should it be reordered? What if the inventory level is 50 units?

2. Suppose an item is reviewed every four weeks. If orders require a 5-week waiting time, and if sales average 3 units per week, should the item be reordered if current inventory is 50 units? What if current inventory is 30?

7.5   The Normal Curve Approximation to the Binomial Distribution

In many practical situations, experiments have only two possible outcomes: *success* or *failure*. Examples of such experiments, called *binomial trials,* or *Bernoulli trials,* include tossing a coin (perhaps *h* would be called a success, with *t* a failure); rolling a die with the two outcomes being, for instance, 5, a success, and a number other than 5, a failure; or choosing a radio from a large batch and deciding if the radio is defective or not. (Bernoulli trials were first discussed in Section 6.7)

A *binomial distribution* must satisfy the following properties. The experiment is a series of independent trials with only two outcomes possible, success and failure. The probability of each outcome must be constant from trial to trial.

As an example, suppose a die is tossed 5 times. Identify a result of 1 or 2 as a success, with any other result a failure. Since each trial (each toss) can result in a success or a failure, the result of the 5 tosses can be any number of successes from 0 through 5. Not all of these six possible outcomes are equally likely. The various probabilities can be found with the result from Section 6.7:

$$P(X = x) = \binom{n}{x} p^x (1 - p)^{n-x},$$

where n is the number of trials, x is the number of successes, p is the probability of success on a single trial, and $P(X = x)$ gives the probability that x of the n trials result in successes. In this example, $n = 5$ and $p = 1/3$, since either a 1 or a 2 results in a success. The results for this experiment are tabulated in Table 14.

Table 14

x	$P(X = x)$
0	$\binom{5}{0}\left(\frac{1}{3}\right)^0\left(\frac{2}{3}\right)^5 = \frac{32}{243}$
1	$\binom{5}{1}\left(\frac{1}{3}\right)^1\left(\frac{2}{3}\right)^4 = \frac{80}{243}$
2	$\binom{5}{2}\left(\frac{1}{3}\right)^2\left(\frac{2}{3}\right)^3 = \frac{80}{243}$
3	$\binom{5}{3}\left(\frac{1}{3}\right)^3\left(\frac{2}{3}\right)^2 = \frac{40}{243}$
4	$\binom{5}{4}\left(\frac{1}{3}\right)^4\left(\frac{2}{3}\right)^1 = \frac{10}{243}$
5	$\binom{5}{5}\left(\frac{1}{3}\right)^5\left(\frac{2}{3}\right)^0 = \frac{1}{243}$

By definition, the mean μ of a probability distribution is given by the expected value of X. Expected value is found by finding the products of outcomes and probabilities. For the distribution of Table 14,

$$\mu = 0\left(\frac{32}{243}\right) + 1\left(\frac{80}{243}\right) + 2\left(\frac{80}{243}\right) + 3\left(\frac{40}{243}\right) + 4\left(\frac{10}{243}\right) + 5\left(\frac{1}{243}\right)$$

$$= \frac{405}{243} = 1\frac{2}{3}.$$

For a binomial distribution, which is a special kind of probability distribution, it can be shown that the method for finding the mean reduces to the formula

$$\mu = np,$$

where n is the number of trials and p is the probability of success on a single trial. Using this simplified formula, the computation of the mean in the example above is

$$\mu = np = 5\left(\frac{1}{3}\right) = 1\frac{2}{3},$$

which agrees with the result obtained using the expected value.

Like the mean, the variance, $\text{Var}(X)$, of a probability distribution is an expected value—the expected value of the squared deviations from the mean, $(x - \mu)^2$. To find the variance for the example given above, first use the mean $\mu = 5/3$ and find the quantities $(x - \mu)^2$. (See Table 15.)

Table 15

x	$P(X = x)$	$x - \mu$	$(x - \mu)^2$
0	$\frac{32}{243}$	$\frac{-5}{3}$	$\frac{25}{9}$
1	$\frac{80}{243}$	$\frac{-2}{3}$	$\frac{4}{9}$
2	$\frac{80}{243}$	$\frac{1}{3}$	$\frac{1}{9}$
3	$\frac{40}{243}$	$\frac{4}{3}$	$\frac{16}{9}$
4	$\frac{10}{243}$	$\frac{7}{3}$	$\frac{49}{9}$
5	$\frac{1}{243}$	$\frac{10}{3}$	$\frac{100}{9}$

Find $\text{Var}(X)$ by finding the sum of the products $[(x - \mu)^2][P(X = x)]$.

$$\text{Var}(X) = \frac{25}{9}\left(\frac{32}{243}\right) + \frac{4}{9}\left(\frac{80}{243}\right) + \frac{1}{9}\left(\frac{80}{243}\right) + \frac{16}{9}\left(\frac{40}{243}\right) + \frac{49}{9}\left(\frac{10}{243}\right) + \frac{100}{9}\left(\frac{1}{243}\right)$$

$$= \frac{10}{9} = 1\frac{1}{9}$$

To find the standard deviation σ, find $\sqrt{10/9}$ or $\sqrt{10}/3$, or approximately 1.05.

Just as with the mean, the variance of a binomial distribution can be found with a relatively simple formula. Again, it can be shown that

$$\text{Var}(X) = np(1 - p) \quad \text{and} \quad \sigma = \sqrt{np(1 - p)}.$$

By substituting the appropriate values for n and p from the example into this new formula,

$$\text{Var}(X) = 5\left(\frac{1}{3}\right)\left(\frac{2}{3}\right) = 10/9 = 1\frac{1}{9},$$

which agrees with our previous result.

A summary of these results is given below.

Binomial

Distribution

Suppose an experiment is a series of n independent repeated trials, where the probability of a success in a single trial is always p. Let x be the number of successes in the n trials. Then the probability that exactly x successes will occur in n trials is given by

$$\binom{n}{x} p^x (1 - p)^{n-x}.$$

The mean μ and variance $\text{Var}(X)$ of this binomial distribution are respectively

$$\mu = np \quad \text{and} \quad \text{Var}(X) = np(1 - p).$$

The standard deviation σ is

$$\sigma = \sqrt{np(1 - p)}.$$

EXAMPLE 1

The probability that a plate selected at random from the assembly line in a china factory will be defective is .01. A sample of three is to be selected. Write the distribution for the number of defective plates in the sample, and give its mean and standard deviation.

Since three plates will be selected, the possible number of defective plates ranges from 0 to 3. Here, n (the number of trials) is 3, and p (the probability of selecting a defective on a single trial) is .01. The distribution and the probability of each outcome are shown in Table 16.

The mean of the distribution is

$$\mu = np = 3(.01) = .03.$$

The standard deviation is

$$\sigma = \sqrt{np(1 - p)} = \sqrt{3(.01)(.99)} = \sqrt{.0297} = .17. \quad \blacksquare$$

The binomial distribution is extremely useful, but its use can lead to complicated calculations if n is large. However, the normal curve of the previous section

Table 16

x	$P(X = x)$
0	$\binom{3}{0}(.01)^0(.99)^3 = .970$
1	$\binom{3}{1}(.01)(.99)^2 = .029$
2	$\binom{3}{2}(.01)^2(.99) = .0003$
3	$\binom{3}{3}(.01)^3(.99)^0 = .000001$

can be used to get a good approximation to the binomial distribution. This approximation was first discovered by Abraham DeMoivre in 1718 for the case $p = 1/2$. The result was generalized by the French mathematician Laplace in a book published in 1812.

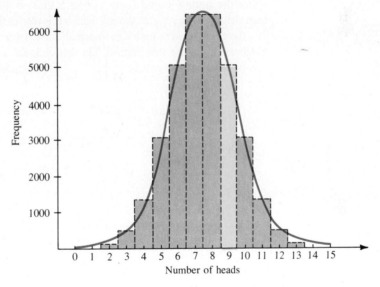

FIGURE 19

To see how the normal curve is used, look at the bar graph and normal curve in Figure 19. This histogram shows the expected number of heads if one coin is tossed 15 times, with the experiment repeated 32,768 times. Since the probability of heads on one toss is 1/2 and $n = 15$, the mean of this distribution is

$$\mu = np = 15\left(\frac{1}{2}\right) = 7.5.$$

The standard deviation is

$$\sigma = \sqrt{15\left(\frac{1}{2}\right)\left(1 - \frac{1}{2}\right)}$$

$$= \sqrt{15\left(\frac{1}{2}\right)\left(\frac{1}{2}\right)}$$

$$= \sqrt{3.75} \approx 1.94.$$

In Figure 19 we have superimposed the normal curve with $\mu = 7.5$ and $\sigma = 1.94$ over the bar graph of the distribution.

Suppose we need to know the fraction of the time that exactly 9 heads would be obtained in the 15 tosses. We could work this out using the methods above. After extensive calculations, we would get .153. This answer is about the same fraction that would be found by dividing the area of the bar in color in Figure 19 by the total area of all 16 bars in the graph. (Some of the bars at the extreme left and right ends of the graph are too short to show up.)

As the graph suggests, the area in color is approximately equal to the area under the normal curve from $x = 8.5$ to $x = 9.5$. The normal curve is higher than the top of the bar in the left half but lower in the right half.

To find the area under the normal curve from $x = 8.5$ to $x = 9.5$, first find z-scores, as in the last section. Do this with the mean and the standard deviation for the distribution, which we have already calculated, to get z-scores for $x = 8.5$ and $x = 9.5$.

For $x = 8.5$

$$z = \frac{8.5 - 7.5}{1.94}$$

$$= \frac{1.00}{1.94}$$

$$z \approx .52$$

For $x = 9.5$

$$z = \frac{9.5 - 7.5}{1.94}$$

$$= \frac{2.00}{1.94}$$

$$z \approx 1.03$$

From the table of normal curves, $z = .52$ gives an area of .6985, while $z = 1.03$ gives .8485. To find the desired result, subtract these two numbers.

$$.8485 - .6985 = .1500$$

This answer (.1500) is not far from the exact answer, .153, found above.

EXAMPLE 2

About 6% of the bolts produced by a certain machine are defective.

(a) Find the probability that in a sample of 100 bolts, 3 or fewer are defective.

This problem satisfies the conditions of the definition of a binomial distribution, so the normal curve approximation can be used. First find the mean and the standard deviation using $n = 100$ and $p = 6\% = .06$.

$$\mu = 100(.06) \qquad \sigma = \sqrt{100(.06)(1 - .06)}$$

$$= 6 \qquad = \sqrt{100(.06)(.94)}$$

$$= \sqrt{5.64} \approx 2.37$$

As the graph of Figure 20 shows, we need to find the area to the left of $x = 3.5$ (since we want 3 or fewer defective bolts). The z-score corresponding to $x = 3.5$ is

$$z = \frac{3.5 - 6}{2.37} = \frac{-2.5}{2.37} \approx -1.05.$$

From the table, $z = -1.05$ leads to an area of .1469, so that the probability of getting 3 or fewer defective bolts in a set of 100 bolts is .1469, or 14.69%.

(b)   Find the probability of getting exactly 11 defective bolts in a sample of 100 bolts.

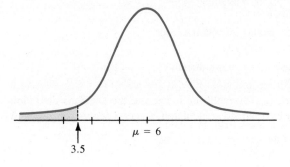

FIGURE 20   **FIGURE 21**

As Figure 21 shows, we need the area between $x = 10.5$ and $x = 11.5$.

$$\text{If } x = 10.5, \text{ then } z = \frac{10.5 - 6}{2.37} \approx 1.90.$$

$$\text{If } x = 11.5, \text{ then } z = \frac{11.5 - 6}{2.37} \approx 2.32.$$

Look in the table; $z = 1.90$ gives an area of .9713, while $z = 2.32$ yields .9898. The final answer is the difference of these numbers, or

$$.9898 - .9713 = .0185.$$

There is about a 1.85% chance of having exactly 11 defective bolts. ▪

The normal curve approximation to the binomial distribution is usually quite accurate, especially for practical problems. For n up to say, 15 or 20, it is usually not too difficult to actually calculate the binomial probabilities directly. For larger values of n, a rule of thumb is that the normal curve approximation can be used as long as both np and $n(1 - p)$ are at least 5.

7.5 EXERCISES

In Exercises 1–6, several binomial experiments are described. For each one, give (a) the distribution; (b) the mean; (c) the standard deviation.

1. A die is rolled six times and the number of 1's that come up is tallied. Write the distribution of 1's that can be expected to occur.

2. A 6-item multiple choice test has 4 possible answers for each item. A student selects all his answers randomly. Give the distribution of correct answers.

3. To maintain quality control on the production line, the Bright Lite Company randomly selects 3 light bulbs each day for testing. Experience has shown a defective rate of .02. Write the distribution for the number of defectives in the daily samples.

4. In a taste test, each member of a panel of 4 is given 2 glasses of Supercola, one made using the old formula and one with the new formula, and asked to identify the new formula. Assuming the panelists operate independently, write the distribution of the number of successful identifications, if each judge actually guesses.

5. The probability that a radish seed will germinate is .7. Joe's mother gives him 4 seeds to plant. Write the distribution for the number of seeds which germinate.

6. Five patients in Ward 8 of Memorial Hospital have a disease with a known mortality rate of .1. Write the distribution of the number who survive.

Work the following problems involving binomial experiments.

7. The probability that an infant will die in the first year of life is about .025. In a group of 500 babies, what are the mean and standard deviation of the number of babies who can be expected to die in their first year of life?

8. The probability that a particular kind of mouse will have a brown coat is 1/4. In a litter of 8, assuming independence, how many could be expected to have a brown coat? With what standard deviation?

9. A certain drug is effective 80% of the time. Give the mean and standard deviation of the number of patients using the drug who recover, out of a group of 64 patients.

10. The probability that a newborn infant will be a girl is .49. If 50 infants are born on Susan B. Anthony's birthday, how many can be expected to be girls? With what standard deviation?

For the remaining exercises, use the normal curve approximation to the binomial distribution.

Suppose 16 coins are tossed. Find the probability of getting exactly

| 11. 8 heads; | 12. 7 heads; | 13. 10 tails; | 14. 12 tails. |

Suppose 1000 coins are tossed. Find the probability of getting each of the following. (Hint: $\sqrt{250} = 15.8$.)

| 15. exactly 500 heads | 16. exactly 510 heads | 17. 480 heads or more |
| 18. less than 470 tails | 19. less than 518 heads | 20. more than 550 tails |

A die is tossed 120 times. Find the probability of getting each of the following. (Hint: $\sigma = 4.08$.)

| 21. exactly 20 fives | 22. exactly 24 sixes | 23. exactly 17 threes |
| 24. exactly 22 twos | 25. more than 18 threes | 26. fewer than 22 sixes |

Two percent of the quartz heaters produced in a certain plant are defective. Suppose the plant produced 10,000 such heaters last month. Find the probability that among these heaters

27. fewer than 170 were defective;

28. more than 222 were defective.

A new drug cures 80% of the patients to whom it is administered. It is given to 25 patients. Find the probability that among these patients

29. exactly 20 are cured;

30. exactly 23 are cured;

31. all are cured;

32. no one is cured;

33. 12 or fewer are cured;

34. between 17 and 23 are cured.

35. An experimental drug causes a rash in 15% of all people taking it. If the drug is given to 12,000 people, find the probability that more than 1700 people will get the rash.

36. In one state, 55% of the voters expect to vote for Jones. Suppose 1400 people are asked for the name of the person they expect to vote for. Find the probability that at least 700 people will say that they expect to vote for Jones.

37. Rework Exercises 30–33 of Section 6.7 using the normal curve to approximate the binomial probabilities. Compare your answers with the results found in Section 6.7 for the binomial distribution.

38. A coin is tossed 100 times. Find the probability of
   (a) exactly 50 heads;   **(b)** at least 55 heads;   **(c)** no more than 40 heads.

KEY WORDS	random variable	fair game
	frequency distribution	variance
	probability distribution	standard deviation
	probability distribution function	Chebyshev's Theorem
	discrete distribution function	skewed distribution
	continuous distribution function	normal distribution
	histogram	normal curve
	mathematical expectation	standard normal distribution
	average	z-score
	arithmetic mean	binomial distribution
	expected value	

Chapter 7   REVIEW EXERCISES

In Exercises 1–5, (a) give a probability distribution and (b) sketch its histogram.

1.

X	1	2	3	4	5		
Frequency	3	7	9	3	2		

2.

X	8	9	10	11	12	13	14
Frequency	1	0	2	5	8	4	3

3. A coin is tossed three times and the number of heads is recorded.

4. A pair of dice are rolled and the number of points showing is recorded.

5. Patients in groups of five were given a new treatment for a fatal disease. The experiment was repeated ten times with the following results.

Number Who Survived	Frequency
0	1
1	1
2	2
3	3
4	3
5	0
Total:	10

In Exercises 6 and 7, give the probability which corresponds to the shaded region of the figure.

6.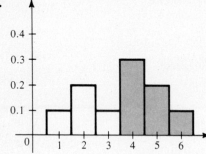

7.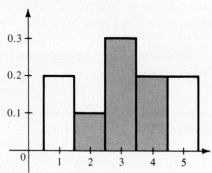

Solve the following problems.

8. You pay $6 to play in a game where you will roll a die, with payoffs as follows: $8 for a 6, $7 for a 5, $4 otherwise. What is your mathematical expectation? Is the game fair?

9. A lottery has a first prize of $5000, two second prizes of $1000 each, and two $100 third prizes. A total of ten thousand tickets is sold, at $1 each. Find the expected winnings of a person buying one ticket.

10. Find the expected number of girls in a family of 5 children.

11. A developer can buy a piece of property that will produce a profit of $16,000 with probability .7, or a loss of $9000 with probability .3. What is the expected profit?

12. Game boards for a recent United Airlines contest could be obtained by sending a self addressed stamped envelope to a certain address. The prize was a ticket for any city to which United flies. Assume that the value of the ticket was $1000 (we might as well go first class), and that the probability that a particular game board would win was 1/4000. If the stamps to enter the contest cost 30¢, and envelopes are 1¢ each, find the expected winnings for a person ordering one game board.

Find the expected value of the random variable in each of the following.

13. the data in Exercise 2

14. the experiment of Exercise 3

15. the experiment of Exercise 5

16. 3 cards are drawn from a standard deck of 52 cards.

(a) What is the expected number of aces?

(b) What is the expected number of clubs?

17. Suppose someone offers to pay you $100 if you draw three cards from a standard deck of 52 cards and all the cards are clubs. What should you pay for the chance to win if it is a fair game?

Find the variance and standard deviation of the random variable in the following.

18. the data in Exercise 3

19. the experiment of Exercise 5

20. The annual returns of two stocks for three years are given below.

	1980	1981	1982
Stock I	11%	−1%	14%
Stock II	9%	5%	10%

(a) Find the mean and standard deviation for each stock over the three-year period.

(b) If you are looking for security with an 8% return, which of these two stocks would you choose?

21. The weight gains of 2 groups of 10 rats fed on two different experimental diets were as follows:

	Weight Gains									
Diet A	1	0	3	7	1	1	5	4	1	4
Diet B	2	1	1	2	3	2	1	0	1	0

Compute the mean and standard deviation for each group.

(a) Which diet produced the greatest mean gain?

(b) Which diet produced the most consistent gain?

22. A probability distribution has an expected value of 28 and a standard deviation of 4. Use Chebyshev's Theorem to decide what percent of the distribution is

(a) between 20 and 36;   (b) less than 23.2 or greater than 32.8.

23. (a) Find the percent of the area under a normal curve within 2.5 standard deviations of the mean.

(b) Compare your answer to part (a) with the result using Chebyshev's Theorem.

24. Find the percent of the total area under the normal curve which corresponds to

(a) $z \geq 2.2$,   (b) between $z = -1.3$ and $z = .2$.

25. Find a z-score such that 8% of the area under the curve is to the right of z.

26. A machine which fills quart milk cartons is set to fill them with 32.1 oz. If the actual contents of the cartons vary normally with a standard deviation of .1 oz., what percent of the cartons contain less than a quart (32 oz.)?

27. The probability that a can of beer from a certain brewery is defective is .005. A sample of 4 cans is selected at random. Write a distribution for the number of defective cans in the sample, and give its mean and standard deviation.

28. Find the probability of getting the following number of heads in 15 tosses of a coin.
    (a) exactly 7
    (b) between 7 and 10
    (c) at least 10

29. The probability that a small business will go bankrupt in its first year is .21. For 50 such small businesses, find the following probabilities.
    (a) exactly 8 go bankrupt.
    (b) no more than 2 go bankrupt.

30. On standard IQ tests, the mean is 100, with a standard deviation of 15. The results are very close to fitting a normal curve. Suppose an IQ test is given to a very large group of people. Find the percentage of those people whose IQ score is
    (a) more than 130;
    (b) less than 85;
    (c) between 85 and 115.

31. The residents of a certain Eastern suburb average 42 minutes a day commuting to work, with a standard deviation of 12 minutes. Assume that commuting times are closely approximated by a normal curve and find the percent of the residents of this suburb who commute
    (a) at least 50 minutes per day;   (b) no more than 35 minutes per day;
    (c) between 32 and 40 minutes per day;   (d) between 38 and 60 minutes per day.

32. About 6% of the frankfurters produced by a certain machine are overstuffed, and thus defective. Find the probability that in a sample of 500 frankfurters,
    (a) 25 or fewer are overstuffed (Hint: $\sigma = 5.3$);
    (b) exactly 30 are overstuffed;
    (c) more than 40 are overstuffed.

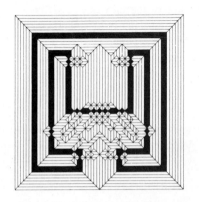 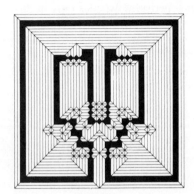 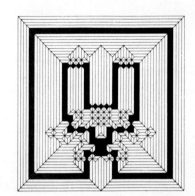

MARKOV CHAINS AND DECISION THEORY

Karl Gerstner. Drawings from *Color Lines C1/L9*, Intro Version, 1957, 1976–77.

In Chapter 6 we briefly studied *stochastic processes,* mathematical models in which the outcome of an experiment depends on the outcome of previous experiments. Now we study a special stochastic process called a **Markov chain;** here the outcome of an experiment depends only on the outcome of the previous experiment. That is, given the present state of the system, future states are independent of past states. Markov chains are named after A. A. Markov, 1856–1922, a Russian mathematician who started the theory of stochastic processes. Decision theory, discussed later, uses matrices and expected value to clarify the options when a difficult decision must be made.

8.1   Basic Properties of Markov Chains

Transition Matrix   In sociology, it is convenient to classify people by income as *lower class, middle class,* and *upper class.* The strongest determinant of the income class of an individual turns out to be the income class of the individual's parents. For example, if we say that an individual in the lower income class is in *state 1,* an individual in the middle income class is in *state 2,* and an individual in the upper income class is in *state 3,* then we might have the following probabilities of change in income class from one generation to the next.

	State	Next Generation 1	2	3
Current	1	.65	.28	.07
Generation	2	.15	.67	.18
	3	.12	.36	.52

This chart shows that if an individual is in state 1 (lower income class) then there is a probability of .65 that any offspring will be in the lower class, a probability of .28 that offspring will be in the middle class, and a probability of .07 that offspring will be in the upper class.

The symbol p_{ij} will be used for the probability of transition from state i to state j, in one generation. For example, p_{23} represents the probability that a person in state 2 will have offspring in state 3; from the table above,

$$p_{23} = .18.$$

Also from the table, $p_{31} = .12$, $p_{22} = .67$, and so on.

The table above can be written as a matrix, with the states indicated at the side and top; this matrix is called a **transition matrix.** If P represents the transition matrix for the table above, then

$$\begin{array}{c} \\ 1 \\ 2 \\ 3 \end{array} \begin{array}{ccc} 1 & 2 & 3 \\ \left[\begin{array}{ccc} .65 & .28 & .07 \\ .15 & .67 & .18 \\ .12 & .36 & .52 \end{array}\right] \end{array} = P.$$

A transition matrix has several features:

1. It is square, since all possible states must be used both as rows and as columns.
2. All entries are between 0 and 1, inclusive; this is because all entries represent probabilities.
3. The sum of the entries in any row must be 1, since the numbers in the row give the probability of changing from the state at the left to one of the states indicated across the top.

Markov Chains   A transition matrix, such as matrix P above, also shows two of the key features of a Markov chain.

Markov Chain

> A sequence of trials of an experiment is a *Markov chain* if
>
> 1. the outcome of each experiment is one of a set of discrete states,
> 2. the outcome of an experiment depends only on the present state, and not on any past states.

For example, in the transition matrix above, a person is assumed to be in one of three discrete states (lower, middle, or upper class) with any offspring in one of these same three discrete states.

EXAMPLE 1

A small town has only two drycleaners, Johnson and NorthClean. Johnson's manager desires to increase the firm's market share by an extensive advertising campaign. After the campaign, a market research firm finds that there is a probability of .8 that a customer of Johnson's will bring their next batch of dirty items to Johnson, and a .35 chance that a NorthClean customer will switch to Johnson for their next batch. Write a transition matrix showing this information.

Here we must assume that the probability that a customer comes to a given cleaners depends only on where the last load of clothes was taken. If there is an .8 chance that a Johnson customer will return to Johnson, then there must be a $1 - .8 = .2$ chance that the customer will switch to NorthClean. In the same way, there is a $1 - .35 = .65$ chance that a NorthClean customer will return to North-Clean. These probabilities give the following transition matrix.

$$\begin{array}{c} \\ \textit{First load} \end{array} \begin{array}{c} \\ \begin{array}{c} \text{Johnson} \\ \text{NorthClean} \end{array} \end{array} \overset{\begin{array}{cc} \textit{Second load} \\ \text{Johnson} \quad \text{NorthClean} \end{array}}{\begin{bmatrix} .8 & .2 \\ .35 & .65 \end{bmatrix}}$$

We shall come back to this transition matrix later in this section (See Example 4). ∎

Look again at transition matrix P for social class changes.

$$
\begin{array}{c}
\\
1 \\
2 \\
3
\end{array}
\begin{array}{ccc}
1 & 2 & 3 \\
\end{array}
\left[
\begin{array}{ccc}
.65 & .28 & .07 \\
.15 & .67 & .18 \\
.12 & .36 & .52
\end{array}
\right] = P
$$

This matrix shows the probability of change in social class from one generation to the next. Now let us investigate the probabilities for changes in social class over *two* generations. For example, if a parent is upper class (state 3), what is the probability that a grandchild will be in state 2?

To find out, start with a tree diagram as shown in Figure 1; the various probabilities come from transition matrix P.

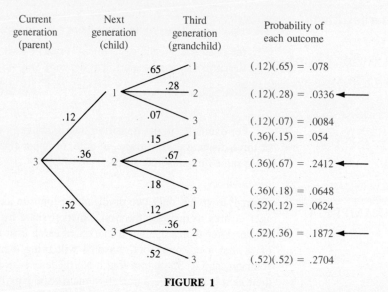

FIGURE 1

The arrows point to the outcomes "grandchild in state 2"; the grandchild can get to state 2 after having had parents in either state 1, state 2, or state 3. The probability that a parent in state 3 will have a grandchild in state 2 is given by the sum of the probabilities indicated with arrows, or

$$.0336 + .2412 + .1872 = .4620.$$

We used p_{ij} to represent the probability of changing from state i to state j in one generation. This notation can be used to write the probability that a parent in state 3 will have a grandchild in state 2:

$$p_{31} \cdot p_{12} + p_{32} \cdot p_{22} + p_{33} \cdot p_{32}.$$

This sum of products of probabilities should remind you of matrix multiplication—it is nothing more than one step in the process of multiplying matrix P by itself.

In particular, it is row 3 of P times column 2 of P. If P^2 represents the matrix product $P \cdot P$, then P^2 gives the probabilities of a transition from one state to another in *two* repetitions of an experiment. Generalizing,

> P^k gives the probabilities of a transition from one state to another in k repetitions of an experiment.

EXAMPLE 2

For transition matrix P (social class changes),

$$P^2 = \begin{bmatrix} .65 & .28 & .07 \\ .15 & .67 & .18 \\ .12 & .36 & .52 \end{bmatrix} \begin{bmatrix} .65 & .28 & .07 \\ .15 & .67 & .18 \\ .12 & .36 & .52 \end{bmatrix} \approx \begin{bmatrix} .47 & .39 & .13 \\ .22 & .56 & .22 \\ .19 & .46 & .34 \end{bmatrix}.$$

(The numbers in the product have been rounded to the same number of decimal places as in matrix P.) The entry in row 3, column 2 of P^2 gives the probability that a person in state 3 will have an offspring in state 2 two generations later. This number, .46, is the result (rounded to 2 decimal places) found through use of the tree diagram.

Row 1, column 3 of P^2 gives the number .13, the probability that a person in state 1 will have an offspring in state 3, but two generations later. How would the entry .47 be interpreted? ▪

EXAMPLE 3

In the same way that matrix P^2 gives the probability of transitions after *two* generations, the matrix $P^3 = P \cdot P^2$ gives the probabilities of change after *three* generations.

For matrix P,

$$P^3 = P \cdot P^2 = \begin{bmatrix} .65 & .28 & .07 \\ .15 & .67 & .18 \\ .12 & .36 & .52 \end{bmatrix} \begin{bmatrix} .47 & .39 & .13 \\ .22 & .56 & .22 \\ .19 & .46 & .34 \end{bmatrix} \approx \begin{bmatrix} .38 & .44 & .17 \\ .25 & .52 & .23 \\ .23 & .49 & .27 \end{bmatrix}.$$

(The rows of P^3 don't necessarily total 1 exactly because of rounding errors.) Matrix P^3 gives a probability of .25 that a person in state 2 will have an offspring in state 1 *three generations* later. The probability is .52 that a person in state 2 will have, three generations later, an offspring in state 2. ▪

EXAMPLE 4

Let us return to the transition matrix for the cleaners.

$$\begin{array}{c} \\ \textit{First load} \end{array} \begin{array}{c} \\ \text{Johnson} \\ \text{NorthClean} \end{array} \overset{\begin{array}{cc} \textit{Second load} \\ \text{Johnson} \quad \text{NorthClean} \end{array}}{\begin{bmatrix} .8 & .2 \\ .35 & .65 \end{bmatrix}}$$

As this matrix shows, there is a .8 chance that persons bringing their first load to Johnson will also bring their second load to Johnson, and so on. To find the probabilities for the third load, the second stage of this Markov chain, find the square of the transition matrix. If C represents the transition matrix, then

$$C^2 = C \cdot C = \begin{bmatrix} .8 & .2 \\ .35 & .65 \end{bmatrix} \begin{bmatrix} .8 & .2 \\ .35 & .65 \end{bmatrix} = \begin{bmatrix} .71 & .29 \\ .51 & .49 \end{bmatrix}.$$

From C^2, the probability that a person bringing their first load of clothes to Johnson will also bring their third load to Johnson is .71; the probability that a person bringing their first load to NorthClean will bring their third load to NorthClean is .49.

The cube of matrix C gives the probabilities for the fourth load, the third step in our experiment.

$$C^3 = C \cdot C^2 = \begin{bmatrix} .67 & .33 \\ .58 & .42 \end{bmatrix}$$

The probability is .58, for example, that persons bringing their first load to North-Clean will bring their fourth load to Johnson. ■

Distribution of States   Look again at the transition matrix for social class changes:

$$P = \begin{bmatrix} .65 & .28 & .07 \\ .15 & .67 & .18 \\ .12 & .36 & .52 \end{bmatrix}.$$

Suppose the following table gives the initial distribution of people in the three social classes.

Class	State	Proportion
lower	1	21%
middle	2	68%
upper	3	11%

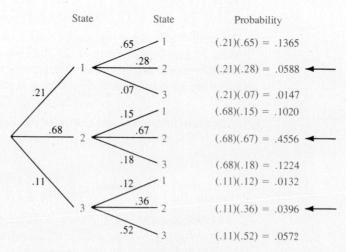

FIGURE 2

To find how these proportions would change after one generation, we use the tree diagram of Figure 2. For example, to find the proportion of people in state 2 after one generation, add the numbers indicated with arrows.

$$.0588 + .4556 + .0396 = .5540$$

In a similar way, the proportion of people in state 1 after one generation is

$$.1365 + .1020 + .0132 = .2517.$$

For state 3, the proportion is

$$.0147 + .1224 + .0572 = .1943.$$

The initial distribution of states, 21%, 68%, and 11%, becomes, after one generation, 25.17% in state 1, 55.4% in state 2, and 19.43% in state 3. These distributions can be written as *probability vectors* (where the percents have been changed to decimals rounded to the nearest hundredth):

$$[.21 \quad .68 \quad .11] \quad \text{and} \quad [.25 \quad .55 \quad .19]$$

respectively. A **probability vector** is a matrix of only one row, having nonnegative entries, with the sum of the entries 1.

The work with the tree diagram to find the distribution of states after one generation is exactly the work required to multiply the initial probability vector, $[.21 \quad .68 \quad .11]$, and the transition matrix P:

$$[.21 \quad .68 \quad .11] \begin{bmatrix} .65 & .28 & .07 \\ .15 & .67 & .18 \\ .12 & .36 & .52 \end{bmatrix} \approx [.25 \quad .55 \quad .19].$$

In a similar way, the distribution of social classes after two generations can be found by multiplying the initial probability vector and the square of P, the matrix P^2. Using P^2 from above,

$$[.21 \quad .68 \quad .11] \begin{bmatrix} .47 & .39 & .13 \\ .22 & .56 & .22 \\ .19 & .46 & .34 \end{bmatrix} \approx [.27 \quad .51 \quad .21]$$

In the next section we shall find a long-range prediction for the proportions of the population in each social class. Our work in this section is summarized below.

Suppose a Markov chain has initial probability vector $I = [i_1 \quad i_2 \quad i_3 \cdot \cdot \cdot \quad i_n]$, and transition matrix P. The probability vector after n repetitions of the experiment is

$$I \cdot P^n.$$

8.1 EXERCISES

Which of the matrices in Exercises 1–9 could be a probability vector?

1. $\left[\begin{array}{cc} \frac{2}{3} & \frac{1}{2} \end{array}\right]$

2. $\left[\begin{array}{cc} \frac{1}{2} & 1 \end{array}\right]$

3. $\left[\begin{array}{cc} 0 & 1 \end{array}\right]$

4. $[.1 \quad .1]$

5. $[.4 \quad .2 \quad 0]$

6. $\left[\begin{array}{ccc} \frac{1}{4} & \frac{1}{8} & \frac{5}{8} \end{array}\right]$

7. $[.07 \quad .04 \quad .37 \quad .52]$

8. $[.3 \quad -.1 \quad .8]$

9. $[0 \quad -.2 \quad .6 \quad .6]$

Which of the matrices in Exercises 10–18 could be transition matrices, by definition?

10. $\left[\begin{array}{cc} .5 & 0 \\ 0 & .5 \end{array}\right]$

11. $\left[\begin{array}{cc} \frac{2}{3} & \frac{1}{3} \\ 1 & 0 \end{array}\right]$

12. $\left[\begin{array}{cc} \frac{1}{4} & \frac{3}{4} \\ \frac{1}{2} & \frac{1}{2} \end{array}\right]$

13. $\left[\begin{array}{ccc} \frac{1}{4} & \frac{3}{4} & 0 \\ 2 & 0 & 1 \\ 1 & \frac{2}{3} & 3 \end{array}\right]$

14. $\left[\begin{array}{ccc} \frac{1}{3} & \frac{1}{3} & \frac{1}{3} \\ 0 & 1 & 0 \\ \frac{1}{2} & 0 & \frac{1}{2} \end{array}\right]$

15. $\left[\begin{array}{ccc} \frac{1}{3} & \frac{1}{3} & 1 \\ 0 & 1 & 0 \\ \frac{1}{2} & \frac{1}{2} & 1 \end{array}\right]$

16. $\left[\begin{array}{ccc} \frac{1}{3} & \frac{1}{2} & 1 \\ \frac{1}{3} & 0 & 0 \\ \frac{1}{3} & \frac{1}{2} & 0 \end{array}\right]$

17. $\left[\begin{array}{ccc} .9 & .1 & 0 \\ .1 & .6 & .3 \\ 0 & .3 & .7 \end{array}\right]$

18. $\left[\begin{array}{ccc} .6 & .2 & .2 \\ .9 & .02 & .08 \\ 0 & 0 & .6 \end{array}\right]$

Find the first three powers of each of the transition matrices in Exercises 19–24, for example, A, A^2 and A^3. For each transition matrix, find the probability that state 1 changes to state 2 after three repetitions of the experiment.

19. $A = \left[\begin{array}{cc} 1 & 0 \\ .8 & .2 \end{array}\right]$

20. $B = \left[\begin{array}{cc} .7 & .3 \\ 0 & 1 \end{array}\right]$

21. $C = \left[\begin{array}{cc} .5 & .5 \\ .72 & .28 \end{array}\right]$

22. $D = \left[\begin{array}{ccc} .3 & .2 & .5 \\ 0 & 0 & 1 \\ .6 & .1 & .3 \end{array}\right]$

23. $E = \left[\begin{array}{ccc} .8 & .1 & .1 \\ .3 & .6 & .1 \\ 0 & 1 & 0 \end{array}\right]$

24. $F = \left[\begin{array}{ccc} .01 & .9 & .09 \\ .72 & .1 & .18 \\ .34 & 0 & .66 \end{array}\right]$

25. Years ago, about 10% of all cars sold were small, while 90% were large. This has changed drastically; now of the people buying a car in a given year, 20% of small car owners will switch to a large car, while 60% of large car owners will switch to a small car.

   (a) Write a transition matrix using this information.

   (b) Write a probability vector for the initial distribution of cars.

   (c) Square the transition matrix and find the distribution of cars after 2 years.

   Find the distribution of cars after

   (d) 3 years.   **(e)** 4 years.   **(f)** 5 years.

26. In the example in the text, we used the transition matrix

$$\begin{array}{c} \\ \text{Johnson} \\ \text{NorthClean} \end{array} \begin{array}{cc} \text{Johnson} & \text{NorthClean} \\ \left[\begin{array}{cc} .8 & .2 \\ .35 & .65 \end{array}\right] \end{array}$$

Suppose now that we assume that each customer brings in one load of clothes each week. Use various powers of the transition matrix to find the probability that a customer bringing a load of clothes to Johnson initially also brings a load to Johnson after

   (a) 1 week   **(b)** 2 weeks   **(c)** 3 weeks   **(d)** 4 weeks.

27. Suppose Johnson has a 40% market share initially, with NorthClean having a 60% share. Use this information to write a probability vector; use this vector along with the transition matrix above to find the share of the market for each firm after

   (a) 1 week   **(b)** 2 weeks   **(c)** 3 weeks   **(d)** 4 weeks.

28. An insurance company classifies its drivers into three groups: G_0 (no accidents), G_1 (one accident), and G_2 (more than one accident). The probability that a driver in G_0 will stay in G_0 after one year is .85, that the driver will become a G_1 is .10, and that the driver will become a G_2 is .05. A driver in G_1 cannot move to G_0 (this company has a long memory). There is a .8 probability that a G_1 driver will stay in G_1. A G_2 driver must stay in G_2. Write a transition matrix using this information.

29. Suppose that the company of Exercise 28 accepts 50,000 new policyholders, all of whom are in G_0. Find the number in each group after

(a) 1 year   (b) 2 years   (c) 3 years   (d) 4 years.

30. The difficulty with the mathematical model of Exercises 28 and 29 is that no "grace period" is provided; there should be a certain positive probability of moving from G_1 or G_2 back to G_0 (say, after four years with no accidents). A new system with this feature might produce the following transition matrix.

$$\begin{bmatrix} .85 & .10 & .05 \\ .15 & .75 & .10 \\ .10 & .30 & .60 \end{bmatrix}$$

Suppose that when this new policy is adopted, the company has 50,000 policyholders, all in G_0. Find the number in each group after

(a) 1 year   (b) 2 years   (c) 3 years.

31. Research done by the Gulf Oil Corporation* produced the following transition matrix for the probability that during a given year a person with one form of home heating would switch to another.

		Will switch to		
		Oil	Gas	Electric
Now has	Oil	.825	.175	0
	Gas	.060	.919	.021
	Electric	.049	0	.951

The current share of the market held by these three types of heat is given by the vector $[.26 \quad .60 \quad .14]$. Find the share of the market held by each type of heat after

(a) 1 year   (b) 2 years   (c) 3 years.

32. In one state, a land use survey showed that 35% of all land was used for agricultural purposes, while 10% was urban. Ten years later, of the agricultural land, 15% had become urban and 80% had remained agricultural. (The remainder lay idle.) Of the idle land, 20% had become urbanized and 10% had been converted for agricultural use. Of the urban land, 90% remained urban and 10% was idle. Assume that these trends continue.

(a) Write a transition matrix using this information.

(b) Write a probability vector for the initial distribution of land.

Find the land use pattern after

(c) ten years   (d) twenty years.

---

*Reprinted by permission of Ali Ezzati, "Forecasting Market Shares of Alternative Home Heating Units," *Management Science*, Vol. 21, No. 4, December 1974, copyright © 1974 The Institute of Management Sciences.

33. In a survey investigating change in housing patterns in one urban area, it was found that 75% of the population lived in single-family dwellings and 25% in multiple housing of some kind. Five years later, in a follow-up survey, of those who had been living in single family dwellings, 90% still did so, but 10% had moved to multiple family dwellings. Of those in multiple family housing, 95% were still living in that type of housing, while 5% had moved to single-family dwellings. Assume that these trends continue.

(a) Write a transition matrix for this information.

(b) Write a probability vector for the initial distribution of housing.

What percent of the population can be expected in each category

(c) five years later   (d) ten years later?

34. At the end of June in a Presidential election year, 40% of the voters were registered as liberal, 45% as conservative, and 15% as independent. Over a one month period, the liberals retained 80% of their constituency, while 15% switched to conservative and 5% to independent. The conservatives retained 70%, and lost 20% to the liberals. The independents retained 60% and lost 20% each to the conservatives and liberals. Assume that these trends continue.

(a) Write a transition matrix using this information.

(b) Write a probability vector for the initial distribution.

Find the percent of each type of voter at the end of

(c) July   (d) August   (e) September   (f) October.

For each of the following transition matrices, find the first five powers of the matrix. Then find the probability that state 2 changes to state 4 after 5 repetitions of the experiment.

35. $\begin{bmatrix} .1 & .2 & .2 & .3 & .2 \\ .2 & .1 & .1 & .2 & .4 \\ .2 & .1 & .4 & .2 & .1 \\ .3 & .1 & .1 & .2 & .3 \\ .1 & .3 & .1 & .1 & .4 \end{bmatrix}$

36. $\begin{bmatrix} .3 & .2 & .3 & .1 & .1 \\ .4 & .2 & .1 & .2 & .1 \\ .1 & .3 & .2 & .2 & .2 \\ .2 & .1 & .3 & .2 & .2 \\ .1 & .1 & .4 & .2 & .2 \end{bmatrix}$

37. A company with a new training program classified each employee in one of the four states: s_1, never in the program; s_2, currently in the program; s_3, discharged; s_4, completed the program. The transition matrix for this company is given below.

$$\begin{array}{c} \\ s_1 \\ s_2 \\ s_3 \\ s_4 \end{array} \begin{array}{cccc} s_1 & s_2 & s_3 & s_4 \\ \begin{bmatrix} .4 & .2 & .05 & .35 \\ 0 & .45 & .05 & .5 \\ 0 & 0 & 1.0 & 0 \\ 0 & 0 & 0 & 1.0 \end{bmatrix} \end{array}$$

(a) What percent of employees who had never been in the program (state s_1) completed the program (state s_4) after the program had been offered five times?

(b) If the initial percent of employees in each state was [.5 .5 0 0], find the corresponding percents after the program had been offered four times.

8.2   Regular Markov Chains

By starting with a transition matrix P and an initial probability vector, the nth power of P makes it possible to find the probability vector for n repetitions of an experiment. In this section we try to decide what happens to an initial probability vector "in the long run," that is, as n gets larger and larger.

For example, let us use the transition matrix associated with the dry cleaners example of the previous section,

$$\begin{bmatrix} .8 & .2 \\ .35 & .65 \end{bmatrix}.$$

The initial probability vector, which gives the market share for each firm at the beginning of the experiment, is $[.4 \quad .6]$. The market shares shown in the following table were found by using powers of the transition matrix. (See Exercise 27 of Section 8.1.)

Week	Johnson	NorthClean
Start	.4	.6
1	.53	.47
2	.59	.41
3	.62	.38
4	.63	.37
5	.63	.37
12	.64	.36

The results seem to approach the numbers in the probability vector $[.64 \quad .36]$.

What happens if the initial probability vector is different from $[.4 \quad .6]$? Suppose $[.75 \quad .25]$ is used; the same powers of the transition matrix as above give the following results.

Week	Johnson	NorthClean
Start	.75	.25
1	.69	.31
2	.66	.34
3	.65	.35
4	.64	.36
5	.64	.36
6	.64	.36

Here the results also seem to be approaching the numbers in the probability vector $[.64 \quad .36]$, the same numbers approached with the initial probability vector $[.4 \quad .6]$. In either case, the long-range trend is for a market share of about 64% for Johnson and 36% for NorthClean. Based on the example above, this long-range trend does not depend on the initial distribution of market shares.

Regular Transition Matrices   One of the many applications of Markov chains is in finding these long-range predictions. It is not possible to make long-range predictions with all transition matrices, but for a large set of transition matrices, long-range predictions *are* possible. Such predictions are always possible with **regular transition matrices.** A transition matrix is **regular** if some power of the matrix contains all positive entries. A Markov chain is a **regular Markov chain** if its transition matrix is regular.

EXAMPLE 1

Decide if the following transition matrices are regular.

(a) $A = \begin{bmatrix} .75 & .25 & 0 \\ 0 & .5 & .5 \\ .6 & .4 & 0 \end{bmatrix}$

Square A.

$A^2 = \begin{bmatrix} .5625 & .3125 & .125 \\ .3 & .45 & .25 \\ .45 & .35 & .2 \end{bmatrix}$

All entries in A^2 are positive, so that matrix A is regular.

(b) $B = \begin{bmatrix} .5 & 0 & .5 \\ 0 & 1 & 0 \\ 0 & 0 & 1 \end{bmatrix}$

Find various powers of B.

$B^2 = \begin{bmatrix} .25 & 0 & .75 \\ 0 & 1 & 0 \\ 0 & 0 & 1 \end{bmatrix}$; $B^3 = \begin{bmatrix} .125 & 0 & .875 \\ 0 & 1 & 0 \\ 0 & 0 & 1 \end{bmatrix}$; $B^4 = \begin{bmatrix} .0625 & 0 & .9375 \\ 0 & 1 & 0 \\ 0 & 0 & 1 \end{bmatrix}$

Further powers of B will still give the same zero entries, so that no power of matrix B contains all positive entries. For this reason, B is not regular.   ■

Suppose that v is a probability vector. It turns out that for a regular Markov chain with a transition matrix P, there exists a single vector V such that $v \cdot P^n$ approaches closer and closer to V as n gets larger and larger.

Equilibrium Vector

of a Markov Chain

If a Markov chain with transition matrix P is regular, then for any probability vector v, there is a unique vector V such that for large values of n,

$$v \cdot P^n \approx V.$$

Vector V is called the **equilibrium vector** or the **fixed vector** of the Markov chain.

In the example with Johnson Cleaners, we found that the equilibrium vector V is approximately [.64 .36]. Vector V can be determined by finding P^n for larger and larger values of n, and then looking for a vector that the product $v \cdot P^n$ approaches. However, such an approach can be very tedious and prone to error. To find a better way, start with the fact that for a large value of n,

$$v \cdot P^n \approx V,$$

as mentioned above. From this result, $v \cdot P^n \cdot P \approx V \cdot P$, so that

$$v \cdot P^n \cdot P = v \cdot P^{n+1} \approx VP.$$

Since $v \cdot P^n \approx V$ for large values of n, it is also true that $v \cdot P^{n+1} \approx V$ for large values of n (the product $v \cdot P^n$ approaches V, so that $v \cdot P^{n+1}$ must also approach V.) Thus, $v \cdot P^{n+1} \approx V$ and $v \cdot P^{n+1} \approx VP$, which suggests that

$$VP = V.$$

> If a Markov chain with transition matrix P is regular, then there exists a probability vector V such that
> $$VP = V.$$

This vector V gives the long-range trend of the Markov chain. Vector V is found by solving a system of linear equations, as shown in the next examples.

EXAMPLE 2

Find the long-range trend for the Markov chain in the dry cleaning example with transition matrix

$$\begin{bmatrix} .8 & .2 \\ .35 & .65 \end{bmatrix}.$$

This matrix is regular since all entries are positive. Let P represent this transition matrix, and let V be the probability vector $[v_1 \quad v_2]$. We want to find V such that

$$VP = V,$$

or

$$[v_1 \quad v_2]\begin{bmatrix} .8 & .2 \\ .35 & .65 \end{bmatrix} = [v_1 \quad v_2].$$

Use matrix multiplication on the left.

$$[.8v_1 + .35v_2 \quad .2v_1 + .65v_2] = [v_1 \quad v_2]$$

Set corresponding entries from the two matrices equal to get

$$.8v_1 + .35v_2 = v_1 \quad \text{and} \quad .2v_1 + .65v_2 = v_2.$$

Simplify each of these equations.

$$-.2v_1 + .35v_2 = 0 \qquad .2v_1 - .35v_2 = 0$$

These last two equations are really the same. (The equations in the system obtained from $VP = V$ are always dependent.) To find the values of v_1 and v_2, recall that $V = [v_1 \quad v_2]$ is a probability vector, so that

$$v_1 + v_2 = 1.$$

To find v_1 and v_2 solve the system

$$-.2v_1 + .35v_2 = 0$$
$$v_1 + v_2 = 1.$$

From the second equation, $v_1 = 1 - v_2$. Substitute $1 - v_2$ for v_1 in the first equation.

$$-.2(1 - v_2) + .35v_2 = 0$$
$$-.2 + .2v_2 + .35v_2 = 0$$
$$.55v_2 = .2$$
$$v_2 = \frac{4}{11} \approx .364$$

Since $v_1 = 1 - v_2$, $v_1 = 7/11 \approx .636$, and the equilibrium vector is $V = [7/11 \quad 4/11] \approx [.636 \quad .364]$. ■

Some powers of the transition matrix P of Example 1 (with entries rounded to two decimal places) are shown here.

$$P^2 = \begin{bmatrix} .71 & .29 \\ .51 & .49 \end{bmatrix} \qquad P^3 = \begin{bmatrix} .67 & .33 \\ .58 & .42 \end{bmatrix} \qquad P^4 = \begin{bmatrix} .65 & .35 \\ .62 & .38 \end{bmatrix}$$

$$P^5 = \begin{bmatrix} .65 & .35 \\ .63 & .37 \end{bmatrix} \qquad P^6 = \begin{bmatrix} .64 & .36 \\ .63 & .37 \end{bmatrix} \qquad P^{10} = \begin{bmatrix} .64 & .36 \\ .64 & .36 \end{bmatrix}$$

As these results suggest, higher and higher powers of the transition matrix P approach a matrix having all rows identical; these identical rows have as entries the entries of the equilibrium vector V. This agrees with the statement above: the initial state doesn't matter. Regardless of the initial probability vector, the system will approach a fixed vector V.

Let us summarize the results of this section.

Properties of Regular Markov Chains	

Suppose a regular Markov chain has a transition matrix P.

1. For any initial probability vector v, the product $v \cdot P^n$ approaches a unique vector V as n gets larger and larger. Vector V is called the *equilibrium* or *fixed vector*.
2. Vector V has the property that $VP = V$.
3. To find V, solve a system of equations obtained from the matrix equation $VP = V$, and from the fact that the sum of the entries of V is 1.
4. The powers P^n approach closer and closer to a matrix whose rows are made up of the entries of the equilibrium vector V.

EXAMPLE 3

Find the equilibrium vector for the transition matrix

$$K = \begin{bmatrix} .2 & .6 & .2 \\ .1 & .1 & .8 \\ .3 & .3 & .4 \end{bmatrix}.$$

Matrix K has all positive entries and thus is regular. For this reason, an equilibrium vector V must exist such that $VK = V$. Let $V = \begin{bmatrix} v_1 & v_2 & v_3 \end{bmatrix}$. Then

$$\begin{bmatrix} v_1 & v_2 & v_3 \end{bmatrix} \begin{bmatrix} .2 & .6 & .2 \\ .1 & .1 & .8 \\ .3 & .3 & .4 \end{bmatrix} = \begin{bmatrix} v_1 & v_2 & v_3 \end{bmatrix}.$$

Use matrix multiplication on the left.

$$\begin{bmatrix} .2v_1 + .1v_2 + .3v_3 & .6v_1 + .1v_2 + .3v_3 & .2v_1 + .8v_2 + .4v_3 \end{bmatrix}$$
$$= \begin{bmatrix} v_1 & v_2 & v_3 \end{bmatrix}$$

Setting corresponding entries equal gives three equations.

$$.2v_1 + .1v_2 + .3v_3 = v_1$$
$$.6v_1 + .1v_2 + .3v_3 = v_2$$
$$.2v_1 + .8v_2 + .4v_3 = v_3$$

Simplifying these equations gives

$$-.8v_1 + .1v_2 + .3v_3 = 0$$
$$.6v_1 - .9v_2 + .3v_3 = 0$$
$$.2v_1 + .8v_2 - .6v_3 = 0.$$

Since V is a probability vector,

$$v_1 + v_2 + v_3 = 1.$$

This gives a system of four equations in three unknowns.

$$-.8v_1 + .1v_2 + .3v_3 = 0$$
$$.6v_1 - .9v_2 + .3v_3 = 0$$
$$.2v_1 + .8v_2 - .6v_3 = 0$$
$$v_1 + v_2 + v_3 = 1.$$

This system can be solved with the Gauss-Jordan method presented earlier. Start with the augmented matrix

$$\begin{bmatrix} -.8 & .1 & .3 & | & 0 \\ .6 & -.9 & .3 & | & 0 \\ .2 & .8 & -.6 & | & 0 \\ 1 & 1 & 1 & | & 1 \end{bmatrix}.$$

The solution of this system is $v_1 = 5/23$, $v_2 = 7/23$, $v_3 = 11/23$, and

$$V = \begin{bmatrix} \dfrac{5}{23} & \dfrac{7}{23} & \dfrac{11}{23} \end{bmatrix} \approx \begin{bmatrix} .22 & .30 & .48 \end{bmatrix}. \quad \blacksquare$$

8.2 EXERCISES

Which of the matrices in Exercises 1–6 are regular?

1. $\begin{bmatrix} .2 & .8 \\ .9 & .1 \end{bmatrix}$

2. $\begin{bmatrix} .22 & .78 \\ .43 & .57 \end{bmatrix}$

3. $\begin{bmatrix} 1 & 0 \\ .6 & .4 \end{bmatrix}$

4. $\begin{bmatrix} .55 & .45 \\ 0 & 1 \end{bmatrix}$

5. $\begin{bmatrix} 0 & 1 & 0 \\ .4 & .2 & .4 \\ 1 & 0 & 0 \end{bmatrix}$

6. $\begin{bmatrix} .3 & .5 & .2 \\ 1 & 0 & 0 \\ .5 & .1 & .4 \end{bmatrix}$

Find the equilibrium vector for each transition matrix in Exercises 7–14.

7. $\begin{bmatrix} \frac{1}{4} & \frac{3}{4} \\ \frac{1}{2} & \frac{1}{2} \end{bmatrix}$

8. $\begin{bmatrix} \frac{2}{3} & \frac{1}{3} \\ \frac{1}{8} & \frac{7}{8} \end{bmatrix}$

9. $\begin{bmatrix} .3 & .7 \\ .4 & .6 \end{bmatrix}$

10. $\begin{bmatrix} .8 & .2 \\ .1 & .9 \end{bmatrix}$

11. $\begin{bmatrix} .1 & .1 & .8 \\ .4 & .4 & .2 \\ .1 & .2 & .7 \end{bmatrix}$

12. $\begin{bmatrix} .5 & .2 & .3 \\ .1 & .4 & .5 \\ .2 & .2 & .6 \end{bmatrix}$

13. $\begin{bmatrix} .25 & .35 & .4 \\ .1 & .3 & .6 \\ .55 & .4 & .05 \end{bmatrix}$

14. $\begin{bmatrix} .16 & .28 & .56 \\ .43 & .12 & .45 \\ .86 & .05 & .09 \end{bmatrix}$

Find the equilibrium vector for each transition matrix in Exercises 15–21. These matrices were first used in the Exercises of Section 8.1. (*Note:* Not all of these transition matrices are regular, but equilibrium vectors still exist. Why doesn't this contradict the work of this section?)

15. car sizes, Exercise 25,

$\begin{bmatrix} .8 & .2 \\ .6 & .4 \end{bmatrix}$

16. housing patterns, Exercise 33,

$\begin{bmatrix} .90 & .10 \\ .05 & .95 \end{bmatrix}$

17. insurance categories, Exercise 28,

$\begin{bmatrix} .85 & .10 & .05 \\ 0 & .80 & .20 \\ 0 & 0 & 1 \end{bmatrix}$

18. "modified" insurance categories, Exercise 30,

$\begin{bmatrix} .85 & .10 & .05 \\ .15 & .75 & .10 \\ .10 & .30 & .60 \end{bmatrix}$

19. land use, Exercise 32,

$\begin{bmatrix} .80 & .15 & .05 \\ 0 & .90 & .10 \\ .10 & .20 & .70 \end{bmatrix}$

20. voting registration, Exercise 34,

$\begin{bmatrix} .80 & .15 & .05 \\ .20 & .70 & .10 \\ .20 & .20 & .60 \end{bmatrix}$

21. home heating systems, Exercise 31,

$\begin{bmatrix} .825 & .175 & 0 \\ .060 & .919 & .021 \\ .049 & 0 & .951 \end{bmatrix}$

22. The probability that a complex assembly line works correctly depends on whether or not the line worked correctly the last time it was used. There is a .9 chance that the line will work correctly if it worked correctly the time before, and a .7 chance that it will work correctly if it did *not* work correctly the time before. Set up a transition matrix with this information and find the long-run probability that the line will work correctly.

23. Suppose improvements are made in the assembly line of Exercise 22, so that the transition matrix becomes

$$\begin{array}{c} \\ \text{Works} \\ \text{Doesn't} \end{array} \begin{array}{cc} \text{Works} & \text{Doesn't} \\ \begin{bmatrix} .95 & .05 \\ .80 & .20 \end{bmatrix} \end{array}$$

Find the long-run probability now that the line will work properly.

24. A certain genetic defect is carried only by males. Suppose the probability is .95 that a male offspring will have the defect if his father did, with the probability .10 that a male offspring will have the defect if his father did not have it. Find the long-range prediction for the fraction of the males in the population who will have the defect.

25. Each month, a sales manager classifies her salespeople as low, medium, or high producers. There is a .4 chance that a low producer one month will become a medium producer the following month, and a .1 chance that a low producer will become a high producer. A medium producer will become a low or high producer, respectively, with probabilities .25 and .3. A high producer will become a low or medium producer, respectively, with probabilities .05 and .4. Find the long-range trend for the proportion of low, medium, and high producers.

26. The weather in a certain spot is classified as fair, cloudy without rain, or rainy. A fair day is followed by a fair day 60% of the time, and by a cloudy day 25% of the time. A cloudy day is followed by a cloudy day 35% of the time, and by a rainy day 25% of the time. A rainy day is followed by a cloudy day 40% of the time, and by another rainy day 25% of the time. Find the long-range prediction for the proportion of fair, cloudy, and rainy days.

27. At one liberal arts college, students are classified as humanities majors, science majors, or undecideds. There is a 20% chance that a humanities major will change to a science major from one year to the next, and a 45% chance that a humanities major will change to undecided. A science major will change to humanities with probability .15, and to undecided with probability .35. An undecided will switch to humanities or science with probabilities of .5 and .3 respectively. Find the long-range prediction for the fraction of students in each of these three majors.

28. A large group of mice is kept in a cage having connected compartments A, B, and C. Mice in compartment A move to B with probability .3 and to C with probability .4. Mice in B move to A or C with probabilities of .15 and .55, respectively. Mice in C move to A and B with probabilities .3 and .6 respectively. Find the long-range prediction for the fraction of mice in each of the compartments.

29. The manager of the slot machines at a major casino makes a decision about whether or not to "loosen up" the slots so that the customers get a larger playback. The manager tells only one other person, a person whose word cannot be trusted. In fact, there is only a probability p, where $0 < p < 1$, that this person will tell the truth. Suppose this person tells several other people, each of whom tell several people, what the manager's decision is. Suppose there is always a probability p that the decision is passed on as heard. Find the long-range prediction for the fraction of the people who will hear the decision correctly. (Hint: use a transition matrix; let the first row be $[p \quad 1 - p]$, with second row $[1 - p \quad p]$.)

30. Find the equilibrium vector for the transition matrix

$$\begin{bmatrix} p & 1 - p \\ 1 - q & q \end{bmatrix}$$

where $0 < p < 1$ and $0 < q < 1$. Under what conditions is this matrix regular?

31. Show that the transition matrix

$$K = \begin{bmatrix} \frac{1}{4} & 0 & \frac{3}{4} \\ 0 & 1 & 0 \\ 0 & 0 & 1 \end{bmatrix}$$

has more than one vector V such that $VK = V$. Why does this not violate the statements of this section?

32. Let

$$P = \begin{bmatrix} a_{11} & a_{12} \\ a_{21} & a_{22} \end{bmatrix}$$

be a regular transition matrix having *column* sums of 1. Show that the equilibrium vector for P is $\begin{bmatrix} 1/2 & 1/2 \end{bmatrix}$.

Find the equilibrium vector for each of the following transition matrices by taking powers of the matrix.

33. $\begin{bmatrix} .1 & .2 & .2 & .3 & .2 \\ .2 & .1 & .1 & .2 & .4 \\ .2 & .1 & .4 & .2 & .1 \\ .3 & .1 & .1 & .2 & .3 \\ .1 & .3 & .1 & .1 & .4 \end{bmatrix}$

34. $\begin{bmatrix} .3 & .2 & .3 & .1 & .1 \\ .4 & .2 & .1 & .2 & .1 \\ .1 & .3 & .2 & .2 & .2 \\ .2 & .1 & .3 & .2 & .2 \\ .1 & .1 & .4 & .2 & .2 \end{bmatrix}$

35. Find the long range prediction for the percent of employees in each state for the company training program from Exercise 37, Section 8.1. The transition matrix is repeated here.

$$\begin{array}{c} \\ s_1 \\ s_2 \\ s_3 \\ s_4 \end{array} \begin{array}{c} \begin{array}{cccc} s_1 & s_2 & s_3 & s_4 \end{array} \\ \begin{bmatrix} .4 & .2 & .05 & .35 \\ 0 & .45 & .05 & .5 \\ 0 & 0 & 1.0 & 0 \\ 0 & 0 & 0 & 1.0 \end{bmatrix} \end{array}$$

8.3   Decision Making

John F. Kennedy once remarked that he had assumed that as President it would be difficult to choose between distinct, opposite alternatives when a decision needed to be made. Actually, however, he said that he found such decisions easy to make; the hard decisions came when he was faced with choices that were not as clear-cut. Most decisions that we are faced with fall in this last category—decisions which must be made under conditions of uncertainty. Decision theory is a mathematical model that provides a systematic way to attack problems of decision making when not all alternatives are clear and unambiguous. The idea of expected value, introduced earlier, is the basis of decision theory. The theory is explained through an example.

Freezing temperatures are endangering the orange crop in central California. A farmer can protect his crop by burning smudge pots—the heat from the pots keeps the oranges from freezing. However, burning the pots is expensive; the cost is $2000. The farmer knows that if he burns smudge pots he will be able to sell his crop for a net profit (after smudge pot costs are deducted) of $5000, provided that the freeze does develop and wipes out many of the other orange growers in California. If he does nothing he will either lose $1000 in planting costs if it does freeze, or make a profit of $4800 if it does not freeze. (If it does not freeze, there will be a large supply of oranges, and thus his profit will be lower than if there was a small supply.)

What should the farmer do? He should begin by carefully defining the problem. First he must decide on the **states of nature,** the possible alternatives over which he has no control. Here there are two: freezing temperatures, or no freezing temperatures. Next, the farmer should list the things he can control—his actions or **strategies.** The farmer has two possible strategies: use smudge pots or not use smudge pots. The consequences of each action under each state of nature, called **payoffs,** can be summarized in a **payoff matrix,** as shown below. The payoffs in this case represent the profit for each possible combination of events.

$$\begin{array}{c} & & \begin{array}{cc} \textit{States of nature} \\ \text{Freeze} & \text{No freeze} \end{array} \\ \textit{Strategies of farmer} & \begin{array}{c} \text{Use smudge pots} \\ \text{Do not use pots} \end{array} & \begin{bmatrix} \$5000 & \$2800 \\ -\$1000 & \$4800 \end{bmatrix} \end{array}$$

To get the $2800 entry in the payoff matrix, we took the profit if there is no freeze, $4800, and subtracted the $2000 cost of using the smudge pots.

Once the farmer makes the payoff matrix, what then? The farmer might be an optimist (some might call him a gambler); in this case he might assume that the best will happen and go for the biggest number on the matrix ($5000). To get this profit, he must adopt the strategy "use smudge pots."

On the other hand, if the farmer is a pessimist, he would want to minimize the worst thing that could happen. If he uses smudge pots, the worst that could happen to him would be a profit of $2800, which will result if there is no freeze. If he does not use smudge pots, he might face a loss of $1000. To minimize the worst, he once again should adopt the strategy "use smudge pots."

Suppose the farmer decides that he is neither an optimist nor a pessimist, but would like further information before choosing a strategy. For example, he might call the weather forecaster and ask for the probability of a freeze. Further, suppose the forecaster says that this probability is only .1. What should the farmer do? He should recall our earlier discussion of expected value and calculate the expected profit for each of his two possible strategies. If the probability of a freeze is .1, then the probability that there will be no freeze is .9. This information gives the following expected values:

$$\text{If smudge pots are used:} \quad 5000(.1) + 2800(.9) = 3020$$

$$\text{If no smudge pots are used:} \quad -1000(.1) + 4800(.9) = 4220$$

Here the maximum expected profit, $4220, is obtained if smudge pots are *not* used. If the probability of a freeze is .6, the expected profit from the strategy "use pots" would be $4120 and from "use no pots," $1320. As the example shows, the farmer's beliefs about the probabilities of a freeze affect his choice of strategy.

EXAMPLE 1

A small Christmas card manufacturer must decide in February about the type of cards she should emphasize in her fall line of cards. She has three possible strategies: emphasize modern cards, emphasize old-fashioned cards, or emphasize a mixture of the two. Her success is dependent on the state of the economy in December. If the economy is strong, she will do well with her modern cards, while in a weak economy people long for the old days and buy old-fashioned cards. In an in-between economy, her mixture of lines would do the best. She first prepares a payoff matrix for all three possibilities. The numbers in the matrix represent her profits in thousands of dollars.

States of nature

		Weak economy	In-between	Strong economy
	Modern	40	85	120
Strategies	Old-fashioned	106	46	83
	Mixture	72	90	68

(a) If the manufacturer is an optimist, she should aim for the biggest number on the matrix, 120 (representing $120,000 in profit). Her strategy in this case would be to produce modern cards.

(b) A pessimistic manufacturer wants to avoid the worst of all bad things that can happen. If she produces modern cards, the worst that can happen is a profit of $40,000. For old-fashioned cards, the worst is a profit of $46,000, while the worst that can happen from a mixture is a profit of $68,000. Her strategy here is to use a mixture.

(c) Suppose the manufacturer reads in a business magazine that leading experts feel there is a 50% chance of a weak economy at Christmas, a 20% chance of an in-between economy, and a 30% chance of a strong economy. The manufacturer should now use this information to find her expected profit for each possible strategy.

Modern: $40(.50) + 85(.20) + 120(.30) = 73$

Old-fashioned: $106(.50) + 46(.20) + 83(.30) = 87.1$

Mixture: $72(.50) + 90(.20) + 68(.30) = 74.4$

Here the best strategy is old-fashioned cards; the expected profit is 87.1, or $87,100. ▨

8.3 EXERCISES

1. An investor has $20,000 to invest in stocks. She has two possible strategies: buy conservative blue-chip stocks or buy highly speculative stocks. There are two states of nature: the market goes up or the market goes down. The following payoff matrix shows the net amounts she will have under the various circumstances.

	Market up	Market down
Buy blue-chip	$25,000	$18,000
Buy speculative	$30,000	$11,000

What should the investor do if she is

(a) an optimist;   **(b)** a pessimist?

(c) Suppose there is a .7 probability of the market going up. What is the best strategy? What is the expected profit?

(d) What is the best strategy if the probability of a market rise is .2?

2. A developer has $100,000 to invest in land. He has a choice of two parcels (at the same price), one on the highway and one on the coast. With both parcels, his ultimate profit depends on whether he faces light opposition from environmental groups or heavy opposition. He estimates that the payoff matrix is as follows (the numbers represent his profit).

$$\begin{array}{c} & & \text{Opposition} \\ & & \text{Light} \quad\quad \text{Heavy} \\ \textit{Parcels} \begin{array}{c} \text{Highway} \\ \text{Coast} \end{array} & \left[\begin{array}{cc} \$70,000 & \$30,000 \\ \$150,000 & -\$40,000 \end{array} \right] \end{array}$$

What should the developer do if he is

(a) an optimist;   **(b)** a pessimist?

(c) Suppose the probability of heavy opposition is .8. What is his best strategy? What is the expected profit?

(d) What is the best strategy if the probability of heavy opposition is only .4?

3. Hillsdale College has sold out all tickets for a jazz concert to be held in the stadium. If it rains, the show will have to be moved to the gym, which has a much smaller capacity. The dean must decide in advance whether to set up the seats and the stage in the gym or in the stadium, or both, just in case. The payoff matrix below shows the net profit in each case.

$$\begin{array}{c} & & \text{States of nature} \\ & & \text{Rain} \quad\quad \text{No rain} \\ \textit{Strategies} \begin{array}{c} \text{Set up in stadium} \\ \text{Set up in gym} \\ \text{Set up both} \end{array} & \left[\begin{array}{cc} -\$1550 & \$1500 \\ \$1000 & \$1000 \\ \$750 & \$1400 \end{array} \right] \end{array}$$

What strategy should the dean choose if she is

(a) an optimist;   **(b)** a pessimist?

(c) If the weather forecaster predicts rain with a probability of .6, what strategy should she choose to maximize expected profit? What is the maximum expected profit?

4. An analyst must decide what fraction of the items produced by a certain machine are defective. He has already decided that there are three possibilities for the fraction of defective items: .01, .10, and .20. He may recommend two courses of action: repair the machine or make no repairs. The payoff matrix below represents the *costs* to the company in each case.

$$\begin{array}{c} & & \text{States of nature} \\ & & .01 \quad\quad .10 \quad\quad .20 \\ \textit{Strategies} \begin{array}{c} \text{Repair} \\ \text{No repair} \end{array} & \left[\begin{array}{ccc} \$130 & \$130 & \$130 \\ \$25 & \$200 & \$500 \end{array} \right] \end{array}$$

What strategy should the analyst recommend if he is

(a) an optimist;   **(b)** a pessimist?

(c) Suppose the analyst is able to estimate probabilities for the three states of nature as follows.

Fraction of defectives	Probability
.01	.70
.10	.20
.20	.10

Which strategy should he recommend? Find the expected cost to the company if this strategy is chosen.

5. The research department of the Allied Manufacturing Company has developed a new process which it believes will result in an improved product. Management must decide whether or not to go ahead and market the new product. The new product may be better than the old or it may not be better. If the new product is better, and the company decides to market it, sales should increase by $50,000. If it is not better and they replace the old product with the new product on the market, they will lose $25,000 to competitors. If they decide not to market the new product they will lose $40,000 if it is better, and research costs of $10,000 if it is not.

   (a) Prepare a payoff matrix.

   (b) If management believes the probability that the new product is better to be .4, find the expected profits under each strategy and determine the best action.

6. A businessman is planning to ship a used machine to his plant in Nigeria. He would like to use it there for the next four years. He must decide whether or not to overhaul the machine before sending it. The cost of overhaul is $2600. If the machine fails when in operation in Nigeria, it will cost him $6000 in lost production and repairs. He estimates the probability that it will fail at .3 if he does not overhaul it, and .1 if he does overhaul it. Neglect the possibility that the machine might fail more than once in the four years.

   (a) Prepare a payoff matrix.

   (b) What should the businessman do to minimize his expected costs?

7. A contractor prepares to bid on a job. If all goes well, his bid should be $30,000, which will cover his costs plus his usual profit margin of $4500. However, if a threatened labor strike actually occurs, his bid should be $40,000 to give him the same profit. If there is a strike and he bids $30,000, he will lose $5500. If his bid is too high, he may lose the job entirely, while if it is too low, he may lose money.

   (a) Prepare a payoff matrix.

   (b) If the contractor believes that the probability of a strike is .6, how much should he bid?

8. A community is considering an anti-smoking campaign.* The city council will choose one of three possible strategies: a campaign for everyone over age 10 in the community, a campaign for youths only, or no campaign at all. The two states of nature are a true cause-effect relationship between smoking and cancer and no cause-effect relationship. The costs to the community (including loss of life and productivity) in each case are as shown below.

| | States of nature | |
	Cause-effect relationship	No cause-effect relationship
Campaign for all	$100,000	$800,000
Strategies Campaign for youth	$2,820,000	$20,000
No campaign	$3,100,100	$0

What action should the city council choose if it is

   (a) optimistic;   (b) pessimistic?

   (c) If the Director of Public Health estimates that the probability of a true cause-effect relationship is .8, which strategy should the city council choose?

---

*This problem is based on an article by B. G. Greenberg in the September 1969 issue of the *Journal of the American Statistical Association*.

Sometimes the numbers (or payoffs) in a payoff matrix do not represent money (profits or costs, for example), but *utility*. A **utility** is a number which measures the satisfaction (or lack of it) that results from a certain action. The numbers must be assigned by each individual, depending on how he or she feels about a situation. For example, one person might assign a utility of $+20$ for a week's vacation in San Francisco, with -6 being assigned if the vacation were moved to Sacramento. Work Exercises 9 and 10 in the same way as those above.

9. A politician must plan her reelection strategy. She can emphasize jobs or she can emphasize the environment. The voters can be concerned about jobs or about the environment. A payoff matrix showing the utility of each possible outcome is shown below.

$$\begin{array}{c} & & \text{\textit{Voters}} \\ & & \text{Jobs} \quad \text{Environment} \\ \textit{Candidate} \begin{array}{c} \text{Jobs} \\ \text{Environment} \end{array} & \left[\begin{array}{cc} +25 & -10 \\ -15 & +30 \end{array} \right] \end{array}$$

The political analysts feel that there is a .35 chance that the voters will emphasize jobs. What strategy should the candidate adopt? What is its expected utility?

10. In an accounting class, the instructor permits the students to bring a calculator or a reference book (but not both) to an examination. The examination itself can emphasize either numerical problems or definitions. In trying to decide which aid to take to an examination, a student first decides on the utilities shown in the following payoff matrix.

$$\begin{array}{c} & & \text{\textit{Exam emphasizes}} \\ & & \text{Numbers} \quad \text{Definitions} \\ \textit{Student chooses} \begin{array}{c} \text{Calculator} \\ \text{Book} \end{array} & \left[\begin{array}{cc} +50 & 0 \\ +10 & +40 \end{array} \right] \end{array}$$

(a) What strategy should the student choose if the probability that the examination will emphasize numbers is .6? What is the expected utility in this case?

(b) Suppose the probability that the examination emphasizes numbers is .4. What strategy should be chosen by the student?

EXTENDED APPLICATION

Decision Making in Life Insurance

When a life insurance company receives an application from an agent requesting insurance on the life of an individual, it knows from experience that the applicant will be in one of three possible states of risk, with proportions as shown.*

States of Risk	Proportions
s_1 = Standard risk	.90
s_2 = Substandard risk (greater risk)	.07
s_3 = Sub-substandard risk (greatest risk)	.03

*This example was supplied by Donald J. vanKeuren, actuary of Metropolitan Life Insurance Company, and Dave Halmstad, senior actuarial assistant. It is based on a paper by Donald Jones.

A particular applicant could be correctly placed if all possible information about the applicant were known. This is not realistic in a practical situation; the company's problem is to obtain the maximum information at the lowest possible cost.

The company can take any of three possible strategies when it receives the application.

Strategies

---

a_1 = Offer a standard policy
a_2 = Offer a substandard policy (higher rates)
a_3 = Offer a sub-substandard policy (highest rates)

The payoff matrix in Table 1 below shows the payoffs associated with the possible strategies of the company and the states of the applicant. Here M represents the face value of the policy in thousands of dollars (for a $30,000 policy we have $M = 30$). For example, if the applicant is substandard (s_2) and the company offers him or her a standard policy (a_1), the company makes a profit of $13M$ (13 times the face value of the policy in thousands). Strategy a_2 would result in a larger profit of $20M$. However, if the prospective customer is a standard risk (s_1) but the company offers a substandard policy (a_2), the company loses $50 (the cost of preparing a policy) since the customer would reject the policy because it has higher rates than he or she could obtain elsewhere.

Table 1		**States of Nature**		
		s_1	s_2	s_3
	a_1	$20M$	$13M$	$3M$
Strategies of company	a_2	-50	$20M$	$10M$
	a_3	-50	-50	$20M$

Before deciding on the policy to be offered, the company can perform any of three experiments to help it decide.

$$e_0 = \text{No inspection report (no cost)}$$

$$e_1 = \text{Regular inspection report (cost: \$5)}$$

$$e_2 = \text{Special life report (cost: \$20)}$$

On the basis of this report, the company can classify the applicant as follows.

$$T_1 = \text{Applicant seems to be a standard risk}$$

$$T_2 = \text{Applicant seems to be a substandard risk}$$

$$T_3 = \text{Applicant seems to be a sub-substandard risk}$$

Let $P(s|T)$ represent the probability that an applicant is in state s when the report indicates that he or she is in state T. For example, $P(s_1|T_2)$ represents the probability that an applicant is a standard risk (s_1) when the report indicates that he or she is a substandard risk (T_2). These probabilities, shown in Table 2, are based on Bayes' formula.

Table 2

	Regular Report			Special Report		
True State	$P(s_i\|T_1)$	$P(s_i\|T_2)$	$P(s_i\|T_3)$	$P(s_i\|T_1)$	$P(s_i\|T_2)$	$P(s_i\|T_3)$
s_1	.9695	.8411	.7377	.9984	.2081	.2299
s_2	.0251	.1309	.1148	.0012	.7850	.0268
s_3	.0054	.0280	.1475	.0004	.0069	.7433

Table 2 shows that $P(s_2|T_2)$, the probability that an applicant actually is substandard (s_2) if the regular report indicates substandard (T_2) is only .1309, while $P(s_2|T_2)$, using the special report, is .7850.

We now have probabilities and payoffs that can be used to find expected values for each possible strategy the company might adopt. There are many possibilities here: the company can use one of three experiments, the experiments can indicate one of three states, the company can offer one of three policies, and the applicant can be in one of three states. The figure shows some of these possibilities in a *decision tree.*

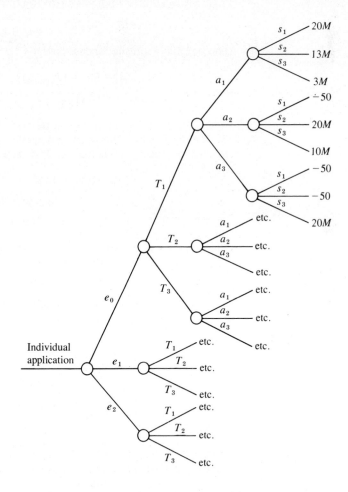

In order to find an optimum strategy for the company, consider an example. Suppose the company decides to perform experiment e_2 (special life report) with the report indicating a substandard risk, T_2. Then the expected values E_1, E_2, E_3 for the three possible actions a_1, a_2, a_3, respectively, are as shown below. (Recall: M is a variable, representing the face amount of the policy in thousands.)

For action a_1 (offer standard policy):

$$E_1 = [P(s_1|T_2)](20M) + [P(s_2|T_2)](13M) + [P(s_3|T_2)](3M)$$
$$= (.2081)(20M) + (.7850)(13M) + (.0069)(3M)$$
$$= 4.162M + 10.205M + .0207M$$
$$\approx 14.388M.$$

For action a_2 (offer a substandard policy):

$$E_2 = [P(s_1|T_2)](-50) + [P(s_2|T_2)](20M) + [P(s_3|T_2)](10M)$$
$$= (.2081)(-50) + (.7850)(20M) + (.0069)(10M)$$
$$= 15.769M - 10.405.$$

For action a_3 (offer a sub-substandard policy):

$$E_3 = [P(s_1|T_2)](-50) + [P(s_2|T_2)](-50) + [P(s_3|T_2)](20M)$$
$$= .138M - 49.655.$$

Strategy a_2 is better than a_3 (for any positive M, $15.769M - 10.405 > .138M - 49.655$). The only choice is between strategies a_1 and a_2. Strategy a_2 is superior if it leads to a higher expected value than a_1. This happens for all values of M such that

$$15.769M - 10.405 > 14.388M$$
$$1.381M > 10.405$$
$$M > 7.535.$$

If the applicant applies for more than $7535 of insurance, the company should use strategy a_2; otherwise it should use a_1.

Similar analyses can be performed for all possible strategies from the decision tree above to find the best strategy. It turns out that the company will maximize its expected profits if it offers a standard policy to all people applying for less than $50,000 in life insurance, with a special report form required for all others.

EXERCISES

1. Find the expected values for each strategy a_1, a_2, and a_3 if the insurance company performs experiment e_1 (a regular report) with the report indicating that the applicant is a substandard risk.

2. Find the expected values for each action if the company performs e_1 with the report indicating that the applicant is a standard risk.

3. Find the expected values for each strategy if e_0 (no report) is selected. (Hint: use the proportions given for the three states s_1, s_2, and s_3 as the probabilities.)

8.4 Strictly Determined Games

The word *game* in the title of this section may have led you to think of checkers or perhaps some card game. While **game theory** does have some application to these recreational games, it was developed in the 1940's to analyze competitive situations in business, warfare, and social situations. Game theory deals with how to make decisions when in competition with an aggressive opponent.

A game can be set up with a payoff matrix, such as the one shown below. This game involves the two players A and B, and is called a **two-person game.** Player A can choose either of the two rows, 1 or 2, while player B can choose either column 1 or column 2. A player's choice is called a **strategy,** just as before. The payoff is at the intersection of the row and column selected. As a general agreement, a positive number represents a payoff from B to A; a negative number represents a payoff from A to B. For example, if A chooses row 2 and B chooses column 2, then B pays $4 to A.

$$\begin{array}{c} & & \text{B} \\ & & \begin{array}{cc} 1 & 2 \end{array} \\ \text{A} \begin{array}{c} 1 \\ 2 \end{array} & \left[\begin{array}{cc} 2 & -1 \\ -3 & 4 \end{array} \right] \end{array}$$

EXAMPLE 1

In the payoff matrix shown above, suppose A chooses row 1 and B chooses column 2. Who gets what?

Row 1 and column 2 lead to the number -1. This number represents a payoff of $1 from A to B. ■

While the numbers in the payoff matrix above represent money, they could just as well represent goods or other property.

In the game above, no money enters the game from the outside; whenever one player wins, the other loses. Such a game model is called a **zero-sum game.** The stock market is not a zero-sum game. Stocks can go up or down according to outside forces. Therefore, it is possible that all investors can make or lose money.

Only two-person zero-sum games are discussed in the rest of this chapter. Each player can have many different options. In particular, an $m \times n$ matrix game is one in which player A has m strategies (rows) and player B has n strategies (columns).

Dominant Strategies In the rest of this section, the best possible strategy for each player is determined. Let us begin with the 3×3 game defined by the following matrix.

$$\begin{array}{c} & \begin{array}{ccc} 1 & 2 & 3 \end{array} \\ \begin{array}{c} 1 \\ 2 \\ 3 \end{array} & \left[\begin{array}{ccc} -3 & -6 & 10 \\ 3 & 0 & -9 \\ 5 & -4 & -8 \end{array} \right] \end{array}$$

From B's viewpoint, strategy 2 is better than strategy 1 no matter which strategy A selects. This can be seen by comparing the two columns. If A chooses row 1, receiving $6 from A is better than receiving $3; in row 2 breaking even is better than paying $3, and in row 3, getting $4 from A is better than paying $5. Therefore, B should never select strategy 1. Strategy 2 is said to *dominate* strategy 1, and strategy 1 (the dominated strategy) can be removed from consideration, producing the following reduced matrix.

$$\begin{array}{c} \\ 1 \\ 2 \\ 3 \end{array} \begin{array}{cc} 2 & 3 \\ \begin{bmatrix} -6 & 10 \\ 0 & -9 \\ -4 & -8 \end{bmatrix} \end{array}$$

Either player may have dominated strategies. In fact, after a dominated strategy for one player is removed, the other player may then have a dominated strategy where there was none before.

Dominant Strategies

A row for A **dominates** another row if every entry in the first row is *larger* than the corresponding entry in the second row. For a column for B to dominate another, each entry must be *smaller*.

In the 3×2 matrix above, neither player now has a dominated strategy. From A's viewpoint strategy 1 is best if B chooses strategy 3, while strategy 2 is best if B chooses strategy 1. Verify that there are no dominated strategies for either player.

EXAMPLE 2

Find any dominated strategies in the games having the following payoff matrices.

(a)

$$\begin{array}{c} \\ 1 \\ 2 \end{array} \begin{array}{cccc} 1 & 2 & 3 & 4 \\ \begin{bmatrix} -8 & -4 & -6 & -9 \\ -3 & 0 & -9 & 12 \end{bmatrix} \end{array}$$

Here every entry in column 3 is smaller than the corresponding entry in column 2. Thus, column 3 dominates column 2. By removing the dominated column 2, the final game is as follows.

$$\begin{array}{c} \\ 1 \\ 2 \end{array} \begin{array}{ccc} 1 & 3 & 4 \\ \begin{bmatrix} -8 & -6 & -9 \\ -3 & -9 & 12 \end{bmatrix} \end{array}$$

(b)

$$\begin{array}{c} \\ 1 \\ 2 \\ 3 \end{array} \begin{array}{cc} 1 & 2 \\ \begin{bmatrix} 3 & -2 \\ 0 & 8 \\ 6 & 4 \end{bmatrix} \end{array}$$

Each entry in row 3 is greater than the corresponding entry in row 1, so that row 3 dominates row 1. Removing row 1 gives the following game.

$$\begin{array}{c} \\ 2 \\ 3 \end{array} \begin{array}{cc} 1 & 2 \\ \begin{bmatrix} 0 & 8 \\ 6 & 4 \end{bmatrix} \end{array}$$

Strictly Determined Games   Which strategies should the players choose in the following game?

$$
A \begin{array}{c} \\ 1 \\ 2 \\ 3 \end{array}
\begin{array}{c}
\\
\begin{array}{ccc} 1 & 2 & 3 \end{array} \\
\left[\begin{array}{ccc}
-9 & 11 & -4 \\
2 & 3 & 5 \\
-1 & -9 & 6
\end{array} \right]
\end{array}
$$

The goal of game theory is to find **optimum strategies,** those which are the most profitable to the respective players. The payoff which results from each player's choosing the optimum strategy is called the **value** of the game.

The simplest strategy for a player is to consistently choose a certain row (or column). Such a strategy is called a **pure strategy,** in contrast to strategies requiring the random choice of a row (or column); these alternate strategies are discussed in the next section.*

To choose a pure strategy in the game above, player A could choose row 1, in hopes of getting the payoff of $11. However, B would quickly discover this, and start playing column 1. By playing column 1, B would receive $9 from A. If A chooses row 2 consistently, then B would again minimize outgo by choosing column 1 (a payoff of $2 by B to A is better than paying $3 or $5, respectively, to A). By choosing row 3 consistently, A would cause B to choose column 2. In summary, by choosing a given row consistently, A would cause the following actions by B.

A Chooses Pure Strategy	Then B Would Choose	With Payoff
row 1	column 1	$9 to B
row 2	column 1	$2 to A
row 3	column 2	$9 to B

Based on these results, A's optimum strategy is to choose row 2; in this way A will guarantee a minimum payoff of $2 per play of the game, no matter what B does.

The optimum pure strategy in this game for A (the *row* player), is found by identifying the *smallest* number in each row of the payoff matrix; the row giving the *largest* such number gives the optimum strategy.

By going through a similar analysis for player B, we find that B should choose that column which will minimize the amount that A can win. In the game above, B will pay $2 to A if B consistently chooses column 1. By choosing column 2 consistently, B will pay $11 to A, and by choosing column 3 player B will pay $6 to A. The optimum strategy for B is thus to choose column 1—with each play of the game B will pay $2 to A.

The optimum pure strategy in this game for B (the column player) is to identify the *largest* number in each column of the payoff matrix, and then choose the column producing the *smallest* such number.

---

*In this section we solve (find the optimum strategies for) only games which have optimum *pure* strategies.

In the game above, the entry 2 is both the *smallest* entry in its *row* and the *largest* entry in its *column*. Such an entry is called a **saddle point.** (See Figure 3.) As Example 3(c) shows, there may be more than one such entry, but then the entries will have the same value.

Optimum Pure

Strategy

> In a game with a saddle point, the optimum pure strategy for player A is to choose the row containing the saddle point, while the optimum pure strategy for B is to choose the column containing the saddle point.

A game with a saddle point is called a **strictly determined game.** By using these optimum strategies, A and B will ensure that the same amount always changes hands with each play of the game; this amount, given by the saddle point, is the value of the game. The value of the game above is $2. A game having a value of 0 is a **fair game;** the game above is not fair.

The name *saddle point* comes from a saddle. The seat of the saddle is the maximum from one direction and the minimum from another direction.

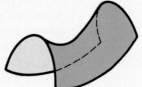

FIGURE 3

EXAMPLE 3

Find the saddle points in the following games.

(a)

$$\begin{array}{c} & \begin{matrix} 1 & 2 \end{matrix} \\ \begin{matrix} 1 \\ 2 \\ 3 \\ 4 \end{matrix} & \begin{bmatrix} 2 & 2 \\ 0 & 4 \\ 1 & 6 \\ 3 & 7 \end{bmatrix} \end{array}$$

The number that is both the smallest number in its row and the largest number in its column is 3. Thus, 3 is the saddle point, and the game has value 3. The strategies producing the saddle point can be written (4, 1). (A's strategy is written first.)

(b)

$$\begin{array}{c} & \begin{matrix} 1 & 2 \end{matrix} \\ \begin{matrix} 1 \\ 2 \end{matrix} & \begin{bmatrix} 6 & 5 \\ 2 & 3 \end{bmatrix} \end{array}$$

The saddle point is 5, at strategies (1, 2).

(c)

$$\begin{array}{c} & \begin{matrix} 1 & 2 & 3 & 4 \end{matrix} \\ \begin{matrix} 1 \\ 2 \end{matrix} & \begin{bmatrix} 4 & 6 & 4 & 12 \\ -8 & -9 & 3 & 2 \end{bmatrix} \end{array}$$

The saddle point, 4, occurs with either of two strategies, (1, 1), or (1, 3). The value of the game is 4. (None of the games in parts (a), (b), or (c) of this example are fair games: none had a value of 0.)

(d)

$$\begin{array}{c} \\ 1 \\ 2 \end{array} \begin{array}{ccc} 1 & 2 & 3 \\ \left[\begin{array}{ccc} 3 & 6 & -2 \\ 8 & -3 & 5 \end{array}\right] \end{array}$$

There is no number which is both the smallest number in its row and the largest number in its column, so that the game has no saddle point. Since the game has no saddle point, it is not strictly determined. In the next section we look at methods for finding optimum strategies for such games. ▪

8.4 EXERCISES

In the following game, decide on the payoff when the strategies of Exercises 1–6 are used.

$$\begin{array}{c} \\ \\ A \end{array} \begin{array}{c} \\ 1 \\ 2 \\ 3 \end{array} \begin{array}{ccc} & \mathbf{B} & \\ 1 & 2 & 3 \\ \left[\begin{array}{ccc} 6 & -4 & 0 \\ 3 & -2 & 6 \\ -1 & 5 & 11 \end{array}\right] \end{array}$$

1. (1, 1) **2.** (1, 2) **3.** (2, 2) **4.** (2, 3) **5.** (3, 1) **6.** (3, 2)

7. Does the game have any dominated strategies?

8. Does it have a saddle point?

Remove any dominated strategies in the games in Exercises 9–14. (From now on, we will save space by deleting the names of the strategies.)

9. $\left[\begin{array}{ccc} 0 & -2 & 8 \\ 3 & -1 & -9 \end{array}\right]$

10. $\left[\begin{array}{cc} 6 & 5 \\ 3 & 8 \\ -1 & -4 \end{array}\right]$

11. $\left[\begin{array}{cc} 1 & 4 \\ 4 & -1 \\ 3 & 5 \\ -4 & 0 \end{array}\right]$

12. $\left[\begin{array}{cccc} 2 & 3 & 1 & -5 \\ -1 & 5 & 4 & 1 \\ 1 & 0 & 2 & -3 \end{array}\right]$

13. $\left[\begin{array}{ccc} 8 & 12 & -7 \\ -2 & 1 & 4 \end{array}\right]$

14. $\left[\begin{array}{cc} 6 & 2 \\ -1 & 10 \\ 3 & 5 \end{array}\right]$

When it exists, find the saddle point and the value of the game in Exercises 15–24. Identify any games that are strictly determined.

15. $\left[\begin{array}{cc} 3 & 5 \\ 2 & -5 \end{array}\right]$

16. $\left[\begin{array}{cc} 7 & 8 \\ -2 & 15 \end{array}\right]$

17. $\left[\begin{array}{ccc} 3 & -4 & 1 \\ 5 & 3 & -2 \end{array}\right]$

18. $\left[\begin{array}{cccc} -4 & 2 & -3 & -7 \\ 4 & 3 & 5 & -9 \end{array}\right]$

19. $\left[\begin{array}{cc} -6 & 2 \\ -1 & -10 \\ 3 & 5 \end{array}\right]$

20. $\left[\begin{array}{ccccc} 1 & 4 & -3 & 1 & -1 \\ 2 & 5 & 0 & 4 & 10 \\ 1 & -3 & 2 & 5 & 2 \end{array}\right]$

21. $\left[\begin{array}{ccc} 2 & 3 & 1 \\ -1 & 4 & -7 \\ 5 & 2 & 0 \\ 8 & -4 & -1 \end{array}\right]$

22. $\left[\begin{array}{cccc} 3 & 8 & -4 & -9 \\ -1 & -2 & -3 & 0 \\ -2 & 6 & -4 & 5 \end{array}\right]$

23. $\begin{bmatrix} -6 & 1 & 4 & 2 \\ 9 & 3 & -8 & -7 \end{bmatrix}$ **24.** $\begin{bmatrix} 6 & -1 \\ 0 & 3 \\ 4 & 0 \end{bmatrix}$

25. When a football team has the ball and is planning its next play, it can choose one of several plays or strategies. The success of the chosen play depends largely on how well the other team "reads" the chosen play. Suppose a team with the ball (team A) can choose from three plays, while the opposition (team B) has four possible strategies. The numbers shown in the following payoff matrix represent yards of gain to team A.

$$\begin{bmatrix} 9 & -3 & -4 & 16 \\ 12 & 9 & 6 & 8 \\ -5 & -2 & 3 & 18 \end{bmatrix}$$

Find the saddle point. Find the value of the game.

26. Two armies, A and B, are involved in a war game. Each army has available three different strategies, with payoffs as shown below. These payoffs represent square kilometers of land with positive numbers representing gains by A.

$$\begin{bmatrix} 3 & -8 & -9 \\ 0 & 6 & -12 \\ -8 & 4 & -10 \end{bmatrix}$$

Find the saddle point and the value of the game.

27. Write a payoff matrix for the child's game *stone, scissors, paper*. Each of two children writes down one of these three words, *stone, scissors,* or *paper*. If the words are the same, the game is a tie. Otherwise, *stone* beats *scissors* (since stone can break scissors), *scissors* beats *paper* (since scissors can cut paper), and *paper* beats *stone* (since paper can hide stone). The winner receives $1 from the loser; no money changes hands in case of a tie. Is the game strictly determined?

28. John and Joann play a finger matching game—each shows one or two fingers at the same time. If the sum of the number of fingers showing is even, Joann pays John that number of dollars; for an odd sum, John pays Joann. Find the payoff matrix for this game. Is the game strictly determined?

29. Two merchants are planning competing stores to serve an area of three small cities. The fraction of the total population that live in each city is shown in the figure. If both merchants locate in the same city, merchant A will get 65% of the total business. If the merchants locate in different cities, each will get 80% of the business in the city it is in, and A will get 60% of the business from the city not containing B. Payoffs are measured by the number of percentage points above or below 50%. Write a payoff matrix for this game. Is this game strictly determined?

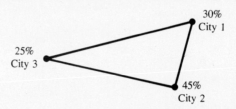

30. Suppose the payoff matrix for a game has at least three rows. Also, suppose that row 1 dominates row 2, and row 2 dominates row 3. Show that row 1 must dominate row 3.

8.5 Mixed Strategies

As we saw earlier, not every game has a saddle point. However, two-person zero-sum games still have optimum strategies, even if the strategy is not as simple as the ones we saw earlier. In a game with a saddle point, the optimum strategy for player A is to pick the row containing the saddle point. Such a strategy is called a *pure strategy,* since the same row is always chosen.

If there is no saddle point, then it will be necessary for both players to mix their strategies. For example, A will sometimes play row 1, sometimes row 2, and so on. If this were done in some specific pattern, the competitor would soon guess it and play accordingly.

For this reason, it is best to mix strategies according to previously determined probabilities. For example, if a player has only two strategies and has decided to play them with equal probability, the random choice could be made by tossing a fair coin, letting heads represent one strategy and tails the other. This would result in each strategy being used about equally over the long run. However, on a particular play it would not be possible to predetermine the strategy to be used. Some other device, such as a spinner, is necessary for more than two strategies, or when the probabilities are not 1/2.

EXAMPLE 1

Suppose a game has payoff matrix

$$\begin{bmatrix} -1 & 2 \\ 1 & 0 \end{bmatrix},$$

where the entries represent dollar winnings. Suppose player A chooses row 1 with probability 1/3 and row 2 with probability 2/3, and player B chooses each column with probability 1/2. Find the expected value of the game.

Assume that rows and columns are chosen independently, so that

$$P(\text{row 1, column 1}) = P(\text{row 1}) \cdot P(\text{column 1}) = \frac{1}{3} \cdot \frac{1}{2} = \frac{1}{6}$$

$$P(\text{row 1, column 2}) = P(\text{row 1}) \cdot P(\text{column 2}) = \frac{1}{3} \cdot \frac{1}{2} = \frac{1}{6}$$

$$P(\text{row 2, column 1}) = P(\text{row 2}) \cdot P(\text{column 1}) = \frac{2}{3} \cdot \frac{1}{2} = \frac{1}{3}$$

$$P(\text{row 2, column 2}) = P(\text{row 2}) \cdot P(\text{column 2}) = \frac{2}{3} \cdot \frac{1}{2} = \frac{1}{3}.$$

The table below lists the probability of each possible outcome, along with the payoff to player A.

Outcome	Probability of Outcome	Payoff for A
row 1, column 1	1/6	−1
row 1, column 2	1/6	2
row 2, column 1	1/3	1
row 2, column 2	1/3	0

The expected value of the game is given by the sum of the products of the probabilities and the payoffs, or

$$\text{expected value} = \frac{1}{6}(-1) + \frac{1}{6}(2) + \frac{1}{3}(1) + \frac{1}{3}(0) = \frac{1}{2}.$$

In the long run, for a great many plays of the game, the payoff to A will average 1/2 dollar per play of the game. It is important to note that as the mixed strategies used by A and B are changed, the expected value of the game may well change. (See Example 2 below.) ■

Let us generalize the work of Example 1. Let the payoff matrix for a 2 × 2 game be

$$M = \begin{bmatrix} a_{11} & a_{12} \\ a_{21} & a_{22} \end{bmatrix}.$$

Let player A choose row 1 with probability p_1 and row 2 with probability p_2, where $p_1 + p_2 = 1$. Write these probabilities as the row matrix

$$A = [p_1 \quad p_2].$$

Let player B choose column 1 with probability q_1 and column 2 with probability q_2, where $q_1 + q_2 = 1$. Write this as the column matrix

$$B = \begin{bmatrix} q_1 \\ q_2 \end{bmatrix}.$$

The probability of choosing row 1 and column 1 is

$$P(\text{row 1, column 1}) = P(\text{row 1}) \cdot P(\text{column 1}) = p_1 \cdot q_1.$$

In the same way, the probabilities of each possible outcome are shown in the table below, along with the payoff matrix for each outcome.

Outcome	Probability of Outcome	Payoff for A
row 1, column 1	$p_1 \cdot q_1$	a_{11}
row 1, column 2	$p_1 \cdot q_2$	a_{12}
row 2, column 1	$p_2 \cdot q_1$	a_{21}
row 2, column 2	$p_2 \cdot q_2$	a_{22}

The expected value for this game is

$$(p_1 \cdot q_1) \cdot a_{11} + (p_1 \cdot q_2) \cdot a_{12} + (p_2 \cdot q_1) \cdot a_{21} + (p_2 \cdot q_2) \cdot a_{22}.$$

This same result can be written as the matrix product

$$\text{expected value} = [p_1 \quad p_2]\begin{bmatrix} a_{11} & a_{12} \\ a_{21} & a_{22} \end{bmatrix}\begin{bmatrix} q_1 \\ q_2 \end{bmatrix} = AMB.$$

The same method works for games larger than 2×2: let the payoff matrix for a game have dimension $m \times n$; call this matrix $M = [a_{ij}]$. Let the mixed strategy for player A be given by the row matrix

$$A = [p_1 \quad p_2 \quad p_3 \cdots p_m],$$

and the mixed strategy for player B be given by the column matrix

$$B = \begin{bmatrix} q_1 \\ q_2 \\ \vdots \\ q_n \end{bmatrix}.$$

The expected value for this game is the product

$$AMB = [p_1 \quad p_2 \cdots p_m] \begin{bmatrix} a_{11} & a_{12} & \cdots & a_{1n} \\ a_{21} & a_{22} & \cdots & a_{2n} \\ \vdots & & & \vdots \\ a_{m1} & a_{m2} & \cdots & a_{mn} \end{bmatrix} \begin{bmatrix} q_1 \\ q_2 \\ \vdots \\ q_n \end{bmatrix}.$$

EXAMPLE 2

In the game of Example 1, having payoff matrix

$$M = \begin{bmatrix} -1 & 2 \\ 1 & 0 \end{bmatrix},$$

suppose player A chooses row 1 with probability .2, and player B chooses column 1 with the probability .6. Find the expected value of the game.

If A chooses row 1 with probability .2, then row 2 is chosen with probability $1 - .2 = .8$, giving

$$A = [.2 \quad .8].$$

In the same way,

$$B = \begin{bmatrix} .6 \\ .4 \end{bmatrix}.$$

The expected value of this game is given by the product AMB, or

$$AMB = [.2 \quad .8] \begin{bmatrix} -1 & 2 \\ 1 & 0 \end{bmatrix} \begin{bmatrix} .6 \\ .4 \end{bmatrix}$$

$$= [.6 \quad .4] \begin{bmatrix} .6 \\ .4 \end{bmatrix}$$

$$= [.52].$$

On the average, these two strategies will produce a payoff of $.52, or 52¢, for A for each play of the game. This is a little better payoff than the 50¢ found in Example 1. ▪

It turns out, however, that B could cause this payoff to decline by a change of strategy. (Check this by choosing different matrices for B.) For this reason, player A needs to develop an *optimum strategy*—a strategy that will produce the best possible payoff no matter what B does. Just as in the previous section, this is done by finding the largest of the smallest possible amounts that can be won.

To find values of p_1 and p_2 so that the probability vector $[p_1 \quad p_2]$ produces an optimum strategy, start with the payoff matrix

$$M = \begin{bmatrix} -1 & 2 \\ 1 & 0 \end{bmatrix}$$

and assume that A chooses row 1 with probability p_1. If player B chooses column 1, then player A's expectation is given by E_1, where

$$E_1 = -1 \cdot p_1 + 1 \cdot p_2 = -p_1 + p_2.$$

Since $p_1 + p_2 = 1$, we have $p_2 = 1 - p_1$, and

$$E_1 = -p_1 + 1 - p_1$$
$$E_1 = 1 - 2p_1.$$

If B chooses column 2, then A's expected value is given by E_2, where

$$E_2 = 2 \cdot p_1 + 0 \cdot p_2$$
$$E_2 = 2p_1.$$

Draw graphs of $E_1 = 1 - 2p_1$ and $E_2 = 2p_1$; see Figure 4.

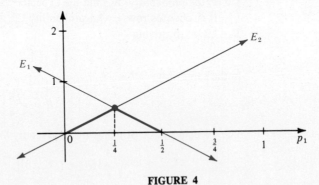

FIGURE 4

As we said, A needs to maximize the smallest amounts that can be won. On the graph, the smallest amounts that can be won are represented by the points of E_2 up to the intersection point. To the right of the intersection point, the smallest amounts that can be won are represented by the points of the line E_1. Player A can maximize the smallest amounts that can be won by choosing the point of intersection itself, the peak of the heavily shaded line in Figure 4.

To find this point of intersection, find the simultaneous solution of the two equations. At the point of intersection, $E_1 = E_2$. Substitute $1 - 2p_1$ for E_1 and $2p_1$ for E_2.

$$E_1 = E_2$$
$$1 - 2p_1 = 2p_1$$
$$1 = 4p_1$$
$$\frac{1}{4} = p_1$$

By this result, player A should choose strategy 1 with probability 1/4, and strategy 2 with probability $1 - 1/4 = 3/4$. By doing so, expected winnings will be maximized. To find the maximum winnings (which is also the value of the game), substitute 1/4 for p_1 in either E_1 or E_2. If we choose E_2,

$$E_2 = 2p_1 = 2\left(\frac{1}{4}\right) = \frac{1}{2},$$

that is, 1/2 dollar, or 50¢. By going through a similar argument for player B, we can find that the optimum strategy for player B is to choose each column with probability 1/2; in this case the value also turns out to be 50¢. In Example 2, A's winnings were 52¢; however, that was because B was not using his optimum strategy.

In the game above, player A can maximize expected winnings by playing row 1 with probability 1/4 and row 2 with probability 3/4. Such a strategy is called a **mixed strategy.** To actually decide which row to use on a given game, player A could use a spinner, such as the one in Figure 5.

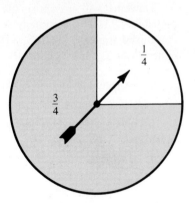

FIGURE 5

EXAMPLE 3

Boll weevils threaten the cotton crop near Hattiesburg. Charles Dawkins owns a small farm; he can protect his crop by spraying with a potent (and expensive) insecticide. In trying to decide what to do, Dawkins first sets up a payoff matrix. The numbers in the matrix represent his profits.

		States of nature	
		Boll weevil attack	No attack
Strategies	Spray	$14,000	$7000
	Don't spray	−$3000	$8000

Let p_1 represent the probability with which Dawkins chooses strategy 1, so that $1 - p_1$ is the probability with which he chooses strategy 2. If nature chooses strategy 1 (an attack), then Dawkins' expected value is

$$E_1 = 14{,}000p_1 - 3000(1 - p_1)$$
$$= 14{,}000p_1 - 3000 + 3000p_1$$
$$E_1 = 17{,}000p_1 - 3000.$$

For nature's strategy 2 (no attack), Dawkins has an expected value of

$$E_2 = 7000p_1 + 8000(1 - p_1)$$
$$= 7000p_1 + 8000 - 8000p_1$$
$$E_2 = 8000 - 1000p_1.$$

As suggested by the work above, to maximize his expected profit, Dawkins should find the value of p_1 for which $E_1 = E_2$.

$$E_1 = E_2$$
$$17{,}000p_1 - 3000 = 8000 - 1000p_1$$
$$18{,}000p_1 = 11{,}000$$
$$p_1 = 11/18$$

Thus, $p_2 = 1 - p_1 = 1 - 11/18 = 7/18$.

Dawkins will maximize his expected profit if he chooses strategy 1 with probability 11/18 and strategy 2 with probability 7/18. His expected profit from this mixed strategy, [11/18 7/18], can be found by substituting 11/18 for p_1 in either E_1 or E_2. If we choose E_1,

$$\text{expected profit} = 17{,}000\left(\frac{11}{18}\right) - 3000 = \frac{133{,}000}{18} \approx \$7400. \quad \blacksquare$$

To obtain a formula for the optimum strategy in a game that is not strictly determined, start with the matrix

$$M = \begin{bmatrix} a_{11} & a_{12} \\ a_{21} & a_{22} \end{bmatrix},$$

the payoff matrix of the game. Assume that A chooses row 1 with probability p_1. The expected value for A, assuming that B plays column 1, is E_1, where

$$E_1 = a_{11} \cdot p_1 + a_{21} \cdot (1 - p_1).$$

The expected value for A if B chooses column 2 is E_2, where

$$E_2 = a_{12} \cdot p_1 + a_{22} \cdot (1 - p_1).$$

As above, the optimum strategy for player A is found by letting $E_1 = E_2$.

$$a_{11} \cdot p_1 + a_{21} \cdot (1 - p_1) = a_{12} \cdot p_1 + a_{22} \cdot (1 - p_1)$$

Solve this equation for p_1.

$$a_{11} \cdot p_1 + a_{21} - a_{21} \cdot p_1 = a_{12} \cdot p_1 + a_{22} - a_{22} \cdot p_1$$

$$a_{11} \cdot p_1 - a_{21} \cdot p_1 - a_{12} \cdot p_1 + a_{22} \cdot p_1 = a_{22} - a_{21}$$

$$p_1(a_{11} - a_{21} - a_{12} + a_{22}) = a_{22} - a_{21}$$

$$p_1 = \frac{a_{22} - a_{21}}{a_{11} - a_{21} - a_{12} + a_{22}}$$

Since $p_2 = 1 - p_1$,

$$p_2 = 1 - \frac{a_{22} - a_{21}}{a_{11} - a_{21} - a_{12} + a_{22}}$$

$$= \frac{a_{11} - a_{21} - a_{12} + a_{22} - (a_{22} - a_{21})}{a_{11} - a_{21} - a_{12} + a_{22}}$$

$$= \frac{a_{11} - a_{12}}{a_{11} - a_{21} - a_{12} + a_{22}}.$$

This result is valid only if $a_{11} - a_{21} - a_{12} + a_{22} \neq 0$; it turns out that this condition is satisfied if the game is not strictly determined.

There is a similar result for player B, which is included in the following summary.

Optimum Strategies in a Non-Strictly Determined Game

Let a non-strictly determined game have payoff matrix

$$\begin{bmatrix} a_{11} & a_{12} \\ a_{21} & a_{22} \end{bmatrix}.$$

The optimum strategy for player A is $[p_1 \quad p_2]$, where

$$p_1 = \frac{a_{22} - a_{21}}{a_{11} - a_{21} - a_{12} + a_{22}} \quad \text{and} \quad p_2 = \frac{a_{11} - a_{12}}{a_{11} - a_{21} - a_{12} + a_{22}}.$$

The optimum strategy for player B is $\begin{bmatrix} q_1 \\ q_2 \end{bmatrix}$, where

$$q_1 = \frac{a_{22} - a_{12}}{a_{11} - a_{21} - a_{12} + a_{22}} \quad \text{and} \quad q_2 = \frac{a_{11} - a_{21}}{a_{11} - a_{21} - a_{12} + a_{22}}.$$

The value of the game is

$$\frac{a_{11}a_{22} - a_{12}a_{21}}{a_{11} - a_{21} - a_{12} + a_{22}}.$$

EXAMPLE 4

Suppose a game has payoff matrix

$$\begin{bmatrix} 5 & -2 \\ -3 & -1 \end{bmatrix}.$$

Here $a_{11} = 5$, $a_{12} = -2$, $a_{21} = -3$, and $a_{22} = -1$. To find the optimum strategy for player A, first find p_1.

$$p_1 = \frac{-1 - (-3)}{5 - (-3) - (-2) + (-1)} = \frac{2}{9}$$

Player A should play row 1 with probability 2/9 and row 2 with probability $1 - 2/9 = 7/9$.

For player B,

$$q_1 = \frac{-1 - (-2)}{5 - (-3) - (-2) + (-1)} = \frac{1}{9}.$$

Player B should choose column 1 with probability 1/9, and column 2 with probability 8/9. The value of the game is

$$\frac{5(-1) - (-2)(-3)}{5 - (-3) - (-2) + (-1)} = \frac{-11}{9}.$$

On the average, B will receive 11/9 dollar from A per play of the game. ■

8.5 EXERCISES

1. Suppose a game has payoff matrix

$$\begin{bmatrix} 3 & -4 \\ -5 & 2 \end{bmatrix}.$$

Suppose that player B uses the strategy $\begin{bmatrix} .3 \\ .7 \end{bmatrix}$. Find the expected value of the game if player A uses the strategy

(a) $[.5 \quad .5]$; (b) $[.1 \quad .9]$; (c) $[.8 \quad .2]$; (d) $[.2 \quad .8]$.

2. Suppose a game has payoff matrix

$$\begin{bmatrix} 0 & -4 & 1 \\ 3 & 2 & -4 \\ 1 & -1 & 0 \end{bmatrix}.$$

Find the expected value of the game for the following strategies for players A and B.

(a) $A = [.1 \quad .4 \quad .5]$; $B = \begin{bmatrix} .2 \\ .4 \\ .4 \end{bmatrix}$ (b) $A = [.3 \quad .4 \quad .3]$; $B = \begin{bmatrix} .8 \\ .1 \\ .1 \end{bmatrix}$

Find the optimum strategy for both player A and player B in the games in Exercises 3–14. Find the value of the game. Be sure to look for a saddle point first.

3. $\begin{bmatrix} 5 & 1 \\ 3 & 4 \end{bmatrix}$ 4. $\begin{bmatrix} -4 & 5 \\ 3 & -4 \end{bmatrix}$ 5. $\begin{bmatrix} -2 & 0 \\ 3 & -4 \end{bmatrix}$ 6. $\begin{bmatrix} 6 & 2 \\ -1 & 10 \end{bmatrix}$

7. $\begin{bmatrix} 4 & -3 \\ -1 & 7 \end{bmatrix}$ 8. $\begin{bmatrix} 0 & 6 \\ 4 & 0 \end{bmatrix}$ 9. $\begin{bmatrix} -2 & \frac{1}{2} \\ 0 & -3 \end{bmatrix}$ 10. $\begin{bmatrix} 6 & \frac{3}{4} \\ \frac{2}{3} & -1 \end{bmatrix}$

11. $\begin{bmatrix} \frac{8}{3} & -\frac{1}{2} \\ \frac{3}{4} & -\frac{5}{12} \end{bmatrix}$ 12. $\begin{bmatrix} -\frac{1}{2} & \frac{2}{3} \\ \frac{7}{8} & -\frac{3}{4} \end{bmatrix}$ 13. $\begin{bmatrix} -1 & 2 \\ 3 & 1 \end{bmatrix}$ 14. $\begin{bmatrix} 8 & 18 \\ -4 & 2 \end{bmatrix}$

Remove any dominated strategies and then find the optimum strategies for each player and the value of the game.

15. $\begin{bmatrix} -4 & 9 \\ 3 & -5 \\ 8 & 7 \end{bmatrix}$

16. $\begin{bmatrix} 3 & 4 & -1 \\ -2 & 1 & 0 \end{bmatrix}$

17. $\begin{bmatrix} 8 & 6 & 3 \\ -1 & -2 & 4 \end{bmatrix}$

18. $\begin{bmatrix} -1 & 6 \\ 8 & 3 \\ -2 & 5 \end{bmatrix}$

19. $\begin{bmatrix} 9 & -1 & 6 \\ 13 & 11 & 8 \\ 6 & 0 & 9 \end{bmatrix}$

20. $\begin{bmatrix} 4 & 8 & -3 \\ 2 & -1 & 1 \\ 7 & 9 & 0 \end{bmatrix}$

21. Suppose Allied Manufacturing Company decides to put its new product on the market with a big television and radio advertising campaign. At the same time, the company finds out that its major competitor, Bates Manufacturing, has also decided to launch a big advertising campaign for a similar product. The payoff matrix below shows the increased sales (in millions) for Allied, as well as the decreased sales for Bates.

$$\begin{array}{cc} & \text{Bates} \\ & \begin{array}{cc} \text{TV} & \text{Radio} \end{array} \\ \text{Allied} \begin{array}{c} \text{TV} \\ \text{Radio} \end{array} & \begin{bmatrix} 1.0 & -.7 \\ -.5 & .5 \end{bmatrix} \end{array}$$

Find the optimum strategy for Allied Manufacturing and the value of the game.

22. The payoffs in the table below represent the differences between Boeing Aircraft Company's profit and its competitor's profit for two prices (in millions) on commercial jet transports, with positive payoffs being in Boeing's favor. What should Boeing's price strategy be?*

$$\begin{array}{cc} & \begin{array}{c} \text{Competitor's} \\ \text{price strategy} \\ \begin{array}{cc} 4.75 & 4.9 \end{array} \end{array} \\ \text{Boeing's strategy} \begin{array}{c} 4.9 \\ 4.75 \end{array} & \begin{bmatrix} -4 & 2 \\ 2 & 0 \end{bmatrix} \end{array}$$

23. The number of cases of African flu has reached epidemic levels. The disease is known to have two strains with similar symptoms. Doctor De Luca has two medicines available: the first is 60% effective against the first strain and 40% effective against the second. The second medicine is completely effective against the second strain but ineffective against the first. Use the matrix below to decide which medicine she should use and the results she can expect.

$$\begin{array}{cc} & \begin{array}{c} \text{Strain} \\ \begin{array}{cc} 1 & 2 \end{array} \end{array} \\ \text{Medicine} \begin{array}{c} 1 \\ 2 \end{array} & \begin{bmatrix} .6 & .4 \\ 0 & 1 \end{bmatrix} \end{array}$$

24. Players A and B play a game in which each show either one or two fingers at the same time. If there is a match, A wins the amount equal to the total number of fingers shown. If there is no match, B wins the amount of dollars equal to the number of fingers shown.

(a) Write the payoff matrix.

(b) Find optimum strategies for A and B and the value of the game.

---

*From "Pricing, Investment, and Games of Strategy," by Georges Brigham in *Management Sciences Models and Techniques*, Vol. 1. Copyright © 1960 Pergamon Press, Ltd. Reprinted with permission.

25. Repeat Exercise 24 if each player may show either 0 or 2 fingers with the same sort of payoffs.

26. In the game of matching coins, two players each flip a coin. If both coins match (both show heads or both show tails), player A wins $1. If there is no match, player B wins $1, as in the payoff matrix. Find the optimum strategies for the two players and the value of the game.

$$\begin{bmatrix} 1 & -1 \\ -1 & 1 \end{bmatrix}$$

27. **The Huckster*** Merrill has a concession at Yankee Stadium for the sale of sunglasses and umbrellas. The business places quite a strain on him, the weather being what it is. He has observed that he can sell about 500 umbrellas when it rains, and about 100 when it is sunny; in the latter case he can also sell 1000 sunglasses. Umbrellas cost him 50 cents and sell for $1; glasses cost 20 cents and sell for 50 cents. He is willing to invest $250 in the project. Everything that is not sold is considered a total loss.

He assembles the facts regarding profit in a table.

		Selling during	
		Rain	Shine
Buying for	Rain	250	−150
	Shine	−150	350

He immediately takes heart, for this is a mixed-strategy game, and he should be able to find a stabilizing strategy which will save him from the vagaries of the weather. Find the best mixed strategy for Merrill.

28. **The Squad Car*** This is a somewhat more harrowing example. A police dispatcher was conveying information and opinion, as fast as she could speak, to Patrol Car 2, cruising on the U.S. Highway: ". . . in a Cadillac; just left Hitch's Tavern on the old Country Road. Direction of flight unknown. Suspect Plesset is seriously wounded but may have an even chance if he finds a good doctor, like Doctor Haydon, soon—even Veterinary Paxson might save him, but his chances would be halved. Plesset shot Officer Flood, who has a large family."

Deputy Henderson finally untangled the microphone from the riot gun and his size 14 shoes. He replied: "Roger. We can cut him off if he heads for Haydon's and we have a fifty-fifty chance of cutting him off at the State Highway if he heads for the vet's. We must cut him off because we can't chase him—Deputy Root got this thing stuck in reverse a while ago, and our cruising has been a disgrace to the department ever since."

The headquarter's carrier-wave again hummed in the speaker, but the dispatcher's musical voice was now replaced by the grating tones of Sheriff Lipp. "If you know anything else, don't tell it. He has a hi-fi radio in that Cad. Get him."

Root suddenly was seized by an idea and stopped struggling with the gearshift. "Henderson, we may not need a gun tonight, but we need a pencil: this is just a two-by-two game. The dispatcher gave us all the dope we need." "You gonna use *her* estimates?" "You got better ones? She's got intuition; besides, that's information from headquarters. Now let's see . . . . . Suppose we head for Haydon's. And suppose Plesset does too; then we rack up one good bandit, if you don't trip on that gun again. But if he heads for Paxson, the chances are three out of four that old doc will kill him."

*From *The Compleat Strategyst* by J. D. Williams. Published 1966, by McGraw-Hill Book Company. Reprinted by permission of The Rand Corporation. This is an excellent nontechnical book on game theory.

"I don't get it." "Well, it didn't come easy. Remember, Haydon would have an even chance—one-half—of saving him. He'd have half as good a chance with Paxson; and half of one-half is one-quarter. So the chance he dies must be three-quarters—subtracting from one, you know."

"Yeah, it's obvious." "Huh. Now if we head for Paxson's it's tougher to figure. First of all, *he* may go to Haydon's, in which case we have to rely on the doc to kill him, of which the chance is only one-half."

"You ought to subtract that from one." "I did. Now suppose he too heads for Paxson's. Either of two things can happen. One is, we catch him, and the chance is one-half. The other is, we don't catch him—and again the chance is one-half—but there is a three-fourths chance that the doc will have a lethal touch. So the overall probability that he will get by us, but not by the doc, is one-half times three-fourths, or three-eighths. Add to that the one-half chance that he doesn't get by us, and we have seven-eighths."

"I don't like this stuff. He's probably getting away while we're doodling." "Relax. He has to figure it out too, doesn't he? And he's in worse shape than we are. Now let's see what we have."

$$\begin{array}{cc} & \textit{Cad goes to} \\ & \text{Haydon} \quad \text{Paxson} \\ \textit{Patrol car goes to} \begin{array}{c} \text{Haydon} \\ \text{Paxson} \end{array} & \left[\begin{array}{cc} 1 & \frac{3}{4} \\ \frac{1}{2} & \frac{7}{8} \end{array} \right] \end{array}$$

"Fractions aren't so good in this light," Root continues. "Let's multiply everything by eight to clean it up. I hear it doesn't hurt anything."

$$\begin{array}{cc} & \textit{Cad} \\ & \text{Haydon} \quad \text{Paxson} \\ \textit{Patrol car} \begin{array}{c} \text{Haydon} \\ \text{Paxson} \end{array} & \left[\begin{array}{cc} 8 & 6 \\ 4 & 7 \end{array} \right] \end{array}$$

"It is now clear that this is a very messy business . . ." "I know." "There is no single strategy which we can safely adopt. I shall therefore compute the best mixed strategy."

What mixed strategy should deputies Root and Henderson pursue?

EXTENDED

APPLICATION

Decision Making in the Military

This example has been reproduced with only minor change from the *Journal of the Operations Research Society of America*, November 1954, pages 365–369.* The article is titled "Military Decision and Game Theory," by O. G. Haywood, Jr. This case is presented unedited so that you can get an idea of the type of articles published in the journals.

A military commander may approach decision with either of two philosophies. He may select his course of action on the basis of his estimate of what his enemy *is able to*

*Reprinted by permission from *Operations Research*, Volume 3, Issue 6, 1954. Copyright 1954 Operations Research Society of America. No further reproduction permitted without the consent of the copyright owner.

do to oppose him. Or, he may make his selection on the basis of his estimate of what his enemy *is going to do.* The former is a doctrine of decision based on enemy capabilities; the latter, on enemy intentions.

The doctrine of decision of the armed forces of the United States is a doctrine based on enemy capabilities. A commander is enjoined to select the course of action which offers the greatest promise of success in view of the enemy capabilities. The process of decision, as approved by the Joint Chiefs of Staff and taught in all service schools, is formalized in a five-step analysis called the *Estimate of the Situation.* These steps are illustrated in the following analysis of an actual World War II battle situation.

General Kenney was Commander of the Allied Air Forces in the Southwest Pacific Area. The struggle for New Guinea reached a critical stage in February 1943. Intelligence reports indicated a Japanese troop and supply convoy was assembling at Rabaul (see Figure 1). Lae was expected to be the unloading point. With this general background Kenney proceeded to make his five-step Estimate of the Situation.

Figure 1 *The Rabaul-Lae Convoy Situation.* The problem is the distribution of reconnaissance to locate a convoy which may sail by either one of two routes.

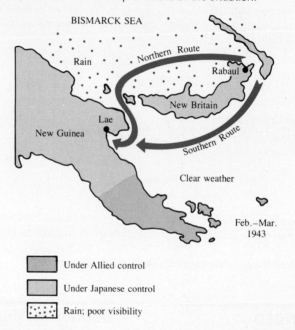

Under Allied control

Under Japanese control

Rain; poor visibility

Step 1. The Mission

General MacArthur as Supreme Commander had ordered Kenney to intercept and inflict maximum destruction on the convoy. This then was Kenney's mission.

Step 2. Situation and Courses of Action

The situation as outlined above was generally known. One new critical factor was pointed out by Kenney's staff. Rain and poor visibility were predicted for the area north of New Britain. Visibility south of the island would be good.

The Japanese commander had two choices for routing his convoy from Rabaul to Lae. He could sail north of New Britain, or he could go south of that island. Either route required three days.

Kenney considered two courses of action, as he discusses in his memoirs. He could concentrate most of his reconnaissance aircraft either along the northern route where visibility would be poor, or along the southern route where clear weather was predicted. Mobility being one of the great advantages of air power, his bombing force could strike the convoy on either route once it was spotted.

Step 3.   Analysis of the Opposing Courses of Action

With each commander having two alternative courses of action, four possible conflicts could ensue. These conflicts are pictured in Figure 2.

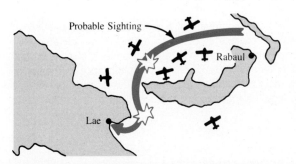

Kenney Strategy: Concentrate reconnaissance on northern route.
Japanese Strategy: Sail northern route.
Estimated Outcome: Although reconnaissance would be hampered by poor visibility, the convoy should be discovered by the second day, which would permit two days of bombing.
TWO DAYS OF BOMBING

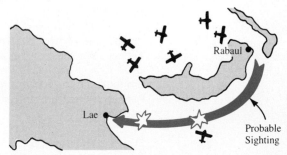

Kenney Strategy: Concentrate reconnaissance on northern route.
Japanese Strategy: Sail southern route.
Estimated Outcome: The convoy would be sailing in clear weather. However, with limited reconnaissance aircraft in this area, the convoy might be missed on the first day. Convoy should be sighted by second day, to permit two days of bombing.
TWO DAYS OF BOMBING

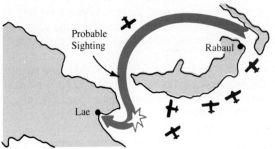

Kenney Strategy: Concentrate reconnaissance on southern route.
Japanese Strategy: Sail northern route.
Estimated Outcome: With poor visibility and limited reconnaissance, Kenney could not expect the convoy to be discovered until it broke out into clear weather on third day. This would permit only one day of bombing.
ONE DAY OF BOMBING

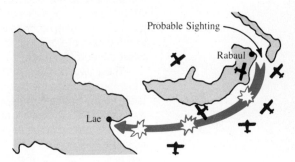

Kenney Strategy: Concentrate reconnaissance on southern route.
Japanese Strategy: Sail southern route.
Estimated Outcome: With good visibility and concentrated reconnaissance in the area, the convoy should be sighted almost as soon as it sailed from Rabaul. This would allow three days of bombing.
THREE DAYS OF BOMBING

Figure 2   *Possible Battles for the Rabaul-Lae Convoy Situation.* Four different engagements of forces may result from the interaction of Kenney's two strategies with the two Japanese from the interaction of Kenney's two strategies with the two Japanese strategies. Neither commander alone can determine which particular battle will result.

Step 4.   Comparison of Available Courses of Action

If Kenney concentrated on the northern route, he ensured one of the two battles of the top row of sketches. However, he alone could not determine which one of these two battles in the top row would result from his decision. Similarly, if Kenney concentrated on the southern route, he ensured one of the battles of the lower row. In the same manner, the Japanese commander could not select a particular battle, but could by his decision assure that the battle would be one of those pictured in the left column or one of those in the right column.

Kenney sought a battle which would provide the maximum opportunity for bombing the convoy. The Japanese commander desired the minimum exposure to bombing. But neither commander could determine the battle which would result from his own decision. Each commander had full and independent freedom to select either one of his alternative strategies. He had to do so with full realization of his opponent's freedom of choice. The particular battle which resulted would be determined by the two independent decisions.

The U.S. doctrine of decision—the doctrine that a commander base his action on his estimate of what the enemy is capable of doing to oppose him—dictated that Kenney select the course of action which offered the greatest promise of success in view of all of the enemy capabilities. If Kenney concentrated his reconnaissance on the northern route, he could expect two days of bombing regardless of his enemy's decision. If Kenney selected his other strategy, he must accept the possibility of a less favorable outcome.

Step 5.   The Decision

Kenney concentrated his reconnaissance aircraft on the northern route.

Discussion

Let us assume that the Japanese commander used a similar philosophy of decision, basing his decision on his enemy's capabilities. Considering the four battles as sketched, the Japanese commander could select either the left or the right column, but could not select the row. If he sailed the northern route, he exposed the convoy to a maximum of two days of bombing. If he sailed the southern route, the convoy might be subjected to three days of bombing. Since he sought minimum exposure to bombing, he should select the northern route.

These two independent choices were the actual decisions which led to the conflict known in history as the Battle of the Bismarck Sea. Kenney concentrated his reconnaissance on the northern route; the Japanese convoy sailed the northern route; the convoy was sighted approximately one day after it sailed; and Allied bombing started shortly thereafter. Although the Battle of the Bismarck Sea ended in a disastrous defeat for the Japanese, we cannot say the Japanese commander erred in his decision. A similar convoy had reached Lae with minor losses two months earlier. The need was critical, and the Japanese were prepared to pay a high price. They did not know that Kenney had modified a number of his aircraft for low-level bombing and had perfected a deadly technique. The U.S. victory was the result of careful planning, thorough training, resolute execution, and tactical surprise of a new weapon—not of error in the Japanese decision.

EXERCISES

1. Use the results of Figure 2 to make a 2 × 2 game. Let the payoffs represent the number of days of bombing.

2. Find any saddle point and optimum strategy for the game.

3. Read the rest of the article used as the source for this example and prepare a discussion of the game theory aspects of the Avranches-Gap situation.

KEY WORDS	state	states of nature	dominated strategy
	transition matrix	strategies	optimum strategy
	Markov chain	payoff matrix	value of the game
	probability vector	utility	pure strategy
	regular transition matrix	decision tree	strictly determined game
	regular Markov chain	two-person game	saddle point
	equilibrium (or fixed) vector	zero-sum game	mixed strategy

Chapter 8   REVIEW EXERCISES

Which of the matrices in Exercises 1–4 could be transition matrices?

1. $\begin{bmatrix} .4 & .6 \\ 1 & 0 \end{bmatrix}$
   2. $\begin{bmatrix} -.2 & 1.2 \\ .8 & .2 \end{bmatrix}$
   3. $\begin{bmatrix} .8 & .2 & 0 \\ 0 & 1 & 0 \\ .1 & .4 & .5 \end{bmatrix}$
   4. $\begin{bmatrix} .6 & .2 & .3 \\ .1 & .5 & .4 \\ .3 & .3 & .4 \end{bmatrix}$

For each of the transition matrices in Exercises 5–8, (a) find the first three powers; (b) find the probability that state 2 changes to state 1 after three repetitions of the experiment.

5. $C = \begin{bmatrix} .6 & .4 \\ 1 & 0 \end{bmatrix}$
   6. $D = \begin{bmatrix} .3 & .7 \\ .5 & .5 \end{bmatrix}$
   7. $E = \begin{bmatrix} .2 & .5 & .3 \\ .1 & .8 & .1 \\ 0 & 1 & 0 \end{bmatrix}$
   8. $F = \begin{bmatrix} .14 & .12 & .74 \\ .35 & .28 & .37 \\ .71 & .24 & .05 \end{bmatrix}$

In Exercises 9–12, use the transition matrices T, along with the given initial distribution D, to find the distribution after two repetitions of the experiment. Also predict the long range distribution.

9. $D = [.3 \quad .7]; T = \begin{bmatrix} .4 & .6 \\ .5 & .5 \end{bmatrix}$

10. $D = [.8 \quad .2]; T = \begin{bmatrix} .7 & .3 \\ .2 & .8 \end{bmatrix}$

11. $D = [.2 \quad .4 \quad .4]; T = \begin{bmatrix} .6 & .2 & .2 \\ .3 & .3 & .4 \\ .5 & .4 & .1 \end{bmatrix}$

12. $D = [.1 \quad .1 \quad .8]; T = \begin{bmatrix} .2 & .3 & .5 \\ .1 & .1 & .8 \\ .7 & .1 & .2 \end{bmatrix}$

13. Currently, 35% of all hot dogs sold in one area are made by Dogkins, while 65% are made by Long Dog. Suppose that Dogkins starts a heavy advertising campaign, with the campaign producing the following transition matrix.

		After campaign	
		Dogkins	Long Dog
Before	Dogkins	.8	.2
campaign	Long Dog	.4	.6

Find the share of the market for each company after

(a) the campaign;   **(b)** three such campaigns.

(c) Predict the long-range market share for Dogkins.

14. A credit card company classifies its customers in three groups, nonusers in a given month, light users, and heavy users. The transition matrix for these states is

$$
\begin{array}{c}
\text{nonuser} \\
\text{light} \\
\text{heavy}
\end{array}
\begin{array}{ccc}
\text{nonuser} & \text{light} & \text{heavy}
\end{array}
\left[
\begin{array}{ccc}
.8 & .15 & .05 \\
.25 & .55 & .2 \\
.04 & .21 & .75
\end{array}
\right].
$$

Suppose the initial distribution for the three states is $[.4 \quad .4 \quad .2]$. Find the distribution after

(a) 1 month;   **(b)** 2 months;   **(c)** 3 months.

(d) What is the long range prediction for the distribution of users?

15. A medical researcher is studying the risk of heart attack in men. She first divides men into three weight categories, thin, normal, and overweight. By studying the ancestors, children, and grandchildren of these men, the researcher comes up with the transition matrix

$$
\begin{array}{c}
\text{thin} \\
\text{normal} \\
\text{overweight}
\end{array}
\begin{array}{ccc}
\text{thin} & \text{normal} & \text{overweight}
\end{array}
\left[
\begin{array}{ccc}
.3 & .5 & .2 \\
.2 & .6 & .2 \\
.1 & .5 & .4
\end{array}
\right].
$$

Find the probability that a person of normal weight has a thin

(a) child;   **(b)** grandchild;   **(c)** great-grandchild.

Find the probability that an overweight man will have an overweight

(d) child;   **(e)** grandchild;   **(f)** great-grandchild.

16. Suppose that in Exercise 15, the distribution of men by weight is initially given by $[.2 \quad .55 \quad .25]$. Find the distribution after

(a) 1 generation;   **(b)** 2 generations;   **(c)** 3 generations.

(d) Find the long range prediction for the distribution of weights.

Which of the following transition matrices are regular?

17. $\begin{bmatrix} .0 & 1 \\ .2 & .8 \end{bmatrix}$

18. $\begin{bmatrix} .4 & .2 & .4 \\ 0 & 1 & 0 \\ .6 & .3 & .1 \end{bmatrix}$

19. $\begin{bmatrix} 1 & 0 & 0 \\ 0 & 1 & 0 \\ .3 & .5 & .2 \end{bmatrix}$

20. In labor-management relations, both labor and management can adopt either a friendly or a hostile attitude. The results are shown in the following payoff matrix. The numbers give the wage gains made by an average worker.

$$
\begin{array}{cc}
& \begin{array}{cc} \textit{Management} \\ \text{Friendly} \quad \text{Hostile} \end{array} \\
\textit{Labor} \begin{array}{c} \text{Friendly} \\ \text{Hostile} \end{array} &
\left[
\begin{array}{cc}
\$600 & \$800 \\
\$400 & \$950
\end{array}
\right]
\end{array}
$$

(a) Suppose the chief negotiator for labor is an optimist. What strategy should he choose?

(b) What strategy should he choose if he is a pessimist?

(c) The chief negotiator for labor feels that there is a 70% chance that the company will be hostile. What strategy should he adopt? What is the expected payoff?

(d) Just before negotiations begin, a new management is installed in the company. There is only a 40% chance that the new management will be hostile. What strategy should be adopted by labor?

21. A candidate for city council can come out in favor of a new factory, be opposed to it, or waffle on the issue. The change in votes for the candidate depends on what her opponent does, with payoffs as shown.

		Opponent		
		favors	waffles	opposes
	favors	0	−1000	−4000
Candidate	waffles	1000	0	−500
	opposes	5000	2000	0

(a) What should the candidate do if she is an optimist?

(b) What should she do if she is a pessimist?

(c) Suppose the candidate's campaign manager feels there is a 40% chance that the opponent will favor the plant, and a 35% chance that he will waffle. What strategy should the candidate adopt? What is the expected change in the number of votes?

(d) The opponent conducts a new poll which shows strong opposition to the new factory. This changes the probability he will favor the factory to 0 and the probability he will waffle to .7. What strategy should our candidate adopt? What is the expected change in the number of votes now?

22. Use the following payoff matrix and decide on the payoff if the given strategies are used.

$$\begin{bmatrix} -2 & 5 & -6 & 3 \\ 0 & -1 & 7 & 5 \\ 2 & 6 & -4 & 4 \end{bmatrix}$$

(a) (1, 1)   (b) (1, 4)   (c) (2, 3)   (d) (3, 4)

(e) Are there any dominated strategies in this game?

(f) Is there a saddle point?

Remove any dominated strategies in the games in Exercises 23–26.

23. $\begin{bmatrix} -11 & 6 & 8 & 9 \\ -10 & -12 & 3 & 2 \end{bmatrix}$ **24.** $\begin{bmatrix} -1 & 9 & 0 \\ 4 & -10 & 6 \\ 8 & -6 & 7 \end{bmatrix}$ **25.** $\begin{bmatrix} -2 & 4 & 1 \\ 3 & 2 & 7 \\ -8 & 1 & 6 \\ 0 & 3 & 9 \end{bmatrix}$ **26.** $\begin{bmatrix} 3 & -1 & 4 \\ 0 & 4 & -1 \\ 1 & 2 & -3 \\ 0 & 0 & 2 \end{bmatrix}$

Find any saddle points for the games in Exercises 27–32. Give the value of the game. Identify any fair games.

27. $\begin{bmatrix} -2 & 3 \\ -4 & 5 \end{bmatrix}$ **28.** $\begin{bmatrix} -4 & 0 & 2 & -5 \\ 6 & 9 & 3 & 8 \end{bmatrix}$ **29.** $\begin{bmatrix} -4 & -1 \\ 6 & 0 \\ 8 & -3 \end{bmatrix}$

30. $\begin{bmatrix} 4 & -1 & 6 \\ -3 & -2 & 0 \\ -1 & -4 & 3 \end{bmatrix}$ **31.** $\begin{bmatrix} 8 & 1 & -7 & 2 \\ -1 & 4 & -3 & 3 \end{bmatrix}$ **32.** $\begin{bmatrix} 2 & -9 \\ 7 & 1 \\ 4 & 2 \end{bmatrix}$

Find the optimum strategies for the games in Exercises 33–36. Find the value of the game.

33. $\begin{bmatrix} 1 & 0 \\ -2 & 3 \end{bmatrix}$

34. $\begin{bmatrix} 2 & -3 \\ -3 & 5 \end{bmatrix}$

35. $\begin{bmatrix} -3 & 5 \\ 1 & 0 \end{bmatrix}$

36. $\begin{bmatrix} 8 & -3 \\ -6 & 2 \end{bmatrix}$

For the games in Exercises 37–40, remove any dominated strategies, then solve the game. Find the value of the game.

37. $\begin{bmatrix} -4 & 8 & 0 \\ -2 & 9 & -3 \end{bmatrix}$

38. $\begin{bmatrix} 1 & 0 & 3 & -3 \\ 4 & -2 & 4 & -1 \end{bmatrix}$

39. $\begin{bmatrix} 2 & -1 \\ -4 & 5 \\ -1 & -2 \end{bmatrix}$

40. $\begin{bmatrix} 8 & -6 \\ 4 & -8 \\ -9 & 9 \end{bmatrix}$

MATHEMATICS OF FINANCE

Karl Gerstner. From the series *Carro 64*, Twenty-one part cycle (Du Clair a l'Obscur a travers le viol), 1960.

Not too many years ago, money could be borrowed by the largest and most secure corporations for 3% (and home mortgages could be had for 4 1/2%). Today, however, even the largest corporations must pay at least 10% or 12% for their money, and over 20% at times. Thus it is important that both the corporation management and consumers (who pay 21% or more to retailers such as Sears or Wards) have a good understanding of the cost of borrowing money. The cost of borrowing money is called **interest.** The formulas for interest are developed in this chapter.

9.1 Simple Interest and Discount

Interest on loans of a year or less is usually calculated as **simple interest;** simple interest is interest that is charged only on the amount borrowed and not on past interest. The amount borrowed is the **principal,** P. The **rate** of interest, r, is given as a percent per year, and t is the **time,** measured in years. Simple interest, I, is the product of the principal, rate, and time. (To use the formula for simple interest, write the rate r in decimal form.)

Simple Interest

> The *simple interest, I,* for t years on an amount of P dollars at a rate of interest r is given by
>
> $$I = Prt.$$

A deposit of P dollars today at a rate of interest r for t years produces interest of $I = Prt$. This interest, added to the original principal P, gives

$$P + Prt = P(1 + rt).$$

This result, called the **future value** of P dollars at an interest rate r for t years, is summarized as follows. (When loans are involved, the future value is often called the *maturity value* of the loan.)

Future or Maturity Value

> The *future value* or *maturity value, A,* of P dollars for t years at a rate of interest r is
>
> $$A = P(1 + rt).$$

EXAMPLE 1

Find the maturity value for each of the following loans.

(a)   a loan of $2500, made on June 5; to be repaid in 8 months with interest of 14%

The loan is for 8 months, or 8/12 = 2/3 of a year. The maturity value is

$$A = P(1 + rt)$$

$$A = 2500\left[1 + .14\left(\frac{2}{3}\right)\right]$$

$$\approx 2500[1 + .09333] \approx 2733.33,$$

or $2733.33. (Here we rounded to the nearest cent, as is customary in financial problems.) Of this maturity value,

$$\$2733.33 - \$2500 = \$233.33$$

represents interest.

(b)   a loan of $11,280 for 85 days at 11% interest

It is common to assume 360 days in a year when working with simple interest. We shall usually make such an assumption in this book. The maturity value in this example is

$$A = 11,280\left[1 + .11\left(\frac{85}{360}\right)\right] \approx 11,280[1.0259722] \approx 11,572.97,$$

or $11,572.97.   ▧

In part (b) of Example 1 we assumed 360 days in a year. Interest found using 360 days is called *ordinary interest,* while interest found using 365 days is *exact interest.*

Present Value   A sum of money that can be deposited today to yield some larger amount in the future is called the **present value** of that future amount. Let P be the present value of some amount A at some time t (in years) in the future. Assume a rate of interest r. As above, the future value of this sum is

$$A = P(1 + rt).$$

Since P is the present value, divide both sides of this last result by $1 + rt$ to get

$$P = \frac{A}{1 + rt}.$$

A summary of present value follows.

Present Value

> The *present value P* of a future amount of A dollars at a rate of interest r for t years is
>
> $$P = \frac{A}{1 + rt}.$$

EXAMPLE 2

Find the present value of the following future amounts.

(a) $10,000 in one year, if interest is 13%

Here $A = 10,000$, $t = 1$, and $r = .13$. Use the formula in the box.

$$P = \frac{10,000}{1 + (.13)(1)} = \frac{10,000}{1.13} \approx 8849.56$$

If $8849.56 were deposited today, at 13% interest, a total of $10,000 would be in the account in one year. These two sums, $8849.56 today, and $10,000 in a year, are equivalent (at 13%); one becomes the other in a year.

(b) $32,000 in four months at 9% interest

$$P = \frac{32,000}{1 + (.09)\left(\frac{4}{12}\right)} = \frac{32,000}{1.03} = 31,067.96 \quad \blacksquare$$

EXAMPLE 3

Because of a court settlement. Charlie Dawkins owes $5000 to Arnold Parker. The money must be paid in ten months, with no interest. Suppose Dawkins wishes to pay the money today. What amount should Parker be willing to accept? Assume an interest rate of 11%.

The amount that Parker should be willing to accept is given by the present value:

$$P = \frac{5000}{1 + (.11)\left(\frac{10}{12}\right)} = \frac{5000}{1.09167} = 4580.14.$$

Parker should be willing to accept $4580.14 in settlement. $\blacksquare$

Simple Discount   It is not an uncommon practice to have interest deducted from the amount of a loan before giving the balance to the borrower. The money that is deducted is called the **discount,** with the money actually received by the borrower called the **proceeds.**

EXAMPLE 4

Elizabeth Thornton agrees to pay $8500 to her banker in nine months. The banker subtracts a discount of 15% and gives the balance to Thornton. Find the amount of the discount and the proceeds.

The discount is found in the same way that simple interest is found.

$$\text{discount} = 8500(.15)\left(\frac{9}{12}\right) = 956.25$$

The proceeds are found by subtracting the discount from the original amount.

$$\text{proceeds} = \$8500 - \$956.25 = \$7543.75 \quad \blacksquare$$

In Example 4, the borrower was charged a discount of 15%. However, 15% is *not* the interest rate paid, since 15% applies to the $8500, while the borrower actually received only $7543.75. To find the rate of interest actually paid by the borrower, work as in the next example.

EXAMPLE 5

Find the actual rate of interest paid by Thornton in Example 4.

The rate of 15% stated in Example 4 is not the actual rate of interest since it applies to the total amount of $8500 and not to the amount actually borrowed, or $7543.75. To find the rate of interest paid by Thornton, use the formula for simple interest, $I = Prt$, with r the unknown. Since the borrower received only $7543.75, $I = 956.25$, $P = 7543.75$, and $t = 9/12$. Substitute these values into $I = Prt$.

$$I = Prt$$

$$956.25 = 7543.75(r)\left(\frac{9}{12}\right)$$

$$\frac{956.25}{7543.75\left(\frac{9}{12}\right)} = r$$

$$.169 \approx r$$

The interest rate paid by the borrower is about 16.9%. (This rate actually paid is called the **effective rate.**) ▰

Let D represent the amount of discount on a loan. Then $D = Art$, where A is the maturity value of the loan (the amount borrowed plus interest), and r is the stated rate of interest. The amount actually received, the proceeds, can be written as $P = A - D$, or $P = A - Art$, from which $P = A(1 - rt)$.

Let us summarize the formulas for discount interest.

Discount Interest

> If D is the discount on a loan having a maturity value A at a rate of interest r for t years, and if P represents the proceeds, then
>
> $$P = A - D, \quad \text{or} \quad P = A(1 - rt).$$

One common use of discount interest is in *discounting a note,* a process by which a promissory note due at some time in the future can be converted to cash now.

EXAMPLE 6

Jim Levy owes $4250 to Jenny Toms. The loan is payable in one year, at 12% interest. Toms needs cash to buy a new car, so three months before the loan is payable she goes to her bank to have the loan discounted. The bank charges a 16% discount fee. Find the amount of cash she will receive from the bank.

First find the maturity value of the loan, the amount Levy must pay to Toms. By the formula for maturity value,

$$A = P(1 + rt)$$

$$A = 4250[1 + (.12)(1)]$$

$$= 4250(1.12) = 4760,$$

or $4760.

The bank applies its discount rate to this total:

$$\text{amount of discount} = 4760(.16)\left(\frac{3}{12}\right) = 190.40.$$

(Remember that the loan was discounted three months before it was due.) Toms actually receives

$$\$4760 - \$190.40 = \$4569.60$$

in cash from the bank. Three months later, the bank would get \$4760 from Levy. ∎

9.1 EXERCISES

Find the simple interest in Exercises 1–6.

1. \$1000 at 12% for one year

2. \$4500 at 16% for one year

3. \$25,000 at 21% for nine months

4. \$3850 at 17% for eight months

5. \$1974 at 16.2% for seven months

6. \$3724 at 14.1% for eleven months

In Exercises 7–12, assume a 360 day year. Also, assume 30 days in each month.

7. \$12,000 at 14% for 72 days

8. \$38,000 at 19% for 216 days

9. \$5147.18 at 17.3% for 58 days

10. \$2930.42 at 13.9% for 123 days

11. \$7980 at 15%; the loan was made May 7 and is due on September 19

12. \$5408 at 20%; the loan was made August 16 and is due on December 30

In Exercises 13–16, assume 365 days in a year, and use the exact number of days in a month. (Assume 28 days in February.)

13. \$7800 at 16%; made on July 7 and due October 25

14. \$11,000 at 15%; made on February 19 and due May 31

15. \$2579 at 17.6%; made on October 4 and due March 15

16. \$37,098 at 19.2%; made on September 12 and due July 30

Find the present value of the future amounts in Exercises 17–22. Assume 360 days in a year.

17. \$15,000 for 8 months, money earns 16%

18. \$48,000 for 9 months, money earns 14%

19. \$5276 for 3 months, money earns 17.4%

20. \$6892 for 7 months, money earns 18.2%

21. \$15,402 for 125 days, money earns 19.3%

22. \$29,764 for 310 days, money earns 21.4%

Find the proceeds for the amounts in Exercises 23–26. Assume 360 days in a year.

23. \$7150, discount rate 16%, length of loan 11 months

24. \$9450, discount rate 18%, length of loan 7 months

25. \$358, discount rate 21.6%, length of loan 183 days

26. \$509, discount rate 23.2%, length of loan 238 days

27. Donna Sharp borrowed \$25,900 from her father to start a flower shop. She repaid him after eleven months, with interest of 18.4%. Find the total amount she repaid.

28. A corporation accountant forgot to pay the firm's income tax of \$725,896.15 on time. The government charged a penalty of 17.7% interest for the 34 days the money was late. Find the total amount, tax and penalty, that was paid. (Use a 365 day year.)

29. Tuition of \$1769 will be due when the spring term begins, in four months. What amount should a student deposit today, at 6.25%, to have enough to pay the tuition?

30. A firm of attorneys has ordered seven new IBM typewriters, at a cost of $2104 each. The machines will not be delivered for seven months. What amount could the firm deposit in an account paying 15.42% to have enough to pay for the machines?

31. Roy Gerard needs $5196 to pay for remodeling work on his house. He plans to repay the loan in 10 months. His bank loans money at a discount rate of 17%. Find the amount of his loan.

32. Mary Collins decides to go back to college. To get to school she buys a small car for $6100. She decides to borrow the money at the bank, where they charge a 19.8% discount rate. If she will repay the loan in 7 months, find the amount of the loan.

33. Marge Prullage signs a $4200 note at the bank. The bank charges a 17.2% discount rate. Find the net proceeds if the note is for ten months. Find the effective interest rate charged by the bank.

34. A bank charges a 23.1% discount rate on a $1000 note for 90 days. Find the effective rate.

35. Helen Spence owes $7000 to the Eastside Music Shop. She has agreed to pay the amount in 7 months, at an interest rate of 21%. Two months before the loan is due to be paid, the store discounts it at the bank. The bank charges a 23.7% discount rate. How much money does the store receive?

36. A building contractor gives a $13,500 note to a plumber. The note is due in nine months, with interest of 19%. Three months after the note is signed, the plumber discounts it at the bank. The bank charges a 21.1% discount rate. How much money does the plumber actually receive?

9.2 Compound Interest

Simple interest is normally used for loans of a year or less; for longer periods **compound interest** is used. With compound interest, interest is charged on interest, as well as principal. To find a formula for compound interest, first suppose that P dollars is deposited at a rate of interest i per year. (While r is used with simple interest, it is common to use i for compound interest.) The interest earned during the first year is found by the formula for simple interest:

$$\text{first year interest} = P \cdot i \cdot 1 = Pi.$$

At the end of one year, the amount on deposit will be the sum of the original principal and the interest earned, or

$$P + Pi = P(1 + i). \tag{1}$$

If the deposit earns compound interest, the interest earned during the second year is found from the total amount on deposit at the end of the first year. Thus, the interest earned during the second year (again found by the formula for simple interest), is given by

$$P(1 + i)(i)(1) = P(1 + i)i, \tag{2}$$

so that the total amount on deposit at the end of the second year is given by the sum of the amounts from (1) and (2) above, or

$$P(1 + i) + P(1 + i)i = P(1 + i) \cdot (1 + i)$$
$$= P(1 + i)^2.$$

In the same way, the total amount on deposit at the end of three years is

$$P(1 + i)^3.$$

Generalizing, in j years the total amount on deposit is $P(1 + i)^j$, called the **compound amount.**

Interest can be compounded more than once a year. Suppose interest is compounded m times per year (m *periods* per year), at a rate i per year, so that i/m is the rate for each period. Suppose that interest is compounded for n years. Then the following formula for the compound amount can be derived in the same way as was the previous formula.

Compound Amount

If P dollars is deposited for n years with interest compounded m periods per year at a rate of interest i per year, the compound amount A is

$$A = P\left(1 + \frac{i}{m}\right)^{mn}.$$

EXAMPLE 1

Suppose $1000 is deposited for 6 years in an account paying 8% per year compounded annually.

(a) Find the compound amount.

In the formula above, $P = 1000$, $i = 8\% = .08$, $m = 1$, and $n = 6$. The compound amount is

$$A = P\left(1 + \frac{i}{m}\right)^{nm}$$
$$A = 1000\left(1 + \frac{.08}{1}\right)^{6(1)} = 1000(1.08)^6.$$

We could find $(1.08)^6$ by using a calculator, or by using special compound interest tables. Such a table is given at the back of this book. To find $(1.08)^6$, look for 8% across the top and 6 (for 6 periods) down the side. You should find 1.58687, thus $(1.08)^6 \approx 1.58687$, and

$$A = 1000(1.58687) = 1586.87,$$

or $1586.87, which represents the final amount on deposit.

(b) Find the actual amount of interest earned.

From the compound amount, subtract the initial deposit.

$$\text{amount of interest} = \$1586.87 - \$1000 = \$586.87 \quad \blacksquare$$

EXAMPLE 2

Find the amount of interest earned by a deposit of $1000 for 6 years at 16% compounded quarterly.

Interest compounded quarterly is compounded four times a year. In 6 years, there are $4 \cdot 6 = 24$ quarters, or 24 periods. Interest of 16% per year is 16%/4, or 4%, per quarter. The compound amount is

$$1000(1 + .04)^{24} = 1000(1.04)^{24}.$$

The value of $(1.04)^{24}$ can be found with a calculator or in the table. Locate 4% across the top of the table and 24 periods at the left. You should find the number 2.56330 with

$$A = 1000(2.56330) = 2563.30,$$

or $2563.30. The compound amount is $2563.30 and the interest earned is $2563.30 − $1000 = $1563.30. ■

EXAMPLE 3

Find the compound amount if $900 is deposited at 16% compounded semiannually for 8 years.

In 8 years there are $8 \cdot 2 = 16$ semiannual periods. If interest is 16% per year, then 16%/2 = 8% is earned per semiannual period. Use a calculator, or look in the table for 8% and 16 periods, finding the number 3.42594. The compound amount is

$$A = 900(1.08)^{16} = 900(3.42594) = 3083.35,$$

or $3083.35. ■

The more often interest is compounded within a given time period, the more interest will be earned. Using a calculator with an x^y key, and using the formula above, we get the results shown in the following chart.

Interest on $1000 at 12% per Year for 10 Years

Compounded	Number of Periods	Compound Amount	Interest
not at all (simple interest)	—	—	$1200.00
annually	10	$1000(1 + .12)^{10} = \$3105.85$	$2105.85
semiannually	20	$1000\left(1 + \frac{.12}{2}\right)^{20} = \$3207.14$	$2207.14
quarterly	40	$1000\left(1 + \frac{.12}{4}\right)^{40} = \$3262.04$	$2262.04
monthly	120	$1000\left(1 + \frac{.12}{12}\right)^{120} = \$3300.39$	$2300.39
daily	3650	$1000\left(1 + \frac{.12}{365}\right)^{3650} = \$3319.46$	$2319.46
hourly	87,600	$1000\left(1 + \frac{.12}{8760}\right)^{87,600} = \$3320.09$	$2320.09
every minute	5,256,000	$1000\left(1 + \frac{.12}{525,600}\right)^{5,256,000} = \$3320.11$	$2320.11

As suggested by the chart, it makes a big difference whether interest is compounded or not. Interest differs by $905.85 when simple interest is compared to interest compounded annually. However, increasing the frequency of compounding makes smaller and smaller differences in the amount of interest earned. In fact, it can be shown that even if interest is compounded at intervals of time as small as one chooses (such as each hour, each minute, or each second), the total amount of interest earned will be only slightly more than for daily compounding. This is true even for a process called **continuous compounding,** which can be loosely described as compounding every instant. The interesting topic of continuous compounding is discussed in more detail in calculus.

EXAMPLE 4

Suppose $24,000 is deposited at 16% for 9 years. Find the interest earned by (a) daily, and (b) hourly compounding.

(a)　In 9 years there are $9 \times 365 = 3285$ days. The compound amount with daily compounding is

$$24{,}000\left(1 + \frac{.16}{365}\right)^{3285} = 101{,}264.60,$$

or $101,264.60. The interest earned is

$$\$101{,}264.60 - \$24{,}000 = \$77{,}264.60.$$

(b)　In one year, there are $365 \times 24 = 8760$ hours, while in 9 years there are $9 \times 8760 = 78{,}840$ hours. The compound amount is

$$24{,}000\left(1 + \frac{.16}{8760}\right)^{78{,}840} = 101{,}295.15,$$

or $101,295.15. This amount includes interest of

$$\$101{,}295.15 - \$24{,}000 = \$77{,}295.15,$$

only $30.55 more than when interest is compounded daily.　■

Effective Rate　If $1 is deposited at 4% compounded quarterly, we can use a calculator or a table to find that at the end of one year, the compound amount is $1.0406, an increase of 4.06% over the original $1. The actual increase of 4.06% in the money is somewhat higher than the stated increase of 4%. To differentiate between these two numbers, 4% is called the **nominal** or **stated** rate of interest, while 4.06% is called the **effective** rate.

EXAMPLE 5

Find the effective rate corresponding to a nominal rate of 6% compounded semi-annually.
　　Look in the compound interest table for an interest rate of 3% for 2 periods. You should find the number 1.06090. Alternatively, use a calculator to find $(1.03)^2$. By either method, $1 will increase to $1.06090, an actual increase of 6.09%. The effective rate is 6.09%.　■

Generalizing from this example, the effective rate of interest is given by the following formula.

Effective Rate

> The effective rate corresponding to a stated rate of interest i compounded m times per year is
> $$\left(1 + \frac{i}{m}\right)^m - 1.$$

EXAMPLE 6

A bank pays interest of 9% compounded monthly. Find the effective rate.

Use the formula in the box, with $i = .09$ and $m = 12$. The effective rate is

$$\left(1 + \frac{.09}{12}\right)^{12} - 1.$$

Use a calculator with an x^y key to get

$$(1.0075)^{12} - 1 = .0938,$$

or 9.38%. ∎

Present Value with Compound Interest   The formula for compound interest, $A = P(1 + i/m)^{nm}$, has five variables, A, P, i, m, and n. If we know the values of any four of these variables, we can then find the value of the fifth. In particular, if we know A, the amount of money we wish to end up with, and also know i, m, and n, then we can find P. Here P is the amount that we should deposit today to produce A dollars in n years. The next example shows this.

EXAMPLE 7

Joan Wilson must pay a lump sum of $6000 in 5 years. What amount deposited today at 8% compounded annually will amount to $6000 in 5 years?

Here $A = 6000$, $i = .08$, $m = 1$, $n = 5$, and P is unknown. Substituting these values into the formula for the compound amount gives

$$6000 = P\left(1 + \frac{.08}{1}\right)^{5(1)} = P(1.08)^5.$$

From a calculator or the table, $(1.08)^5 \approx 1.46933$, with

$$6000 \approx P(1.46933)$$

and
$$P = \frac{6000}{1.46933} \approx 4083.49,$$

or $4083.49. If Wilson deposits $4083.49 for 5 years in an account paying 8% compounded annually, she will have $6000 when she needs it. ∎

As the last example shows, $6000 in 5 years is the same as $4083.49 today (if money can be deposited at 8% compounded annually.) Recall from the first section that an amount that can be deposited today to yield a given sum in the future is called the *present value* of this future sum.

EXAMPLE 8

Find the present value of $16,000 in 9 years if money can be deposited at 12% compounded semiannually.

In 9 years there are $2 \cdot 9 = 18$ semiannual periods. A rate of 12% per year is 6% each semiannual period. Use a calculator, or look in the table (6% across the top and 18 periods down the side). You should find 2.85434. The present value is

$$\frac{16,000}{2.85434} \approx 5605.50.$$

A deposit of $5605.50 today, at 12% compounded semiannually, will produce a total of $16,000 in 9 years. ■

We can also solve the formula for the compound amount for n, as the following example shows.

EXAMPLE 9

Suppose the general level of inflation in the economy averages 8% per year. Find the number of years it would take for the overall level of prices to double.

We want to find the number of years it will take for $1 worth of goods or services to cost $2. That is, we want to find n in the equation

$$2 = 1(1 + .08)^{n},$$

where $A = 2$, $P = 1$, and $i = .08$. This equation simplifies to

$$2 = (1.08)^{n}.$$

We could find n by using logarithms or certain calculators, but we can find a reasonable approximation by reading down the 8% column of the table. Read down this column until you come to the number closest to 2, which is 1.99900. This number corresponds to 9 periods. The general level of prices will double in about 9 years. ■

9.2 EXERCISES

Find the compound amount when the deposits in Exercises 1–12 are made.

1. $1000 at 6% compounded annually for 8 years

2. $1000 at 8% compounded annually for 10 years

3. $4500 at 8% compounded annually for 20 years

4. $810 at 8% compounded annually for 12 years

5. $470 at 12% compounded semiannually for 12 years

6. $15,000 at 16% compounded semiannually for 11 years

7. $46,000 at 12% compounded semiannually for 5 years

8. $1050 at 16% compounded semiannually for 13 years

9. $7500 at 16% compounded quarterly for 9 years

10. $8000 at 16% compounded quarterly for 4 years

11. $6500 at 12% compounded quarterly for 6 years

12. $9100 at 12% compounded quarterly for 4 years

Find the amount of interest earned by the deposits in Exercises 13–18.

13. $6000 at 8% compounded annually for 8 years

14. $21,000 at 6% compounded annually for 5 years

15. $43,000 at 10% compounded semiannually for 9 years

16. $7500 at 8% compounded semiannually for 5 years

17. $2196.58 at 20.8% compounded quarterly for 4 years

18. $4915.73 at 21.6% compounded quarterly for 3 years

Find the present value of the sums in Exercises 19–26.

19. $4500 at 8% compounded annually for 9 years

20. $11,500 at 8% compounded annually for 12 years

21. $15,902.74 at 19.8% compounded annually for 7 years

22. $27,159.68 at 21.3% compounded annually for 11 years

23. $2000 at 16% compounded semiannually for 8 years

24. $2000 at 12% compounded semiannually for 8 years

25. $8800 at 16% compounded quarterly for 5 years

26. $7500 at 12% compounded quarterly for 9 years

27. If money can be invested at 8% compounded quarterly, which is larger, $1000 now or $1210 in 5 years?

28. If money can be invested at 6% compounded annually, which is larger, $10,000 now or $15,000 in 10 years?

Find the effective rate corresponding to each of the following nominal rates.

29. 4% compounded semiannually

30. 8% compounded quarterly

31. 8% compounded semiannually

32. 10% compounded semiannually

33. 12% compounded semiannually

34. 12% compounded quarterly

Use the ideas of Example 9 in the text to answer questions 35–37. Find the time it would take for the general level of prices in the economy to double if the average annual inflation rate is

35. 4%   **36.** 5%   **37.** 6%.

38. **(a)** The consumption of electricity has increased historically at 6% per year. If it continues to increase at this rate indefinitely, find the number of years before the electric utilities would need to double their generating capacity.

  (b) Suppose a conservation campaign coupled with higher rates caused the demand for electricity to increase at only 2% per year, as it has recently. Find the number of years before the utilities would need to double generating capacity.

Under certain conditions, Swiss banks pay *negative interest*—they charge you. (You didn't think all that secrecy was free?) Suppose a bank "pays" −2.4% interest compounded annually. Use a calculator and find the compound amount for a deposit of $150,000 after

39. 2 years   **40.** 4 years   **41.** 8 years   **42.** 12 years.

Find the compound amount for each of the following deposits.

43. $40,552 at 9.13% compounded quarterly for 5 years.

44. $11,641.10 at 10.9% compounded monthly for 8 years.

45. $673.27 at 8.6% compounded semi-annually for 3.5 years.

46. $2964.93 at 11.4% compounded monthly for 4.25 years.

9.3   Sequences (Optional)

So far in our discussion of mathematics of finance, we have discussed only lump sums—a lump sum deposit today that produces a lump sum compound amount in the future, or the present value of a lump sum amount in the future. In practice, however, it is very common to deal with a sequence of *periodic payments,* such as a car payment or house payment. We shall develop formulas for these payments in the next sections. To develop these formulas, we need some of the results of this section, on sequences.

A **sequence** is a function whose domain is the set of positive integers. For example,

$$a(n) = 2n, \qquad n = 1, 2, 3, 4, \ldots$$

is a sequence. The letter n is used as a variable instead of x to emphasize the fact that the domain includes only positive integers. For the same reason, a is used to name the function instead of f.

The range values of a sequence function, such as

$$a(1) = 2, \qquad a(2) = 4, \qquad a(3) = 6, \ldots$$

from the sequence given above, are called the **terms** of the sequence. Instead of writing $a(5)$ for the fifth term of the sequence, for example, it is customary to write

$$a_5 = 10.$$

In the same way, for the sequence above, $a_1 = 2$, $a_2 = 4$, $a_8 = 16$, $a_{20} = 40$, and $a_{51} = 102$.

The symbol a_n is often used for the **general** or **nth term** of a sequence. For example, for the sequence 4, 7, 10, 13, 16, . . . the general term is given by $a_n = 1 + 3n$. This formula for a_n can be used to find any desired term of the sequence. For example, the first three terms of the sequence having $a_n = 1 + 3n$ are

$$a_1 = 1 + 3(1) = 4, \quad a_2 = 1 + 3(2) = 7, \quad a_3 = 1 + 3(3) = 10.$$

Also, $a_8 = 25$ and $a_{12} = 37$.

EXAMPLE 1

Find the first four terms for the sequence having the general term $a_n = -4n + 2$.
Replace n, in turn, with 1, 2, 3, and 4. If $n = 1$,

$$a_1 = -4(1) + 2 = -4 + 2 = -2. \qquad \text{Let } n = 1$$

Also, $\qquad a_2 = -4(2) + 2 = -6.$ $\qquad\qquad$ Let $n = 2$

When $n = 3$, then $a_3 = -10$; finally, $a_4 = -4(4) + 2 = -14$. The first four terms of this sequence are -2, -6, -10, and -14. ■

Arithmetic Sequences   A sequence in which each term after the first is found by adding the same number to the preceding term is called an **arithmetic sequence.**

The sequence of Example 1 above is an arithmetic sequence; -4 is added to any term to get the next term.

The sequence

$$8, 13, 18, 23, 28, \ldots$$

is an arithmetic sequence since each term after the first is found by adding 5 to the previous term. The number 5, the difference between any two adjacent terms, is called the **common difference.**

If a_1 is the first term of an arithmetic sequence and d is the common difference, then the second term can be found by adding the common difference d to the first term: $a_2 = a_1 + d$. The third term is found by adding d to the second term.

$$a_3 = a_2 + d = (a_1 + d) + d = a_1 + 2d$$

In the same way, $a_4 = a_1 + 3d$ and $a_5 = a_1 + 4d$. Generalizing, the nth term of an arithmetic sequence is given by $a_n = a_1 + (n - 1)d$.

---

nth Term

If an arithmetic sequence has first term a_1 and common difference d, then a_n, the nth term of the sequence, is given by

$$a_n = a_1 + (n - 1)d.$$

EXAMPLE 2

A company had sales of \$50,000 during its first year of operation. If the sales increase by \$6000 per year, find its sales in the eleventh year.

Since the sales for each year after the first are found by adding \$6000 to the sales of the previous year, the sales form an arithmetic sequence with $a_1 = 50,000$ and $d = 6000$. Using the formula for the nth term of an arithmetic sequence, sales during the eleventh year are given by

$$a_{11} = 50,000 + (11 - 1)6000 = 50,000 + 60,000 = 110,000,$$

or \$110,000. ▪

The formula above gives the nth term of an arithmetic sequence. We can now find a formula for the *sum* of the first n terms of an arithmetic sequence. To find this formula, let an arithmetic sequence have first term a_1 and common difference d. Let S_n represent the sum of the first n terms of the sequence. Start by writing a formula for S_n as follows:

$$S_n = a_1 + [a_1 + d] + [a_1 + 2d] + \cdots + [a_1 + (n - 1)d].$$

Next, write this same sum in reverse order.

$$S_n = [a_1 + (n - 1)d] + [a_1 + (n - 2)d] + \cdots + [a_1 + d] + a_1$$

Now add the respective sides of these last two equations.

$$S_n + S_n = (a_1 + [a_1 + (n - 1)d]) + ([a_1 + d] + [a_1 + (n - 2)d])$$
$$+ \cdots + ([a_1 + (n - 1)d] + a_1)$$

From this,

$$2S_n = [2a_1 + (n - 1)d] + [2a_1 + (n - 1)d]$$
$$+ \cdots + [2a_1 + (n - 1)d].$$

There are n of the $[2a_1 + (n - 1)d]$ terms on the right, making

$$2S_n = n[2a_1 + (n - 1)d],$$

$$S_n = \frac{n}{2}[2a_1 + (n - 1)d].$$

Since $a_n = a_1 + (n - 1)d$, also $S_n = \frac{n}{2}[a_1 + a_1 + (n - 1)d]$, or

$$S_n = \frac{n}{2}(a_1 + a_n).$$

The following box summarizes this work with arithmetic sequences.

Sum of Terms

Suppose an arithmetic sequence has first term a_1, common difference d, and nth term a_n. Then the sum S_n of the first n terms of the sequence is given by

$$S_n = \frac{n}{2}[2a_1 + (n - 1)d]$$

or

$$S_n = \frac{n}{2}(a_1 + a_n).$$

Either of these two formulas can be used to find the sum of the first n terms of an arithmetic sequence.

EXAMPLE 3

Find the sum of the first 25 terms of the arithmetic sequence

$$3, 8, 13, 18, 23, \ldots .$$

In this sequence, $a_1 = 3$ and $d = 5$. If we use the first formula from above, we get

$$S_{25} = \frac{25}{2}[2(3) + (25 - 1)5] \qquad \text{Let } n = 25, \quad a_1 = 3, \quad d = 5$$

$$= \frac{25}{2}[6 + 120]$$

$$= 1575. \quad \blacksquare$$

EXAMPLE 4

Find the total sales of the company of Example 2 during its first 11 years.

From Example 2, $a_1 = 50,000$, $a_{11} = 110,000$, and $n = 11$. By the second formula above,

$$S_{11} = \frac{11}{2}(50,000 + 110,000) = 880,000.$$

The total sales for 11 years are $880,000. ◼

Geometric Sequences In an arithmetic sequence, each term after the first is found by adding the same number to the preceding term. In a **geometric sequence,** each term after the first is found by *multiplying* the preceding term by the same number. For example,

$$3, -6, 12, -24, 48, -96, \ldots$$

is a geometric sequence with each term after the first found by multiplying the preceding term by the number -2. The number -2 is called the **common ratio.**

If a_1 is the first term of a geometric sequence and r is the common ratio, then the second term is given by $a_2 = a_1 r$ and the third term by $a_3 = a_2 r = a_1 r^2$. Also, $a_4 = a_1 r^3$, and $a_5 = a_1 r^4$. The next box generalizes from these results.

*n*th Term

> If a geometric sequence has first term a_1 and common ratio r, then
>
> $$a_n = a_1 r^{n-1}.$$

EXAMPLE 5

Find the indicated term for each of the following geometric sequences.

(a) $6, 24, 96, 384, \ldots$; find a_7.

Here $a_1 = 6$. To find r, choose any term except the first and divide it by the preceding term. If we choose 96,

$$r = \frac{96}{24} = 4.$$

Now use the formula for the *n*th term.

$$
\begin{aligned}
a_7 &= 6(4)^{7-1} \quad &&\text{Let } n = 7,\ a_1 = 6,\ r = 4 \\
&= 6(4)^6 \\
&= 6(4096) \quad &&4^6 = 4096 \\
&= 24,576
\end{aligned}
$$

(b) $8, -16, 32, -64, 128, \ldots$; find a_6.

In this sequence $a_1 = 8$ and $r = -2$.

$$
\begin{aligned}
a_6 &= 8(-2)^{6-1} \quad &&\text{Let } n = 6,\ a_1 = 8,\ r = -2 \\
&= 8(-2)^5 \\
&= 8(-32) \\
&= -256 \quad ◼
\end{aligned}
$$

Often we need to find the sum of the first n terms of a geometric sequence. We can find a formula for this sum, just as we did with arithmetic sequences. To find this formula, let a geometric sequence have first term a_1 and common ratio r. Write the sum S_n of the first n terms as

$$S_n = a_1 + a_2 + a_3 + \cdots + a_n.$$

This sum can also be written as

$$S_n = a_1 + a_1 r + a_1 r^2 + \cdots + a_1 r^{n-1}. \tag{1}$$

If $r = 1$, then $S_n = na_1$, the correct result for this case. If $r \neq 1$, multiply both sides of equation (1) by r, obtaining

$$rS_n = a_1 r + a_1 r^2 + a_1 r^3 + \cdots + a_1 r_n. \tag{2}$$

Now subtract corresponding sides of equation (1) from equation (2);

$$rS_n - S_n = a_1 r_n - a_1$$
$$S_n(r - 1) = a_1(r_n - 1),$$

or finally

$$S_n = \frac{a_1(r_n - 1)}{r - 1}.$$

The next box summarizes this result.

Sum of Terms

If a geometric sequence has first term a_1 and common ratio r, then the sum S_n of the first n terms is given by

$$S_n = \frac{a_1(r^n - 1)}{r - 1}, \qquad r \neq 1.$$

EXAMPLE 6

Find the sum of the first six terms of the geometric sequence 3, 12, 48, ...
Here $a_1 = 3$ and $r = 4$. Find S_6 by the formula above.

$$S_6 = \frac{3(4^6 - 1)}{4 - 1} \qquad \text{Let } n = 6, \, a_1 = 3, \, r = 4$$

$$= \frac{3(4096 - 1)}{3}$$

$$= 4095 \quad \blacksquare$$

9.3 EXERCISES

In Exercises 1–16, a formula for the general term of a sequence is given. Use the formula to find the first five terms of the sequence. Identify each sequence as *arithmetic, geometric,* or *neither*.

1. $a_n = 6n + 5$

2. $a_n = 12n - 3$

3. $a_n = 3n - 7$

4. $a_n = 5n - 12$

5. $a_n = -6n + 4$

6. $a_n = -11n + 10$

7. $a_n = 2^n$

8. $a_n = 3^n$

9. $a_n = (-2)^n$

10. $a_n = (-3)^n$

11. $a_n = 3(2^n)$

12. $a_n = -4(2^n)$

13. $a_n = \dfrac{n + 1}{n + 5}$

14. $a_n = \dfrac{2n}{n + 1}$

15. $a_n = \dfrac{1}{n + 1}$

16. $a_n = \dfrac{1}{n + 8}$

Identify each sequence in Exercises 17–32 as *arithmetic, geometric,* or *neither*. For an arithmetic sequence, give the common difference. For a geometric sequence, give the common ratio.

17. 6, 14, 22, 30, 38, 46, . . .

18. 40, 46, 52, 58, 64, . . .

19. 5, 8, 11, 14, 17, 20, 23, . . .

20. 23, 34, 45, 54, 63, 72, . . .

21. 4, 12, 36, 108, . . .

22. 7, 14, 28, 56, 112, . . .

23. 2, 5, 9, 14, 20, 27, . . .

24. 1, 4, 9, 16, 25, 36, . . .

25. 12, 9, 6, 3, 0, -3, -6, . . .

26. 37, 31, 25, 19, 13, 7, . . .

27. -18, -15, -12, -9, -6, . . .

28. -21, -17, -13, -9, -5, . . .

29. 3, -6, 12, -24, 48, -96, . . .

30. -5, 10, -20, 40, -80, . . .

31. -5, 6, -7, 8, -9, 10, -11, . . .

32. -12, 9, -6, 3, . . .

In Exercises 33–40, find the indicated term for each arithmetic sequence.

33. $a_1 = 10$, $d = 5$; find a_{13}

34. $a_1 = 6$, $d = 9$; find a_8

35. $a_1 = 8$, $d = 3$; find a_{20}

36. $a_1 = 13$, $d = 7$; find a_{11}

37. 6, 9, 12, 15, 18, . . . ; find a_{25}

38. 14, 17, 20, 23, 26, 29, . . . ; find a_{13}

39. -9, -13, -17, -21, -25, . . . ; find a_{15}

40. -4, -11, -18, -25, -32, . . . ; find a_{18}

Find the sum of the first six terms for each of the arithmetic sequences in Exercises 41–48.

41. 3, 6, 9, 12, . . .

42. 11, 13, 15, 17, . . .

43. 88, 98, 108, . . .

44. 92, 95, 98, . . .

45. $a_1 = 8$, $d = 9$

46. $a_1 = 12$, $d = 6$

47. $a_1 = 7$, $d = -4$

48. $a_1 = 13$, $d = -5$

Find a_5 for each of the geometric sequences in Exercises 49–56.

49. $a_1 = 3$, $r = 2$

50. $a_1 = 5$, $r = 3$

51. $a_1 = -8$, $r = 3$

52. $a_1 = -6$, $r = 2$

53. $a_1 = 1$, $r = -3$

54. $a_1 = 12$, $r = -2$

55. $a_1 = 1024$, $r = 1/2$

56. $a_1 = 729$, $r = 1/3$

Find the sum of the first four terms for each of the geometric sequences in Exercises 57–62.

57. $a_1 = 1$, $r = 2$

58. $a_1 = 3$, $r = 3$

59. $a_1 = 5$, $r = 1/5$

60. $a_1 = 6$, $r = 1/2$

61. $a_1 = 128$, $r = -3/2$

62. $a_1 = 81$, $r = -2/3$

Sums of the terms of a sequence are often written in *sigma notation* (also used in statistics). For example, to evaluate

$$\sum_{i=1}^{4} (3i + 7)$$

(where Σ is the capital Greek letter *sigma*), first evaluate $3i + 7$ for $i = 1$, then for $i = 2$, $i = 3$, and finally, $i = 4$. Then add the results to get

$$\sum_{i=1}^{4} (3i + 7) = [3(1) + 7] + [3(2) + 7] + [3(3) + 7] + [3(4) + 7]$$
$$= 10 + 13 + 16 + 19 = 58.$$

Evaluate each of the sums in Exercises 63–70.

63. $\displaystyle\sum_{i=1}^{5} (3 - 2i)$ **64.** $\displaystyle\sum_{i=1}^{4} (2i - 5)$ **65.** $\displaystyle\sum_{i=1}^{8} (2i + 1)$

66. $\displaystyle\sum_{i=1}^{4} (-6i + 8)$ **67.** $\displaystyle\sum_{i=1}^{5} i(2i + 1)$ **68.** $\displaystyle\sum_{i=1}^{4} (2i - 1)(i + 2)$

69. $\displaystyle\sum_{i=1}^{4} (3i + 1)(i + 1)$ **70.** $\displaystyle\sum_{i=1}^{5} (i - 3)(i + 5)$

A sum in the form

$$\sum_{i=1}^{n} (ai + b),$$

where a and b are real numbers, represents the sum of the first n terms of an arithmetic sequence. The first term is $a_1 = a(1) + b = a + b$ and the common difference is a. The nth term is $a_n = an + b$. Using these numbers, the sum can be found by using the formula for the sum of the first n terms. Use this method to find the sums in Exercises 71–76.

71. $\displaystyle\sum_{i=1}^{5} (2i + 8)$ **72.** $\displaystyle\sum_{i=1}^{6} (4i - 5)$ **73.** $\displaystyle\sum_{i=1}^{4} (-8i + 6)$

74. $\displaystyle\sum_{i=1}^{9} (2i - 3)$ **75.** $\displaystyle\sum_{i=1}^{500} i$ **76.** $\displaystyle\sum_{i=1}^{1000} i$

Sigma notation can also be used for geometric sequences. A sum in the form

$$\sum_{i=1}^{n} a(b^i)$$

represents the sum of the first n terms of a geometric sequence having first term $a_1 = ab$ and common ratio b. These sums can thus be found by applying the formula for the sum of the first n terms of a geometric sequence. Use this method to find the sums in Exercises 77–82.

77. $\displaystyle\sum_{i=1}^{4} 3(2^i)$ **78.** $\displaystyle\sum_{i=1}^{3} 2(3^i)$ **79.** $\displaystyle\sum_{i=1}^{4} \frac{1}{2}(4^i)$

80. $\displaystyle\sum_{i=1}^{4} \frac{3}{2}(2^i)$ **81.** $\displaystyle\sum_{i=1}^{4} \frac{4}{3}(3^i)$ **82.** $\displaystyle\sum_{i=1}^{4} \frac{5}{3}(3^i)$

83. Joy Watt is hired for $11,400 per year, with annual raises of $600. What will she earn during her eighth year with the company?

84. What will be the total income received by Watt (see Exercise 83) during her first eight years with the company?

85. A certain machine annually loses 30% of the value it had at the beginning of that year. If its initial value is $10,000, use a calculator to find its value (a) at the end of the fifth year, (b) at the end of the eighth year.

86. A certain colony of bacteria increases in number by 10% per hour. After five hours, what is the percentage increase in the population over the initial population?

9.4   Annuities

In the first two sections of this chapter we studied *lump sum* payments; now we study a *sequence* of equal payments. For example, suppose $1500 is deposited at the end of each year for the next six years, in an account paying 8% per year, compounded annually. How much would be in the account after the six years?

A sequence of equal payments made at equal periods of time is called an **annuity.** If the payments are made at the end of the time period, and if the frequency of payments is the same as the frequency of compounding, the annuity is called an **ordinary annuity.** The time between payments is the **payment period,** with the time from the beginning of the first payment period to the end of the last called the **term** of the annuity. The **future value** of the annuity, the final sum on deposit, is defined as the sum of the compound amounts of all the payments, compounded to the end of the term.

Figure 1 shows our annuity of $1500 at the end of each year for six years. To find the future value of this annuity, look separately at each of the $1500 payments. The first of these payments will produce a compound amount of

$$1500(1 + .08)^5 = 1500(1.08)^5.$$

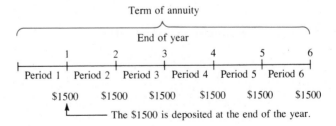

FIGURE 1

Use 5 as the exponent instead of 6 since the money is deposited at the *end* of the first year, and earns interest for only five years. The second payment of $1500 will produce a compound amount of $1500(1.08)^4$. As shown in Figure 2, the future value of the annuity is

$$1500(1.08)^5 + 1500(1.08)^4 + 1500(1.08)^3 + 1500(1.08)^2 + 1500(1.08)^1 + 1500.$$

(The last payment earns no interest at all.) From the compound interest table, this sum is

$$1500(1.46933) + 1500(1.36049) + 1500(1.25971) + 1500(1.16640)$$
$$+ 1500(1.08000) + 1500$$

$$\approx \$2204.00 + \$2040.74 + \$1889.57 + \$1749.60 + \$1620 + \$1500$$

$$= \$11,003.91.$$

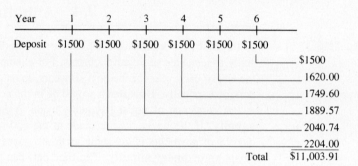

FIGURE 2

To generalize this result, suppose that a payment of R dollars is paid into an account at the end of each period for n periods, at a rate of interest i per period. The first payment of R dollars will produce a compound amount of $R(1 + i)^{n-1}$ dollars, the second payment produces $R(1 + i)^{n-2}$ dollars, and so on; the final payment earns no interest and contributes just R dollars to the total. If A represents the future value of the annuity, then (as shown in Figure 3),

$$A = R(1 + i)^{n-1} + R(1 + i)^{n-2} + R(1 + i)^{n-3} + \cdots + R(1 + i) + R$$

or, written in reverse order,

$$A = R + R(1 + i)^1 + R(1 + i)^2 + \cdots + R(1 + i)^{n-1}.$$

This sum is the sum of the first n terms of the geometric sequence having first term R and common ratio $1 + i$. Using the formula for the sum of the first n terms of a geometric sequence from the previous section,

$$A = \frac{R[(1 + i)^n - 1]}{(1 + i) - 1} = \frac{R[(1 + i)^n - 1]}{i} = R\left[\frac{(1 + i)^n - 1}{i}\right].$$

The quantity in brackets is commonly written $s_{\overline{n}|i}$ (read "s-angle-n at i"), so that

$$A = R \cdot s_{\overline{n}|i}.$$

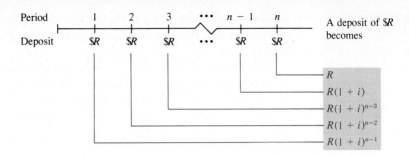

The sum of these
is the amount
of the annuity.

FIGURE 3

Values of $s_{\overline{n}|i}$ can be found by a calculator or from the table "Amount of an Annuity," at the back of this book.

To check the result above, go back to the annuity of $1500 at the end of each year for 6 years; interest was 8% per year compounded annually. In the table, these values give the number 7.33593. Multiply this number and 1500:

$$\text{future value} = 1500(7.33593) \approx 11{,}003.90,$$

or $11,003.90. The results differ by 1¢ due to rounding error.

The next box summarizes this work.

Future Value of an Annuity

> The future value, A, of an annuity of n payments of R dollars each at the end of each consecutive interest period, with interest compounded at a rate i per period, is
>
> $$A = R\left[\frac{(1 + i)^n - 1}{i}\right], \quad \text{or} \quad A = R \cdot s_{\overline{n}|i}.$$

EXAMPLE 1

Tom Bleser is an athlete who feels that his playing career will last 7 years. To prepare for his future, he deposits $22,000 at the end of each year for 7 years in an account paying 6% compounded annually. How much will he have on deposit after 7 years?

His payments form an ordinary annuity with $R = 22{,}000$, $n = 7$, and $i = .06$. The future value of this annuity is (by the formula above)

$$A = 22{,}000\left[\frac{(1.06)^7 - 1}{.06}\right].$$

From the table or a calculator, the number in brackets, $s_{\overline{7}|.06}$, is 8.39384, so that

$$A = 22{,}000(8.39384) = 184{,}664.48,$$

or $184,664.48. ∎

EXAMPLE 2

Suppose $1000 is deposited at the end of each six-month period for 5 years in an account paying 16% compounded semiannually. Find the future value of the annuity.

Interest of 16%/2 = 8% is earned semiannually. In 5 years there are $5 \cdot 2 = 10$ semiannual periods. Find $s_{\overline{10}|.08}$ from the table or a calculator. By looking in the 8% column and down 10 periods, we find $s_{\overline{10}|.08} = 14.48656$, with a future value of

$$A = 1000(14.48656) = 14{,}486.56,$$

or $14,486.56. ∎

Our results so far have been developed for *ordinary annuities*—those with payments made at the *end* of each time period. These results can be modified slightly to apply to **annuities due**—an annuity where payments are made at the *beginning* of each time period. To find the future value of an annuity due, treat each payment as if it were made at the *end* of the *preceding* period. That is, use the table or a calculator to find $s_{\overline{n}|i}$ for *one additional period;* to compensate for this, subtract the amount of one payment.

EXAMPLE 3

Find the future value of an annuity due if payments of $500 are made at the beginning of each quarter for 7 years, in an account paying 12% compounded quarterly.

In 7 years, there are 28 quarterly periods. Look in row 29 (28 + 1) of the table. Use the 12%/4 = 3% column of the table. You should find the number 45.21885. Multiply this number by 500, the amount of each payment.

$$500(45.21885) \approx 22{,}609.43$$

Subtract the amount of one payment from this result.

$$\$22{,}609.43 - \$500 = \$22{,}109.43$$

The account will contain a total of $22,109.43 after 7 years. ∎

Just as the formula $A = P(1 + i)^n$ can be solved for any of its variables, the formula for the future value of an annuity can be used to find the values of variables other than A. In Example 4 below we are given A, the amount of money wanted at the end, and we need to find R, the amount of each payment.

EXAMPLE 4

Betsy Martens wants to buy an expensive video camera three years from now. She wants to deposit an equal amount at the end of each quarter for three years in order to accumulate enough money to pay for the camera. The camera costs $2400, and the bank pays 12% interest compounded quarterly. Find the amount of each of the twelve deposits she will make.

This example describes an ordinary annuity with $A = 2400$, $i = .03$ (12%/4 = 3%) and $n = 3 \cdot 4 = 12$ periods. The unknown here is the amount of each payment, R. By the formula for the amount of an annuity from above,

$$2400 = R \cdot s_{\overline{12}|.03}.$$

From the table or a calculator,

$$2400 = R(14.19203)$$

$$R \approx 169.11,$$

or $169.11 (dividing both sides by 14.19203). ▪

Sinking Fund   The annuity in Example 4 is a *sinking fund:* a fund set up to receive periodic payments. These periodic payments ($169.11 in the example) together with the interest earned by the payments, are designed to produce a given sum at some time in the future. As another example, a sinking fund might be set up to receive money that will be needed to pay off the principal on a loan at some time in the future.

EXAMPLE 5

The Stockdales are close to retirement. They agree to sell an antique urn to the local museum for $17,000. Their tax adviser suggests that they defer receipt of this money until they retire, 5 years in the future. (At that time, they might well be in a lower tax bracket.) Find the amount of each payment the museum must make into a sinking fund so that it will have the necessary $17,000 in 5 years. Assume that the museum can earn 8% compounded annually on its money. Also, assume that the payments are made annually.

These payments are the periodic payments into an ordinary annuity. The annuity will amount to $17,000 in 5 years at 8% compounded annually. Using the formula,

$$17,000 = R \cdot s_{\overline{5}|.08}$$

or

$$R = \frac{17,000}{s_{\overline{5}|.08}}$$

$$R = \frac{17,000}{5.86660} \qquad \textbf{From the table}$$

$$R \approx 2897.76,$$

or $2897.76. If the museum deposits $2897.76 at the end of each year for 5 years in an account paying 8% compounded annually, it will have the total amount that it needs. This result is shown in the following table. In these tables, the last payment might well differ slightly from the others because of rounding errors.

Payment number	Amount of deposit	Interest earned	Total in account
1	$2897.76	$0	$2897.76
2	$2897.76	$231.82	$6027.34
3	$2897.76	$482.19	$9407.29
4	$2897.76	$752.58	$13,057.63
5	$2897.76	$1044.61	$17,000.00	▪

9.4 EXERCISES

Find each of the values in Exercises 1–8.

1. $s_{\overline{12}|.05}$ 2. $s_{\overline{20}|.06}$ 3. $s_{\overline{16}|.04}$ 4. $s_{\overline{40}|.02}$

5. $s_{\overline{20}|.01}$ 6. $s_{\overline{18}|.015}$ 7. $s_{\overline{15}|.04}$ 8. $s_{\overline{30}|.015}$

Find the future value of the ordinary annuities in Exercises 9–16. Interest is compounded annually.

9. $R = 100$, $i = .06$, $n = 10$ 10. $R = 1000$, $i = .06$, $n = 12$

11. $R = 10,000$, $i = .05$, $n = 19$ 12. $R = 100,000$, $i = .08$, $n = 23$

13. $R = 8500$, $i = .06$, $n = 30$ 14. $R = 11,200$, $i = .08$, $n = 25$

15. $R = 46,000$, $i = .06$, $n = 32$ 16. $R = 29,500$, $i = .05$, $n = 15$

Find the future value of each of the ordinary annuities in Exercises 17–22. Payments are made and interest is compounded as given.

17. $R = 9200$, 16% interest compounded semiannually for 7 years

18. $R = 3700$, 12% interest compounded semiannually for 11 years

19. $R = 800$, 12% interest compounded semiannually for 12 years

20. $R = 4600$, 16% interest compounded quarterly for 9 years

21. $R = 15,000$, 12% interest compounded quarterly for 6 years

22. $R = 42,000$, 16% interest compounded semiannually for 12 years

In Exercises 23–26, find the future value of each annuity due. Assume that interest is compounded annually.

23. $R = 600$, $i = .06$, $n = 8$ 24. $R = 1400$, $i = .08$, $n = 10$

25. $R = 20,000$, $i = .08$, $n = 6$ 26. $R = 4000$, $i = .06$, $n = 11$

In Exercises 27–30, find the future value of each annuity due.

27. payments of $1000 made at the beginning of each year for 9 years at 8% compounded annually

28. $750 deposited at the beginning of each year for 15 years at 6% compounded annually

29. $100 deposited at the beginning of each quarter for 9 years at 16% compounded quarterly

30. $1500 deposited at the beginning of each semiannual period for 11 years at 16% compounded semiannually

In Exercises 31–33, find the periodic payment that will amount to the given sums under the given conditions.

31. $A = \$10,000$, interest is 8% compounded annually, payments made at the end of each year for 12 years

32. $A = \$100,000$, interest is 16% compounded semiannually, payments made at the end of each semiannual period for 9 years

33. $A = \$50,000$, interest is 12% compounded quarterly, payments made at the end of each quarter for 8 years

34. Pat Dillon deposits $12,000 at the end of each year for 9 years in an account paying 8% interest compounded annually. Find the final amount she will have on deposit.

35. Pat's brother-in-law works in a bank which pays 6% compounded annually. If she deposits her money in this bank, instead of the one of Exercise 34, how much will she have in her account?

36. How much would Pat lose over 9 years by using her brother-in-law's bank? (See Exercises 34 and 35.)

37. Pam Parker deposits $2435 at the beginning of each semiannual period for 8 years in an account paying 12% compounded semiannually. She then leaves that money alone, with no further deposits, for an additional 5 years. Find the final amount on deposit after the entire 13-year period.

38. Chuck deposits $10,000 at the beginning of each year for 12 years in an account paying 8% compounded annually. He then puts the total amount on deposit in another account paying 12% compounded semiannually for another 9 years. Find the final amount on deposit after the entire 21-year period.

39. Ray Berkowitz needs $10,000 in 8 years. What amount can he deposit at the end of each quarter at 16% compounded quarterly so that he will have his $10,000?

40. Find Berkowitz's quarterly deposit (see Exercise 39) if the money is deposited at 12% compounded quarterly.

41. Barb Silverman wants to buy an $18,000 car in 6 years. How much money must she deposit at the end of each quarter in an account paying 12% compounded quarterly, so that she will have enough to pay for her car?

42. Harv's Meats knows that it must buy a new deboner machine in 4 years. The machine costs $12,000. In order to accumulate enough money to pay for the machine, Harv decides to deposit a sum of money at the end of each six months in an account paying 16% compounded semiannually. How much should each payment be?

Recent tax law changes have made Individual Retirement Accounts (IRA's) available to a great many workers. Under these plans, a person can currently deposit $2000 annually, with taxes deferred on the principal and interest. To attract these deposits, banks have been advertising the amount that will accumulate at retirement. Suppose a 40-year-old deposits $2000 per year until age 65. Find the total in the account with the following assumptions of interest rates. (Assume semiannual compounding with payment made at the end of each semiannual period.)

43. 6%   44. 8%   45. 10%   46. 12%

Find the amount of each payment to be made into a sinking fund so that enough will be present to pay off the indicated loans.

47. loan $2000, money earns 6% compounded annually, 5 annual payments

48. loan $8500, money earns 8% compounded annually, 7 annual payments

49. loan $11,000, money earns 16% compounded semiannually, for 6 years

50. loan $75,000, money earns 12% compounded semiannually, for 4 1/2 years

51. loan $50,000, money earns 16% compounded quarterly, for 2 1/2 years

52. loan $25,000, money earns 12% compounded quarterly, for 3 1/2 years

53. loan $6000, money earns 18% compounded monthly, for 3 years

54. loan $9000, money earns 18% compounded monthly, for 2 1/2 years

Find the final amount of the annuities in Exercises 55 and 56.

55. $892.17 a month for 2 years in an account paying 7.5% interest compounded monthly

56. $2476.32 each quarter for 5.5 years at 7.81% interest compounded quarterly.

57. Jill Streitzel sells some land in Nevada. She will be paid a lump sum of $60,000 in 7 years. Until then, the buyer pays 8% interest, quarterly.

  (a) Find the amount of each quarterly interest payment.

  (b) The buyer sets up a sinking fund so that enough money will be present to pay off the $60,000. The buyer wants to make semiannual payments into the sinking fund; the account pays 6% compounded semiannually. Find the amount of each payment into the fund.

  (c) Prepare a table showing the amount in the sinking fund after each deposit.

58. Jeff Reschke bought a rare stamp for his collection. He agreed to pay a lump sum of $4000 after 5 years. Until then, he pays 6% interest, compounded semiannually.

  (a) Find the amount of each semiannual interest payment.

  (b) Reschke sets up a sinking fund so that enough money will be present to pay off the $4000. He wants to make annual payments into the fund. The account pays 8% compounded annually. Find the amount of each payment into the fund.

  (c) Prepare a table showing the amount in the sinking fund after each deposit.

9.5 Present Value of an Annuity; Amortization

As shown in the previous section, if deposits of R dollars are made at the end of each period for n periods, at a rate of interest i per period, then the account will contain

$$A = R \cdot s_{\overline{n}|i} = R\left[\frac{(1 + i)^n - 1}{i}\right]$$

dollars after n periods. Let us now find the *lump sum P* that can be deposited today at a rate of interest i per period which will amount to the same A dollars in n periods.

First recall that P dollars deposited today will amount to $P(1 + i)^n$ dollars after n periods at a rate of interest i per period. We want this amount, $P(1 + i)^n$, to be the same as A, the future value of the annuity. Substituting $P(1 + i)^n$ for A in the formula above gives

$$P(1 + i)^n = R\left[\frac{(1 + i)^n - 1}{i}\right].$$

To solve this equation for P, multiply both sides by $(1 + i)^{-n}$.

$$P = R(1 + i)^{-n}\left[\frac{(1 + i)^n - 1}{i}\right]$$

Use the distributive property; also recall $(1 + i)^{-n}(1 + i)^n = 1$.

$$P = R\left[\frac{(1 + i)^{-n}(1 + i)^n - (1 + i)^{-n}}{i}\right]$$

$$P = R\left[\frac{1 - (1 + i)^{-n}}{i}\right]$$

The amount P is called the **present value of the annuity.** The quantity in brackets is abbreviated as $a_{\overline{n}|i}$, so

$$a_{\overline{n}|i} = \frac{1 - (1 + i)^{-n}}{i}.$$

Values of $a_{\overline{n}|i}$ are given in the table "Present Value of an Annuity," at the back of this text. The next box summarizes the formula for the present value of an annuity.

Present Value of an

Annuity

The present value, P, of an annuity of n payments of R dollars each at the end of consecutive interest periods with interest compounded at a rate of interest i per period is

$$P = R\left[\frac{1 - (1 + i)^{-n}}{i}\right] \quad \text{or} \quad P = R \cdot a_{\overline{n}|i}$$

EXAMPLE 1

What lump sum deposited today at 8% interest compounded annually will yield the same total amount as payments of $1500 at the end of each year for 12 years, also at 8% interest compounded annually?

We want to find the present value of an annuity of $1500 per year for 12 years at 8% compounded annually. Using the table or a calculator, $a_{\overline{12}|.08} = 7.53608$, so

$$P = 1500(7.53608) \approx 11,304.12$$

or $11,304.12. A lump sum deposit of $11,304.12 today at 8% compounded annually will yield the same total after 12 years as deposits of $1500 at the end of each year for 12 years at 8% compounded annually.

Let's check this result. The compound amount in 12 years of a deposit of $11,304.12 today at 8% compounded annually can be found by the formula $A = P(1 + i)^n$. From the compound interest table, $11,304.12 will produce a total of

$$(11,304.12)(2.51817) \approx 28,465.70,$$

or $28,465.70. On the other hand, from the table for $s_{\overline{n}|i}$, deposits of $1500 at the end of each year for 12 years, at 8% compounded annually, give an amount of

$$1500(18.97713) \approx 28,465.70,$$

or $28,465.70, the same amount found above.

In summary, there are two ways to have $28,465.70 in 12 years at 8% compounded annually—a single deposit of $11,304.12 today, or payments of $1500 at the end of each year for 12 years.

EXAMPLE 2

Mr. Jones and Ms. Gonsalez are both graduates of the Forestvire Institute of Technology. They both agree to contribute to the endowment fund of FIT. Mr. Jones says that he will give $500 at the end of each year for 9 years. Ms. Gonsalez would rather give a lump sum today. What lump sum can she give that will be equivalent to Mr. Jones' annual gifts, if the endowment fund earns 8% compounded annually?

Here $R = 500$, $n = 9$, and $i = .08$. The necessary number from the present value table or a calculator is $a_{\overline{9}|.08} = 6.24689$. Ms. Gonsalez must therefore donate a lump sum of

$$500(6.24689) \approx 3123.45,$$

or $3123.45, today. ∎

We can also use the formula above if we know the lump sum and want to find the periodic payment of the annuity. The next example shows how to do this.

EXAMPLE 3

A car costs $6000. After a down payment of $1000, the balance will be paid off in 36 monthly payments with interest of 12% per year, compounded monthly. Find the amount of each payment.

A single lump sum payment of $5000 today would pay off the loan. Thus, $5000 is the present value of an annuity of 36 monthly payments with interest of $12\%/12 = 1\%$ per month. We need to find R, the amount of each payment. Start with $P = R \cdot a_{\overline{n}|i}$; replace P with 5000, n with 36, and i with .01. From the table or a calculator, $a_{\overline{36}|.01} = 30.10751$, so

$$5000 = R(30.10751)$$
$$R \approx 166.07,$$

or $166.07. A monthly payment of $166.07 will be needed. ∎

Amortization   A loan is **amortized** if both the principal and interest are paid by a sequence of equal periodic payments. In Example 3 above, a loan of $5000 at 12% interest compounded monthly could be amortized by paying $166.07 per month for 36 months.

EXAMPLE 4

A speculator agrees to pay $15,000 for a parcel of land; this amount, with interest, will be paid over 4 years, with semiannual payments, at an interest rate of 12% compounded semiannually.

(a)   Find the amount of each payment.

If the speculator were to pay $15,000 immediately, there would be no need for any payments at all, making $15,000 the present value of an annuity of R dollars, $2 \cdot 4 = 8$ periods, and $i = 12\%/2 = 6\% = .06$ per period. Using $P = R \cdot a_{\overline{n}|i}$, in our example $P = 15,000$, with

$$15,000 = R \cdot a_{\overline{8}|.06}$$

or

$$R = \frac{15,000}{a_{\overline{8}|.06}}.$$

From the table or a calculator, $a_{\overline{8}|.06} = 6.20979$, and

$$R = \frac{15,000}{6.20979} \approx 2415.54,$$

or $2415.54. Each payment is $2415.54.

(b) Find the portion of the first payment that is applied to the reduction of the debt.

Interest is 12% per year, compounded semiannually, or 6% per semiannual period. During the first period, the entire $15,000 is owed. Interest on this amount for 6 months (1/2 year) is found by the formula for simple interest:

$$I = Prt = 15,000(.12)\left(\frac{1}{2}\right) = 900,$$

or $900. At the end of 6 months, the speculator makes a payment of $2415.54; since $900 of this represents interest, a total of

$$\$2415.54 - \$900 = \$1515.54$$

is applied to the reduction of the original debt.

(c) Find the balance due after 6 months.

The original balance due is $15,000. After 6 months, $1515.54 is applied to reduction of the debt. The debt owed after 6 months is

$$\$15,000 - \$1515.54 = \$13,484.46.$$

(d) How much interest is owed for the second six-month period?

A total of $13,484.46 is owed for the second 6 months. Interest on it is

$$I = 13,484.46\,(.12)\left(\frac{1}{2}\right) = 809.07,$$

or $809.07. A payment of $2415.54 is made at the end of this period; a total of

$$\$2415.54 - \$809.07 = \$1606.47$$

is applied to reduction of the debt.

By continuing this process, we get the **amortization schedule** shown below. As the schedule shows, the payment is always the same, except perhaps for a small adjustment in the final payment. Payment 0 is the original amount of the loan.

Amortization Schedule

Payment number	Amount of payment	Interest for period	Portion to principal	Principal at end of period
0	—	—	—	$15,000.00
1	$2415.54	$900.00	$1515.54	$13,484.46
2	$2415.54	$809.07	$1606.47	$11,877.99
3	$2415.54	$712.68	$1702.86	$10,175.13
4	$2415.54	$610.51	$1805.03	$8370.10
5	$2415.54	$502.21	$1913.33	$6456.77
6	$2415.54	$387.41	$2028.13	$4428.64
7	$2415.54	$265.72	$2149.82	$2278.82
8	$2415.55	$136.73	$2278.82	$0

EXAMPLE 5

A house is bought for $74,000, with a down payment of $16,000. Interest is charged at 10.25% per year for 30 years. Find the amount of each monthly payment to amortize the loan.

Here, the present value, P, is 58,000 (or 74,000 − 16,000). Also, $i = .1025/12 = .0085416667$, and $n = 12 \cdot 30 = 360$. We must find R. From the formula for the present value of an annuity,

$$58,000 = R \cdot a_{\overline{360}|.0085416667}$$

or

$$58,000 = R \left[\frac{1 - (1 + .0085416667)^{-360}}{.0085416667} \right].$$

Use a financial calculator, or a calculator with an x^y key to get

$$58,000 = R \left[\frac{1 - .0467967624}{.0085416667} \right]$$

$$58,000 = R \left[\frac{.9532032376}{.0085416667} \right]$$

$$58,000 = R[111.5945249]$$

or

$$R = 519.74.$$

Monthly payments of $519.74 will be required to amortize the loan.   ∎

9.5 EXERCISES

Find each of the values in Exercises 1–8.

1. $a_{\overline{15}|.06}$ **2.** $a_{\overline{10}|.03}$ **3.** $a_{\overline{18}|.04}$ **4.** $a_{\overline{30}|.01}$

5. $a_{\overline{16}|.01}$ **6.** $a_{\overline{32}|.02}$ **7.** $a_{\overline{6}|.015}$ **8.** $a_{\overline{18}|.015}$

Find the present value of each ordinary annuity in Exercises 9–16.

9. Payments of $1000 are made annually for 9 years at 8% compounded annually.

10. Payments of $5000 are made annually for 11 years at 6% compounded annually.

11. Payments of $890 are made annually for 16 years at 8% compounded annually.

12. Payments of $1400 are made annually for 8 years at 8% compounded annually.

13. Payments of $10,000 are made semiannually for 15 years at 10% compounded semiannually.

14. Payments of $50,000 are made quarterly for 10 years at 8% compounded quarterly.

15. Payments of $15,806 are made quarterly for 3 years at 15.8% compounded quarterly.

16. Payments of $18,579 are made every six months for 8 years at 19.4% compounded semiannually.

In Exercises 17–22, find the lump sum deposited today that will yield the same total amount as payments of $10,000 at the end of each year for 15 years, at each of the given interest rates.

17. 4%, compounded annually

19. 6%, compounded annually

21. 12%, compounded annually

18. 5%, compounded annually

20. 8%, compounded annually

22. 16%, compounded annually

23. In his will the late Mr. Hudspeth said that each child in his family could have an annuity of $2000 at the end of each year for 9 years, or the equivalent present value. If money can be deposited at 8% compounded annually, what is the present value?

24. In the "Million Dollar Lottery," a winner is paid a million dollars at the rate of $50,000 per year for 20 years. Assume that these payments form an ordinary annuity, and that the lottery managers can invest money at 6% compounded annually. Find the lump sum that the management must put away to pay off the "million dollar" winner.

25. Lynn Meyers buys a new car costing $6000. She agrees to make payments at the end of each monthly period for 4 years. If she pays 12% interest, compounded monthly, what is the amount of each payment?

26. Find the total amount of interest Meyers will pay. (See Exercise 25.)

27. What sum deposited today at 5% compounded annually for 8 years will provide the same amount as $1000 deposited at the end of each year for 8 years at 6% compounded annually?

28. What lump sum deposited today at 8% compounded quarterly for 10 years will yield the same final amount as deposits of $4000 at the end of each six month period for 10 years at 6% compounded semiannually?

Find the payment necessary to amortize each of the loans in Exercises 29–36.

29. $1000, 8% compounded annually, 9 annual payments

30. $2500, 16% compounded quarterly, 6 quarterly payments

31. $41,000, 12% compounded semiannually, 10 semiannual payments

32. $90,000, 8% compounded annually, 12 annual payments

33. $140,000, 12% compounded quarterly, 15 quarterly payments

34. $7400, 16% compounded semiannuallly, 18 semiannual payments

35. $5500, 18% compounded monthly, 24 monthly payments

36. $45,000, 18% compounded monthly, 36 monthly payments

Find the monthly house payment necessary to amortize the loans in Exercises 37–40. You will need a financial calculator or one with an x^y key.

37. $49,560 at 15.75% for 25 years

38. $70,892 at 14.11% for 30 years

39. $53,762 at 16.45% for 30 years

40. $96,511 at 15.57% for 25 years

41. An insurance firm pays $4000 for a new printer for its computer. It amortizes the loan for the printer in 4 annual payments at 8% compounded annually. Prepare an amortization schedule for this machine.

42. Large semitrailer trucks cost $72,000 each. Ace Trucking buys such a truck and agrees to pay for it by a loan which will be amortized with 9 semiannual payments at 16% compounded semiannually. Prepare an amortization schedule for this truck.

43. One retailer charges $1048 for a correcting electric typewriter. A firm of tax accountants buys 8 of these machines. They make a down payment of $1200 and agree to amortize the balance with monthly payments at 18% compounded monthly for 4 years. Prepare an amortization schedule showing the first six payments.

44. When Denise Sullivan opened her law office, she bought $14,000 worth of law books and $7200 worth of office furniture. She paid $1200 down and agreed to amortize the balance with semiannual payments for 5 years, at 16% compounded semiannually. Prepare an amortization schedule for this purchase.

45. When Ms. Thompson died, she left $25,000 for her husband. He deposits the money at 6% compounded annually. He wants to make annual withdrawals from the account so that the money (principal and interest) is gone in exactly 8 years.

  (a) Find the amount of each withdrawal.

  (b) Find the amount of each withdrawal if the money must last 12 years.

46. The trustees of a college have accepted a gift of $150,000. The donor has directed the trustees to deposit the money in an account paying 12% per year, compounded semiannually. The trustees may withdraw money at the end of each 6-month period; the money must last 5 years.

  (a) Find the amount of each withdrawal.

  (b) Find the amount of each withdrawal if the money must last 6 years.

Prepare an amortization schedule for each of the following problems.

47. A loan of $37,947.50 with interest at 8.5% compounded annually, to be paid with equal annual payments over 10 years.

48. A loan of $4835.80 at 9.25% interest compounded semiannually, to be repaid in 5 years in equal semiannual payments.

EXTENDED

APPLICATION

A New Look at Athletes' Contracts*

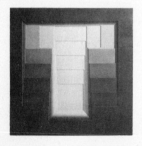

There has been a lot of controversy lately about big-buck contracts with athletes and how this affects the nature of the sports business.

Indeed, the recent headlines of a $40 million contract with Steve Young from Brigham Young University to play football for the USFL has opened Pandora's box. Club owners in all sports are wondering when all of this is going to stop.

To put the issue in its proper perspective, however, it seems to me that the $40 million contract is misleading. Just mentioning dollars misses several points. For one, the USFL has got to be around long enough to pay off. Two, the present value of million dollar payments that stretch 43 years into the future is reduced considerably.

In order to assess the effective value of these kinds of contracts, two important questions must be answered. First, what is the risk of the company to pay off on the periodic principal payments; and second, what is the present value of the return when parlayed into future cash benefits?

Recently, I conducted a survey among a number of sports-minded educators and students here on the campus. The survey was similar to the rating survey conducted by Wall Street rating firms when they evaluate risk of a corporation.

Specifically, the question was: "On a scale of 1 to 10, give me your estimate of the team's ability to continue in business and to meet the commitments of its contracts."

---

*From "A New Look at Athletes' Contracts" by Richard F. Kaufman in *The Sacramento Bee*, April 30, 1984. Reprinted by permission of the author.

I was surprised to find that the baseball teams were rated with the lowest risk; the National Football League teams next; then the National Basketball Association teams; and then the United States Football League teams coming in last.

The cash flows which these athletes receive in the future have a present value today in total dollars based upon about an 8 percent discount factor each year for expected inflation. By determining the expected present value, the average per annum return of Athlete A who receives megabucks in the future can be compared with Athlete B who receives megabucks not so far into the future.

When risk of paying these megabucks is considered, we arrive at a completely different picture than just the dollar signs on the contract portray.

The following chart of the highly paid athletes, recently taken from a newspaper article, shows the athletes' names in sequence according to the best deal when risk and expected yearly return are assessed. A lesser coefficient of variation provides a statistical ratio of lesser risk to the per annum return for each athlete for each dollar of present value.

Notice that these risk assumptions show George Foster of the New York Mets with the best deal. Dave Winfield and Gary Carter are close behind. Steve Young is last, yet it is claimed that he received the most attractive sports contract ever signed.

Some Highly Paid Athletes

	Present Value		Per Annum	
	of Contract (In Millions)	Expected Value	Risk Assessment	Coefficient of Variation
George Foster NL (Mets) $10 million, 5 years	$ 7.985	$1.597	2.3	1.44
Dave Winfield AL (Yankees) $21 million, 10 years	$14.091	$1.409	2.6	1.85
Gary Carter NL (Expos) $15 million, 8 years	$10.775	$1.347	3.0	2.23
Moses Malone NBA (76ers) $13.2 million, 6 years	$10.170	$1.695	5.4	3.19
Larry Bird NBA (Celtics) $15 million, 7 years	$11.157	$1.594	5.2	3.26
Wayne Gretzky NHL (Edmonton Oilers) $21 million, 21 years	$10.170	$ .477	5.8	12.16
Magic Johnson NBA (Lakers) $25 million, 25 years	$10.675	$ .427	5.6	13.12
Steve Young USFL (Express) $40 million, 43 years	$11.267	$ .262	7.2	27.48

It is true that risk is only our perception of the uncertainties of future events, and many times our judgment is wrong. But let's face it. It is the only game in town, unless you are gifted with extrasensory perception or have a crystal ball. In that case, I would appreciate your contacting me because I have work for you.

Anytime we purchase a bond or a like security, we make judgments about the future ability of the firm or municipality to meet its interest and principal payments. We employ expert rating agencies like Moody's or Standard & Poor's to professionally rate these securities. Indeed, the market price of the bond depends upon the judgments of these agencies.

It would seem to me that the time is long overdue for a similar rating system to be implemented to determine the risk of sports organizations—if for no other reason than to help the athlete decide where he would like to hang his hat. But more importantly, to provide a truer financial picture to the fans and broadcasting companies who are asked to pick up the tab. What do you think?

EXTENDED	Present Value*
APPLICATION	

The Southern Pacific Railroad, with lines running from Oregon to Louisiana, is one of the country's most profitable railroads. The railroad has vast landholdings (granted by the government in the last half of the nineteenth century) and is diversified into trucking, pipelines, and data transmission.

The railroad was recently faced with a decision on the fate of an old bridge which crosses the Kings River in central California. The bridge is on a minor line which carries very little traffic. Just north of the Southern Pacific bridge is another bridge, owned by the Santa Fe Railroad; it too carries little traffic. The Southern Pacific had two alternatives: it could replace its own bridge or it could negotiate with the Santa Fe for the rights to run trains over its bridge. In the second alternative a yearly fee would be paid to the Santa Fe, and new connecting tracks would be built. The situation is shown in the figure.

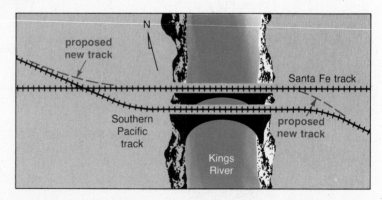

---

*Based on information supplied by The Southern Pacific Transportation Company, San Francisco.

To find the better of these two alternatives, the railroad used the following approach.

1. Calculate estimated expenses for each alternative.
2. Calculate annual cash flows in after tax dollars. At a 48% corporate tax rate, $1 of expenses actually costs the railroad $.52, and $1 of revenue can bring a maximum of $.52 in profit. Cash flow for a given year is found by the following formula.

$$\text{cash flow} = -.52 \text{ (operating and maintenance expenses)}$$
$$+ .52 \text{ (savings and revenue)} + .48 \text{ (depreciation)}$$

3. Calculate the net present values of all cash flows for future years. The formula used is

$$\text{net present value} = \Sigma\,(\text{cash flow in year } i)(1 + k)^{1-i},$$

where i is a particular year in the life of the project and k is the assumed annual rate of interest. (Recall: Σ indicates a sum.) The net present value is found for interest rates from 0% to 20%.
4. The interest rate that leads to a net present value of $0 is called the **rate of return** on the project.

Let us now see how these steps worked out in practice.

Alternative 1: Operate over the Santa Fe bridge First, estimated expenses were calculated.

1976	Work done by Southern Pacific on Santa Fe track	$27,000
1976	Work by Southern Pacific on its own track	11,600
1976	Undepreciated portion of cost of current bridge	97,410
1976	Salvage value of bridge	12,690
1977	Annual maintenance of Santa Fe track	16,717
1977	Annual rental fee to Santa Fe	7,382

From these figures and others not given here, annual cash flows and net present values were calculated. The following table was then prepared.

Interest Rate, %	Net Present Value
0	$85,731
4	67,566
8	53,332
12	42,008
16	32,875
20	25,414

Although the table does not show a net present value of $0, the interest rate that leads to that value is 44%. This is the rate of return for this alternative.

Alternative 2: Build a new bridge   Again, estimated expenses were calculated.

1976	Annual maintenance	$2,870
1976	Annual inspection	120
1976	Repair trestle	17,920
1977	Install bridge	189,943
1977	Install walks and handrails	15,060
1978	Repaint steel (every 10 years)	10,000
1978	Repair trusses (every 10 years, increases by $200)	2,000
1981	Replace ties	31,000
1988	Repair concrete (every 10 years)	400
2021	Replace ties	31,000

After cash flows and net present values were calculated, the following table was prepared.

Interest Rate, %	Net Present Value
0	$399,577
4	96,784
7.8	0
8	−3,151
12	−43,688
16	−62,615
20	−72,126

In this alternative the net present value is $0 at 7.8%, the rate of return.

Based on this analysis, the first alternative, renting from the Santa Fe, is clearly preferable.

EXERCISES

Find the cash flow in each of the following years. Use the formula given above.

1. Alternative 1, year 1977, operating expenses $6228, maintenance expenses $2976, savings $26,251, depreciation $10,778

2. Alternative 1, year 1984, same as Exercise 1, but depreciation is only $1347

3. Alternative 2, year 1976, maintenance $2870, operating expenses $6386, savings $26,251, no depreciation

4. Alternative 2, year 1980, operating expenses $6228, maintenance expenses $2976, savings $10,618, depreciation $6736

KEY WORDS	simple interest	discount interest	common difference
	principal	proceeds	geometric sequence
	rate	compound interest	common ratio
	time	compound amount	annuity
	future value	effective rate	ordinary annuity
	maturity value	sequence	term of an annuity
	ordinary interest	terms	annuity due
	exact interest	general term	sinking fund
	present value	arithmetic sequence	amortization

Chapter 9   REVIEW EXERCISES

Many of these exercises will require a calculator with an x^y key.

Find the simple interest in Exercises 1–6.

1. $15,903 at 18% for 8 months

2. $4902 at 19.5% for 11 months

3. $42,368 at 15.22% for 5 months

4. $3478 at 17.4% for 88 days (assume a 360-day year)

5. $2390 at 18.7% from May 3 to July 28 (assume 365 days in a year)

6. $69,056.12 at 15.5% from September 13 to March 25 of the following year (assume a 365-day year)

Find the present value of the future amounts in Exercises 7–9. Assume 360 days in a year; use simple interest.

7. $25,000 for 10 months, money earns 17%

8. $459.57 for 7 months, money earns 18.5%

9. $80,612 for 128 days, money earns 16.77%

Find the proceeds in Exercises 10–12. Assume 360 days in a year.

10. $56,882, discount rate 19%, length of loan 5 months

11. $802.34, discount rate 18.6%, length of loan 11 months

12. $12,000, discount rate 17.09%, length of loan 145 days

13. Tom Wilson owes $5800 to his mother. He has agreed to pay the money in 10 months, at an interest rate of 14%. Three months before the loan is due, the mother discounts the loan at the bank. The bank charges a 17.45% discount rate. How much money does the mother receive?

14. Larry DiCenso needs $9812 to buy new equipment for his business. The bank charges a discount of 14%. Find the amount of DiCenso's loan, if he borrows the money for 7 months.

Find the effective annual rate for the bank discount rates in Exercise 15 and 16. (Assume a one-year loan of $1000.)

15. 14%   **16.** 17.5%

Find the compound amounts in Exercises 17–24.

17. $1000 at 8% compounded annually for 9 years

18. $2800 at 6% compounded annually for 10 years

19. $19,456.11 at 12% compounded semiannually for 7 years

20. $312.45 at 16% compounded semiannually for 16 years

21. $1900 at 16% compounded quarterly for 9 years

22. $57,809.34 at 12% compounded quarterly for 5 years

23. $2500 at 18% compounded monthly for 3 years

24. $11,702.55 at 18% compounded monthly for 4 years

Find the amount of interest earned by each deposit in Exercises 25–30.

25. $3954 at 8% compounded annually for 12 years

26. $12,699.36 at 16% compounded semiannually for 7 years

27. $7801.72 at 12% compounded quarterly for 5 years

28. $48,121.91 at 18% compounded monthly for 2 years

29. $12,903.45 at 12.37% compounded quarterly for 29 quarters

30. $34,677.23 at 14.72% compounded monthly for 32 months

Find the present value of the amounts given in Exercises 31–36 if money can be invested at the given rate.

31. $5000 in 9 years, 8% compounded annually

32. $12,250 in 5 years, 12% compounded semiannually

33. $42,000 in 7 years, 18% compounded monthly

34. $17,650 in 4 years, 16% compounded quarterly

35. $1347.89 in 3.5 years, 13.77% compounded semiannually

36. $2388.90 in 44 months, 12.93% compounded monthly

37. In four years, Mr. Heeren must pay a pledge of $5000 to his church's building fund. What lump sum can he invest today, at 12% compounded semiannually, so that he will have enough to pay his pledge?

38. Joann Hudspeth must make an alimony payment of $1500 in 15 months. What lump sum can she invest today, at 18% compounded monthly, so that she will have enough to make the payment?

Write the first five terms for each of the sequences in Exercises 39–42. Identify any which are arithmetic or geometric.

39. $a_n = -4n + 2$ **40.** $a_n = (-2)^n$

41. $a_n = \dfrac{n + 2}{n + 5}$ **42.** $a_n = (n - 7)(n + 5)$

43. Find a_{12} for the arithmetic sequence having $a_1 = 6$ and $d = 5$.

44. Find the sum of the first 20 terms for the arithmetic sequence having $a_1 = -6$ and $d = 8$.

45. Find a_4 for the geometric sequence with $a_1 = -3$ and $r = 2$.

46. Find the sum of the first 6 terms for the geometric sequence with $a_1 = 8000$ and $r = -1/2$.

Find the value of each of the annuities in Exercises 47–52.

47. $500 is deposited at the end of each six month period for 8 years; money earns 16% compounded semiannually

48. $1288 is deposited at the end of each year for 14 years; money earns 8% compounded annually

49. $4000 is deposited at the end of each quarter for 7 years; money earns 16% compounded quarterly

50. $233 is deposited at the end of each month for 4 years; money earns 18% compounded monthly

51. $672 is deposited at the beginning of each quarter for 7 years; money earns 20% compounded quarterly

52. $11,900 is deposited at the beginning of each month for 13 months; money earns 18% compounded monthly

53. Georgette Dahl deposits $491 at the end of each quarter for 9 years. If the account pays 19.4% compounded quarterly, find the final amount in the account.

54. J. Euclid deposits $1526.38 at the beginning of each six-month period in an account paying 20.6% compounded semiannually. How much will be in the account after five years?

In Exercises 55–58 find the amount of each payment to be made into a sinking fund so that enough money will be available to pay off the indicated loan.

55. $6500 loan, money earns 8% compounded annually, 6 annual payments

56. $57,000 loan, money earns 16% compounded semiannually, for 8 1/2 years

57. $233,188 loan, money earns 19.7% compounded quarterly, for 7 3/4 years

58. $1,056,788 loan, money earns 18.12% compounded monthly, for 4 1/2 years

Find the present value of each ordinary annuity in Exercises 59–62.

59. Payments of $850 are made annually for 4 years at 8% compounded annually.

60. Payments of $1500 are made quarterly for 7 years, at 16% compounded quarterly.

61. Payments of $4210 are made semiannually for 8 years, at 18.6% compounded semiannually.

62. Payments of $877.34 are made monthly for 17 months, at 22.4% compounded monthly.

63. Vicki Manchester borrows $20,000 from the bank to help her expand her business. She agrees to repay the money in equal payments at the end of each year for 9 years. Interest is at 18.9% compounded annually. Find the amount of each payment.

64. Ken Murrill wants to expand his pharmacy. To do this, he takes out a loan of $49,275 from the bank, and agrees to repay it at 24.2% compounded monthly, over 48 months. Find the amount of each payment necessary to amortize this loan.

Find the amount of the payment necessary to amortize the loans in Exercises 65–68.

65. $80,000 loan, 8% compounded annually, 9 annual payments

66. $3200 loan, 16% compounded quarterly, 10 quarterly payments

67. $32,000 loan, 19.4% compounded quarterly, 17 quarterly payments

68. $51,607 loan, 23.6% compounded monthly, 32 monthly payments

Find the monthly house payments for the mortgages in Exercises 69 and 70.

69. $56,890 at 14.74% for 25 years

70. $77,110 at 16.45% for 30 years

Prepare amortization schedules for the following loans.

71. $5000 at 10% compounded semiannually, for 3 years

72. $12,500 at 12% compounded quarterly, for 2 years

 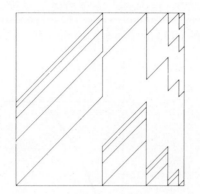 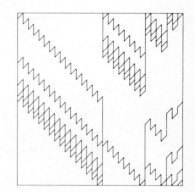

THE DERIVATIVE

Karl Gerstner. Drawings from *Diagon 31²*, *Red/Green*, alterable object, 1956.

The graph of Figure 1 shows the profit earned by a firm from the production of x hundred items. The graph shows that profit increases quickly to the point where $x = 3$. At this point, the profit is $4000. For the firm to produce more than $x = 3$ (or 300) items, a second factory must be reopened, with the additional costs for the opening causing profits to fall. The graph shows that only after 600 items are produced does profit again reach $4000.

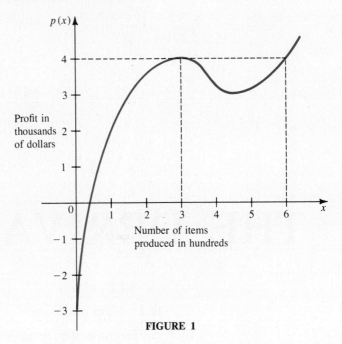

FIGURE 1

Optimum profit depends on estimated sales—if the sales manager says that only 500 items can be sold, then the optimum profit is found when $x = 3$. On the other hand, if a sudden demand means that well over 600 items can be sold, then the second factory should be opened.

In this chapter we will see how one branch of calculus, called **differential calculus,** is used to find the optimum values of functions giving profits, costs, nutritional values, and so on. In addition, we will see how differential calculus is used to describe *rates of change* in management, social science, and biology.

The basic concept of differential calculus is the **derivative,** which we begin discussing in Section 3 of this chapter. The definition of derivative involves the idea of a limit, which we discuss first.

10.1 Limits

The idea of a limit arises when we consider a function $y = f(x)$ defined on some interval and ask "What happens to the values of $f(x)$ as x gets closer and closer to some fixed number?" For example, Figure 2 shows the graph of a function f. The arrowheads suggest that as x gets closer and closer to the number 5 (on the x-axis), the values of $f(x)$ get closer and closer to the number 4 (on the y-axis). That is, the *limit* of $f(x)$ as x approaches 5 is the number 4, written

$$f(x) \to 4 \text{ when } x \to 5, \qquad \text{or, more commonly,} \qquad \lim_{x \to 5} f(x) = 4.$$

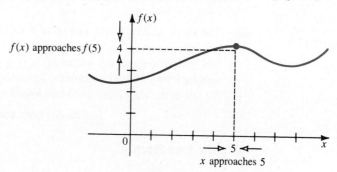

FIGURE 2

EXAMPLE 1

(a) The graph in Figure 3 is that of a function g. The open circle at $(3, -1)$ means that the function is not defined at $x = 3$. Since $g(3)$ is not defined, it is meaningless to ask about the value of g *at* 3. However, we can ask how the values of g behave when x is *close to* 3. The graph suggests that as x gets closer and closer to 3 (but doesn't *equal* 3), the values of $g(x)$ get closer and closer to -1. As above, this is written

$$\lim_{x \to 3} g(x) = -1.$$

For values of x near 3, the function g never takes on the value -1. However, as x gets as close as desired to 3, the values of g get as close as desired to -1.

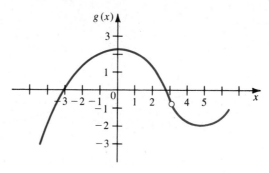

FIGURE 3

This example suggests that $x \to a$ means that x approaches as close as desired to a, without necessarily reaching a.

(b) The graph of Figure 3 also shows that as x gets closer and closer to -3, the values of $g(x)$ get closer and closer to 0, or

$$\lim_{x \to -3} g(x) = 0.$$

Here $g(-3)$ is defined and equals 0. ∎

EXAMPLE 2

(a) The graph of function h in Figure 4 shows that as x approaches 4 from the left, the values of $h(x)$ approach 3. However, as x gets closer and closer to 4 from the right, the values of $h(x)$ approach 5. Since the values of $h(x)$ approach two different numbers depending on whether x approaches 4 from the left or the right, and since one would want a limit to be only one number,

$$\lim_{x \to 4} h(x) \quad \text{does not exist.}$$

(b) Also from Figure 4,

$$\lim_{x \to 1} h(x) = -1 \quad \text{and} \quad \lim_{x \to 8} h(x) = 5. \quad ∎$$

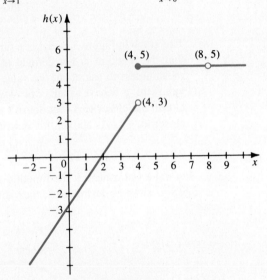

FIGURE 4

The examples above suggest the following intuitive definition of limit.

Limit

If the values $f(x)$ of a function f can be made as close as desired to a single number L for all values of x sufficiently close to the number a, with $x \neq a$, then L is the **limit** of $f(x)$ as x approaches a, written

$$\lim_{x \to a} f(x) = L.$$

This definition is *intuitive* because we have not defined "as close as desired." A more formal definition of limit would be needed for proving the rules for limits given later in the section.

The definition of limit implies that the values of a function cannot approach two different limits at the same time, so that if a limit exists, it is unique. Also, Example 2(a) shows that a limit need not always exist. In Figure 5, both at -4 and at 3 the values of $f(x)$ do not approach some fixed number, so that both

$$\lim_{x \to -4} f(x) \quad \text{and} \quad \lim_{x \to 3} f(x) \quad \text{do not exist.}$$

A final observation is that a limit can exist, even if the function is not defined. Again in Figure 5, $\lim_{x \to 4} f(x) = 1$, even though $f(4)$ is not defined (because of the hole in the graph).

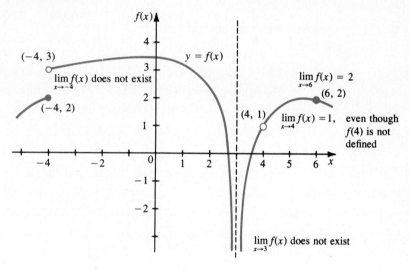

FIGURE 5

In the examples above, we found limits by examining a graph. Other methods may be used for finding limits; for example, we can find several values of the function as x approaches the given number. The next few examples show how this process works. (A calculator is very helpful for these examples.)

EXAMPLE 3   **(a)**   Find $\lim_{x \to 1} \dfrac{x^2 - 4}{x - 2}$.

To find this limit, choose several values of x close to 1 and on either side of 1. The results for several different values of x are shown in the following table.

Closer and closer to 1 ↓

x	0.8	0.9	0.99	0.9999	1	1.0000001	1.0001	1.001	1.01	1.05	1.1
$f(x)$	2.8	2.9	2.99	2.9999	3	3.0000001	3.0001	3.001	3.01	3.05	3.1

↑ Closer and closer to 3

The table suggests that the values of $f(x)$ get closer and closer to 3 as the values of x get closer and closer to 1, or

$$\lim_{x \to 1} \frac{x^2 - 4}{x - 2} = 3.$$

(b)   Find $\lim\limits_{x \to 2} \dfrac{x^2 - 4}{x - 2}$.

The value $x = 2$ is not in the domain of $f(x) = (x^2 - 4)/(x - 2)$, since 2 makes the denominator equal 0. However, f may still have a limit as x approaches 2. (Recall Example 1(a) above: the limit existed, even though the function was not defined.) Start with a table of values.

Closer and closer to 2
↓

x	1.8	1.9	1.99	1.9999	2	2.0000001	2.00001	2.001	2.05	2.1
$f(x)$	3.8	3.9	3.99	3.9999	4	4.0000001	4.00001	4.001	4.05	4.1

↑
Closer and closer to 4

The table suggests that the values of $f(x)$ get closer and closer to 4 as x gets closer and closer to 2. Therefore, it seems likely that

$$\lim_{x \to 2} \frac{x^2 - 4}{x - 2} = 4. \quad \blacksquare$$

In Example 3, you may have noticed that, if $x \neq 2$,

$$\frac{x^2 - 4}{x - 2} = \frac{(x + 2)(x - 2)}{x - 2} = x + 2.$$

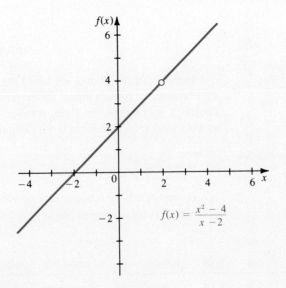

FIGURE 6

The values in the tables could have been found more easily by evaluating $x + 2$ instead of $(x^2 - 4)/(x - 2)$; the limits also could have been found in this way. For example,

$$\lim_{x \to 2} \frac{x^2 - 4}{x - 2} = \lim_{x \to 2} (x + 2).$$

As x gets closer and closer to 2, the expression $x + 2$ will get closer and closer to $2 + 2 = 4$, with

$$\lim_{x \to 2} \frac{x^2 - 4}{x - 2} = \lim_{x \to 2} (x + 2) = 4.$$

A graph of $f(x) = (x^2 - 4)/(x - 2)$ is shown in Figure 6.

EXAMPLE 4   Let $g(x) = \dfrac{x^2 + 4}{x - 2}$ and find $\displaystyle\lim_{x \to 2} \dfrac{x^2 + 4}{x - 2}$.

Make a table of values as in the previous example.

x	1.8	1.9	1.99	1.999	2	2.001	2.01	2.05
$g(x)$	-36.2	-76.1	-796	-7996		8004	804	164

does not exist

Both the table and the graph of Figure 7 suggest that

$$\lim_{x \to 2} \frac{x^2 + 4}{x - 2} \quad \text{does not exist.} \quad \blacksquare$$

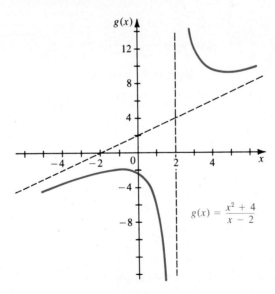

$$g(x) = \frac{x^2 + 4}{x - 2}$$

FIGURE 7

Rules for Limits The rules for limits given in the following box are often helpful in evaluating limits. (The proof of these rules requires a formal definition of limit, which we have not given.)

Rules for Limits

Let a, k, n, A, and B be real numbers, and let f and g be functions such that
$$\lim_{x \to a} f(x) = A \qquad \text{and} \qquad \lim_{x \to a} g(x) = B.$$

1. If k is a constant, then $\lim_{x \to a} k = k$ and $\lim_{x \to a} k \cdot f(x) = k \cdot \lim_{x \to a} f(x)$.

2. $\lim_{x \to a} [f(x) \pm g(x)] = \lim_{x \to a} f(x) \pm \lim_{x \to a} g(x) = A \pm B$

   (The limit of a sum or difference is the sum or difference of the limits.)

3. $\lim_{x \to a} [f(x) \cdot g(x)] = [\lim_{x \to a} f(x)] \cdot [\lim_{x \to a} g(x)] = A \cdot B$

   (The limit of a product is the product of the limits.)

4. $\lim_{x \to a} \dfrac{f(x)}{g(x)} = \dfrac{\lim_{x \to a} f(x)}{\lim_{x \to a} g(x)} = \dfrac{A}{B}$ if $B \neq 0$

   (The limit of a quotient is the quotient of the limits, provided the limit of the denominator is not zero.)

5. For any real number n, $[\lim_{x \to a} f(x)]^n = A^n$.

6. $\lim_{x \to a} f(x) = \lim_{x \to a} g(x)$ if $f(x) = g(x)$ for all $x \neq a$.

EXAMPLE 5

(a) Find $\lim_{x \to 2} (4x^2 - 2x + 3)$.

By Rule 2 above,
$$\lim_{x \to 2} (4x^2 - 2x + 3) = \lim_{x \to 2} 4x^2 + \lim_{x \to 2} (-2x) + \lim_{x \to 2} 3$$

Rules 1, 3, and 5 give
$$\lim_{x \to 2} 4x^2 + \lim_{x \to 2} (-2x) + \lim_{x \to 2} 3 = (\lim_{x \to 2} 4)(\lim_{x \to 2} x^2) + (\lim_{x \to 2} -2)(\lim_{x \to 2} x) + \lim_{x \to 2} 3$$
$$= 4(2^2) + (-2)(2) + 3 = 15.$$

In practice, many of these steps may be omitted.

(b) Find $\lim_{x \to 9} \sqrt{4x - 11}$.

As $x \to 9$, the expression $4x - 11$ approaches $4 \cdot 9 - 11 = 25$. Using Rule 5, with $n = 1/2$, gives
$$\lim_{x \to 9} \sqrt{4x - 11} = \sqrt{25} = 5. \quad \blacksquare$$

EXAMPLE 6   Find $\lim\limits_{x \to 4} \dfrac{\sqrt{x} - 2}{x - 4}$

As $x \to 4$, the numerator approaches 0 and the denominator also approaches 0, giving the meaningless expression 0/0. Here we may use algebra to rationalize the numerator by multiplying numerator and denominator by $\sqrt{x} + 2$. This gives

$$\frac{\sqrt{x} - 2}{x - 4} \cdot \frac{\sqrt{x} + 2}{\sqrt{x} + 2} = \frac{\sqrt{x} \cdot \sqrt{x} - 2\sqrt{x} + 2\sqrt{x} - 4}{(x - 4)(\sqrt{x} + 2)}$$

$$= \frac{x - 4}{(x - 4)(\sqrt{x} + 2)} = \frac{1}{\sqrt{x} + 2}.$$

Now use rules for limits.

$$\lim_{x \to 4} \frac{\sqrt{x} - 2}{x - 4} = \lim_{x \to 4} \frac{1}{\sqrt{x} + 2} = \frac{1}{\sqrt{4} + 2} = \frac{1}{2 + 2} = \frac{1}{4}.$$

(b) $\lim\limits_{x \to -1} \dfrac{x^2 - x - 2}{x + 1}$

Replacing x with -1 again gives the meaningless expression 0/0. Factor the numerator to get

$$\lim_{x \to -1} \frac{x^2 - x - 2}{x + 1} = \lim_{x \to -1} \frac{(x - 2)(x + 1)}{x + 1} = \lim_{x \to -1} (x - 2).$$

By the rules for limits, this result is

$$\lim_{x \to -1} (x - 2) = -3. \quad \blacksquare$$

EXAMPLE 7   The graph of Figure 8 shows the profit from producing x units of a certain product in a given day. If one shift of workers can produce no more than 25 items, a second shift must be called to work when more than 25 items are needed. This second shift increases the fixed costs and causes a drop in profits (indicated by a break in the

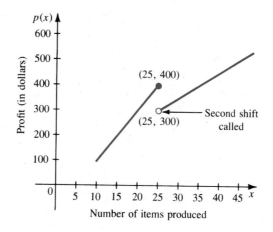

FIGURE 8

graph at $x = 25$) unless many more than 25 items are needed. (The graph shows that on 30 items, for example, the profit is about \$340, and that production must increase to 35 items before profit returns to \$400 and the second shift produces an increase in profits.) Profit when production is near 25 items depends on whether or not the second shift has been called in. As the graph suggests,

$$\lim_{x \to 25} p(x) \quad \text{does not exist.} \quad \blacksquare$$

Limits at Infinity Suppose a small pond normally contains 12 units of dissolved oxygen in a fixed volume of water. Suppose also that at time $t = 0$ a quantity of organic waste is introduced into the pond, with the oxygen concentration t weeks later given by

$$f(t) = \frac{12t^2 - 15t + 12}{t^2 + 1}.$$

For example, after 2 weeks, the pond contains

$$f(2) = \frac{12 \cdot 2^2 - 15 \cdot 2 + 12}{2^2 + 1} = \frac{30}{5} = 6$$

units of oxygen; and after 4 weeks,

$$f(4) = \frac{12 \cdot 4^2 - 15 \cdot 4 + 12}{4^2 + 1} \approx 8.5$$

units. Choosing several values of t and finding the corresponding values of $f(t)$ leads to the graph in Figure 9.

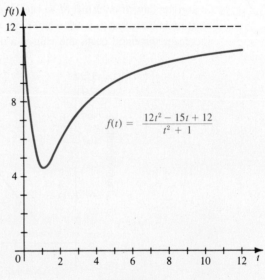

FIGURE 9

The graph suggests that as time goes on, the oxygen level returns closer and closer to the original 12 units. Because of this, the limit of $f(t)$ as t increases without bound is 12, written

$$\lim_{t \to \infty} f(t) = 12.$$

The symbol ∞ is read "infinity," while $t \to \infty$ is read "t increases without bound." (Also, $-\infty$ is read "negative infinity," with $t \to -\infty$ read "t decreases without bound.")

The graphs of $f(x) = 1/x$ (in black), and $g(x) = 1/x^2$ (in color), shown in Figure 10 lead to examples of such *limits at infinity*. The graph indicates that both $\lim_{x \to \infty} (1/x) = 0$ and $\lim_{x \to \infty} (1/x^2) = 0$, suggesting the following rule.

For any positive real number n and any real number k,

$$\lim_{x \to \infty} \frac{k}{x^n} = 0.$$

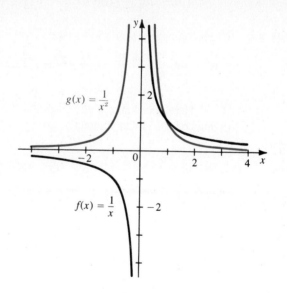

FIGURE 10

x	-100	-10	-1	1	10	100
$f(x) = \dfrac{1}{x}$	$-.01$	$-.1$	-1	1	$.1$	$.01$
$g(x) = \dfrac{1}{x^2}$	$.0001$	$.01$	1	1	$.01$	$.0001$

The rules for limits given earlier in this section remain unchanged when a is replaced with ∞.

EXAMPLE 8

Find each limit.

(a) $\lim\limits_{x \to \infty} \dfrac{8x + 6}{3x - 1}$

By the rule in the box, $\lim\limits_{x \to \infty} k/x^n = 0$ for any real number k. To make use of this rule, divide numerator and denominator by x to get

$$\lim_{x \to \infty} \frac{8x + 6}{3x - 1} = \lim_{x \to \infty} \frac{\dfrac{8x}{x} + \dfrac{6}{x}}{\dfrac{3x}{x} - \dfrac{1}{x}} = \lim_{x \to \infty} \frac{8 + \dfrac{6}{x}}{3 - \dfrac{1}{x}} = \frac{8 + 0}{3 - 0} = \frac{8}{3}.$$

(b) $\lim\limits_{x \to \infty} \dfrac{4x^2 - 6x + 3}{2x^2 - x + 4}$

Divide each term of the numerator and denominator by x^2, the highest power of x.

$$\lim_{x \to \infty} \frac{4x^2 - 6x + 3}{2x^2 - x + 4} = \lim_{x \to \infty} \frac{4 - \dfrac{6}{x} + \dfrac{3}{x^2}}{2 - \dfrac{1}{x} + \dfrac{4}{x^2}} = \frac{4 - 0 + 0}{2 - 0 + 0} = \frac{4}{2} = 2$$

(c) $\lim\limits_{x \to \infty} \dfrac{3x + 2}{4x^3 - 1} = \lim\limits_{x \to \infty} \dfrac{\dfrac{3}{x^2} + \dfrac{2}{x^3}}{4 - \dfrac{1}{x^3}} = \dfrac{0 + 0}{4 - 0} = \dfrac{0}{4} = 0$

Here, the highest power of x is x^3, which is used to divide each term in numerator and denominator. ∎

10.1 EXERCISES

Decide if the limits in Exercises 1–9 exist. If a limit exists, find its value.

1. $\lim\limits_{x \to 3} f(x)$

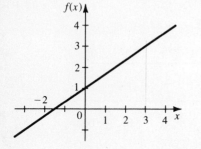

2. $\lim\limits_{x \to 2} F(x)$

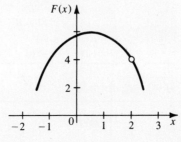

3. $\lim\limits_{x \to -2} f(x)$

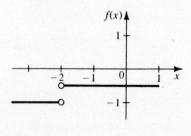

4. $\lim\limits_{x\to 3} g(x)$

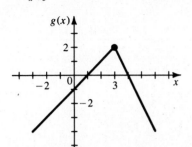

5. $\lim\limits_{x\to 0} f(x)$

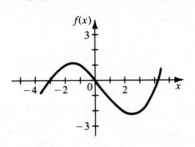

6. $\lim\limits_{x\to 1} g(x)$

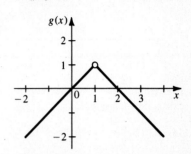

7. $\lim\limits_{x\to 3} F(x)$

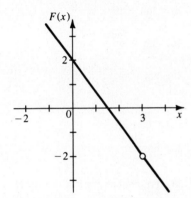

8. $\lim\limits_{x\to\infty} f(x)$

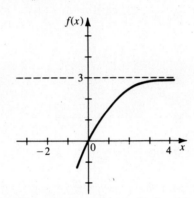

9. $\lim\limits_{x\to\infty} g(x)$

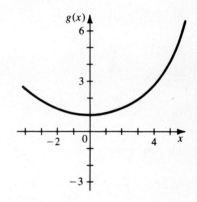

In Exercises 10–14, complete the tables and use the results to find the indicated limits. You will need a calculator with a $\sqrt{x}$ key or a computer for Exercises 13 and 14.

10. $f(x) = 2x^2 - 4x + 3$, find $\lim\limits_{x\to 1} f(x)$.

x	.9	.99	.999	1.001	1.01	1.1
$f(x)$			1.000002	1.000002		

11. $k(x) = \dfrac{x^3 - 2x - 4}{x - 2}$, find $\lim\limits_{x\to 2} k(x)$.

x	1.9	1.99	1.999	2.001	2.01	2.1
$k(x)$						

12. $f(x) = \dfrac{2x^3 + 3x^2 - 4x - 5}{x + 1}$, find $\lim\limits_{x\to -1} f(x)$.

x	−1.1	−1.01	−1.001	−.999	−.99	−.9
$f(x)$						

13. $h(x) = \dfrac{\sqrt{x} - 2}{x - 1}$, find $\lim\limits_{x \to 1} h(x)$.

x	.9	.99	.999	1.001	1.01	1.1
$h(x)$						

14. $f(x) = \dfrac{\sqrt{x} - 3}{x - 3}$, find $\lim\limits_{x \to 3} f(x)$.

x	2.999	2.99	2.9	3.001	3.01	3.1
$f(x)$						

In Exercises 15–38, use the properties of limits to help decide if the limits exist. If a limit exists, find its value.

15. $\lim\limits_{x \to 2} (2x^3 + 5x^2 + 2x + 1)$

16. $\lim\limits_{x \to -1} (4x^3 - x^2 + 3x - 1)$

17. $\lim\limits_{x \to 3} \dfrac{5x - 6}{2x + 1}$

18. $\lim\limits_{x \to -2} \dfrac{2x + 1}{3x - 4}$

19. $\lim\limits_{x \to 1} \dfrac{2x^2 - 6x + 3}{3x^2 - 4x + 2}$

20. $\lim\limits_{x \to 2} \dfrac{-4x^2 + 6x - 8}{3x^2 + 7x - 2}$

21. $\lim\limits_{x \to 3} \dfrac{x^2 - 9}{x - 3}$

22. $\lim\limits_{x \to -2} \dfrac{x^2 - 4}{x + 2}$

23. $\lim\limits_{x \to -2} \dfrac{x^2 - x - 6}{x + 2}$

24. $\lim\limits_{x \to 5} \dfrac{x^2 - 3x - 10}{x - 5}$

25. $\lim\limits_{x \to 3} \sqrt{x^2 - 4}$

26. $\lim\limits_{x \to 3} \sqrt{x^2 - 5}$

27. $\lim\limits_{x \to 4} \dfrac{-6}{(x - 4)^2}$

28. $\lim\limits_{x \to -2} \dfrac{3x}{(x + 2)^3}$

29. $\lim\limits_{x \to 0} \dfrac{x^3 - 4x^2 + 8x}{2x}$

30. $\lim\limits_{x \to 0} \dfrac{-x^5 - 9x^3 + 8x^2}{5x}$

31. $\lim\limits_{x \to 0} \dfrac{[1/(x + 3)] - 1/3}{x}$

32. $\lim\limits_{x \to 0} \dfrac{[-1/(x + 2)] + 1/2}{x}$

33. $\lim\limits_{x \to 25} \dfrac{\sqrt{x} - 5}{x - 25}$

34. $\lim\limits_{x \to 36} \dfrac{\sqrt{x} - 6}{x - 36}$

35. $\lim\limits_{x \to 5} \dfrac{\sqrt{x} - \sqrt{5}}{x - 5}$

36. $\lim\limits_{x \to 8} \dfrac{\sqrt{x} - \sqrt{8}}{x - 8}$

37. $\lim\limits_{h \to 0} \dfrac{(x + h)^2 - x^2}{h}$

38. $\lim\limits_{h \to 0} \dfrac{(x + h)^3 - x^3}{h}$

39. The accompanying graph shows the profit from the daily production of x thousand kilograms of an industrial chemical. Use the graph to decide if the limits in (a)–(c) exist. Find the value of the limits that exist.

(a) $\lim\limits_{x \to 6} P(x)$ (b) $\lim\limits_{x \to 10} P(x)$ (c) $\lim\limits_{x \to 15} P(x)$

(d) Use the graph to estimate the number of units of the chemical that must be produced before the second shift is profitable.

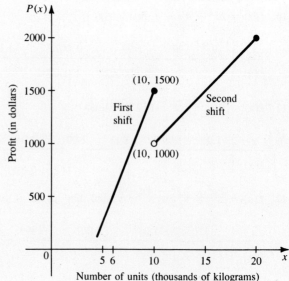

40. According to some economists, when the price of an essential commodity (such as gasoline) rises rapidly, consumption drops slowly at first. However, if the price rise continues, a "tipping" point may be reached, at which consumption takes a sudden, substantial drop. Suppose the graph on the right shows the consumption of gasoline, $G(t)$, in millions of gallons, in a certain area. We assume that the price is rising rapidly. Here t is time in months after the price began rising. Use the graph to find the following.

(a) $\lim\limits_{t \to 12} G(t)$ (b) $\lim\limits_{t \to 16} G(t)$

(c) the tipping point (in months).

Decide if the limits in Exercises 41–50 exist. If a limit exists, find its value.

41. $\lim\limits_{x \to \infty} \dfrac{3x}{5x - 1}$

42. $\lim\limits_{x \to \infty} \dfrac{5x}{3x - 1}$

43. $\lim\limits_{x \to \infty} \dfrac{2x + 3}{4x - 7}$

44. $\lim\limits_{x \to \infty} \dfrac{8x + 2}{2x - 5}$

45. $\lim\limits_{x \to \infty} \dfrac{x^2 + 2x}{2x^2 - 2x + 1}$

46. $\lim\limits_{x \to \infty} \dfrac{x^2 + 2x - 5}{3x^2 + 2}$

47. $\lim\limits_{x \to \infty} \dfrac{3x^3 + 2x - 1}{2x^4 - 3x^3 - 2}$

48. $\lim\limits_{x \to \infty} \dfrac{2x^2 - 1}{3x^4 + 2}$

49. $\lim\limits_{x \to \infty} (\sqrt{x^2 + 4} - x)$

50. $\lim\limits_{x \to \infty} (x - \sqrt{x^2 - 9})$

51. Members of a legislature must often vote repeatedly on the same issue. As time goes on, the members may change their vote. A formula* for the chance that a legislator will vote *yes* on the *n*th roll call vote on the same issue is

$$p_n = \frac{1}{2} + \left(p_0 - \frac{1}{2}\right)(1 - 2p)^n,$$

where n is the number of roll calls taken, p_n is the chance that the member will vote *yes* on the *n*th roll call vote, p is the chance that the legislator will change his or her position on successive roll calls, and p_0 is the chance that the member favors the issue at the beginning (p_n, p, and p_0 are always between 0 and 1, inclusive). Suppose that $p_0 = .7$ and $p = .2$. Use a calculator or a computer to find p_n for

(a) $n = 2$ (b) $n = 4$ (c) $n = 8$.   (d) Find $\lim\limits_{n \to \infty} p_n$.

Use a table of values to find the following limits.

52. $\lim\limits_{x \to 1.3} \dfrac{x^3 - 2x^2 + 5x - 8}{2x^4 - 3x^2}$

53. $\lim\limits_{x \to 5.2} \dfrac{x^4 - 6x^3 - 10x + 5}{4x^3 + 6x^2 - 12x - 6}$

54. $\lim\limits_{x \to 0} \dfrac{x^3 - 4x^2 + 2x}{x^4 + 5x^3 + 4x}$

55. $\lim\limits_{x \to 1} \dfrac{3.1x^3 + 5.2\sqrt{x}}{-2x^3 + 12.3x - 2\sqrt{x}}$

If $\lim\limits_{x \to a} f(x) = L$, how close must x be to a for $f(x)$ to be within .01 of L in the limits in Exercises 56 and 57?

56. $\lim\limits_{x \to -1} (3x - 4) = -7$

57. $\lim\limits_{x \to -2} \dfrac{x^2 - 4}{x + 2} = -4$

---

*See John W. Bishir and Donald W. Drewes, *Mathematics in the Behavioral and Social Sciences* (New York: Harcourt Brace Jovanovich, 1970), p. 538.

10.2   Rates of Change

One of the main applications of calculus is telling how one variable changes in relation to another. A person in business wants to know how profit changes with respect to advertising, while a person in medicine wants to know how a patient's reaction to a drug changes with respect to the dose.

For example, the graph in Figure 11 shows the profit $P(x)$ for a certain product when x hundred dollars is spent on advertising. The graph suggests that as advertising expenditures increase, profit also increases, but the rate of increase slows down, as shown by the "flattening" of the profit curve. For example, when spending on advertising increases from $0 to $100, profit increases by $1000 (from $1000 to $2000), but a further expenditure of $200 on advertising is necessary for the next $1000 increase in profit.

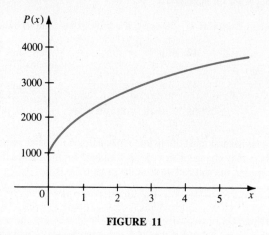

FIGURE 11

The **average rate of change** of profit with respect to advertising on some interval is defined as the change in profit divided by the change in advertising costs on that interval. For example, on the interval $[1, 3]$,

$$\text{average rate of change} = \frac{\text{change in profit}}{\text{change in advertising costs}}$$

$$= \frac{3000 - 2000}{3 - 1} = \frac{1000}{2} = 500.$$

On the interval $[1, 3]$, an increase of $100 in advertising produces an average increase of $500 in profit.

EXAMPLE 1

The graph of Figure 12 shows the profit, $P(x)$, in hundreds of thousands of dollars, from a highly profitable new video game x months after its introduction on the market. The graph shows that profit increases until the game has been on the market for 25 months, and then decreases as the popularity of the game goes down. Here the average rate of change of profit with respect to *time* on some interval is defined as the change in profit divided by the change in time on the interval.

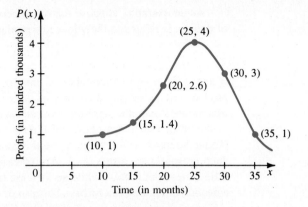

FIGURE 12

(a) On the interval from 15 to 25 months the average rate of change of the profits from the game is given by

$$\frac{4 - 1.4}{25 - 15} = \frac{2.6}{10} = .26.$$

On the average, from 15 months to 25 months each month shows an increase in profit of .26 hundred thousand dollars, or $26,000.

(b) From 25 months to 30 months, the average rate of change is

$$\frac{3 - 4}{30 - 25} = \frac{-1}{5} = -.20,$$

with each month in this interval showing an average *decline* in profits of .20 hundred thousand dollars, or $20,000.

(c) From 10 months to 35 months, the average rate of change of profit is

$$\frac{1 - 1}{35 - 10} = \frac{0}{25} = 0, \qquad \text{or } \$0. \quad \blacksquare$$

Average Rate of Change

> The **average rate of change** for a function $f(x)$ as x changes from a to b, where $a < b$, is
>
> $$\frac{f(b) - f(a)}{b - a}.$$

As Example 1(c) suggests, finding the average rate of change of a function over a large interval can lead to answers that aren't very helpful.

The results are often more useful if the average rate of change is found over a fairly narrow interval, with the usefulness generally increasing as the width of the interval decreases. In fact, the most useful result comes from taking the limit of the average rate of change as the width of the interval approaches 0.

As an example, suppose that for a certain firm, the profit, $P(x)$ in thousands of dollars, is related to the volume of production by the mathematical model

$$P(x) = 16x - x^2,$$

where x represents the number of units produced. Assume that the company can produce any nonnegative number of units. (A *unit* here can represent any number of a product; x might represent thousands or tens of thousands of an item.) A graph of the profit function is shown in Figure 13. The graph shows that an increase in production from $x = 1$ to $x = 2$ will increase profits more than an increase in production from $x = 6$ to $x = 7$. An increase from $x = 7$ to $x = 8$ produces very little increase in profits, while an increase from $x = 8$ to $x = 9$ actually produces a decline in total profit (perhaps because of additional production costs).

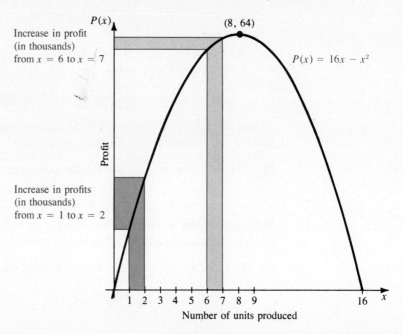

FIGURE 13

Using the profit function $P(x) = 16x - x^2$, the profit from producing 1 unit is

$$P(1) = 16(1) - 1^2 = 15, \qquad \text{or } \$15,000.$$

The profit from producing 2 units is

$$P(2) = 16(2) - 2^2 = 28, \qquad \text{or } \$28,000.$$

This 1-unit increase in production (from 1 unit to 2 units) increases profit by $28 - 15 = 13$ thousand dollars.

Use the profit function P to show that if production increases from 1 unit to 4 units, profit increases by 33 thousand dollars. The average rate of change in profit for this 3-unit increase in production is found by dividing the change in profits by the change in production, or

$$\text{average rate of increase} = \frac{P(4) - P(1)}{4 - 1} = \frac{48 - 15}{3}$$

$$= 11 \quad \text{thousand dollars per unit.}$$

We have seen that an increase in production from 1 unit to 4 units leads to an average rate of increase in profit of 11 thousand dollars per unit, while an increase from 1 unit to 2 units leads to an average rate of increase of profit of 13 thousand dollars per unit. Suppose that production changes from 1 unit to $1 + h$ units, where h is a small number; what would then happen to the average rate of change in profit? To find out, make a table for some selected values of h.

Average Rate of Change in Profit (in Thousands of Dollars) for a Production Level of 1

h	$-.1$	$-.001$	$.001$	$.1$
$1 + h$	$.9$	$.999$	1.001	1.1
$P(1 + h)$	13.59	14.985999	15.013999	16.39
$P(1)$	15	15	15	15
Change in Profit $= P(1 + h) - P(1)$	-1.41	$-.014001$	$.013999$	1.39
Average Rate of Change in Profit $= \dfrac{P(1 + h) - P(1)}{h}$	14.1	14.001	13.999	13.9

Average rate of change approaches 14

The numbers in the bottom row of the table are found by dividing the change in profit (row 5) by the change in production (row 1); that is, by evaluating the quotient

$$\frac{P(1 + h) - P(1)}{(1 + h) - 1} = \frac{P(1 + h) - P(1)}{h}$$

for the different values of h.

The table suggests that as h approaches 0 (or, as production gets closer and closer to $1 + 0 = 1$), the average rate of change of profit approaches the limit 14. This limit,

$$\lim_{h \to 0} \frac{P(1 + h) - P(1)}{h},$$

is called the *instantaneous rate of change,* or just the *rate of change,* of the profit at a production level of $x = 1$.

The rate of change in profit varies as the level of production varies. However, at the exact instant when production is 1 unit, the rate of change in profit is 14 thousand dollars per unit.

Instantaneous Rate of Change

The **instantaneous rate of change** for a function f when $x = x_0$ is

$$\lim_{h \to 0} \frac{f(x_0 + h) - f(x_0)}{h},$$

provided this limit exists.

Velocity   A good example of an instantaneous rate of change comes from *velocity*. Suppose a car leaves a city at time $t = 0$ and travels due west. Let $s(t)$ represent the position of the car (its distance from the city in kilometers) at time t. Suppose $s(t)$ is given by

$$s(t) = 10t^2 + 30t.$$

The average velocity during the second hour of driving (between time $t = 1$ and $t = 2$) is given by the quotient of the change in distance and the change in time, or

$$\frac{s(2) - s(1)}{2 - 1} = \frac{(10 \cdot 2^2 + 30 \cdot 2) - (10 \cdot 1^2 + 30 \cdot 1)}{1}$$

$$= \frac{100 - 40}{1} = 60 \quad \text{kilometers per hour.}$$

To find the instantaneous velocity for a particular value of t, use the definition of instantaneous rate of change given above. The instantaneous velocity when $t = 2$ is

$$\lim_{h \to 0} \frac{s(2 + h) - s(2)}{h}.$$

In this example,

$$s(2 + h) = 10(2 + h)^2 + 30(2 + h)$$
$$= 10(4 + 4h + h^2) + 30(2 + h)$$
$$= 40 + 40h + 10h^2 + 60 + 30h$$
$$= 100 + 70h + 10h^2.$$

Also, $s(2) = 100$. Now find the limit.

$$\lim_{h \to 0} \frac{s(2 + h) - s(2)}{h} = \lim_{h \to 0} \frac{(100 + 70h + 10h^2) - 100}{h}$$

$$= \lim_{h \to 0} \frac{70h + 10h^2}{h}$$

$$= \lim_{h \to 0} (70 + 10h) = 70$$

At the instant that the car is 2 hours out of town, its velocity is 70 kilometers per hour.

Suppose an object is moving is a straight line, with its position (distance from some fixed point) given by $s(t)$, where t represents time. The quotient

$$\frac{s(t + h) - s(t)}{h}$$

represents the average rate of change of the distance, or the **average velocity** of the object. The **instantaneous velocity at time** t (often called just the **velocity** at time t) is the limit of the quotient above as h approaches 0.

Velocity

If $v(t)$ represents the velocity at time t of an object moving in a straight line with position $s(t)$, then

$$v(t) = \lim_{h \to 0} \frac{s(t + h) - s(t)}{h},$$

provided this limit exists.

EXAMPLE 2

The position of a red blood cell in the capillaries is given by

$$s(t) = 1.2t + 5,$$

where $s(t)$ gives the position of a cell in millimeters from some initial point and t is time in seconds. Find the velocity of this red blood cell at time t.

Evaluate the limit given above. To find $s(t + h)$, replace t in $s(t) = 1.2t + 5$ with $t + h$.

$$s(t + h) = 1.2(t + h) + 5$$

Now use the definition of velocity.

$$v(t) = \lim_{h \to 0} \frac{s(t + h) - s(t)}{h}$$

$$= \lim_{h \to 0} \frac{1.2(t + h) + 5 - (1.2t + 5)}{h}$$

$$= \lim_{h \to 0} \frac{1.2t + 1.2h + 5 - 1.2t - 5}{h}$$

$$= \lim_{h \to 0} \frac{1.2h}{h} = 1.2$$

The velocity of the red blood cell is a constant 1.2 millimeters per second. ■

10.2 EXERCISES

1. The graph shows the total sales in thousands
   of dollars from the distribution of x
   thousand catalogs. Find the average rate of
   change of sales with respect to the number
   of catalogs distributed for the following
   changes in x.
   (a) 10 to 20
   (b) 10 to 40
   (c) 20 to 30
   (d) 30 to 40.

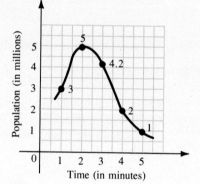

2. The graph shows the population in millions
   of bacteria t minutes after a bactericide is
   introduced into the culture. Find the average
   rate of change of population with respect to
   time for the following time intervals.
   (a) 1 to 2
   (b) 1 to 3
   (c) 2 to 3
   (d) 2 to 5
   (e) 3 to 4
   (f) 4 to 5

3. The graph shows annual sales (in units) of a
   typical product. Sales increase slowly at first
   to some peak, hold steady for a while, and
   then decline as the product goes out of style.
   Find the average annual rate of change in
   sales for the following changes in years.
   (a) 1 to 3
   (b) 2 to 4
   (c) 3 to 6
   (d) 5 to 7
   (e) 7 to 9
   (f) 8 to 11
   (g) 9 to 10
   (h) 10 to 12

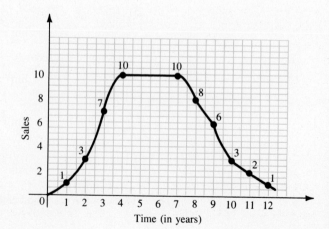

4. The graph shows the share of the total United States automobile market held by small cars during the years 1973–83.* Estimate the average rate of change for the market share between the following years.

(a) 1973 and 1983

(b) 1975 and 1979

(c) 1977 and 1981

(d) 1981 and 1983

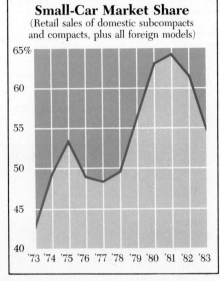

Small-Car Market Share
(Retail sales of domestic subcompacts and compacts, plus all foreign models)

5. The graph shows the temperature in degrees Celsius as a function of the altitude h in feet when an inversion layer is over Southern California. (An inversion layer is formed when air at a higher altitude, say 3000 feet, is warmer than air at sea level, even though air normally is cooler with increasing altitude.) Find the average rate of change in temperature as the altitude changes from

(a) 1000 to 3000 feet

(b) 1000 to 5000 feet

(c) 3000 to 9000 feet

(d) 1000 to 9000 feet

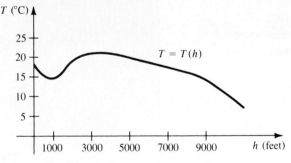

$T = T(h)$

6. A car is moving along a straight test track. The position in feet of the car, $s(t)$, at various times t is measured, with the following results.

t (seconds)	0	2	6	10	12	18	20
$s(t)$ (feet)	0	10	14	18	30	36	40

Find the average velocity as the time in seconds changes from

(a) 0 to 6   **(b)** 2 to 10   **(c)** 2 to 12

(d) 6 to 10   **(e)** 6 to 18   **(f)** 12 to 20

7. The graph* shows the Consumer Price Index for the last several years. Use the midpoint of each year to estimate the average annual rate of change in the Index from

(a) 1976 to 1982

(b) 1980 to 1983

(c) 1975 to 1983

(d) 1982 to 1983

8. The graph† shows the Federal government deficit for the last few months. Estimate the average rate of change in the deficit from

(a) January to December, 1983

(b) July to December, 1983

(c) September 1983 to January 1984

(d) November 1983 to January 1984

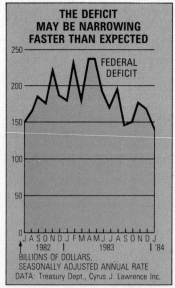

---

*Source: Bureau of Labor Statistics. Courtesy of *Fortune* Art Dept.

†"The Deficit May Be Narrowing Faster Than Expected" reprinted from the March 12, 1984 issue of *Business Week* by special permission, © 1984 by McGraw-Hill, Inc.

In Exercises 9–16, find the average rate of change for the functions over the given intervals.

9. $y = x^2 + 2x$ between $x = 0$ and $x = 3$

10. $y = -4x^2 - 6$ between $x = 2$ and $x = 5$

11. $y = 2x^3 - 4x^2 + 6x$ between $x = -1$ and $x = 1$

12. $y = -3x^3 + 2x^2 - 4x + 1$ between $x = 0$ and $x = 1$

13. $y = \sqrt{x}$ between $x = 1$ and $x = 4$

14. $y = \sqrt{3x - 2}$ between $x = 1$ and $x = 2$

15. $y = \dfrac{1}{x - 1}$ between $x = -2$ and $x = 0$

16. $y = \dfrac{-5}{2x - 3}$ between $x = 2$ and $x = 4$

17. Suppose that the total cost in dollars to produce x items is given by

$$C(x) = 2x^2 - 5x + 6.$$

Find the average rate of change of cost as x increases from

(a) 2 to 4;   **(b)** 2 to 3.

(c) Use $C(x) = 2x^2 - 5x + 6$ to complete the following table.

h	1	0.1	0.01	0.001	0.0001
$2 + h$	3	2.1	2.01	2.001	2.0001
$C(2 + h)$	9	4.32	4.0302	4.003002	4.00030002
$C(2)$	4	4	4	4	4
$C(2 + h) - C(2)$	5	.32	.0302	.003002	.00030002
$\dfrac{C(2 + h) - C(2)}{h}$	5	3.2	____	____	____

(d) Use the bottom row of the chart to find $\displaystyle\lim_{h \to 0} \frac{C(2 + h) - C(2)}{h}$.

18. Use the properties of limits of Section 1 of this chapter to find the limit of Exercise 17(d),

$$\lim_{h \to 0} \frac{C(2 + h) - C(2)}{h}.$$

Also find

$$\lim_{h \to 0} \frac{C(6 + h) - C(6)}{h} \quad \text{and} \quad \lim_{h \to 0} \frac{C(10 + h) - C(10)}{h}.$$

19. In Exercise 17, what is the instantaneous rate of change of cost with respect to the number of items produced when $x = 2$? (This number, called the *marginal cost* at $x = 2$, is the approximate cost of producing the third item.)

20. Redo the chart of Exercise 17. This time, change the second line to $4 + h$, the third line to $C(4 + h)$, and so on. Then find

$$\lim_{h \to 0} \frac{C(4 + h) - C(4)}{h}.$$

(As in Exercise 19, this result is the marginal cost, the approximate cost of producing the fifth item.)

21. The distance of a particle from some fixed point is given by

$$s(t) = t^2 + 5t + 2,$$

where t is time measured in seconds. Find the average velocity of the particle from

(a) 4 seconds to 6 seconds   **(b)** 4 seconds to 5 seconds

(c) Complete the following table.

h	1	0.1	0.01	0.001	0.0001
$4 + h$	5	4.1	4.01	4.001	4.0001
$s(4 + h)$	52	39.31	38.1301	38.013001	38.00130001
$s(4)$	38	38	38	38	38
$s(4 + h) - s(4)$	14	1.31	.1301	.013001	.00130001
$\dfrac{s(4 + h) - s(4)}{h}$	14	13.1	_____	_____	_____

(d) Find $\lim\limits_{h \to 0} \dfrac{s(4 + h) - s(4)}{h}$, and give the instantaneous velocity of the particle when $x = 4$.

Use the properties of limits to find the limits in Exercises 22–24 for $s(t) = t^2 + 5t + 2$.

22. $\lim\limits_{h \to 0} \dfrac{s(6 + h) - s(6)}{h}$ **23.** $\lim\limits_{h \to 0} \dfrac{s(1 + h) - s(1)}{h}$

24. $\lim\limits_{h \to 0} \dfrac{s(10 + h) - s(10)}{h}$

Use the properties of limits to find the following for $s(t) = t^3 + 2t + 9$.

25. $\lim\limits_{h \to 0} \dfrac{s(1 + h) - s(1)}{h}$ **26.** $\lim\limits_{h \to 0} \dfrac{s(4 + h) - s(4)}{h}$

In each of the following exercises, tell which graph, **(a)** or **(b)**, represents velocity and which represents position.

27. (a)   **(b)**

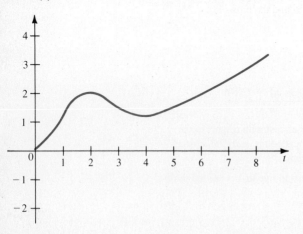
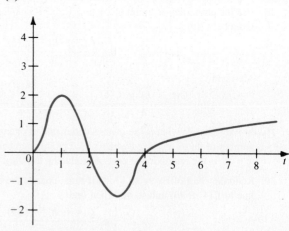

28. (a)   **(b)**

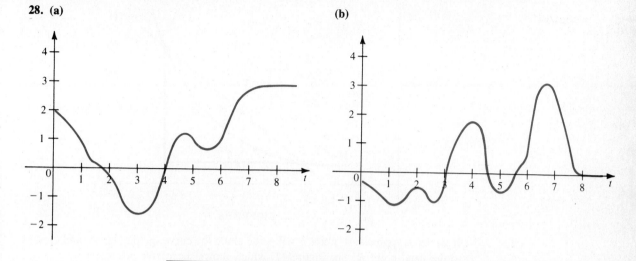

10.3 Definition of the Derivative

Tangent Lines   One of the key problems of calculus is to find a line **tangent** to the graph of a function. We shall see how to define the tangent line to a curve in this section.

In geometry, a tangent line to a circle is defined as a line that touches the circle at only one point, as in Figure 14. Tangent lines to more complicated curves are not as easy to define. In Figure 15, we would probably agree that the lines at P_1, P_3, and P_4 are tangent lines to the curve, while the lines at P_2 and P_5 are not.

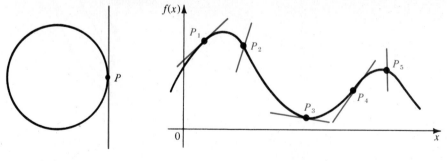

FIGURE 14   **FIGURE 15**

The definition of a tangent line for more general graphs is obtained from the slope of a line. For this definition, select a fixed point R, with coordinates $(x_0, f(x_0))$ on the graph of a function $y = f(x)$, as in Figure 16. Choose a different point S on the graph and draw the line through R and S: this line is called a **secant line.** If S has coordinates $(x_0 + h, f(x_0 + h))$, then by the definition of slope, the slope of the secant line RS is

$$\text{slope of secant} = \frac{f(x_0 + h) - f(x_0)}{x_0 + h - x_0} = \frac{f(x_0 + h) - f(x_0)}{h}.$$

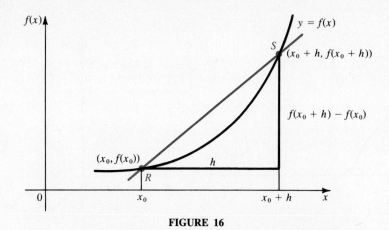

FIGURE 16

If we let h approach 0, point S will slide along the curve, getting closer and closer to the fixed point R. See Figure 17, which shows successive positions s_1, s_2, s_3, s_4 of the point S. If the slopes of these secant lines approach a limit as h approaches 0, then this limit is defined to be the slope of the tangent line at point R.

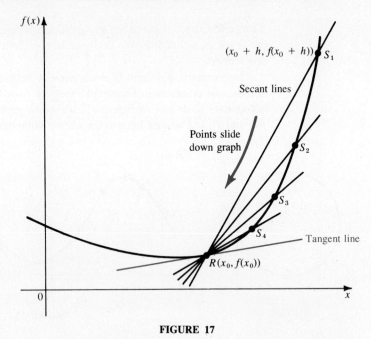

FIGURE 17

Tangent Line

The **tangent line** to the graph of $y = f(x)$ at the point $(x_0, f(x_0))$ is the line through this point having slope

$$\lim_{h \to 0} \frac{f(x_0 + h) - f(x_0)}{h},$$

provided this limit exists.

The slope of this line at a point is also called the **slope of the curve** at the point.

EXAMPLE 1

Find the slope of the tangent line to the graph of $y = x^2 + 2$ when $x = -1$. Find the equation of the tangent line.

   Use the definition above, with $f(x) = x^2 + 2$ and $x_0 = -1$. The slope of the tangent line is

$$\text{slope of tangent} = \lim_{h \to 0} \frac{f(x_0 + h) - f(x_0)}{h}$$

$$= \lim_{h \to 0} \frac{[(-1 + h)^2 + 2] - [(-1)^2 + 2]}{h}$$

$$= \lim_{h \to 0} \frac{[1 - 2h + h^2 + 2] - [1 + 2]}{h}$$

$$= \lim_{h \to 0} \frac{-2h + h^2}{h} = \lim_{h \to 0} (-2 + h) = -2.$$

The slope of the tangent line at $(-1, f(-1)) = (-1, 3)$ is -2. The equation of the tangent line can be found with the point-slope form of the equation of a line from Chapter 1.

$$y - y_1 = m(x - x_1)$$

$$y - 3 = -2[x - (-1)]$$

$$y - 3 = -2(x + 1)$$

$$y - 3 = -2x - 2$$

$$y = -2x + 1$$

Figure 18 shows a graph of $f(x) = x^2 + 2$, along with a graph of the tangent line at $x = -1$. ▨

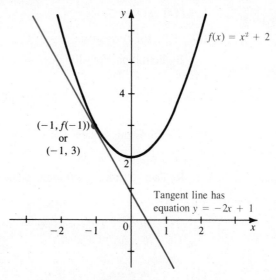

$f(x) = x^2 + 2$

$(-1, f(-1))$ or $(-1, 3)$

Tangent line has equation $y = -2x + 1$

FIGURE 18

The Derivative   We have now seen

$$\lim_{h \to 0} \frac{f(x_0 + h) - f(x_0)}{h}$$

used in two different ways—as the instantaneous rate of change and also as the slope of a tangent line. This particular limit is so important that it is given a special name, the *derivative*.

Derivative

The **derivative of the function** f, at x, written $f'(x)$, is defined as

$$f'(x) = \lim_{h \to 0} \frac{f(x + h) - f(x)}{h},$$

provided this limit exists.

An alternate notation, y', is sometimes used for the derivative of the function $y = f(x)$.

A new function $y' = f'(x)$ can be obtained from a function $y = f(x)$. This new function has as domain all the points at which the limit in the box exists, and its value at x is $f'(x)$. This new function $y' = f'(x)$ is called the **derivative** of $y = f(x)$. If x is a value in the domain of f, and if $f'(x)$ exists, then f is **differentiable** at x.

The next few examples show how to use the definition to find the derivative of a function by means of a four-step procedure summarized after Example 4.

EXAMPLE 2

Let $f(x) = x^2$.

(a)   Find the derivative.

By definition, for all values of x where the following limit exists, the derivative is

$$f'(x) = \lim_{h \to 0} \frac{f(x + h) - f(x)}{h}.$$

Use the following sequence of steps to evaluate this limit.

Step 1.   Find $f(x + h)$.

Replace x with $x + h$ in the equation for $f(x)$. Simplify the result.

$$f(x) = x^2$$

$$f(x + h) = (x + h)^2$$

$$= x^2 + 2xh + h^2$$

Step 2. Find $f(x + h) - f(x)$.
  Since $f(x) = x^2$,

$$f(x + h) - f(x) = (x^2 + 2xh + h^2) - x^2 = 2xh + h^2.$$

Step 3. Form and simplify the quotient $\dfrac{f(x + h) - f(x)}{h}$.

$$\frac{f(x + h) - f(x)}{h} = \frac{2xh + h^2}{h} = \frac{h(2x + h)}{h} = 2x + h$$

Step 4. Finally, find the limit as h approaches 0.

$$f'(x) = \lim_{h \to 0} \frac{f(x + h) - f(x)}{h} = \lim_{h \to 0} (2x + h) = 2x + 0 = 2x$$

By this result, the derivative of $f(x) = x^2$ is $f'(x) = 2x$. (In using these four steps, always think of x as fixed and h as the variable.)

(b) Calculate and interpret $f'(3)$.

$$f'(3) = 2 \cdot 3 = 6$$

The number 6 is the slope of the tangent line to the graph of $f(x) = x^2$ at the point where $x = 3$, that is, at $(3, f(3)) = (3, 9)$. See Figure 19. ■

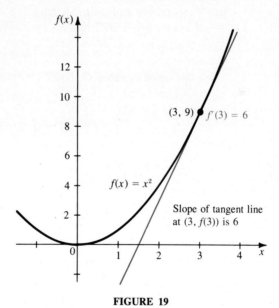

FIGURE 19

In Example 2(b), do not confuse $f(3)$ and $f'(3)$. The value $f(3)$ is found by substituting 3 for x in $f(x)$; doing so gives $f(3) = 3^2 = 9$. On the other hand, $f'(3)$ is the slope of the tangent line to the curve at $x = 3$; as Example 1 shows, $f'(3) = 2 \cdot 3 = 6$.

EXAMPLE 3

Let $f(x) = 2x^3 + 4x$. Find $f'(x)$. Then find $f'(2)$ and $f'(-3)$.
Go through the four steps used above.

Step 1. Find $f(x + h)$ by replacing x with $x + h$.

$$f(x + h) = 2(x + h)^3 + 4(x + h)$$

$$= 2(x^3 + 3x^2h + 3xh^2 + h^3) + 4(x + h)$$

$$= 2x^3 + 6x^2h + 6xh^2 + 2h^3 + 4x + 4h.$$

Step 2. $f(x + h) - f(x) = 2x^3 + 6x^2h + 6xh^2 + 2h^3 + 4x + 4h - 2x^3 - 4$

$$= 6x^2h + 6xh^2 + 2h^3 + 4h.$$

Step 3. $\dfrac{f(x + h) - f(x)}{h} = \dfrac{6x^2h + 6xh^2 + 2h^3 + 4h}{h}$

$$= \dfrac{h(6x^2 + 6xh + 2h^2 + 4)}{h}$$

$$= 6x^2 + 6xh + 2h^2 + 4.$$

Step 4.   Now use the rules for limits to get

$$f'(x) = \lim_{h \to 0} \frac{f(x + h) - f(x)}{h} = \lim_{h \to 0} (6x^2 + 6xh + 2h^2 + 4)$$

$$= 6x^2 + 6x(0) + 2(0)^2 + 4 = 6x^2 + 4$$

Use this result to find $f'(2)$ and $f'(-3)$.

$$f'(2) = 6 \cdot 2^2 + 4 = 28$$

$$f'(-3) = 6 \cdot (-3)^2 + 4 = 58 \quad \blacksquare$$

EXAMPLE 4

Let $f(x) = \dfrac{4}{x}$. Find $f'(x)$.

Step 1. $f(x + h) = \dfrac{4}{x + h}$

Step 2. $f(x + h) - f(x) = \dfrac{4}{x + h} - \dfrac{4}{x}$

$$= \dfrac{4x - 4(x + h)}{x(x + h)} \qquad \text{Find a common denominator}$$

$$= \dfrac{4x - 4x - 4h}{x(x + h)} \qquad \text{Simplify the numerator}$$

$$= \dfrac{-4h}{x(x + h)}$$

Step 3. $\dfrac{f(x+h)-f(x)}{h} = \dfrac{\dfrac{-4h}{x(x+h)}}{h}$

$$= \frac{-4h}{x(x+h)} \cdot \frac{1}{h} \qquad \text{Invert and multiply}$$

$$= \frac{-4}{x(x+h)}$$

Step 4. $f'(x) = \lim_{h\to 0} \dfrac{f(x+h)-f(x)}{h} = \lim_{h\to 0} \dfrac{-4}{x(x+h)}$

$$= \frac{-4}{x(x+0)}$$

$$= \frac{-4}{x(x)} = \frac{-4}{x^2} \quad \blacksquare$$

Notice that in this example neither $f(x)$ nor $f'(x)$ is defined when $x = 0$.

Finding $f'(x)$ from

the Definition of

Derivative

Let us summarize the four steps used when finding the derivative $f'(x)$ for a function $y = f(x)$.

1. Find $f(x+h)$.
2. Find $f(x+h) - f(x)$.
3. Divide by h to get $\dfrac{f(x+h)-f(x)}{h}$.
4. Let $h \to 0$;

$$f'(x) = \lim_{h\to 0} \frac{f(x+h)-f(x)}{h} \quad \text{if this limit exists.}$$

The next example shows how to find a point on a graph where the slope of the tangent line equals a given number.

EXAMPLE 5

Find all points on the graph of $f(x) = x^2 + 6x + 5$ where the slope of the tangent line is 0.

Go through the four steps given above to find that

$$f'(x) = 2x + 6.$$

Find all values of x where the slope of the tangent is 0 by finding values of x that make $f'(x) = 0$.

$$f'(x) = 0$$
$$2x + 6 = 0$$
$$2x = -6$$
$$x = -3$$

When $x = -3$, the slope of the tangent is 0. Since only horizontal lines have a slope of 0, the tangent to $f(x) = x^2 + 6x + 5$ at $x = -3$ is horizontal, as shown in Figure 20. When $x = -3$, then $f(-3) = -4$, making the slope of the tangent line 0 at the point $(-3, -4)$. The equation of this tangent line is $y = -4$. ■

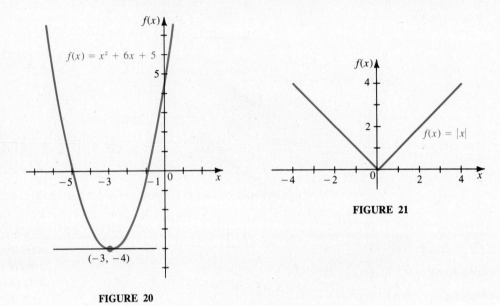

FIGURE 20

FIGURE 21

The derivative was defined with the limit

$$\lim_{h \to 0} \frac{f(x + h) - f(x)}{h}.$$

This is exactly the same limit that we used in the previous section to define the instantaneous rate of change of one variable with respect to another.

Instantaneous Rate of Change

For a function $y = f(x)$, the **instantaneous rate of change** of y with respect to x is given by the derivative $f'(x)$.

From now on, we will use "rate of change" to mean "instantaneous rate of change."

EXAMPLE 6

The cost in dollars to manufacture x electronic calculators is given by $C(x) = x^3 - 4x^2 + 3x$. Find the rate of change of cost with respect to the number manufactured when 5 electronic calculators are made.

The rate of change of cost is given by the derivative of the cost function. Going through the four steps for finding $f'(x)$ leads to

$$C'(x) = 3x^2 - 8x + 3.$$

When $x = 5$,

$$C'(5) = 3(5)^2 - 8(5) + 3 = 38.$$

At the point when exactly 5 electronic calculators are made, the rate of change of cost is \$38. As we shall see, this means that the approximate cost of manufacturing a sixth calculator is \$38. ■

Existence of the Derivative   The definition of the derivative included the phrase "provided this limit exists." If the limit used to define the derivative does not exist, then of course the derivative does not exist. For example, a derivative cannot exist at a point where the function itself is not defined. If there is no function value for a particular value of x, there can be no tangent line for that value. This was the case in Example 4—there was no tangent line when $x = 0$.

Derivatives also do not exist at "corners" or "sharp points" on a graph. For example, Figure 21 shows the graph of $f(x) = |x|$ (recall: $|x|$ represents the absolute value of x). By the definition of derivative, the derivative at x is given by

$$\lim_{h \to 0} \frac{f(x + h) - f(x)}{h},$$

provided this limit exists. To find the derivative at 0 for $f(x) = |x|$, replace x with 0 and $f(x)$ with $|0|$ to get

$$\lim_{h \to 0} \frac{|0 + h| - |0|}{h} = \lim_{h \to 0} \frac{|h|}{h}.$$

If $h > 0$, then $|h| = h$, and

$$\frac{|h|}{h} = \frac{h}{h} = 1,$$

while if $h < 0$, then $|h| = -h$, and

$$\frac{|h|}{h} = \frac{-h}{h} = -1.$$

For positive values of h, the quotient $|h|/h$ is 1, while it is -1 for negative values of h. For this reason,

$$\lim_{h \to 0} \frac{|h|}{h} \quad \text{does not exist,}$$

and there is no derivative at 0.

The derivative of $f(x) = |x|$ does exist for all values of x other than 0. In fact, $f'(x) = 1$ if $x > 0$ and $f'(x) = -1$ if $x < 0$. A graph of $f'(x)$ is shown in Figure 22.

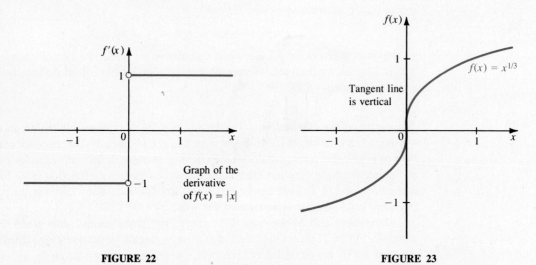

FIGURE 22

FIGURE 23

A graph of the function $f(x) = x^{1/3}$ is shown in Figure 23. As the graph suggests, the tangent line is vertical when $x = 0$. Since a vertical line has an undefined slope, the derivative of $f(x) = x^{1/3}$ cannot exist when $x = 0$.

Figure 24 summarizes the various ways that a derivative can fail to exist.

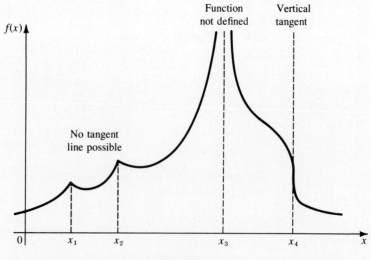

FIGURE 24

10.3 EXERCISES

Find the slope of the tangent line to the curves in Exercises 1–6 when x has the given value. (Hint for Exercise 5: In Step 3, multiply numerator and denominator by $\sqrt{16 + h} + \sqrt{16}$.)

1. $f(x) = -4x^2 + 11x$; $x = -2$
2. $f(x) = 6x^2 - 4x$; $x = -1$
3. $f(x) = -2/x$; $x = 4$

4. $f(x) = 6/x$; $x = -1$
5. $f(x) = \sqrt{x}$; $x = 16$
6. $f(x) = -3\sqrt{x}$; $x = 1$

Find the equation of the tangent line to the curves in Exercises 7–12 when x has the given value.

7. $f(x) = x^2 + 2x$; $x = 3$
8. $f(x) = 6 - x^2$; $x = -1$
9. $f(x) = 5/x$; $x = 2$

10. $f(x) = -3/(x + 1)$; $x = 1$
11. $f(x) = 4\sqrt{x}$; $x = 9$
12. $f(x) = \sqrt{x}$; $x = 25$

In Exercises 13–18 estimate the slope of the tangent line at the given point (x, y).

13.

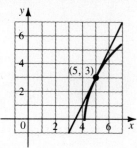

14.

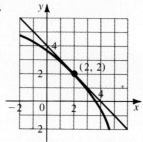

15.

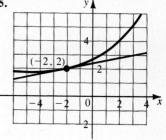

16.

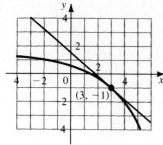

17.

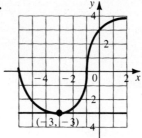

18.

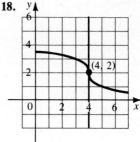

Find $f'(x)$ for Exercises 19–30. Then find $f'(2)$, $f'(0)$, and $f'(-3)$.

19. $f(x) = -4x^2 + 11x$
20. $f(x) = 6x^2 - 4x$
21. $f(x) = 8x + 6$

22. $f(x) = -9x - 5$
23. $f(x) = x^3 + 3x$
24. $f(x) = 2x^3 - 14x$

25. $f(x) = -\dfrac{2}{x}$
26. $f(x) = \dfrac{6}{x}$
27. $f(x) = \dfrac{4}{x - 1}$

28. $f(x) = \dfrac{3}{x + 2}$
29. $f(x) = \sqrt{x}$
30. $f(x) = -3\sqrt{x}$

Find all points where the following do not have derivatives.

31.

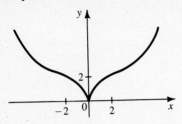

32.

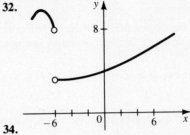

33.

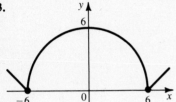

34.

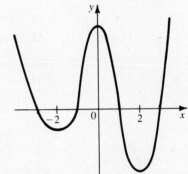

35.

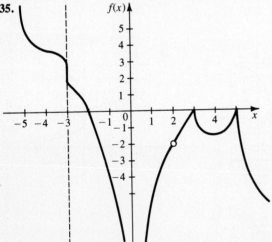

36.

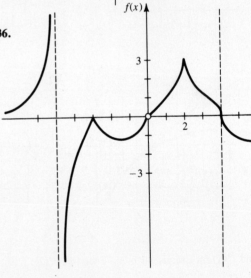

Find all points (if there are any) where the functions in Exercises 37–46 have tangent lines with a slope of 0. (In Exercises 41–44 it is necessary to factor.)

37. $f(x) = 9x^2$

38. $f(x) = -2x^2$

39. $f(x) = 8x^2 + 32x$

40. $f(x) = 2x^2 + 6x$

41. $f(x) = 2x^3 - 3x^2 - 12x$

42. $f(x) = 2x^3 - 6x^2 + 6x$

43. $f(x) = 4x^3 + 24x^2$

44. $f(x) = 4x^3 - 18x^2$

45. $f(x) = \dfrac{1}{x}$

46. $f(x) = \dfrac{-2}{x-1}$

47. Suppose the demand for a certain item is given by
$$D(x) = -2x^2 + 4x + 6,$$
where x represents the price of the item. Find the rate of change of demand with respect to price for the following values of x.

(a) 1   (b) 2   (c) 3

48. The profit from the expenditure of x thousand dollars on advertising is given by
$$P(x) = 1000 + 32x - 2x^2.$$
Find the rate of change of profit with respect to the expenditure on advertising for the following amounts. In each case, decide if the firm should increase the expenditure.

(a) $x = 8$ (b) $x = 6$ (c) $x = 12$ (d) $x = 20$

49. A biologist has estimated that if a bactericide is introduced into a culture of bacteria, the number of bacteria, $B(t)$, present at time t (in hours) is given by
$$B(t) = 1000 + 50t - 5t^2 \quad \text{million.}$$
Find the rate of change of the number of bacteria with respect to time for the following values of t.

(a) 2   (b) 3   (c) 4   (d) 5   (e) 6.

50. When does the population of bacteria in Exercise 49 start to decline?

51. (Continuation of Exercise 5 from the previous section.) The graph on the right shows the temperature in degrees Celsius as a function of the altitude h in feet when an inversion layer is over Southern California. Estimate the derivatives of $T(h)$ at the marked points.

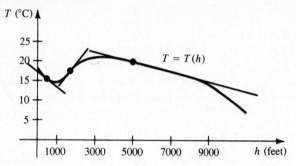

52. In one research study, the population of a certain shellfish in an area at time t was closely approximated by the graph on the right. Estimate the derivative at the marked points.

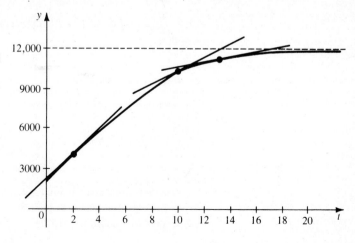

Find the slope of the tangent line to the graph of each of the functions in Exercises 53–58.

53. $f(x) = \dfrac{x^2 + 4.9}{3x^2 - 1.7x}$ at 4.9

54. $f(x) = \dfrac{3x - 7.2}{x^2 + 5x + 2.3}$ at -6.2

55. $f(x) = \sqrt{x^3 + 4.8}$ at 8.17

56. $f(x) = \sqrt{6x^2 + 3.5}$ at 3.49

57. $f(x) = \dfrac{2.8}{\sqrt{x} + 1.2}$ at 2.65

58. $f(x) = \dfrac{-3.7}{4.1 + 2\sqrt{x}}$ at 1.23

10.4   Techniques for Finding Derivatives

The process of finding the derivative of a function is called **differentiation.** In the previous section we used the symbols y' and $f'(x)$ to represent the derivative of the function $y = f(x)$. Sometimes it is important to show that the derivative is taken with respect to a particular variable; for example, if y is a function of x, use the notation

$$\frac{dy}{dx}$$

for the derivative of y with respect to x.

Another notation is used to write a derivative without functional symbols such as f or f'. With this notation, the derivative of $y = 2x^3 + 4x$, for example, which we found in the last section to be $y' = 6x^2 + 4$, would be written

$$\frac{d}{dx}[2x^3 + 4x] = 6x^2 + 4,$$

or $$D_x[2x^3 + 4x] = 6x^2 + 4.$$

Either $\frac{d}{dx}[f(x)]$ or $D_x[f(x)]$ represents the derivative of the function f with respect to x.

Notations for the

Derivative

The derivative of $y = f(x)$ may be written in any of the following ways:

$$f'(x), \quad y', \quad \frac{dy}{dx}, \quad \frac{d}{dx}[f(x)], \quad \text{or} \quad D_x[f(x)].$$

Variables other than x often are used as the independent variable. For example, if $y = f(t)$ gives population growth as a function of time, then the derivative of y with respect to t could be written

$$f'(t), \quad \frac{dy}{dt}, \quad \frac{d}{dt}[f(t)], \quad \text{or} \quad D_t[f(t)].$$

In this section we use the definition

$$f'(x) = \lim_{h \to 0} \frac{f(x + h) - f(x)}{h}$$

to develop some rules for finding derivatives more easily than by the four-step process of the previous section.

The first rule tells how to find the derivative of a constant function $f(x) = k$, where k is a constant real number. Since $f(x + h)$ is also k, by definition $f'(x)$ is

$$f'(x) = \lim_{h \to 0} \frac{f(x + h) - f(x)}{h}$$

$$= \lim_{h \to 0} \frac{k - k}{h} = \lim_{h \to 0} \frac{0}{h}$$

$$= \lim_{h \to 0} 0 = 0.$$

We have proved the following rule.

Constant Rule

> If $f(x) = k$ where k is any real number, then
>
> $$f'(x) = 0.$$
>
> (The derivative of a constant is 0.)

(For reference, a summary of all the formulas for derivatives is given at the end of Section 6 of this chapter.)

Figure 25 illustrates this constant rule geometrically; it shows a graph of the horizontal line $y = k$. At any point P on this line, the tangent line at P is the line itself. Since a horizontal line has a slope of 0, the slope of the tangent line is 0. This agrees with the result above: the derivative of a constant is 0.

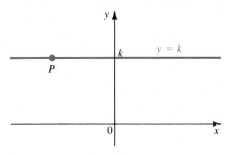

FIGURE 25

EXAMPLE 1

(a)   If $f(x) = 9$, then $f'(x) = 0$.

(b)   If $y = \pi$, then $y' = 0$.

(c)   If $y = 2^3$, then $dy/dx = 0$.   ▨

Functions of the form $y = x^n$, where n is a real number, are very common in applications. To find a rule for the derivative of these functions, we first use the definition to work out the derivatives for various special values of n, with results as given in the following table. (These results are modifications of some of the examples and exercises from the previous section.)

Function	n	Derivative
$y = x^2$	2	$y' = 2x = 2x^1$
$y = x^3$	3	$y' = 3x^2$
$y = x^4$	4	$y' = 4x^3$
$y = x^{-1}$	-1	$y' = -1 \cdot x^{-2} = \dfrac{-1}{x^2}$
$y = x^{1/2}$	1/2	$y' = \dfrac{1}{2}x^{-1/2} = \dfrac{1}{2x^{1/2}}$

These results suggest the following rule.

Power Rule

If $f(x) = x^n$, for any real number n, then
$$f'(x) = nx^{n-1}.$$
(The derivative of $f(x) = x^n$ is found by multiplying by the exponent n and decreasing the exponent on x by 1.)

While the power rule is true for every real number value of n, we shall prove it only for positive integer values of n. This proof depends on the **binomial theorem**, discussed in most intermediate and college algebra texts: for any real numbers p and q,

$$(p + q)^n = p^n + np^{n-1}q + \frac{n(n-1)}{2}p^{n-2}q^2 + \cdots + npq^{n-1} + q^n.$$

Replacing p with x and q with h gives

$$(x + h)^n = x^n + nx^{n-1}h + \frac{n(n-1)}{2}x^{n-2}h^2 + \cdots + nxh^{n-1} + h^n$$

from which

$$(x + h)^n - x^n = nx^{n-1}h + \frac{n(n-1)}{2}x^{n-2}h^2 + \cdots + nxh^{n-1} + h^n.$$

Dividing each term by h yields

$$\frac{(x + h)^n - x^n}{h} = nx^{n-1} + \frac{n(n - 1)}{2}x^{n-2}h + \cdots + nxh^{n-2} + h^{n-1}.$$

Use the definition of derivative, and the fact that each term except the first contains h as a factor, and thus approaches 0 as h approaches 0, to get

$$f'(x) = \lim_{h \to 0} \frac{(x + h)^n - x^n}{h}$$

$$= nx^{n-1} + \frac{n(n - 1)}{2}x^{n-2}0 + \cdots + nx0^{n-2} + 0^{n-1}$$

$$= nx^{n-1}.$$

This shows that the derivative of $f(x) = x^n$ is $f'(x) = nx^{n-1}$, proving the power rule for positive integer values of n.

EXAMPLE 2

(a)   If $y = x^6$, then $y' = 6x^{6-1} = 6x^5$.

(b)   If $y = x = x^1$, then $y' = 1x^{1-1} = x^0 = 1$.

(c) $y = \dfrac{1}{x^3}$

Use a negative exponent to rewrite this as $y = x^{-3}$; then $dy/dx = -3x^{-3-1} = -3x^{-4}$ or $\dfrac{-3}{x^4}$.

(d) $D_x[x^{4/3}] = \dfrac{4}{3}x^{4/3-1} = \dfrac{4}{3}x^{1/3}$.

(e) $y = \sqrt{x}$

Rewrite this as $y = x^{1/2}$; then $y' = \dfrac{1}{2}x^{1/2-1} = \dfrac{1}{2}x^{-1/2}$ or $\dfrac{1}{2x^{1/2}}$ or $\dfrac{1}{2\sqrt{x}}$.   ■

The next rule shows how to find the derivative of the product of a constant and a function.

Constant Times a Function

Let k be a real number. If $g(x) = kf(x)$, and if $f'(x)$ exists, then

$$g'(x) = kf'(x).$$

(The derivative of a constant times a function is the constant times the derivative of the function.)

This rule is proved with the definition of the derivative and rules for limits. If $g(x) = kf(x)$, then

$$g'(x) = \lim_{h \to 0} \frac{g(x + h) - g(x)}{h}$$

$$= \lim_{h \to 0} \frac{kf(x + h) - kf(x)}{h}$$

$$= \lim_{h \to 0} k \frac{[f(x + h) - f(x)]}{h}$$

$$= k \lim_{h \to 0} \frac{f(x + h) - f(x)}{h}$$

$$= kf'(x).$$

EXAMPLE 3

(a) If $y = 8x^4$, then $y' = 8(4x^3) = 32x^3$.

(b) If $y = -\frac{3}{4}x^{12}$, then $dy/dx = -\frac{3}{4}(12x^{11}) = -9x^{11}$.

(c) If $y = -8x$, then $y' = -8(1) = -8$.

(d) $D_x[10x^{3/2}] = 10\left(\frac{3}{2}x^{1/2}\right) = 15x^{1/2}$.

(e) $y = \frac{6}{x}$

Rewrite this as $y = 6x^{-1}$; then

$$y' = 6(-1x^{-2}) = -6x^{-2} \text{ or } \frac{-6}{x^2}. \quad \blacksquare$$

The final rule in this section is for the derivative of a function which is a sum or difference of terms.

Sum or Difference Rule

If $y = f(x) \pm g(x)$, and if $f'(x)$ and $g'(x)$ exist, then

$$y' = f'(x) \pm g'(x).$$

(The derivative of a sum or difference of functions is the sum or difference of the derivatives.)

The proof of the sum part of this rule is as follows: If $y = f(x) + g(x)$, then

$$y' = \lim_{h \to 0} \frac{[f(x + h) + g(x + h)] - [f(x) + g(x)]}{h}$$

$$= \lim_{h \to 0} \frac{[f(x + h) - f(x)] + [g(x + h) - g(x)]}{h}$$

$$= \lim_{h \to 0} \left[\frac{f(x + h) - f(x)}{h} + \frac{g(x + h) - g(x)}{h} \right]$$

$$= \lim_{h \to 0} \frac{f(x + h) - f(x)}{h} + \lim_{h \to 0} \frac{g(x + h) - g(x)}{h}$$

$$= f'(x) + g'(x).$$

A similar proof can be given for the difference of two functions.

EXAMPLE 4

Find the derivative of each function.

(a) $y = 6x^3 + 15x^2$

Let $f(x) = 6x^3$ and $g(x) = 15x^2$; then $y = f(x) + g(x)$. Since $f'(x) = 18x^2$ and $g'(x) = 30x$,

$$\frac{dy}{dx} = 18x^2 + 30x.$$

(b) $p(t) = 12t^4 - 6\sqrt{t} + \dfrac{5}{t}$

Rewrite $p(t)$ as $p(t) = 12t^4 - 6t^{1/2} + 5t^{-1}$; then

$$p'(t) = 48t^3 - 3t^{-1/2} - 5t^{-2}.$$

Also, $p'(t)$ may be written as $p'(t) = 48t^3 - 3/\sqrt{t} - 5/t^2$. ∎

As we saw in the previous section, the derivative of a function gives the rate of change of the function.

EXAMPLE 5

A tumor has the approximate shape of a cone (see Figure 26). The radius of the base of the tumor is fixed by the bone structure at 2 centimeters, but the tumor is growing along the height of the cone (the volume of the tumor therefore being a function of its height). The formula for the volume of a cone is $V = \frac{1}{3}\pi r^2 h$, where r is the radius of the base and h is the height of the cone. Find the rate of change in the volume of the tumor with respect to the height.

The symbol dV/dh (instead of V') emphasizes that the rate of change of volume is with respect to the height. For this tumor, r is fixed at 2 centimeters. By substituting 2 for r,

$$V = \frac{1}{3}\pi r^2 h \qquad \text{becomes} \qquad V = \frac{1}{3}\pi 2^2 \cdot h \qquad \text{or} \qquad V = \frac{4}{3}\pi h.$$

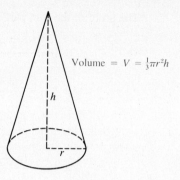

FIGURE 26

Since $4\pi/3$ is a constant,

$$\frac{dV}{dh} = \frac{4\pi}{3} \approx 4.2 \text{ cu cm per cm.}$$

For each additional centimeter that the tumor grows in height, its volume will increase approximately 4.2 cubic centimeters. ∎

Marginal Cost   In business and economics the rates of change of such variables as cost, revenue, and profits are important considerations. Economists use the word **marginal** to refer to rates of change: for example, *marginal cost* refers to the rate of change of cost. Since the derivative of a function gives the rate of change of the function, a marginal cost (or revenue, or profit) function is found by taking the derivative of the cost (or revenue, or profit) function. Roughly speaking, the marginal cost at some level of production x is the cost to produce the $(x + 1)$st item. (Similar statements could be made for revenue or profit.)

EXAMPLE 6

Suppose that the total cost in hundreds of dollars to produce x thousand barrels of a beverage is given by

$$C(x) = 4x^2 + 100x + 500.$$

Find the marginal cost for the following values of x.

(a) $x = 5$

To find the marginal cost, first find $C'(x)$, the derivative of the total cost function.

$$C'(x) = 8x + 100$$

When $x = 5$,

$$C'(5) = 8(5) + 100 = 140.$$

After 5 thousand barrels of the beverage have been produced, the cost to produce one thousand more barrels will be *approximately* 140 hundred dollars, or \$14,000.

The *actual* cost to produce one thousand more barrels is $C(6) - C(5)$:

$$C(6) - C(5) = (4 \cdot 6^2 + 100 \cdot 6 + 500) - (4 \cdot 5^2 + 100 \cdot 5 + 500)$$

$$= 1244 - 1100$$

$$= 144 \quad \text{hundred dollars, or } \$14,400.$$

(b) $x = 30$

After 30 thousand barrels have been produced, the cost to produce one thousand more barrels will be approximately

$$C'(30) = 8(30) + 100 = 340, \quad \text{or } \$34,000. \quad \blacksquare$$

Management must be careful to keep track of marginal costs. If the marginal cost of producing an extra unit exceeds the revenue received from selling it, then the company will lose money on that unit.

The following box summarizes this work with marginal cost, revenue, and profit.

Marginal Cost, Revenue, and Profit

If $C(x)$ is the total cost to produce x units, then $C'(x)$ is the **marginal cost,** the approximate cost of the $(x + 1)$st unit.

If $R(x)$ is the total revenue from selling x units, then $R'(x)$ is the **marginal revenue,** the approximate revenue from the $(x + 1)$st unit.

If $P(x) = R(x) - C(x)$ is the total profit from selling x units, then $P'(x) = R'(x) - C'(x)$ is the **marginal profit,** the approximate profit on the $(x + 1)$st unit.

10.4 EXERCISES

Find the derivatives of each of the functions in Exercises 1–32.

1. $f(x) = 9x^2 - 8x + 4$

2. $f(x) = 10x^2 + 4x - 9$

3. $y = 10x^3 - 9x^2 + 6x$

4. $y = 3x^3 - x^2 - 12x$

5. $y = x^4 - 5x^3 + 9x^2 + 5$

6. $y = 3x^4 + 11x^3 + 2x^2 - 4x$

7. $f(x) = 6x^{1.5} - 4x^{.5}$

8. $f(x) = -2x^{2.5} + 8x^{.5}$

9. $y = -15x^{3.2} + 2x^{1.9}$

10. $y = 18x^{1.6} - 4x^{3.1}$

11. $y = 24t^{3/2} + 4t^{1/2}$

12. $y = -24t^{5/2} - 6t^{1/2}$

13. $y = 8\sqrt{x} + 6x^{3/4}$

14. $y = -100\sqrt{x} - 11x^{2/3}$

15. $g(x) = 6x^{-5} - x^{-1}$

16. $y = -2x^{-4} + x^{-1}$

17. $y = -4x^{-2} + 3x^{-3}$

18. $g(x) = 8x^{-4} - 9x^{-2}$

19. $y = 10x^{-2} + 3x^{-4} - 6x$

20. $y = x^{-5} - x^{-2} + 5x^{-1}$

21. $f(t) = \dfrac{6}{t} - \dfrac{8}{t^2}$

22. $f(t) = \dfrac{4}{t} + \dfrac{2}{t^3}$

23. $y = \dfrac{9}{x^4} - \dfrac{8}{x^3} + \dfrac{2}{x}$

24. $y = \dfrac{3}{x^6} + \dfrac{1}{x^5} - \dfrac{7}{x^2}$

25. $f(x) = 12x^{-1/2} - 3x^{1/2}$

26. $r(x) = -30x^{-1/2} + 5x^{1/2}$

27. $p(x) = -10x^{-1/2} + 8x^{-3/2}$

28. $h(x) = x^{-1/2} - 14x^{-3/2}$

29. $y = \dfrac{6}{\sqrt[4]{x}}$

30. $y = \dfrac{-2}{\sqrt[3]{x}}$

31. $y = \dfrac{-5t}{\sqrt[3]{t^2}}$

32. $g(t) = \dfrac{9t}{\sqrt{t^3}}$

Find each of the following.

33. $\dfrac{dy}{dx}$ if $y = 8x^{-5} - 9x^{-4}$

34. $\dfrac{dy}{dx}$ if $y = -3x^{-2} - 4x^{-5}$

35. $D_x\left[9x^{-1/2} + \dfrac{2}{x^{3/2}}\right]$

36. $D_x\left[\dfrac{8}{\sqrt[4]{x}} - \dfrac{3}{\sqrt{x^3}}\right]$

37. $f'(-2)$ if $f(x) = 6x^2 - 4x$

38. $f'(3)$ if $f(x) = 9x^3 - 8x^2$

39. $f'(4)$ if $f(t) = 2\sqrt{t} - \dfrac{3}{\sqrt{t}}$

40. $f'(8)$ if $f(t) = -5\sqrt[3]{t} + \dfrac{6}{\sqrt[3]{t}}$

For the functions in Exercises 41–50, find any points where the tangent line is horizontal. (Recall: find the x-values of points where the derivative is 0.)

41. $y = 6x^2 - 20x + 5$

42. $y = 9x^2 - 18x - 4$

43. $y = x^3 - \dfrac{5}{2}x^2 + 2x - 1$

44. $y = \dfrac{4}{3}x^3 - 13x^2 + 12x - 6$

45. $y = \dfrac{2}{3}x^3 - \dfrac{3}{2}x^2 - 5x + 8$

46. $y = x^3 - 2x^2 - 15x + 6$

47. $y = x^4 - 16x$

48. $y = x^4 - 256x$

49. $y = \dfrac{1}{x}$

50. $y = \dfrac{-4}{x^2}$

In Exercises 51–56, find the slope of the tangent line to the graph of the given function at the given value of x. Find the equation of the tangent line in Exercises 51 and 52.

51. $y = x^4 - 5x^3 + 2;\ x = 2$

52. $y = -2x^5 - 7x^3 + 8x^2;\ x = 1$

53. $y = 3x^{3/2} - 2x^{1/2};\ x = 9$

54. $y = -2x^{1/2} + x^{3/2};\ x = 4$

55. $y = 5x^{-1} - 2x^{-2};\ x = 3$

56. $y = -x^{-3} + x^{-2};\ x = 1$

57. If the price of a product is given by

$$P(x) = \dfrac{-1000}{x} + 1000,$$

where x represents the demand for the product, find the rate of change of price when the demand is 10.

58. Often sales of a new product grow rapidly at first and then level off with time. This is the case with the sales represented by the function

$$S(t) = 100 - 100t^{-1},$$

where t represents time in years. Find the rate of change of sales for the following values of t.

(a) $t = 1$ (b) $t = 10$

59. Suppose $P(t) = 100/t$ represents the percent of acid in a chemical solution after t days of exposure to an ultraviolet light source. Find the percent of acid in the solution after the following number of days.

(a) 1 day   (b) 100 days   (c) Find and interpret $P'(100)$.

60. Insulin affects the glucose, or blood sugar, level of some diabetics according to the function

$$G(x) = -.2x^2 + 450,$$

where $G(x)$ is the blood sugar level one hour after x units of insulin are injected. (This mathematical model is only approximate and valid only for values of x less than about 40.)

(a) Find $G(0)$.   (b) Find $G(25)$.

61. Use the function G of Exercise 60 and find dG/dx for the following values of x. Interpret your answers.

(a) $x = 10$ (b) $x = 25$

62. A short length of blood vessel has a cylindrical shape. The volume of a cylinder is given by $V = \pi r^2 h$. Suppose an experimental device is set up to measure the volume of blood in a blood vessel of fixed length 80 mm.

(a) Find dV/dr.

Suppose a drug is administered which causes the blood vessel to expand. Evaluate dV/dr for the following values of r.

(b) 4 mm   (c) 6 mm   (d) 8 mm

63. The profit in dollars from the sale of x expensive cassette recorders is
$$P(x) = x^3 - 5x^2 + 7x + 10.$$
Find the marginal profit for the following values of x.

(a) $x = 4$ (b) $x = 8$ (c) $x = 10$ (d) $x = 12$

64. The total cost to produce x handcrafted weathervanes is
$$C(x) = 100 + 8x - x^2 + 4x^3.$$
Find the marginal cost for the following values of x.

(a) $x = 0$ (b) $x = 4$ (c) $x = 6$ (d) $x = 8$

65. An analyst has found that a company's costs and revenues for one product are given by
$$C(x) = 2x \quad \text{and} \quad R(x) = 6x - \frac{x^2}{1000},$$
respectively, where x is the number of items produced.

(a) Find the marginal cost function.

(b) Find the marginal revenue function.

(c) Using the fact that profit is the difference between revenue and costs, find the marginal profit function.

(d) What value of x makes marginal profit equal 0?

(e) Find the profit when the marginal profit is 0.

(As we shall see in the next chapter, this process is used to find *maximum* profit.)

66. In an experiment testing methods of sexually attracting male insects to sterile females, equal numbers of males and females of a certain species are permitted to intermingle. Assume that
$$M(t) = 4t^{3/2} + 2t^{1/2}$$
approximates the number of matings observed among the insects in an hour, where t is the temperature in degrees Celsius. (This formula is only valid for certain temperature ranges.) Find each of the following.

(a) $M(16)$ (b) $M(25)$ (c) the rate of change of M when $t = 16$.

We saw earlier in this chapter that the velocity of a particle moving in a straight line is given by

$$\lim_{h \to 0} \frac{s(t + h) - s(t)}{h},$$

where $s(t)$ gives the position of the particle at time t. This limit is actually the derivative of $s(t)$, so the velocity of the particle is given by $s'(t)$. If $v(t)$ represents velocity at time t,

then $v(t) = s'(t)$. For each of the position functions in Exercises 67–74, find (a) $v(t)$;
(b) the velocity when $t = 0$; $t = 5$; and $t = 10$.

67. $s(t) = 6t + 5$ **68.** $s(t) = 9 - 2t$ **69.** $s(t) = 11t^2 + 4t + 2$

70. $s(t) = 25t^2 - 9t + 8$ **71.** $s(t) = 4t^3 + 8t^2$ **72.** $s(t) = -2t^3 + 4t^2 - 1$

73. $s(t) = 4\sqrt{t}$ **74.** $s(t) = -t^{3/2}$

10.5   Derivatives of Products and Quotients

The derivative of a sum of two functions is found from the sum of the derivatives. What about products? Is the derivative of a product equal to the product of the derivatives? Let's try an example:

$$\text{Let } g(x) = 2x + 3 \quad \text{and} \quad k(x) = 3x^2,$$
$$\text{then } g'(x) = 2 \quad \text{and} \quad k'(x) = 6x.$$

Let $f(x)$ be the product of g and k; that is, $f(x) = (2x + 3)(3x^2) = 6x^3 + 9x^2$. By the rules of the preceding section, $f'(x) = 18x^2 + 18x$. On the other hand, $g'(x) = 2$ and $k'(x) = 6x$, with the product $g'(x) \cdot k'(x) = 2(6x) = 12x \neq f'(x)$. In this example, the derivative of a product is *not* equal to the product of the derivatives, nor is this usually the case.

The rule for finding derivatives of products is given in the next box.

Product Rule

If $f(x) = g(x) \cdot k(x)$, and if $g'(x)$ and $k'(x)$ both exist, then
$$f'(x) = g(x) \cdot k'(x) + k(x) \cdot g'(x).$$

(The derivative of a product of two functions is the first function times the derivative of the second, plus the second times the derivative of the first.)

To sketch the method used to prove the product rule, let

$$f(x) = g(x) \cdot k(x).$$

Then $f(x + h) = g(x + h) \cdot k(x + h)$, and, by definition, $f'(x)$ is given by

$$f'(x) = \lim_{h \to 0} \frac{f(x + h) - f(x)}{h}$$

$$= \lim_{h \to 0} \frac{g(x + h) \cdot k(x + h) - g(x) \cdot k(x)}{h}.$$

Now we use an algebraic procedure: add and subtract $g(x + h) \cdot k(x)$ in the numerator, giving

$$f'(x) = \lim_{h \to 0} \frac{g(x + h) \cdot k(x + h) - g(x + h) \cdot k(x) + g(x + h) \cdot k(x) - g(x) \cdot k(x)}{h}$$

$$= \lim_{h \to 0} \frac{g(x + h)[k(x + h) - k(x)] + k(x)[g(x + h) - g(x)]}{h}$$

$$= \lim_{h \to 0} g(x + h)\left[\frac{k(x + h) - k(x)}{h}\right] + \lim_{h \to 0} k(x)\left[\frac{g(x + h) - g(x)}{h}\right]$$

$$= \lim_{h \to 0} g(x + h) \cdot \lim_{h \to 0} \frac{k(x + h) - k(x)}{h} + \lim_{h \to 0} k(x) \cdot \lim_{h \to 0} \frac{g(x + h) - g(x)}{h} \qquad (*)$$

If g' and k' both exist, then

$$\lim_{h \to 0} \frac{g(x + h) - g(x)}{h} = g'(x) \qquad \text{and} \qquad \lim_{h \to 0} \frac{k(x + h) - k(x)}{h} = k'(x).$$

The fact that g' exists can be used to prove

$$\lim_{h \to 0} g(x + h) = g(x),$$

and since no h is involved in $k(x)$,

$$\lim_{h \to 0} k(x) = k(x).$$

Substituting these results into equation (*) gives

$$f'(x) = g(x) \cdot k'(x) + k(x) \cdot g'(x),$$

the desired result.

EXAMPLE 1

Let $f(x) = (2x + 3)(3x^2)$. Use the product rule to find $f'(x)$.
  Here f is given as the product of $g(x) = 2x + 3$ and $k(x) = 3x^2$. By the product rule and the fact that $g'(x) = 2$ and $k'(x) = 6x$,

$$f'(x) = g(x) \cdot k'(x) + k(x) \cdot g'(x) = (2x + 3)(6x) + (3x^2)(2)$$
$$= 12x^2 + 18x + 6x^2 = 18x^2 + 18x.$$

This result is the same as that found at the beginning of the section. ∎

EXAMPLE 2

Find the derivative of $y = (\sqrt{x} + 3)(x^2 - 5x)$.
  Let $g(x) = \sqrt{x} + 3 = x^{1/2} + 3$, and $k(x) = x^2 - 5x$. Then

$$y' = g(x) \cdot k'(x) + k(x) \cdot g'(x)$$

$$= (x^{1/2} + 3)(2x - 5) + (x^2 - 5x)\left(\frac{1}{2}x^{-1/2}\right).$$

Simplify by multiplying and combining terms.

$$y' = (2x)(x^{1/2}) + 6x - 5x^{1/2} - 15 + (x^2)\left(\frac{1}{2}x^{-1/2}\right) - (5x)\left(\frac{1}{2}x^{-1/2}\right)$$

$$= 2x^{3/2} + 6x - 5x^{1/2} - 15 + \frac{1}{2}x^{3/2} - \frac{5}{2}x^{1/2}$$

$$= \frac{5}{2}x^{3/2} + 6x - \frac{15}{2}x^{1/2} - 15. \quad \blacksquare$$

The problems above could have been worked by multiplying out the original functions. The product rule would then not be needed. However, in the next section we shall see products of functions where this cannot be done—where the product rule is essential.

What about *quotients* of functions? To find the derivative of the quotient of two functions, use the next result.

Quotient Rule

If $f(x) = \dfrac{g(x)}{k(x)}$, if all indicated derivatives exist, and if $k(x) \neq 0$, then

$$f'(x) = \frac{k(x) \cdot g'(x) - g(x) \cdot k'(x)}{[k(x)]^2}.$$

(The derivative of a quotient is the denominator times the derivative of the numerator, minus the numerator times the derivative of the denominator, all divided by the square of the denominator.)

The proof of the quotient rule is similar to that of the product rule and is omitted.

EXAMPLE 3

Find $f'(x)$ if $f(x) = \dfrac{2x - 1}{4x + 3}$.

Let $g(x) = 2x - 1$, with $g'(x) = 2$. Also, let $k(x) = 4x + 3$, and $k'(x) = 4$. Then, by the quotient rule,

$$f'(x) = \frac{k(x) \cdot g'(x) - g(x) \cdot k'(x)}{[k(x)]^2}$$

$$= \frac{(4x + 3)(2) - (2x - 1)(4)}{(4x + 3)^2}$$

$$= \frac{8x + 6 - 8x + 4}{(4x + 3)^2}$$

$$= \frac{10}{(4x + 3)^2}. \quad \blacksquare$$

EXAMPLE 4   Find $D_x\left(\dfrac{x^{-1} - 2}{x^{-2} + 4}\right)$.

Use the quotient rule.

$$D_x\left(\frac{x^{-1} - 2}{x^{-2} + 4}\right) = \frac{(x^{-2} + 4)(-x^{-2}) - (x^{-1} - 2)(-2x^{-3})}{(x^{-2} + 4)^2}$$

$$= \frac{-x^{-4} - 4x^{-2} + 2x^{-4} - 4x^{-3}}{(x^{-2} + 4)^2}$$

$$= \frac{x^{-4} - 4x^{-3} - 4x^{-2}}{(x^{-2} + 4)^2}$$

In the next chapter we use derivatives to solve practical problems. That work will be easier if the derivatives are first simplified. This derivative, for example, can be simplified if the negative exponents are removed by multiplying numerator and denominator by x^4, and using $(x^{-2} + 4)^2 = x^{-4} + 8x^{-2} + 16$.

$$\frac{x^{-4} - 4x^{-3} - 4x^{-2}}{(x^{-2} + 4)^2} = \frac{1 - 4x - 4x^2}{x^4(x^{-4} + 8x^{-2} + 16)} = \frac{1 - 4x - 4x^2}{1 + 8x^2 + 16x^4} \quad \blacksquare$$

Average Cost   Suppose $y = C(x)$ gives the total cost to manufacture x items. Then the *average cost per item* is found by dividing the total cost by the number of items. The rate of change of average cost is called the **marginal average cost,** and is the derivative of the average cost.

Average Cost

> If the total cost to manufacture x items is given by $C(x)$, then the **average cost per item** is
> $$\text{average cost} = \frac{C(x)}{x}.$$
> The **marginal average cost** is the derivative of the average cost function.

A company naturally would be interested in making the average cost as small as possible. We will see in the next chapter that this can be done by using the derivative of $C(x)/x$. This derivative often can be found by means of the quotient rule, as in the next example.

EXAMPLE 5   The total cost in thousands of dollars to manufacture x electrical generators is given by $C(x)$, where

$$C(x) = x^3 + 15x^2 + 1000.$$

(a)   Find the average cost per generator.

Ical average cost is given by the total cost divided by the number of items, or

$$\frac{C(x)}{x} = \frac{x^3 + 15x^2 + 1000}{x}.$$

(b)   Find the marginal average cost.

The marginal average cost is the derivative of the average cost function. Using the quotient rule,

$$\frac{d}{dx}\left[\frac{C(x)}{x}\right] = \frac{x(3x^2 + 30x) - (x^3 + 15x^2 + 1000)(1)}{x^2}$$

$$= \frac{3x^3 + 30x^2 - x^3 - 15x^2 - 1000}{x^2}$$

$$= \frac{2x^3 + 15x^2 - 1000}{x^2}. \quad \blacksquare$$

10.5 EXERCISES

Use the product rule to find the derivatives for each of the functions in Exercises 1–18.
(Hint for Exercise 11: $a^2 = a \cdot a$.)

1. $y = (2x - 5)(x + 4)$

2. $y = (3x + 7)(x - 1)$

3. $f(x) = (8x - 2)(3x + 9)$

4. $f(x) = (4x + 1)(7x + 12)$

5. $y = (3x^2 + 2)(2x - 1)$

6. $y = (5x^2 - 1)(4x + 3)$

7. $y = (t^2 + t)(3t - 5)$

8. $y = (2t^2 - 6t)(t + 2)$

9. $y = (9x^2 + 7x)(x^2 - 1)$

10. $y = (2x^2 - 4x)(5x^2 + 4)$

11. $y = (2x - 5)^2$

12. $y = (7x - 6)^2$

13. $k(t) = (t^2 - 1)^2$

14. $g(t) = (3t^2 + 2)^2$

15. $y = (x + 1)(\sqrt{x} + 2)$

16. $y = (2x - 3)(\sqrt{x} - 1)$

17. $g(x) = (5\sqrt{x} - 1)(2\sqrt{x} + 1)$

18. $g(x) = (-3\sqrt{x} + 6)(4\sqrt{x} - 2)$

Use the quotient rule to find the derivatives of each of the functions in Exercises 19–38.

19. $y = \dfrac{x + 1}{2x - 1}$

20. $y = \dfrac{3x - 5}{x - 4}$

21. $f(x) = \dfrac{7x + 1}{3x + 8}$

22. $f(x) = \dfrac{6x - 11}{8x + 1}$

23. $y = \dfrac{2}{3x - 5}$

24. $y = \dfrac{-4}{2x - 11}$

25. $y = \dfrac{5 - 3t}{4 + t}$

26. $y = \dfrac{9 - 7t}{1 - t}$

27. $y = \dfrac{x^2 + x}{x - 1}$

28. $y = \dfrac{x^2 - 4x}{x + 3}$

29. $f(t) = \dfrac{t - 2}{t^2 + 1}$

30. $f(t) = \dfrac{4t + 11}{t^2 - 3}$

31. $y = \dfrac{3x^2 + x}{2x^2 - 1}$

32. $y = \dfrac{-x^2 + 6x}{4x^2 + 1}$

33. $g(x) = \dfrac{x^2 - 4x + 2}{x + 3}$

34. $k(x) = \dfrac{x^2 + 7x - 2}{x - 2}$

35. $p(t) = \dfrac{\sqrt{t}}{t - 1}$

36. $r(t) = \dfrac{\sqrt{t}}{2t + 3}$

37. $y = \dfrac{5x + 6}{\sqrt{x}}$

38. $y = \dfrac{9x - 8}{\sqrt{x}}$

39. The total cost to produce x units of perfume is
$$C(x) = 9x^2 - 4x + 8.$$
Find the average cost to produce
(a) 10 units   **(b)** 20 units   **(c)** x units
(d) Find the marginal average cost function.

40. The total profit from selling x units of self-help books is
$$P(x) = 10x^2 - 5x - 18.$$
Find the average profit from selling
(a) 8 units   **(b)** 15 units   **(c)** x units   **(d)** Find the marginal average profit function.

41. Suppose you are the manager of a trucking firm, and one of your drivers reports that, according to her calculations, her truck burns fuel at the rate of

$$G(x) = \frac{1}{200}\left(\frac{800 + x^2}{x}\right)$$

gallons per mile when traveling at x miles per hour on a smooth, dry road.

(a) If the driver tells you that she wants to travel 20 miles per hour, what should you tell her? (Hint: Take the derivative of G and evaluate it for $x = 20$. Then interpret your results.)

(b) If the driver wants to go 40 miles per hour, what should you say? (Hint: Find $G'(40)$.)

42. Assume that the total number (in millions) of bacteria present in a culture at a certain time t is given by

$$N(t) = (t - 10)^2(2t) + 50$$

(a) Find $N'(t)$.

At what rate is the population of bacteria changing when

(b) $t = 8$?   (c) $t = 11$?

(d) The answer in part (b) is negative, while the answer in part (c) is positive. What does this mean in terms of the population of bacteria?

43. When a certain drug is introduced into a muscle, the muscle responds by contracting. The amount of contraction, s, in millimeters, is related to the concentration of the drug, x, in milliliters, by

$$s(x) = \frac{x}{m + nx},$$

where m and n are constants.

(a) Find $s'(x)$.   (b) Evaluate $s'(x)$ when $x = 50$, $m = 10$, and $n = 3$.

44. According to the psychologist L. L. Thurstone, the number of facts of a certain type that are remembered after t hours is given by

$$f(t) = \frac{kt}{at - m}$$

where k, m, and a are constants. Find $f'(t)$ if $a = 99$, $k = 90$, $m = 90$, and

(a) $t = 1$;   (b) $t = 10$.

10.6   The Chain Rule

In an exercise in Chapter 1 we discussed a leaking oil well off the Gulf Coast from which a circular film of oil is spreading over the water surface. At any time t, in minutes, after the beginning of the leak, the radius of the circular oil slick is given by

$$r(t) = 4t, \qquad \text{with} \qquad \frac{dr}{dt} = 4.$$

The area of the oil slick is given by

$$A = \pi r^2, \qquad \text{with} \qquad \frac{dA}{dr} = 2\pi r.$$

As these derivatives show, the radius is increasing 4 times as fast as the time t, and the area is increasing $2\pi r$ times as fast as the radius r. It seems reasonable, then, that the area is increasing $2\pi r \cdot 4 = 8\pi r$ times as fast as time. That is,

$$\frac{dA}{dt} = \frac{dA}{dr} \cdot \frac{dr}{dt} = 2\pi r \cdot 4 = 8\pi r.$$

Since $r = 4t$,

$$\frac{dA}{dt} = 8\pi(4t) = 32\pi t.$$

To check this, use the fact that $r = 4t$ and $A = \pi r^2$ to get the same result:

$$A = \pi(4t)^2 = 16\pi t^2, \qquad \text{with} \qquad \frac{dA}{dt} = 32\pi t.$$

The product used above,

$$\frac{dA}{dt} = \frac{dA}{dr} \cdot \frac{dr}{dt},$$

is an example of the **chain rule,** which is used to find the derivative of a *composite function* (a function of a function—see Chapter 1).

Chain Rule

If y is a function of u, say $y = f(u)$, and if u is a function of x, say $u = g(x)$, then $y = f(u) = f[g(x)]$, and

$$\frac{dy}{dx} = \frac{dy}{du} \cdot \frac{du}{dx}.$$

One way to remember the chain rule is to pretend that dy/du and du/dx are fractions, with du "canceling out." The proof of the chain rule requires advanced concepts, and is not given here.

EXAMPLE 1

Find dy/dx if $y = (3x^2 - 5x)^{1/2}$.

Let $y = u^{1/2}$, and $u = 3x^2 - 5x$. Then

$$\frac{dy}{dx} = \frac{dy}{du} \cdot \frac{du}{dx}$$

$$= \frac{1}{2}u^{-1/2} \cdot (6x - 5).$$

Replacing u with $3x^2 - 5x$ gives

$$\frac{dy}{dx} = \frac{1}{2}(3x^2 - 5x)^{-1/2}(6x - 5) = \frac{6x - 5}{2(3x^2 - 5x)^{1/2}}. \quad \blacksquare$$

The next box gives an alternate statement of the chain rule, in terms of composite functions.

Chain Rule	If $y = f[g(x)]$, then
(Alternate Form)	$$y' = f'[g(x)] \cdot g'(x).$$

(To find the derivative of $f[g(x)]$, find the derivative of $f(x)$, replace each x with $g(x)$, and then multiply the result by the derivative of $g(x)$.)

EXAMPLE 2

Use the chain rule to find the derivative of $y = \sqrt{15x^2 + 1}$.

Since $y = (15x^2 + 1)^{1/2}$, let $f(x) = x^{1/2}$ and $g(x) = 15x^2 + 1$. Then $y = f[g(x)]$, and

$$y' = f'[g(x)] \cdot g'(x).$$

Here $f'(x) = \frac{1}{2}x^{-1/2}$, with $f'[g(x)] = \frac{1}{2}[g(x)]^{-1/2} = \frac{1}{2}(15x^2 + 1)^{-1/2}$, and

$$y' = \frac{1}{2}[g(x)]^{-1/2} \cdot g'(x) = \frac{1}{2}(15x^2 + 1)^{-1/2} \cdot (30x)$$

$$= \frac{15x}{(15x^2 + 1)^{1/2}}. \quad \blacksquare$$

While the chain rule is essential for finding the derivatives of some of the functions discussed later, the derivatives of the algebraic functions we have seen so far can be found by the following *generalized power rule*, a special case of the chain rule.

Generalized Power	Let u be a function of x, and let $y = u^n$, for any real number n. Then
Rule	$$y' = n \cdot u^{n-1} \cdot u'.$$

(The derivative of $y = u^n$ is found by decreasing the exponent on u by 1 and multiplying the result by the exponent n and by the derivative of u with respect to x.)

EXAMPLE 3

(a) Use the generalized power rule to find the derivative of $y = (3 + 5x)^2$.

Let $u = 3 + 5x$, and $n = 2$. Then $u' = 5$. By the generalized power rule,

$$y' = \frac{dy}{dx} = n \cdot u^{n-1} \cdot u'$$

$$= \overset{n}{2} \cdot \overset{u}{(3 + 5x)}^{\overset{n-1}{2-1}} \cdot \overset{u'}{\frac{d}{dx}(3 + 5x)}$$

$$= 2(3 + 5x)^{2-1} \cdot 5 = 10(3 + 5x)$$

$$= 30 + 50x.$$

(b) Find y' if $y = (3 + 5x)^{-3/4}$.

Use the generalized power rule, with $u = 3 + 5x$, $n = -3/4$, and $u' = 5$.

$$y' = -\frac{3}{4}(3 + 5x)^{-3/4-1} \cdot 5 = -\frac{15}{4}(3 + 5x)^{-7/4}$$

This result could not have been found by any of the rules given in previous sections. ■

EXAMPLE 4

Find the derivative of each function.

(a) $y = 2(7x^2 + 5)^4$

Let $u = 7x^2 + 5$. Then $u' = 14x$, and

$$y' = 2 \cdot \overset{n}{4}(7\overset{u}{x^2} + 5)^{\overset{n-1}{4-1}} \cdot \overbrace{\frac{d}{dx}(7x^2 + 5)}^{u'}$$

$$= 2 \cdot 4(7x^2 + 5)^3(14x)$$

$$= 112x(7x^2 + 5)^3.$$

(b) $y = \sqrt{9x + 2}$

Write $y = \sqrt{9x + 2}$ as $y = (9x + 2)^{1/2}$. Then

$$y' = \frac{1}{2}(9x + 2)^{-1/2}(9) = \frac{9}{2}(9x + 2)^{-1/2}.$$

The derivative also can be written as

$$y' = \frac{9}{2(9x + 2)^{1/2}} \quad \text{or} \quad y' = \frac{9}{2\sqrt{9x + 2}}. \quad ■$$

EXAMPLE 5

Suppose the revenue, $R(x)$, produced by selling x units of a biological nutrient is given by

$$R(x) = 4\sqrt{3x + 1} + \frac{4}{x}.$$

Assume that $x > 0$. Find the marginal revenue when $x = 5$.

As mentioned earlier, the marginal revenue is given by the derivative of the revenue function. By the generalized power rule,

$$R'(x) = \frac{6}{\sqrt{3x + 1}} - \frac{4}{x^2}.$$

When $x = 5$,

$$R'(5) = \frac{6}{\sqrt{3(5) + 1}} - \frac{4}{5^2} = \frac{6}{\sqrt{16}} - \frac{4}{25}$$

$$= \frac{6}{4} - \frac{4}{25} = 1.34.$$

After 5 units have been sold, the sale of one more unit will increase revenue by about $1.34. ■

Sometimes we need both the generalized power rule and either the product or quotient rule, as the next examples show.

EXAMPLE 6

Find the derivative of $y = 4x(3x + 5)^5$.

Write $4x(3x + 5)^5$ as the product

$$(4x) \cdot (3x + 5)^5.$$

To find the derivative of $(3x + 5)^5$, let $u = 3x + 5$, with $u' = 3$. Now use the product rule and the generalized power rule.

$$\overset{\text{derivative of }(3x + 5)^5}{\overbrace{\qquad\qquad}} \qquad \overset{\text{derivative of }4x}{\overbrace{\qquad}}$$

$$y' = 4x[5(3x + 5)^4 \cdot 3] + (3x + 5)^5(4)$$

$$= 60x(3x + 5)^4 + 4(3x + 5)^5$$

$$= 4(3x + 5)^4[15x + (3x + 5)^1] \qquad \text{Factor out the greatest}$$

$$= 4(3x + 5)^4(18x + 5). \quad ▨ \qquad\qquad \text{common factor, } 4(3x + 5)^4$$

EXAMPLE 7

Find the derivative of $y = \dfrac{(3x + 2)^7}{x - 1}$.

Use the quotient rule and the generalized power rule.

$$y' = \frac{(x - 1)[7(3x + 2)^6 \cdot 3] - (3x + 2)^7(1)}{(x - 1)^2}$$

$$= \frac{21(x - 1)(3x + 2)^6 - (3x + 2)^7}{(x - 1)^2}$$

$$= \frac{(3x + 2)^6[21(x - 1) - (3x + 2)]}{(x - 1)^2}$$

$$= \frac{(3x + 2)^6[21x - 21 - 3x - 2]}{(x - 1)^2}$$

$$= \frac{(3x + 2)^6(18x - 23)}{(x - 1)^2} \quad ▨$$

For reference, we now list the definition and the rules for derivatives developed in this chapter.

Definition of

Derivative

The derivative of the function $y = f(x)$ is

$$f'(x) = \lim_{h \to 0} \frac{f(x + h) - f(x)}{h}$$

provided this limit exists. Alternative notations for the derivative include dy/dx, $D_x y$, $D_x[f(x)]$, and y'.

The following rules for derivatives are valid when all the indicated derivatives exist.

Summary of Rules for Derivatives

Constant Function   If $f(x) = k$, where k is any real number, then $f'(x) = 0$.

Power Rule   If $f(x) = x^n$, for any real number n, then $f'(x) = n \cdot x^{n-1}$.

Constant times a Function   Let k be a real number. Then the derivative of $y = k \cdot f(x)$ is $y' = k \cdot f'(x)$.

Sum or Difference Rule   If $y = f(x) \pm g(x)$, then $y' = f'(x) \pm g'(x)$.

Product Rule   If $f(x) = g(x) \cdot k(x)$, then

$$f'(x) = g(x) \cdot k'(x) + k(x) \cdot g'(x).$$

Quotient Rule   If $f(x) = \dfrac{g(x)}{k(x)}$, and $k(x) \neq 0$, then

$$f'(x) = \frac{k(x) \cdot g'(x) - g(x) \cdot k'(x)}{[k(x)]^2}.$$

Chain Rule   Let y be a function of u, say $y = f(u)$, and let u be a function of x, say $u = g(x)$. Then $y = f(u) = f[g(x)]$, and

$$\frac{dy}{dx} = \frac{dy}{du} \cdot \frac{du}{dx}.$$

Chain Rule (alternate form)   Let $y = f[g(x)]$. Then $y' = f'[g(x)] \cdot g'(x)$.

Generalized Power Rule   Let u be a function of x, and let $y = u^n$. Then $y' = n \cdot u^{n-1} \cdot u'$.

10.6 EXERCISES

As a review of composite functions from Chapter 1, find $f[g(x)]$ and $g[f(x)]$.

1. $f(x) = x^{1/3}$; $g(x) = 2x + 5$

2. $f(x) = x^{-3/4}$; $g(x) = 8x - 3$

3. $f(x) = \dfrac{2}{\sqrt{x}}$; $g(x) = 4 - 3x$

4. $f(x) = \dfrac{5}{\sqrt[4]{x}}$; $g(x) = 9 + 5x$

5. $f(x) = 5x^2 - x$; $g(x) = 5x + 3$

6. $f(x) = 2x + 3x^2$; $g(x) = 9x - 1$

7. $f(x) = \sqrt{x + 5}$; $g(x) = x^2 + 7$

8. $f(x) = 8 - x^2$; $g(x) = \sqrt{3 - x}$

Write each function in Exercises 9–16 as the composition of two functions. (There may be more than one way to do this.)

9. $y = (3x - 7)^{1/3}$

10. $y = (5 - x)^{2/5}$

11. $y = \sqrt{9 - 4x}$

12. $y = -\sqrt{13 + 7x}$

13. $y = \dfrac{\sqrt{x} + 3}{\sqrt{x} - 3}$

14. $y = \dfrac{2}{\sqrt{x} + 5}$

15. $y = (x^{1/2} - 3)^2 + (x^{1/2} - 3) + 5$

16. $y = (x^2 + 5x)^{1/3} - 2(x^2 + 5x)^{2/3} + 7$

Find the derivatives of the functions in Exercises 17–48.

17. $y = (2x + 9)^2$

18. $y = (8x - 3)^2$

19. $f(x) = 6(5x - 1)^3$

20. $f(x) = -8(3x + 2)^3$

21. $k(x) = -2(12x^2 + 5)^3$

22. $g(x) = 5(3x^2 - 5)^3$

23. $y = 9(x^2 + 5x)^4$

24. $y = -3(x^2 - 5x)^4$

25. $s(t) = 12(2t + 5)^{3/2}$

26. $s(t) = 45(3t - 8)^{3/2}$

27. $y = -7(4x^2 + 9x)^{3/2}$

28. $y = 11(5x^2 + 6x)^{3/2}$

29. $f(t) = 8\sqrt{4t + 7}$

30. $g(t) = -3\sqrt{7t - 1}$

31. $y = -2\sqrt{x^2 + 4x}$

32. $y = 4\sqrt{2x^2 + 3}$

33. $r(t) = 4t(2t + 3)^2$

34. $m(t) = -6t(5t - 1)^2$

35. $y = (x + 2)(x - 1)^2$

36. $y = (3x + 1)^2(x + 4)$

37. $f(x) = 5(x + 3)^2(x - 1)^2$

38. $g(x) = -9(x + 4)^2(2x - 3)^2$

39. $y = (x + 1)^2\sqrt{x}$

40. $y = (3x + 5)^2\sqrt{x}$

41. $y = \dfrac{1}{(x - 4)^2}$

42. $y = \dfrac{-5}{(2x + 1)^2}$

43. $p(t) = \dfrac{(t + 3)^2}{t - 1}$

44. $r(t) = \dfrac{(t - 6)^2}{t + 4}$

45. $y = \dfrac{x^2 + 4x}{(x + 2)^2}$

46. $y = \dfrac{3x^2 - x}{(x - 1)^2}$

47. $y = (x^{1/2} + 1)(x^{1/2} - 1)^{1/2}$

48. $y = (3 - x^{2/3})(x^{2/3} + 2)^{1/2}$

49. Assume that the total revenue from the sale of x television sets is given by

$$R(x) = 1000\left(1 - \frac{x}{500}\right)^2.$$

Find the marginal revenue for the following values of x.

(a) $x = 100$ (b) $x = 150$ (c) $x = 200$ (d) $x = 400$

(e) Find the average revenue from the sale of x sets.

(f) Find the marginal average revenue.

50. The total number of bacteria (in millions) present in a culture is given by

$$N(t) = 2t(5t + 9)^{1/2} + 12,$$

where t represents time in hours after the beginning of an experiment. Find the rate of change of the population of bacteria with respect to time when

(a) $t = 0$ (b) $t = 7/5$ (c) $t = 8$ (d) $t = 11$.

51. To test an individual's use of calcium, a researcher injects a small amount of radioactive calcium into the person's bloodstream. The calcium remaining in the bloodstream is measured each day for several days. Suppose the amount of the calcium remaining in the bloodstream in milligrams per cubic centimeter t days after the initial injection is approximated by

$$C(t) = \frac{1}{2}(2t + 1)^{-1/2}.$$

Find the rate of change of C with respect to time when

(a) $t = 0$;   (b) $t = 4$;   (c) $t = 6$ (use a calculator);   (d) $t = 7.5$.

52. The strength of a person's reaction to a certain drug is given by

$$R(Q) = Q\left(C - \frac{Q}{3}\right)^{1/2},$$

where Q represents the quantity of the drug given to the patient and C is a constant.

(a) The derivative $R'(Q)$ is called the *sensitivity* to the drug. Find $R'(Q)$.

(b) Find $R'(Q)$ if $Q = 87$ and $C = 59$.

10.7   Continuity and Differentiability

Most of the graphs of functions we have used so far were drawn by selecting several values of x and finding the corresponding values of y. The resulting ordered pairs were plotted and a smooth curve drawn through them. This process worked reasonably well because most of the functions graphed were **continuous**—the graph could be drawn without lifting pencil from paper. A function that is not continuous at some point is **discontinuous** at the point.

In order to clarify the idea of continuity at a point, we shall first look at graphs having points of discontinuity. Studying the reasons why the functions are discontinuous at various points will lead to a reasonable definition of continuity. For example, the function shown in Figure 27(a) is discontinuous at $x = 2$ because of the "hole" in the graph at $(2, 3)$. The function of Figure 27(b) is discontinuous at $x = -3$ because of the "jump" in the graph when $x = -3$.

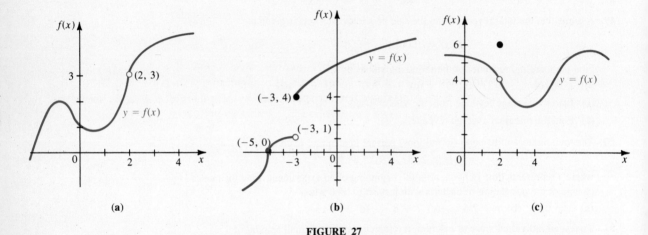

(a)   (b)   (c)

FIGURE 27

Finally, the function in Figure 27(c) is discontinuous when $x = 2$. Even though $f(2)$ is defined (here $f(2) = 6$), the value of $f(2)$ is not "close" to the values of $f(x)$ for values of x "close" to 2. That is,

$$\lim_{x \to 2} f(x) \neq f(2).$$

Now that we have seen some different ways for a function to have a point of discontinuity, look again at Figure 27(b). The function shown in Figure 27(b), which is *not* continuous when $x = -3$, *is* continuous when $x = -5$. To see the difference, note first that $f(-5)$ is defined, so that a point on the graph corresponds to $x = -5$. Second, $\lim_{x \to -5} f(x)$ exists. As x approaches -5 from either side of -5, the values of $f(x)$ approach one particular number, $f(-5)$, which is 0. These examples suggest the following definition.

Definition of	A function f is **continuous at c** if all the following three conditions are satisfied:
Continuity at a	
Point	**1.** $f(c)$ is defined;

1. $f(c)$ is defined;

2. $\lim\limits_{x \to c} f(x)$ exists;

3. $\lim\limits_{x \to c} f(x) = f(c)$.

If f is not continuous at c, it is **discontinuous** there.

EXAMPLE 1

Tell why the following functions are discontinuous at the indicated points.

(a) $f(x)$ in Figure 28 at $x = 3$

The open circle on the graph of Figure 28 at the point where $x = 3$ means that $f(3)$ is not defined. Because of this, part (1) of the definition fails.

(b) $h(x)$ in Figure 29 at $x = 0$

According to the graph of Figure 29, $h(0) = -1$. Also, as x approaches 0 from the left, $h(x)$ is -1. However, as x approaches 0 from the right, $h(x)$ is 1. Since there is no single number approached by the values of $h(x)$ as x approaches 0, $\lim\limits_{x \to 0} h(x)$ does not exist, and part (2) of the definition fails.

(c) $g(x)$ in Figure 30 at $x = 4$

In Figure 30, the heavy dot above 4 shows that $g(4)$ is defined. In fact, $g(4) = 1$. However, the graph also shows that

$$\lim_{x \to 4} g(x) = -2,$$

so $\lim\limits_{x \to 4} g(x) \neq g(4)$ and part (3) of the definition fails.

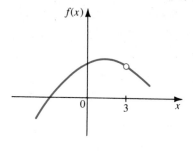

FIGURE 28

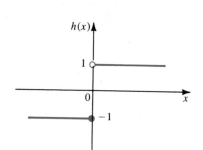

FIGURE 29

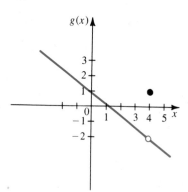

FIGURE 30

(d) $f(x)$ in Figure 31 at $x = -2$

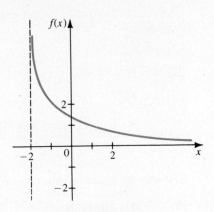

FIGURE 31

The function of Figure 31 is not defined at -2, and

$$\lim_{x \to -2} f(x) \text{ does not exist.}$$

Either of these reasons is sufficient to show that f is not continuous at -2. (However, f *is* continuous at any value of x greater than -2.) ■

The properties of continuous functions given in the next box may be used to construct other continuous functions.

Properties of Continuous Functions	
	$f(x) = k$ is continuous for all x.
	$f(x) = x^n$ and $g(x) = \sqrt[n]{x}$ are continuous for all positive integers n and all real numbers x in the domain of the functions.
	If $f(x)$ and $g(x)$ are continuous at a point, then so are $f(x) + g(x)$, $f(x) - g(x)$, and $f(x) \cdot g(x)$.
	If $f(x)$ and $g(x)$ are continuous at a point, and if $g(x) \neq 0$, then $f(x)/g(x)$ is continuous at the point.

The next table lists some key functions and tells where each is continuous.

Continuous Functions

Type of function	Where continuous	Graphic example
Polynomial Function $y = a_n x^n + a_{n-1} x^{n-1} + \cdots + a_1 x + a_0$ $a_n, a_{n-1}, \cdots, a_1, a_0$ are real numbers, not all 0	for all x	
Rational Function $y = \dfrac{p(x)}{q(x)}$ $p(x),\ q(x)$ are polynomials, with $q(x) \neq 0$	for all x where $q(x) \neq 0$	
Root Function $y = \sqrt{ax + b}$ a, b are real numbers, with $a \neq 0$ and $ax + b \geq 0$	for all x where $ax + b > 0$	

Finally, in addition to continuity at a point, we can define continuity on an open interval.*

Continuous on an Open Interval

> If a function f is continuous at each point of an open interval, f is said to be **continuous on that interval.**

EXAMPLE 2

Is the function of Figure 32 continuous on the following intervals?

(a) $(-2, -1)$

The function is discontinuous only at $x = -2, 0,$ and 2. Thus, it is continuous at every point of the open interval $(-2, -1)$. The function is continuous on the open interval.

---

*In a few places later in the book we need the idea of continuity on a closed interval. While it is perhaps intuitively clear when a function is continuous on a closed interval, a precise definition requires more work than we have given.

(b)   (1, 3)

This interval includes the point of discontinuity $x = 2$, so that the function is not continuous on the open interval (1, 3). ■

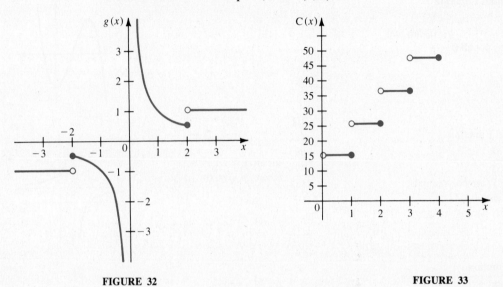

FIGURE 32   FIGURE 33

EXAMPLE 3

A trailer rental firm charges a flat \$4 to rent a hitch. The trailer itself is rented for \$11 per day or fraction of a day. Let $C(x)$ represent the cost of renting a hitch and trailer for x days.

(a)   Graph C.

The charge for one day is \$4 for the hitch and \$11 for the trailer, or \$15. In fact, if $0 < x \le 1$, then $C(x) = 15$. To rent the trailer for more than one day, but not more than two days, the charge is $4 + 2 \cdot 11 = 26$ dollars. For any value of x satisfying $1 < x \le 2$, $C(x) = 26$. Also, if $2 < x \le 3$, then $C(x) = 37$. These results lead to the graph of Figure 33.

(b)   Find any points of discontinuity for C.

As the graph suggests, C is discontinuous at $x = 1, 2, 3, 4$, and all other positive integers. ■

Continuity and Differentiability   We saw earlier in this chapter that a function fails to have a derivative at a point where the function is not defined, where the graph of the function has a "sharp point," or where the graph has a vertical tangent line. (See Figure 34.)

The function graphed in Figure 34 is continuous on the interval (x_1, x_2) and has a derivative at each point of this interval. On the other hand, the function is also continuous on the interval $(0, x_2)$, but does *not* have a derivative at each point in the interval. While a function continuous at a point need not have a derivative at that point (see x_1 on the graph),

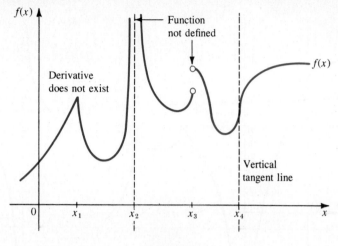

FIGURE 34

if the derivative of a function exists at a point, then the function is continuous at that point.

Intuitively, this means that a graph can have a derivative at a point only if the graph is "smooth" in the vicinity of the point.

10.7 EXERCISES

In Exercises 1–6, find all points of discontinuity. Tell where the derivatives would fail to exist.

1.

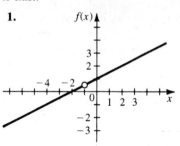

2.

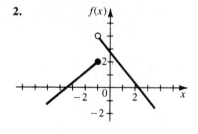

3.

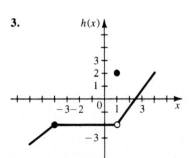

4.

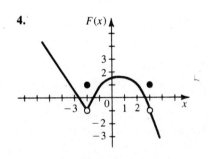

5.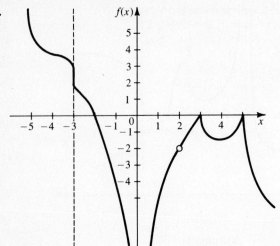

6.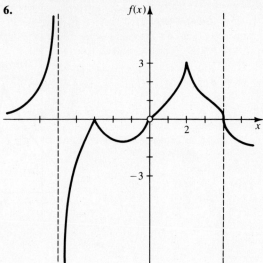

Are the functions in Exercises 7–20 continuous at the given values of x?

7. $f(x) = \dfrac{2}{x - 3}$; $x = 0$, $x = 3$

8. $f(x) = \dfrac{6}{x}$; $x = 0$, $x = -1$

9. $g(x) = \dfrac{1}{x(x - 2)}$; $x = 0$, $x = 2$, $x = 4$

10. $h(x) = \dfrac{-2}{3x(x + 5)}$; $x = 0$, $x = 3$, $x = -5$

11. $h(x) = \dfrac{1 + x}{(x - 3)(x + 1)}$; $x = 0$, $x = 3$, $x = -1$

12. $g(x) = \dfrac{-2x}{(2x + 1)(3x + 6)}$; $x = 0$, $x = -1/2$, $x = -2$

13. $k(x) = \dfrac{5 + x}{2 + x}$; $x = 0$, $x = -2$, $x = -5$

14. $f(x) = \dfrac{4 - x}{x - 9}$; $x = 0$, $x = 4$, $x = 9$

15. $g(x) = \dfrac{x^2 - 4}{x - 2}$; $x = 0$, $x = 2$, $x = -2$

16. $h(x) = \dfrac{x^2 - 25}{x + 5}$; $x = 0$, $x = 5$, $x = -5$

17. $p(x) = x^2 - 4x + 11$; $x = 0$, $x = 2$, $x = -1$

18. $q(x) = -3x^3 + 2x^2 - 4x + 1$; $x = -2$, $x = 3$, $x =$

19. $p(x) = \dfrac{|x + 2|}{x + 2}$; $x = -2$, $x = 0$, $x = 2$

20. $r(x) = \dfrac{|5 - x|}{x - 5}$; $x = -5$, $x = 0$, $x = 5$

21. A company charges $1.20 per pound for a certain fertilizer on all orders not over 100 pounds, and $1 per pound for orders over 100 pounds. Let $F(x)$ represent the cost for buying x pounds of the fertilizer.

(a) Find $F(80)$.   (b) Find $F(150)$.

(c) Graph $y = F(x)$.   (d) Where is F discontinuous?

22. The cost to transport a mobile home depends on the distance, x, in miles that the home is moved. Let $C(x)$ represent the cost to move a mobile home x miles. One firm charges as follows.

Cost Per Mile	Distance in Miles
$2	if $0 < x \le 150$
$1.50	if $150 < x \le 400$
$1.25	if $400 < x$

(a) Find $C(130)$.   (b) Find $C(210)$.

(c) Find $C(350)$.   (d) Find $C(500)$.

(e) Graph $y = C(x)$.

(f) Where is C discontinuous?

23. Recently, a car rental firm charged $30 per day to rent a car for a period of 1 to 5 days. Days 6 and 7 were then "free," while the charge for days 8 through 12 was again $30 per day. Let $A(t)$ represent the average cost per day to rent the car for t days, where $0 < t \le 12$. Find each of the following.

(a) $A(4)$ (b) $A(5)$ (c) $A(6)$ (d) $A(7)$

(e) $A(8)$ (f) $\lim\limits_{t \to 5} A(t)$ (g) $\lim\limits_{t \to 6} A(t)$

24. With certain skills (such as musical skills), learning is rapid at first and then levels off, with sudden insights causing learning to take a jump. A typical graph of such learning is shown in the figure. Where is the function discontinuous?

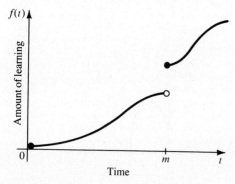

25. Suppose a gram of ice is at a temperature of $-100°C$. The graph on the left shows the temperature of the ice as an increasing number of calories of heat are applied. It takes 80 calories to melt one gram of ice at $0°C$ into water, and 539 calories to boil one gram of water at $100°C$ into steam. Where is this graph discontinuous?

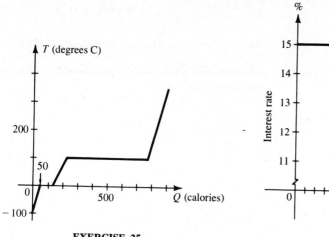

EXERCISE 25

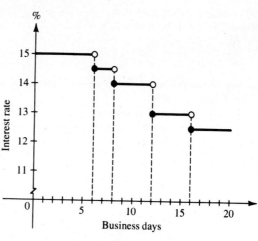

EXERCISE 26

26. The graph on the right shows the prime interest rate for business loans for the business days of a recent month. Where is the graph discontinuous?

Are the functions in Exercises 27–30 continuous on the indicated intervals?

27. $(-3, 0); (0, 3); (0, 4)$

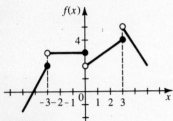

28. $(-6, 0); (0, 6); (4, 8)$

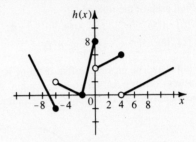

29. $(-12, 6); (0, 6); (6, 12)$

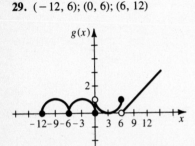

30. $(-4, 0); (0, 3); (0, 5)$

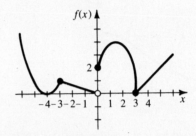

31. Let $f(x) = x + 5$ and $g(x) = \sqrt{x}$. Tell if the following functions are continuous when $x = -4$, $x = 0$, or $x = 4$.

  (a) $f[g(x)]$ **(b)** $g[f(x)]$

32. Let $f(x) = 2/(3 - x)$ and $g(x) = 4 - x^2$. Tell if the following functions are continuous when $x = -3$, $x = -2$, $x = 0$, $x = 2$, $x = 3$.

  (a) $f[g(x)]$ **(b)** $g[f(x)]$

KEY WORDS

limit
limit at infinity
average rate of change
instantaneous rate of change
rate of change
velocity
tangent line
secant line
slope of a curve
derivative
differentiable

differentiation
marginal cost
product rule
quotient rule
average cost
chain rule
generalized power rule
continuous
discontinuous
continuous on an open interval

Chapter 10   REVIEW EXERCISES

Decide if the limits in Exercises 1–18 exist. If a limit exists, find its value.

1. $\lim_{x \to -3} f(x)$

2. $\lim_{x \to -1} g(x)$

3. $\lim_{x \to \infty} f(x)$

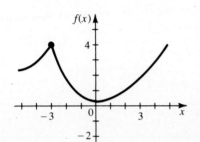

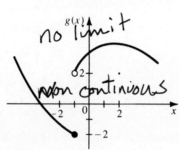

no limit

non continious

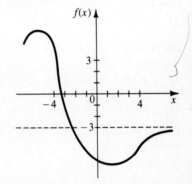

4. $\lim_{x \to 0} \dfrac{x^2 - 5}{2x}$

5. $\lim_{x \to -1} (2x^2 + 3x + 5)$

6. $\lim_{x \to 2} (-x^2 + 4x + 1)$

7. $\lim_{x \to 6} \dfrac{2x + 5}{x - 3}$

8. $\lim_{x \to 3} \dfrac{2x + 5}{x - 3}$

9. $\lim_{x \to 4} \dfrac{x^2 - 16}{x - 4}$

10. $\lim_{x \to 2} \dfrac{x^2 + 3x - 10}{x - 2}$

11. $\lim_{x \to -4} \dfrac{2x^2 + 3x - 20}{x + 4}$

12. $\lim_{x \to 3} \dfrac{3x^2 - 2x - 21}{x - 3}$

13. $\lim_{x \to 9} \dfrac{\sqrt{x} - 3}{x - 9}$

14. $\lim_{x \to 16} \dfrac{\sqrt{x} - 4}{x - 16}$

15. $\lim_{x \to \infty} \dfrac{x^2 + 5}{5x^2 - 1}$

16. $\lim_{x \to \infty} \dfrac{x^2 + 6x + 8}{x^3 + 2x + 1}$

17. $\lim_{x \to \infty} \left(\dfrac{3}{4} + \dfrac{2}{x} - \dfrac{5}{x^2} \right)$

18. $\lim_{x \to \infty} \left(\dfrac{9}{x^4} + \dfrac{1}{x^2} - 3 \right)$

Use the graph to find the average rate of change of f on the intervals in Exercises 19–22.

19. $x = 0$ to $x = 4$

20. $x = 2$ to $x = 8$

21. $x = 2$ to $x = 4$

22. $x = 0$ to $x = 6$

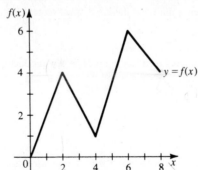

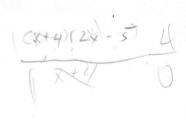

Find the average rate of change for the functions in Exercises 23–26 on the given intervals.

23. $y = 6x^2 + 2$; from $x = 1$ to $x = 4$

24. $y = -2x^3 - x^2 + 5$; from $x = -2$ to $x = 6$

25. $y = \dfrac{-6}{3x - 5}$; from $x = 4$ to $x = 9$

26. $y = \dfrac{x + 4}{x - 1}$; from $x = 2$ to $x = 5$

Use the definition of the derivative to find the derivative of each of the functions in Exercises 27–30.

27. $y = 4x + 3$

28. $y = 5x^2 + 6x$

29. $y = -x^3 + 7x$

30. $y = 11x^2 - x^3$

In Exercises 31–38, find the slope of the tangent line to the given curve at the given value of x. Find the equation of each tangent line.

31. $y = x^2 - 6x$; at $x = 2$

32. $y = 8 - x^2$; at $x = 1$

33. $y = \dfrac{3}{x - 1}$; at $x = -1$

34. $y = \dfrac{-2}{x + 5}$; at $x = -2$

35. $y = (3x^2 - 5x)(2x)$; at $x = -1$

36. $y = \dfrac{3}{x^2 - 1}$; at $x = 2$

37. $y = \sqrt{6x - 2}$; at $x = 3$

38. $y = -\sqrt{8x + 1}$; at $x = 3$

Find all values of x (if any) at which the functions in Exercises 39–44 have tangent lines whose slope is 0.

39. $f(x) = -5x^2$

40. $f(x) = 4x^2 - 6x$

41. $f(x) = 3x - 9x^2$

42. $f(x) = \frac{1}{3}x^3 + \frac{1}{2}x^2 - 2x$

43. $f(x) = \dfrac{-6}{x}$

44. $f(x) = x^3 - 4x^2$

45. Suppose the profit in cents from selling x pounds of potatoes is given by
$$P(x) = 15x + 25x^2.$$
Find the marginal profit when

   (a) $x = 6$ **(b)** $x = 20$ **(c)** $x = 30$

46. In Exercise 45, find the average profit function and the marginal average profit function.

47. The sales of a company are related to its expenditures on research by
$$S(x) = 1000 + 50\sqrt{x} + 10x,$$
where $S(x)$ gives sales in millions when x thousand dollars is spent on research. Find dS/dx when

   (a) $x = 9$ **(b)** $x = 16$ **(c)** $x = 25$.

48. Suppose that the profit in hundreds of dollars from selling x units of a product is given by $P(x)$, where
$$P(x) = \frac{x^2}{x - 1}.$$
Find the marginal profit when

   (a) $x = 4$ **(b)** $x = 12$ **(c)** $x = 20$.

49. A company finds that its sales are related to the amount spent on training programs by
$$T(x) = \frac{1000 + 50x}{x + 1},$$
where $T(x)$ is sales in thousands of dollars when x hundred dollars are spent on training. Find $T'(x)$ when

   (a) $x = 9$;   **(b)** $x = 19$.

50. Waverly Products has found that its profits are related to advertising expenditures by the function

$$P(x) = 5000 + 16x - 3x^2,$$

where $P(x)$ is the profit when x hundred dollars are spent on advertising.

(a) Find the marginal profit function.

(b) Find the marginal profit when $x = 10$.

Find the derivative of each of the functions in Exercises 51–80.

51. $y = 5x^2 - 7x - 9$

52. $y = x^3 - 4x^2$

53. $y = 6x^{7/3}$

54. $y = -3x^{-2}$

55. $f(x) = x^{-3} + \sqrt{x}$

56. $f(x) = 6x^{-1} - 2\sqrt{x}$

57. $y = (3t^2 + 7)(t^3 - t)$

58. $y = (-5t + 4)(t^3 - 2t^2)$

59. $y = 4\sqrt{x}(2x - 3)$

60. $y = -3\sqrt{x}(8 - 5x)$

61. $g(t) = -3t^{1/3}(5t + 7)$

62. $p(t) = 8t^{3/4}(7t - 2)$

63. $y = 12x^{-3/4}(3x + 5)$

64. $y = 15x^{-3/5}(x + 6)$

65. $k(x) = \dfrac{3x}{x + 5}$

66. $r(x) = \dfrac{-8}{2x + 1}$

67. $y = \dfrac{\sqrt{x} - 1}{x + 2}$

68. $y = \dfrac{\sqrt{x} + 6}{x - 3}$

69. $y = \dfrac{x^2 - x + 1}{x - 1}$

70. $y = \dfrac{2x^3 - 5x^2}{x + 2}$

71. $f(x) = (3x - 2)^4$

72. $k(x) = (5x - 1)^6$

73. $y = \sqrt{2t - 5}$

74. $y = -3\sqrt{8t - 1}$

75. $y = 3x(2x + 1)^3$

76. $y = 4x^2(3x - 2)^5$

77. $r(t) = \dfrac{5t^2 - 7t}{(3t + 1)^3}$

78. $s(t) = \dfrac{t^3 - 2t}{(4t - 3)^4}$

79. $y = \dfrac{x^2 + 3x - 10}{x - 2}$

80. $y = \dfrac{x^2 - x - 6}{x - 3}$

Find each of the following.

81. $D_x \left[\dfrac{\sqrt{x} + 1}{\sqrt{x} - 1} \right]$

82. $D_x \left[\dfrac{2x + \sqrt{x}}{1 - x} \right]$

83. $\dfrac{dy}{dt}$ if $y = \sqrt{t^{1/2} + t}$

84. $\dfrac{dy}{dx}$ if $y = \dfrac{\sqrt{x} - 1}{x}$

85. $f'(1)$ if $f(x) = \dfrac{\sqrt{8 + x}}{x + 1}$

86. $f'(-2)$ if $f(t) = \dfrac{2 - 3t}{\sqrt{2 + t}}$

In Exercises 87–94, are the functions continuous at the given values of x?

87. $f(x) = \dfrac{6x + 1}{2x - 3}$; $x = 3/2$; $x = -1/6$; $x = 0$

88. $f(x) = \dfrac{2}{x(x + 4)}$; $x = 2$; $x = 0$; $x = -4$

89. $f(x) = \dfrac{-5}{3x(2x - 1)}$; $x = -5$; $x = 0$; $x = -1/3$; $x = 1/2$

90. $f(x) = \dfrac{2 - 3x}{(1 + x)(2 - x)}$; $x = 2/3$; $x = -1$; $x = 2$; $x = 0$

91. $f(x) = \dfrac{x - 6}{x + 5}$; $x = 6$; $x = -5$; $x = 0$

92. $f(x) = \dfrac{x^2 - 9}{x + 3}$; $x = 3$; $x = -3$; $x = 0$

93. $f(x) = x^2 + 3x - 4$; $x = 1$; $x = -4$; $x = 0$

94. $f(x) = 2x^2 - 5x - 3$; $x = -1/2$; $x = 3$; $x = 0$

Are the functions in Exercises 95 and 96 continuous on the given intervals?

95. $(-3, 0)$; $(-3, 3)$; $(0, 4)$

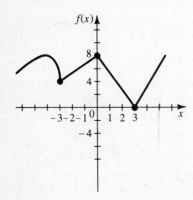

96. $(-4, 2)$; $(-4, 6)$; $(2, 6)$

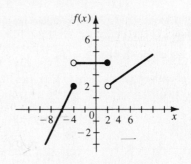

97. A company charges $1.50 per pound when a certain chemical is bought in lots of 125 pounds or less, with a price per pound of $1.35 if more than 125 pounds are purchased. Let $C(x)$ represent the cost of x pounds. Find

(a) $C(100)$ (b) $C(125)$ (c) $C(140)$.   (d) Graph $y = C(x)$.

(e) Where is C discontinuous?

98. Use the information of Exercise 97 to find the average cost per pound if the following number of pounds are bought.

(a) 100   (b) 125   (c) 140   (d) 200

Where does the derivative fail to exist for the following functions? Where are the functions discontinuous?

99.

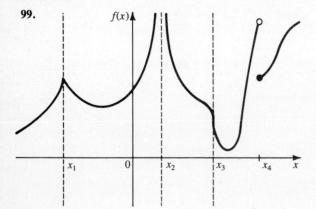

100.

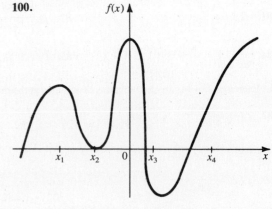

APPLICATIONS
OF THE DERIVATIVE

Karl Gerstner. From the series *AlgoRhythm 3*, 1973. Roche AG, Basel.

The graph of Figure 1 shows the population of deer on the Kaibab Plateau on the North Rim of the Grand Canyon between 1905 and 1930. In the early years of the 20th century, hunters were very effective in reducing the population of predators. With few predators, the deer population increased rapidly and this increase in population caused a depletion of food resources. Deer population peaked around 1925, and then rapidly dropped.

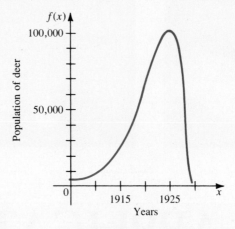

FIGURE 1

Given a graph such as the one in Figure 1, maximum and minimum values can usually be read directly. (Also, we saw in Chapter 1 how to find maximum and minimum values for quadratic functions by finding the vertex of a parabola.) For more complicated functions with graphs that may be difficult to draw, derivatives can be used to find maximum and minimum values. The procedure for doing this is discussed in the first part of this chapter, which begins with a discussion of increasing and decreasing functions.

11.1   Increasing and Decreasing Functions

According to the graph of Figure 1 above, deer population increased from 1905 to 1925, and then decreased from 1925 until about 1930. Intuitively, a function is *increasing* if the graph goes *up* from left to right. A function is *decreasing* if its graph goes *down* from left to right. Examples of increasing functions are shown in Figure 2, with examples of decreasing functions in Figure 3.

Increasing and

Decreasing

Functions

Let f be a function defined on some interval. Then for any two numbers x_1 and x_2 in the interval, f is **increasing** on the interval if

$$f(x_1) < f(x_2) \quad \text{whenever} \quad x_1 < x_2;$$

f is **decreasing** on the interval if

$$f(x_1) > f(x_2) \quad \text{whenever} \quad x_1 < x_2.$$

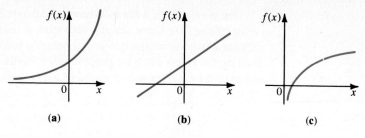

FIGURE 2

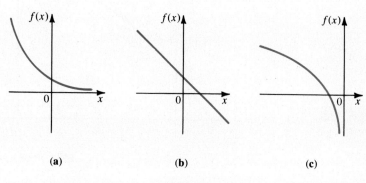

FIGURE 3

EXAMPLE 1

Where is the function graphed in Figure 4 increasing? Where is it decreasing?

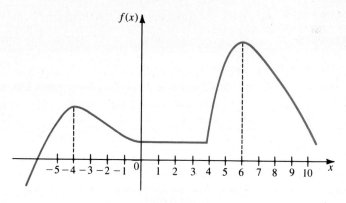

FIGURE 4

Moving from left to right, the function is increasing up to -4, then decreasing from -4 to 0, constant (neither increasing nor decreasing) from 0 to 4, increasing from 4 to 6, and finally, decreasing from 6 on. In interval notation, the function is increasing on $(-\infty, -4)$ and $(4, 6)$, decreasing on $(-4, 0)$ and $(6, \infty)$, and constant on $(0, 4)$. ▪

The derivative of a function can be used to tell whether a function is increasing or decreasing. We know that the derivative gives the slope of the tangent line to a curve at any point on the curve. If a function is increasing, the tangent line at any point on the graph will have positive slope, while if the function is decreasing, the slopes of the tangents will be negative. See Figure 5.

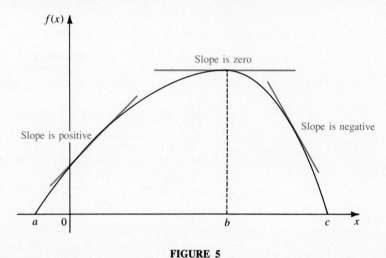

FIGURE 5

Test for Intervals where $f(x)$ is Increasing and Decreasing	Suppose a function f has a derivative at each point in an open interval; then if $f'(x) > 0$ for each x in the interval, f is *increasing* on the interval; if $f'(x) < 0$ for each x in the interval, f is *decreasing* on the interval; if $f'(x) = 0$ for each x in the interval, f is *constant* on the interval.

The derivative $f'(x)$ can change signs from positive to negative at points where $f'(x) = 0$, and also at points where $f'(x)$ does not exist. This suggests that the test for increasing and decreasing functions be applied as follows. (We are assuming that no open intervals exist where the function is constant.)

Applying The Test	**1.** Locate on a number line those values of x that make $f'(x) = 0$ and where $f'(x)$ does not exist. These points determine several open intervals. **2.** Choose a value of x in each of the intervals determined in Step 1. Use these values to decide if $f'(x) > 0$ or $f'(x) < 0$ in that interval. **3.** Use the test above to decide if f is increasing or decreasing on the interval.

EXAMPLE 2

Find where the following functions are increasing or decreasing. Locate all points where the tangent line is horizontal. Graph the function.

(a) $f(x) = 2x^2 + 6x - 5$

The derivative $f'(x) = 4x + 6$ is 0 when

$$4x + 6 = 0$$

$$x = -\frac{3}{2}.$$

There are no values of x where $f'(x)$ fails to exist. Locate $x = -3/2$ on a number line, as in Figure 6. This point determines two intervals, $(-\infty, -3/2)$ and $(-3/2, \infty)$.

Now, choose any value of x in the interval $(-3/2, \infty)$. If we choose $x = 0$, then

$$f'(0) = 4 \cdot 0 + 6 = 6,$$

which is positive. Since one value of x in this interval makes $f'(x) > 0$, all values will do so, with f therefore increasing on $(-3/2, \infty)$. Use -2 as a test point in the interval $(-\infty, -3/2)$:

$$f'(-2) = 4(-2) + 6 = -2,$$

which is negative. This means that f is decreasing on the interval $(-\infty, -3/2)$.

Since a horizontal line has a slope of 0, horizontal tangents can be found by solving the equation $f'(x) = 0$. As we saw above, $f'(x) = 0$ when $x = -3/2$. The arrows in each interval in Figure 6 indicate where f is increasing or decreasing.

Our only method of graphing most functions so far has been by plotting several points that lie on the graph. Now we have an additional tool: the test for determining where a function is increasing or decreasing. (Other tools are discussed in the next few sections.) Using the intervals where $f(x) = 2x^2 + 6x - 5$ is increasing or decreasing, along with the fact (from Chapter 1) that the graph is a parabola, leads to the graph of Figure 7.

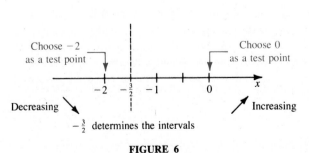

FIGURE 6

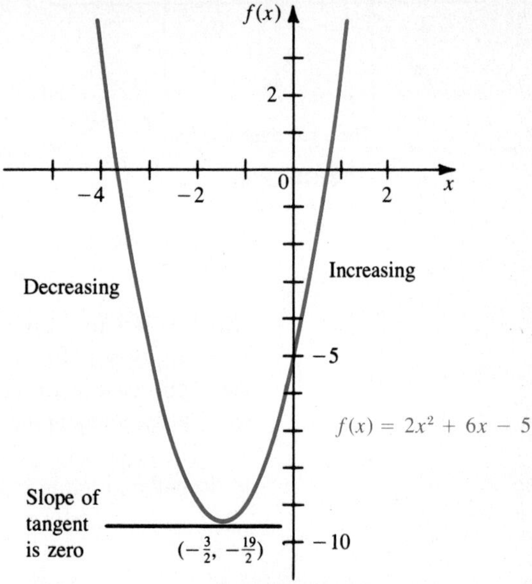

FIGURE 7

(b) $f(x) = x^3 + 3x^2 - 9x + 4$.

Here $f'(x) = 3x^2 + 6x - 9$. Set this derivative equal to 0, and solve the resulting equation by factoring.

$$3x^2 + 6x - 9 = 0$$
$$3(x^2 + 2x - 3) = 0$$
$$3(x + 3)(x - 1) = 0$$
$$x = -3 \quad \text{or} \quad x = 1$$

The tangent line is horizontal at $x = -3$ or $x = 1$. There are no values of x where $f'(x)$ fails to exist. To determine where the function is increasing or decreasing, locate -3 and 1 on a number line, as in Figure 8. (Be sure to place the values on the number line in numerical order.)

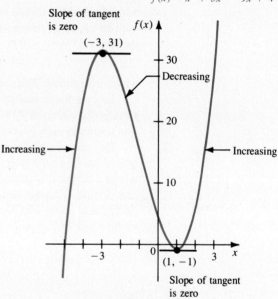

FIGURE 9

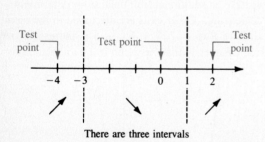

There are three intervals

FIGURE 8

Choosing the test point -4 from the left interval gives

$$f'(-4) = 3(-4)^2 + 6(-4) - 9 = 15,$$

which is positive, so f is increasing on $(-\infty, -3)$. Selecting 0 from the middle interval gives $f'(0) = -9$, so f is decreasing on $(-3, 1)$. Finally, choosing 2 in the right-hand region gives $f'(2) = 15$, with f increasing on $(-1, \infty)$. The intervals where f is increasing or decreasing are shown with arrows in Figure 8.

The information found above, along with point plotting as necessary, was used to draw the graph in Figure 9.

(c) $f(x) = \dfrac{x-1}{x+1}$

Use the quotient rule to find $f'(x)$.

$$f'(x) = \frac{(x+1)(1) - (x-1)(1)}{(x+1)^2}$$

$$= \frac{x+1-x+1}{(x+1)^2} = \frac{2}{(x+1)^2}$$

This derivative is never 0, but it fails to exist when $x = -1$. Locate -1 on a number line, and use test points to find that $f'(x) > 0$ for *all* x except -1. This means that the function f is increasing on both $(-\infty, -1)$ and $(-1, \infty)$. The graph of f has a vertical asymptote at -1. Since

$$\lim_{x \to \infty} \frac{x-1}{x+1} = 1,$$

the graph has the line $y = 1$ as a horizontal asymptote. Using all this information and plotting a few points as necessary gives the graph in Figure 10. ▨

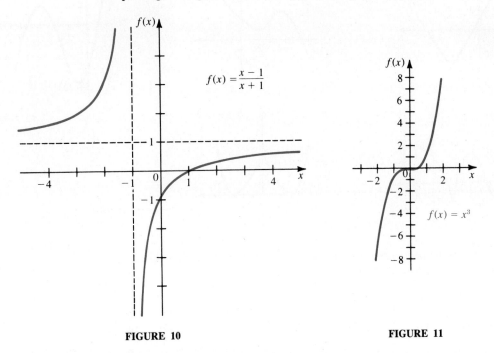

FIGURE 10   FIGURE 11

We close this section by mentioning that the reverse of the test for increasing and decreasing functions is not true—it is possible for a function to be increasing on an interval even though the derivative is not positive at every point in the interval. A good example is given by $f(x) = x^3$, which is increasing on every interval, even though $f'(x) = 0$ when $x = 0$. See Figure 11.

We shall refer to the function $f(x) = x^3$ several times in this chapter. This function shows that many of the results we give do not work in reverse. If you think you have developed a new rule of calculus, see if it works with $f(x) = x^3$.

11.1 EXERCISES

Find the largest open intervals where the following functions are **(a)** increasing; **(b)** decreasing.

1.

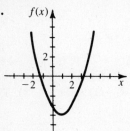

2.

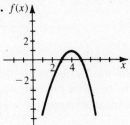

3.

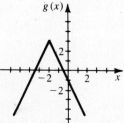

4.

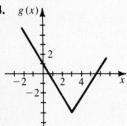

5.

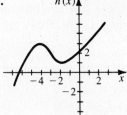

6.

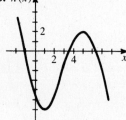

7.

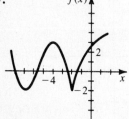

8.

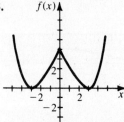

Find the largest open intervals where the functions in Exercises 9–26 are **(a)** increasing; **(b)** decreasing. **(c)** Graph each function.

9. $f(x) = x^2 + 12x - 6$

10. $f(x) = x^2 - 9x + 4$

11. $y = 5 + 9x - 3x^2$

12. $y = 3 + 4x - 2x^2$

13. $f(x) = 2x^3 - 3x^2 - 72x - 4$

14. $f(x) = 2x^3 - 3x^2 - 12x + 2$

15. $f(x) = 4x^3 - 15x^2 - 72x + 5$

16. $f(x) = 4x^3 - 9x^2 - 30x + 6$

17. $y = -3x + 6$

18. $y = 6x - 9$

19. $f(x) = \dfrac{x + 2}{x + 1}$

20. $f(x) = \dfrac{x + 3}{x - 4}$

21. $y = |x + 4|$

22. $y = -|x - 3|$

23. $f(x) = -\sqrt{x - 1}$

24. $f(x) = \sqrt{5 - x}$

25. $y = \sqrt{x^2 + 1}$

26. $y = x\sqrt{9 - x^2}$

27. The number of people, $P(t)$, in hundreds, infected t days after an epidemic begins is approximated by

$$P(t) = 2 + 50t - \frac{5}{2}t^2.$$

When will the number of people infected start to decline?

28. In Chapter 1 we gave the function
$$y = -0.015x^3 + 1.058x$$
as the approximate alcohol concentration in tenths of a percent in an average person's bloodstream x hours after drinking eight ounces of 100-proof whiskey. The function applies only for the interval $[0, 8]$. On which open intervals is the function (a) increasing? (b) decreasing?

29. The percent of concentration of a drug in the bloodstream x hours after the drug is administered is given by
$$K(x) = \frac{4x}{3x^2 + 27}.$$
For what open intervals is the concentration (a) increasing? (b) decreasing?

30. Suppose a certain drug is administered to a patient, with the percent of concentration of the drug in the bloodstream t hours later given by
$$K(t) = \frac{5t}{t^2 + 1}.$$
For what open intervals of t is the concentration (a) increasing? (b) decreasing?

31. Suppose the total cost to manufacture x liters of a weed killer is given by
$$C(x) = x^3 - 2x^2 + 8x.$$
Define the average cost to manufacture x liters as $C(x)/x$. Where is the average cost (a) decreasing? (b) increasing?

32. The cost to manufacture x units of an item is given by
$$C(x) = x^3 - 3x^2 + 5x.$$
Find the average cost per item to manufacture x items. Where is the average cost (a) increasing? (b) decreasing?

11.2 Extrema

Business people are interested in finding a production level that will produce a minimum cost of manufacturing an item, while biologists must predict the maximum size of a population of organisms. The need to find a maximum or a minimum value of a function comes up in a great many different situations, as we shall see. Calculus is a very useful tool for finding these maxima or minima.

Relative Maximum or Minimum

Let c be a number in the domain of a function f. Then
$f(c)$ is a **relative maximum** for f if there exists an open interval (a, b) containing c such that
$$f(x) \le f(c)$$
for all x in (a, b);
$f(c)$ is a **relative minimum** for f if there exists an open interval (a, b) containing c such that
$$f(x) \ge f(c)$$
for all x in (a, b).

Think of a relative maximum as a peak (not necessarily the highest peak) and a relative minimum as a valley (not necessarily the lowest valley) on the graph of the function.

A function has a **relative extremum** at c if it has either a relative maximum or a relative minimum there.

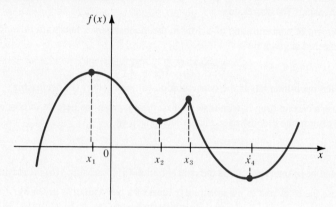

FIGURE 12

EXAMPLE 1

Identify the x-values of all points where the graph of Figure 12 has relative extrema.

The graph has relative maxima when $x = x_1$ or $x = x_3$ and relative minima when $x = x_2$ or $x = x_4$. ▪

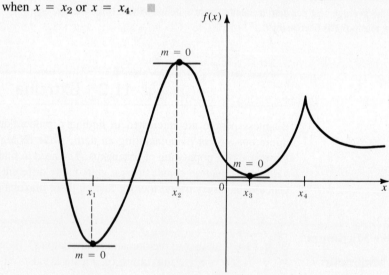

FIGURE 13

How can the equation for a function be used to find its extrema? Figure 13 suggests a method. The function graphed in Figure 13 has relative maxima when $x = x_2$ or $x = x_4$, with relative minima when $x = x_1$ or $x = x_3$. The tangents at the points having x-values x_1, x_2, and x_3, respectively, are drawn in Figure 13: all three of these tangents are horizontal and have a slope of 0. Since the derivative gives the slope of a tangent line, one way to find relative extrema for a function is to find all points where the derivative (the slope of the tangent) is 0. These points *might* lead to relative extrema.

However, a function can have relative extrema even when the derivative does not exist. For example, the function of Figure 13 also has a relative maximum when $x = x_4$, even though no derivative exists at the point where $x = x_4$ (as we saw in the previous chapter, no tangent line can be drawn).

In summary, when looking for relative extrema, check all values that make the derivative equal 0 and all values where the function exists but the derivative does not exist. Any of these values might lead to relative extrema. (A rough sketch of the graph of the function is often enough to tell if an extremum has been found.) The points where a derivative equals 0 or does not exist (but the function is defined) are called **critical points** of the function. The following result summarizes these facts.

If a function f has a relative extremum at a number c, then either $f'(c) = 0$ or $f'(c)$ does not exist.

Be very careful not to get this result backward. It does *not* say that a function has relative extrema at all critical points of the function. For example, Figure 14 shows the graph of $f(x) = x^3$. The derivative, $f'(x) = 3x^2$, is 0 when $x = 0$, so that the function has a critical point when $x = 0$. However, as suggested by the graph of Figure 14, $f(x) = x^3$ has neither a relative maximum nor a relative minimum at $x = 0$ (or anywhere else, for that matter).

First Derivative Test   Suppose all critical points have been found for some function f. How can we then tell from the equation of the function if these critical points lead to relative maxima, relative minima, or neither a relative maximum nor a relative minimum? One way is suggested by the graph in Figure 15.

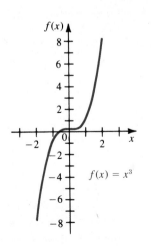

FIGURE 14

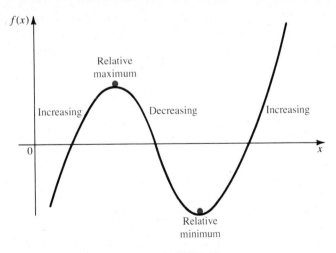

FIGURE 15

As shown in Figure 15, a function is increasing on an interval just to the left of a relative maximum and decreasing on an interval just to the right. A function is decreasing on an interval just to the left of a relative minimum and increasing on an interval just to the right.

Putting this together with the methods from Section 1 for identifying intervals where a function is increasing or decreasing gives the following *first derivative test* for locating relative extrema.

First Derivative Test

Let c be a critical point for a function f. Suppose that f is differentiable on (a, b), and that c is the only critical point of f in (a, b).

1. $f(c)$ is a relative maximum of f if the derivative $f'(x)$ is positive in an open interval extending left from c and negative in an open interval extending right from c.

2. $f(c)$ is a relative minimum of f if the derivative $f'(x)$ is negative in an interval extending left from c and positive in an interval extending right from c.

The sketches in the following table show how the first derivative test works. Assume the same conditions on a, b, and c as given above.

$f(x)$ has:	Sign of f' in (a, c)	Sign of f' in (c, b)	Sketch
Relative maximum	$+$	$-$	
Relative minimum	$-$	$+$	
No relative extrema	$+$	$+$	
No relative extrema	$-$	$-$	

EXAMPLE 2   Find all relative extrema for the following functions. Graph each function.

(a) $f(x) = 2x^3 - 3x^2 - 72x + 15$

The derivative is $f'(x) = 6x^2 - 6x - 72$. There are no points where $f'(x)$ fails to exist, so the only critical values will be where the derivative equals 0. Setting the derivative equal to 0 gives

$$6x^2 - 6x - 72 = 0$$

$$6(x^2 - x - 12) = 0$$

$$6(x - 4)(x + 3) = 0$$

$$x - 4 = 0 \quad \text{or} \quad x + 3 = 0$$

$$x = 4 \quad \text{or} \quad x = -3.$$

The critical values, 4 and -3, are used to locate the intervals shown on the number line of Figure 16.

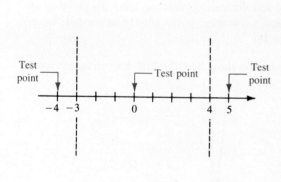

FIGURE 16

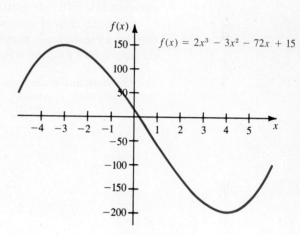

FIGURE 16A

Using -4, 0, and 5 as test points shows that the derivative is positive on $(-\infty, -3)$, negative on $(-3, 4)$, and positive on $(4, \infty)$. By part 1 of the first derivative test, this means that the function has a relative maximum of $f(-3) = 150$ when $x = -3$; by part 2, f has a relative minimum of $f(4) = -193$ when $x = 4$. From the information found above and by plotting a few points, we get the graph in Figure 16A.

(b) $f(x) = 6x^{2/3} - 4x$

Find $f'(x)$:

$$f'(x) = 4x^{-1/3} - 4 = \frac{4}{x^{1/3}} - 4.$$

The derivative fails to exist when $x = 0$, but the function itself is defined when $x = 0$, making 0 a critical value for f. To find other critical values, set $f'(x) = 0$.

$$f'(x) = 0$$

$$\frac{4}{x^{1/3}} - 4 = 0$$

$$\frac{4}{x^{1/3}} = 4$$

$$4 = 4x^{1/3}$$

$$1 = x^{1/3}$$

$$1 = x$$

The critical values of f, 0 and 1, are used to locate intervals on a number line, as in Figure 17.

Test points, and the first derivative test, show that f has a relative maximum at $x = 1$; the value of this relative maximum is $f(1) = 2$. Also, f has a relative minimum at $x = 0$; this relative minimum is $f(0) = 0$.

Using the ideas of increasing and decreasing functions from the previous section, the extrema found above, and a few other points plotted as needed, we can get the graph of f shown in Figure 18.

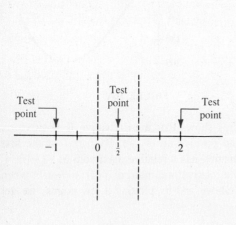

FIGURE 17

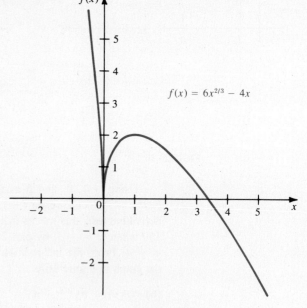

$f(x) = 6x^{2/3} - 4x$

FIGURE 18

(c) $f(x) = x^{2/3}$

The derivative is $f'(x) = \frac{2}{3}x^{-1/3} = \frac{2}{3x^{1/3}}.$

The derivative is never 0, but it does fail to exist when $x = 0$. Since $f(0)$ *does* exist, but $f'(0)$ does not, 0 is a critical point. Use a sketch of a number line, test points, and the first derivative test to see that the function has a relative minimum at 0. The value of this relative minimum is $f(0) = 0^{2/3} = 0$. The function is decreasing on the interval $(-\infty, 0)$ and increasing on $(0, \infty)$. Using this information, and perhaps plotting a few points, we get the graph of Figure 19.

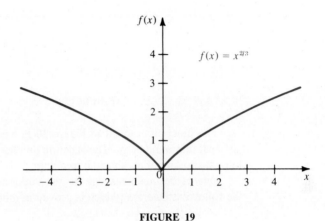

FIGURE 19

(d) $f(x) = x^3$

As we have said, this function (graphed in Figure 14) has a critical point at 0, but no extremum there. The first derivative test shows why. The derivative, $f'(x) = 3x^2$, is positive for all numbers on either side of the critical point 0. Since the sign of the derivative does not change at 0, there is no extremum there. ■

Absolute Extrema   As we have seen, a function might well have several relative maxima or relative minima. However, a function never has more than one *absolute maximum or absolute minimum*.

Absolute Maximum
or Minimum

Let f be a function defined on some interval. Let c be a number in the interval. Then

$f(c)$ is the **absolute maximum** of f on the interval if

$$f(x) \leq f(c)$$

for every x in the interval;

$f(c)$ is the **absolute minimum** of f on the interval if

$$f(x) \geq f(c)$$

for every x in the interval.

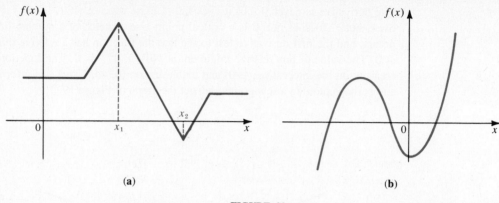

FIGURE 20

The function graphed in Figure 20(a) has an absolute maximum at x_1 and an absolute minimum at x_2. The function graphed in Figure 20(b) has neither an absolute maximum nor an absolute minimum.

One of the main reasons for the importance of absolute extrema is given by the following theorem (which is proved in more advanced courses).

Extreme Value Theorem

A function f continuous on a closed interval $[a, b]$ will have both an absolute maximum and an absolute minimum on the interval.

This extreme value theorem guarantees the existence of absolute extrema. To find these extrema, use the following steps.

Finding Absolute Extrema

To find absolute extrema for a function f continuous on an interval $[a, b]$:

1. Find f' and solve $f'(x) = 0$ to find all critical points $c_1, c_2, \ldots$ in (a, b).

2. Evaluate $f(c_1), f(c_2), \ldots$ for all critical points in (a, b).

3. Evaluate $f(a)$ and $f(b)$ for the endpoints a and b of the interval $[a, b]$.

4. The largest value found in Steps 2 or 3 is the absolute maximum for f on $[a, b]$; the smallest value found is the absolute minimum.

EXAMPLE 3

Find the absolute extrema of the function
$$f(x) = 2x^3 - x^2 - 20x - 10$$
on the interval $[-2, 4]$.

First look for critical points in the interval $(-2, 4)$. Set the derivative $f'(x) = 6x^2 - 2x - 20$ equal to 0.

$$6x^2 - 2x - 20 = 0$$
$$2(3x^2 - x - 10) = 0$$
$$2(3x + 5)(x - 2) = 0$$
$$3x + 5 = 0 \quad \text{or} \quad x - 2 = 0$$
$$x = -5/3 \quad \text{or} \quad x = 2$$

Since there are no values of x where $f'(x)$ does not exist, the only critical values are $-5/3$ and 2. Both of these critical values are in the interval $(-2, 4)$. Now evaluate the function at $-5/3$ and 2, and at the end points of its domain, -2 and 4.

x-value	Value of Function	
-2	10	
$-5/3$	11.296	
2	-38	←absolute minimum
4	22	←absolute maximum

The absolute maximum, 22, occurs when $x = 4$, and the absolute minimum, -38, occurs when $x = 2$. A graph of f on $[-2, 4]$ is shown in Figure 21. ■

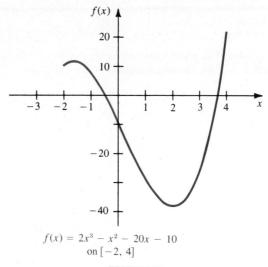

$$f(x) = 2x^3 - x^2 - 20x - 10$$
on $[-2, 4]$

FIGURE 21

EXAMPLE 4

A company has found that its profit from the sale of x units of an auto part is given by

$$P(x) = x^4 - 8x^2 + 100.$$

Production bottlenecks limit the number of units that can be made to no more than

5, while a long-term contract requires that at least one unit be made. Find the maximum possible profit that the firm can make.

Because of the restrictions, the profit function is defined only for the domain [1, 5]. Look first for critical points of the function in the open interval (1, 5). Here $f'(x) = 4x^3 - 16x$. Now set this derivative equal to 0.

$$4x^3 - 16x = 0$$
$$4x(x^2 - 4) = 0$$
$$4x(x + 2)(x - 2) = 0$$

$$4x = 0 \quad \text{or} \quad x + 2 = 0 \quad \text{or} \quad x - 2 = 0$$
$$x = 0 \quad \text{or} \quad x = -2 \quad \text{or} \quad x = 2$$

Since $x = 0$ and $x = -2$ are not in the interval (1, 5), disregard them. Now evaluate the function at the remaining critical point 2, and at the endpoints of the domain, 1 and 5.

x-value	Value of Function
1	93
2	84
5	525 ←absolute maximum

Maximum profit of $525 occurs when 5 units are made. ▦

11.2 EXERCISES

Find the location and value of all relative extrema for the functions in Exercises 1–8.
Compare to Exercises 1–8 of the previous section.

1. $f(x)$
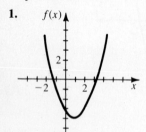

2. $f(x)$
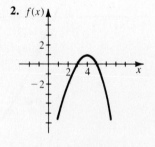

3. $g(x)$
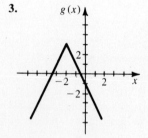

4. $g(x)$
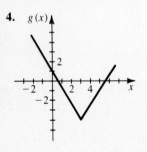

5. $h(x)$
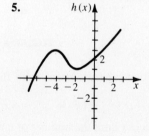

6. $h(x)$
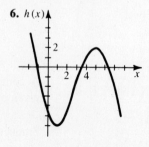

7.

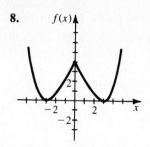

8.

Find the x-values of all points where the functions in Exercises 9–30 have any relative extrema. Find the value of any relative extrema.

9. $f(x) = x^2 + 12x - 8$

10. $f(x) = x^2 - 4x + 6$

11. $f(x) = 8 - 6x - x^2$

12. $f(x) = 3 - 4x - 2x^2$

13. $f(x) = x^3 + 6x^2 + 9x - 8$

14. $f(x) = x^3 + 3x^2 - 24x + 2$

15. $f(x) = -\frac{4}{3}x^3 - \frac{21}{2}x^2 - 5x + 8$

16. $f(x) = -\frac{2}{3}x^3 - \frac{1}{2}x^2 + 3x - 4$

17. $f(x) = 2x^3 - 21x^2 + 60x + 5$

18. $f(x) = 2x^3 + 15x^2 + 36x - 4$

19. $f(x) = x^4 - 18x^2 - 4$

20. $f(x) = x^4 - 8x^2 + 9$

21. $f(x) = -(8 - 5x)^{2/3}$

22. $f(x) = (2 - 9x)^{2/3}$

23. $f(x) = 2x + 3x^{2/3}$

24. $f(x) = 3x^{5/3} - 15x^{2/3}$

25. $f(x) = x - \dfrac{1}{x}$

26. $f(x) = x^2 + \dfrac{1}{x}$

27. $f(x) = \dfrac{x^2}{x^2 + 1}$

28. $f(x) = \dfrac{x^2}{x - 3}$

29. $f(x) = \dfrac{x^2 - 2x + 1}{x - 3}$

30. $f(x) = \dfrac{x^2 - 6x + 9}{x + 2}$

Use the derivative to find the vertex of the parabolas in Exercises 31–34.

31. $y = -2x^2 + 8x - 1$

32. $y = 3x^2 - 12x + 2$

33. $y = 2x^2 - 5x + 2$

34. $y = -x^2 - 2x + 1$

35. A professor has found that the number of biology students attending class is approximated by

$$S(x) = -x^2 + 20x + 80,$$

where x is the number of daily hours that the student union is open. Find the number of hours that the union should be open so that the number of students attending class is a maximum. Find the maximum number of such students.

36. The total profit in dollars from the sale of x units of a certain prescription drug is given by

$$P(x) = -x^3 + 3x^2 + 72x + 1280.$$

(a) Find the number of units that should be sold in order to maximize the total profit.

(b) What is the maximum profit?

Find the location of any absolute extrema for the functions in Exercises 37–44.

37.
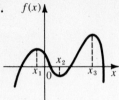

38.
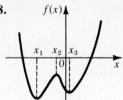

39.
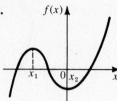

40.
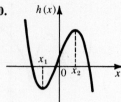

41.
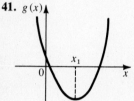

42.
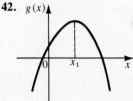

43.
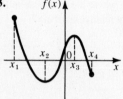

44.
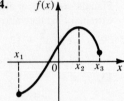

Find the location of all absolute extrema for the functions having domains as specified in Exercises 45–66. A calculator will be helpful for many of these problems.

45. $f(x) = x^2 + 6x + 2; [-4, 0]$

46. $f(x) = x^2 - 4x + 1; [-6, 5]$

47. $f(x) = 5 - 8x - 4x^2; [-5, 1]$

48. $f(x) = 9 - 6x - 3x^2; [-4, 3]$

49. $f(x) = x^3 - 3x^2 - 24x + 5; [-3, 6]$

50. $f(x) = x^3 - 6x^2 + 9x - 8; [0, 5]$

51. $f(x) = \frac{1}{3}x^3 - \frac{1}{2}x^2 - 6x + 3; [-4, 4]$

52. $f(x) = \frac{1}{3}x^3 + \frac{3}{2}x^2 - 4x + 1; [-5, 2]$

53. $f(x) = x^4 - 32x^2 - 7; [-5, 6]$

54. $f(x) = x^4 - 18x^2 + 1; [-4, 4]$

55. $f(x) = \frac{1}{1 + x}; [0, 2]$

56. $f(x) = \frac{-2}{x + 3}; [1, 4]$

57. $f(x) = \frac{8 + x}{8 - x}; [4, 6]$

58. $f(x) = \frac{1 - x}{3 + x}; [0, 3]$

59. $f(x) = \frac{x}{x^2 + 2}; [0, 4]$

60. $f(x) = \frac{x - 1}{x^2 + 1}; [1, 5]$

61. $f(x) = (x^2 + 18)^{2/3}; [-3, 3]$

62. $f(x) = (x^2 + 4)^{1/3}; [-2, 2]$

63. $f(x) = (x + 1)(x + 2)^2; [-4, 0]$

64. $f(x) = (x - 3)(x - 1)^3; [-2, 3]$

65. $f(x) = \frac{1}{\sqrt{x^2 + 1}}; [-1, 1]$

66. $f(x) = \frac{3}{\sqrt{x^2 + 4}}; [-2, 2]$

67. The total profit in thousands of dollars from the sale of x hundred thousand automobile tires is approximated by

$$P(x) = -x^3 + 9x^2 + 120x - 400, \qquad x \geq 5.$$

Find the number of hundred thousands of tires that must be sold to maximize profit. Find the maximum profit.

68. The number of salmon swimming upstream to spawn is approximated by

$$S(x) = -x^3 + 3x^2 + 360x + 5000, \qquad 6 \leq x \leq 20,$$

where x represents the temperature of the water in degrees Celsius. Find the water temperature that produces the maximum number of salmon swimming upstream.

69. From information given in a recent business publication we constructed the mathematical model

$$M(x) = -\frac{1}{45}x^2 + 2x - 20, \qquad 30 \le x \le 65,$$

to represent the miles per gallon used by a certain car at a speed of x miles per hour. Find the absolute maximum miles per gallon and the absolute minimum.

70. For a certain compact car,

$$M(x) = -.018x^2 + 1.24x + 6.2, \qquad 30 \le x \le 60,$$

represents the miles per gallon obtained at a speed of x miles per hour. Find the absolute maximum miles per gallon and the absolute minimum.

A piece of wire of length 12 feet is cut into two pieces. One piece is made into a circle and the other piece is made into a square. (See the figure.)

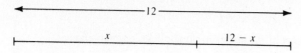

Let the piece of length x be formed into a circle.

Radius of circle $= \dfrac{x}{2\pi}$; Area of circle $= \pi \left(\dfrac{x}{2\pi}\right)^2$;

Side of square $= \dfrac{12 - x}{4}$; Area of square $= \left(\dfrac{12 - x}{4}\right)^2$.

71. Where should the cut be made in order to make the sum of the areas enclosed by both figures minimum? (Hint: Use 3.14 as an approximation for π. Have a calculator handy.)

72. Where should the cut be made in order to make the sum of the areas maximum? (Hint: Remember to use the endpoints of a domain when looking for absolute maxima and minima.)

EXTENDED APPLICATION

The Effect of Oil Price on the Optimal Speed of Ships*

With the major increase in fuel prices during the past decade, choosing an optimum speed for a large ocean-going ship has become a major concern of ship operators. Sailing slowly uses less fuel, but causes increased costs for salaries and interest on the value of the cargo.

The speed of sailing has a great effect on the amount of fuel used, the major expense in operating a ship. Past empirical studies have shown that the amount of fuel used by a ship is approximately proportional to the cube of the speed. This means that a

*From ''The Effect of Oil Price on the Optimal Speed of Ships'' by David Ronen from *Journal of the Operations Research Society*, Vol. 33, 1982, pp. 1035–1040. Copyright © 1982 Operational Research Society Ltd. Reprinted by permission.

20% change in cruising speed produces about a 50% change in fuel consumption. As an example, a medium sized ship that burns 40 tons of fuel per day at a certain speed could save 50% of this amount, or 20 tons, with a 20% reduction in speed. At a cost of $250 per ton, this 20% speed reduction would save $5000 per day in fuel costs.

To find the optimal sailing speed for one leg of a journey (a one-way trip with a given cargo between two points), let

R = income from the leg

P = profit from the leg

D_s = number of days at sea in the leg

D_p = number of days in port in the leg

L = distance of the leg in nautical miles

V = actual cruising speed

V_0 = normal cruising speed

C = daily cost of the vessel (excluding fuel for main engines)

F = actual daily fuel consumption in tons per day

F_0 = daily fuel consumption at normal cruising speed

F_c = cost of fuel in dollars per ton

V_m = minimum cruising speed

The duration of the leg, D, is

$$D = D_s + D_p,\tag{1}$$

where

$$D_s = \frac{L}{24V}.\tag{2}$$

The profit from the leg is

$$P = R - (DC + FF_c D_s).\tag{3}$$

As we mentioned above, the amount of fuel used is proportional to the cube of the speed, or

$$F = \left(\frac{V}{V_0}\right)^3 \cdot F_0.\tag{4}$$

Our goal is to maximize the daily profit, Z, given by

$$Z = \frac{P}{D}.$$

Substituting equations (1), (2), and (4) into the equation for profit, (3), and dividing by D as given by equations (1) and (2) yields

$$Z = \frac{R - D_p C - \dfrac{LC}{24V} - \left(\dfrac{V}{V_0}\right)^3 F_0 F_c \left(\dfrac{L}{24V}\right)}{D_p + \dfrac{L}{24V}}.\tag{5}$$

It is not possible for a ship to sail at just any speed between 0 and its normal cruising speed, V_0. The design of the ship usually imposes some minimum cruising speed, V_m. This restriction forces V to be in the interval $[V_m, V_0]$.

To find the optimum value of V, take the derivative dZ/dV in equation (5), and place the derivative equal to 0. This gives the cubic equation

$$V^3 + V^2\frac{L}{16D_p} - \frac{RV_0^3}{2F_0F_cD_p} = 0. \tag{6}$$

Any real solutions of this equation are potential critical values. As mentioned above, these critical values must lie in the interval $[V_m, V_0]$ to be useful. To maximize Z, therefore, we must use our work with absolute extrema and check all critical values in $[V_m, V_0]$, as well as both endpoints, V_m and V_0.

EXERCISES

1. Find the optimum sailing speed for a voyage of 1536 miles, with 8 days in port, a normal cruising speed of 20 knots, a minimum speed of 10 knots, income from the leg of $86,400, fuel costs of $250 per ton, 50 tons of fuel consumed daily at normal cruising speed, and a daily cost for the vessel of $1000. (Hint: try $V = 12$.)

2. Why does the variable C not appear in equation (6) above?

11.3   Concavity, The Second Derivative Test, and

Curve Sketching

Knowing that a function is increasing on an interval does not necessarily tell the *rate* at which the function is increasing. For example, the graphs in Figure 22 show two possible ways that inflation might occur over a period of time. While both graphs are increasing, the *rate* of inflation is *increasing* in the graph on the left, while in the graph on the right the rate is *decreasing*. Government policies to deal with inflation might be quite different depending on the change in the rate of increase.

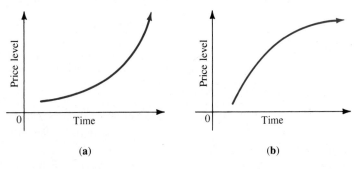

(a)   (b)

FIGURE 22

As shown later in this section, the graph on the left in Figure 22 is *concave upward*, while the one on the right is *concave downward*. A detailed discussion of concavity requires *second derivatives*.

Higher Derivatives   If a function f has a derivative f', then the derivative of f', if it exists, is the **second derivative** of f, written $f''(x)$. The derivative of $f''(x)$, if it exists, is called the **third derivative** of f, and so on. By continuing this process, **fourth derivatives** and other higher derivatives may be found. For example, if $f(x) = x^4 + 2x^3 + 3x^2 - 5x + 7$, then

$$f'(x) = 4x^3 + 6x^2 + 6x - 5, \qquad \text{first derivative of } f$$
$$f''(x) = 12x^2 + 12x + 6, \qquad \text{second derivative of } f$$
$$f'''(x) = 24x + 12, \qquad \text{third derivative of } f$$
$$f^{(4)}(x) = 24. \qquad \text{fourth derivative of } f$$

Notation for Higher Derivatives	The second derivative of $y = f(x)$ can be written with any of the following notations: $$f''(x), \qquad y'', \qquad \frac{d^2 y}{dx^2}, \qquad \text{or} \qquad D_x^2[f(x)].$$ The third derivative can be written in a similar way. For $n \geq 4$, the nth derivative is written $f^{(n)}(x)$.

EXAMPLE 1

Let $f(x) = x^3 + 6x^2 - 9x + 8$. Find the following.

(a) $f''(0)$

Here $f'(x) = 3x^2 + 12x - 9$, so that $f''(x) = 6x + 12$. Then

$$f''(0) = 6(0) + 12 = 12.$$

(b) $f''(-3) = 6(-3) + 12 = -6$ ▪

The next example shows how the second derivative is used to give the rate of change of a derivative.

EXAMPLE 2

In the last chapter we saw that the velocity of a particle is given by the derivative of the position function for the particle. That is, if $y = s(t)$ describes the position (along a straight line) of the particle at time t, then $v(t) = s'(t)$ gives the velocity at time t.

The rate of change of the velocity is called the **acceleration.** By this definition, the acceleration is the derivative of the velocity; if $a(t)$ represents the acceleration at time t, then

$$a(t) = \frac{d}{dt} v(t) = s''(t).$$

If a particle is moving along a line with its position at time t given by

$$s(t) = t^3 + 2t^2 - 7t + 9,$$

then
$$v(t) = s'(t) = 3t^2 + 4t - 7,$$

and
$$a(t) = v'(t) = s''(t) = 6t + 4.$$

The acceleration is positive if $6t + 4 > 0$ (or $t > -2/3$), which means that the particle is speeding up, and negative if $t < -2/3$ when it is slowing down. ▨

Concave Upward and Downward   Now we can continue the discussion of concavity started at the beginning of this section. Intuitively, a graph is *concave upward* on an interval if it "holds water"; it is *concave downward* if it "spills water." (See Figure 23.)

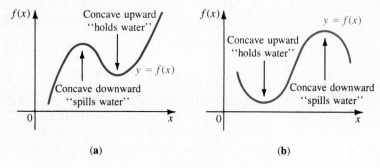

(a)   **(b)**

FIGURE 23

More precisely, a function is **concave upward** on an interval (a, b) if the graph of the function lies above its tangent line at each point of (a, b); a function is **concave downward** on (a, b) if the graph of the function lies below its tangent line at each point of (a, b). A point where a graph changes concavity is called a **point of inflection.** See Figure 24.

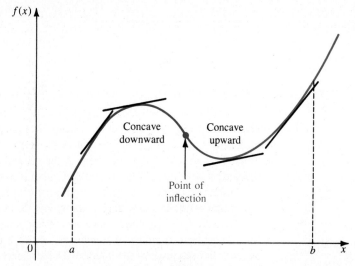

FIGURE 24

A function can be either increasing or decreasing, and either concave upward or concave downward on an interval. Examples of various combinations are shown in Figure 25.

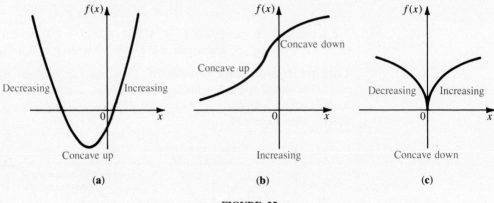

FIGURE 25

Figure 26 shows two functions that are concave upward on an interval (a, b). Several tangent lines are also shown. In Figure 26(a), the slopes of these tangent lines (moving from left to right) are first negative, then 0, and then positive. In Figure 26(b), the slopes are all positive, but getting larger.

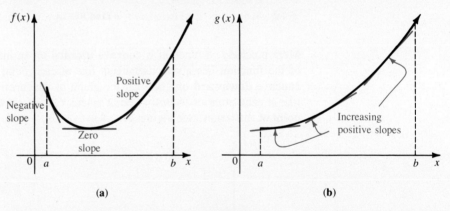

FIGURE 26

In both cases, the slopes are *increasing*. The slope at a point on a curve is given by the derivative. Since a function is increasing if its derivative is positive, the slope is increasing if the derivative of the function giving the slopes is positive. Since the derivative of a derivative is the second derivative, a function is concave upward on an interval if its second derivative is positive at each point of the interval.

A similar result is suggested by Figure 27 for functions whose graphs are concave downward. In both graphs, the slopes of the tangent lines are *decreasing* as we move from left to right. Since a function is decreasing if its derivative is negative, a function is concave downward on an interval if its second derivative is negative at each point of the interval. These observations suggest the following test.

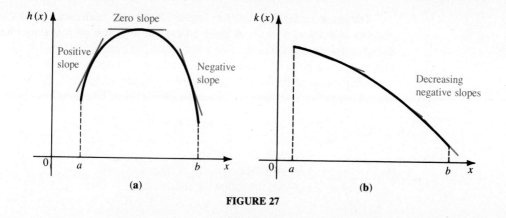

FIGURE 27

Test for Concavity

Let f be a function with derivatives f' and f'' existing at all points in an interval (a, b). Then f is **concave upward** on (a, b) if $f''(x) > 0$ for all x in (a, b) and **concave downward** on (a, b) if $f''(x) < 0$ for all x in (a, b).

EXAMPLE 3

Find all intervals where $f(x) = x^3 - 3x^2 + 5x - 4$ is concave upward or downward.

The first derivative is $f'(x) = 3x^2 - 6x + 5$, and the second derivative is $f''(x) = 6x - 6$. The function f is concave upward whenever $f''(x) > 0$, or

$$6x - 6 > 0$$

$$6x > 6$$

$$x > 1.$$

Also, f is concave downward if $f''(x) < 0$, or $x < 1$. In interval notation, f is concave upward on $(1, \infty)$ and concave downward on $(-\infty, 1)$. A graph of f is shown in Figure 28. ◼

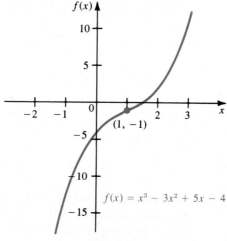

$$f(x) = x^3 - 3x^2 + 5x - 4$$

FIGURE 28

The graph of the function f in Figure 28 changes from concave downward to concave upward at $x = 1$. A point where the direction of concavity changes is called a **point of inflection.** This means that the point $(1, f(1))$, or $(1, -1)$ in Figure 28, is a point of inflection. This point can be located by finding values of x where the second derivative changes from negative to positive, that is, where the second derivative is 0. Setting the second derivative of Example 2 equal to 0 gives

$$6x - 6 = 0$$
$$x = 1.$$

As before, the point of inflection is $(1, f(1))$ or $(1, -1)$.

Example 2 suggests the following result:

> At a point of inflection for a function f, the second derivative is 0 or it does not exist.

Be careful with the statement in the box: just because $f''(x_0) = 0$, we have no assurance that a point of inflection has been located. For example, if $f(x) = (x - 1)^4$, then $f''(x) = 12(x - 1)^2$, which is 0 at $x = 1$. However, the graph of $f(x) = (x - 1)^4$ is always concave upward and has no point of inflection. See Figure 29.

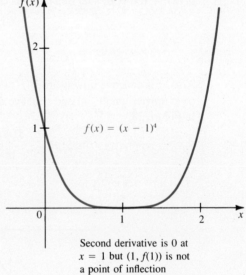

Second derivative is 0 at
$x = 1$ but $(1, f(1))$ is not
a point of inflection

FIGURE 29

EXAMPLE 4

The graph of Figure 30 shows the population of catfish in a commercial catfish farm as a function of time. As the graph shows, the population increases rapidly up to a point, and then increases at a slower rate. The horizontal dashed line shows that the

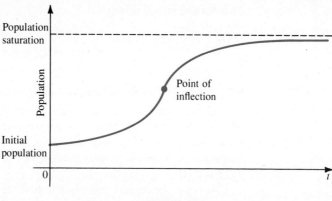

FIGURE 30

population will approach some upper limit determined by the capacity of the farm. The point at which the rate of population growth starts to slow is the point of inflection for the graph.

To produce maximum yield of catfish, it turns out that harvest should take place at the point of fastest possible growth of the population—here, this is at the point of inflection. ■

Curve Sketching   Concavity, along with our discussion of increasing and decreasing functions, helps in more accurately sketching the graphs of a variety of functions. This process, called *curve sketching,* uses the following steps.

Curve Sketching

To sketch the graph of a function f:

1. Find f'. Solve the equation $f'(x) = 0$. Also determine where f' does not exist (but f does). This locates any critical points. Find any relative extrema and determine where f is increasing or decreasing.

2. Find f''. Solve the equation $f''(x) = 0$ and determine where f'' does not exist. This helps locate any points of inflection. Determine where f is concave upward or concave downward.

3. Plot a few carefully chosen points as needed.

EXAMPLE 5

Graph each function.

(a) $f(x) = 2x^3 - 3x^2 - 12x + 1.$

To find the intervals where the function is increasing or decreasing, find the first derivative

$$f'(x) = 6x^2 - 6x - 12.$$

This derivative is 0 when

$$6(x^2 - x - 2) = 0$$
$$6(x - 2)(x + 1) = 0$$
$$x = 2 \quad \text{or} \quad x = -1.$$

These values divide the number line of Figure 31 into three regions. Testing a point from each region in $f'(x)$ shows that f is increasing on $(-\infty, -1)$ and $(2, \infty)$, and decreasing on $(-1, 2)$. This is shown with the arrows of Figure 31. By the first derivative test, f has a relative maximum when $x = -1$ and a relative minimum when $x = 2$. The relative maximum is $f(-1) = 8$, while the relative minimum is $f(2) = -19$.

Now use the second derivative to find the intervals where the function is concave upward or downward. Here

$$f''(x) = 12x - 6,$$

which is 0 when $x = 1/2$. Testing a point with x less than $1/2$, and one with x greater than $1/2$, shows that f is concave downward on $(-\infty, 1/2)$ and concave upward on $(1/2, \infty)$. (See Figure 32.) The graph has an inflection point at $(1/2, f(1/2)) = (1/2, -11/2)$.

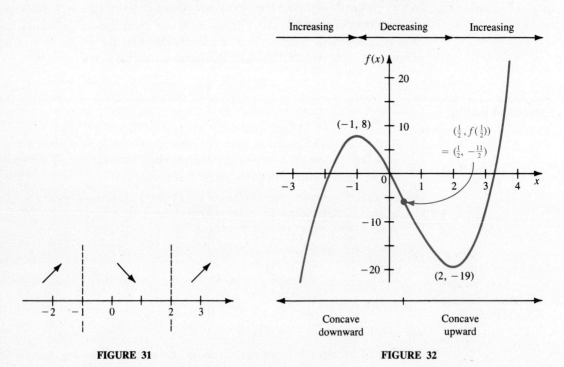

FIGURE 31

FIGURE 32

Using all this information and plotting a few points gives the graph of Figure 32.

(b) $f(x) = x + 1/x$

Here $f'(x) = 1 - \dfrac{1}{x^2}$, which is 0 when

$$\frac{1}{x^2} = 1$$

$$x^2 = 1$$

$$x = 1 \quad \text{or} \quad x = -1.$$

The derivative fails to exist at 0 (where the function itself is undefined). Substitute test points into $f'(x)$ to decide that f is increasing on $(-\infty, -1)$ and $(1, \infty)$ and decreasing on $(-1, 0)$ and $(0, 1)$. By the first derivative test, f has a relative maximum when $x = -1$ and a relative minimum when $x = 1$.

The second derivative is

$$f''(x) = \frac{2}{x^3},$$

which is never equal to 0 and does not exist when $x = 0$. (The function itself also does not exist at 0.) Because of this, there may be a change of concavity, but not an inflection point, when $x = 0$. The second derivative is negative when x is negative, making f concave downward on $(-\infty, 0)$. Also, $f''(x) > 0$ when $x > 0$, making f concave upward on $(0, \infty)$. Use this information and plot points as necessary to get the graph of Figure 33. ■

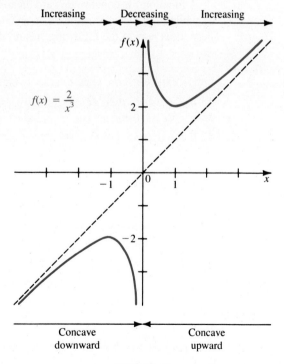

FIGURE 33

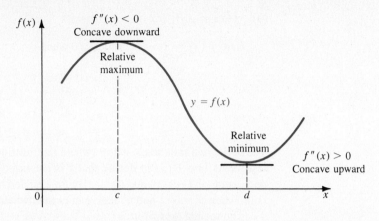

FIGURE 34

Second Derivative Test The idea of concavity can be used to find whether a given critical point leads to a relative maximum or a relative minimum. This test, an alternative to the first derivative test, is based on the fact that a curve that has a horizontal tangent at a point c and is concave downward on an open interval containing c also has a relative maximum at c. Also, a relative minimum occurs when a graph has a horizontal tangent line at a point d and is concave upward on an open interval containing d. (See Figure 34.)

A function f is concave upward on an interval if $f''(x) > 0$ for all x in the interval, while f is concave downward on an interval if $f''(x) < 0$ for all x in the interval. These ideas lead to the following **second derivative test** for relative extrema.

Second Derivative Test

> Let f'' exist on some open interval containing c, and let $f'(c) = 0$.
>
> **1.** If $f''(c) > 0$, then $f(c)$ is a relative minimum.
> **2.** If $f''(c) < 0$, then $f(c)$ is a relative maximum.
> **3.** If $f''(c) = 0$, then the test gives no information about extrema.

EXAMPLE 6

Find all relative extrema for
$$f(x) = 4x^3 + 7x^2 - 10x + 8.$$

First, find the points where the derivative is 0. Here $f'(x) = 12x^2 + 14x - 10$. Solve the equation $f'(x) = 0$ to get

$$12x^2 + 14x - 10 = 0$$
$$2(6x^2 + 7x - 5) = 0$$
$$2(3x + 5)(2x - 1) = 0$$
$$3x + 5 = 0 \quad \text{or} \quad 2x - 1 = 0$$
$$3x = -5 \qquad\qquad 2x = 1$$
$$x = -\frac{5}{3} \qquad\qquad x = \frac{1}{2}$$

Now use the second derivative test. The second derivative is $f''(x) = 24x + 14$. Evaluate $f''(x)$ first at $-5/3$, getting

$$f''\left(-\frac{5}{3}\right) = 24\left(-\frac{5}{3}\right) + 14 = -40 + 14 = -26 < 0,$$

so that by part 2 of the second derivative test, $-5/3$ leads to a relative maximum of $f(-\frac{5}{3}) = \frac{691}{27}$. Also, when $x = 1/2$,

$$f''\left(\frac{1}{2}\right) = 24\left(\frac{1}{2}\right) + 14 = 12 + 14 = 26 > 0,$$

with $1/2$ leading to a relative minimum of $f(\frac{1}{2}) = \frac{21}{4}$. ■

The second derivative test works only for those critical points c that make $f'(c) = 0$. This test does not work for those critical points c for which $f'(c)$ does not exist (since $f''(c)$ would not exist either). Also, the second derivative test does not work for critical points c that make $f''(c) = 0$. In both of these cases, use the first derivative test.

11.3 EXERCISES

For each of the functions in Exercises 1–16, find f''. Then find $f''(0)$, $f''(2)$, and $f''(-3)$.

1. $f(x) = 3x^3 - 4x + 5$

2. $f(x) = x^3 + 4x^2 + 2$

3. $f(x) = 3x^4 - 5x^3 + 2x^2$

4. $f(x) = -x^4 + 2x^3 - x^2$

5. $f(x) = 3x^2 - 4x + 8$

6. $f(x) = 8x^2 + 6x + 5$

7. $f(x) = (x + 4)^3$

8. $f(x) = (x - 2)^3$

9. $f(x) = \dfrac{2x + 1}{x - 2}$

10. $f(x) = \dfrac{x + 1}{x - 1}$

11. $f(x) = \dfrac{x^2}{1 + x}$

12. $f(x) = \dfrac{-x}{1 - x^2}$

13. $f(x) = \sqrt{x + 4}$

14. $f(x) = \sqrt{2x + 9}$

15. $f(x) = 5x^{3/5}$

16. $f(x) = -2x^{2/3}$

For the functions in Exercises 17–24, find $f'''(x)$, the third derivative of f, and $f^{(4)}(x)$, the fourth derivative.

17. $f(x) = -x^4 + 2x^2 + 8$

18. $f(x) = 2x^4 - 3x^3 + x^2$

19. $f(x) = 4x^5 + 6x^4 - x^2 + 2$

20. $f(x) = 3x^5 - x^4 + 2x^3 - 7x$

21. $f(x) = \dfrac{x - 1}{x + 2}$

22. $f(x) = \dfrac{x + 1}{x}$

23. $f(x) = \dfrac{3x}{x - 2}$

24. $f(x) = \dfrac{x}{2x + 1}$

In Exercises 25–42, find the largest open intervals where the functions are concave upward or concave downward. Find any points of inflection.

25.

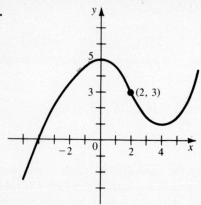

26.

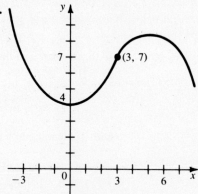

27.

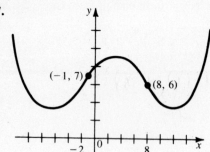

28.

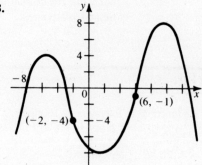

29.

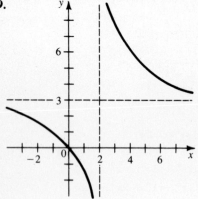

30.

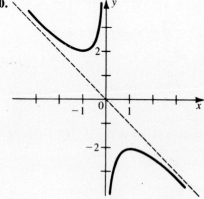

31. $f(x) = x^2 + 10x - 9$

32. $f(x) = x^2 - 4x + 3$

33. $f(x) = -3 + 8x - x^2$

34. $f(x) = 8 - 6x - x^2$

35. $f(x) = x^3 + 3x^2 - 45x - 3$

36. $f(x) = 2x^3 - 3x^2 - 12x + 1$

37. $f(x) = -2x^3 + 9x^2 + 168x - 3$

38. $f(x) = -x^3 - 12x^2 - 45x + 2$

39. $f(x) = \dfrac{3}{x - 5}$

40. $f(x) = \dfrac{-2}{x + 1}$

41. $f(x) = x(x + 5)^2$

42. $f(x) = -x(x - 3)^2$

Find any critical points for the functions in Exercises 43–60 and then use the second
derivative test to decide if the critical points lead to relative maxima or relative minima. If
$f''(c) = 0$ for a critical point c, then the second derivative test gives no information. In this
case, use the first derivative test instead. Sketch the graph of each function.

43. $f(x) = -x^2 - 10x - 25$ **44.** $f(x) = x^2 - 12x + 36$ **45.** $f(x) = 3x^3 - 3x^2 + 1$

46. $f(x) = 2x^3 - 4x^2 + 2$ **47.** $f(x) = -2x^3 - 9x^2 + 108x - 10$ **48.** $f(x) = -2x^3 - 9x^2 + 60x - 8$

49. $f(x) = 2x^3 + \frac{7}{2}x^2 - 5x + 3$ **50.** $f(x) = x^3 - \frac{15}{2}x^2 - 18x - 1$ **51.** $f(x) = (x + 3)^4$

52. $f(x) = x^3$ **53.** $f(x) = x^4 - 18x^2 + 5$ **54.** $f(x) = x^4 - 8x^2$

55. $f(x) = x + \frac{1}{x}$ **56.** $f(x) = 2x + \frac{8}{x}$ **57.** $f(x) = \frac{x^2 + 25}{x}$

58. $f(x) = \frac{x^2 + 4}{x}$ **59.** $f(x) = \frac{x - 1}{x + 1}$ **60.** $f(x) = \frac{x}{1 + x}$

61. The accompanying figure shows the *product life cycle* graph, with typical products
marked on it.*

(a) Where would you place home
videotape recorders on this graph?

(b) Where would you place light bulbs?

(c) Which products are closest to the
point of inflection on the left of the
graph? What does the point of
inflection mean here?

(d) Which products are closest to the
point of inflection on the right of the
graph? What does the point of
inflection mean here?

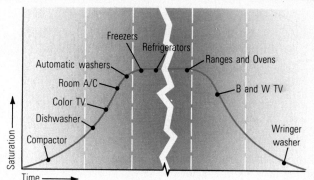

62. When a hardy new species is introduced into an area, the population often increases as
shown.

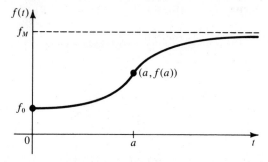

Explain the significance of the following points on the graph.

(a) f_0 **(b)** $(a, f(a))$ **(c)** f_M

---

*From "The Product Life Cycle: A Key to Strategic Marketing Planning" in *MSU Business Topics*
(Winter 1973), p. 30. Reprinted by permission of the publisher, Graduate School of Business
Administration, Michigan State University.

63. An autocatalytic chemical reaction is one in which the product being formed causes the rate of formation to increase. The rate of a certain autocatalytic reaction is given by

$$V(x) = 12x(100 - x),$$

where x is the quantity of the product present and 100 represents the quantity of chemical present initially. For what value of x is the rate of the reaction a maximum?

64. The percent of concentration of a certain drug in the bloodstream x hours after the drug is administered is given by

$$K(x) = \frac{3x}{x^2 + 4}.$$

For example, after one hour the concentration is given by $K(1) = 3(1)/(1^2 + 4) = \frac{3}{5}\% = .6\% = .006.$

(a) Find the time at which concentration is a maximum.

(b) Find the maximum concentration.

65. The percent of concentration of another drug in the bloodstream x hours after the drug is administered is given by

$$K(x) = \frac{4x}{3x^2 + 27}.$$

(a) Find the time at which the concentration is a maximum.

(b) Find the maximum concentration.

66. Assume that the number of bacteria, in millions, present in a certain culture at time t is given by

$$R(t) = t^2(t - 18) + 96t + 1000.$$

(a) At what time before 8 hours will the population be maximized?

(b) Find the maximum population.

Each of the functions in Exercises 67–72 gives the displacement at time t of a particle moving along a line. Find the velocity and acceleration functions. Then find the velocity and acceleration at $t = 0$ and $t = 4$. Assume that time is measured in seconds and distance is measured in centimeters. Velocity will be in centimeters per second (cm/sec) and acceleration in centimeters per second per second (cm/sec^2).

67. $s(t) = 8t^2 + 4t$ **68.** $s(t) = -3t^2 - 6t + 2$ **69.** $s(t) = -5t^3 - 8t^2 + 6t - 3$

70. $s(t) = 3t^3 - 4t^2 + 8t - 9$ **71.** $s(t) = \dfrac{-2}{3t + 4}$ **72.** $s(t) = \dfrac{1}{t + 3}$

73. When an object is dropped straight down, the distance in feet that it travels in t seconds is given by

$$s(t) = -16t^2.$$

Find the velocity of an object **(a)** after 3 seconds; **(b)** after 5 seconds; **(c)** after 8 seconds. **(d)** Find the acceleration. (The answer here is a constant, the acceleration due to the influence of gravity alone.)

74. If an object is thrown directly upward with a velocity of 256 feet per second, its height above the ground after t seconds is given by $s(t) = 256t - 16t^2$. Find the velocity and the acceleration after t seconds. What is the maximum height the object reaches? When does it hit the ground?

In Exercises 75–78 get a list of values for $f'(x)$ and $f''(x)$ for each function on the given interval as indicated. **(a)** By looking at the sign of $f'(x)$, give the (approximate) intervals where $f(x)$ is increasing and any intervals where $f(x)$ is decreasing. **(b)** Give the (approximate) x-value where any maximums or minimums occur. **(c)** By looking at the sign of $f''(x)$, give the intervals where $f(x)$ is concave up and where it is concave down. **(d)** Give the (approximate) x-value of any inflection points.

75. $f(x) = .25x^4 - 2x^3 + 3.5x^2 + 4x - 1;$ $(-5, 5)$ in steps of .5

76. $f(x) = 10x^3(x - 1)^2;$ $(-2, 2)$ in steps of .3

77. $f(x) = 3.1x^4 - 4.3x^3 + 5.82; (-1, 2)$ in steps of .2

78. $f(x) = \dfrac{x}{x^2 + 1}; (-3, 3)$ in steps of .4

11.4 Applications of Extrema

Finding extrema for realistic problems requires an accurate mathematical model of the problem. For example, suppose the number of units that can be produced on a production line can be closely approximated by the mathematical model

$$T(x) = 8x^{1/2} + 2x^{3/2} + 50,$$

where x is the number of employees on the line. Once this mathematical model has been established, we can use it to produce information about the production line. For example, the derivative $T'(x)$ could be used to estimate the change in production resulting from the addition of an extra worker to the line.

However, in writing the mathematical model itself, we must be aware of restrictions on the values of the variables. For example, since x represents the number of employees on a production line, x must certainly be restricted to the positive integers, or perhaps to a few common fractional values (we can conceive of half-time employees, but probably not 1/32-time employees).

On the other hand, to apply the tools of calculus to obtain an extremum for some function, the function must be defined and be meaningful at every real-number point in some interval. Because of this, the answer obtained by using a mathematical model of a practical problem might be a number that is not feasible in the setting of the problem.

Usually, the requirement that we use a continuous function instead of a function which can take on only certain selected values is of theoretical interest only. In most cases, calculus gives results which *are* acceptable in a given situation. And if the methods of calculus should be used on a function f and lead to the conclusion that $80\sqrt{2}$ units should be produced in order to get the lowest possible cost, it is usually only necessary to calculate $f(80\sqrt{2})$, and then compare this result to various values of $f(x)$ where x is an acceptable number close to $80\sqrt{2}$. The lowest of these values of $f(x)$ then gives minimum cost. In most cases, the result obtained will be very close to the theoretical minimum.

In this section we give several examples showing applications of calculus to maximum and minimum problems. To solve these examples, go through the following steps.

Solving Applied Problems

1. Read the problem carefully. Make sure you understand what is given and what is unknown.
2. If possible, sketch a diagram. Label the various parts.
3. Decide on the variable that must be maximized or minimized. Express that variable as a function of *one* other variable.
4. Find the critical points for the function of Step 3. Test each of these for maxima or minima.
5. Check for extrema at any endpoints of the domain of the function of Step 3.

EXAMPLE 1

For a semiconductor manufacturer to sell x new style memory chips, the price per chip must be

$$p(x) = 4 - \frac{x}{25}.$$

(a) Find an expression for the total revenue $T(x)$ from the sale of x memory chips.

The total revenue is given by the product of the number of chips sold, x, and the price per chip, $4 - x/25$, so

$$T(x) = x\left(4 - \frac{x}{25}\right) = 4x - \frac{x^2}{25}.$$

(b) Find the value of x that leads to maximum revenue.

Here $$T'(x) = 4 - \frac{2x}{25}.$$

Set this derivative equal to 0.

$$4 - \frac{2x}{25} = 0$$

$$-\frac{2x}{25} = -4$$

$$2x = 100$$

$$x = 50$$

Use the second derivative test to decide if $x = 50$ leads to maximum revenue or minimum revenue. Since $T'(x) = 4 - 2x/25$, the second derivative is $T''(x) = -2/25$, which is negative. Thus $x = 50$ gives maximum revenue, as desired.

(c) Find the maximum revenue.

$$T(50) = 4(50) - \frac{50^2}{25} = 200 - 100 = 100 \text{ dollars.} \quad \blacksquare$$

EXAMPLE 2

When Power and Money, Inc. charges $600 for a seminar on management techniques, it attracts 1000 people. For each $20-decrease in the charge, an additional 100 people will attend the seminar.

(a) Find an expression for the total revenue if there are x \$20-decreases in the price.

The price charged will be

$$\text{price per person} = 600 - 20x,$$

and the number of people in the seminar will be

$$\text{number of people} = 1000 + 100x.$$

The total revenue, $R(x)$, is given by the product of the price and the number of people attending, or

$$R(x) = (600 - 20x)(1000 + 100x)$$
$$= 600,000 + 40,000x - 2000x^2.$$

(b) Find the value of x that maximizes revenue.

Here $R'(x) = 40,000 - 4000x$. Set this derivative equal to 0.

$$40,000 - 4000x = 0$$
$$-4000x = -40,000$$
$$x = 10$$

Since $R''(x) = -4000$, $x = 10$ leads to maximum revenue.

(c) Find the maximum revenue.

Use the function $R(x)$ from part (a).

$$R(10) = 600,000 + 40,000(10) - 2000(10)^2 = 800,000$$

dollars. To get this level of revenue, $1000 + 100(10) = 2000$ people must attend the seminar; each person will pay $600 - 20(10) = \$400$. ∎

EXAMPLE 3

A truck burns fuel at the rate of

$$G(x) = \frac{1}{200}\left(\frac{800 + x^2}{x}\right)$$

gallons per mile when traveling x miles per hour on a straight, level road. If fuel costs \$2 per gallon, find the speed that will produce the minimum total cost for a 1000-mile trip. Find the minimum total cost. (This is an extension of Exercise 41 in Section 5 of the previous chapter.)

The total cost of the trip, in dollars, is the product of the number of gallons per mile, the number of miles, and the cost per gallon. If $C(x)$ represents this cost, then

$$C(x) = \left[\frac{1}{200}\left(\frac{800 + x^2}{x}\right)\right](1000)(2)$$
$$= \frac{2000}{200}\left(\frac{800 + x^2}{x}\right)$$
$$C(x) = \frac{8000 + 10x^2}{x}.$$

To find the value of x that will minimize cost, first find the derivative:

$$C'(x) = \frac{10x^2 - 8000}{x^2}.$$

Set this derivative equal to 0.

$$\frac{10x^2 - 8000}{x^2} = 0$$

$$10x^2 - 8000 = 0$$

$$10x^2 = 8000$$

$$x^2 = 800$$

Take the square root on both sides to get

$$x \approx \pm 28.3 \text{ mph}.$$

Reject -28.3 as a speed, leaving $x = 28.3$ as the only critical value. To see if 28.3 leads to a minimum cost, find $C''(x)$.

$$C''(x) = \frac{16{,}000}{x^3}$$

Since $C''(28.3) > 0$, the critical value 28.3 leads to a minimum. (It is not necessary to actually calculate $C''(28.3)$; just check that $C''(28.3) > 0$.)

The minimum total cost is

$$C(28.3) = \frac{8000 + 10(28.3)^2}{28.3} = 565.69 \text{ dollars.} \quad \blacksquare$$

EXAMPLE 4

An open box is to be made by cutting squares from each corner of a 12 inch by 12 inch piece of metal and then folding up the sides. What size square should be cut from each corner in order to produce the box of maximum volume?

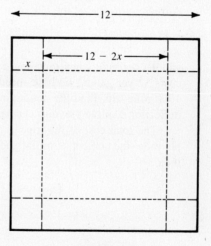

FIGURE 35

Let x represent the length of a side of the square that is cut from each corner, as shown in Figure 35. The width of the box is $12 - 2x$, with the length also $12 - 2x$. The volume of the box is given by the product of the length, width, and height. In this example, the volume, $V(x)$, depends on x:

$$V(x) = x(12 - 2x)(12 - 2x) = 144x - 48x^2 + 4x^3.$$

The derivative is $V'(x) = 144 - 96x + 12x^2$. Set this derivative equal to 0.

$$12x^2 - 96x + 144 = 0$$
$$12(x^2 - 8x + 12) = 0$$
$$12(x - 2)(x - 6) = 0$$
$$x - 2 = 0 \quad \text{or} \quad x - 6 = 0$$
$$x = 2 \quad \text{or} \quad x = 6$$

Since $V''(x) = -96 + 24x$, we have $V''(2) = -96 + 24(2) = -48$, which is negative. This means the box will have maximum volume when $x = 2$, with the maximum volume

$$V(2) = 144(2) - 48(2)^2 + 4(2)^3 = 128$$

cubic inches. The function $V(x)$ is defined only on the interval $[0, 6]$. Both the end-points of this domain, $x = 0$ and $x = 6$, lead to *minimum* volumes of 0. ▪

11.4 EXERCISES

Exercises 1–8 involve maximizing and minimizing products and sums of numbers. Work all these problems using the steps shown in Exercise 1.

1. We want to find two numbers x and y such that $x + y = 100$ and the product $P = xy$ is as large as possible.
   (a) We know $x + y = 100$. Solve this equation for y.
   (b) Substitute this result for y into $P = xy$.
   (c) Find P'. Solve the equation $P' = 0$.
   (d) What are the two numbers?
   (e) What is the maximum value of P?

2. Find two numbers whose sum is 250 and whose product is as large as possible. What is the maximum product?

3. Find two numbers whose sum is 200 such that the sum of the squares of the two numbers is minimized.

4. Find two numbers whose sum is 30 such that the sum of the squares of the numbers is minimized.

In Exercises 5–8, use the steps of Exercise 1 to find numbers x and y such that

5. $x + y = 150$ and x^2y is maximized.

6. $x + y = 45$ and xy^2 is maximized.

7. $x - y = 10$ and xy is minimized.

8. $x - y = 3$ and xy is minimized.

9. If the price charged for a candy bar is $p(x)$ cents, then x thousand candy bars will be sold in a certain city, where

$$p(x) = 100 - \frac{x}{10}.$$

(a) Find an expression for the total revenue from the sale of x thousand candy bars.

(b) Find the value of x that leads to maximum revenue.

(c) Find the maximum revenue.

10. The sale of cassette tapes of "lesser" performers is very sensitive to price. If a tape manufacturer charges $p(x)$ dollars per tape, where

$$p(x) = 6 - \frac{x}{8},$$

then x thousand tapes will be sold.

(a) Find an expression for the total revenue from the sale of x thousand tapes.

(b) Find the value of x that leads to maximum revenue.

(c) Find the maximum revenue.

11. A truck burns fuel at the rate of $G(x)$ gallons per mile, where

$$G(x) = \frac{1}{32}\left(\frac{64}{x} + \frac{x}{50}\right),$$

while traveling x miles per hour.

(a) If fuel costs $1.60 per gallon, find the speed that will produce minimum total cost for a 400-mile trip. (See Example 3.)

(b) Find the minimum total cost.

12. A rock and roll band travels from engagement to engagement in a large bus. This bus burns fuel at the rate of $G(x)$ gallons per mile, where

$$G(x) = \frac{1}{50}\left(\frac{200}{x} + \frac{x}{15}\right),$$

while traveling x miles per hour.

(a) If fuel costs $2 per gallon, find the speed that will produce minimum total cost for a 250-mile trip.

(b) Find the minimum total cost.

13. A farmer has 1200 meters of fencing. He wants to enclose a rectangular field bordering a river, with no fencing needed along the river. (See the sketch.) Let x represent the width of the field.

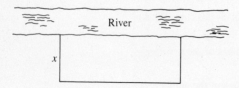

(a) Write an expression for the length of the field.

(b) Find the area of the field (area = length × width).

(c) Find the value of x leading to the maximum area.

(d) Find the maximum area.

14. Find the dimensions of the rectangular field of maximum area that can be made from 200 meters of fencing material. (This fence has four sides.)

15. An ecologist is conducting a research project on breeding pheasants in captivity. She first must construct suitable pens. She wants a rectangular area with two additional fences across its width, as shown in the sketch. Find the maximum area she can enclose with 3600 meters of fencing.

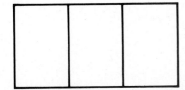

16. A rectangular field is to be enclosed with a fence. One side of the field is against an existing fence, so that no fence is needed on that side. If material for the fence costs $2 per foot for the two ends and $4 per foot for the side parallel to the existing fence, find the dimensions of the field of largest area that can be enclosed for $1000.

17. A rectangular field is to be enclosed on all four sides with a fence. Fencing material costs $3 per foot for two opposite sides, and $6 per foot for the other two sides. Find the maximum area that can be enclosed for $2400.

18. The manager of an 80-unit apartment complex is trying to decide on the rent to charge. It is known from experience that at a rent of $200, all the units will be full. However, on the average, one additional unit will remain vacant for each $10 increase in rent.

    (a) Let x represent the number of $10 increases. Find the amount of rent per apartment. (See Example 2.)

    (b) Find the number of apartments rented.

    (c) Find the total revenue from all rented apartments.

    (d) What value of x leads to maximum revenue?

    (e) What is the maximum revenue?

19. The manager of a peach orchard is trying to decide when to arrange for picking the peaches. If they are picked now, the average yield per tree will be 100 pounds, which can be sold for 40¢ per pound. Past experience shows that the yield per tree will increase about 5 pounds per week, while the price will decrease about 2¢ per pound per week.

    (a) Let x represent the number of weeks that the manager should wait. Find the income per pound.

    (b) Find the number of pounds per tree.

    (c) Find the total revenue from a tree.

    (d) When should the peaches be picked in order to produce maximum revenue?

    (e) What is the maximum revenue?

20. A local group of scouts has been collecting old aluminum cans for recycling. The group has already collected 12,000 pounds of cans, for which they could currently receive $4 per hundred pounds. The group can continue to collect cans at the rate of 400 pounds per day. However, a glut in the old-can market has caused the recycling company to announce that it will lower its price, starting immediately, by $.10 per hundred pounds per day. The scouts can make only one trip to the recycling center. Find the best time for that single trip. What total income will be received?

21. In planning a small restaurant, it is estimated that a profit of $5 per seat will be made if the number of seats is between 60 and 80, inclusive. On the other hand, the profit on each seat will decrease by 5¢ for each seat above 80.

(a) Find the number of seats that will produce the maximum profit.

(b) What is the maximum profit?

22. A local club is arranging a charter flight to Hawaii. The cost of the trip is $425 each for 75 passengers, with a refund of $5 per passenger for each passenger in excess of 75.

(a) Find the number of passengers that will maximize the revenue received from the flight.

(b) Find the maximum revenue.

23. A television manufacturing firm needs to design an open-topped box with a square base. The box must hold 32 cubic inches. Find the dimensions of the box that can be built with the minimum amount of materials. (See the figure.)

24. A closed box with a square base is to have a volume of 16,000 cubic centimeters. The material for the top and bottom of the box costs $3 per square centimeter, while the material for the sides costs $1.50 per square centimeter. Find the dimensions of the box that will lead to minimum total cost. What is the minimum total cost?

25. A company wishes to manufacture a box with a volume of 36 cubic feet which is open on top and which is twice as long as it is wide. Find the dimensions of the box produced from the minimum amount of material.

26. A mathematics book is to contain 36 square inches of printed matter per page, with margins of 1 inch along the sides, and $1\frac{1}{2}$ inches along the top and bottom. Find the dimensions of the page that will lead to the minimum amount of paper being used for a page. (See the figure.)

27. In Example 3, we found the speed in miles per hour that minimized cost when we considered only the cost of the fuel. Rework the problem taking into account the driver's salary of $12 per hour. (Hint: If the trip is 1000 miles at x miles per hour, the driver will be paid for $1000/x$ hours.)

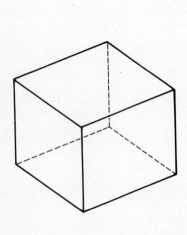

EXERCISE 23

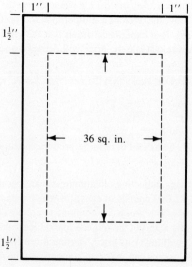

EXERCISE 26

28. Decide what you would do if your assistant brought you the following contract for your signature:

> Your firm offers to deliver 300 tables to a dealer, at $90 per table, and to reduce the price per table on the entire order by 25¢ for each additional table over 300.

Find the dollar total involved in the largest possible transaction between the manufacturer and the dealer; find the smallest possible dollar amount.

29. A company wishes to run a utility cable from point A on the shore (see the figure) to an installation at point B on the island. The island is 6 miles from the shore. It costs $400 per mile to run the cable on land and $500 per mile underwater. Assume that the cable starts at A and runs along the shoreline, then angles and runs underwater to the island. Find the point at which the line should begin to angle in order to yield the minimum total cost. (Hint: The length of the line underwater is $\sqrt{x^2 + 36}$.)

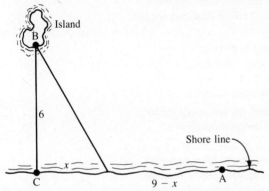

30. A hunter is at a point on a river bank. He wants to get to his cabin, located three miles north and eight miles west. (See the figure.) He can travel 5 miles per hour on the river but only 2 miles per hour on this very rocky land. How far up river should he go in order to reach the cabin in minimum time? (Hint: Distance = rate × time.)

31. Homing pigeons are very careful to avoid flying over large bodies of water—they will go around them if at all possible. This may be due to the extra energy required to fly over water, due to the fact that air pressure drops over water in daytime. Assume that a pigeon is released from a boat in a lake 1 mile from shore (see the figure), then flies to point P on the shore and then along the straight edge of the lake to reach its home, at L. If L is 2 miles from point A, the point on the shore closest to the boat, and a pigeon needs 4/3 as much energy to fly over water as over land, find the location of point P.

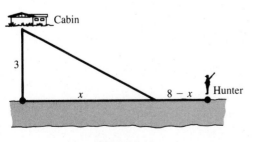

EXERCISE 30

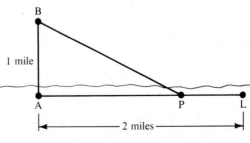

EXERCISE 31

32. When salmon* struggle upstream to their spawning grounds, it is essential that they conserve energy, for they no longer feed once they have left the ocean. Let $v_0 =$ speed (in mph) of the current, $d =$ distance the salmon must travel, and $v =$ speed of the salmon. Hence, $(v - v_0)$ is the net velocity of the salmon upstream. (See the figure.)

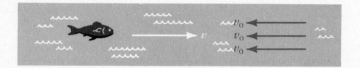

(a) Show that if the journey takes t hours, then $t = d/(v - v_0)$.

We next will assume that the amount of energy expended per hour when the speed of the salmon is v is directly proportional to v^α for some $\alpha > 1$. (Empirical data suggest this.)

(b) Show that the total energy T expended over the journey is given by

$$T = k\frac{v^\alpha}{v - v_0} \quad \text{for } v > v_0.$$

(c) Show that T is minimized by selecting velocity $v = \alpha v_0/(\alpha - 1)$.

(d) If $v_0 = 2$ mph and the salmon make the 20-mile journey by swimming for 40 hours, estimate α. What must you assume in order to do the computations?

33. For most living things, reproduction is *seasonal*—it can take place only at selected times of the year. Large whales, for example, reproduce every two years during a relatively short time span of about two months. Shown on the time axis in the figure are the reproductive periods. Let $S =$ number of adults present during the reproductive period and let $R =$ number of adults that return the next season to reproduce.

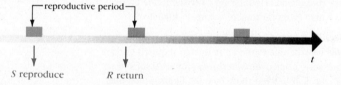

If we find a relationship between R and S, $R = f(S)$, then we have formed a *spawner-recruit* function or *parent-progeny* function. These functions are notoriously hard to develop because of the difficulty of obtaining accurate counts and because of the many hypotheses that can be made about the life stages. We will simply suppose that the function f takes various forms.

If $R > S$, we can presumably harvest $H = R - S$ individuals, leaving S to reproduce. Next season, $R = f(S)$ will return and the harvesting process can again be repeated, as shown in the figure. Find the number of spawners S that will maximize the harvest

$$H = R - S = f(S) - S$$

*Exercises 32–34 from *Mathematics for the Biosciences* by Michael R. Cullen. Copyright © 1983 PWS Publishers. Reprinted by permission.

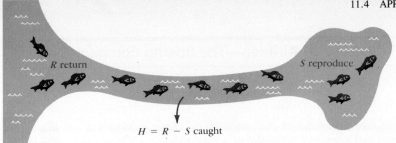

$H = R - S$ caught

for:

(a) $f(S) = -.1S^2 + 11S$ **(b)** $f(S) = -S^2 + 2.2S$ **(c)** $f(S) = 15\sqrt{S}$

(d) $f(S) = 12S^{.25}$ **(e)** $f(S) = 25S/(S + 2)$ **(f)** $f(S) = .999S$

Both R and S are measured in thousands.

34. It is well known that during coughing, the diameters of the trachea and bronchi decrease. Let r_0 be the normal radius of an airway at atmospheric pressure P_0. For the trachea, $r_0 \approx .5$ inch. The glottis is the opening at the entrance of the trachea through which air must pass as it either enters or leaves the lungs, as depicted in the illustration. Assume that, after a deep inspiration of air, the glottis is closed. Then pressure develops in the airways and the radius of the airway decreases. We will assume a simple linear relation between r and P:

$$r - r_0 = a(P - P_0)$$

$$\text{or} \quad \Delta r = a\Delta P$$

where $a < 0$ and $r_0/2 \le r \le r_0$.

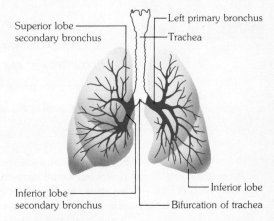

Left primary bronchus
Trachea
Superior lobe secondary bronchus
Inferior lobe
Inferior lobe secondary bronchus
Bifurcation of trachea

(Adapted from Barbara R. Landau, *Essential Anatomy and Physiology*, 2nd ed. Glenview, Ill.: Scott, Foresman and Co., Copyright 1980.)

When the glottis is opened, how does the air flow through these passages? We will assume that the flow is governed by **Poiseuille's Laws:**

$$\textbf{(i)} \quad v = \frac{P - P_0}{k}(r^2 - x^2), \quad 0 \le x \le r$$

$$\textbf{(ii)} \quad F = \frac{dV}{dt} = \frac{\pi(P - P_0)}{2k}r^4$$

Here, v is the velocity at a distance x from the center of the airway (in cm/sec, e.g.) and F is the flow rate (in cm^3/sec, e.g.). The average velocity $\bar{v}$ over the circular cross section is given by

$$\textbf{(iii)} \quad \bar{v} = F/(\pi r^2) = \frac{P - P_0}{2k}r^2.$$

(a) Write the flow rate as a function of r only. Find the value of r that maximizes the rate of flow.

(b) Write both the average velocity $\bar{v}$ and $v(0)$, the velocity in the center of the airway, as functions of r alone. Find the value of r that maximizes these two velocities.

(c) Use the results of parts (a) and (b) to discuss how a given quantity of air can be expelled from the lungs as efficiently as possible.

EXTENDED	**Pricing an Airliner—The Boeing Company***
APPLICATION	

The Boeing Company is one of the United States' largest producers of civilian airliners. It has developed a series of successful jet aircraft, starting with the 707 in 1955. In this application we discuss the mathematics involved in determining the optimum price for a new model jet airliner. It is helpful to summarize here the variables to be used in this case.

p = price per airliner, in millions of dollars

$N(p)$ = total number of airliners that will be sold by the industry at a price of p

x = total number of airliners to be produced by Boeing

$C(x)$ = total cost to manufacture x airliners

h = share of the total market to be won by Boeing

P^* = total profit for Boeing

For the airliner in question, Boeing had only one competitor. The price charged by both Boeing and its competitor would have to be the same—any attempt by one firm to lower the price would of necessity be met by the other firm. Thus, the price charged by Boeing would have no effect on the share of the total market to be won by Boeing. However, the price charged by Boeing (and the competitor) would have considerable effect on the *size* of the total market. In fact, Boeing sales analysts made predictions of the total market at various price levels and found that the function

$$N(p) = -78p^2 + 655p - 1125$$

gave a reasonable estimate of the total market; that is, $N(p)$ is the total number of planes that will be sold, by both Boeing and its competitor, at a price p, in millions of dollars per plane. A graph of $N(p)$ is shown in Figure 1.

Production analysts at Boeing estimated that if $C(x)$ is the total cost to manufacture x airplanes, then

$$C(x) = 50 + 1.5x + 8x^{3/4},$$

where $C(x)$ is measured in millions of dollars.

The company desires to know the price, p, it should charge per plane so that the total profit, P^*, will be a maximum. Profit is given as the numerical product of the price per plane, p, and the total number of planes sold by Boeing, x, minus the cost to manufacture x planes, $C(x)$. Thus, the profit function is

$$P^* = p \cdot x - C(x). \tag{1}$$

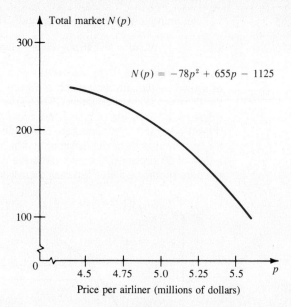

$$N(p) = -78p^2 + 655p - 1125$$

FIGURE 1

If h is the fractional share of the total market for this plane that will be won by Boeing (note: $0 \le h \le 1$), then

$$x = h \cdot N(p).$$

(The number of planes sold by Boeing equals its share of the market times the total market.) Substituting $h \cdot N(p)$ for x in the profit function, equation (1), gives

$$P^* = p \cdot h \cdot N(p) - C[h \cdot N(p)].$$

To find the maximum profit, we must take the derivative of this function with respect to p. Assume h is a constant; treat $p \cdot h \cdot N(p)$ as the product $(ph) \cdot N(p)$, and use the chain rule on $C[h \cdot N(p)]$. This gives

$$(P^*)' = (ph) \cdot N'(p) + N(p) \cdot h - C'[h \cdot N(p)] \cdot h \cdot N'(p).$$

For convenience, replace $h \cdot N(p)$ by x in the expression $C'[h \cdot N(p)]$. Then put the derivative equal to 0 and simplify:

$$(ph) \cdot N'(p) + N(p) \cdot h - C'(x) \cdot h \cdot N'(p) = 0,$$
$$p \cdot N'(p) + N(p) = C'(x) \cdot N'(p),$$

from which

$$p + \frac{N(p)}{N'(p)} = C'(x). \tag{2}$$

Thus, the optimum price, p, must satisfy equation (2). (It is necessary to verify that this value of p leads to a *maximum* profit and not a minimum. This calculation, using the second derivative test, is left for the energetic reader.)

Returning to the functions $N(p)$ and $C(x)$ given above, verify that

$$N'(p) = -156p + 655 \qquad \text{and} \qquad C'(x) = 1.5 + 6x^{-1/4}.$$

Using p, $N(p)$, and $N'(p)$, we can sketch a graph of the left-hand side of equation (2), as shown by the left-hand graph of Figure 2. On the right in Figure 2 is the graph of the right-hand side of equation (2), $C'(x) = 1.5 + 6x^{-1/4}$, for various values of x considered feasible by the company. We know that the maximum profit is produced when the left-hand and right-hand sides of equation (2) are equal. Using this fact, we can read the price that leads to the maximum profit from Figure 2. If $x = 60$ (the company sells a total of 60 airplanes), the price per plane will be about $5.1 million, while if $x = 120$, the price should be a little less than $5 million.

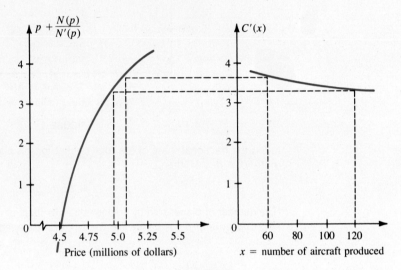

FIGURE 2

EXERCISES

1. (a) Find the total cost of manufacturing 120 planes. (Hint: $8 \cdot 120^{3/4} \approx 290$)
   (b) Assume each plane sells for $5 million, and find the total profit from the sale of 120 planes, using equation (1).

2. (a) Find the total market at a price of $5 million per plane.
   (b) If Boeing sells 120 planes at a price of $5 million each, how many will be sold by the competitor?

3. (a) Find $C(60)$. (Hint: $8 \cdot 60^{3/4} \approx 170$)
   (b) Assume each plane is sold for $5.1 million, and find the total profit from the sale of 60 planes, using equation (1).

11.5   Further Management Applications (Optional)

Suppose that a company manufactures a constant number of units of a product per year, and that the product can be manufactured in a number of batches of equal size during the year. The company could manufacture the item only once per year to minimize setup costs, but they would then have much higher warehouse costs. On the other hand, they might make many small batches, but this would increase setup cost. Calculus can be used to find the number of batches per year that should be manufactured in order to minimize total cost.

Figure 36 shows several of the possibilities for a product having an annual demand of 12,000 units. The top graph shows the results if only one batch of the product is made annually: in this case an average of 6000 items will be held in a warehouse. If four batches (of 3000 each) are made at equal time intervals during a year, the average number of units in the warehouse falls to only 1500. If twelve batches are made, an average of 500 items will be in the warehouse.

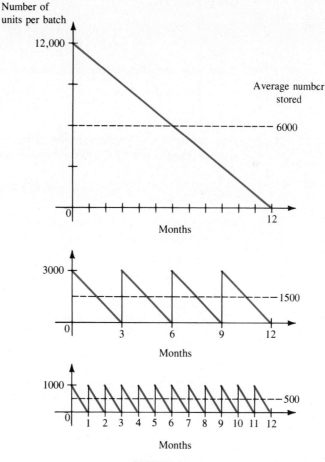

FIGURE 36

In this section, the following variables are used:

x = number of batches to be manufactured annually

k = cost of storing one unit of the product for one year

f = fixed setup cost to manufacture the product

g = variable cost of manufacturing a single unit of the product

M = total number of units produced annually.

The company has two types of costs associated with the production of its product: a cost associated with manufacturing the item, and a cost associated with storing the finished product.

Let us start with manufacturing costs. During a year the company will produce x batches of the product, with M/x units of the product produced per batch. Each batch has a fixed cost f and a variable cost g per unit, so that the manufacturing cost per batch is

$$f + \frac{gM}{x}.$$

Since there are x batches per year, the total annual manufacturing cost is

$$\left(f + \frac{gM}{x}\right)x. \tag{1}$$

Now we must find the storage cost. Since each batch consists of M/x units, and since demand is constant, it is common to assume an average inventory of

$$\frac{1}{2}\left(\frac{M}{x}\right) = \frac{M}{2x}$$

units per year. It costs k to store one unit of the product for a year, making a total storage cost of

$$k\left(\frac{M}{2x}\right) = \frac{kM}{2x}. \tag{2}$$

The total production cost is the sum of the manufacturing and storage costs, or the sum of expressions (1) and (2). If $T(x)$ is the total cost of producing x batches,

$$T(x) = \left(f + \frac{gM}{x}\right)x + \frac{kM}{2x} = fx + gM + \frac{kM}{2x}.$$

To find the value of x that will minimize $T(x)$, remember that f, g, k, and M are constants and find $T'(x)$.

$$T'(x) = f - \frac{kM}{2}x^{-2}.$$

Place this derivative equal to 0.

$$f - \frac{kM}{2}x^{-2} = 0$$

$$f = \frac{kM}{2x^2}$$

$$2fx^2 = kM$$

$$x^2 = \frac{kM}{2f}$$

$$x = \sqrt{\frac{kM}{2f}} \qquad (3)$$

The second derivative test can be used to show that $\sqrt{kM/(2f)}$ is the annual number of batches that gives minimum total production cost. (See Exercise 7.)

EXAMPLE 1

A paint company has a steady annual demand for 24,500 cans of automobile primer. The cost accountant for the company says that it costs $2 to hold one can of paint for one year and $500 to set up the plant for the production of the primer. Find the number of batches of primer that should be produced for the minimum total production cost.

Use equation (3) above.

$$x = \sqrt{\frac{kM}{2f}}$$

$$x = \sqrt{\frac{2(24,500)}{2(500)}}$$

$$x = \sqrt{49} = 7$$

Seven batches of primer per year will lead to minimum production costs. ▪

The analysis above also applies to reordering an item that is used at a constant rate throughout the year, as the next example shows.

EXAMPLE 2

A large pharmacy has an annual need for 200 units of a certain antibiotic. It costs $10 to store one unit for one year. The fixed cost of placing an order (clerical time, mailing, and so on) amounts to $40. Find the number of orders that should be placed annually.

Here $k = 10$, $M = 200$, and $f = 40$. We have

$$x = \sqrt{\frac{10(200)}{2(40)}} = \sqrt{25} = 5.$$

The drug should be ordered 5 times a year. ▪

11.5 EXERCISES

1. Find the approximate number of batches that should be produced annually if 100,000 units are to be manufactured. It costs $1 to store a unit for one year and it costs $500 to set up the factory to produce each batch.

2. How many units per batch will be manufactured in Exercise 1?

3. A market has a steady annual demand for 16,800 cases of sugar. It costs $3 to store one case for one year. The market pays $7 for each order that is placed. Find the number of orders for sugar that should be placed each year.

4. Find the number of cases per order in Exercise 3.

5. The publisher of a best-selling book has an annual demand for 100,000 copies. It costs 50¢ to store one copy for one year. Setup of the press for a new printing costs $1000. Find the number of batches that should be printed annually.

6. A restaurant has an annual demand for 810 bottles of a California wine. It costs $1 to store one bottle for one year, and it costs $5 to place a reorder. Find the number of orders that should be placed annually.

7. Use the second derivative to show that the value of x obtained in the text [equation (3)] really leads to the minimum cost.

8. Why do you think that the variable cost g does not appear in the answer for x [equation (3)]?

EXTENDED

APPLICATION

A Total Cost Model for a Training Program*

In this application, we set up a mathematical model for determining the total costs in setting up a training program. Then we use calculus to find the time between training programs that produces the minimum total cost. The model assumes that the demand for trainees is constant and that the fixed cost of training a batch of trainees is known. Also, it is assumed that people who are trained, but for whom no job is readily available, will be paid a fixed amount per month while waiting for a job to open up.

The model uses the following variables.

D = demand for trainees per month
N = number of trainees per batch
C_1 = fixed cost of training a batch of trainees
C_2 = variable cost of training per trainee per month
C_3 = salary paid monthly to a trainee who has not yet been given a job after training
m = time interval in months between successive batches of trainees
t = length of training program in months
$Z(m)$ = total monthly cost of program

---

*Based on "A Total Cost Model for a Training Program" by P. L. Goyal and S. K. Goyal, Faculty of Commerce and Administration, Concordia University. Used with permission.

The total cost of training a batch of trainees is given by $C_1 + NtC_2$. However, $N = mD$, so that the total cost per batch is $C_1 + mDtC_2$.

After training, personnel are given jobs at the rate of D per month. Thus, $N - D$ of the trainees will not get a job the first month, $N - 2D$ will not get a job the second month, and so on. The $N - D$ trainees who do not get a job the first month produce total costs of $(N - D)C_3$, those not getting jobs during the second month produce costs of $(N - 2D)C_3$, and so on. Since $N = mD$, the costs during the first month can be written as

$$(N - D)C_3 = (mD - D)C_3 = (m - 1)DC_3,$$

while the costs during the second month are $(m - 2)DC_3$, and so on. The total cost for keeping the trainees without a job is thus

$$(m - 1)DC_3 + (m - 2)DC_3 + (m - 3)DC_3 + \cdots + 2DC_3 + DC_3,$$

which can be factored to give

$$DC_3[(m - 1) + (m - 2) + (m - 3) + \cdots + 2 + 1].$$

The expression in brackets is the sum of the terms of an arithmetic sequence, discussed in most algebra texts. Using formulas for arithmetic sequences, the expression in brackets can be shown to equal $m(m - 1)/2$, so that we have

$$DC_3\left[\frac{m(m - 1)}{2}\right] \tag{1}$$

as the total cost for keeping jobless trainees.

The total cost per batch is the sum of the training cost per batch, $C_1 + mDtC_2$, and the cost of keeping trainees without a proper job, given by (1). Since we assume that a batch of trainees is trained every m months, the total cost per month, $Z(m)$, is given by

$$Z(m) = \frac{C_1 + mDtC_2}{m} + \frac{DC_3\left[\dfrac{m(m - 1)}{2}\right]}{m} = \frac{C_1}{m} + DtC_2 + DC_3\left(\frac{m - 1}{2}\right).$$

EXERCISES

1. Find $Z'(m)$.

2. Solve the equation $Z'(m) = 0$.
   As a practical matter, it is usually required that m be a whole number. If m does not come out to be a whole number in Exercise 2, then m^+ and m^-, the two whole numbers closest to m, must be chosen. Calculate both $Z(m^+)$ and $Z(m^-)$; the smaller of the two provides the optimum value of Z.

3. Suppose a company finds that its demand for trainees is 3 per month, that a training program requires 12 months, that the fixed cost of training a batch of trainees is $15,000, that the variable cost per trainee per month is $100, and that trainees are paid $900 per month after training but before going to work. Use your result from Exercise 2 and find m.

4. Since m is not a whole number, find m^+ and m^-.

5. Calculate $Z(m^+)$ and $Z(m^-)$.

6. What is the optimum time interval between successive batches of trainees? How many trainees should be in a batch?

11.6   Implicit Differentiation

In almost all the examples and applications so far, any necessary functions have been written in the form

$$y = f(x),$$

with y given **explicitly** in terms of x, or as an **explicit function** of x. For example,

$$y = 3x - 2, \quad y = x^2 + x + 6, \quad \text{and} \quad y = -x^3 + 2$$

are all explicit functions of x. We can express $4xy - 3x = 6$ as an explicit function of x by solving for y. This gives

$$4xy - 3x = 6$$

$$4xy = 3x + 6$$

$$y = \frac{3x + 6}{4x}.$$

On the other hand, some equations in x and y cannot be readily solved for y, and some equations cannot be solved for y at all. For example, while it would be possible (but tedious) to use the quadratic formula to solve for y in the equation $y^2 + 2yx + 4x^2 = 0$, it is not possible to solve for y in the equation $y^5 + 8y^3 + 6y^2x^2 + 2yx^3 + 6 = 0$. In equations such as these last two, y is said to be given **implicitly** in terms of x.

In such cases, we may still be able to find the derivative dy/dx by a process called **implicit differentiation.** In doing so, we assume that there exists some function or functions f, which we may or may not be able to find, such that $y = f(x)$ and dy/dx exists. We will use dy/dx here rather than $f'(x)$.

EXAMPLE 1

Find $\dfrac{dy}{dx}$ if $3xy + 4y^2 = 10$.

Differentiate with respect to x on both sides of the equation:

$$3xy + 4y^2 = 10$$

$$\frac{d}{dx}(3xy + 4y^2) = \frac{d}{dx}(10). \tag{1}$$

On the left, think of $3xy$ as the product $(3x)(y)$ and use the product rule. Since

$$\frac{d}{dx}(3x) = 3 \quad \text{and} \quad \frac{d}{dx}(y) = \frac{dy}{dx},$$

the derivative of $(3x)(y)$ is

$$(3x)\frac{dy}{dx} + (y)3 = 3x\frac{dy}{dx} + 3y.$$

To differentiate the second term, $4y^2$, use the generalized power rule, since y is assumed to be some function of x.

$$\frac{d}{dx}(4y^2) = 4(2y^1)\frac{dy}{dx} = 8y\frac{dy}{dx}$$

On the right side of equation (1), the derivative of 10 is 0. Taking the indicated derivatives in equation (1) term by term gives

$$3x\frac{dy}{dx} + 3y + 8y\frac{dy}{dx} = 0.$$

Now solve this result for dy/dx.

$$(3x + 8y)\frac{dy}{dx} = -3y$$

$$\frac{dy}{dx} = \frac{-3y}{3x + 8y} \quad \blacksquare$$

EXAMPLE 2

Find dy/dx for $x^2 + 2xy^2 + 3x^2y = 0$.

Again, differentiate on each side with respect to x.

$$\frac{d}{dx}(x^2 + 2xy^2 + 3x^2y) = \frac{d}{dx}(0)$$

Use the product rule to find the derivatives of $2xy^2$ and of $3x^2y$.

derivative of x^2	derivative of $2xy^2$	derivative of $3x^2y$	derivative of 0
↓			↓

$$2x \quad + 2x\left(2y\frac{dy}{dx}\right) + 2y^2 + 3x^2\left(\frac{dy}{dx}\right) + 6xy = \quad 0$$

Simplify to get

$$2x + 4xy\left(\frac{dy}{dx}\right) + 2y^2 + 3x^2\left(\frac{dy}{dx}\right) + 6xy = 0,$$

from which

$$(4xy + 3x^2)\frac{dy}{dx} = -2x - 2y^2 - 6xy,$$

or, finally,

$$\frac{dy}{dx} = \frac{-2x - 2y^2 - 6xy}{4xy + 3x^2}. \quad \blacksquare$$

EXAMPLE 3

Find dy/dx for $x + \sqrt{xy} = y^2$.

Take the derivative on each side.

$$\frac{d}{dx}(x + \sqrt{xy}) = \frac{d}{dx}(y^2)$$

Since $\sqrt{xy} = \sqrt{x} \cdot \sqrt{y} = x^{1/2} \cdot y^{1/2}$ for nonnegative values of x and y, taking derivatives gives

$$1 + x^{1/2}\left(\frac{1}{2}y^{-1/2} \cdot \frac{dy}{dx}\right) + y^{1/2}\left(\frac{1}{2}x^{-1/2}\right) = 2y\frac{dy}{dx}$$

$$1 + \frac{x^{1/2}}{2y^{1/2}} \cdot \frac{dy}{dx} + \frac{y^{1/2}}{2x^{1/2}} = 2y\frac{dy}{dx}.$$

Multiply both sides by $2x^{1/2} \cdot y^{1/2}$.

$$2x^{1/2} \cdot y^{1/2} + x\frac{dy}{dx} + y = 4x^{1/2} \cdot y^{3/2} \cdot \frac{dy}{dx}$$

Combine terms and solve for dy/dx.

$$2x^{1/2} \cdot y^{1/2} + y = (4x^{1/2} \cdot y^{3/2} - x)\frac{dy}{dx}$$

$$\frac{dy}{dx} = \frac{2x^{1/2} \cdot y^{1/2} + y}{4x^{1/2} \cdot y^{3/2} - x} \quad \blacksquare$$

EXAMPLE 4

The graph of $x^2 + 5y^2 = 36$ is the ellipse shown in Figure 37. Find the equation of the tangent line at the point $(4, 2)$.

A vertical line can cut the graph of the ellipse of Figure 37 in more than one point, so the graph is not the graph of a function. This means that y *cannot* be written as a function of x, so that dy/dx would not exist. However, it seems intuitive that a tangent line could be drawn to the graph at the point $(4, 2)$. To get around this difficulty, we try to decide if a function f does exist whose graph is exactly the same as our graph in the "vicinity" of the point $(4, 2)$. We can then say that the tangent line to f at $(4, 2)$ is also the tangent line to the ellipse. See Figure 38.

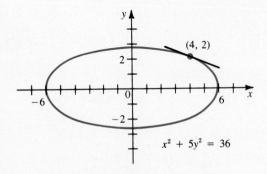

$x^2 + 5y^2 = 36$

FIGURE 37

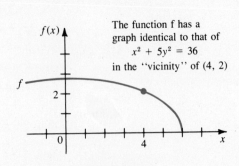

The function f has a graph identical to that of $x^2 + 5y^2 = 36$ in the "vicinity" of $(4, 2)$

FIGURE 38

Assuming that such a function f exists, we can find dy/dx by implicit differentiation.

$$2x + 10y \cdot \frac{dy}{dx} = 0$$

$$\frac{dy}{dx} = \frac{-2x}{10y} = -\frac{x}{5y}$$

To find the slope of the tangent line at the point $(4, 2)$, let $x = 4$ and $y = 2$. The slope, m, is

$$m = -\frac{x}{5y} = -\frac{4}{5 \cdot 2} = -\frac{2}{5}.$$

The equation of the tangent line is then found by using the point-slope form of the equation of a line.

$$y - y_1 = m(x - x_1)$$

$$y - 2 = -\frac{2}{5}(x - 4)$$

$$5y - 10 = -2x + 8$$

$$2x + 5y = 18$$

This tangent line is graphed in Figure 37. ∎

Let us summarize the steps used in implicit differentiation.

Implicit	To find dy/dx for an equation containing x and y:
Differentiation	1. Differentiate on both sides with respect to x.
	2. Place all terms with dy/dx on one side of the equals sign, and all terms without dy/dx on the other side.
	3. Factor out dy/dx, and then solve for dy/dx.

11.6 EXERCISES

Find dy/dx by implicit differentiation for Exercises 1–28.

1. $4x^2 + 3y^2 = 6$

2. $2x^2 - 5y^2 = 4$

3. $2xy + y^2 = 8$

4. $-3xy - 4y^2 = 2$

5. $y^2 = 4x + 1$

6. $y^2 - 2x = 6$

7. $6xy^2 - 8y + 1 = 0$

8. $-4y^2x^2 - 3x + 2 = 0$

9. $x^2 + 2xy = 6$

10. $2x^2 - 3xy = 10$

11. $6x^2 + 8xy + y^2 = 6$

12. $8x^2 = 6y^2 + 2xy$

13. $x^3 = y^2 + 4$

14. $x^3 - 6y^2 = 10$

15. $\dfrac{1}{x} - \dfrac{1}{y} = 2$

16. $\dfrac{3}{2x} + \dfrac{1}{y} = y$

17. $3x^2 = \dfrac{2 - y}{2 + y}$

18. $2y^2 = \dfrac{5 + x}{5 - x}$

19. $x^2 y + y^3 = 4$

20. $2xy^2 + 2y^3 + 5x = 0$

21. $\sqrt{x} + \sqrt{y} = 4$

22. $2\sqrt{x} - \sqrt{y} = 1$

23. $\sqrt{xy} + y = 1$

24. $\sqrt{2xy} - 1 = 3y^2$

25. $(x^2 + 4y^3)^{3/4} = x$

26. $(2y^2 - 4x)^{2/3} = 5y$

27. $\dfrac{1 + \sqrt{x}}{1 + \sqrt{y}} = 2y$

28. $\dfrac{5 - \sqrt{y}}{2 + \sqrt{x}} = -3x$

Find the equation of the tangent line at the given point on each curve in Exercises 29–36.

29. $x^2 + y^2 = 25$; $(-3, 4)$

30. $x^2 + y^2 = 100$; $(8, -6)$

31. $x^2 y^2 = 1$; $(-1, 1)$

32. $x^2 y^3 = 8$; $(-1, 2)$

33. $x^2 + \sqrt{y} = 7$; $(2, 9)$

34. $2y^2 - \sqrt{x} = 4$; $(16, 2)$

35. $y + \dfrac{\sqrt{x}}{y} = 3$; $(4, 2)$

36. $x + \dfrac{\sqrt{y}}{3x} = 2$; $(1, 9)$

37. The graph of $x^2 + y^2 = 100$ is a circle having center at the origin and radius 10.
(a) Write the equations of the tangent lines at the points where $x = 6$. (b) Graph the circle and the tangent lines.

38. The graph of $xy = 1$, shown in the figure, is a *hyperbola*.
(a) Write the equations of the tangent lines when $x = -1$ and when $x = 1$.
(b) Graph the hyperbola and the tangent lines.

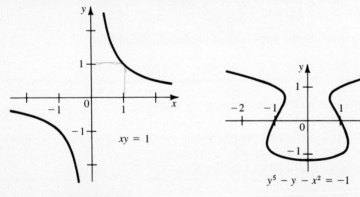

EXERCISE 38   EXERCISE 39

39. The graph of $y^5 - y - x^2 = -1$ is shown in the figure. Find the equation of the tangent line to the graph at the point $(1, 1)$.

40. The graph of $3(x^2 + y^2)^2 = 25(x^2 - y^2)$ is shown in the figure. Find the equation of the tangent line at the point $(2, 1)$.

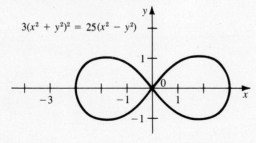

41. Suppose $x^2 + y^2 + 1 = 0$. Use implicit differentiation to find dy/dx. Then explain why the result you got is meaningless. (Hint: can $x^2 + y^2 + 1$ equal 0?)

42. The position of a particle at time t is given by s, where $s^3 - 4st + 2t^3 - 5t = 0$. Find ds/dt.

Let $\sqrt{u} + \sqrt{2v + 1} = 5$. Find the derivatives in Exercises 43–44.

43. du/dv **44.** dv/du

11.7   Related Rates

It is common for variables to be functions of time—for example, sales of an item may depend on the season of the year, or a population of animals may be increasing at a certain rate several months after being introduced into an area. Time is often present implicitly in a mathematical model, meaning that derivatives with respect to time must be found by the method of implicit differentiation discussed in the previous section. For example, if a particular mathematical model leads to the equation

$$x^2 + 5y - 3x + 1 = 0,$$

differentiating on both sides with respect to t gives

$$\frac{d}{dt}(x^2 + 5y - 3x + 1) = \frac{d}{dt}(0)$$

$$2x \cdot \frac{dx}{dt} + 5 \cdot \frac{dy}{dt} - 3 \cdot \frac{dx}{dt} = 0$$

$$(2x - 3)\frac{dx}{dt} + 5\frac{dy}{dt} = 0.$$

The derivatives (or rates of change) dx/dt and dy/dt are related by this last equation; for this reason they are called **related rates.**

EXAMPLE 1

A small rock is dropped into a lake. Circular ripples spread over the surface of the water, with the radius increasing at the rate of 3/2 feet per second. Find the rate of change of the area at the instant that the radius is 4 feet.

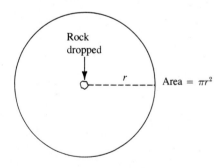

FIGURE 39

As shown in Figure 39, the area A and the radius r are related by

$$A = \pi r^2.$$

Take the derivative of each side with respect to time.

$$\frac{d}{dt}(A) = \frac{d}{dt}(\pi r^2)$$

$$\frac{dA}{dt} = 2\pi r \cdot \frac{dr}{dt} \tag{1}$$

Since the radius is increasing at the rate of 3/2 feet per second,

$$\frac{dr}{dt} = \frac{3}{2}.$$

We want to find dA/dt at the instant when $r = 4$. Substituting into equation (1) gives

$$\frac{dA}{dt} = 2\pi \cdot 4 \cdot \frac{3}{2}$$

$$\frac{dA}{dt} = 12\pi \approx 37.7 \text{ square feet per second.} \quad \blacksquare$$

As suggested by Example 1, four basic steps are involved in solving problems about related rates.

Solving Related Rate Problems

1. Identify all given quantities, as well as the quantities to be found. Draw a sketch when possible.
2. Write an equation relating the variables of the problem.
3. Use implicit differentiation to find the derivative of both sides of the equation in Step 2 with respect to time.
4. Solve for the derivative giving the unknown rate of change and substitute the given values.

Note: differentiate *first,* and *then* substitute values for the variables. If the substitutions were performed first, differentiating would not lead to useful results.

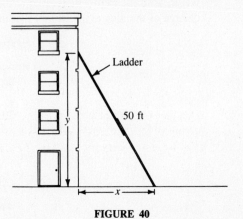

Ladder

50 ft

y

x

FIGURE 40

EXAMPLE 2

A 50-foot ladder is placed against a large building. The base of the ladder is resting on an oil spill, and slips (to the right in Figure 40) at the rate of 3 feet per minute. Find the rate of change of the height of the top of the ladder above the ground at the instant when the base of the ladder is 30 feet from the base of the building.

Let y be the height of the top of the ladder above the ground, and let x be the distance of the base of the ladder from the base of the building. By the Pythagorean theorem,

$$x^2 + y^2 = 50^2. \tag{2}$$

Both x and y are functions of time, t, measured from the moment that the ladder starts slipping. Take the derivative of both sides of equation (2) with respect to time, getting

$$\frac{d}{dt}(x^2 + y^2) = \frac{d}{dt}(50^2)$$

$$2x\frac{dx}{dt} + 2y\frac{dy}{dt} = 0. \tag{3}$$

Since the base is sliding at the rate of 3 feet per minute,

$$\frac{dx}{dt} = 3.$$

Also, the base of the ladder is 30 feet from the base of the building. Use this to find y.

$$50^2 = 30^2 + y^2$$
$$2500 = 900 + y^2$$
$$1600 = y^2$$
$$y = 40$$

In summary, $y = 40$, $x = 30$, and $dx/dt = 3$. Substituting these values into equation (3) gives

$$2(30)(3) + 2(40)\frac{dy}{dt} = 0$$

$$180 + 80\frac{dy}{dt} = 0$$

$$80\frac{dy}{dt} = -180$$

$$\frac{dy}{dt} = \frac{-180}{80} = \frac{-9}{4} = -2.25 \text{ feet per minute.}$$

At the instant when the base of the ladder is 30 feet from the base of the building, the top of the ladder is sliding down the building at the rate of 2.25 feet per minute. (The minus sign shows that the ladder is sliding *down*.) ■

EXAMPLE 3

Industrial waste is collected in a conical storage tank, as shown in Figure 41. The waste runs into the tank at the rate of 5 cubic feet per minute. How fast is the level of waste rising at the instant the waste is 4 feet deep?

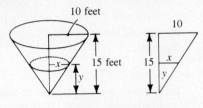

FIGURE 41

Let V be the volume of waste in the tank at time t, with x the radius of the surface of the waste at time t, and y the depth of the waste at time t. We know $dV/dt = 5$ cubic feet per minute, and we want to find dy/dt when $y = 4$.

Using the formula for the volume of a cone, the volume of the waste is

$$V = \frac{1}{3}\pi x^2 y. \tag{4}$$

Before we can find dy/dt, it is necessary to express V as a function of y only, and not of both y and x. To find a connection between x and y, look at the similar triangles of Figure 41 above. Since similar triangles have their corresponding sides in proportion,

$$\frac{x}{10} = \frac{y}{15},$$

or

$$x = \frac{10}{15}y = \frac{2}{3}y.$$

Substituting into equation (4) gives

$$V = \frac{1}{3}\pi\left(\frac{2}{3}y\right)^2 y = \frac{1}{3}\pi \cdot \frac{4}{9}y^2 \cdot y = \frac{4}{27}\pi y^3.$$

Now take the derivative of both sides with respect to t and solve for dy/dt.

$$\frac{dV}{dt} = \frac{4}{9}\pi y^2 \cdot \frac{dy}{dt},$$

or

$$\frac{dy}{dt} = \frac{9}{4\pi y^2} \cdot \frac{dV}{dt}.$$

Substituting $dV/dt = 5$ and $y = 4$ gives

$$\frac{dy}{dt} = \frac{9}{4\pi(4)^2} \cdot 5 = \frac{45}{64\pi} \approx .22$$

feet per minute. At the instant the depth of the waste is 4 feet, the depth is increasing at a rate of about .22 feet per minute. ■

11.7 EXERCISES

Find dy/dt in Exercises 1–8.

1. $y = 9x^2 + 2x$, $dx/dt = 4$, $x = 6$

2. $y = \dfrac{3x + 2}{1 - x}$, $dx/dt = -1$, $x = 3$

3. $y^2 - 5x^2 = -1$, $dx/dt = -3$, $x = 1$, $y = 2$

4. $8y^3 + x^2 = 1$, $dx/dt = 2$, $x = 3$, $y = -1$

5. $xy - 5x + 2y^3 = -70$, $dx/dt = -5$, $x = 2$, $y = -3$

6. $4x^3 - 9xy^2 + y = -80$, $dx/dt = 4$, $x = -3$, $y = 1$

7. $\dfrac{x^2 + y}{x - y} = 9$, $dx/dt = 2$, $x = 4$, $y = 2$

8. $\dfrac{y^3 - x^2}{x + 2y} = \dfrac{17}{7}$, $dx/dt = 1$, $x = -3$, $y = -2$

9. A 25-foot ladder is placed against a building. The base of the ladder is slipping away from the building at the rate of 4 feet per minute. Find the rate at which the top of the ladder is sliding down the building at the instant when the bottom of the ladder is 7 feet from the base of the building.

10. One car leaves a given point and travels north at 30 miles per hour. Another car leaves the same point at the same time and travels west at 40 miles per hour. At what rate is the distance between the two cars changing at the instant when the cars have traveled 2 hours?

11. A rock is thrown into a still pond. The circular ripples move outward from the point of impact of the rock so that the radius of the area of ripples increases at the rate of 2 feet per minute. Find the rate at which the area is changing at the instant the radius is 4 feet.

12. A spherical snowball is placed in the sun. The sun melts the snowball so that its radius decreases 1/4 inch per hour. Find the rate of change of the volume with respect to time at the instant the radius is 4 inches.

13. A sand storage tank used by the highway department for winter storms is leaking. As the sand leaks out, it forms a conical pile. The radius of the base of the pile increases at the rate of 1 inch per minute. The height of the pile is always twice the radius of the base. Find the rate at which the volume of the pile is increasing at the instant the radius of the base is 5 inches.

14. A man 6 feet tall is walking away from a lamp post at the rate of 50 feet per minute. When the man is 8 feet from the lamp post, his shadow is 10 feet long. Find the rate at which the length of the shadow is increasing when he is 25 feet from the lamp post.

15. A trough has a triangular cross section. The trough is 6 feet across the top, 6 feet deep, and 16 feet long. Water is being pumped into the trough at the rate of 4 cubic feet per minute. Find the rate at which the height of water is increasing at the instant that the height is 4 feet.

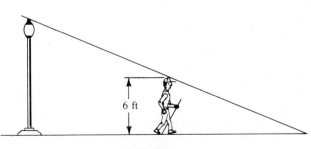

EXERCISE 14

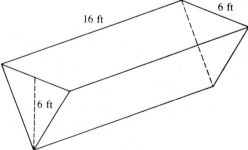

EXERCISE 15

16. A pulley is on the edge of a dock, 8 feet above the water level. A rope is being used to pull in a boat. The rope is attached to the boat at water level. The rope is being pulled in at the rate of 1 foot per second. Find the rate at which the boat is approaching the dock at the instant the boat is 8 feet from the dock.

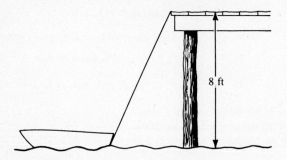

Blood flows faster the closer it is to the center of a blood vessel. According to Poiseuille's Law, the velocity of blood, V, is given by

$$V = k(R^2 - r^2),$$

when R is the radius of the blood vessel, r is the distance from the center of the vessel, and k is a constant.

17. Find dV/dt when $r = 2$ mm, if $k = 3$, $dr/dt = .02$ mm per minute, and R is fixed.

18. Find dV/dt when $r = 1$ mm, if $k = 4$, $dr/dt = .004$ mm per minute, and R is fixed.

19. A person just learning a certain assembly line task takes

$$T(x) = \frac{2 + x}{2 + x^2}$$

minutes to perform a task after x repetitions of the task. Find dT/dt if dx/dt is 4, and 4 repetitions of the task have been performed.

20. Under certain conditions, a person can memorize W words in t minutes, when

$$W(t) = \frac{-.02t^2 + t}{t + 1}.$$

Find dW/dt when $t = 5$.

11.8   Differentials

As we saw when discussing slope in Chapter 1, the symbol Δx represents a change in the variable x; that is,

$$\Delta x = x_2 - x_1$$

for values x_1 and x_2. Solving for x_2 gives

$$x_2 = x_1 + \Delta x.$$

For a function $y = f(x)$, the symbol Δy represents a change in y:

$$\Delta y = f(x_2) - f(x_1).$$

Replacing x_2 with $x_1 + \Delta x$ gives

$$\Delta y = f(x_1 + \Delta x) - f(x_1).$$

If we used Δx instead of h, the derivative of a function f at x_1 could be defined as

$$\frac{dy}{dx} = \lim_{\Delta x \to 0} \frac{\Delta y}{\Delta x}.$$

If the derivative exists, then

$$\frac{dy}{dx} \approx \frac{\Delta y}{\Delta x}$$

as long as Δx is close to 0. Multiplying both sides by Δx (which we assume is not 0) gives

$$\Delta y \approx \frac{dy}{dx} \cdot \Delta x.$$

Up until now we have used dy/dx as a single symbol representing the derivative of y with respect to x. In this section we introduce separate meanings for dy and dx, in such a way that their quotient, when $dx \neq 0$, is the derivative of y with respect to x. We use these meanings of dy and of dx to find an approximate value of Δy.

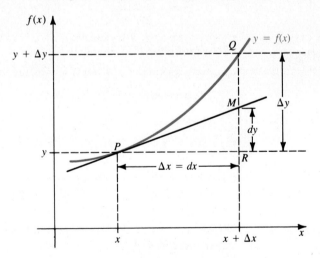

FIGURE 42

To define dy and dx, look at Figure 42, which shows the graph of a function $y = f(x)$. The tangent line to the graph has been drawn at the point P. Let Δx be any nonzero real number (in practical problems, Δx is a small number) and locate the point $x + \Delta x$ on the x-axis. Draw a vertical line through $x + \Delta x$. Let this vertical line cut the tangent line at M and the graph of the function at Q.

Define the new symbol dx to be the same as Δx. Define the new symbol dy to equal the length MR. The slope of PM is $f'(x)$. By the definition of slope, the slope of PM is also dy/dx, so that

$$f'(x) = \frac{dy}{dx},$$

or $\qquad\qquad\qquad\qquad\qquad dy = f'(x)\,dx.$

Let us summarize the definitions of the symbols dy and dx.

Differentials

> For a function $y = f(x)$ whose derivative exists,
> the **differential** of x, written dx, is an arbitrary real number (usually small);
> the **differential** of y, written dy, is the product of $f'(x)$ and dx, or
> $$dy = f'(x)\,dx.$$

The usefulness of the differential is suggested by Figure 42. As dx approaches 0, the value of dy gets closer and closer to that of Δy, so that for small nonzero values of dx

$$dy \approx \Delta y,$$

or $\qquad\qquad\qquad\qquad\qquad \Delta y \approx f'(x)\,dx.$

EXAMPLE 1

Find dy for the following functions.

(a) $y = 6x^2$

The derivative is $y' = 12x$, so that

$$dy = 12x\,dx.$$

(b)   If $y = 8x^{-3/4}$, then $dy = -6x^{-7/4}\,dx$.

(c)   If $f(x) = \dfrac{2 + x}{2 - x}$, then $dy = \dfrac{4}{(2 - x)^2}\,dx$. ∎

EXAMPLE 2

Suppose $y = 5x - x^2 + 4$. Find dy for the following values of x and dx.

(a) $x = -3,\ dx = .05$

First, by definition

$$dy = (5 - 2x)\,dx.$$

If $x = -3$ and $dx = .05$, then

$$dy = (5 - 2(-3))(.05) = 11(.05) = .55.$$

(b) $x = 0,\ dx = -.004$

$$dy = (5 - 2 \cdot 0)(-.004) = 5(-.004) = -.02. \quad \blacksquare$$

Differential Approximation   As we know,

$$\Delta y = f(x + \Delta x) - f(x).$$

For small nonzero values of Δx, we know that $\Delta y \approx dy$, so that

$$dy \approx f(x + \Delta x) - f(x),$$

or

$$f(x) + dy \approx f(x + \Delta x). \tag{1}$$

Since $dy = f'(x)\,dx$, we have the following result.

Differential Approximation

> Let f be a function whose derivative exists. For small nonzero values of Δx,
> $$dy \approx \Delta y,$$
> and $\qquad f(x + \Delta x) \approx f(x) + dy = f(x) + f'(x)\,dx.$

Differential approximations can be used to estimate various radicals, as shown by the next example.

EXAMPLE 3

Approximate $\sqrt{38}$.

To approximate $\sqrt{38}$, use the function $y = f(x) = \sqrt{x} = x^{1/2}$. The differential dy is $f'(x)\,dx$, or

$$dy = \frac{1}{2}x^{-1/2}\,dx.$$

From the box above,

$$f(x + \Delta x) \approx f(x) + f'(x)\,dx,$$

or, since $f(x) = x^{1/2}$,

$$(x + \Delta x)^{1/2} \approx x^{1/2} + \frac{1}{2}x^{-1/2}\,dx.$$

The closest perfect square to 38 is 36. Let $x = 36$ and $dx = \Delta x = 38 - 36 = 2$. This gives

$$\sqrt{38} = (36 + 2)^{1/2} \approx 36^{1/2} + \frac{1}{2}(36^{-1/2})(2) = 6 + \frac{1}{6} = 6.167.$$

From a square root table or calculator, $\sqrt{38} \approx 6.164$, so that the approximation is fairly close. $\blacksquare$

While calculators have made this particular application of differential approximations less important than in the past, the approach shown by this example does have applications in other areas.

EXAMPLE 4

A tumor is in the shape of a cone of height 3 centimeters. Find the approximate increase in the volume of the tumor if the radius of the base increases from 1 cm to 1.1 cm.

The volume of a cone is given by $V = \frac{1}{3}\pi r^2 h$. In this example, $h = 3$, so that

$$V = \frac{1}{3}\pi r^2 \cdot 3 = \pi r^2.$$

The increase in volume is approximated by dV, where

$$dV = 2\pi r \cdot dr.$$

Since $r = 1$ and $dr = 1.1 - 1 = .1$,

$$dV = 2\pi(1)(.1) \approx 2(3.14)(1)(.1) = .628.$$

The approximate increase in volume is .628 cubic centimeters. ∎

EXAMPLE 5

The mathematical model

$$y = A(x) = \frac{-7}{480}x^3 + \frac{127}{120}x, \qquad 0 \le x < 9,$$

gives the approximate alcohol concentration (in tenths of a percent) in an average person's bloodstream x hours after drinking 8 ounces of 100-proof whiskey.

(a)   Approximate the change in y as x changes from 3 to 3.5. Use dy as an approximation of Δy. Here

$$dy = \left(\frac{-7}{160}x^2 + \frac{127}{120}\right)dx.$$

In this example, $x = 3$ and $dx = \Delta x = 3.5 - 3 = .5$. Substitution gives

$$\Delta y \approx dy = \left(\frac{-7}{160} \cdot 3^2 + \frac{127}{120}\right)(.5) \approx .33,$$

so $\Delta y \approx .33$. This means that the alcohol concentration increases by about .33 tenths of a percent as x changes from 3 hours to 3.5 hours. (The *exact* increase, found by calculating $A(3.5) - A(3)$, is .30 tenths of a percent.)

(b)   Approximate the change in y as x changes from 6 to 6.25 hours.

Let $x = 6$ and $dx = 6.25 - 6 = .25$.

$$\Delta y \approx dy = \left(-\frac{7}{160} \cdot 6^2 + \frac{127}{120}\right)(.25) \approx -.13$$

The minus sign shows that alcohol concentration decreases by .13 tenths of a percent as x changes from 6 to 6.25 hours. ∎

Our final example shows how differentials are used to estimate errors that might enter into measurements of a physical quantity.

EXAMPLE 6

In a precision manufacturing process, ball bearings must be made with a radius of .6 mm, with a maximum error in the radius of ± .015 mm. Estimate the maximum error in the volume of the ball bearing.

The formula for the volume of a sphere is

$$V = \frac{4}{3}\pi r^3.$$

If an error of Δr is made in measuring the radius of the sphere, the maximum error in the volume is

$$\Delta V = \frac{4}{3}\pi(r + \Delta r)^3 - \frac{4}{3}\pi r^3.$$

We can approximate ΔV with dV, where

$$dV = 4\pi r^2 dr.$$

Replacing r with .6 and $dr = \Delta r$ with ± .015 gives

$$dV = 4\pi(.6)^2(\pm.015) \approx \pm.0679.$$

The maximum error in the volume is about .0679 cu mm. ∎

11.8 EXERCISES

Find dy for the functions in Exercises 1–12.

1. $y = 6x^2$

2. $y = -8x^4$

3. $y = 7x^2 - 9x + 6$

4. $y = -3x^3 + 2x^2$

5. $y = 2\sqrt{x}$

6. $y = 8\sqrt{2x - 1}$

7. $y = \dfrac{8x - 2}{x - 3}$

8. $y = \dfrac{-4x + 7}{3x - 1}$

9. $y = x^2\left(x - \dfrac{1}{x} + 2\right)$

10. $y = -x^3\left(2 + \dfrac{3}{x^2} - \dfrac{5}{x}\right)$

11. $y = \left(2 - \dfrac{3}{x}\right)\left(1 + \dfrac{1}{x}\right)$

12. $y = \left(9 - \dfrac{2}{x^2}\right)\left(3 + \dfrac{1}{x}\right)$

For the functions in Exercises 13–24, find dy for the given values of x and Δx.

13. $y = 2x^2 - 5x$; $x = -2, \Delta x = .2$

14. $y = x^2 - 3x$; $x = 3, \Delta x = .1$

15. $y = x^3 - 2x^2 + 3$; $x = 1, \Delta x = -.1$

16. $y = 2x^3 + x^2 - 4x$; $x = 2, \Delta x = -.2$

17. $y = \sqrt{3x}$; $x = 1, \Delta x = .15$

18. $y = \sqrt{4x - 1}$; $x = 5, \Delta x = .08$

19. $y = \dfrac{2x - 5}{x + 1}$; $x = 2, \Delta x = -.03$

20. $y = \dfrac{6x - 3}{2x + 1}$; $x = 3, \Delta x = -.04$

21. $y = -6\left(2 - \dfrac{1}{x^2}\right)$; $x = -1, \Delta x = .02$

22. $y = 9\left(3 + \dfrac{1}{x^4}\right)$; $x = -2, \Delta x = -.015$

23. $y = \dfrac{1 + x}{\sqrt{x}}$; $x = 9, \Delta x = -.03$

24. $y = \dfrac{2 - 5x}{\sqrt{x + 1}}$; $x = 3, \Delta x = .02$

Use differentials to find approximations for the numbers in Exercises 25–40.

25. $\sqrt{10}$

26. $\sqrt{26}$

27. $\sqrt{15}$

28. $\sqrt{63}$

29. $\sqrt{123}$

30. $\sqrt{146}$

31. $\sqrt[3]{7}$

32. $\sqrt[3]{25}$

33. $\sqrt[3]{65}$

34. $\sqrt[3]{127}$

35. $\sqrt[4]{17}$

36. $\sqrt[4]{83}$

37. $\sqrt{4.02}$

38. $\sqrt{16.08}$

39. $\sqrt[3]{7.9}$

40. $\sqrt[3]{124.75}$

41. A spherical beachball is being inflated. Find the approximate change in volume if the radius increases from 4 cm to 4.2 cm.

42. A spherical snowball is melting; find the approximate change in volume if the radius decreases from 3 cm to 2.8 cm.

43. An oil slick is in the shape of a circle. Find the approximate increase in the area of the slick if its radius increases from 1.2 miles to 1.4 miles.

44. The shape of a colony of bacteria on a Petri dish is circular. Find the approximate increase in its area if the radius increases from 20 mm to 22 mm.

45. A cube 4 inches on an edge is given a protective coating .1 inch thick. About how much coating should a production manager order for 1000 such cubes?

46. Beach balls 1 foot in diameter have a thickness of .03 inch. How much material would be needed to make 5000 beach balls?

47. The radius of a blood vessel is 17 millimeters. A drug causes the radius to change to 16 millimeters. Find the approximate change in the area of a cross section of the vessel.

48. A tumor is approximately spherical in shape. If the radius of the tumor changes from 14 millimeters to 16 millimeters, find the approximate change in volume.

49. The edge of a square is measured as 3.45 inches with a possible error of $\pm.002$ inches. Estimate the maximum error in the area of the square.

50. The radius of a circle is measured as 4.87 inches, with a possible error of $\pm.040$ inches. Estimate the maximum error in the area of the circle.

51. A sphere has a radius of 5.81 inches with a possible error of $\pm.003$ inches. Estimate the maximum error in the volume of the sphere.

52. A cone has a known height of 7.284 inches. The radius of the base is measured as 1.09 inches, with a possible error of $\pm.007$ inch. Estimate the maximum error in the volume of the cone.

Use differential approximations in Exercises 53–56.

53. The demand in thousands of pounds at a price of x dollars for grass seed is
$$d(x) = -5x^3 - 2x^2 + 1500.$$
Approximate the change in demand as the price changes from
   (a) $2 to $2.50   (b) $6 to $6.30.

54. The average cost to manufacture x dozen marking pencils is
$$A(x) = .04x^3 + .1x^2 + .5x + 6.$$
Approximate the change in the average cost as x changes from
   (a) 3 to 4   (b) 5 to 6.

55. The concentration of a certain drug in the blood stream x hours after being administered is approximately
$$C(x) = \frac{5x}{9 + x^2}.$$
Approximate the change in concentration as x changes from
   (a) 1 to 1.5   (b) 2 to 2.25

56. The population in millions of bacteria in a certain culture x hours after an experimental nutrient is introduced into the culture is

$$P(x) = \frac{25x}{8 + x^2}.$$

Approximate the change in P as x changes from
(a) 2 to 2.5   (b) 3 to 3.25.

KEY WORDS

increasing function	absolute minimum	second derivative test
decreasing function	extreme value theorem	implicit differentiation
relative maximum	concavity	explicit differentiation
relative minimum	second derivative	related rates
critical point	acceleration	differentials
first derivative test	concave upward and downward	differential
absolute maximum	point of inflection	approximation

Chapter 11   REVIEW EXERCISES

In Exercises 1–6, find the largest open intervals where the functions are increasing or decreasing.

1. $f(x) = x^2 - 5x + 3$

2. $f(x) = -2x^2 - 3x + 4$

3. $f(x) = -x^3 - 5x^2 + 8x - 6$

4. $f(x) = 4x^3 + 3x^2 - 18x + 1$

5. $f(x) = \frac{6}{x - 4}$

6. $f(x) = \frac{5}{2x + 1}$

In Exercises 7–18, find the location and value of all relative maxima and minima.

7. $f(x) = -x^2 + 4x - 8$

8. $f(x) = x^2 - 6x + 4$

9. $f(x) = 2x^2 - 8x + 1$

10. $f(x) = -3x^2 + 2x - 5$

11. $f(x) = 2x^3 + 3x^2 - 36x + 20$

12. $f(x) = 2x^3 + 3x^2 - 12x + 5$

13. $f(x) = -2x^3 - \frac{1}{2}x^2 + x - 3$

14. $f(x) = -\frac{4}{3}x^3 + x^2 + 30x - 7$

15. $f(x) = x^4 - \frac{4}{3}x^3 - 4x^2 + 1$

16. $f(x) = -\frac{2}{3}x^3 + \frac{9}{2}x^2 + 5x + 1$

17. $f(x) = \frac{x - 1}{2x + 1}$

18. $f(x) = \frac{2x - 5}{x + 3}$

In Exercises 19–26, find the largest open intervals where the functions are concave upward or concave downward. Find the location of any points of inflection. Graph each function.

19. $f(x) = -4x^3 - x^2 + 4x + 5$

20. $f(x) = x^3 + \frac{5}{2}x^2 - 2x - 3$

21. $f(x) = x^4 + 2x^2$

22. $f(x) = 6x^3 - x^4$

23. $f(x) = \frac{x^2 + 4}{x}$

24. $f(x) = x + \frac{8}{x}$

25. $f(x) = \frac{2x}{3 - x}$

26. $f(x) = \frac{-4x}{1 + 2x}$

Find the second derivative of the functions in Exercises 27–32, then find $f''(1)$ and $f''(-3)$.

27. $f(x) = 3x^4 - 5x^2 - 11x$

28. $f(x) = 9x^3 + \dfrac{1}{x}$

29. $f(x) = \dfrac{5x - 1}{2x + 3}$

30. $f(x) = \dfrac{4 - 3x}{x + 1}$

31. $f(t) = \sqrt{t^2 + 1}$

32. $f(t) = -\sqrt{5 - t^2}$

In Exercises 33–36, find the location of all absolute maxima and minima on the given intervals.

33. $f(x) = -x^2 + 5x + 1; [1, 4]$

34. $f(x) = 4x^2 - 8x - 3; [-1, 2]$

35. $f(x) = x^3 + 2x^2 - 15x + 3; [-4, 2]$

36. $f(x) = -2x^3 - 2x^2 + 2x - 1; [-3, 1]$

37. Find two numbers whose sum is 25 and whose product is a maximum.

38. Find x and y such that $x = 2 + y$, and xy^2 is minimized.

39. Suppose the profit from a product is $P(x) = 16 + 4x - x^2$, where x is the price in dollars.

    (a) At what price will the maximum profit occur?

    (b) What is the maximum profit?

40. The total profit in dollars from the sale of x hundred boxes of candy is given by
$$P(x) = -x^3 + 10x^2 - 12x + 106.$$

    (a) Find the number of boxes of candy that should be sold in order to produce maximum profit.

    (b) Find the maximum profit.

41. The city park department is planning an enclosed play area in a new park. One side of the area will be against an existing building, with no fence needed there. Find the dimensions of the maximum rectangular area that can be made with 900 meters of fence.

42. A company plans to package its product in a cylinder which is open at one end. The cylinder is to have a volume of 27π cubic inches. What radius should the circular bottom of the cylinder have to minimize the cost of the material? (Hint: The volume of a circular cylinder is $\pi r^2 h$ where r is the radius of the circular base and h is the height; the surface area of the open cylinder is $2\pi rh + \pi r^2$.)

43. A box is to be built with a square base and no top. The volume is to be 32 cubic meters. Find the dimensions of the box with minimum surface area.

44. A closed cylindrical tin can is to have a volume of 54π cubic inches. Find the radius and height of the can if it is to have minimum surface area.

45. A very large camera store sells 320,000 rolls of film annually. It costs 10¢ to store one roll for one year and $10 to place a reorder. Find the number of orders that should be placed annually.

46. A store sells 980,000 cases of a product annually. It costs $2 to store one case for a year and $20 to place a reorder. Find the number of orders that should be placed annually.

47. A supermarket chain sells 128,000 cases of soft drink annually. It costs $1 to store a case for one year and $10 to place a reorder. Find the number of orders that should be placed annually.

48. In one year, a health food chain sells 240,000 cases of vitamins. It costs $2 to store a case for one year and $15 to place a reorder. Find the number of orders that should be placed annually.

Find dy/dx for the functions in Exercises 49–56.

49. $x^2y^3 + 4xy = 2$

50. $\dfrac{x}{y} - 4y = 3x$

51. $9\sqrt{x} + 4y^3 = \dfrac{2}{x}$

52. $2\sqrt{y - 1} = 8x^{2/3}$

53. $\dfrac{x + 2y}{x - 3y} = y^{1/2}$

54. $\dfrac{6 + 5x}{2 - 3y} = \dfrac{1}{5x}$

55. $(4y^2 - 3x)^{2/3} = 6x$

56. $(8x + y^{1/2})^3 = 9y^2$

57. Find the equation of the tangent to the graph of $\sqrt{2x} - 4yx = -22$ at the point $(2, 3)$.

58. The graph of $x^2 + y^2 = 25$ is a circle of radius 5 with center at the origin. Find the equation of the tangent lines when $x = -3$. Graph the circle and the tangent lines.

Find dy/dt in Exercises 59–62.

59. $y = 8x^3 - 7x^2$, $dx/dt = 4$, $x = 2$

60. $y = \dfrac{9 - 4x}{3 + 2x}$, $dx/dt = -1$, $x = -3$

61. $y = \dfrac{1 + \sqrt{x}}{1 - \sqrt{x}}$, $dx/dt = -4$, $x = 4$

62. $\dfrac{x^2 + 5y}{x - 2y} = 2$, $dx/dt = 1$, $x = 2$, $y = 0$

63. A circle of pollution is spreading from a broken underwater waste disposal pipe, with the radius increasing at the rate of 4 feet per minute. Find the rate of change of the area of the circle when the radius is 7 feet.

64. A 50-foot ladder is placed against a building. The top of the ladder is sliding down the building at the rate of 2 feet per minute. Find the rate at which the base of the ladder is slipping away from the building at the instant that the base is 30 feet from the building.

65. A large weather balloon is being inflated at the rate of 1.2 cubic feet of air per minute. Find the rate of change of the radius when the radius is 1.2 feet.

66. A water trough 2 feet across, 4 feet long, and 1 foot deep has ends in the shape of isosceles triangles. (See the figure.) It is being filled with 3.5 cubic feet of water per minute. Find the rate at which the depth of water in the tank is changing when the water is 1/3 foot deep.

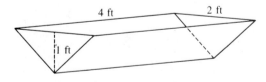

4 ft   2 ft

1 ft

Find dy in Exercises 67–70.

67. $y = 8x^3 - 2x^2$

68. $y = 4(x^2 - 1)^3$

69. $y = \dfrac{6 - 5x}{2 + x}$

70. $y = \sqrt{9 + x^3}$

Find the value of dy in Exercises 71 and 72.

71. $y = 8 - x^2 + x^3$, $x = -1$, $\Delta x = .02$

72. $y = \dfrac{3x - 7}{2x + 1}$, $x = 2$, $\Delta x = .003$

Use differentials to approximate the following numbers.

73. $\sqrt{120}$

74. $\sqrt[3]{27.5}$

75. Approximate the volume of coating on a sphere of radius 4 inches if the coating is .02 inch thick.

76. A square has an edge of 9.2 inches, with a possible error in the measurement of $\pm .04$ inch. Estimate the possible error in the area of the square.

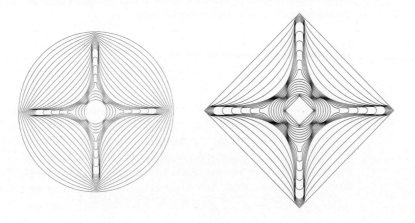

EXPONENTIAL AND LOGARITHMIC FUNCTIONS

Karl Gerstner. Color-Form continuum drawings.

593

Exponential functions are probably the single most important type of function used in practical applications. Exponential functions, and the closely related logarithmic functions, are used to describe growth and decay, which are important ideas in management, social science, and biology.

12.1   Exponential Functions

In earlier chapters we worked with functions involving terms like x^2, $(2x + 1)^3$, or $x^{3/4}$, where the variable or variable expression is the base of an exponential expression with a constant exponent. In an exponential function, the variable is in the exponent and the base is a constant.

In this chapter we first discuss the properties and graphs of these important functions. Then we show how to differentiate them, and in the last two sections we look at some of the many applications involving such functions.

Exponential

Function

An **exponential function** with base a is defined as

$$f(x) = a^x, \qquad a > 0 \quad \text{and} \quad a \neq 1.$$

(If $a = 1$, the function is the constant function $f(x) = 1$.)

To graph the exponential function $y = 2^x$, make a table of values of x and y, as shown in Figure 1. Plot these points and draw a smooth curve through them, to get the graph shown in Figure 1. The graph approaches the negative x-axis but will never actually touch it, since y cannot be 0. This makes the x-axis a horizontal asymptote. The graph suggests that the domain is the set of all real numbers, and the range is the set of all positive real numbers. This graph is typical of the graphs of exponential functions of the form $y = a^x$, where $a > 1$.

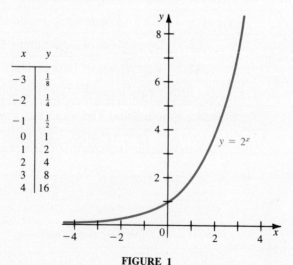

x	y
-3	$\frac{1}{8}$
-2	$\frac{1}{4}$
-1	$\frac{1}{2}$
0	1
1	2
2	4
3	8
4	16

$y = 2^x$

FIGURE 1

EXAMPLE 1

Graph $y = 2^{-x}$.

By the properties of exponents,

$$2^{-x} = \frac{1}{2^x} = \left(\frac{1}{2}\right)^x.$$

Construct a table of values and draw a smooth curve through the resulting points (see Figure 2). This graph is typical of the graphs of exponential functions of the form $y = a^x$ where $0 < a < 1$. Again the domain includes all real numbers and the range includes all positive numbers. ■

In the definition of an exponential function, notice that the base a is restricted to positive values, with negative or zero bases not allowed. For example, if we tried to graph $y = (-4)^x$, the domain could not include such numbers as $x = 1/2$ or $x = 1/4$. The resulting graph would at best be a series of separate points having little practical use.

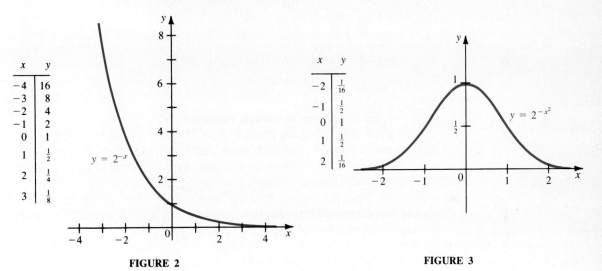

x	y
-4	16
-3	8
-2	4
-1	2
0	1
1	$\frac{1}{2}$
2	$\frac{1}{4}$
3	$\frac{1}{8}$

$y = 2^{-x}$

FIGURE 2

x	y
-2	$\frac{1}{16}$
-1	$\frac{1}{2}$
0	1
1	$\frac{1}{2}$
2	$\frac{1}{16}$

$y = 2^{-x^2}$

FIGURE 3

EXAMPLE 2

Graph $y = 2^{-x^2}$.

Plotting several values of x and y gives the graph in Figure 3. Both the negative sign and the fact that x is squared affect the shape of the graph, with the final result looking quite different from the typical graphs of exponential functions in Figures 1 and 2. Graphs such as this are important in probability, where the normal curve has an equation similar to the one in this example. ■

Figure 1 and Figure 2, typical graphs of exponential functions, suggest that a given value of x leads to exactly one value of a^x. Because of this, an equation with a variable in the exponent, called an **exponential equation,** can often be solved using the following property.

If $a \neq 1$ and $a^x = a^y$, then $x = y$.

(Both bases must be the same.) The value $a = 1$ is excluded since $1^2 = 1^3$, for example, even though $2 \neq 3$. To solve $2^{3x} = 2^7$ using this property, work as follows:

$$2^{3x} = 2^7$$
$$3x = 7$$
$$x = \frac{7}{3}.$$

EXAMPLE 3

(a) Solve $9^x = 27$.

First rewrite both sides of the equation so the bases are the same. Since $9 = 3^2$ and $27 = 3^3$,

$$(3^2)^x = 3^3$$
$$3^{2x} = 3^3$$
$$2x = 3$$
$$x = \frac{3}{2}.$$

(b) Solve $32^{2x-1} = 128^{x+3}$

Since the bases must be the same, write 32 as 2^5 and 128 as 2^7, giving

$$32^{2x-1} = 128^{x+3}$$
$$(2^5)^{2x-1} = (2^7)^{x+3}$$
$$2^{10x-5} = 2^{7x+21}.$$

Now use the property above to get

$$10x - 5 = 7x + 21$$
$$3x = 26$$
$$x = \frac{26}{3}.$$

Verify this solution in the original equation. ▪

The Number e   Perhaps the single most useful base for an exponential function is the number e, an irrational number that occurs often in practical applications. To see how the number e comes up in an application, let us begin with the formula for compound interest (interest paid on both principal and interest). If P dollars is deposited in an account paying a rate of interest i compounded m times per year, the account will contain

$$P\left(1 + \frac{i}{m}\right)^{nm}$$

dollars after n years. (We shall derive this formula later in this chapter.)

For example, suppose $1000 is deposited into an account paying 8% per year compounded quarterly, or four times a year. After 10 years the account will contain

$$P\left(1 + \frac{i}{m}\right)^{nm} = 1000\left(1 + \frac{.08}{4}\right)^{10(4)} = 1000(1 + .02)^{40} = 1000(1.02)^{40}$$

dollars. The number $(1.02)^{40}$ can be found in financial tables, or by using a calculator with a y^x key. To five decimal places, $(1.02)^{40} = 2.20804$. The amount on deposit after 10 years is

$$1000(1.02)^{40} = 1000(2.20804) = 2208.04,$$

or $2208.04.

Suppose now that a lucky investment produces annual interest of 100%, so that $i = 1.00 = 1$. Suppose also that you can deposit only $1 at this rate, and for only one year. Then $P = 1$ and $n = 1$. Substituting these values into the formula for compound interest gives

$$P\left(1 + \frac{i}{m}\right)^{nm} = 1\left(1 + \frac{1}{m}\right)^{1(m)} = \left(1 + \frac{1}{m}\right)^{m}.$$

As interest is compounded more and more often, m gets larger and the value of this expression will increase. For example, if $m = 1$ (interest is compounded annually),

$$\left(1 + \frac{1}{m}\right)^{m} = \left(1 + \frac{1}{1}\right)^{1} = 2^1 = 2,$$

so that your $1 becomes $2 in one year. Using a calculator with a y^x key, we get the results shown in the following table for larger and larger values of m. These results have been rounded to five decimal places.

m	$\left(1 + \dfrac{1}{m}\right)^{m}$
1	2
2	2.25
5	2.48832
10	2.59374
25	2.66584
50	2.69159
100	2.70481
500	2.71557
1000	2.71692
10,000	2.71815
1,000,000	2.71828

The table suggests that as m increases, the value of $(1 + 1/m)^{m}$ gets closer and closer to some fixed number. It turns out that this is indeed the case. This fixed number is called e.

Definition of *e*

$$\lim_{m \to \infty} \left(1 + \frac{1}{m}\right)^m = e \approx 2.718281828.$$

(This last approximation gives the value of *e* to nine decimal places.) A table in this book gives various powers of *e*. Also, some calculators give values of e^x. In Figure 4, the functions $y = 2^x$, $y = e^x$, and $y = 3^x$ are graphed for comparison.

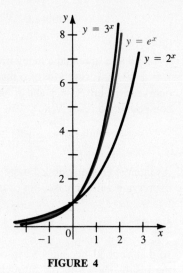

FIGURE 4

Any exponential function $y = a^x$ can be written as an exponential function with base *e*. For example, there exists a real number *k* such that

$$2 = e^k.$$

Raising both sides to the power *x* gives

$$2^x = e^{kx},$$

so that powers of 2 can be found by evaluating appropriate powers of *e*. To find the necessary number *k*, use the table. Look down the e^x column for the number closest to 2. You should find that

$$e^{.70} \approx 2.01375,$$

so that $k \approx .70$ and

$$2^x = e^{kx} \approx e^{.70x}.$$

Better accuracy could be obtained with a calculator or a more complete table. In Section 4 of this chapter we will see why this change of base may be useful. A general statement can be drawn from this example.

For every positive real number a with $a \neq 1$, there is a real number k such that
$$a^x = e^{kx}.$$

EXAMPLE 4

Use the table to approximate the value of each exponential.

(a) $e^{1.5}$

Use the first two columns of the table to find
$$e^{1.5} \approx 4.48168.$$

(b) $e^{-3} \approx 0.04978$

Look up 3 in the first column and read across to find e^{-3} in the third column.

(c) $2^{3.57}$

Use the result found above,
$$2^x \approx e^{.70x}$$
with $x = 3.57$. Then
$$2^{3.57} \approx e^{(.70)(3.57)} = e^{2.499} \approx e^{2.5} \approx 12.18248.$$

(d) $5^{-1.38}$

Let $5^x = e^{kx}$ so that $5 = e^k$. From the table, $k \approx 1.60$ and $5^x \approx e^{1.60x}$. Then, with a calculator
$$5^{-1.38} \approx e^{1.60(-1.38)} \approx e^{-2.208} \approx .10992.$$
Using the table, approximate $e^{-2.208}$ as $e^{-2.2} \approx .11080.$ ∎

As we have said, exponential functions have many practical applications. In situations which involve growth or decay of a population, the size of the population at a given time t often is determined by an exponential function of t.

EXAMPLE 5

The oxygen consumption of yearling salmon (in appropriate units) increases exponentially with speed of swimming according to the function
$$f(x) = 100(3)^{.6x},$$
where x is the speed in feet per second. Find each of the following.

(a) $f(0)$

Substitute 0 for x:
$$f(0) = 100(3)^{(.6)(0)} = 100(3)^0$$
$$= 100 \cdot 1 = 100.$$

When the fish are still (their speed is 0) their oxygen consumption is 100 units.

(b) $f(5)$

Replace x with 5.

$$f(5) = 100(3)^{(.6)(5)} = 100(3)^3 = 2700$$

A speed of 5 feet per second increases the oxygen consumption to 2700 units.

(c) $f(2)$

Find $f(2)$ as follows.

$$f(2) = 100(3)^{(.6)(2)} = 100(3)^{1.2}.$$

Use the table to find $3^x \approx e^{1.1x}$, so that $3^{1.2} \approx e^{1.32}$. The closest entry in the table is for $e^{1.30}$. Using that entry,

$$3^{1.2} \approx e^{1.3} \approx 3.66929.$$

Now find $f(2)$.

$$f(2) = 100(3)^{1.2} \approx 100(3.7) = 370$$

At a speed of 2 feet per second, the oxygen consumption is about 370 units. ∎

12.1 EXERCISES

Graph the exponential functions in Exercises 1–18. (In Exercises 15–17, the domain is $x \geq 0$.)

1. $y = 3^x$

2. $y = 4^x$

3. $y = 3^{-x}$

4. $y = 4^{-x}$

5. $y = \left(\dfrac{1}{4}\right)^x$

6. $y = \left(\dfrac{1}{3}\right)^x$

7. $y = \left(\dfrac{1}{3}\right)^{-x}$

8. $y = \left(\dfrac{1}{4}\right)^{-x}$

9. $y = 3^{2x}$

10. $y = 3^{-2x}$

11. $y = 2^{x^2}$

12. $y = 3^{x^2}$

13. $y = e^{-x^2}$

14. $y = e^{x+1}$

15. $y = 10 - 5e^{-x}$

16. $y = 100 - 80e^{-x}$

17. $y = 25 - 25e^{-.5x}$

18. $y = 40 - 40e^{-.2x}$

Use a calculator, if necessary, to find enough ordered pairs to graph the functions in Exercises 19–22.

19. $y = x \cdot 2^x$

20. $y = x^2 \cdot 2^x$

21. $y = \dfrac{e^x - e^{-x}}{2}$

22. $y = \dfrac{e^x + e^{-x}}{2}$

Solve the equations in Exercises 23–46.

23. $2^x = \dfrac{1}{8}$

24. $4^x = 64$

25. $e^x = e^2$

26. $e^x = \dfrac{1}{e^2}$

27. $4^x = 8$

28. $25^x = 125$

29. $16^x = 64$

30. $\left(\dfrac{1}{8}\right)^x = 8$

31. $\left(\dfrac{3}{4}\right)^x = \dfrac{16}{9}$

32. $5^{-2x} = \dfrac{1}{25}$

33. $3^{x-1} = 9$

34. $16^{-x+1} = 8$

35. $25^{-2x} = 3125$

36. $16^{x+2} = 64^{2x-1}$

37. $(e^4)^{-2x} = e^{-x+1}$

38. $e^{-x} = (e^2)^{x+3}$

39. $2^{|x|} = 16$

40. $5^{-|x|} = \dfrac{1}{25}$

41. $\left(\dfrac{1}{3}\right)^{|x-4|} = \dfrac{1}{81}$

42. $\left(\dfrac{3}{2}\right)^{|x+5|} = \dfrac{27}{8}$

43. $2^{x^2-4x} = \dfrac{1}{16}$

44. $5^{x^2+x} = 1$

45. $8^{x^2} = 2^{5x}$

46. $9^x = 3^{x^2}$

Approximate the value of the expressions in Exercises 47–54.

47. $e^{2.5}$

48. $e^{-0.04}$

49. $e^{-0.13}$

50. $e^{-2.8}$

51. $6^{0.5}$

52. $4^{3.2}$

53. $1.1^{-2.4}$

54. $4.5^{-0.8}$

Generally speaking, the larger an organism, the greater its complexity (as measured by counting the number of different types of cells present). The figure shows an estimate of the maximum number of cells (or the largest volume) in various organisms plotted against the number of types of cells found in those organisms.*

55. Use the graph to estimate the maximum number of cells and the corresponding volume for each of the following organisms.

    (a) whale   **(b)** sponge   **(c)** green alga

56. From the graph estimate the number of cell types in each of the following organisms.

    (a) mushroom   **(b)** kelp   **(c)** sequoia

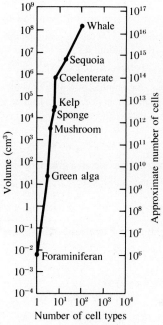

57. If \$1 is deposited into an account paying 12% per year compounded annually, then after t years the account will contain

$$y = (1 + .12)^t = (1.12)^t$$

dollars.

    (a) Use a calculator to help you complete the following table.

t	0	1	2	3	4	5	6	7	8	9	10
y	1					1.76					3.11

    (b) Graph $y = (1.12)^t$.

*From *On Size and Life* by Thomas A. McMahon and John Tyler Bonner. Copyright © 1983 by Thomas A. McMahon and John Tyler Bonner. Reprinted by permission of W. H. Freeman and Company.

58. If money loses value at the rate of 8% per year, the value of $1 in t years is given by

$$y = (1 - .08)^t \doteq (.92)^t.$$

(a) Use a calculator to help complete the following table.

t	0	1	2	3	4	5	6	7	8	9	10
y	1					.66					.43

(b) Graph $y = (.92)^t$.

59. Use the results of Exercise 58(a) to answer the following questions.

(a) Suppose a house costs $65,000 today. Estimate the cost of a similar house in 10 years. (Hint: solve the equation $.43x = \$65,000$.)

(b) Find the cost of a $20 textbook in 8 years.

60. Under certain conditions, the number of individuals of a species that is newly introduced into an area can double every year. That is, if t represents the number of years since the species was introduced into the area, and y represents the number of individuals, then

$$y = 6 \cdot 2^t$$

if 6 animals were introduced into the area originally.

(a) Complete the following table.

t	0	1	2	3	4	5	6	7	8	9	10
y	6					192					6144

(b) Graph $y = 6 \cdot 2^t$.

61. Suppose the population of a city is

$$P(t) = 1,000,000(2^{.2t}),$$

where t represents time measured in years. Find each of the following values.

(a) $P(0)$ (b) $P\left(\dfrac{5}{2}\right)$ (c) $P(5)$ (d) $P(10)$ (e) Graph $P(t)$.

62. Suppose the quantity in grams of a radioactive substance present at time t is

$$Q(t) = 500(3^{-.5t}),$$

where t is measured in months. Find the quantity present at each of the following times.

(a) $t = 0$ (b) $t = 2$ (c) $t = 4$ (d) $t = 10$ (e) Graph $Q(t)$.

63. *Escherichia coli* is a strain of bacteria that occurs naturally in many different situations. Under certain conditions, the number of these bacteria present in a colony is given by

$$E(t) = E_0 \cdot 2^{t/30},$$

where $E(t)$ is the number of bacteria present t minutes after the beginning of an experiment, and E_0 is the number present when $t = 0$. Let $E_0 = 1,000,000$, and use a calculator with a y^x key to find the number of bacteria at the following times.

(a) $t = 5$ (b) $t = 10$ (c) $t = 15$ (d) $t = 20$

(e) $t = 30$ (f) $t = 60$ (g) $t = 90$ (h) $t = 120$

64. A person learning certain skills involving repetition tends to learn quickly at first. Then learning tapers off and approaches some upper limit. Suppose the number of symbols per minute a keypunch operator can produce is given by

$$p(t) = 250 - 120(2.8)^{-.5t}$$

where t is the number of months the operator has been in training. Find each of the following.

(a) $p(2)$ (b) $p(4)$

(c) $p(10)$ (d) Graph $p(t)$.

65. Suppose the domain of $y = 2^x$ is restricted to include only rational values of x (which are the only values discussed prior to this section.) Describe in words the resulting graph.

66. In our definition of exponential function, we ruled out negative values of a. However, in a textbook on mathematical economics, published by a well-known publisher, the author obtained a "graph" of $y = (-2)^x$ by plotting the following points and drawing a smooth curve through them.

x	-4	-3	-2	-1	0	1	2	3
y	1/16	$-1/8$	1/4	$-1/2$	1	-2	4	-8

The graph oscillates very neatly from positive to negative values of y. Comment on this approach. (This example shows the dangers of point plotting when drawing graphs.)

12.2   Logarithmic Functions

In the previous section we discussed exponential functions. In this section, we discuss *logarithmic functions,* which can be obtained from exponential expressions using the following definition.

Definition of Logarithm

For $a > 0$ and $a \neq 1$,

$$y = \log_a x \text{ means } a^y = x.$$

(Read $y = \log_a x$ as "y is the logarithm of x to the base a.") For example, the exponential statement $2^4 = 16$ can be translated into a logarithmic statement using the definition: $4 = \log_2 16$. Think of a logarithm as an exponent: $\log_a x$ is the exponent to be used with the base a to get x.

EXAMPLE 1

This example shows the same statement written in both exponential and logarithmic form.

Exponential form	Logarithmic form
(a) $3^2 = 9$	$\log_3 9 = 2$
(b) $(1/5)^{-2} = 25$	$\log_{1/5} 25 = -2$
(c) $10^5 = 100,000$	$\log_{10} 100,000 = 5$
(d) $4^{-3} = 1/64$	$\log_4 1/64 = -3$
(e) $2^{-4} = 1/16$	$\log_2 1/16 = -4$
(f) $e^0 = 1$	$\log_e 1 = 0$ ▪

For a given positive value of x, the definition above leads to exactly one value of y, making $y = \log_a x$ the *logarithmic function* of base a (the base a must be positive, with $a \neq 1$).

Logarithmic Function

> If $a > 0$ and $a \neq 1$, then the logarithmic function of base a is
> $$f(x) = \log_a x.$$

The graphs of the exponential function $f(x) = 2^x$ and the logarithmic function $g(x) = \log_2 x$ are shown in Figure 5. The graph shows that $f(3) = 2^3 = 8$, while $g(8) = \log_2 8 = 3$. Thus, $f(3) = 8$ and $g(8) = 3$. Also, $f(5) = 32$ and $g(32) = 5$. In fact, for any number m, if $f(m) = p$, then $g(p) = m$. Functions related in this way are called *inverses* of each other. The graphs also show that the domain of the exponential function (the real numbers) is the range of the logarithmic function. Also, the range of the exponential function (the positive real numbers) is the domain of the logarithmic function. Every logarithmic function is the inverse of some exponential function. The graphs in Figure 5 show a characteristic of inverse functions: their graphs are mirror images about the 45° line, $y = x$. A more complete discussion of inverse functions is given in most standard intermediate algebra and college algebra books.

By plotting points and connecting them with a smooth curve, we get the graph of $y = \log_{1/2} x$ shown in Figure 6, which also includes the graph of $y = (1/2)^x$. Again, the logarithmic and exponential graphs are mirror images with respect to the line $y = x$.

The graph of $y = \log_2 x$ shown in Figure 5 is typical of the graphs of logarithmic functions $y = \log_a x$, where $a > 1$. The graph of $y = \log_{1/2} x$, shown in Figure 6, is typical of logarithmic functions of the form $y = \log_a x$, where $0 < a < 1$. For both logarithmic graphs, the y-axis is a vertical asymptote.

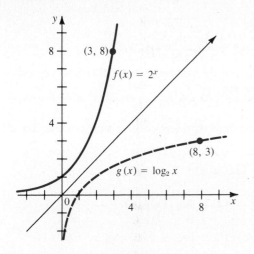

FIGURE 5

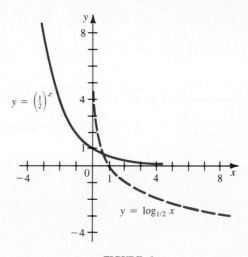

FIGURE 6

Properties of Logarithms The usefulness of logarithmic functions depends in large part on the following **properties of logarithms.**

Properties of	Let x and y be any positive real numbers and r be any real number. Let a be a positive real number, $a \neq 1$. Then
Logarithms	

(a) $\log_a xy = \log_a x + \log_a y;$ (product rule)

(b) $\log_a \dfrac{x}{y} = \log_a x - \log_a y;$ (quotient rule)

(c) $\log_a x^r = r \log_a x;$ (power rule)

(d) $\log_a a = 1;$

(e) $\log_a 1 = 0.$

To prove property (a), let $m = \log_a x$ and $n = \log_a y$. Then, by the definition of logarithm,

$$a^m = x \quad \text{and} \quad a^n = y.$$

Hence,

$$a^m a^n = xy.$$

By a property of exponents, $a^m a^n = a^{m+n}$, so

$$a^{m+n} = xy.$$

Now use the definition of logarithm to write

$$\log_a xy = m + n.$$

Since $m = \log_a x$ and $n = \log_a y$,

$$\log_a xy = \log_a x + \log_a y.$$

Proofs of parts (b) and (c) are left for the exercises. Parts (d) and (e) depend on the definition of the logarithmic function.

EXAMPLE 2

If all the following variable expressions represent positive numbers, then for $a > 0$, $a \neq 1$,

(a) $\log_a x + \log_a (x - 1) = \log_a x(x - 1)$

(b) $\log_a \dfrac{x^2 - 4x}{x + 6} = \log_a (x^2 - 4x) - \log_a (x + 6)$

(c) $\log_a (9x^5) = \log_a 9 + \log_a (x^5) = \log_a 9 + 5 \cdot \log_a x.$ ▪

Historically, one of the main applications of logarithms has been as an aid to numerical calculation. By using the properties and a table of logarithms, many numerical problems can be simplified. Since our number system has base 10, logarithms to base 10 are most convenient for numerical calculations. Such logarithms are called **common logarithms.** For simplicity, $\log_{10} x$ is abbreviated $\log x$. With this notation,

$$\log 1000 = \log 10^3 = 3$$
$$\log 100 = \log 10^2 = 2$$
$$\log 1 = \log 10^0 = 0$$
$$\log .01 = \log 10^{-2} = -2,$$

and so on.

Most practical applications of logarithms use the number e as base. (Recall: To seven decimal places, $e = 2.7182818$.) Logarithms to base e are called **natural logarithms,** written with the abbreviation ln x. While common logarithms may seem more "natural" than logarithms to base e, there are several good reasons for using natural logarithms instead. The most important reason is discussed in Section 4 of this chapter.

A table of natural logarithms is given in the back of the book. From this table, for example,

$$\ln 55 = 4.0073$$
$$\ln 1.9 = 0.6419$$

and $\ln 0.4 = -.9163.$

EXAMPLE 3

Use a calculator or the table of natural logarithms to find the following logarithms.

(a) ln 85

With a calculator, simply press the keys for 85, then press the ln key, and read the result, 4.4427.

The table of natural logarithms gives $\ln 85 = 4.4427$, the same as the answer found when using a calculator. The results may differ sometimes due to rounding error.

(b) $\ln 36$

A calculator gives $\ln 36 = 3.5835$. To use the table, first use properties of logarithms, since 36 is not listed.

$$\ln 36 = \ln 6^2 = 2 \ln 6 \approx 2(1.7918) = 3.5836.$$

Alternatively, find $\ln 36$ as follows:

$$\ln 36 = \ln 9 \cdot 4 = \ln 9 + \ln 4 = 2.1972 + 1.3863 = 3.5835. \quad \blacksquare$$

Just as any exponential function can be expressed with base e, a logarithmic function to any base can be expressed as a natural (base e) logarithmic function. The following theorem is used to change logarithms from one base to another.

Change of Base

If x is any positive number and if a and b are positive real numbers, $a \neq 1$, $b \neq 1$, then

$$\log_a x = \frac{\log_b x}{\log_b a}.$$

To prove this result, use the definition of logarithm to write $y = \log_a x$ as $x = a^y$ or $x = a^{\log_a x}$ (for positive x and positive a, $a \neq 1$). Now take base b logarithms of both sides of this last equation. This gives

$$\log_b x = \log_b a^{\log_a x}$$

or

$$\log_b x = (\log_a x)(\log_b a),$$

from which

$$\log_a x = \frac{\log_b x}{\log_b a}.$$

If the base b is equal to e, then by the change of base theorem

$$\log_a x = \frac{\log_e x}{\log_e a}.$$

Using $\ln x$ for $\log_e x$ gives the special case of the theorem using natural logarithms.

For any positive numbers a and x, $a \neq 1$,

$$\log_a x = \frac{\ln x}{\ln a}.$$

EXAMPLE 4

Use natural logarithms to find each of the following. Round to the nearest hundredth.

(a) $\log_5 27$

Let $x = 27$ and $a = 5$. Using the second form of the theorem gives

$$\log_5 27 = \frac{\ln 27}{\ln 5}.$$

Now use a calculator or the table of natural logarithms.

$$\log_5 27 \approx \frac{3.2958}{1.6094} \approx 2.05$$

To check, use a calculator with a y^x key, along with the definition of logarithm, to verify that $5^{2.05} \approx 27$.

(b) $\log_2 0.1$

$$\log_2 0.1 = \frac{\ln 0.1}{\ln 2} \approx \frac{-2.3026}{.6931} = -3.32 \quad \blacksquare$$

The next example shows how to solve equations involving logarithms.

EXAMPLE 5

Solve each of the following equations for x.

(a) $\log_x \frac{8}{27} = 3$

First, use the definition of logarithm and write the expression in exponential form. To solve for x, take the cube root on both sides.

$$x^3 = \frac{8}{27}$$

$$x = \frac{2}{3}$$

(b) $\log_4 x = \frac{5}{2}$

In exponential form, the given statement becomes

$$4^{5/2} = x$$
$$(4^{1/2})^5 = x$$
$$2^5 = x$$
$$32 = x.$$

(c) $\log_2 x - \log_2 (x - 1) = 1$

By a property of logarithms,

$$\log_2 x - \log_2 (x - 1) = \log_2 \frac{x}{x - 1},$$

so the original equation becomes

$$\log_2 \frac{x}{x - 1} = 1.$$

Use the definition of logarithms to write this result in exponential form:

$$\frac{x}{x-1} = 2^1 = 2.$$

Solve this equation:

$$\frac{x}{x-1}(x-1) = 2(x-1)$$

$$x = 2(x-1)$$

$$x = 2x - 2$$

$$-x = -2$$

$$x = 2.$$

It is important to check solutions when solving equations involving logarithms because $\log_a u$, where u is an expression in x, has domain $u > 0$. ■

In the previous section we solved exponential equations like $(1/3)^x = 81$ by writing each side of the equation as a power of 3. However, we can't use that method to solve an equation such as $3^x = 5$, since 5 cannot easily be written as a power of 3. A more general method for solving these equations depends on the following property of logarithms, which is supported by the graphs of the logarithmic functions (Figures 5 and 6).

For $x > 0$, $y > 0$, $b > 0$, and $b \neq 1$,

if $x = y$, then $\log_b x = \log_b y$, and if $\log_b x = \log_b y$, then $x = y$.

EXAMPLE 6

Solve $3^{2x} = 4^{x+1}$.

Taking natural logarithms (we could use logarithms to any base) on both sides gives

$$\ln 3^{2x} = \ln 4^{x+1}.$$

Now use the power rule for logarithms.

$$2x \ln 3 = (x+1)\ln 4$$

$$(2 \ln 3)x = (\ln 4)x + \ln 4$$

$$(2 \ln 3)x - (\ln 4)x = \ln 4$$

$$(2 \ln 3 - \ln 4)x = \ln 4$$

$$x = \frac{\ln 4}{2 \ln 3 - \ln 4}$$

Use the table or a calculator to evaluate the logarithms, then divide, to get

$$x \approx \frac{1.3863}{2(1.0986) - 1.3863} \approx 1.710. ■$$

The last example illustrates a use of logarithms in a practical problem.

EXAMPLE 7

One measure of the diversity of the species in an ecological community is given by the index of diversity, H, where

$$H = \frac{-1}{\ln 2} [P_1 \ln P_1 + P_2 \ln P_2 + \ldots + P_n \ln P_n],$$

and $P_1, P_2, \ldots, P_n$ are the proportions of a sample belonging to each of n species found in the sample. For example, in a community with two species, where there are 90 of one species and 10 of the other, $P_1 = 90/100 = 0.9$ and $P_2 = 10/100 = 0.1$, with

$$H = \frac{-1}{\ln 2} [0.9 \ln 0.9 + 0.1 \ln 0.1].$$

From the table or a calculator,

$$\ln 2 = .6931, \qquad \ln 0.9 = -.1054, \qquad \text{and} \qquad \ln 0.1 = -2.3026.$$

Therefore,

$$H \approx \frac{-1}{.6931} [(0.9)(-.1054) + (0.1)(-2.3026)] \approx .469. \quad \blacksquare$$

12.2 EXERCISES

Write Exercises 1–6 in logarithmic form.

1. $2^3 = 8$
2. $5^2 = 25$
3. $3^4 = 81$

4. $6^3 = 216$
5. $\left(\frac{1}{3}\right)^{-2} = 9$
6. $\left(\frac{3}{4}\right)^{-2} = \frac{16}{9}$

Write Exercises 7–12 in exponential form.

7. $\log_2 128 = 7$
8. $\log_3 81 = 4$
9. $\log_{25} \frac{1}{25} = -1$

10. $\log_2 \frac{1}{8} = -3$
11. $\log 10,000 = 4$
12. $\log 0.00001 = -5$

Use the definition to evaluate Exercises 13–20.

13. $\log_5 25$
14. $\log_9 81$
15. $\log_4 64$
16. $\log_6 216$

17. $\log_2 \frac{1}{4}$
18. $\log_3 \frac{1}{27}$
19. $\log_2 \sqrt[3]{\frac{1}{4}}$
20. $\log_8 \sqrt[4]{\frac{1}{2}}$

21. Complete the following table of values for $y = \log_3 x$.

x	1/27						9
y	-3	-2	-1	0	1	2	3

Graph the function using the same scale on both axes.

22. Complete the following table of values for $y = 3^x$.

x	-3	-2	-1	0	1	2	3
y		1/9					27

Graph the function on the same axes you used in Exercise 21. Compare the two graphs. How are they related?

Graph the functions in Exercises 23–28.

23. $y = \log_4 x$

24. $y = \log x$

25. $y = \log_3 (x - 1)$

26. $y = \log_2 (1 + x)$

27. $y = \log_2 x^2$

28. $y = \log_2 |x|$

Use the properties of logarithms to write Exercises 29–34 as a sum, difference, or product.

29. $\log_9 (7m)$

30. $\log_5 (8p)$

31. $\log_3 \dfrac{3p}{5k}$

32. $\log_7 \dfrac{11p}{13y}$

33. $\log_3 \dfrac{5\sqrt{2}}{\sqrt[4]{7}}$

34. $\log_2 \dfrac{9\sqrt[3]{5}}{\sqrt[4]{3}}$

Suppose $\log_b 2 = a$ and $\log_b 3 = c$. Use the properties of logarithms to find the logarithms in Exercises 35–40.

35. $\log_b 8$

36. $\log_b 24$

37. $\log_b 54$

38. $\log_b 144$

39. $\log_b (72b)$

40. $\log_b (4b^2)$

Find the natural logarithms in Exercises 41–50.

41. ln 20

42. ln 35

43. ln 800

44. ln 920

45. ln 1800

46. ln 250

47. ln 55,000

48. ln 12,000

49. ln 0.45

50. ln 0.39

In Exercises 51–56, use natural logarithms to evaluate the logarithms to the nearest hundredth.

51. $\log_5 20$

52. $\log_{12} 170$

53. $\log_{1.2} 5.5$

54. $\log_{2.8} 0.12$

55. $\log_{10} 420$

56. $\log_{10} 0.008$

Solve the equations in Exercises 57–74. Round decimal answers to the nearest hundredth.

57. $\log_x 25 = -2$

58. $\log_x \dfrac{1}{16} = -2$

59. $\log_9 27 = m$

60. $\log_8 4 = z$

61. $\log_y 8 = \dfrac{3}{4}$

62. $\log_r 7 = \dfrac{1}{2}$

63. $\log_3 (5x + 1) = 2$

64. $\log_5 (9x - 4) = 1$

65. $\log_4 x - \log_4 (x + 3) = -1$

66. $\log_9 m - \log_9 (m - 4) = -2$

67. $3^x = 5$

68. $4^x = 12$

69. $e^{k-1} = 4$

70. $e^{2y} = 12$

71. $2e^{5a+2} = 8$

72. $10e^{3z-7} = 5$

73. $\left(1 + \dfrac{k}{2}\right)^4 = 8$

74. $\left(1 + \dfrac{a}{5}\right)^3 = 9$

For Exercises 75 and 76, refer to Example 7.

75. Suppose a sample of a small community shows two species with 50 individuals each. Find the index of diversity H.

76. A virgin forest in northwestern Pennsylvania has 4 species of large trees with the following proportions of each: hemlock, .521; beech, .324; birch, .081; maple, .074. Find the index of diversity H.

77. The number of species in a sample is given by

$$S(n) = a \ln \left(1 + \frac{n}{a} \right).$$

Here n is the number of individuals in the sample and a is a constant that indicates the diversity of species in the community. If $a = .36$, find $S(n)$ for the following values of n.

   (a) 100   **(b)** 200   **(c)** 150   **(d)** 10.

78. In Exercise 77, find n if $S(n) = 9$ and $a = .36$.

79. The population of an animal species that is introduced into a certain area may grow rapidly at first but then grow more slowly as time goes on. A logarithmic function can provide an excellent model of such growth. Suppose that the population of foxes, $F(t)$, in an area t months after the foxes were introduced there, is

$$F(t) = 500 \log (2t + 3).$$

Find the population of foxes at the following times:

   (a) when they are first released into the area (that is, when $t = 0$)   **(b)** after 3 months
   (c) after 15 months   **(d)** Graph $y = F(t)$.

80. The number of years, $N(r)$, since two independently evolving languages split off from a common ancestral language is approximated by

$$N(r) = -5000 \ln r,$$

where r is the proportion of the words from the ancestral language that are common to both languages now. Find each of the following.

   (a) $N(.9)$ **(b)** $N(.5)$ **(c)** $N(.3)$
   (d) How many years have elapsed since the split if 70% of the words of the ancestral language are common to both languages today?
   (e) If two languages split off from a common ancestral language about 1000 years ago, find r.

For Exercises 81–84, recall that log x represents the common (base 10) logarithm of x.

81. The loudness of sounds is measured in a unit called a *decibel*. To do this, a very faint sound, called the **threshold sound,** is assigned an intensity I_0. If a particular sound has intensity I, then the decibel rating of this louder sound is

$$10 \cdot \log \frac{I}{I_0}.$$

Find the decibel ratings of sounds having the following intensities.

   (a) $100 I_0$ **(b)** $1000 I_0$ **(c)** $100,000 I_0$ **(d)** $1,000,000 I_0$

82. Find the decibel ratings of the following sounds, having intensities as given. Round answers to the nearest whole number.

   (a) whisper, $115 I_0$
   (b) busy street, $9,500,000 I_0$
   (c) heavy truck, 20 m away, $1,200,000,000 I_0$
   (d) rock music, $895,000,000,000 I_0$
   (e) jetliner at takeoff, $109,000,000,000,000 I_0$

83. The intensity of an earthquake, measured on the **Richter Scale,** is given by

$$\log \frac{I}{I_0},$$

where I_0 is the intensity of an earthquake of a certain (small) size. Find the Richter Scale ratings of earthquakes having intensity

(a) $1000I_0$ (b) $1,000,000I_0$ (c) $100,000,000I_0$.

84. The San Francisco earthquake of 1906 had a Richter Scale rating of 8.6. Use a calculator with a y^x key to express the intensity of this earthquake as a multiple of I_0. (See Exercise 83.)

The graphs below are plotted on a *logarithmic scale*, where differences between successive measurements are not always the same. Data that do not plot in a linear pattern on the usual Cartesian axes often form a linear pattern when plotted on a logarithmic scale. Notice that on the vertical scale, the distance from 1 to 2 is not the same as the distance from 2 to 3, and so on. This is characteristic of a graph drawn with logarithmic scales.

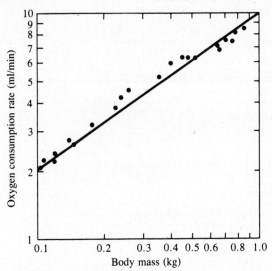 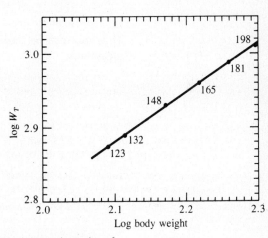

85. The graph on the left gives the rate of oxygen consumption for resting guinea pigs of various sizes. This rate is proportional to body mass raised to the power 0.67.* Estimate the oxygen consumption for a guinea pig with body mass of .3 kg. Do the same for one with body mass of .7.

86. The graph on the right gives the world weight-lifting records, as log W_T, plotted against the logarithm of body weight. Here W_T is the total weight lifted in three lifts: the press, the snatch, and the clean-and-jerk. The numbers beside each point indicate the body weight class, in pounds.*

(a) Find the record for a weight of 150 pounds and for a weight of 165 pounds. (Use base 10 logarithms.)

(b) Find the body weight that corresponds to a record of 750 pounds.

87. Prove: $\log_a \dfrac{x}{y} = \log_a x - \log_a y$

88. Prove: $\log_a x^r = r \log_a x$

---

*From *On Size and Life* by Thomas A. McMahon and John Tyler Bonner. Copyright © 1983 by Thomas A. McMahon and John Tyler Bonner. Reprinted by permission of W. H. Freeman and Company.

12.3   Derivatives of Logarithmic Functions

In this section formulas will be developed for the derivatives of $y = \ln x$ and other logarithmic functions. To find the derivative of the function $y = \ln x$, assuming $x > 0$, go back to the definition of the derivative given earlier: if $y = f(x)$, then

$$y' = f'(x) = \lim_{h \to 0} \frac{f(x + h) - f(x)}{h},$$

provided this limit exists. (Remember that h represents the variable in this expression, while x is constant.)

Here, $f(x) = \ln x$, with

$$y' = f'(x) = \lim_{h \to 0} \frac{\ln (x + h) - \ln x}{h}.$$

This limit can be found using properties of logarithms. By the quotient rule for logarithms,

$$y' = \lim_{h \to 0} \frac{\ln (x + h) - \ln x}{h} = \lim_{h \to 0} \frac{\ln \left(\dfrac{x + h}{x} \right)}{h}$$

$$= \lim_{h \to 0} \left[\frac{1}{h} \ln \left(\frac{x + h}{x} \right) \right].$$

The power rule for logarithms is used to get

$$y' = \lim_{h \to 0} \ln \left(\frac{x + h}{x} \right)^{1/h}$$

$$= \lim_{h \to 0} \ln \left(1 + \frac{h}{x} \right)^{1/h}.$$

Now make a substitution: let $m = x/h$, so that $h/x = 1/m$. As $h \to 0$, with x fixed, $m \to \infty$ (since $x > 0$), so

$$\lim_{h \to 0} \ln \left(1 + \frac{h}{x} \right)^{1/h} = \lim_{m \to \infty} \ln \left(1 + \frac{1}{m} \right)^{m/x}$$

$$= \lim_{m \to \infty} \ln \left[\left(1 + \frac{1}{m} \right)^{m} \right]^{1/x}.$$

By the power rule for logarithms, this becomes

$$= \lim_{m \to \infty} \left[\frac{1}{x} \cdot \ln \left(1 + \frac{1}{m} \right)^{m} \right].$$

Since x is fixed here (a constant), by the product rule for limits, this last limit becomes

$$\lim_{m \to \infty} \left[\frac{1}{x} \cdot \ln \left(1 + \frac{1}{m} \right)^{m} \right] = \left(\lim_{m \to \infty} \frac{1}{x} \right) \lim_{m \to \infty} \left[\ln \left(1 + \frac{1}{m} \right)^{m} \right]$$

$$= \frac{1}{x} \cdot \lim_{m \to \infty} \left[\ln \left(1 + \frac{1}{m} \right)^{m} \right].$$

Since the logarithmic function is continuous,

$$\frac{1}{x} \cdot \lim_{m \to \infty} \left[\ln \left(1 + \frac{1}{m} \right)^m \right] = \frac{1}{x} \cdot \ln \left[\lim_{m \to \infty} \left(1 + \frac{1}{m} \right)^m \right].$$

In the previous section we saw that the limit on the right equals e, so that

$$\frac{1}{x} \cdot \ln \left[\lim_{m \to \infty} \left(1 + \frac{1}{m} \right)^m \right] = \frac{1}{x} \ln e = \frac{1}{x} \cdot 1 = \frac{1}{x}.$$

Summarizing, if $y = \ln x$, then $y' = \frac{1}{x}$.

EXAMPLE 1

Find the derivative of $y = \ln 6x$. Assume $x > 0$.

Use the properties of logarithms and the rules for derivatives.

$$y' = \frac{d}{dx} (\ln 6x)$$

$$= \frac{d}{dx} (\ln 6 + \ln x)$$

$$= \frac{d}{dx} (\ln 6) + \frac{d}{dx} (\ln x)$$

$$= 0 + \frac{1}{x}$$

$$= \frac{1}{x}.$$

We can use the chain rule to find the derivative of the more general logarithmic function $y = \ln g(x)$. Recall the chain rule:

$$\text{if } y = f[g(x)] \text{ then } y' = f'[g(x)] \cdot g'(x).$$

Let $y = f(u) = \ln u$ and $u = g(x)$, so that $f[g(x)] = \ln g(x)$. Then

$$f'[g(x)] = f'(u) = \frac{1}{u} = \frac{1}{g(x)},$$

and by the chain rule,

$$y' = f'[g(x)] \cdot g'(x)$$

$$= \frac{1}{g(x)} \cdot g'(x)$$

$$y' = \frac{g'(x)}{g(x)}. \quad \blacksquare$$

EXAMPLE 2

Find the derivative of $y = \ln (x^2 + 1)$.

Here $g(x) = x^2 + 1$ and $g'(x) = 2x$. Thus

$$y' = \frac{g'(x)}{g(x)} = \frac{2x}{x^2 + 1}. \quad \blacksquare$$

If $y = \ln(-x)$, where $x < 0$, the chain rule with $g(x) = -x$ and $g'(x) = -1$ gives

$$y' = \frac{g'(x)}{g(x)} = \frac{-1}{-x} = \frac{1}{x}.$$

The derivative of $y = \ln(-x)$ is the same as the derivative of $y = \ln x$. For this reason, these two results can be combined into one rule using the absolute value of x. A similar situation holds true for $y = \ln[g(x)]$ and $y = \ln[-g(x)]$. The next box summarizes all these results.

Derivatives of $\ln|x|$ and $\ln|g(x)|$

$$\frac{d}{dx} \ln|x| = \frac{1}{x}$$

$$\frac{d}{dx} \ln|g(x)| = \frac{g'(x)}{g(x)}$$

EXAMPLE 3

Find the derivative of each function.

(a) $y = \ln|5x|$

Let $g(x) = 5x$, so that $g'(x) = 5$. From the box above,

$$y' = \frac{g'(x)}{g(x)} = \frac{5}{5x} = \frac{1}{x}.$$

Notice that the derivative of $\ln|5x|$ is the same as the derivative of $\ln|x|$. Also, in Example 1, we found the derivative of $\ln 6x$ to be the same as that for $\ln x$. This suggests that for any constant a,

$$\frac{d}{dx} \ln|ax| = \frac{d}{dx} \ln|x| = \frac{1}{x}.$$

For a proof of this result, see Exercise 47.

(b) $y = \ln|3x^2 - 4x|$

$$y' = \frac{6x - 4}{3x^2 - 4x}$$

(c) $y = 3x \ln x^2$

This function is the product of the two functions $3x$ and $\ln x^2$, so use the product rule.

$$y' = (3x)\left[\frac{d}{dx} \ln x^2\right] + (\ln x^2)\left[\frac{d}{dx} 3x\right]$$

$$= 3x\left(\frac{2x}{x^2}\right) + (\ln x^2)(3)$$

$$= 6 + 3 \ln x^2$$

By the power rule for logarithms,

$$y' = 6 + \ln (x^2)^3$$
$$= 6 + \ln x^6.$$

Alternatively, write the answer as $y' = 6 + 6 \ln x$. ∎

EXAMPLE 4

Find the derivative of $y = \log |3x + 2|$.

This is a base 10 logarithm, while the derivative rule we have developed applies only to natural logarithms. To find the derivative, first use the change of base rule to convert the function to one involving natural logarithms.

$$y = \log_{10} |3x + 2|$$

$$= \frac{\ln |3x + 2|}{\ln 10}$$

$$= \frac{1}{\ln 10} \ln |3x + 2|$$

Now find the derivative. (Remember: 1/ln 10 is a constant.)

$$y' = \frac{1}{\ln 10} \cdot \frac{d}{dx}[\ln |3x + 2|]$$

$$= \frac{1}{\ln 10} \cdot \frac{3}{3x + 2}$$

$$= \frac{3}{\ln 10 (3x + 2)} \quad ∎$$

Following the procedure of Example 4, we could derive the following formula.

Derivatives with Other Bases

For any suitable value of a,

$$D_x(\log_a |x|) = \frac{1}{\ln a} \cdot \frac{1}{x}.$$

When $y = \log_a |g(x)|$, the chain rule gives

$$D_x(\log_a |g(x)|) = \frac{1}{\ln a} \cdot \frac{g'(x)}{g(x)}.$$

EXAMPLE 5

Find any extrema or inflection points and sketch the graph of $y = (\ln x)/x^2$, $x > 0$.

To locate any extrema, begin by finding the first derivative.

$$y' = \frac{x^2(1/x) - 2x \ln x}{x^4} = \frac{x - 2x \ln x}{x^4}$$

$$= \frac{x(1 - 2 \ln x)}{x^4} = \frac{1 - 2 \ln x}{x^3}$$

The derivative function exists everywhere on the domain ($x > 0$), so any maxima or minima will occur only at points where the derivative equals 0.

$$\frac{1 - 2 \ln x}{x^3} = 0$$

$$1 - 2 \ln x = 0$$

$$2 \ln x = 1$$

$$\ln x = \frac{1}{2}$$

Use the definition of logarithm to get the equivalent exponential statement

$$x = e^{1/2} \approx 1.65.$$

To locate inflection points and determine whether $x = e^{1/2}$ represents a maximum or a minimum, find the second derivative.

$$y'' = \frac{x^3(-2/x) - 3x^2(1 - 2 \ln x)}{x^6}$$

$$= \frac{-2x^2 - 3x^2 + 6x^2 \ln x}{x^6} = \frac{-5x^2 + 6x^2 \ln x}{x^6}$$

$$= \frac{x^2(-5 + 6 \ln x)}{x^6} = \frac{-5 + 6 \ln x}{x^4}$$

Use a calculator to show that the second derivative is negative for $x = e^{1/2}$ with a maximum where $x = e^{1/2}$. Set the second derivative equal to 0 and solve the resulting equation to identify any inflection points.

$$\frac{-5 + 6 \ln x}{x^4} = 0$$

$$-5 + 6 \ln x = 0$$

$$6 \ln x = 5$$

$$\ln x = 5/6$$

$$x = e^{5/6} \approx 2.30$$

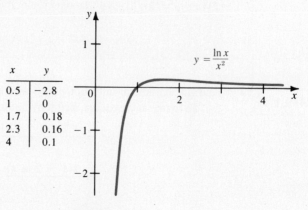

x	y
0.5	−2.8
1	0
1.7	0.18
2.3	0.16
4	0.1

$$y = \frac{\ln x}{x^2}$$

FIGURE 7

Verify that $f''(1) < 0$ and $f''(3) > 0$, with an inflection point when $x = e^{5/6} \approx$ 2.3. Also, verify that the graph is concave downward for $x < e^{5/6}$ and concave upward for $x > e^{5/6}$. Use this information and plot a few points as necessary to get the graph of Figure 7. ▪

12.3 EXERCISES

Find derivatives of each function in Exercises 1–32.

1. $y = \ln |8x|$

2. $y = \ln |-4x|$

3. $y = \ln |3 - x|$

4. $y = \ln |1 + x^2|$

5. $y = \ln |2x^2 - 7x|$

6. $y = \ln |-8x^2 + 6x|$

7. $y = \ln \sqrt{x + 5}$

8. $y = \ln \sqrt{2x + 1}$

9. $y = \ln (x^4 + 5x^2)^{3/2}$

10. $y = \ln |(5x^3 - 2x)^{3/2}|$

11. $y = -3x \ln |x + 2|$

12. $y = (3x + 1) \ln |x - 1|$

13. $y = x^2 \ln |x|$

14. $y = x \ln |2 - x^2|$

15. $y = \dfrac{2 \ln |x + 3|}{x^2}$

16. $y = \dfrac{\ln |x|}{x^3}$

17. $y = \dfrac{\ln |x|}{4x + 7}$

18. $y = \dfrac{-2 \ln |x|}{3x - 1}$

19. $y = \dfrac{3x^2}{\ln |x|}$

20. $y = \dfrac{x^3 - 1}{2 \ln |x|}$

21. $y = (\ln |x + 1|)^4$

22. $y = \sqrt{\ln |x - 3|}$

23. $y = \ln |\ln |x||$

24. $y = (\ln 4)(\ln |3x|)$

25. $y = \log |6x|$

26. $y = \log |2x - 3|$

27. $y = \log |1 - x|$

28. $y = \log |-3x|$

29. $y = \log_5 \sqrt{5x + 2}$

30. $y = \log_7 \sqrt{2x - 3}$

31. $y = \log_3 |(x^2 + 2x)^{3/2}|$

32. $y = \log_2 |(2x^2 - x)^{5/2}|$

Find all relative maxima or minima for the functions in Exercises 33–40. Sketch the graphs.

33. $y = x \cdot \ln x, \ x > 0$

34. $y = x - \ln x, \ x > 0$

35. $y = x \cdot \ln |x|$

36. $y = x - \ln |x|$

37. $y = (\ln |x|)^2$

38. $y = (\ln |x|)^3$

39. $y = \dfrac{\ln x}{x}, \ x > 0$

40. $y = \dfrac{\ln x^2}{x^2}$

41. Suppose that the population of a certain collection of rare Brazilian ants is given by
$$P(t) = (t + 100) \ln (t + 2),$$
where t represents the time in days. Find the rate of change of the population when $t = 2$; when $t = 8$.

42. Consider an experiment in which equal numbers of male and female insects of a certain species are permitted to intermingle. Assume that
$$M(t) = (0.1t + 1) \ln \sqrt{t}$$
represents the number of matings observed among the insects in an hour, where t is the temperature in degrees Celsius. (Note: The formula is an approximation at best and holds only for specific temperature intervals.) Find

(a) $M(15)$;   (b) $M(25)$.

(c) Find the rate of change of $M(t)$ when $t = 15$.

43. Assume that the total revenue received from the sale of x items is given by
$$R(x) = 30 \cdot \ln (2x + 1),$$
while the total cost to produce x items is $C(x) = x/2$. Find the number of items that should be manufactured so that profit, $R(x) - C(x)$, is a maximum.

44. Suppose dots and dashes are transmitted over a telegraph line so that dots occur a fraction p of the time (where $0 \le p \le 1$) and dashes occur a fraction $1 - p$ of the time. The **information content** of the telegraph line is given by $I(p)$, where
$$I(p) = -p \cdot \ln p - (1 - p) \cdot \ln (1 - p).$$

(a) Show that $I'(p) = -\ln p + \ln (1 - p)$.

(b) Let $I'(p) = 0$ and find the value of p that maximizes $I(p)$.

45. What is true about the slope of the tangent line to the graph of $f(x) = \ln x$ as $x \to \infty$? as $x \to 0$?

46. Let $f(x) = \ln x$.

(a) Compute $f'(x)$, $f''(x)$, $f'''(x)$, $f^{(4)}(x)$, and $f^{(5)}(x)$.

(b) Guess a formula for $f^{(n)}(x)$, where n is any positive integer.

47. Prove $\dfrac{d}{dx} \ln |ax| = \dfrac{d}{dx} \ln |x|$ for any constant a.

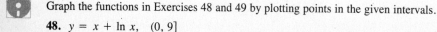

Graph the functions in Exercises 48 and 49 by plotting points in the given intervals.

48. $y = x + \ln x$, $(0, 9]$

49. $y = \ln x - \dfrac{1}{x}$, $(0, 9]$

12.4   Derivatives of Exponential Functions

Now that we have formulas for the derivatives of natural logarithmic functions, we turn to exponential functions. To find the derivative of the function $y = e^x$, start with $y = e^x$ and take the natural logarithm of each side.

$$y = e^x$$
$$\ln y = \ln e^x$$

By the power rule for logarithms and the fact that $\ln e = 1$,

$$\ln y = x \cdot \ln e$$

$$\ln y = x.$$

Now, using implicit differentiation, take the derivative of each side. (Remember, y is a function of x, so use the chain rule.)

$$\frac{1}{y} \cdot \frac{dy}{dx} = 1$$

$$\frac{dy}{dx} = y.$$

or

Since $y = e^x$,

$$\frac{d}{dx}(e^x) = e^x, \text{ or } y' = e^x.$$

This result shows one of the main reasons for the widespread use of e as a base— the function $y = e^x$ is its own derivative. Furthermore, it is the *only* useful function with this property. For a more general result let $y = e^u$ and $u = g(x)$, so that $y = e^{g(x)}$. Then

$$\frac{dy}{du} = e^u \qquad \text{and} \qquad \frac{du}{dx} = g'(x).$$

By the chain rule,

$$\frac{dy}{dx} = \frac{dy}{du} \cdot \frac{du}{dx}$$

$$= e^u \cdot g'(x)$$

$$= e^{g(x)} \cdot g'(x).$$

Now replace y with $e^{g(x)}$ to get

$$\frac{d}{dx} e^{g(x)} = e^{g(x)} \cdot g'(x).$$

The next box summarizes these results.

Derivatives of e^x and $e^{g(x)}$

$$\frac{d}{dx} e^x = e^x$$

$$\frac{d}{dx} e^{g(x)} = g'(x) e^{g(x)}$$

EXAMPLE 1

Find derivatives of the following functions.

(a) $y = e^{5x}$

Let $g(x) = 5x$, with $g'(x) = 5$. Then
$$y' = 5e^{5x}.$$

(b) $y = 3e^{-4x}$
$$y' = 3 \cdot e^{-4x}(-4) = -12e^{-4x}$$

(c) $y = 10e^{3x^2}$
$$y' = 10(e^{3x^2})(6x) = 60xe^{3x^2} \quad \blacksquare$$

EXAMPLE 2

Let $y = e^x(\ln |x|)$. Find y'.
Use the product rule.
$$y' = e^x\left(\frac{1}{x}\right) + (\ln |x|)e^x$$
$$y' = e^x\left(\frac{1}{x} + \ln |x|\right). \quad \blacksquare$$

EXAMPLE 3

Let $y = \dfrac{100,000}{1 + 100e^{-0.3x}}$. Find y'.
Use the quotient rule.
$$y' = \frac{(1 + 100e^{-0.3x})(0) - 100,000(-30e^{-0.3x})}{(1 + 100e^{-0.3x})^2}$$
$$= \frac{3,000,000e^{-0.3x}}{(1 + 100e^{-0.3x})^2} \quad \blacksquare$$

EXAMPLE 4

Find $D_x(3^x)$.
Change 3^x to e^{kx}. From the table of powers of e, $k = 1.10$ and $3^x \approx e^{1.10x}$, so
$$D_x(3^x) \approx D_x(e^{1.10x}) = 1.10e^{1.10x}. \quad \blacksquare$$

In Example 4, we found $e^{1.10} \approx 3$. Taking natural logarithms on both sides gives

$$e^{1.10} \approx 3$$
$$\ln e^{1.10} \approx \ln 3$$
$$1.10 \ln e \approx \ln 3$$
$$1.10 \approx \ln 3.$$

By this result, the derivative of $f(x) = 3^x$ can also be written as

$$D_x(3^x) = (\ln 3)e^{x \ln 3}$$

Extending this idea gives the following general rule for the derivative of an exponential function with any appropriate base a.

$$D_x(a^x) = (\ln a)e^{x \ln a}.$$

By the chain rule,

$$D_x[a^{g(x)}] = (\ln a)e^{(\ln a)g(x)} g'(x).$$

Frequently a population, or the sales of a certain product, will start growing slowly, then grow more rapidly, and then gradually level off. Such growth can often be approximated by a mathematical model of the form

$$f(x) = \frac{b}{1 + ae^{kx}}$$

for appropriate constants a, b, and k.

EXAMPLE 5

Suppose that the sales of a new product can be approximated for its first few years on the market by the function

$$S(x) = \frac{100,000}{1 + 100e^{-0.3x}},$$

where x is time in years since the introduction of the product. Find the rate of change of sales when $x = 4$.

The derivative of this sales function, which gives the rate of change of sales, was found in the previous example. Using that derivative,

$$S'(4) = \frac{3,000,000e^{-0.3(4)}}{[1 + 100e^{-0.3(4)}]^2}$$

$$= \frac{3,000,000e^{-1.2}}{(1 + 100e^{-1.2})^2}.$$

By using a calculator or the table of powers of e, $e^{-1.2} \approx 0.301$, and

$$S'(4) \approx \frac{3,000,000(0.301)}{[1 + 100(0.301)]^2}$$

$$\approx \frac{903,000}{(1 + 30.1)^2}$$

$$= \frac{903,000}{967.21} \approx 934.$$

The rate of change of sales at time $x = 4$ is about 934 units per year. The positive number indicates that sales are increasing at this time.   ∎

EXAMPLE 6

Graph $S(x)$ from Example 5.

Use the first derivative to check for extrema. Set $S'(x) = 0$ and solve for x.

$$S'(x) = \frac{3,000,000\,e^{-0.3x}}{(1 + 100\,e^{-0.3x})^2} = 0$$

$$3,000,000\,e^{-0.3x} = 0$$

$$\frac{3,000,000}{e^{0.3x}} = 0$$

The expression on the left can never equal 0, so $S'(x) = 0$ leads to no extrema. Next, find any critical values for which $S'(x)$ does not exist; that is, values that make the denominator equal 0.

$$1 + 100\,e^{-0.3x} = 0$$

$$100\,e^{-0.3x} = -1$$

$$\frac{100}{e^{0.3x}} = -1$$

Since the expression on the left is always positive, it cannot equal -1. There are no critical values and no extrema. Further, $e^{-0.3x}$ is always positive, so $S'(x)$ is always positive. This means the graph is always increasing over the domain of the function. Use the second derivative to verify that the graph has an inflection point at approximately 15.4 and is concave upward on $(-\infty, 15.4)$ and concave downward on $(15.4, \infty)$. Plotting a few points leads to the graph in Figure 8. ■

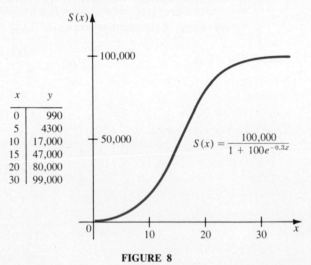

x	y
0	990
5	4300
10	17,000
15	47,000
20	80,000
30	99,000

$$S(x) = \frac{100,000}{1 + 100\,e^{-0.3x}}$$

FIGURE 8

12.4 EXERCISES

Find derivatives of the functions in Exercises 1–32.

1. $y = e^{4x}$

2. $y = e^{-2x}$

3. $y = -6e^{-2x}$

4. $y = 8e^{4x}$

5. $y = -8e^{2x}$

6. $y = 0.2e^{5x}$

7. $y = -16e^{x+1}$

8. $y = -4e^{-0.1x}$

9. $y = e^{x^2}$

10. $y = e^{-x^2}$

11. $y = 3e^{2x^2}$

12. $y = -5e^{4x^3}$

13. $y = 4e^{2x^2-4}$

14. $y = -3e^{3x^2+5}$

15. $y = xe^x$

16. $y = x^2e^{-2x}$

17. $y = (x-3)^2e^{2x}$

18. $y = (3x^2 - 4x)e^{-3x}$

19. $y = e^{x^2} \ln x, \ x > 0$

20. $y = e^{2x-1} \ln (2x - 1), \ x > \dfrac{1}{2}$

21. $y = \dfrac{e^x}{\ln x}, \ x > 0$

22. $y = \dfrac{\ln x}{e^x}, \ x > 0$

23. $y = \dfrac{x^2}{e^x}$

24. $y = \dfrac{e^x}{2x + 1}$

25. $y = \dfrac{e^x + e^{-x}}{x}$

26. $y = \dfrac{e^x - e^{-x}}{x}$

27. $y = \dfrac{5000}{1 + 10e^{0.4x}}$

28. $y = \dfrac{600}{1 - 50e^{0.2x}}$

29. $y = \dfrac{10,000}{9 + 4e^{-0.2x}}$

30. $y = \dfrac{500}{12 + 5e^{-0.5x}}$

31. $y = (2x + e^{-x^2})^2$

32. $y = (e^{2x} - \ln x)^3, \ x > 0$

Find the derivative of each function in Exercises 33–38.

33. $y = 8^{5x}$

34. $y = 2^{-x}$

35. $y = 3 \cdot 4^{x^2+2}$

36. $y = -10^{3x^2-4}$

37. $y = 2 \cdot 3^{\sqrt{x}}$

38. $y = 5 \cdot 7^{\sqrt{x-2}}$

39. The sales of a new personal computer, in thousands, are given by
$$S(t) = 100 - 90e^{-0.3t},$$
where t represents time in years. Find the rate of change of sales when **(a)** $t = 1$; **(b)** $t = 5$.

40. Suppose $P(x) = e^{-0.02x}$ represents the proportion of shoes manufactured by a given company that are still wearable after x days of use. Find the proportion of shoes wearable after

(a) 1 day; **(b)** 10 days; **(c)** 100 days.

(d) Calculate and interpret $P'(100)$.

41. The concentration of pollutants, in grams per liter, in the east fork of the Big Weasel River is approximated by
$$P(x) = 0.04e^{-4x},$$
where x is the number of miles downstream from a paper mill that the measurement is taken. Find

(a) $P(0.5)$; **(b)** $P(1)$; **(c)** $P(2)$.

Find the rate of change of the concentration with respect to distance at

(d) $x = 0.5$; **(e)** $x = 1$; **(f)** $x = 2$.

42. Using data in a car magazine, we constructed the mathematical model
$$y = 100e^{-0.03045t}$$
for the percent of cars of a certain type still on the road after t years. Find the percent of cars on the road after the following number of years.

(a) 0 **(b)** 2 **(c)** 4 **(d)** 6

Find y' for the following values of t.

(e) 0 **(f)** 2

(g) Interpret your answers to (e) and (f).

43. Assume that the amount of a radioactive substance present at time t is given by

$$A(t) = 500e^{-0.25t}$$

grams. Find the rate of change of the quantity present when

(a) $t = 0$ **(b)** $t = 4$ **(c)** $t = 6$ **(d)** $t = 10$.

44. According to work by the psychologist C. L. Hull, the strength of a habit is a function of the number of times the habit is repeated. If N is the number of repetitions and $H(N)$ is the strength of the habit, then

$$H(N) = 1000(1 - e^{-kN})$$

where k is a constant. Find $H'(N)$ if $k = .1$ and

(a) $N = 10$;   **(b)** $N = 100$;   **(c)** $N = 1000$.

(d) Show that $H'(N)$ is always positive. What does this mean?

Find all relative maxima or minima for the functions in Exercises 45–50. Sketch the graphs.

45. $y = -xe^x$ **46.** $y = xe^{-x}$

47. $y = x^2e^{-x}$ **48.** $y = (x - 1)e^{-x}$

49. $y = e^x + e^{-x}$ **50.** $y = -x^2e^x$

51. What is true of the slope of the tangent line to the graph of $f(x) = e^x$

(a) as $x \rightarrow -\infty$?   **(b)** as $x \rightarrow 0$?

52. Prove: $\dfrac{d}{dx}e^{ax} = ae^{ax}$ for any constant a.

Graph the functions in Exercises 53 and 54 by plotting points in the given intervals.

53. $y = e^x \ln x$, $(0, 5]$

54. $y = \dfrac{5 \ln 10x}{e^{.5x}}$, $(0, 10]$

12.5   Applications—Growth and Decay

In many situations that occur in biology, economics, and the social sciences, a quantity changes at a rate proportional to the amount present. In such cases the amount present at time t is a function of t called the **exponential growth function.***

Exponential
Growth Function

> Let y_0 be the amount or number of a quantity present at time $t = 0$. Then, under certain conditions, the amount present at any time t is given by
>
> $$y = y_0e^{kt},$$
>
> where k is a constant.

---

*The derivation of this function is presented in a later chapter.

If $k > 0$, then k is called the **growth constant**; if $k < 0$, then k is called the **decay constant.** A common example is the growth of bacteria in a culture. The more bacteria present, the faster the population increases.

EXAMPLE 1

Yeast in a sugar solution is growing at a rate such that 1 gram becomes 1.5 grams after 20 hours. Find the growth function, assuming exponential growth.

We must find values for y_0 and k in the exponential growth function $y = y_0 e^{kt}$. Since y_0 is the amount present at time $t = 0$, the value of $y_0 = 1$ here. To find k, substitute $y = 1.5$, $t = 20$, and $y_0 = 1$ into the equation.

$$y = y_0 e^{kt}$$
$$1.5 = 1 e^{k(20)}$$

Now take natural logarithms on both sides and use the power rule for logarithms and the fact that $\ln e = 1$.

$$1.5 = e^{20k}$$
$$\ln 1.5 = \ln e^{20k}$$
$$\ln 1.5 = 20k \ln e$$
$$\ln 1.5 = 20k$$
$$\frac{\ln 1.5}{20} = k$$
$$k \approx .02 \text{ (to the nearest hundredth)}$$

The exponential growth function is

$$y = e^{.02t},$$

where y is the weight of yeast present after t hours.   ▪

EXAMPLE 2

A population of fruit flies is contained in a large glass jar which can hold 1000 flies. The population, y, is increasing according to the function

$$y = 100 e^{.03t},$$

where t is time in days.

(a)   What was the initial population?

In the equation $y = y_0 e^{kt}$, the initial population is given by y_0. In the given function, $y_0 = 100$, so there were 100 fruit flies in the jar initially.

(b)   How long will it take for the fruit fly population to fill the jar to capacity?

The maximum population is 1000. To find the value of t that corresponds to $y = 1000$, solve the equation

$$1000 = 100 e^{.03t}$$

for t. First divide both sides by 100:

$$10 = e^{.03t}.$$

Take natural logarithms on both sides.

$$\ln 10 = \ln e^{.03t}.$$

By the power rule for logarithms, and using the fact that $\ln e = 1$,

$$\ln 10 = .03t \ln e$$

$$\ln 10 = .03t$$

$$t = \frac{\ln 10}{.03}.$$

Use a calculator or the table of natural logarithms to find $\ln 10 \approx 2.3026$, so that

$$t \approx 76.8.$$

It will take about 76.8 days for the jar to be filled to capacity. ■

The decline of a population or decay of a substance may also be described by the exponential growth function. In this case the decay constant k is negative, since an increase in time leads to a decrease in the quantity present. Radioactive substances provide a good example of exponential decay. By definition, the **half-life** of a radioactive substance is the time it takes for exactly half of the initial quantity to decay.

EXAMPLE 3

Suppose that $A(t)$, the amount of a certain radioactive substance present at time t, is given by

$$A(t) = 1000\,e^{-.1t},$$

where t is measured in days and $A(t)$ in grams.

To find the half-life, we must find a value of t such that $A(t) = \frac{1}{2}(1000) = 500$ grams. That is, we must solve the equation

$$500 = 1000\,e^{-.1t}.$$

To solve this equation, first divide through by 1000, obtaining

$$\frac{1}{2} = e^{-.1t}.$$

Now take natural logarithms of both sides:

$$\ln \frac{1}{2} = \ln e^{-.1t}.$$

Using the power rule of logarithms and the fact that $\ln e = 1$,

$$\ln \frac{1}{2} = -.1t,$$

and

$$t = \frac{\ln \frac{1}{2}}{-.1}.$$

Since $\ln \frac{1}{2} = \ln .5$, use the table of natural logarithms or a calculator to get

$$t \approx \frac{-.6931}{-.1} \approx 6.9.$$

It will take about 6.9 days for half the sample to decay. ■

EXAMPLE 4

Carbon 14 is a radioactive isotope of carbon which has a half-life of about 5600 years. The earth's atmosphere contains much carbon, mostly in the form of carbon dioxide gas, with small traces of carbon 14. Most atmospheric carbon is the nonradioactive isotope, carbon 12. The ratio of carbon 14 to carbon 12 is virtually constant in the atmosphere. However, as a plant absorbs carbon dioxide from the air in the process of photosynthesis, the carbon 12 stays in the plant while the carbon 14 is converted into nitrogen. Thus, in a plant, the ratio of carbon 14 to carbon 12 is smaller than the ratio in the atmosphere. Even when the plant dies, this ratio will continue to decrease. Based on these facts, a method of dating objects called **carbon-14 dating** has been developed.

(a) Suppose a mummy has been discovered in which the ratio of carbon 14 to carbon 12 is only about half the ratio found in the atmosphere. How long ago did the individual who became the mummy die?

As mentioned above, in 5600 years half the carbon 14 in a specimen will decay. This means the individual who became the mummy died about 5600 years ago.

(b) Let R be the (nearly constant) ratio of carbon 14 to carbon 12 in the atmosphere, and let r be the ratio in an observed specimen. What is the relationship between R and r?

Assuming that R and r are related by an exponential growth function, the value of r, where R is the ratio at time $t = 0$, is

$$r = Re^{kt}.$$

To find k, use the fact that $r = R/2$ if $t = 5600$. Substitution gives

$$\frac{1}{2}R = Re^{5600k}, \quad \text{or} \quad \frac{1}{2} = e^{5600k}.$$

Taking natural logarithms on both sides and using the power rule on the right,

$$\ln \frac{1}{2} = 5600k \ln e$$

or
$$\ln 1 - \ln 2 = 5600k \ln e.$$

Since $\ln 1 = 0$ and $\ln e = 1$,

$$-\ln 2 = 5600k$$

$$k = -\frac{\ln 2}{5600}.$$

The relationship between R and r is given by

$$r = Re^{(-t \ln 2)/5600}. \qquad (*)$$

(c) Verify equation (*) for $t = 0$.

Substitute 0 for t in the equation (*). This gives

$$r = Re^{(-0 \cdot \ln 2)/5600}$$

$$= R \cdot e^0 = R \cdot 1 = R$$

This result is correct; when $t = 0$, the specimen has just died, so that R and r should be the same.

(d) Suppose a specimen is found in which $r = \frac{2}{3}R$. Estimate the age of the specimen.

Use equation (*) and substitute $\frac{2}{3}R$ for r.

$$r = Re^{(-t \ln 2)/5600}$$

$$\frac{2}{3}R = Re^{(-t \ln 2)/5600}$$

Dividing through by R gives

$$\frac{2}{3} = e^{(-t \ln 2)/5600}.$$

Take natural logarithms on both sides:

$$\ln \frac{2}{3} = \ln e^{(-t \ln 2)/5600}.$$

Using properties of logarithms gives

$$\ln 2 - \ln 3 = \frac{-t \ln 2}{5600}.$$

To solve this equation for t, the age of the specimen, multiply both sides by $-5600/\ln 2$. This gives

$$\frac{-5600(\ln 2 - \ln 3)}{\ln 2} = t.$$

Using the table or a calculator, $\ln 3 \approx 1.0986$ and $\ln 2 \approx .6931$. These values lead to

$$t \approx \frac{-5600(.6931 - 1.0986)}{.6931} \approx 3280,$$

so the specimen is about 3280 years old. ■

The exponential growth functions discussed so far all continued to grow without bound. Many populations, however, grow exponentially for a while, but then the growth is slowed by some external constraint which eventually limits the growth. For example, an animal population may grow to the point where its habitat can no longer support the population and the growth rate begins to dwindle until a stable population size is reached. Models which reflect this pattern are called **limited growth functions.** The next two examples discuss functions of this type.

EXAMPLE 5

Suppose the sales, $S(x)$, in some appropriate unit, of a new model typewriter are approximated by the function

$$S(x) = 1000 - 800e^{-x},$$

where x represents the number of years the typewriter has been on the market.

(a) In how many years will sales reach 500 units?

Replace $S(x)$ with 500 and solve the equation for x.

$$500 = 1000 - 800e^{-x}$$

$$-500 = -800e^{-x}$$

$$.625 = e^{-x}$$

Take natural logarithms on both sides.

$$\ln .625 = \ln e^{-x}$$
$$\ln .625 = -x \ln e$$
$$\ln .625 = -x$$
$$x = -\ln .625 \approx .47$$

Sales will reach 500 units in about 1/2 year or 6 months.

(b) Will sales ever reach 1000 units?

Replacing $S(x)$ with 1000 gives

$$1000 = 1000 - 800 e^{-x}$$
$$0 = -800 e^{-x}$$
$$e^{-x} = 0.$$

Since $e^{-x} > 0$ for all x, sales will never reach 1000 units. As x gets larger and larger, $800 e^{-x} = 800/e^x$ will get smaller and smaller. This means sales will tend to level off with time and gradually approach a limit of 1000. The horizontal line $y = 1000$ is an asymptote to the graph of the function as shown in Figure 9. ■

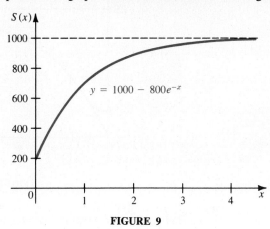

FIGURE 9

EXAMPLE 6

Assembly line operations tend to have a high turnover of employees forcing companies to spend much time and effort in training new workers. It has been found that a worker new to a task on the line will produce items according to the function

$$P(x) = 25 - 25 e^{-.3x},$$

where $P(x)$ items are produced by the worker on day x.

(a) What is the limit on the number of items a worker on this assembly line can produce?

Since the exponent on e is negative, write the function as

$$P(x) = 25 - \frac{25}{e^{.3x}}.$$

As $x \rightarrow \infty$, the term $(25/e^{.3x}) \rightarrow 0$, so $P(x) \rightarrow 25$. The limit is 25 items.

(b) How many days will it take for a new worker to produce 20 items?

Let $P(x) = 20$ and solve for x.

$$P(x) = 25 - 25e^{-.3x}$$
$$20 = 25 - 25e^{-.3x}$$
$$-5 = -25e^{-.3x}$$
$$.2 = e^{-.3x}$$

Now take natural logarithms of both sides and use properties of logarithms.

$$\ln .2 = -.3x \ln e$$
$$\ln .2 = -.3x$$
$$x = \frac{\ln .2}{-.3} \approx 5.4$$

In about 5 1/2 days on the job a new worker will be producing 20 items. A graph of the function P is shown in Figure 10. ■

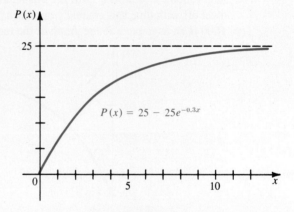

$P(x) = 25 - 25e^{-0.3x}$

FIGURE 10

Graphs such as the one in Figure 10 are called **learning curves.** According to such a graph, a new worker tends to learn quickly at first; then learning tapers off and approaches some upper limit. This is characteristic of the learning of certain types of skills involving the repetitive performance of the same task.

The last example discusses still another type of exponential function.

EXAMPLE 7

Under certain conditions the total number of facts of a certain kind that are remembered is approximated by

$$N(t) = y_0\left(\frac{1 + e}{1 + e^{t+1}}\right)$$

where $N(t)$ is the number of facts remembered at time t, measured in days, and y_0 is the number of facts remembered initially. Graph the function.

The graph of $N(t)$ has no vertical asymptotes, since $1 + e^{t+1} > 0$ for all t. The numerator is constant and the denominator increases as t increases, so $y = 0$ is a horizontal asymptote. The first derivative is

$$N'(t) = \frac{-y_0(1 + e)e^{t+1}}{(1 + e^{t+1})^2}.$$

Neither the numerator nor denominator of $N'(t)$ can equal 0, so there are no extrema. Since $N'(t) < 0$ for all values of t, the graph is always decreasing. Plotting a few points will complete the graph. For example, if $t = 0$

$$N(0) = y_0\left(\frac{1 + e}{1 + e^1}\right) = y_0(1) = y_0.$$

If $t = 1$,

$$N(1) = y_0\left(\frac{1 + e}{1 + e^2}\right) \approx y_0\left(\frac{3.718}{8.389}\right) = .44 y_0.$$

The graph, shown in Figure 11, is called a **forgetting curve.**

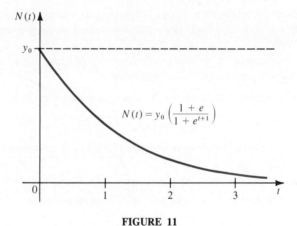

FIGURE 11

12.5 EXERCISES

1. A population of 100 lice is growing exponentially. After 2 months the population has increased to 125.
   (a) Write an exponential equation to express the exponential growth function y in terms of time t in months.
   (b) How long will it take for the population to reach 500?

2. A culture contains 25,000 bacteria, with the population increasing exponentially. The culture contains 40,000 bacteria after 10 hours.
   (a) Write an exponential equation to express the growth function y in terms of time t in hours.
   (b) How long will it be until there are 60,000 bacteria?

3. Five hundred grams of a radioactive substance is decaying exponentially. The substance is reduced to 400 grams after 4 days.

  (a) Write an exponential equation to express the decay function y in terms of time t in days.

  (b) Find the half-life of the substance.

4. When a bactericide is introduced into a culture of 50,000 bacteria, the number of bacteria decreases exponentially. After 9 hours, there are only 20,000 bacteria.

  (a) Write an exponential equation to express the decay function y in terms of time t in hours.

  (b) In how many hours will half the number of bacteria remain?

5. The amount of chemical that will dissolve in a solution increases exponentially as the temperature is increased. At $0°$ C 10 grams dissolved and at a temperature of $10°$ C 11 grams dissolved.

  (a) Write an equation to express the amount of chemical dissolved, y, in terms of temperature, t, in degrees Celsius.

  (b) At what temperature will 15 grams dissolve?

6. The population of a boomtown in Alaska is increasing exponentially. There were 10,000 people in town when the boom began. Two years later the population had reached 12,000.

  (a) Write an equation to express the growth function y in terms of time t in years.

  (b) How long will it be until the population doubles?

7. The amount of a certain radioactive specimen present at time t (measured in seconds) is given by

$$A(t) = 5000\,e^{-.02t},$$

where $A(t)$ is the amount measured in grams. Find each of the following.

  (a) $A(0)$ **(b)** $A(5)$

  (c) $A(20)$ **(d)** the half-life of the specimen

8. The number of bacteria in a certain culture, $B(t)$, is approximated by

$$B(t) = 250{,}000\,e^{-.04t}$$

where t is time measured in hours. Find each of the following.

  (a) B_0 **(b)** $B(5)$ **(c)** $B(20)$

  (d) the time it will take until only 125,000 bacteria are present

  (e) the time it will take until only 25,000 bacteria are present

Using Example 4, find the age of a specimen for each of the following.

9. $r = .8R$ **10.** $r = .4R$ **11.** $r = .1R$ **12.** $r = .01R$

13. A large cloud of radioactive debris from a nuclear explosion has floated over the Pacific Northwest, contaminating much of the hay supply. Consequently, farmers in the area are concerned that the cows who eat this hay will give contaminated milk. (The tolerance level for radioactive iodine in milk is 0.) The percent of the initial amount of radioactive iodine still present in the hay after t days is approximated by $P(t)$, which is given by the mathematical model

$$P(t) = 100\,e^{-.1t}.$$

  (a) Find the percent remaining after 4 days.

  (b) Find the percent remaining after 10 days.

(c) Some scientists feel that the hay is safe after the percent of radioactive iodine has declined to 10% of the original amount. Solve the equation $10 = 100\,e^{-.1t}$ to find the number of days before the hay may be used.

(d) Other scientists believe that the hay is not safe until the level of radioactive iodine has declined to only 1% of the original level. Find the number of days that this would take.

14. Experiments have shown that sales of a product, under relatively stable market conditions, but in the absence of promotional activities such as advertising, tend to decline at a constant yearly rate. This sales decline, which varies considerably from product to product, can often be expressed by an exponential function of the form

$$S(t) = S_0 e^{-at},$$

where $S(t)$ is the sales at time t measured in years, S_0 is sales at time $t = 0$, and a is the sales decay constant. Suppose a certain product had sales of 50,000 at the beginning of the year and 45,000 at the end of the year.

(a) Write an equation for the sales decline.

(b) Find $S(2)$.

(c) How long will it take for sales to decline to 40,000?

15. Under certain conditions, the number of a type of bacteria present in a colony is given by

$$E(t) = E_0 e^{kt},$$

where $E(t)$ is the number of bacteria present t minutes after the beginning of an experiment, and E_0 is the number present when $t = 0$. Suppose there were 10^6 bacteria present initially and 1.8×10^6 bacteria present after 60 minutes.

(a) Write an equation for the number of bacteria present at time t.

(b) Find $E(10)$.

(c) How long will it take for the population to reach 1,500,000?

16. The higher a student's grade-point average, the fewer applications the student must send to medical schools (other things being equal). Using information given in a guidebook for prospective medical school students, we constructed the following mathematical model of the number of applications that a student should send out:

$$y = 540\,e^{-1.3x},$$

where y is the number of applications that should be sent out by a person whose grade-point average is x. Here $2.0 \le x \le 4.0$. Use a calculator with a y^x key to find the number of applications that should be sent out by students having a grade-point average of

(a) 2.0;   (b) 2.5;   (c) 3.0.

What grade-point average requires the following number of applications?

(d) 15   (e) 3

17. Suppose the number of symbols per minute a keypunch operator can produce is given by

$$p(t) = 350 - 80\,e^{-.3t}$$

where t is the number of months the operator has been training. Find each of the following.

(a) $p(2)$ (b) $p(4)$ (c) $p(10)$

(d) When will an operator produce 300 symbols per minute?

(e) What is the limit on the number of symbols produced per minute?

(f) Graph $p(t)$.

18. The number of words per minute that an average typist can type is given by
$$W(x) = 60 - 30e^{-.5t},$$
where t is time in months after the beginning of a typing class. Find each of the following.

  (a) $W_0 = W(0)$ **(b)** $W(1)$ **(c)** $W(4)$

  (d) When will the average typist type 45 words per minute?

  (e) What is the upper limit on the number of words that can be typed according to this model?

  (f) Graph $W(x)$.

19. Sales of a new model can opener are approximated by
$$S(x) = 5000 - 4000e^{-x},$$
where x represents the number of years that the can opener has been on the market, and $S(x)$ represents sales in thousands. Find each of the following.

  (a) $S_0 = S(0)$ **(b)** $S(2)$ **(c)** $S(10)$

  (d) When will sales reach 4,500,000?

  (e) Find the limit on sales.

  (f) Graph $S(x)$.

20. Assume that a person new to an assembly line will produce
$$P(x) = 500 - 500e^{-x}$$
items per day, where x is time measured in days. Find each of the following.

  (a) $P_0 = P(0)$ **(b)** $P(2)$ **(c)** $P(5)$

  (d) When will a new person produce 400 items?

  (e) Find the limit on the number of items produced per day.

  (f) Graph $P(x)$.

Newton's Law of Cooling says that the rate at which a body cools is proportional to the difference in temperature between the body and an environment into which it is introduced. This leads to an equation where the temperature $f(t)$ of the body at time t after being introduced into an environment having constant temperature T_0 is
$$f(t) = T_0 + Ce^{-kt},$$
where C and k are constants. Use this result in Exercises 21–24.

21. Find the temperature of an object when $t = 4$ if $T_0 = 125$, $C = 8$, and $k = .2$.

22. Find the temperature of an object when $t = 9$ if $T_0 = 18$, $C = 5$, and $k = .6$

23. If $C = 100$, $k = .1$, and t is in minutes, how long will it take a hot cup of coffee to cool to a temperature of 25° Celsius in a room at 20° Celsius?

24. If $C = -14.6$ and $k = .6$ and t is in hours, how long will it take a frozen pizza to thaw to 10° Celsius in a room at 18° Celsius?

A sociologist has shown that the fraction $y(t)$ of people who have heard a rumor after t days is approximated by
$$y(t) = \frac{y_0 e^{kt}}{1 - y_0(1 - e^{kt})},$$
where y_0 is the fraction of people who have heard the rumor at time $t = 0$, and k is a constant. A graph of $y(t)$ for a particular value of k is shown in the figure on the next page.

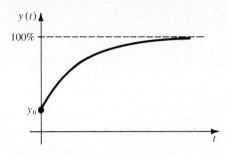

25. If $k = 0.1$ and $y_0 = .05$, find $y(10)$.

26. If $k = .2$ and $y_0 = 0.10$, find $y(5)$.

27. If $k = 0.1$ and $y_0 = 0.02$, find the number of days until half the people have heard the rumor.

28. Environmental situations place effective limits on the population growth of an organism in an area. Many such limited growth situations are described by the *logistic function:*

$$G(t) = \frac{mG_0}{G_0 + (m - G_0)e^{-kmt}},$$

where G_0 is the initial number present, m is the maximum possible size of the population, and k is a positive constant. Assume $G_0 = 1000$, $m = 2500$, $k = .0004$, and t is time in decades (10-year periods).

(a) Find $G(.2)$.   **(b)** Find $G(1)$.   **(c)** Find $G(3)$.

(d) At what time t will the population reach 2000?

(e) Graph $G(t)$. (*Hint:* There is an inflection point at $t \approx .4$. What does this mean in terms of population?)

EXTENDED

APPLICATION

The Van Meegeren Art Forgeries*

After the liberation of Belgium at the end of World War II, officials began a search for Nazi collaborators. One person arrested as a collaborator was a minor painter, H. A. Van Meegeren; he was charged with selling a valuable painting by the Dutch artist Vermeer (1632–1675) to the Nazi Hermann Goering. He defended himself from the very serious charge of collaboration by claiming that the painting was a fake—he had forged it himself.

He also claimed that the beautiful and famous painting "Disciples at Emmaus," as well as several other supposed Vermeers, was his own work. To prove this, he did another "Vermeer" in his prison cell. An international panel of experts was assembled, which pronounced as forgeries all the "Vermeers" in question.

*From "The Van Meegeren Art Forgeries" by Martin Braun from *Applied Mathematical Sciences*, Vol. 15. Copyright © 1975. Published by Springer-Verlag New York, Inc. Reprinted by permission.

Many people would not accept the verdict of this panel for the painting "Disciples at Emmaus"; it was felt to be too beautiful to be the work of a minor talent such as Van Meegeren. In fact, the painting was declared genuine by a noted art scholar and sold for $170,000. The question of the authenticity of this painting continued to trouble art historians, who began to insist on conclusive proof one way or the other. This proof was given by a group of scientists at Carnegie-Mellon University, using the idea of radioactive decay.

The dating of objects is based on radioactivity; the atoms of certain radioactive elements are unstable, and within a given time period a fixed fraction of such atoms will spontaneously disintegrate, forming atoms of a new element. If t_0 represents some initial time, N_0 represents the number of atoms present at time t_0, and N represents the number present at some later time t, then it can be shown (using physics and calculus) that

$$t - t_0 = \frac{1}{\lambda} \cdot \ln \frac{N_0}{N}$$

where λ is a "decay constant" that depends on the radioactive substance under consideration.

If t_0 is the time that the substance was formed or made, then $t - t_0$ is the age of the item. Thus, the age of an item is given by

$$\frac{1}{\lambda} \cdot \ln \frac{N_0}{N}.$$

The decay constant λ can be readily found, as can N, the number of atoms present now. The problem is N_0—we can't find a value for this variable. However, it is possible to get reasonable ranges for the values of N_0. This is done by studying the white lead in the painting. This pigment has been used by artists for over 2000 years. It contains a small amount of the radioactive substance lead 210 and an even smaller amount of radium 226.

Radium 226 disintegrates through a series of intermediate steps to produce lead 210. The lead 210, in turn, decays to form polonium 210. This last process, lead 210 to polonium 210, has a half-life of 22 years. That is, in 22 years half the initial quantity of lead 210 will decay to polonium 210.

When lead ore is processed to form white lead, most of the radium is removed with other waste products. Thus, most of the supply of lead 210 is cut off, with the remainder beginning to decay very rapidly. This process continues until the lead 210 in the white lead is once more in equilibrium with the small amount of radium then present. Let $y(t)$ be the amount of lead 210 per gram of white lead present at time of manufacture of the pigment, t_0. Let r represent the number of disintegrations of radium 226 per minute per gram of white lead. (Actually, r is a function of time, but the half-life of radium 226 is so long in comparison to the time interval in question that we assume it to be a constant.) If λ is the decay constant for lead 210, then it can be shown that

$$y(t) = \frac{r}{\lambda}[1 - e^{-\lambda(t-t_0)}] + y_0 e^{-\lambda(t-t_0)}. \tag{1}$$

All variables in this result can be evaluated except y_0. To get around this problem, we use the fact that the original amount of lead 210 was in radioactive equilibrium with the larger amount of radium 226 in the ore from which the metal was extracted. We therefore take samples of different ores and compute the rate of disintegration of radium 226. The results are as shown in the table.

Location of Ore	Disintegrations of Radium 226 Per Minute Per Gram of White Lead
Oklahoma	4.5
S.E. Missouri	.7
Idaho	.18
Idaho	2.2
Washington	140
British Columbia	.4

The numbers in the table vary from .18 to 140—quite a range. Since the number of disintegrations is proportional to the amount of lead 210 present originally, we must conclude that y_0 also varies over a tremendous range. Thus, equation (1) cannot be used to obtain even a crude estimate of the age of a painting. However, we want to distinguish only between a modern forgery and a genuine painting 300 years old.

To do this, we observe that if the painting is very old compared to the 22-year half-life of lead 210, then the amount of radioactivity from the lead 210 will almost equal the amount of radioactivity from the radium 226. On the other hand, if the painting is modern, then the amount of radioactivity from the lead 210 will be much greater than the amount from the radium 226.

We want to know if the painting is modern or 300 years old. To find out, let $t - t_0 = 300$ in equation (1), getting

$$\lambda y_0 = \lambda \cdot y(t) \cdot e^{300\lambda} + r(e^{300\lambda} - 1) \tag{2}$$

after some rearrangement of terms. If the painting is modern, then λy_0 should be a very large number; λy_0 represents the number of disintegrations of the lead 210 per minute per gram of white lead at the time of manufacture. By studying samples of white lead, we can conclude that λy_0 should never be anywhere near as large as 30,000. Thus, we use equation (2) to calculate λy_0; if our result is greater than 30,000 we conclude that the painting is a modern forgery. The details of this calculation are left for the exercises.

EXERCISES

1. To calculate λ, use the formula

$$\lambda = \frac{\ln 2}{\text{half-life}}$$

Find λ for lead 210, whose half-life is 22 years.

2. For the painting "Disciples at Emmaus," the current rate of disintegration of the lead 210 was measured and found to be $\lambda \cdot y(t) = 8.5$. Also, r was found to be .8. Use this information and equation (2) to calculate λy_0. Based on your results, what do you conclude about the age of the painting?

The table below lists several other possible forgeries. Decide which of them must be modern forgeries.

Title	$\lambda \cdot y(t)$	r
3. "Washing of Feet"	12.6	.26
4. "Lace Maker"	1.5	.4
5. "Laughing Girl"	5.2	6
6. "Woman Reading Music"	10.3	.3

12.6   Compound Interest

An important application of exponential functions comes when calculating **compound interest.** The cost of borrowing money or the return on an investment is called **interest.** The amount borrowed or invested is the **principal,** P. The **rate of interest,** r, is given as a percent per year, and t is the **time,** measured in years.

Simple Interest

> The product of the principal P, rate r, and time t gives **simple interest,** I:
> $$I = Prt.$$

With **compound interest,** interest is charged (or paid) on interest, as well as on principal. To find a formula for compound interest, first suppose that P dollars, the principal, is deposited at a rate of interest i per year. The interest earned during the first year is found by the formula for simple interest:

$$\text{first-year interest} = P \cdot i \cdot 1 = Pi.$$

At the end of one year, the amount on deposit will be the sum of the original principal and the interest earned, or

$$P + Pi = P(1 + i). \tag{1}$$

If the deposit earns compound interest, the interest earned during the second year is found from the total amount on deposit at the end of the first year. Thus, the interest earned during the second year (again found by the formula for simple interest), is given by

$$[P(1 + i)](i)(1) = P(1 + i)i, \tag{2}$$

so that the total amount on deposit at the end of the second year is given by the sum of the amounts from (1) and (2) above, or

$$P(1 + i) + P(1 + i)i = P(1 + i)(1 + i)$$
$$= P(1 + i)^2.$$

In the same way, the total amount on deposit at the end of three years is

$$P(1 + i)^3.$$

Generalizing, in j years, the total amount on deposit, called the **compound amount,** is $P(1 + i)^j$.

When interest is compounded more than once a year, the compound interest formula is adjusted as follows.

Compound Interest

> The compound amount if P dollars is deposited at a yearly rate of interest i compounded m times per year for n years is
>
> $$A = P\left(1 + \frac{i}{m}\right)^{mn}.$$

EXAMPLE 1

Find the amount of interest paid on a loan of $9,000 at 12% compounded quarterly for 8 years.

Use the formula for compound interest with $P = 9000$, $i = .12$, $m = 4$ (quarterly means 4 times a year), and $n = 8$.

$$A = P\left(1 + \frac{i}{m}\right)^{mn}$$

$$= 9000\left(1 + \frac{.12}{4}\right)^{4(8)}$$

$$= 9000(1 + .03)^{32}$$

$$= 9000(1.03)^{32}$$

To find $(1.03)^{32}$, use a calculator or the compound interest table given at the back of this book. Look for 3% across the top and 32 down the side. You should find 2.57508 which gives

$$A = 9000(2.57508) = 23,175.72.$$

The loan plus the interest is $23,175.72 and the interest is $23,175.72 − $9,000 = $14,175.72. ■

The more often interest is compounded within a given time period, the greater the interest earned. Using a calculator with a y^x key, or a compound interest table more complete than the one in this text, and using the formula above, we can get the results shown in the table on the next page.

As suggested by the table, it makes a big difference whether interest is compounded or not. Interest differs by $905.85 when simple interest is compared to interest compounded annually. However, increasing the frequency of compounding makes smaller and smaller differences in the amount of interest earned. In fact, it can be shown that even if interest is compounded at intervals of time as small as one chooses (such as each hour, each minute, or each second), the total amount of interest earned will be only slightly more than for daily compounding. This is true even for a process called **continuous compounding** which can be loosely described as compounding every instant. (See Examples 2 and 3.)

Interest on $1000 at 12% per year for 10 years

Compounded	Number of periods	Compound amount	Interest
not at all (simple interest)	—	—	$1200.00
annually	10	$1000(1 + .12)^{10} = \$3105.85$	$2105.85
semiannually	20	$1000\left(1 + \dfrac{.12}{2}\right)^{20} = \$3207.14$	$2207.14
quarterly	40	$1000\left(1 + \dfrac{.12}{4}\right)^{40} = \$3262.04$	$2262.04
monthly	120	$1000\left(1 + \dfrac{.12}{12}\right)^{120} = \$3300.39$	$2300.39
daily	3650	$1000\left(1 + \dfrac{.12}{365}\right)^{3650} = \$3319.46$	$2319.46
hourly	87,600	$1000\left(1 + \dfrac{.12}{8760}\right)^{87,600} = \$3320.09$	$2320.09
every minute	5,256,000	$1000\left(1 + \dfrac{.12}{525,600}\right)^{5,256,000} = \$3320.11$	$2320.11

In the table above, if we consider the interest for just one year, instead of for 10 years, the compound amounts are

$$1000(1 + .12)^1, \qquad 1000\left(1 + \frac{.12}{2}\right)^2, \qquad 1000\left(1 + \frac{.12}{3}\right)^3,$$

and so on. These numbers are the terms of a sequence with general term

$$1000\left(1 + \frac{i}{m}\right)^m.$$

If we let

$$\frac{i}{m} = \frac{1}{s}, \quad \text{so that} \quad m = si,$$

then

$$\lim_{m \to \infty} \left(1 + \frac{i}{m}\right)^m = \lim_{s \to \infty} \left(1 + \frac{1}{s}\right)^{si}$$

$$= \lim_{s \to \infty} \left[\left(1 + \frac{1}{s}\right)^s\right]^i$$

$$= \left[\lim_{s \to \infty} \left(1 + \frac{1}{s}\right)^s\right]^i.$$

In Section 2 of this chapter, we showed that

$$\lim_{m \to \infty} \left(1 + \frac{1}{m}\right)^m = e.$$

Using s as the variable instead of m gives

$$\lim_{s \to \infty} \left(1 + \frac{1}{s}\right)^{s} = e.$$

Thus,

$$\left[\lim_{s \to \infty} \left(1 + \frac{1}{s}\right)^{s}\right]^{i} = e^{i},$$

and

$$\lim_{m \to \infty} \left(1 + \frac{i}{m}\right)^{m} = e^{i}.$$

Generalizing from this example, we get the following formula for continuous compounding.

Continuous Compounding

If P dollars is deposited at a rate of interest i compounded continuously for n years, the compound amount is

$$A = Pe^{ni} \quad \text{dollars.}$$

EXAMPLE 2

Suppose $1000 is deposited in an account paying 12% compounded continuously for 10 years. Find the compound amount.

Let $P = 1000$, $n = 10$, and $i = .12$. Then

$$A = 1000\,e^{10(.12)} = 1000\,e^{1.2}.$$

From the table of powers of e, or a calculator, $e^{1.2} \approx 3.32012$, and

$$A = 1000(3.32012) = 3320.12$$

or $3320.12. Compare this amount with the results in the chart given above. Daily compounding produces only 66¢ less. ▪

EXAMPLE 3

Assuming continuous compounding, if the inflation rate averaged 6% a year for 5 years, how much would a $1 item cost at the end of the 5 years?

In the formula for continuous compounding, let $P = 1$, $n = 5$, and $i = .06$, to get

$$A = 1\,e^{5(.06)} = e^{.3} \approx 1.34986.$$

An item that cost $1 at the beginning of the 5-year period would cost $1.35 at the end of the period, an increase of 35% or about 1/3. ▪

Effective Rate   From the compound interest table or a calculator, we find that $1 at 8% interest (per year) compounded semiannually is $1(1.04)^{2} = 1.0816$ or $1.0816. The actual increase of $.0816 is 8.16% rather than the 8% that would be earned with interest compounded annually. To distinguish between these two amounts, 8% (the annual interest rate) is called the **nominal** or **stated** interest rate, and 8.16% is called the **effective** interest rate.

Effective Rate

> If i is the annual stated rate of interest and m is the number of compounding periods per year, the effective rate of interest is
>
> $$\left(1 + \frac{i}{m}\right)^m - 1.$$

EXAMPLE 4

Find the effective rate corresponding to a nominal interest rate of 8% compounded quarterly.

We could use the formula from the box above, but it is simpler to look in the compound interest table for $8\%/4 = 2\%$ for 4 periods. From the table we find the effective rate is $1.08243 - 1 = .08243$ or 8.243%. ▧

The formula for interest compounded m times a year, $A = P(1 + i/m)^{nm}$, has five variables, $A, P, i, m,$ and n. If we know the values of any four, we can then find the value of the fifth. In particular, if we know A, the amount of money we wish to end up with, and also know $i, m,$ and n, then we can find P. Here P is the amount that we should deposit today to produce A dollars in n years. The amount P is called the **present value** of A dollars. The next example shows how this works.

EXAMPLE 5

Ed Calvin has a balloon payment of \$100,000 due in 3 years. What is the present value of that amount if the money earns interest at 12% annually?

Here P in the compound interest formula is unknown, with $A = 100{,}000$, $i = .12$, $n = 3$, and $m = 1$. Substitute the known values into the formula to get $100{,}000 = P(1.12)^3$. Solve for P using a calculator to find $(1.12)^3$.

$$P = \frac{100{,}000}{(1.12)^3} = 71{,}178.03$$

The present value of \$100,000 in 3 years at 12% a year is \$71,178.03. ▧

In solving the equation of Example 5, we could have proceeded as follows.

$$100{,}000 = P(1.12)^3$$

Multiply both sides by $(1.12)^{-3}$ to solve for P, so

$$P = 100{,}000(1.12)^{-3}.$$

This suggests a general formula for present value.

Present Value

> The present value of A dollars at a rate of interest i compounded m times per year for n years is
>
> $$P = A\left(1 + \frac{i}{m}\right)^{-mn}.$$

We can also solve $A = Pe^{ni}$ for any of the variables A, P, n, or i, as the following example shows.

EXAMPLE 6

Suppose the rate of inflation in the economy averages 8% per year, assuming continuous compounding. Find the number of years it would take for the general level of prices to double.

We want to find the number of years it will take for $1 worth of goods or services to cost $2. That is, we want to find n in the equation

$$A = Pe^{ni}$$

or

$$2 = 1e^{.08n}.$$

Taking natural logarithms on both sides,

$$\ln 2 = \ln e^{.08n}.$$

Using the power rule for logarithms and the fact that $\ln e = 1$ gives

$$\ln 2 = .08n$$

$$n = \frac{\ln 2}{.08} \approx 8.7.$$

The general level of prices will double in about 9 years. ▮

12.6 EXERCISES

In Exercises 1–8, find the compound amount when the given deposits are made.

1. $4000 at 6% compounded annually for 10 years

2. $950 at 9% compounded annually for 15 years

3. $1500 at 13.5% compounded semiannually for 11 semiannual periods

4. $45,675 at 13.2% compounded quarterly for 9 years

5. $3256 at 14% compounded quarterly for 13 quarters

6. $13,675 at 14.4% compounded monthly for 36 months

7. $2398.45 at 13.2% compounded monthly for 48 months

8. $2964.58 at 11.25% compounded daily (ignoring leap years) for 9 years of 365 days

Find the compound amount if $20,000 is invested at 8% compounded continuously for the number of years given in Exercises 9–14.

9. 1   **10.** 5   **11.** 10   **12.** 15   **13.** 3   **14.** 7

Find the compound amount of the deposits in Exercises 15–20 compounded continuously.

15. $10,000 at 12% for 5 years

16. $8900 at 10% for 3 years

17. $1593 at 15% for 8 years

18. $23,675 at 9% for 2 years

19. $5670 at 12% for 10 years

20. $68,000 at 10% for 8 years

Find the effective rate corresponding to each of the nominal rates given in Exercises 21–26.

21. 5% compounded monthly

22. 15% compounded quarterly

23. 18% compounded semiannually

24. 10% compounded monthly

25. 11% compounded quarterly

26. 13% compounded semiannually

27. Find the number of years it will take for $1000 at 12% compounded annually to
   (a) double   **(b)** triple

28. If interest is compounded quarterly, how long will it take in Exercise 27 for the account to
   (a) double?   **(b)** triple?

29. Assuming continuous compounding, find the time it would take for the general level of prices in the economy to double if the average annual inflation rate is
   (a) 6%   **(b)** 8%   **(c)** 12%

30. Find the interest rate required for an investment of $5000 to grow to $8000 in 4 years under the following conditions.
   (a) interest is compounded annually
   (b) interest is compounded quarterly
   (c) interest is compounded continuously

Find the present value of each amount in Exercises 31–38.

31. $2000 at 6% compounded semiannually for 11 years

32. $5000 at 8% compounded annually for 12 years

33. $10,000 at 10% compounded quarterly for 8 years

34. $7300 at 11% compounded semiannually for 15 years

35. $10,000, if interest is 12% compounded semiannually for 5 years

36. $25,000, if interest is 16% compounded quarterly for 11 quarters

37. $45,678.93 if interest is 12.6% compounded monthly for 11 months

38. $123,788 if interest is 14.7% compounded daily for 195 days (Assume 365 days in a year.)

Find the final amount for each of the following deposits.

39. $2758.32 at 5 1/2% compounded quarterly for 8 years

40. $173,000 at 6 1/4% compounded semiannually for 5 years

41. $6293 at 8 3/4% compounded annually for 25 years

42. $47,230 at 9 1/4% compounded semiannually for 22 years

Find the present value of each of the following amounts.

43. $5270, interest at 4 3/4% compounded annually for 18 years

44. $36,950, interest at 7.2% compounded semiannually for 15.5 years

45. $12,650, interest at 8.15% compounded quarterly for 25 years

46. $7516.28, interest at 6.3% compounded monthly for 8 years

Find the effective rate for a nominal rate of 7 1/2% compounded as follows.

47. semiannually

48. quarterly

49. monthly

50. 360 times per year

51. 365 times per year

52. Jacob can invest an inheritance of $10,000 at 6 1/2%. How much will it be worth in five years if interest is compounded semiannually?

<table>
<tr><td>**KEY WORDS**</td><td>exponential function</td><td>limited growth function</td></tr>
<tr><td></td><td>exponential equation</td><td>learning curve</td></tr>
<tr><td></td><td>*e*</td><td>forgetting curve</td></tr>
<tr><td></td><td>logarithm</td><td>simple interest</td></tr>
<tr><td></td><td>logarithmic function</td><td>compound interest</td></tr>
<tr><td></td><td>properties of logarithms</td><td>compound amount</td></tr>
<tr><td></td><td>common logarithms</td><td>continuous compounding</td></tr>
<tr><td></td><td>natural logarithms</td><td>effective rate</td></tr>
<tr><td></td><td>exponential growth function</td><td>nominal (stated) rate</td></tr>
<tr><td></td><td>growth constant</td><td>present value</td></tr>
<tr><td></td><td>decay constant</td><td></td></tr>
</table>

Chapter 12 REVIEW EXERCISES

Solve the equations in Exercises 1–4.

1. $2^{3x} = \dfrac{1}{8}$ **2.** $\left(\dfrac{9}{16}\right)^x = \dfrac{3}{4}$ **3.** $9^{2y-1} = 27^y$ **4.** $\dfrac{1}{2} = \left(\dfrac{b}{4}\right)^{1/4}$

Graph the functions in Exercises 5–8.

5. $y = 5^x$ **6.** $y = 5^{-x}$ **7.** $y = \left(\dfrac{1}{5}\right)^x$ **8.** $y = \left(\dfrac{1}{2}\right)^{x+1}$

Write the equations in Exercises 9–12 using logarithms.

9. $2^6 = 64$ **10.** $3^{1/2} = \sqrt{3}$

11. $e^{0.09} = 1.09417$ **12.** $10^{1.07918} = 12$

Write the equations in Exercises 13–16 using exponents.

13. $\log_2 32 = 5$ **14.** $\log_{10} 100 = 2$

15. $\ln 82.9 = 4.41763$ **16.** $\log 15.46 = 1.18921$

Evaluate the expressions in Exercises 17–22.

17. $\log_3 81$ **18.** $\log_{1/3} 81$ **19.** $\log_{32} 16$

20. $\log_{25} 5$ **21.** $\log_{100} 1000$ **22.** $\log_{1/2} 4$

Find the natural logarithms in Exercises 23–26.

23. $\ln 6.2$ **24.** $\ln 700$ **25.** $\ln 483$ **26.** $\ln 0.504$

Simplify Exercises 27–30 using the properties of logarithms.

27. $\log_5 3k + \log_5 7k^3$ **28.** $\log_3 2y^3 - \log_3 8y^2$

29. $2 \log_2 x - 3 \log_2 m$ **30.** $5 \log_4 r - 3 \log_4 r^2$

Solve each equation in Exercises 31–38. Round to the nearest thousandth.

31. $8^p = 19$ **32.** $3^z = 11$ **33.** $2^{-m} = 7$

34. $15^{-k} = 9$ **35.** $e^{-5-2x} = 5$ **36.** $e^{3x-1} = 12$

37. $\left(1 + \dfrac{m}{3}\right)^5 = 10$ **38.** $\left(1 + \dfrac{2p}{5}\right)^2 = 3$

39. The average height, in meters, of the members of a certain tribe is approximated by

$$h = 0.5 + \log t,$$

where t is the tribe member's age in years, and $1 < t < 20$. Find the height of a tribe member of age

(a) 2 years   **(b)** 5 years

(c) 10 years   **(d)** 20 years.

(e) Graph h.

40. The turnover of legislators is a problem of interest to political scientists. One model of legislative turnover in the U.S. House of Representatives is given by the exponential function

$$M = 434\,e^{-.08t},$$

where M is the number of continuously serving members at time t.* This model is based on the 1965 membership of the House. Thus, 1965 corresponds to $t = 0$, 1966 to $t = 1$, and so on. Find the number of continuously serving members in each of the following years.

(a) 1969   **(b)** 1973   **(c)** 1979

Find the derivatives of the functions in Exercises 41–54.

41. $y = -6e^{2x}$ **42.** $y = 8e^{.5x}$ **43.** $y = e^{-2x^3}$

44. $y = -4e^{x^2}$ **45.** $y = 5x \cdot e^{2x}$ **46.** $y = -7x^2 \cdot e^{-3x}$

47. $y = \ln |2 + x^2|$ **48.** $y = \ln |5x + 3|$ **49.** $y = \dfrac{\ln |3x|}{x - 3}$

50. $y = \dfrac{\ln |2x - 1|}{x + 3}$ **51.** $y = \dfrac{x\,e^x}{\ln |x^2 - 1|}$ **52.** $y = \dfrac{(x^2 + 1)e^{2x}}{\ln |x|}$

53. $y = (x^2 + e^x)^2$ **54.** $y = (e^{2x+1} - 2)^4$

Find all relative maxima or minima for the functions in Exercises 55–58. Graph each function.

55. $y = x \cdot e^x$ **56.** $y = 3x \cdot e^{-x}$

57. $y = \dfrac{e^x}{x - 1}$ **58.** $y = \dfrac{\ln |5x|}{2x}$

59. The production of an oil well has decreased exponentially from 128,000 barrels per year five years ago to 100,000 barrels per year at present. Letting $t = 0$ represent the present time, find the following:

(a) an exponential equation for production y in terms of time t in years

(b) the time it will take for production to fall to 70,000 barrels per year

---

*From UMAP Unit 296, "Exponential Models of Legislative Turnover" by Thomas W. Casstevens, published by Birkhauser Boston, Inc. Reprinted by permission of COMAP, Inc.

60. A population of 15,000 small deer in a specific region has grown exponentially to 17,000 in 4 years.

(a) Write an exponential equation to express the population growth y in terms of time t in years.

(b) At this rate, how long will it take for the population to reach 45,000?

61. Radium-228 decays exponentially. A sample which contained 100 grams 6 years ago ($t = 0$) has decreased to 25 grams at present.

(a) Write an exponential equation to express the amount y present after t years.

(b) What is the half-life of radium-228?

62. The intensity of light (in appropriate units) passing through water decreases exponentially with the depth it penetrates into the liquid according to the function

$$I(x) = 10e^{-.3x},$$

where x is the depth in meters. A certain water plant requires light of an intensity of 1 unit. What is the greatest depth of water in which it will grow?

63. A company finds that its new workers produce

$$P(x) = 100 - 100e^{-.8x}$$

items per day, after x days on the job. Find each of the following.

(a) $P_0 = P(0)$ (b) $P(1)$ (c) $P(5)$

(d) How many items per day would you expect an experienced worker to produce?

(e) How long will it be before a new employee will produce 50 items per day?

(f) Graph $P(x)$.

64. The concentration of a certain drug in the bloodstream at time t in minutes is given by

$$c(t) = e^{-t} - e^{-2t}.$$

Find the concentration at the following times.

(a) $t = 0$ (b) $t = 1$ (c) $t = 5$

(d) Find the maximum concentration and the value of t where it occurs.

(e) Graph $c(t)$.

65. When glucose is infused into the bloodstream at a constant rate of c grams per minute, the glucose is converted and removed from the bloodstream at a rate proportional to the amount present. The amount of glucose in the bloodstream at time t (in minutes) is given by

$$g(t) = \frac{c}{a} + \left(g_0 - \frac{c}{a}\right)e^{-at}$$

where a is a positive constant. Assume $g_0 = .08$, $c = .1$, and $a = 1.3$. Find

(a) $g(5)$;   (b) $g(10)$;   (c) $g(20)$.

(d) At what time is the amount of glucose in the bloodstream .1 gram?

Find the compound amounts in Exercises 66–69.

66. $3000 at 6% compounded annually for 12 years

67. $512.78 at 16% compounded semiannually for 4 years

68. $12,000 at 8% compounded quarterly for 11 years

69. $11,702.55 at 18% compounded monthly for 10 years

Find the amount of interest earned by the deposits given in Exercises 70–71.

70. $6902 at 12% compounded semiannually for 8 years

71. $2781.36 at 8% compounded quarterly for 6 years

Find the compound amount if $12,104 is invested at 8% compounded continuously for the following number of years.

72. 2   **73.** 4   **74.** 7   **75.** 9   **76.** 12

Find the compound amount for the deposits in Exercises 77–80 if interest is compounded continuously.

77. $1500 at 10% for 9 years

78. $12,000 at 5% for 8 years

79. $68,100 at 9% for 2 years

80. $7590 at 15% for 4 years

81. Find the interest rate needed for $6000 to grow to $8000 in 3 years with continuous compounding.

82. How long will it take for $1 to triple at an average annual inflation rate of 8% compounded continuously?

Find the present value of each of the following amounts.

83. $2000 at 6% interest compounded annually for 5 years.

84. $10,000 at 8% interest compounded semiannually for 6 years.

85. $43,200 at 8% interest compounded quarterly for 4 years.

86. $9,760 at 12% interest compounded monthly for 3 years.

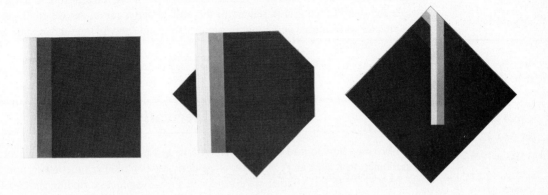

INTEGRATION

Karl Gerstner. From the series *Progressive Penetration* (Finite-Infinite Series), 1960. Pierburg Collection, Neus, West Germany.

Calculus is divided into *differential calculus,* which we discussed earlier, and *integral calculus,* which we consider in this chapter. Like the derivative of a function, the definite integral of a function is a special limit with many diverse applications. Geometrically, the derivative is related to the slope of the tangent line to a curve, while the definite integral is related to the area under a curve. As we shall see in this chapter, differential and integral calculus are connected by the fundamental theorem of calculus.

13.1   Antiderivatives

We have seen how to find the derivative of a large variety of functions. However, if some function f, such as $f(x) = 2x$, is the derivative of another function F, how do we find $F(x)$? In this chapter we consider this reverse process: finding *antiderivatives.*

Antiderivative

> If $F'(x) = f(x)$, then $F(x)$ is an **antiderivative** of $f(x)$.

EXAMPLE 1

(a) If $F(x) = 10x$, then $F'(x) = 10$, so $F(x) = 10x$ is an antiderivative of $f(x) = 10$.

(b) For $F(x) = x^2$, $F'(x) = 2x$, making $F(x) = x^2$ an antiderivative of $f(x) = 2x$. ■

EXAMPLE 2

Find an antiderivative of $f(x) = 5x^4$.

  To find a function $F(x)$ whose derivative is $5x^4$, work backwards. Recall that the derivative of x^n is nx^{n-1}. If

$$nx^{n-1} \quad \text{is} \quad 5x^4,$$

then $n - 1 = 4$ and $n = 5$, so x^5 is an antiderivative of $5x^4$. ■

  The function $F(x) = x^2$ is not the only function whose derivative is $f(x) = 2x$; for example, both $G(x) = x^2 + 2$ and $H(x) = x^2 - 7$ have $f(x) = 2x$ as a derivative. In fact, for any real number C, the function $f(x) = x^2 + C$ has $f(x) = 2x$ as its derivative. This means that there is a *family* or *class* of functions each of which is an antiderivative of $f(x)$. However, as the next theorem states, if two functions $F(x)$ and $G(x)$ are each antiderivatives of $f(x)$, then $F(x)$ and $G(x)$ can differ only by a constant.

Theorem

> If $F(x)$ and $G(x)$ are both antiderivatives of a function $f(x)$, then there is a constant C such that
>
> $$F(x) - G(x) = C.$$
>
> (Two antiderivatives of a function can differ only by a constant.)

For example,

$$F(x) = x^2 + 2, \qquad G(x) = x^2, \qquad \text{and} \qquad H(x) = x^2 - 4$$

are all antiderivatives of $f(x) = 2x$, and any two of them differ only by a constant. The derivative of a function gives the slope of the tangent line at any x-value. The fact that these three functions have the same derivative, $f(x) = 2x$, means that their slopes at any particular value of x are the same, as shown in Figure 1.

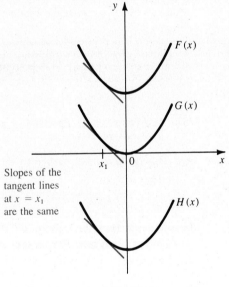

FIGURE 1

The family of all antiderivatives of the function f is indicated by

$$\int f(x)\ dx.$$

The symbol $\int$ is the **integral sign,** $f(x)$ is the **integrand,** and $\int f(x)\ dx$ is called an **indefinite integral,** the most general antiderivative of f.

The dx in the indefinite integral indicates that $\int f(x)\ dx$ is the "integral of $f(x)$ *with respect to x*" just as the symbol dy/dx denotes the "derivative of y with respect to x."

Indefinite Integral

If $F'(x) = f(x)$, then

$$\int f(x)\, dx = F(x) + C,$$

for any real number C.

For example, using this notation,

$$\int (2x)\, dx = x^2 + C.$$

Working backwards, as above, to find an antiderivative is not very satisfactory. We need some rules for finding antiderivatives. Since finding an indefinite integral is the inverse of finding a derivative, each formula for derivatives leads to a rule for indefinite integrals.

As mentioned above, the derivative of x^n is found by multiplying x by n and reducing the exponent on x by 1. To find an indefinite integral, that is, to undo what was done, *increase* the exponent by 1 and *divide* by the new exponent, $n + 1$.

Power Rule for Indefinite Integrals

For any real number $n \neq -1$,

$$\int x^n\, dx = \frac{1}{n+1} x^{n+1} + C.$$

This result can be verified by differentiating the expression on the right above:

$$\frac{d}{dx}\left(\frac{1}{n+1} x^{n+1} + C \right) = \frac{n+1}{n+1} x^{(n+1)-1} + 0 = x^n.$$

(If $n = -1$, the expression in the denominator is 0, and the above rule cannot be used. We will see later how to find an antiderivative in this case.)

EXAMPLE 3

Find each indefinite integral.

(a) $\int t^3\, dt$

Use the power rule with $n = 3$.

$$\int t^3\, dt = \frac{1}{3+1} t^{3+1} + C = \frac{1}{4} t^4 + C$$

(b) $\int \frac{1}{t^2}\, dt$

First, write $1/t^2$ as t^{-2}. Then

$$\int \frac{1}{t^2}\, dt = \int t^{-2}\, dt = \frac{t^{-1}}{-1} + C = \frac{-1}{t} + C.$$

(c) $\int \sqrt{u}\ du$

Since $\sqrt{u} = u^{1/2}$,

$$\int \sqrt{u}\ du = \int u^{1/2}\ du = \frac{1}{1/2 + 1} u^{3/2} + C = \frac{2}{3} u^{3/2} + C.$$

To check this, differentiate $(2/3)\,u^{3/2} + C$; the derivative is $u^{1/2}$, the original function.

(d) $\int dx$

Writing dx as $1 \cdot dx$, and using the fact that $x^0 = 1$ for any nonzero number x,

$$\int dx = \int 1\,dx = \int x^0\,dx = \frac{1}{1}\,x^1 + C = x + C. \quad \blacksquare$$

As shown earlier, the derivative of the product of a constant and a function is the product of the constant and the derivative of the function. A similar rule applies to indefinite integrals. Also, since derivatives of sums or differences are found term by term, indefinite integrals can also be found term by term. The next box states these rules for indefinite integrals.

Rules for Indefinite Integrals:	If all indicated integrals exist,
Constant Multiple	$\int k \cdot f(x)\,dx = k\int f(x)\ dx,$ for any real number k
Sum or Difference	$\int [f(x) \pm g(x)]\,dx = \int f(x)\ dx \pm \int g(x)\,dx.$

EXAMPLE 4

Find each of the following.

(a) $\int 2v^3\,dv$

By the constant multiple rule and the power rule,

$$\int 2v^3\ dv = 2\int v^3\ dv = 2\left(\frac{1}{4}v^4\right) + C = \frac{1}{2}v^4 + C.$$

(b) $\int \frac{12}{z^5}\ dz$

Use negative exponents.

$$\int \frac{12}{z^5}\ dz = \int 12z^{-5}\ dz = 12\int z^{-5}\ dz = 12\left(\frac{z^{-4}}{-4}\right) + C = -3z^{-4} + C = \frac{-3}{z^4} + C.$$

(c) $\int (3z^2 - 4z + 5)\,dz$

Using the results of this section,

$$\int (3z^2 - 4z + 5)\,dz = 3\int z^2\,dz - 4\int z\,dz + 5\int dz$$

$$= 3\left(\frac{1}{3}z^3\right) - 4\left(\frac{1}{2}z^2\right) + 5z + C$$

$$= z^3 - 2z^2 + 5z + C.$$

Only one constant C is needed in the answer: the three constants from integrating term by term are combined. In Example 4(a), C represents any real number, it is not necessary to multiply it by 2 in the next-to-last step. ∎

Integration can always be checked by taking the derivative of the result. For instance, in Example 4(c) check that $z^3 - 2z^2 + 5z + C$ is the required indefinite integral by taking the derivative

$$\frac{d}{dz}(z^3 - 2z^2 + 5z + C) = 3z^2 - 4z + 5,$$

the given function we started with.

As we know, the derivative of $f(x) = e^x$ is $f'(x) = e^x$. Also, the derivative of $f(x) = e^{kx}$ is $f'(x) = k \cdot e^{kx}$. These results lead to the following formulas for indefinite integrals of exponential functions.

Indefinite Integrals **of Exponential** **Functions**	$$\int e^x\,dx = e^x + C$$ $$\int e^{kx}\,dx = \frac{1}{k} \cdot e^{kx} + C, \quad k \neq 0$$

EXAMPLE 5

(a) $\displaystyle\int 9e^t\,dt = 9\int e^t\,dt = 9e^t + C$

(b) $\displaystyle\int e^{9t}\,dt = \frac{1}{9}\,e^{9t} + C$

(c) $\displaystyle\int 3e^{(5/4)u}\,du = 3\left(\frac{1}{5/4}\,e^{(5/4)u}\right) + C$

$$= 3\left(\frac{4}{5}\right)\,e^{(5/4)u} + C$$

$$= \frac{12}{5}\,e^{(5/4)u} + C \quad \blacksquare$$

The restriction $n \neq -1$ was necessary in the formula for $\int x^n\,dx$ since $n = -1$ made the denominator of $1/(n + 1)$ equal to 0. To find $\int x^n\,dx$ when $n = -1$, that is, to find $\int x^{-1}\,dx$, recall the differentiation formula for the logarithmic function: the derivative of $f(x) = \ln|x|$, where $x \neq 0$, is $f'(x) = 1/x = x^{-1}$. This formula for the derivative of $f(x) = \ln|x|$ gives a formula for $\int x^{-1}\,dx$.

Indefinite Integral

of x^{-1}

$$\int x^{-1}\,dx = \int \frac{1}{x}\,dx = \ln |x| + C$$

EXAMPLE 6

(a) $\int \frac{4}{x}\,dx = 4\int \frac{1}{x}\,dx = 4 \ln |x| + C$

(b) $\int \left(-\frac{5}{x} + e^{-2x} \right) dx = -5 \ln |x| - \frac{1}{2}e^{-2x} + C$ ▪

Integrals have many applications. Often it is possible to find a function that expresses the rate of change of a quantity, rather than the quantity itself. Since the rate of change of a function is given by its derivative, if we know the derivative of a function, the function itself can be found by integrating. For example, a marginal cost function is the derivative of a cost function, so a cost function must be an antiderivative of a marginal cost function. The next example illustrates this.

EXAMPLE 7

Suppose a publishing company has found that the marginal cost at a level of production of x thousand books is given by

$$C'(x) = \frac{50}{\sqrt{x}}$$

and that the fixed cost (the costs before the first book can be produced) is $25,000. Find the cost function $C(x)$.

Write $50/\sqrt{x}$ as $50/x^{1/2}$ or $50x^{-1/2}$, and then use the indefinite integral rules to integrate the function.

$$\int \frac{50}{\sqrt{x}}\,dx = \int 50x^{-1/2}\,dx = 50(2x^{1/2}) + k = 100x^{1/2} + k$$

(Here k is used instead of C to avoid confusion with the cost function $C(x)$.) To find the value of k, use the fact that $C(0)$ is 25,000.

$$C(x) = 100x^{1/2} + k$$
$$25,000 = 100 \cdot 0 + k$$
$$k = 25,000.$$

With this result, the cost function is $C(x) = 100x^{1/2} + 25,000$ ▪

The next example shows how integrals are used to find the position of a particle when the acceleration of the particle is given.

EXAMPLE 8

We saw earlier that if the function $s(t)$ gives the position of a particle at time t, then the velocity of the particle, $v(t)$, and its acceleration, $a(t)$, are given by

$$v(t) = s'(t)$$
$$a(t) = v'(t) = s''(t).$$

(a) Suppose the velocity of an object is $v(t) = 6t^2 - 8t$, with a position of -5 when time is 0. Find $s(t)$.

Since $v(t) = s'(t)$, the function $s(t)$ is an antiderivative of $v(t)$:

$$s(t) = \int v(t)\,dt = \int (6t^2 - 8t)\,dt$$
$$= 2t^3 - 4t^2 + C$$

for some constant C. Find C from the given information that $s = -5$ when $t = 0$.

$$s(t) = 2t^3 - 4t^2 + C$$
$$-5 = 2(0)^3 - 4(0)^2 + C$$
$$-5 = C$$
$$s(t) = 2t^3 - 4t^2 - 5$$

(b) Many experiments have shown that when an object is dropped, its acceleration (ignoring air resistance) is constant. This constant has been found to be approximately 32 feet per second every second; that is,

$$a(t) = -32.$$

The negative sign is used because the object is falling. Suppose an object is thrown down from the top of the 1100-foot tall Sears Tower in Chicago. If the initial velocity of the object is -20 feet per second, find $s(t)$.

First find $v(t)$ by integrating $a(t)$:

$$v(t) = \int (-32)\,dt = -32t + k.$$

When $t = 0$, $v(t) = -20$:

$$-20 = -32(0) + k$$
$$-20 = k$$

and

$$v(t) = -32t - 20.$$

Now integrate $v(t)$ to find $s(t)$.

$$s(t) = \int (-32t - 20)\,dt = -16t^2 - 20t + C$$

We know that $s(t) = 1100$ when $t = 0$. Substituting these values into the equation for $s(t)$ gives $C = 1100$ and

$$s(t) = -16t^2 - 20t + 1100$$

as the distance of the object from the ground after t seconds.

(c) Use the equations derived in (b) to find out how fast the object was falling when it hit the ground and how long it took to strike the ground.

When the object strikes the ground, $s = 0$, so

$$0 = -16t^2 - 20t + 1100.$$

To solve this equation for t, factor out the common factor of -4 and then use the quadratic formula.

$$0 = -4(4t^2 + 5t - 275)$$

$$t = \frac{-5 \pm \sqrt{25 + 4400}}{8} \approx \frac{-5 \pm 66.5}{8}$$

Only the positive value of t is meaningful here: $t \approx 7.69$. It takes the object about 7.69 seconds to strike the ground. From the velocity equation, with $t = 7.69$, we find

$$v(t) = -32t - 20$$

$$v(7.69) = -32(7.69) - 20 \approx -266,$$

so the object was falling at about 266 feet per second when it hit the ground. ▨

EXAMPLE 9

Find a function f whose graph has slope $f'(x) = 6x^2 + 4$ and goes through the point $(1, 1)$.

Since $f'(x) = 6x^2 + 4$,

$$f(x) = \int (6x^2 + 4)\,dx = 2x^3 + 4x + C.$$

The graph of f goes through $(1, 1)$, so C can be found by substituting 1 for x and 1 for $f(x)$.

$$1 = 2(1)^3 + 4(1) + C$$

$$1 = 6 + C$$

$$C = -5.$$

Finally, $f(x) = 2x^3 + 4x - 5$. ▨

13.1 EXERCISES

Find each of the following.

1. $\int 4x\,dx$

2. $\int 8x\,dx$

3. $\int 5t^2\,dt$

4. $\int 6x^3\,dx$

5. $\int 6\,dk$

6. $\int 2\,dy$

7. $\int (2z + 3)\,dz$

8. $\int (3x - 5)\,dx$

9. $\int (x^2 + 6x)\,dx$

10. $\int (t^2 - 2t)\,dt$

11. $\int (t^2 - 4t + 5)\,dt$

12. $\int (5x^2 - 6x + 3)\,dx$

13. $\int (4z^3 + 3z^2 + 2z - 6)\,dz$

14. $\int (12y^3 + 6y^2 - 8y + 5)\,dy$

15. $\int 5\sqrt{z}\,dz$

16. $\int t^{1/4}\,dt$

17. $\int (u^{1/2} + u^{3/2})\,du$

18. $\int (4\sqrt{v} - 3v^{3/2})\,dv$

19. $\int (15x\sqrt{x} + 2\sqrt{x})\,dx$

20. $\int (x^{1/2} - x^{-1/2})\,dx$

21. $\int (10u^{3/2} - 14u^{5/2})\,du$

22. $\int (56t^{5/2} + 18t^{7/2})\,dt$

23. $\int \left(\frac{1}{z^2}\right)dz$

24. $\int \left(\frac{4}{x^3}\right)dx$

25. $\int \left(\dfrac{1}{y^3} - \dfrac{1}{\sqrt{y}} \right) dy$

26. $\int \left(\sqrt{u} + \dfrac{1}{u^2} \right) du$

27. $\int (-9t^{-2} - 2t^{-1}) dt$

28. $\int (8x^{-3} + 4x^{-1}) dx$

29. $\int e^{2t} dt$

30. $\int e^{-3y} dy$

31. $\int 3e^{-0.2x} dx$

32. $\int -4e^{0.2v} dv$

33. $\int \left(\dfrac{3}{x} + 4e^{-0.5x} \right) dx$

34. $\int \left(\dfrac{9}{x} - 3e^{-0.4x} \right) dx$

35. $\int \dfrac{1 + 2t^3}{t} dt$

36. $\int \dfrac{2y^{1/2} - 3y^2}{y} dy$

37. $\int (e^{2u} + 4u) du$

38. $\int (v^2 - e^{3v}) dv$

39. $\int (x + 1)^2 dx$

40. $\int (2y - 1)^2 dy$

41. $\int \dfrac{\sqrt{x} + 1}{\sqrt[3]{x}} dx$

42. $\int \dfrac{1 - 2\sqrt[3]{z}}{\sqrt[3]{z}} dz$

Find the cost function for the marginal cost functions in Exercises 43–52.

43. $C'(x) = 4x - 5$, fixed cost is $8

44. $C'(x) = 2x + 3x^2$, fixed cost is $15

45. $C'(x) = 0.2x^2 + 5x$, fixed cost is $10

46. $C'(x) = 0.8x^2 - x$, fixed cost is $5

47. $C'(x) = x^{1/2}$, 16 units cost $40

48. $C'(x) = x^{2/3} + 2$, 8 units cost $58

49. $C'(x) = x^2 - 2x + 3$, 3 units cost $15

50. $C'(x) = x + 1/x^2$, 2 units cost $5.50

51. $C'(x) = 1/x + 2x$, 7 units cost $58.40

52. $C'(x) = 5x - 1/x$, 10 units cost $94.20

53. The marginal profit of a small fast-food stand is given by

$$P'(x) = 2x + 20,$$

where x is the sales volume in thousands of hamburgers. The "profit" is -50 dollars when no hamburgers are sold. Find the profit function.

54. Suppose the marginal profit from the sale of x hundred items is

$$P'(x) = 4 - 6x + 3x^2,$$

and the profit on 0 items is $-\$40$. Find the profit function.

In Exercises 55–57, refer to Example 8.

55. For a particular object, $a(t) = t^2 + 1$ and $v(0) = 6$. Find $v(t)$.

56. Suppose $v(t) = 6t^2 - 2/t^2$ and $s(1) = 8$. Find $s(t)$.

57. An object is dropped from a small plane flying at 6400 feet. Assume that $a(t) = -32$ feet per second per second and $v(0)$ is 0, and find $s(t)$. How long will it take the object to hit the ground?

58. The slope of the tangent line to a curve is given by

$$f'(x) = 6x^2 - 4x + 3.$$

If the point $(0, 1)$ is on the curve, find the equation of the curve.

59. Find the equation of the curve whose tangent line has a slope of

$$f'(x) = x^{2/3},$$

if the point $(1, 3/5)$ is on the curve.

60. According to Fick's Law, the diffusion of a solute across a cell membrane is given by

$$c'(t) = \dfrac{kA}{V}(C - c(t)), \tag{1}$$

where A is the area of the cell membrane, V is the volume of the cell, $c(t)$ is the concentration inside the cell at time t, C is the concentration outside the cell, and k is a constant. If c_0 represents the concentration of the solute inside the cell when $t = 0$, then it can be shown that

$$c(t) = (c_0 - C)e^{-kAt/V} + M. \tag{2}$$

(a) Use this last result to find $c'(t)$.

(b) Substitute back into equation (1) to show that (2) is indeed the correct antiderivative of (1).

13.2   Area and the Definite Integral

This section shows how to find the area of a region bounded on one side by a curve. Finding the area under a curve is very important in a great many applications. For example, the graph and caption in Figure 2 is from a test report in *Modern Photography**** magazine on the Minolta X-700 camera. The area under the curve gives the total noise made by the camera.

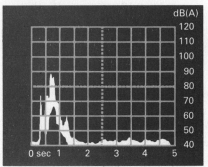

On the quiet side for a 35mm SLR, the X – 700 measured a relatively low 70 dB(A) at 1/125 sec. despite having one sound peak at around 88 dB(A). Total area under curve is small due to relatively short sound duration.

FIGURE 2

Figure 3 shows the region bounded by the lines $x = 0$, the x-axis, and the graph of

$$f(x) = \sqrt{4 - x^2}.$$

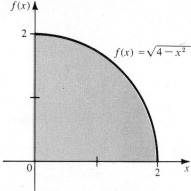

FIGURE 3

---

*From ''Sounding out the Minolta X-700'' in *Modern Photography*, June 1982. Copyright © 1981 by ABC Leisure Magazines, Inc. Reprinted by permission.

A very rough approximation of the area of this region can be found by using two rectangles as in Figure 4. The height of the rectangle on the left is $f(0) = 2$ and the height of the rectangle on the right is $f(1) = \sqrt{3}$. The width of each rectangle is 1, making the total area of the two rectangles

$$1 \cdot f(0) + 1 \cdot f(1) = 2 + \sqrt{3} \approx 3.7321 \text{ square units.}$$

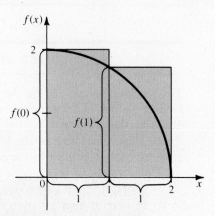

FIGURE 4

As shown in Figure 4, this approximation is greater than the actual area. To improve the accuracy of the approximation, we could divide the interval from $x = 0$ to $x = 2$ into four equal parts, each of width 1/2, as shown in Figure 5. As before, the height of each rectangle is given by the value of f at the left-hand side of the rectangle, and its area is the width, 1/2, multiplied by the height. The total area of the four rectangles is

$$\frac{1}{2} \cdot f(0) + \frac{1}{2} \cdot f\left(\frac{1}{2}\right) + \frac{1}{2} \cdot f(1) + \frac{1}{2} \cdot f\left(1\frac{1}{2}\right)$$

$$= \frac{1}{2}(2) + \frac{1}{2}\left(\frac{\sqrt{15}}{2}\right) + \frac{1}{2}(\sqrt{3}) + \frac{1}{2}\left(\frac{\sqrt{7}}{2}\right)$$

$$= 1 + \frac{\sqrt{15}}{4} + \frac{\sqrt{3}}{2} + \frac{\sqrt{7}}{4} \approx 3.4957 \text{ square units.}$$

This approximation looks better, but it is still greater than the actual area desired. To improve the approximation, divide the interval from $x = 0$ to $x = 2$ into 8 parts with equal widths of 1/4. (See Figure 6.) The total area of all these rectangles is

$$\frac{1}{4} \cdot f(0) + \frac{1}{4} \cdot f\left(\frac{1}{4}\right) + \frac{1}{4} \cdot f\left(\frac{1}{2}\right) + \frac{1}{4} \cdot f\left(\frac{3}{4}\right) + \frac{1}{4} \cdot f(1) + \frac{1}{4} \cdot f\left(\frac{5}{4}\right)$$

$$+ \frac{1}{4} \cdot f\left(\frac{3}{2}\right) + \frac{1}{4} \cdot f\left(\frac{7}{4}\right)$$

$$\approx 3.3398 \text{ square units.}$$

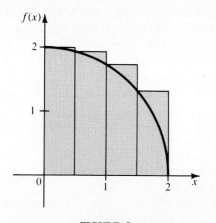

FIGURE 5

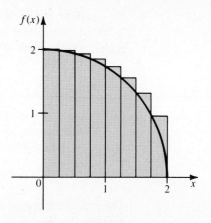

FIGURE 6

This process of approximating the area under a curve by using more and more rectangles to get a better and better approximation can be generalized. To do this, divide the interval from $x = 0$ to $x = 2$ into n equal parts. Each of these n intervals has width

$$\frac{2 - 0}{n} = \frac{2}{n},$$

so each rectangle has width $2/n$ and height determined by the function-value at the left side of the rectangle. A computer was used to find approximations to the area for several values of n, with the results given in the table.

n	Area
2	3.7321
4	3.4957
8	3.3398
10	3.3045
20	3.2285
50	3.1783
100	3.1512
500	3.1455

The areas in the last column in the table are approximations of the area under the curve, above the x-axis, and between the lines $x = 0$ and $x = 2$. As n becomes larger and larger, the approximation is better and better, getting closer to the actual area. In this example, the exact area can be found by a formula from plane geometry. Write the given function as

$$y = \sqrt{4 - x^2},$$

then square both sides to get

$$y^2 = 4 - x^2$$
$$x^2 + y^2 = 4,$$

the equation of a circle centered at the origin with radius 2. The region in Figure 3 is the quarter of this circle that lies in the first quadrant. The actual area of this region is one-quarter of the area of the entire circle, or

$$\frac{1}{4}\pi(2)^2 = \pi \approx 3.1416.$$

(The value of π was originally found by a process similar to this.)

It turns out that as the number of rectangles increases without bound, that is, as $n \rightarrow \infty$, for our region,

$$\lim_{n \to \infty}(\text{sum of areas of } n \text{ rectangles}) = \pi.$$

The area of the region under the graph of $f(x) = \sqrt{4 - x^2}$ and above the x-axis, between the lines $x = 0$ and $x = 2$, is defined to be this limit. This limit is the **definite integral** of $f(x) = \sqrt{4 - x^2}$ from $x = 0$ to $x = 2$, written

$$\int_0^2 \sqrt{4 - x^2} \; dx = \pi.$$

The 2 above the integral sign is the **upper limit** of integration, and 0 is the **lower limit** of integration. This use of the word "limit" has nothing to do with the limit of the sum; it refers to the limits, or boundaries, of the region. In the next section we shall see how antiderivatives are used in finding the definite integral and thus the area under a curve.

Sigma Notation At this point, some new notation and terminology is needed to write sums concisely. To indicate addition, or summation, the Greek letter sigma, Σ, is used as shown in the next example.

EXAMPLE 1

Find the following sums.

(a) $\displaystyle\sum_{i=1}^{5} i$

Replace i in turn with the integers 1 through 5 and add the resulting terms.

$$\sum_{i=1}^{5} i = 1 + 2 + 3 + 4 + 5 = 15$$

(b) $\displaystyle\sum_{i=1}^{4} a_i = a_1 + a_2 + a_3 + a_4$

(c) $\displaystyle\sum_{i=1}^{3} (6x_i - 2)$ if $x_1 = 2, x_2 = 4, x_3 = 6$

Letting $i = 1, 2$, and 3 respectively gives

$$\sum_{i=1}^{3} (6x_i - 2) = (6x_1 - 2) + (6x_2 - 2) + (6x_3 - 2).$$

Now substitute the given values for x_1, x_2, and x_3.

$$\sum_{i=1}^{3} (6x_i - 2) = (6 \cdot 2 - 2) + (6 \cdot 4 - 2) + (6 \cdot 6 - 2)$$

$$= 10 + 22 + 34$$

$$= 66$$

(d) $\sum_{i=1}^{4} f(x_i)\Delta x$ if $f(x) = x^2$, $x_1 = 0$, $x_2 = 2$, $x_3 = 4$, $x_4 = 6$, and $\Delta x = 2$

$$\sum_{i=1}^{4} f(x_i)\Delta x = f(x_1)\Delta x + f(x_2)\Delta x + f(x_3)\Delta x + f(x_4)\Delta x$$

$$= x_1^2\Delta x + x_2^2\Delta x + x_3^2\Delta x + x_4^2\Delta x$$

$$= 0^2(2) + 2^2(2) + 4^2(2) + 6^2(2)$$

$$= 0 + 8 + 32 + 72 = 112 \quad \blacksquare$$

Now we can generalize the idea of the definite integral from the example discussed in the text above. Figure 7 on the next page shows the area bounded by the curve $y = f(x)$, the x-axis, and the vertical lines $x = a$ and $x = b$. To approximate this area, we might divide the region under the curve first into ten rectangles (Figure 7 (a)) and then into 20 rectangles (Figure 7 (b)). The sums of the areas of the rectangles give approximations to the area under the curve.

To get a number which can be defined as the **exact** area, begin by dividing the interval from a to b into n pieces of equal width, using each of these n pieces as the base of a rectangle. (See Figure 7 (c).)

The left endpoints of the n intervals are labeled x_1, x_2, x_3, . . . , x_{n+1}, where $a = x_1$ and $b = x_{n+1}$. In the graph of Figure 7(c), the symbol Δx is used to represent the width of each of the intervals. The darker rectangle is an arbitrary rectangle called the ith rectangle. Its area is the product of its length and width. Since the width of the ith rectangle is Δx and the length of the ith rectangle is given by the height $f(x_i)$,

$$\text{area of } i\text{th rectangle} = f(x_i) \cdot \Delta x.$$

The total area under the curve is approximated by the sum of the areas of all n of the rectangles. With sigma notation, the approximation to the total area becomes

$$\text{area of all } n \text{ rectangles} = \sum_{i=1}^{n} f(x_i) \cdot \Delta x.$$

The exact area is defined to be the limit of this sum (if the limit exists) as the number of rectangles increases without bound.

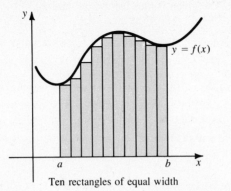

Ten rectangles of equal width

(a)

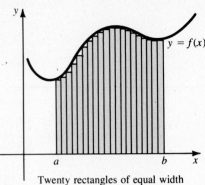

Twenty rectangles of equal width

(b)

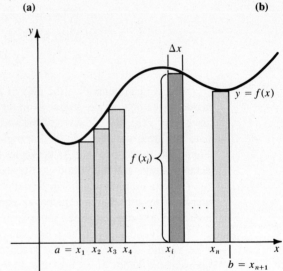

n rectangles of equal width

(c)

FIGURE 7

Area Under a

Curve

> If $f(x) \geq 0$ for all x in the interval $[a, b]$, then the area between $f(x)$, the x-axis, $x = a$, and $x = b$ is given by
>
> $$\lim_{n \to \infty} \sum_{i=1}^{n} f(x_i)\Delta x = \int_a^b f(x)\, dx$$
>
> provided the limit exists, where $\Delta x = \dfrac{b - a}{n}$ and x_i is any value of x in the ith subinterval.

As indicated in this definition any number in the ith interval can be used to find the height of the ith rectangle. Also, we might mention that a more general definition is possible in which the rectangles do not necessarily all have the same width.

EXAMPLE 2

Approximate $\int_0^4 2x \, dx$ by finding the area of the region under the graph of $f(x) = 2x$, above the x-axis, and between $x = 0$ and $x = 4$, using four rectangles of equal width whose heights are the values of the function at the midpoint of each rectangle.

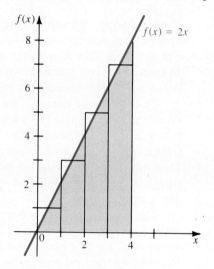

FIGURE 8

As shown in Figure 8, the heights of the four rectangles, given by $f(x_i)$ for $i = 1, 2, 3, 4$, are as follows.

i	x_i	$f(x_i)$
1	$x_1 = .5$	$f(.5) = 1.0$
2	$x_2 = 1.5$	$f(1.5) = 3.0$
3	$x_3 = 2.5$	$f(2.5) = 5.0$
4	$x_4 = 3.5$	$f(3.5) = 7.0$

The width of each rectangle is $\Delta x = \dfrac{4 - 0}{4} = 1$. The sum of the areas of the four rectangles is

$$\sum_{i=1}^{4} f(x_i)\Delta x = f(x_1)\Delta x + f(x_2)\Delta x + f(x_3)\Delta x + f(x_4)\Delta x$$

$$= f(.5)\Delta x + f(1.5)\Delta x + f(2.5)\Delta x + f(3.5)\Delta x$$

$$= (1)(1) + (3)(1) + 5(1) + 7(1)$$

$$= 16.$$

Using the formula for the area of a triangle, $A = (1/2)bh$, with b, the length of the base, equal to 4 and h, the height, equal to 8, gives

$$A = \frac{1}{2} bh = \frac{1}{2}(4)(8) = 16,$$

the exact value of the area. Our approximation equals the exact area in this case since the use of the midpoints of each subinterval distributed the error evenly above and below the graph.

Total Change Suppose the function $f(x) = x^2 + 20$ gives the marginal cost of some item at a particular x-value. Then $f(2) = 24$ gives the rate of change of cost at $x = 2$. That is, a unit change in x (at this point) will produce a change of 24 units in the cost function. Also, $f(3) = 29$ means that a unit of change in x (when $x = 3$) will produce a change of 29 units in the cost function.

To find the *total* change in the cost function as x changes from 2 to 3, we could divide the interval from 2 to 3 into n equal parts, using each part as the base of a rectangle as we did above. The area of each rectangle would approximate the change in cost at the x-value which is the left endpoint of the base of the rectangle. Then the sum of the areas of these rectangles would approximate the net total change in cost from $x = 2$ to $x = 3$. The limit of this sum as $n \to \infty$ would give the exact total change.

This result produces another application of the area under a curve: the area under the graph of the marginal cost function $f(x)$, above the x-axis, between $x = a$ and $x = b$ gives the net total change in the cost as x goes from a to b. Generalizing, the total change in a quantity can be approximated from the function which gives the rate of change of the quantity, using the same methods used to find the approximate area under a curve.

EXAMPLE 3

Figure 9 shows the rate of change of the annual maintenance charges for a certain machine. To approximate the total maintenance charges over the 10-year life of the machine, we can use approximating rectangles, dividing the interval from 0 to 10 into ten equal subdivisions. Each rectangle has width 1; if we use the left endpoint of each rectangle to determine the height of the rectangle, the approximation becomes

$$1 \cdot 0 + 1 \cdot 500 + 1 \cdot 750 + 1 \cdot 1800 + 1 \cdot 1800 + 1 \cdot 3000 + 1 \cdot 3000$$
$$+ 1 \cdot 3400 + 1 \cdot 4200 + 1 \cdot 5100 = 23{,}550.$$

About \$23,550 will be spent on maintenance over the 10-year life of the machine.

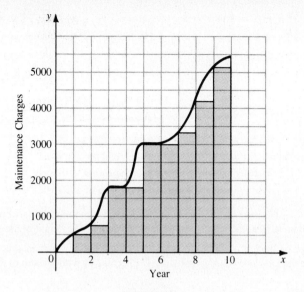

FIGURE 9

13.2 EXERCISES

Evaluate the sums in Exercises 1–10.

1. $\displaystyle\sum_{i=1}^{3} 3i$

2. $\displaystyle\sum_{i=1}^{6} (-5i)$

3. $\displaystyle\sum_{i=1}^{5} (2i + 7)$

4. $\displaystyle\sum_{i=1}^{10} (5i - 8)$

5. Let $x_1 = -5$, $x_2 = 8$, $x_3 = 7$, and $x_4 = 10$. Find $\displaystyle\sum_{i=1}^{4} x_i$.

6. Let $x_1 = 10$, $x_2 = 15$, $x_3 = -8$, $x_4 = -12$, and $x_5 = 0$. Find $\displaystyle\sum_{i=1}^{5} x_i$.

7. Let $f(x) = x - 3$ and $x_1 = 4$, $x_2 = 6$, $x_3 = 7$. Find $\displaystyle\sum_{i=1}^{3} f(x_i)$.

8. Let $f(x) = x^2 + 1$ and $x_1 = -2$, $x_2 = 0$, $x_3 = 2$, $x_4 = 4$. Find $\displaystyle\sum_{i=1}^{4} f(x_i)$.

9. Let $f(x) = 2x + 1$, $x_1 = 0$, $x_2 = 2$, $x_3 = 4$, $x_4 = 6$, and $\Delta x = 2$. Find $\displaystyle\sum_{i=1}^{4} f(x_i)\Delta x$.

10. Let $f(x) = 1/x$, $x_1 = 1/2$, $x_2 = 1$, $x_3 = 3/2$, $x_4 = 2$, and $\Delta x = 1/2$. Find $\displaystyle\sum_{i=1}^{4} f(x_i)\Delta x$.

In Exercises 11–22, first approximate the area under the given curve and above the x-axis by using two rectangles. Let the height of the rectangle be given by the value of the function at the left side of the rectangle. Then repeat the process and approximate the area using four rectangles.

11. $f(x) = 3x + 2$ from $x = 1$ to $x = 5$

12. $f(x) = -2x + 1$ from $x = -4$ to $x = 0$

13. $f(x) = x + 5$ from $x = 2$ to $x = 4$

14. $f(x) = 3 + x$ from $x = 1$ to $x = 3$

15. $f(x) = x^2$ from $x = 1$ to $x = 5$

16. $f(x) = x^2$ from $x = 0$ to $x = 4$

17. $f(x) = x^2 + 2$ from $x = -2$ to $x = 2$

18. $f(x) = -x^2 + 4$ from $x = -2$ to $x = 2$

19. $f(x) = e^x - 1$ from $x = 0$ to $x = 4$

20. $f(x) = e^x + 1$ from $x = -2$ to $x = 2$

21. $f(x) = \dfrac{1}{x}$ from $x = 1$ to $x = 5$

22. $f(x) = \dfrac{2}{x}$ from $x = 1$ to $x = 9$

23. Consider the region below $f(x) = x/2$, above the x-axis, between $x = 0$ and $x = 4$.
   Let x_i be the left endpoint of the ith subinterval.

   (a) Approximate the area of the region using four rectangles.

   (b) Approximate the area of the region using eight rectangles.

   (c) Find $\int_0^4 f(x)\,dx$ by using the formula for the area of a triangle.

24. Find $\int_0^5 (5 - x)\,dx$ by using the formula for the area of a triangle.

In Exercises 25–28, estimate the area under the curve by summing the area of rectangles.
Let the function value at the left side of each rectangle give the height of the rectangle.

25. The graph on the left *(below)* shows the rate of sales of new cars in a recent year.
   Estimate the total sales during that year. Use rectangles with a width of 1.

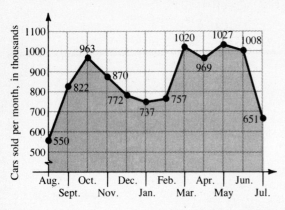 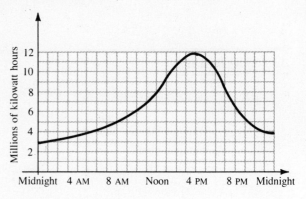

26. The graph on the right *(above)* shows the rate of use of electrical energy (in kilowatt
   hours) in a certain city on a very hot day. Estimate the total usage of electricity on that
   day. Let the width of each rectangle be 2 hours.

27. The graph on the left *(below)* shows the approximate concentration of alcohol in a
   person's bloodstream t hours after drinking 2 ounces of alcohol. Estimate the total
   amount of alcohol in the bloodstream by estimating the area under the curve. Use
   rectangles of width 1.

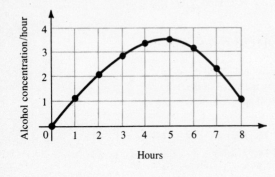 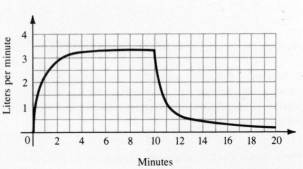

28. The graph on the right *(bottom of previous page)* shows the rate of inhalation of oxygen by a person riding a bicycle very rapidly for 10 minutes. Estimate the total volume of oxygen inhaled in the first 20 minutes after the beginning of the ride. Use rectangles of width 1.

The next two graphs are from *Road and Track* magazine.* The curve shows the velocity at time t, in seconds, when the car accelerates from a dead stop. To find the total distance traveled by the car in reaching 100 miles per hour, we must estimate the definite integral

$$\int_0^T v(t)\,dt,$$

where T represents the number of seconds it takes for the car to reach 100 mph.

Use the graphs to estimate this distance by adding the areas of rectangles with widths of 3 seconds. The last rectangle will have a width of 1 second. To adjust your answer to miles per hour, divide by 3600 (the number of seconds in an hour). You then have the number of miles that the car traveled in reaching 100 mph. Finally, multiply by 5280 feet per mile to convert the answers to feet.

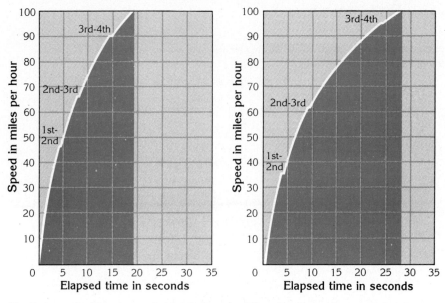

29. Estimate the distance traveled by the Porsche 928, using the graph on the left *(above)*.

30. Estimate the distance traveled by the BMW 733i using the graph on the right *(above)*.

When doing research on the wolf-moose relationships in Michigan's Isle Royale National Park, the biologist Rolf Peterson needed a snow-depth index to help correlate populations with snow levels. The graph shown at the right is given a snow depth index of 1.0. The vertical scale gives snow depth in inches, and the horizontal scale gives months.†

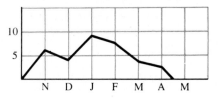

---

*From *Road & Track,* April and May, 1978. Reprinted with permission of Road & Track.
†From *Wolf Ecology and Prey Relationships on Isle Royale* by Rolf Olin Peterson. Copyright © 1977 by the U.S. Government Printing Office, p. 187.

Find the snow depth index for the following years by forming the ratio of the areas under the given curves to the area under the curve on the previous page.

31.

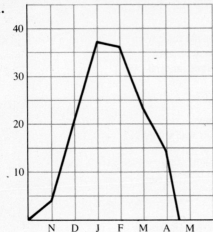

32.

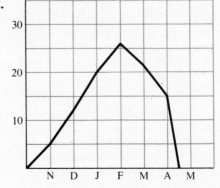

In Exercises 33–36, use the method of the text to approximate the area between the *x*-axis and the graph of each function on the given interval.

33. $f(x) = x \ln x; [1, 5]$

34. $f(x) = x^2 e^{-x}; [-1, 3]$

35. $f(x) = \dfrac{\ln x}{x}; [1, 5]$

36. $f(x) = \dfrac{e^x - e^{-x}}{2}; [0, 4]$

13.3   The Fundamental Theorem of Calculus

The work from the last two sections can now be put together. We have seen that, if $f(x) > 0$,

$$\int_a^b f(x)\, dx$$

gives the area between the graph of $f(x)$ and the *x*-axis, from $x = a$ to $x = b$. We will see that this definite integral can be found using the antiderivatives discussed earlier. The connection between antiderivatives and definite integrals is given by the fundamental theorem of calculus.

Fundamental Theorem of Calculus	Let f be continuous on the interval $[a, b]$, and let F be *any* antiderivative of f. Then $$\int_a^b f(x)\, dx = F(b) - F(a) = F(x)\bigg]_a^b.$$

The symbol $F(x)]_a^b$ is used to represent $F(b) - F(a)$. It is important to note that the fundamental theorem does not require $f(x) > 0$. The condition $f(x) > 0$ is necessary only when using the fundamental theorem to find area.

EXAMPLE 1

Find $\int_0^3 (x^2 - 4)\, dx$.

First find an antiderivative of $x^2 - 4$.

$$F(x) = \int (x^2 - 4)\, dx$$

$$= \frac{x^3}{3} - 4x.$$

We let $C = 0$ since the fundamental theorem says that *any* antiderivative can be used. Then, by the fundamental theorem,

$$\int_0^3 (x^2 - 4)\, dx = \left(\frac{x^3}{3} - 4x \right) \Big]_0^3$$

$$= \left[\frac{3^3}{3} - 4(3) \right] - \left[\frac{0^3}{3} - 4(0) \right]$$

$$= -3. \quad \blacksquare$$

Figure 10 shows the graph of $f(x) = x^2 - 4$ from Example 1. Here, the value of the definite integral, -3, *does not* represent the area between the graph of $f(x)$ and the x-axis from $x = 0$ to $x = 3$. This is because $f(x) < 0$ in part of $[0, 3]$. The definite integral is a real number and represents area only when $f(x) > 0$ for all x in $[a, b]$.

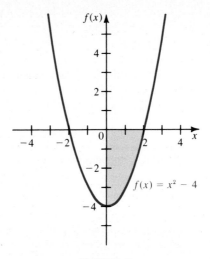

$f(x) = x^2 - 4$

FIGURE 10

EXAMPLE 2

First find $\int 4t^3\,dt$ and then find $\int_1^2 4t^3\,dt$.

By the rules given earlier,

$$\int 4t^3\,dt = t^4 + C.$$

By the fundamental theorem, the value of $\int_1^2 4t^3\,dt$ is found by evaluating $t^4\Big]_1^2$, with no constant C required.

$$\int_1^2 4t^3\,dt = t^4\Big]_1^2 = 2^4 - 1^4 = 15. \quad \blacksquare$$

Example 2 illustrates the difference between the definite integral and the indefinite integral. A definite integral is a real number; an indefinite integral is a family of functions—all the functions which are antiderivatives of a function f.

To see why the fundamental theorem of calculus is true for $f(x) > 0$, look at Figure 11. Define the function $A(x)$ as the area between the x-axis and the graph of $y = f(x)$ from a to x. We first show that A is an antiderivative of f, that is, $A' = f$.

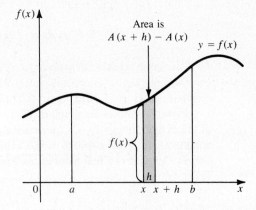

FIGURE 11

To do this, let h be a small positive number. Then $A(x + h) - A(x)$ is the shaded area of Figure 11. This area can be approximated with a rectangle having width h and height $f(x)$. The area of the rectangle is $h \cdot f(x)$, and

$$A(x + h) - A(x) \approx h \cdot f(x).$$

Dividing both sides by h gives

$$\frac{A(x + h) - A(x)}{h} \approx f(x).$$

This approximation improves as h gets smaller and smaller. Take the limit on the left as h approaches 0, getting

$$\lim_{h \to 0} \frac{A(x + h) - A(x)}{h} = f(x).$$

This limit is simply $A'(x)$, so

$$A'(x) = f(x).$$

This result means that A is an antiderivative of f, as we set out to show.

Since $A(x)$ is the area under the curve $y = f(x)$ from a to x, $A(a) = 0$. The expression $A(b)$ is the area from a to b, the desired area. Since A is an antiderivative of f,

$$\int_a^b f(x)\,dx = A(x)\Big]_a^b = A(b) - A(a) = A(b) - 0 = A(b).$$

This suggests the proof of the fundamental theorem—for $f(x) > 0$ the area under the curve $y = f(x)$ from a to b is given by $\int_a^b f(x)\,dx$.

The fundamental theorem of calculus certainly deserves its name, which sets it apart as the most important theorem of calculus. It is the key connection between differential calculus and integral calculus, which originally were developed separately without knowledge of this connection between them.

The variable used in the integrand does not matter; that is,

$$\int_a^b f(x)\,dx = \int_a^b f(t)\,dt = \int_a^b f(u)\,du.$$

Each of these definite integrals represents the number $F(b) - F(a)$.

Key properties of definite integrals are listed below. Some of them are just restatements of properties from Section 1.

Properties of Definite Integrals

If all indicated definite integrals exist,

1. $\displaystyle\int_a^a f(x)\,dx = 0$

2. $\displaystyle\int_a^b k \cdot f(x)\,dx = k \cdot \int_a^b f(x)\,dx$, for any real constant k.
   (constant multiple of a function)

3. $\displaystyle\int_a^b [f(x) \pm g(x)]\,dx = \int_a^b f(x)\,dx \pm \int_a^b g(x)\,dx$
   (sum or difference of functions)

4. $\displaystyle\int_a^b f(x)\,dx = \int_a^c f(x)\,dx + \int_c^b f(x)\,dx$
   for any real number c.

Since the distance from a to a is 0, the first property says that the "area" under the graph of f bounded by $x = a$ and $x = a$ is 0. Also, since $\int_a^c f(x)\,dx$ represents the darker region in Figure 12, and $\int_c^b f(x)\,dx$ represents the lighter region,

$$\int_a^b f(x)\,dx = \int_a^c f(x)\,dx + \int_c^b f(x)\,dx,$$

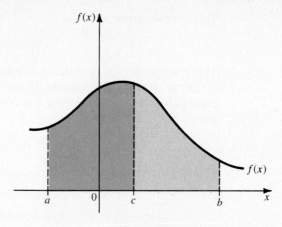

FIGURE 12

as stated in the fourth property. While the figure shows $a < c < b$, the property is true for any value of c where both $f(x)$ and $F(x)$ are defined.

An algebraic proof is given here for the third property; proofs of the other properties are left for the exercises. If $F(x)$ and $G(x)$ are antiderivatives of $f(x)$ and $g(x)$ respectively,

$$\int_a^b [f(x) + g(x)]dx = [F(x) + G(x)]\Big]_a^b$$

$$= [F(b) + G(b)] - [F(a) + G(a)]$$

$$= [F(b) - F(a)] + [G(b) - G(a)]$$

$$= \int_a^b f(x) \, dx + \int_a^b g(x) \, dx.$$

EXAMPLE 3 Find $\int_2^5 (6x^2 - 3x + 5) \, dx$.

Use the properties above, and the fundamental theorem, along with properties from Section 1.

$$\int_2^5 (6x^2 - 3x + 5) \, dx = 6 \int_2^5 x^2 dx - 3 \int_2^5 xdx + 5 \int_2^5 dx$$

$$= 2x^3 \Big]_2^5 - \frac{3}{2}x^2 \Big]_2^5 + 5x \Big]_2^5$$

$$= 2(5^3 - 2^3) - \frac{3}{2}(5^2 - 2^2) + 5(5 - 2)$$

$$= 2(125 - 8) - \frac{3}{2}(25 - 4) + 5(3)$$

$$= 234 - \frac{63}{2} + 15 = \frac{435}{2}. \quad \blacksquare$$

EXAMPLE 4 $\int_1^2 \dfrac{dy}{y} = \ln|y| \Big]_1^2 = \ln|2| - \ln|1|$

$$= \ln 2 - \ln 1 \approx .6931 - 0 = .6931 \quad \blacksquare$$

Area   In the previous section we saw that, if $f(x) > 0$ in $[a, b]$, the definite integral $\int_a^b f(x)\,dx$ gives the area below the graph of the function $y = f(x)$, above the x-axis, and between the lines $x = a$ and $x = b$.

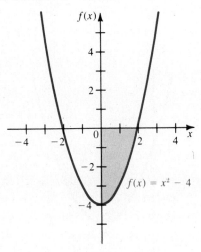

FIGURE 13

To see how to work around the requirement that $f(x) > 0$, look at Figure 13 which shows the graph of $f(x) = x^2 - 4$. As Figure 13 shows, the area bounded by the graph of f, the x-axis, and the vertical lines $x = 0$ and $x = 2$ lies below the x-axis. Using the fundamental theorem to find this area gives

$$\int_0^2 (x^2 - 4)\,dx = \left(\frac{x^3}{3} - 4x\right)\Big]_0^2 = \left(\frac{8}{3} - 8\right) - (0 - 0) = \frac{-16}{3}.$$

The result is a negative number because $f(x)$ is negative for values of x in the interval $[0, 2]$. Since Δx is always positive, $f(x) < 0$ makes the product $f(x) \cdot \Delta x$ negative, so $\int_0^2 f(x)\,dx$ is negative. Since area is nonnegative, the required area is given by $|-16/3|$ or $16/3$. Using a definite integral, the area could be written as

$$\left| \int_0^2 (x^2 - 4)\,dx \right|.$$

EXAMPLE 5   Find the area of the region between the x-axis and the graph of $f(x) = x^2 - 3x$ from $x = 1$ to $x = 3$.

The region is shown in Figure 14 on the next page. Since the region lies below the x-axis, the area is given by

$$\left| \int_1^3 (x^2 - 3x)\,dx \right|.$$

By the fundamental theorem,

$$\int_1^3 (x^2 - 3x)\,dx = \left(\frac{x^3}{3} - \frac{3x^2}{2}\right)\Big]_1^3 = \left(\frac{27}{3} - \frac{27}{2}\right) - \left(\frac{1}{3} - \frac{3}{2}\right) = -\frac{10}{3}.$$

The required area is $|-10/3| = 10/3$ square units. ■

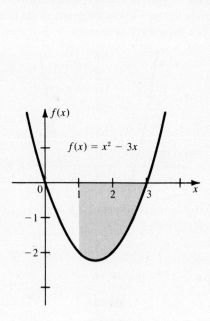

FIGURE 14   FIGURE 15

EXAMPLE 6

Find the area between the x-axis and the graph of $f(x) = x^2 - 4$ from $x = 0$ to $x = 4$.

Figure 15 shows the required region. Part of the region is below the x-axis. The definite integral over that interval will have a negative value. To find the area, integrate the negative and positive portions separately and take the absolute value of the first result before combining the two results to get the total area. Start by finding the point where the graph crosses the x-axis. This is done by solving the equation

$$x^2 - 4 = 0.$$

The solutions of this equation are 2 and -2. The only solution in the interval $[0, 4]$ is 2. The total area of the region in Figure 15 is given by

$$\left|\int_0^2 (x^2 - 4)\,dx\right| + \int_2^4 (x^2 - 4)\,dx = \left|\left(\frac{1}{3}x^3 - 4x\right)\Big]_0^2\right| + \left(\frac{1}{3}x^3 - 4x\right)\Big]_2^4$$

$$= \left|\frac{8}{3} - 8\right| + \left(\frac{64}{3} - 16\right) - \left(\frac{8}{3} - 8\right)$$

$$= 16 \text{ square units.} ■$$

Incorrectly using one integral over the entire interval to find the area would give

$$\int_0^4 (x^2 - 4)\,dx = \left(\frac{x^3}{3} - 4x\right)\Big]_0^4 = \left(\frac{64}{3} - 16\right) - 0 = \frac{16}{3},$$

which is not the correct area. This definite integral represents no area, but is just a real number.

Finding Area

> In summary, find the area bounded by $f(x)$, $x = a$, $x = b$, and the x-axis with the following steps:
>
> 1. Sketch a graph.
> 2. Find any x-intercepts in $[a, b]$. These divide the total region into subregions.
> 3. The definite integral will be *positive* for subregions above the x-axis and *negative* for subregions below the x-axis. Use separate integrals to find the areas of the subregions.
> 4. The total area is the sum of the absolute values of the definite integrals for all of the subregions.

In the last section, we saw that the area under a rate of change function $f'(x)$ from $x = a$ to $x = b$ gives the total value of $f(x)$ on $[a, b]$. Now we can use the definite integral to solve these problems.

EXAMPLE 7

The yearly rate of consumption of natural gas in trillions of cubic feet for a certain city is

$$C'(t) = t + e^{0.01t},$$

when $t = 0$ corresponds to 1980. At this consumption rate, what is the total amount the city will use in the 10-year period of the eighties?

To find the consumption over the ten-year period from 1980 through 1989, use the definite integral.

$$\int_0^{10} (t + e^{0.01t})\,dt = \left(\frac{t^2}{2} + \frac{e^{0.01t}}{.01}\right)\Big]_0^{10}$$

$$\approx (50 + 100e^{.1}) - (0 + 100)$$

$$\approx -50 + 100(1.10517) \approx 60.5$$

Therefore, a total of 60.5 trillion cubic feet of natural gas will be used during the eighties if the consumption rate remains the same. ∎

13.3 EXERCISES

Evaluate each definite integral in Exercises 1–24.

1. $\int_{-2}^{4} (-dp)$

2. $\int_{-4}^{1} 6x \, dx$

3. $\int_{-1}^{2} (3t - 1) \, dt$

4. $\int_{-2}^{2} (4z + 3) \, dz$

5. $\int_{0}^{2} (5x^2 - 4x + 2) \, dx$

6. $\int_{-2}^{3} (-x^2 - 3x + 5) \, dx$

7. $\int_{4}^{9} 3\sqrt{u} \, du$

8. $\int_{2}^{8} \sqrt{2r} \, dr$

9. $\int_{0}^{1} 2(t^{1/2} - t) \, dt$

10. $\int_{0}^{4} -(3x^{3/2} + x^{1/2}) \, dx$

11. $\int_{1}^{4} (5y\sqrt{y} + 3\sqrt{y}) \, dy$

12. $\int_{4}^{9} (4\sqrt{r} - 3r\sqrt{r}) \, dr$

13. $\int_{1}^{3} \frac{2}{x^2} \, dx$

14. $\int_{1}^{4} \frac{-3}{u^2} \, du$

15. $\int_{1}^{5} (5n^{-2} + n^{-3}) \, dn$

16. $\int_{2}^{3} (3x^{-2} - x^{-4}) \, dx$

17. $\int_{2}^{3} \left(2e^{-0.1A} + \frac{3}{A}\right) dA$

18. $\int_{1}^{2} \left(\frac{-1}{B} + 3e^{0.2B}\right) dB$

19. $\int_{1}^{2} \left(e^{5u} - \frac{1}{u^2}\right) du$

20. $\int_{.5}^{1} (p^3 - e^{4p}) \, dp$

21. $\int_{-1}^{0} (2y - 3)^2 \, dy$

22. $\int_{0}^{3} (4m + 2)^2 \, dm$

23. $\int_{1}^{64} \frac{\sqrt{z} - 2}{\sqrt[3]{z}} \, dz$

24. $\int_{1}^{8} \frac{3 - y^{1/3}}{y^{2/3}} \, dy$

In Exercises 25–36, use the definite integral to find the area between the x-axis and $f(x)$ over the indicated interval. Check first to see if the graph crosses the x-axis in the given interval.

25. $f(x) = 2x + 3; [8, 10]$

26. $f(x) = 4x - 7; [5, 10]$

27. $f(x) = 2 - 2x^2; [0, 5]$

28. $f(x) = 9 - x^2; [0, 6]$

29. $f(x) = x^2 + 4x - 5; [-1, 3]$

30. $f(x) = x^2 - 6x + 5; [-1, 4]$

31. $f(x) = x^3; [-1, 3]$

32. $f(x) = x^3 - 2x; [-2, 4]$

33. $f(x) = e^x - 1; [-1, 2]$

34. $f(x) = 1 - e^{-x}; [-1, 2]$

35. $f(x) = \frac{1}{x}; [1, e]$

36. $f(x) = \frac{1}{x}; [e, e^2]$

Find the area of each shaded region.

37.

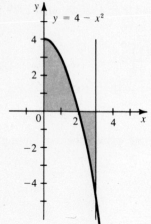

$y = 4 - x^2$

38.

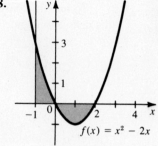

$f(x) = x^2 - 2x$

39.

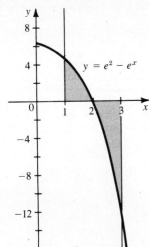

$y = e^2 - e^x$

40.

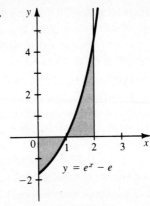

$y = e^x - e$

41. Pollution from a factory is entering a lake. The rate of concentration of the pollutant at time t is given by
$$P(t) = 140t^{5/2},$$
where t is the number of years since the factory started introducing pollutants into the lake. Ecologists estimate that the lake can accept a total level of pollution of 4850 units before all the fish life in the lake ends. Can the factory operate for 4 years without killing all the fish in the lake?

42. An oil tanker is leaking oil at the rate of $20t + 50$ barrels per hour, where t is time in hours after the tanker hits a hidden rock (when $t = 0$).

(a) Find the total number of barrels that the ship will leak on the first day.

(b) Find the number of barrels that the ship will leak on the second day.

43. De Win Enterprises has found that its expenditure rate per day (in hundreds of dollars) on a certain type of job is given by
$$E(x) = 4x + 2,$$
where x is the number of days since the start of the job.

(a) Find the total expenditure if the job takes 10 days.

(b) How much will be spent on the job from the 10th to the 20th day?

(c) If the company wants to spend no more than $5000 on the job, in how many days must they complete it?

44. De Win Enterprises (see Exercise 43) also knows that the rate of income per day (in hundreds of dollars) for the same job is
$$I(x) = 100 - x,$$
where x is the number of days since the job was started.

(a) Find the total income for the first 10 days.

(b) Find the income from the 10th to the 20th day.

(c) How many days must the job last for the total income to be at least $5000?

45. After a new firm starts in business, it finds that its rate of profits (in hundreds of dollars) after t years of operation, is given by

$$P(t) = 6t^2 + 4t + 5.$$

(a) Find the total profits in the first three years.

(b) Find the profit in the fourth year of operation.

46. A worker new to a job will improve his efficiency with time so that it takes him fewer hours to produce an item with each day on the job up to a certain point. Suppose the rate of change of the number of hours it takes a worker in a certain factory to produce the xth item is given by

$$H(x) = 20 - 2x.$$

(a) What is the total number of hours required to produce the first 5 items?

(b) What is the total number of hours required to produce the first 10 items?

47. After long study, tree scientists conclude that a eucalyptus tree will grow at the rate of $.2 + 4t^{-4}$ feet per year, where t is time in years.

(a) Find the number of feet that the tree will grow in the second year.

(b) Find the number of feet the tree will grow in the third year.

48. The rate at which a substance grows is given by

$$R(x) = 200e^x,$$

where x is the time in days. What is the total accumulated growth after 2.5 days?

49. For a certain drug, the rate of reaction in appropriate units is given by

$$R(t) = \frac{5}{t} + \frac{2}{t^2},$$

where t is measured in hours after the drug is administered. Find the total reaction to the drug

(a) from $t = 1$ to $t = 12$

(b) from $t = 12$ to $t = 24$.

50. For another drug, the rate of reaction in appropriate units is

$$R(t) = \frac{4}{t^2} + 1,$$

where t is measured in hours after the drug is administered. Find the total reaction to the drug

(a) from $t = \frac{1}{4}$ to $t = 1$

(b) from $t = 12$ to $t = 24$.

51. Most of the numbers in this exercise come from a recent article in *The Wall Street Journal*. Suppose that the rate of consumption of a natural resource is $c(t)$, where

$$c(t) = ke^{rt}.$$

Here t is time in years, r is constant, and k is the consumption in the year when $t = 0$. In 1984, Texaco sold 1.2 billion barrels of oil. Assume that $r = .04$.

(a) Write $c(t)$ for Texaco, letting $t = 0$ represent 1984.

(b) Set up a definite integral for the amount of oil that Texaco will sell in the next ten years.

(c) Evaluate the definite integral of part (b).

(d) Texaco has about 20 billion barrels of oil in reserve. To find the number of years that this amount will last, solve the equation

$$\int_0^T 1.2\,e^{0.04t}\,dt \,=\, 20.$$

(e) Rework part (d) assuming that $r = .02$.

52. A mine begins producing at time $t = 0$. After t years, the mine is producing at the rate of

$$P'(t) \,=\, 10t \,-\, \frac{15}{\sqrt{t}}$$

tons per year. Write an expression for the total output of the mine from year 1 to year T.

53. The rate of consumption of one natural resource in one country is

$$C'(t) \,=\, 72\,e^{0.014t},$$

where $t = 0$ corresponds to 1985. How much of the resource will be used, altogether, from 1985 to year T?

54. In Exercise 51, the rate of consumption of oil (in billions of barrels) by Texaco was given as

$$1.2\,e^{0.04t},$$

where $t = 0$ corresponds to 1984. Find the total amount of oil used by Texaco from 1984 to year T. At this rate, how much will be used in 5 years?

Show that each of the following is true.

55. $\displaystyle\int_a^a f(x)\,dx = 0$ **56.** $\displaystyle\int_a^b k f(x)\,dx = k\int_a^b f(x)\,dx$ **57.** $\displaystyle\int_a^b f(x)\,dx = \int_a^c f(x)\,dx + \int_c^b f(x)\,dx$

58. Use Exercise 57 to find $\displaystyle\int_{-1}^4 f(x)\,dx$ given

$$f(x) \,=\, \begin{cases} 2x + 3 & \text{if } x \le 0 \\ -\dfrac{x}{4} - 3 & \text{if } x > 0. \end{cases}$$

EXTENDED

Estimating Depletion Dates for Minerals

APPLICATION

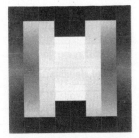

It is becoming more and more obvious that the earth contains only a finite quantity of minerals. The "easy and cheap" sources of minerals are being used up, forcing an ever more expensive search for new sources. For example, oil from the North Slope of Alaska would never have been used in the United States during the 1930's since there was so much Texas and California oil readily available.

We said in an earlier chapter that population tends to follow an exponential growth curve. Mineral usage also follows such a curve. Thus, if q represents the rate of consumption of a certain mineral at time t, while q_0 represents consumption when $t = 0$, then

$$q = q_0 e^{kt},$$

where k is the growth constant. For example, the world consumption of petroleum in a recent year was about 19,600 million barrels, with the value of k about 6%. If we let $t = 0$ correspond to this base year, then $q_0 = 19,600$, $k = 0.06$, and

$$q = 19,600\, e^{0.06t}$$

is the rate of consumption at time t, assuming that all present trends continue.

Based on estimates of the National Academy of Science, we shall use 2,000,000 as the number of millions of barrels of oil that are now in provable reserves or that are likely to be discovered in the future. At the present rate of consumption, how many years would be necessary to deplete these estimated reserves? We can use the integral calculus of this chapter to find out.

To begin, we need to know the total quantity of petroleum that would be used between time $t = 0$ and some future time $t = t_1$. The figure below shows a typical graph of the function $q = q_0 e^{kt}$.

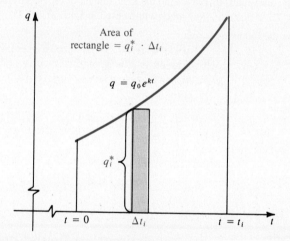

Following the work we did in Section 2, divide the time interval from $t = 0$ to $t = t_1$ into n subintervals. Let the ith subinterval have width Δt_i. Let the rate of consumption for the ith subinterval be approximated by q_i^*. Thus, the approximate total consumption for the subinterval is given by

$$q_i^* \cdot \Delta t_i,$$

and the total consumption over the interval from time $t = 0$ to $t = t_1$ is approximated by

$$\sum_{i=1}^{n} q_i^* \cdot \Delta t_i.$$

The limit of this sum as each of the Δt_i's approaches 0 gives the total consumption from time $t = 0$ to $t = t_1$. That is,

$$\text{total consumption} = \lim_{\Delta t_i \to 0} \sum q_i^* \cdot \Delta t_i.$$

However, we have seen that this limit is the definite integral of the function $q = q_0 e^{kt}$ from $t = 0$ to $t = t_1$, or

$$\text{total consumption} = \int_0^{t_1} q_0 e^{kt} \, dt.$$

We can now evaluate this definite integral.

$$\int_0^{t_1} q_0 e^{kt} \, dt = q_0 \int_0^{t_1} e^{kt} \, dt = q_0 \left(\frac{1}{k} e^{kt} \right) \Big]_0^{t_1}$$

$$= \frac{q_0}{k} e^{kt} \Big]_0^{t_1} = \frac{q_0}{k} e^{kt_1} - \frac{q_0}{k} e^0$$

$$= \frac{q_0}{k} e^{kt_1} - \frac{q_0}{k}(1)$$

$$= \frac{q^0}{k}(e^{kt_1} - 1) \tag{1}$$

Now let us return to the numbers we gave for petroleum. We said that $q_0 = 19,600$ million barrels where q_0 represents consumption in the base year. We have $k = 0.06$, with total petroleum reserves estimated as 2,000,000 million barrels. Thus, using equation (1) we have

$$2,000,000 = \frac{19,600}{0.06}(e^{0.06t_1} - 1).$$

Multiply both sides of the equation by 0.06:

$$120,000 = 19,600(e^{0.06t_1} - 1).$$

Divide both sides of the equation by 19,600.

$$6.1 = e^{0.06t_1} - 1$$

Add 1 to both sides.

$$7.1 = e^{0.06t_1}$$

Take natural logarithms of both sides:

$$\ln 7.1 = \ln e^{0.06t_1} = 0.06 t_1 \ln e$$

$$= 0.06 t_1 \quad (\text{since } \ln e = 1).$$

Finally,

$$t_1 = \frac{\ln 7.1}{0.06}.$$

From the table of natural logarithms or a calculator, estimate ln 7.1 as about 1.96. Thus,

$$t_1 = \frac{1.96}{0.06} = 33.$$

By this result, petroleum reserves will last the world for thirty-three years.

The results of mathematical analyses such as this must be used with great caution. By the analysis above, the world would use all the petroleum that it wants in the thirty-second year after the base year, but there would be none at all in thirty-four years. This is not at all realistic. As petroleum reserves decline, the price will increase, causing demand to decline and supplies to increase.

EXERCISES

1. Find the number of years that the estimated petroleum reserves would last if used at the same rate as in the base year.

2. How long would the estimated petroleum reserves last if the growth constant was only 2% instead of 6%?

Estimate the length of time until depletion for each of the following minerals.

3. Bauxite (the ore from which aluminum is obtained), estimated reserves in base year 15,000,000 thousand tons, rate of consumption 63,000 thousand tons, growth constant 6%.

4. Bituminous coal, estimated world reserves 2,000,000 million tons, rate of consumption 2200 million tons, growth constant 4%.

EXTENDED

APPLICATION

Evaluating Voting Power*

A problem from political science is how to numerically evaluate the power of voters in a **weighted voting body.** A weighted voting body can be represented by the symbol

$$[q;\ w_1,\ w_2,\ .\ .\ .,\ w_n],$$

where there are n voters, the ith voter casts w_i votes, and a quota of q votes is necessary to pass a bill. For example, the symbol

$$[7;\ 4,\ 3,\ 2,\ 1]$$
$$\text{A}\quad\text{B}\quad\text{C}\quad\text{D}$$

represents a body in which there are four voters (call them A, B, C, D) casting 4, 3, 2, 1 votes respectively, and 7 votes are necessary to pass a bill.

*From "Using Integrals to Evaluate Voting Power," by Philip D. Straffin, Jr. from *The Two-Year College Mathematics Journal,* Vol. 10, No. 3, June 1979. Reprinted by permission of The Mathematical Association of America and the author.

Weighted voting bodies are fairly common in political situations. Classic examples include voting by shareholders in a corporation, several United Nations organizations, the World Bank, the European Economic Community, the New Mexico legislature, and many county governments in New York State.

A legislature in which each member casts only one vote, but where members belong to different political parties and vote under strict party discipline, can also be thought of as a weighted voting body. In this interpretation, the example just given might represent a legislature of 10 members, with 4 belonging to party A, 3 to party B, 2 to party C, and 1 to party D.

The naive way to think of the distribution of power in a weighted voting body like that of the example is to suppose that power is in strict proportion to number of votes. Thus, A has 40% of the votes and hence should have 40% of the power. A little reflection should convince students of the naivete of this supposition. For instance, note that A has *veto power:* even if B, C, and D all favor a bill, it cannot pass without A's approval. This observation should lead us to believe that A might have considerably more than 40% of the power. Two other compelling examples follow.

Example 1

[6; 7, 1, 1, 1]
Here A has 70% of the vote, but she clearly has all the power. A is a *dictator,* in the sense that a bill passes if and only if A votes for it.

Example 2

[6; 3, 3, 3, 1]
Here D has 10% of the vote, but no power. D's vote can never make any difference to the outcome, and D is called a *dummy.*

To obtain a more realistic measure of power than just proportion of votes, consider the following model. Let us suppose that each bill which comes before the voting body can be assigned a number $p \in [0, 1]$, where p is the probability that any member of the body will vote for the bill. We can think of p as the "level of acceptability" of the bill. Some bills will be generally unacceptable (p near 0) and will usually (but not always) be overwhelmingly defeated; others will be generally acceptable (p near 1) and will usually pass; and others will be controversial (p near 1/2).

We think of each member of the voting body as being concerned with the question "What is the probability that my vote will *make a difference* to the outcome on a bill?" This probability will, in general, vary as a function of p. We define power as follows:

Definition.   The *power* of a member in a weighted voting body is the probability that that member's vote will make a difference to the outcome on a bill with acceptability p, averaged over all p between 0 and 1.

The notion of integration comes in, of course, when we take the average on [0, 1]. An example should make clear how this works. Consider

$$[3; 2, 1, 1]$$

$$A \ B \ C$$

Suppose a bill with acceptability p comes before this body. Thus each member votes for the bill with probability p. Notice that A's vote will make a difference to the outcome if either B or C, or both, vote for the bill. (If they both vote against it, it will fail regardless of what A does.) Thus the probability that A's vote will make a difference is

$$f_A(p) = \underset{\text{B yes, C no}}{p(1-p)} + \underset{\text{B no, C yes}}{(1-p)p} + \underset{\text{B, C yes}}{p^2} = 2p - p^2.$$

Similarly, B's vote will make a difference if A votes "yes" and C votes "no." (If A votes no, the bill will fail regardless of what B does; if A and C both vote yes, the bill will pass regardless of what B does.) Thus

$$f_B(p) = \underset{\text{A yes, C no}}{p(1-p)} = p - p^2.$$

By symmetry, we also have

$$f_C(p) = p - p^2.$$

Our measure of power is traditionally denoted by the letter ϕ. Thus we have, according to our definition,

$$\phi_A = \int_0^1 f_A(p)\,dp = \int_0^1 (2p - p^2)\,dp = 2/3$$

$$\phi_B = \phi_C = \int_0^1 (p - p^2)\,dp = 1/6.$$

A has two-thirds of the power, with B and C having one-sixth. This seems reasonable if we note that A has veto power in this example.

The power index ϕ calculated according to our definition above has an interesting history in political science. It was first defined by Lloyd Shapley, a mathematical game theorist at the RAND Corporation, and Martin Shubik, an economist at Yale, in a classic paper in 1954. It has been known since as the Shapley-Shubik power index and has become the most widely accepted measure of voting power in political science.

EXERCISES

Find the voting power for each voter in each of the following weighted voting bodies.

1. [6; 4, 3, 2]
    A B C

2. [5; 5, 1, 1]
    A B C

3. [5; 3, 3, 2]
    A B C

13.4   Substitution

In Section 1 we saw how to integrate a few simple functions. More complicated functions can sometimes be integrated by *substitution*. The technique depends on the idea of a differential, discussed in an earlier chapter. If $u = f(x)$, the *differential* of u, written du, is defined as

$$du = f'(x)\,dx.$$

For example, if $u = 6x^4$, then $du = 24x^3 \, dx$.

Recall the chain rule for derivatives as used in the following example:

$$\frac{d}{dx}(x^2 - 1)^5 = 5(x^2 - 1)^4(2x) = 10x(x^2 - 1)^4.$$

As in this example, the result of using the chain rule is often a product of two functions. Because of this, functions formed by the product of two functions can sometimes be integrated by using the chain rule in reverse. In the example above, working backwards from the derivative gives

$$\int 10x(x^2 - 1)^4 \, dx = (x^2 - 1)^5 + C.$$

To find an antiderivative involving products, it often helps to make a substitution: let $u = x^2 - 1$, then $du = 2x \, dx$. Now substitute u for $x^2 - 1$ and du for $2x \, dx$ in the indefinite integral above.

$$\int 10x(x^2 - 1)^4 \, dx = \int 5 \cdot 2x(x^2 - 1)^4 \, dx$$
$$= 5 \int (x^2 - 1)^4 \, (2x \, dx)$$
$$= 5 \int u^4 \, du$$

This last integral can now be found by the power rule.

$$5 \int u^4 \, du = 5 \cdot \frac{1}{5}u^5 + C = u^5 + C$$

Finally, substitute $x^2 - 1$ for u.

$$\int 10x(x^2 - 1)^4 \, dx = (x^2 - 1)^5 + C$$

This method of integration is called **integration by substitution.** As shown above, it is simply the chain rule for derivatives in reverse. The results can always be verified by differentiation.

EXAMPLE 1

Find $\int 6x(3x^2 + 4)^4 \, dx$.

A certain amount of trial and error may be needed to decide on the expression to set equal to u. The integrand must be written as two factors, one of which is the derivative of the other. In this example, if $u = 3x^2 + 4$, then $du = 6x \, dx$. Now substitute.

$$\int 6x(3x^2 + 4)^4 \, dx = \int (3x^2 + 4)^4(6x \, dx) = \int u^4 \, du$$

Find this last indefinite integral.

$$\int u^4 \, du = \frac{u^5}{5} + C$$

Now replace u with $3x^2 + 4$.

$$\int 6x(3x^2 + 4)^4 \, dx = \frac{u^5}{5} + C = \frac{(3x^2 + 4)^5}{5} + C$$

To verify this result, find the derivative:

$$\frac{d}{dx}\left[\frac{(3x^2 + 4)^5}{5} + C\right] = \frac{5}{5}(3x^2 + 4)^4(6x) + 0 = (3x^2 + 4)^4(6x),$$

which is the original function. ■

EXAMPLE 2

Find $\int x^2 \sqrt{x^3 + 1}\ dx$.

An expression raised to a power is usually a good choice for u, so because of the square root or 1/2 power, let $u = x^3 + 1$; then $du = 3x^2\ dx$. The integrand does not contain the constant 3, which is needed for du. To take care of this, multiply by 3/3, placing 3 inside the integral sign and 1/3 outside.

$$\int x^2 \sqrt{x^3 + 1}\ dx = \frac{1}{3}\int 3x^2 \sqrt{x^3 + 1}\ dx = \frac{1}{3}\int \sqrt{x^3 + 1}\ (3x^2\ dx)$$

Now substitute u for $x^3 + 1$ and du for $3x^2\ dx$, and integrate.

$$\frac{1}{3}\int \sqrt{x^3 + 1}\ 3x^2\ dx = \frac{1}{3}\int \sqrt{u}\ du = \frac{1}{3}\int u^{1/2}\ du$$

$$= \frac{1}{3}\cdot\frac{u^{3/2}}{3/2} + C = \frac{2}{9}u^{3/2} + C$$

Since $u = x^3 + 1$,

$$\int x^2 \sqrt{x^3 + 1}\ dx = \frac{2}{9}(x^3 + 1)^{3/2} + C.\quad ■$$

The substitution method given in the examples above will not always work. For example, we might try to find

$$\int x^3 \sqrt{x^3 + 1}\ dx$$

by substituting $u = x^3 + 1$, so that $du = 3x^2\ dx$. However, there is no constant which can be inserted inside the integral sign to give $3x^2$. This integral, and a great many others, cannot be evaluated by substitution.

Integration by substitution may also be needed to evaluate definite integrals. First find the necessary antiderivatives and then evaluate them at the upper and lower limits of integration.

EXAMPLE 3

Find the value of $\int_1^4 \frac{2x + 5}{(x^2 + 5x)^2}dx$.

To evaluate this definite integral, first find the indefinite integral

$$\int \frac{2x + 5}{(x^2 + 5x)^2}dx.$$

Let $u = x^2 + 5x$, so that $du = (2x + 5)dx$. This gives

$$\int \frac{2x + 5}{(x^2 + 5x)^2} dx = \int \frac{du}{u^2} = \int u^{-2} \, du$$

$$= \frac{u^{-1}}{-1} + C = \frac{-1}{u} + C.$$

Substituting $x^2 + 5x$ for u gives

$$\int \frac{2x + 5}{(x^2 + 5x)^2} dx = \frac{-1}{(x^2 + 5x)} + C.$$

This antiderivative can now be used to evaluate the given definite integral. Using the fundamental theorem of calculus,

$$\int_1^4 \frac{2x + 5}{(x^2 + 5x)^2} dx = \frac{-1}{x^2 + 5x}\Bigg]_1^4$$

$$= \frac{-1}{4^2 + 5 \cdot 4} - \frac{-1}{1^2 + 5 \cdot 1}$$

$$= \frac{-1}{36} + \frac{1}{6} = \frac{5}{36}.$$

Remember, it is not necessary to include the constant C when evaluating a definite integral. ■

Recall the formula for $\frac{d}{dx}(e^u)$, where $u = f(x)$:

$$\frac{d}{dx}(e^u) = e^u \frac{d}{dx} u.$$

For example, if $u = x^2$ then $\frac{d}{dx} u = \frac{d}{dx}(x^2) = 2x$, and

$$\frac{d}{dx}(e^{x^2}) = e^{x^2} \cdot 2x.$$

Working backwards, if $u = x^2$, then $du = 2x \, dx$, so

$$\int e^{x^2} \cdot 2x \, dx = \int e^u \, du = e^u + C = e^{x^2} + C.$$

Summarizing, we have the following rule for the indefinite integral of e^u, where $u = f(x)$.

Indefinite Integral **of e^u**	If $u = f(x)$, then $$\int e^u \, du = e^u + C.$$

EXAMPLE 4

Find $\int x^2 \cdot e^{x^3} \, dx$.

Let $u = x^3$, the exponent on e. Then $du = 3x^2 \, dx$. Multiplying by 3/3 gives

$$\int x^2 \cdot e^{x^3} \, dx = \frac{1}{3} \int e^{x^3} (3x^2 \, dx)$$

$$= \frac{1}{3} \int e^u \, du$$

$$= \frac{1}{3} e^u + C$$

$$= \frac{1}{3} e^{x^3} + C. \quad \blacksquare$$

Recall that the antiderivative of $f(x) = 1/x$ is $\ln |x|$. The next example uses $\int x^{-1} \, dx = \ln |x| + C$, and the method of substitution.

EXAMPLE 5

Find $\int \dfrac{(2x - 3) \, dx}{x^2 - 3x}$.

Let $u = x^2 - 3x$, so that $du = (2x - 3) \, dx$. Then

$$\int \frac{(2x - 3) \, dx}{x^2 - 3x} = \int \frac{du}{u} = \ln |u| + C = \ln |x^2 - 3x| + C. \quad \blacksquare$$

Generalizing from Example 5 gives the rule for finding the indefinite integral of u^{-1}, where $u = f(x)$.

Indefinite Integral
of u^{-1}

If $u = f(x)$, then

$$\int u^{-1} \, du = \int \frac{du}{u} = \ln |u| + C.$$

The next example shows a more complicated integral evaluated by the method of substitution.

EXAMPLE 6

Find $\int x \sqrt{1 - x} \, dx$.

Let $u = 1 - x$. Then $x = 1 - u$ and $dx = -du$. Now substitute:

$$\int x\sqrt{1 - x} \, dx = \int (1 - u)\sqrt{u}(-du)$$

$$= -\int (1 - u) u^{1/2} \, du$$

$$= \int (u^{3/2} - u^{1/2}) \, du$$

$$= \frac{2}{5} u^{5/2} - \frac{2}{3} u^{3/2} + C$$

$$= \frac{2}{5} (1 - x)^{5/2} - \frac{2}{3} (1 - x)^{3/2} + C. \quad \blacksquare$$

The substitution method is useful if the integral can be written in one of the following forms, where $u(x)$ is some function of x.

Substitution Method	Form of the Integral	Form of the Antiderivative
	1. $\int [u(x)]^n \cdot u'(x)\, dx,\ n \neq -1$	$\dfrac{[u(x)]^{n+1}}{n+1} + C$
	2. $\int e^{u(x)} \cdot u'(x)\, dx$	$e^{u(x)} + C$
	3. $\int \dfrac{u'(x)\, dx}{u(x)}$	$\ln |u(x)| + C$

13.4 EXERCISES

Use substitution to find the indefinite integrals in Exercises 1–36.

1. $\int 4(2x + 3)^4\, dx$

2. $\int (-4t + 1)^3\, dt$

3. $\int \dfrac{4}{(y - 2)^3}\, dy$

4. $\int \dfrac{-3}{(x + 1)^4}\, dx$

5. $\int \dfrac{2\, dm}{(2m + 1)^3}$

6. $\int \dfrac{3\, du}{\sqrt{3u - 5}}$

7. $\int \dfrac{2x + 2}{(x^2 + 2x - 4)^4}\, dx$

8. $\int \dfrac{6x^2\, dx}{(2x^3 + 7)^{3/2}}$

9. $\int z\sqrt{z^2 - 5}\, dz$

10. $\int r\sqrt{r^2 + 2}\, dr$

11. $\int (-4e^{2p})\, dp$

12. $\int 5e^{-0.3g}\, dg$

13. $\int 3x^2 e^{2x^3}\, dx$

14. $\int re^{-r^2}\, dr$

15. $\int (1 - t)e^{2t - t^2}\, dt$

16. $\int (x^2 - 1)e^{x^3 - 3x}\, dx$

17. $\int \dfrac{e^{1/z}}{z^2}\, dz$

18. $\int \dfrac{e^{\sqrt{y}}}{2\sqrt{y}}\, dy$

19. $\int \dfrac{-8}{1 + 3x}\, dx$

20. $\int \dfrac{9}{2 + 5t}\, dt$

21. $\int \dfrac{dt}{2t + 1}$

22. $\int \dfrac{dw}{5w - 2}$

23. $\int \dfrac{v\, dv}{(3v^2 + 2)^4}$

24. $\int \dfrac{x\, dx}{(2x^2 - 5)^3}$

25. $\int \dfrac{x - 1}{(2x^2 - 4x)^2}\, dx$

26. $\int \dfrac{2x + 1}{(x^2 + x)^3}\, dx$

27. $\int \left(\dfrac{1}{r} + r\right)\left(1 - \dfrac{1}{r^2}\right) dr$

28. $\int \left(\dfrac{2}{A} - A\right)\left(\dfrac{-2}{A^2} - 1\right) dA$

29. $\int \dfrac{x^2 + 1}{(x^3 + 3x)^{2/3}}\, dx$

30. $\int \dfrac{B^3 - 1}{(2B^4 - 8B)^{3/2}}\, dB$

31. $\int p(p + 1)^5\, dp$

32. $\int x^3(1 + x^2)^{1/4}\, dx$

33. $\int t\sqrt{5t - 1}\, dt$

34. $\int 4r\sqrt{8 - r}\, dr$

35. $\int \dfrac{u}{\sqrt{u - 1}}\, du$

36. $\int \dfrac{2x}{(x + 5)^6}\, dx$

Use substitution to find the definite integrals in Exercises 37–44.

37. $\int_0^1 2x(x^2 + 1)^3\, dx$

38. $\int_0^1 y^2(y^3 - 4)^3\, dy$

39. $\int_0^4 (\sqrt{x^2 + 12x})(x + 6)\, dx$

40. $\int_0^8 (\sqrt{x^2 - 6x})(x - 3)\, dx$

41. $\int_{-1}^{e-2} \dfrac{t}{t^2 + 2}\, dt$

42. $\int_{-2}^{0} \dfrac{-4x}{x^2 + 3}\, dx$

43. $\int_{0}^{1} ze^{2z^2}\, dz$

44. $\int_{1}^{2} x^2 e^{-x^3}\, dx$

45. Suppose the marginal revenue in hundred thousands of dollars from the sale of x jet planes is

$$R'(x) = 2x(x^2 + 50)^3.$$

Find the total revenue from the sale of 3 planes.

46. The rate of expenditure for maintenance for a particular machine is given by

$$M'(x) = \sqrt{x^2 + 12x}\,(2x + 12),$$

where x is time measured in years. Find the total maintenance charge for the first 5 years of the machine's life.

47. The rate of growth of the profit (in millions of dollars) from a new technology is approximated by

$$p'(x) = xe^{-x^2},$$

where x represents time measured in years. Find the total profit from the first 3 years that the new technology is in operation.

48. If x milligrams of a certain drug are administered to a person, the rate of change in the person's temperature, in degrees Celsius, with respect to the dosage (the person's *sensitivity* to the drug) is given by

$$D'(x) = \frac{2}{x + 9}.$$

Find the total change in body temperature if 3 milligrams of the drug are administered.

13.5   The Area Between Two Curves

The method used in previous sections to find the area between the graph of a function and the x-axis from $x = a$ to $x = b$ can be generalized to find the area between two graphs. For example, the area between the graphs of $f(x)$ and $g(x)$ from $x = a$ to $x = b$ in Figure 16(a) is the same as the difference of the area from a to b between $f(x)$ and the x-axis, shown in Figure 16(b), and the area from a to b between $g(x)$ and the x-axis (see Figure 16(c)). That is, the area between the graphs is given by

$$\int_{a}^{b} f(x)\, dx - \int_{a}^{b} g(x)\, dx,$$

which can be written as

$$\int_{a}^{b} [f(x) - g(x)]\, dx.$$

Area Between Two Curves	If f and g are continuous functions and $f(x) \geq g(x)$ on $[a, b]$, then the area between the curves $f(x)$ and $g(x)$ from $x = a$ to $x = b$ is given by $$\int_{a}^{b} [f(x) - g(x)]\, dx.$$

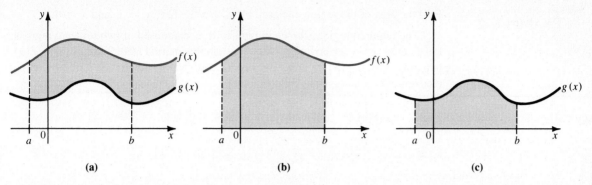

(a)   (b)   (c)

FIGURE 16

EXAMPLE 1

Find the area between the curves $y = x^{1/2}$ and $y = x^3$ from $x = 0$ to $x = 1$.

As shown in Figure 17, $f(x) = x^{1/2}$, $g(x) = x^3$, and the area between these two curves is given by

$$\int_a^b [f(x) - g(x)]\, dx = \int_0^1 (x^{1/2} - x^3)\, dx.$$

Using the fundamental theorem,

$$\int_0^1 (x^{1/2} - x^3)\, dx = \left(\frac{x^{3/2}}{3/2} - \frac{x^4}{4}\right)\Big]_0^1$$

$$= \left(\frac{2}{3}x^{3/2} - \frac{x^4}{4}\right)\Big]_0^1$$

$$= \frac{2}{3}\cdot 1 - \frac{1}{4} - 0 = \frac{5}{12} \text{ square units.} \quad \blacksquare$$

The difference between two integrals can be used to find the area between the graphs of two functions even if one graph lies below the x-axis or if both graphs lie below the x-axis. In fact, if $f(x) \geq g(x)$ for all values of x in the interval $[a, b]$, then the area between the two graphs is always given by

$$\int_a^b [f(x) - g(x)]\, dx.$$

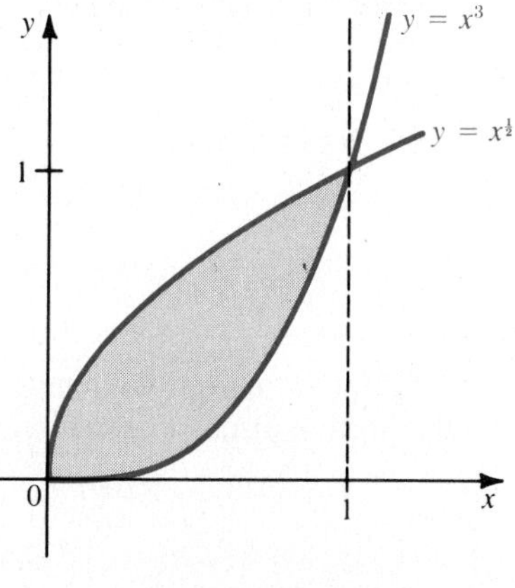

$y = x^3$

$y = x^{\frac{1}{2}}$

FIGURE 17

EXAMPLE 2

Find the area of the region enclosed by $y = x^2 - 2x$, $y = x$, and $x = 4$.

The required region, shown in Figure 18, is composed of two separate regions. Let $f(x) = x^2 - 2x$ and $g(x) = x$. Then, in the interval from 0 to 3, $g(x) \geq f(x)$, but from 3 to 4, $f(x) \geq g(x)$. Because of this switch, the area is found by taking the sum of two integrals as follows.

$$\text{Area} = \int_0^3 [x - (x^2 - 2x)] \, dx + \int_3^4 [(x^2 - 2x) - x] \, dx$$

$$= \int_0^3 (-x^2 + 3x) \, dx + \int_3^4 (x^2 - 3x) \, dx$$

$$= \left(\frac{-x^3}{3} + \frac{3x^2}{2} \right) \Bigg]_0^3 + \left(\frac{x^3}{3} - \frac{3x^2}{2} \right) \Bigg]_3^4$$

$$= \left(-9 + \frac{27}{2} - 0 \right) + \left(\frac{64}{3} - 24 - 9 + \frac{27}{2} \right)$$

$$= \frac{19}{3}$$

This example illustrates the importance of a sketch when using the definite integral to find the area between two curves. ▨

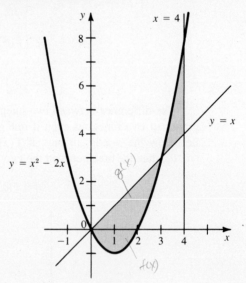

FIGURE 18

Many applications require finding the area between two curves. The rest of this section discusses some typical applications of this type.

EXAMPLE 3

A company is considering a new manufacturing process in one of its plants. The new process provides substantial initial savings, with the savings declining with time x according to the rate-of-savings function

$$S(x) = 100 - x^2,$$

where $S(x)$ is in thousands of dollars. At the same time, the cost of operating the new process increases with time x, according to the rate-of-cost function (in thousands of dollars)

$$C(x) = x^2 + \frac{14}{3}x.$$

(a) For how many years will the company realize savings?

Figure 19 shows the graphs of the rate-of-savings and the rate-of-cost functions. The rate-of-cost (marginal cost) is increasing, while the rate-of-savings (marginal savings) is decreasing. The company should use this new process until the difference between these quantities is zero—that is, until the time at which these graphs intersect. The graphs intersect when

$$C(x) = S(x),$$

or

$$100 - x^2 = x^2 + \frac{14}{3}x.$$

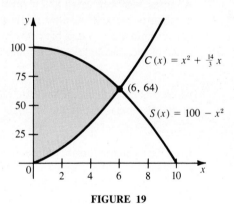

FIGURE 19

Solve this equation as follows.

$$0 = 2x^2 + \frac{14}{3}x - 100$$

$$= 3x^2 + 7x - 150 \qquad \text{Multiply by 3/2}$$

$$= (x - 6)(3x + 25) \qquad \text{Factor}$$

Set each factor equal to 0 separately to get

$$x = 6 \qquad \text{or} \qquad x = -25/3.$$

Only 6 is a meaningful solution here. The company should use the new process for 6 years.

(b)   What will be the net total savings during this period?

Since the total savings over the six-year period is given by the area under the rate-of-savings curve and the total additional cost by the area under the rate-of-cost curve, the net total savings over the 6-year period is given by the area between the rate of cost and the rate of savings curves and the lines $x = 0$ and $x = 6$. This area can be evaluated with a definite integral as follows:

$$\text{total savings} = \int_0^6 \left[(100 - x^2) - \left(x^2 + \frac{14}{3}x \right) \right] dx$$

$$= \int_0^6 \left(100 - \frac{14}{3}x - 2x^2 \right) dx$$

$$= 100x - \frac{7}{3}x^2 - \frac{2}{3}x^3 \Big]_0^6$$

$$= 100(6) - \frac{7}{3}(36) - \frac{2}{3}(216) = 372.$$

The company will save a total of $372,000 over the 6-year period. ▪

EXAMPLE 4

A farmer has been using a new fertilizer that gives him a better yield, but because it exhausts the soil of other nutrients he must use other fertilizers in greater and greater amounts, so that his costs increase each year. The new fertilizer produces a rate of increase in revenue (in hundreds of dollars) given by

$$R(t) = -0.4t^2 + 8t + 10,$$

where t is measured in years. The rate of increase in yearly costs (also in hundreds of dollars) due to use of the fertilizer is given by

$$C(t) = 2t + 5.$$

How long can the farmer profitably use the fertilizer? What will be his net increase in revenue over this period?

The farmer should use the new fertilizer until the marginal costs equal the marginal revenue. Find this point by solving the equation $R(t) = C(t)$ as follows.

$$-0.4t^2 + 8t + 10 = 2t + 5$$
$$-4t^2 + 80t + 100 = 20t + 50$$
$$-4t^2 + 60t + 50 = 0$$

Use the quadratic formula to get

$$t = 15.8$$

The new fertilizer will be profitable for about 15.8 years.

To find the total amount of additional revenue over the 15.8-year period, find the area between the graphs of the rate of revenue and the rate of cost functions, as shown in Figure 20.

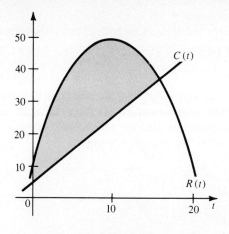

FIGURE 20

FIGURE 21

$$\text{Total savings} = \int_0^{15.8} [R(t) - C(t)]\, dt$$

$$= \int_0^{15.8} [(-0.4t^2 + 8t + 10) - (2t + 5)]\, dt$$

$$= \int_0^{15.8} (-0.4t^2 + 6t + 5)\, dt$$

$$= \left(\frac{-0.4t^3}{3} + \frac{6t^2}{2} + 5t \right) \Bigg]_0^{15.8}$$

$$= 302.01$$

The total savings will amount to about \$30,000 over the 15.8-year period.

It is not realistic to say that the farmer will need to use the new process for 15.8 years—he will probably have to use it for 15 years or for 16 years. In this case, when the mathematical model produces results that are not in the domain of the function, it will be necessary to find the total savings after 15 years and after 16 years and then select the best result. ■

EXAMPLE 5

Suppose the price, in cents, for a certain product is

$$p(x) = 900 - 20x - x^2,$$

when the demand for the product is x units. Also, suppose the function

$$p(x) = x^2 + 10x$$

gives the price, in cents, when the supply is x units. The graphs of both functions are shown in Figure 21 along with the equilibrium point at which supply and demand are equal. To find the equilibrium supply or demand x, solve the equation

$$900 - 20x - x^2 = x^2 + 10x$$

$$0 = 2x^2 + 30x - 900$$

$$0 = x^2 + 15x - 450.$$

The only positive solution of the equation is $x = 15$.

At the equilibrium point where supply and demand are both 15 units, the price is

$$p(15) = 900 - 20(15) - 15^2 = 375,$$

or $3.75.

As the demand graph shows, there are consumers who are willing to pay more than the equilibrium price, so they benefit from the equilibrium price. Some benefit a lot, some less, and so on. Their total benefit, called the **consumer's surplus,** is represented by the area shown in Figure 21. The consumer's surplus is

$$\int_0^{15} (900 - 20x - x^2)\,dx - \int_0^{15} 375\,dx.$$

Evaluating these definite integrals gives

$$\left(900x - 10x^2 - \frac{1}{3}x^3\right)\Big]_0^{15} - 375x\Big]_0^{15}$$

$$= \left[900(15) - 10(15)^2 - \frac{1}{3}(15)^3 - 0\right] - [(375)(15) - 0]$$

$$= 4500.$$

Here the consumer's surplus is 4500 cents, or $45.

On the other hand, some suppliers would have offered the product at a price below the equilibrium price, so they too gain from the equilibrium price. The total of the supplier's gains, called the **producer's surplus,** is also represented by an area shown in Figure 21. The producer's surplus is given by

$$\int_0^{15} 375\,dx - \int_0^{15} (x^2 + 10x)\,dx = 375x\Big]_0^{15} - \left(\frac{1}{3}x^3 + 5x^2\right)\Big]_0^{15}$$

$$= 5625 - \left[\frac{1}{3}(15)^3 + 5(15)^2\right]$$

$$= 3375.$$

The producer's surplus is $33.75. ■

13.5 EXERCISES

Find the area between the curves in Exercises 1–16.

1. $x = -2$, $x = 1$, $y = x^2 + 4$, $y = 0$

2. $x = 1$, $x = 2$, $y = x^3$, $y = 0$

3. $x = -3$, $x = 1$, $y = x + 1$, $y = 0$

4. $x = -2$, $x = 0$, $y = 1 - x^2$, $y = 0$

5. $x = 0$, $x = 6$, $y = 5x$, $y = 3x + 10$

6. $x = -2$, $x = 1$, $y = 2x$, $y = x^2 - 3$

7. $y = x^2 - 30$, $y = 10 - 3x$

8. $y = x^2 - 18$, $y = x - 6$

9. $y = x^2$, $y = 2x$

10. $y = x^2$, $y = x^3$

11. $x = 1$, $x = 6$, $y = \dfrac{1}{x}$, $y = -1$

12. $x = 0$, $x = 4$, $y = \dfrac{1}{x + 1}$, $y = \dfrac{x - 1}{2}$

13. $x = -1$, $x = 1$, $y = e^x - 2$, $y = x + 1$

14. $x = 0$, $x = 2$, $y = e^{-x}$, $y = e^x$

15. $x = 1$, $x = 2$, $y = e^x$, $y = \dfrac{1}{x}$

16. $x = 2$, $x = 4$, $y = \dfrac{x}{2} + 3$, $y = \dfrac{1}{x - 1}$

17. Suppose a company wants to introduce a new machine which will produce a rate of annual savings given by

$$S(x) = 150 - x^2,$$

where x is the number of years of operation of the machine, while producing a rate of annual costs of

$$C(x) = x^2 + \frac{11}{4}x.$$

(a) For how many years will it be profitable to use this new machine?

(b) What are the net total savings during the first year of the use of the machine?

(c) What are the net total savings over the entire period of use of the machine?

18. A new smog-control device will reduce the output of oxides of sulfur from automobile exhausts. It is estimated that the rate of savings to the community from the use of this device will be approximated by

$$S(x) = -x^2 + 4x + 8,$$

where $S(x)$ is the rate of savings in millions of dollars after x years of use of the device. The new device cuts down on the production of oxides of sulfur, but it causes an increase in the production of oxides of nitrogen. The rate of additional costs in millions to the community after x years is approximated by

$$C(x) = \frac{3}{25}x^2.$$

(a) For how many years will it pay to use the new device?

(b) What will be the net total savings over this period of time?

19. De Win Enterprises had an expenditure rate (in hundreds of dollars) of $E(x) = 4x + 2$, and an income rate (in hundreds of dollars of $I(x) = 100 - x$ on a particular job, where x was the number of days from the start of the job. Their profit on that job will equal total income less total expenditure. Profit will be maximized if the job ends at the optimum time, which is the point where the two curves meet. Find the following.

(a) The optimum number of days for the job to last.

(b) The total income for the optimum number of days.

(c) The total expenditure for the optimum number of days.

(d) The maximum profit for the job.

20. A factory has installed a new process that will produce an increased rate of revenue (in thousands of dollars) of
$$R(t) = -t^2 + 15.5t + 16,$$
where t is measured in years. The new process produces additional costs (in thousands of dollars) at the rate of
$$C(t) = .25t + 4.$$
(a) When will it no longer be profitable to use this new process?
(b) Find the total net savings.

For Exercises 21–26 refer to Example 5.

21. Find the producer's surplus if the supply function of some item is given by
$$p(x) = x^2 + 2x + 50.$$
Assume supply and demand are in equilibrium at $x = 20$.

22. Suppose the supply function for a certain commodity is given by
$$p(x) = 100 + 3x + x^2.$$
Suppose that supply and demand are in equilibrium at $x = 3$. Find the producer's surplus.

23. Find the consumer's surplus if the demand function for an item is given by
$$p(x) = 50 - x^2,$$
assuming supply and demand are in equilibrium at $x = 5$.

24. Find the consumer's surplus if the demand for an item is given by
$$p(x) = -(x + 4)^2 + 66,$$
if supply and demand are in equilibrium at $x = 3$.

25. Suppose the supply function of a certain item is given by
$$p(x) = \frac{7}{5}x,$$
and the demand function is
$$p(x) = -\frac{3}{5}x + 10.$$
(a) Graph the supply and demand curves.
(b) Find the point at which supply and demand are in equilibrium.
(c) Find the consumer's surplus.
(d) Find the producer's surplus.

26. Repeat the four steps in Exercise 25 for the supply function
$$p(x) = x^2 + \frac{11}{4}x$$
and the demand function
$$p(x) = 150 - x^2.$$

27. Suppose that all the people in a country are ranked according to their incomes, starting at the bottom. Let x represent the fraction of the community making the lowest income $(0 \le x \le 1)$; $x = .4$, therefore, represents the lower 40% of all income producers. Let

$I(x)$ represent the proportion of the total income earned by the lowest x of all people. Thus, $I(.4)$ represents the fraction of total income earned by the lowest 40% of the population. Suppose

$$I(x) = .9x^2 + .1x.$$

Find and interpret the following.

(a) $I(.1)$ (b) $I(.4)$ (c) $I(.6)$ (d) $I(.9)$

If income were distributed uniformly, we would have $I(x) = x$. The area between the curves $I(x) = x$ and the particular function $I(x)$ for a given country is called the *coefficient of inequality* for that country.

(e) Graph $I(x) = x$ and $I(x) = .9x^2 + .1x$ for $0 \le x \le 1$ on the same axes.

(f) Find the area between the curves.

In Exercises 28–31, approximate the area between the graphs of the given functions on the given interval.

28. $y = \ln x$ and $y = xe^x$; $[1, 4]$

29. $y = \ln x$ and $y = 4 - x^2$; $[2, 4]$

30. $y = \sqrt{9 - x^2}$ and $y = \sqrt{x + 1}$; $[-1, 3]$

31. $y = \sqrt{4 - 4x^2}$ and $y = \sqrt{\dfrac{9 - x^2}{3}}$; $[-1, 1]$

KEY WORDS	antiderivative	area under a curve	integration by substitution
	integral sign	definite integral	area between two curves
	integrand	limits of integration	consumer's surplus
	indefinite integral	fundamental theorem of calculus	producer's surplus

Chapter 13   REVIEW EXERCISES

Find each indefinite integral in Exercises 1–20.

1. $\int 6 \, dx$

2. $\int (-4) \, dx$

3. $\int (2x + 3) \, dx$

4. $\int (5x - 1) \, dx$

5. $\int (x^2 - 3x + 2) \, dx$

6. $\int (6 - x^2) \, dx$

7. $\int 3\sqrt{x} \, dx$

8. $\int \dfrac{\sqrt{x}}{2} \, dx$

9. $\int (x^{1/2} + 3x^{-2/3}) \, dx$

10. $\int (2x^{4/3} + x^{-1/2}) \, dx$

11. $\int \dfrac{-4}{x^3} \, dx$

12. $\int \dfrac{5}{x^4} \, dx$

13. $\int -3e^{2x} \, dx$

14. $\int 5e^{-x} \, dx$

15. $\int \dfrac{2}{x-1}\,dx$

16. $\int \dfrac{-4}{x+2}\,dx$

17. $\int xe^{3x^2}\,dx$

18. $\int 2xe^{x^2}\,dx$

19. $\int \dfrac{3x}{x^2-1}\,dx$

20. $\int \dfrac{-x}{2-x^2}\,dx$

Find the cost function for each of the marginal cost functions in Exercises 21–24.

21. $C'(x) = 10 - 2x$, fixed cost is \$4.

22. $C'(x) = 2x + 3x^2$, 2 units cost \$12.

23. $C'(x) = 3\sqrt{2x-1}$, 13 units cost \$270.

24. $C'(x) = \dfrac{1}{x+1}$, fixed cost is \$18.

25. A particle is moving along a straight line with velocity $v(t) = t^2 - 2t$. Its distance from the starting point after 3 seconds is 8 cm. Find $s(t)$, the distance of the particle from the starting point after t seconds.

26. Evaluate $\displaystyle\sum_{i=1}^{4}(i^2 - i)$.

27. Let $f(x) = 3x + 1$ and $x_1 = -1$, $x_2 = 0$, $x_3 = 1$, $x_4 = 2$, $x_5 = 3$. Find

$$\sum_{i=1}^{5} f(x_i).$$

28. Approximate the area under the graph of $f(x) = 2x + 3$ and above the x-axis from $x = 0$ to $x = 4$ using four rectangles. Let the height of each rectangle be the function value on the left side.

29. Find $\int_0^4 (2x + 3)\,dx$ by using the formula for the area of a trapezoid: $A = \dfrac{1}{2}(B + b)h$, where B and b are the lengths of the parallel sides and h is the distance between them. (See Exercise 28.)

30. The two curves in the figure below give the rate of change of principal in each year of the loan for two different types of 30-year mortgages of \$50,000 at 15% interest. Use rectangles with a width of 2 units and height determined by the function value on the left side to find the following:

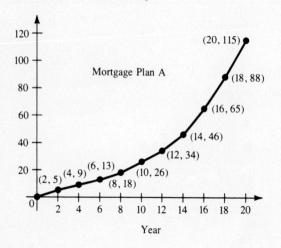

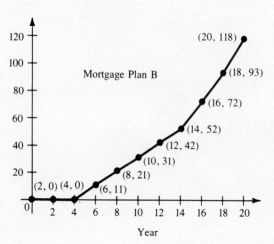

(a) The total amount of principal accumulated in the first 20 years under mortgage plan A.

(b) The total amount of principal accumulated in the first 20 years of mortgage plan B.

Find each definite integral in Exercises 31–38.

31. $\int_1^2 (3x^2 + 5)\,dx$

32. $\int_1^6 (2x^2 + x)\,dx$

33. $\int_1^5 (3x^{-2} + x^{-3})\,dx$

34. $\int_2^3 (5x^{-2} + x^{-4})\,dx$

35. $\int_1^3 2x^{-1}\,dx$

36. $\int_1^6 8x^{-1}\,dx$

37. $\int_0^4 2e^x\,dx$

38. $\int_1^6 \frac{5}{2} e^{4x}\,dx$

In Exercises 39–42, find the area between the x-axis and $f(x)$ over the given interval.

39. $f(x) = \sqrt{x - 1}$; $[1, 10]$

40. $f(x) = 9 - x^2$; $[-2, 2]$

41. $f(x) = e^x$; $[0, 2]$

42. $f(x) = 1 + e^{-x}$; $[0, 4]$

43. The rate of change of sales of a new brand of tomato soup, in thousands, is given by
$$S(x) = \sqrt{x} + 2,$$
where x is the time in months that the new product has been on the market. Find the total sales after 9 months.

44. The rate of change of a population of prairie dogs, in terms of the number of coyotes, x, which prey on them, is given by
$$P(x) = 25 - .1x.$$
Find the total number of prairie dogs as the coyote population grows from 100 to 200.

45. The rate of change of the population of a rare species of Australian spider is given by
$$y' = 100 - .2x,$$
where y is the number of spiders present at time x, measured in months. Find the total number of spiders in the first 10 months.

46. A manufacturer of electronic equipment requires a certain rare metal. He has a reserve supply of 4,000,000 units which he will not be able to replace. If the rate at which the metal is used is given by
$$f(t) = 100,000\,e^{0.03t},$$
where t is the time in years, how long will it be before he uses up the supply? (Hint: Find an expression for the total amount used in t years and set it equal to the known reserve supply.)

Use substitution to find the indefinite integrals in Exercises 47–56.

47. $\int 2x\sqrt{x^2 - 3}\,dx$

48. $\int x\sqrt{5x^2 + 6}\,dx$

49. $\int \frac{x^2\,dx}{(x^3 + 5)^4}$

50. $\int (x^2 - 5x)^4 (2x - 5)\,dx$

51. $\int \frac{4x - 5}{2x^2 - 5x}\,dx$

52. $\int \frac{12(2x + 9)}{x^2 + 9x + 1}\,dx$

53. $\displaystyle\int \frac{x^3}{e^{3x^4}} \, dx$

54. $\displaystyle\int e^{3x^2} \, x \, dx$

55. $\displaystyle\int -2e^{-5x} \, dx$

56. $\displaystyle\int e^{-4x} \, dx$

Find the area of the region enclosed by the given curves in Exercises 57–60.

57. $f(x) = 5 - x^2$, $g(x) = x^2 - 3$

58. $f(x) = x^2 - 4x$, $g(x) = x + 1$, $x = 2$, $x = 4$

59. $f(x) = x^2 - 4x$, $g(x) = x - 6$

60. $f(x) = 5 - x^2$, $g(x) = x^2 - 3$, $x = 0$, $x = 4$

61. A company has installed new machinery which will produce a savings rate (in thousands of dollars) of

$$S(x) = 225 - x^2,$$

where x is the number of years the machinery is to be used. The rate of additional costs to the company due to the new machinery is expected to be

$$C(x) = x^2 + 25x + 150.$$

For how many years should the company use the new machinery? Find the net savings in thousands of dollars over this period.

62. Suppose that the supply function of some commodity is

$$p(x) = x^2 + 5x + 100$$

and the demand function for the commodity is

$$p(x) = 350 - x^2.$$

(a) Find the producer's surplus.

(b) Find the consumer's surplus.

FURTHER TECHNIQUES AND APPLICATIONS OF INTEGRATION

Karl Gerstner. From the series *Aperspective 3* (The Large Sliding Mirror Picture), 1953/55.

In this chapter we develop additional methods of integrating functions. We also look at numerical methods of integration, which are often used with experimental data or with a function that cannot be integrated by other methods. Then we see how to evaluate an integral with one or both limits at infinity. The chapter also includes applications of integration: continuous money flow, volumes of solids of revolution, average value of a function, and differential equations.

14.1   Integration by Parts; Tables of Integrals

The technique of integration by parts often makes it possible to reduce a complicated integral to a simpler integral. If u and v are both differentiable functions, then uv is also differentiable and, by the product rule for derivatives,

$$\frac{d(uv)}{dx} = u\frac{dv}{dx} + v\frac{du}{dx}.$$

This expression can be rewritten, using differentials, as

$$d(uv) = u\,dv + v\,du.$$

Integrating both sides of this last equation gives

$$\int d(uv) = \int u\,dv + \int v\,du,$$

or

$$uv = \int u\,dv + \int v\,du.$$

Rearranging terms gives the following formula.

Integration by Parts

> If u and v are differentiable functions, then
> $$\int u\,dv = uv - \int v\,du.$$

The process of finding integrals by this formula is called **integration by parts.** The method is shown in the following examples.

EXAMPLE 1

Find $\int xe^{5x}\,dx$.

While this integral cannot be found by any method studied so far, it can be found by integration by parts. To do this, first write the expression $xe^{5x}\,dx$ as a product of functions u and dv in such a way that $\int dv = v$ can be found. Let

$$dv = e^{5x}\,dx \qquad \text{and} \qquad u = x.$$

Then

$$du = dx,$$

with v found by integrating dv:

$$v = \int dv = \int e^{5x} \, dx = \frac{1}{5}e^{5x} + C.$$

For simplicity, ignore the constant C and add it at the end of the integration by parts. Now substitute $e^{5x}/5$ into the formula for integration by parts and complete the integration.

$$\int u \, dv = uv - \int v \, du$$

$$\underbrace{\int x}_{u} \underbrace{e^{5x} \, dx}_{dv} = \underbrace{x}_{u}\underbrace{\left(\frac{1}{5}e^{5x}\right)}_{v} - \int \underbrace{\frac{1}{5}e^{5x}}_{v} \underbrace{dx}_{du}$$

$$= \frac{1}{5}xe^{5x} - \frac{1}{25}e^{5x} + C$$

The constant C was added in the last step. As before, check the answer by taking its derivative. ■

EXAMPLE 2

Find $\int \ln x \, dx$ for $x > 0$.
Let

$$u = \ln x \quad \text{and} \quad dv = dx.$$

Then

$$du = \frac{1}{x}dx \quad \text{and} \quad v = x,$$

and

$$\int u \cdot dv = v \cdot u - \int v \cdot du$$

$$\int \ln x \, dx = x \ln x - \int x \cdot \frac{1}{x}dx$$

$$= x \ln x - \int dx$$

$$= x \ln x - x + C. \quad ■$$

EXAMPLE 3

Find $\int_0^3 x\sqrt{1 + x} \, dx$.
First find the indefinite integral, $\int x\sqrt{1 + x} \, dx$. Let

$$u = x \quad \text{and} \quad dv = \sqrt{1 + x} \, dx = (1 + x)^{1/2} \, dx.$$

Then $\quad du = dx \quad$ and $\quad v = \frac{2}{3}(1 + x)^{3/2}.$

Substitute these values into the formula for integration by parts and integrate the second term on the right.

$$\int u \, dv = uv - \int v \, du$$

$$\int x\sqrt{1 + x} \, dx = \frac{2}{3}x(1 + x)^{3/2} - \int \frac{2}{3}(1 + x)^{3/2} \, dx$$

$$= \frac{2}{3}x(1 + x)^{3/2} - \frac{2}{3} \cdot \frac{2}{5}(1 + x)^{5/2} + C$$

Now find the definite integral.

$$\int_0^3 x\sqrt{1 + x}\, dx = \left[\frac{2}{3}x(1 + x)^{3/2} - \frac{4}{15}(1 + x)^{5/2}\right]_0^3$$

$$= \left[\frac{2}{3}(3)(1 + 3)^{3/2} - \frac{4}{15}(1 + 3)^{5/2}\right] -$$

$$\left[\frac{2}{3}(0)(1 + 0)^{3/2} - \frac{4}{15}(1 + 0)^{5/2}\right]$$

$$= \left[2(4)^{3/2} - \frac{4}{15}(4)^{5/2}\right] - \left[0 - \frac{4}{15}\right]$$

$$= 16 - \frac{128}{15} + \frac{4}{15} = \frac{116}{15} \quad\blacksquare$$

The preceding examples illustrate the following general principles for identifying integrals that can be found by integration by parts.

Integrating by Parts

> 1. The integrand can be written as the product of two factors, u and dv.
> 2. It is possible to integrate dv to get v and to differentiate u to get du.
> 3. The integral $\int v\, du$ can be found.

Sometimes it is necessary to use the technique of integrating by parts more than once as in the following example.

EXAMPLE 4

Find $\int 2x^2 e^x\, dx$.

Since $\int e^x\, dx$ can be found, choose $dv = e^x\, dx$, so that $v = e^x$. Then $u = 2x^2$ and $du = 4x\, dx$. Now substitute into the formula for integrating by parts.

$$\int u\, dv = uv - \int v\, du$$

$$\int \underbrace{2x^2}_{u}\, \underbrace{e^x\, dx}_{dv} = \underbrace{2x^2}_{u}\,\underbrace{e^x}_{v} - \int \underbrace{e^x}_{v}\underbrace{(4x\, dx)}_{du} \tag{1}$$

We must find $\int e^x(4x\, dx)$ by parts. Start over, choosing $dv = e^x\, dx$, which gives $v = e^x$, $u = 4x$, and $du = 4\, dx$. Substituting again into the formula for integrating by parts gives

$$\int \underbrace{4x}_{u}\,\underbrace{e^x\, dx}_{dv} = \underbrace{4x}_{u}\,\underbrace{e^x}_{v} - \int \underbrace{e^x}_{v}\underbrace{(4\, dx)}_{du}$$

$$= 4xe^x - 4e^x.$$

Now substitute this antiderivative back into equation (1) to get the desired integral.

$$\int 2x^2 e^x\, dx = 2x^2 e^x - (4xe^x - 4e^x) = 2x^2 e^x - 4xe^x + 4e^x + C$$

(A constant C was added at the last step.) $\quad\blacksquare$

Tables of Integrals   The method of integration by parts requires choosing the factor dv so that $\int dv$ can be found. If this is not possible, or if the remaining factor, which becomes u, does not have a differential du such that $\int v\,du$ can be found, the technique cannot be used. For example, to integrate

$$\int \frac{1}{4-x^2}\,dx$$

we might choose $dv = dx$ and $u = (4-x^2)^{-1}$. Then integration gives $v = x$ and differentiation gives $du = 2x\,dx/(4-x^2)^2$, with

$$\int \frac{1}{4-x^2}\,dx = \frac{x}{4-x^2} - \int \frac{2x^2\,dx}{(4-x^2)^2}.$$

However, the integral on the right is more complicated than the original integral. A second use of integration by parts on the new integral would make matters even worse. Since we cannot choose $dv = (4-x^2)^{-1}\,dx$ because we cannot integrate it by the methods we have studied so far, integration by parts is not possible for this problem. In fact, there are many functions whose integrals cannot be found by any of the methods we have described. Many of these can be found by more advanced methods and are listed in **tables of integrals.** Such a table is given at the back of this book. The next examples show how to use this table.

EXAMPLE 5   Find $\displaystyle\int \frac{1}{\sqrt{x^2+16}}\,dx$.

If $a = 4$, this antiderivative is the same as entry 5 of the table,

$$\int \frac{1}{\sqrt{x^2+a^2}}\,dx = \ln\left| \frac{x+\sqrt{x^2+a^2}}{a} \right| + C.$$

Substituting 4 for a gives

$$\int \frac{1}{\sqrt{x^2+16}}\,dx = \ln\left| \frac{x+\sqrt{x^2+16}}{4} \right| + C.$$

This result could be verified by taking the derivative of the right-hand side of this last equation.   ■

EXAMPLE 6   Find $\displaystyle\int \frac{8}{16-x^2}\,dx$.

Convert this antiderivative into the one given in entry 7 of the table by writing the 8 in front of the integral sign (permissible only with constants) and by letting $a = 4$. Doing this gives

$$8\int \frac{1}{16-x^2}\,dx = 8\left[\frac{1}{2\cdot 4}\ln\left(\frac{4+x}{4-x} \right) \right] + C$$

$$= \ln\left(\frac{4+x}{4-x} \right) + C.$$

In entry 7 of the table, the condition $x^2 < a^2$ is given. Since $a = 4$ in this example, the result given above is valid only for $x^2 < 16$, so that the final answer should be written

$$\int \frac{8}{16 - x^2} dx = \ln \left(\frac{4 + x}{4 - x} \right) + C, \qquad \text{for } x^2 < 16.$$

Because of the condition $x^2 < 16$, the expression in parentheses is always positive, so that absolute value bars are not needed. ∎

EXAMPLE 7

Find $\int \sqrt{9x^2 + 1} \, dx$.

This antiderivative seems most similar to entry 15 of the table. However, entry 15 requires that the coefficient of the x^2 term be 1. That requirement can be satisfied here by factoring out the 9.

$$\int \sqrt{9x^2 + 1} \, dx = \int \sqrt{9 \left(x^2 + \frac{1}{9} \right)} \, dx$$

$$= \int 3 \sqrt{x^2 + \frac{1}{9}} \, dx$$

$$= 3 \int \sqrt{x^2 + \frac{1}{9}} \, dx$$

Now, use entry 15 with $a = 1/3$.

$$\int \sqrt{9x^2 + 1} \, dx = 3 \left[\frac{x}{2} \sqrt{x^2 + \frac{1}{9}} + \frac{\left(\frac{1}{3} \right)^2}{2} \ln \left| x + \sqrt{x^2 + \frac{1}{9}} \right| \right] + C$$

$$= \frac{3x}{2} \sqrt{x^2 + \frac{1}{9}} + \frac{1}{6} \ln \left| x + \sqrt{x^2 + \frac{1}{9}} \right| + C. \; ∎$$

14.1 EXERCISES

Use integration by parts to find the integrals in Exercises 1–10.

1. $\int x e^x \, dx$

2. $\int (x + 1) e^x \, dx$

3. $\int (5x - 9) e^{-3x} \, dx$

4. $\int (6x + 3) e^{-2x} \, dx$

5. $\int_0^1 \frac{2x + 1}{e^x} dx$

6. $\int_0^1 \frac{1 - x}{3 e^x} dx$

7. $\int_1^4 \ln x \, dx$

8. $\int_1^2 \ln(5x - 1) dx$

9. $\int x \ln x \, dx, \; x > 0$

10. $\int x^2 \ln x \, dx, \; x > 0$

11. Find the area between $y = (x - 2) e^x$ and the x-axis from $x = 2$ to $x = 4$.

12. Find the area between $y = x e^x$ and the x-axis from $x = 0$ to $x = 1$.

13. The velocity of revenue from the sale of x units of small desk calculators is
$$R'(x) = 20x(2x + 3)^{1/2}.$$
Find the total revenue from the sale of the first 39 calculators. (Recall that velocity of revenue was defined earlier as the first derivative of the revenue function.)

Exercises 14–23 are mixed—some require integration by parts, others can be found by using techniques discussed earlier. Some problems may require integration by parts more than once.

14. $\displaystyle\int \frac{x^2\ dx}{2x^3 + 1}$

15. $\displaystyle\int x^2 e^{2x}\ dx$

16. $\displaystyle\int_1^2 (1 - x^2)e^{2x}\ dx$

17. $\displaystyle\int_0^5 x \sqrt[3]{x^2 + 2}\ dx$

18. $\displaystyle\int (2x - 1)\ln(3x)\,dx,\ x > 0$

19. $\displaystyle\int (8x + 7)\ln(5x)\,dx,\ x > 0$

20. $\displaystyle\int xe^{x^2}\ dx$

21. $\displaystyle\int x^2 \sqrt{x + 2}\ dx$

22. $\displaystyle\int_0^1 \frac{x^2\ dx}{2x^3 + 1}$

23. $\displaystyle\int_0^1 \frac{x^3\ dx}{\sqrt{3 + x^2}}$

24. The rate (in hours per item) at which a worker in a certain job produces the xth item is
$$h'(x) = \sqrt[3]{1 + x}.$$
What is the total number of hours it will take this worker to produce the first 7 items?

25. The rate at which a microbe population grows is given by
$$m'(x) = 30xe^{2x},$$
where x is time in days. What is the total accumulated growth after 3 days?

26. The rate of reaction to a drug is given by
$$r'(x) = 2x^2 e^{-x},$$
where x is the number of hours since the drug was administered. Find the total reaction to the drug from $x = 1$ to $x = 6$.

Use the table of integrals to find each indefinite integral in Exercises 27–44.

27. $\displaystyle\int \frac{-4}{\sqrt{x^2 + 36}}\,dx$

28. $\displaystyle\int \frac{9}{\sqrt{x^2 + 9}}\,dx$

29. $\displaystyle\int \frac{6}{x^2 - 9}\,dx$

30. $\displaystyle\int \frac{-12}{x^2 - 16}\,dx$

31. $\displaystyle\int \frac{-4}{x\sqrt{9 - x^2}}\,dx$

32. $\displaystyle\int \frac{3}{x\sqrt{121 - x^2}}\,dx$

33. $\displaystyle\int \frac{-2x}{3x + 1}\,dx$

34. $\displaystyle\int \frac{6x}{4x - 5}\,dx$

35. $\displaystyle\int \frac{2}{3x(3x - 5)}\,dx$

36. $\displaystyle\int \frac{-4}{3x(2x + 7)}\,dx$

37. $\displaystyle\int \frac{4}{4x^2 - 1}\,dx$

38. $\displaystyle\int \frac{-6}{9x^2 - 1}\,dx$

39. $\displaystyle\int \frac{3}{x\sqrt{1 - 9x^2}}\,dx$

40. $\displaystyle\int \frac{-2}{x\sqrt{1 - 16x^2}}\,dx$

41. $\displaystyle\int \frac{4x}{2x + 3}\,dx$

42. $\displaystyle\int \frac{4x}{6 - x}\,dx$

43. $\displaystyle\int \frac{-x}{(5x - 1)^2}\,dx$

44. $\displaystyle\int \frac{-3}{x(4x + 3)^2}\,dx$

EXTENDED

APPLICATION

How Much Does a Warranty Cost?*

This application uses some of the ideas of probability. The probability of an event is a number p, where $0 \le p \le 1$, such that p is the ratio of the number of ways that the event can happen divided by the total number of possible outcomes. For example, the probability of drawing a red card from a deck of 52 cards (of which 26 are red) is given by

$$P(\text{red card}) = \frac{26}{52} = \frac{1}{2}.$$

In the same way, the probability of drawing a black queen from a deck of 52 cards is

$$P(\text{black queen}) = \frac{2}{52} = \frac{1}{26}.$$

In this application we find the cost of a warranty program to a manufacturer. This cost depends on the quality of the products made, as we might expect. We use the following variables.

$\quad c$ = constant product price, per unit, including cost of warranty (We assume the price charged per unit is constant, since this price is likely to be fixed by competition.)

$\quad m$ = expected lifetime of the product

$\quad w$ = length of the warranty period

$\quad N$ = size of a production lot, such as a year's production

$\quad r$ = warranty cost per unit

$C(t)$ = pro rata customer rebate at time t

$P(t)$ = probability of product failure at any time t

$F(t)$ = number of failures occurring at time t.

We assume that the warranty is of the pro rata customer rebate type, in which the customer is paid for the proportion of the warranty left. Hence, if the product has a warranty period of w, and fails at time t, then the product worked for the fraction t/w of the warranty period. The customer is reimbursed for the unused portion of the warranty, or the fraction

$$1 - \frac{t}{w}.$$

If we assume the product cost c originally, and if we use $C(t)$ to represent the customer rebate at time t, we have

$$C(t) = c\left(1 - \frac{t}{w}\right).$$

For many different types of products, it has been shown by experience that

$$P(t) = 1 - e^{-t/m}$$

*Reprinted by permission of Warren W. Menke, "Determination of Warranty Reserves," *Management Sciences*, Volume 15, Number 10, June 1969. Copyright © 1969 The Institute of Management Sciences.

provides a good estimate of the probability of product failure at time t. The total number of failures at time t is given by the product of $P(t)$ and N, the total number of items per batch. If we use $F(t)$ to represent this total, we have

$$F(t) = N \cdot P(t) = N(1 - e^{-t/m}).$$

The total number of failures in some "tiny time interval" of width dt can be shown to be the derivative of $F(t)$,

$$F'(t) = \left(\frac{N}{m}\right) e^{-t/m},$$

while the cost for the failures in this "tiny time interval" is

$$C(t) \cdot F'(t) = c\left(1 - \frac{t}{w}\right)\left(\frac{N}{m}\right) e^{-t/m}.$$

The total cost for all failures during the warranty period is thus given by the definite integral

$$\int_0^w c\left(1 - \frac{t}{w}\right)\left(\frac{N}{m}\right) e^{-t/m}\, dt.$$

Using integration by parts, this definite integral can be shown to equal

$$Nc\left[-e^{-t/m} + \frac{t}{w} \cdot e^{-t/m} + \frac{m}{w}(e^{-t/m}) \right]\Bigg|_0^w \quad \text{or} \quad Nc\left(1 - \frac{m}{w} + \frac{m}{w}e^{-w/m}\right).$$

This last quantity is the total warranty cost for all the units manufactured. Since there are N units per batch, the warranty cost per item is

$$r = \frac{1}{N}\left[Nc\left(1 - \frac{m}{w} + \frac{m}{w}e^{-w/m}\right) \right] = c\left(1 - \frac{m}{w} + \frac{m}{w}e^{-w/m}\right).$$

For example, suppose a product which costs $100 has an expected life of 24 months, with a 12-month warranty. Then we have $c = \$100$, $m = 24$, $w = 12$, with r, the warranty cost per unit, given by

$$r = 100(1 - 2 + 2e^{-0.5}) = 100[-1 + 2(0.6065)] = 100(0.2130) = 21.30,$$

where we found $e^{-0.5}$ from the table of powers of e.

EXERCISES

Find r for each of the following.

1. $c = \$50$, $m = 48$ months, $w = 24$ months
2. $c = \$1000$, $m = 60$ months, $w = 24$ months
3. $c = \$1200$, $m = 30$ months, $w = 30$ months

14.2   Numerical Integration

As mentioned in the previous section, some integrals cannot be evaluated by any technique or found in any table. Since $\int_a^b f(x)\,dx$ represents an area when $f(x) > 0$, any approximation of that area also approximates the definite integral. In Section 2 of the previous chapter, the region under a curve was divided into rectangles and the sum of the areas of the rectangles was used as an approximation of the area under the curve. Many methods of approximating definite integrals by areas have been made feasible by the availability of pocket calculators and high-speed computers. These methods are referred to as **numerical integration** methods. We shall discuss two methods of numerical integration, the trapezoidal rule and Simpson's rule.

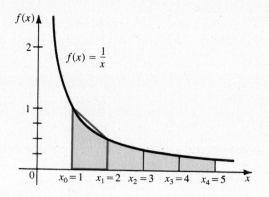

Left-hand trapezoid

$B = f(x_0) = f(1) = 1$

$b = f(x_1) = f(2) = \dfrac{1}{2}$

$h = 2 - 1 = 1$

$\text{Area} = \dfrac{1}{2}(B + b)h = \dfrac{1}{2}\left(1 + \dfrac{1}{2}\right)1$

$\qquad = \dfrac{1}{2} \cdot \dfrac{3}{2}$

$\qquad = \dfrac{3}{4}$

FIGURE 1

As an example, let us approximate

$$\int_1^5 \frac{1}{x}\,dx.$$

The shaded region in Figure 1 shows the area representing that integral, the area under the graph of $f(x) = 1/x$, above the x-axis, and between the lines $x = 1$ and $x = 5$. Since $\int(1/x)\,dx = \ln|x| + C$,

$$\int_1^5 \frac{1}{x}\,dx = \ln|x|\Big]_1^5 = \ln 5 - \ln 1 = \ln 5 - 0 = \ln 5.$$

From the table of natural logarithms or a calculator, $\ln 5 \approx 1.609438$.

Now let us use numerical methods to approximate this area, and then compare the results with the exact area, $\ln 5$. As in our earlier work, divide the interval $[1, 5]$ into subintervals of equal width. To get a first approximation to $\ln 5$ by the trapezoidal rule, find the sum of the areas of the four trapezoids shown in Figure 1. From geometry, the area of a trapezoid is half the product of the sum of the bases and the altitude. Each of the trapezoids in Figure 1 has altitude 1. (In this case, the bases of the trapezoid are vertical and so the altitudes are horizontal.) Adding the areas gives

$$\ln 5 = \int_1^5 \frac{1}{x} dx \approx \frac{1}{2}\left(\frac{1}{1} + \frac{1}{2}\right)(1) + \frac{1}{2}\left(\frac{1}{2} + \frac{1}{3}\right)(1) + \frac{1}{2}\left(\frac{1}{3} + \frac{1}{4}\right)(1) + \frac{1}{2}\left(\frac{1}{4} + \frac{1}{5}\right)(1)$$

$$= \frac{1}{2}\left(\frac{3}{2} + \frac{5}{6} + \frac{7}{12} + \frac{9}{20}\right) \approx 1.68333.$$

To get a better approximation, divide the interval $[1, 5]$ into more subintervals. Generally speaking, the larger the number of subintervals, the better the approximation. The results for selected values of n are shown below to 5 decimal places.

n	$\int_1^5 \frac{1}{x} dx = \ln 5$
6	1.64360
8	1.62897
10	1.62204
20	1.61263
100	1.60957
1000	1.60944

When $n = 1000$, the approximation agrees with the table value to 5 decimal places.

Generalizing from this example, let f be a continuous function on an interval $[a, b]$. Divide the interval from a to b into n equal subintervals by the points $a = x_0, x_1, x_2, \ldots, x_n = b$, as shown in Figure 2. Use the subintervals to make trapezoids which approximately fill in the region under the curve. The approximate value of the definite integral $\int_a^b f(x) \, dx$ is given by the sum of the areas of the trapezoids, or

$$\int_a^b f(x) \, dx \approx \frac{1}{2}\left[f(x_0) + f(x_1) \right]\left(\frac{b-a}{n}\right) + \frac{1}{2}\left[f(x_1) + f(x_2) \right]\left(\frac{b-a}{n}\right) + \cdots$$

$$+ \frac{1}{2}\left[f(x_{n-1}) + f(x_n) \right]\left(\frac{b-a}{n}\right)$$

$$= \left(\frac{b-a}{n}\right)\left[\frac{1}{2}f(x_0) + \frac{1}{2}f(x_1) + \frac{1}{2}f(x_1) + \frac{1}{2}f(x_2) + \frac{1}{2}f(x_2) + \cdots \right.$$

$$\left. + \frac{1}{2}f(x_{n-1}) + \frac{1}{2}f(x_n) \right]$$

$$= \left(\frac{b-a}{n}\right)\left[\frac{1}{2}f(x_0) + f(x_1) + f(x_2) + \cdots + f(x_{n-1}) + \frac{1}{2}f(x_n) \right].$$

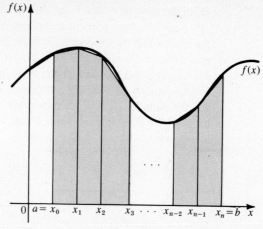

FIGURE 2

Trapezoidal Rule	Let f be a continuous function on $[a, b]$ and let $[a, b]$ be divided into n equal subintervals by the points $a = x_0, x_1, x_2, \ldots, x_n = b$. Then, by the **trapezoidal rule**, $$\int_a^b f(x)\, dx \approx \left(\frac{b - a}{n}\right)\left[\frac{1}{2} f(x_0) + f(x_1) + \cdots + f(x_{n-1}) + \frac{1}{2} f(x_n)\right].$$

EXAMPLE 1

Use the trapezoidal rule with $n = 4$ to approximate

$$\int_3^7 \frac{1}{x - 2}\, dx.$$

Here $a = 3$, $b = 7$, and $n = 4$, with $(b - a)/n = (7 - 3)/4 = 1$ as the altitude of each trapezoid. Then $x_0 = 3$, $x_1 = 4$, $x_2 = 5$, $x_3 = 6$, and $x_4 = 7$. Now find the corresponding function values. The work can be organized into a table, as follows.

i	x_i	$f(x_i)$
0	3	$\dfrac{1}{3 - 2} = 1$
1	4	$\dfrac{1}{4 - 2} = \dfrac{1}{2}$
2	5	$\dfrac{1}{5 - 2} = \dfrac{1}{3}$
3	6	$\dfrac{1}{6 - 2} = \dfrac{1}{4}$
4	7	$\dfrac{1}{7 - 2} = \dfrac{1}{5}$

Substitution into the trapezoidal rule gives

$$\int_3^7 \frac{1}{x-2}\,dx \approx \frac{7-3}{4}\left[\frac{1}{2}(1) + \frac{1}{2} + \frac{1}{3} + \frac{1}{4} + \frac{1}{2}\left(\frac{1}{5}\right)\right]$$

$$= 1\left(\frac{1}{2} + \frac{1}{2} + \frac{1}{3} + \frac{1}{4} + \frac{1}{10}\right) \approx 1.6833.$$

In this case, we can find the integral and evaluate it from a table or calculator.

$$\int_3^7 \frac{1}{x-2}\,dx = \ln(x-2)\Big]_3^7 = \ln 5 - \ln 1$$

$$\approx 1.6094 - 0 = 1.6094$$

The approximation 1.6833 that we found using $n = 4$ differs from the value in the table by .0739. As mentioned above, this error would be reduced if larger values of n were used. Techniques for estimating such errors are considered in more advanced courses. ▪

Simpson's Rule   Another numerical method, *Simpson's rule,* approximates consecutive portions of the curve with portions of parabolas rather than the line segments of the trapezoidal rule. Simpson's rule usually gives a better approximation than the trapezoidal rule for the same number of subintervals. As shown in Figure 3, one parabola is fitted through points A, B, and C, another through C, D, and E, and so on. Then the sum of the areas under these parabolas will approximate the area under the graph of the function. Because of the way the parabolas overlap, it is necessary to have an even number of intervals to apply Simpson's Rule.

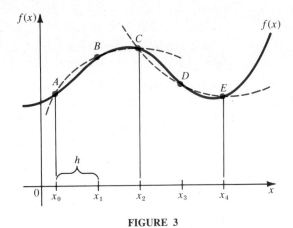

FIGURE 3

If h, the length of each subinterval, is $(b - a)/n$, the area under the parabola through points A, B, and C can be found by a definite integral. The details are omitted; the result is

$$\frac{h}{3}\Big[f(x_0) + 4f(x_1) + f(x_2)\Big].$$

Similarly, the area under the parabola through points C, D, and E is

$$\frac{h}{3}\left[f(x_2) + 4f(x_3) + f(x_4)\right].$$

When these expressions are added, the last term of one expression will be equal to the first term of the next. For example, the sum of the two areas given above is

$$\frac{h}{3}\left[f(x_0) + 4f(x_1) + 2f(x_2) + 4f(x_3) + f(x_4)\right].$$

This illustrates the origin of the pattern of the terms in the general rule given below.

Simpson's Rule

Let f be a continuous function on $[a, b]$ and let $[a, b]$ be divided into an even number n of equal subintervals by the points $a = x_0, x_1, x_2, \ldots, x_n = b$. Then by **Simpson's rule,**

$$\int_a^b f(x)\, dx \approx \frac{b - a}{3n}[f(x_0) + 4f(x_1) + 2f(x_2) + 4f(x_3) + \cdots$$
$$+ 2f(x_{n-2}) + 4f(x_{n-1}) + f(x_n)].$$

EXAMPLE 2

Use Simpson's rule with $n = 4$ to evaluate

$$\int_0^4 \sqrt{x^2 + 1}\, dx.$$

Here $a = 0$, $b = 4$, and $n = 4$, so $(b - a)/(3n) = 4/12 = 1/3$. The endpoints of the four intervals are $x_0 = 0$, $x_1 = 1$, $x_2 = 2$, $x_3 = 3$, and $x_4 = 4$. Set up a table and find the function values for each endpoint.

i	x_i	$f(x_i)$
0	0	1
1	1	1.4142
2	2	2.2361
3	3	3.1623
4	4	4.1231

Now substitute into Simpson's rule to get

$$\int_0^4 \sqrt{x^2 + 1}\, dx \approx \frac{1}{3}[1 + 4(1.4142) + 2(2.2361) + 4(3.1623) + 4.1231]$$

$$= \frac{1}{3}(27.9013)$$

$$= 9.3004. \quad \blacksquare$$

Numerical methods make it possible to approximate

$$\int_a^b f(x) \ dx$$

even when $f(x)$ is not known. The next example shows how this is done.

EXAMPLE 3

As we have seen, the velocity, $v(t)$, gives the rate of change of distance, $s(t)$, with respect to time t. Suppose a vehicle travels an unknown distance. The passengers keep track of the velocity at 10-minute intervals (every 1/6 of an hour) with the following results.

time in hours, t	1/6	2/6	3/6	4/6	5/6	1	7/6
velocity, miles per hour, $v(t)$	45	55	52	60	64	58	47

What is the total distance traveled in the sixty-minute period from $t = 1/6$ to $t = 7/6$?

The distance traveled in t hours is $s(t)$, with $s'(t) = v(t)$. The total distance traveled between $t = 1/6$ and $t = 7/6$ is given by

$$\int_{1/6}^{7/6} v(t) \ dt.$$

Even though this integral cannot be evaluated since we do not have an expression for $v(t)$, either the trapezoidal rule or Simpson's rule can be used to approximate its value and give the total distance traveled. In either case, let $n = 6$, $a = t_0 = 1/6$, and $b = t_6 = 7/6$. By the trapezoidal rule,

$$\int_{1/6}^{7/6} v(t) \ dt \approx \frac{7/6 - 1/6}{6} \left[\frac{1}{2}(45) + 55 + 52 + 60 + 64 + 58 + \frac{1}{2}(47) \right]$$

$$\approx 55.83.$$

By Simpson's rule,

$$\int_{1/6}^{7/6} v(t) \ dt \approx \frac{7/6 - 1/6}{3(6)} [45 + 4(55) + 2(52) + 4(60) + 2(64) + 4(58) + 47]$$

$$= \frac{1}{18}(45 + 220 + 104 + 240 + 128 + 232 + 47)$$

$$= 56.44.$$

As mentioned above, Simpson's rule generally gives a better approximation than the trapezoidal rule. As n increases, the two approximations differ by less and less. However, for the same accuracy, a smaller value of n can generally be used with Simpson's rule so that less computation is necessary. ▨

14.2 EXERCISES

In Exercises 1–10, use $n = 4$ to approximate the value of each of the given integrals (a) by the trapezoidal rule; (b) by Simpson's rule. (c) In Exercises 1–8, find the exact value by integration.

1. $\int_0^2 x^2 \, dx$

2. $\int_0^2 (2x + 1) \, dx$

3. $\int_{-1}^3 \frac{1}{4 - x} \, dx$

4. $\int_1^5 \frac{1}{x + 1} \, dx$

5. $\int_{-2}^2 (2x^2 + 1) \, dx$

6. $\int_0^3 (2x^2 + 1) \, dx$

7. $\int_1^5 \frac{1}{x^2} \, dx$

8. $\int_2^4 \frac{1}{x^3} \, dx$

9. $\int_0^4 \sqrt{x^2 + 1} \, dx$

10. $\int_1^4 x\sqrt{2x - 1} \, dx$

11. Find the area under the semicircle $y = \sqrt{4 - x^2}$ and above the x-axis using $n = 8$ (a) by the trapezoidal rule; (b) by Simpson's rule. (c) Compare the results with the area found by the formula for the area of a circle. Which of the two approximation techniques was more accurate?

12. Find the area between the x-axis and the ellipse $4x^2 + 9y^2 = 36$ using $n = 12$ (a) by the trapezoidal rule; (b) by Simpson's rule. (Hint: Solve the equation for y and find the area of the semiellipse.) (c) Compare the results with the actual area, $6\pi \approx 18.8496$ (which can be found by methods not considered in this text). Which approximation technique was more accurate?

13. The reaction rate to a new drug is given by

$$y = e^{-t^2} + \frac{1}{t}$$

where t is measured in hours after the drug is administered. Find the total reaction to the drug from $t = 1$ to $t = 9$ by letting $n = 8$ and (a) using the trapezoidal rule; (b) using Simpson's rule.

14. The growth rate of a certain tree in feet is given by

$$y = \frac{2}{t} + e^{-t^2/2},$$

where t is time in years. Find the total growth from the first to the sixth year, using $n = 12$, (a) by the trapezoidal rule; (b) by Simpson's rule.

In the following applications, values of $f(x)$ are given.

15. The table below shows the results from a chemical experiment.

Concentration of chemical A, x	1	2	3	4	5	6	7
Rate of formation of chemical B, $f(x)$	12	16	18	21	24	27	32

(a) Plot these points. Connect the points with line segments.

(b) Use the trapezoidal rule to find the area bounded by the broken line of part (a), the x-axis, the line $x = 1$, and the line $x = 7$.

(c) Find the same area using Simpson's rule.

16. The results from a research study in psychology were as follows.

Number of hours of study, x	1	2	3	4	5	6	7
Rate of extra points earned on a test, $f(x)$	4	7	11	9	15	16	23

Repeat steps (a)–(c) of Exercise 15 for this data.

17. A sales manager presented the following results at a sales meeting.

Year, x	1	2	3	4	5	6	7
Rate of sales, $f(x)$	.4	.6	.9	1.1	1.3	1.4	1.6

Repeat steps (a)–(c) of Exercise 15 for this data to find the total sales over the 7-year period.

18. A company's marginal costs in hundreds of dollars were as follows over a 7-year period.

Year, x	1	2	3	4	5	6	7
Marginal cost, $f(x)$	9.0	9.2	9.5	9.4	9.8	10.1	10.5

Repeat steps (a)–(c) of Exercise 15 for this data to find the total sales over the 7-year period.

In the study of *bioavailability* in pharmacy, a drug is given to a patient. The level of concentration of the drug is then measured periodically, producing *blood level* curves such as the ones shown in the figures. The areas under the curves give the total amount of the drug available to the patient. Use the trapezoidal rule to find the following areas. Break the problem into two parts: find the area from 0 to 4 using 1-hour intervals, and find the area from 4 to 20 using 2-hour intervals. You will have to estimate the height for many of the values of time. Refer to the graphs below for Exercises 19–22. (These graphs are from *Basics of Bioavailability*, by D. J. Chodos and A. R. DeSantos. Copyright © 1978 by The Upjohn Company. Reproduced with permission of the Upjohn Company.)

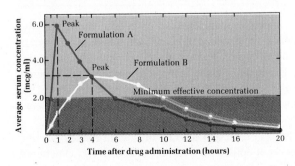

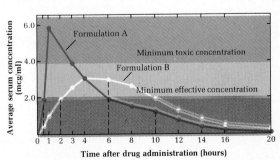

19. Find the area between the curve for Formulation A and the minimum effective concentration line. What does your answer represent?

20. Find the area between the curve for Formulation B and the minimum effective concentration line. What does this area represent?

21. Find the area under the curve between the minimum toxic concentration line and the minimum effective concentration line for Formulation A. Use triangles for the areas from 1/2 to 1 and from 4 to 6.

22. Find the area under the curve and above the minimum effective concentration line for Formulation B.

Use the trapezoidal rule and then use Simpson's rule to approximate each of the following integrals. Use $n = 100$.

23. $\int_{4}^{8} \ln (x^2 - 10) \, dx$

24. $\int_{-2}^{2} e^{-x^2} \, dx$

25. $\int_{-2}^{2} \sqrt{9 - 2x^2} \, dx$

26. $\int_{-1}^{1} \sqrt{16 + 5x^2} \, dx$

27. $\int_{1}^{5} (2x^2 + 3x - 1)^{2/5} \, dx$

28. $\int_{1}^{4} (x^3 + 4)^{5/4} \, dx$

Use either the trapezoidal rule or Simpson's rule with $n = 100$ for Exercises 29 and 30.

29. An electronics company analyst has determined that the rate per month at which revenue comes in from the calculator division is given by

$$R(x) = 105 \, e^{.01x} + 32,$$

where x is the number of months the division has been in operation. Find the total revenue between the 12th and 36th months.

30. Blood pressure in an artery changes rapidly over a very short time for a healthy young adult, from a high of about 120 to a low of about 80. Suppose the blood pressure function over a 1.5 second interval is given by

$$f(x) = .2x^5 - .68x^4 + .8x^3 - .39x^2 + .055x + 100,$$

where x is the time in seconds after a peak reading. The area under the curve for one cycle is important in some blood pressure studies. Find the area under $f(x)$ from .1 seconds to 1.1 seconds.

14.3   Continuous Money Flow

In another chapter we discuss interest payments, loan payments, mortgage payments, and other payments which are made periodically at scheduled times. In some situations, however, money flows in and out of an account almost continuously over a period of time. Examples include income in a store, bank receipts and dispersals, and highway tolls. Although the flow of money in such cases is not exactly continuous, it can be treated, with useful results, as though it were continuous.

Let the continuous function $f(x)$ represent the rate of flow of money per unit of time. If x is in years and $f(x)$ is in dollars per year, the area under $f(x)$ between two points in time gives the total dollar flow over the given time interval.

The function $f(x) = 2000$, shown in Figure 4, represents a uniform rate of money flow of \$2000 per year. The graph of this money flow is a horizontal line and the total money flow over a specified time t is given by the rectangular area below the graph of $f(x)$ and above the x-axis between $x = 0$ and $x = t$. For example, the total money flow over $t = 5$ years would be $2000(5) = 10,000$, or \$10,000.

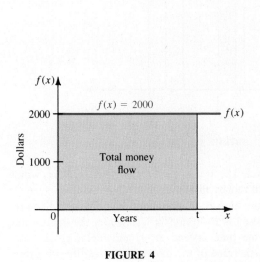

FIGURE 4

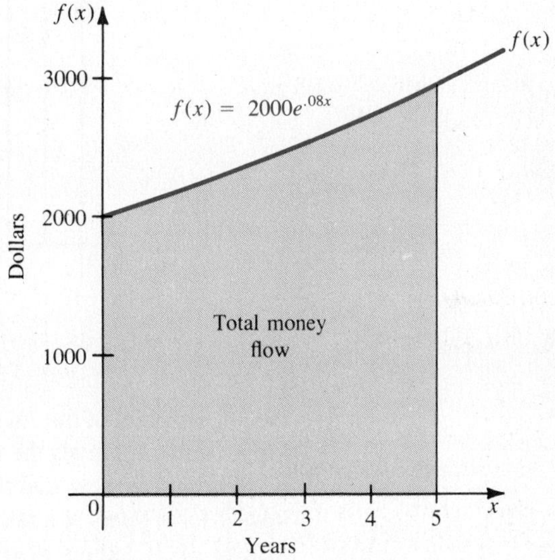

FIGURE 5

A definite integral is needed to find the total money flow over a specific time interval for a variable function. For the function $f(x) = 2000\,e^{0.08x}$, for example, the total money flow over a five-year period would be given by

$$\int_0^5 2000\,e^{0.08x}\;dx \approx 12{,}295.62,$$

or \$12,295,62. See Figure 5.

Total Money Flow

> If $f(x)$ is the rate of money flow, then the total money flow over the time interval from $x = 0$ to $x = t$ is given by
>
> $$\int_0^t f(x)\;dx.$$

To find the present value of a continuous money flow with interest compounded continuously, let $f(x)$ represent the rate of the continuous flow. In Figure 6, the time axis from 0 to x is divided into n subintervals, each of width Δx. The amount of money that flows over any interval of time is given by the area between the x-axis and the graph of $f(x)$ over the specified time interval. The area of each subinterval is approximated by the area of a rectangle with height $f(x_i)$, where x_i is

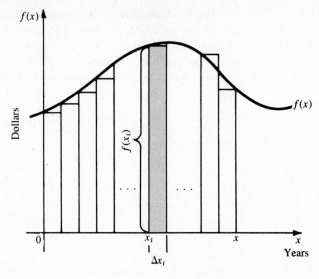

FIGURE 6

the left endpoint of the ith subinterval. The area of each rectangle is $f(x_i)\Delta x$, which (approximately) gives the amount of money flow over that subinterval.

Earlier, we saw that the present value P of an amount A compounded continuously for n years at a rate of interest i is $P = Ae^{-ni}$. Using j for the interest rate instead of i, letting x_i represent the time instead of n, and replacing Δx with Δx_i and A with $f(x_i)\Delta x_i$, the present value of the money flow over the ith subinterval is approximately equal to

$$P_i = f(x_i)\Delta x_i e^{-jx_i}.$$

The total present value is approximately equal to the sum

$$\sum_{i=1}^{n} f(x_i)\Delta x_i e^{-jx_i}.$$

This approximation is improved as n is increased, and if we take the limit of the sum as n increases without bound, we have the present value

$$P = \lim_{n \to \infty} \sum_{i=1}^{n} f(x_i)\Delta x_i e^{-jx_i}.$$

This limit of a summation is given by the definite integral below.

Present Value of	If $f(x)$ is the rate of continuous money flow at an interest rate j at time x, then the present value is
Money Flow	$$P = \int_0^t f(x)\, e^{-jx}\, dx.$$

To find the amount of the flow at any time t, use $A = Pe^{ni}$ with $n = t$, $i = j$, and $P = \int_0^t f(x) e^{-jx} dx$.

Amount of Money

Flow at Time t

> If $f(x)$ is the rate of money flow at an interest rate j at time x, the amount of flow at time t is
>
> $$A = e^{jt} \int_0^t f(x) e^{-jx} dx.$$

It turns out that most money flows can be expressed as exponential or polynomial functions. When these are multiplied by e^{-jx}, the result is a function which can be integrated. The next example illustrates uniform flow, where $f(x)$ is a constant function. (This is a special case of the polynomial function.)

EXAMPLE 1

If money is flowing continuously at a constant rate of $2000 over 5 years, at 12% compounded continuously, find each of the following.

(a) The total amount of the flow over the 5-year period

The total amount is given by $\int_0^t f(x) dx$. Here $f(x) = 2000$ and $t = 5$.

$$\int_0^5 2000 \, dx = 2000x \Big]_0^5 = 2000(5) = 10,000.$$

The total money flow over the five-year period is $10,000.

(b) The amount, compounded continuously, at time $t = 5$

At $t = 5$ with $j = .12$, the amount is

$$A = e^{jt} \int_0^t f(x) e^{-jx} dx = e^{(0.12)5} \int_0^5 (2000) e^{-0.12x} dx$$

$$= (e^{0.6})(2000) \int_0^5 e^{-0.12x} dx = (e^{0.6})(2000) \left(\frac{1}{-.12}\right)\left(e^{-0.12x} \Big]_0^5\right)$$

$$= \frac{2000 e^{0.6}}{-.12}(e^{-0.6} - 1) = \frac{2000}{-.12}(1 - e^{0.6}) \qquad (e^{0.6})(e^{-0.6}) = 1$$

$$= 13,701.98,$$

or $13,701.98. The answer to part (a), $10,000.00, was the amount of money flow over the 5-year period. The $13,701.98 gives that amount with interest compounded continuously over the 5-year period.

(c) The present value of the amount with interest

Use $P = \int_0^t f(x) e^{-jx} dx$ with $f(x) = 2000$, $j = .12$, and $t = 5$.

$$P = \int_0^5 2000 e^{-0.12x} dx = 2000 \left(\frac{e^{-0.12x}}{-.12}\right) \Big]_0^5$$

$$= \frac{2000}{-.12}(e^{-0.6} - 1) = 7519.81$$

The present value of the amount in 5 years is $7519.81, which can be checked by substituting $13,701.98 for A in $A = Pe^{jt}$. We could have found the present value, P, by dividing the amount found in (b) by $e^{jt} = e^{0.6}$. Check that this would give the same result. ■

If the money flow is increasing or decreasing exponentially, then $f(x) = Ce^{kx}$, where C is a constant which represents the initial amount and k is the (nominal) continuous rate of change which may be positive or negative.

EXAMPLE 2

A continuous money flow starts at $1000 and increases exponentially at 2% a year.

(a) Find the amount at the end of 5 years at 10% compounded continuously.

Here $C = 1000$ and $k = .02$, so that $f(x) = 1000e^{0.02x}$. Using $j = .10$ and $t = 5$,

$$A = e^{(0.10)5} \int_0^5 1000 e^{0.02x} e^{-0.10x} \, dx$$

$$= (e^{0.5})(1000) \int_0^5 e^{-0.08x} \, dx \qquad e^{0.02x} \cdot e^{-0.10x} = e^{-0.08x}$$

$$= 1000 e^{0.5} \left(\frac{1}{-.08} e^{-0.08x} \right) \Big]_0^5$$

$$= \frac{1000 e^{0.5}}{-.08} (e^{-0.4} - 1)$$

$$= \frac{1000}{-.08} (e^{0.1} - e^{0.5}) = 6794.38,$$

or $6794.38.

(b) Find the present value at 15% compounded continuously.

Using $f(x) = 1000e^{0.02x}$ with $j = .15$ and $t = 5$ in the present value expression,

$$P = \int_0^5 1000 e^{0.02x} e^{-0.15x} \, dx$$

$$= 1000 \int_0^5 e^{-0.13x} \, dx$$

$$= 1000 \left(\frac{1}{-.13} e^{-0.13x} \Big]_0^5 \right)$$

$$= \frac{1000}{-.13} (e^{-0.65} - 1)$$

$$= 3676.57,$$

or $3676.57. ■

If the rate of change of the continuous money flow is given by the polynomial function $f(x) = a_n x^n + a_{n-1} x^{n-1} + \cdots + a_0$, the expressions for present value and amount can be integrated term by term using integration by parts.

EXAMPLE 3

The rate of change of a continuous flow of money is given by $f(x) = 1000x^2 + 100x$. Find the present value of this money flow at the end of 10 years at 10% compounded continuously.

Evaluate

$$P = \int_0^{10} (1000x^2 + 100x)e^{-0.10x}\, dx$$

$$= \int_0^{10} 1000x^2 e^{-0.10x}\, dx + \int_0^{10} 100xe^{-0.10x}\, dx.$$

First find each indefinite integral using integration by parts. Let $u = x^2$ and $dv = e^{-0.10x}\, dx$ in the first integral. (Two integrations will be needed in this first integral.)

$$1000 \int x^2 e^{-0.1x}\, dx = 1000\left[\frac{1}{-.1}x^2 e^{-0.1x} - \frac{2}{-.1}\int xe^{-0.1x}\, dx\right]$$

Now let $u = x$ and $dv = e^{-0.1x}\, dx$.

$$1000 \int x^2 e^{-0.1x}\, dx = 1000\left[\frac{1}{-.1}x^2 e^{-0.1x} - \frac{2}{-.1}\left(\frac{1}{-.1}xe^{-0.1x} - \frac{1}{-.1}\int e^{-0.1x}\, dx\right)\right]$$

Use this result to find the definite integral.

$$1000 \int_0^{10} x^2 e^{-0.1x}\, dx = 1000\left[\frac{1}{-.1}x^2 e^{-0.1x} - \frac{2}{(-.1)^2}\left(xe^{-0.1x} - \frac{1}{-.1}e^{-0.1x}\right)\right]_0^{10}$$

$$= 1000[(-1000e^{-1} - 4000e^{-1}) - (0 - 2000)]$$

$$= 160{,}602.79.$$

For the second integral, let $u = x$ and $dv = e^{-0.1x}\, dx$.

$$100 \int_0^{10} xe^{-0.1x}\, dx = 100\left(\frac{1}{(-.1)^2}(-.1x - 1)e^{-0.1x}\right)_0^{10}$$

$$= 100[100(-2)e^{-1} - 100(-1)]$$

$$= 2642.41$$

The present value is

$$P = 160{,}602.79 + 2642.41 = 163{,}245.20,$$

or \$163,245.20. ▪

14.3 EXERCISES

Each of the functions in Exercises 1–14 represents the rate of flow of money per unit of time. Assume a ten-year period at 12% compounded continuously and find each of the following: **(a)** the present value; **(b)** the amount at $t = 10$.

1. $f(x) = 1000$

2. $f(x) = 300$

3. $f(x) = 500$

4. $f(x) = 2000$

5. $f(x) = 400 e^{0.03x}$

6. $f(x) = 800 e^{0.05x}$

7. $f(x) = 5000 e^{-0.01x}$

8. $f(x) = 1000 e^{-0.02x}$

9. $f(x) = .1x$

10. $f(x) = .5x$

11. $f(x) = .01x + 100$

12. $f(x) = .05x + 500$

13. $f(x) = 1000 - 100x$

14. $f(x) = 2000 - 150x$

15. An investment is expected to yield a uniform continuous income flow of $20,000 a year for 3 years. Find the final amount at an interest rate of 14% compounded continuously.

16. A real estate investment is expected to produce a uniform continuous income flow of $8000 a year for 6 years. Find the present value at the following rates compounded continuously.

   (a) 12%   **(b)** 10%   **(c)** 15%

17. A continuous flow of money starts at $5000 and decreases exponentially at 1% a year for 8 years. Find the present value and final amount at an interest rate of 18% compounded continuously.

18. A continuous money flow starts at $1000 and increases exponentially at 5% a year for 4 years. Find the present value and final amount if interest earned is 11% compounded continuously.

19. A money market fund has a continuous flow of money which changes at a rate of $f(x) = 1500 - 60x^2$, reaching 0 in 5 years. Find the present value of this flow if interest is 10% compounded continuously.

20. Find the amount of a continuous money flow in 3 years if the rate of change is given by $f(x) = 1000 - x^2$ and if interest is 10% compounded continuously.

14.4   Two Applications of Integration:
Volume and Average Value

This section discusses two very useful topics—finding the volume of a solid by integration, and finding the average value of a function.

Volume   Figure 7 shows the region below the graph of some function $y = f(x)$, above the x-axis, and between $x = a$ and $x = b$. We have already used integrals to find the area of such a region. Now, suppose this region is revolved about the x-axis as shown in Figure 8. The resulting figure is called a **solid of revolution.** In many cases, the volume of a solid of revolution can be found by integration.

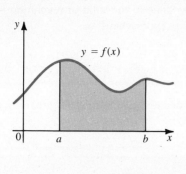

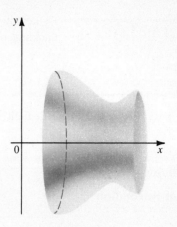

FIGURE 7   **FIGURE 8**

To do this, start as in finding area and divide the interval $[a, b]$ into n subintervals of equal width Δx by the points $x_0 = a, x_1, x_2, \ldots, x_i, \ldots, x_n = b$. Then think of slicing the solid into n slices of equal thickness Δx, as shown in Figure 9. If the slices are thin enough, each slice is very close to being a right circular cylinder. The formula for the volume of a right circular cylinder is $\pi r^2 h$, where r is the radius of the circular base and h is the height of the cylinder. As shown in Figure 10, the height of each slice is Δx. (The height is horizontal here, since the cylinder is on its side.) The radius of the circular base of each slice is $f(x_i)$. Thus, the volume of the slice is closely approximated by $\pi[f(x_i)]^2 \Delta x$. The volume of the solid of revolution will be approximated by the sum of the volumes of the slices:

$$V \approx \sum_{i=1}^{n} \pi[f(x_i)]^2 \Delta x.$$

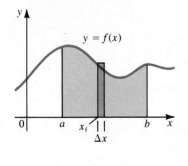

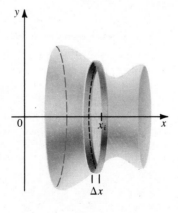

(a)   **(b)**

FIGURE 9   **FIGURE 10**

By definition, the volume of the solid of revolution is the limit of this sum as the thickness of the slices approaches 0 or,

$$V = \lim_{\Delta x \to 0} \sum_{i=1}^{n} \pi[f(x_i)]^2 \, \Delta x.$$

This limit, like the one discussed earlier for area, is a definite integral:

Volume of a Solid of Revolution

$$V = \lim_{\Delta x \to 0} \sum_{i=1}^{n} \pi[f(x_i)]^2 \, \Delta x = \int_a^b \pi[f(x)]^2 \, dx.$$

EXAMPLE 1

Find the volume of the solid of revolution formed by rotating about the x-axis the region bounded by $y = x + 1$, $y = 0$, $x = 1$, and $x = 4$. (See Figure 11(a).)

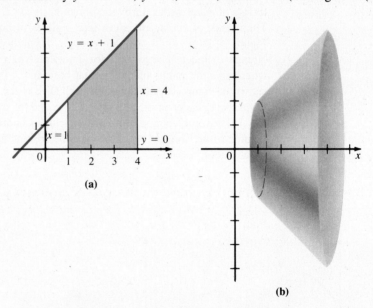

FIGURE 11

The solid is shown in Figure 11(b). Use the formula given above for the volume, with $a = 1$, $b = 4$, and $f(x) = x + 1$.

$$V = \int_1^4 \pi(x + 1)^2 \, dx = \pi\left(\frac{(x + 1)^3}{3}\right)\Bigg]_1^4$$

$$= \frac{\pi}{3}(5^3 - 2^3) = \frac{117\pi}{3} \quad \blacksquare$$

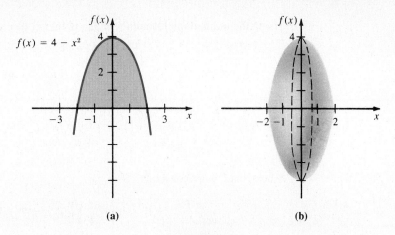

(a)

(b)

FIGURE 12

EXAMPLE 2

Find the volume of the solid of revolution formed by rotating about the x-axis the area bounded by $f(x) = 4 - x^2$ and the x-axis. (See Figure 12(a).)

The solid is shown in Figure 12(b). Find a and b from the x-intercepts. If $y = 0$, then $x = 2$ or $x = -2$, so that $a = -2$ and $b = 2$. The volume is

$$V = \int_{-2}^{2} \pi(4 - x^2)^2 \, dx = \int_{-2}^{2} \pi(16 - 8x^2 + x^4) \, dx$$

$$= \pi\left(16x - \frac{8x^3}{3} + \frac{x^5}{5}\right)\bigg]_{-2}^{2} = \frac{512\pi}{15}. \quad \blacksquare$$

EXAMPLE 3

Find the volume of a right circular cone with height h and base radius r.

Figure 13(a) shows the required cone, while Figure 13(b) shows an area which could be rotated about the x-axis to get such a cone. Here $y = f(x)$ is the equation (in slope-intercept form) of the line through $(0, r)$ and $(h, 0)$. The slope of this line is

$$\frac{0 - r}{h - 0} = -\frac{r}{h}.$$

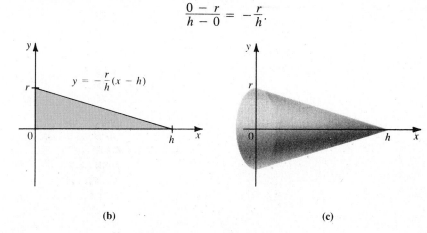

(a)

(b)

(c)

FIGURE 13

Using the point-slope formula with the point $(h, 0)$ gives

$$y - y_1 = m(x - x_1)$$

$$y = -\frac{r}{h}(x - h)$$

as the equation of the line. Then the volume is

$$V = \int_0^h \pi\left[-\frac{r}{h}(x - h)\right]^2 dx = \pi\int_0^h \frac{r^2}{h^2}(x - h)^2 \, dx.$$

Since r and h are constants,

$$V = \frac{\pi r^2}{h^2}\int_0^h (x - h)^2 \, dx.$$

Using substitution with $u = x - h$ and $du = dx$ gives

$$V = \frac{\pi r^2}{h^2}\left[\frac{(x - h)^3}{3}\right]_0^h = \frac{\pi r^2}{3h^2}[0 - (-h)^3] = \frac{\pi r^2 h}{3}.$$

This is the familiar formula for the volume of a right circular cone.   ▨

Average Value of a Function   The average of the n numbers $v_1, v_2, v_3, \ldots,$ v_n is given by

$$\frac{v_1 + v_2 + v_3 + \cdots + v_n}{n}.$$

We can define an average value of a function f on $[a, b]$ in a similar manner: divide the interval $[a, b]$ into n subintervals each of width Δx. Then choose an x-value, x_i, in each interval, and find $f(x_i)$. The average function value for the n subintervals and the given choices of x_i is

$$\frac{f(x_1) + f(x_2) + f(x_3) + \cdots + f(x_n)}{n} = \frac{\sum_{i=1}^{n} f(x_i)}{n}.$$

Since $(b - a)/n = \Delta x$, multiply the sum by $(b - a)/(b - a)$ and rearrange the expression to get

$$\frac{b - a}{b - a} \cdot \frac{\sum_{i=1}^{n} f(x_i)}{n} = \frac{b - a}{n} \cdot \frac{\sum_{i=1}^{n} f(x_i)}{b - a}$$

$$= \Delta x \cdot \frac{\sum_{i=1}^{n} f(x_i)}{b - a}$$

$$= \frac{1}{b - a}\sum_{i=1}^{n} f(x_i) \, \Delta x.$$

Now, take the limit as $n \to \infty$. If the limit exists, then

$$\lim_{n \to \infty} \frac{1}{b-a} \sum_{i=1}^{n} f(x_i) \, \Delta x = \frac{1}{b-a} \lim_{n \to \infty} \sum_{i=1}^{n} f(x_i) \, \Delta x$$

$$= \frac{1}{b-a} \int_{a}^{b} f(x) \, dx$$

Summarizing, we have the following definition.

Average Value of a Function

The **average value** of a function f on the interval $[a, b]$ is

$$\frac{1}{b-a} \int_{a}^{b} f(x) \, dx,$$

provided the indicated definite integral exists.

EXAMPLE 4

An analyst determines that the cost (in dollars) to produce x units of a new product is given by

$$f(x) = 3\sqrt{x} + 8.$$

Find the average cost per unit of the first 100 units produced.
With $a = 0$ and $b = 100$, the average cost is

$$\frac{1}{100} \int_{0}^{100} (3\sqrt{x} + 8) \, dx = \frac{1}{100}(2x^{3/2} + 8x) \Big]_{0}^{100}$$

$$= \frac{1}{100}(2000 + 800 - 0) = 28,$$

for an average cost of $28 per unit. ▪

14.4 EXERCISES

Find the volume of the solid of revolution formed by rotating about the x-axis the regions bounded by the graphs in Exercises 1–18.

1. $f(x) = x$, $y = 0$, $x = 0$, $x = 2$
2. $f(x) = 2x$, $y = 0$, $x = 0$, $x = 3$
3. $f(x) = 2x + 1$, $y = 0$, $x = 0$, $x = 4$
4. $f(x) = x - 4$, $y = 0$, $x = 4$, $x = 10$
5. $f(x) = \frac{1}{3}x + 2$, $y = 0$, $x = 1$, $x = 3$
6. $f(x) = \frac{1}{2}x + 4$, $y = 0$, $x = 0$, $x = 5$
7. $f(x) = \sqrt{x}$, $y = 0$, $x = 1$, $x = 2$
8. $f(x) = \sqrt{x + 1}$, $y = 0$, $x = 0$, $x = 3$
9. $f(x) = \sqrt{2x + 1}$, $y = 0$, $x = 1$, $x = 4$
10. $f(x) = \sqrt{3x + 2}$, $y = 0$, $x = 1$, $x = 2$
11. $f(x) = e^x$, $y = 0$, $x = 0$, $x = 2$
12. $f(x) = 2e^x$, $y = 0$, $x = -2$, $x = 1$

13. $f(x) = \dfrac{1}{\sqrt{x}}$, $y = 0$, $x = 1$, $x = 4$

14. $f(x) = \dfrac{1}{\sqrt{x+1}}$, $y = 0$, $x = 0$, $x = 2$

15. $f(x) = x^2$, $y = 0$, $x = 1$, $x = 5$

16. $f(x) = \dfrac{x^2}{2}$, $y = 0$, $x = 0$, $x = 4$

17. $f(x) = 1 - x^2$, $y = 0$

18. $f(x) = 2 - x^2$, $y = 0$

The function $y = \sqrt{r^2 - x^2}$ has as its graph a semicircle of radius r with center at $(0, 0)$. (See the figure.) In Exercises 19–21, find the volume that results when this semicircle is rotated about the x-axis. (The result gives a formula for the volume of a sphere with radius r.)

19. $f(x) = \sqrt{1 - x^2}$

20. $f(x) = \sqrt{16 - x^2}$

21. $f(x) = \sqrt{r^2 - x^2}$

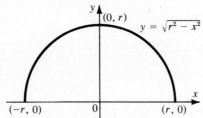

22. Find a formula for the volume of an ellipsoid. See Exercises 19–21 and the figure.

Ellipsoid

23. The figure shows the blood flow in a small artery of the body. The flow of blood is *laminar* (in layers), with the velocity very low near the artery walls and highest in the center of the artery. To calculate the total flow in the artery we think of the flow as being made up of many layers of concentric tubes sliding one on the other.

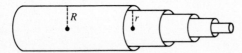

   Suppose R is the radius of an artery and r is the distance from a given layer to the center. Then the velocity of blood in a given layer can be shown to equal

$$v(r) = k(R^2 - r^2),$$

where k is a numerical constant.

   Since the area of a circle is $A = \pi r^2$, the change in the area of the cross section of one of the layers, corresponding to a small change in the radius, Δr, can be approximated by differentials. For $dr = \Delta r$, the differential of the area A is

$$dA = 2\pi r\, dr = 2\pi r \Delta r,$$

where Δr is the thickness of the layer. The total flow in the layer is defined to be the product of volume and cross-section area, or

$$F(r) = 2\pi r k(R^2 - r^2)\Delta r.$$

(a) Set up a definite integral to find the total flow in the artery.

(b) Evaluate this definite integral.

Find the average value of each function on the interval $[a, b]$.

24. $f(x) = x^2 - 2$; $a = 0$, $b = 5$

25. $f(x) = 3 - 2x^2$, $a = 1$, $b = 9$

26. $f(x) = \sqrt{x + 1}$; $a = 3$, $b = 8$

27. $f(x) = (2x - 1)^{1/2}$; $a = 1$, $b = 13$

28. $f(x) = e^{x/5}$; $a = 0$, $b = 5$

29. $f(x) = e^{0.1x}$; $a = 0$, $b = 10$

30. Suppose the number of items a new worker on an assembly line produces after t days on the job is given by

$$I(t) = 35 + 2t.$$

Find the average number of items produced by this employee after the following number of days.

(a) 5 **(b)** 10 **(c)** 15

31. The reaction to a certain drug in appropriate units is given by

$$R(t) = \frac{1}{t} + \frac{2}{t^2},$$

where t is time in hours after the drug is administered. Find the average reaction during each of the following hours.

(a) 2nd hour **(b)** 12th hour **(c)** 24th hour

14.5 Improper Integrals

The graph in Figure 14(a) shows the area bounded by the curve $f(x) = x^{-3/2}$, the x-axis, and the vertical line $x = 1$. Think of the shaded region below the curve as extending indefinitely to the right. Does this shaded region have an area?

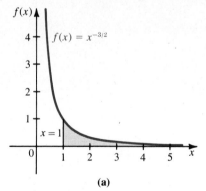
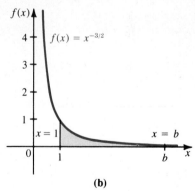

(a) (b)

FIGURE 14

To see if the area of this region can be defined, introduce a vertical line at $x = b$, as shown in Figure 14(b). This vertical line gives a region with both upper and lower limits of integration. The area of this new region is given by the definite integral

$$\int_1^b x^{-3/2} \, dx.$$

By the fundamental theorem of calculus,

$$\int_1^b x^{-3/2} \, dx = (-2x^{-1/2}) \Big]_1^b$$

$$= -2b^{-1/2} - (-2 \cdot 1^{-1/2})$$

$$= -2b^{-1/2} + 2 = 2 - \frac{2}{b^{1/2}}.$$

Suppose we now let the vertical line $x = b$ of Figure 14(b) move further to the right. That is, suppose we let $b \to \infty$. The expression $-2/b^{1/2}$ would then approach 0, and

$$\lim_{b \to \infty} \left(2 - \frac{2}{b^{1/2}} \right) = 2 - 0 = 2.$$

This limit is defined to be the *area* of the region shown in Figure 14(a), so that

$$\int_1^\infty x^{-3/2} \, dx = 2.$$

An integral of the form

$$\int_a^\infty f(x) \, dx, \qquad \int_{-\infty}^b f(x) \, dx, \qquad \text{or} \qquad \int_{-\infty}^\infty f(x) \, dx$$

is called an improper integral. These **improper integrals** are defined as follows.

Improper Integrals

> If f is continuous on the indicated interval and if the indicated limits exist, then
>
> $$\int_a^\infty f(x) \, dx = \lim_{b \to \infty} \int_a^b f(x) \, dx,$$
>
> $$\int_{-\infty}^b f(x) \, dx = \lim_{a \to -\infty} \int_a^b f(x) \, dx,$$
>
> $$\int_{-\infty}^\infty f(x) \, dx = \int_{-\infty}^c f(x) \, dx + \int_c^\infty f(x) \, dx,$$
>
> for real numbers a, b, and c.

If the expressions on the right side exist, the integrals are **convergent**; otherwise, they are **divergent**.

EXAMPLE 1

Find the following integrals.

(a) $\displaystyle\int_1^\infty \frac{dx}{x}$

A graph of this region is shown in Figure 15. By the definition of an improper integral,

$$\int_1^\infty \frac{dx}{x} = \lim_{b \to \infty} \int_1^b \frac{dx}{x}.$$

Find $\int_1^b \dfrac{dx}{x}$ by the fundamental theorem of calculus.

$$\int_1^b \frac{dx}{x} = \ln |x| \Big]_1^b = \ln |b| - \ln |1| = \ln |b| - 0 = \ln |b|$$

As $b \to \infty$, $\ln |b| \to \infty$, so

$$\lim_{b \to \infty} \ln |b| \text{ does not exist.}$$

Since the limit does not exist, $\int_1^\infty \dfrac{dx}{x}$ is divergent.

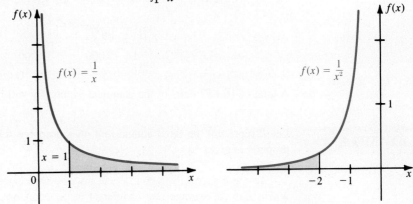

FIGURE 15   **FIGURE 16**

(b) $\displaystyle \int_{-\infty}^{-2} \frac{1}{x^2} dx = \lim_{a \to -\infty} \int_a^{-2} \frac{1}{x^2} dx = \lim_{a \to -\infty} \left(\frac{-1}{x} \right) \Big]_a^{-2} = \lim_{a \to -\infty} \left(\frac{1}{2} + \frac{1}{a} \right) = \frac{1}{2}$

A graph of this region is shown in Figure 16. Since the limit exists, this integral converges. ▨

EXAMPLE 2

Find $\displaystyle \int_0^\infty 4e^{-3x} \, dx$.

By definition,

$$\int_0^\infty 4e^{-3x} \, dx = \lim_{b \to \infty} \int_0^b 4e^{-3x} \, dx$$

$$= \lim_{b \to \infty} \left(-\frac{4}{3} e^{-3x} \right) \Big]_0^b$$

$$= \lim_{b \to \infty} \left[-\frac{4}{3} e^{-3b} - \left(-\frac{4}{3} e^{-0} \right) \right]$$

$$= \lim_{b \to \infty} \left[\frac{-4}{3 e^{3b}} + \frac{4}{3} \right] = 0 + \frac{4}{3} = \frac{4}{3}.$$

This integral converges. ▨

Probability density functions, discussed in a later chapter, are an important application of improper integrals. The last two examples illustrate other applications.

EXAMPLE 3

The rate at which a chemical is being released into a small stream at time t is given by $P_0 e^{-kt}$, where P_0 is the amount of chemical released into the stream initially. Suppose $P_0 = 1000$ and $k = .06$. Find the total amount of the chemical that will be released into the stream into the indefinite future.

We need to find

$$\int_0^\infty P_0 e^{-kt}\, dt = \int_0^\infty 1000 e^{-0.06t}\, dt.$$

Work as above.

$$\int_0^\infty 1000 e^{-0.06t}\, dt = \lim_{b\to\infty} \int_0^b 1000 e^{-0.06t}\, dt$$

$$= \lim_{b\to\infty} \left(\frac{1000}{-.06} e^{-0.06t} \right) \Big]_0^b$$

$$= \lim_{b\to\infty} \left[\frac{1000}{-.06\, e^{0.06b}} - \frac{1000}{-.06} e^0 \right] = \frac{-1000}{-.06} = 16{,}667$$

A total of 16,667 units of the chemical eventually will be released. ▪

EXAMPLE 4

Let R represent the fixed annual rent on a property. The **capitalized value** of the property is given by

$$\int_0^b R e^{-kt}\, dt,$$

where k is the average rate of interest in the economy. Find the capitalized value of property when rent is paid perpetually if $k = .04$ and $R = 5000$.*

The capitalized value will be

$$\int_0^\infty 5000 e^{-0.04t}\, dt.$$

Find this improper integral as follows.

$$\int_0^\infty 5000 e^{-0.04t}\, dt = \lim_{b\to\infty} \int_0^b 5000 e^{-0.04t}\, dt = \lim_{b\to\infty} \left(\frac{5000}{-.04} e^{-0.04t} \right) \Big]_0^b$$

$$= \lim_{b\to\infty} (-125{,}000 e^{-0.04b} + 125{,}000) = 125{,}000$$

The capitalized value is $125,000. ▪

14.5 EXERCISES

Determine whether the improper integrals in Exercises 1–22 converge or diverge, and find the value of those that converge.

1. $\int_2^\infty \frac{1}{x^2}\, dx$

2. $\int_5^\infty \frac{1}{x^2}\, dx$

3. $\int_1^\infty \frac{1}{\sqrt{x}}\, dx$

4. $\int_{16}^\infty \frac{-3}{\sqrt{x}}\, dx$

5. $\int_{-\infty}^{-1} \frac{2}{x^3}\, dx$

6. $\int_{-\infty}^{-4} \frac{3}{x^4}\, dx$

7. $\int_1^\infty \frac{1}{x^{1.001}}\, dx$

8. $\int_1^\infty \frac{1}{x^{.999}}\, dx$

*There are historical situations where governments have agreed to pay a fixed rent perpetually.

9. $\int_{-\infty}^{-1} x^{-2} \, dx$

10. $\int_{-\infty}^{-4} x^{-2} \, dx$

11. $\int_{-\infty}^{-1} x^{-8/3} \, dx$

12. $\int_{-\infty}^{27} x^{-5/3} \, dx$

13. $\int_{0}^{\infty} 4e^{-4x} \, dx$

14. $\int_{0}^{\infty} 10e^{-10x} \, dx$

15. $\int_{-\infty}^{0} 4e^{x} \, dx$

16. $\int_{-\infty}^{0} 3e^{4x} \, dx$

17. $\int_{-\infty}^{-1} \ln |x| \, dx$

18. $\int_{1}^{\infty} \ln |x| \, dx$

19. $\int_{0}^{\infty} \frac{dx}{(x + 1)^2}$

20. $\int_{0}^{\infty} \frac{dx}{(2x + 1)^3}$

21. $\int_{-\infty}^{-1} \frac{2x - 1}{x^2 - x} \, dx$

22. $\int_{0}^{\infty} \frac{2x + 3}{x^2 + 3x} \, dx$

Use the table of integrals as necessary to evaluate Exercises 23–28.

23. $\int_{-\infty}^{1} \frac{2}{3x(2x - 7)} \, dx$

24. $\int_{1}^{\infty} \frac{7}{2x(5x + 1)} \, dx$

25. $\int_{1}^{\infty} \frac{4}{9x(x + 1)^2} \, dx$

26. $\int_{-\infty}^{5} \frac{5}{4x(x + 2)^2} \, dx$

27. $\int_{0}^{\infty} \ln |2x| \, dx$

28. $\int_{0}^{\infty} \ln |3x| \, dx$

For Exercises 29–32, find the area between the graph of the given function and the x-axis over the given interval, if possible.

29. $f(x) = \dfrac{1}{x - 1}$ for $(-\infty, 0]$

30. $f(x) = e^{-x}$ for $(-\infty, e]$

31. $f(x) = \dfrac{1}{(x - 1)^2}$ for $(-\infty, 0]$

32. $f(x) = \dfrac{1}{(x - 1)^3}$ for $(-\infty, 0]$.

Find the capitalized values of the properties in Exercises 33 and 34.

33. A castle for which annual rent of $60,000 will be paid in perpetuity; the interest rate is 8%

34. A fort on a strategic peninsula in the North Sea, annual rent $500,000, paid in perpetuity; the interest rate is 6%

Radioactive waste is entering the atmosphere over an area at a decreasing rate. Use the improper integral

$$\int_{0}^{\infty} Pe^{-kt} \, dt$$

with $P = 50$ to find the total amount of the waste that will enter the atmosphere for each of the following values of k.

35. $k = .04$

36. $k = .06$

37. Find $\int_{-\infty}^{\infty} xe^{-x^2} \, dx$.

38. Find $\int_{-\infty}^{\infty} \frac{x}{(1 + x^2)^2} \, dx$.

EXTENDED

APPLICATION

Flow Systems*

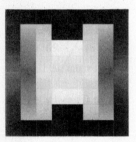

One of the most important biological applications of integration is the determination of properties of flow systems. Among the significant characteristics of a flow system are its flow rate (a heart's output in liters per minute, for example), its volume (for blood, the vascular volume), and the quantity of a substance flowing through it (a pollutant in a stream, perhaps).

A flow system can be anything from a river to an oil pipeline to an artery. We assume that the system has some well defined volume between two points, and a more or less constant flow rate between them. In arteries the blood pulses, but we shall measure the flow over long enough time intervals for the flow rate to be regarded as constant.

The standard method for analyzing flow system behavior is the so-called indicator dilution method, but we shall also discuss the more recent thermodilution technique for determining cardiac output. In the indicator dilution method, a known or unknown quantity of a substance such as a dye, a pollutant, or a radioactive tracer is injected or seeps into a flow system at some entry point. The substance is assumed to mix well with the fluid, and at some downstream measuring point its concentration is sampled either serially or continuously. The concentration function $c(t)$ is then integrated over an appropriate time interval, either by numerical approximation, or a planimeter, or electronically, or by curve-fitting and the fundamental theorem of calculus. As we shall see, the integral

$$\int_0^T c(t) \, dt$$

(whose units are mass × time/volume) is extremely useful for finding unknown flow system properties.

The basis for the analysis of flow systems is the principle of mass conservation, or "what goes in must come out." We are going to assume that the indicator does not leak from the stream (for example, by diffusion into tissue), and that the time interval is over before any of the indicator recirculates (less than a minute in the case of blood). What goes *into* the system is a (known or unknown) quantity Q_{in} of indicator. What comes *out* of the system, or more precisely, what passes by the downstream measuring point at a flow rate F, is a volume of fluid with a variable concentration $c(t)$ of the indicator. The product of F and $c(t)$ is called the **mass rate** of indicator flowing past the measuring point. The total quantity Q_{out} of indicator flowing by during the time interval from 0 to T is the integral of the mass rate from 0 to T:

$$Q_{out} = \int_0^T F \, c(t) \, dt.$$

By our assumption of mass conservation (no leakage and no recirculation), we must have $Q_{in} = Q_{out}$, or

$$Q_{in} = \int_0^T F \, c(t) \, dt = F \int_0^T c(t) \, dt, \tag{1}$$

provided of course that F is essentially constant.

Equation (1) is the basic relationship of indicator dilution. We shall illustrate its use with an example.

Example 1

Suppose that an industrial plant is discharging toxic Kryptonite into the Cahaba River at an unknown variable rate. Downriver, a field station of the Environmental Protection Agency measures the following concentrations:

Time	Concentration
2 A.M.	3.0 mg/m^3
6 A.M.	3.5 mg/m^3
10 A.M.	2.5 mg/m^3
2 P.M.	1.0 mg/m^3
6 P.M.	0.5 mg/m^3
10 P.M.	1.0 mg/m^3

The EPA has found the flow rate of the Cahaba in the vicinity to be 1000 ft^3/sec = 1.02×10^5 m^3/hr. How much Kryptonite is being discharged?

We use Equation (1) to estimate the total amount of Kryptonite discharged during a 24-hour day by approximating the concentration integral. Dividing the day into six 4-hour subintervals (so that $\Delta t = 4$) and using the EPA data as our function values $c(t)_i$, we compute as follows:

$$\int_0^{24} c(t) \, dt \approx \sum_{i=1}^{6} c(t_i)\Delta t$$

$$= \Delta t \sum_{i=1}^{6} c(t_i)$$

$$= 4(3 + 3.5 + 2.5 + 1.0 + 0.5 + 1.0)$$

$$= 4(11.5) = 46,$$

or 46 mg × hrs/m^3. Hence, by equation (1), the total daily discharge is

$$Q_{in} = F \int_0^{24} c(t) \, dt$$

$$\approx \left(1.02 \times 10^5 \frac{m^3}{hour}\right)\left(46\frac{mg \times hour}{m^3}\right)$$

$$= 4.7 \times 10^6 \text{ mg}$$

$$= 4.7 \text{ kilograms of Kryptonite.} \quad \blacksquare$$

DETERMINING CARDIAC OUTPUT BY THERMODILUTION

Knowledge of a patient's cardiac output is a valuable aid to diagnosis and treatment of heart damage. By cardiac output we mean the volume flow rate of venous blood pumped by the right ventricle through the pulmonary artery to the lungs (to be oxygenated). Normal resting cardiac output is 4 to 5 liters per minute, but in critically ill patients it may fall well below 3 liters per minute.

Unfortunately, cardiac output is difficult to determine by dye dilution, owing to the need to calibrate the dye and to sample the blood repeatedly. There are also problems with dye instability, recirculation, and slow dissipation. With the development in 1970 of a suitable pulmonary artery catheter, it became possible to make rapid and routine bedside measurements of cardiac output by thermodilution, and to do so with very few patient complications.

In a coronary intensive care unit (typically), a balloon-tipped catheter is inserted in an arm vein and guided to the superior vena cava or right atrium (upper chamber of the heart). A temperature sensing device called a thermistor is moved through the right side of the heart and positioned a few centimeters into the pulmonary artery. Then, 10 ml of cold D5W (5% dextrose in water) is injected into the vena cava or atrium. As the cold D5W mixes with blood in the right heart, temperature variations in the flow are detected by the thermistor. Figure 1 shows a typical record of temperature change as a function of time. With computerized equipment, cardiac output can be displayed within a minute after injection. Since the cold D5W is warmed by the body before it recirculates, repeated measurements can be made reliably.

We now derive an equation for thermodilution comparable to equation (1). First, we need to define the thermal equivalent of mass. We define the "quantity of cold" injected to be

$$Q_{in} = V_i(T_b - T_i)$$

where V_i is the volume of injectate, T_i is its temperature, and T_b is body temperature. Thus, "quantity of cold" injected is jointly proportional to how cold the injectate is (below body) and to how much is injected.

As with indicator dilution, we shall assume "conservation of cold," that is, no loss and no recirculation. (Actually, there is some loss of cold as the injectate travels up through the catheter to the injection point, but that can be corrected for.) The quantity of cold passing by the thermistor in a short time interval dt can be calculated by multiplying the flow volume $F\,dt$ and the temperature variation ΔT during the interval. The total quantity of cold flowing by is

$$Q_{out} = \int_0^\infty F\Delta T\,dt = F\int_0^\infty \Delta T\,dt.$$

Equating Q_{in} to Q_{out} and solving for the flow rate F produces the analog of equation (1):

$$Q_{out} = Q_{in} = V_i(T_b - T_i)$$

$$F\int_0^\infty \Delta T\,dt = V_i(T_b - T_i)$$

$$F = \frac{V_i(T_b - T_i)}{\int_0^\infty \Delta T\,dt}.$$

If time is measured in seconds and temperature in degrees Celsius, then the denominator of equation (2) has units of (°C)(sec) and the numerator has units of (ml)(°C). Hence F has units ml/sec, which can be converted to liters/minute by multiplying by $60/1000 = 0.06$.

Although thermistor signals are usually calibrated and integrated electronically, we shall illustrate equation (2) with an example.

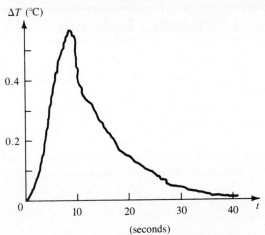

ΔT (°C)

(seconds)

FIGURE 1. This curve shows the temperature variation in the pulmonary artery that resulted from injecting a few milliliters of cold dextrose solution into the right atrium of the heart.

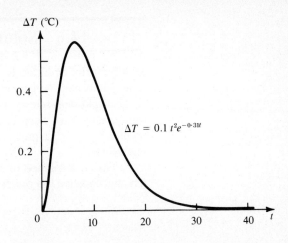

ΔT (°C)

$\Delta T = 0.1\, t^2 e^{-0.31t}$

FIGURE 2. The illustration of Equation 2 uses this smooth curve in place of the thermodilution curve of Figure 1.

Example 2

Suppose $T_b = 37°C$, $T_i = 0°C$, and $V_i = 10$ ml. Suppose that the change in temperature with respect to time is represented by the curve $\Delta T = 0.1\, t^2 e^{-0.31t}$, shown in Figure 2. Finally, suppose that the net effect of all the correction factors is to multiply the right side of Equation (2) by 0.891. Then integration by parts gives

$$F = \frac{(10)(37 - 0)(0.891)}{\int_0^{\infty} (0.1) t^2 e^{-0.31t}\, dt} = \frac{330}{(0.1)\dfrac{2}{(0.31)^3}}$$

$$= 49.16 \text{ ml/sec} = 2.95 \text{ liters/minute.} \quad \blacksquare$$

EXERCISES

1. Approximate the integral in Example 1 using (a) the trapezoidal rule; (b) Simpson's rule. Let t represent the number of hours after 2 A.M., so that 2 A.M. = 0, 6 A.M. = 4, and so on. Assume the reading after 24 hours is 3.0 mg/m³ again.

2. A dye dilution technique for measuring cardiac output involves injection of a dye into a main vein near the heart and measurement by a catheter in the aorta at regular intervals. Suppose the results from such measurements are as given in the table.

time (seconds)	0	4	8	12	16	20	24
concentration (ml/liter)	0	0.6	2.7	4.1	2.9	0.9	0

   If 8 ml of dye is injected, approximate the cardiac output F, in the equation

   $$Q_{in} = F \int_0^t c(t)\, dt$$

   by **(a)** the trapezoidal rule; **(b)** Simpson's rule.

3. In Example 2 let $T_b = 37.1°C$, $T_i = 5°C$ and $v_i = 8$ ml. Find the cardiac output, F.

14.6   Solutions of Differential Equations

A **differential equation** is an equation which involves an unknown function and a finite number of its derivatives. Differential equations have been important in the study of physical science and engineering since the eighteenth century. More recently, they have become useful in the life sciences, social sciences, and economics for solving problems about population growth, ecological balance, and interest rates.

Usually, a solution of an equation is a *number*. However, a solution of a differential equation is a *function*. For example, to solve a differential equation such as

$$\frac{dy}{dx} = 3x^2 - 2x, \tag{1}$$

we must find all functions y which satisfy the equation. Since the left side of the equation is the derivative of y with respect to x, solve the equation for y by finding an antiderivative on each side. On the left, the antiderivative is $y + C_1$. On the right,

$$\int (3x^2 - 2x)\,dx = x^3 - x^2 + C_2.$$

The solutions of equation (1) are given by

$$y + C_1 = x^3 - x^2 + C_2$$

or $\qquad\qquad\qquad\qquad y = x^3 - x^2 + C_2 - C_1.$

Replacing the constant $C_2 - C_1$ with the single constant C gives

$$y = x^3 - x^2 + C. \tag{2}$$

(From now on we will add just one constant with the understanding that it represents the difference between the two constants obtained in the two integrations.)

Each different value of C in equation (2) leads to a different solution of equation (1), showing that a differential equation can have an infinite number of solutions. Equation (2) is the **general solution** of the differential equation (1). Some of the solutions to equation (1) are graphed in Figure 17.

The simplest kind of differential equation has the form

$$\frac{dy}{dx} = f(x).$$

Since equation (1) has this form, the solution of equation (1) suggests the following generalization.

General Solution of

$$\frac{dy}{dx} = f(x)$$

The general solution of the differential equation

$$\frac{dy}{dx} = f(x) \text{ is } y = \int f(x)\,dx.$$

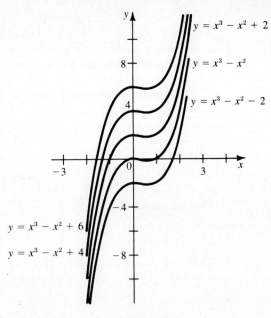

FIGURE 17

EXAMPLE 1

The time-dating of dairy products depends on the solution of a differential equation. Suppose, for some product, that y is the number of bacteria (in thousands) present at a time t (in days) and

$$\frac{dy}{dt} = 10t. \qquad (3)$$

Further, suppose at $t = 0$, $y = 50$ (in thousands). Find an equation for y in terms of t.

We need to solve the differential equation $dy/dt = 10t$. By the general solution given above,

$$y = \int 10t \, dt,$$

$$y = \frac{10t^2}{2} + C$$

$$y = 5t^2 + C,$$

which is the general solution of equation (3). Because of the given information that $y = 50$ when $t = 0$, a specific value of C can be found here. Replacing t with 0 and y with 50 in the general solution gives

$$50 = 5 \cdot 0^2 + C$$

$$50 = C.$$

Let $C = 50$ in the general solution to get

$$y = 5t^2 + 50.$$

In this solution, the given information has been used to produce a solution with a specific value of C. Such a solution is called a **particular solution** of the given differential equation. The given information, $y = 50$ when $t = 0$, is called an **initial condition** because $t = 0$. ■

Sometimes a differential equation must be rewritten in the form

$$\frac{dy}{dx} = f(x)$$

before it can be solved.

EXAMPLE 2

Find the particular solution of

$$\frac{dy}{dx} - 2x = 5,$$

given that $y = 2$ when $x = -1$.

Add $2x$ to both sides of the equation to get

$$\frac{dy}{dx} = 2x + 5.$$

The solution is the antiderivative of the left side of the equation.

$$y = \frac{2x^2}{2} + 5x + C = x^2 + 5x + C.$$

Substituting 2 for y and -1 for x gives

$$2 = (-1)^2 + 5(-1) + C$$
$$C = 6.$$

The particular solution is $y = x^2 + 5x + 6$. ■

EXAMPLE 3

The population P of a flock of birds is growing exponentially so that

$$\frac{dP}{dx} = 20e^{0.05x},$$

where x is time in years. Find P in terms of x if there were 20 birds in the flock initially.

Solve the differential equation:

$$P = \int 20e^{0.05x}\, dx = \frac{20}{.05}e^{0.05x} + C = 400e^{0.05x} + C.$$

Since P is 20 when x is 0,

$$20 = 400e^0 + C$$
$$-380 = C$$

and

$$P = 400e^{0.05x} - 380. \quad ■$$

14.6 EXERCISES

Find general solutions for the differential equations in Exercises 1–12.

1. $\dfrac{dy}{dx} = x^2$

2. $\dfrac{dy}{dx} = -x + 2$

3. $\dfrac{dy}{dx} = -2x + 3x^2$

4. $\dfrac{dy}{dx} = 6x^2 - 4x$

5. $\dfrac{dy}{dx} = e^x$

6. $\dfrac{dy}{dx} = e^{3x}$

7. $\dfrac{dy}{dx} = 2e^{-x}$

8. $\dfrac{dy}{dx} = 3e^{-2x}$

9. $3\dfrac{dy}{dx} = -4x^2$

10. $4\dfrac{dy}{dx} - x = 0$

11. $3x^3 - 2\dfrac{dy}{dx} = 0$

12. $3x^2 - 3\dfrac{dy}{dx} = 2$

Find particular solutions for the differential equations in Exercises 13–20.

13. $\dfrac{dy}{dx} + 2x = 3x^2$; $y = 2$ when $x = 0$

14. $\dfrac{dy}{dx} = 4x + 3$; $y = -4$ when $x = 0$

15. $\dfrac{dy}{dx} = 3x^2 - 4x + 2$; $y = 3$ when $x = -1$

16. $\dfrac{dy}{dx} = 4x^3 - 3x^2 + x$; $y = 0$ when $x = 1$

17. $\dfrac{dy}{dx} = \dfrac{1}{x}$; $y = 10$ when $x = 1$

18. $\dfrac{dy}{dx} = \dfrac{1}{x - 2}$; $y = 50$ when $x = 3$

19. $2\dfrac{dy}{dx} = 4xe^{-x}$; $y = 42$ when $x = 0$

20. $x\dfrac{dy}{dx} = x^2 e^{3x}$; $y = 8/9$ when $x = 0$

21. The marginal profit of a certain company is given by

$$\frac{dy}{dx} = \frac{100}{32 - 4x},$$

where x represents the amount in thousands of dollars spent on advertising. Find the profit for each of the following advertising expenditures if the profit is $1000 when nothing is spent for advertising.

(a) $3000   **(b)** $5000

(c) Can advertising expenditures ever reach $8000 according to this model? Why?

22. The average rate of decline of a bacteria population after the introduction of a bactericide is given by

$$\frac{dy}{dt} = \frac{-200}{1 + 2t},$$

where t is time in hours after the bactericide is introduced. If there are 10,000 bacteria initially, what is the population after

(a) 4 hours?   **(b)** 12 hours?

23. Assume the rate of change of the population of a certain city is given by

$$\frac{dy}{dt} = 6000\,e^{0.06t},$$

where y is the population at time t, measured in years. If the population was 100,000 in 1980 (assume $t = 0$ in 1980), predict the population in the year 2000.

24. A company has found that the rate of change of sales during an advertising campaign is

$$\frac{dy}{dx} = 30e^{0.03x},$$

where y is the sales in thousands of dollars at time x in months. If the sales are $200,000 when $x = 0$, find the sales at the end of 6 months.

The **elasticity** $e(x)$ of a cost function is the ratio of the marginal cost to the average cost. For the cost function $y = C(x)$, the elasticity is

$$e(x) = \frac{C'(x)}{\dfrac{C(x)}{x}} = \frac{\dfrac{dy}{dx}}{\dfrac{y}{x}} = \frac{x}{y}\left(\frac{dy}{dx}\right).$$

Find the general cost function for the following elasticity functions. (Hint: set each elasticity function equal to $\dfrac{x}{y}\left(\dfrac{dy}{dx}\right)$, then solve for y.)

25. $e(x) = \dfrac{2x + 1}{y}$

26. $e(x) = \dfrac{6x^3 - x}{x^2 y}$

14.7   Separation of Variables

Interest on an investment is sometimes compounded continuously*, which means that the investment grows at a rate proportional to the amount present. If A is the amount in an account at time t, then, for some constant k, the differential equation

$$\frac{dA}{dt} = kA$$

gives the rate of growth of A with respect to t. This differential equation is different from those discussed in the previous section, which had the form

$$\frac{dy}{dx} = f(x).$$

A more general differential equation is one which can be written in the form

$$\frac{dy}{dx} = \frac{f(x)}{g(y)}.$$

Using differentials and multiplying on both sides by $g(y)\,dx$ gives

$$g(y)\,dy = f(x)\,dx.$$

In this form all terms involving y (including dy) are on one side of the equation, and all terms involving x (and dx) are on the other side. A differential equation in

---

*See Section 6 in the chapter, Exponential and Logarithmic Functions.

this form is said to be **separable,** since the variables x and y can be separated. A separable differential equation may be solved by integrating each side.

EXAMPLE 1

Find the general solution of $y \dfrac{dy}{dx} = x^2$.

Begin by separating the variables to get

$$y \, dy = x^2 \, dx.$$

The general solution is found by taking antiderivatives on each side.

$$\int y \, dy = \int x^2 \, dx$$

$$\frac{y^2}{2} = \frac{x^3}{3} + C$$

$$y^2 = \frac{2}{3}x^3 + 2C = \frac{2}{3}x^3 + K \quad \blacksquare$$

The constant K was substituted for $2C$ in the last step. The solution is left in implicit form, not solved explicitly for y.

EXAMPLE 2

Find the general solution of $\dfrac{dy}{dx} = ky$, where k is a constant.

Separating variables leads to

$$\frac{1}{y} \, dy = k \, dx.$$

To solve this equation, take antiderivatives on each side.

$$\int \frac{1}{y} \, dy = \int k \, dx$$

$$\ln |y| = kx + C.$$

Use the definition of logarithm to write the equation in exponential form as

$$|y| = e^{kx+C}.$$

By properties of exponents,

$$|y| = e^{kx} e^{C}.$$

Finally, use the definition of absolute value to get

$$y = e^{kx} e^{C} \qquad \text{or} \qquad y = -e^{kx} e^{C}.$$

Since e^{C} and $-e^{C}$ are constants, we replace them with the constant M, which may have any real number value, to get the single equation

$$y = M e^{kx}.$$

This equation, $y = M e^{kx}$, is the exponential growth or decay function which we discussed earlier (in the chapter on exponential and logarithmic functions).

Recall that such equations arise in situations where the rate of change of a quantity is proportional to the amount present at time x; that is, where

$$\frac{dy}{dx} = ky.$$

The constant k is the growth (or decay) constant, while M represents the amount present at time $x = 0$. ▪

Applying the results of Example 2 to the equation discussed at the beginning of this section,

$$\frac{dA}{dt} = kA,$$

shows that the amount in the account at time t is

$$A = A_0 e^{kt},$$

where A_0 is the amount originally invested.

As a model of population growth, the equation $y = Me^{kx}$ is not realistic over the long run for most populations. As shown by graphs of functions of the form $y = Me^{kx}$, with both M and k positive, growth would be unbounded. Additional factors, such as space restrictions or a limited amount of food, tend to inhibit growth of populations as time goes on. In an alternative model that assumes a maximum population of size N, the rate of growth of a population is proportional to how close the population is to that maximum. These assumptions lead to the differential equation

$$\frac{dy}{dx} = k(N - y),$$

the **limited growth function** mentioned in the earlier chapter. Graphs of limited growth functions look like the graph in Figure 18, where y_0 is the initial population.

EXAMPLE 3

A certain area can support at most 4000 mountain goats. There are 1000 goats in the area at present, with a growth constant of .20.

(a)   Write a differential equation for the rate of growth of this population.

Let $N = 4000$ and $k = .20$. The rate of change of the population is given by

$$\frac{dy}{dx} = .20(4000 - y).$$

To solve for y, first separate the variables.

$$\frac{dy}{4000 - y} = .2\, dx$$

$$\int \frac{dy}{4000 - y} = \int .2\, dx$$

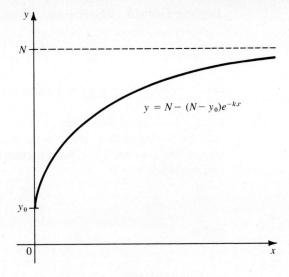

FIGURE 18

$$-\ln(4000 - y) = .2x + C$$
$$\ln(4000 - y) = -.2x - C$$
$$4000 - y = e^{-0.2x-C} = (e^{-0.2x})(e^{-C})$$

The absolute value bars are not needed for $\ln(4000 - y)$ since we know $y < 4000$. Let $e^{-C} = B$. Then

$$4000 - y = Be^{-0.2x}$$
$$y = 4000 - Be^{-0.2x}$$

To find B, use the fact that $y = 1000$ when $x = 0$.

$$1000 = 4000 - B$$
$$B = 3000.$$

The value of B is the difference between the maximum population and the initial population.

Substituting 3000 for B in the equation for y gives

$$y = 4000 - 3000e^{-0.2x}.$$

(b) What will the goat population be in 5 years?

In 5 years, the population will be

$$y = 4000 - 3000e^{-(0.2)(5)} = 4000 - 3000e^{-1}$$
$$= 4000 - 1103.6 = 2896.4$$

or about 2900 goats. ▪

Logistic Growth   This important model of biological growth has the form

$$\frac{dy}{dx} = ry\left(1 - \frac{y}{k}\right) = ry\left(\frac{k - y}{k}\right)$$

or

$$\frac{dy}{dx} = \frac{r}{k}y(k - y).$$

Here, y is the population at time x, r is the difference between the birth and death rates for the population, and k is the maximum population that the environment allows. The constant k is called the **carrying capacity** of the environment for the species. When $y \to 0$,

$$\frac{k - y}{k} \to 1,$$

so that

$$\frac{dy}{dx} = ry\left(\frac{k - y}{k}\right) \to ry.$$

This is our original exponential growth model.

On the other hand, when $y \to k$, $k - y \to 0$,

making

$$\frac{k - y}{k} \to 0,$$

and

$$\frac{dy}{dx} = ry\left(\frac{k - y}{k}\right) \to 0.$$

That is, the growth rate slows to 0 as y approaches k. These effects are shown in Figure 19 for the cases where $y > k$ initially, and where $y < k$ initially.

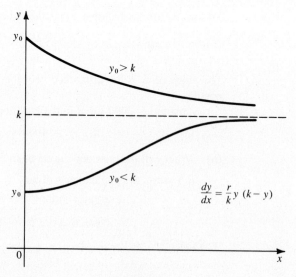

FIGURE 19

Examples of populations which seem to grow logistically include *E. coli* (a common intestinal bacterium), certain fruit flies, and the population of the United States.

In economics, **marginal productivity** is the rate at which production changes (increases or decreases) for a unit change in investment. Just as with marginal cost and marginal revenue, discussed earlier, marginal productivity can be approximated by the first derivative of the function which gives production in terms of investment.

EXAMPLE 4

Suppose the marginal productivity of a manufacturing process is given by

$$\frac{dy}{dx} = .1(500 - y), \tag{1}$$

where x is the amount of the investment in hundreds of thousands of dollars. Maximum production is limited to 500 units per month. If the process produces 100 units per month with its present investment of $300,000 (that is, $x = 3$), by how much would production increase if the investment were increased to $500,000?

To obtain an equation for production, separate the variables, and then integrate on both sides of equation (1) to get

$$\int \frac{dy}{500 - y} = \int .1 \ dx$$

$$-\ln(500 - y) = .1x + C$$

$$\ln(500 - y) = -.1x - C$$

$$500 - y = e^{-0.1x} e^{-C}.$$

Letting $B = e^{-C}$ gives

$$500 - y = Be^{-0.1x}$$

$$y = 500 - Be^{-0.1x}. \tag{2}$$

To find B, use the given initial values, $y = 100$ when $x = 3$.

$$100 = 500 - Be^{-0.3}$$

$$400 = Be^{-0.3}$$

$$B = 400e^{0.3} \approx 540$$

Substituting 540 for B in equation (2) gives the production function

$$y = 500 - 540e^{-0.1x}.$$

If investment is increased to $500,000, production becomes

$$y = 500 - 540e^{-0.5} \approx 172.$$

An increase to $500,000 in investment will increase production from 100 units to 172 units. To decide whether or not investment should be increased to $500,000, management would need to consider other factors as well as this increase in production. ▪

14.7 EXERCISES

Find general solutions for the differential equations in Exercises 1–12.

1. $y\dfrac{dy}{dx} = x$

2. $y\dfrac{dy}{dx} = x^2 - 1$

3. $\dfrac{dy}{dx} = 2xy$

4. $\dfrac{dy}{dx} = x^2 y$

5. $\dfrac{dy}{dx} = 3x^2 y - 2xy$

6. $(y^2 - y)\dfrac{dy}{dx} = x$

7. $\dfrac{dy}{dx} = \dfrac{y}{x}, \; x > 0$

8. $\dfrac{dy}{dx} = \dfrac{y}{x^2}$

9. $\dfrac{dy}{dx} = y - 5$

10. $\dfrac{dy}{dx} = 3 - y$

11. $\dfrac{dy}{dx} = y^2 e^x$

12. $\dfrac{dy}{dx} = \dfrac{e^x}{e^y}$

Find particular solutions for Exercises 13–22.

13. $\dfrac{dy}{dx} = \dfrac{x^2}{y}; \quad y = 3$ when $x = 0$

14. $x^2 \dfrac{dy}{dx} = y; \quad y = -1$ when $x = 1$

15. $(2x + 3)y = \dfrac{dy}{dx}; \quad y = 1$ when $x = 0$

16. $x\dfrac{dy}{dx} - y\sqrt{x} = 0; \quad y = 1$ when $x = 0$

17. $\dfrac{dy}{dx} = \dfrac{y^2}{x}; \quad y = 5$ when $x = e$

18. $\dfrac{dy}{dx} = x^{1/2} y^2; \quad y = 12$ when $x = 4$

19. $\dfrac{dy}{dx} = \dfrac{2x + 1}{y - 3}; \quad y = 4$ when $x = 0$

20. $\dfrac{dy}{dx} = \dfrac{x^2 + 5}{2y - 1}; \quad y = 11$ when $x = 0$

21. $\dfrac{dy}{dx} = (y - 1)^2 e^x; \quad y = 2$ when $x = 0$

22. $\dfrac{dy}{dx} = (x + 2)^2 e^y; \quad y = 0$ when $x = 1$

23. Suppose the rate at which a rumor spreads—that is, the number of people who have heard the rumor over a period of time—increases with the number of people who have heard it. If y is the number of people who have heard the rumor, then

$$\frac{dy}{dt} = ky,$$

where t is the time in days.

(a) If y is 1 when $t = 0$, and y is 5 when $t = 2$, find k.
Using the value of k from part (a), find y when

(b) $t = 3$ (c) $t = 5$ (d) $t = 10$.

24. The rate at which the number of bacteria (in thousands) in a culture is changing after the introduction of a bactericide is given by

$$\frac{dy}{dx} = 50 - y,$$

where y is the number of bacteria (in thousands) present at time x. Find the number of bacteria present at each of the following times if there were 1000 thousand bacteria present at time $x = 0$.

(a) $x = 2$ (b) $x = 5$ (c) $x = 10$ (d) $x = 15$

25. Suppose the marginal cost of producing x copies of a book is given by

$$\frac{dy}{dx} = \frac{50}{y\sqrt{x}}.$$

If $y = 150$ when $x = 4$, find the cost of producing the following number of books.

(a) 100 books   (b) 400 books   (c) 625 books

26. A company has found that the rate at which a person new to the assembly line produces items is

$$\frac{dy}{dx} = 7.5e^{-0.3y},$$

where x is the number of days the person has worked on the line. How many items can a new worker be expected to produce on the 8th day if he produces none when $x = 0$?

27. The amount of a radioactive substance decreases exponentially with a decay constant of 5% a month.

    (a) Write a differential equation to express the rate of change.

    (b) Find a general solution to the differential equation of part (a).

    (c) If there are 90 grams at the start of the decay process, find a particular solution for the differential equation of part (a).

    (d) Find the amount left at 10 months.

28. Sales (in thousands) of a certain product are declining exponentially with a decay constant of 25% a year.

    (a) Write a differential equation to express the rate of sales decline.

    (b) Find a general solution to the equation in part (a).

29. If inflation grows continuously at a rate of 6% per year, how long will it take for $1 to lose half its value?

30. Suppose that the Gross National Product (GNP) of a particular country increases exponentially with a growth constant of 2% per year. Ten years ago, the GNP was 10^5 dollars. What will be the GNP in 5 years?

31. The amount of a tracer dye injected into the bloodstream decreases exponentially with a decay constant of 3% per minute. If 6 cc are present initially, how many cc are present after 10 minutes? (Here k will be negative.)

32. A population of mites (in hundreds) increases exponentially with a growth constant of 5% per week. At the beginning of an observation period there were 3000 mites. How many are present 4 weeks later?

33. An isolated fish population is limited to 5000 by the amount of food available. If there are presently 150 fish and the population is growing with a growth constant of 1% a year, find the number present at the end of 5 years.

34. In a certain area, 1500 small business firms are threatened by bankruptcy. Assume the rate of change in the number of bankruptcies is proportional to the number of these firms which are not yet bankrupt. If the growth constant is 6%, and 100 firms are bankrupt initially, how many will be bankrupt in 2 years?

35. An influenza epidemic spreads at a rate proportional to the product of the number of people infected and the number not yet infected. If 50 people are infected at the beginning of the epidemic in a community of 10,000 people, and 300 are infected 10 days later,

    (a) write an equation for the number of people infected, y, after t days.

    (b) When will half the community be infected?

$$\text{Hint: } \frac{1}{y(10{,}000 - y)} = \frac{1}{10{,}000}\left(\frac{1}{y} + \frac{1}{10{,}000 - y}\right).$$

36. The Gompertz growth law,

$$\frac{dy}{dt} = kye^{-at},$$

for constants k and a, is another model used to describe the growth of an epidemic. Repeat Exercise 35, using this differential equation with $a = .02$.

37. A rumor spreads at a rate proportional to the product of the number of people who have heard it and the number who have not heard it. If 5 people in an office with 50 employees heard the rumor initially, and if 15 people have heard it 3 days later,

   (a) write an equation for the number, y, that have heard the rumor in t days.

   (b) When will 30 employees have heard the rumor?

$$\text{Hint: } \frac{1}{y(50 - y)} = \frac{1}{50}\left(\frac{1}{y} + \frac{1}{50 - y}\right).$$

38. Repeat Exercise 37 using the Gompertz growth law,

$$\frac{dy}{dt} = kye^{-at},$$

for constants k and a, with $a = .1$.

KEY WORDS

integration by parts
tables of integrals
numerical integration
trapezoidal rule
Simpson's rule
continuous money flow
solid of revolution
average value of a function
improper integral
convergent integral

divergent integral
differential equation
general solution of a differential equation
particular solution of a differential equation
initial condition
separable differential equation
limited growth function
logistic growth
carrying capacity

Chapter 14   REVIEW EXERCISES

Use integration by parts to find the integrals in Exercises 1–6.

1. $\int x(8 - x)^{3/2}\, dx$

2. $\int \frac{3x}{\sqrt{x - 2}}\, dx$

3. $\int xe^x\, dx$

4. $\int (x + 2)e^{-3x}\, dx$

5. $\int \ln |2x + 3|\, dx$

6. $\int (x - 1) \ln |x|\, dx$

7. Find the area between $y = (3 + x^2)e^{2x}$ and the x-axis from $x = 0$ to $x = 1$.

8. Find the area between $y = x^3(x^2 - 1)^{1/3}$ and the x-axis from $x = 1$ to $x = 3$.

9. The velocity of revenue from the sale of x units of toaster ovens is

$$R'(x) = x(x - 50)^{1/2}.$$

Find the total revenue from the sale of the 50th to the 75th ovens.

10. The reaction rate to a new drug x hours after the drug is administered is

$$r'(x) = .5xe^{-x}.$$

Find the total reaction over the first 5 hours.

In Exercises 11–13 use the trapezoidal rule with $n = 4$ to approximate the value of each integral.

11. $\displaystyle\int_2^6 \frac{dx}{x^2 - 1}$ 　　　　　 **12.** $\displaystyle\int_2^{10} \frac{x\,dx}{x - 1}$ 　　　　　 **13.** $\displaystyle\int_1^5 \ln x\,dx$

In Exercises 14–16 use Simpson's rule with $n = 4$ to approximate the value of each integral.

14. $\displaystyle\int_2^6 \frac{dx}{x^2 - 1}$ 　　　　　 **15.** $\displaystyle\int_2^{10} \frac{x\,dx}{x - 1}$ 　　　　　 **16.** $\displaystyle\int_1^5 \ln x\,dx$

17. Find the area under the semicircle $y = \sqrt{1 - x^2}$ and above the x-axis by the trapezoidal rule, using $n = 6$.

18. Repeat Exercise 17 using Simpson's rule.

19. Use the values of $f(x)$ given in the table to find total sales for the 6-year period by the trapezoidal rule, using $n = 6$.

year, x	1	2	3	4	5	6	7
rate of sales $f(x)$	.7	1.2	1.5	1.9	2.2	2.4	2.0

20. Repeat Exercise 19 using Simpson's rule.

Each of the functions in Exercises 21–24 represents the rate of flow of money per unit of time over the given time period, compounded continuously at the given annual interest rate. Find the present value in each case.

21. $f(x) = 5000;$ 　8 years; 　9%

22. $f(x) = 25{,}000;$ 　12 years; 　10%

23. $f(x) = 100\,e^{.02x};$ 　5 years; 　11%

24. $f(x) = 30x;$ 　18 months; 　15%

Assume the following functions give the rate of flow of money per unit of time over the given period, with continuous compounding at the given rate. Find the amount at the end of the time period.

25. $f(x) = 2000;$ 　5 months; 　1% per month

26. $f(x) = 500\,e^{-.03x};$ 　8 years; 　10% per year

27. $f(x) = 20x;$ 　6 years; 　12% per year

28. $f(x) = 1000 + 200x;$ 　10 years; 　9% per year

29. An investment scheme is expected to produce a continuous flow of money, starting at $1000 and increasing exponentially at 5% a year for 7 years. Find the present value at an interest rate of 11% compounded continuously.

30. The proceeds from the sale of a building will yield a uniform continuous flow of $10,000 a year for 10 years. Find the final amount at an interest rate of 10.5% compounded continuously.

Find the volume of the solid of revolution formed by rotating each of the following bounded regions about the x-axis.

31. $f(x) = 2x - 1$, $y = 0$, $x = 3$

32. $f(x) = \sqrt{x - 2}$, $y = 0$, $x = 11$

33. $f(x) = e^{-x}$, $y = 0$, $x = -2$, $x = 1$

34. $f(x) = \dfrac{1}{\sqrt{x - 1}}$, $y = 0$, $x = 2$, $x = 4$

35. $f(x) = 4 - x^2$, $y = 0$, $x = -1$, $x = 1$

36. $f(x) = \dfrac{x^2}{4}$, $y = 0$, $x = 4$

37. Use Simpson's rule with $n = 8$ to approximate the volume of the *ellipsoid* formed by rotating the region between the graph of $f(x) = \dfrac{3}{2}\sqrt{4 - x^2}$ and the x-axis about the x-axis.

38. Find a formula for the volume of the right circular cylinder formed by rotating the area below the line $y = r$ from $x = 0$ to $x = h$ and above the x-axis, around the x-axis.

39. Find the average value of $f(x) = \sqrt{x + 1}$ over the interval $[0, 8]$.

40. Suppose the temperature in a river at a point x meters downstream from a factory that is discharging hot water into the river is given by
$$T(x) = 400 - .25x^2.$$
Find the average temperature over the following intervals.

(a) $[0, 10]$ (b) $[10, 40]$ (c) $[0, 40]$

In Exercises 41–46, find the value of each integral which converges.

41. $\displaystyle\int_{-\infty}^{-2} x^{-2}\, dx$

42. $\displaystyle\int_{1}^{\infty} x^{-1}\, dx$

43. $\displaystyle\int_{1}^{\infty} 6e^{-x}\, dx$

44. $\displaystyle\int_{0}^{\infty} \dfrac{dx}{(5x + 2)^2}$

45. $\displaystyle\int_{10}^{\infty} \ln(2x)\, dx$

46. $\displaystyle\int_{-\infty}^{0} \dfrac{x}{x^2 + 3}\, dx$

Find the area between the graph of each function and the x-axis over the given interval, if possible.

47. $f(x) = 3e^{-x}$ for $[0, \infty)$

48. $f(x) = \dfrac{3}{(x - 2)^2}$ for $(-\infty, 1]$

49. Find the capitalized value of an office building for which annual rent of $50,000 will be paid in perpetuity, if the interest rate is 9%.

50. An oil leak from an uncapped well is polluting a bay at a rate of $f(x) = 100e^{-0.05x}$ gallons per year. Use an improper integral to find the total amount of oil that will enter the bay, assuming the well is never capped.

Find general solutions for the differential equations in Exercises 51–54.

51. $\dfrac{dy}{dx} = 2x^3 + 6x$

52. $\dfrac{dy}{dx} = x^2 + 5x^4$

53. $\dfrac{dy}{dx} = 4e^x$

54. $\dfrac{dy}{dx} = \dfrac{1}{2x + 3}$

Find particular solutions for the differential equations in Exercises 55–58.

55. $\dfrac{dy}{dx} = x^2 - 5x;\quad y = 1$ when $x = 0$

56. $\dfrac{dy}{dx} = 4x^3 + 2;\quad y = 3$ when $x = 1$

57. $\dfrac{dy}{dx} = 5(e^{-x} - 1);\quad y = 17$ when $x = 0$

58. $\dfrac{dy}{dx} = \dfrac{x}{x^2 - 3};\quad y = 52$ when $x = 2$

59. The marginal sales (in hundreds of dollars) of a computer software company are given by

$$\frac{dy}{dx} = 5e^{.2x},$$

where x is the number of months the company has been in business. Find the sales after the following number of months, if sales were 0 initially.

(a) 6   **(b)** 12

60. After use of an experimental insecticide, the rate of decline of an insect population is

$$\frac{dy}{dt} = \frac{-10}{1 + 5t},$$

where t is the number of hours after the insecticide is applied. If there were 50 insects initially,

(a) how many are left after 24 hours?

(b) How long will it take for the entire population to die?

Find general solutions for the following differential equations.

61. $\dfrac{dy}{dx} = \dfrac{3x + 1}{y}$

62. $\dfrac{dy}{dx} = \dfrac{e^x + x}{y - 1}$

63. $\dfrac{dy}{dx} = \dfrac{2y + 1}{x}$

64. $\dfrac{dy}{dx} = \dfrac{3 - y}{e^x}$

Find particular solutions for the following differential equations. (Some solutions may give y implicitly.)

65. $(5 - 2x)y = \dfrac{dy}{dx};\quad y = 2$ when $x = 0$

66. $\sqrt{x}\,\dfrac{dy}{dx} = xy;\quad y = 4$ when $x = 1$

67. $\dfrac{dy}{dx} = \dfrac{1 - 2x}{y + 3};\quad y = 16$ when $x = 0$

68. $\dfrac{dy}{dx} = (3x + 2)^2\, e^y;\quad y = 0$ when $x = 0$

69. A population of mites grows at a rate proportional to the number present, y. If the growth constant is 10% and 120 mites are present at time $t = 0$, in weeks, find the number present after 6 weeks.

70. The rate at which a new worker in a certain factory produces items is given by

$$\frac{dy}{dx} = .2(125 - y),$$

where y is the number of items produced by the worker per day, x is the number of days worked, and the maximum production per day is 125 items. Assume the worker produced 20 items at the beginning of the first day on the job ($x = 0$).

(a) Find the number of items the worker will produce in 10 days.

(b) According to the function which is the solution of the differential equation, can the worker ever produce 125 items in a day?

FUNCTIONS OF SEVERAL VARIABLES

Karl Gerstner. From the series *Carro 64*, Twenty-one part cycle (Du Clair a l'Obscur a travers le viol), 1960.

If a company produces x items at a cost of \$10 per item, then $C(x)$, the total cost of producing the items, is given by

$$C(x) = 10x.$$

The cost is a function of one independent variable. If the company produces two products, with x of one product at a cost of \$10 each, and y of another product at a cost of \$15 each, then the total cost to the firm is a function of *two* independent variables, x and y. By generalizing $f(x)$ notation, the total cost can be written as $C(x, y)$ where

$$C(x, y) = 10x + 15y.$$

In this chapter we discuss such functions of more than one independent variable. We shall see that many of the ideas developed for functions of one variable also apply to functions of more than one variable. In particular, the fundamental idea of derivative generalizes in a very natural way to functions of more than one variable.

15.1   Functions of Several Variables

The total cost for the firm above is given by

$$C(x, y) = 10x + 15y.$$

When $x = 5$ and $y = 12$ the total cost is written $C(5, 12)$, with

$$C(5, 12) = 10 \cdot 5 + 15 \cdot 12 = 230.$$

EXAMPLE 1

Let $f(x, y) = 4x^2 + 2xy + 3/y$ and find each of the following.

(a) $f(-1, 3)$.

Replace x with -1 and y with 3.

$$f(-1, 3) = 4(-1)^2 + 2(-1)(3) + \frac{3}{3} = 4 - 6 + 1 = -1$$

(b) $f(2, 0)$

Because of the quotient $3/y$, it is not possible to replace y with 0, so that $f(2, 0)$ does not exist.   ▬

Function of Two Variables

> $z = f(x, y)$ is a **function of two variables** if a unique value of z is obtained from each ordered pair of real numbers (x, y). The variables x and y are **independent variables**; z is the **dependent variable**. The set of all ordered pairs of real numbers (x, y) such that $f(x, y)$ exists is the **domain** of f; the set of all values of $f(x, y)$ is the **range**.

Unless otherwise stated, we shall assume that the domain of the functions we study is the largest set of ordered pairs of real numbers (x, y) for which $f(x, y)$ exists.

EXAMPLE 2

Let x represent the number of milliliters (ml) of carbon dioxide released by the lungs in one minute. Let y be the change in the carbon dioxide content of the blood as it leaves the lungs (y is measured in ml of carbon dioxide per 100 ml of blood). Let C be the total output of blood from the heart in one minute (measured in ml). It turns out that C is a function of x and y, with

$$C = C(x, y) = \frac{100x}{y}.$$

Find $C(320, 6)$.

Replace x with 320 and y with 6 to get

$$C(320, 6) = \frac{100(320)}{6} \approx 5333 \text{ ml of blood per minute.} \quad \blacksquare$$

The definition above was for a function of two independent variables, but similar definitions could be given for functions of three, four, or more independent variables.

EXAMPLE 3

Let $f(x, y, z) = 4xz - 3yx^2 + 2z^2$. Find the following.

(a) $f(2, -3, 1)$

Replace x with 2, y with -3, and z with 1.

$$f(2, -3, 1) = 4(2)(1) - 3(-3)(2)^2 + 2(1)^2 = 8 + 36 + 2 = 46$$

(b) $f(-4, 3, -2) = 4(-4)(-2) - 3(3)(-4)^2 + 2(-2)^2$
$$= 32 - 144 + 8 = -104 \quad \blacksquare$$

Graphing Functions of Two Variables   Functions of one independent variable are graphed by using an x-axis and a y-axis to locate points in a plane. The plane determined by the x- and y-axes is called the *xy-plane*. A third axis is needed to graph functions of two independent variables—the z-axis, which goes through the origin in the xy-plane, and is perpendicular to both the x-axis and the y-axis.

Figure 1 shows one possible way to draw the three axes. In Figure 1, the yz-plane is in the plane of the page, with the x-axis perpendicular to the plane of the page.

Just as ordered pairs were graphed earlier, we can now graph *ordered triples* of the form (x, y, z). For example, to locate the point corresponding to the ordered triple $(2, -4, 3)$, start at the origin and go 2 units along the positive x-axis. Then go 4 units in a negative direction (to the left), parallel to the y-axis. Finally, go up 3 units, parallel to the z-axis. The point representing $(2, -4, 3)$ and several other

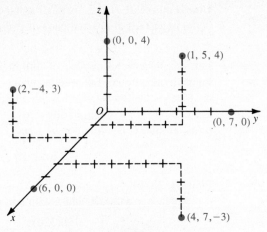

FIGURE 1

sample points are shown in Figure 1. The region of three-dimensional space where all coordinates are positive is called the **first octant.**

Many of the results from two dimensions suggest similar results for three dimensions. For example, the distance formula from previous work generalizes in a natural way. By the Pythagorean theorem, the diagonal of the base of the box on the left in Figure 2 has length $\sqrt{a^2 + b^2}$. The diagonal of the box itself is the hypotenuse of a right triangle having the diagonal of the base as one side and a vertical edge as the other side. Again by the Pythagorean theorem, the length of the diagonal of the box is the square root of $(\sqrt{a^2 + b^2})^2 + c^2$, or $\sqrt{a^2 + b^2 + c^2}$.

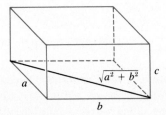
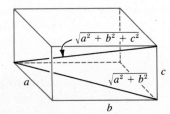

FIGURE 2

Generalizing this approach leads to the *distance formula*.

Distance Formula

The distance d between (x_1, y_1, z_1) and (x_2, y_2, z_2) is

$$d = \sqrt{(x_2 - x_1)^2 + (y_2 - y_1)^2 + (z_2 - z_1)^2}.$$

A *sphere* is the set of all points in space a fixed distance from a fixed point. The distance formula leads to the equation of a sphere.

Equation of a

Sphere

> An equation of the **sphere** with center at (h, k, j) and radius r is
> $$(x - h)^2 + (y - k)^2 + (z - j)^2 = r^2.$$

EXAMPLE 4

Graph $(x - 2)^2 + (y + 3)^2 + (z - 4)^2 = 4$.

The graph of this equation is a sphere of radius 2 with center at $(2, -3, 4)$. See Figure 3. ■

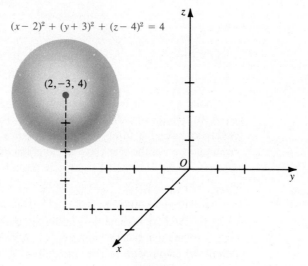

FIGURE 3

In Chapter 1 we found that the graph of $ax + by = c$ (where a and b are not both 0) is a straight line. This result generalizes to three dimensions.

Plane

> The graph of
> $$ax + by + cz = d$$
> is a **plane** if a, b, and c are not all 0.

EXAMPLE 5

Graph $2x + y + z = 6$.

By the result in the box, the graph of this equation is a plane. Earlier, we graphed straight lines by finding x- and y-intercepts. A similar idea helps graph a plane. To find the x-intercept, the point where the graph crosses the x-axis, let $y = 0$ and $z = 0$.

$$2x + 0 + 0 = 6$$
$$x = 3.$$

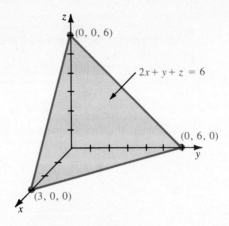

FIGURE 4

The point $(3, 0, 0)$ is on the graph. Letting $x = 0$ and $z = 0$ gives the point $(0, 6, 0)$, while $x = 0$ and $y = 0$ lead to $(0, 0, 6)$. The plane through these three points includes the triangular surface shown in Figure 4. This region is the first-octant portion of the plane that is the graph of $2x + y + z = 6$. ▨

EXAMPLE 6

Graph $x + z = 6$.
    To find the x-intercept, let $z = 0$, giving $(6, 0, 0)$. If $x = 0$, we get the point $(0, 0, 6)$. Because there is no y in the equation $x + z = 6$, there can be no y-intercept. A plane that has no y-intercept is parallel to the y-axis. The first-octant portion of the graph of $x + z = 6$ is shown in Figure 5. ▨

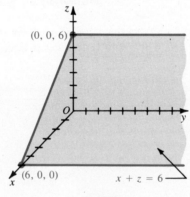

FIGURE 5

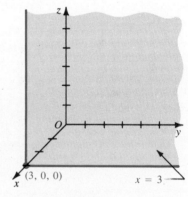

FIGURE 6

EXAMPLE 7

Graph $x = 3$.
    This graph, which goes through $(3, 0, 0)$, can have no y-intercept and no z-intercept. It is therefore a plane parallel to the y-axis and the z-axis and, therefore, to the yz plane. The first-octant portion of the graph is shown in Figure 6. ▨

The graph of a function $z = f(x, y)$ is called a **surface.** It may be difficult to draw the surface resulting from a function of two variables. One useful way of picturing these graphs is by finding various **traces**—the curves that result when a surface is cut by a plane. For example, the sphere $x^2 + y^2 + z^2 = 25$ is graphed in Figure 7. The **xy-trace,** the intersection of the sphere and the xy-plane, is a circle of radius 5. The **yz-trace** and the **xz-trace,** defined in a similar manner, are also circles of radius 5.

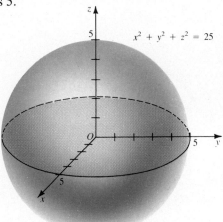

$$x^2 + y^2 + z^2 = 25$$

FIGURE 7

Because of the difficulty of drawing the graphs of more complicated functions, we shall now merely list some common equations and their graphs. These graphs were drawn by computer, a very useful method of drawing such graphs.

paraboloid, $z = x^2 + y^2$

xy-trace	point
yz-trace	parabola
xz-trace	parabola

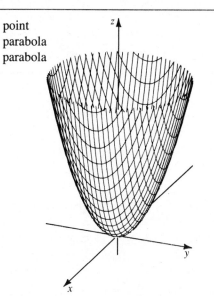

ellipsoid, $\dfrac{x^2}{a^2} + \dfrac{y^2}{b^2} + \dfrac{z^2}{c^2} = 1$

xy-trace	ellipse
yz-trace	ellipse
xz-trace	ellipse

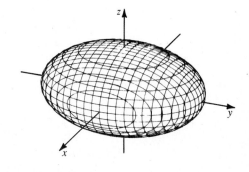

hyperbolic paraboloid, $x^2 - y^2 = z$
(sometimes called a saddle)

xy-trace	two intersecting lines
yz-trace	parabola
xz-trace	parabola

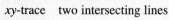

hyperboloid of two sheets,
$-x^2 - y^2 + z^2 = 1$

xy-trace	none
yz-trace	hyperbola
xz-trace	hyperbola

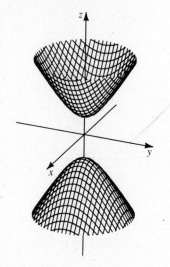

15.1 EXERCISES

1. Let $f(x, y) = 4x + 5y + 3$. Find the following.

   (a) $f(2, -1)$ (b) $f(-4, 1)$ (c) $f(-2, -3)$ (d) $f(0, 8)$

2. Let $g(x, y) = -x^2 - 4xy + y^3$. Find the following.

   (a) $g(-2, 4)$ (b) $g(-1, -2)$ (c) $g(-2, 3)$ (d) $g(5, 1)$

3. Let $h(x, y) = \sqrt{x^2 + 2y^2}$. Find the following.

   (a) $h(5, 3)$ (b) $h(2, 4)$ (c) $h(-1, -3)$ (d) $h(-3, -1)$

4. Let $f(x, y) = \dfrac{\sqrt{9x + 5y}}{\log x}$. Find the following.

   (a) $f(10, 2)$ (b) $f(100, 1)$ (c) $f(1000, 0)$ (d) $f\left(\dfrac{1}{10}, 5\right)$

5. The number of cows that can graze on a certain farm without causing overgrazing is approximated by

$$c(x, y) = 9x + 5y - 4,$$

where x is the number of acres of tall grass and y is the number of acres of short grass. Find the following.

   (a) $C(50, 0)$ (b) $C(30, 4)$

   (c) How many cows may graze if there are 80 acres of tall grass and 20 acres of short grass?

   (d) If the farm has 10 acres of short grass and 5 acres of tall grass, how many cows may graze?

6. The labor charge for assembling a precision camera is given by
$$L(x, y) = 12x + 6y + 2xy + 40,$$
where x is the number of work hours required by a skilled worker and y is the number of hours required by a semiskilled worker. Find the following.

(a) $L(3, 5)$ (b) $L(5, 2)$

(c) If a skilled worker requires 7 hours and a semiskilled worker needs 9 hours, find the total labor charge.

(d) Find the total labor charge if a skilled worker needs 12 hours and a semiskilled worker requires 4 hours.

Use a calculator with a y^x key to work the following problems.*

7. The oxygen consumption of a well-insulated mammal which is not sweating is approximated by
$$m = \frac{2.5(T - F)}{w^{.67}},$$
where T is the internal body temperature of the animal (in °C), F is the temperature of the outside of the animal's fur (in °C), and w is the animal's weight in kilograms. Find m for the following data.

(a) $T = 38°$, $F = 6°$, $w = 32$ kg   (b) $T = 40°$, $F = 20°$, $w = 43$ kg

8. The surface area of a human (in square meters) is approximated by
$$A = .202 W^{0.425} H^{0.725}$$
where W is the weight of the person in kilograms and H is the height in meters. Find A for the following data.

(a) $W = 72$, $H = 1.78$ (b) $W = 65$, $H = 1.40$

(c) $W = 70$, $H = 1.60$ (d) Find your own surface area.

Graph the first-octant portion of each plane in Exercises 9–18.

9. $x + y + z = 6$ **10.** $x + y + z = 12$ **11.** $2x + 3y + 4z = 12$

12. $4x + 2y + 3z = 24$ **13.** $3x + 2y + z = 18$ **14.** $x + 3y + 2z = 9$

15. $x + y = 4$ **16.** $y + z = 5$ **17.** $x = 2$

18. $z = 3$

Find the distance between the pairs of points in Exercises 19–24.

19. $(1, 4, 2)$ and $(0, 3, 1)$ **20.** $(3, 7, 9)$ and $(1, 5, 3)$

21. $(-2, 1, 7)$ and $(3, -4, 0)$ **22.** $(-5, -3, -8)$ and $(-2, -4, -6)$

23. $(1, 0, -4)$ and $(-2, 1, 3)$ **24.** $(5, 8, -6)$ and $(-3, 0, 4)$

Find an equation for each sphere in Exercises 25–28.

25. center $(-1, 4, 2)$, radius 3   **26.** center $(2, -5, 8)$, radius 1

27. center $(2, 0, -3)$, radius 4   **28.** center $(0, 0, 3)$, radius 5

Complete the square to find the center and radius of each sphere in Exercises 29–32.

29. $x^2 - 10x + y^2 - 6y + z^2 + 8z = -41$ **30.** $x^2 - 4x + y^2 - 10y + z^2 + 6z = -13$

31. $x^2 + 6x + y^2 + z^2 - 2z = 2$ **32.** $x^2 + 2x + y^2 - 6y + z^2 - 4z = -13$

---

*From *Mathematics in Biology* by Duane J. Clow and N. Scott Urquhart. Copyright © 1974 by W. W. Norton & Company, Inc. Used by permission.

Match each equation of Exercises 33–38 with its graph.

33. $z = x^2 + y^2$

34. $z^2 - y^2 - x^2 = 1$

35. $x^2 - y^2 = z$

36. $z = x^2 - y^2$

37. $\dfrac{x^2}{16} + \dfrac{y^2}{25} + \dfrac{z^2}{4} = 1$

38. $z = 5(x^2 + y^2)^{-1/2}$

(a)   **(b)**   **(c)**

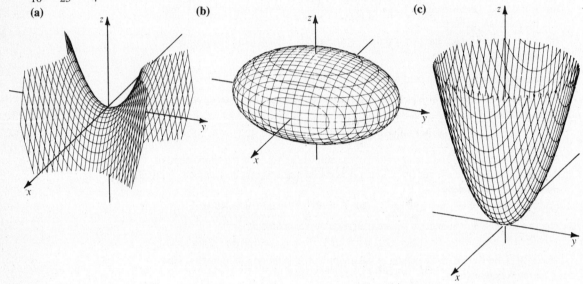

(d)   **(e)**   **(f)**

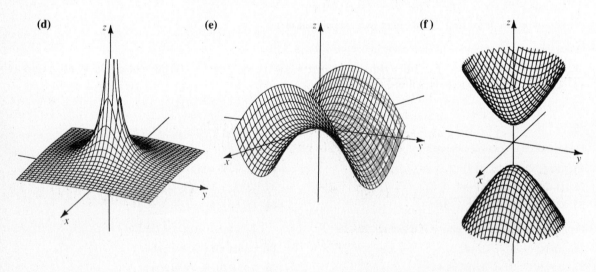

39. Let $f(x, y) = 9x^2 - 3y^2$. Find **(a)** $\dfrac{f(x + h, y) - f(x, y)}{h}$ **(b)** $\dfrac{f(x, y + h) - f(x, y)}{h}$.

40. Let $f(x, y) = 7x^3 + 8y^2$. Find **(a)** $\dfrac{f(x + h, y) - f(x, y)}{h}$ **(b)** $\dfrac{f(x, y + h) - f(x, y)}{h}$.

15.2 Partial Derivatives

The derivative of a function $y = f(x)$ gives the rate of change of y with respect to x. Suppose now we have a function of two independent variables, say $z = f(x, y)$, and want to know how a change in x or y will affect z. To find out, take the derivative of $f(x, y)$ with respect to one variable, while holding the other constant.

As an example of this process, suppose that a small firm makes only two products, radios and cassette recorders, with the profit of the firm given by

$$P(x, y) = 40x^2 - 10xy + 5y^2 - 80,$$

where x is the number of units of radios sold and y is the number of units of cassette recorders sold. Lately, sales of radios have been steady at 10 units; only the sales of recorders vary. The management would like to know the marginal profit when $y = 12$.

Recall that marginal profit is given by the derivative of the profit function. Here, x is fixed at 10. Using this information, begin by finding a new function, $f(y) = P(10, y)$. Let $x = 10$ and get

$$f(y) = P(10, y) = 40(10)^2 - 10(10)y + 5y^2 - 80$$
$$= 3920 - 100y + 5y^2.$$

The function $f(y)$ shows the profit from the sale of y recorders, assuming that x is fixed at 10. To find the marginal profit when $y = 12$, first find the derivative df/dy.

$$\frac{df}{dy} = -100 + 10y$$

When $y = 12$, we have $-100 + 10(12) = -100 + 120 = 20$, so the marginal profit is 20 when $y = 12$.

The derivative of the function $f(y)$ was taken with respect to y only; we assumed that x was fixed. To generalize this example, let $z = f(x, y)$. An intuitive definition of the partial derivatives of f with respect to x and y follows.

Partial Derivatives **(Informal** **Definition)**	The **partial derivative of f with respect to x** is the derivative of f obtained by treating x as a variable and y as a constant. The **partial derivative of f with respect to y** is the derivative of f obtained by treating y as a variable and x as a constant.

The symbols $f_x(x, y)$ (no prime is used), $\partial z/\partial x$, and $\partial f/\partial x$ are used to represent the partial derivative of $z = f(x, y)$ with respect to x, with similar symbols used for the partial derivative with respect to y. The symbol $f_x(x, y)$ is often abbreviated as just f_x, with $f_y(x, y)$ abbreviated f_y.

Generalizing from the definition of derivative given earlier, partial derivatives of a function $z = f(x, y)$ are defined as follows.

Partial Derivatives

(Formal Definition)

Let $z = f(x, y)$ be a function of two variables. Let all indicated limits exist. Then the **partial derivative of f with respect to x** is

$$f_x = \frac{\partial f}{\partial x} = \lim_{h \to 0} \frac{f(x + h, y) - f(x, y)}{h};$$

the **partial derivative of f with respect to y** is

$$f_y = \frac{\partial f}{\partial y} = \lim_{h \to 0} \frac{f(x, y + h) - f(x, y)}{h}.$$

If the indicated limits do not exist, then the partial derivatives do not exist.

Similar definitions could be given for functions of more than two independent variables.

EXAMPLE 1

Let $f(x, y) = 4x^2 - 9xy + 6y^3$. Find f_x and f_y.

To find f_x, treat y as a constant and x as a variable. This gives

$$f_x = 8x - 9y.$$

Now treat y as a variable and x as a constant, to find f_y.

$$f_y = -9x + 18y^2. \quad \blacksquare$$

The next example shows how the chain rule can be used to find partial derivatives.

EXAMPLE 2

Let $f(x, y) = \ln|x^2 + y|$. Find f_x and f_y.

Recall the formula for the derivative of a natural logarithm function. If $g(x) = \ln|x|$, then $g'(x) = 1/x$. Using this formula and the chain rule,

$$f_x = \frac{2x}{x^2 + y} \quad \text{and} \quad f_y = \frac{1}{x^2 + y}. \quad \blacksquare$$

The notation

$$f_x(a, b) \quad \text{or} \quad \frac{\partial f}{\partial x}(a, b)$$

represents the value of a partial derivative when $x = a$ and $y = b$, as shown in the next example.

EXAMPLE 3

Let $f(x, y) = 2x^2 + 3xy^3 + 2y + 5$. Find the following.

(a) $f_x(-1, 2)$

First, find f_x by holding y constant.

$$f_x = 4x + 3y^3.$$

Now let $x = -1$ and $y = 2$.

$$f_x(-1, 2) = 4(-1) + 3(2)^3 = -4 + 24 = 20.$$

(b) $\dfrac{\partial f}{\partial y}(-4, -3)$

Since $\partial f/\partial y = 9xy^2 + 2$,

$$\frac{\partial f}{\partial y}(-4, -3) = 9(-4)(-3)^2 + 2 = 9(-36) + 2 = -322. \quad ■$$

The derivative of a function f gives the slope of the tangent line to the graph of f. A similar interpretation can be given for partial derivatives. If y is held fixed, say $y = a$, then $f_x(x, a)$ gives the slope of the tangent line to the curve obtained by intersecting the plane $y = a$ and the surface $z = f(x, y)$. See Figure 8.

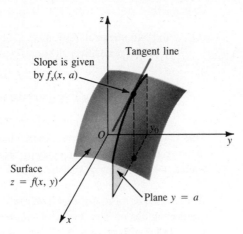

FIGURE 8

The derivative of $y = f(x)$ gives the rate of change of y with respect to x. In the same way, if $z = f(x, y)$, then f_x' gives the rate of change of z with respect to x, provided that y is held constant.

EXAMPLE 4

Suppose that the temperature of the water at the point on a river where a nuclear power plant discharges its hot waste water is approximated by

$$T(x, y) = 2x + 5y + xy - 40,$$

where x represents the temperature of the river water in degrees Celsius before it reaches the power plant and y is the number of megawatts (in hundreds) of electricity being produced by the plant.

(a) Find the temperature of the discharged water if the water reaching the plant has a temperature of 8°C and if 300 megawatts of electricity are being produced.

Here $x = 8$ and $y = 3$ (since 300 megawatts of electricity are being produced), with

$$T(8, 3) = 2(8) + 5(3) + 8(3) - 40 = 15.$$

The water at the outlet of the plant is at a temperature of 15°C.

(b) Find and interpret $T_x(9, 5)$.

First, find the partial derivative T_x.

$$T_x = 2 + y$$

This partial derivative gives the rate of change of T with respect to x. Replacing x with 9 and y with 5 gives

$$T_x(9, 5) = 2 + 5 = 7.$$

Just as marginal cost is the approximate cost of one more item, this result, 7, is the approximate change in temperature of the output water if input water temperature changes by 1 degree, from $x = 9$ to $x = 9 + 1 = 10$, while y remains constant.

(c) Find and interpret $T_y(9, 5)$.

The partial derivative T_y is

$$T_y = 5 + x.$$

This partial derivative gives the rate of change of T with respect to y, with

$$T_y(9, 5) = 5 + 9 = 14.$$

This result, 14, is the approximate change in temperature resulting from a 1-unit increase in production of electricity from $y = 5$ to $y = 5 + 1 = 6$ (600 megawatts), while x remains constant. ■

Second-Order Partial Derivatives   Earlier we found second derivatives, which are derivatives of derivatives. A similar method can be used to find **second-order partial derivatives,** which are defined as follows.

Second-Order Partial Derivatives

For a function $z = f(x, y)$, if all indicated partial derivatives exist, then

$$\frac{\partial}{\partial x}\left(\frac{\partial z}{\partial x}\right) = \frac{\partial^2 z}{\partial x^2} = f_{xx} \qquad \frac{\partial}{\partial y}\left(\frac{\partial z}{\partial y}\right) = \frac{\partial^2 z}{\partial y^2} = f_{yy}$$

$$\frac{\partial}{\partial y}\left(\frac{\partial z}{\partial x}\right) = \frac{\partial^2 z}{\partial y \partial x} = f_{xy} \qquad \frac{\partial}{\partial x}\left(\frac{\partial z}{\partial y}\right) = \frac{\partial^2 z}{\partial x \partial y} = f_{yx}.$$

As seen above, f_{xx} is used as an abbreviation for $f_{xx}(x, y)$, with f_{yy}, f_{xy}, and f_{yx} used in a similar way.

Be careful with a mixed partial derivative such as

$$\frac{\partial^2 z}{\partial y \partial x}.$$

This symbol says to start with a function $z = f(x, y)$ and find f_x or $\partial z/\partial x$, the partial derivative with respect to x. Then find the derivative of f_x (or $\partial z/\partial x$) with respect to y, producing f_{xy} (or $\partial^2 z/\partial y\partial x$). Based on this order of finding partial derivatives,

$$\frac{\partial^2 z}{\partial y\partial x} = f_{xy}.$$

Notice that the order of x and y in the two symbols is reversed.

EXAMPLE 5

Find all second-order partial derivatives for
$$f(x, y) = -4x^3 - 3x^2y^3 + 2y^2.$$

First find f_x and f_y.
$$f_x = -12x^2 - 6xy^3 \quad \text{and} \quad f_y = -9x^2y^2 + 4y$$
To find f_{xx}, take the partial derivative of f_x with respect to x.
$$f_{xx} = -24x - 6y^3$$
Take the partial derivative of f_y with respect to y; this gives f_{yy}.
$$f_{yy} = -18x^2y + 4$$
Find f_{xy} by starting with f_x, then taking the partial derivative of f_x with respect to y.
$$f_{xy} = -18xy^2$$
Finally, find f_{yx} by starting with f_y; take its partial derivative with respect to x.
$$f_{yx} = -18xy^2 \quad \blacksquare$$

EXAMPLE 6

Let $f(x, y) = 2e^x - 8x^3y^2$. Find all second-order partial derivatives.
 Here $f_x = 2e^x - 24x^2y^2$ and $f_y = -16x^3y$. [Recall: If $g(x) = e^x$, then $g'(x) = e^x$.] Now find the second partial derivatives.
$$f_{xx} = 2e^x - 48xy^2 \quad f_{xy} = -48x^2y$$
$$f_{yy} = -16x^3 \qquad\qquad f_{yx} = -48x^2y \quad \blacksquare$$

In both our examples of second-order partial derivatives, $f_{xy} = f_{yx}$. It can be proved that this happens for many functions, including most functions found in applications, and all the functions in this book.

15.2 EXERCISES

1. Let $z = f(x, y) = 12x^2 - 8xy + 3y^2$. Find each of the following.

(a) $\dfrac{\partial z}{\partial x}$ (b) $\dfrac{\partial z}{\partial y}$ (c) $\left(\dfrac{\partial f}{\partial x}\right)(2, 3)$ (d) $f_y(1, -2)$

2. Let $z = g(x, y) = 5x + 9x^2y + y^2$. Find each of the following.

(a) $\dfrac{\partial g}{\partial x}$ (b) $\dfrac{\partial g}{\partial y}$ (c) $\left(\dfrac{\partial z}{\partial y}\right)(-3, 0)$ (d) $g_x(2, 1)$

In Exercises 3–16, find f_x and f_y. Then find $f_x(2, -1)$ and $f_y(-4, 3)$. Leave the answers in terms of e in Exercises 7–10 and 15–16.

3. $f(x, y) = -2xy + 6y^3 + 2$

4. $f(x, y) = 4x^2y - 9y^2$

5. $f(x, y) = 3x^3y^2$

6. $f(x, y) = -2x^2y^4$

7. $f(x, y) = e^{x+y}$

8. $f(x, y) = 3e^{2x+y}$

9. $f(x, y) = -5e^{3x-4y}$

10. $f(x, y) = 8e^{7x-y}$

11. $f(x, y) = \dfrac{x^2 + y^3}{x^3 - y^2}$

12. $f(x, y) = \dfrac{3x^2y^3}{x^2 + y^2}$

13. $f(x, y) = \ln|1 + 3x^2y^3|$

14. $f(x, y) = \ln|2x^5 - xy^4|$

15. $f(x, y) = xe^{x^2y}$

16. $f(x, y) = y^2e^{(x+3y)}$

Find all second-order partial derivatives for Exercises 17–28.

17. $f(x, y) = 6x^3y - 9y^2 + 2x$

18. $g(x, y) = 5xy^4 + 8x^3 - 3y$

19. $R(x, y) = 4x^2 - 5xy^3 + 12y^2x^2$

20. $h(x, y) = 30y + 5x^2y + 12xy^2$

21. $r(x, y) = \dfrac{4x}{x + y}$

22. $k(x, y) = \dfrac{-5y}{x + 2y}$

23. $z = 4xe^y$

24. $z = -3ye^x$

25. $r = \ln|x + y|$

26. $k = \ln|5x - 7y|$

27. $z = x \ln|xy|$

28. $z = (y + 1) \ln|x^3y|$

For the functions in Exercises 29–32, find values of x and y such that both $f_x(x, y) = 0$ and $f_y(x, y) = 0$.

29. $f(x, y) = 6x^2 + 6y^2 + 6xy + 36x - 5$

30. $f(x, y) = 50 + 4x - 5y + x^2 + y^2 + xy$

31. $f(x, y) = 9xy - x^3 - y^3 - 6$

32. $f(x, y) = 2200 + 27x^3 + 72xy + 8y^2$

Find f_x, f_y, f_z, and f_{yz} for Exercises 33–38.

33. $f(x, y, z) = x^2 + yz + z^4$

34. $f(x, y, z) = 3x^5 - x^2 + y^5$

35. $f(x, y, z) = \dfrac{6x - 5y}{4z + 5}$

36. $f(x, y, z) = \dfrac{2x^2 + xy}{yz - 2}$

37. $f(x, y, z) = \ln|x^2 - 5xz^2 + y^4|$

38. $f(x, y, z) = \ln|8xy + 5yz - x^3|$

39. Suppose that the manufacturing cost of a precision electronic calculator is approximated by

$$M(x, y) = 40x^2 + 30y^2 - 10xy + 30,$$

where x is the cost of electronic chips and y is the cost of labor. Find the following.

(a) $M_y(4, 2)$ (b) $M_x(3, 6)$

(c) $(\partial M/\partial x)_{(2,5)}$ (d) $(\partial M/\partial y)_{(6,7)}$

40. The revenue from the sale of x units of a tranquilizer and y units of an antibiotic is given by

$$R(x, y) = 5x^2 + 9y^2 - 4xy.$$

(a) Suppose $x = 9$ and $y = 5$. What is the approximate effect on revenue if x is increased to 10, while y is fixed?

(b) Suppose $x = 9$ and $y = 5$. What is the approximate effect on revenue if y is increased to 6, while x is fixed?

A **production function** $z = f(x, y)$ is a function which gives the quantity of an item produced, z, as a function of two other variables, x and y.

41. The production function z for the United States was once estimated as
$$z = x^{0.7}y^{0.3},$$
where x stands for the amount of labor and y stands for the amount of capital. (This is an example of a **Cobb-Douglas production function.**) Find the marginal productivity of labor (find $\partial z/\partial x$) and of capital.

42. A similar production function for Canada is
$$z = x^{0.4}y^{0.6},$$
with x, y, and z as in Exercise 41. Find the marginal productivity of labor and of capital.

43. The total number of matings per day between individuals of a certain species of grasshoppers is approximated by
$$M(x, y) = 2xy + 10xy^2 + 30y^2 + 20,$$
where x represents the temperature in °C and y represents the number of days since the last rain. Find the following.
    (a) $(\partial M/\partial x)_{(20,4)}$ (b) $(\partial M/\partial y)_{(24,10)}$ (c) $M_x(17, 3)$ (d) $M_y(21, 8)$

44. (The next two exercises were first discussed in Section 1 of this chapter.) The oxygen consumption of a well-insulated mammal which is not sweating is approximated by
$$m = m(T, F, w) = \frac{2.5(T - F)}{w^{0.67}} = 2.5(T - F)w^{-0.67},$$
where T is the internal body temperature of the animal (in °C), F is the temperature of the outside of the animal's fur (in °C), and w is the animal's weight in kilograms.
    (a) Find m_T.   (b) Suppose $T = 38°$, $F = 12°$, and $w = 30$ kg. Find $m_T(38, 12, 30)$.
    (c) Find m_w.   (d) Suppose $T = 40°$, $F = 20°$, and $w = 40$ kg. Find $m_w(40, 20, 40)$.
    (e) Find m_F.   (f) Suppose $T = 36°$, $F = 14°$, and $w = 25$ kg. Find $m_F(36, 14, 25)$.

45. The surface area of a human, in square meters, is approximated by
$$A(W, H) = 0.202\,W^{0.425}H^{0.725},$$
where W is the weight of the person in kilograms and H is the height in meters.
    (a) Find $\partial A/\partial W$.   (b) Suppose $W = 72$ and $H = 1.8$. Find $(\partial A/\partial W)_{(72,\ 1.8)}$.
    (c) Find $\partial A/\partial H$.   (d) Suppose $W = 70$ and $H = 1.6$. Find $(\partial A/\partial H)_{(70,\ 1.6)}$.

46. In one method of computing the quantity of blood pumped through the lungs in one minute, a researcher first finds each of the following (in milliliters).
    b = quantity of oxygen used by body in one minute
    a = quantity of oxygen per liter of blood that has just gone through the lungs
    v = quantity of oxygen per liter of blood that is about to enter the lungs
In one minute,
amount of oxygen used = amount of oxygen per liter × number of liters of blood pumped
    If C is the number of liters pumped through the blood in one minute, then
$$b = (a - v) \cdot C \quad \text{or} \quad C = \frac{b}{a - v}.$$
    (a) Find C if $a = 160$, $b = 200$, and $v = 125$.
    (b) Find C if $a = 180$, $b = 260$, and $v = 142$.
    Find the following partial derivatives.
    (c) $\partial C/\partial b$ (d) $\partial C/\partial v$

15.3   Maxima and Minima

One of the most important applications of calculus is in finding maxima and minima for functions. Earlier, this idea was studied extensively for functions of a single independent variable, and now we find extrema for functions of two variables. In particular, we discuss an extension of the second derivative test which is used to identify maxima or minima. We begin with the definition of relative maxima and minima.

Relative Maxima and Minima

Let (a, b) be the center of a circular region contained in the xy-plane. Then, for a function $z = f(x, y)$ defined for every (x, y) in the region, $f(a, b)$ is a **relative maximum** if

$$f(a, b) \geq f(x, y)$$

for all points (x, y) in the circular region, and $f(a, b)$ is a **relative minimum** if

$$f(a, b) \leq f(x, y)$$

for all points (x, y) in the circular region.

As before, the word *extremum* is used for either a relative maximum or a relative minimum. Examples of a relative maximum and a relative minimum are given in Figures 9 and 10.

When we discussed functions of a single variable, we made a distinction between relative extrema and absolute extrema. It turns out that the methods for finding absolute extrema are quite involved for functions of two variables, so we

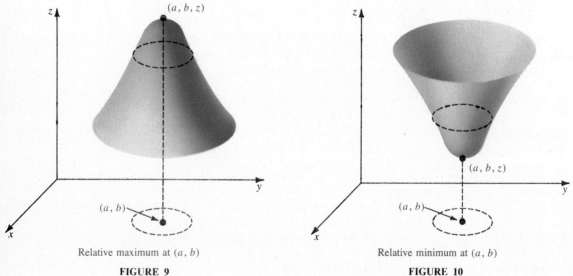

Relative maximum at (a, b)

FIGURE 9

Relative minimum at (a, b)

FIGURE 10

shall discuss only relative extrema. However, in most practical applications the relative extrema coincide with the absolute extrema.

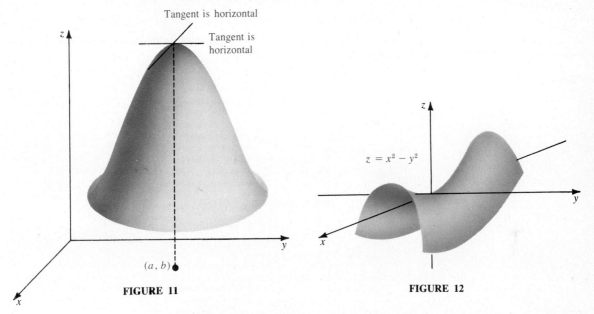

FIGURE 11

FIGURE 12

As suggested by Figure 11, at a relative maximum the tangent line parallel to the x-axis has a slope of 0, as does the tangent line parallel to the y-axis. (Notice the similarity to functions of one variable.) That is, if the function $z = f(x, y)$ has a relative extremum at (a, b), then $f_x(a, b) = 0$ and $f_y(a, b) = 0$, as stated in the following theorem.

Location of

Extrema

> Let a function $z = f(x, y)$ have a relative maximum or relative minimum at the point (a, b). Let $f_x(a, b)$ and $f_y(a, b)$ both exist. Then
>
> $$f_x(a, b) = 0 \quad \text{and} \quad f_y(a, b) = 0.$$

Just as with functions of one variable, the fact that the slopes of the tangent lines are 0 is no guarantee that a relative extremum has been located. For example, Figure 12 shows the graph of $z = f(x, y) = x^2 - y^2$. Both $f_x(0, 0) = 0$ and $f_y(0, 0) = 0$, and yet $(0, 0)$ leads to neither a relative maximum nor a relative minimum for the function. The point $(0, 0, 0)$ on the graph of this function is called a **saddle point**; it is a minimum when approached from one direction but a maximum when approached from another direction. A saddle point is neither a maximum nor a minimum.

The theorem on location of extrema suggests a useful strategy for finding extrema. First, locate all points (a, b) where $f_x(a, b) = 0$ and $f_y(a, b) = 0$. Then test each of these points separately, using the test given after the next example. For a function $f(x, y)$, the points (a, b) such that $f_x(a, b) = 0$ and $f_y(a, b) = 0$ are called **critical points**.

EXAMPLE 1

Find all critical points for
$$f(x, y) = 6x^2 + 6y^2 + 6xy + 36x - 5.$$
We want all points (a, b) such that $f_x(a, b) = 0$ and $f_y(a, b) = 0$. Here
$$f_x = 12x + 6y + 36 \quad \text{and} \quad f_y = 12y + 6x.$$
Place each of these two partial derivatives equal to 0.
$$12x + 6y + 36 = 0 \quad \text{and} \quad 12y + 6x = 0.$$
These two equations make up a system of linear equations. To solve this system, rewrite $12y + 6x = 0$ as follows.
$$12y + 6x = 0$$
$$6x = -12y$$
$$x = -2y$$
Now substitute $-2y$ for x in the other equation.
$$12x + 6y + 36 = 0$$
$$12(-2y) + 6y + 36 = 0$$
$$-24y + 6y + 36 = 0$$
$$-18y + 36 = 0$$
$$-18y = -36$$
$$y = 2$$
The equation $x = -2y$ leads to $x = -2(2) = -4$. The solution of the system of equations is $(-4, 2)$. Since this is the only solution of the system, $(-4, 2)$ is the only critical point for the given function. By the theorem above, if the function of Example 1 has a relative extremum, it will occur at $(-4, 2)$. ■

The results of the next theorem can be used to decide whether $(-4, 2)$ in Example 1 leads to a relative maximum, a relative minimum, or neither.

Test for Relative Extrema

For a function $z = f(x, y)$, let f_{xx}, f_{yy}, and f_{xy} all exist. Let (a, b) be a point for which
$$f_x(a, b) = 0 \quad \text{and} \quad f_y(a, b) = 0.$$
Define the number M by
$$M = f_{xx}(a, b) \cdot f_{yy}(a, b) - [f_{xy}(a, b)]^2.$$
Then
(a) $f(a, b)$ is a relative maximum if $M > 0$ and $f_{xx}(a, b) < 0$.
(b) $f(a, b)$ is a relative minimum if $M > 0$ and $f_{xx}(a, b) > 0$.
(c) $f(a, b)$ is a saddle point (neither a maximum nor a minimum) if $M < 0$.
(d) If $M = 0$, the test gives no information.

EXAMPLE 2

The previous example showed that the only critical point for the function

$$f(x, y) = 6x^2 + 6y^2 + 6xy + 36x - 5$$

is $(-4, 2)$. Does $(-4, 2)$ lead to a relative maximum, a relative minimum, or neither?

Find out by using the test above. We already know that

$$f_x(-4, 2) = 0 \quad \text{and} \quad f_y(-4, 2) = 0.$$

Now find the various second partial derivatives used in finding M. From $f_x = 12x + 6y + 36$ and $f_y = 12y + 6x$,

$$f_{xx} = 12, \quad f_{yy} = 12, \quad \text{and} \quad f_{xy} = 6.$$

(If these second order partial derivatives had not all been constants, we would have had to evaluate them at the point $(-4, 2)$.) Now

$$M = f_{xx}(-4, 2) \cdot f_{yy}(-4, 2) - [f_{xy}(-4, 2)]^2 = 12 \cdot 12 - 6^2 = 108.$$

Since $M > 0$ and $f_{xx}(-4, 2) = 12 > 0$, part (b) of the theorem applies, showing that $f(x, y) = 6x^2 + 6y^2 + 6xy + 36x - 5$ has a relative minimum at $(-4, 2)$. This relative minimum is $f(-4, 2) = -77$. ■

EXAMPLE 3

Find all points where the function

$$f(x, y) = 9xy - x^3 - y^3 - 6$$

has any relative maxima or relative minima.

First find any critical points. Here

$$f_x = 9y - 3x^2 \quad \text{and} \quad f_y = 9x - 3y^2.$$

Place each of these partial derivatives equal to 0.

$$
\begin{array}{ll}
f_x = 0 & f_y = 0 \\
9y - 3x^2 = 0 & 9x - 3y^2 = 0 \\
9y = 3x^2 & 9x = 3y^2 \\
3y = x^2 & 3x = y^2
\end{array}
$$

The final equation on the left, $3y = x^2$, can be rewritten as $y = x^2/3$. Substitute this into the final equation on the right.

$$3x = y^2 = \left(\frac{x^2}{3}\right)^2$$

$$3x = \frac{x^4}{9}$$

Rewrite this equation as

$$27x = x^4$$

$$x^4 - 27x = 0$$

$$x(x^3 - 27) = 0 \quad \text{Factor}$$

$$x = 0 \quad \text{or} \quad x^3 - 27 = 0$$

$$x^3 = 27$$

$$x = 3.$$

Use these values of x, along with the equation $3x = y^2$, to find y.

If $x = 0$,	If $x = 3$,
$3x = y^2$	$3x = y^2$
$3(0) = y^2$	$3(3) = y^2$
$0 = y^2$	$9 = y^2$
$0 = y$	$3 = y$ or $-3 = y$.

The points $(0, 0)$, $(3, 3)$, and $(3, -3)$ appear to be critical points; however, $(3, -3)$ does not make $f_y = 0$. The only possible relative extrema for $f(x, y) = 9xy - x^3 - y^3 - 6$ occur at the critical points $(0, 0)$ or $(3, 3)$. To identify any extrema, use the test. Here

$$f_{xx} = -6x, \qquad f_{yy} = -6y, \qquad \text{and} \qquad f_{xy} = 9.$$

Test each of the possible critical points.

For $(0, 0)$:

$f_{xx}(0, 0) = -6(0) = 0$
$f_{yy}(0, 0) = -6(0) = 0$
$f_{xy}(0, 0) = 9$
$M = 0 \cdot 0 - 9^2 = -81.$

Since $M < 0$, there is a saddle point at $(0, 0)$.

For $(3, 3)$:

$f_{xx}(3, 3) = -6(3) = -18$
$f_{yy}(3, 3) = -6(3) = -18$
$f_{xy}(3, 3) = 9$
$M = -18(-18) - 9^2 = 243.$

Here $M > 0$ and $f_{xx}(3, 3) = -18 < 0$; there is a relative maximum at $(3, 3)$. ▨

EXAMPLE 4

A company is developing a new soft drink. The cost in dollars to produce a batch of the drink is approximated by

$$C(x, y) = 2200 + 27x^3 - 72xy + 8y^2,$$

where x is the number of kilograms of sugar per batch and y is the number of grams of flavoring per batch.

(a) Find the amounts of sugar and flavoring that result in minimum cost for a batch.

Start with the following partial derivatives.

$$C_x = 81x^2 - 72y \qquad \text{and} \qquad C_y = -72x + 16y$$

Set each of these equal to 0 and solve for y.

$81x^2 - 72y = 0$	$-72x + 16y = 0$
$-72y = -81x^2$	$16y = 72x$
$y = \dfrac{9}{8}x^2$	$y = \dfrac{9}{2}x$

Since $(9/8)x^2$ and $(9/2)x$ both are equal to y, they are equal to each other. Place $(9/8)x^2$ and $(9/2)x$ equal and solve the resulting equation for x.

$$\frac{9}{8}x^2 = \frac{9}{2}x$$

$$9x^2 = 36x$$

$$9x^2 - 36x = 0$$

$$9x(x - 4) = 0$$

$$9x = 0 \quad \text{or} \quad x - 4 = 0$$

The equation $9x = 0$ leads to $x = 0$ which is not a useful answer for our problem. Substitute $x = 4$ into $y = (9/2)x$ to find y.

$$y = \frac{9}{2}x = \frac{9}{2}(4) = 18$$

Now check to see if the critical point $(4, 18)$ leads to a relative minimum. For $(4, 18)$,

$$C_{xx} = 162x = 162(4) = 648, \qquad C_{yy} = 16, \qquad \text{and} \qquad C_{xy} = -72.$$

Also, $$M = (648)(16) - (-72)^2 = 5184.$$

Since $M > 0$ and $C_{xx}(4, 18) > 0$, the cost at $(4, 18)$ is a minimum.

(b) What is the minimum cost?

To find the minimum cost, go back to the cost function and evaluate $C(4, 18)$.

$$C(x, y) = 2200 + 27x^3 - 72xy + 8y^2$$

$$C(4, 18) = 2200 + 27(4)^3 - 72(4)(18) + 8(18)^2 = 1336$$

The minimum cost for a batch is $1336.00. ■

15.3 EXERCISES

Find all points where the functions in Exercises 1–20 have any relative extrema. Identify any saddle points.

1. $f(x, y) = xy + x - y$

2. $f(x, y) = 4xy + 8x - 9y$

3. $f(x, y) = x^2 - 2xy + 2y^2 + x - 5$

4. $f(x, y) = x^2 + xy + y^2 - 6x - 3$

5. $f(x, y) = x^2 - xy + y^2 + 2x + 2y + 6$

6. $f(x, y) = x^2 + xy + y^2 + 3x - 3y$

7. $f(x, y) = x^2 + 3xy + 3y^2 - 6x + 3y$

8. $f(x, y) = 5xy - 7x^2 - y^2 + 3x - 6y - 4$

9. $f(x, y) = 4xy - 10x^2 - 4y^2 + 8x + 8y + 9$

10. $f(x, y) = x^2 + xy + 3x + 2y - 6$

11. $f(x, y) = x^2 + xy - 2x - 2y + 2$

12. $f(x, y) = x^2 + xy + y^2 - 3x - 5$

13. $f(x, y) = x^2 - y^2 - 2x + 4y - 7$

14. $f(x, y) = 4x + 2y - x^2 + xy - y^2 + 3$

15. $f(x, y) = 2x^3 + 3y^2 - 12xy + 4$

16. $f(x, y) = 5x^3 + 2y^2 - 60xy - 3$

17. $f(x, y) = x^2 + 4y^3 - 6xy - 1$

18. $f(x, y) = 3x^2 + 7y^3 - 42xy + 5$

19. $f(x, y) = e^{xy}$

20. $f(x, y) = x^2 + e^y$

Figures (a)–(f) show the graphs of the functions of Exercises 21–26. Find all relative
extrema for each function and then match the function to the graphs.

21. $z = 3xy - x^3 - y^3 + \dfrac{1}{8}$

22. $z = \dfrac{3}{2}x - \dfrac{1}{2}x^3 - xy^2 + \dfrac{1}{16}$

23. $z = x^4 - 2x^2 + y^2 + \dfrac{17}{16}$

24. $z = 2y^3 - 3x^4 - 6x^2y + \dfrac{1}{16}$

25. $z = x^4 - y^4 - 2x^2 + 2y^2 + \dfrac{1}{16}$

26. $z = -x^4 + 4xy - 2y^2 + \dfrac{1}{16}$

(a)   **(b)**   **(c)**

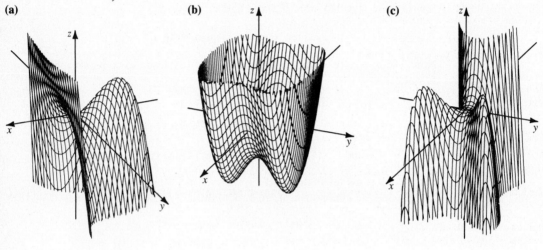

(d)   **(e)**   **(f)**

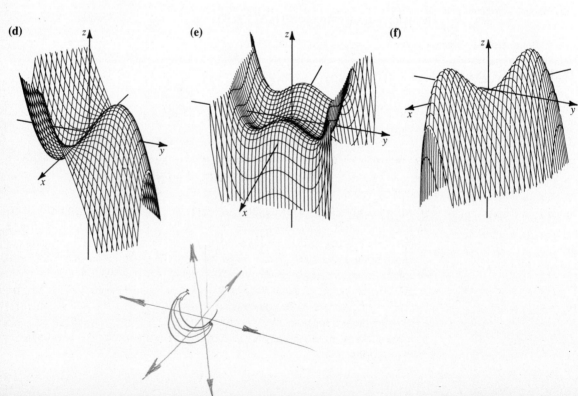

27. Suppose that the profit of a certain firm is approximated by
$$P(x, y) = 1000 + 24x - x^2 + 80y - y^2,$$
where x is the cost of a unit of labor and y is the cost of a unit of goods. Find values of x and y that maximize profit. Find the maximum profit.

28. The labor cost for manufacturing a precision camera can be approximated by
$$L(x, y) = \frac{3}{2}x^2 + y^2 - 2x - 2y - 2xy + 68,$$
where x is the number of hours required by a skilled craftsperson and y is the number of hours required by a semiskilled person. Find values of x and y that minimize the labor charge. Find the minimum labor charge.

29. The number of roosters that can be fed from x pounds of Super-Hen chicken feed and y pounds of Super-Rooster feed is given by
$$R(x, y) = 800 - 2x^3 + 12xy - y^2.$$
Find the number of pounds of each kind of feed that produces the maximum number of roosters.

30. The total profit from one acre of a certain crop depends on the amount spent on fertilizer, x, and hybrid seed, y, according to the model
$$P(x, y) = -x^2 + 3xy + 160x - 5y^2 + 200y + 2,600,000.$$
Find values of x and y that lead to maximum profit. Find the maximum profit.

31. The total cost to produce x units of electrical tape and y units of packing tape is given by
$$C(x, y) = 2x^2 + 3y^2 - 2xy + 2x - 126y + 3800.$$
Find the number of units of each kind of tape that should be produced so that the total cost is a minimum. Find the minimum total cost.

32. The total revenue from the sale of x spas and y solar heaters is approximated by
$$R(x, y) = 12 + 74x + 85y - 3x^2 - 5y^2 - 5xy.$$
Find the number of each that should be sold to produce maximum revenue. Find the maximum revenue.

33. Show that $f(x, y) = 1 - x^4 - y^4$ has a relative maximum, even though M in the theorem is 0.

34. Show that $M = 0$ for $f(x, y) = x^3 + (x - y)^2$, and that the function has neither a relative maximum nor minimum.

15.4 Lagrange Multipliers

In the previous section we saw how to find relative extrema for functions of two variables. In practice, many such functions are given with a secondary condition or **constraint.** For example, a problem might require that we find the maximum area that can be enclosed with a given length of fence (Exercise 17), or that we find the optimum dimensions of a can that will hold a given volume (Exercise 22).

A typical problem might require the smallest possible value of the function $z = x^2 + y^2$, subject to the constraint $x + y = 4$. To find this smallest value, first graph both the surface $z = x^2 + y^2$ and the plane $x + y = 4$, as in Figure 13. The necessary lowest value would be found on the curve formed by the intersection of the two graphs.

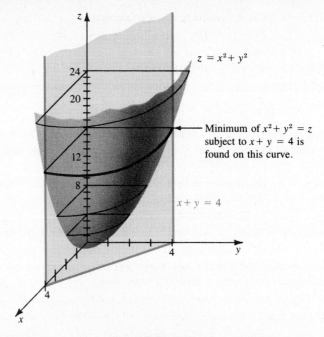

FIGURE 13

Problems with constraints are often solved by the method of *Lagrange multipliers*, named for the French mathematician Joseph Louis Lagrange (1736–1813). The proof for the method is complicated and is not given here. The method of Lagrange multipliers is used for problems of the form

$$\text{Find the relative extrema for } \quad z = f(x, y)$$

$$\text{subject to} \quad g(x, y) = 0.$$

We state the method only for functions of two independent variables, but it is valid for any number *n* of variables.

Lagrange Multipliers

All relative extrema of the function $z = f(x, y)$, subject to a constraint $g(x, y) = 0$, will be found among those points (x, y) for which there exists a value of λ such that

$$F_x(x, y, \lambda) = 0$$
$$F_y(x, y, \lambda) = 0$$
$$F_\lambda(x, y, \lambda) = 0,$$

where $\qquad F(x, y, \lambda) = f(x, y) + \lambda \cdot g(x, y).$

We assume that all indicated partial derivatives exist.

In the theorem, the function $F(x, y, \lambda) = f(x, y) + \lambda \cdot g(x, y)$ is called the Lagrange function; λ, the Greek letter *lambda,* is called a **Lagrange multiplier.**

EXAMPLE 1

Find the minimum value of
$$f(x, y) = 5x^2 + 6y^2 - xy,$$
subject to the constraint $x + 2y = 24$.
   Go through the following steps.

1. Rewrite the constraint in the form $g(x, y) = 0$. In this example the constraint
$$x + 2y = 24 \qquad \text{becomes} \qquad x + 2y - 24 = 0,$$
with
$$g(x, y) = x + 2y - 24.$$

2. Form the Lagrange function $F(x, y, \lambda)$, the sum of the function $f(x, y)$ and the product of λ and $g(x, y)$. Here,
$$\begin{aligned} F(x, y, \lambda) &= f(x, y) + \lambda \cdot g(x, y) \\ &= 5x^2 + 6y^2 - xy + \lambda(x + 2y - 24) \\ &= 5x^2 + 6y^2 - xy + \lambda x + 2\lambda y - 24\lambda. \end{aligned}$$

3. Find F_x, F_y, and F_λ. Form the system of equations $F_x = 0$, $F_y = 0$, and $F_\lambda = 0$.
$$F_x = 10x - y + \lambda = 0 \tag{1}$$
$$F_y = 12y - x + 2\lambda = 0 \tag{2}$$
$$F_\lambda = x + 2y - 24 = 0. \tag{3}$$

4. Solve the system of equations from Step 3 for x, y, and λ.
   To solve the system, multiply both sides of equation (1) by 12 and add the result to equation (2). Doing this, and rearranging terms, gives
$$\begin{aligned} 120x - 12y + 12\lambda &= 0 \\ -x + 12y + 2\lambda &= 0 \\ \hline 119x \qquad\quad + 14\lambda &= 0. \end{aligned} \tag{4}$$

To eliminate y from equations (2) and (3), rearrange terms, multiply both sides of equation (3) by -6 and add the result to equation (2) to get
$$\begin{aligned} -x + 12y + 2\lambda &= 0 \\ -6x - 12y \qquad\quad &= -144 \\ \hline -7x \qquad\quad + 2\lambda &= -144. \end{aligned} \tag{5}$$

Now find x by solving the systems of equations (4) and (5). Multiply both sides of equation (5) by -7, and add to equation (4).
$$\begin{aligned} 119x + 14\lambda &= 0 \\ 49x - 14\lambda &= 1008 \\ \hline 168x \qquad\quad &= 1008, \end{aligned}$$

from which $x = 6$. Substituting 6 for x in equation (3) gives $y = 9$. Also, although we don't use this number, $\lambda = -51$.

Finally, the minimum value for $f(x, y) = 5x^2 + 6y^2 - xy$, subject to the constraint $x + 2y = 24$, is at the point $(6, 9)$. The minimum value is $f(6, 9) = 612$. The second derivative test for relative extrema from the previous section can be used to verify that 612 is indeed a minimum: since $f_{xx} = 10$, $f_{yy} = 12$, and $f_{xy} = -1$, $M = 10 \cdot 12 - (-1)^2 > 0$, so part (b) applies and indicates a minimum. ■

Before looking at applications of Lagrange multipliers, let us summarize the steps involved in solving a problem by this method.

Using Lagrange Multipliers

1. Write the constraint in the form $g(x, y) = 0$.
2. Form the Lagrange function

$$F(x, y, \lambda) = f(x, y) + \lambda \cdot g(x, y).$$

3. Form the system of equations

$$F_x = 0, \qquad F_y = 0, \qquad F_\lambda = 0.$$

4. Solve the system in Step 3; the relative extrema for f are among the solutions of the system.

EXAMPLE 2

Find two numbers whose sum is 50 and whose product is a maximum.

Let x and y represent the two numbers. We must maximize the product

$$f(x, y) = xy,$$

subject to the constraint $x + y = 50$. Go through the four steps presented above.

1. $g(x, y) = x + y - 50$
2. $F(x, y, \lambda) = xy + \lambda(x + y - 50)$
3. $F_x = y + \lambda = 0$ (6)
   $F_y = x + \lambda = 0$ (7)
   $F_\lambda = x + y - 50 = 0$ (8)
4. From equation (6), $\lambda = -y$. Substituting $-y$ for λ in equation (7) gives

$$x + \lambda = 0$$

$$x + (-y) = 0$$

$$x = y.$$

Substituting y for x in equation (8) gives

$$x + y - 50 = 0$$

$$y + y - 50 = 0$$

$$2y = 50$$

$$y = 25.$$

Since $x = y$, $x = 25$.

The numbers 25 and 25 have a sum of 50 and produce the maximum product of all pairs of numbers satisfying $x + y = 50$. This product is $25 \cdot 25 = 625$. To check this, choose other numbers near 25 and 25 (having a sum of 50). The product of these other numbers should be less than 625. ■

As mentioned earlier, the method of Lagrange multipliers works for more than two independent variables. The next example shows how to find extrema for a function of three independent variables.

EXAMPLE 3

Find the dimensions of the closed rectangular box of maximum volume that can be produced from 6 square feet of material.

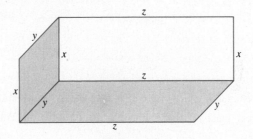

FIGURE 14

Let x, y, and z represent the dimensions of the box, as shown in Figure 14. The volume of the box is given by

$$f(x, y, z) = xyz.$$

As shown in Figure 14, the total amount of material required for the two ends of the box is $2xy$, the total needed for the sides is $2xz$, and the total needed for the top and bottom is $2yz$. Since 6 square feet of material is available,

$$2xy + 2xz + 2yz = 6 \quad \text{or} \quad xy + xz + yz = 3.$$

In summary, we must maximize $f(x, y, z) = xyz$ subject to the constraint $xy + xz + yz = 3$. Go through the steps above.

1. $g(x, y, z) = xy + xz + yz - 3$
2. $F(x, y, z, \lambda) = xyz + \lambda(xy + xz + yz - 3)$
3. $F_x = yz + \lambda y + \lambda z = 0$
   $F_y = xz + \lambda x + \lambda z = 0$
   $F_z = xy + \lambda x + \lambda y = 0$
   $F_\lambda = xy + xz + yz - 3 = 0$
4. The solution of the system of equations of Step 3 is $x = 1$, $y = 1$, $z = 1$. In other words, the box is a cube, 1 foot on a side. ■

15.4 EXERCISES

Find the relative maxima or minima in Exercises 1–10.

1. Maximum of $f(x, y) = 2xy$, subject to $x + y = 12$.
2. Maximum of $f(x, y) = 4xy + 2$, subject to $x + y = 24$.
3. Maximum of $f(x, y) = x^2y$, subject to $2x + y = 4$.
4. Maximum of $f(x, y) = 4xy^2$, subject to $3x - 2y = 5$.
5. Minimum of $f(x, y) = x^2 + 2y^2 - xy$, subject to $x + y = 8$.
6. Minimum of $f(x, y) = 3x^2 + 4y^2 - xy - 2$, subject to $2x + y = 21$.
7. Maximum of $f(x, y) = x^2 - 10y^2$, subject to $x - y = 18$.
8. Maximum of $f(x, y) = 12xy - x^2 - 3y^2$, subject to $x + y = 16$.
9. Maximum of $f(x, y, z) = xyz^2$, subject to $x + y + z = 6$.
10. Maximum of $f(x, y, z) = xy + 2xz + 2yz$ subject to $xyz = 32$.
11. Find two numbers whose sum is 20 and whose product is a maximum.
12. Find two numbers whose sum is 100 and whose product is a maximum.
13. Find two numbers x and y such that $x + y = 18$ and xy^2 is maximized.
14. Find two numbers x and y such that $x + y = 36$ and x^2y is maximized.
15. Find three numbers whose sum is 90 and whose product is a maximum.
16. Find three numbers whose sum is 240 and whose product is a maximum.
17. A farmer has 200 meters of fencing. Find the dimensions of the rectangular field of maximum area that can be enclosed by this amount of fencing.
18. Because of terrain difficulties, two sides of a fence can be built for $6 a foot, while the other two sides cost $4 per foot. (See the sketch.) Find the field of maximum area that can be enclosed for $1200.

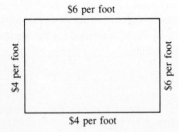

$6 per foot

$4 per foot $6 per foot

$4 per foot

19. Find the area of the largest rectangular field that can be enclosed with 600 meters of fencing. Assume that no fencing is needed along one side of the field.
20. A fence is built against a large building, so that no fencing material is used on that one side. Material for the ends costs $8 a foot; the side can be built for $6 per foot. Find the dimensions of the field of maximum area that can be enclosed for $1200.
21. A cylindrical can is to be made that will hold 250π cubic inches of candy. Find the dimensions of the can with minimum surface area.
22. An ordinary 12-ounce beer or soda pop can holds about 25 cubic inches. Use a calculator and find the dimensions of a can with minimum surface area. Measure a can and see how close its dimensions are to the results you found.

23. A rectangular box with no top is to be built from 500 square meters of material. Find the dimensions of such a box that will enclose the maximum volume.

24. A one-pound soda cracker box has a volume of 185 cubic inches. The end of the box is square. Find the dimensions of such a box that has minimum surface area.

25. The total cost to produce x large needlepoint kits and y small ones is given by

$$C(x, y) = 2x^2 + 6y^2 + 4xy + 10.$$

If a total of ten kits must be made, how should production be allocated so that total cost is minimized?

26. The profit from the sale of x units of radiators for automobiles and y units of radiators for generators is given by

$$P(x, y) = -x^2 - y^2 + 4x + 8y.$$

Find values of x and y that lead to a maximum profit if the firm must produce a total of 6 units of radiators.

27. The production of nails depends on the cost of steel and the price of labor. Suppose that the number of units of nails manufactured is given by

$$f(x, y) = -60x + 100y - x^2 - 2y^2 - 3xy + 390,000$$

where x is the number of units of steel and y is the number of units of labor. Assume that steel costs $8 per unit and labor is $10 per unit. Find the maximum number of units of nails that can be made if the total budget for steel and labor is $4600.

15.5   The Least Squares Line

In trying to predict the future sales of a product or the total number of matings between two species of insects, it is common to gather as much data as possible and then draw a graph showing the data. This graph, called a **scatter diagram,** can then be inspected to see if a reasonably simple mathematical curve can be found which fits fairly well through all the given data points.

As an example, suppose a firm gathers data showing the relationship between the price in dollars of an item, y, and the number of units of the item that are sold, x, with results as follows.

units sold, x	10	15	20
price, y	80	68	62

A graph of this data is shown in Figure 15.

The graph suggests that a straight line fits reasonably well through these data points. If all the data points were to lie on the straight line, the point-slope form of the equation of a line (Chapter 1) could be used to find the equation of the line through the points.

In practice, the points on a scatter diagram almost never fit a straight line exactly. Then we must decide on the "best" straight line through the points. One

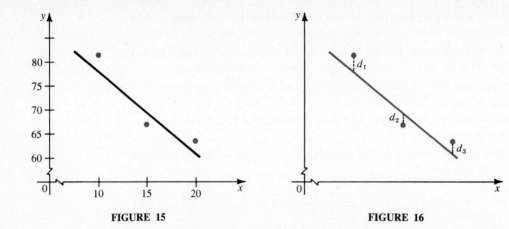

FIGURE 15   **FIGURE 16**

way to define the "best" line is as follows. Figure 16 shows just the points from Figure 15, without the numerical scale. Vertical line segments indicate the distances of these points from a possible line. The "best" straight line is often defined as the one for which the sum of the squares of the distances, $d_1{}^2 + d_2{}^2 + d_3{}^2$ here, is minimized.

To find the equation of the "best" line, let $y = mx + b$ be the equation of the line in Figure 16. Then for point d_1, we have $x = 10$ and $y = 80$ (from Figure 15), with $y = mx + b$ becoming $y = 10m + b$, and

$$d_1{}^2 = [80 - (10m + b)]^2.$$

Also, $$d_2{}^2 = [68 - (15m + b)]^2$$

and $$d_3{}^2 = [62 - (20m + b)]^2.$$

We want to find values of m and b that will minimize $d_1{}^2 + d_2{}^2 + d_3{}^2$; that is, we want to minimize

$$S = [80 - (10m + b)]^2 + [68 - (15m + b)]^2 + [62 - (20m + b)]^2.$$

To minimize S we need $\partial S/\partial m$ and $\partial S/\partial b$. Here

$$\frac{\partial S}{\partial m} = -20[80 - (10m + b)] - 30[68 - (15m + b)] - 40[62 - (20m + b)]$$

$$\frac{\partial S}{\partial b} = -2[80 - (10m + b)] - 2[68 - (15m + b)] - 2[62 - (20m + b)].$$

Simplify each of these, obtaining

$$\frac{\partial S}{\partial m} = -6120 + 1450m + 90b$$

$$\frac{\partial S}{\partial b} = -420 + 90m + 6b.$$

Place $\partial S/\partial m = 0$ and $\partial S/\partial b = 0$ and simplify.

$$-6120 + 1450m + 90b = 0 \quad \text{or} \quad 145m + 9b = 612$$
$$-420 + 90m + 6b = 0 \quad \text{or} \quad 15m + b = 70$$

Solve the system on the right by multiplying both sides of the second equation by -9. The solution is $m = -1.8$, $b = 97$. The equation that best fits through the points of Figure 15 is $y = mx + b$, or

$$y = -1.8x + 97.$$

The methods given earlier can be used to show that this line *minimizes* the sum of the squares of the distances. By the definition we have given, $y = -1.8x + 97$ is the "best" straight line that will fit through the data points. This line is called the **least squares line,** or sometimes the **regression line.**

Once a least squares line is obtained from a set of data, the equation can be used to predict a value of one variable, given a value of the other. In the example above, management might want an estimate of the number of units that would be sold at a price of $75. To find out, replace y with 75.

$$y = -1.8x + 97$$
$$75 = -1.8x + 97$$
$$-22 = -1.8x$$
$$12.2 \approx x$$

As an estimate, about 12 units would be sold at a price of 75.

The example above used three data points on the scatter diagram. A practical problem, however, might well involve a very large number of points. We shall now use the method above to find the least squares line for any finite number of data points. To simplify the notation for this more complicated case, we use *summation notation,* or *sigma notation.* As explained in the chapter on integration,

$$\sum_{i=1}^{n} x_i = x_1 + x_2 + x_3 + \cdots + x_n.$$

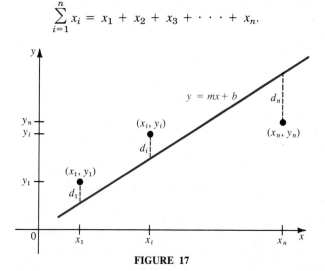

FIGURE 17

Let $y = mx + b$ be the least squares line for the set of known data points $(x_1, y_1), (x_2, y_2), \ldots, (x_n, y_n)$. (See **Figure 17.**) As above, we want to minimize the sum of squares

$$d_1{}^2 + d_2{}^2 + \cdots + d_n{}^2.$$

The square of the distance of the first point (x_1, y_1) from the line is given by

$$d_1{}^2 = [y_1 - (mx_1 + b)]^2.$$

The square of the distance of the point (x_i, y_i) from the line is

$$d_i{}^2 = [y_i - (mx_i + b)]^2.$$

We want to minimize the sum

$$\sum_{i=1}^{n} [y_i - (mx_i + b)]^2.$$

Since the x_i and y_i values represent known data points, the unknowns in this sum are the numbers m and b. To emphasize this fact, write the sum as a function of m and b:

$$f(m, b) = \sum_{i=1}^{n} [y_i - (mx_i + b)]^2$$

$$= \sum_{i=1}^{n} [y_i - mx_i - b]^2$$

$$= (y_1 - mx_1 - b)^2 + (y_2 - mx_2 - b)^2$$
$$+ \cdots + (y_n - mx_n - b)^2.$$

To find the minimum value of this function, find the partial derivatives with respect to m and to b and place each equal to 0. (Recall that all the x's and y's are constants.)

$$\frac{\partial f}{\partial m} = -2x_1(y_1 - mx_1 - b) - 2x_2(y_2 - mx_2 - b) - \cdots$$

$$-2x_n(y_n - mx_n - b) = 0$$

$$\frac{\partial f}{\partial b} = -2(y_1 - mx_1 - b) - 2(y_2 - mx_2 - b) - \cdots$$

$$- 2(y_n - mx_n - b) = 0.$$

Using some algebra and rearranging terms, these two equations become

$$(x_1{}^2 + x_2{}^2 + \cdots + x_n{}^2)m + (x_1 + x_2 + \cdots + x_n)b$$
$$= x_1y_1 + x_2y_2 + \cdots + x_ny_n$$
$$(x_1 + x_2 + \cdots + x_n)m + nb = y_1 + y_2 + \cdots + y_n.$$

Rewrite these last two equations using abbreviated sigma notation as follows. (Remember that n terms are being added.)

$$\left(\sum x^2\right)m + \left(\sum x\right)b = \sum xy \tag{1}$$

$$\left(\sum x\right)m + nb = \sum y \tag{2}$$

To solve this system of equations, multiply the first on both sides by $-n$ and the second on both sides by $\sum x$ and then add to eliminate the term with b. This gives

$$-n\left(\sum x^2\right)m - n\left(\sum x\right)b = -n\left(\sum xy\right)$$

$$\underline{\left(\sum x\right)\left(\sum x\right)m + \left(\sum x\right)nb = \left(\sum x\right)\left(\sum y\right)}$$

$$\left(\sum x\right)\left(\sum x\right)m - n\left(\sum x^2\right)m = \left(\sum x\right)\left(\sum y\right) - n\left(\sum xy\right)$$

Write the product $(\sum x)(\sum x)$ as $(\sum x)^2$. Using this notation and solving the last equation for m gives

$$m = \frac{\left(\sum x\right)\left(\sum y\right) - n\left(\sum xy\right)}{\left(\sum x\right)^2 - n\left(\sum x^2\right)}. \tag{3}$$

The easiest way to find b is to solve equation (2) for b:

$$\left(\sum x\right)m + nb = \sum y \tag{2}$$

$$nb = \sum y - \left(\sum x\right)m$$

$$b = \frac{\sum y - m\left(\sum x\right)}{n}.$$

A summary of the formulas for m and b in the least squares equation follows.

Least Squares Equation

> The **least squares equation** for the n points (x_1, y_1), (x_2, y_2), . . . , (x_n, y_n) is given by
> $$y = mx + b,$$
> where
> $$m = \frac{(\sum x)(\sum y) - n(\sum xy)}{(\sum x)^2 - n(\sum x^2)} \quad \text{and} \quad b = \frac{\sum y - m(\sum x)}{n}.$$

As the formulas in the box suggest, find m first. Then use the value of m and the second formula to find b.

EXAMPLE 1

Find the least squares line for the data in the following chart.

x	1	2	3	5	6
y	−2	2	5	12	14

Start by drawing the scatter diagram of Figure 18. Since the points in the scatter diagram lie approximately in a straight line, it is appropriate to find the least squares line for the data.

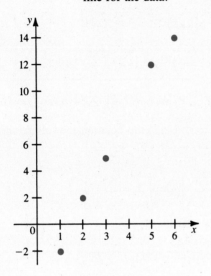

FIGURE 18

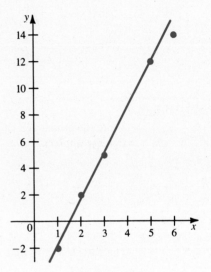

FIGURE 19

The formulas in the box above require Σx, Σy, Σx^2, and Σxy. Organize the work as follows.

x	y	x^2	xy
1	−2	1	−2
2	2	4	4
3	5	9	15
5	12	25	60
6	14	36	84
Totals 17	31	75	161

The chart shows that $\Sigma x = 17$, $\Sigma y = 31$, $\Sigma x^2 = 75$, $\Sigma xy = 161$, and $n = 5$. Using the equation for m given in the box gives

$$m = \frac{17(31) - 5(161)}{17^2 - 5(75)} = \frac{527 - 805}{289 - 375} = \frac{-278}{-86} \approx 3.2.$$

Now find b:

$$b = \frac{\Sigma y - m(\Sigma x)}{n} = \frac{31 - 3.2(17)}{5} \approx -4.7.$$

The least squares equation for the given data is $y = mx + b$, or

$$y = 3.2x - 4.7.$$

This line is graphed in Figure 19.

The equation $y = 3.2x - 4.7$ can be used to estimate values of y for given values of x. For example, if $x = 4$,

$$y = 3.2x - 4.7 = 3.2(4) - 4.7 = 12.8 - 4.7 = 8.1.$$

Also, if $x = 7$, then $y = 3.2(7) - 4.7 = 17.7.$ ■

15.5 EXERCISES

In Exercises 1–4, draw a scatter diagram for the given set of data points and then find the least squares equation.

1.

x	1	2	3	5	9
y	9	13	18	25	41

Estimate y when x is 4; 7.

2.

x	2	3	5	6	8
y	8	13	23	28	38

Estimate y when x is 7; 9.

3.

x	4	5	8	12	14
y	3	7	17	28	35

Estimate x when y is 12; 32.

4.

x	3	4	5	6	8
y	8	12	16	18	28

Estimate x when y is 17; 26.

5. In a study to determine the linear relationship between y, the size (in decimeters) of an ear of corn, and x, the amount (in tons per acre) of fertilizer used, the following data were collected.

$$n = 10 \qquad \Sigma x = 30 \qquad \Sigma y = 24$$
$$\Sigma xy = 75 \qquad \Sigma x^2 = 100 \qquad \Sigma y^2 = 80$$

(a) Find an equation for the least squares line.

(b) If 3 tons per acre of fertilizer are used, what length (in decimeters) would the equation in (a) predict for an ear of corn?

6. In an experiment to determine the linear relationship between temperatures on the Celsius scale (y) and on the Fahrenheit scale (x), a student got the following results.

$$n = 5 \qquad \Sigma x = 376 \qquad \Sigma y = 120$$
$$\Sigma xy = 28,050 \qquad \Sigma x^2 = 62,522 \qquad \Sigma y^2 = 13,450$$

(a) Find an equation for the least squares line.

(b) Find the reading on the Celsius scale that corresponds to a reading of 120° Fahrenheit, using the equation of part (a).

7. The ACT test scores of eight students were compared to their GPA's after one year in college, with the following results.

ACT score, x	19	20	22	24	25	26	27	29
GPA, y	2.2	2.4	2.7	2.6	3.0	3.5	3.4	3.8

   (a) Plot the eight points on a scatter diagram.

   (b) Find the least squares equation and graph it on the scatter diagram of part (a).

   (c) Using the results of (b), predict the GPA of a student with an ACT score of 28.

8. Records show that the annual sales for the Sweet Palms Life Insurance Company in 5-year periods for the last 20 years were as follows.

Year	Year in Coded Form, x	Sales in Millions, y
1964	1	1.0
1969	2	1.3
1974	3	1.7
1979	4	1.9
1984	5	2.1

   (a) Plot the five points on a scatter diagram.

   (b) Find the least squares equation and graph it on the scatter diagram of part (a).

   (c) Predict the company's sales for 1989.

9. A sample of 10 adult men gave the following data on their heights (in inches) and weights (in pounds).

Height, x	62	62	63	65	66	67	68	68	70	72
Weight, y	120	140	130	150	142	130	135	175	149	168

   (a) Find the equation of the least squares line.

   Using the results of (a), predict the weight of a man whose height is

   (b) 60 inches;   (c) 70 inches.

10. A fast-food chain wishes to find the relationship between annual store sales (in thousands of dollars) and percent of pretax profit in order to estimate increases in profit due to increased sales volume. The data shown below was obtained from a sample of stores across the country.

Annual sales, x	250	300	375	425	450	475	500	575	600	650
Pretax profit, y	9.3	10.8	14.8	14.0	14.2	15.3	15.9	19.1	19.2	21.0

   (a) Plot the ten pairs of values on a scatter diagram.

   (b) Find the equation of the least squares line and graph it on the scatter diagram of part (a).

   (c) Using the equation of part (b), predict the percent of pretax profit for annual sales of $700,000; of $750,000.

11. Sales (in thousands of dollars) of a certain company are shown here.

Year, x	0	1	2	3	4	5
Sales, y	48	59	66	75	80	90

Find the equation of the least squares line.

12. The following data, furnished by a major brewery, which asked that its name not be given, were used to determine if there is a relationship between repair costs and barrels of beer produced. The data (in thousands) are given for a 10-month period.

Month	Barrels of Beer x	Repairs y
Jan	369	299
Feb	379	280
Mar	482	393
April	493	388
May	496	385
June	567	423
July	521	374
Aug	482	357
Sept	391	106
Oct	417	332

(a) Find the equation of the least squares line.

(b) If 500,000 barrels of beer are produced, what will the equation from part (a) give as the predicted repair costs?

Exercise 13 is for students who have studied logarithms.

13. Sometimes the scatter diagram of the data does not have a linear pattern. This is particularly true in some biological and chemical applications. In these applications, however, often the scatter diagram of the *logarithms* of the data has a linear pattern. A least squares line then can be used to predict the logarithm of any desired value from which the value itself can be found. Suppose that a certain kind of bacterium grows in number as shown in Table A. The actual number of bacteria present at each time period is replaced with the common logarithm of that number in Table B.

Table A		Table B	
Time in Hours	Number of Bacteria	Time x	Log y
0	1000	0	3.0000
1	1649	1	3.2172
2	2718	2	3.4343
3	4482	3	3.6515
4	7389	4	3.8686
5	12182	5	4.0857

We can now find a least squares line which will predict y, given x.

(a) Plot the original pairs of numbers. The pattern should be nonlinear.

(b) Plot the log values against the time values. The pattern should be almost linear.

(c) Find the equation of the least squares line. (First round off the log values to the nearest hundredth.)

(d) Predict the log value for a time of 7 hours. Find the number whose logarithm is your answer. This will be the predicted number of bacteria.

It is sometimes possible to get a better prediction for a variable by considering its relationship with more than one other variable. For example, one should be able to predict college GPAs more precisely if both high school GPAs and scores on the ACT are considered. To do this, we alter the equation used to find a least squares line by adding a term for the new variable as follows. If y represents college GPAs, x_1 high school GPAs, and x_2 ACT scores, then y', the predicted GPA, is given by

$$y' = ax_1 + bx_2 + c.$$

This equation represents a **least squares plane.** The equations for the constants a, b, and c are more complicated than those given in the text for m and b, so that calculating a least squares equation for three variables is more likely to require the aid of a computer.

14. Alcoa* used a least squares line with two independent variables, x_1 and x_2, to predict the effect on revenue of the price of aluminum forged truck wheels, as follows.

x_1 = the average price per wheel
x_2 = large truck production in thousands
y = sales of aluminum forged truck wheels in thousands

Using data for the past eleven years, the company found the equation of the least squares plane to be

$$y' = 49.2755 - 1.1924x_1 + 0.1631x_2.$$

The following figures were then forecast for truck production.

1982	1983	1984	1985	1986	1987
160.0	165.0	170.0	175.0	180.0	185.0

Three possible price levels per wheel were considered: $42, $45, and $48.

(a) Use the least squares plane equation given above to find the estimated sales of wheels (y') for 1984 at each of the three price levels.

(b) Repeat part (a) for 1987.

(c) For which price level, on the basis of the 1984 and 1987 figures, are total estimated sales greatest?

(By comparing total estimated sales for the years 1982 through 1987 at each of the three price levels, the company found that the selling price of $42 per wheel would generate the greatest sales volume over the six-year period.)

15.6   Total Differentials and Approximations

Recall from an earlier chapter that the differential of a function $y = f(x)$, written dy, is defined as

$$dy = f'(x) \cdot dx,$$

where dx, the differential of x, is any real number (usually small). This definition shows that dy is a function of *two* variables, x and dx. This idea can be extended to three dimensions by defining a *total differential*.

---

*This example supplied by John H. Van Denender, Public Relations Department, Aluminum Company of America.

Total Differential for Two Variables

> Let $z = f(x, y)$ be a function of x and y. Let dx and dy be real numbers. Then the **total differential** of f is
>
> $$df = f_x(x, y) \cdot dx + f_y(x, y) \cdot dy.$$
>
> Sometimes, df is written dz.

By this definition, df is a function of *four* variables, x, dx, y, and dy.

EXAMPLE 1

Find df for each function.

(a) $f(x, y) = 9x^3 - 8x^2y + 4y^3$.

First find f_x and f_y.

$$f_x = 27x^2 - 16xy \qquad \text{and} \qquad f_y = -8x^2 + 12y^2.$$

By the definition,

$$df = (27x^2 - 16xy)\,dx + (-8x^2 + 12y^2)\,dy.$$

(b) $z = f(x, y) = \ln(x^3 + y^2)$

Since

$$f_x = \frac{3x^2}{x^3 + y^2} \qquad \text{and} \qquad f_y = \frac{2y}{x^3 + y^2},$$

the total differential is

$$dz = df = \left(\frac{3x^2}{x^3 + y^2}\right)dx + \left(\frac{2y}{x^3 + y^2}\right)dy. \quad \blacksquare$$

EXAMPLE 2

Let $f(x, y) = 9x^3 - 8x^2y + 4y^3$. Find df when $x = 1$, $y = 3$, $dx = .01$, and $dy = -.02$.

Example 1 gave the total differential

$$df = (27x^2 - 16xy)\,dx + (-8x^2 + 12y^2)\,dy.$$

Replace x with 1, y with 3, dx with .01, and dy with $-.02$.

$$df = [27 \cdot 1^2 - 16(1)(3)](.01) + (-8 \cdot 1^2 + 12 \cdot 3^2)(-.02)$$

$$= (27 - 48)(.01) + (-8 + 108)(-.02)$$

$$= (-21)(.01) + (100)(-.02)$$

$$df = -2.21. \quad \blacksquare$$

The idea of a total differential can be extended to include functions of three independent variables.

Total Differential

for Three Variables

If $w = f(x, y, z)$, then the **total differential, dw**, is

$$dw = f_x(x, y, z)dx + f_y(x, y, z)dy + f_z(x, y, z)dz,$$

provided all indicated partial derivatives exist.

As this definition shows, dw is a function of six variables, x, y, z, dx, dy, and dz. Similar definitions could be given for functions of more than three independent variables.

EXAMPLE 3

Let $w = f(x, y, z) = x^2 + yz^4$.

(a) Find dw.

Find the necessary three partial derivatives.

$$f_x = 2x, \qquad f_y = z^4, \qquad f_z = 4yz^3.$$

By the definition of the total differential,

$$dw = 2xdx + z^4dy + 4yz^3dz.$$

(b) Evaluate dw for $x = -1$, $y = 2$, $z = -3$, $dx = .02$, $dy = -.03$, and $dz = .05$.

Substitute these values into the total differential, dw.

$$dw = 2(-1)(.02) + (-3)^4(-.03) + 4(2)(-3)^3(.05) = -13.27. \quad \blacksquare$$

Approximations Recall that with a function of one variable, $y = f(x)$, the differential dy can be used to approximate Δy, the change in y corresponding to a change in x, Δx. A similar approximation can be made for a function of two variables. Define Δz as $f(x + \Delta x, y + \Delta y) - f(x, y)$; then

For small values of Δx and Δy,

$$dz \approx \Delta z$$

where $\Delta z = f(x + \Delta x, y + \Delta y) - f(x, y)$.

EXAMPLE 4

Let $f(x, y) = 6x^2 + xy + y^3$. Find Δz and dz when $x = 2$, $y = -1$, $\Delta x = -.03$, and $\Delta y = .02$.

Here $x + \Delta x = 2 + (-.03) = 1.97$ and $y + \Delta y = -1 + .02 = -.98$. Find Δz with the definition above.

$$\Delta z = f(x + \Delta x, y + \Delta y) - f(x, y)$$
$$= f(1.97, -.98) - f(2, -1)$$
$$= [6(1.97)^2 + (1.97)(-.98) + (-.98)^3] - [6(2)^2 + 2(-1) + (-1)^3]$$
$$= [23.2854 - 1.9306 - .941192] - [24 - 2 - 1]$$
$$= 20.413608 - 21$$
$$\Delta z = -.586392$$

To find dz, the total differential, we need

$$f_x = 12x + y \quad \text{and} \quad f_y = x + 3y^2.$$

Then

$$dz = (12x + y)dx + (x + 3y^2)dy.$$

Since $dx = \Delta x$ and $dy = \Delta y$, substitution gives

$$dz = [12 \cdot 2 + (-1)](-.03) + [2 + 3 \cdot (-1)^2](.02)$$
$$= (23)(-.03) + (5)(.02)$$
$$dz = -.59.$$

In this example the values of Δz and dz are very close. (Compare the amount of work needed to find dz with that needed for Δz.) ∎

For small values of dx and dy the values of Δz and dz are approximately equal. Since $\Delta z = f(x + dx, y + dy) - f(x, y)$, we have

$$f(x + dx, y + dy) = f(x, y) + \Delta z$$

or

$$f(x + dx, y + dy) \approx f(x, y) + dz.$$

Replacing dz by the expression for the total differential gives the result in the next box.

Approximations by Differentials

For a function f having all indicated partial derivatives, and for small values of dx and dy,

$$f(x + dx, y + dy) \approx f(x, y) + dz,$$

or

$$f(x + dx, y + dy) \approx f(x, y) + f_x(x, y) \cdot dx + f_y(x, y) \cdot dy.$$

EXAMPLE 5

The total profit in hundreds of dollars from the sale of x tons of fertilizer for wheat and y tons of fertilizer for corn is given by

$$P(x, y) = 6x^{1/2} + 9y^{2/3} + \frac{5000}{xy}.$$

Suppose a firm is producing 64 tons of fertilizer for wheat and 125 tons of fertilizer for corn. Find the approximate change in profit if production is changed to 63 tons and 127 tons, respectively. Use this result to estimate the total profit from the sale of 63 tons and 127 tons.

The approximate change in profit, dP, is

$$dP = P_x(x, y) \cdot dx + P_y(x, y) \cdot dy.$$

Finding the necessary partial derivatives gives

$$dP = \left(3x^{-1/2} - \frac{5000}{x^2 y}\right) dx + \left(6y^{-1/3} - \frac{5000}{xy^2}\right) dy.$$

Substitute 64 for x, 125 for y, -1 for dx, and 2 for dy.

$$dP = \left(3 \cdot 64^{-1/2} - \frac{5000}{64^2 \cdot 125}\right)(-1) + \left(6 \cdot 125^{-1/3} - \frac{5000}{64 \cdot 125^2}\right)(2)$$

$$= \left(3 \cdot \frac{1}{8} - \frac{5000}{512,000}\right)(-1) + \left(6 \cdot \frac{1}{5} - \frac{5000}{1,000,000}\right)(2)$$

$$= (.375 - .0098)(-1) + (1.2 - .005)(2)$$

$$dP \approx 2.0248$$

A change in production from 64 tons of fertilizer for wheat and 125 tons for corn, to 63 and 127 tons respectively, will increase profits by about 2.02 hundred dollars, or $202.

To estimate the total profit from the production of 63 tons and 127 tons, use the approximation formula in the box.

$$P(63, 127) \approx P(64, 125) + dP$$

$$= \left(6 \cdot 64^{1/2} + 9 \cdot 125^{2/3} + \frac{5000}{64 \cdot 125}\right) + 2.0248$$

$$= \left(6 \cdot 8 + 9 \cdot 25 + \frac{5000}{8000}\right) + 2.0248 = 275.65$$

hundred dollars, or a total profit of $27,565. ■

EXAMPLE 6

A short length of blood vessel is in the shape of a right circular cylinder. (See Figure 20.) The length of the vessel is measured as 42 millimeters, and the radius is measured as 2.5 millimeters. Suppose the maximum error in the measurement of the length is .9 millimeters, with an error of no more than .2 millimeters in the measurement of the radius. Find the maximum possible error in calculating the volume of the blood vessel.

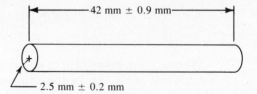

42 mm ± 0.9 mm

2.5 mm ± 0.2 mm

FIGURE 20

The volume of a right circular cylinder is given by $V = \pi r^2 h$. To approximate the error in the volume, find the total differential, dV.

$$dV = (2\pi rh) \cdot dr + (\pi r^2) \cdot dh.$$

Here, $r = 2.5$, $h = 42$, $dr = .2$, and $dh = .9$. Substitution gives

$$dV = [(2\pi)(2.5)(42)](.2) + [\pi(2.5)^2](.9) \approx 149.6$$

The maximum possible error in calculating the volume is 149.6 cubic millimeters.   ▦

15.6 EXERCISES

Find dz or dw, as appropriate, for each function in Exercises 1–20.

1. $z = 9x^4 - 5y^3$

2. $z = x^2 + 7y^4$

3. $z = x^2y^3 + y$

4. $z = 8x^2 - xy^2$

5. $z = \dfrac{x + y}{x - y}$

6. $z = \dfrac{x + y^2}{y - 2}$

7. $z = 2\sqrt{xy} - \sqrt{x + y}$

8. $z = \sqrt{x^2 + y^2} + \sqrt{xy}$

9. $z = (3x + 2)\sqrt{1 - 2y}$

10. $z = (5x^2 + 6)\sqrt{4 + 3y}$

11. $z = \ln(x^2 + 2y^4)$

12. $z = \ln\left(\dfrac{8 + x}{8 - y}\right)$

13. $z = xy^2 e^{x+y}$

14. $z = (x + y)e^{-x^2}$

15. $z = x^2 - y \ln x$

16. $z = x^2 + 3y - x \ln y$

17. $w = x^4yz^3$

18. $w = 6x^3y^2z^5$

19. $w = 6\left(1 - \dfrac{2}{y} + \dfrac{1}{x} - \dfrac{3}{z}\right)$

20. $w = 8\left(\dfrac{4 + x}{y + z}\right)$

In Exercises 21–28, evaluate dz using the given functions and values.

21. $z = x^2 + 3xy + y^2$; $x = 4$, $y = -2$, $dx = .02$, $dy = -.03$

22. $z = 8x^3 + 2x^2y - y$; $x = 1$, $y = 3$, $dx = .01$, $dy = .02$

23. $z = \dfrac{x - 4y}{x + 2y}$; $x = 0$, $y = 5$, $dx = -.03$, $dy = .05$

24. $z = \dfrac{y^2 + 3x}{y^2 - x}$; $x = 4$, $y = -4$, $dx = .01$, $dy = .03$

25. $z = \sqrt{x + y} + \sqrt{x(y + 1)}$; $x = 2$, $y = 1$, $dx = -.03$, $dy = -.02$

26. $z = (6x + y) + \sqrt{x^2 + y^2}$; $x = 1$, $y = 2$, $dx = -.01$, $dy = .04$

27. $z = \ln(x^2 + y^2)$; $x = 2$, $y = 3$, $dx = .02$, $dy = -.03$

28. $z = \ln\left(\dfrac{x + y}{x - y}\right)$; $x = 4$, $y = -2$, $dx = .03$, $dy = .02$

In Exercises 29–32, evaluate dw using the given functions and values.

29. $w = x^4y + z^2x$; $x = 1$, $y = -1$, $z = 2$, $dx = .01$, $dy = .03$, $dz = .02$

30. $w = x^2y^3 - x^3y^4z$; $x = 2$, $y = 3$, $z = -1$, $dx = -.03$, $dy = -.01$, $dz = .01$

31. $w = \dfrac{5x^2 + y^2}{z + 1}$; $x = -2$, $y = 1$, $z = 1$, $dx = .02$, $dy = -.03$, $dz = .02$

32. $w = x \ln(yz) - y \ln\dfrac{x}{z}$; $x = 2$, $y = 1$, $z = 4$, $dx = .03$, $dy = .02$, $dz = -.01$

33. Approximate the amount of material needed to make a water tumbler of diameter 3 cm and height 9 cm. Assume the walls of the tumbler are .2 cm thick.

34. Approximate the amount of aluminum needed for a beverage can of radius 2.5 cm and height 14 cm. Assume the walls of the can are .08 cm thick.

35. An industrial coating .2 inches thick is applied to all sides of a box of dimensions 10 inches by 9 inches by 14 inches. Estimate the volume of the coating used.

36. A piece of bone in the shape of a right circular cylinder is 7 cm long and has a radius of 1.4 cm. It is coated with a layer of preservative .09 cm thick. Estimate the volume of preservative used.

37. The width of a rectangle is measured as 15.8 cm, while the length is measured as 29.6 cm. The width measurement could be off by .8 cm, and the length could be off by 1.1 cm. Estimate the maximum possible error in calculating the area of the rectangle.

38. The height of a triangle is measured as 42.6 cm, with the base measured as 23.4 cm. The measurement of the height can be off as much as 1.2 cm, and that of the base off by no more than .9 cm. Estimate the maximum possible error in calculating the area of the triangle.

39. A portion of a blood vessel is measured to have length 7.9 cm and radius .8 cm. If each measurement could be off by as much as .15 cm, estimate the maximum possible error in calculating the volume of the vessel.

40. The height of a cone is measured to be 8.4 cm, with a radius of 2.9 cm. Each measurement could be off by as much as .1 cm. Estimate the maximum possible error in calculating the volume of the cone.

41. The manufacturing cost of a precision electronic calculator is approximated by
$$M(x, y) = 40x^2 + 30y^2 - 10xy + 30,$$
where x is the cost of the chips and y is the cost of labor. Right now, the company spends \$4 on chips and \$7 on labor. Use differentials to approximate the change in cost if the company spends \$5 on chips and \$6.50 on labor.

42. The total number of matings per day between individuals of a certain species of grasshoppers is approximated by
$$M(x, y) = 2xy + 10xy^2 + 30y^2 + 20,$$
where x represents the temperature in °C and y represents the number of days since the last rain. Currently, the temperature is 20°C, and it has been 7 days since the last rain. Use differentials to approximate the change in M if the temperature changes to 18°C, and it has been 8 days since the last rain.

43. The profit from the sale of x small computers and y electronic games is given by
$$P(x, y) = \frac{x}{x + 5y} + \frac{y + x}{y}.$$
Right now, 75 small computers and 50 games are being sold. Use differentials to approximate the change in profit if 3 fewer computers and 2 more games were sold.

44. The cost to produce x satellite receiving dishes and y transmitters is given by
$$C(x, y) = \ln(x^2 + y) + e^{xy/20}.$$
Production schedules now call for 15 receiving dishes and 9 transmitters. Use differentials to approximate the change in costs if 1 more dish and 1 fewer transmitter are made.

45. The production function for one country is
$$z = x^{0.8} y^{0.2},$$
where x stands for units of labor and y for units of capital. At present, x is 20 and y is 18. Use differentials to estimate the change in z if x becomes 21 and y becomes 16.

46. The production function for another country is
$$z = x^{0.65} y^{0.35},$$
where x stands for units of labor and y for units of capital. At present, x is 50 and y is 29. Use differentials to estimate the change in z if x becomes 52 and y becomes 27.

47. In Exercise 46 of Section 2 of this chapter, we found that the number of liters pumped through the lungs in one minute is given by
$$C = \frac{b}{a - v}.$$
Suppose $a = 160$, $b = 200$, and $v = 125$. Estimate the change in C if a becomes 145, b becomes 190, and v changes to 130.

48. In Exercise 44 of Section 2 of this chapter, we found that the oxygen consumption of a mammal is
$$m = \frac{2.5(T - F)}{w^{0.67}}.$$
Suppose T is 38°, F is 12°, and w is 30 kg. Approximate the change in m if T changes to 36°, F changes to 13°, and w becomes 31 kg.

15.7 Double Integrals

Earlier in this chapter we found partial derivatives of functions of two or more variables by holding constant all variables except one. In this section we begin by considering a similar process for antiderivatives of functions of two or more variables. For example, to find
$$\int (5x^3 y^4 - 6x^2 y + 2)\,dy,$$
treat x as a constant and y as a variable. (We know y is the variable, and x the constant, because of the symbol dy.) The rules for antiderivatives give
$$\int (5x^3 y^4 - 6x^2 y + 2)\,dy = x^3 y^5 - 3x^2 y^2 + 2y + C(x).$$
The constant C used earlier must be replaced with $C(x)$ to show that the "constant of integration" here can be any function involving only the variable x. Just as before, check this work by taking the derivative (actually the partial derivative) of the answer:
$$\frac{\partial}{\partial y}\left[x^3 y^5 - 3x^2 y^2 + 2y + C(x) \right] = 5x^3 y^4 - 6x^2 y + 2 + 0,$$
which shows that the answer is correct.

EXAMPLE 1

Find $\int(5x^3y^4 - 6x^2y + 2)\,dx$.

Because of the dx, treat y as a constant, with x the variable.

$$\int(5x^3y^4 - 6x^2y + 2)\,dx = \frac{5}{4}x^4y^4 - 2x^3y + 2x + C(y). \quad \blacksquare$$

EXAMPLE 2

(a) Find $\int x(x^2 + y)\,dx$.

Use substitution. Let $u = x^2 + y$, with $du = 2x\,dx + 0\,dy = 2x\,dx$. Then

$$\int x(x^2 + y)\,dx = \frac{1}{2}\int(x^2 + y)(2x\,dx)$$

$$= \frac{1}{2}\int u\,du$$

$$= \frac{1}{2}\left(\frac{1}{2}u^2\right) + f(y)$$

$$= \frac{1}{4}u^2 + f(y)$$

$$= \frac{1}{4}(x^2 + y)^2 + f(y).$$

(b) Find $\int x(x^2 + y)\,dy$.

Since y is a variable and x is held constant,

$$\int x(x^2 + y)\,dy = \int(x^3 + xy)\,dy = x^3y + \frac{1}{2}xy^2 + g(x). \quad \blacksquare$$

We can continue our analogy to integration of functions of one variable by evaluating definite integrals. Do this by holding one variable constant, and using the fundamental theorem of calculus with the other variable.

EXAMPLE 3

(a) Evaluate $\int_3^5 (6xy^2 + 12x^2y + 4y)\,dx$.

First, find an antiderivative:

$$\int(6xy^2 + 12x^2y + 4y)\,dx = 3x^2y^2 + 4x^3y + 4xy + h(y).$$

Now replace each x with 5, and then with 3, and subtract the results.

$$(3x^2y^2 + 4x^3y + 4xy + h(y))\Big|_3^5 = [3 \cdot 5^2 \cdot y^2 + 4 \cdot 5^3 \cdot y + 4 \cdot 5 \cdot y + h(y)]$$
$$- [3 \cdot 3^2 \cdot y^2 + 4 \cdot 3^3 \cdot y + 4 \cdot 3 \cdot y + h(y)]$$
$$= 75y^2 + 500y + 20y + h(y)$$
$$- (27y^2 + 108y + 12y + h(y))$$
$$= 48y^2 + 400y.$$

The "function of integration," $h(y)$, drops out, just as the constant of integration does with definite integrals.

(b) Evaluate $\int_1^2 (6xy^2 + 12x^2y + 4y)\,dy$.

Integrate with respect to y; then substitute 2 and 1.

$$\int_1^2 (6xy^2 + 12x^2y + 4y)\,dy = (2xy^3 + 6x^2y^2 + 2y^2)\Big]_1^2$$
$$= (2x \cdot 2^3 + 6x^2 \cdot 2^2 + 2 \cdot 2^2)$$
$$- (2x \cdot 1^3 + 6x^2 \cdot 1^2 + 2 \cdot 1^2)$$
$$= 16x + 24x^2 + 8 - (2x + 6x^2 + 2)$$
$$= 14x + 18x^2 + 6 \quad \blacksquare$$

As Example 3 suggests, an integral of the form

$$\int_a^b f(x,\,y)\,dy$$

produces a result which is a function of x, while

$$\int_a^b f(x,\,y)\,dx$$

produces a function of y. These resulting functions of one variable can themselves be integrated, as in the next example.

EXAMPLE 4

(a) Find $\int_1^2 \left[\int_3^5 (6xy^2 + 12x^2y + 4y)\,dx \right] dy$.

In Example 3(a), we found the quantity in brackets to be $48y^2 + 400y$. Thus,

$$\int_1^2 \left[\int_3^5 (6xy^2 + 12x^2y + 4y)\,dx \right] dy = \int_1^2 (48y^2 + 400y)\,dy$$
$$= (16y^3 + 200y^2)\Big]_1^2$$
$$= 16 \cdot 2^3 + 200 \cdot 2^2 - (16 \cdot 1^3 + 200 \cdot 1^2)$$
$$= 128 + 800 - (16 + 200)$$
$$= 712.$$

(b) Evaluate $\int_3^5 \left[\int_1^2 (6xy^2 + 12x^2y + 4y)\,dy \right] dx$. (This is the same integrand, with the same limits of integration as in part (a), but the order of integration is reversed.)

Use the result of Example 3(b).

$$\int_3^5 \left[\int_1^2 (6xy^2 + 12x^2y + 4y)\,dy \right] dx = \int_3^5 (14x + 18x^2 + 6)\,dx$$
$$= (7x^2 + 6x^3 + 6x)\Big]_3^5$$
$$= 7 \cdot 5^2 + 6 \cdot 5^3 + 6 \cdot 5 - (7 \cdot 3^2 + 6 \cdot 3^3 + 6 \cdot 3)$$
$$= 175 + 750 + 30 - (63 + 162 + 18)$$
$$= 712. \quad \blacksquare$$

The answers in the two parts of Example 4 are equal. It can be proved that for a large class of functions, including most functions that occur in applications,

$$\int_a^b \left[\int_c^d f(x, y)\, dx \right] dy = \int_c^d \left[\int_a^b f(x, y)\, dy \right] dx.$$

Because these two integrals are equal, the brackets are not needed, and either of the integrals in the box is given by

$$\int_a^b \int_c^d f(x, y)\, dx\, dy.$$

This integral is called an **iterated integral** since it is evaluated by integrating twice, first using one variable and then using the other. (The order in which dx and dy are written tells the order of integration.)

The fact that the iterated integrals in the preceding box are equal makes it possible to define a *double integral*. First, the set of points (x, y) with $c \le x \le d$ and $a \le y \le b$ defines a rectangular region R in the plane, as shown in Figure 21. Then, the *double integral over R* is defined as follows.

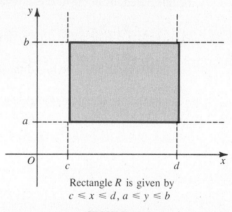

Rectangle R is given by
$c \le x \le d, a \le y \le b$

FIGURE 21

Double Integral

The **double integral** of $f(x, y)$ over a rectangular region R is written

$$\iint_R f(x, y)\, dx\, dy \qquad \text{or} \qquad \iint_R f(x, y)\, dy\, dx,$$

and equals either

$$\int_a^b \int_c^d f(x, y)\, dx\, dy \qquad \text{or} \qquad \int_c^d \int_a^b f(x, y)\, dy\, dx.$$

Extending earlier definitions, $f(x, y)$ is the **integrand** and R is the **region of integration**.

EXAMPLE 5

Find $\iint\limits_{R} \sqrt{x} \cdot \sqrt{y-2} \, dx \, dy$ over the rectangular region R defined by $0 \le x \le 4$, $3 \le y \le 11$.

We integrate first with respect to x; then, as a check, we use y first. Values of x for (x, y) in R go from 0 to 4; values of y from 3 to 11.

$$\iint\limits_{R} \sqrt{x} \cdot \sqrt{y-2} \, dx \, dy = \int_3^{11} \left[\int_0^4 \sqrt{x} \cdot \sqrt{y-2} \, dx \right] dy$$

$$= \int_3^{11} \left(\frac{2}{3} x^{3/2} \sqrt{y-2} \right) \Big|_0^4 \, dy$$

$$= \int_3^{11} \left[\frac{2}{3}(4^{3/2}\sqrt{y-2}) - \frac{2}{3}(0^{3/2})\sqrt{y-2} \right] dy$$

$$= \int_3^{11} \left(\frac{16}{3}\sqrt{y-2} - 0 \right) dy = \int_3^{11} \left(\frac{16}{3}\sqrt{y-2} \right) dy$$

$$= \frac{32}{9}(y-2)^{3/2} \Big|_3^{11} = \frac{32}{9}(9)^{3/2} - \frac{32}{9}(1)^{3/2}$$

$$= 96 - \frac{32}{9} = \frac{832}{9}.$$

Now rework the problem by integrating with respect to y first.

$$\iint\limits_{R} \sqrt{x} \cdot \sqrt{y-2} \, dx \, dy = \int_0^4 \left[\int_3^{11} \sqrt{x} \cdot \sqrt{y-2} \, dy \right] dx$$

$$= \int_0^4 \left(\frac{2}{3}\sqrt{x}(y-2)^{3/2} \right) \Big|_3^{11} \, dx$$

$$= \int_0^4 \left[\frac{2}{3}\sqrt{x}(9)^{3/2} - \frac{2}{3}\sqrt{x}(1)^{3/2} \right] dx$$

$$= \int_0^4 \left(18\sqrt{x} - \frac{2}{3}\sqrt{x} \right) dx$$

$$= \int_0^4 \frac{52}{3}\sqrt{x} \, dx = \frac{104}{9} x^{3/2} \Big|_0^4$$

$$= \frac{104}{9}(4)^{3/2} - \frac{104}{9}(0)^{3/2} = \frac{832}{9}.$$

As expected, both answers are the same. ▨

Volume As shown earlier, the definite integral $\int_a^b f(x) \, dx$ can be used to find the area under a curve. In a similar manner, double integrals are used to find the *volume under a surface*. Figure 22 shows that portion of a surface $f(x, y)$ directly over a rectangle R in the xy-plane. Just as areas were approximated by a large number of small rectangles, volume could be approximated by adding the volumes of a large number of properly drawn small boxes. The height of a typical box would be $f(x, y)$ with the length and width given by dx and dy. The formula for the volume of a box would then suggest the following result.

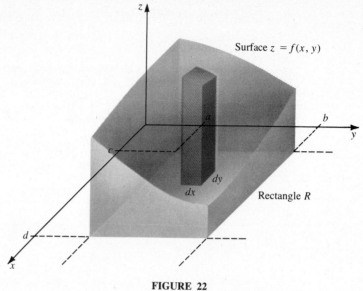

FIGURE 22

Volume

Let $z = f(x, y)$ be a function that is never negative on the rectangular region R defined by $c \leq x \leq d$, $a \leq y \leq b$. The volume of the solid under the graph of f and over the region R is

$$\iint\limits_{R} f(x, y)\, dx\, dy.$$

EXAMPLE 6   Find the volume under the surface $z = x^2 + y^2$ shown in Figure 23.

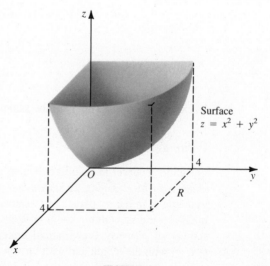

FIGURE 23

By the results in the box, this volume is

$$\iint_R f(x, y)\, dx\, dy,$$

where $f(x, y) = x^2 + y^2$, and R is the region $0 \le x \le 4, 0 \le y \le 4$. By definition,

$$\iint_R f(x, y)\, dx\, dy = \int_0^4 \left[\int_0^4 (x^2 + y^2)\, dx \right] dy$$

$$= \int_0^4 \left(\frac{1}{3}x^3 + xy^2 \right)\Big]_0^4 \, dy$$

$$= \int_0^4 \left(\frac{64}{3} + 4y^2 \right) dy = \left(\frac{64}{3}y + \frac{4}{3}y^3 \right)\Big]_0^4$$

$$= \frac{64}{3} \cdot 4 + \frac{4}{3} \cdot 4^3 - 0 = \frac{512}{3}. \quad \blacksquare$$

Double Integrals Over Other Regions In the work in this section, we found double integrals over rectangular regions, with constant limits of integration. Now this work can be extended to include *variable* limits of integration. (Notice in the examples that follow that the variable limits always go on the *inner* integral sign.)

EXAMPLE 7

Evaluate $\displaystyle\int_1^2 \int_y^{y^2} xy \, dx \, dy$.

Integrate first with respect to x, then with respect to y.

$$\int_1^2 \int_y^{y^2} xy \, dx \, dy = \int_1^2 \left[\int_y^{y^2} xy \, dx \right] dy = \int_1^2 \left[\frac{1}{2}x^2 y \right]_y^{y^2} dy$$

Replace x first with y^2 and then with y, and subtract.

$$\int_1^2 \int_y^{y^2} xy \, dx \, dy = \int_1^2 \left[\frac{1}{2}(y^2)^2 y - \frac{1}{2}(y)^2 y \right] dy$$

$$= \int_1^2 \left(\frac{1}{2}y^5 - \frac{1}{2}y^3 \right) dy = \left(\frac{1}{12}y^6 - \frac{1}{8}y^4 \right)\Big]_1^2$$

$$= \left(\frac{1}{12} \cdot 2^6 - \frac{1}{8} \cdot 2^4 \right) - \left(\frac{1}{12} \cdot 1^6 - \frac{1}{8} \cdot 1^4 \right)$$

$$= \frac{64}{12} - \frac{16}{8} - \frac{1}{12} + \frac{1}{8} = \frac{27}{8} \quad \blacksquare$$

The use of variable limits of integration permits evaluation of double integrals over the types of regions shown in Figure 24.

Double integrals over more complicated regions are discussed in more advanced books. Integration over regions such as those of Figure 24 is done with the results of the following theorem.

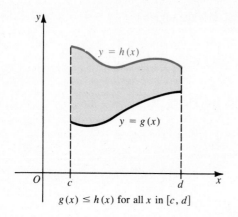

$g(x) \le h(x)$ for all x in $[c, d]$

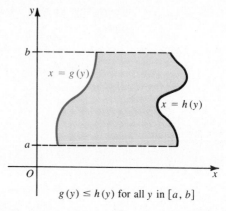

$g(y) \le h(y)$ for all y in $[a, b]$

FIGURE 24

Double Integrals Over Variable Regions

Let $z = f(x, y)$ be a function of two variables.
If R is the region (on the left in Figure 24) defined by $c \le x \le d$, $g(x) \le y \le h(x)$, then

$$\iint\limits_{R} f(x, y) \, dy \, dx = \int_{c}^{d} \left[\int_{g(x)}^{h(x)} f(x, y) \, dy \right] dx.$$

If R is the region (on the right in Figure 24) defined by $g(y) \le x \le h(y)$, $a \le y \le b$, then

$$\iint\limits_{R} f(x, y) \, dx \, dy = \int_{a}^{b} \left[\int_{g(y)}^{h(y)} f(x, y) \, dx \right] dy.$$

EXAMPLE 8

Let R be the region shown in Figure 25, and evaluate

$$\iint\limits_{R} (x + 2y) \, dy \, dx.$$

Region R is bounded by $h(x) = 2x$ and $g(x) = x^2$, with $0 \le x \le 2$. By the first result in the box above,

$$\iint\limits_R (x + 2y) \, dydx = \int_0^2 \int_{x^2}^{2x} (x + 2y) \, dy \, dx$$

$$= \int_0^2 (xy + y^2) \Big]_{x^2}^{2x} \, dx$$

$$= \int_0^2 \left[x(2x) + (2x)^2 - (x \cdot x^2 + (x^2)^2) \right] dx$$

$$= \int_0^2 \left[2x^2 + 4x^2 - (x^3 + x^4) \right] dx$$

$$= \int_0^2 (6x^2 - x^3 - x^4) \, dx$$

$$= \left(2x^3 - \frac{1}{4}x^4 - \frac{1}{5}x^5 \right) \Big]_0^2$$

$$= 2 \cdot 2^3 - \frac{1}{4} \cdot 2^4 - \frac{1}{5} \cdot 2^5 - 0$$

$$= 16 - 4 - \frac{32}{5}$$

$$= \frac{28}{5}. \quad \blacksquare$$

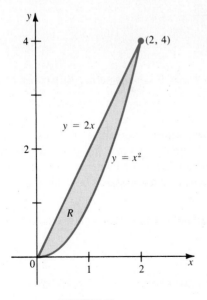

FIGURE 25

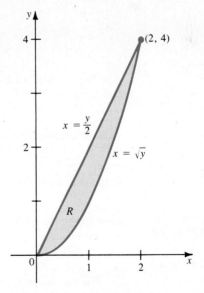

FIGURE 26

EXAMPLE 9

Let R be the region of Figure 26, and evaluate

$$\iint_R (x + 2y) \, dx \, dy.$$

This is the same region shown in Figure 25, with the equations of the boundaries given in terms of x rather than y. That is, R is defined by $y/2 \le x \le \sqrt{y}$, $0 \le y \le 4$, and

$$\iint_R (x + 2y) \, dxdy = \int_0^4 \int_{y/2}^{\sqrt{y}} (x + 2y) \, dx \, dy$$

$$= \int_0^4 \left(\tfrac{1}{2}x^2 + 2xy\right)\Big]_{y/2}^{\sqrt{y}} \, dy$$

$$= \int_0^4 \left[\left(\tfrac{1}{2}(\sqrt{y})^2 + 2(\sqrt{y})\,y - \left(\tfrac{1}{2}\left(\tfrac{1}{2}y\right)^2 + 2\left(\tfrac{1}{2}y\right)y\right)\right)\right] dy$$

$$= \int_0^4 \left[\tfrac{1}{2}y + 2y^{3/2} - \left(\tfrac{1}{8}y^2 + y^2\right)\right] dy$$

$$= \int_0^4 \left[\tfrac{1}{2}y + 2y^{3/2} - \tfrac{9}{8}y^2\right] dy$$

$$= \left(\tfrac{1}{4}y^2 + \tfrac{4}{5}y^{5/2} - \tfrac{3}{8}y^3\right)\Big]_0^4$$

$$= \tfrac{1}{4} \cdot 4^2 + \tfrac{4}{5} \cdot 4^{5/2} - \tfrac{3}{8} \cdot 4^3 - 0$$

$$= 4 + \frac{128}{5} - 24$$

$$= \frac{28}{5}.$$

The answers in Examples 8 and 9 are the same, as we would expect them to be. ■

Interchanging Limits of Integration   Sometimes it is easier to integrate first with respect to x, and then y, while with other integrals the reverse process is easier. The limits of integration can be reversed whenever the region R is like one of the regions in Figure 24. The next example shows how this process works.

EXAMPLE 10

Interchange the limits of integration in

$$\int_0^{16} \int_{\sqrt{y}}^4 f(x, y) \, dx \, dy.$$

For this integral, region R is given by $\sqrt{y} \le x \le 4, 0 \le y \le 16$. A graph of R is shown in Figure 27.

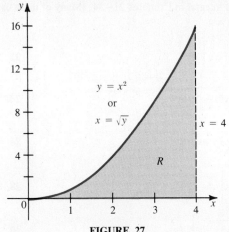

FIGURE 27

The same region R can be written in an alternate way. As Figure 27 shows, one boundary of R is $x = \sqrt{y}$. Solving for y gives $y = x^2$. Also, Figure 27 shows that $0 \le x \le 4$. Since R can be written as $0 \le y \le x^2$, $0 \le x \le 4$, the double integral above can be written

$$\int_0^4 \int_0^{x^2} f(x, y) \, dy \, dx. \quad \blacksquare$$

15.7 EXERCISES

Evaluate the integrals in Exercises 1–20.

1. $\int_0^3 (x^3 y + y) \, dx$

2. $\int_1^4 (xy^2 - x) \, dy$

3. $\int_2^5 (x + y^3 x^2 - 2) \, dy$

4. $\int_1^3 (x^3 - 2x^2 y^2 + 5) \, dx$

5. $\int_4^8 \sqrt{6x + y} \, dx$

6. $\int_3^7 \sqrt{x + 5y} \, dy$

7. $\int_3^6 x\sqrt{x^2 + 3y} \, dx$

8. $\int_4^5 x\sqrt{x^2 + 3y} \, dy$

9. $\int_4^9 \frac{3 + 5y}{\sqrt{x}} \, dx$

10. $\int_2^7 \frac{3 + 5y}{\sqrt{x}} \, dy$

11. $\int_3^5 \frac{6x + 2y}{3x^2 + 2xy} \, dx$

12. $\int_1^4 \frac{30y^2 + 16yx^2}{10y^3 + 8y^2 x^2} \, dy$

13. $\int_{-1}^1 e^{x+4y} \, dy$

14. $\int_2^6 e^{x+4y} \, dx$

15. $\int_0^5 xe^{x^2+9y} \, dx$

16. $\int_1^6 xe^{x^2+9y} \, dy$

17. $\int_0^4 y\sqrt{y^2 + 3x} \, dy$

18. $\int_1^5 y\sqrt{y^2 + 3x} \, dy$

19. $\int_3^6 \frac{10y}{\sqrt{3x + 5y^2}} \, dx$

20. $\int_0^2 \frac{10y}{\sqrt{3x + 5y^2}} \, dy$

Evaluate each iterated integral in Exercises 21–34. (Many of these use results from Exercises 1–20.)

21. $\int_{1}^{2}\left[\int_{0}^{3}(x^3y + y)\,dx\right]dy$

22. $\int_{0}^{3}\left[\int_{1}^{4}(xy^2 - x)\,dy\right]dx$

23. $\int_{-1}^{1}\left[\int_{2}^{5}(x + y^3x^2 - 2)\,dy\right]dx$

24. $\int_{-2}^{2}\left[\int_{1}^{3}(x^3 - 2x^2y^2 + 5)\,dx\right]dy$

25. $\int_{0}^{1}\left[\int_{3}^{6}x\sqrt{x^2 + 3y}\,dx\right]dy$

26. $\int_{0}^{3}\left[\int_{4}^{5}x\sqrt{x^2 + 3y}\,dy\right]dx$

27. $\int_{1}^{2}\left[\int_{4}^{9}\frac{3 + 5y}{\sqrt{x}}\,dx\right]dy$

28. $\int_{16}^{25}\left[\int_{2}^{7}\frac{3 + 5y}{\sqrt{x}}\,dy\right]dx$

29. $\int_{0}^{3}\left[\int_{0}^{4}y\sqrt{y^2 + 3x}\,dy\right]dx$

30. $\int_{0}^{2}\left[\int_{2}^{6}e^{x+4y}\,dx\right]dy$

31. $\int_{1}^{2}\int_{1}^{2}\frac{dx\,dy}{xy}$

32. $\int_{1}^{4}\int_{2}^{5}\frac{dy\,dx}{x}$

33. $\int_{2}^{4}\int_{3}^{5}\left(\frac{x}{y} + \frac{y}{3}\right)dx\,dy$

34. $\int_{3}^{4}\int_{1}^{2}\left(\frac{6x}{5} + \frac{y}{x}\right)dx\,dy$

In Exercises 35–42, find each double integral over the rectangular region R with the given boundaries.

35. $\iint_{R}(x + 3y^2)\,dx\,dy; \quad 0 \le x \le 2, 1 \le y \le 5$

36. $\iint_{R}(4x^3 + y^2)\,dx\,dy; \quad 1 \le x \le 4, 0 \le y \le 2$

37. $\iint_{R}\sqrt{x + y}\,dy\,dx; \quad 1 \le x \le 3, 0 \le y \le 1$

38. $\iint_{R}x^2\sqrt{x^3 + 2y}\,dx\,dy; \quad 0 \le x \le 2, 0 \le y \le 3$

39. $\iint_{R}\frac{2}{(x + y)^2}\,dy\,dx; \quad 2 \le x \le 3, 1 \le y \le 5$

40. $\iint_{R}\frac{y}{\sqrt{6x + 5y^2}}\,dx\,dy; \quad 0 \le x \le 3, 1 \le y \le 2$

41. $\iint_{R}ye^{(x+y^2)}\,dx\,dy; \quad 2 \le x \le 3, 0 \le y \le 2$

42. $\iint_{R}x^2e^{(x^3+2y)}\,dx\,dy; \quad 1 \le x \le 2, 1 \le y \le 3$

Find the volume under the given surface $z = f(x, y)$ and above the rectangle with given boundaries.

43. $z = 6x + 2y + 5; \quad -1 \le x \le 1, 0 \le y \le 3$

44. $z = 9x + 5y + 12; \quad 0 \le x \le 3, -2 \le y \le 1$

45. $z = x^2; \quad 0 \le x \le 1, 0 \le y \le 4$

46. $z = \sqrt{y}; \quad 0 \le x \le 4, 0 \le y \le 9$

47. $z = x\sqrt{x^2 + y}; \quad 0 \le x \le 1, 0 \le y \le 1$

48. $z = yx\sqrt{x^2 + y^2}; \quad 0 \le x \le 4, 0 \le y \le 1$

49. $z = \frac{xy}{(x^2 + y^2)^2}; \quad 1 \le x \le 2, 1 \le y \le 4$

50. $z = e^{x+y}; \quad 0 \le x \le 1, 0 \le y \le 1$

While it is true that a double integral can be evaluated by using either dx or dy first, sometimes one choice over the other makes the work easier. Evaluate the double integrals in Exercises 51 and 52 in the easiest way possible.

51. $\displaystyle\iint_R xe^{xy}\ dx\ dy;\quad 0 \le x \le 2, 0 \le y \le 1$

52. $\displaystyle\iint_R x^2 e^{2x^3+6y}\ dx\ dy;\quad 0 \le x \le 1, 0 \le y \le 1$

Evaluate each double integral in Exercises 53–64.

53. $\displaystyle\int_1^4 \int_0^y (x + 4y)\ dx\ dy$

54. $\displaystyle\int_0^2 \int_1^x (3x + 5y)\ dy\ dx$

55. $\displaystyle\int_2^4 \int_2^{x^2} (x^2 + y^2)\ dy\ dx$

56. $\displaystyle\int_0^5 \int_0^{2y} (x^2 + y)\ dx\ dy$

57. $\displaystyle\int_0^4 \int_0^x \sqrt{xy}\ dy\ dx$

58. $\displaystyle\int_1^4 \int_0^x \sqrt{x + y}\ dy\ dx$

59. $\displaystyle\int_1^2 \int_0^{x^2-1} xy^2\ dy\ dx$

60. $\displaystyle\int_2^4 \int_{1+y}^{2+3y} (x - y^2)\ dx\ dy$

61. $\displaystyle\int_1^2 \int_y^{3y} \frac{1}{x}dx\ dy$

62. $\displaystyle\int_1^4 \int_x^{x^2} \frac{1}{y}dy\ dx$

63. $\displaystyle\int_0^4 \int_1^{e^x} \frac{x}{y}dy\ dx$

64. $\displaystyle\int_0^1 \int_{2x}^{4x} e^{x+y}\ dy\ dx$

Use the region R with the indicated boundaries to evaluate the given double integral.

65. $\displaystyle\iint_R (4x + 7y)\ dy\ dx;\quad 1 \le x \le 3, 0 \le y \le x + 1$

66. $\displaystyle\iint_R (3x + 9y)\ dy\ dx;\quad 2 \le x \le 4, 2 \le y \le 3x$

67. $\displaystyle\iint_R (4 - 4x^2)\ dy\ dx;\quad 0 \le x \le 1, 0 \le y \le 2 - 2x$

68. $\displaystyle\iint_R \frac{dy\ dx}{x};\quad 1 \le x \le 2, 0 \le y \le x - 1$

69. $\displaystyle\iint_R e^{x/y^2}\ dx\ dy;\quad 1 \le y \le 2, 0 \le x \le y^2$

70. $\displaystyle\iint_R (x^2 - y)\ dy\ dx;\quad -1 \le x \le 1, -x^2 \le y \le x^2$

71. $\displaystyle\iint_R x^3 y\ dx\ dy;\quad R \text{ bounded by } y = x^2,\ y = 2x$

72. $\displaystyle\iint_R x^2 y^2\ dx\ dy;\quad R \text{ bounded by } y = x,\ y = 2x,\ x = 1$

73. $\displaystyle\iint_R (x + y)\ dy\ dx;\quad R \text{ bounded by } 4y = x^2,\ x = 2y - 4$

74. $\displaystyle\iint_R xy^2\ dy\ dx;\quad R \text{ bounded by } y = 2x,\ y = 3 - x,\ y = 0$

75. $\displaystyle\iint_R \frac{dy\ dx}{y};\quad R \text{ bounded by } y = x,\ y = \frac{1}{x},\ x = 2$

76. *The Effects of Nuclear Weapons,* prepared by the U.S. Department of Defense, contains these remarks on the computation of the radioactive dose after a 1-kiloton atomic explosion.*

"If all the residues from 1-kiloton fission yield were deposited on a smooth surface in varying concentrations typical of an early fallout pattern, instead of uniformly, the product of the dose rate at 1 hour and the area would be replaced by the "area integral" of the 1-hour dose rate defined by

$$\text{Area Integral} = \int_A R_1 \, dA,$$

where R_1 is the 1-hour dose rate over an element of area dA and A square miles is the total area covered by the residues."

Explain why an integral is involved. (Note that in this case R_1 denotes the function and A the region. In the diverse applications of integrals many notations are employed.)

The idea of the *average value* of a function, discussed earlier for functions of the form $y = f(x)$, can be extended to functions of more than one independent variable. For a function $z = f(x, y)$, the **average value** of f over a region R is defined as

$$\frac{1}{A}\iint\limits_R f(x, y) \, dx \, dy,$$

where A is the area of the region R. Find the average value for the following functions over regions R having the given boundaries.

77. $f(x, y) = x^2 + y^2$; $0 \le x \le 2, 0 \le y \le 3$

78. $f(x, y) = 5xy + 2y$; $1 \le x \le 4, 1 \le y \le 2$

79. $f(x, y) = e^{2x+y}$; $1 \le x \le 2, 2 \le y \le 3$

80. $f(x, y) = e^{-5y+3x}$; $0 \le x \le 2, 0 \le y \le 2$

81. A company's total cost for operating its two warehouses is

$$C(x, y) = \frac{1}{9}x^2 + 2x + y^2 + 5y + 100$$

dollars, where x represents the number of units stored at the first warehouse, and y represents the number of units stored at the second. Find the average cost to store a unit if the first warehouse has between 48 and 75 units, and the second has between 20 and 60 units.

82. A production function is given by

$$P(x, y) = 500x^{0.2}y^{0.8},$$

where x is the number of units of labor and y is the number of units of capital. Find the average production level if x varies between 10 and 50, and y varies from 20 to 40.

KEY WORDS	functions of several variables	surface	**Lagrange multiplier**
	domain	**trace**	**scatter diagram**
	range	**partial derivative**	**least squares line**
	***xy*-plane**	**second-order partial**	**regression line**
	ordered triple	**derivative**	**total differential**
	first octant	**mixed partial derivative**	**iterated integral**
	distance formula	**extrema**	**double integral**
	sphere	**critical point**	**region of integration**
	plane	**constraint**	**volume**

---

*Exercise 76 from *Calculus and Analytic Geometry,* Third Edition, by Sherman K. Stein. Copyright © 1982 by McGraw-Hill, Inc. Reprinted by permission.

Chapter 15   REVIEW EXERCISES

In Exercises 1–4, find $f(-1, 2)$ and $f(6, -3)$.

1. $f(x, y) = -4x^2 + 6xy - 3$

2. $f(x, y) = 3x^2y^2 - 5x + 2y$

3. $f(x, y) = \dfrac{x - 3y}{x + 4y}$

4. $f(x, y) = \dfrac{\sqrt{x^2 + y^2}}{x - y}$

Find the distance between the pairs of points in Exercises 5–8.

5. $(-1, 4, 0)$ and $(2, -1, 3)$

6. $(-2, 1, 5)$ and $(1, 1, 4)$

7. $(0, -2, 5)$ and $(3, 2, -1)$

8. $(5, 0, 3)$ and $(-2, 4, 3)$

9. The number of foxes and birds that can coexist in an area is approximated by

$$N(x, y) = 5x^2 - 3x + y^2 + xy,$$

where x is the average temperature in degrees Celsius and y is the annual rainfall in centimeters. Find

   (a) $N(20, 30)$ **(b)** $N(24, 50)$ **(c)** $N(14, 70)$.

10. The charge for painting a sports car is given by

$$C(x, y) = 2x^2 + 4y^2 - 3xy + \sqrt{x},$$

where x is the number of hours of labor needed, and y is the number of gallons of paint and sealer used. Find

   (a) $C(10, 5)$ **(b)** $C(15, 10)$ **(c)** $C(20, 20)$.

Graph the first octant portion of each plane in Exercises 11–16.

11. $x + y + z = 4$

12. $x + y + 4z = 8$

13. $5x + 2y = 10$

14. $3x + 5z = 15$

15. $x = 3$

16. $y = 2$

Find the center and radius of each sphere in Exercises 17–18.

17. $x^2 - 4x + y^2 + 6y + z^2 - 8z + 20 = 0$

18. $x^2 + 6x + y^2 - 10y + z^2 + 12z + 54 = 0$

19. Let $z = f(x, y) = -5x^2 + 7xy - y^2$. Find

   (a) $\dfrac{\partial z}{\partial x}$ **(b)** $\left(\dfrac{\partial z}{\partial y}\right)(-1, 4)$ **(c)** $f_{xy}(2, -1)$

20. Let $z = f(x, y) = \dfrac{x + y^2}{x - y^2}$. Find

   (a) $\dfrac{\partial z}{\partial y}$ **(b)** $\left(\dfrac{\partial z}{\partial x}\right)(0, 2)$ **(c)** $f_{xx}(-1, 0)$

In Exercises 21–28, find f_x and f_y.

21. $f(x, y) = 9x^3y^2 - 5x$

22. $f(x, y) = 6x^5y - 8xy^9$

23. $f(x, y) = \sqrt{4x^2 + y^2}$

24. $f(x, y) = \dfrac{2x + 5y^2}{3x^2 + y^2}$

25. $f(x, y) = x^2 \cdot e^{2y}$

26. $f(x, y) = (y - 2)^2 \cdot e^{(x+2y)}$

27. $f(x, y) = \ln|2x^2 + y^2|$

28. $f(x, y) = \ln|2 - x^2y^3|$

In Exercises 29–36, find f_{xx} and f_{xy}.

29. $f(x, y) = 4x^3y^2 - 8xy$

30. $f(x, y) = -6xy^4 + x^2y$

31. $f(x, y) = \dfrac{2x}{x - 2y}$

32. $f(x, y) = \dfrac{3x + y}{x - 1}$

33. $f(x, y) = x^2 e^y$

34. $f(x, y) = y e^{x^2}$

35. $f(x, y) = \ln|2 - x^2 y|$

36. $f(x, y) = \ln|1 + 3xy^2|$

37. The production function z for one country is

$$z = x^{0.6} y^{0.4},$$

where x represents the amount of labor and y the amount of capital. Find the marginal productivity of

(a) labor   **(b)** capital.

38. The manufacturing cost for a medium-sized business computer is given by

$$c(x, y) = 2x + y^2 + 4xy + 25,$$

where x is the memory capacity of the computer in kilobytes and y is the number of hours of labor required. Find

(a) $\dfrac{\partial c}{\partial x}(64, 6)$ **(b)** $\dfrac{\partial c}{\partial y}(128, 12)$.

Find all points where the functions in Exercises 39–46 have any relative extrema. Find any saddle points.

39. $z = x^2 + 2y^2 - 4y$

40. $z = x^2 + y^2 + 9x - 8y + 1$

41. $f(x, y) = x^2 + 5xy - 10x + 3y^2 - 12y$

42. $z = x^3 - 8y^2 + 6xy + 4$

43. $z = \dfrac{1}{2}x^2 + \dfrac{1}{2}y^2 + 2xy - 5x - 7y + 10$

44. $f(x, y) = 3x^2 + 2xy + 2y^2 - 3x + 2y - 9$

45. $z = x^3 + y^2 + 2xy - 4x - 3y - 2$

46. $f(x, y) = 7x^2 + y^2 - 3x + 6y - 5xy$

The total cost to manufacture x solar cells and y solar collectors is

$$c(x, y) = x^2 + 5y^2 + 4xy - 70x - 164y + 1800.$$

47. Find values of x and y that produce minimum total cost.

48. Find the minimum total cost.

In Exercises 49–56, use Lagrange multipliers to find the extrema of the functions, subject to the given constraints.

49. $f(x, y) = x^2 y$; $x + y = 4$

50. $f(x, y) = x^2 + y^2$; $x = y + 2$

51. $z = 3x^2 - 2y^2$; $y - 5x = 0$

52. $z = x^2 + 2xy + 2y^2$; $x + y = 1$

53. Find two numbers x and y whose sum is 80 such that $x^2 y$ is maximized.

54. Find two numbers x and y whose sum is 50 such that xy^2 is maximized.

55. A closed box with square ends must have a volume of 125 cubic inches. Find the dimensions of such a box that has minimum surface area.

56. Find the maximum rectangular area that can be enclosed with 400 feet of fencing, if no fencing is needed along one side.

57. **(a)** Find the least squares line for the following data.

x	3	5	7	8
y	4	11	20	23

(b) Predict y when x is 6.

58. The following data show the connection between blood sugar levels, x, and cholesterol levels, y, for 8 different diabetic patients.

Patient	1	2	3	4	5	6	7	8
Blood sugar level, x	130	138	142	159	165	200	210	250
Cholesterol level, y	170	160	173	181	201	192	240	290

For this data, $\Sigma x = 1394$, $\Sigma y = 1607$, $\Sigma xy = 291{,}990$, $\Sigma x^2 = 255{,}214$, and $\Sigma y^2 = 336{,}155$.

(a) Find the equation of the least squares line.

(b) Predict the cholesterol level for a person whose blood sugar level is 190.

Find dz or dw, as appropriate, for each function in Exercises 59–66.

59. $z = 6x^3 - 10y^2$

60. $z = 7x^3y - 4y^3$

61. $z = \dfrac{x - 2y}{x + 2y}$

62. $z = 3x^2 + \sqrt{x + y}$

63. $z = x^2 y e^{x-y}$

64. $z = \ln|x + 4y| + y^2 \ln|x|$

65. $w = x^5 + y^4 - z^3$

66. $w = \dfrac{3 + 5xy}{2 - z}$

In Exercises 67–68, evaluate dz using the given functions and values.

67. $z = 2x^2 - 4y^2 + 6xy$; $x = 2$, $y = -3$, $dx = .01$, $dy = .05$

68. $z = \dfrac{x + 5y}{x - 2y}$; $x = 1$, $y = -2$, $dx = -.04$, $dy = .02$

69. Approximate the amount of material needed for a cone of radius 2 cm, height 8 cm, and wall thickness of .21 cm.

70. A sphere of radius 2 feet is to receive an insulating coating 1 inch thick. Approximate the volume of the coating needed.

71. A length of blood vessel is measured as 2.7 cm, with the radius measured as .7 cm. If each of these measurements could be off by .1 cm, estimate the maximum possible error in the volume of the vessel.

72. The height of a cone is measured as 11.4 cm, while the radius is measured as 2.9 cm. Each of these measurements could be off by .2 cm. Approximate the maximum possible error in the volume of the cone.

Evaluate each of the following.

73. $\displaystyle\int_0^4 (x^2y^2 + 5x)\,dx$

74. $\displaystyle\int_0^3 (x + 5y + y^2)\,dy$

75. $\displaystyle\int_2^5 \sqrt{6x + 3y}\,dx$

76. $\displaystyle\int_1^3 6y^4\sqrt{8x + 3y}\,dx$

77. $\displaystyle\int_4^9 \dfrac{6y - 8}{\sqrt{x}}\,dx$

78. $\displaystyle\int_3^5 e^{2x-7y}\,dx$

79. $\displaystyle\int_0^5 \dfrac{6x}{\sqrt{4x^2 + 2y^2}}\,dx$

80. $\displaystyle\int_1^3 \dfrac{y^2}{\sqrt{7x + 11y^3}}\,dy$

Evaluate each iterated integral in Exercises 81–86.

81. $\int_0^2 \left[\int_0^4 (x^2 y^2 + 5x) \, dx \right] dy$

82. $\int_0^2 \left[\int_0^3 (x + 5y + y^2) \, dy \right] dx$

83. $\int_3^4 \left[\int_2^5 \sqrt{6x + 3y} \, dx \right] dy$

84. $\int_1^2 \left[\int_3^5 e^{2x-7y} \, dx \right] dy$

85. $\int_2^4 \int_2^4 \frac{dx \, dy}{y}$

86. $\int_1^2 \int_1^2 \frac{dx \, dy}{x}$

In Exercises 87–90, find each double integral over the region R with boundaries as indicated.

87. $\iint_R (x^2 + y^2) \, dx \, dy; \quad 0 \le x \le 2, 0 \le y \le 3$

88. $\iint_R \sqrt{2x + y} \, dx \, dy; \quad 1 \le x \le 3, 2 \le y \le 5$

89. $\iint_R \sqrt{y + x} \, dx \, dy; \quad 0 \le x \le 7, 1 \le y \le 9$

90. $\iint_R y \, e^{(y^2+x)} \, dx \, dy; \quad 0 \le x \le 1, 0 \le y \le 1$

Find the volume under the given surface $z = f(x, y)$ and above the given rectangle.

91. $z = x + 9y + 8; \quad 1 \le x \le 6, 0 \le y \le 8$

92. $z = x^2 + y^2; \quad 3 \le x \le 5, 2 \le y \le 4$

Evaluate each double integral in Exercises 93–96.

93. $\int_0^1 \int_0^{2x} xy \, dy \, dx$

94. $\int_0^1 \int_0^{x^3} y \, dy \, dx$

95. $\int_0^1 \int_{x^2}^{x} x^3 y \, dy \, dx$

96. $\int_0^1 \int_y^{\sqrt{y}} x \, dx \, dy$

In Exercises 97 and 98, use the region R, with boundaries as indicated, to evaluate the given double integral.

97. $\iint_R (2x + 3y) \, dx \, dy; \quad 0 \le y \le 1, y \le x \le 2 - y$

98. $\iint_R (2 - x^2 - y^2) \, dy \, dx; \quad 0 \le x \le 1, x^2 \le y \le x$

PROBABILITY AND CALCULUS

Karl Gerstner. From the series *Aperspective 1* (The Endless Spiral at a Right Angle), 1952–1956.

Probability has become an increasingly useful tool in a variety of fields—for example, in manufacturing, government, agriculture, medicine, the social and life sciences—and in all types of research. In this chapter we give a brief introduction to the use of calculus in probability.

16.1   Finite Probability Models

In families with four children the possible number of boys may be any of the numbers 0, 1, 2, 3, or 4. Because the occurrence of a boy on any birth is a random event, the number of boys in a four-child family is a *random variable*.

Random Variable

> A **random variable** is a function that assigns a real number to each outcome of an experiment.

Upper case letters, such as X or Y, are used for random variables. Lower case letters, such as x or y, represent a particular value of the random variable.

Suppose that at each birth, the probability of a boy is somewhat greater than .5 (which is actually the case), and that Table 1 gives the probabilities for the number of boys in a four-child family.

Table 1

Number of Boys X	Probability $P(X)$
0	.06
1	.24
2	.37
3	.26
4	.07

A table that gives a set of outcomes, along with the corresponding probabilities (like Table 1), is a **probability distribution.** The sum of the probabilities in a probability distribution must always be 1, since at least one of the outcomes must occur.

Instead of writing in a table the probability distribution of the number of boys in a four-child family, the same information could be written as a set of ordered pairs:

$$\{(0, .06), (1, .24), (2, .37), (3, .26), (4, .07)\}.$$

Because each value of the random variable has just one probability, a probability distribution defines a function, called a **probability distribution function,** or simply a **probability function.** The special properties of a probability function are given in the box.

Probability Function of a Random Variable

If $f(x)$ is a probability function with domain $\{x_1, x_2, \ldots, x_n\}$, then for $1 \le i \le n$,

$$0 \le f(x_i) \le 1,$$

and

$$f(x_1) + f(x_2) + \cdots + f(x_n) = 1.$$

We shall use the terms "probability distribution" and "probability function" interchangeably. The function described above is a *discrete* function, since it has a finite number of ordered pairs. A *continuous* probability function has an infinite number of values of the random variable, corresponding to an interval on the number line. Continuous probability functions are discussed in the next three sections.

The information in a discrete probability distribution is often displayed graphically with a special kind of bar graph called a **histogram.** The bars of a histogram all have the same width. The heights of the bars are determined by the frequencies. A histogram for the data of Table 1 is shown in Figure 1. A histogram often shows important characteristics of a distribution which may not be evident in tabular form. For example, a histogram shows at a glance the relative sizes of the probabilities and any symmetry in the distribution.

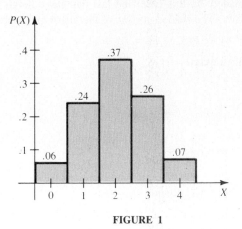

FIGURE 1

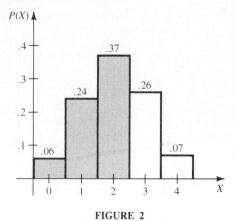

FIGURE 2

The area of the bar above $X = 1$ in Figure 1 is given by the product of 1 and .24, or .24 $\times$ 1 = .24. Since each bar has a width of 1, its area is equal to the probability that corresponds to the value of X. The total area of the five bars is 1, the sum of the five probabilities. The probability of fewer than three boys in a four-child family, for example, is given by the sum of the areas for $X = 0$, $X = 1$, and $X = 2$. This area, which is shaded in Figure 2, corresponds to 67% of the total area, since

$$P(X < 3) = P(X = 0) + P(X = 1) + P(X = 2)$$
$$= .06 + .24 + .37 = .67.$$

EXAMPLE 1

In an experiment to determine how the common cold is transmitted, 10 groups of 5 volunteers each were given nasal injections of cold viruses. The random variable is the number in each group (from 0 to 5) who caught cold. The results are given in Table 2; the probabilities were determined by the relative frequencies of the outcomes.

Table 2

Number who Caught Cold	Frequency	Probability
0	1	.1
1	2	.2
2	3	.3
3	3	.3
4	1	.1
5	0	0

Sketch a histogram for this data. Then show the area which gives the probability that the number of colds will be more than 2.

A histogram for this distribution is shown in Figure 3. Since

$$P(X > 2) = P(X = 3) + P(X = 4) + P(X = 5),$$

the last three bars should be shaded. In this case, the last bar has a height of 0, and adds nothing to the probability. The shaded portion of the histogram represents

$$P(X = 3) + P(X = 4) + P(X = 5) = .3 + .1 + 0 = .4,$$

or 40% of the total area of the histogram. ■

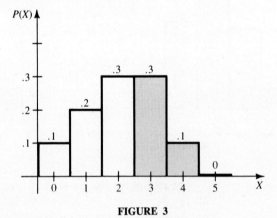

FIGURE 3

Expected Value In working with experimental data, it is often useful to have a single number, a typical or "average" number, which is representative of the entire set of data. Just about everyone is familiar with some type of average. For example, we compare our heights and weights to those of the typical or "average" person on weight charts. Students are familiar with the "class average" and their own "average" at any time in a given course.

The **arithmetic mean,** or **average,** of a set of numbers is the sum of all the numbers in the set, divided by the total number of numbers in the set. To write the sum of the n numbers $x_1, x_2, x_3, \ldots, x_n$ in a compact way, it is customary to use the *summation notation* presented earlier: using the Greek letter Σ (sigma), the sum $x_1 + x_2 + x_3 + \cdots + x_n$ is written

$$x_1 + x_2 + x_3 + \cdots + x_n = \sum_{i=1}^{n} x_i.$$

The Greek letter μ (mu) is used to represent the mean, so that the mean of the n numbers $x_1, x_2, x_3, \cdots, x_n$ is

$$\mu = \frac{\sum_{i=1}^{n} x_i}{n}.$$

This formula for the mean is sometimes abbreviated

$$\mu = \frac{\Sigma x}{n}.$$

For example, the mean of the set of numbers 2, 3, 5, 6, 8 is

$$\frac{2 + 3 + 5 + 6 + 8}{5} = \frac{24}{5} = 4.8.$$

If the random variable X takes the values $x_1, x_2, x_3, \ldots, x_n$ with equal probability, then the probability of each x_i is $1/n$. The average value is the mean

$$\mu = \frac{\Sigma x}{n} = \frac{x_1 + x_2 + x_3 + \cdots + x_n}{n}$$

$$= x_1 \cdot \frac{1}{n} + x_2 \cdot \frac{1}{n} + x_3 \cdot \frac{1}{n} + \cdots + x_n \cdot \frac{1}{n}.$$

This result shows that an average or *expected value* for a random variable is found by multiplying each value of the random variable by its corresponding probability. If the probabilities are different, the result is generalized as follows.

Expected Value

Suppose the random variable X can take on the n values $x_1, x_2, x_3, \cdots, x_n$. Also, suppose the probabilities that each of these values occurs are respectively $p_1, p_2, p_3, \cdots, p_n$. Then the **expected value** of the random variable is

$$E(X) = x_1 p_1 + x_2 p_2 + x_3 p_3 + \cdots + x_n p_n = \sum_{i=1}^{n} x_i p_i.$$

Since the expected value is the mean of the distribution, the symbol μ is also used for the expected value of the random variable X. The expected value of a random variable may be a number which can never occur on any one trial of the experiment; it gives the theoretical result of averaging the outcomes of a great many trials.

EXAMPLE 2

Find the expected number of colds per group of five in the distribution of Example 1.

Using the values of X and their corresponding probabilities from Table 2 in the definition of expected value gives

$$\mu = E(X) = 0(.1) + 1(.2) + 2(.3) + 3(.3) + 4(.1) + 5(0)$$

$$= 2.1,$$

so the expected value, or average number of colds per group of five, is 2.1. ∎

EXAMPLE 3

Find the expected value of the number of boys in a four-child family using the probability distribution given in Table 1.

By the definition of expected value, the expected number of boys is

$$\mu = 0(.06) + 1(.24) + 2(.37) + 3(.26) + 4(.07) = 2.04.$$

As mentioned above, this number represents the average number of boys in a large number of four-child families. ∎

Variance   The mean or expected value of a probability distribution gives an average value for the distribution, but tells nothing about the *spread* of the values in the distribution. For example, look at the two distributions I and II.

I		II	
x_i	p_i	x_i	p_i
3	.6	0	.4
5	.2	1	.2
6	.2	9	.2
		10	.2

Each distribution has a mean of 4.0, yet the distributions are quite different; the dispersion or variation of the values of the random variable differs. In addition to the expected value we need a number which describes the variation of the numbers in a probability distribution.

One way to measure the variation within a set of numbers might be to find the average of their distances from the expected value. That is, if the numbers are $x_1, x_2, \ldots, x_n$ and the expected value is μ, find the differences $x_1 - \mu$, $x_2 - \mu$, $\ldots, x_n - \mu$, and then find the expected value of the differences. However, it turns out that the sum of these differences is always 0, so that the expected value also would be 0, and would not be a good measure of the variability of a distribution.

A simple example illustrates why the sum is 0. The values of a random variable with $\mu = 4$ are given in Table 3. The table also shows the differences between each value of X and the mean μ. Because of the way μ is calculated, the sum of the negative entries equals the sum of the positive entries, so the sum of all entries is always 0.

A useful measure of variability can be found by *squaring* the differences from the mean, as in the third column of Table 3.

Table 3

x_i	$x_i - \mu$	$(x_i - \mu)^2$
2	-2	4
3	-1	1
4	0	0
5	1	1
6	2	4
Totals:	0	10

The expected value of the squares of the differences is called the *variance* of the probability distribution. If X is the random variable for the distribution, then the variance is written Var(X). The variance gives a measure of the variation of the numbers in the distribution and is useful for comparing two distributions. However, since *squared* differences are used to get it, the size of the variance does not reflect the actual amount of variation. To correct this problem, another measure of variation is used, the *standard deviation,* the square root of the variance. The symbol σ (the Greek lower case sigma) is used for standard deviation.

Variance and

Standard Deviation

If a random variable X takes on the n values $x_1, x_2, x_3, \cdots, x_n$ with respective probabilities $p_1, p_2, p_3, \cdots, p_n$, and if the expected value of X is $E(X) = \mu$, then the **variance** of X is

$$\text{Var}(X) = \sum p_i(x_i - \mu)^2.$$

The **standard deviation** of X is

$$\sigma = \sqrt{\text{Var}(X)}.$$

EXAMPLE 4

Find the variance and standard deviation of distributions I and II.

I		II	
x_i	p_i	x_i	p_i
3	.6	0	.4
5	.2	1	.2
6	.2	9	.2
		10	.2

Recall that the mean of both distributions is 4. For distribution I, the variance is

$$V(X) = (3 - 4)^2(.6) + (5 - 4)^2(.2) + (6 - 4)^2(.2)$$
$$= .6 + .2 + .8 = 1.6,$$

and the standard deviation is

$$\sigma = \sqrt{1.6} \approx 1.26.$$

For distribution II, the variance is

$$V(X) = (0 - 4)^2(.4) + (1 - 4)^2(.2) + (9 - 4)^2(.2) + (10 - 4)^2(.2)$$
$$= 6.4 + 1.8 + 5.0 + 7.2 = 20.4,$$

and the standard deviation is

$$\sigma = \sqrt{20.4} \approx 4.52.$$

The second distribution has the larger standard deviation, indicating the greater dispersion of the values of the random variable in that distribution. The histograms of the two distributions in Figure 4 also show this difference. ■

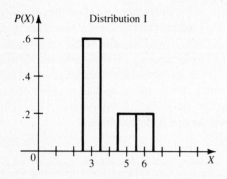
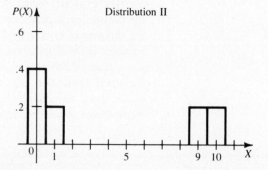

FIGURE 4

EXAMPLE 5

Find the variance and the standard deviation of the following probability distribution.

x_i	p_i
0	.08
1	.14
2	.29
3	.32
4	.17

The expected value of the distribution is

$$\mu = 0(.08) + 1(.14) + 2(.29) + 3(.32) + 4(.17) = 2.36.$$

To use the formula for variance it is easiest to work in columns as shown in Table 4.

Table 4

x_i	p_i	$x_i - \mu$	$(x_i - \mu)^2$	$p_i(x_i - \mu)^2$
0	.08	−2.36	5.57	.45
1	.14	−1.36	1.85	.26
2	.29	−.36	.13	.04
3	.32	.64	.41	.13
4	.17	1.64	2.69	.46
				$\mathrm{Var}(X) = 1.34$

The total of the last column gives the variance, 1.34. To find the standard deviation, take the square root of the variance.

$$\sigma = \sqrt{1.34} \approx 1.16 \quad \blacksquare$$

EXAMPLE 6

Find the variance and standard deviation of the number of colds in the distribution of Example 1, shown in Table 2.

From Example 2, we have $\mu = 2.1$. Table 5 shows the steps in calculating the value of $\displaystyle\sum_{i=1}^{6} p_i(x_i - \mu)^2$.

Table 5

x_i	p_i	$x_i - \mu$	$(x_i - \mu)^2$	$p_i(x_i - \mu)^2$
0	.1	−2.1	4.41	.441
1	.2	−1.1	1.21	.242
2	.3	−.1	.01	.003
3	.3	.9	.81	.243
4	.1	1.9	3.61	.361
5	0	2.9	8.41	0
			Var(X) =	1.290

The variance is 1.290 and the standard deviation is

$$\sigma = \sqrt{1.290} \approx 1.14. \quad \blacksquare$$

16.1 EXERCISES

For the probability distributions in Exercises 1–6, **(a)** draw a histogram; **(b)** find the expected value; **(c)** find the standard deviation.

1.

X	4	5	6	7	8
$P(X)$	.1	0	.2	.5	.2

2.

Y	10	11	12	13	14
$P(Y)$	.1	.1	.4	.3	.1

3.

Z	1	2	3	4	5	6
$P(Z)$	.2	.2	.3	.2	0	.1

4.

X	3	4	5	6	7	8
$P(X)$	.05	0	.23	.34	.28	.10

5.

Y	10	11	12	13	14
$P(Y)$	.12	.24	.18	.31	.15

6.

Z	21	22	23	24	25	26
$P(Z)$	.48	0	0	.36	.12	.04

Find the expected value and standard deviation for the random variables X having the probability functions graphed in Exercises 7–10.

7.

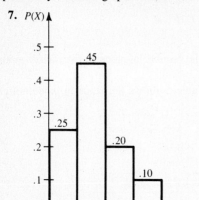

8.

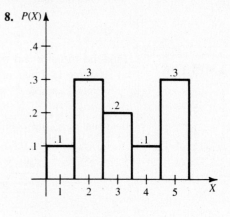

9.

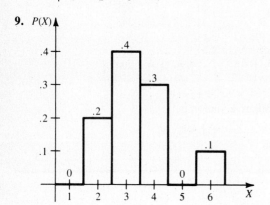

10.

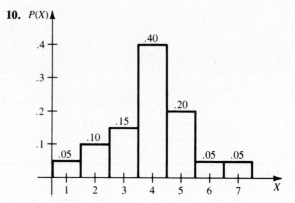

Exercises 11 and 12 give histograms of two probability distributions. Decide from the graphs without any calculations which distribution—**(a)** or **(b)**—has the greater variance.

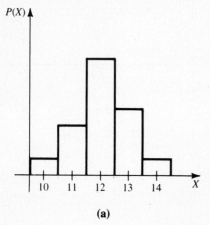

(a)

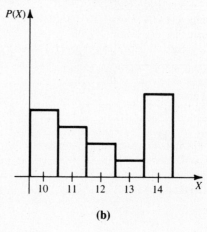

(b)

12.

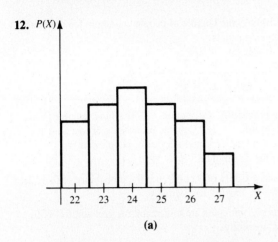

(a)

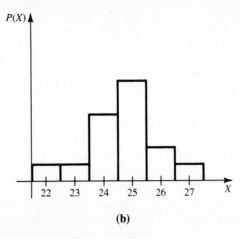

(b)

13. A basketball player with a free-throw shooting average of .6 gets a two-shot foul. Her probabilities of getting 0, 1, or 2 points respectively are .16, .48, and .36.

(a) What is her probability of scoring at least one point?   (b) What is the expected number of points?   (c) What is the standard deviation?

14. Four blood cells are selected randomly from plasma with red and white blood cells. The number of red blood cells is observed. The probabilities of getting 0, 1, 2, 3, or 4 red blood cells are .1, .2, .4, .2, and .1, respectively.

(a) What is the probability of getting at most 2 red blood cells?   (b) What is the expected number of red blood cells?   (c) What is the standard deviation?

15. In a laboratory experiment 4 mice are drawn from a cage containing 5 white and 5 brown mice. The probability of 0, 1, 2, 3, or 4 white mice in the sample is 1/42, 5/21, 10/21, 5/21, and 1/42, respectively.

(a) Find the probability of at least 2 white mice in the sample.   (b) Find the probability of 2 or 3 white mice in the sample.   (c) Find the expected number of white mice in the sample.   (d) Find the standard deviation of the distribution.

16. An office force consists of 6 women and 4 men. Three people from the group are selected at random to go to a conference. The probabilities of 0, 1, 2, or 3 men being selected are .1667, .5, .3, and .0333, respectively.

(a) Find the probability that at least one man is in the group.   (b) Find the probability that no more than one woman is in the group.   (c) Find the expected number of men in the group.   (d) Find the standard deviation of the distribution.

17. A class of 36 students received the following scores on a 10-point quiz.

Number of Points	4	5	6	7	8	9	10
Frequency	1	0	4	10	13	6	2

(a) Use the frequencies to write a probability distribution.   (b) Find the probability of getting 8 or more on the quiz.   (c) Find the probability of getting less than 6 on the quiz.   (d) Find the expected score on the quiz.   (e) Find the standard deviation of the distribution.

18. For a survey taken in a medical building, the number of people waiting in ten doctors' offices were counted with the following results.

Number Waiting	0	1	2	3	4
Frequency	2	4	3	0	1

(a) Use the frequencies to write a probability distribution.   (b) Find the probability of more than 2 people in a waiting room.   (c) Find the probability of less than 1 person in a waiting room.   (d) Find the expected number of people waiting. (e) Find the standard deviation of the distribution.

19. Find the expected number of boys in a family of 3 children if the probability of 0, 1, 2, or 3 boys in the family is 1/8, 3/8, 3/8, and 1/8, respectively.

20. Find the expected number of heads if 2 fair coins are tossed and the probabilities of 0, 1, or 2 heads are 1/4, 1/2, and 1/4, respectively.

21. Find the expected number of spots showing if 2 fair dice are rolled, given the following distribution.

X	2	3	4	5	6	7	8	9	10	11	12
$P(X)$	$\dfrac{1}{36}$	$\dfrac{1}{18}$	$\dfrac{1}{12}$	$\dfrac{1}{9}$	$\dfrac{5}{36}$	$\dfrac{1}{6}$	$\dfrac{5}{36}$	$\dfrac{1}{9}$	$\dfrac{1}{12}$	$\dfrac{1}{18}$	$\dfrac{1}{36}$

22. Find the expected number of kings if 3 cards are drawn from a deck of 52 cards and the probabilities of 0, 1, 2, or 3 kings being drawn are .783, .204, .013, and .000, respectively.

23. Find the expected number of white marbles if 3 marbles are drawn from a jar with 4 white and 5 black marbles, and the probability of 0, 1, 2, or 3 white marbles is 5/42, 10/21, 5/14, and 1/21, respectively.

24. Find the expected number of black marbles in the experiment of Exercise 23, if the probability of 0, 1, 2, or 3 black marbles is 1/21, 5/14, 10/21, and 5/42, respectively.

25. In a study of amounts paid out, an insurance company found that it had $500,000 of insurance on a person with probability .05 of dying, $250,000 of insurance on a person with probability .50 of dying, and $100,000 of insurance on a person with probability .45 of dying. What is the expected pay-out on these policies?

26. A contest offers a first prize worth $1000, a second prize worth $500, and three third prizes worth $100 each. Find the expected winnings for one entry if 10,000 entries are received.

16.2 Continuous Probability Models

In the last section we discussed discrete probability distribution functions with finite domains. Many distributions, however, have infinite domains. For example, the distribution of heights (in inches) of college women includes infinitely many possible measurements, such as 53, 58 1/2, 66.5, 72.33. . ., and so on. Distributions with infinite domains are called *continuous probability distributions*.

Continuous Probability Distribution

> A **continuous random variable** can take on any value in some interval of real numbers. The distribution of this random variable is called a **continuous probability distribution.**

For example, suppose that a study of bank transaction times is made, and the time spent on each transaction, to the nearest minute, is as shown in Table 6.

Table 6

Time	1	2	3	4	5	6	7	8	9	10	
Frequency	3	5	9	12	15	11	10	6	3	1	(Total: 75)
Probability	.04	.07	.12	.16	.20	.15	.13	.08	.04	.01	

It would have been possible to time the transactions more accurately—to the nearest tenth of a minute or even to the nearest second (1/60th of a minute) if desired. Theoretically, at least, the transaction times t could take on any positive real-number value (between, say, 0 and 11 minutes). This allows us to think of the graph of the relative frequency of transaction times as the continuous curve shown in Figure 5. As indicated in Figure 5, the curve was derived from Table 6 by connecting the points at the top of the bars in the corresponding histogram and smoothing the resulting polygon into a curve.

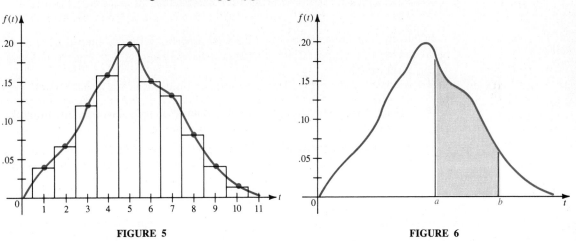

FIGURE 5   **FIGURE 6**

For a discrete probability function, the area of each bar (or rectangle) gives the probability of a particular transaction time. Thus, if we prefer to think of the possible transaction times as all the real numbers between 0 and 11, the area under the curve of Figure 6 between any two values of T can be interpreted as the probability that a transaction time will be between those two numbers. For example, the shaded region in Figure 6 corresponds to the probability that T is between a and b, written $P(a \leq T \leq b)$.

We have seen that the definite integral of a continuous function $f(x)$, where $f(x) \geq 0$, gives the area under the graph of $f(x)$ from $x = a$ to $x = b$. If a function $f(x)$ can be found to describe a continuous probability function, then the definite integral can be used to find the area under the curve from a to b. Since that area represents the probability that X will be between a and b,

$$P(a \leq X \leq b) = \int_a^b f(x) \, dx.$$

A function $f(x)$ which describes a continuous probability distribution is called a *probability density function*. Such a function must satisfy the conditions given in the next box.

Probability Density Function

The function $f(x)$ is a **probability density function** of a random variable X with x in the interval $[a, b]$, if

1. $\int_a^b f(x) \, dx = 1$,   and

2. $f(x) \geq 0$ for all x in the interval $[a, b]$.

Intuitively, condition (1) says that the total probability for the interval must be 1; *something* must happen. Condition (2) says that the probability of a particular event can never be negative.

EXAMPLE 1

(a) Show that $f(x) = (3/26)x^2$ is a probability density function for the interval $[1, 3]$.

First, show that condition 1 holds.

$$\int_1^3 \frac{3}{26}x^2 \, dx = \frac{3}{26}\left(\frac{x^3}{3}\right)\Bigg]_1^3 = \frac{3}{26}\left(9 - \frac{1}{3}\right) = 1$$

Next, show that $f(x) \geq 0$ for the interval $[1, 3]$. Since x^2 is always positive, condition (2) also holds, making $f(x)$ a probability density function.

(b) Find the probability that x will be between 1 and 2.

The desired probability is given by the area under the graph of $f(x)$ between $x = 1$ and $x = 2$ as shown in Figure 7. The area is found by using a definite integral.

$$P(1 \leq X \leq 2) = \int_1^2 \frac{3}{26}x^2 \, dx = \frac{3}{26}\left(\frac{x^3}{3}\right)\Bigg]_1^2 = \frac{7}{26} \quad \blacksquare$$

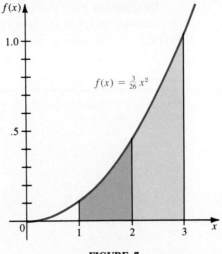

FIGURE 7

EXAMPLE 2

Is $f(x) = 3x^2$ a probability density function for the interval $[0, 4]$? If not, convert it to one.

First,

$$\int_0^4 3x^2 \, dx = x^3 \Big]_0^4 = 64.$$

Since the integral is not equal to 1, the function is not a probability density function. To convert it to one, multiply $f(x)$ by $\frac{1}{64}$. The function $\frac{3}{64}x^2$ for $[0, 4]$ will be a probability density function since

$$\int_0^4 \frac{3}{64}x^2 = 1,$$

and $\frac{3}{64}x^2 \geq 0$ for all x in $[0, 4]$. ▨

An important distinction is made between a discrete probability distribution and a probability density function (which is continuous). In a discrete distribution, the probability that the random variable X will assume a specific value is given in the distribution for every possible value of X. However, in a probability density function, the probability that X equals a specific value, say c, is

$$P(X = c) = \int_c^c f(x) \, dx = 0.$$

For a probability density function, only probabilities of *intervals* can be found. For example, suppose the random variable is the annual rainfall for a given area. The amount of rainfall in one year can take on any value within some continuous interval which depends on the area. However, the probability that the rainfall in a given year will be some specific amount, say 33.25 inches, is actually zero.

The definition of a probability density function given above is extended to intervals such as $(-\infty, b]$, $[a, \infty)$, or $(-\infty, \infty)$ by using improper integrals as follows.

Probability Density

Functions on

$(-\infty, \infty)$

If $f(x)$ is a probability density function for a continuous random variable X on $(-\infty, \infty)$, then

$$P(x \le b) = \int_{-\infty}^{b} f(x) \, dx,$$

$$P(x \ge a) = \int_{a}^{\infty} f(x) \, dx,$$

$$P(-\infty \le x \le \infty) = \int_{-\infty}^{\infty} f(x) \, dx.$$

The total area under the graph of a probability density function of this type must still equal 1.

EXAMPLE 3

Suppose the random variable X is the distance (in kilometers) from a given point to the nearest bird's nest, with the probability density function of the distribution given by $f(x) = 2xe^{-x^2}$ for $x \ge 0$.

(a) Show that $f(x)$ is a probability density function.

Since $e^{-x^2} = 1/e^{x^2}$ is always positive, and $x \ge 0$,

$$f(x) = 2xe^{-x^2} \ge 0.$$

Use substitution to evaluate the definite integral $\int_{0}^{\infty} 2xe^{-x^2} \, dx$. Let $u = -x^2$, so that $du = -2x \, dx$, and

$$\int 2xe^{-x^2} \, dx = -\int e^{-x^2}(-2x \, dx) = -\int e^u \, du = -e^u = -e^{-x^2}.$$

Then $\int_{0}^{\infty} 2xe^{-x^2} \, dx = \lim_{a \to \infty} \int_{0}^{a} 2xe^{-x^2} \, dx = \lim_{a \to \infty}(-e^{-x^2}) \Big]_{0}^{a}$

$$= \lim_{a \to \infty}\left(-\frac{1}{e^{a^2}} + e^0\right) = 0 + 1 = 1$$

The function $f(x) = 2xe^{-x^2}$ satisfies the two conditions required of a probability density function.

(b) Find the probability that there is a bird's nest within 0.5 kilometers of the given point.

We want $P(X \leq 0.5)$ where $x \geq 0$. This probability is given by

$$P(0 \leq X \leq 0.5) = \int_0^{0.5} 2xe^{-x^2} \, dx.$$

Now evalute the integral.

$$P(0 \leq X \leq 0.5) = \int_0^{0.5} 2xe^{-x^2} \, dx = (-e^{-x^2}) \Big]_0^{0.5}$$

$$= -e^{-(0.5)^2} - (-e^0) = -e^{-.25} + 1$$

$$\approx -.78 + 1 = .22$$

There is a 22% chance of a bird's nest within 0.5 kilometers of the point.

16.2 EXERCISES

Decide if the functions in Exercises 1–10 are probability density functions on the indicated intervals. If not, tell why.

1. $f(x) = \frac{1}{9}x - \frac{1}{18}, [2, 5]$

2. $f(x) = \frac{1}{3}x - \frac{1}{6}, [3, 4]$

3. $f(x) = \frac{3}{63}x^2, [1, 4]$

4. $f(x) = \frac{3}{98}x^2, [3, 5]$

5. $f(x) = 4x^3, [0, 3]$

6. $f(x) = \frac{x^3}{81}, [0, 3]$

7. $f(x) = \frac{x^2}{16}, [-2, 2]$

8. $f(x) = 2x^2, [-1, 1]$

9. $f(x) = 2x, [-2, \sqrt{5}]$

10. $f(x) = 4x^3, [-1, \sqrt[4]{2}]$

For Exercises 11–20, find a value of k which will make $f(x)$ a probability density function on the indicated interval.

11. $f(x) = kx^{1/2}, [1, 4]$

12. $f(x) = kx^{3/2}, [4, 9]$

13. $f(x) = kx^2, [0, 5]$

14. $f(x) = kx^2, [-1, 2]$

15. $f(x) = kx, [0, 3]$

16. $f(x) = kx, [2, 3]$

17. $f(x) = kx, [1, 5]$

18. $f(x) = kx, [0, 4]$

19. $f(x) = kx^2, [1, 3]$

20. $f(x) = kx^3, [2, 4]$

21. The probability density function of a random variable X is

$$f(x) = 1 - \frac{1}{\sqrt{x}} \quad \text{for } [1, 4].$$

Find the following probabilities.

(a) $P(X \geq 3)$ (b) $P(X \leq 2)$ (c) $P(2 \leq X \leq 3)$

22. The probability density function of a random variable X is

$$f(x) = \frac{1}{11}\left(1 + \frac{3}{\sqrt{x}}\right) \quad \text{for } [4, 9].$$

Find the following probabilities.

(a) $P(X \geq 6)$ (b) $P(X \leq 5)$ (c) $P(4 \leq X \leq 7)$

23. The probability density function of a random variable X is

$$f(x) = \frac{1}{15}\left(x + \frac{1}{2}\right) \qquad \text{for } [0, 5].$$

Find the following probabilities.

(a) $P(X \geq 3)$ (b) $P(X \leq 2)$ (c) $P(1 \leq X \leq 4)$

24. The probability density function of a random variable X is

$$f(x) = \frac{1}{2} \qquad \text{for } [1, 3].$$

Find the following probabilities.

(a) $P(X \geq 2)$ (b) $P(X \leq 3/2)$ (c) $P(1 \leq X \leq 5/2)$

For Exercises 25–28, show that the function is a probability density function on the given interval. Then find the indicated probabilities.

25. $f(x) = \frac{1}{2}(1 + x)^{-3/2}$, $[0, \infty)$

(a) $P(0 \leq X \leq 2)$ (b) $P(1 \leq X \leq 3)$ (c) $P(X \geq 5)$

26. $f(x) = e^{-x}$, $[0, \infty)$

(a) $P(0 \leq X \leq 1)$ (b) $P(1 \leq X \leq 2)$ (c) $P(X \leq 2)$

27. $f(x) = (1/2)e^{-x/2}$, $[0, \infty)$

(a) $P(0 \leq X \leq 1)$ (b) $P(1 \leq X \leq 3)$ (c) $P(X \geq 2)$

28. $f(x) = \dfrac{20}{(x + 20)^2}$, $[0, \infty)$

(a) $P(0 \leq X \leq 1)$ (b) $P(1 \leq X \leq 5)$ (c) $P(X \geq 5)$

29. The time X required to learn a certain task is a random variable with probability density function

$$f(x) = \frac{8}{7(x - 2)^2}.$$

The time required to learn the task is between 3 and 10 minutes. Find the probability that a randomly selected person will learn the task in (a) less than 4 minutes; (b) more than 5 minutes.

30. The clotting time of blood is a random variable X with values from 1 to 20 seconds and probability density function

$$f(x) = \frac{1}{(\ln 20)x}.$$

Find the following probabilities for a person selected at random.

(a) $P(1 \leq X \leq 5)$ (b) $P(X \geq 10)$

31. The life in months of a certain electronic computer part has the probability density function

$$f(x) = \frac{1}{2}e^{-x/2} \qquad \text{for } [0, \infty).$$

Find the probability that a randomly selected component will last (a) for at most 12 months; (b) between 12 and 20 months.

32. The length of a telephone call (in minutes) for a certain town is a continuous random variable with probability density function

$$f(x) = 3x^{-4}, \qquad \text{for } [1, \infty).$$

Find the following probabilities.

(a) $P(1 \leq X \leq 2)$ (b) $P(3 \leq X \leq 5)$ (c) $P(X \geq 3)$

16.3   Expected Value and Variance of Continuous Random Variables

We used finite sums to define the expected value and variance for a discrete random variable. For continuous random variables, integrals are used to define these concepts. Standard deviation is defined to be the square root of the variance.

Expected Value, Variance, and Standard Deviation

If X is a continuous random variable with probability density function $f(x)$ on $[a, b]$, then the **expected value** of X is

$$E(X) = \mu = \int_a^b x f(x) \, dx.$$

The **variance** of X is

$$\text{Var}(X) = \int_a^b (x - \mu)^2 f(x) \, dx,$$

and the **standard deviation** of X is

$$\sigma = \sqrt{\text{Var}(X)}.$$

The expected value and variance have the same interpretation as in the discrete case. Geometrically, the expected value, or mean, of the distribution represents the "center" of the distribution. If a fulcrum were placed at μ on the x-axis the figure would be in balance. See Figure 8.

The variance or standard deviation indicates how closely the values of the distribution cluster about the mean. As we saw in Section 1, these measures are most useful for comparing different distributions, as shown in Figure 9.

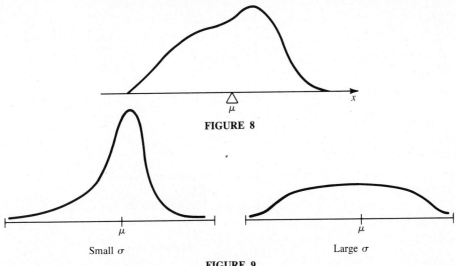

FIGURE 8

Small σ Large σ

FIGURE 9

EXAMPLE 1

Find the expected value and variance of the random variable with probability density function $f(x) = (3/26)x^2$ on $[1, 3]$.

By the definition given above,

$$\mu = \int_1^3 x f(x) \, dx = \int_1^3 x \left(\frac{3}{26} x^2 \right) dx = \frac{3}{26} \int_1^3 x^3 \, dx$$

$$= \frac{3}{26} \left(\frac{x^4}{4} \right) \Bigg]_1^3 = \frac{3}{104} (81 - 1) = \frac{30}{13}$$

or about 2.31.

The variance is

$$\text{Var}(X) = \int_1^3 \left(x - \frac{30}{13} \right)^2 \left(\frac{3}{26} x^2 \right) dx$$

$$= \int_1^3 \left(x^2 - \frac{60}{13} x + \frac{900}{169} \right) \left(\frac{3}{26} x^2 \right) dx$$

$$= \frac{3}{26} \int_1^3 \left(x^4 - \frac{60}{13} x^3 + \frac{900}{169} x^2 \right) dx$$

$$= \frac{3}{26} \left(\frac{x^5}{5} - \frac{60}{13} \cdot \frac{x^4}{4} + \frac{900}{169} \cdot \frac{x^3}{3} \right) \Bigg]_1^3$$

$$= \frac{3}{26} \left[\left(\frac{243}{5} - \frac{60(81)}{52} + \frac{300(27)}{169} \right) - \left(\frac{1}{5} - \frac{60}{52} + \frac{300}{169} \right) \right]$$

$$\approx .259$$

From the variance, the standard deviation is $\sigma \approx \sqrt{.259} \approx .51$. The expected value and standard deviation are shown on the graph of the probability density function in Figure 10. ■

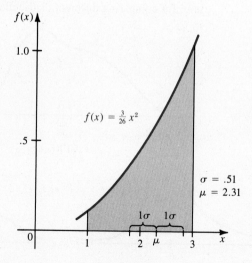

FIGURE 10

Calculating the variance in the last example was a messy job. An alternate form of the formula for the variance is easier to compute. This alternate formula is derived as follows.

$$\text{Var}(X) = \int_a^b (x - \mu)^2 f(x) \, dx$$

$$= \int_a^b (x^2 - 2\mu x + \mu^2) f(x) \, dx$$

$$= \int_a^b x^2 f(x) \, dx - 2\mu \int_a^b x f(x) \, dx + \mu^2 \int_a^b f(x) \, dx \qquad (1)$$

We know that

$$\int_a^b x f(x) \, dx = \mu,$$

and, since $f(x)$ is a probability density function,

$$\int_a^b f(x) \, dx = 1.$$

Substitute back into equation (1) to get the alternate formula,

$$\text{Var}(X) = \int_a^b x^2 f(x) \, dx - 2\mu^2 + \mu^2 = \int_a^b x^2 f(x) \, dx - \mu^2.$$

Alternate Formula

For Variance

If X is a random variable with probability density function $f(x)$ on $[a, b]$ and $E(X) = \mu$, then

$$\text{Var}(X) = \int_a^b x^2 f(x) \, dx - \mu^2.$$

EXAMPLE 2

Use the alternate formula for variance to compute the variance of the random variable X with probability density function $f(x) = 3/x^4$ for $x \geq 1$.

To find the variance, first find the expected value.

$$\mu = \int_1^\infty x f(x) \, dx = \int_1^\infty x \cdot \frac{3}{x^4} dx = \int_1^\infty \frac{3}{x^3} dx$$

$$= \lim_{a \to \infty} \int_1^a \frac{3}{x^3} dx = \lim_{a \to \infty} \left(\frac{3}{-2x^2} \right) \Big]_1^a = \frac{3}{2} \text{ or } 1.5$$

Now find the variance by the alternate formula for variance.

$$\text{Var}(X) = \int_1^\infty x^2 \left(\frac{3}{x^4}\right) dx - \left(\frac{3}{2}\right)^2$$

$$= \int_1^\infty \frac{3}{x^2} dx - \frac{9}{4}$$

$$= \lim_{a \to \infty} \int_1^a \frac{3}{x^2} dx - \frac{9}{4}$$

$$= \lim_{a \to \infty} \left(\frac{-3}{x}\right)\Big]_1^a - \frac{9}{4}$$

$$= 3 - \frac{9}{4} = \frac{3}{4} \text{ or } 0.75 \quad \blacksquare$$

EXAMPLE 3

A recent study has shown that on any given day the proportion of airline passengers who rent a car at their destination is a random variable with probability density function $f(x) = 6x - 6x^2$, for $0 \le x \le 1$.

(a) Find and interpret the expected value for this distribution.

The expected value is

$$\mu = \int_0^1 x(6x - 6x^2) dx = \int_0^1 (6x^2 - 6x^3) dx$$

$$= \left(2x^3 - \frac{3}{2}x^4\right)\Big]_0^1 = \frac{1}{2} \text{ or } 0.5.$$

This result indicates that over a long period of time, about 1/2 of all airline passengers rent a car at their destination.

(b) Compute the standard deviation.

First compute the variance. We use the alternate formula.

$$\text{Var}(X) = \int_0^1 x^2(6x - 6x^2) dx - \left(\frac{1}{2}\right)^2$$

$$= \int_0^1 (6x^3 - 6x^4) dx - \left(\frac{1}{2}\right)^2$$

$$= \left(\frac{3}{2}x^4 - \frac{6}{5}x^5\right)\Big]_0^1 - \frac{1}{4}$$

$$= \frac{3}{10} - \frac{1}{4} = \frac{1}{20} = .05$$

The standard deviation is $\sigma = \sqrt{.05} \approx .22.$ $\quad \blacksquare$

16.3 EXERCISES

In Exercises 1–8 a probability density function of a random variable is given. Find the expected value, the variance, and the standard deviation. Round answers to the nearest hundredth.

1. $f(x) = \frac{1}{4}, [3, 7]$

2. $f(x) = \frac{1}{10}, [0, 10]$

3. $f(x) = \frac{x}{8} - \frac{1}{4}, [2, 6]$

4. $f(x) = 2(1 - x), [0, 1]$

5. $f(x) = 1 - \frac{1}{\sqrt{x}}, [1, 4]$

6. $f(x) = \frac{1}{11}\left(1 + \frac{3}{\sqrt{x}}\right), [4, 9]$

7. $f(x) = 4x^{-5}, [1, \infty)$

8. $f(x) = 3x^{-4}, [1, \infty)$

In Exercises 9–12, the probability density function of a random variable is given.

(a) Find the expected value to the nearest hundredth.   **(b)** Find the variance to the nearest hundredth.   **(c)** Find the standard deviation. Round to the nearest hundredth.
(d) Find the probability that the random variable has a value greater than the mean.
(e) Find the probability that the value of the random variable is within one standard deviation of the mean.

9. $f(x) = \frac{\sqrt{x}}{18}, [0, 9]$

10. $f(x) = \frac{x^{-1/3}}{6}, [0, 8]$

11. $f(x) = \frac{1}{2}x, [0, 2]$

12. $f(x) = \frac{3}{2}(1 - x^2), [0, 1]$

If X is a random variable with probability density function $f(x)$ on $[a, b]$, then the **median** of X is the number m such that

$$\int_a^m f(x) \, dx = \frac{1}{2}.$$

(a) Find the median of each random variable for the probability density functions in Exercises 13–18.   **(b)** In each case, find the probability that the random variable is between the expected value (mean) and the median. The expected value for each of these functions was found in Exercises 1–8.

13. $f(x) = \frac{1}{4}, [3, 7]$

14. $f(x) = \frac{1}{10}, [0, 10]$

15. $f(x) = \frac{x}{8} - \frac{1}{4}, [2, 6]$

16. $f(x) = 2(1 - x), [0, 1]$

17. $f(x) = 4x^{-5}, [1, \infty)$

18. $f(x) = 3x^{-4}, [1, \infty)$

19. The length of a leaf on a tree is a random variable with a probability density function

$$f(x) = \frac{3}{32}(4x - x^2) \qquad \text{for } [0, 4].$$

(a) What is the average leaf length?   **(b)** Find σ for this distribution.
(c) Find the probability that the length of a given leaf would be within one standard deviation of the expected value.

20. The length of life (in hours) of a certain kind of light bulb is a random variable with probability density function

$$f(x) = \frac{1}{58\sqrt{x}} \qquad \text{for } [1, 900].$$

(a) What is the average or expected life of such a bulb?   **(b)** Find σ.   **(c)** Find the probability that one of these bulbs lasts longer than one standard deviation above the mean.

16.4   Special Probability Density Functions

In practice, it is not feasible to construct a probability density function for each experiment. Instead, a researcher uses one of several probability density functions that are well known, matching the shape of the experimental distribution to one of the known distributions. In this section we discuss some of the most commonly used probability distributions.

Uniform Distribution   This probability density function is given by

$$f(x) = \frac{1}{b - a} \quad \text{for } [a, b],$$

where a and b are nonnegative real numbers. The graph of $f(x)$ is shown in Figure 11.

Since $b - a$ is positive, $f(x) \geq 0$, and

$$\int_a^b \frac{1}{b - a} dx = \frac{1}{b - a} x \Big]_a^b = \frac{1}{b - a}(b - a) = 1.$$

Therefore, the function is a probability density function.

The expected value for the uniform distribution is

$$\mu = \int_a^b \left(\frac{1}{b - a}\right) x \, dx = \left(\frac{1}{b - a}\right) \frac{x^2}{2} \Big]_a^b$$

$$= \frac{1}{2(b - a)}(b^2 - a^2) = \frac{1}{2}(b + a).$$

The variance is given by

$$\text{Var}(X) = \int_a^b \left(\frac{1}{b - a}\right) x^2 \, dx - \left(\frac{b + a}{2}\right)^2$$

$$= \left(\frac{1}{b - a}\right) \frac{x^3}{3} \Big]_a^b - \frac{(b + a)^2}{4}$$

$$= \frac{1}{3(b - a)}(b^3 - a^3) - \frac{1}{4}(b + a)^2$$

$$= \frac{b^2 + ab + a^2}{3} - \frac{b^2 + 2ab + a^2}{4}$$

$$= \frac{b^2 - 2ab + a^2}{12}.$$

Thus, $$\text{Var}(X) = \frac{1}{12}(b - a)^2,$$

and $$\sigma = \frac{1}{\sqrt{12}}(b - a).$$

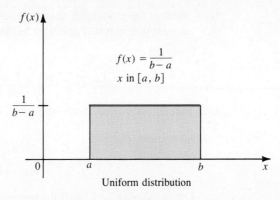

Uniform distribution

FIGURE 11

These properties of the uniform distribution are summarized in the box.

Uniform Distribution	If X is a random variable with probability density function $$f(x) = \frac{1}{b-a} \quad \text{for } [a, b],$$ then $$\mu = \frac{1}{2}(b + a) \quad \text{and} \quad \sigma = \frac{1}{\sqrt{12}}(b - a).$$

EXAMPLE 1

A couple is planning to vacation in San Francisco. They have been told that the maximum daily temperature during the time they plan to be there ranges from 15°C to 27°C. Assume that the probability of any temperature between 15°C and 27°C is equally likely for any given day during the specified time period.

(a) What is the probability that the maximum temperature on the day they arrive will be greater than 24°C?

If the random variable T represents the maximum temperature on a given day, then the uniform probability density function for T is $f(t) = 1/12$ for the interval $[15, 27]$. By definition,

$$P(T > 24) = \int_{24}^{27} \frac{1}{12} dt = \frac{1}{12} t \Big]_{24}^{27} = \frac{1}{4}.$$

(b) What average maximum temperature can they expect?

The expected maximum temperature is

$$\mu = \frac{1}{2}(27 + 15) = 21$$

or 21°C.

(c)   What is the probability that the maximum temperature on a given day will be at least one standard deviation below the mean?

First find σ:

$$\sigma = \frac{1}{\sqrt{12}}(27 - 15) = \frac{12}{\sqrt{12}} = \sqrt{12} = 2\sqrt{3} \approx 3.5.$$

One standard deviation below the mean indicates a temperature of $21 - 3.5 = 17.5°C$.

$$P(T \le 17.5°) = \int_{15}^{17.5} \frac{1}{12} dt = \frac{1}{12}t \Big]_{15}^{17.5} \approx .21$$

The probability is .21 that the temperature will not exceed 17.5°C.   ▨

Exponential Distribution   The exponential probability density function is given by

$$f(x) = ae^{-ax} \quad \text{for } [0, \infty),$$

where a is a positive real number. The graph of $f(x)$ is shown in Figure 12.

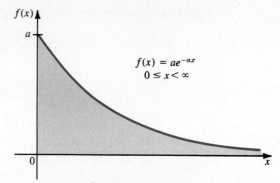

Exponential distribution

FIGURE 12

Here $f(x) \ge 0$ since e^{-ax} and a are both positive for all values of x. Also,

$$\int_0^\infty ae^{-ax} \, dx = \lim_{b \to \infty} \int_0^b ae^{-ax} \, dx$$

$$= \lim_{b \to \infty} (-e^{-ax}) \Big]_0^b$$

$$= \lim_{b \to \infty} \left(\frac{-1}{e^{ab}} + \frac{1}{e^0} \right) = 1,$$

so the function is a probability density function.

The expected value and standard deviation of the exponential distribution can be found using integration by parts. The results are given in the next box.

Exponential

Distribution

If X is a random variable with probability density function

$$f(x) = ae^{-ax} \qquad \text{for } [0, \infty),$$

then

$$\mu = \frac{1}{a} \qquad \text{and} \qquad \sigma = \frac{1}{a}.$$

EXAMPLE 2

Suppose the useful life (in hours) of a flashlight battery is the random variable T, with probability density function given by the exponential distribution

$$f(t) = \frac{1}{20}e^{-t/20} \qquad \text{for } t \geq 0.$$

(a) Find the probability that a particular battery, selected at random, has a useful life of less than 100 hours.

The probability is given by

$$P(T \leq 100) = \int_0^{100} \frac{1}{20}e^{-t/20}\,dt = \frac{1}{20}\left(-20e^{-t/20}\right)\Big]_0^{100}$$

$$= -(e^{-100/20} - e^0) = -(e^{-5} - 1)$$

$$\approx 1 - .0067 = .9933.$$

(b) Find the expected value and standard deviation of the distribution.

Use the formulas given in the box. Both μ and σ equal $1/a$ and since $a = 1/20$ here,

$$\mu = 20 \qquad \text{and} \qquad \sigma = 20.$$

This means that the average life of a battery is 20 hours and no battery lasts less than one standard deviation below the mean.

(c) What is the probability that a battery will last more than 40 hours?

The probability is given by

$$P(T > 40) = \int_{40}^{\infty} \frac{1}{20}e^{-t/20}\,dt = \lim_{b \to \infty}(-e^{-t/20})\Big]_{40}^{\infty} = \frac{1}{e^2} \approx .1353$$

or about 14%. ∎

Normal Distribution The normal distribution, with its well known bell-shaped graph, is undoubtedly the most important probability density function. It is widely used in various applications of statistics. The characteristics of the normal distribution function are given in the next box.

Normal Distribution

If μ and σ are real numbers, $\sigma \geq 0$, and X is a random variable with probability density function

$$f(x) = \frac{1}{\sigma\sqrt{2\pi}}e^{-(x-\mu)^2/(2\sigma^2)} \qquad \text{for } (-\infty, \infty),$$

then

$$E(X) = \mu, \qquad \text{Var}(X) = \sigma^2, \qquad \textbf{Standard Deviation} = \sigma.$$

Using advanced techniques, it can be shown that

$$\int_{-\infty}^{\infty} \frac{1}{\sigma\sqrt{2\pi}}e^{-(x-\mu)^2/(2\sigma^2)}\, dx = 1.$$

Deriving the expected value and standard deviation for the normal distribution also requires techniques beyond the scope of this text.

Each normal probability distribution has associated with it a bell-shaped curve, called a **normal curve,** such as the one in Figure 13. Each normal curve is symmetric about a vertical line drawn through the mean, μ. Vertical lines drawn at points $+1\sigma$ and -1σ from the mean show the inflection points of the graph. A normal curve never touches the x-axis; it extends indefinitely in both directions.

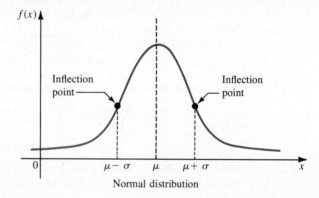

Normal distribution

FIGURE 13

Many different normal curves have the same mean. For example, a larger value of σ produces a "flatter" normal curve, while smaller values of σ produce more values near the mean, resulting in a "taller" normal curve. See Figure 14.

It would be far too much work to calculate values for the normal probability distribution for various values of μ and σ. Instead, values are calculated for the **standard normal distribution,** which has $\mu = 0$ and $\sigma = 1$. The graph of the standard normal distribution is shown in Figure 15.

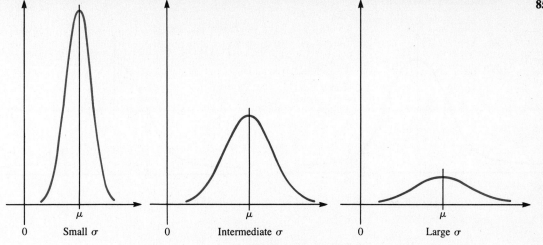

FIGURE 14

Probabilities for the standard normal distribution come from the definite integral

$$\int_a^b \frac{1}{\sqrt{2\pi}} e^{-x^2/2} \, dx.$$

Since $f(x) = e^{-x^2/2}$ does not have an antiderivative that can be expressed in terms of functions used in this course, numerical methods are used to find values of this definite integral. A table in the back of the book gives areas under the standard normal curve, along with a sketch of the curve. Each value in this table is the total area under the standard normal curve to the left of the number z.

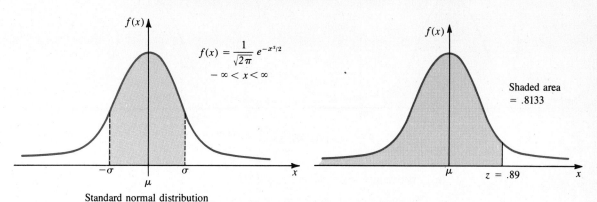

FIGURE 15

FIGURE 16

EXAMPLE 3

Find the following areas from the table for the standard normal curve.

(a) to the left of $z = 0.89$

Look up 0.89 in the normal curve table. The corresponding area is .8133. Thus the shaded area shown in Figure 16 is .8133. This area represents 81.33% of the total area under the normal curve.

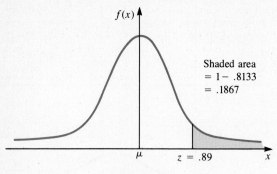

FIGURE 17

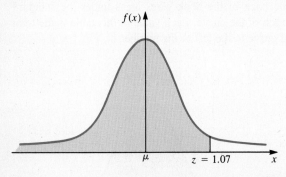

FIGURE 18

(b)   to the right of $z = .89$

In part (a) of this example we found that the area to the left of $z = .89$ is .8133. The total area under the normal curve is 1, so that the area to the right of $z = .89$ is

$$1 - .8133 = .1867.$$

See Figure 17, where the shaded area represents 18.67% of the total area under the normal curve.

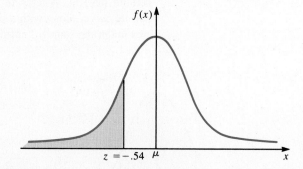

FIGURE 19

(c)   between $z = -.54$ and $z = 1.07$

To find this area, shaded in Figure 18, start with the area to the left of $z = 1.07$ and subtract the area to the left of $z = -.54$. See Figure 19. This gives .8577 − .2946 = .5631. ∎

If a normal distribution does not have $\mu = 0$ and $\sigma = 1$, the following theorem, which is stated without proof, is used.

z-scores Theorem

> Suppose a normal distribution has mean μ and standard deviation σ. The area under the associated normal curve that is to the left of the value x is exactly the same as the area to the left of
>
> $$z = \frac{x - \mu}{\sigma}$$
>
> for the standard normal curve.

Using this result, the table can be used for *any* normal distribution, no matter the values of μ and σ. The number z in the theorem is called a **z-score.**

EXAMPLE 4

A normal distribution has mean 35 and standard deviation 5.9. Find the following areas under the associated normal curve.

(a)   to the left of 40

Find the appropriate z-score using $x = 40$, $\mu = 35$, and $\sigma = 5.9$. Round to the nearest hundredth.

$$z = \frac{40 - 35}{5.9} = \frac{5}{5.9} \approx .85$$

From the table, the desired area is .8023.

(b)   to the right of 32

$$z = \frac{32 - 35}{5.9} = \frac{-3}{5.9} \approx -.51$$

The area to the *left* of $z = -.51$ is .3050, so the area to the *right* is $1 - .3050 = .6950$.

(c)   between 30 and 33

Find z-scores for both values.

$$z = \frac{30 - 35}{5.9} = \frac{-5}{5.9} \approx -.85 \quad \text{and} \quad z = \frac{33 - 35}{5.9} = \frac{-2}{5.9} \approx -.34$$

Start with the area to the left of $z = -.34$ and subtract the area to the left of $z = -.85$ which gives

$$.3669 - .1977 = .1692. \quad \blacksquare$$

The z-scores are actually standard deviation multiples—that is, a z-score of 2.5 corresponds to a value 2.5 standard deviations above the mean. For example, looking up $z = 1.00$ and $z = -1.00$ in the table shows that

$$.8413 - .1587 = .6826,$$

with 68.26% of the area under a normal curve within one standard deviation of the mean. Also, using $z = 2.00$ and $z = -2.00$,

$$.9772 - .0228 = .9544,$$

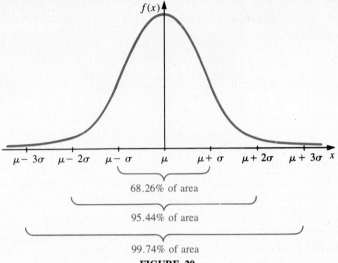

FIGURE 20

with 95.44% of the area within two standard deviations of the mean. These results, summarized in Figure 20, can be used to get a quick estimate of results when working with normal curves.

16.4 EXERCISES

For Exercises 1–6, find

(a) the mean of the distribution;   (b) the standard deviation of the distribution;

(c) the probability that the random variable is between the mean and one standard deviation above the mean.

1. The length (in centimeters) of the leaf of a certain plant is a continuous random variable with probability density function

$$f(x) = \frac{5}{4} \quad \text{for } [4, 4.8].$$

2. The price of an item in dollars is a continuous random variable with probability density function

$$f(x) = 2 \quad \text{for } [1.25, 1.75].$$

3. The length of time in years until a particular radioactive particle decays is a random variable T with probability density function

$$f(t) = 0.03 e^{-0.03t} \quad \text{for } [0, \infty).$$

4. The length of time (in years) that a seedling tree survives is a random variable T with probability density function

$$f(t) = 0.05 e^{-0.05t} \quad \text{for } [0, \infty).$$

5. The length of time (in days) required to learn a certain task is a random variable T with probability density function

$$f(t) = e^{-t} \quad \text{for } [0, \infty).$$

6. The distance (in meters) that seeds are dispersed from a certain kind of plant is a random variable X with probability density function

$$f(x) = 0.1 e^{-0.1x} \quad \text{for } [0, \infty).$$

7. The life span of a certain insect in days is uniformly distributed over the interval [20, 36].

(a) What is the expected life of the insect?   (b) Find the probability that one of these insects, randomly selected, lives longer than 30 days.

8. The rainfall in inches in a certain region is uniformly distributed over the interval [32, 44].

(a) What is the expected number of inches of rainfall?   (b) What is the probability that the rainfall will be between 38 and 40 inches?

9. The amount of insurance (in thousands of dollars) sold in a day by a particular agent is uniformly distributed over the interval [10, 85].

(a) What amount of insurance does the agent sell on an average day?   (b) Find the probability that the agent sells more than $50,000 of insurance on a particular day.

10. The number of emergency room patients at a certain hospital is uniformly distributed over the interval [8, 25].

(a) What is the expected number of patients on any given day?   (b) What is the probability that the number of patients will be within one standard deviation of the mean?

11. A swarm of bees is released from a certain point. The proportion of the swarm located at least 2 meters from the point of release after one hour is a random variable which is exponentially distributed with $a = 2$ over the interval $[0, \infty)$.

(a) Find the expected proportion.   (b) Find the probability that fewer than 1/3 of the bees are located at least 2 meters from the release point.

12. The digestion time in hours of a fixed amount of food is exponentially distributed with $a = 1$.

(a) Find the mean digestion time.   (b) Find the probability that the digestion time is less than 30 minutes.

13. A salesperson's monthly expenses (in thousands of dollars) are exponentially distributed with an average of 4.25 (thousand).

(a) Give the probability density function for the expenses.   (b) Find the probability that the expenses are more than $10,000.

14. The number of new fast-food outlets opening during June in a certain city is exponentially distributed with a mean of 5.

(a) Give the probability density function for this distribution.   (b) What is the probability that the number opening is between 2 and 6?

Find the percent of the area under a normal curve between the mean and the number of standard deviations above the mean given in Exercises 15–18.

15. 3.50   **16.** 1.68   **17.** 0.45   **18.** 1.71

Find the percent of the total area under the normal curve between the z-scores given in Exercises 19–22.

19. 1.28 and 2.05   **20.** −2.13 and −0.04   **21.** −3.05 and 1.27   **22.** −0.53 and 0.53

Find a z-score satisfying the conditions given in Exercises 23–26. (Hint: use the table backwards.)

23. 10% of the total area is to the left of z **24.** 2% of the total area is to the left of z

25. 18% of the total area is to the right of z **26.** 22% of the total area is to the right of z

In Exercises 27–30, assume a normal distribution.

27. A machine produces screws with a mean length of 2.5 cm and a standard deviation of .2 cm. Find the probability that a screw is produced with a length **(a)** greater than 2.7 cm;   **(b)** within 1.2 standard deviations of the mean.

28. A machine that fills quart bottles with apple juice averages 32.8 ounces per bottle with a standard deviation of 1.1 ounces. What is the probability that a bottle contains **(a)** less than a quart of juice?   **(b)** at least one ounce more than a quart of juice?

29. Customers at a certain pharmacy spend an average of $12.20 with a standard deviation of $6.50. What are the largest and smallest amounts spent by the middle 50% of these customers?

30. The average height of a member of a certain tribe of pygmies is 3.2 feet with a standard deviation of .2 feet. What are the largest and smallest heights of the middle 50% of this population?

31. Find an expression for the median m of the uniform distribution.

32. Find an expression for the median m of the exponential distribution.

Use Simpson's rule with $n = 100$ to approximate the following integrals.

33. $\displaystyle\int_0^{50} .5e^{-.5x}\, dx$ **34.** $\displaystyle\int_0^{50} .5xe^{-.5x}\, dx$ **35.** $\displaystyle\int_0^{50} .5x^2 e^{-.5x}\, dx - 4$

36. Use your results from Exercises 33 and 34 to verify that, for the exponential distribution, $\mu = 1/a$ and $\sigma = 1/a$.

37. The standard normal probability density function is

$$f(x) = \int_{-\infty}^{\infty} \frac{1}{\sqrt{2\pi}} e^{-x^2/2}\, dx.$$

Use Simpson's rule with $n = 100$ and the formulas for the mean and standard deviation of a probability density function to approximate **(a)** the mean and **(b)** the standard deviation of the standard normal probability distribution. Use limits of -4 and 4 (instead of $-\infty$ and ∞).

EXTENDED   A Crop-Planting Model*

APPLICATION

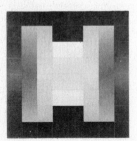

Many firms in food processing, seed production, and similar industries face a problem every year deciding how many acres of land to plant in each of various crops. Demand for the crop is unknown, as is the actual yield per acre. In this application, we set up a mathematical model for determining the optimum number of acres to plant in a crop.

This model is designed to tell the company the number of acres of seed that it should plant. The model uses the following variables.

---

*Based on work by David P. Rutten, Senior Mathematician, The Upjohn Company, Kalamazoo, Michigan. Reprinted with permission.

D = number of tons of seed demanded

$f(D)$ = continuous probability density function for the quantity of seed demanded, D

X = quantity of seed produced per acre of land

Q = quantity of seed carried over in inventory from previous years

S = selling price per ton of seed

C_p = variable costs of production, marketing, etc., per ton of seed

C_c = cost to carry over a ton of seed from previous years

A = number of acres of land to be planted

C_A = variable cost per acre of land contracted

T = total number of tons of seed available for sale

a = lower limit of the domain of $f(D)$

b = upper limit of the domain of $f(D)$

To decide on the optimum number of acres to plant, it is necessary to calculate the expected value of the profit from the planting of A acres.

Based on the definition of the variables above, the total number of tons of seed that will be available for sale is given by the product of the number of acres planted, A, and the yield per acre, X, added to the carryover, Q. If T represents this total, then

$$T = AX + Q.$$

The variable here is A; we assume X and Q are known and fixed.

The expected profit can be broken down into several parts. The first portion comes from multiplying the profit per ton and the average number of tons demanded. The profit per ton is found by subtracting the variable cost per ton, C_p, from the selling price per ton, S:

$$\text{profit per ton} = S - C_p.$$

The average number of tons demanded for our interval of concern is given by

$$\int_a^T D \cdot f(D)\,dD.$$

Thus, this portion of the expected profit is

$$(S - C_p) \cdot \int_a^T D \cdot f(D)\,dD. \tag{1}$$

A second portion of expected profit is found by multiplying the profit per ton, $S - C_p$, the total number of tons available, T (recall that this is a variable), and the probability that T or more tons will be demanded by the marketplace.

$$(S - C_p)(T)\int_T^b f(D)\,dD \tag{2}$$

If T is greater than D, there will be costs associated with carrying over the excess seeds. The expected value of these costs is given by the product of the carrying cost per ton, C_c, and the number of tons to be carried over, or

$$- C_c\int_a^T (T - D)f(D)\,dD. \tag{3}$$

The minus sign shows that these costs reduce profit. If $T < D$, this term would be omitted.

Finally, the total cost of producing the seeds is given by the product of the variable cost per acre and the number of acres:

$$- C_A \cdot A. \tag{4}$$

The expected profit is the sum of the expressions in (1)–(4), or

$$\text{expected profit} = (S - C_p) \cdot \int_a^T D \cdot f(D)\, dD + (S - C_p)(T)\int_T^b f(D)\, dD$$

$$- C_c \int_a^T (T - D) f(D)\, dD - C_A \cdot A. \tag{5}$$

As an example, suppose that

$$\text{probability density function} = f(D) = \frac{1}{1000} \quad \text{for } 500 \le D \le 1500 \text{ tons}$$

$$a = 500$$
$$b = 1500$$
$$\text{selling price} = S = \$10{,}000 \text{ per ton}$$
$$\text{variable cost} = C_p = \$5000 \text{ per ton}$$
$$\text{carrying cost} = C_c = \$3000 \text{ per ton}$$
$$\text{variable cost per acre} = C_A = \$100$$
$$\text{inventory carryover} = Q = 200 \text{ tons}$$
$$\text{yield per acre} = X = .1 \text{ ton}$$
$$T = AX + Q = .1A + 200.$$

Substitute all this into equation (5).

$$\text{expected profit} = (10{,}000 - 5000)\int_{500}^{.1A+200} D \cdot \frac{1}{1000}\, dD$$

$$+ (10{,}000 - 5000)(.1A + 200)\int_{.1A+200}^{1500} \frac{1}{1000}\, dD$$

$$- 3000\int_{500}^{.1A+200} (.1A + 200 - D) \cdot \frac{1}{1000}\, dD - 100A$$

Simplify all this.

$$\text{expected profit} = \frac{5000}{1000} \cdot \frac{D^2}{2}\Bigg]_{500}^{.1A+200} + (5000)(.1A + 200)\frac{D}{1000}\Bigg]_{.1A+200}^{1500}$$

$$- 3000\left(\frac{.1AD}{1000} + \frac{200D}{1000} - \frac{D^2}{2000}\right)\Bigg]_{500}^{.1A+200} - 100A$$

$$= \frac{5}{2}(.1A + 200)^2 - \frac{5}{2} \cdot 500^2 + 5(.1A + 200)1500$$

$$- 5(.1A + 200)(.1A + 200) - .3A(.1A + 200)$$

$$- 600(.1A + 200) + \frac{3}{2}(.1A + 200)^2 + 150A$$

$$+ 600(500) - \frac{3}{2}(500)^2 - 100A$$

$$= -(.1A + 200)^2 + 6900(.1A + 200) - .3A(.1A + 200)$$

$$+ 50A - 700{,}000$$

To find the maximum expected profit, take the derivative of this function with respect to A and then place it equal to 0.

$$D_A[\text{expected profit}] = -2(.1A + 200)(.1) + 690 - .06A - 60 + 50$$
$$= -.02A - 40 + 690 - .06A - 10$$
$$= -.08A + 640$$

Place this derivative equal to 0.

$$-.08A + 640 = 0$$
$$8000 = A$$

If 8000 acres are planted, the maximum profit will be obtained.

KEY WORDS

random variable	continuous probability distribution
probability distribution	probability density function
probability distribution function	uniform distribution
histogram	exponential distribution
expected value	normal distribution
variance	normal curve
standard deviation	standard normal distribution
continuous random variable	z-score

Chapter 16   REVIEW EXERCISES

For Exercises 1–4, (a) give a probability distribution and (b) sketch its histogram.

1.

X	2	3	4	5	6
Frequency	7	9	3	2	3

2.

X	10	11	12	13	14	15	16
Frequency	1	0	2	5	8	4	3

3. Eight laboratory animals were given a new treatment for a disease. The experiment was repeated ten times with the following results.

Number Who Improved	0	1	2	3	4	5	6	7	8
Frequency	1	0	1	2	3	1	0	2	0

4. An airline company kept track for one month of the number of people with reservations for a certain flight who did not show up for the flight. The results are shown below.

Number of No-shows	2	3	4	5	6	7	8	9	10
Frequency	3	2	5	4	4	8	0	3	1

In Exercises 5–8, for each distribution **(a)** draw a histogram and shade the region which gives the indicated probability; **(b)** find the probability.

5. The distribution of Exercise 1, $P(X < 3)$

6. The distribution of Exercise 2, $P(X \geq 15)$

7. The distribution of Exercise 3, $P(4 \leq X \leq 7)$

8. The distribution of Exercise 4, $P(4 \leq X \leq 8)$

In Exercises 9–12, for each distribution, find **(a)** the expected value; **(b)** the variance; **(c)** the standard deviation.

9. The distribution of Exercise 1

10. The distribution of Exercise 2

11. The distribution of Exercise 3

12. The distribution of Exercise 4

13. The prices per share of two mutual funds for two (5-day) weeks were as follows.

Fund I

Price	8.00	8.10	8.12	8.13	8.15
Frequency	2	1	3	2	2

Fund II

Price	3.21	3.25	3.32	3.36	4.01
Frequency	2	3	3	1	1

(a) Find the mean and standard deviation for each fund price.

(b) Which fund had the more stable price per share for that two-week period?

14. The weight losses (in pounds) of 2 groups of 10 people following two different experimental new diets were as follows.

Diet A

Weight Loss	0	4	10	12	18	22
Frequency	1	1	3	2	2	1

Diet B

Weight Loss	1	6	9	14	21	25
Frequency	1	3	2	1	2	1

(a) Compute the mean and standard deviation for each group.

(b) Which diet produced the greatest average loss?

(c) Which diet produced the most variable loss?

Which of the functions in Exercises 15–18 are probability density functions for the given intervals?

15. $f(x) = \dfrac{1}{27}(2x + 4)$, $[1, 4]$

16. $f(x) = \sqrt{x}$, $[4, 9]$

17. $f(x) = .1$, $[0, 10]$

18. $f(x) = e^{-x}$, $[0, \infty)$

In Exercises 19 and 20, find a value of k which will make $f(x)$ a probability density function for the indicated interval.

19. $f(x) = k\sqrt{x}$, $[1, 4]$

20. $f(x) = kx^2$, $[0, 3]$

21. The probability density function of a random variable X is

$$f(x) = 1 - \frac{1}{\sqrt{x - 1}} \quad \text{for } [2, 5].$$

Find the following probabilities.

(a) $P(X \geq 3)$ **(b)** $P(X \leq 4)$ **(c)** $P(3 \leq X \leq 4)$

22. The probability density function of a random variable X is

$$f(x) = \frac{1}{10} \quad \text{for } [10, 20].$$

Find the following probabilities.

(a) $P(X \leq 12)$ **(b)** $P(X \geq 31/2)$ **(c)** $P(10.8 \leq X \leq 16.2)$

23. The time (in years) until a certain machine requires repairs is a random variable T with probability density function

$$f(t) = \frac{5}{112}(1 - t^{-3/2}) \quad \text{for } [1, 25].$$

Find the probability that no repairs are required in the first three years by finding the probability that a repair will be needed in years 4 through 25.

24. The distance (in meters) that a certain animal moves away from a release point is a random variable with probability density function

$$f(x) = .01 e^{-.01x} \quad \text{for } [0, \infty).$$

Find the probability that the animal will move no farther than 100 meters away.

For the probability density functions in Exercises 25–28, find the expected value, the variance, and the standard deviation.

25. $f(x) = \frac{1}{5}, \quad [4, 9]$

26. $f(x) = \frac{2}{9}(x - 2), \quad [2, 5]$

27. $f(x) = \frac{1}{7}\left(1 + \frac{2}{\sqrt{x}}\right), \quad [1, 4]$

28. $f(x) = 5x^{-6}, \quad [1, \infty)$

29. The probability density function of a random variable is $f(x) = 4x - 3x^2$ for $[0, 1]$. Find each of the following for the distribution:

(a) the mean;   **(b)** the standard deviation;   **(c)** the probability that the value of the random variable will be less than the mean;   **(d)** the probability that the value of the random variable will be within one standard deviation of the mean.

30. Find the median of the random variable of Exercise 29. Then find the probability that the value of the random variable will be between the median and the mean of the distribution.

For Exercises 31–34, find **(a)** the mean of the distribution; **(b)** the standard deviation of the distribution, **(c)** the probability that the value of the random variable is within one standard deviation of the mean.

31. $f(x) = \frac{5}{112}(1 - x^{-3/2})$ for $[1, 25]$.

32. $f(x) = .01 e^{-0.01x}$ for $[0, \infty)$.

33. The weight gain (in grams) of rats fed a certain vitamin supplement is a continuous random variable with probability density function

$$f(x) = \frac{8}{7}x^{-2} \quad \text{for } [1, 8].$$

34. The body temperature (in degrees Celsius) of a particular species of bird is a continuous random variable with probability density function

$$f(x) = \frac{6}{15{,}925}(x^2 + x) \qquad \text{for } [20, 25].$$

   (a) What is the expected body temperature of this species?

   (b) Find the probability of a body temperature below the mean.

35. The snowfall in inches in a certain area is uniformly distributed over the interval [2, 40].

   (a) What is the expected snowfall?

   (b) What is the probability of getting more than 20 inches of snow?

36. The number of repairs required by a new product each month is exponentially distributed with an average of 8.

   (a) What is the probability density function for this distribution?

   (b) What is the probability that the number of repairs per month will be between 5 and 10?

In Exercises 37–42, find the percent of the area under a normal curve for each of the following.

37. above $z = 1.53$

38. below $z = -.49$

39. between $z = -1.47$ and $z = 1.03$

40. between $z = -.98$ and $z = -.15$

41. up to 2.5 standard deviations above the mean

42. up to 1.2 standard deviations below the mean

43. Find a z-score so that 21% of the area under the normal curve is to the left of z.

44. Find a z-score so that 52% of the area under the normal curve is to the right of z.

Assume a normal distribution in Exercises 45–48.

45. The average state "take" on lotteries is 40% with a standard deviation of 13%. What is the probability that a state-run lottery will have a "take" of more than 50%?

46. In a pilot study on tension of the heart muscle in dogs, the mean developed tension was 2.4 grams with a standard deviation of .4 grams. Find the probability of a tension of less than 1.9 grams.

47. The useful life of a certain appliance part (in hundreds of hours) is 46.2 with a standard deviation of 15.8. Find the probability that one such part would last for at least 6000 (60 hundred) hours.

48. The average weight at birth of infants in the United States is 7.2 pounds with a standard deviation of 1.1 pounds. What is the probability that a newborn will weigh more than 9 pounds?

APPENDIX: TABLES

Combinations

n	$\binom{n}{0}$	$\binom{n}{1}$	$\binom{n}{2}$	$\binom{n}{3}$	$\binom{n}{4}$	$\binom{n}{5}$	$\binom{n}{6}$	$\binom{n}{7}$	$\binom{n}{8}$	$\binom{n}{9}$	$\binom{n}{10}$
0	1										
1	1	1									
2	1	2	1								
3	1	3	3	1							
4	1	4	6	4	1						
5	1	5	10	10	5	1					
6	1	6	15	20	15	6	1				
7	1	7	21	35	35	21	7	1			
8	1	8	28	56	70	56	28	8	1		
9	1	9	36	84	126	126	84	36	9	1	
10	1	10	45	120	210	252	210	120	45	10	1
11	1	11	55	165	330	462	462	330	165	55	11
12	1	12	66	220	495	792	924	792	495	220	66
13	1	13	78	286	715	1287	1716	1716	1287	715	286
14	1	14	91	364	1001	2002	3003	3432	3003	2002	1001
15	1	15	105	455	1365	3003	5005	6435	6435	5005	3003
16	1	16	120	560	1820	4368	8008	11440	12870	11440	8008
17	1	17	136	680	2380	6188	12376	19448	24310	24310	19448
18	1	18	153	816	3060	8658	18564	31824	43758	48620	43758
19	1	19	171	969	3876	11628	27132	50388	75582	92378	92378
20	1	20	190	1140	4845	15504	38760	77520	125970	167960	184756

For $r > 10$, it may be necessary to use the identity

$$\binom{n}{r} = \binom{n}{n-r}.$$

Area Under a Normal Curve to the Left of z, Where $z = \dfrac{x - \mu}{\sigma}$

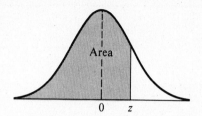

z	0.00	0.01	0.02	0.03	0.04	0.05	0.06	0.07	0.08	0.09
−3.4	0.0003	0.0003	0.0003	0.0003	0.0003	0.0003	0.0003	0.0003	0.0003	0.0002
−3.3	0.0005	0.0005	0.0005	0.0004	0.0004	0.0004	0.0004	0.0004	0.0004	0.0003
−3.2	0.0007	0.0007	0.0006	0.0006	0.0006	0.0006	0.0006	0.0005	0.0005	0.0005
−3.1	0.0010	0.0009	0.0009	0.0009	0.0008	0.0008	0.0008	0.0008	0.0007	0.0007
−3.0	0.0013	0.0013	0.0013	0.0012	0.0012	0.0011	0.0011	0.0011	0.0010	0.0010
−2.9	0.0019	0.0018	0.0017	0.0017	0.0016	0.0016	0.0015	0.0015	0.0014	0.0014
−2.8	0.0026	0.0025	0.0024	0.0023	0.0023	0.0022	0.0021	0.0021	0.0020	0.0019
−2.7	0.0035	0.0034	0.0033	0.0032	0.0031	0.0030	0.0029	0.0028	0.0027	0.0026
−2.6	0.0047	0.0045	0.0044	0.0043	0.0041	0.0040	0.0039	0.0038	0.0037	0.0036
−2.5	0.0062	0.0060	0.0059	0.0057	0.0055	0.0054	0.0052	0.0051	0.0049	0.0048
−2.4	0.0082	0.0080	0.0078	0.0075	0.0073	0.0071	0.0069	0.0068	0.0066	0.0064
−2.3	0.0107	0.0104	0.0102	0.0099	0.0096	0.0094	0.0091	0.0089	0.0087	0.0084
−2.2	0.0139	0.0136	0.0132	0.0129	0.0125	0.0122	0.0119	0.0116	0.0113	0.0110
−2.1	0.0179	0.0174	0.0170	0.0166	0.0162	0.0158	0.0154	0.0150	0.0146	0.0143
−2.0	0.0228	0.0222	0.0217	0.0212	0.0207	0.0202	0.0197	0.0192	0.0188	0.0183
−1.9	0.0287	0.0281	0.0274	0.0268	0.0262	0.0256	0.0250	0.0244	0.0239	0.0233
−1.8	0.0359	0.0352	0.0344	0.0336	0.0329	0.0322	0.0314	0.0307	0.0301	0.0294
−1.7	0.0446	0.0436	0.0427	0.0418	0.0409	0.0401	0.0392	0.0384	0.0375	0.0367
−1.6	0.0548	0.0537	0.0526	0.0516	0.0505	0.0495	0.0485	0.0475	0.0465	0.0455
−1.5	0.0668	0.0655	0.0643	0.0630	0.0618	0.0606	0.0594	0.0582	0.0571	0.0559
−1.4	0.0808	0.0793	0.0778	0.0764	0.0749	0.0735	0.0722	0.0708	0.0694	0.0681
−1.3	0.0968	0.0951	0.0934	0.0918	0.0901	0.0885	0.0869	0.0853	0.0838	0.0823
−1.2	0.1151	0.1131	0.1112	0.1093	0.1075	0.1056	0.1038	0.1020	0.1003	0.0985
−1.1	0.1357	0.1335	0.1314	0.1292	0.1271	0.1251	0.1230	0.1210	0.1190	0.1170
−1.0	0.1587	0.1562	0.1539	0.1515	0.1492	0.1469	0.1446	0.1423	0.1401	0.1379

Area Under a Normal Curve (Continued)

z	0.00	0.01	0.02	0.03	0.04	0.05	0.06	0.07	0.08	0.09
−0.9	0.1841	0.1814	0.1788	0.1762	0.1736	0.1711	0.1685	0.1660	0.1635	0.1611
−0.8	0.2119	0.2090	0.2061	0.2033	0.2005	0.1977	0.1949	0.1922	0.1894	0.1867
−0.7	0.2420	0.2389	0.2358	0.2327	0.2296	0.2266	0.2236	0.2206	0.2177	0.2148
−0.6	0.2743	0.2709	0.2676	0.2643	0.2611	0.2578	0.2546	0.2514	0.2483	0.2451
−0.5	0.3085	0.3050	0.3015	0.2981	0.2946	0.2912	0.2877	0.2843	0.2810	0.2776
−0.4	0.3446	0.3409	0.3372	0.3336	0.3300	0.3264	0.3228	0.3192	0.3156	0.3121
−0.3	0.3821	0.3783	0.3745	0.3707	0.3669	0.3632	0.3594	0.3557	0.3520	0.3483
−0.2	0.4207	0.4168	0.4129	0.4090	0.4052	0.4013	0.3974	0.3936	0.3897	0.3859
−0.1	0.4602	0.4562	0.4522	0.4483	0.4443	0.4404	0.4364	0.4325	0.4286	0.4247
−0.0	0.5000	0.4960	0.4920	0.4880	0.4840	0.4801	0.4761	0.4721	0.4681	0.4641
0.0	0.5000	0.5040	0.5080	0.5120	0.5160	0.5199	0.5239	0.5279	0.5319	0.5359
0.1	0.5398	0.5438	0.5478	0.5517	0.5557	0.5596	0.5636	0.5675	0.5714	0.5753
0.2	0.5793	0.5832	0.5871	0.5910	0.5948	0.5987	0.6026	0.6064	0.6103	0.6141
0.3	0.6179	0.6217	0.6255	0.6293	0.6331	0.6368	0.6406	0.6443	0.6480	0.6517
0.4	0.6554	0.6591	0.6628	0.6664	0.6700	0.6736	0.6772	0.6808	0.6844	0.6879
0.5	0.6915	0.6950	0.6985	0.7019	0.7054	0.7088	0.7123	0.7157	0.7190	0.7224
0.6	0.7257	0.7291	0.7324	0.7357	0.7389	0.7422	0.7454	0.7486	0.7517	0.7549
0.7	0.7580	0.7611	0.7642	0.7673	0.7704	0.7734	0.7764	0.7794	0.7823	0.7852
0.8	0.7881	0.7910	0.7939	0.7967	0.7995	0.8023	0.8051	0.8078	0.8106	0.8133
0.9	0.8159	0.8186	0.8212	0.8238	0.8264	0.8289	0.8315	0.8340	0.8365	0.8389
1.0	0.8413	0.8438	0.8461	0.8485	0.8508	0.8531	0.8554	0.8577	0.8599	0.8621
1.1	0.8643	0.8665	0.8686	0.8708	0.8729	0.8749	0.8770	0.8790	0.8810	0.8830
1.2	0.8849	0.8869	0.8888	0.8907	0.8925	0.8944	0.8962	0.8980	0.8997	0.9015
1.3	0.9032	0.9049	0.9066	0.9082	0.9099	0.9115	0.9131	0.9147	0.9162	0.9177
1.4	0.9192	0.9207	0.9222	0.9236	0.9251	0.9265	0.9278	0.9292	0.9306	0.9319
1.5	0.9332	0.9345	0.9357	0.9370	0.9382	0.9394	0.9406	0.9418	0.9429	0.9441
1.6	0.9452	0.9463	0.9474	0.9484	0.9495	0.9505	0.9515	0.9525	0.9535	0.9545
1.7	0.9554	0.9564	0.9573	0.9582	0.9591	0.9599	0.9608	0.9616	0.9625	0.9633
1.8	0.9641	0.9649	0.9656	0.9664	0.9671	0.9678	0.9686	0.9693	0.9699	0.9706
1.9	0.9713	0.9719	0.9726	0.9732	0.9738	0.9744	0.9750	0.9756	0.9761	0.9767
2.0	0.9772	0.9778	0.9783	0.9788	0.9793	0.9798	0.9803	0.9808	0.9812	0.9817
2.1	0.9821	0.9826	0.9830	0.9834	0.9838	0.9842	0.9846	0.9850	0.9854	0.9857
2.2	0.9861	0.9864	0.9868	0.9871	0.9875	0.9878	0.9881	0.9884	0.9887	0.9890
2.3	0.9893	0.9896	0.9898	0.9901	0.9904	0.9906	0.9909	0.9911	0.9913	0.9916
2.4	0.9918	0.9920	0.9922	0.9925	0.9927	0.9929	0.9931	0.9932	0.9934	0.9936
2.5	0.9938	0.9940	0.9941	0.9943	0.9945	0.9946	0.9948	0.9949	0.9951	0.9952
2.6	0.9953	0.9955	0.9956	0.9957	0.9959	0.9960	0.9961	0.9962	0.9963	0.9964
2.7	0.9965	0.9966	0.9967	0.9968	0.9969	0.9970	0.9971	0.9972	0.9973	0.9974
2.8	0.9974	0.9975	0.9976	0.9977	0.9977	0.9978	0.9979	0.9979	0.9980	0.9981
2.9	0.9981	0.9982	0.9982	0.9983	0.9984	0.9984	0.9985	0.9985	0.9986	0.9986
3.0	0.9987	0.9987	0.9987	0.9988	0.9988	0.9989	0.9989	0.9989	0.9990	0.9990
3.1	0.9990	0.9991	0.9991	0.9991	0.9992	0.9992	0.9992	0.9992	0.9993	0.9993
3.2	0.9993	0.9993	0.9994	0.9994	0.9994	0.9994	0.9994	0.9995	0.9995	0.9995
3.3	0.9995	0.9995	0.9995	0.9996	0.9996	0.9996	0.9996	0.9996	0.9996	0.9997
3.4	0.9997	0.9997	0.9997	0.9997	0.9997	0.9997	0.9997	0.9997	0.9997	0.9998

Compound Interest

$(1 + i)^n$

n \ i	1%	$1\frac{1}{2}$%	2%	3%	4%	5%	6%	8%
1	1.01000	1.01500	1.02000	1.03000	1.04000	1.05000	1.06000	1.08000
2	1.02010	1.03023	1.04040	1.06090	1.08160	1.10250	1.12360	1.16640
3	1.03030	1.04568	1.06121	1.09273	1.12486	1.15763	1.19102	1.25971
4	1.04060	1.06136	1.08243	1.12551	1.16986	1.21551	1.26248	1.36049
5	1.05101	1.07728	1.10408	1.15927	1.21665	1.27628	1.33823	1.46933
6	1.06152	1.09344	1.12616	1.19405	1.26532	1.34010	1.41852	1.58687
7	1.07214	1.10984	1.14869	1.22987	1.31593	1.40710	1.50363	1.71382
8	1.08286	1.12649	1.17166	1.26677	1.36857	1.47746	1.59385	1.85093
9	1.09369	1.14339	1.19509	1.30477	1.42331	1.55133	1.68948	1.99900
10	1.10462	1.16054	1.21899	1.34392	1.48024	1.62889	1.79085	2.15892
11	1.11567	1.17795	1.24337	1.38423	1.53945	1.71034	1.89830	2.33164
12	1.12683	1.19562	1.26824	1.42576	1.60103	1.79586	2.01220	2.51817
13	1.13809	1.21355	1.29361	1.46853	1.66507	1.88565	2.13293	2.71962
14	1.14947	1.23176	1.31948	1.51259	1.73168	1.97993	2.26090	2.93719
15	1.16097	1.25023	1.34587	1.55797	1.80094	2.07893	2.39656	3.17217
16	1.17258	1.26899	1.37279	1.60471	1.87298	2.18287	2.54035	3.42594
17	1.18430	1.28802	1.40024	1.65285	1.94790	2.29202	2.69277	3.70002
18	1.19615	1.30734	1.42825	1.70243	2.02582	2.40662	2.85434	3.99602
19	1.20811	1.32695	1.45681	1.75351	2.10685	2.52695	3.02560	4.31570
20	1.22019	1.34686	1.48595	1.80611	2.19112	2.65330	3.20714	4.66096
21	1.23239	1.36706	1.51567	1.86029	2.27877	2.78596	3.39956	5.03383
22	1.24472	1.38756	1.54598	1.91610	2.36992	2.92526	3.60354	5.43654
23	1.25716	1.40838	1.57690	1.97359	2.46472	3.07152	3.81975	5.87146
24	1.26973	1.42950	1.60844	2.03279	2.56330	3.22510	4.04893	6.34118
25	1.28243	1.45095	1.64061	2.09378	2.66584	3.38635	4.29187	6.84848
26	1.29526	1.47271	1.67342	2.15659	2.77247	3.55567	4.54938	7.39635
27	1.30821	1.49480	1.70689	2.22129	2.88337	3.73346	4.82235	7.98806
28	1.32129	1.51722	1.74102	2.28793	2.99870	3.92013	5.11169	8.62711
29	1.33450	1.53998	1.77584	2.35657	3.11865	4.11614	5.41839	9.31727
30	1.34785	1.56308	1.81136	2.42726	3.24340	4.32194	5.74349	10.06266
31	1.36133	1.58653	1.84759	2.50008	3.37313	4.53804	6.08810	10.86767
32	1.37494	1.61032	1.88454	2.57508	3.50806	4.76494	6.45339	11.73708
33	1.38869	1.63448	1.92223	2.65234	3.64838	5.00319	6.84059	12.67605
34	1.40258	1.65900	1.96068	2.73191	3.79432	5.25335	7.25103	13.69013
35	1.41660	1.68388	1.99989	2.81386	3.94609	5.51602	7.68609	14.78534
36	1.43077	1.70914	2.03989	2.89828	4.10393	5.79182	8.14725	15.96817
37	1.44508	1.73478	2.08069	2.98523	4.26809	6.08141	8.63609	17.24563
38	1.45953	1.76080	2.12230	3.07478	4.43881	6.38548	9.15425	18.62528
39	1.47412	1.78721	2.16474	3.16703	4.61637	6.70475	9.70351	20.11530
40	1.48886	1.81402	2.20804	3.26204	4.80102	7.03999	10.28572	21.72452
41	1.50375	1.84123	2.25220	3.35990	4.99306	7.39199	10.90286	23.46248
42	1.51879	1.86885	2.29724	3.46070	5.19278	7.76159	11.55703	25.33948
43	1.53398	1.89688	2.34319	3.56452	5.40050	8.14967	12.25045	27.36664
44	1.54932	1.92533	2.39005	3.67145	5.61652	8.55715	12.98548	29.55597
45	1.56481	1.95421	2.43785	3.78160	5.84118	8.98501	13.76461	31.92045
46	1.58046	1.98353	2.48661	3.89504	6.07482	9.43426	14.59049	34.47409
47	1.59626	2.01328	2.53634	4.01190	6.31782	9.90597	15.46592	37.23201
48	1.61223	2.04348	2.58707	4.13225	6.57053	10.40127	16.39387	40.21057
49	1.62835	2.07413	2.63881	4.25622	6.83335	10.92133	17.37750	43.42742
50	1.64463	2.10524	2.69159	4.38391	7.10668	11.46740	18.42015	46.90161

Amount of an Annuity

$$s_{\overline{n}|i} = \frac{(1 + i)^n - 1}{i}$$

i / n	1%	$1\frac{1}{2}$%	2%	3%	4%	5%	6%	8%
1	1.00000	1.00000	1.00000	1.00000	1.00000	1.00000	1.00000	1.00000
2	2.01000	2.01500	2.02000	2.03000	2.04000	2.05000	2.06000	2.08000
3	3.03010	3.04523	3.06040	3.09090	3.12160	3.15250	3.18360	3.24640
4	4.06040	4.09090	4.12161	4.18363	4.24646	4.31013	4.37462	4.50611
5	5.10101	5.15227	5.20404	5.30914	5.41632	5.52563	5.63709	5.86660
6	6.15202	6.22955	6.30812	6.46841	6.63298	6.80191	6.97532	7.33593
7	7.21354	7.32299	7.43428	7.66246	7.89829	8.14201	8.39384	8.92280
8	8.28567	8.43284	8.58297	8.89234	9.21423	9.54911	9.89747	10.63663
9	9.36853	9.55933	9.75463	10.15911	10.58280	11.02656	11.49132	12.48756
10	10.46221	10.70272	10.94972	11.46388	12.00611	12.57789	13.18079	14.48656
11	11.56683	11.86326	12.16872	12.80780	13.48635	14.20679	14.97164	16.64549
12	12.68250	13.04121	13.41209	14.19203	15.02581	15.91713	16.86994	18.97713
13	13.80933	14.23683	14.68033	15.61779	16.62684	17.71298	18.88214	21.49530
14	14.94742	15.45038	15.97394	17.08632	18.29191	19.59863	21.01507	24.21492
15	16.09690	16.68214	17.29342	18.59891	20.02359	21.57856	23.27597	27.15211
16	17.25786	17.93237	18.63929	20.15688	21.82453	23.65749	25.67253	30.32428
17	18.43044	19.20136	20.01207	21.76159	23.69751	25.84037	28.21288	33.75023
18	19.61475	20.48938	21.41231	23.41444	25.64541	28.13238	30.90565	37.45024
19	20.81090	21.79672	22.84056	25.11687	27.67123	30.53900	33.75999	41.44626
20	22.01900	23.12367	24.29737	26.87037	29.77808	33.06595	36.78559	45.76196
21	23.23919	24.47052	25.78332	28.67649	31.96920	35.71925	39.99273	50.42292
22	24.47159	25.83758	27.29898	30.53678	34.24797	38.50521	43.39229	55.45676
23	25.71630	27.22514	28.84496	32.45288	36.61789	41.43048	46.99583	60.89330
24	26.97346	28.63352	30.42186	34.42647	39.08260	44.50200	50.81558	66.76476
25	28.24320	30.06302	32.03030	36.45926	41.64591	47.72710	54.86451	73.10594
26	29.52563	31.51397	33.67091	38.55304	44.31174	51.11345	59.15638	79.95442
27	30.82089	32.98668	35.34432	40.70963	47.08421	54.66913	63.70577	87.35077
28	32.12910	34.48148	37.05121	42.93092	49.96758	58.40258	68.52811	95.33883
29	33.45039	35.99870	38.79223	45.21885	52.96629	62.32271	73.63980	103.96594
30	34.78489	37.53868	40.56808	47.57542	56.08494	66.43885	79.05819	113.28321
31	36.13274	39.10176	42.37944	50.00268	59.32834	70.76079	84.80168	123.34587
32	37.49407	40.68829	44.22703	52.50276	62.70147	75.29883	90.88978	134.21354
33	38.86901	42.29861	46.11157	55.07784	66.20953	80.06377	97.34316	145.95062
34	40.25770	43.93309	48.03380	57.73018	69.85791	85.06696	104.18375	158.62667
35	41.66028	45.59209	49.99448	60.46208	73.65222	90.32031	111.43478	172.31680
36	43.07688	47.27597	51.99437	63.27594	77.59831	95.83632	119.12087	187.10215
37	44.50765	48.98511	54.03425	66.17422	81.70225	101.62814	127.26812	203.07032
38	45.95272	50.71989	56.11494	69.15945	85.97034	107.70955	135.90421	220.31595
39	47.41225	52.48068	58.23724	72.23423	90.40915	114.09502	145.05846	238.94122
40	48.88637	54.26789	60.40198	75.40126	95.02552	120.79977	154.76197	259.05652
41	50.37524	56.08191	62.61002	78.66330	99.82654	127.83976	165.04768	280.78104
42	51.87899	57.92314	64.86222	82.02320	104.81960	135.23175	175.95054	304.24352
43	53.39778	59.79199	67.15947	85.48389	110.01238	142.99334	187.50758	329.58301
44	54.93176	61.68887	69.50266	89.04841	115.41288	151.14301	199.75803	356.94965
45	56.48107	63.61420	71.89271	92.71986	121.02939	159.70016	212.74351	386.50562
46	58.04589	65.56841	74.33056	96.50146	126.87057	168.68516	226.50812	418.42607
47	59.62634	67.55194	76.81718	100.39650	132.94539	178.11942	241.09861	452.90015
48	61.22261	69.56522	79.35352	104.40840	139.26321	188.02539	256.56453	490.13216
49	62.83483	71.60870	81.94059	108.54065	145.83373	198.42666	272.95840	530.34274
50	64.46318	73.68283	84.57940	112.79687	152.66708	209.34800	290.33590	573.77016

Present Value of an Annuity

$$a_{\overline{n}|i} = \frac{1 - (1 + i)^{-n}}{i}$$

n \ i	1%	$1\frac{1}{2}$%	2%	3%	4%	5%	6%	8%
1	0.99010	0.98522	0.98039	0.97087	0.96154	0.95238	0.94340	0.92593
2	1.97040	1.95588	1.94156	1.91347	1.88609	1.85941	1.83339	1.78326
3	2.94099	2.91220	2.88388	2.82861	2.77509	2.72325	2.67301	2.57710
4	3.90197	3.85438	3.80773	3.71710	3.62990	3.54595	3.46511	3.31213
5	4.85343	4.78264	4.71346	4.57971	4.45182	4.32948	4.21236	3.99271
6	5.79548	5.69719	5.60143	5.41719	5.24214	5.07569	4.91732	4.62288
7	6.72819	6.59821	6.47199	6.23028	6.00205	5.78637	5.58238	5.20637
8	7.65168	7.48593	7.32548	7.01969	6.73274	6.46321	6.20979	5.74664
9	8.56602	8.36052	8.16224	7.78611	7.43533	7.10782	6.80169	6.24689
10	9.47130	9.22218	8.98259	8.53020	8.11090	7.72173	7.36009	6.71008
11	10.36763	10.07112	9.78685	9.25262	8.76048	8.30641	7.88687	7.13896
12	11.25508	10.90751	10.57534	9.95400	9.38507	8.86325	8.38384	7.53608
13	12.13374	11.73153	11.34837	10.63496	9.98565	9.39357	8.85268	7.90378
14	13.00370	12.54338	12.10625	11.29607	10.56312	9.89864	9.29498	8.24424
15	13.86505	13.34323	12.84926	11.93794	11.11839	10.37966	9.71225	8.55948
16	14.71787	14.13126	13.57771	12.56110	11.65230	10.83777	10.10590	8.85137
17	15.56225	14.90765	14.29187	13.16612	12.16567	11.27407	10.47726	9.12164
18	16.39827	15.67256	14.99203	13.75351	12.65930	11.68959	10.82760	9.37189
19	17.22601	16.42617	15.67846	14.32380	13.13394	12.08532	11.15812	9.60360
20	18.04555	17.16864	16.35143	14.87747	13.59033	12.46221	11.46992	9.81815
21	18.85698	17.90014	17.01121	15.41502	14.02916	12.82115	11.76408	10.01680
22	19.66038	18.62082	17.65805	15.93692	14.45112	13.16300	12.04158	10.20074
23	20.45582	19.33086	18.29220	16.44361	14.85684	13.48857	12.30338	10.37106
24	21.24339	20.03041	18.91393	16.93554	15.24696	13.79864	12.55036	10.52876
25	22.02316	20.71961	19.52346	17.41315	15.62208	14.09394	12.78336	10.67478
26	22.79520	21.39863	20.12104	17.87684	15.98277	14.37519	13.00317	10.80998
27	23.55961	22.06762	20.70690	18.32703	16.32959	14.64303	13.21053	10.93516
28	24.31644	22.72672	21.28127	18.76411	16.66306	14.89813	13.40616	11.05108
29	25.06579	23.37608	21.84438	19.18845	16.98371	15.14107	13.59072	11.15841
30	25.80771	24.01584	22.39646	19.60044	17.29203	15.37245	13.76483	11.25778
31	26.54229	24.64615	22.93770	20.00043	17.58849	15.59281	13.92909	11.34980
32	27.26959	25.26714	23.46833	20.38877	17.87355	15.80268	14.08404	11.43500
33	27.98969	25.87895	23.98856	20.76579	18.14765	16.00255	14.23023	11.51389
34	28.70267	26.48173	24.49859	21.13184	18.41120	16.19290	14.36814	11.58693
35	29.40858	27.07559	24.99862	21.48722	18.66461	16.37419	14.49825	11.65457
36	30.10751	27.66068	25.48884	21.83225	18.90828	16.54685	14.62099	11.71719
37	30.79951	28.23713	25.96945	22.16724	19.14258	16.71129	14.73678	11.77518
38	31.48466	28.80505	26.44064	22.49246	19.36786	16.86789	14.84602	11.82887
39	32.16303	29.36458	26.90259	22.80822	19.58448	17.01704	14.94907	11.87858
40	32.83469	29.91585	27.35548	23.11477	19.79277	17.15909	15.04630	11.92461
41	33.49969	30.45896	27.79949	23.41240	19.99305	17.29437	15.13802	11.96723
42	34.15811	30.99405	28.23479	23.70136	20.18563	17.42321	15.22454	12.00670
43	34.81001	31.52123	28.66156	23.98190	20.37079	17.54591	15.30617	12.04324
44	35.45545	32.04062	29.07996	24.25427	20.54884	17.66277	15.38318	12.07707
45	36.09451	32.55234	29.49016	24.51871	20.72004	17.77407	15.45583	12.10840
46	36.72724	33.05649	29.89231	24.77545	20.88465	17.88007	15.52437	12.13741
47	37.35370	33.55319	30.28658	25.02471	21.04294	17.98102	15.58903	12.16427
48	37.97396	34.04255	30.67312	25.26671	21.19513	18.07716	15.65003	12.18914
49	38.58808	34.52468	31.05208	25.50166	21.34147	18.16872	15.70757	12.21216
50	39.19612	34.99969	31.42361	25.72976	21.48218	18.25593	15.76186	12.23348

ANSWERS TO SELECTED EXERCISES

Review of Algebra (page xi)

1. -21 **2.** 150 **3.** 37 **4.** 28 **5.** $-6/7$ **6.** 6/5 **7.** Not a real number **8.** Not a real number **9.** 2.22
10. -5.617 **11.** 2 **12.** -4 **13.** 17 **14.** 4 **15.** -19 **16.** 14 **17.** 21 **18.** 1 **19.** -3
20. -22 **21.** 12 **22.** $-2/7$ **23.** $-7/8$ **24.** -1 **25.** 3 **26.** 12 **27.** $-12/5$ **28.** $-48/71$
29. $-59/6$ **30.** $-11/5$ **31.** .72 **32.** 1.6 **33.** 6.53 **34.** 3.19 **35.** -13.26 **36.** 1.02 **37.** $<$
38. $>$ **39.** $<$ **40.** $=$ **41.** $=$ **42.** $=$ **43.** $=$ **44.** $=$ **45.** $=$ **46.** $=$ **47.** $p \le -1$
48. $k < 1$ **49.** $m > -1$ **50.** $y \le 1$ **51.** $p > 1/5$ **52.** $x > 1/3$ **53.** $-5 < y < 6$ **54.** $7/3 \le r \le 4$
55. $-11/2 \le k \le 7/2$ **56.** $-1 \le y \le 2$ **57.** $p \ge -17/7$ **58.** $z \le 50/9$ **59.** $z < 1.5$ **60.** $k > .7$
61. $-x^2 + x + 9$ **62.** $-6y^2 + 3y + 10$ **63.** $-14q^2 + 11q - 14$ **64.** $9r^2 - 4r + 19$
65. $-0.327x^2 - 2.805x - 1.458$ **66.** $-2.97r^2 - 8.083r + 7.81$ **67.** $-18m^3 - 27m^2 + 9m$

68. $12k^2 - 20k + 3$ **69.** $25r^2 + 5rs - 12s^2$ **70.** $18k^2 - 7kq - q^2$ **71.** $\frac{6}{25}y^2 + \frac{11}{40}yz + \frac{1}{16}z^2$

72. $\frac{15}{16}r^2 - \frac{7}{12}rs - \frac{2}{9}s^2$ **73.** $0.0036x^2 - 0.04452x - 0.0918$ **74.** $4.34m^2 + 5.68m - 4.42$ **75.** $27p^3 - 1$

76. $6p^3 - 11p^2 + 14p - 5$ **77.** $8m^3 + 1$ **78.** $12k^4 + 21k^3 - 5k^2 + 3k + 2$
79. $m^2 + mn - 2n^2 - 2km + 5kn - 3k^2$ **80.** $2r^2 - 7rs + 3s^2 + 3rt - 4st + t^2$ **81.** $8a(a^2 - 2a + 3)$
82. $3y(y^2 + 8y + 3)$ **83.** $5p^2(5p^2 - 4pq + 20q^2)$ **84.** $10m^2(6m^2 - 12mn + 5n^2)$ **85.** $(m + 7)(m + 2)$
86. $(x + 5)(x - 1)$ **87.** $(z + 4)(z + 5)$ **88.** $(b - 7)(b - 1)$ **89.** $(a - 5b)(a - b)$ **90.** $(s - 5t)(s + 7t)$
91. $(y - 7z)(y + 3z)$ **92.** $6(a - 10)(a + 2)$ **93.** $3m(m + 3)(m + 1)$ **94.** $(2x + 1)(x - 3)$
95. $(3a + 7)(a + 1)$ **96.** $(2a - 5)(a - 6)$ **97.** $(5y + 2)(3y - 1)$ **98.** $(7m + 2n)(3m + n)$
99. $2a^2(4a - b)(3a + 2b)$ **100.** $4z^3(8z + 3a)(z - a)$ **101.** $(x + 8)(x - 8)$ **102.** $(3m + 5)(3m - 5)$
103. $(11a + 10)(11a - 10)$ **104.** Cannot be factored **105.** $(z + 7y)^2$ **106.** $(m - 3n)^2$ **107.** $(3p - 4)^2$
108. $(a - 6)(a^2 + 6a + 36)$ **109.** $(2r - 3s)(4r^2 + 6rs + 9s^2)$ **110.** $(4m + 5)(16m^2 - 20m + 25)$ **111.** $5, -4$
112. $-2, -3$ **113.** $6, -1$ **114.** $-8, 3$ **115.** $3, -1$ **116.** 4 **117.** $5/2, -2$ **118.** $4/3, -1/2$
119. $5, 2$ **120.** $4/3, -4/3$ **121.** $1/2, -4$ **122.** $0, 4$ **123.** $(5 + \sqrt{13})/6 \approx 1.434, (5 - \sqrt{13})/6 \approx 0.232$
124. $(1 + \sqrt{33})/4 \approx 1.686, (1 - \sqrt{33})/4 \approx -1.186$ **125.** $(-1 + \sqrt{5})/2 \approx 0.618, (-1 - \sqrt{5})/2 \approx -1.618$
126. $5 + \sqrt{5} \approx 7.236, 5 - \sqrt{5} \approx 2.764$ **127.** $(-6 + \sqrt{26})/2 \approx -0.450, (-6 - \sqrt{26})/2 \approx -5.550$ **128.** $5/2, 1$
129. $4/3, 1/2$ **130.** $-5, 2$ **131.** $5/2, -1$ **132.** No real number solutions **133.** $(-1 + \sqrt{73})/6 \approx 1.257,$
$(-1 - \sqrt{73})/6 \approx -1.591$ **134.** $0, -1$
135. $-2 < m < 4$ **136.** $t \le -6$ or $t \ge 1$ **137.** $1 < y < 2$

138. $k < -4$ or $k > 1/2$

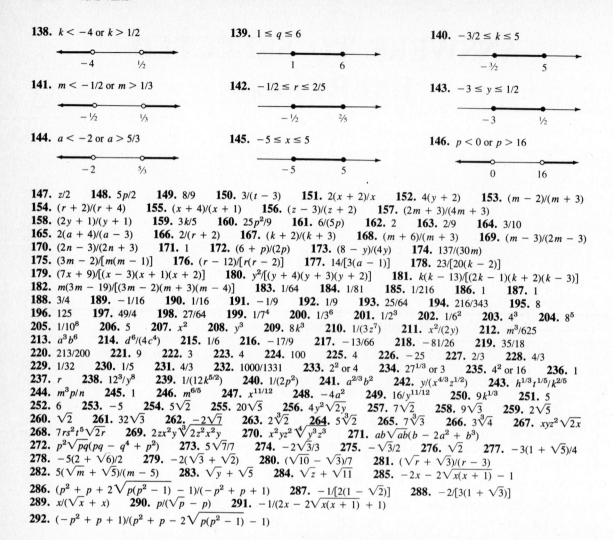

139. $1 \le q \le 6$

140. $-3/2 \le k \le 5$

141. $m < -1/2$ or $m > 1/3$

142. $-1/2 \le r \le 2/5$

143. $-3 \le y \le 1/2$

144. $a < -2$ or $a > 5/3$

145. $-5 \le x \le 5$

146. $p < 0$ or $p > 16$

147. $z/2$ **148.** $5p/2$ **149.** $8/9$ **150.** $3/(t-3)$ **151.** $2(x+2)/x$ **152.** $4(y+2)$ **153.** $(m-2)/(m+3)$
154. $(r+2)/(r+4)$ **155.** $(x+4)/(x+1)$ **156.** $(z-3)/(z+2)$ **157.** $(2m+3)/(4m+3)$
158. $(2y+1)/(y+1)$ **159.** $3k/5$ **160.** $25p^2/9$ **161.** $6/(5p)$ **162.** 2 **163.** $2/9$ **164.** $3/10$
165. $2(a+4)/(a-3)$ **166.** $2/(r+2)$ **167.** $(k+2)/(k+3)$ **168.** $(m+6)/(m+3)$ **169.** $(m-3)/(2m-3)$
170. $(2n-3)/(2n+3)$ **171.** 1 **172.** $(6+p)/(2p)$ **173.** $(8-y)/(4y)$ **174.** $137/(30m)$
175. $(3m-2)/[m(m-1)]$ **176.** $(r-12)/[r(r-2)]$ **177.** $14/[3(a-1)]$ **178.** $23/[20(k-2)]$
179. $(7x+9)/[(x-3)(x+1)(x+2)]$ **180.** $y^2/[(y+4)(y+3)(y+2)]$ **181.** $k(k-13)/[(2k-1)(k+2)(k-3)]$
182. $m(3m-19)/[(3m-2)(m+3)(m-4)]$ **183.** $1/64$ **184.** $1/81$ **185.** $1/216$ **186.** 1 **187.** 1
188. $3/4$ **189.** $-1/16$ **190.** $1/16$ **191.** $-1/9$ **192.** $1/9$ **193.** $25/64$ **194.** $216/343$ **195.** 8
196. 125 **197.** $49/4$ **198.** $27/64$ **199.** $1/7^4$ **200.** $1/3^6$ **201.** $1/2^3$ **202.** $1/6^2$ **203.** 4^3 **204.** 8^5
205. $1/10^8$ **206.** 5 **207.** x^2 **208.** y^3 **209.** $8k^3$ **210.** $1/(3z^7)$ **211.** $x^2/(2y)$ **212.** $m^3/625$
213. $a^3 b^6$ **214.** $d^6/(4c^4)$ **215.** $1/6$ **216.** $-17/9$ **217.** $-13/66$ **218.** $-81/26$ **219.** $35/18$
220. $213/200$ **221.** 9 **222.** 3 **223.** 4 **224.** 100 **225.** 4 **226.** -25 **227.** $2/3$ **228.** $4/3$
229. $1/32$ **230.** $1/5$ **231.** $4/3$ **232.** $1000/1331$ **233.** 2^2 or 4 **234.** $27^{1/3}$ or 3 **235.** 4^2 or 16 **236.** 1
237. r **238.** $12^3/y^8$ **239.** $1/(12k^{5/2})$ **240.** $1/(2p^2)$ **241.** $a^{2/3}b^2$ **242.** $y/(x^{4/3}z^{1/2})$ **243.** $h^{1/3}t^{1/5}/k^{2/5}$
244. $m^3 p/n$ **245.** 1 **246.** $m^{6/5}$ **247.** $x^{11/12}$ **248.** $-4a^2$ **249.** $16/y^{11/12}$ **250.** $9k^{1/3}$ **251.** 5
252. 6 **253.** -5 **254.** $5\sqrt{2}$ **255.** $20\sqrt{5}$ **256.** $4y^2\sqrt{2y}$ **257.** $7\sqrt{2}$ **258.** $9\sqrt{3}$ **259.** $2\sqrt{5}$
260. $\sqrt{2}$ **261.** $32\sqrt{3}$ **262.** $-2\sqrt{7}$ **263.** $2\sqrt[3]{2}$ **264.** $5\sqrt[3]{2}$ **265.** $7\sqrt[3]{3}$ **266.** $3\sqrt[3]{4}$ **267.** $xyz^2\sqrt{2x}$
268. $7rs^2t^5\sqrt{2r}$ **269.** $2zx^2y\sqrt[3]{2z^2x^2y}$ **270.** $x^2yz^2\sqrt[4]{y^3z^3}$ **271.** $ab\sqrt{ab}(b-2a^2+b^3)$
272. $p^2\sqrt{pq}(pq-q^4+p^2)$ **273.** $5\sqrt{7}/7$ **274.** $-2\sqrt{3}/3$ **275.** $-\sqrt{3}/2$ **276.** $\sqrt{2}$ **277.** $-3(1+\sqrt{5})/4$
278. $-5(2+\sqrt{6})/2$ **279.** $-2(\sqrt{3}+\sqrt{2})$ **280.** $(\sqrt{10}-\sqrt{3})/7$ **281.** $(\sqrt{r}+\sqrt{3})/(r-3)$
282. $5(\sqrt{m}+\sqrt{5})/(m-5)$ **283.** $\sqrt{y}+\sqrt{5}$ **284.** $\sqrt{z}+\sqrt{11}$ **285.** $-2x-2\sqrt{x(x+1)}-1$
286. $(p^2+p+2\sqrt{p(p^2-1)}-1)/(-p^2+p+1)$ **287.** $-1/[2(1-\sqrt{2})]$ **288.** $-2/[3(1+\sqrt{3})]$
289. $x/(\sqrt{x}+x)$ **290.** $p/(\sqrt{p}-p)$ **291.** $-1/(2x-2\sqrt{x(x+1)}+1)$
292. $(-p^2+p+1)/(p^2+p-2\sqrt{p(p^2-1)}-1)$

Chapter 1   Section 1.1   (page 9)

1. $(-2, -3), (-1, -2), (0, -1), (1, 0), (2, 1), (3, 2)$;
range: $\{-3, -2, -1, 0, 1, 2\}$

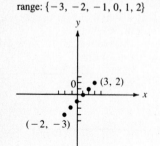

3. $(-2, 17), (-1, 13), (0, 9), (1, 5), (2, 1), (3, -3)$;
range: $\{-3, 1, 5, 9, 13, 17\}$

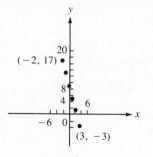

5. $(-2, -3), (-1, -4), (0, -5), (1, -6), (2, -7), (3, -8)$;
range: $\{-8, -7, -6, -5, -4, -3\}$

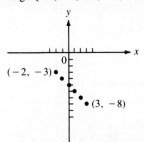

7. $(-2, 13), (-1, 11), (0, 9), (1, 7), (2, 5), (3, 3)$;
range: $\{3, 5, 7, 9, 11, 13\}$

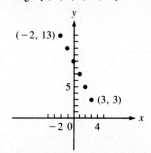

9. $(-2, 3/2), (-1, 2), (0, 5/2), (1, 3), (2, 7/2), (3, 4)$;
range: $\{3/2, 2, 5/2, 3, 7/2, 4\}$

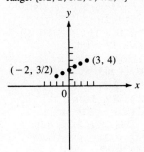

11. $(-2, 2), (-1, 0), (0, 0), (1, 2), (2, 6), (3, 12)$;
range: $\{0, 2, 6, 12\}$

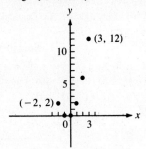

13. $(-2, 4), (-1, 1), (0, 0), (1, 1), (2, 4), (3, 9)$;
range: $\{0, 1, 4, 9\}$

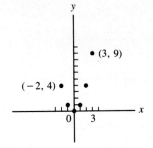

15. $(-2, 1), (-1, 1/2), (0, 1/3), (1, 1/4), (2, 1/5), (3, 1/6)$;
range: $\{1, 1/2, 1/3, 1/4, 1/5, 1/6\}$

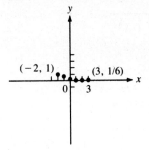

17. $(-2, -3), (-1, -3/2), (0, -3/5), (1, 0), (2, 3/7), (3, 3/4)$; range: $\{-3, -3/2, -3/5, 0, 3/7, 3/4\}$

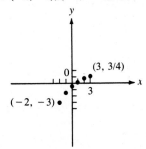

19. Function   **21.** Not a function   **23.** Function   **25.** (a) 14   (b) -7 (c) 1/2   (d) $3a + 2$ (e) $6/m + 2$ **27.** (a) 5
(b) -23 (c) $-7/4$ (d) $-a^2 + 5a + 1$ (e) $-4/m^2 + 10/m + 1$ or $(-4 + 10m + m^2)/m^2$ **29.** (a) 9/2   (b) 1   (c) 0
(d) $(2a + 1)/(a - 2)$ (e) $(4 + m)/(2 - 2m)$ **31.** (a) 30   (b) 2   (c) 3/4   (d) $(a + 1)(a + 2)$ or $a^2 + 3a + 2$
(e) $(4 + 6m + 2m^2)/m^2$ **33.** (a) 0   (b) 4   (c) 3   (d) 4   **35.** (a) -3 (b) -2 (c) -1 (d) 2   **37.** $6m - 20$
39. $r^2 + 2rh + h^2 - 2r - 2h + 5$ **41.** $9/q^2 - 6/q + 5$ or $(9 - 6q + 5q^2)/q^2$ **43.** 28   **45.** 4
47. $(-1, 4)$

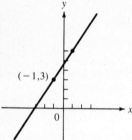

49. $(-\infty, 0)$

51. $[1, 2)$

53. $(-\infty, -9)$

55. $-4 < x < 3$ **57.** $x \le -1$ **59.** $-2 \le x < 6$ **61.** $x \le -4$ **63.** $(-\infty, \infty)$ **65.** $(-\infty, \infty)$
67. $[-4, 4]$ **69.** $[3, \infty)$ **71.** $x \ne \pm 2$, or $(-\infty, -2) \cup (-2, 2) \cup (2, \infty)$ **73.** $(-\infty, \infty)$ **75.** $(-\infty, \infty)$
77. $(-\infty, -1] \cup [5, \infty)$ **79.** $(-\infty, -5/3] \cup [1/2, \infty)$ **81.** Domain: $[-5, 4]$; Range: $[-2, 6]$
83. Domain: $(-\infty, \infty)$; Range: $(-\infty, 12]$ **85.** (a) $x^2 + 2xh + h^2 - 4$ (b) $2xh + h^2$ (c) $2x + h$ **87.** (a) $6x + 6h + 2$
(b) $6h$ (c) 6   **89.** (a) $2x^3 + 6x^2h + 6xh^2 + 2h^3 + x^2 + 2xh + h^2$ (b) $6x^2h + 6xh^2 + 2h^3 + 2xh + h^2$
(c) $6x^2 + 6xh + 2h^2 + 2x + h$ **91.** (a) $1/(x + h)$ (b) $-h/[x(x + h)]$ (c) $-1/[x(x + h)]$ **93.** (a) \$11   (b) \$11
(c) \$18   (d) \$32   (e) \$32   (f) \$39   (g) \$39   (h) Continue the horizontal bars up and to the right.

Section 1.2   (page 21)

1. 3/5   **3.** Not defined   **5.** 2   **7.** 5/9   **9.** Not defined   **11.** 2   **13.** .5785   **15.** $2x + y = 5$ **17.** $y = 1$
19. $x + 3y = 10$ **21.** $3x + 4y = 12$ **23.** $2x - 3y = 6$ **25.** $x = -6$ **27.** $5.081x + y = -4.69$

29.

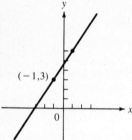

31.

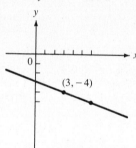

33.

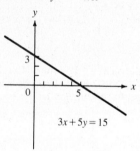

35.

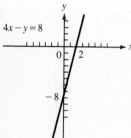

37.

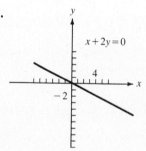

39.

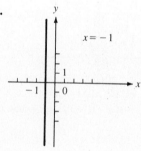

41.

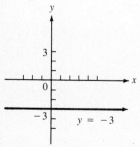

43. $x + 3y = 11$
45. $x - y = 7$
47. $-2x + y = 4$
49. $2x - 3y = -6$
51. No

55. (a)

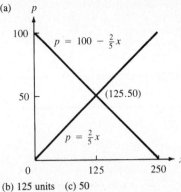

$p = 100 - \frac{2}{5}x$

$p = \frac{2}{5}x$

(125.50)

(b) 125 units   (c) 50

57. $y = 640x + 1100$; $m = 640$
59. $y = 2.5x - 70$; $m = 2.5$
61. (a) $h = (8/3)t + 211/3$; $m = 8/3$
   (b) About 172 cm; about 190 cm
   (c) About 45 cm
63. (a) \$52   (b) \$52   (c) \$52
   (d) \$79   (e) \$106
   (g) Yes   (h) No

63. (f)

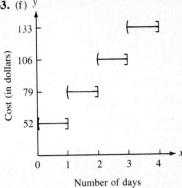

Cost (in dollars)

Number of days

Section 1.3   (page 28)

1. (a) 2600   (b) 2900   (c) 3200   (d) 2000   (e) 300   **3.** (a) 240   (b) 200   (c) 160   (d) -8; more required study produces fewer students   (e) 28 hours   **5.** (a) $y = (800,000/7)x + 200,000$ (b) About \$429,000   (c) About \$1,230,000   **7.** If $C(x)$ is the cost of renting a saw for x hours, then $C(x) = 12 + x$.   **9.** If $P(x)$ is the cost in cents of parking for x half-hours, then $P(x) = 35x + 50$.   **11.** $C(x) = 30x + 100$ **13.** $C(x) = 25x + 1000$ **15.** $C(x) = 50x + 500$
17. $C(x) = 90x + 2500$ **19.** (a) \$97   (b) \$97.097   (c) \$.097 or 9.7¢   (d) \$.097 or 9.7¢   **21.** (a) \$100   (b) \$36   (c) \$24
23. 500 units; \$30,000   **25.** Break-even point is 45 units; don't produce   **27.** Break-even point is -50 units; impossible to make a profit here   **29.** about 2,000,000 cars   **31.** (a) 32.5   (b) 70   (c) 145   (d) 220

Extended Application   (page 33)

1. 4.8 million units   **2.** Portion of a straight line going through (3.1, 10.50) and (5.7, 10.67)   **3.** In the interval under discussion (3.1 to 5.7 million units), the marginal cost always exceeds the selling price.   **4.** (a) 9.87; 10.22   (b) portion of a straight line through (3.1, 9.87) and (5.7, 10.22)   (c) .83 million units, which is not in the interval under discussion

Section 1.4   (page 38)

1.

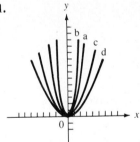

3.

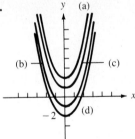

5.

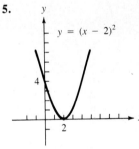

$y = (x - 2)^2$

7.

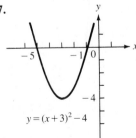

$y = (x+3)^2 - 4$

9.

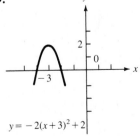

$y = -2(x+3)^2 + 2$

11.

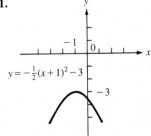

$y = -\frac{1}{2}(x+1)^2 - 3$

13.

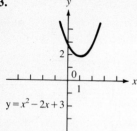

$y = x^2 - 2x + 3$

15.

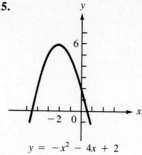

$y = -x^2 - 4x + 2$

17.

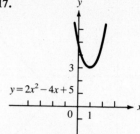

$y = 2x^2 - 4x + 5$

19.

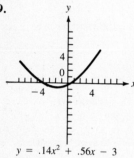

$y = .14x^2 + .56x - 3$

21.

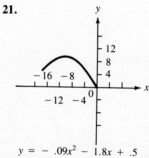

$y = -.09x^2 - 1.8x + .5$

23. 80 ft by 160 ft
25. 5 units of sandwiches; $310
27. 5 in   **29.** 10, 10

31. (a) $x(500 - x) = 500x - x^2$
  (b) $R(x)$

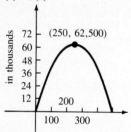

(250, 62,500)

33.

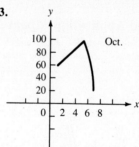

Oct.

35. $6\sqrt{3}$ cm

Section 1.5   (page 47)

1.

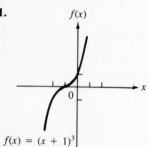

$f(x) = (x + 1)^3$

3.

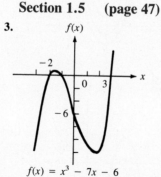

$f(x) = x^3 - 7x - 6$

5.

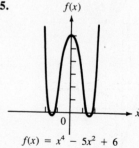

$f(x) = x^4 - 5x^2 + 6$

7.

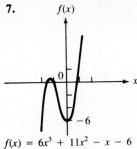

$f(x) = 6x^3 + 11x^2 - x - 6$

9.

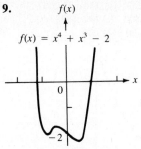

$f(x) = x^4 + x^3 - 2$

11.

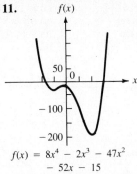

$f(x) = 8x^4 - 2x^3 - 47x^2 - 52x - 15$

13.

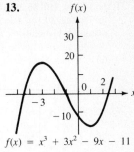

$f(x) = x^3 + 3x^2 - 9x - 11$

15.

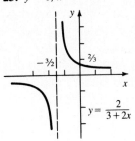

$f(x) = -x^3 + 6x^2 - x - 14$

17.

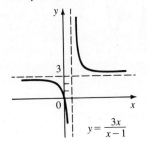

$f(x) = 2x^3 + 4x + 1$

19.

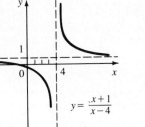

$f(x) = 2x^4 - 3x^3 + 4x^2 + 5x - 1$

21. $y = 0; x = 3$

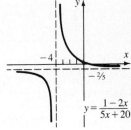

$y = \dfrac{-4}{x-3}$

23. $y = 0; x = -3/2$

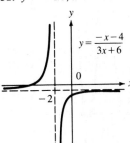

$y = \dfrac{2}{3+2x}$

25. $y = 3; x = 1$

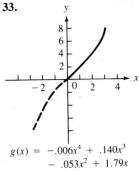

$y = \dfrac{3x}{x-1}$

27. $y = 1; x = 4$

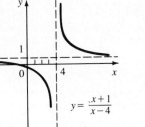

$y = \dfrac{x+1}{x-4}$

29. $y = -2/5; x = -4$

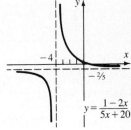

$y = \dfrac{1-2x}{5x+20}$

31. $y = -1/3; x = -2$

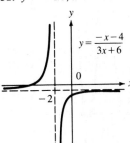

$y = \dfrac{-x-4}{3x+6}$

33.

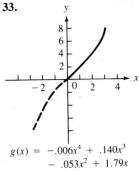

$g(x) = -.006x^4 + .140x^3 - .053x^2 + 1.79x$

35. (a)   (b) Between 4 and 5 hours, closer to 5 hours

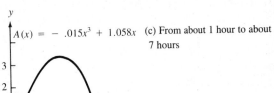

$A(x) = -.015x^3 + 1.058x$ (c) From about 1 hour to about 7 hours

37. (a) $12.50; $10; $6.25; $4.76; $3.85
(b) Probably $(0, \infty)$; doesn't seem reasonable to discuss the average cost per unit of no unit.
(c)

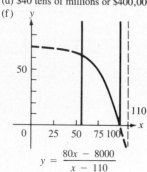

$$C(x) = \frac{500}{x+30}$$

39. (a) $0 (b) $6250 (c) About $24,000
(d) About $48,800 (e) About $88,000
(f) $214,500 (g) $325,000
(h) y

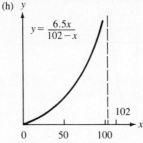

$$y = \frac{6.5x}{102-x}$$

41. (a) About $10,000
(b) About $20,000

43. (a) $R = -1000$ (b) $y = 1$
(c)

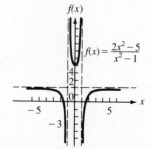

$$G(R) = \frac{R}{1000+R}$$

45. (a) $65.5 tens of millions, or $655,000,000
(b) $64 tens of millions, or $640,000,000
(c) $60 tens of millions or $600,000,000
(d) $40 tens of millions or $400,000,000 (e) $0
(f) y

47. Maximum of -10.013 when $x = .3$; minimum of -11.328 when $x = .8$
49. Maximum is 84 when $x = -2$; minimum is -13 when $x = -1$

51.

x	-3	-2.5	-2	-1.5	-1	$-.5$	0	$.5$	1	1.5
$f(x)$	7	9.125	9	7.375	5	2.625	1	.875	3	8.125

$f(x) = x^3 + 3x^2 - 2x + 1$

$$y = \frac{80x - 8000}{x - 110}$$

53.

x	-6	-5.5	-5	-4.5	-4	-3.5	-3	-2.5	-1.5	-1	$-.5$	0	$.5$
$f(x)$	-2.769	-2.988	-3.333	-3.951	-5.333	-10.889	18	3.333	.581	.222	.051	0	.051

x	1	1.5	2
$f(x)$	.222	.581	1.333

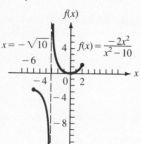

$$x = -\sqrt{10} \qquad f(x) = \frac{-2x^2}{x^2 - 10}$$

55. No horizontal asymptote

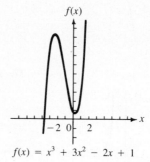

$$f(x) = \frac{-2x^2 + x - 1}{2x + 3}$$

57. $y = 2$

$$f(x) = \frac{2x^2 - 5}{x^2 - 1}$$

Section 1.6   (page 55)

1. $10x + 2$; $-2x - 4$; $24x^2 + 6x - 3$; $(4x - 1)/(6x + 3)$; all domains are $(-\infty, \infty)$, except for f/g, which is $(-\infty, -1/2) \cup (-1/2, \infty)$ **3.** $4x^2 - 4x + 1$; $2x^2 - 1$; $(3x^2 - 2x)(x^2 - 2x + 1)$; $(3x^2 - 2x)/(x^2 - 2x + 1)$; all domains are $(-\infty, \infty)$, except for f/g, which is $(-\infty, 1) \cup (1, \infty)$ **5.** $\sqrt{2x + 5} + \sqrt{4x - 9}$; $\sqrt{2x + 5} - \sqrt{4x - 9}$; $\sqrt{(2x + 5)(4x - 9)}$; $\sqrt{(2x + 5)/(4x - 9)}$; all domains are $[9/4, \infty)$, except f/g, which is $(9/4, \infty)$ **7.** $5x^2 - 11x + 7$; $3x^2 - 11x - 3$; $(4x^2 - 11x + 2)(x^2 + 5)$; $(4x^2 - 11x + 2)/(x^2 + 5)$; all domains (including f/g) are $(-\infty, \infty)$ **9.** 55   **11.** 1848   **13.** $-6/7$ **15.** $4m^2 + 6m + 1$ **17.** 1122   **19.** 97   **21.** $256k^2 + 48k + 2$ **23.** $24x + 4$; $24x + 35$ **25.** $-5x^2 + 20x + 18$; $-25x^2 - 10x + 6$ **27.** $-64x^3 + 2$; $-4x^3 + 8$ **39.** $1/x^2$; $1/x^2$ **31.** $\sqrt{8x^2 - 4}$; $8x + 10$ **33.** $x/(2 - 5x)$; $2(x - 5)$ **35.** $\sqrt{(x - 1)/x}$; $-1/\sqrt{x + 1}$ **49.** $18a^2 + 24a + 9$ **51.** $16\pi t^2$ **53.** No greater than 4   **55.** No greater than 8   **57.** Even   **59.** Odd   **61.** Neither   **63.** Neither

Chapter 1   Review Exercises   (page 57)

1. $(-3, -16/5)$, $(-2, -14/5)$, $(-1, -12/5)$, $(0, -2)$, $(1, -8/5)$, $(2, -6/5)$, $(3, -4/5)$; range: $\{-16/5, -14/5, -12/5, -2, -8/5, -6/5, -4/5\}$

3. $(-3, 20)$, $(-2, 9)$, $(-1, 2)$, $(0, -1)$, $(1, 0)$, $(2, 5)$, $(3, 14)$; range: $\{-1, 0, 2, 5, 9, 14, 20\}$

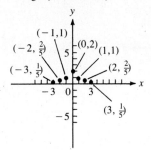

5. $(-3, 7)$, $(-2, 2)$, $(-1, -1)$, $(0, -2)$, $(1, -1)$, $(2, 2)$, $(3, 7)$; range: $\{-2, -1, 2, 7\}$

7. $(-3, 1/5)$, $(-2, 2/5)$, $(-1, 1)$, $(0, 2)$, $(1, 1)$, $(2, 2/5)$, $(3, 1/5)$; range: $\{1/5, 2/5, 1, 2\}$

9. $(-3, -1)$, $(-2, -1)$, $(-1, -1)$, $(0, -1)$, $(1, -1)$, $(2, -1)$, $(3, -1)$; range: $\{-1\}$

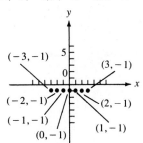

11. (a) 23 (b) -9 (c) -17 (d) $4r + 3$ **13.** (a) -28 (b) -12 (c) -28 (d) $-r^2 - 3$ **15.** (a) -13 (b) 3 (c) -32
(d) 22 (e) $-k^2 - 4k$ (f) $-9m^2 + 12m$ (g) $-k^2 + 14k - 45$ (h) $12 - 5p$ (i) -28 (j) -21

17.

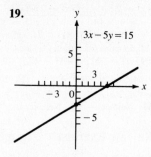

19.

21.

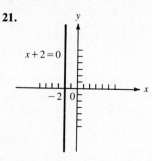

23.

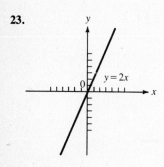

25. (a) 7/6; 9/2 (b) 2; 2 (c) 5/2; 1/2 (d)
(e) 15 (f) 2; 2

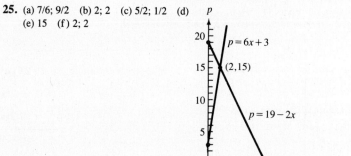

27. 1/3   **29.** $-2/11$ **31.** $-2/3$ **33.** Not defined   **35.** $3y = 2x - 13$ **37.** $5x + 4y = 17$ **39.** $x = -1$
41. $y = 3/4$ **43.** $5x - 8y = -40$ **45.** $y = -5$
47.   **49.**   **51.** $C(x) = 30x + 60$
53. $C(x) = 46x + 120$

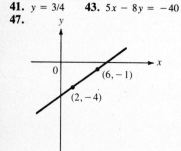

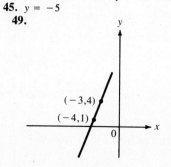

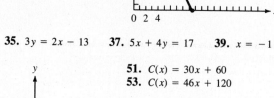

55.

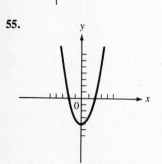

57.

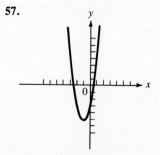

59.

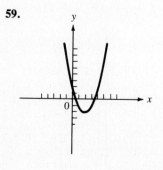

61.

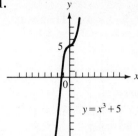

$y = x^3 + 5$

63.

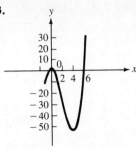

65. $f(x) = x^4 - 4x^3 - 5x^2 + 14x - 15$

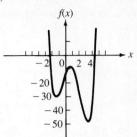

67.

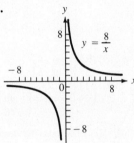

$y = \dfrac{8}{x}$

69.

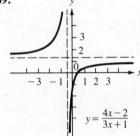

$y = \dfrac{4x - 2}{3x + 1}$

71. $4x^2 - 3x - 8$ **73.** 44   **75.** $16k^2 - 6k - 8$ **77.** $-23/4$ **79.** $(-\infty, \infty)$ **81.** $\sqrt{x^2 - 2}$ **83.** $\sqrt{34}$ **85.** 1

Chapter 2   Section 2.1   (page 72)

---

1. $(3, 6)$ **3.** $(-1, 4)$ **5.** $(-2, 0)$ **7.** $(1, 3)$ **9.** $(4, -2)$ **11.** $(2, -2)$ **13.** No solution   **15.** Same line
17. $(12, 6)$ **19.** $(7, -2)$ **21.** $(1, 2, -1)$ **23.** $(2, 0, 3)$ **25.** No solution   **27.** $(0, 2, 4)$ **29.** $(1, 2, 3)$
31. $(-1, 2, 1)$ **33.** $(4, 1, 2)$ **35.** x arbitrary, $y = x + 5$, $z = -2x + 1$ **37.** x arbitrary, $y = x + 1$, $z = -x + 3$
39. x arbitrary, $y = 4x - 7$, $z = 3x + 7$, $w = -x - 3$ **41.** $(3, -4)$ **43.** No solution   **45.** No solution   **47.** Wife:
40 days; husband: 32 days   **49.** 5 model 201; 8 model 301   **51.** \$10,000 at 16%; \$7000 at 20%; \$8000 at 18%   **53.** $k = 3$;
solution is $(-1, 0, 2)$

Section 2.2   (page 80)

1. $\begin{bmatrix} 2 & 3 & | & 11 \\ 1 & 2 & | & 8 \end{bmatrix}$ **3.** $\begin{bmatrix} 1 & 5 & | & 6 \\ 0 & 1 & | & 1 \end{bmatrix}$ **5.** $\begin{bmatrix} 2 & 1 & 1 & | & 3 \\ 3 & -4 & 2 & | & -7 \\ 1 & 1 & 1 & | & 2 \end{bmatrix}$ **7.** $\begin{bmatrix} 1 & 1 & 0 & | & 2 \\ 0 & 2 & 1 & | & -4 \\ 0 & 0 & 1 & | & 2 \end{bmatrix}$ **9.** $\begin{bmatrix} 1 & 0 & 0 & | & 5 \\ 0 & 1 & 0 & | & -2 \\ 0 & 0 & 1 & | & 3 \end{bmatrix}$

11. $x = 2$ **13.** $2x + y = 1$ **15.** $x = 2$ **17.** $(2, 3)$ **19.** $(-3, 0)$ **21.** $(7/2, -1)$ **23.** $(5/2, -1)$
$\quad\ y = 3$ $\quad\ 3x - 2y = -9$ $\quad\ y = 3$
$\qquad\qquad\qquad\qquad\qquad\qquad z = -2$
25. No solution   **27.** Same line   **29.** $(-2, 1, 3)$ **31.** $(-1, 23, 16)$ **33.** $(3, 2, -4)$ **35.** No solution
37. $(-1, 3, 2)$ **39.** $(2, 4, 5)$ **41.** $(0, 2, -2, 1)$ The answers are given in the order x, y, z, w.
43. (a) $\begin{bmatrix} 1 & 0 & 0 & 1 & | & 1000 \\ 1 & 1 & 0 & 0 & | & 1100 \\ 0 & 1 & 1 & 0 & | & 700 \\ 0 & 0 & 1 & 1 & | & 600 \end{bmatrix}$; $\begin{bmatrix} 1 & 0 & 0 & 1 & | & 1000 \\ 0 & 1 & 0 & -1 & | & 100 \\ 0 & 0 & 1 & 1 & | & 600 \\ 0 & 0 & 0 & 0 & | & 0 \end{bmatrix}$ (b) $x_1 + x_4 = 1000$; $x_2 - x_4 = 100$; $x_3 + x_4 = 600$
(c) $x_4 = 1000 - x_1$; $x_4 = x_2 - 100$; $x_4 = 600 - x_3$
(d) 1000; 1000   (e) 100   (f) 600; 600
(g) $x_4 = 600$; $x_3 = 600$; $x_2 = 700$; $x_1 = 1000$
45. $(4.12062, 1.66866, .117699)$ **47.** $(30.7209, 39.6513, 31.386, 50.3966)$ **49.** 81 kg of the first chemical, 382.286 kg of
the second, 286.714 kg of the third   **51.** 243 of A, 38 of B, 101 of C (rounded)

Section 2.3   (page 89)

1. False; not all corresponding elements are equal.   **3.** True   **5.** True   **7.** 2×2; square   **9.** 3×4 **11.** 2×1; column   **13.** $x = 2, y = 4, z = 8$ **15.** $x = -15, y = 5, k = 3$ **17.** $z = 18, r = 3, s = 3, p = 3, a = 3/4$

19. $\begin{bmatrix} 9 & 12 & 0 & 2 \\ 1 & -1 & 2 & -4 \end{bmatrix}$ **21.** $\begin{bmatrix} 5 & 13 & 0 \\ 3 & 1 & 8 \end{bmatrix}$ **23.** Not possible   **25.** $\begin{bmatrix} 1 & 5 & 6 & -9 \\ 5 & 7 & 2 & 1 \\ -7 & 2 & 2 & -7 \end{bmatrix}$

27. $\begin{bmatrix} -12x + 8y & -x + y \\ x & 8x - y \end{bmatrix}$ **29.** $\begin{bmatrix} x & y \\ z & w \end{bmatrix} + \begin{bmatrix} r & s \\ t & u \end{bmatrix} = \begin{bmatrix} x + r & y + s \\ z + t & w + u \end{bmatrix}$ (a 2×2 matrix)

31. $\begin{bmatrix} x + (r + m) & y + (s + n) \\ z + (t + p) & w + (u + q) \end{bmatrix} = \begin{bmatrix} (x + r) + m & (y + s) + n \\ (z + t) + p & (w + u) + q \end{bmatrix}$ **33.** $\begin{bmatrix} m + 0 & n + 0 \\ p + 0 & q + 0 \end{bmatrix} = \begin{bmatrix} m & n \\ p & q \end{bmatrix}$

35. $\begin{bmatrix} 7 & 2 \\ 9 & 0 \\ 8 & 6 \end{bmatrix}; \begin{bmatrix} 7 & 9 & 8 \\ 2 & 0 & 6 \end{bmatrix}$ **37.** (a) $\begin{bmatrix} 2 & 1 & 2 & 1 \\ 3 & 2 & 2 & 1 \\ 4 & 3 & 2 & 1 \end{bmatrix}$ (b) $\begin{bmatrix} 5 & 0 & 7 \\ 0 & 10 & 1 \\ 0 & 15 & 2 \\ 10 & 12 & 8 \end{bmatrix}$ (c) $\begin{bmatrix} 8 \\ 4 \\ 5 \end{bmatrix}$

Section 2.4   (page 97)

1. 2×2; 2×2 **3.** 4×4; 2×2 **5.** 3×2; BA does not exist   **7.** AB does not exist; 3×2 **9.** $\begin{bmatrix} -4 & 8 \\ 0 & 6 \end{bmatrix}$

11. $\begin{bmatrix} 24 & -8 \\ -16 & 0 \end{bmatrix}$ **13.** $\begin{bmatrix} -22 & -6 \\ 20 & -12 \end{bmatrix}$ **15.** $\begin{bmatrix} 13 \\ 25 \end{bmatrix}$ **17.** $\begin{bmatrix} -2 & 10 \\ 0 & 8 \end{bmatrix}$ **19.** $\begin{bmatrix} 13 & 5 \\ 25 & 15 \end{bmatrix}$ **21.** $\begin{bmatrix} 13 \\ 29 \end{bmatrix}$ **23.** $\begin{bmatrix} 110 \\ 40 \\ -50 \end{bmatrix}$

25. $\begin{bmatrix} 22 & -8 \\ 11 & -4 \end{bmatrix}$ **27.** (a) $\begin{bmatrix} 16 & 22 \\ 7 & 19 \end{bmatrix}$ (b) $\begin{bmatrix} 5 & -5 \\ 0 & 30 \end{bmatrix}$ (c) No; no   (d) No   **33.** (a) P, P, X (b) T (c) I maintains the identity of any 2×2 matrix under multiplication.   **35.** (a) $\begin{bmatrix} 20 & 52 & 27 \\ 25 & 62 & 35 \\ 30 & 72 & 43 \end{bmatrix}$ The rows represent the amounts of fat, carbohydrate, and protein, respectively, in each of the daily meals.

(b) $\begin{bmatrix} 75 \\ 45 \\ 70 \\ 168 \end{bmatrix}$ The rows give the number of calories in one exchange of each of the food groups.   **39.** $\begin{bmatrix} 44 & 75 & -60 & -33 & 11 \\ 20 & 169 & -164 & 18 & 105 \\ 113 & -82 & 239 & 218 & -55 \\ 119 & 83 & 7 & 82 & 106 \\ 162 & 20 & 175 & 143 & 74 \end{bmatrix}$

41. Cannot be found   **43.** No

Extended Application   (page 100)

1. (a) 3   (b) 3   (c) 5   (d) 3   **2.** (a) 21   (b) 25   **3.** (a) $B = \begin{bmatrix} 0 & 2 & 3 \\ 2 & 0 & 4 \\ 3 & 4 & 0 \end{bmatrix}$ (b) $\begin{bmatrix} 13 & 12 & 8 \\ 12 & 20 & 6 \\ 8 & 6 & 25 \end{bmatrix}$ (c) 12   (d) 14

4. (a)

	S	J	NO	H
S	0	1	2	1
J	1	0	1	0
NO	2	1	0	1
H	1	0	1	0

(b) 2   (c) 2   (d) 2   **5.** (a)

	dogs	rats	cats	mice
dogs	0	1	1	1
rats	0	0	0	1
cats	0	1	0	1
mice	0	0	0	0

$C = $

6. See Exercises 1, 3(b), and 5(b).

(b)

$C^2 = \begin{bmatrix} 0 & 1 & 0 & 2 \\ 0 & 0 & 0 & 0 \\ 0 & 0 & 0 & 1 \\ 0 & 0 & 0 & 0 \end{bmatrix}$ C^2 gives the number of food sources once removed from the feeder. Thus, since dogs eat rats and rats eat mice, mice are an indirect as well as a direct food source.

Extended Application   (page 102)

1. $PQ = \begin{bmatrix} 1 & 2 & 0 & 2 & 1 & 1 \\ 0 & 1 & 0 & 1 & 0 & 0 \\ 1 & 1 & 0 & 1 & 2 & 1 \end{bmatrix}$ **2.** None   **3.** Yes, the third person

4. The second and fourth persons in the third group each had four contacts in all.

Section 2.5   (page 109)

1. Yes   **3.** No   **5.** No   **7.** Yes   **9.** $\begin{bmatrix} 0 & 1/2 \\ -1 & 1/2 \end{bmatrix}$ **11.** $\begin{bmatrix} 2 & 1 \\ 5 & 3 \end{bmatrix}$ **13.** None   **15.** $\begin{bmatrix} 1 & 0 & 0 \\ 0 & -1 & 0 \\ -1 & 0 & 1 \end{bmatrix}$

17. $\begin{bmatrix} 15 & 4 & -5 \\ -12 & -3 & 4 \\ -4 & -1 & 1 \end{bmatrix}$ **19.** None   **21.** $\begin{bmatrix} 7/4 & 5/2 & 3 \\ -1/4 & -1/2 & 0 \\ -1/4 & -1/2 & -1 \end{bmatrix}$ **23.** $\begin{bmatrix} 1/2 & 1/2 & -1/4 & 1/2 \\ -1 & 4 & -1/2 & -2 \\ -1/2 & 5/2 & -1/4 & -3/2 \\ 1/2 & -1/2 & 1/4 & 1/2 \end{bmatrix}$

25. $(-1, 4)$ **27.** $(2, 1)$ **29.** $(2, 3)$ **31.** Same line   **33.** $(-8, 6, 1)$ **35.** $(15, -5, -1)$ **37.** $(-31, 24, -4)$

39. No inverse, no solution for system   **41.** $(-7, -34, -19, 7)$

49. (a) $\begin{bmatrix} 72 \\ 48 \\ 60 \end{bmatrix}$ (b) $\begin{bmatrix} 2 & 4 & 2 \\ 2 & 1 & 2 \\ 2 & 1 & 3 \end{bmatrix} \begin{bmatrix} x_1 \\ x_2 \\ x_3 \end{bmatrix} = \begin{bmatrix} 72 \\ 48 \\ 60 \end{bmatrix}$ (c) 8, 8, 12

In (51) and (53), results are rounded to four decimal places.

51. $\begin{bmatrix} -.0047 & -.0230 & .0292 & .0895 & -.0402 \\ .0921 & .0150 & .0321 & .0209 & -.0276 \\ -.0678 & .0315 & -.0404 & .0326 & .0373 \\ .0171 & -.0248 & .0069 & -.0003 & .0246 \\ -.0208 & .0740 & .0096 & -.1018 & .0646 \end{bmatrix}$ **53.** $\begin{bmatrix} .0394 & .0880 & .0033 & .0530 & -.1499 \\ -.1492 & .0289 & .0187 & .1033 & .1668 \\ -.1330 & -.0543 & .0356 & .1768 & .1055 \\ .1407 & .0175 & -.0453 & -.1344 & .0655 \\ .0102 & -.0653 & .0993 & .0085 & -.0388 \end{bmatrix}$

55. $\begin{bmatrix} .62963 \\ .148148 \\ .259259 \end{bmatrix}$ **57.** $\begin{bmatrix} .489558 \\ 1.00104 \\ 2.11853 \\ -1.20793 \\ -.961346 \end{bmatrix}$

Extended Application   (page 113)

1. (a) $\begin{bmatrix} 47 \\ 56 \end{bmatrix}$ $\begin{bmatrix} 0 \\ 130 \end{bmatrix}$ $\begin{bmatrix} 107 \\ 60 \end{bmatrix}$ $\begin{bmatrix} 53 \\ 202 \end{bmatrix}$ $\begin{bmatrix} 72 \\ 88 \end{bmatrix}$ $\begin{bmatrix} -7 \\ 172 \end{bmatrix}$ $\begin{bmatrix} 11 \\ 12 \end{bmatrix}$ $\begin{bmatrix} 83 \\ 74 \end{bmatrix}$ (b) $M^{-1} = \begin{bmatrix} 3/13 & 1/26 \\ -1/13 & 2/13 \end{bmatrix}$

2. $\begin{bmatrix} 39 \\ -98 \end{bmatrix}$ $\begin{bmatrix} -18 \\ 35 \end{bmatrix}$ $\begin{bmatrix} 19 \\ -49 \end{bmatrix}$ $\begin{bmatrix} -25 \\ 49 \end{bmatrix}$ $\begin{bmatrix} 34 \\ -95 \end{bmatrix}$ $\begin{bmatrix} -2 \\ 3 \end{bmatrix}$ $\begin{bmatrix} 5 \\ -24 \end{bmatrix}$ $\begin{bmatrix} 15 \\ -51 \end{bmatrix}$ $\begin{bmatrix} 10 \\ -32 \end{bmatrix}$ $\begin{bmatrix} 33 \\ -85 \end{bmatrix}$ $\begin{bmatrix} 35 \\ -97 \end{bmatrix}$ $\begin{bmatrix} 10 \\ -35 \end{bmatrix}$ $\begin{bmatrix} 39 \\ -105 \end{bmatrix}$ $\begin{bmatrix} 27 \\ -69 \end{bmatrix}$ $\begin{bmatrix} -4 \\ 4 \end{bmatrix}$

3. Santa Claus is fat   **4.** $\begin{bmatrix} 76 \\ 77 \\ 96 \end{bmatrix}$ $\begin{bmatrix} 62 \\ 67 \\ 75 \end{bmatrix}$ $\begin{bmatrix} 88 \\ 108 \\ 97 \end{bmatrix}$ $\begin{bmatrix} 141 \\ 160 \\ 168 \end{bmatrix}$ $\begin{bmatrix} 147 \\ 166 \\ 174 \end{bmatrix}$ $\begin{bmatrix} 105 \\ 120 \\ 123 \end{bmatrix}$ $\begin{bmatrix} 111 \\ 131 \\ 119 \end{bmatrix}$ $\begin{bmatrix} 92 \\ 119 \\ 94 \end{bmatrix}$ $\begin{bmatrix} 75 \\ 93 \\ 79 \end{bmatrix}$ $\begin{bmatrix} 181 \\ 208 \\ 208 \end{bmatrix}$

Section 2.6   (page 118)

1. $\begin{bmatrix} 32/3 \\ 25/3 \end{bmatrix}$ **3.** $\begin{bmatrix} 23,000/3579 \\ 93,500/3579 \end{bmatrix}$ or $\begin{bmatrix} 6.43 \\ 26.12 \end{bmatrix}$ **5.** $\begin{bmatrix} 20/3 \\ 20 \\ 10 \end{bmatrix}$ **7.** 1079 metric tons of wheat, 1428 metric tons of oil

9. 1285 units of agriculture, 1455 units of manufacturing, and 1202 units of transportation   **11.** 3077 units of agriculture, 2564 units of manufacturing, and 3179 units of transportation   **13.** (a) 7/4 bushels of yams, 15/8 pigs (b) 167.5 bushels of yams, 153.75 pigs   **15.** 33:47:23   **17.** $\begin{bmatrix} 2930 \\ 3570 \\ 2300 \\ 580 \end{bmatrix}$ **19.** $\begin{bmatrix} 1583.91 \\ 1529.54 \\ 1196.09 \end{bmatrix}$

Extended Application   (page 123)

1. (a) $A = \begin{bmatrix} 0.245 & 0.102 & 0.051 \\ 0.099 & 0.291 & 0.279 \\ 0.433 & 0.372 & 0.011 \end{bmatrix}$ $D = \begin{bmatrix} 2.88 \\ 31.45 \\ 30.91 \end{bmatrix}$ $X = \begin{bmatrix} x_1 \\ x_2 \\ x_3 \end{bmatrix}$ (b) $I - A = \begin{bmatrix} 0.755 & -0.102 & -0.051 \\ -0.099 & 0.709 & -0.279 \\ -0.433 & -0.372 & 0.989 \end{bmatrix}$ (d) $\begin{bmatrix} 18.2 \\ 73.2 \\ 66.8 \end{bmatrix}$

(e) \$18.2 billion of agriculture, \$73.2 billion of manufacturing, and \$66.8 billion of household would be required (rounded to three significant digits).   **2.** (a) $A = \begin{bmatrix} 0.293 & 0 & 0 \\ 0.014 & 0.207 & 0.017 \\ 0.044 & 0.010 & 0.216 \end{bmatrix}$ $D = \begin{bmatrix} 138,213 \\ 17,597 \\ 1,786 \end{bmatrix}$ (b) $I - A = \begin{bmatrix} .707 & 0 & 0 \\ -0.014 & 0.793 & -0.017 \\ -0.044 & -0.010 & 0.784 \end{bmatrix}$

(c) Agriculture 195,000 million pounds; manufacture 26,000 million pounds; energy 13,600 million pounds

Chapter 2 Review Exercises (page 125)

1. $(-4, 6)$ **3.** $(-1, 2, 3)$ **5.** 8 thousand standard, 6 thousand extra large **7.** 5 blankets, 3 rugs, 8 skirts **9.** $(-9, 3)$

11. $(7, -9, -1)$ **13.** $x = 6 - (7/3)z$, $y = 1 + (1/3)z$, z arbitrary **15.** 3×2; $a = 2$, $x = -1$, $y = 4$, $p = 5$, $z = 7$

17. 3×3 (square); $a = -12$, $b = 1$, $k = 9/2$, $c = 3/4$, $d = 3$, $l = -3/4$, $m = -1$, $p = 3$, $q = 9$

19. $\begin{bmatrix} 5 & 7 & 2532 & 52\frac{3}{8} & -\frac{1}{4} \\ 3 & 9 & 1464 & 56 & \frac{1}{8} \\ 2.50 & 5 & 4974 & 41 & -1\frac{1}{2} \\ 1.36 & 10 & 1754 & 18\frac{7}{8} & \frac{1}{2} \end{bmatrix}$ **21.** $\begin{bmatrix} 8 & -6 \\ -10 & -16 \end{bmatrix}$ **23.** Not possible **25.** $\begin{bmatrix} 26 & 86 \\ -7 & -29 \\ 21 & 87 \end{bmatrix}$

27. $\begin{bmatrix} 6 & 18 & -24 \\ 1 & 3 & -4 \\ 0 & 0 & 0 \end{bmatrix}$ **29.** $\begin{bmatrix} 15 \\ 16 \\ 1 \end{bmatrix}$ **31.** $\begin{bmatrix} -7/19 & 4/19 \\ 3/19 & 1/19 \end{bmatrix}$ **33.** Not possible **35.** $\begin{bmatrix} -\frac{1}{4} & \frac{1}{6} \\ 0 & \frac{1}{3} \end{bmatrix}$ **37.** No inverse

39. $\begin{bmatrix} \frac{1}{4} & \frac{1}{2} & \frac{1}{2} \\ \frac{1}{4} & -\frac{1}{2} & \frac{1}{2} \\ \frac{1}{8} & -\frac{1}{4} & -\frac{1}{4} \end{bmatrix}$ **41.** No inverse **43.** $X = \begin{bmatrix} 3 \\ 4 \end{bmatrix}$ **45.** $X = \begin{bmatrix} 6 \\ 15 \\ 16 \end{bmatrix}$ **47.** $(2, 1)$ **49.** $(-1, 0, 2)$

51. $\begin{bmatrix} 725.7 \\ 305.9 \\ 166.7 \end{bmatrix}$

Chapter 3 Section 3.1 (page 137)

1.
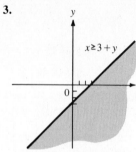
$x + y \leq 2$

3.
$x \geq 3 + y$

5.
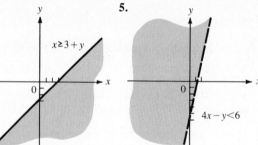
$4x - y < 6$

7.
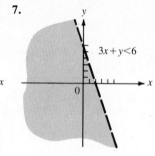
$3x + y < 6$

9.
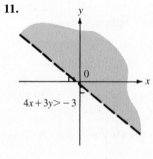
$x + 3y \geq -2$

11.
$4x + 3y > -3$

13.
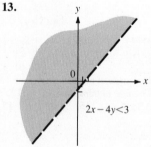
$2x - 4y < 3$

15.
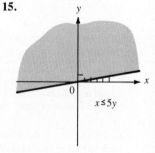
$x \leq 5y$

17.
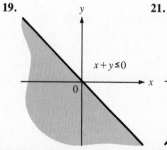
$-3x < y$

19.
$x + y \leq 0$

21.
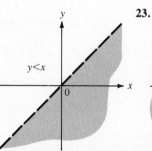
$y < x$

23.
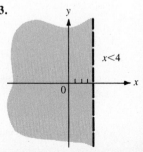
$x < 4$

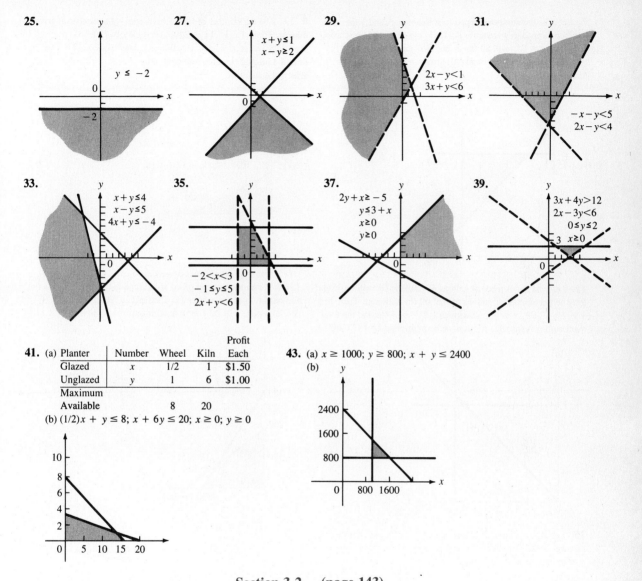

25. $y \leq -2$

27. $x + y \leq 1$
$x - y \geq 2$

29. $2x - y < 1$
$3x + y < 6$

31. $-x - y < 5$
$2x - y < 4$

33. $x + y \leq 4$
$x - y \leq 5$
$4x + y \leq -4$

35. $-2 < x < 3$
$-1 \leq y \leq 5$
$2x + y < 6$

37. $2y + x \geq -5$
$y \leq 3 + x$
$x \geq 0$
$y \geq 0$

39. $3x + 4y > 12$
$2x - 3y < 6$
$0 \leq y \leq 2$
$x \geq 0$

41. (a)

Planter	Number	Wheel	Kiln	Profit Each
Glazed	x	1/2	1	$1.50
Unglazed	y	1	6	$1.00
Maximum Available		8	20	

(b) $(1/2)x + y \leq 8$; $x + 6y \leq 20$; $x \geq 0$; $y \geq 0$

43. (a) $x \geq 1000$; $y \geq 800$; $x + y \leq 2400$

(b)

Section 3.2   (page 143)

1. Let x be the number of product A made, and y the number of B. Then $2x + 3y \leq 45$.   **3.** Let x be the number of green pills, and y be the number of red. Then $4x + y \geq 25$.   **5.** Let x be the number of pounds of $6 coffee, and y the number of $5 coffee. Then $x + y \geq 50$.

7. Let x be the number shipped to warehouse A and y the number shipped to warehouse B. Then $x + y \geq 100$, $x \leq 100$, $y \leq 100$, $x \leq 75$, $y \leq 80$ (these last two constraints make $x \leq 100$ and $y \leq 100$ redundant); also $x \geq 0$ and $y \geq 0$; minimize $12x + 10y$.

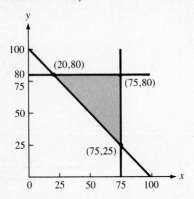

9. Let x be the number of type 1 bolts and y the number of type 2 bolts. Then $.1x + .1y \leq 240$, $.1x + .4y \leq 720$. $.1x + .5y \leq 160$, $x \geq 0$, $y \geq 0$; maximize $.10x + .12y$. The first two inequalities are redundant; only $.1x + .5y \leq 160$ affects the solution.

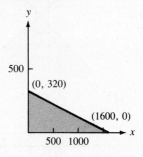

11. Let x be the number of gallons of gasoline (in millions), and let y be the number of gallons of fuel oil (in millions). Then $x \geq 2y$, $y \geq 3$, $x \leq 6.4$; maximize $1.25x + y$ (to find the total maximum revenue; this result must be multiplied by 1,000,000.)

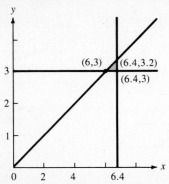

13. Let x be the number of kg of half and half mix, and y be the number of kg of the other mix. Then $x/2 + y/3 \leq 100$, $x/2 + (2y/3) \leq 125$, $x \geq 0$, $y \geq 0$; maximize $6x + 4.80y$.

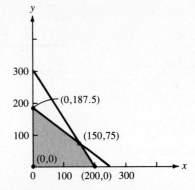

15. Let x be the number of servings of A and y the number of servings of B. Then $3x + 2y \geq 15$, $2x + 4y \geq 15$, $x \geq 0$, $y \geq 0$; minimize $.25x + .40y$.

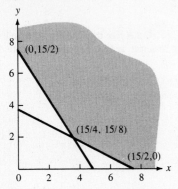

Section 3.3   (page 151)

1. Maximum of 65 at (5, 10); minimum of 8 at (1, 1)   **3.** Maximum of 9 at (0, 12); minimum of 0 at (0, 0)   **5.** No maximum; minimum of 18 at (3, 4)   **7.** $x = 6/5$; $y = 6/5$ **9.** $x = 10$; $y = 5$ **11.** $x = 105/8$; $y = 25/8$ **13.** (a) Maximum of 204; $x = 18$, $y = 2$ (b) Maximum of 117 3/5; $x = 12/5$, $y = 39/5$ (c) Maximum of 102; $x = 0$, $y = 17/2$ **15.** Ship 20 to A and 80 to B; $1040   **17.** 1600 Type 1 and 0 Type 2 for maximum revenue of $160   **19.** 6.4 million gallons of gasoline and 3.2 million gallons of fuel oil, for maximum revenue of $11,200,000   **21.** 150 kg half-and-half mix, 75 kg other mix; $1260   **23.** 3 3/4 servings of A, 1 7/8 servings of B; $1.6875   **25.** (b)   **27.** (c)

Chapter 3   Review Exercises   (page 155)

1.
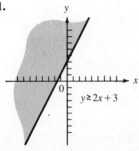

3.
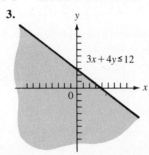

5.
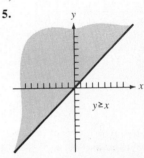

7.
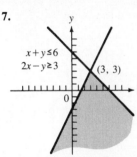

9.
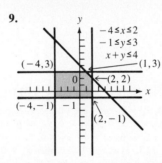

11.
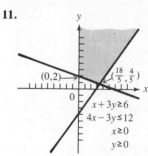

13. Let x = number of batches of cakes and y = number of batches of cookies. Then $x \geq 0$, $y \geq 0$, and $2x + (3/2)y \leq 15$
$$3x + (2/3)y \leq 13.$$

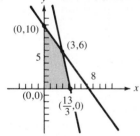

15. Minimum of 8 at (2, 1); maximum of 40 at (6, 7)   **17.** Maximum of 24 at (0, 6)
19. Minimum of 40 at any point on the segment connecting (0, 20) and (10/3, 40/3)
21. Make 3 batches of cakes, and 6 of cookies, for a maximum profit of $210

Chapter 4   Section 4.1   (page 163)

1. $x_1 + 2x_2 + x_3 = 6$ **3.** $2x_1 + 4x_2 + 3x_3 + x_4 = 100$ **5.** (a) 3   (b) x_3, x_4, x_5 (c) $4x_1 + 2x_2 + x_3 = 20$
$$5x_1 + x_2 + x_4 = 50$$
$$2x_1 + 3x_2 + x_5 = 25$$

7. (a) 2   (b) x_4, x_5 (c) $7x_1 + 6x_2 + 8x_3 + x_4 = 118$ **9.** $x_1 = 0$, $x_2 = 0$, $x_3 = 20$, $x_4 = 0$, $x_5 = 15$ **11.** $x_1 = 0$,
$$4x_1 + 5x_2 + 10x_3 + x_5 = 220$$
$x_2 = 0$, $x_3 = 8$, $x_4 = 0$, $x_5 = 6$, $x_6 = 7$ **13.** $x_1 = 0$, $x_2 = 20$, $x_3 = 0$, $x_4 = 16$, $x_5 = 0$ **15.** $x_1 = 0$, $x_2 = 0$,
$x_3 = 12$, $x_4 = 0$, $x_5 = 9$, $x_6 = 8$ **17.** $x_1 = 0$, $x_2 = 0$, $x_3 = 50$, $x_4 = 10$, $x_5 = 0$, $x_6 = 50$

19.

$$\begin{array}{cccc} x_1 & x_2 & x_3 & x_4 \end{array}$$
$$\begin{bmatrix} 2 & 3 & 1 & 0 & 6 \\ 4 & 1 & 0 & 1 & 6 \\ \hline -5 & -1 & 0 & 0 & 0 \end{bmatrix}$$

21.

$$\begin{array}{ccccc} x_1 & x_2 & x_3 & x_4 & x_5 \end{array}$$
$$\begin{bmatrix} 1 & 1 & 1 & 0 & 0 & 10 \\ 5 & 2 & 0 & 1 & 0 & 20 \\ 1 & 2 & 0 & 0 & 1 & 36 \\ \hline -1 & -3 & 0 & 0 & 0 & 0 \end{bmatrix}$$

23.

$$\begin{array}{cccc} x_1 & x_2 & x_3 & x_4 \end{array}$$
$$\begin{bmatrix} 3 & 1 & 1 & 0 & 12 \\ 1 & 1 & 0 & 1 & 15 \\ \hline -2 & -1 & 0 & 0 & 0 \end{bmatrix}$$

25. If x_1 is the number of kg of half-and-half mix and x_2 is the number of kg of the other mix, find $x_1 \geq 0$, $x_2 \geq 0$, $x_3 \geq 0$, $x_4 \geq 0$ so that $(1/2)x_1 + (1/3)x_2 + x_3 = 100$, $(1/2)x_1 + (2/3)x_2 + x_4 = 125$, and $z = 6x_1 + 4.8x_2$ is maximized.

$$\begin{array}{cccc} x_1 & x_2 & x_3 & x_4 \end{array}$$
$$\begin{bmatrix} 1/2 & 1/3 & 1 & 0 & 100 \\ 1/2 & 2/3 & 0 & 1 & 125 \\ \hline -6 & -4.8 & 0 & 0 & 0 \end{bmatrix}$$

27. If x_1 is the number of prams, x_2 is the number of runabouts, and x_3 is the number of trimarans, find $x_1 \geq 0$, $x_2 \geq 0$, $x_3 \geq 0$, $x_4 \geq 0$, $x_5 \geq 0$, $x_6 \geq 0$ so that $x_1 + 2x_2 + 3x_3 + x_4 = 6240$, $2x_1 + 5x_2 + 4x_3 + x_5 = 10,800$, $x_1 + x_2 + x_3 + x_6 = 3000$, and $z = 75x_1 + 90x_2 + 100x_3$ is maximized.

$$\begin{array}{cccccc} x_1 & x_2 & x_3 & x_4 & x_5 & x_6 \end{array}$$
$$\begin{bmatrix} 1 & 2 & 3 & 1 & 0 & 0 & 6,240 \\ 2 & 5 & 4 & 0 & 1 & 0 & 10,800 \\ 1 & 1 & 1 & 0 & 0 & 1 & 3,000 \\ \hline -75 & -90 & -100 & 0 & 0 & 0 & 0 \end{bmatrix}$$

29. If x_1 is the number of Siamese cats and x_2 is the number of Persian cats, find $x_1 \geq 0$, $x_2 \geq 0$, $x_3 \geq 0$, $x_4 \geq 0$, $x_5 \geq 0$ so that $2x_1 + x_2 + x_3 = 90$, $x_1 + 2x_2 + x_4 = 80$, $x_1 + x_2 + x_5 = 50$, and $z = 12x_1 + 10x_2$ is maximized.

$$\begin{array}{ccccc} x_1 & x_2 & x_3 & x_4 & x_5 \end{array}$$
$$\begin{bmatrix} 2 & 1 & 1 & 0 & 0 & 90 \\ 1 & 2 & 0 & 1 & 0 & 80 \\ 1 & 1 & 0 & 0 & 1 & 50 \\ \hline -12 & -10 & 0 & 0 & 0 & 0 \end{bmatrix}$$

Section 4.2 (page 171)

1. Maximum is 20 when $x_1 = 0$, $x_2 = 4$, $x_3 = 0$, $x_4 = 0$, $x_5 = 2$ **3.** Maximum is 8 when $x_1 = 4$, $x_2 = 0$, $x_3 = 8$, $x_4 = 2$, $x_5 = 0$ **5.** Maximum is 264 when $x_1 = 16$, $x_2 = 4$, $x_3 = 0$, $x_4 = 0$, $x_5 = 16$ **7.** Maximum is 22 when $x_1 = 5.5$, $x_2 = 0$, $x_3 = 0$ and $x_4 = .5$ **9.** Maximum is 120 when $x_1 = 0$, $x_2 = 10$, $x_3 = 0$, $x_4 = 40$, $x_5 = 4$ **11.** Maximum is 944 when $x_1 = 118$, $x_2 = 0$, $x_3 = 0$, $x_4 = 0$, $x_5 = 102$ **13.** Maximum is 250 when $x_1 = 0$, $x_2 = 0$, $x_3 = 0$, $x_4 = 50$, $x_5 = 0$, $x_6 = 50$ **15.** 163.6 kg of food P; none of Q; 1090.9 kg of R; 145.5 kg of S; maximum is 87,454.5   **17.** 150 kg of the half-and-half mix; 75 kg of the other; maximum revenue is $1260   **19.** Make no 1-speed or 3-speed bicycles; make 2700 10-speed bicycles; maximum profit is $59,400   **21.** (a) 3 (b) 4 (c) 3   **23.** 6700 trucks and 4467 fire engines for a maximum profit of $110,997

Section 4.3 (page 181)

1. $2x_1 + 3x_2 + x_3 = 8$
$x_1 + 4x_2 - x_4 = 7$ **3.** $x_1 + x_2 + x_3 + x_4 = 100$
$x_1 + x_2 + x_3 - x_5 = 75$
$x_1 + x_2 - x_6 = 27$ **5.** Change the objective function to maximize $z = -4x_1 - 3x_2 - 2x_3$.

7. Change the objective function to maximize $z = -x_1 - 2x_2 - x_3 - 5x_4$.   **9.** Maximum is 480 when $x_1 = 40$ and $x_3 = 16$.   **11.** Maximum is 750 when $x_2 = 150$ and $x_5 = 50$ **13.** Maximum is 300 when $x_2 = 100$, $x_4 = 50$, and $x_5 = 10$ **15.** Minimum is 40 when $x_1 = 10$ and $x_4 = 50$ **17.** Minimum is 100 when $x_2 = 100$ and $x_5 = 50$ **19.** 800,000 for whole tomatoes and 80,000 for sauce for a minimum cost of $3,460,000   **21.** 3 of pill #1 and 2 of pill #2 for a minimum cost of 70¢   **23.** Buy 1000 small and 500 large for a minimum cost of $210   **25.** 2 2/3 units of I, none of II, and 4 of III for a minimum cost of $30.67   **27.** 1 2/3 ounces of I, 6 2/3 ounces of II, 1 2/3 ounces of III, for a minimum cost of $1.55 per gallon

Section 4.4 (page 191)

1. $\begin{bmatrix} 1 & 3 & 1 \\ 2 & 2 & 10 \\ 3 & 1 & 0 \end{bmatrix}$ **3.** $\begin{bmatrix} -1 & 13 & -2 \\ 4 & 25 & -1 \\ 6 & 0 & 11 \\ 12 & 4 & 3 \end{bmatrix}$

5. Minimize $5y_1 + 4y_2 + 15y_3$ subject to $y_1 + y_2 + 2y_3 \geq 4$, $y_1 + y_2 + y_3 \geq$

3, $y_1 + 3y_3 \geq 2$, $y_1 \geq 0$, $y_2 \geq 0$, $y_3 \geq 0$. **7.** Maximize $50x_1 + 100x_2$ subject to $x_1 + 3x_2 \leq 1$; $x_1 + x_2 \leq 2$; $x_1 + 2x_2 \leq 1$; $x_1 + x_2 \leq 5$; $x_1 \geq 0$; $x_2 \geq 0$. **9.** $y_1 = 0$, $y_2 = 7$; minimum is 14 **11.** $y_1 = 10$, $y_2 = 0$; minimum is 40 **13.** $y_1 = 0$, $y_2 = 100$, $y_3 = 0$; minimum is 100 **15.** 800,000 for whole tomatoes and 80,000 for sauce for a minimum cost of \$3,460,000 **17.** 3 of pill #1, 2 of pill #2 for a minimum cost of 70 cents **19.** (a) Minimize $200y_1 + 600y_2 + 90y_3 = w$ subject to $y_1 + 4y_2 \geq 1$, $2y_1 + 3y_2 + y_3 \geq 1.5$, $y_1 \geq 0$, $y_2 \geq 0$, $y_3 \geq 0$ (b) $y_1 = .6$, $y_2 = .1$, $y_3 = 0$, $w = 180$ (c) \$186 ($x_1 = 114$, $x_2 = 48$) (d) \$179 ($x_1 = 116$, $x_2 = 42$) **21.** Use 81 kg of the first chemical, 382.3 kg of the second, and 286.7 kg of the third for a minimum cost of \$3652.25.

Extended Application   (page 195)

1. (a) $x_4 = 16.9$, $x_8 = 5.8$, $x_9 = 22.5$, $x_{10} = 1$ (b) $x_2 = 84.8$, $x_8 = 4.3$, $x_9 = 28.2$, $x_{10} = 1$

Extended Application   (page 197)

1. 1: .95; 2: .83; 3: .75; 4: 1.00; 5: .87; 6: .94 **2.** $x_1 = 100$; $x_2 = 0$; $x_3 = 0$; $x_4 = 90$; $x_5 = 0$; $x_6 = 210$

Chapter 4   Review Exercises   (page 198)

1. (a) Let x_1 = number of item A, x_2 = number of item B, and x_3 = number of item C she should buy (b) $z = 4x_1 + 3x_2 + 3x_3$ (c) $5x_1 + 3x_2 + 6x_3 \leq 1200$ **3.** (a) Let x_1 = number of gallons of fruity wine and x_2 = number of gallons of crystal wine to be
$$x_1 + 2x_2 + 2x_3 \leq 800$$
$$2x_1 + x_2 + 5x_3 \leq 500$$
made (b) $z = 12x_1 + 15x_2$ (c) $2x_1 + x_2 \leq 110$
$$2x_1 + 3x_2 \leq 125$$
$$2x_1 + x_2 \leq 90$$

5. (a) $2x_1 + 5x_2 + x_3 = 50$; (b)
$$x_1 + 3x_2 + x_4 = 25;$$
$$4x_1 + x_2 + x_5 = 18;$$
$$x_1 + x_2 + x_6 = 12$$

x_1	x_2	x_3	x_4	x_5	x_6	
2	5	1	0	0	0	50
1	3	0	1	0	0	25
4	1	0	0	1	0	18
1	1	0	0	0	1	12
-5	-3	0	0	0	0	0

7. (a) $x_1 + x_2 + x_3 + x_4 = 90$; (b)
$$2x_1 + 5x_2 + x_3 + x_5 = 120;$$
$$x_1 + 3x_2 - x_6 = 80$$

x_1	x_2	x_3	x_4	x_5	x_6	
1	1	1	1	0	0	90
2	5	1	0	1	0	120
1	3	0	0	0	-1	80
-5	-8	-6	0	0	0	0

9. (68/5, 0, 24/5, 0, 0,); maximum is 412/5; or (13.6, 0, 4.8, 0, 0); maximum is 82.4 **11.** (20/3, 0, 65/3, 35, 0, 0); maximum is 76 2/3 **13.** Change the objective function to maximize $z = -10x_1 - 15x_2$ **15.** Change the objective function to maximize $z = -7x_1 - 2x_2 - 3x_3$ **17.** (8, 12, 0, 1, 0, 2); minimum is 62 **19.** None of A; 400 of B; none of C; maximum profit is \$1200 **21.** Produce 36.25 gallons of fruity and 17.5 gallons of crystal for a maximum profit of \$697.50

Chapter 5   Section 5.1   (page 206)

1. False **3.** True **5.** True **7.** True **9.** False **11.** False **13.** False **15.** True **17.** False **19.** True **21.** True **23.** False **25.** True **27.** True **29.** False **31.** False **33.** False **35.** 8 **37.** 32 **39.** 2 **41.** 32 **43.** 4 **45.** 3 **47.** 0 **49.** (a) All except $\varnothing$, {s}, {l}, {m}, {s, l}, {s, m} (b) All except $\varnothing$, {s}, {l}

Section 5.2   (page 210)

1. True **3.** False **5.** True **7.** False **9.** True **11.** True **13.** {3, 5} **15.** U, or {2, 3, 4, 5, 7, 9} **17.** U, or {2, 3, 4, 5, 7, 9} **19.** {7, 9} **21.** $\varnothing$ **23.** $\varnothing$ **25.** U, or {2, 3, 4, 5, 7, 9} **27.** All students in this school not taking this course **29.** All students in this school taking accounting and zoology **31.** All students in this school taking this course or zoology **33.** 6 **35.** 5 **37.** 1 **39.** 5 **41.** $B' = $ {stocks having a price to earnings ratio of less than 10}; $B' = $ {ATT, GE, Hershey, Mobil, RCA} **43.** $B \cap C = $ {stocks having a price to earnings ratio of 10 or more, *and* having a positive price change}; $B \cap C = \varnothing$ **45.** $(A \cap B)'$ is made up of the stocks that are *not* in the set {stock with a dividend greater than \$3 and a price to earnings ratio of at least 10}; $(A \cap B)' = $ {ATT, GE, Hershey, Mobil, RCA} **47.** (a) {s, d, c, g, i, m, h} (b) {s, d, c} (c) {i, m, h} (d) {g} (e) {s, d, c, g, i, m, h} (f) {s, d, c}

Section 5.3 (page 215)

1.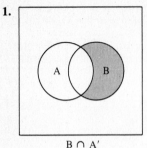

$B \cap A'$

3.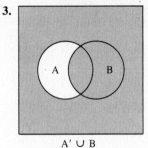

$A' \cup B$

5.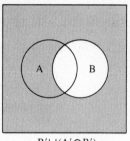

$B' \cup (A' \cap B')$

7. $\varnothing$

9.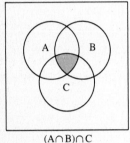

$(A \cap B) \cap C$

11.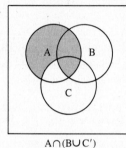

$A \cap (B \cup C')$

13.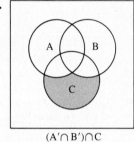

$(A' \cap B') \cap C$

15.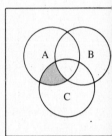

$(A \cap B') \cap C$

17. 9   **19.** 16

21.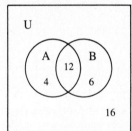

23.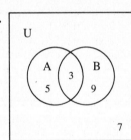

25.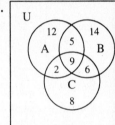

27.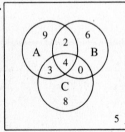

29. Yes; his data add up to 142 people   **31.** (a) 37   (b) 22   (c) 50   (d) 11   (e) 25   (f) 11

33. (a) 50   (b) 2   (c) 14   **35.** (a) 54   (b) 17   (c) 10   (d) 7   (e) 15   (f) 3   (g) 12   (h) 1

37. (a) 40   (b) 30   (c) 95   (d) 110   (e) 160   (f) 65

Section 5.4 (page 225)

1. 12   **3.** 56   **5.** 8   **7.** 24   **9.** 792   **11.** 156   **13.** 2.490952×10^{15} **15.** 240,240   **17.** 352,716

19. 2,042,975   **21.** $\binom{52}{2} = 1326$ **23.** 10   **25.** (a) $5^7 = 78,125$ (b) $9 \cdot 10^5 \cdot 1 = 900,000$ (c) $9 \cdot 10^4 \cdot 1^2 = 90,000$

(d) $1^3 \cdot 10^4 = 10,000$ (e) $9 \cdot 9 \cdot 8 \cdot 7 \cdot 6 \cdot 5 \cdot 4 = 544,320$ **27.** (a) $\binom{8}{5} = 56$ (b) $\binom{11}{5} = 462$ (c) $\binom{8}{3} \cdot \binom{11}{2} = 56 \cdot 55 =$

3080   **29.** $\binom{5}{2} \cdot \binom{4}{1} + \binom{5}{3} \cdot \binom{4}{0} = 40 + 10 = 50$ **31.** (a) $\binom{5}{3} = 10$ (b) 0   (c) $\binom{3}{3} = 1$ (d) $\binom{5}{2} \cdot \binom{1}{1} = 10$ (e) $\binom{5}{2} \cdot \binom{3}{1} =$

30   (f) $\binom{5}{1} \cdot \binom{3}{2} = 15$ (g) 0   **33.** $5 \cdot 3 \cdot 2 = 30$ **35.** (a) $2 \cdot 25 \cdot 24 \cdot 23 = 27,600$ (b) $2 \cdot 26 \cdot 26 \cdot 26 = 35,152$

(c) $2 \cdot 24 \cdot 23 \cdot 1 = 1104$ **37.** $\binom{4}{2} = 6$ **39.** (a) $\binom{7}{2} = 21$ (b) $1 \cdot \binom{6}{1} = 6$ (c) $\binom{2}{1} \cdot \binom{5}{1} + \binom{2}{2} \cdot \binom{5}{0} = 11$

41. (a) $\binom{12}{3} = 220$ (b) $\binom{12}{9} = 220$ **43.** $6! = 720$ **45.** $5! = 120$ **47.** $2 \cdot 26 \cdot 25 \cdot 24 \cdot 10 \cdot 9 \cdot 8 = 22,464,000$

49. (a) $\binom{9}{3} = 84$ (b) $\binom{5}{3} = 10$ (c) $\binom{5}{2} \cdot \binom{4}{1} = 40$ (d) $1 \cdot \binom{8}{2} = 28$ **51.** 2,598,960   **53.** 6.3501356×10^{11}

55. 55,440

Section 5.5   (page 231)

1. $m^4 + 4m^3n + 6m^2n^2 + 4mn^3 + n^4$ **3.** $729x^6 - 2916x^5y + 4860x^4y^2 - 4320x^3y^3 + 2160x^2y^4 - 576xy^5 + 64y^6$
5. $m^5/32 - 15m^4n/16 + 45m^3n^2/4 - 135m^2n^3/2 + 405mn^4/2 - 243n^5$ **7.** $p^{10} + 10p^9q + 45p^8q^2 + 120p^7q^3$
9. $a^{15} + 30a^{14}b + 420a^{13}b^2 + 3640a^{12}b^3$ **11.** $2^{10} = 1024$ **13.** $2^6 = 64$ (This result includes a pizza made with *none* of
the six toppings.)   **15.** $\binom{20}{2} + \binom{20}{3} + \binom{20}{4} + \binom{20}{5} + \binom{20}{6} = 60{,}439$ **17.** 64

Chapter 5   Review Exercises   (page 232)

1. False   **3.** False   **5.** True   **7.** False   **9.** False   **11.** {6, 7}; 2   **13.** {1, 2, 3, 4}; 4   **15.** $2^4 = 16$
17. {a, b, e}   **19.** {c, d, g}   **21.** {a, b, e, f}   **23.** U **25.** All employees in the accounting department who also have at
least 10 years with the company   **27.** All employees who are in the accounting department or who have MBA degrees   **29.** All
employees who are not in the sales department and who have worked less than 10 years with the company
31.   **33.**

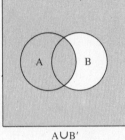

$A \cup B'$

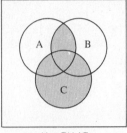

$(A \cap B) \cup C$

35. 52   **37.** 12   **39.** $6! = 720$ **41.** $5 \cdot 4 = 20$ **43.** $\binom{8}{3} \cdot \binom{6}{2} = 840$ **45.** $32m^5 + 80m^4n + 80m^3n^2 +$
$40m^2n^3 + 10mn^4 + n^5$ **47.** $x^{20} - 10x^{19}y + 95x^{18}y^2/2 - 285x^{17}y^3/2$ **49.** $2^8 - 8 - 1 = 247$

Chapter 6   Section 6.1   (page 241)

1. {January, February, March, $\cdots$, December}   **3.** $\{0, 1, 2, \cdots, 80\}$ **5.** {go ahead, cancel}
7. $\{0, 1, 2, 3, \cdots, 5000\}$ **9.** {hhhh, hhht, hhth, hthh, thhh, hhtt, htth, tthh, thth, thht, htht, httt, thtt, ttht, ttth, tttt}
11. {h, th, tth, ttth, tttth, $\cdots$}   **13.** (a) {(1, 1), (1, 2), (1, 3), (1, 4), (1, 5), (1, 6), (2, 1), (2, 2), (2, 3), (2, 4), (2, 5), (2, 6),
(3, 1), (3, 2), (3, 3), (3, 4), (3, 5), (3, 6), (4, 1), (4, 2), (4, 3), (4, 4), (4, 5), (4, 6), (5, 1), (5, 2), (5, 3), (5, 4), (5, 5), (5, 6), (6, 1),
(6, 2), (6, 3), (6, 4), (6, 5), (6, 6)}   (b) $F = \{(3, 1), (3, 2), (3, 3), (3, 4), (3, 5), (3, 6)\}$ (c) $G = \{(2, 6), (3, 5), (4, 4), (5, 3), (6, 2)\}$
(d) $H = \varnothing$ **15.** (a) {hh, hth, thh, htth, thth, tthh, ttthh, thtth, thtth, htthh, htttt, thttt, tthht, ttthh, ttttt, tttttt} (b) $E = \{hh\}$ (c) $F =$
{hth, thh}   (d) $G = \{ttttt, ttttth, ttht, ttht, thttt, htttt\}$ **17.** (a) Worker is male   (b) Worker has worked five years or more
(c) Worker is female and has worked less than five years   (d) Worker has worked less than five years or has contributed to a voluntary
retirement plan   (e) Worker is female or does not contribute to a voluntary retirement plan   (f) Worker has worked five years or more
and does not contribute to a voluntary retirement plan   **19.** No   **21.** No   **23.** Yes   **25.** Yes   **27.** No   **29.** (a) E'
(b) $E \cap F$ (c) $E' \cap F'$ or $(E \cup F)'$ (d) $E \cap F'$ (e) $(E \cup F) \cap (E \cap F)'$ (f) $E \cup F$ **31.** {r, s, t}; {r, s}; {r, t}; {s, t}; {r};
{s}; {t}; $\varnothing$

Section 6.2   (page 250)

1. 1/6   **3.** 2/3   **5.** 1/13   **7.** 1/26   **9.** 1/52   **11.** 1 to 5   **13.** 2 to 1   **15.** {2}; {4}; {6}   **17.** {up}; {down};
{stays the same}   **19.** Feasible   **21.** Not feasible; sum of probabilities is less than 1   **23.** Not feasible; $P(s_2) < 0$
25. .12   **27.** .50   **29.** .77   **31.** 6 to 19   **33.** .15   **35.** .85   **37.** .70   **39.** 1/5   **41.** 4/15   **43.** 8 to 7
45. 11 to 4   **47.** 4/11   **49.** .41   **51.** .21   **53.** .79   **55.** Not subjective   **57.** Subjective   **59.** Subjective
61. Not subjective   **63.** Not subjective   **65.** "Odds *in favor* of a direct hit . . . ." For 67 and 69 theoretical probabilities are
given. Answers using the Monte Carlo method will vary.   **67.** $1/32 = .03125$ **69.** .0249995

Extended Application　(page 253)

1. .715; .569; .410; .321; .271

Section 6.3　(page 257)

1. 1/36　**3.** 1/9　**5.** 5/36　**7.** 1/12　**9.** 5/18　**11.** 11/36　**13.** 5/12　**15.** 2/13　**17.** 3/26　**19.** 3/13
21. 7/13　**23.** 1/2　**25.** 3/10　**27.** 7/10　**29.** 1/10　**31.** 2/5　**33.** 7/20　**35.** .88　**37.** .25　**39.** .38
41. .89　**43.** .50　**45.** .09　**47.** .39　**49.** .77　**51.** .951　**53.** .473　**55.** .007　**57.** 3/4　**59.** 1/4
61. 1/4　**63.** .23　**65.** 2/3　**67.** The theoretical answer is 7/8. Answers using the Monte Carlo method will vary.

Section 6.4　(page 264)

1. $\binom{7}{1}/\binom{9}{1} = 7/9$　**3.** $\binom{7}{3}/\binom{9}{3} = 35/84$　**5.** .424　**7.** $\binom{6}{3}/\binom{10}{3} = 1/6$　**9.** $\binom{4}{1}\binom{6}{1}/\binom{10}{3} = 3/10$　**11.** $\binom{52}{2} = 1326$
13. $(4 \cdot 48 + 6)/\binom{52}{2} = 33/221$　**15.** $4 \cdot \binom{13}{2}/\binom{52}{2} = 52/221$　**17.** $\binom{40}{2}/\binom{52}{2} = 130/221$　**19.** $(1/26)^5$　**21.** $1 \cdot 25 \cdot$
$24 \cdot 23 \cdot 22/(26)^4 = 18{,}975/28{,}561$　**23.** $4/\binom{52}{5} = 1/649{,}740$　**25.** $13 \cdot \binom{4}{4}\binom{48}{1}/\binom{52}{5} = 1/4165$　**27.** $1/\binom{52}{13}$
29. $\binom{4}{3}\binom{4}{3}\binom{44}{7}/\binom{52}{13}$　**31.** $1 - P(365, 39)/(365)^{39} \approx .8782$　**33.** 1　**35.** 3/8; 1/4　**37.** $120/343 \approx .3498$　**39.** $3! = 6$
41. $9! = 362{,}880$　**43.** 1/3

Section 6.5　(page 275)

1. 0　**3.** 1　**5.** 1/6　**7.** 4/17　**9.** 25/51　**11.** $\frac{13}{52} \cdot \frac{12}{51} \cdot \frac{11}{50} \cdot \frac{10}{49} \cdot \frac{9}{48} \approx .00050$　**13.** $9/48 = .1875$

15. $4\left(\frac{13}{52} \cdot \frac{12}{51} \cdot \frac{11}{50} \cdot \frac{10}{49} \cdot \frac{9}{48}\right) \approx .00198$　**17.** $(2/3)^3 \approx .296$　**19.** 1/10　**21.** 0　**23.** 2/7　**25.** 2/7　**27.** The
probability of a customer cashing a check given that the customer made a deposit is 5/7.　**29.** The probability of a customer not
cashing a check given that the customer did not make a deposit is 1/4.　**31.** The probability of a customer not both cashing a check
and making a deposit is 6/11　**33.** 1/6　**35.** 0　**37.** 2/3　**39.** .06　**41.** 1/4　**43.** 1/4　**45.** 1/7　**47.** .049
49. .534　**51.** 42/527 or .080　**53.** Yes　**55.** .05　**57.** .25　**59.** Not very reasonable　**61.** $1 - .000015 = .999985$
63. $1/2000 = .0005$　**65.** $(1999/2000)^a$　**67.** $(1999/2000)^{Nc}$　**69.** $1 - .741 = .259$　**71.** True　**73.** True
75. True　**77.** False　**79.** 0

Section 6.6　(page 283)

1. 1/3　**3.** 2/41　**5.** 21/41　**7.** 8/17　**9.** .146　**11.** .082　**13.** $119/131 \approx .908$　**15.** .824　**17.** $1/176 \approx$
.006　**19.** 1/11　**21.** 5/9　**23.** 5/26　**25.** 72/73　**27.** 165/343

Extended Application　(page 287)

1. .076　**2.** .542　**3.** .051

Section 6.7　(page 292)

1. $\binom{5}{2}\left(\frac{1}{2}\right)^2\left(\frac{1}{2}\right)^3 = 5/16$　**3.** $\binom{5}{0}\left(\frac{1}{2}\right)^0\left(\frac{1}{2}\right)^5 = 1/32$　**5.** $\binom{5}{4}\left(\frac{1}{2}\right)^4\left(\frac{1}{2}\right)^1 + \binom{5}{5}\left(\frac{1}{2}\right)^5\left(\frac{1}{2}\right)^0 = 3/16$　**7.** $\binom{5}{0}\left(\frac{1}{2}\right)^0\left(\frac{1}{2}\right)^5 +$
$\binom{5}{1}\left(\frac{1}{2}\right)^1\left(\frac{1}{2}\right)^4 + \binom{5}{2}\left(\frac{1}{2}\right)^2\left(\quad\right.$　$\binom{5}{3}\left(\frac{1}{2}\right)^3\left(\frac{1}{2}\right)^2 = 13/16$　**9.** $\binom{12}{12}\left(\frac{1}{6}\right)^{12}\left(\frac{5}{6}\right)^0 \approx .0000000005$　**11.** $\binom{12}{1}\left(\frac{1}{6}\right)^1\left(\frac{5}{6}\right)^{11} \approx .269$
13. $\binom{12}{0}\left(\frac{1}{6}\right)^0\left(\frac{5}{6}\right)^{12} + \binom{12}{1}\left(\frac{1}{6}\right)^1\left(\frac{5}{6}\right)^{11} + \binom{12}{2}\left(\frac{1}{6}\right)^2\left(\frac{5}{6}\right)^{10} + \binom{12}{3}\left(\frac{1}{6}\right)^3\left(\frac{5}{6}\right)^9 \approx .875$　**15.** $\binom{5}{5}\left(\frac{1}{2}\right)^5\left(\frac{1}{2}\right)^0 = 1/32$
17. $\binom{5}{0}\left(\frac{1}{2}\right)^0\left(\frac{1}{2}\right)^5 + \binom{5}{1}\left(\frac{1}{2}\right)^1\left(\frac{1}{2}\right)^4 + \binom{5}{2}\left(\frac{1}{2}\right)^2\left(\frac{1}{2}\right)^3 + \binom{5}{3}\left(\frac{1}{2}\right)^3\left(\frac{1}{2}\right)^2 = 13/16$　**19.** $\binom{20}{0}(.05)^0(.95)^{20} \approx .358$
21. $\binom{6}{2}\left(\frac{1}{5}\right)^2\left(\frac{4}{5}\right)^4 \approx .246$　**23.** $\binom{6}{4}\left(\frac{1}{5}\right)^4\left(\frac{4}{5}\right)^2 + \binom{6}{5}\left(\frac{1}{5}\right)^5\left(\frac{4}{5}\right)^1 + \binom{6}{6}\left(\frac{1}{5}\right)^6\left(\frac{4}{5}\right)^0 \approx .017$　**25.** $\binom{3}{1}\left(\frac{5}{50}\right)^1\left(\frac{45}{50}\right)^2 \approx .243$
27. $\binom{10}{5}(.20)^5(.80)^5 \approx .026$　**29.** .999　**31.** $\binom{20}{17}(.70)^{17}(.30)^3 \approx .072$　**33.** .035　**35.** $\binom{10}{7}\left(\frac{1}{5}\right)^7\left(\frac{4}{5}\right)^3 \approx .00079$
37. $\approx .999922$　**39.** $\binom{3}{1}(.80)^1(.20)^2 = .096$　**41.** $\binom{3}{0}(.80)^0(.20)^3 + \binom{3}{1}(.80)^1(.20)^2 = .104$　**43.** .185　**45.** .256

47. $1 - (.99999975)^{10,000} \approx .0025$ **49.** $\binom{12}{4}(.2)^4(.8)^8 \approx .133$ **51.** .795 **53.** 3/16 **55.** 21/256 **57.** 125/23,328
59. $(165(5)^8)/6^{12}$ **61.** 6 teams **63.** 10 teams **65.** (a) .000036 (b) .999912 (c) 0 **67.** (a) .148774 (b) .021344
(c) .978656

Chapter 6   Review Exercises   (page 295)

1. $\{1, 2, 3, 4, 5, 6\}$ **3.** $\{0, .5, 1, 1.5, 2, \cdots, 299.5, 300\}$ **5.** $\{(3, R), (3, G), (5, R), (5, G), (7, R), (7, G), (9, R), (9, G),$
$(11, R), (11, G)\}$ **7.** $\{(3, G), (5, G), (7, G), (9, G), (11, G)\}$ **9.** $E' \cap F'$ **11.** 1/4 **13.** 3/13 **15.** 1/2 **17.** 1
19. 1 to 25 **21.** .86 **23.**

	N_2	T_2
N_1	N_1N_2	N_1T_2
T_1	T_1N_2	T_1T_2

25. 1/2 **27.** 5/36 **29.** 1/6 **31.** 1/6 **33.** 2/11
35. .66 **37.** .71 **39.** $\binom{4}{3}/\binom{11}{3} = 4/165$ **41.** $\binom{4}{2}\binom{5}{1}/\binom{11}{3} = 2/11$ **43.** $\binom{5}{2}\binom{2}{1}/\binom{11}{3} = 4/33$ **45.** 25/102
47. 15/34 **49.** 4/17 **51.** 3/10 **53.** 2/5 or .4 **55.** 3/4 or .75 **57.** 19/22 **59.** 1/3 **61.** 1/7 **63.** 5/16
65. 11/32 **67.** $\binom{20}{4}(.01)^4(.99)^{16} \approx .00004$ **69.** $.81791 + .16523 + .01586 + .00096 + .00004 = 1.0000$
71. (a) 8 wells (b) 10 wells

Chapter 7   Section 7.1   (page 305)

1. (a)

Number	0	1	2	3	4	5
Probability	0	0	.1	.3	.4	.2

(b)

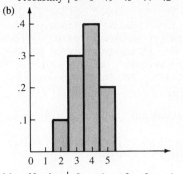

3. (a)

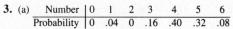

Number	0	1	2	3	4	5	6
Probability	0	.04	0	.16	.40	.32	.08

(b)

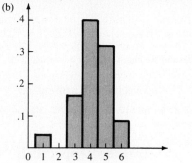

5. (a)

Number	0	1	2	3	4	5
Probability	.15	.25	.3	.15	.1	.05

(b)

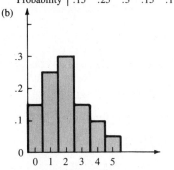

7.

Number of heads	0	1	2	3	4
Probability	1/16	1/4	3/8	1/4	1/16

9.

Number of aces	0	1	2	3
Probability	$4324/5525 \approx .783$	$1128/5525 \approx .204$	$72/5525 \approx .013$	$1/5525 \approx .0002$

11.

Number of hits	0	1	2	3	4
Probability	.254	.415	.254	.069	.007

13. 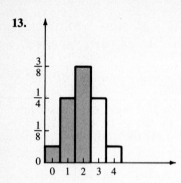   **15.** 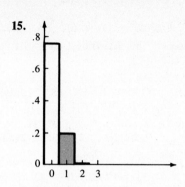   **17.**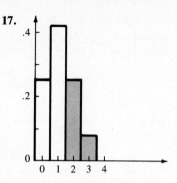

19. E: 18.1%; T: 8.8%; A: 6.2%; O: 4.4%; N: 7.5%; I: 7.1%; R: 5.8%; S: 5.8%; H: 5.8%; D: 2.2%; L: 5.3%; C: 4.9%; U: 4.0%;
M: 1.8%; F: 4.0%; P: 1.8%; Y: 1.3%; W: 1.8%; G: 4.0%; B: 0%; V: .4%; K: 0%; X: 0%; J: 0%; Q: 1.3%; Z: 0%

Section 7.2   (page 312)

1. 3.6   **3.** 14.64   **5.** 2.7   **7.** 18   **9.** -64¢; no   **11.** $9/7 \approx 1.3$ **13.** (a) $5/3 \approx 1.67$ (b) $4/3 \approx 1.33$ **15.** 1
17. No, the expected value is about -21¢.   **19.** -2.7¢   **21.** -20¢   **23.** (a) Yes, the probability of a match is still 1/2.
(b) 40¢   (c) -40¢   **25.** 2.5   **27.** $4500   **29.** 118   **31.** 3.51   **33.**

Account	EV	Total	Class
3	$2000	$22,000	C
4	1000	51,000	B
5	25,000	30,000	C
6	60,000	60,000	A
7	16,000	46,000	B

35. 1.58   **37.** (a) $94.0 million for seeding; $116.0 for not seeding   (b) "Seed"

Extended Application   (page 318)

1. (a) $69.01   (b) $79.64   (c) $58.96   (d) $82.54   (e) $62.88   (f) $64.00   **2.** Stock only part 3 on the truck   **3.** p_1, p_2, p_3
are not the only events in the sample space   **4.** 2^n

Extended Application   (page 320)

1. .9886 million dollars   **2.** $-.9714$ million dollars

Section 7.3   (page 325)

1. $\sqrt{407.4} \approx 20.2$ **3.** $\sqrt{215.3} \approx 14.7$ **5.** $\sqrt{59.4} \approx 7.7$ **7.** Variance is .81; $\sigma = .9$
9. Variance is .000124; $\sigma = 0.011$ **11.** .700   **13.** .745   **15.** (a)   **17.** 2.41   **19.** (a) At least 3/4 (b) At least 15/16
(c) At least 24/25   **21.** (a) Mean is 320; standard deviation is 170.8 (b) 6 (c) 6 (d) At least 3/4   **23.** (a) 12.5 (b) -3.0
(c) 4.3 (d) 3.7 (e) 15.5 (f) 7.55 and 23.45   **25.** Mean is 5.0876; standard deviation is .1065   **27.** Mean is 46.6807;
standard deviation is .9223

Section 7.4   (page 336)

1. 49.38%   **3.** 17.36%   **5.** 45.64%   **7.** 49.91%   **9.** 7.7%   **11.** 47.35%   **13.** 92.42%   **15.** 32.56%
17. -1.64 or -1.65 **19.** 1.04   **21.** 5000   **23.** 4332   **25.** 642   **27.** 9918   **29.** 19   **31.** 15.87%
33. .62%   **35.** 84.13%   **37.** 37.79%   **39.** 2.28%   **41.** 99.38%   **43.** 189   **45.** .0062   **47.** .4325
49. $38.62 and $25.89   **51.** .0823   **53.** 6.68%   **55.** 38.3%   **57.** 82   **59.** 70   **61.** .079614   **63.** .993333
65. .317246   **67.** .152730   **69.** .005107

Extended Application   (page 339)

1. No; yes   **2.** No; yes

Section 7.5   (page 346)

1. (a)

X	0	1	2	3	4	5	6
P(X)	.335	.402	.201	.054	.008	.001	.000

(b) 1.00   (c) .91

3. (a)

X	0	1	2	3
P(X)	.941	.058	.001	.000

(b) .06   (c) .24

5. (a)

X	0	1	2	3	4
P(X)	.0081	.0756	.2646	.4116	.2401

(b) 2.8   (c) .92

7. 12.5; 3.49   **9.** 51.2; 3.2   **11.** .1974   **13.** .1210   **15.** .0240   **17.** .9032   **19.** .8665   **21.** .0956
23. .0760   **25.** .6443   **27.** .0146   **29.** .1974   **31.** .0092   **33.** .0001   **35.** .9945
37. For Exercise 30: .029784; for Exercise 31: .068924; for Exercise 32: .110495; for Exercise 33: .028682

Chapter 7   Review Exercises   (page 347)

1. (a)

Number	1	2	3	4	5
Probability	.125	.292	.375	.125	.083

(b)

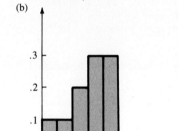

3. (a)

Number	0	1	2	3
Probability	$\frac{1}{8} = .125$	$\frac{3}{8} = .375$	$\frac{3}{8} = .375$	$\frac{1}{8} = .125$

(b)

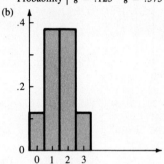

5. (a)

Number	0	1	2	3	4	5
Probability	.1	.1	.2	.3	.3	0

(b)

7. .6   **9.** −28¢   **11.** $8500   **13.** 11.87   **15.** 2.6   **17.** $1.29

19. Variance is 1.64; standard deviation is 1.28   **21.** (a) Diet A   (b) Diet B
23. (a) 98.76%   (b) Chebyshev's inequality would give ''at least 84%''
25. $z = 1.41$
27. (a)

x	0	1	2	3	4
Probability	.9801	.0197	.0001485	.0000004975	6×10^{-10}

(b) Mean = .02, $\sigma = .141$
29. (a) .1019   (b) .0008   **31.** (a) 25.14%   (b) 28.10%   (c) 22.92%   (d) 56.25%

Chapter 8   Section 8.1   (page 358)

1. No   **3.** Yes   **5.** No   **7.** Yes   **9.** No   **11.** Yes   **13.** No   **15.** No   **17.** Yes   **19.** $A^1 = \begin{bmatrix} 1 & 0 \\ .8 & .2 \end{bmatrix}$;

$A^2 = \begin{bmatrix} 1 & .0 \\ .96 & .04 \end{bmatrix}$; $A^3 = \begin{bmatrix} 1 & 0 \\ .992 & .008 \end{bmatrix}$; 0   **21.** $C^1 = \begin{bmatrix} .5 & .5 \\ .72 & .28 \end{bmatrix}$; $C^2 = \begin{bmatrix} .61 & .39 \\ .5616 & .4384 \end{bmatrix}$;

$C^3 = \begin{bmatrix} .5858 & .4142 \\ .596448 & .403552 \end{bmatrix}$; .4142   **23.** $E^1 = \begin{bmatrix} .8 & .1 & .1 \\ .3 & .6 & .1 \\ 0 & 1 & 0 \end{bmatrix}$; $E^2 = \begin{bmatrix} .67 & .24 & .09 \\ .42 & .49 & .09 \\ .3 & .6 & .1 \end{bmatrix}$; $E^3 = \begin{bmatrix} .608 & .301 & .091 \\ .483 & .426 & .091 \\ .42 & .49 & .09 \end{bmatrix}$; .301

25. (a)

	Small	Large
Small	.80	.20
Large	.60	.40

(b) [.10 .90] (c) [.724 .276] (d) [.7448 .2552] (e) [.7490 .2510] (f) [.7498 .2502]

27. (a) [.53 .47] (b) [.5885 .4115] (c) [.6148 .3852] (d) [.62666 .37334] **29.** (a) 42,500; 5000; 2500
(b) 36,125; 8250; 5625 (c) 30,706; 10,213; 9081 (d) 26,100; 11,241; 12,659 **31.** (a) [.257 .597 .146]

(b) [.255 .594 .151] (c) [.254 .590 .156] **33.** (a)

	Single	Multiple
Single	.90	.10
Multiple	.05	.95

(b) [.75 .25] (c) [68.8% 31.3%]

(d) [63.4% 36.6%] **35.** The first power is the given transition matrix;

$$\begin{bmatrix} .2 & .15 & .17 & .19 & .29 \\ .16 & .2 & .15 & .18 & .31 \\ .19 & .14 & .24 & .21 & .22 \\ .16 & .19 & .16 & .2 & .29 \\ .16 & .19 & .14 & .17 & .34 \end{bmatrix};$$

$$\begin{bmatrix} .17 & .178 & .171 & .191 & .29 \\ .171 & .178 & .161 & .185 & .305 \\ .18 & .163 & .191 & .197 & .269 \\ .175 & .174 & .164 & .187 & .3 \\ .167 & .184 & .158 & .182 & .309 \end{bmatrix};\quad \begin{bmatrix} .1731 & .175 & .1683 & .188 & .2956 \\ .1709 & .1781 & .1654 & .1866 & .299 \\ .1748 & .1718 & .1753 & .1911 & .287 \\ .1712 & .1775 & .1667 & .1875 & .2971 \\ .1706 & .1785 & .1641 & .1858 & .301 \end{bmatrix};$$

$$\begin{bmatrix} .17193 & .17643 & .1678 & .18775 & .29609 \\ .17167 & .17689 & .16671 & .18719 & .29754 \\ .17293 & .17488 & .17007 & .18878 & .29334 \\ .17192 & .17654 & .16713 & .18741 & .297 \\ .17142 & .17726 & .16629 & .18696 & .29807 \end{bmatrix};\ .18719$$

37. (a) .847423 or about 85% (b) [.032 .0998125 .0895625 .778625]

Section 8.2 (page 366)

1. Regular **3.** Not regular **5.** Regular **7.** [2/5 3/5] **9.** [4/11 7/11] **11.** [14/83 19/83 50/83]
13. [170/563 197/563 196/563] **15.** [3/4 1/4] **17.** [0 0 1] **19.** [2/17 11/17 4/17]
21. [.244 .529 .227] **23.** 16/17 **25.** [51/209 88/209 70/209] **27.** [1/3 1/3 1/3] **29.** 1/2
33. [.171898 .176519 .167414 .187526 .296644] **35.** [0 0 .113636 .886364]

Section 8.3 (page 370)

1. (a) Buy speculative (b) Buy blue-chip (c) Buy speculative; $24,300 (d) Buy blue-chip **3.** (a) Set up in the stadium
(b) Set up in the gym (c) Set up both; $1010 **5.** (a)

	Better	Not better
Market	50,000	−25,000
Don't market	−40,000	−10,000

(b) $5000 if they market new product, −$22,000 if they don't; market the new product.

7. (a)

	Strike	No strike
Bid $30,000	−5500	4500
Bid $40,000	4500	0

(b) $40,000 **9.** Emphasize environment; 14.25

Extended Application (page 376)

1. $E_1 = 18.61M$, $E_2 = 2.898M - 42.055$, $E_3 = .56M - 48.6$
2. $E_1 = 19.7325M$, $E_2 = .054M - 47.973$, $E_3 = .108M - 49.73$ **3.** $E_1 = 19M$, $E_2 = 1.7M - 45$, $E_3 = .6M - 48.5$

Section 8.4 (page 381)

1. $6 from B to A **3.** $2 from A to B **5.** $1 from A to B **7.** Yes **9.** $\begin{bmatrix} -2 & 8 \\ -1 & -9 \end{bmatrix}$ **11.** $\begin{bmatrix} 4 & -1 \\ 3 & 5 \end{bmatrix}$

13. $\begin{bmatrix} 8 & -7 \\ -2 & 4 \end{bmatrix}$ **15.** (1, 1); 3; strictly determined **17.** No saddle point; not strictly determined **19.** (3, 1); 3; strictly
determined **21.** (1, 3); 1; strictly determined **23.** No saddle point; not strictly determined **25.** (2, 3); 6

	stone	scissors	paper
stone	0	1	−1
scissors	−1	0	1
paper	1	−1	0

27. (above) ; no

29. A

	B: 1	2	3
1	15	−2	6
2	7	15	9
3	3	−3	15

; no

Section 8.5   (page 390)

1. (a) −1   (b) −.28   (c) −1.54   (d) −.46   **3.** Player A: 1: 1/5, 2: 4/5; player B: 1: 3/5, 2: 2/5; value 17/5   **5.** Player A: 1: 7/9, 2: 2/9; player B: 1: 4/9, 2: 5/9; value −8/9   **7.** Player A: 1: 8/15, 2: 7/15; player B: 1: 2/3, 2: 1/3; value 5/3   **9.** Player A: 1: 6/11, 2: 5/11; player B: 1: 7/11, 2: 4/11; value −12/11   **11.** Strictly determined game; saddle point at (2, 2); value is −5/12   **13.** Player A: 1: 2/5, 2: 3/5; player B: 1: 1/5, 2: 4/5; value 7/5   **15.** Player A: 1: 1/14, 2: 0, 3: 13/14; player B: 1: 1/7, 2: 6/7; value 50/7   **17.** Player A: 1: 2/3, 2: 1/3; player B: 1: 0, 2: 1/9, 3: 8/9; value: 10/3   **19.** Player A: 1: 0; 2: 3/4; 3: 1/4; player B: 1: 0, 2: 1/12, 3: 11/12; value 33/4   **21.** Allied should use TV with probability 10/27 and use radio with probability 17/27. The value of the game is 1/18, which represents increased sales of $55,556.   **23.** The doctor should prescribe medicine 1 about 5/6 of the time and medicine 2 about 1/6 of the time. The effectiveness will be about 50%.   **25.** (a)

		Number of fingers	
		0	2
Number	0	0	−2
of fingers	2	−2	4

(b) For both players A and B: choose 0 with probability 3/4 and 2 with probability 1/4. The value of the game is −1/2.

27. He should invest in rainy day goods about 5/9 of the time and sunny day goods about 4/9 of the time for a steady profit of $72.22.

Extended Application   (page 396)

1. $\begin{bmatrix} 2 & 2 \\ 1 & 3 \end{bmatrix}$ **2.** Both (1, 1) and (1, 2) are saddle points.

Chapter 8   Review Exercises   (page 397)

1. Yes   **3.** Yes   **5.** (a) $C^1 = \begin{bmatrix} .6 & .4 \\ 1 & 0 \end{bmatrix}$; $C^2 = \begin{bmatrix} .76 & .24 \\ .6 & .4 \end{bmatrix}$; $C^3 = \begin{bmatrix} .696 & .304 \\ .76 & .24 \end{bmatrix}$ (b) .76

7. (a) $E^1 = \begin{bmatrix} .2 & .5 & .3 \\ .1 & .8 & .1 \\ 0 & 1 & 0 \end{bmatrix}$; $E^2 = \begin{bmatrix} .09 & .8 & .11 \\ .1 & .79 & .11 \\ .1 & .8 & .1 \end{bmatrix}$; $E^3 = \begin{bmatrix} .098 & .795 & .107 \\ .099 & .792 & .109 \\ .1 & .79 & .11 \end{bmatrix}$ (b) .099   **9.** [.453   .547];
[5/11   6/11] ≈ [.455   .545]   **11.** [.48   .28   .24]; [47/95   26/95   22/95] ≈ [.495   .274   .232]   **13.** (a) [.54   .46]
(b) [.6464   .3536]   (c) 2/3 of the market   **15.** (a) .2   (b) .2   (c) .196   (d) .4   (e) .28   (f) .256   **17.** Regular
19. Not regular   **21.** (a) Oppose   (b) Oppose   (c) Oppose; 2700   (d) Oppose; +1400 votes   **23.** $\begin{bmatrix} −11 & 6 \\ −10 & −12 \end{bmatrix}$

25. $\begin{bmatrix} −2 & 4 \\ 3 & 2 \\ 0 & 3 \end{bmatrix}$ **27.** (1, 1); value is −2   **29.** (2, 2); value is 0; fair game   **31.** (2, 3); value is −3   **33.** Player A: 1: 5/6, 2: 1/6; player B: 1: 1/2, 2: 1/2; value 1/2   **35.** Player A: 1: 1/9, 2: 8/9; player B: 1: 5/9, 2: 4/9; value 5/9   **37.** Player A: 1: 1/5, 2: 4/5; player B: 1: 3/5, 2: 0; 3: 2/5; value −12/5   **39.** Player A: 1: 3/4, 2: 1/4, 3: 0; player B: 1: 1/2, 2: 1/2; value 1/2

Chapter 9   Section 9.1   (page 406)

1. $120   **3.** $3937.50   **5.** $186.54   **7.** $336   **9.** $143.46   **11.** $438.90   **13.** $376.11   **15.** $201.46
17. $13,554.22   **19.** $5056.06   **21.** $14,434.68   **23.** $6101.33   **25.** $318.69   **27.** $30,268.47   **29.** $1732.90
31. $6053.59   **33.** $3598; 20.1%   **35.** $7547.13

Answers in the remainder of this chapter may differ by a few cents depending on whether tables or a calculator is used.

Section 9.2 (page 412)

1. $1593.85 **3.** $20,974.32 **5.** $1903.00 **7.** $82,379.10 **9.** $30,779.48 **11.** $13,213.14 **13.** $5105.58
15. $60,484.66 **17.** $2746.51 **19.** $2551.13 **21.** $4490.29 **23.** $583.78 **25.** $4016.21 **27.** $1000 now
29. 4.04% **31.** 8.16% **33.** 12.36% **35.** About 18 years **37.** About 12 years **39.** $142,886.40
41. $123,506.50 **43.** $63,685.27 **45.** $904.02

Section 9.3 (page 419)

1. 11, 17, 23, 29, 35; arithmetic **3.** $-4, -1, 2, 5, 8$; arithmetic **5.** $-2, -8, -14, -20, -26$; arithmetic
7. 2, 4, 8, 16, 32; geometric **9.** $-2, 4, -8, 16, -32$; geometric **11.** 6, 12, 24, 48, 96; geometric
13. 1/3, 3/7, 1/2, 5/9, 3/5; neither **15.** 1/2, 1/3, 1/4, 1/5, 1/6; neither **17.** Arithmetic, $d = 8$ **19.** Arithmetic, $d = 3$
21. Geometric, $r = 3$ **23.** Neither **25.** Arithmetic, $d = -3$ **27.** Arithmetic, $d = 3$ **29.** Geometric, $r = -2$
31. Neither **33.** 70 **35.** 65 **37.** 78 **39.** -65 **41.** 63 **43.** 678 **45.** 183 **47.** -18 **49.** 48
51. -648 **53.** 81 **55.** 64 **57.** 15 **59.** 156/25 **61.** -208 **63.** -15 **65.** 80 **67.** 125 **69.** 134
71. 70 **73.** -56 **75.** 125,250 **77.** 90 **79.** 170 **81.** 160 **83.** $15,600 **85.** (a) $1681 (b) $576

Section 9.4 (page 426)

1. 15.91713 **3.** 21.82453 **5.** 22.01900 **7.** 20.02359 **9.** $1318.08 **11.** $305,390.00 **13.** $671,994.62
15. $4,180,929.88 **17.** $222,777.26 **19.** $40,652.46 **21.** $516,397.05 **23.** $6294.79 **25.** $158,456.00
27. $13,486.56 **29.** $8070.23 **31.** $526.95 **33.** $952.33 **35.** $137,895.84 **37.** $118,667.74 **39.** $159.49
41. $522.85 **43.** $112,796.87 **45.** $209,348.00 **47.** $354.79 **49.** $579.65 **51.** $4164.55 **53.** $126.91
55. $23,023.98 **57.** (a) $1200 (b) $3511.58 (c)

Payment Number	Amount of Deposit	Interest Earned	Total
1	$3511.58	$0	$3511.58
2	3511.58	105.35	7128.51
3	3511.58	213.86	10,853.95
4	3511.58	325.62	14,691.15
5	3511.58	440.73	18,643.46
6	3511.58	559.30	22,714.34
7	3511.58	681.43	26,907.35
8	3511.58	807.22	31,226.15
9	3511.58	936.78	35,674.51
10	3511.58	1070.24	40,256.33
11	3511.58	1207.69	44,975.60
12	3511.58	1349.27	49,836.45
13	3511.58	1495.09	54,843.12
14	3511.59	1645.29	60,000.00

Section 9.5 (page 432)

1. 9.71225 **3.** 12.65930 **5.** 14.71787 **7.** 5.69719 **9.** $6246.89 **11.** $7877.72 **13.** $153,724.50
15. $148,771.76 **17.** $111,183.90 **19.** $97,122.50 **21.** $68,108.64 **23.** $12,493.78 **25.** $158.00
27. $6698.98 **29.** $160.08 **31.** $5570.58 **33.** $11,727.32 **35.** $274.58 **37.** $663.75 **39.** $742.51
41.

Payment Number	Amount of Payment	Interest for Period	Portion to Principal	Principal at End of Period
0	—	—	—	$4000
1	$1207.68	$320.00	$887.68	$3112.32
2	1207.68	248.99	958.69	2153.63
3	1207.68	172.29	1035.39	1118.24
4	1207.70	89.46	1118.24	0

43.

Payment Number	Amount of Payment	Interest for Period	Portion to Principal	Principal at End of Period
0	—	—	—	$7184
1	$211.03	$107.76	$103.27	$7080.73
2	211.03	106.21	104.82	6975.91
3	211.03	$104.64	106.39	6869.52
4	211.03	103.04	107.99	6761.53
5	211.03	101.42	109.61	6651.92
6	211.03	99.78	111.25	6540.67

45. (a) $4025.90 (b) $2981.93

47.

End of Year	To Interest	To Principal	Total Interest	Total Principal	Balance
1	$3225.54	$2557.95	$ 3225.54	$ 2557.95	$35389.50
2	3008.11	2775.38	6233.64	5333.34	32614.20
3	2772.21	3011.29	9005.85	8344.62	29602.90
4	2516.24	3267.25	11522.10	11611.90	26335.60
5	2238.53	3544.96	13760.60	15156.80	22790.70
6	1937.20	3846.29	15697.80	19003.10	18944.40
7	1610.28	4173.22	17308.10	23176.30	14771.20
8	1255.54	4527.95	18563.60	27704.30	10243.20
9	870.67	4912.82	19434.30	32617.10	5330.39
10	453.07	5330.42	19887.40	37947.50	−0.02

Extended Application   (page 438)

1. $14,038   **2.** $9511   **3.** $8837   **4.** $3968

Chapter 9   Review Exercises   (page 439)

1. $1908.36   **3.** $2686.84   **5.** $105.30   **7.** $21,897.81   **9.** $76,075.85   **11.** $665.54   **13.** $6194.13
15. 16.3%   **17.** $1999.00   **19.** $43,988.32   **21.** $7797.47   **23.** $4272.85   **25.** $6002.84   **27.** $6289.04
29. $18,306.34   **31.** $2501.24   **33.** $12,025.46   **35.** $845.74   **37.** $3137.06   **39.** −2, −6, −10, −14, −18;
arithmetic   **41.** 1/2, 4/7, 5/8, 2/3, 7/10   **43.** 61   **45.** −24   **47.** $15,162.14   **49.** $199,870.32   **51.** $41,208.86
53. $45,569.65   **55.** $886.05   **57.** $3339.86   **59.** $2815.31   **61.** $34,357.52   **63.** $4788.17   **65.** $12,806.37
67. $2806.66   **69.** $717.21

71.

Payment Number	Amount of Payment	Interest for Period	Portion to Principal	Principal at End of Period
0	—	—	—	$5000
1	$985.09	$250.00	$735.09	$4264.91
2	985.09	213.25	771.84	3493.07
3	985.09	174.65	810.44	2682.63
4	985.09	134.13	850.96	1831.67
5	985.09	91.58	893.51	938.16
6	985.07	46.91	938.16	0

Chapter 10   Section 10.1   (page 454)

1. 3   **3.** Does not exist   **5.** 0   **7.** −2   **9.** Does not exist   **11.** 10   **13.** Does not exist   **15.** 41   **17.** 9/7
19. −1   **21.** 6   **23.** −5   **25.** $\sqrt{5}$ **27.** Does not exist   **29.** 4   **31.** −1/9   **33.** 1/10   **35.** $1/(2\sqrt{5})$
37. 2x   **39.** (a) $500 (b) Does not exist (c) $1500 (d) 15 units   **41.** 3/5   **43.** 1/2   **45.** 1/2   **47.** 0   **49.** 0
51. (a) .57 (b) .53 (c) .5 (d) .5   **53.** −.24302   **55.** 1.000   **57.** −2.01 < x < −1.99

Section 10.2 (page 464)

1. (a) 1 (b) 2/3 (c) 3/5 (d) 2/5 **3.** (a) 3 (b) 7/2 (c) 1 (d) 0 (e) -2 (f) -2 (g) -3 (h) -1 **5.** (a) 3° per thousand feet (b) 1.25° per thousand feet (c) $-7/6°$ per thousand feet (d) about $-1/8°$ per thousand feet **7.** (a) almost 0 (b) -4% per year (c) about -1% per year (d) about $-3\ 1/2\%$ per year **9.** 5 **11.** 8 **13.** 1/3 **15.** $-1/3$ **17.** (a) 7 (b) 5 (c) 3.02; 3.002; 3.0002 (d) 3 **19.** 3 **21.** (a) 15 (b) 14 (c) 13.01; 13.001; 13.0001 (d) 13 **23.** 7 **25.** 5 **27.** Graph (a) gives total distance and (b) gives velocity.

Section 10.3 (page 479)

1. 27 **3.** 1/8 **5.** 1/8 **7.** $y = 8x - 9$ **9.** $5x + 4y = 20$ **11.** $3y = 2x + 18$ **13.** 2 **15.** 1/5 **17.** 0 **19.** $f'(x) = -8x + 11$; -5; 11; 35 **21.** $f'(x) = 8$; 8; 8; 8 **23.** $f'(x) = 3x^2 + 3$; 15; 3; 30 **25.** $f'(x) = 2/x^2$; 1/2; does not exist; 2/9 **27.** $f'(x) = -4/(x - 1)^2$; -4; -4; $-1/4$ **29.** $f'(x) = 1/(2\sqrt{x})$; $1/(2\sqrt{2})$; does not exist; does not exist **31.** 0 **33.** -6; 6 **35.** -3; 0; 2; 3; 5 **37.** 0 **39.** -2 **41.** -1; 2 **43.** -4; 0 **45.** Derivative is never 0 **47.** (a) 0 (b) -4 (c) -8 **49.** (a) 30 (b) 20 (c) 10 (d) 0 (e) -10 **51.** From the left, our estimates are $-.005$; .008; $-.00125$. **53.** .0435 **55.** 4.269 **57.** 1.075

Section 10.4 (page 489)

1. $f'(x) = 18x - 8$ **3.** $y' = 30x^2 - 18x + 6$ **5.** $y' = 4x^3 - 15x^2 + 18x$ **7.** $f'(x) = 9x^5 - 2x^{-.5}$ or $9x^5 - 2/x^{.5}$ **9.** $y' = -48x^{2.2} + 3.8x^9$ **11.** $y' = 36t^{1/2} + 2t^{-1/2}$ or $36t^{1/2} + 2/t^{1/2}$ **13.** $y' = 4x^{-1/2} + (9/2)x^{-1/4}$ or $4/x^{1/2} + 9/(2x^{1/4})$ **15.** $g'(x) = -30x^{-6} + x^{-2}$ or $-30/x^6 + 1/x^2$ **17.** $y' = 8x^{-3} - 9x^{-4}$ or $8/x^3 - 9/x^4$ **19.** $y' = -20x^{-3} - 12x^{-5} - 6$ or $-20/x^3 - 12/x^5 - 6$ **21.** $f'(t) = -6t^{-2} + 16t^{-3}$ or $-6/t^2 + 16/t^3$ **23.** $y' = -36x^{-5} + 24x^{-4} - 2x^{-2}$ or $-36/x^5 + 24/x^4 - 2/x^2$ **25.** $f'(x) = -6x^{-3/2} - (3/2)x^{-1/2}$ or $-6/x^{3/2} - 3/(2x^{1/2})$ **27.** $p'(x) = 5x^{-3/2} - 12x^{-5/2}$ or $5/x^{3/2} - 12/x^{5/2}$ **29.** $y' = (-3/2)x^{-5/4}$ or $-3/(2x^{5/4})$ **31.** $y' = (-5/3)t^{-2/3}$ or $-5/(3t^{2/3})$ **33.** $dy/dx = -40x^{-6} + 36x^{-5}$ or $-40/x^6 + 36/x^5$ **35.** $(-9/2)x^{-3/2} - 3x^{-5/2}$ or $-9/(2x^{3/2}) - 3/x^{5/2}$ **37.** -28 **39.** 11/16 **41.** When $x = 5/3$ **43.** When $x = 2/3$ or 1 **45.** When $x = 5/2$ or -1 **47.** When $x = \sqrt[3]{4}$ **49.** Tangent line is never horizontal **51.** -28; $28x + y = 34$ **53.** 79/6 **55.** $-11/27$ **57.** 10 **59.** (a) 100 (b) 1 (c) $-.01$; the percent of acid is decreasing at the rate of .01 per day after 100 days **61.** (a) The blood sugar level is decreasing at a rate of 4 points per unit of insulin. (b) The blood sugar level is decreasing at a rate of 10 points per unit of insulin. **63.** (a) 15 (b) 119 (c) 207 (d) 319 **65.** (a) $C'(x) = 2$ (b) $R'(x) = 6 - x/500$ (c) $P'(x) = 4 - x/500$ (d) $x = 2000$ (e) $4000 **67.** (a) $v(t) = 6$ (b) 6; 6; 6 **69.** (a) $v(t) = 22t + 4$ (b) 4; 114; 224 **71.** (a) $v(t) = 12t^2 + 16t$ (b) 0; 380; 1360 **73.** (a) $v(t) = 2t^{-1/2}$ or $2/t^{1/2}$ (b) Does not exist; $2/\sqrt{5}$ or $2\sqrt{5}/5$; $2/\sqrt{10}$ or $\sqrt{10}/5$

Section 10.5 (page 496)

1. $y' = 4x + 3$ **3.** $f'(x) = 48x + 66$ **5.** $y' = 18x^2 - 6x + 4$ **7.** $y' = 9t^2 - 4t - 5$ **9.** $y' = 36x^3 + 21x^2 - 18x - 7$ **11.** $y' = 4(2x - 5)$ or $8x - 20$ **13.** $k'(t) = 4t(t^2 - 1)$ or $4t^3 - 4t$ **15.** $y' = (3/2)x^{1/2} + (1/2)x^{-1/2} + 2$ or $3x^{1/2}/2 + 1/(2\sqrt{x}) + 2$ **17.** $g'(x) = 10 + (3/2)x^{-1/2}$ or $10 + 3/(2\sqrt{x})$ **19.** $y' = -3/(2x - 1)^2$ **21.** $f'(x) = 53/(3x + 8)^2$ **23.** $y' = -6/(3x - 5)^2$ **25.** $y' = -17/(4 + t)^2$ **27.** $y' = (x^2 - 2x - 1)/(x - 1)^2$ **29.** $f'(t) = (-t^2 + 4t + 1)/(t^2 + 1)^2$ **31.** $y' = (-2x^2 - 6x - 1)/(2x^2 - 1)^2$ **33.** $g'(x) = (x^2 + 6x - 14)/(x + 3)^2$ **35.** $p'(t) = [-\sqrt{t}/2 - 1/(2\sqrt{t})]/(t - 1)^2$ or $(-t - 1)/[2\sqrt{t}(t - 1)^2]$ **37.** $y' = (5\sqrt{x}/2 - 3/\sqrt{x})/x$ or $(5x - 6)/(2x\sqrt{x})$ **39.** (a) 86.8 (b) 176.4 (c) $A(x) = (9x^2 - 4x + 8)/x$ (d) $A'(x) = (9x^2 - 8)/x^2$ **41.** (a) $G'(20) = -1/200$; go faster (b) $G'(40) = 1/400$; go slower **43.** (a) $s'(x) = m/(m + nx)^2$ (b) $1/2560 \approx .000391$

Section 10.6 (page 502)

1. $(2x + 5)^{1/3}$; $2x^{1/3} + 5$ **3.** $2/\sqrt{4 - 3x}$; $4 - 6/\sqrt{x}$ **5.** $125x^2 + 145x + 42$; $25x^2 - 5x + 3$ **7.** $\sqrt{x^2 + 12}$; $x + 12$ **9.** If $f(x) = x^{1/3}$ and $g(x) = 3x - 7$, then $y = f[g(x)]$ **11.** If $f(x) = x^{1/2}$ and $g(x) = 9 - 4x$, then $y = f[g(x)]$ **13.** If $f(x) = (x + 3)/(x - 3)$ and $g(x) = \sqrt{x}$, then $y = f[g(x)]$ **15.** If $f(x) = x^2 + x + 5$ and $g(x) = x^{1/2} - 3$, then $y = f[g(x)]$ **17.** $y' = 4(2x + 9)$ **19.** $f'(x) = 90(5x - 1)^2$ **21.** $k'(x) = -144x(12x^2 + 5)^2$ **23.** $y' = 36(2x + 5)(x^2 + 5x)^3$ **25.** $s'(t) = 36(2t + 5)^{1/2}$ **27.** $y' = -21(8x + 9)(4x^2 + 9x)^{1/2}/2$ **29.** $f'(t) = 16(4t + 7)^{-1/2}$ or $16/(4t + 7)^{1/2}$ **31.** $y' = -(2x + 4)(x^2 + 4x)^{-1/2}$ or $-(2x + 4)/(x^2 + 4x)^{1/2}$ **33.** $r'(t) = 16t(2t + 3)^2 + 4(2t + 3)^3$ or $12(2t + 3)(2t + 1)$ **35.** $y' = 2(x + 2)(x - 1) + (x - 1)^2$ or $3(x - 1)(x + 1)$ **37.** $f'(x) = 10(x + 3)^2(x - 1) + 10(x - 1)^2(x + 3)$ or $20(x + 3)(x - 1)(x + 1)$ **39.** $y' = (x + 1)^2 \cdot x^{-1/2}/2 + 2x^{1/2}(x + 1)$ or $(x + 1)(5x + 1)/(2x^{1/2})$ **41.** $y' = -2(x - 4)^{-3}$ or $-2/(x - 4)^3$ **43.** $p'(t) = (t^2 - 2t - 15)/(t - 1)^2$ **45.** $y' = 8/(x + 2)^3$ **47.** $y' = x^{-1/2}(x^{1/2} - 1)^{-1/2}(3x^{1/2} - 1)/4$ **49.** (a) -3.2 (b) -2.8 (c) -2.4 (d) $-.8$ (e) $A(x) = 1000/x - 4 + x/250$ (f) $A'(x) = -1000/x^2 + 1/250$ **51.** (a) $-.5$ (b) $-1/54 \approx -.02$ (c) $-.011$ (d) $-1/128 \approx -.008$

Section 10.7   (page 509)

1. Discontinuous at -1; derivative fails to exist at -1 **3.** Discontinuous at 1; derivative fails to exist at -4 and 1
5. Discontinuous at 0 and 2; derivative fails to exist at -3, 0, 2, 3 and 5   **7.** Yes; no   **9.** No; no; yes   **11.** Yes; no; no
13. Yes; no; yes   **15.** Yes; no; yes   **17.** Yes; yes; yes   **19.** No; yes; yes
21. (a) \$96 (b) \$150 (d) when $x = 100$ **23.** (a) 30 (b) 30 (c) 25 (d) 21.43 (e) 22.50 (f) 30 (g) 25
(c) F(x)   **25.** For no value of Q **27.** Yes; yes; no   **29.** No; yes; yes
31. (a) -4 is not in the domain of $f[g(x)]$; yes; yes (b) Yes; yes; yes

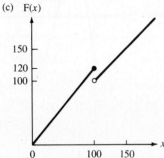

Chapter 10   Review Exercises   (page 513)

1. 4   **3.** -3 **5.** 4   **7.** 17/3   **9.** 8   **11.** -13 **13.** 1/6   **15.** 1/5   **17.** 3/4   **19.** 1/4   **21.** $-3/2$
23. 30   **25.** 9/77   **27.** $y' = 4$ **29.** $y' = -3x^2 + 7$ **31.** $-2; y + 2x = -4$ **33.** $-3/4; 3x + 4y = -9$
35. 38; $y = 38x + 22$ **37.** 3/4; $4y = 3x + 7$ **39.** $x = 0$ **41.** $x = 1/6$ **43.** Tangent lines never have a slope of 0.
45. (a) 315 (b) 1015 (c) 1515   **47.** (a) 55/3 $\approx$ 18.3 (b) 65/4 or 16.25 (c) 15   **49.** (a) -9.5 (b) -2.375 **51.** $y' = 10x - 7$ **53.** $y' = 14x^{4/3}$ **55.** $f'(x) = -3x^{-4} + (1/2)x^{-1/2}$ or $-3/x^4 + 1/(2x^{1/2})$ **57.** $y' = 15t^4 + 12t^2 - 7$
59. $y' = 12x^{1/2} - 6x^{-1/2}$ or $12x^{1/2} - 6/x^{1/2}$ **61.** $g'(t) = -20t^{1/3} - 7t^{-2/3}$ or $-20t^{1/3} - 7/t^{2/3}$ **63.** $y' = 9x^{-3/4} - 45x^{-7/4}$ or $9/x^{3/4} - 45/x^{7/4}$ **65.** $k'(x) = 15/(x + 5)^2$ **67.** $y' = (2 - x + 2x^{1/2})/[2x^{1/2}(x + 2)^2]$ **69.** $y' = (x^2 - 2x)/(x - 1)^2$ **71.** $f'(x) = 12(3x - 2)^3$ **73.** $y' = 1/(2t - 5)^{1/2}$ **75.** $y' = 3(2x + 1)^2(8x + 1)$ **77.** $r'(t) = (-15t^2 + 52t - 7)(3t + 1)^4$ **79.** $y' = (x^2 - 4x + 4)(x - 2)^2 = 1$ **81.** $-1/[x^{1/2}(x^{1/2} - 1)^2]$ **83.** $dy/dt = (1 + 2t^{1/2})/[4t^{1/2}(t^{1/2} + t)^{1/2}]$ **85.** $-2/3$ **87.** No; yes; yes   **89.** Yes; no; yes; no   **91.** Yes; no; yes   **93.** Yes; yes; yes
95. Yes; yes; yes   **97.** (a) 150 (b) 187.5 (c) 189 (d) C(x)
(e) when $x = 125$

99. Derivative fails to exist at x_1, x_2, and x_4; function
is discontinuous at x_2 and x_4

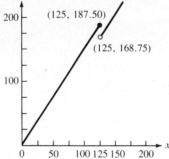

Chapter 11   Section 11.1   (page 524)

1. Decreasing on $(-\infty, 1)$; increasing on $(1, \infty)$ **3.** Increasing on $(-\infty, -2)$; decreasing on $(-2, \infty)$ **5.** Increasing on $(-\infty, -4)$ and $(-2, \infty)$; decreasing on $(-4, -2)$ **7.** Decreasing on $(-\infty, -7)$ and $(-4, -2)$; increasing on $(-7, -4)$ and $(-2, \infty)$

9. (a) $(-6, \infty)$ (b) $(-\infty, -6)$
(c)

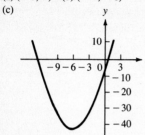

11. (a) $(-\infty, 3/2)$ (b) $(3/2, \infty)$
(c)

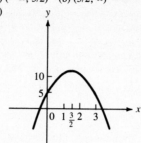

13. (a) $(-\infty, -3), (4, \infty)$ (b) $(-3, 4)$
(c)

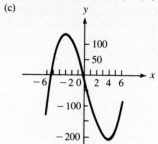

15. (a) $(-\infty, -3/2), (4, \infty)$
(b) $(-3/2, 4)$
(c)

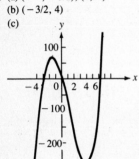

17. (a) Never (b) Always
(c)

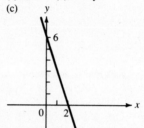

19. (a) Never (b) Always
(c)

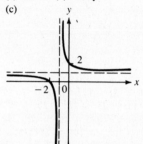

21. (a) $(-4, \infty)$ (b) $(-\infty, -4)$
(c)

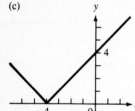

23. (a) Never (b) Always
(c)

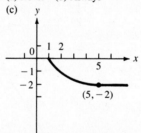

25. (a) $(0, \infty)$ (b) $(-\infty, 0)$
(c)

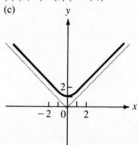

27. After 10 days. **29.** Increasing on $(0, 3)$, decreasing on $(3, \infty)$ (Remember: x must be at least 0) **31.** $(0, 1); (1, \infty)$

Section 11.2   (page 534)

1. Relative minimum of -4 at 1 **3.** Relative maximum of 3 at -2 **5.** Relative maximum of 3 at -4; relative minimum of 1 at -2 **7.** Relative maximum of 3 at -4; relative minimum of -2 at -7 and -2 **9.** Relative minimum of -44 at -6
11. Relative maximum of 17 at -3 **13.** Relative maximum of -8 at -3; relative minimum of -12 at -1 **15.** Relative maximum of 827/96 at $-1/4$; relative minimum of $-377/6$ at -5 **17.** Relative maximum of 57 at 2; relative minimum of 30 at 5
19. Relative maximum of -4 at 0; relative minimum of -85 at 3 and -3 **21.** Relative maximum of 0 at 8/5 **23.** Relative maximum of 1 at -1; relative minimum of 0 at 0 **25.** No relative extrema **27.** Relative minimum of 0 at 0 **29.** Relative maximum of 0 at 1; relative minimum of 8 at 5 **31.** $(2, 7)$ **33.** $(5/4, -9/8)$ **35.** 10; 180 **37.** Absolute maximum at x_3; no absolute minimum **39.** No absolute extrema **41.** Absolute minimum at x_1; no absolute maximum **43.** Absolute maximum at x_1; absolute minimum at x_2 **45.** Absolute maximum at 0; absolute minimum at -3 **47.** Absolute maximum at -1; absolute minimum at -5 **49.** Absolute maximum at -2; absolute minimum at 4 **51.** Absolute maximum at -2; absolute

minimum at 3   **53.** Absolute maximum at 6; absolute minimum at -4 and 4   **55.** Absolute maximum at 0; absolute minimum at 2   **57.** Absolute maximum at 6; absolute minimum at 4   **59.** Absolute maximum at $\sqrt{2}$; absolute minimum at 0   **61.** Absolute maximum at -3 and 3, absolute minimum at 0   **63.** Absolute maximum at 0; absolute minimum at -4 **65.** Absolute maximum at 0; absolute minimum at -1 and 1   **67.** 10 hundred thousand tires; $700 thousand, or $700,000   **69.** 45; 65   **71.** The piece formed into a circle should have length $12\pi/(4 + \pi)$

Extended Application   (page 539)

1. Maximum profit of $6535.71 comes from traveling at 20 knots.

Section 11.3   (page 549)

1. $f''(x) = 18x; 0; 36; -54$ **3.** $f''(x) = 36x^2 - 30x + 4; 4; 28; 418$ **5.** $f''(x) = 6; 6; 6; 6$ **7.** $f''(x) = 6(x + 4); 24;$ 36; 6   **9.** $f''(x) = 10/(x - 2)^3; -5/4; f''(2)$ does not exist; $-2/25$ **11.** $f''(x) = 2/(1 + x)^3; 2; 2/27; -1/4$ **13.** $f''(x) = -1/[4(x + 4)^{3/2}]; -1/32; -1/(4 \cdot 6^{3/2}) \approx -.0170; -1/4$ **15.** $f''(x) = (-6/5)x^{-7/5}$ or $-6/(5x^{7/5}); f''(0)$ does not exist; $-6/(5 \cdot 2^{7/5}) \approx -.4547; -6/[5 \cdot (-3)^{7/5}] \approx .2578$ **17.** $f'''(x) = -24x; f^{(4)}(x) = -24$ **19.** $f'''(x) = 240x^2 + 144x;$ $f^{(4)}(x) = 480x + 144$ **21.** $f'''(x) = 18(x + 2)^{-4}$ or $18/(x + 2)^4; f^{(4)}(x) = -72(x + 2)^{-5}$ or $-72/(x + 2)^5$ **23.** $f'''(x) = -36(x - 2)^{-4}$ or $-36/(x - 2)^4; f^{(4)}(x) = 144(x - 2)^{-5}$ or $144/(x - 2)^5$ **25.** Concave upward on $(2, \infty)$; concave downward on $(-\infty, 2)$; point of inflection at $(2, 3)$ **27.** Concave upward on $(-\infty, -1)$ and $(8, \infty)$; concave downward on $(-1, 8)$; points of inflection at $(-1, 7)$ and $(8, 6)$ **29.** Concave upward on $(2, \infty)$; concave downward on $(-\infty, 2)$; no points of inflection   **31.** Always concave upward; no points of inflection   **33.** Always concave downward; no points of inflection   **35.** Concave upward on $(-1, \infty)$; concave downward on $(-\infty, -1)$; point of inflection at $(-1, 44)$ **37.** Concave upward on $(-\infty, 3/2)$; concave downward on $(3/2, \infty)$; point of inflection at $(3/2, 525/2)$ **39.** Concave upward on $(5, \infty)$; concave downward on $(-\infty, 5)$; no points of inflection   **41.** Concave upward on $(-10/3, \infty)$; concave downward on $(-\infty, -10/3)$; point of inflection at $(-10/3, -250/27)$

43. Relative maximum at -5

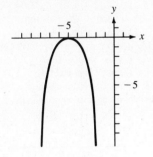

45. Relative maximum at 0, relative minimum at 2/3

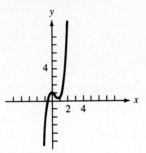

47. Relative maximum at 3, relative minimum at -6

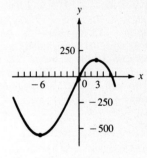

49. Relative maximum at $-5/3$, relative minimum at 1/2

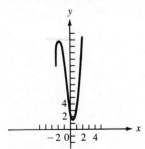

51. Relative minimum at -3

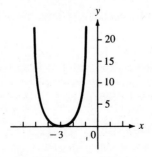

53. Relative maximum at 0, relative minimum at -3 and 3

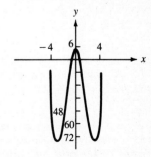

55. Relative maximum at -1, relative minimum at 1

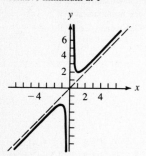

57. Relative maximum at -5, relative minimum at 5

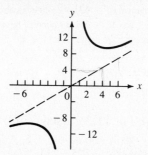

59. No critical values, no maximum or minimum

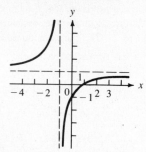

61. (a) Near trash compactors (b) Near wringer washers (c) Color tv's, room air conditioners: rate of growth of sales will now decline (d) Black and white tv's and wringer washers: the rate of decline is starting to slow **63.** 50 **65.** (a) After 3 hours (b) 2/9% **67.** $v(t) = 16t + 4$; $a(t) = 16$; 4; 68; 16; 16 **69.** $v(t) = -15t^2 - 16t + 6$; $a(t) = -30t - 16$; 6; -298; -16; -136 **71.** $v(t) = 6(3t + 4)^{-2}$ or $6/(3t + 4)^2$; $a(t) = -36(3t + 4)^{-3}$ or $-36/(3t + 4)^3$; 3/8; 3/128; $-9/16$; $-9/1024$ **73.** (a) -96 ft per sec (b) -160 ft per sec (c) -256 ft per sec (d) -32 ft per sec per sec **75.** (a) Increasing on $(0, 2)$ and $(4, 5)$; decreasing on $(-5, -.5)$ and $(2.5, 3.5)$ (b) Minima between $-.5$ and 0 and between 3.5 and 4; a maximum between 2 and 2.5 (c) Concave up on $(-5, .5)$ and $(3.5, 22)$; concave down on $(1, 3)$ (d) Inflection points between .5 and 1 and between 3 and 3.5 **77.** (a) Decreasing on $(-2, 1)$; increasing on $(1.3, 2)$ (b) Minimum between 1 and 1.3 (c) Concave up on $(-2, -.2)$ and $(.7, 2)$; concave down on $(.1, .4)$ (d) Inflection points between $-.2$ and .1 and between .4 and .7

Section 11.4 (page 557)

1. (a) $y = 100 - x$ (b) $P = x(100 - x)$ (c) $P' = 100 - 2x$; $x = 50$ (d) 50 and 50 (e) $50 \cdot 50 = 2500$ **3.** 100; 100 **5.** 100; 50 **7.** 5; -5 **9.** (a) $R(x) = 100,000x - 100x^2$ (b) 500 (c) 25,000,000 cents **11.** (a) $\sqrt{3200} \approx 56.6$ mph (b) $45.24 **13.** (a) $1200 - 2x$ (b) $A(x) = 1200x - 2x^2$ (c) 300 m (d) 180,000 sq m **15.** 405,000 sq m **17.** 200 feet on the $3 sides; 100 feet on the $6 sides; area is 20,000 sq ft **19.** (a) $40 - 2x$ (b) $100 + 5x$ (c) $R(x) = 4000 - 10x^2$ (d) pick now (e) $40 per tree **21.** (a) 90 (b) $405 **23.** 4 by 4 by 2 **25.** 3 by 6 by 2 **27.** 44.7 mph gives the minimum cost of $894 **29.** 1 mile from point A **31.** point P is $3\sqrt{7}/7 \approx 1.134$ miles from A **33.** (a) 50 thousand (b) .6 thousand (c) 56.25 thousand (d) 4.327 thousand (e) 5.071 thousand (f) no harvest is possible; the population is naturally declining

Extended Application (page 566)

1. (a) $520 million, or $4.33 million per plane (b) 80 million **2.** (a) 200 planes (b) 80 **3.** (a) $310 million (b) -4 million, or a loss of $4 million

Section 11.5 (page 570)

1. 10 **3.** 60 **5.** 5

Extended Application (page 571)

1. $-C_1/m^2 + DC_3/2$ **2.** $m = \sqrt{2C_1/(DC_3)}$ **3.** About 3.33 **4.** $m^+ = 4$ and $m^- = 3$ **5.** $Z(m^+) = Z(4) = $11,400$; $Z(m^-) = Z(3) = $11,300$ **6.** 3 months; 9 trainees per batch

Section 11.6 (page 575)

1. $dy/dx = -4x/(3y)$ **3.** $dy/dx = -y/(y + x)$ **5.** $dy/dx = 2/y$ **7.** $dy/dx = -3y^2/(6xy - 4)$ **9.** $dy/dx = (-y - x)/x$ **11.** $dy/dx = (-6x - 4y)/(4x + y)$ **13.** $dy/dx = 3x^2/(2y)$ **15.** $dy/dx = y^2/x^2$ **17.** $dy/dx = -3x(2 + y)^2/2$ **19.** $dy/dx = -2xy/(x^2 + 3y^2)$ **21.** $dy/dx = -y^{1/2}/x^{1/2}$ **23.** $dy/dx = -y^{1/2}x^{-1/2}/(x^{1/2}y^{-1/2} + 2)$ or $-y/(x + 2x^{1/2}y^{1/2})$ **25.** $dy/dx = [2(x^2 + 4y^3)^{1/4} - 3x]/(18y^2)$ **27.** $dy/dx = (x^{-1/2} + y^{1/2}x^{-1/2})/[4(1 + y^{1/2})^2 + y^{-1/2} + x^{1/2}y^{-1/2}]$ or $(y^{1/2} + y)/[4x^{1/2}y^{1/2}(1 + y^{1/2})^2 + x^{1/2} + x]$ **29.** $4y = 3x + 25$ **31.** $y = x + 2$ **33.** $24x + y = 57$ **35.** $x + 4y = 12$

37. (a) $3x + 4y = 50$; $-3x + 4y = -50$ **39.** $2y = x + 1$ **43.** $du/dv = -2u^{1/2}/(2v + 1)^{1/2}$

(b)

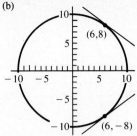

Section 11.7   (page 581)

1. 440   **3.** $-15/2$ **5.** $-5/7$ **7.** $1/5$ **9.** 7/6 ft per min   **11.** 16π sq ft per min   **13.** 50π cu in per min
15. 1/16 ft per min   **17.** .24 mm per min   **19.** $-.370$

Section 11.8   (page 587)

1. $dy = 12x\,dx$ **3.** $dy = (14x - 9)\,dx$ **5.** $dy = x^{-1/2}\,dx$ **7.** $dy = [-22/(x - 3)^2]\,dx$ **9.** $dy = (3x^2 - 1 + 4x)\,dx$
11. $dy = (x^{-2} + 6x^{-3})\,dx$ or $(1/x^2 + 6/x^3)\,dx$ **13.** -2.6 **15.** .1   **17.** .130   **19.** $-.023$ **21.** .24
23. $-.00444$ **25.** 3 1/6   **27.** 3 7/8   **29.** 11 1/11   **31.** 1 11/12   **33.** 4 1/48   **35.** 2 1/32   **37.** 2.005
39. 1 119/120 ≈ 1.992 **41.** 12.8π cu cm   **43.** $.48\pi$ sq mi   **45.** About 4800 cu in   **47.** -34π sq mm
49. $\pm.0138$ sq in   **51.** $\pm.405\pi \approx \pm1.273$ cu in   **53.** (a) -34 thousand pounds (b) -169.2 thousand pounds   **55.** (a) .2
(b) $-.037$

Chapter 11   Review Exercises   (page 589)

1. Increasing on $(5/2, \infty)$; decreasing on $(-\infty, 5/2)$ **3.** Increasing on $(-4, 2/3)$; decreasing on $(-\infty, -4)$ and $(2/3, \infty)$
5. Decreasing on $(-\infty, 4)$ and $(4, \infty)$ **7.** Relative maximum of -4 at 2   **9.** Relative minimum of -7 at 2   **11.** Relative
maximum of 101 at -3; relative minimum of -24 at 2   **13.** Relative maximum of $-151/54$ at 1/3; relative minimum of $-27/8$ at
$-1/2$ **15.** Relative maximum of 1 at 0; relative minimum of $-2/3$ at -1 and $-29/3$ at 2   **17.** No extrema
19. Concave upward on $(-\infty, -1/12)$; concave downward on $(-1/12, \infty)$; point of inflection at $(-1/12, 1007/216)$

21. Always concave upward; no points of inflection   **23.** Concave upward on $(0, \infty)$;
concave downward on $(-\infty, 0)$;
no point of inflection

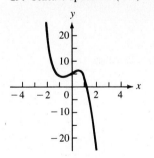

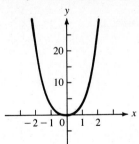

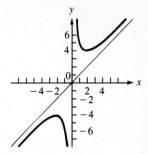

25. Concave upward on $(-\infty, 3)$; concave downward on $(3, \infty)$; no point of inflection

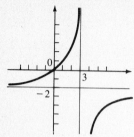

27. $f''(x) = 36x^2 - 10; 26; 314$ **29.** $f''(x) = -68(2x + 3)^{-3}$ or $-68/(2x + 3)^3; -68/125; 68/27$ **31.** $f''(t) = -(2t^2 + 1)/(t^2 + 1)^{3/2}; -3/2^{3/2} \approx -1.061; -19/10^{3/2} \approx -.601$ **33.** Absolute maximum of 29/4 at 5/2; absolute minimum of 5 at 1 and 4 **35.** Absolute maximum of 39 at -3; absolute minimum of $-319/27$ at 5/3 **37.** 25/2 and 25/2 **39.** (a) when $x = 2$ (b) 20 dollars **41.** 225 m by 450 m **43.** 4 m by 4 m by 2 m **45.** 40 **47.** 80 **49.** $dy/dx = (-4y - 2xy^3)/(3x^2y^2 + 4x)$ **51.** $dy/dx = (-4 - 9x^{3/2})/(24x^2y^2)$ **53.** $dy/dx = (2y - 2y^{1/2})/(4y^{1/2} - x + 9y)$ (This form of the answer was obtained by multiplying both sides of the given function by $x - 3y$.) **55.** $dy/dx = [9(4y^2 - 3x)^{1/3} + 3]/(8y)$ **57.** $23x + 16y = 94$ **59.** 272 **61.** -2 **63.** 56π sq ft per min **65.** $1/(4.8\pi) \approx .0663$ ft per min **67.** $dy = (24x^2 - 4x)dx$ **69.** $dy = [-16/(2 + x)^2]dx$ **71.** .1 **73.** 10 21/22 ≈ 10.955 **75.** 1.28π cu in or about 4.021 cu in

Chapter 12 Section 12.1 (page 600)

1.

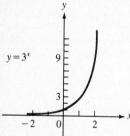

3.

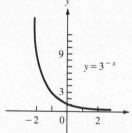

5.

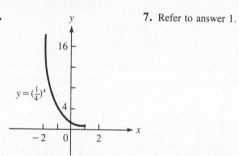

7. Refer to answer 1.

9.

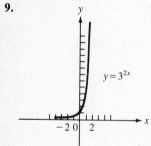

11.

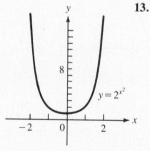

13.

15.

17.

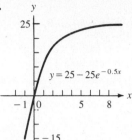

$y = 25 - 25e^{-0.5x}$

19.

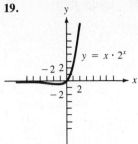

$y = x \cdot 2^x$

21.

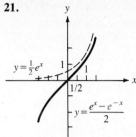

$y = \frac{1}{2}e^x$

$y = \dfrac{e^x - e^{-x}}{2}$

23. -3 **25.** 2
27. 3/2   **29.** 3/2
31. -2 **33.** 3
35. $-5/4$ **37.** $-1/7$
39. 4, -4 **41.** 0, 8
43. 2   **45.** 0, 5/3

The answers to Exercises 47–53 were found on a calculator. Values from the table may differ slightly.   **47.** 12.18249   **49.** .87810
51. 2.44948   **53.** .79553   **55.** (a) 2.8×10^{16}, 3.7×10^8 cm³   (b) 5.5×10^{12} cm³, 3.25×10^4 (c) 5.5×10^9 cm³, 32.5
57. (a) 1.12, 1.25, 1.40, 1.57,   **59.** (a) About \$151,000   **61.** (a) 1,000,000   (b) About 1,410,000   (c) 2,000,000
1.97, 2.21, 2.48, 2.77   (b) About \$39   (d) 4,000,000   (e) $P(t)$
(b) y **63.** (a) About 1,120,000   (b) About 1,260,000
(c) About 1,410,000   (d) About 1,590,000
(e) 2,000,000   (f) 4,000,000
(g) 8,000,000   (h) 16,000,000
65. A sequence of points, one for each
rational number

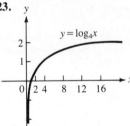

$y = (1.12)^t$

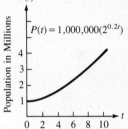

$P(t) = 1,000,000(2^{0.2t})$

Section 12.2   (page 610)

1. $\log_2 8 = 3$ **3.** $\log_3 81 = 4$ **5.** $\log_{1/3} 9 = -2$ **7.** $2^7 = 128$ **9.** $25^{-1} = 1/25$ **11.** $10^4 = 10,000$ **13.** 2
15. 3   **17.** -2 **19.** $-2/3$
21. 1/9, 1/3, 1, 3, 27   **23.** y **25.** y **27.** y

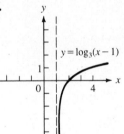

$y = \log_3 x$

$y = \log_4 x$

$y = \log_3(x - 1)$

$y = \log_2 x^2$

29. $\log_9 7 + \log_9 m$ **31.** $1 + \log_3 p - \log_3 5 - \log_3 k$ **33.** $\log_3 5 + (1/2)\log_3 2 - (1/4)\log_3 7$ **35.** $3a$
37. $a + 3c$ **39.** $2c + 3a + 1$ **41.** 2.9957   **43.** 6.6846   **45.** 7.4956   **47.** 10.9151   **49.** $-.7985$
51. 1.86   **53.** 9.35   **55.** 2.62   **57.** $x = 1/5$ **59.** $m = 3/2$ **61.** $y = 16$ **63.** $x = 8/5$ **65.** $x = 1$
67. $x = 1.47$ **69.** $k = 2.39$ **71.** $a = -.12$ **73.** $k = 1.36$ **75.** 1   **77.** (a) 2.03   (b) 2.28   (c) 2.17   (d) 1.21
79. (a) About 240   (b) About 480   (c) About 760   (d) $F(t)$ **81.** (a) 20   (b) 30   (c) 50   (d) 60
83. (a) 3   (b) 6   (c) 8
85. 4.3 ml/min; 7.8 ml/min

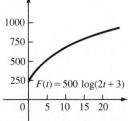

$F(t) = 500 \log(2t + 3)$

Section 12.3   (page 619)

1. $y' = 1/x$ **3.** $y' = -1/(3 - x)$ or $1/(x - 3)$ **5.** $y' = (4x - 7)/(2x^2 - 7x)$ **7.** $y' = 1/[2(x + 5)]$ **9.** $y' = 3(2x^2 + 5)/[x(x^2 + 5)]$ **11.** $y' = -3x/(x + 2) - 3\ln|x + 2|$ **13.** $y' = x + 2x\ln|x|$ **15.** $y' = [2x - 4(x + 3)\ln|x + 3|]/[x^3(x + 3)]$ **17.** $y' = (4x + 7 - 4x\ln|x|)/[x(4x + 7)^2]$ **19.** $y' = (6x\ln|x| - 3x)/(\ln|x|)^2$ **21.** $y' = 4(\ln|x + 1|)^3/(x + 1)$ **23.** $1/(x\ln|x|)$ **25.** $1/(x\ln 10)$ **27.** $-1/[(\ln 10)(1 - x)]$ or $1/[(\ln 10)(x - 1)]$ **29.** $5/[2(\ln 5)(5x + 2)]$ **31.** $3(x + 1)/[(\ln 3)(x^2 + 2x)]$

33. Minimum of $-1/e \approx -.3679$ at $1/e \approx .3679$.

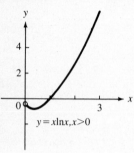
$y = x\ln x, x > 0$

35. Minimum of $-1/e \approx -.3679$ at $1/e \approx .3679$; maximum of $1/e$ at $-1/e$

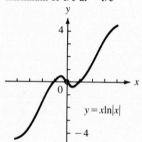
$y = x\ln|x|$

37. Minimum of 0 at $x = 1$ and $x = -1$

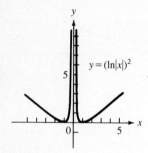
$y = (\ln|x|)^2$

39. Maximum of $1/e \approx .3679$ at $x = e \approx 2.718$

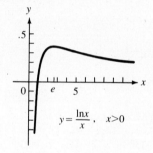
$y = \dfrac{\ln x}{x}, \quad x > 0$

41. 26.9; 13.1   **43.** 119/2 items, or, as a practical matter, 60 items

45. As $x \to \infty$, the slope approaches 0; as $x \to 0$, the slope becomes infinitely large.

49.

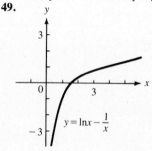
$y = \ln x - \dfrac{1}{x}$

Section 12.4   (page 624)

1. $y' = 4e^{4x}$ **3.** $y' = 12e^{-2x}$ **5.** $y' = -16e^{2x}$ **7.** $y' = -16e^{x+1}$ **9.** $y' = 2xe^{x^2}$ **11.** $y' = 12xe^{2x^2}$ **13.** $y' = 16xe^{2x^2-4}$ **15.** $y' = xe^x + e^x = e^x(x + 1)$ **17.** $y' = 2(x - 3)(x - 2)e^{2x}$ **19.** $y' = e^{x^2}/x + 2xe^{x^2}\ln x$ **21.** $y' = (xe^x\ln x - e^x)/[x(\ln x)^2]$ **23.** $y' = (2xe^x - x^2e^x)/e^{2x} = x(2 - x)/e^x$ **25.** $y' = [x(e^x - e^{-x}) - (e^x + e^{-x})]/x^2$ **27.** $y' = -20,000e^{0.4x}/(1 + 10e^{0.4x})^2$ **29.** $y' = 8,000e^{-0.2x}/(9 + 4e^{-0.2x})^2$ **31.** $y' = 2(2x + e^{-x^2})(2 - 2xe^{-x^2})$ **33.** $y' = 5\ln 8\,e^{5x\ln 8}$ **35.** $y' = 6x(\ln 4)e^{(x^2+2)\ln 4}$ **37.** $y' = [(\ln 3)e^{\sqrt{x}\ln 3}]/\sqrt{x}$ **39.** (a) 20 (b) 6   **41.** (a) .005 (b) .0007 (c) .000013 (d) $-.022$ (e) $-.0029$ (f) $-.000054$ **43.** (a) -125 (b) -46.0 (c) -27.9 (d) -10.3

45. Maximum of $1/e$ at $x = -1$

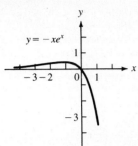

47. Minimum of 0 at $x = 0$;
maximum of $4/e^2 \approx .54$ at $x = 2$

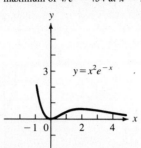

49. Minimum of 2 at $x = 0$

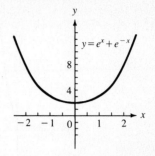

51. (a) As $x \to -\infty$, the slope approaches 0.
(b) As $x \to 0$, the slope approaches 1, the slope of a 45° line.

53.

![Graph of y = e^x ln x with y-axis marked 50, 100, 150, 200, 250 and x-axis marked 1 2 3 4 5, labeled $y = e^x \ln x$]

Section 12.5   (page 633)

1. (a) $y = 100e^{0.11t}$ (b) About 15 months   **3.** (a) $y = 500e^{-0.056t}$ (b) About 12.4 days   **5.** (a) $y = 10e^{0.0095t}$
(b) 42.7° C   **7.** (a) 5000   (b) About 1840   (c) About 91.6   (d) 3.47 seconds   **9.** About 1800 years   **11.** About 18,600
years   **13.** (a) 67%   (b) 37%   (c) 23 days   (d) 46 days   **15.** (a) $E(t) = 10^6 e^{0.0098t}$ (b) About 1.1×10^6 (c) About 41 minutes
17. (a) 306   (b) 326   (c) 346   **19.** (a) 1000   (b) 4500   (c) 4999.8   **21.** 128.6°   **23.** About 30 minutes
(d) After 1.6 months   (e) 350   (d) At about 2 years   (e) 5000   **25.** .125   **27.** 39 days
(f)

![Graph of p(t) with y-axis marked 100, 200, 300, 400 and t-axis marked 2 4 6 8 10, labeled $p(t) = 350 - 80e^{0.3t}$]

(f)

![Graph of S(x) with y-axis marked 1000, 5000 and x-axis marked 2, 10, labeled $S(x) = 5000 - 4000e^{-x}$]

Extended Application   (page 639)

1. .0315   **2.** λy_0 is about 118,000; painting is a forgery.   **3.** $\lambda y_0 = 163,000$; forgery   **4.** 24,000; cannot be modern forgery
5. $\lambda y_0 = 142,000$; forgery   **6.** 134,000; forgery

Section 12.6   (page 645)

1. $7163.39   **3.** $3077.07   **5.** $5092.24   **7.** $4054.96   **9.** $21,665.74   **11.** $44,510.82   **13.** $25,424.98
15. $18,221.19   **17.** $5288.95   **19.** $18,825.06   **21.** 5.11619%   **23.** 18.81%   **25.** 11.46213%   **27.** (a) about
6.1 years   (b) about 9.7 years   **29.** (a) about 11.5 years   (b) about 8.7 years   (c) about 5.8 years   **31.** $1043.79
33. $4537.71   **35.** $5583.95   **37.** $40,720.81   **39.** $4270.04   **41.** $51,237.67   **43.** $2285.80   **45.** $1683.10
47. 7.64063%   **49.** 7.76326%   **51.** 7.78758%

Chapter 12   Review Exercises   (page 647)

1. -1 **3.** 2   **5.**

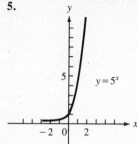

$y = 5^x$

7.

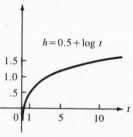

$y = \left(\frac{1}{5}\right)^x$

9. $\log_2 64 = 6$ **11.** $\ln 1.09417 = 0.09$ **13.** $2^5 = 32$ **15.** $e^{4.41763} = 82.9$ **17.** 4   **19.** 4/5   **21.** 3/2
23. 1.8245   **25.** 6.1800   **27.** $\log_5(21k^4)$ **29.** $\log_2(x^2/m^3)$ **31.** $p = 1.416$ **33.** $m = -2.807$ **35.** $x =$
-3.305 **37.** $m = 1.7547$ **39.** (a) .8 m   (b) 1.2 m   (c) 1.5 m   (d) 1.8 m   (e)

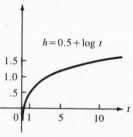

$h = 0.5 + \log t$

41. $y' = -12e^{2x}$ **43.** $y' = -6x^2 e^{-2x^3}$
45. $y' = 10xe^{2x} + 5e^{2x} = 5e^{2x}(2x + 1)$ **47.** $y' = 2x/(2 + x^2)$
49. $y' = (x - 3 - x \ln|3x|)/[x(x - 3)^2]$
51. $y' = [e^x(x + 1)(x^2 - 1)\ln|x^2 - 1| - 2x^2 e^x]/[(x^2 - 1)(\ln|x^2 - 1|)^2]$
53. $y' = 2(x^2 + e^x)(2x + e^x)$
55. Relative minimum of $-.368$ at $x = -1$

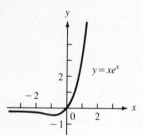

$y = xe^x$

57. Relative minimum at $x = 2$ **59.** (a) $y = 100,000e^{-0.05t}$ (b) About 7.1 years   **61.** (a) $y = 100e^{-0.23t}$ (b) About 3 years
63. (a) 0   (b) 55   (c) 98   (d) 100   (e) One day   (f)

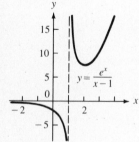

$y = \dfrac{e^x}{x - 1}$

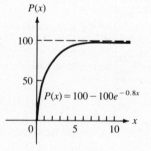

$P(x) = 100 - 100e^{-0.8x}$

65. (a) .0769277   (b) .0769231   (c) .0769231   (d) At .807556 minutes   **67.** $949.12   **69.** $69,856.30   **71.** $1692.28
73. $16,668.75   **75.** $24,866.86   **77.** $3689.40   **79.** $81,530.50   **81.** About 9.59%   **83.** $1494.52
85. $31,468.86

Chapter 13   Section 13.1   (page 659)

1. $2x^2 + C$ **3.** $5t^3/3 + C$ **5.** $6k + C$ **7.** $z^2 + 3z + C$ **9.** $x^3/3 + 3x^2 + C$ **11.** $t^3/3 - 2t^2 + 5t + C$
13. $z^4 + z^3 + z^2 - 6z + C$ **15.** $10z^{3/2}/3 + C$ **17.** $2u^{3/2}/3 + 2u^{5/2}/5 + C$ **19.** $6x^{5/2} + 4x^{3/2}/3 + C$
21. $4u^{5/2} - 4u^{7/2} + C$ **23.** $-1/z + C$ **25.** $-1/(2y^2) - 2y^{1/2} + C$ **27.** $9/t - 2\ln|t| + C$ **29.** $e^{2t}/2 + C$
31. $-15e^{-0.2x} + C$ **33.** $3\ln|x| - 8e^{-0.5x} + C$ **35.** $\ln|t| + 2t^3/3 + C$ **37.** $e^{2u}/2 + 2u^2 + C$ **39.** $x^3/3 +$
$x^2 + x + C$ **41.** $6x^{7/6}/7 + 3x^{2/3}/2 + C$ **43.** $C(x) = 2x^2 - 5x + 8$ **45.** $C(x) = .2x^3/3 + 5x^2/2 + 10$
47. $C(x) = 2x^{3/2}/3 - 8/3$ **49.** $C(x) = x^3/3 - x^2 + 3x + 6$ **51.** $C(x) = \ln|x| + x^2 + 7.45$ **53.** $P(x) = x^2 +$
$20x - 50$ **55.** $v(t) = t^3/3 + t + 6$ **57.** $s(t) = -16t^2 + 6400$; 20 seconds   **59.** $f(t) = 3x^{5/3}/5$

Section 13.2   (page 669)

1. 18   **3.** 65   **5.** 20   **7.** 8   **9.** 56   **11.** 32; 38   **13.** 15; 31/2   **15.** 20; 30   **17.** 16; 14   **19.** 12.8; 27.2
21. 2.67; 2.08   **23.** (a) 3 (b) 3.5 (c) 4   **25.** About 10,000,000 cars   **27.** A concentration of about 19 units
29. About 1622 feet   **31.** about 4   **33.** 13.9572   **35.** 1.28857

Section 13.3   (page 680)

1. -6 **3.** 3/2   **5.** 28/3   **7.** 38   **9.** 1/3   **11.** 76   **13.** 4/3   **15.** 112/25   **17.** $20e^{-0.2} - 20e^{-0.3} +$
$3\ln 3 - 3\ln 2 \approx 2.775$ **19.** $c^{10}/5 - e^5/5 - 1/2 \approx 4375.1$ **21.** 49/3   **23.** $447/7 \approx 63.857$
25. 42   **27.** 76   **29.** 24   **31.** 41/2   **33.** $e^2 - 3 + 1/e \approx 4.757$ **35.** 1   **37.** 16   **39.** $e^3 - 2e^2 +$
$e \approx 8.026$ **41.** No   **43.** (a) \$22,000 (b) \$62,000 (c) 49.5 days   **45.** (a) \$8700 (b) \$9300   **47.** (a) 1.37 (b) .32

49. (a) 14.26 (b) 3.55   **51.** (a) $c(t) = 1.2e^{0.04t}$ (b) $\int_0^{10} 1.2e^{0.04t}\,dt$ (c) $30e^{0.4} - 30 \approx 14.75$ billion (d) About 12.8 years
(e) About 14.4 years   **53.** $(72/.014)(e^{0.014T} - 1)$

Extended Application   (page 686)

1. About 102 years   **2.** About 98 years   **3.** About 45.5 years   **4.** About 90 years

Extended Application   (page 688)

1. A:1/3, B:1/6, C:1/6   **2.** A:1, B:0, C:0   **3.** A:1/3, B:1/3, C:1/3

Section 13.4   (page 693)

1. $2(2x + 3)^{5/5} + C$ **3.** $-2(y - 2)^{-2} + C$ **5.** $-(2m + 1)^{-2}/2 + C$ **7.** $-(x^2 + 2x - 4)^{-3}/3 + C$
9. $(z^2 - 5)^{3/2}/3 + C$ **11.** $-2e^{2p} + C$ **13.** $e^{2x^3}/2 + C$ **15.** $e^{2t-t^2}/2 + C$ **17.** $-e^{1/z} + C$
19. $-8\ln|1 + 3x|/3 + C$ **21.** $(\ln|2t + 1|)/2 + C$ **23.** $-(3v^2 + 2)^{-3}/18 + C$ **25.** $-(2x^2 - 4x)^{-1}/4 + C$
27. $[(1/r) + r]^2/2 + C$ **29.** $(x^3 + 3x)^{1/3} + C$ **31.** $(p + 1)^7/7 - (p + 1)^6/6 + C$
33. $2(5t - 1)^{5/2}/125 + 2(5t - 1)^{3/2}/75 + C$ **35.** $2(u - 1)^{3/2}/3 + 2(u - 1)^{1/2} + C$ **37.** 15/4   **39.** 512/3
41. $[\ln(e^2 - 4e + 6) - \ln 3]/2$ or $\ln[(e^2 - 4e + 6)/3]^{1/2} \approx -.0880$ **43.** $(e^2 - 1)/4 \approx 1.597$ **45.** \$1,466,840
47. .5 million dollars

Section 13.5   (page 700)

1. 15   **3.** 4   **5.** 26   **7.** 366.1667   **9.** 4/3   **11.** $5 + \ln 6 \approx 6.792$ **13.** $6 - e + 1/e \approx 3.650$ **15.** $e^2 -$
$e - \ln 2 \approx 3.978$ **17.** (a) 8 years (b) about 148 (c) about 771   **19.** (a) 19.6 days (b) \$176,792 (c) \$80,752 (d) \$96,040
21. 5733.33   **23.** 83.33   **25.** (a) (b) $x = 5$ (c) 7.50 (d) 17.50

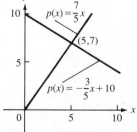

27. (a) .019; the lower 10% of the income producers earn 1.9% of the total income of the population. (b) .184; the lower 40% of the income producers earn 18.4% of the total income of the population. (c) .384; the lower 60% of the income producers earn 38.4% of the total income of the population. (d) .819; the lower 90% of the income producers earn 81.9% of the total income of the population. (e) See graph at right. (f) .15
29. 12.8256 **31.** 1.17596

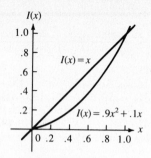

Chapter 13 Review Exercises (page 703)

1. $6x + C$ **3.** $x^2 + 3x + C$ **5.** $x^3/3 - 3x^2/2 + 2x + C$ **7.** $2x^{3/2} + C$ **9.** $2x^{3/2}/3 + 9x^{1/3} + C$
11. $2x^{-2} + C$ **13.** $-3e^{2x}/2 + C$ **15.** $2\ln|x - 1| + C$ **17.** $e^{3x}/6 + C$ **19.** $(3\ln|x^2 - 1|)/2 + C$
21. $C(x) = 10x - x^2 + 4$ **23.** $C(x) = (2x - 1)^{3/2} + 145$ **25.** $s(t) = t^3/3 - t^2 + 8$ **27.** 20 **29.** 28
31. 12 **33.** $72/25 \approx 2.88$ **35.** $2\ln 3$ or $\ln 9 \approx 2.1972$ **37.** $2e^4 - 2 \approx 107.1963$ **39.** 18 **41.** $e^2 - 1 \approx 6.3891$
43. 36,000 **45.** 990 **47.** $2(x^2 - 3)^{3/2}/3 + C$ **49.** $-(x^3 + 5)^{-3}/9 + C$ **51.** $\ln|2x^2 - 5x| + C$
53. $-e^{-3x^4}/12 + C$ **55.** $2e^{-5x}/5 + C$ **57.** 64/3 **59.** 1/6 **61.** 2.5 years; about $99,000

Chapter 14 Section 14.1 (page 712)

1. $xe^x - e^x + C$ **3.** $(-5xe^{-3x})/3 - (5e^{-3x})/9 + 3e^{-3x} + C$ **5.** $-5e^{-1} + 3 \approx 1.1606$ **7.** $4\ln 4 - 3 \approx 2.5452$
9. $(x^2 \ln x)/2 - x^2/4 + C$ **11.** $e^4 + e^2 \approx 61.9872$ **13.** About 110,829 **15.** $(x^2e^{2x})/2 - (xe^{2x})/2 + (e^{2x})/4 + C$
17. $243/8 - [3(2)^{4/3}]/8$ **19.** $4x^2 \ln(5x) + 7x \ln(5x) - 2x^2 - 7x + C$ **21.** $[2x^2(x + 2)^{3/2}]/3 - [8x(x + 2)^{5/2}]/15 + [16(x + 2)^{7/2}]/105 + C$ **23.** .13077 **25.** $15(5e^6 + 1)/2 \approx 15,136.08$ **27.** $-4\ln|(x + \sqrt{x^2 + 36})/6| + C$
29. $\ln|(x - 3)/(x + 3)| + C$ $(x^2 > 9)$ **31.** $(4/3)\ln|(3 + \sqrt{9 - x^2})/x| + C$, $0 < x < 3$
33. $-2x/3 + 2\ln|3x + 1|/9 + C$ **35.** $(-2/15)\ln|x/(3x - 5)| + C$ **37.** $\ln|(2x - 1)/(2x + 1)| + C$
39. $-3\ln|(1 + \sqrt{1 - 9x^2})/(3x)| + C$ **41.** $2x - 3\ln|2x + 3| + C$ **43.** $1/[25(5x - 1)] - (\ln|5x - 1|)/25 + C$

Extended Application (page 715)

1. 10.65 **2.** 175.8 **3.** 441.46

Section 14.2 (page 722)

1. (a) 2.7500 (b) 2.6667 (c) $8/3 \approx 2.6667$ **3.** (a) 1.6833 (b) 1.6222 (c) $\ln 5 \approx 1.6094$ **5.** (a) 16 (b) 14.6667
(c) $44/3 \approx 14.6667$ **7.** (a) .9436 (b) .8374 (c) $4/5 = .8$ **9.** (a) 9.3741 (b) 9.3004 **11.** (a) 5.9914 (b) 6.1672
(c) 6.2832; Simpson's rule is more accurate. **13.** (a) 2.4759 (b) 2.3572
15. (a) $f(x)$ (b) 128 **17.** (a) $f(x)$ (b) 6.3
(c) 128 (c) 6.27

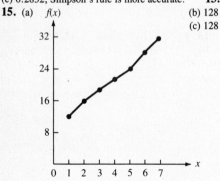

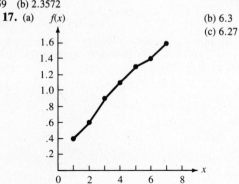

19. about 20; this represents the total effective amount of the drug available to the patient.   **21.** 7.5   **23.** Trapezoidal: 12.6027; Simpson: 12.6029   **25.** Trapezoidal: 9.79271; Simpson: 9.83377   **27.** Trapezoidal: 14.5192; Simpson: 14.5193   **29.** Trapezoidal: 3935.44; Simpson: 3979.24

Section 14.3   (page 730)

1. (a) \$5823.38   (b) \$19,334.31   **3.** (a) \$2911.69   (b) \$9667.16   **5.** (a) \$2637.47   (b) \$8756.70   **7.** (a) \$27,979.55   (b) \$92,895.37   **9.** (a) \$2.34   (b) \$7.78   **11.** (a) \$582.57   (b) \$1934.20   **13.** (a) \$3480.51   (b) \$11,555.70   **15.** \$74,565.94   **17.** \$20,560.21; \$86,778.41   **19.** \$4175.52

Section 14.4   (page 735)

1. $8\pi/3$ **3.** $364\pi/3$ **5.** $386\pi/27$ **7.** $3\pi/2$ **9.** 18π **11.** $\pi(e^4 - 1)/2 \approx 84.19$ **13.** $\pi\ln 4 \approx 4.36$

15. $3124\pi/5$ **17.** $16\pi/15$ **19.** $4\pi/3$ **21.** $4\pi r^3/3$ **23.** (a) $2\pi k \int_0^R r(R^2 - r^2)\,dr$ (b) $\pi kR^4/2$ **25.** -57.67 **27.** $31/9 \approx 3.44$ **29.** $e - 1 \approx 1.72$ **31.** (a) 1.69   (b) .10   (c) .046

Section 14.5   (page 740)

1. 1/2   **3.** Divergent   **5.** -1 **7.** 1000   **9.** 1   **11.** 3/5   **13.** 1   **15.** 4   **17.** Divergent   **19.** 1   **21.** Divergent   **23.** $(2 \ln 2.5)/21 \approx .087$ **25.** $4(\ln 2 - 1/2)/9 \approx .086$ **27.** Divergent   **29.** Not possible   **31.** 1   **33.** \$750,000   **35.** 1250   **37.** 0

Extended Application   (page 745)

1. (a) 46   (b) 45.33   **2.** (a) .0002 liters/sec   (b) .0002 liters/sec   **3.** 34.08 ml/sec

Section 14.6   (page 749)

1. $y = x^3/3 + C$ **3.** $y = -x^2 + x^3 + C$ **5.** $y = e^x + C$ **7.** $y = -2e^{-x} + C$ **9.** $y = -4x^3/9 + C$ **11.** $y = 3x^4/8 + C$ **13.** $y = x^3 - x^2 + 2$ **15.** $y = x^3 - 2x^2 + 2x + 8$ **17.** $y = \ln x + 10$ **19.** $y = -2xe^{-x} - 2e^{-x} + 44$ **21.** (a) \$1011.75   (b) \$1024.52   (c) No; if $x = 8$, the denominator becomes 0.   **23.** About 332,000   **25.** $y = C(x) = 2x + \ln|x| + C$

Section 14.7   (page 756)

1. $y^2 = x^2 + C$ **3.** $y = ke^{x^2}$ **5.** $y = ke^{(x^3 - x^2)}$ **7.** $y = Mx$ **9.** $y = Me^x + 5$ **11.** $y = -1/(e^x + C)$ **13.** $y^2 = 2x^3/3 + 9$ **15.** $y = e^{x^2 + 3x}$ **17.** $y = -5/(5 \ln x - 6)$ **19.** $y^2/2 - 3y = x^2 + x - 4$ **21.** $y = (e^x - 3)/(e^x - 2)$ **23.** (a) $k \approx .8$ (b) 11   (c) 55   (d) 2981   **25.** (a) \$155.24   (b) \$161.55   (c) \$164.62   **27.** (a) $dy/dt = -.05y$ (b) $y = Me^{-0.05t}$ (c) $y = 90e^{-0.05t}$ (d) About 55 grams   **29.** About 11.6 years   **31.** About 4.4 cc   **33.** About 387   **35.** (a) $y = (50e^{0.18t})/(1 + .005e^{0.18t})$ (b) In about 29 days   **37.** (a) $y = (5.55e^{0.45t})/(1 + .111e^{0.45t})$ (b) In about 6 days

Chapter 14   Review Exercises   (page 758)

1. $[-2x(8 - x)^{5/2}]/5 - [4(8 - x)^{7/2}]/35 + C$ **3.** $xe^x - e^x + C$ **5.** $[(2x + 3)(\ln|2x + 3| - 1)]/2 + C$ **7.** $7(e^2 - 1)/4 \approx 11.181$ **9.** $16250/3 \approx 5416.67$ **11.** .4143   **13.** 3.9828   **15.** 10.2773   **17.** 1.4588   **19.** 10.55   **21.** \$28,513.76   **23.** \$402.64   **25.** \$10,254.22   **27.** \$464.49   **29.** \$5715.89   **31.** $125\pi/6 \approx 65.45$ **33.** $\pi(e^4 - e^{-2})/2 \approx 85.55$ **35.** $406\pi/15 \approx 85.03$ **37.** 9.2508   **39.** 13/6   **41.** 1/2   **43.** $6/e \approx 2.207$ **45.** Divergent   **47.** 3   **49.** \$555,555.56   **51.** $y = x^4/2 + 3x^2 + C$ **53.** $y = 4e^x + C$ **55.** $y = x^3/3 - 5x^2/2 + 1$ **57.** $y = -5e^{-x} - 5x + 22$ **59.** (a) About \$5800   (b) About \$25,000   **61.** $y^2 = 3x^2 + 2x + K$ **63.** $y = (Mx^2 - 1)/2$ **65.** $y = 2e^{5x - x^2}$ **67.** $y^2 + 6y = 2x - 2x^2 + 352$ **69.** About 219

Chapter 15 Section 15.1 (page 770)

1. (a) 6 (b) -8 (c) -20 (d) 43 **3.** (a) $\sqrt{43}$ (b) 6 (c) $\sqrt{19}$ (d) $\sqrt{11}$ **5.** (a) 446 (b) 286 (c) 816 (d) 91
7. (a) 7.85 (b) 4.02
9.

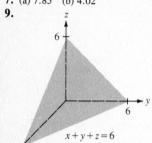

11.

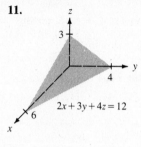

$2x + 3y + 4z = 12$

13.

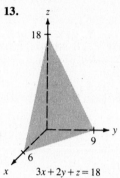

$3x + 2y + z = 18$

15.

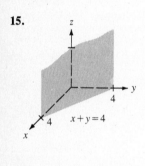

$x + y = 4$

17.

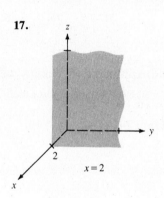

$x = 2$

19. $\sqrt{3}$ **21.** $\sqrt{99}$ or $3\sqrt{11}$ **23.** $\sqrt{59}$ **25.** $(x + 1)^2 + (y - 4)^2 + (z - 2)^2 = 9$ **27.** $(x - 2)^2 + y^2 +$
$(z + 3)^2 = 16$ **29.** $(5, 3, -4)$; $r = 3$ **31.** $(-3, 0, 1)$; $r = \sqrt{12}$ or $2\sqrt{3}$ **33.** (c) **35.** (e) **37.** (b)
39. (a) $18x + 9h$ (b) $-6y - 3h$

Section 15.2 (page 777)

1. (a) $24x - 8y$ (b) $-8x + 6y$ (c) 24 (d) -20 **3.** $f_x = -2y$; $f_y = -2x + 18y^2$; 2; 170 **5.** $f_x = 9x^2y^2$; $f_y = 6x^3y$;
36; -1152 **7.** $f_x = e^{x+y}$; $f_y = e^{x+y}$; e^1 or e; e^{-1} or $1/e$ **9.** $f_x = -15e^{3x-4y}$; $f_y = 20e^{3x-4y}$; $-15e^{10}$; $20e^{-24}$
11. $f_x = (-x^4 - 2xy^2 - 3x^2y^3)/(x^3 - y^2)^2$; $f_y = (3x^3y^2 - y^4 + 2x^2y)/(x^3 - y^2)^2$; $-8/49$; $-1713/5329$ **13.** $f_x = 6xy^3/$
$(1 + 3x^2y^3)$; $f_y = 9x^2y^2/(1 + 3x^2y^3)$; $12/11$; $1296/1297$ **15.** $f_x = e^{x^2y}(2x^2y + 1)$; $f_y = x^3e^{x^2y}$; $-7e^{-4}$; $-64e^{48}$
17. $f_{xx} = 36xy$; $f_{yy} = -18$; $f_{xy} = f_{yx} = 18x^2$ **19.** $R_{xx} = 8 + 24y^2$; $R_{yy} = -30xy + 24x^2$; $R_{xy} = R_{yx} = -15y^2 + 48yx$
21. $r_{xx} = -8y/(x + y)^3$; $r_{yy} = 8x/(x + y)^3$; $r_{xy} = r_{yx} = (4x - 4y)/(x + y)^3$ **23.** $z_{xx} = 0$; $z_{yy} = 4xe^y$; $z_{xy} = z_{yx} = 4e^y$
25. $r_{xx} = -1/(x + y)^2$; $r_{yy} = -1/(x + y)^2$; $r_{xy} = r_{yx} = -1/(x + y)^2$ **27.** $z_{xx} = 1/x$; $z_{yy} = -x/y^2$; $z_{xy} = 1/y$
29. $x = -4$; $y = 2$ **31.** $x = 0$, $y = 0$, or $x = 3$, $y = 3$ **33.** $f_x = 2x$; $f_y = z$; $f_z = y + 4z^3$; $f_{yz} = 1$ **35.** $f_x =$
$6/(4z + 5)$; $f_y = -5/(4z + 5)$; $f_z = -4(6x - 5y)/(4z + 5)^2$; $f_{yz} = 20/(4z + 5)^2$ **37.** $f_x = (2x - 5z^2)/(x^2 - 5xz^2 + y^4)$;
$f_y = 4y^3/(x^2 - 5xz^2 + y^4)$; $f_z = -10xz/(x^2 - 5xz^2 + y^4)$; $f_{yz} = 40xy^3z/(x^2 - 5xz^2 + y^4)^2$ **39.** (a) 80 (b) 180 (c) 110
(d) 360 **41.** $.7x^{-.3}y^{.3}$ or $.7y^{.3}/x^{.3}$; $.3x^{.7}y^{-.7}$ or $.3x^{.7}/y^{.7}$ **43.** (a) 168 (b) 5448 (c) 96 (d) 3882
45. (a) $.08585W^{-.575}H^{.725}$ (b) $.0112$ (c) $.14645W^{.425}H^{-.275}$ (d) $.783$

Section 15.3 (page 785)

1. Saddle point at $(1, -1)$ **3.** Relative minimum at $(-1, -1/2)$ **5.** Relative minimum at $(-2, -2)$ **7.** Relative
minimum at $(15, -8)$ **9.** Relative maximum at $(2/3, 4/3)$ **11.** Saddle point at $(2, -2)$ **13.** Saddle point at $(1, 2)$
15. Saddle point at $(0, 0)$; relative minimum at $(4, 8)$ **17.** Saddle point at $(0, 0)$; relative minimum at $(9/2, 3/2)$ **19.** Saddle
point at $(0, 0)$ **21.** (a) **23.** (b) **25.** (e) **27.** $P(12, 40) = 2744$ **29.** $x = 12$, $y = 72$ **31.** $C(12, 25) = 2237$

Section 15.4   (page 792)

1. $f(6, 6) = 72$ **3.** $f(4/3, 4/3) = 64/27$ **5.** $f(5, 3) = 28$ **7.** $f(20, 2) = 360$ **9.** $f(3/2, 3/2, 3) = 81/4$ **11.** 10, 10   **13.** $x = 6, y = 12$ **15.** 30, 30, 30   **17.** 50 m by 50 m   **19.** 150 m by 300 m   **21.** $r = 5$ in, $h = 10$ in   **23.** 12.91 m by 12.91 m by 6.46 m   **25.** Make 10 large, no small   **27.** $x = 200, y = 300$

Section 15.5   (page 799)

1. $y = 3.98x + 5.28$; 21.2; 33.14   **3.** $y = 3.125x - 8.875$; 6.68; 13.08   **5.** (a) $y = .3x + 1.5$ (b) 2.4

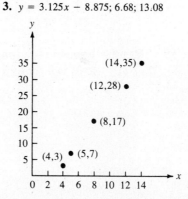

7. (a) See graph below.
(b) $y = .16x - .89$ (c) 3.6

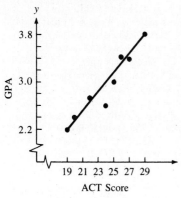

9. (a) $y = 3.35x - 78.2$ (b) 123   (c) 156

11. $y = 8.06x + 49.52$

13. (a)

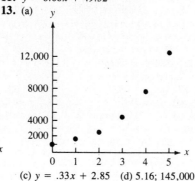

(c) $y = .33x + 2.85$ (d) 5.16; 145,000

15. $y = 1.003077x + 8.486716$; $r = .879913$ **17.** $y = .027980x + 2.489262$; $r = .978365$

Section 15.6   (page 807)

1. $dz = 36x^3 \, dx - 15y^2 \, dy$ **3.** $dz = 2xy^3 \, dx + (3x^2y^2 + 1) \, dy$ **5.** $dz = [-2y/(x - y)^2] \, dx + [2x/(x - y)^2] \, dy$
7. $dz = [y^{1/2}/x^{1/2} - 1/[2(x + y)^{1/2}]] \, dx + [x^{1/2}/y^{1/2} - 1/[2(x + y)^{1/2}]] \, dy$ **9.** $dz = (3\sqrt{1 - 2y}) \, dx + [-(3x + 2)/(1 - 2y)^{1/2}] \, dy$ **11.** $dz = [2x/(x^2 + 2y^4)] \, dx + [8y^3/(x^2 + 2y^4)] \, dy$ **13.** $dz = [y^2 e^{x+y}(x + 1)] \, dx + [xye^{x+y}(y + 2)] \, dy$
15. $dz = (2x - y/x) \, dx + (-\ln x) \, dy$ **17.** $dw = (4x^3yz^3) \, dx + (x^4z^3) \, dy + (3x^4yz^2) \, dz$ **19.** $dw = (-6/x^2) \, dx + (12/y^2) \, dy + (18/z^2) \, dz$ **21.** -0.2 **23.** -0.009 **25.** -0.0394 **27.** -0.00769 **29.** 0.11   **31.** -0.335
33. 15.1 cu cm   **35.** 71.2 cu in   **37.** 41.06 sq cm   **39.** 6.26 cu cm   **41.** \$60   **43.** $-.134$ dollars   **45.** .348
47. 2.980

Section 15.7 (page 819)

1. $93y/4$ **3.** $3x + 609x^2/4 - 6$ **5.** $(1/9)(48 + y)^{3/2} - (1/9)(24 + y)^{3/2}$ **7.** $(1/3)(36 + 3y)^{3/2} - (1/3)(9 + 3y)^{3/2}$
9. $6 + 10y$ **11.** $\ln|75 + 10y| - \ln|27 + 6y|$ or $\ln|(75 + 10y)/(27 + 6y)|$ **13.** $(1/4)e^{x+4} - (1/4)e^{x-4}$
15. $(1/2)e^{25+9y} - (1/2)e^{9y}$ **17.** $(1/3)(16 + 3x)^{3/2} - (1/3)(3x)^{3/2}$ **19.** $(20y/3)(18 + 5y^2)^{1/2} - (20y/3)(9 + 5y^2)^{1/2}$
21. $279/8$ **23.** $179/2$ **25.** $(2/45)(39^{5/2} - 12^{5/2} - 7533)$ **27.** 21 **29.** $3716/45$ **31.** $(\ln 2)^2$
33. $8 \ln 2 + 4$ **35.** 256 **37.** $(4/15)[33 - 2^{5/2} - 3^{5/2}]$ **39.** $-2 \ln 6/7$ **41.** $(1/2)(e^7 - e^6 - e^3 + e^2)$ **43.** 48
45. $4/3$ **47.** $(2/15)(2^{5/2} - 2)$ **49.** $(1/4) \ln (17/8)$ **51.** $e^2 - 3$ **53.** $189/2$ **55.** $97{,}632/105$ **57.** $128/9$
59. $27/8$ **61.** $\ln 3$ **63.** $64/3$ **65.** 116 **67.** $10/3$ **69.** $7(e - 1)/3$ **71.** $16/3$ **73.** $117/5$
75. $4 \ln 2 - 2$ **77.** $13/3$ **79.** $(e^7 - e^6 - e^5 + e^4)/2$ **81.** $\$2583$

Chapter 15 Review Exercises (page 823)

1. $-19; -255$ **3.** $-1; -5/2$ **5.** $\sqrt{43}$ **7.** $\sqrt{61}$ **9.** (a) 3440 (b) 6508 (c) 6818
11.

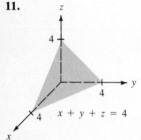

13.

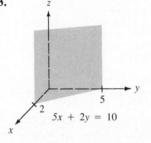

15.

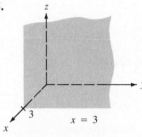

17. $(2, -3, 4); r = 3$ **19.** (a) $-10x + 7y$ (b) -15 (c) 7 **21.** $f_x = 27x^2y^2 - 5; f_y = 18x^3y$ **23.** $f_x = 4x/(4x^2 + y^2)^{1/2}; f_y = y/(4x^2 + y^2)^{1/2}$ **25.** $f_x = 2x \cdot e^{2y}; f_y = 2x^2 \cdot e^{2y}$ **27.** $f_x = 4x/(2x^2 + y^2); f_y = 2y/(2x^2 + y^2)$
29. $f_{xx} = 24xy^2; f_{xy} = 24x^2y - 8$ **31.** $f_{xx} = 8y/(x - 2y)^3; f_{xy} = (-4x - 8y)/(x - 2y)^3$ **33.** $f_{xx} = 2e^y; f_{xy} = 2xe^y$
35. $f_{xx} = (-2x^2y^2 - 4y)/(2 - x^2y)^2; f_{xy} = -4x/(2 - x^2y)^2$ **37.** (a) $.6x^{-.4}y^{.4}$ or $.6y^{.4}/x^{.4}$ (b) $.4x^{.6}y^{-.6}$ or $.4x^{.6}/y^{.6}$
39. Relative minimum when $x = 0$, $y = 1$ **41.** Saddle point when $x = 0$, $y = 2$ **43.** Saddle point when $x = 3$, $y = 1$
45. Relative minimum when $x = 1$, $y = 1/2$; Saddle point when $x = -1/3$, $y = 11/6$ **47.** Relative minimum when $x = 11$, $y = 12$ **49.** Minimum when $x = 0$, $y = 4$; maximum when $x = 8/3$, $y = 4/3$ **51.** Extremum when $x = 0$, $y = 0$
53. $80/3$ and $160/3$ **55.** 5 by 5 by 5 **57.** (a) $y = 3.9x - 7.9$ (b) 15.5 **59.** $dz = 18x^2 \, dx - 20y \, dy$ **61.** $dz = [4y/(x + 2)^2]dx + [-4x/(x + 2)^2]dy$ **63.** $dz = [xye^{x-y}(x + 2)]dx + [x^2e^{x-y}(1 - y)]dy$ **65.** $dw = 5x^4 \, dx + 4y^3 \, dy - 3z^2 \, dz$ **67.** 1.7 **69.** 7.92 cu cm **71.** 1.34 cu cm **73.** $64y^2/3 + 40$ **75.** $(1/9)[(30 + 3y)^{3/2} - (12 + 3y)^{3/2}]$ **77.** $12y - 16$ **79.** $(3/2)[(100 + 2y^2)^{1/2} - (2y^2)^{1/2}]$ **81.** $1232/9$ **83.** $2[(42)^{5/2} - (24)^{5/2} - (39)^{5/2} + (21)^{5/2}]/135$ **85.** $2 \ln 2$ or $\ln 4$ **87.** 26 **89.** $(4/15)(782 - 8^{5/2})$ **91.** 1900 **93.** $1/2$ **95.** $1/48$
97. 3

Chapter 16 Section 16.1 (page 835)

1. (a) $P(X)$ (b) 6.7 (c) 1.1 **3.** (a) $P(Z)$ (b) 2.9 (c) 1.45

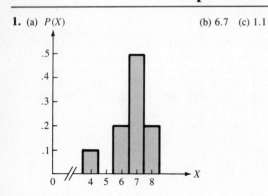

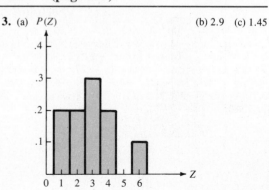

5. (a) P(Y)   (b) 12.13   (c) 1.27

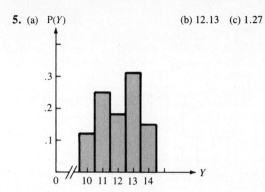

7. $E(X) = 2.15, \sigma = .91$ **9.** $E(X) = 3.4, \sigma = 1.11$
11. (b)   **13.** (a) .84   (b) 1.2   (c) .69   **15.** (a) 31/42
(b) 5/7   (c) 2   (d) $\sqrt{6}/3 \approx .82$
17. (a)

Number of Points	4	5	6	7	8	9	10
Probability	1/36	0	1/9	5/18	13/36	1/6	1/18

(b) 7/12   (c) 1/36   (d) 23/3   (e) $\sqrt{13}/3 \approx 1.20$ **19.** 1.5
21. 7   **23.** 4/3   **25.** \$195,000

Section 16.2   (page 843)

1. Yes   **3.** Yes   **5.** No; $\int_0^3 4x^3\, dx \neq 1$ **7.** No; $\int_{-2}^2 \frac{x^2}{16} dx \neq 1$ **9.** No; $f(x) < 0$ on $[-2, 0)$ **11.** $k = 3/14$
13. $k = 3/125$ **15.** $k = 2/9$ **17.** $k = 1/12$ **19.** $k = 3/26$ **21.** (a) .4641   (b) .1716   (c) .3643   **23.** (a) 3/5 = .6
(b) 1/5 = .2   (c) 3/5 = .6   **25.** (a) .4226   (b) .2071   (c) .4082   **27.** (a) .3935   (b) .3834   (c) .3679   **29.** (a) 4/7 $\approx$
.5714   (b) 5/21 $\approx$ .2381   **31.** (a) .9975   (b) .0025

Section 16.3   (page 849)

1. $\mu = 5$, Var$(X) = 1.33$, $\sigma = 1.15$ **3.** $\mu = 14/3 = 4.67$, Var$(X) = .89$, $\sigma = .94$ **5.** $\mu = 2.83$, Var$(X) = .59$, $\sigma = .77$
7. $\mu = 4/3 = 1.33$, Var$(X) = 2/9 = .22$, $\sigma = .47$ **9.** (a) 5.40   (b) 5.55   (c) 2.36   (d) .54   (e) .60   **11.** (a) 4/3 = 1.33
(b) .22   (c) .47   (d) .56   (e) .63   **13.** (a) 5   (b) 0   **15.** (a) 4.83   (b) .055   **17.** (a) $\sqrt[4]{2} \approx 1.19$ (b) .18
19. (a) 2   (b) .89   (c) .62

Section 16.4   (page 858)

1. (a) 4.4   (b) .23   (c) .29   **3.** (a) 33.33   (b) 33.33   (c) .23   **5.** (a) 1   (b) 1   (c) .23   **7.** (a) 28   (b) .375
9. (a) \$47,500   (b) .47   **11.** (a) 1/2   (b) .49   **13.** (a) $f(x) = .235e^{-.235x}$ on $[0, \infty)$ (b) .095   **15.** 49.98%
17. 17.36%   **19.** 8.01%   **21.** 89.69%   **23.** -1.28 **25.** .92   **27.** (a) .1587   (b) .7698   **29.** \$16.56; \$7.85
31. $m = (b + a)/2$ **33.** 1.00002   **35.** 4.09032   **37.** $\mu = -8.02538 \times 10^{-11} \approx 0$; Var$(X) = .998866$; $\sigma = .999433 \approx 1$

Chapter 16   Review Exercises   (page 863)

1. (a)

X	2	3	4	5	6
P(X)	.292	.375	.125	.083	.125

(b) P(X)

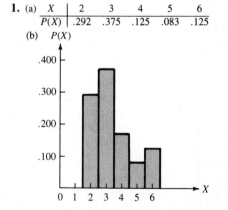

3. (a)

X	0	1	2	3	4	5	6	7	8
P(X)	.1	0	.1	.2	.3	.1	0	.2	0

(b) P(X)

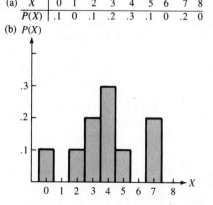

5. (a) P(X)   (b) .292

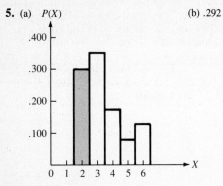

7. (a) P(X)   (b) .6

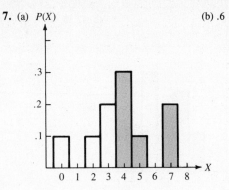

9. (a) 3.374   (b) 1.734   (c) 1.317   **11.** (a) 3.9   (b) 4.09   (c) 2.02   **13.** (a) *I*: $\mu = 8.012$, $\sigma = .053$; *II*: $\mu = 3.35$, $\sigma = .225$ (b) Fund I   **15.** Probability density function   **17.** Probability density function   **19.** $k = 3/14$
21. (a) .828   (b) .536   (c) .364   **23.** .911   **25.** $\mu = 6.5$, Var(X) = 2.083, $\sigma = 1.443$ **27.** $\mu = 2.405$, Var(X) = .759, $\sigma = .871$ **29.** (a) $7/12 \approx .583$ (b) .244   (c) .482   (d) .611   **31.** (a) 13.571   (b) 6.681   (c) .582   **33.** (a) 2.377
(b) 1.533   (c) .851   **35.** (a) 21 inches   (b) .526   **37.** 6.3%   **39.** 77.77%   **41.** 99.38%   **43.** $-.81$ **45.** .2206
47. .1921

INDEX

---

*Page references in Roman numerals refer to topics introduced in the "Review of Algebra" before Chapter 1.